Whitman Encyclopedia of Obsolete Paper Money

Whitman Encyclopedia of Obsolete Paper Money

Notes Issued by United States Banks, 1782–1866

Q. David Bowers

States, districts, and territories covered in this series, in order:

Connecticut, Maine, New Hampshire, Massachusetts, Rhode Island, Vermont, Florida, Georgia, South Carolina, North Carolina, Alabama, Arkansas, Kentucky, Louisiana, Mississippi, Tennessee, Texas, Delaware, District of Columbia, Maryland, Virginia, New Jersey, Pennsylvania, New York, Illinois, Indiana, Michigan, Ohio, Iowa, Kansas, Minnesota, Missouri, Nebraska, Utah, and Wisconsin

Also see volume 1, *An Introduction for Collectors and Historians.*

For news (or announcements) and more information, refer to www.Whitman.com.

Volume 4

New England Region, Part 2

Massachusetts, Book 2

From Hallowell to Yarmouth

Edited by C. John Ferreri

Whitman Publishing, LLC
PUBLISHING SINCE 1934
www.whitman.com

WHITMAN ENCYCLOPEDIA OF OBSOLETE PAPER MONEY

NOTES ISSUED BY UNITED STATES BANKS, 1782–1866

VOLUME 4: NEW ENGLAND REGION, PART 2

MASSACHUSETTS, BOOK 2

Whitman Publishing, LLC
PUBLISHING SINCE 1934
www.whitman.com

3101 Clairmont Road • Suite G • Atlanta, GA 30329

ISBN: 0794843131
Printed in China

If you have new information about any banks or notes listed in this volume, contact Whitman Publishing, Attn: Obsolete Paper Money, 3101 Clairmont Road, Suite G, Atlanta, GA 30329.

OCG™ COLLECTING GUIDE

WHITMAN®

Contents

Foreword

by Anne E. Bentley, Curator, Massachusetts Historical Society

Prolific author Q. David Bowers's latest project, the *Whitman Encyclopedia of Obsolete Paper Money,* truly embodies the very definition of the word *encyclopedia:* a book, or set of books, covering all branches of knowledge or all aspects of one subject—in this case, the wonderfully decorative and colorful currency issued by American banks from 1782 to 1866.

As a fledgling numismatist back in the early 1980s, facing the task of re-cataloging the obsolete currency in the collections of the Massachusetts Historical Society, my first reference was David C. Wismer's *The Obsolete Bank Notes of New England,* a descriptive catalog that served its purpose . . . just. In 1988 I welcomed James A. Haxby's four-volume set, the *Standard Catalog of United States Obsolete Bank Notes, 1782–1866,* with its miniature half-tone reproductions and new numbering system. It was a terrific step forward in reference works on the subject.

Then Dave Bowers and Whitman Publishing joined forces in 2006 to produce *Obsolete Paper Money Issued by Banks in the United States 1782–1866,* which gave us an impressively comprehensive overview of the banking and paper-money history of that period—along with illustrations that spoiled me forever for anything less than digital, high-resolution imagery as a reference tool.

Now, I am delighted to have been asked to play a role in a new and eagerly awaited series, the *Whitman Encyclopedia of Obsolete Paper Money.*

Massachusetts issued her first paper notes in 1690 to pay soldiers involved in the failed Phips Expedition to take Quebec. From that time to the institution of a federal currency, Massachusetts was an enthusiastic partner in the production and circulation of paper notes of all descriptions—the better to support her very active role as a center of commerce, especially during the early 19th century. In this time period the banking system was ripe for exploitation by greedy and unscrupulous characters. The sheer volume of Massachusetts obsolete bank notes stamped "counterfeit" or "spurious" bears witness to that fact. Even Newburyport native Jacob Perkins, with his Patent Stereotype Steel Plate, couldn't stem the tide of fraudulent issues. The Panic of 1837 saw many of the larger banks in the state fail during the ensuing depression that lasted until 1844, leaving us with the notes that we collect so enthusiastically today.

The Massachusetts Historical Society's obsolete section of paper currency spans from Connecticut to Tennessee, with the larger sections pertaining to Massachusetts and New York. I confess that the wonderfully engraved vignettes provide our chief purpose in using them as illustrations in exhibitions and online features. From village greens to portraits to whaling scenes, these exquisite miniature views are fascinating to examine, detailed, and sometimes puzzling. For example, why did the Harvard Bank choose to place an engraved copy of the portrait that the Historical Society commissioned of our benefactor Thomas Dowse on its 1861 $1 note? He was neither an officer of the bank nor an elected official—yet there he is, seated in the library he donated to us in 1856.

As you examine these pages with their vivid illustrations, you'll find a host of interesting stories about the banks, their notes, and the era they represent. This encyclopedic series is designed not just for specialists and collectors of paper currency, but also for all who enjoy learning more about various aspects of our nation's financial history, as well as for those of us who are entrusted with the cataloging and care of such material. Gentle Reader, you hold in your hands a treasure trove of information and images to enjoy at your leisure. Now if you'll excuse me, I'm off to add the Whitman numbers to our catalog records. . . .

—Boston, Massachusetts

Credits and Acknowledgements

For global and general credits for the *Whitman Encyclopedia of Obsolete Paper Money,* see volume 1. For volume 4's study of Massachusetts, specific credit goes to:

American Bank Note Co.; American Numismatic Association; American Numismatic Society; Irene Axelrod; Georgia Barnhill; Anne E. Bentley; Steve Blum; Wynn Bowers; Karen Bridges; Mark Carter; Ashley Clark; Rich Deming; Thomas Denly; Richard Doty; C. John Ferreri; Jeffrey M. Feuerman; Roberta French; Bruce Hagen; James A. Haxby; Heritage Auctions; Danielle Hill; Wayne Homren; Peter Huntoon; Christine Karstedt; Michael Keane; Kevin Lafond; Littleton Coin Co.; Massachusetts Historical Society; Don Munro; Eric P. Newman; Steve Noyes; Gary Parietti; Phillips Library at the Peabody-Essex Museum; Michael Rocco; Smithsonian Institution; Stack's Bowers Galleries; David M. Sundman; John and Nancy Wilson.

Valuations editors for volume 4: C. John Ferreri, Bruce Hagen, John Rowe, and Peter Treglia.

Image Credits

AAS	American Antiquarian Society, Worcester, Massachusetts
ABNCo	American Bank Note Co. Archives
ANS	American Numismatic Society, New York City, New York
BC	Bob Casper
CC	Caine Collection
CJF	C. John Ferreri Collection
HA	Heritage Auction Archives
HS	Hugh Shull Collection
HSPA	Historical Society of Pennsylvania, Philadelphia, Pennsylvania
JF	Jeffrey M. Feuerman Collection
MC	Mark Carter Collection
MHS	Massachusetts Historical Society, Boston, Massachusetts
MK	Michael Keane Collection
MR	Michael Rocco Collection
NJW	Nancy and John Wilson Collection
PEM	Peabody-Essex Museum, Salem, Massachusetts
QDB	Q. David Bowers Archives
RD	Rich Deming Collection
RMS	R.M. Smythe Collection
SBG	Stack's Bowers Galleries
SI	Smithsonian Institution, National Numismatic Collection
SN	Steve Noyes Collection
TD	Tom Denly Archives

How to Use This Book

When considering the purchase or sale of a note, two main considerations are grade and price. Beyond that, there are other aspects that are important in study and set one note apart from another. In certain aspects the study of notes is different from that of coins. Notes that are spurious (not official) can have significant value, as can counterfeits of standard notes. In some instances, a note in Extremely Fine-40 (EF-40) grade can be more valuable than an Uncirculated or unused note.

This guide explains the different aspects of typical bank listings in this book—covering the state of Massachusetts. Volume 1 of this series contains a thoroughly detailed study of the entire field of obsolete state bank notes issued from 1782 to 1866, including a glossary of bank-note engravers, information on how currency was designed, printed, and distributed, and much more. If read even casually, Volume 1 will set you on your way to becoming an expert. In the meantime, "How to Use This Book" will explain the current listings in the volume at hand.

Types of Notes

There are several classes of collectible notes in this series. Their status affects their collectability and desirability.

Valid Issues

Valid issues are notes that were printed from plates made by skilled engravers and produced by bank-note companies or other authorized sources. In their time, they were paid out at face value by banks. Such bills were often later redeemed for face value and replaced by new issues. If a bank failed and its notes could not be redeemed, today its notes are still considered to be valid issues by collectors. Valid notes form the main focus of collecting obsolete currency.

A valid issue from the North River Banking Co., New York.

Non-Valid Issues

These exist in several categories:

Counterfeit notes: Illegally issued notes from false plates that imitated genuine bills. They are collectible as "fillers" in some instances but generally sell for low prices. They are collectible mainly as curiosities.

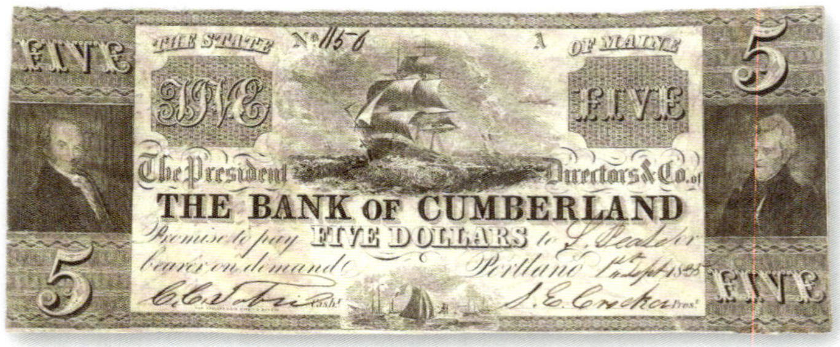

Note counterfeited to be passed as an issue from the Bank of Cumberland, Maine.

Raised notes: It was a common deceptive practice to raise the value of a low-denomination note to a higher one by chemically removing the counters (as they are called) or denomination ornaments and altering them to read as a higher value. Such notes have nominal values as collectibles today.

Original note of the Merchants & Manufacturers Bank.

Raised note.

Altered notes: Notes that were valid or spurious when first printed but then fell into the hands of criminals who altered them. When a bank failed, its notes became worthless and could not be redeemed for face value. There was a market for such, often at 2 percent or 3 percent of face value. Criminals bought them and, by the use of chemicals, removed certain information such as the town, state, and sometimes even the name of the bank. New information was then printed in the blank spaces. As an example, quantities of worthless $10 notes of the Egg Harbor Bank, Egg Harbor, New Jersey, were altered to appear as $10 notes of the active and strong Valley Bank, Hillsborough, New Hampshire. Altered notes are collectible, but their values are considerably less than the genuine.

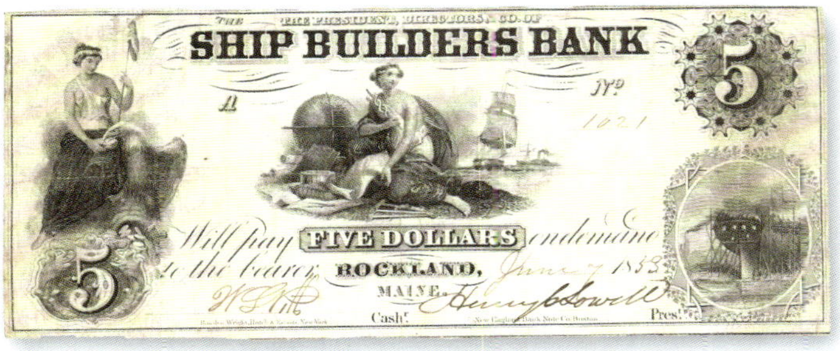

Original note of the Ship Builders Bank.

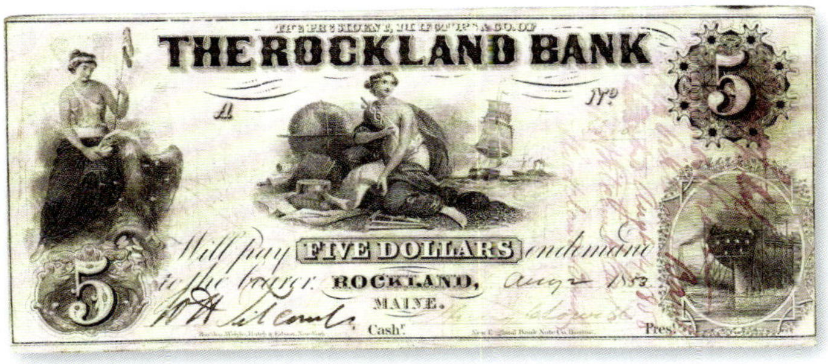

Altered note.

Spurious Issues

Spurious issues are notes from established engravers and printers that were delivered to banks that never opened their doors or to fraudsters who issued notes bearing the names of banks that never existed. Often these have fascinating stories. These are a basic part of collecting and in many instances are valued for as much as, or higher than, valid issues.

In this text Spurious issues are located in one of two places—under Valid Issues if the bank as a whole never opened or was fraudulently run, but the notes were genuinely printed, or under Non-Valid issues if notes from a genuine bank were taken into the hands of fraudsters and illegally distributed in a similar fashion to other Non-Valid notes such as counterfeits and altered notes.

Spurious note from a non-existent bank in a non-existent town. Fraudsters intended to alter it to represent the BOSTON bank of the same name.

Signed and Issued Notes

Banks typically received notes from the printer in sheets, most often a four-subject sheet bearing one to four denominations. Certain features needed to be added once the notes were received. Law cases affirmed that a bill was monetized only after the cashier affixed his signature. It was standard practice in small banks for the cashier to prepare the sheets in advance and then sign them only when the sheets were cut apart and ready to be issued. These features were added to prepare a note for distribution:

Date: Each note needed to bear a year, month, and day of when it was issued. Some notes had printed dates, such as *Jany 1st, 1854*, and did not require hand entry. Sometimes these referred to the charter date or were an annual date. It was not unusual for a note to be issued later than the date shown. Accordingly, if a note with a printed date of *Jany 1st, 1854*, was signed by cashier John Doe, who was named to that office on May 6, 1856, this was not an extraordinary situation. Many other notes had the number partially printed, such as 18__ or 185_, with the remainder to be inked in.

Partially printed date with the remainder inked in by hand.

Serial number: Serial numbers were usually added by hand in ink. Some notes had the same serial number twice on a note. The combination of the serial number, the date, and the plate letter defines a note as one of a kind.

To cut down on the work involved, serial-number sequences were often started anew when the date changed. This kept the numbers low. Unlike the situation for federal paper money, it is not unusual for an obsolete note to have a serial number below 100. Very few were higher than four digits. Sometimes colored ink was used for serial numbers. Certain notes of larger banks have the serial numbers printed by machine, but these are unusual.

Printed serial number.

President's signature: The primary duty of the president was to conduct meetings of the board of directors and the annual meeting of stockholders. Many directors lived at a distance from the bank and visited it infrequently. Accordingly, it was the custom of the president to sign large quantities of notes far in advance. The president of a small bank usually received a nominal salary, say $100 or $200 per year, or none at all.

Cashier's signature on the left. President's signature on the right.

Cashier's signature: The cashier was the person in charge. Often, for small banks, he was the only employee. It was not unusual for banks in small villages to be kept in the house of the cashier or, if the bank had its own building, for the cashier and his family to live on the premises. Security systems usually consisted only of locks and bolts. The cashier could keep watch at all times, including when the bank was closed.

The cashier was the highest-paid person, often $1,000 per year, more or less. The cashier opened the bank and closed it, kept the books, and took charge of money receipts and payments. Loans were usually arranged with another person on hand, such as one or two directors. Loans were given on "discount days," usually one or two days a week. This made it easier for one or more directors to attend. The discount day schedule was published in local papers. When the cashier affixed his signature to a note, it was officially monetized. That way, if notes were stolen but lacked the signature, the bank could simply declare them to be worthless.

Cashier's signature *D. Holmes*.

Notes in Circulation

Most bills circulated at face value locally or regionally. A $10 bill issued in New Haven, Connecticut, by a sound bank would be received at par with a slight discount for handling in Providence, Boston, or New York City. In Pittsburgh, Richmond, or another distant place, it would be taken in at a discount. Many earned extra profits by selling notes at a discount to brokers or runners who put them into circulation in distant places. The Hillsborough Bank of Amherst, New Hampshire, shipped bundles of notes to Marietta, Ohio, where they were placed into circulation easily. Storekeepers would buy them at a discount. The recipients would spend them, as would others. Hardly anyone went back to New Hampshire to exchange them for coins. Brokers in New York City handled large quantities of discounted notes.

Printed bank-note reporters and counterfeit detectors, as they were called, were published in many forms. These usually told of new counterfeits as well as of banks that had failed or were in financial difficulty. Long lists were presented by state, town, and bank, rating the notes and stating the discount from par at which banks and merchants should be valued.

Grading of Notes

There are no hard and fast rules for grading obsolete currency. Interpretations can vary, sometimes widely. Most old-time dealers and experienced auction houses tend to be more conservative than many who list in Internet sales or who are otherwise not part of the profession. A "Fine" note to one dealer may be another's "Very Fine." Similar to the situation for coins, grading has become looser over the years. A bill bought in the 1960s as Fine will easily be Very Fine today. Years ago, a bill with even a slight trace of a fold or crease was automatically excluded from the Uncirculated category. Today, bills described as such can have these traces, and, perhaps, one without such traces would be given a loftier designation such as Choice Uncirculated or Gem Uncirculated. And so it goes. The methodology is not as consistent or as well developed as is the grading of coins. Two commercial grading services are prominent in grading notes. PCGS Currency, once a part of the Professional Coin Grading Service but now independently owned, and PMG (Paper Money Grading), a division of the Numismatic Guaranty Corporation, have found wide acceptance in the marketplace. As of today they have published no standards, but they seem to more or less follow the guidelines given below.

These categories reflect the author's observations of current grading methods by many dealers and collectors. Beginning in the early 21st century, numbers have been attached to grades by some sellers based on the American Numismatic Association Grading Standards for United States Coins. However, as bills were printed, not minted, the term "Mint State" is not used for paper money.

Grading System

Choice or Gem Uncirculated

Unc-63 and 64 (Choice), Unc-65 (Gem).

A crisp, bright bill with no evidence of creases, folds, or stains. Tom Denly commented in 2004: "I consider centering to be a most important part of grade. For instance, a poorly centered note possibly cut into the design can never be called Gem or even Choice, no matter how nice it otherwise is." Most notes in this category are remainders.

Uncirculated

Unc-60.

A new, never circulated bill, but perhaps with slight evidences of a fold, a crease, or smudges from handling (presumably by bank officers). If part of the margin is trimmed away, this should be mentioned, but often is not. Most notes in this category are remainders.

About Uncirculated

AU-53, 55, and 58.

A bright, attractive note, with some creases, folds, or light discoloration, but with only slight evidences of use in commerce or, in the case of remainders, numismatic or bank handling. If signed and issued for circulation, this is a top-of-the-line grade in great demand.

Extremely Fine

EF-40 and 45.

Bright and attractive but with some slight stains or discoloration, perhaps with a pinhole or two or some small defect. Overall excellent appearance. A bill in this grade saw limited service in circulation.

Very Fine

VF-20 and 30.

This is a widely used grade for a "nice" note, worn but with nice features. Such a bill may be somewhat faded, but the printing and vignettes will be clear and with an attractive overall appearance. There may be an edge chip or two or perhaps a tiny piece off of a corner (but not into the printed part of the note). As most bank tellers and users were right-handed, the right side of a note usually has some discoloration from everyday handling.

Fine

Fine-12.

A note with even more wear, often limp or flimsy from extended use in commerce, but with all printed areas intact and most of them sharply defined. May be stained or discolored in areas.

Very Good

VG-8.

Well circulated, usually with some problems, tears, perhaps a small piece missing from the border, etc. Flimsy and often faded or discolored.

Good

G-4.

Extensively circulated and with evidence of such, including small tears, perhaps edge pieces missing, areas of the printing and vignettes indistinct, and, often, old writing on the face of the note.

Poor, Fair, and About Good

Poor-1, Fair-2, AG-3.

Notes that have been in circulation for a very long time, now with ragged edges or pieces missing and often with significant areas of the note faded or otherwise indiscernible. A filler note. There are quite a few very early bills from the late 18th and early 19th century for which these grades may represent the finest known.

Grade as a Determinant of Value

Remainder notes: Surprise! In the field of bank notes, a well-worn example is often worth more than an Uncirculated bill of the same variety! However, the explanation is simple: most Uncirculated bills are remainders that were never distributed. Most have no officers' signatures. Years after certain banks closed, large quantities of their unissued notes became available. In most instances, a nice Very Fine bill of the same denomination and design, signed and serially numbered, is worth more. Remainder notes of this kind are designated as Unc-Rem. A signed and dated Uncirculated note is designated as Unc-S&D.

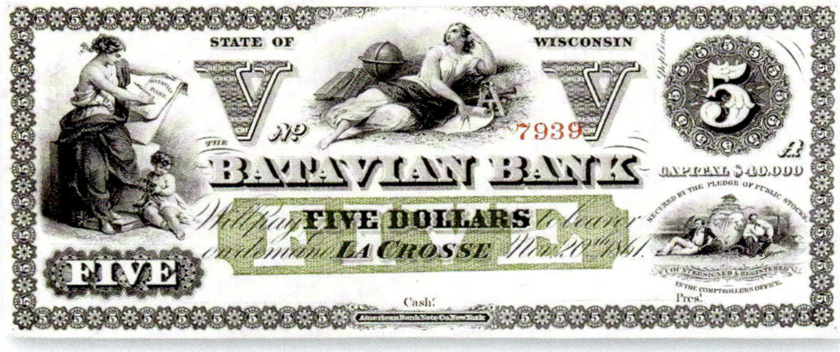

An Uncirculated remainder note.

Circulated notes: Among signed and numbered notes, higher-grade examples are more desirable than those in lower levels of preservation. In all instances, an About Uncirculated bill is worth more than an Extremely Fine one, and an EF is worth more than a Very Fine, and on down the line. Among the most desirable of circulated notes are those that are serially numbered, dated, and signed in ink by the cashier and president and which are in a high grade today.

A signed, dated, circulated note.

Cancelled notes: When worn notes were redeemed to be exchanged for others, banks often destroyed them. In many instances, however, they were saved but "canceled" to prevent them from being placed into circulation again. Several small, circular punch holes will either not affect the value of a note or will affect it only slightly, unless uncancelled notes are readily available. Large holes, notches cut out from the border, signatures cut off, and other cancellations that are unattractive are viewed negatively, as are stamped overprints, such as the common WORTHLESS and COUNTERFEIT.

A note cancelled to prevent further circulation.

Proof notes: Proof notes are special printings on special paper or light card stock, are usually found Uncirculated, and can be very valuable, if they are contemporary (made in the 19th century). Modern Proof reprints are worth varying lesser amounts. Beware of scanned or photographic modern copies.

A Proof note, without signatures, printed on special stock.

Valuation of Notes

Explanation of Values

Values assigned to notes in given grades have been compiled by consulting with dealers and collectors and by studying listed prices and auction results. Unlike coins, which often have values determined by "bid" prices and, for some such as gold, trade on close margins, the valuation of paper currency is much more subjective. In a way, the pricing can be compared to that in the fields of tokens and medals.

Many notes are infrequently traded. This is especially true for rare early issues. Sometimes, years can elapse between offerings. In such instances the values here are "educated guesses." Actual sale results such as an offering at auction may differ widely. For that reason values in this book should be considered as estimates compiled at the time of publication. Although the future is unknown, in past decades the price trends have been upward. Many notes valued at $100 a decade ago may be valued at $125 to $175 or more now. Few if any valid-issue notes have decreased in value. When contemplating a purchase or sale it is recommended that you check with experts and other sources for current values.

Even for common remainder notes and for certain common circulated bills in a given grade, prices can vary in the same time frame. One note might be priced at $200, another at $175, and a third at $250. It may be worthwhile to say that the same variations are seen in many other collectibles markets—such as Currier & Ives prints, postcards, colonial coins, ancient coins, antique furniture, tokens and medals, and more. The point here is that federal coins of the past 200 years are often quite common, trade frequently, and have bid and ask prices—a situation not comparable to other collectible specialties as mentioned.

To aid in current valuation we recommend subscribing to publications about paper money and checking auction and sale listings, often available on the Internet.

If a long-sought rarity is offered, many if not most experienced dealers and collectors will "reach" for it. A rarity listed for $1,000 may be a good buy for $2,000 if it is the only one to be offered in recent years.

With some experience, you will get a grasp for pricing—just as collectors of tokens, medals, prints, and other things have. What starts as being esoteric will in time become familiar.

Factors Affecting Values

Grade or condition: Among notes that were signed, numbered, dated, and placed into circulation, the higher the grade, the more valuable the note is. Uncirculated notes or remainders can be worth less than a circulated signed note.

Location: Notes of certain states or territories can be worth a premium. Western notes of a given rarity, such as from Utah, Kansas Terrritory, or Arkansas can be worth more than notes from New York, Pennsylvania, or New Jersey.

Rarity: In a given series, a rare note is worth more a common one.

Demand and popularity: Notes of certain towns and states can be worth more if there are more collectors desiring to buy them. Notes from Florida are more widely collected than are those of Vermont. Accordingly, a note of a given rarity can be worth more if from Florida. Such popularity may change over a period of time. If two or three well-financed buyers each seek to build a collection of a state, there will be great competition for rarities, and prices will be much higher than if this competition were not present. In addition, the publication of a new reference work on a particular state or category can serve to increase the number of people desiring such notes.

Denomination: Within a given rarity, an unusual denomination such as $4, $6, $7, $8, or $9 will be worth more than a $1, $2, $3, $5, $10, or $20 (these being the most often seen). On their own, $3 notes have always attracted a following; once common in circulation, the denomination is considered unusual today. It has not been used since the federal government began issuing notes in quantity in 1861, despite being very popular with state-chartered banks. $50 and $100 notes are scarce for most banks, and with relatively few exceptions, $500 and $1,000 notes are great rarities.

Vignette topic: The illustration or vignette of a note can add value. A Connecticut note showing Iranistan, the palatial home of P.T. Barnum, or "the Battle of the Frogs" is worth more than one showing a train or buildings. Notes showing Santa Claus are extremely popular and often sell for much more than what a comparable-rarity bill of a miscellaneous subject might command.

"Battle of the Frogs."

Santa Claus at upper left.

Proofs: Proof notes printed on special paper and intended as samples or for reference are usually found in Uncirculated preservation and will sell for many multiples of the price of common remainder notes.

Market and economic trends: The general market for obsolete paper money has been quite strong in recent decades. However, it was rather quiet before then. Market strength is based on the number of buyers at a given time and how much money they have to spend.

Imaging of Notes

Given their age and extensive circulation, obsolete bank notes are sometimes found with a high level of wear and tear. Within this encyclopedia, some images have been digitally enhanced to mitigate the effects of rust, water damage, stains, age, circulation wear, color fading, and other environmental stresses. Where necessary, they have been conceptually restored to more closely resemble their original form in an attempt to aid collectors and historians in identifying and analyzing the various issues, vignettes, engravings, and styles of the bank notes.

Printed Features of Note Designs

A typical note includes these printed features:

Name of bank: The name of the bank is usually the most prominently printed figure and can be found either high on the center of the note face or in a position about half way down. New Haven Bank, Derby Bank, Cochituate Bank, Bank of Commerce, Warner Bank, and Butchers and Drovers Bank are examples. Such titles often reflect the location of the bank, an industry such as farming or manufacturing, a geographical feature such as an ocean or river, or a proper name from history Among the latter there are banks named Franklin, Washington, Lafayette, and Indian names such as Amoskeag, Oneida, Quinnipiack, and Mohawk. At any given time there was only one bank of a certain name in operation in a given state.

Location of bank: Every note gives the town and state. The town often appears near the bank name or is sometimes tagged on to it, such as the Tradesmens Bank of New Haven. The name of the state often appears away from the town name, perhaps in the field of the note or at a border.

Denomination: This is the face value of a note. The most popular values were $1, $2, $3, $5, and $10 among the lower denominations and were made in the largest quantities. $20, $50, and $100 values were made in smaller quantities. Only a few banks issued $500 or $1,000 notes. There are also fractional notes such as 25¢, 50¢, and 75¢ in existence, issued by banks as part of a series that included higher denominations. The more times a denomination was printed on a note, the harder it was to alter by raising. Many notes have the denomination given dozens of times in micro-letters in addition to larger digits. Odd-value notes such as $1.25, $1.50, $1.75, $4, and $6 to $9 were issued by a few banks.

Scattered small notes denominated in cents were sometimes issued, usually but not always privately, in times of economic distress and are called scrip. Scrip notes were usually made by local printers. They are not studied herein.

Denomination counters: While the denominations of many notes, especially early ones, were lettered or in script, most bills after about 1810 had the value as a number surrounded with an oval, circle, or fancy engraving. These are referred to as counters. Volume 1 gives many examples.

Main vignette: Most notes have a large vignette at the center or to one side extending to the center. These are often scenic in nature—a seated figure, laborers at work, a train and cars, capitols and commercial buildings, figures from mythology, seascapes, and more. After 1820 vignettes became increasingly ornate.

Other vignettes: Most notes also had two or more smaller vignettes. Portraits of people ranging from well-known, such as a national president, to obscure, such as a bank president, were popular. Others show standing or seated figures, people in various activities, etc. Medallion vignettes reproduce medals, cameos, or plaques by means of a medal-ruling machine.

Ornaments and borders: Various geometric figures and engraved ornaments add to the complexity of many notes, as do ornamental borders.

Seals and arms: State arms, seals stating that a note was backed by securities or liens on real estate, etc., were added to many notes.

The state arms of Connecticut can be seen in the upper left corner.

Plate letter: It was common practice to assign a letter such as A, B, or C to the face of a note. A sheet of four notes might include, as an example, $1-$1-$1-$2. The three $1 notes would bear letters A, B, and C, and the $2 note would start again with A.

Engraver's imprint: The name of the bank-note printing company was nearly always stated in the face, usually in tiny letters at the bottom border but sometimes elsewhere. On some occasions ornamental vignettes were signed in micro-letters by engravers.

Place of redemption: While most bank notes could be redeemed over the counter of the banks that issued them, some others gave distant places where they could be redeemed, as at an office in another state, often in New York City. Such notes were frequently of questionable value.

Time of redemption: Most notes could be redeemed on demand, but many had a printed inscription stating that they could be redeemed only at a specified time later than the date on the note—six months, a year, or some other interval. Later-payment bills are called post notes, a term printed on some of them. Confederate States of America notes were redeemable two years after a peace treaty was signed with the United States, which, of course, never happened.

Overprints: Many notes, especially those after the 1820s, have overprints in color. These often give the denomination, such as ONE, FIVE, or TWENTY. Some later notes have grillwork, the denomination in micro-printing, or other features added in panels of color printing. On some the entire face can be overprinted in color.

Backs of notes: With only scattered exceptions, the backs of notes have not been discussed in reference books or auction catalogs. Hence, there are many notes listed in this book that have ornate backs not described.

Security features: Security features to deter counterfeiting or altering are seen on many notes. The most common is the "Canada green" or "Patent Green Tint" used on notes of Rawdon, Wright, Hatch & Edson in 1857 and by the American Bank Note Co. from 1858 onward. This color was said to deter copying by photographic means. Jacob Perkins's Patented Stereotype Steel Plate (PSSP) used micro-lettering to deter counterfeiting.

Other information: Ruled spaces and lettering were provided to indicate where the bank officers should sign and where the serial number should be placed. Various inscriptions, monograms, and other elements were sometimes added.

Listings of Notes

There are various elements to each bank and note in this book. Not every note will have the same or all of these characteristics. For ease of communication, description, and inventory, "Whitman numbers" have been assigned to the various notes.

Town / Town information: The name of and a brief historical sketch of the city or town in which the bank was located.

Bank name: The name of the bank. This is usually the name as imprinted on notes. Often on a note "The" will be the preface. "And" in a bank title is used in bank charters and is used here, as in Farmers and Merchants Bank. However, some notes and many numismatic listings use an ampersand (&) instead. It is numismatic practice to drop punctuation, to use Citizens instead of Citizens', for example. On some notes the name of the town is added to the title, such as the Farmers Bank of River City or the Farmers Bank in River City. Some notes of a given bank have such suffixes and others do not. They are not used here unless they are a main part of the title as boldly printed on a note, such as Smithville Bank of Commerce or Greenville Grocers Bank.

Date of operation: Years of existence, from the bank's charter date until it ceased operations, such as 1851–1865. Sometimes a bank did not begin operations until a year or two after it was chartered.

History: A synopsis of the history of the bank during its note-issuing period. Often much additional information can be found in historical texts or on the Internet and makes an interesting pursuit.

Numismatic commentary: Comments on the bank, the notes' overall availability, and more. In this volume C. John Ferreri was among those who assisted with this content.

Note listing: Divided into sections by Valid Issues (genuine notes from functioning banks), Issues (spurious notes from non-functioning or fraudulent banks), and Non-Valid Issues (notes from genuine banks that were later counterfeited, raised, made spurious by fraudsters, altered, etc.). The sample listing below is from the Abington Bank, Abington, Massachusetts:

$1 • W-MA-010-001-G010a TD

Overprint: Red ONE. ***Engraver:*** Rawdon, Wright, Hatch & Edson / New England Bank Note Co. ***Comments:*** H-Unlisted. Similar to W-MA-010-001-G010. Oct. __, 185_. 1850s.

Rarity: URS-1
G $1,000

$1: Denomination of the note shown.

W-MA-010-001-G010a

W: Whitman number. This number is a sortable code unique to each bank and note.

MA: Abbreviation for the state under study.

010: Numerical designation for the Abington Bank, Abington. Other banks have different numbers.

001: The denomination in dollars.

G010a: G indicates a good or valid note. Other categories are indicated thus: C (counterfeit); R (raised); S (spurious); N (not-attributed); A (altered). 010a is the specific note shown. Notes are listed in a bank-series by increments of 10 in order of denomination—a "porous" system so new discoveries can be added if needed. Terminal letters following the numerical designation, in this example "a," indicate variations of a note: a series of different colored overprints, tints, payees, etc., all on the same design of note. Thus the first type of a note will have no letter, the second an "a," the third a "b," the fourth a "c," and so on as necessary.

TD: Photographic image of an actual note in a collection, museum, or other location. Each photograph shown identifies its original source, when known, by an abbreviation at the upper right-hand corner of the image. A list of these creditors can be found at the front of the volume.

Vignette description: Primarily divided into Left, Center, Bottom center, and Right, these describe what is seen on the face of the note. Other descriptors include Overprint, Tint, Back, Payee, Engraver, and Comments, which includes other details about the note. For notes that are not illustrated, descriptions are given—based on information, when available, from contemporary bank-note reporters, counterfeit detectors, and other listings. Some are partial or may even prove to be inaccurate if an actual note is discovered. PSSP refers to a note of the Patent Stereotype Steel Plate by Jacob Perkins or his successor, the New England Bank Note Co. (see volume 1 for details). Illustrated notes will not have the primary descriptions included.

Rarity and Value: Estimate of the number of notes in existence today and the typical market value of a note at the time of publication. The figure indicates the center of a range. As an example, $400 suggests a range of about $350 to $450. Included as available.

Rarity (URS) Ratings

The Universal Rarity Scale

The Universal Rarity Scale uses a simple geometric progression of numbers by doubling the preceding value for each successive "rank": 1, 2, 4, 8, 16, 32, etc. (see the rightmost of each number pair), with the higher numbers rounded off for simplicity. Introduced in 1993, this has been widely used in various publications since that time. It is not copyrighted.

URS-1 = 1 known, unique
URS-2 = 2 known
URS-3 = 3 or 4
URS-4 = 5 to 8
URS-5 = 9 to 16
URS-6 = 17 to 32
URS-7 = 33 to 64
URS-8 = 65 to 124
URS-9 = 125 to 249
URS-10 = 250 to 499
URS-11 = 500 to 999
URS-12 = 1,000 to 1,999
URS-13 = 2,000 to 3,999
URS-14 = 4,000 to 7,999

Population Estimates

Drawing from authoritative catalogs, input from dealers and collectors, and other sources, rarity estimates have been given for many notes. In the past there have been many instances in which additional examples of previously rare notes have been found or new information has been learned. This will continue to be the case. Accordingly, some notes may become more plentiful than now listed. Many estates and other holdings with notes have not as of yet been examined or surveyed. To paraphrase an old comment, if Jones was not seen at a football game, he still might have been there.

Factors Affecting Present-Day Rarity

Some obsolete notes are very common. Others are so rare that only one or two exist. In some cases, a note may have been described in a bank-note reporter or other early reference, but no physical examples are known to exist. Such notes are assigned a Rarity listing of *None known*. Still others are so intangible that a guess has not been made as to their rarity; these are given a dash (—) as their Rarity listing.

If a bank was well-run and had no difficulties, its notes were usually redeemed at par. Sometimes these were burned—as mandated for banks in the state of Maine. There are many Maine notes that were once in circulation by the thousand but for which few are known today. In other states, notes were burned or were canceled at the option of the directors. In many instances quantities of canceled notes were saved, and later generations of collectors and dealers obtained them.

Many banks failed or otherwise could not redeem their notes. Spurious banks did not redeem any currency. Bills of such banks can be very common today. Quantities of unissued remainder notes, often as original sheets, exist for some banks. With increasing demand, many of the sheets have been cut apart. Notes of certain banks are extremely common as Uncirculated remainders, but signed and issued notes are rare and much more valuable. Original sheets can be collected as a specialty and are listed in this book. However, as they are not convenient to display and as the four notes to a sheet have been worth more individually in the past, most have been cut apart, as noted.

Learning More

Collecting obsolete bank notes can be a fascinating pursuit. Scarce and rare bills can often be obtained for fractions of the cost of comparably rare coins. With modest financial means it is often possible to build a first-class collection of notes from a particular area or with a particular theme.

As you have read to this point, you know that notes can be complex—and to an enthusiast, wonderfully so. Your enjoyment can be enriched by learning more. Whitman Publishing offers three key volumes that are guaranteed to please:

Volume 1 of the *Whitman Encyclopedia of Obsolete Paper Money* series is an in-depth study of obsolete paper money, how it was conceived, created, and distributed. Chapters go into great detail concerning engravers, vignettes, counterfeiting, and more. It is probably correct to say that if you spend a few evenings with your copy, you will be well on your way to becoming an expert. This book is a companion to the volume you are now holding and has been designed to complement it with much additional information.

Obsolete Paper Money Issued by Banks in the United States 1782–1866, published in 2006, is another essential volume on your way to becoming an expert and smart buyer.

The third book in the Whitman suite is *100 Greatest American Currency Notes*, a "for fun" volume that includes many different types of paper money with many obsolete bills featured.

Bank Note Reporter, issued monthly by Krause Publications, is filled with news and offerings. *Paper Money*, the journal of the Society of Paper Money Collectors, has much valuable information and many research articles.

The Professional Currency Dealers Association (PCDA) has dozens of members and opens the door to buying notes. It is strongly recommended that unless you are aware of special qualifications, you avoid buying notes on the Internet or other nonprofessional sources without an iron-clad money-back guarantee.

Obsolete notes are meant to be enjoyed. With some study of historical books and newspapers on the Internet or in a library, a single note can be your passport to a lot of ownership pleasure.

The Obsolete Bank Notes of Massachusetts

State Banking in Massachusetts

The Colonial Era

The Massachusetts Bay Colony, which incorporated much of what is now New England, was a pioneer in the American monetary system. The Massachusetts General Court authorized the first coinage of our country in 1652. From that year until the early 1780s, various silver denominations were struck at a mint in Boston. Perhaps the most familiar of these to numismatists are the Pine Tree shillings.

There seem to have been banks, or at least projected banks, in Massachusetts during the early days, according to scattered accounts. In 1688 John Blackwell was granted the privilege of erecting and managing a bank of credit. He was also permitted to issue bills on the security of real and personal estate. However, no such bills are known today.[1]

The first paper money issued by an American colony consisted of notes authorized December 10, 1690, by the Massachusetts Bay Colony. Before that time there were other types of money in use, ranging from corn to musket balls and cows to furs. Wampum beads used in trade with Indians (Native Americans) had assigned values as well. Silver and gold coins from Europe and the Spanish-controlled colonies in Central and South America facilitated commerce. The colony also issued many of its own notes in various series during the 18th century, including bills from plates engraved by Paul Revere.

In 1740 a large number of Boston merchants and others banded together to create the Land Bank, which seems to have issued £120,000 in bills and to have arranged dozens of mortgages, among other banking activities. The royal governor frowned on the action and warned citizens not to accept the currency. This was to no avail, and the court and other papers from that point up to 1760 show that many transactions occurred.[2]

Early State-Chartered Banks

This state had an early entry into American banking: the Massachusetts Bank was chartered on February 7, 1784, the backers having been inspired by the success of the Bank of North America in Philadelphia, which had been chartered on March 8, 1782, two months after it had actually commenced business. The Massachusetts Bank was thus the second banking institution to be established in the United States. Business began on July 5, 1784, by which time $253,500 of the authorized $300,000 capital had been paid in. Shares were priced at $500, a very large figure at the time, to restrict wide ownership by the general public. The Manufactory House, a building that had been used for other purposes, was purchased for $4,000 and became the bank's headquarters. It was well situated with 125 feet fronting on Common (now Tremont) Street. The bank issued bills in denominations of $1.50, $2.50, $3.50, $4.50, $6, $7, $8, $9, $15, $25, $30, $35, and $40. Certain of the denominations were familiar to the public, as some of the Continental Currency notes, by then nearly worthless, had similar imprints.

In 1791 Congress chartered the Bank of the United States. Headquartered in Philadelphia, it was to have branches in the larger cities, including Boston. The Boston branch opened in 1792 with offices on State Street. The cashier drew a salary of $1,600 per year. Notes printed in Philadelphia—which were of a common design that was used for all branches—were issued by the Boston office. These are extreme rarities today. Among the directors was Joseph Barrell, who in 1787 had been a backer of the famous voyages of the *Columbia* and *Lady Washington*, which sailed out of Boston Harbor to the Pacific. Commemorative medals were issued for the occasion.

The next Massachusetts state charter was for the Union Bank, Boston, which was granted in 1792 with $1,200,000 in capital to be paid in specie (gold or silver coins). The state took $400,000 worth and named it as the official depository for its funds. The bank was required to loan funds to the state in an amount up to $100,000 at an interest rate not to exceed 5 percent. In the same year the state mandated that no bank could issue bills with a face value of less than $5. This law was the first of many regulations over the years designed to promote the use of coins for small transactions.

That same year, the new Philadelphia Mint of 1792 had yet to strike any coins for circulation, Continental Currency bills were in disrepute, and most commercial transactions were conducted in gold and silver coins, especially of Spanish-American and European countries. Newspapers published lists of "prices current" giving exchange values for the foreign coins.

In 1795 two more banks were incorporated. The Nantucket Bank, located on an island off the coast famed for its whaling industry, was chartered for $100,000. On June 20 of that year, someone with false keys entered the bank and made off with "a considerable sum of money in dollars, crowns, and some gold." A reward of $1,000 was posted.[3] In 1796 two men were arrested in Philadelphia, implicated in the burglary, and put in jail. One escaped soon afterward. They said they had buried the money on a nearby island and later dug it up, but none was recovered. The crime was a sensation and widely reported. The loss was placed at about $10,000—a fortune in those times.

The Merrimac Bank in Newburyport, a busy maritime trading center, had a capital authorized to be at least $70,000 but not more than $150,000. This bank remained important for decades afterward. By special exception, both this bank and the Nantucket Bank were permitted to issue bills as low as $2.

Bills of this early era were issued from hand-engraved copper plates and were rather crude in their design compared to later issues. They were easily counterfeited by making false plates or by hand-drawing with pen and ink. Typical of many newspaper notices on this subject is this from the *Hampshire Gazette*, published in Northampton, Massachusetts, on October 18, 1797:

A Caution

> The public are cautioned against counterfeit five dollar bills of the Massachusetts Bank, dated January the 1st, 1795; two of which have been exhibited to the directors of said bank, and are so badly executed as to must render their detection easy to anyone in the smallest degree conversant with bank bills. The paper is thin and ordinary, even as to suffer the ink to soak through and cause an appearance on the back very different from the true bills; while the general face and complexion of them must excite instant apprehension and lead directly to the discovery of the forgery. . . .
>
> Ten dollar counterfeit bills of the Union Bank have also been discovered and brought to that bank. They appear to be executed by the same engraver as those of the Massachusetts Bank and were found in the hands of the same person. The description of the false bills of the Massachusetts Bank applies in almost every particular to the false bills of the Union Bank. Those of the Union Bank which have been detected are of the date October 1, 1792. . . .

Banking in the Early 19th Century

In the early years of the new century, other banks were chartered. By June 1805, there were 16 authorized banks in business in the state with a combined capital of $5,760,000 (of which $5,460,000 had been paid in). Banks were allowed to issue paper money amounting to double their paid-in capital.

The Embargo Act of 1807, later remembered by many historians as one of the greatest mistakes of the Jefferson administration, restricted maritime commerce. At the time American vessels were being intercepted by British and some French ships; their sailors were captured and their cargos summarily stolen. As a result, the act forbade ships from engaging in anything other than coastal trade. This decision wreaked hardship on all coastal areas and on New England in particular. Along with the ensuing Non-Intercourse Act, the Embargo Act forced the failure of many New England banks, among which was the Nantucket Bank earlier mentioned.

Meanwhile, many coins disappeared from circulation and went into the hands of hoarders. Many small-denomination bills, some legitimate, others not, flooded the channels of commerce. Counterfeiting became endemic. In 1809 the discounts on legitimate bank notes in terms of coins ranged from 10 percent to 50 percent or more in Boston. On January 1, 1810, the state Legislature enacted a law providing a penalty of 2 percent per month, payable by banks to holders of their bills, if they failed to redeem the notes promptly in coins. As a general rule, this and other regulations regarding currency over the years were loosely enforced. In 1811 a rechartering of most banks in the state reduced the amount of notes a bank could issue to 150 percent of its capital.

Jacob Perkins

In Newburyport, Jacob Perkins, a skilled engraver and artisan, entered the bank-note printing business at the turn of the century. By 1803 he had devised a method of engraving on soft steel and then hardening it, a method which permitted plates to produce many more impressions than the copper versions then in wide use. He also devised a transfer press whereby engravings could be reproduced, a process known as siderography. Later, he made a cylinder die in circular form, patented in 1813, which was a great improvement in siderography.

In the *Newburyport Herald*, March 8, 1805, an advertisement by Perkins included this:

Stereotype Plates for Banks

> The patentee of the Stereotype Plates for the impression of bank bills informs the public that he has constantly on hand ready-made plates (the name of the bank and town excepted), and will be happy to supply banks on the shortest notice. His terms are reasonable and uniform, the plates well executed, and he has the authority of many eminent artists, as well as the sanction of experience, to say that bills impressed from these plates cannot be counterfeited. No attempts of the kind have ever yet been made, tho' it has been adopted and is now used by sixteen banks in New England.
>
> Encouraged by the success of his principle, and the increasing demand for his plates, he has at a great expense improved his former invention by adding beauty to security. He has formed a steel plate of sixty-four dies, impressed by the same dies now used for copperplates, neatly fitted and keyed together in a strong iron frame. The name of the bank and town and the denomination of the bill are removed and substituted at pleasure.
>
> The standing parts of the plates are elegantly engraved by Mr. James Akin. When completed there will be from six to seven hundred days' work in the plate, and being

> well hardened, it will, without injury, print more paper than will be used by the United States. It is now nearly finished, and any orders addressed to him at Newburyport will be punctually honored.
>
> *Jacob Perkins*

No patent for the above has been located. Seemingly, by this time Perkins was involved in multiple businesses. James Akin, the engraver of what would be billed as the Perkins Patent Stereotype Steel Plate, had recently moved from Salem to Newburyport, where he would remain until about 1808.

The basic Perkins bank-note innovation consisted of a plate of rectangular shape on which a design was impressed, the design being more ornate than used earlier. Although there were variations, a popular early motif consisted of an approximately elliptical ("watermelon" shaped) border composed of lettering for the denomination and floral decorations, outside of which the denomination was given as a number in each of the four corners. Within the ellipse was standard lettering, often a plate letter (sometimes designated as Check Plate A, etc.), and a place for the number, payee, date, and signatures of the bank officers.

Rectangular openings in the plate provided spaces where steel slugs could be inserted with the bank name, town, and state. By switching the slugs, notes could be made for many different banks. Later versions had large areas on the face of the note filled with tiny repeated letters indicating the denomination, in italic type, such as *Five Dollars Five Dollars Five Dollars*, etc.

In 1806 Perkins addressed a memorial to the Massachusetts General Court suggesting that the state mandate use of his plates to deter counterfeiting. The idea met with a warm reception, and although it was not enacted into law at the time, much favorable publicity resulted.

In 1808 Jacob's brother Abraham, a storekeeper in Newburyport, relinquished that trade and joined in the bank-note engraving and printing business. Soon, a small three-story brick factory was erected on land behind Jacob's home on Fruit Street.[4]

In 1809 the Massachusetts Banking Act was passed, mandating use, beginning in July, of the Perkins plate for denominations from $1 to $5. The $5 denomination was to have the Perkins check plate on the back. The use of this extra security was optional for other denominations. In actual practice, some $5 notes were made with this feature, but many were not. Higher denominations were made as well. This type of note is known as a Patent Stereotype Steel Plate bill, abbreviated as PSSP.

Many New England banks used PSSP notes, with Connecticut being an exception. The most distant bank was in Detroit.

Perkins filled orders for all comers, it seems, including from bank officers who ordered quantities of currency far in excess of the amounts permitted by their charters The Berkshire Bank of Pittsfield and the Northampton Bank, both controlled by the scheming Andrew Dexter Jr. (of the Farmers Exchange Bank of Gloucester, Rhode Island, infamy), were good customers of Perkins. These two banks failed: upon examination, one bank was found to have about $30 in its vaults and the other absolutely nothing.

Despite a lot of publicity to the contrary, the PSSP notes proved to be a boon to counterfeiters, who made up their own plates with slugs to be inserted, creating false notes for multiple banks.

Effects of the War of 1812

The despised Embargo Act and the Non-Intercourse Act continued to cause hardships for all New England ports and, consequently, the banks in port towns. British (and to a lesser extent French) interference with American shipping, now on a reduced scale due to restrictions, reached a breaking point. On June 18, 1814, Congress declared war against Great Britain. For most citizens in New England, economic matters went from bad to worse.

For the next three years, the War of 1812, as it became known, saw many military engagements, including naval battles fought in the Atlantic Ocean, Lake Champlain, and Lake Erie. For many Americans this was a war that few wanted. It was felt that the maritime problems with England had been blown far out of proportion and that other means could have been used to settle them.

Countless gold coins were exported despite the blockade of American ports at various times by British ships.[5] Certain banking interests were charged with aiding the enemy by making coins available to them under various subterfuges, including shipments to Canada, which was prohibited, as it was considered trade with "the contiguous British provinces."

Niles' Weekly Register, February 5, 1814, included this:

> The *Albany Argus* says, "Such has been the demand for specie in this city, for the Canada market, and for the banks, that ten percent premium has been paid for it in exchange for paper."
>
> We are satisfied that mighty efforts will be made to supply the enemy with this needful article; but would hope the vigilance of our officer may render the commerce too hazardous. British government bills are at a great discount in Canada, as, indeed, they are in all parts of Europe and America, and the bait is tempting.

A related article in the same issue reported:

> A quantity of specie, about $140,000, was boxed up in New-York some days ago and forwarded for Boston, ostensibly for the "New-England Bank." Mr. Gelston, collector of the port of New-York, seized it, under a clause of the embargo law, had it brought back and deposited in the Manhattan Bank. When the collector shall be satisfied that the money was really destined for Boston, he will, doubtless restore it.
>
> In the meantime the stockholders of the New-England Bank have petitioned the Legislature of Massachusetts to demand of the president of the United States the restitution of the money illegally seized by the collector of the port of New York, and the punishment of the offender. . . .

In the summer of 1814, British troops fought on land in Maryland and continued to Washington, where the Capitol, Executive Mansion (White House), and other buildings were burned. The troops boarded their ships and headed to Baltimore, where a bombardment of Fort McHenry ensued (inspiring "The Star Spangled Banner"). The effort was not a success, and the ships headed back to England. The war was over, and in December a peace treaty was signed. News traveled slowly, and on January 8, 1815, General Andrew Jackson was successful against British forces in the Battle of New Orleans. The combatants were not aware that the conflict had officially ended.

During the war the various Massachusetts banks were under pressure to redeem their notes in coins, which was nearly always done. Unlike the situation elsewhere in America, none suspended payments, mainly because of the penalty to be levied if this was done. In 1814 there were 21 banks in operation in the state.

Later in the Decade

It was thought that peace and the removal of shipping restrictions would bring a revival of the economy. This did not happen, and many banks across America were in trouble. Coins disappeared into the hands of hoarders, resulting in a flood of fractional bills issued by banks, usually printed in haste at a local or regional shop.

In August 1816, the Dedham Bank, Massachusetts, issued a large quantity of bills payable at par at the Middletown Bank in the Connecticut town of the same name. Bills could be exchanged for coins at the Dedham facility but only at a 1 percent discount. This idea, as strange as it may seem, was widely practiced by various American banks over a long period of years. The Massachusetts Legislature effectively put an end to the practice in December by passing a law prohibiting distant places being used as redemption centers unless the bills were also exchanged at the bank's home office at the same rate.

Coins remained scarce. As bills had to be redeemed promptly in coins by law, the banks issued a relatively low amount of currency. In June 1816, the capital of banks in the state was $11,475,000, but only $2,134,690 in bills was in circulation, a tiny fraction of the 150 percent of capital that was legally authorized.[6]

These strict rules resulted in great strength among Massachusetts banks in comparison to the situation in nearly all other states, most of which were dotted with bank failures. The numismatic result is that bills of Massachusetts banks of this decade range from scarce to rare as a class, while those of failed banks in other states are common.

In 1816 Congress chartered the second Bank of the United States for a period of 20 years, at which time the charter might be extended. In July of that year, subscription offices to raise $28,000,000 in capital were opened in various cities, including Boston. The Boston branch opened on January 1, 1817, and began giving loans on February 10 to those who had revenue bonds as collateral. The general public was accommodated beginning on February 20. President William Gray drew a salary of $1,500 per year, and cashier Samuel Frothingham received $3,000. The Boston branch offered paper money of a common design used by other branches and printed in Philadelphia. Today these notes are extremely rare.

The Suffolk Bank System

Boston was the focal point of banking in New England. Bills from the other states—Maine, New Hampshire, Vermont, Rhode Island, and Connecticut—were actively traded there at a discount from their value in the towns and cities of issue. New York City was another trading venue for New England notes at even deeper discounts.

In April 1824, the Suffolk Bank in Boston proposed setting up a clearing house for New England bills. A committee met with other Boston banks in a successful effort to gain their cooperation. A letter of proposal stated:

> Of the whole incorporated banking capital of New England, amounting to less than twenty millions of dollars, the eleven banks in this city possess ten million one hundred and fifty thousand. That estimating the circulation of the country banks at only seventy-five percent, of their capital, which they believe to be a moderate computation, these banks furnish seven million five hundred thousand dollars of the circulating medium, while the banks in the city with a capital equal to all the rest, keep in what may be fairly termed permanent circulation only three hundred thousand dollars.

The Suffolk Bank stated that in the space of three months it had received for exchange nearly $1,000,000 in notes from "country banks" (the term used for banks that were not in large cities or were distant from Boston). These were received at a discount and then given to agents who would travel over sometimes difficult roads to redeem the bills in coins at the offices of the issuing banks. This was a profitable enterprise for the Suffolk Bank.

If other banks would sign up with Suffolk, there would be a great economy in transporting and redeeming the bills. Six Boston banks did this and set up a fund of $300,000 to implement it. Bills received by the other banks were sent to Suffolk under an agreement perfected on May 24, 1824.

This news caused great consternation among distant banks, as the longer their bills could remain in circulation, the more money a bank could use for other purposes such as loans. It was common practice to ship notes in bulk, discounted, to distant banks, with the expectation that it would be a long time until they were presented for redemption. As an example, the Hillsborough Bank in Amherst, New Hampshire, made a point to ship large quantities of its bills to the Marietta Bank in distant Ohio, hoping that few would be returned.

The Suffolk Bank system, as it was known, was eventually viewed with favor by most New England banks, once they realized that having a clearing house in Boston that received its bills at only a small discount was a boon to their business. Most banks joined the system, placing deposits of $2,000 or more (depending upon capital and volume of notes) with the Suffolk Bank to make it possible to redeem their bills near face value. Banks shipped bundles of miscellaneous bills to Boston at frequent intervals and were immediately credited with the proceeds.[7]

The Suffolk Bank system was unique in America at the time and facilitated the public's acceptance of bills from distant banks and gave the notes a greater exchange value. Whenever a shipment of notes contained a counterfeit, the Suffolk Bank prominently stamped it as such and returned it to the bank that sent it. This policy had the benefit of forcing bank tellers to be alert in order to detect fraudulent bills.

Elsewhere on the Banking Scene

The American monetary system underwent several crises in the late 1810s and early 1820s, mainly due to variations in agriculture, commerce, and international trade. In 1820 the international value of gold bullion rose, and it cost more than face value to mint the two gold coin denominations then in use—the $2.50 quarter eagle and the $5 half eagle. From 1821 until the authorized weight of gold coins was reduced by the Act of June 28, 1834, no such coins were seen in circulation. Production continued at the Philadelphia Mint on behalf of depositors who valued the coins at their intrinsic worth and used them in international trade. If a $5 gold coin cost $5.05 to mint, it was of no consequence, as it was valued at the increased amount when it was received in another country.

As a result of this, the largest circulating federal coins in the United States from 1821 to 1834 were half dollars. In addition, various silver and gold coins of Spanish-American and European countries were legal tender at various assigned values.

By January 1, 1825, 49 banks had been chartered in Massachusetts with a total authorized capital of $20,800,000. Six of these had failed, and three others never opened for business. In operation were 40 banks with a combined authorized capital of $14,305,000, of which $13,300,000 was said to have been paid in.

From 1824 to 1829 there were only seven new banks chartered in the state. Although Massachusetts had strict laws on the books, enforcement was casual at best. Capital was to be paid in gold or silver coins (specie) but was often in the form of promissory notes from stockholders. There was no system of audit or verification.

This laxness changed with the Banking Law of February 28, 1829, which would apply to all future charters as well as to any existing bank extending its charter or changing its capital. Under the new regulations, banks were to have at least 50 percent of their capital paid in verifiable specie before they could commence business. Specie included any legal-tender gold or silver coins, American or foreign. No loans could be made to shareholders unless their stock subscriptions had been paid in full. Total loans secured by pledging shares of the bank's own stock could not exceed 50 percent of the paid-in capital. Currency could be circulated to the extent of 125 percent of paid-in capital. By this time most Massachusetts banks had been extremely conservative in this regard, in the aggregate issuing only a small fraction of the bills they could have paid out.

Under state law, banks continued to use only Patent Stereotype Steel Plate (PSSP) notes printed in Newburyport. Jacob Perkins had left Massachusetts in the early 1810s and had gone to Philadelphia, then on to London. The business was conducted by his brother along with staff engravers and printers.

The Farmers Bank of Belchertown

In 1825 the Farmers Bank of Belchertown, Massachusetts, was chartered by the Legislature. The authorized capital was $100,000. Its bills were printed by Perkins and were well received in commerce. At first they typically traded at a 2 percent discount from face value in places other than its home town. After it joined the Suffolk Bank system, the discount was only 1/2 of 1%. In New York City they could be exchanged at a discount ranging from 3/4 of 1% to 1%. This was the typical rate for nearly all Massachusetts banks. The following from the *Evening Post* in New York City was reprinted from the *Journal of Commerce*:

Another Bank Failure

News was received yesterday that the Farmers Bank at Belchertown has stopped payment. We were apprised of the circumstances which led to this result, but it may be sufficient to state in general that the bank having received the paper of certain gentlemen (still supposed to be responsible) to a large amount, was unable to realize the money when it was need, and was thus compelled to yield to the pressure of circumstances.

One of the principal merchants of Northampton (8 miles from Belchertown) tells us that he should be happy to purchase a quantity of the notes at 75 cents on the dollar. He is confident only that all the bills will eventually be redeemed, but also a considerable percentage paid on the stock.—*Journal of Commerce.*

An investigation held by state authorities in January 1830 revealed that the bank was insolvent by early 1829, but this was disguised by paying a three percent dividend on the stock. Rather than loaning money, the directors of the bank had borrowed large sums from local and regional people. In January 1830, the hard assets consisted of $1.25 in specie! The cashier, Theodore D. Lyman, stated that $27,822.90 in bills was in circulation, but the actual figure is unknown and was probably much larger. Perkins had a history of supplying huge quantities of unrecorded notes to fraudulent banks, no questions asked.[8]

In March 1830, the editor of the *Belchertown Sentinel* advertised that he had $2,500 in such bills "for sale at a great discount for cash" or "to be exchanged for real estate in Belchertown or its vicinity."

As was true of other worthless notes, the bills of the Farmers Bank continued to be bought and sold by exchange houses and brokers, particularly in New York City. These were bought by crooks who would peddle them in small amounts to merchants and others who either were not aware of their nature or who simply took in bills regardless of quality and then paid them out again to other customers.

The Jacksonian Era

The decade of the 1830s was very tumultuous. Andrew Jackson, who was inaugurated as president on March 4, 1829, was strongly challenged by his opponents under different party designations, including Whigs beginning in 1833. The Indian Removal Act of 1830 ejected Cherokees and other Native Americans from their traditional tribal lands in the Carolinas and forced them to relocate in the Midwest. Thousands died, especially on the infamous "Trail of Tears."

The second Bank of the United States, chartered in 1816, was called "The Monster" by many, especially those in the banking community who resented that its currency traded at par everywhere in America, including at its many branches, while bills of state-chartered banks were exchanged at a discount. Jackson took a stand against the bank, and it seemed that its future would be in doubt when its charter came up for renewal or extension in 1836. To settle the matter, certain of Jackson's adversaries, including Daniel Webster and Henry Clay, had Congress pass legislation in 1832 to authorize the renewal far in advance. Although it passed both houses, Jackson vetoed it. The fate of the Bank of the United States was sealed, and for the next several years certain operations were wound down, including the Boston office. Amid much criticism, federal deposits were moved to "pet banks" selected by the administration. In 1836 the remaining branches closed their doors. Jackson's actions were lampooned by dozens of cartoons. He was unpopular with much of the "establishment," including educators and moneyed interests, but was loved by the general public.

In the meantime, during the early 1830s, the economy was robust in most of America, including in Massachusetts where the benefits of restrictive tariffs in 1828 decreased imports and spurred manufacturing, such as in the many mills in the state. In 1832 the New England Bank Note Co. was formed in Boston and assumed the business conducted by the Perkins interests in Newburyport. The PSSP notes continued to be made for all Massachusetts banks as mandated by law and for any banks in other states that desired them.

Steam power came into increasing use in factories, and railroads were a growth industry as construction of new canals faded. In contrast, there was a chill in the commerce of Eastern cities that seemed to have no cure. In January 1834, a mass meeting of merchants was held in Boston, after which a petition was sent to Congress urging the prompt restoration of deposits to the Bank of the United States.

On the frontier—the land west of Pennsylvania—the government opened up millions of acres of land to settlers, who could buy acreage cheaply, usually paying for it in various bank bills or promissory notes. While much land was bought by settlers who planned to operate farms or set up residences in towns, speculators were the dominant force in the market. Deeds changed hands at ever-increasing prices. This brought great prosperity to the Midwest, mainly to the speculators. To stop the cycle, on July 11, 1836, President Jackson issued the Specie Circular, a document stating that henceforth federal lands had to be paid for in gold and silver coins.

Despite generally good times, the mercantile interests in some larger cities including Boston and New York saw a softening of business. On the other hand, the closing of the Bank of the United States spurred the chartering of many new banks by various state legislatures. Most citizens felt secure. In November 1836, Martin Van Buren, Jackson's vice president, was elected president on the Democratic ticket.

During 1836, as stated in a memorial of the Boston Chamber of Commerce to the Legislature in January 1837, the mercantile community was "subjected to a pressure in their financial operations unexampled in its severity and duration." For more than a year the rate of interest "ranged from twelve to thirty-six percent per annum." The memorialists believed the chief cause was to be found in the operation of the usury laws and recommended their total or partial repeal. "It is well known," said the memorial, "that they are publicly and generally evaded by circuitous transactions through agents; the difficulty of obtaining money has been thereby increased, and the price of it enhanced." "Many of our capitalists, from an unwillingness to evade these laws, have sent large sums to other states, particularly New York, where the legal rate of interest is higher. Large amounts have thus been withdrawn when most needed."[9] It was hardly to be expected that such a memorial would be heeded.

Uncertainty prevailed. With speculators no longer on the scene, the business atmosphere in the Midwest was one of insecurity. Unrest increased in cities as employment declined while prices rose. New York City in particular was distressed. In December 1835, a huge conflagration leveled much of the financial district: nearly 700 buildings were destroyed, and many businesses were wiped out. The premises of Rawdon, Wright, Hatch & Edson, America's leading bank-note printer, located in the Merchants Exchange, was a total loss. The next year was unsettled in the city. In early 1837 business and employment worsened while prices of commodities rose. Barrels of flour that had once sold for $7 and had already risen in price up to $12 jumped to $20. Bread, an essential of life, became unaffordable to many. Rumors spread, meetings were held, and speakers encouraged action. On February 10, a crowd assembled in Chatham Square and marched to storm the premises of Eli Hart & Co. and S.H. Herrick & Co., flour dealers who were accused of hoarding and driving up prices. Quantities of warehoused flour and wheat were destroyed.

Hard Times

On March 4, 1837, Martin Van Buren was inaugurated as president. Jackson left Washington and headed for The Hermitage, his plantation near Nashville, Tennessee. He left behind an era that, for the most part, was prosperous. In the same month, the prices of many stocks on Wall Street fell. Holders of paper money became increasingly concerned with the news of bankruptcies, increased unemployment, and generally unsettled conditions; they redeemed many bills for gold and silver coins.

In Massachusetts the Legislature set about investigating several new banks that had been chartered in 1836 but whose operations seemed questionable: the Chelsea, Kilby, Middling Interest, and Lafayette banks. The bank cashiers must have presented documents that satisfied the examiners, for all were allowed to continue business. However, each of these banks closed its doors in the next few years with losses to the holders of their currency. The Chelsea Bank folded on April 12, 1837, with just $36.71 in cash available to redeem over $110,000 of its bills![10] This caused great concern in Boston, and many business activities were curtailed.

Officially inaugurating what became known as the Hard Times era, New York City banks suspended specie payments on May 10, 1837. The next day, Boston bankers met in Faneuil Hall and reluctantly agreed to do the same thing. On May 12, the suspension took effect. Almost immediately, gold and silver coins became worth a premium of 10 to 13 percent. To facilitate trade, many merchants and others issued copper tokens with advertising or political messages. Most were the size of a copper cent and traded for that value but cost just $6 to $7 per 1,000 wholesale. Paper scrip notes were also issued in abundance. Massachusetts law prohibited banks from issuing bills for less than $1. In 1837 the state enacted a penalty of $50 per note for any individual issuing fractional bills. To facilitate making change, this spawned such unusual denominations as $1.25, $1.50, and $1.75. Terry, Pelton & Co., relatively new on the

Boston bank-note printing scene, produced many of these in addition to the output of the New England Bank Note Co.

On September 1, 1837, the *New York Journal of Commerce* ran this:

> Banks have been more freely incorporated in Massachusetts than in any other state, if we except Rhode Island. Charters have been given so freely that the necessity of getting them was but a form, for they have been granted whenever asked under circumstances which gave any tolerable warrant for the grant. Charters have been granted until chartered monopolies have been brought upon the ground of free trade; for the charters are so numerous that anybody can have one.
>
> The business has in fact been overdone, and free trade will probably cause a considerable number of the charters to be given up, and the capitals divided. So there will be charters to be had gratis. We know that a considerable number of the Massachusetts banks are seriously considering the question of winding up their affairs. . . .

The large and important Lafayette Bank folded in July 1837. The legislature appointed a special committee to investigate the affairs of this bank. A report issued on January 6, 1838, related that very little of the stated $150,000 in capital was ever paid in. $124,558.50 worth of bills were reported to have been circulated in addition to unstated amounts not recorded. False reports had been filed, the books of the bank "had been in disarray since the beginning of business," and at the time of collapse, the officers of the bank were trying to work out a currency distribution scheme with a New York City bank.[11] In July the Franklin Bank also collapsed.

On January 11, 1838, the Commonwealth Bank of Boston failed. With outstanding paper money and other liabilities worth $915,946, this was the greatest loss to the public to date in the state's history. To make matters worse, the Commonwealth Bank was a "pet bank" that the Treasury Department had designated as a depository for federal funds. Contemporary accounts laid part of the problem to the recent death of bank president John K. Simpson, who was heavily indebted to the institution. Simpson, in collusion with the cashier, had issued $120,000 in bills for which no record had been kept and had secretly reissued $40,000 in notes that were stated to have been burned.[12] On January 16, the Middlesex Bank of Cambridge closed up. Many others experienced difficulties. In 1837 the Legislature revoked the charters of three banks, followed by 10 more in 1838, but this did not stop the flood of worthless notes. The prime supplier was the New England Bank Note Co., successor to the Perkins interests, which accepted orders for bills and never asked questions. In 1838 the Board of Bank Commissioners was established to audit and analyze the financial documents of banks in the state.

In 1838 many Massachusetts banks began to redeem their smaller bills (up to $3) in coin. The City Bank of Lowell was chartered at $75,000 and immediately set about ordering quantities of bills from the New England Bank Note Co. Soon, banking authorities learned that it had borrowed on short term some specie from Boston and had IOUs for the rest of its capital, and there were no assets at all. In July 1838, an injunction was issued forbidding it to open. That same month the Roxbury Bank, a phony operation run by swindlers in New York City, was enjoined from continuing. However, this did not deter its owners from passing out a further $50,000 or so of bills, including some of the popular $1.25, $1.50, and $1.75 denominations. By August 1838, nearly all banks in Massachusetts had resumed exchanging coins for their paper money.

From 1837 to 1844, the latter year seeing the resumption of strong economic conditions in America, 32 Massachusetts banks failed or forfeited their charters, a sorry showing among New England states. These defunct institutions included five of the 15 incorporated in 1831, two of the 16 chartered in 1832, six of the 14 new banks of 1833, and 11 of the 32 incorporated in 1836. During this time only two new banks were chartered—the Cabot in Springfield (1837) and the Fishermens Bank, Provincetown (1839). Neither ever went into operation. Bills from these failed banks form a sizeable proportion of the collectible notes in numismatic hands today. In 1844 there were 103 active banks in the state, a reduction from the number a decade earlier.

Recovery

After the Hard Times era there was not much interest in forming new banks. Noted by historian Dudley P. Bailey Jr.:

> For the five years 1845–49, little new capital was asked for or authorized for banking purposes. Twenty-five new banks were incorporated with $3,300,000 of capital. Of these 25 banks, three, the Hampshire and Franklin, of Amherst, the Bank of Barre, and the Cape Cod Bank, of Provincetown, with $300,000 of capital, never went into operation.[13]

The Legislature mandated that all banks chartered before 1849 had to apply for new charters in 1851, at which time their affairs could be studied. At that time, of the 115 banks involved, all but the Manufacturers Bank of Georgetown (which was first located in Rowley and then in 1838 moved to nearby Georgetown) continued in business. This bank was solvent, liquidated its affairs, and returned a profit to its shareholders.

In 1851 the Free Banking Law was passed, permitting any group of 50 or more stockholders to set up a bank with capital to be at least $100,000 and no more than $1,000,000. Half the capital had to be paid in before the bank could commence business. Bills could be issued, backed in part with securities posted with the state, totaling no less than $50,000 or no more than 25 percent of the face value, whichever amount was larger. In 1852 the number of people needed to form a bank was reduced to just 10.

Unlike the situation in many other states, in Massachusetts the new law elicited no interest from investors. It was not until the Bank of the Metropolis, Boston, opened in November 1858 that an institution was organized under its provisions. It folded in November 1863. No more than half a dozen other banks were founded under the law.[14]

By the early 1850s, the state of Massachusetts had on its books a long list of banking rules and regulations dating back many years, including these:

No bill or note can be issued by or on account of any bank, at any other place than its banking-house.

No bank is allowed to pay out from its own counter any other bills than its own.

All bills are to be issued in the name of the president, directors, and company of the bank issuing them, and to be signed by the president and cashier of the bank; but all bills signed by either the president or cashier, in circulation through the agency or neglect of any officer of the bank, must be redeemed by the corporation.

Banks are liable to pay to any bona fide holder the original amount of any of their bills which may have been altered to a larger amount in the course of circulation, notwithstanding the alteration.

Banks may issue bills under five dollars to the amount of one quarter part of their capital actually paid in; but no bank can issue bills of a less denomination than one dollar, under a penalty of one hundred dollars for each offense.

The amount of bills issued by a bank must not at any time exceed its capital actually paid in more than twenty-five per cent.

If the officers of any bank refuse or delay payment in gold or silver money of any note or bill of the bank, presented for payment in their usual hours of business, the bank will be liable to pay to the holder, as damages, at the rate of 24% a year during such delay or refusal.

As might be imagined, many rules were overlooked in practice or were not enforced. By this time the state had racked up the worst banking record by far in the Northeast in terms of problems, mainly due to there being more banks to supervise.

At the same time, 110 banks in New England conducted the Association of Banks for the Suppression of Counterfeiting to track down the passers of false bills and, among other challenges, persuade the Massachusetts Legislature to outlaw use of the easily counterfeited PSSP bills. *Banker's Magazine*, February 1852, told of a curious situation:

Counterfeiting

A singular development has taken place in regard to the special agency in Boston, for the detection of counterfeiters. An association of the banks has, for some years, appropriated quite a liberal sum annually for the suppression of counterfeiting. The Legislature of Massachusetts granted last year the sum of $2,500, annually for five years, in aid of this object.

The special agent appointed by the banks to discover the source or sources of counterfeiting, has himself been detected in engraving and printing spurious notes. He has been in the habit of buying the spurious plates from professional counterfeiters, and selling them to the Banking Association, with a view to the plates being destroyed. Sufficient evidence is brought forward to show that the agent has deceived his employers, and has contributed very largely to the numerous counterfeits that have been afloat within a year or two past. The name of this person is William W. Wilson, who is charged with counterfeiting on the Merchants' Bank, Boston, and the Tradesman's Bank, Chelsea, and having in his possession dies and bank plates for that purpose.

His case came up in the Police Court on Tuesday, 18th January, per assignment. A fifth complaint was entered against him, charging the same offences of the Housatonic Bank, after which the examination upon the previous complaint proceeded. The government produced about a dozen witnesses. Police officer Galen Holmes and Constable Wm. K. Jones detailed the circumstances of the arrest, and what implements, counterfeit bills, &c., were seized; and Mr. Pelton, an engraver, testified concerning certain bank plates and dies made by him, which passed into Wilson's possession. and by the use of which, it is alleged by the prosecution, he counterfeited bank bills.

Other News of the 1850s

In the meantime, during the 1850s there were scattered failures, the most prominent of which was the Cochituate Bank of Boston in 1854, for which the bank president had made poor investments in the South and West. Thousands of worthless notes were preserved, much to the delight of a later generation of numismatists. Several subsequent failures prompted the Legislature to revise banking laws that permitted secrecy, requiring banks to publish weekly figures of condition if located in Boston and monthly if elsewhere.

In April 1855, "some few" banks in the state omitted their quarterly dividends, as they were short of funds. The culprit proved to be unwise or slow-paying investments in the distant Midwest, where speculation in lands and businesses was active again. Such banks did little in the way of loans locally and were viewed by some to be in violation of their chartered purpose.[15] Loaning funds outside of the state in order to gain high rates of interest had been practiced by other banks for a long time.

The Panic of 1857 was precipitated by the failure of the Ohio Life Insurance and Trust Co. branch office in New York City, which handled many bank transfers and loans. Concern spread, and other banks, brokerage offices, and businesses in the financial district became distressed. "Runs" on banks took place, and a shortage of coins forced all but one bank in New York City (the Chemical Bank) to suspend specie payments on October 13. The next day all Boston banks stopped paying out coins. The malaise spread to other institutions. In Massachusetts, only one bank failed, the Western Bank of Springfield, which was closed by injunction on October 6 in the face of long-standing problems unrelated to the panic.

Banks nationwide scaled down their operations, uncertain if this was to be a repetition of the Hard Times era of the 1830s. Faced with diminished business, most of the leading bank-note printers consolidated and formed the American Bank Note Co. in March 1858. Its ABNCo. monogram was added to printing plates of the founding partners when new bills were ordered by past clients.

In 1858 there was a big fight between proponents of the Suffolk Bank system and the perceived upstart Bank of Mutual Redemption, which had been chartered in 1855 but did not begin business until three years later. The latter drew much business from banks outside of Boston. In the city of Boston, the leading banks banded together to deny the Bank of Mutual Redemption membership in the Clearing House Association. Not long after, the Suffolk Bank stated that as of November 30 it would no longer do business with "country banks," these being small institutions. By April 1859, the Bank of Mutual Redemption had 143 banks as members, about half of the institutions in New England.

The *Boston Advertiser*, August 25, 1859, told of a burglary of the house that belonged to the president of an unnamed bank, in which 200 sheets of bank bills awaiting his signature were stolen. Apparently this was far from being an isolated occurrence, as Thompson & Brothers, exchange brokers in New York City, reported that thousands of genuine notes from various banks with forged signatures had turned up in Wall Street.[16]

After the Panic of 1857, only a few new banks were formed in Massachusetts. By 1862 there were 183 of them in operation, just 10 more than at the onset of the financial crisis. After the Civil War commenced in 1861, the banks of the state continued business as normal with no problems of significance. Statewide, the banks had a surplus of $5,902,598 and held specie in their vaults to the amount of $8,877,193.[17] Both the Confederacy and the Union had a share of military victories. By December, with the war in progress and no clear conclusion in sight, many citizens began to hoard coins. By late in the month gold coins were no longer being paid out at par by banks.

After Legal Tender Notes were authorized in March 1862, these not redeemable in gold or silver coins, public concern increased. By late spring silver coins were no longer available at par, and in the second week of July one-cent pieces, with little intrinsic value, disappeared as well. Although the Massachusetts banks no longer redeemed their notes in specie, all were financially sound. Business from the summer of 1862 through 1863 was conducted by various monetary substitutes, including Postage Currency notes issued by the Treasury Department, ordinary postage stamps, which were given legal-tender status, encased postage stamps, bronze and brass cent-size tokens, and paper scrip.

Federal cents returned to circulation in 1864, but silver coins did not appear until 1876 and gold until late 1878. In 1863 the National Banking Act allowed the directors of state-chartered banks in sound condition to apply for a charter to become a National Banking Association. The state banks were dissolved and their businesses assumed by new National Banks, often with similar names. The October 1865 report of the Bank Commissioners stated that beginning with the Safety Fund Bank in 1863, 178 state-chartered banks had evolved into National Banks. Four had surrendered their charters and discontinued business. The sole exception remaining under state charter was the North Bridgewater Bank.

Notes of state banks were redeemed by their successors for a period of several years. The government enacted a law stating that after July 1, 1866, there would be a tax of 10 percent on any transactions involving state-bank notes. This tax effectively ended their circulation, although redemptions continued. Thus concluded the era of currency issued by state-chartered banks.

Most redeemed notes were burned. Others were punch canceled. Some of the latter survived to enter numismatic circles years later.

Numismatic Comments

The state of Massachusetts offers a vast panorama of obsolete bank bills ranging from prior to 1800 up to 1866. In addition to banks located in what is today considered Massachusetts, several banks that existed in the Maine District of Massachusetts, in towns such as Castine, Hallowell, and Portland, have Massachusetts imprints. After Maine became a state on March 15, 1820, banks doing business there adopted Maine addresses. Accordingly, currency issued before March 1820 is of interest to specialists in Maine as well as in Massachusetts.

Study of the Amherst Bank, Amherst, revealed that it was preceded by the formerly unknown Sunderland Bank, Sunderland, a short distance away. In 1831 the bank changed its name and moved to Amherst. Today, no bills of the Sunderland Bank have been located. In 1862 there was a boundary line adjustment in Fall River with the result that two banks that had been in Rhode Island previously were now located in Massachusetts without moving. The history of a bank can be endlessly fascinating!

As noted above, in 1809 the state mandated that all banks use PSSP notes printed by Perkins in Newburyport. This gave the currency a uniform appearance for many years afterward, in contrast to the varied motifs used by banks in other states. It became the case that the Perkins system was easy to counterfeit, causing many problems. In 1829 the Farmers Bank of Belchertown exploded (to use a popular word of the time for fraudulent banks being exposed and failing) with the result that countless tens of thousands of dollars in bills remained in circulation with no possibility of being redeemed. Today, these bills are the earliest of the state that are very common in numismatic hands.

In 1832 the Perkins business was merged into the New England Bank Note Co. in Boston, after which the PSSP notes carry that imprint. By the late 1830s, other companies were making currency for Massachusetts banks, most notably the short-lived Terry, Pelton & Co. with offices in Boston and in Providence, Rhode Island.

The Hard Times of the late 1830s caused other banks to fail, some simply because of economic conditions, others through fraud. From this point forward currency of failed banks is easily obtained by collectors today. Many of such surviving bills are in higher grades such as Fine, Very Fine, and Extremely Fine. From the 1850s through the 1860s, bills became much more varied in appearance as different firms began supplying currency, using ornate vignettes not different in concept from those used in other Eastern states at the time. Most later bills have colored overprints giving the denominations.

In 1854 the Cochituate Bank of Boston collapsed, leaving being a large quantity of bills—easily enough found today. In contrast, of the nearly 300 state-chartered banks in Massachusetts that were in operation from the late 18th century through the 1860s, 80 percent or more redeemed and destroyed their paper money. This widescale destruction is much different from the scenario for many banks of other states, where in many instances redeemed bills were canceled but kept on hand and later fell into the hands of numismatists. The unusual result is that today the signed and issued bills of the vast majority of Massachusetts banks are those that somehow were saved by chance and are in lower grades. In some instances the finest known bills exist in grades such as About Good and Good.

Some very early bills survive only as tattered paper. As noted, bills of failed banks are usually available in grades of Fine to Extremely Fine.

It is frustrating to read the accounts of many banks issuing bills of denominations from $1 to $100 or more, only to realize that not a single example is known of many varieties that were once circulated by the thousands. Among the New England states, Massachusetts differs from the other five in this regard.

Proof impressions are known for many varieties, most of which came on the market beginning with the dispersal of the long-stored American Bank Note Co. archives in Christie's memorable sales of 1990 and 1991, followed by other distributions. These offerings brought to light many designs unknown to earlier generations of numismatists. Proofs appear with regularity in auctions and always draw enthusiastic competition.

This volume covers the cities of Hallowell through Yarmouth. For Abington through Greenfield, see volume 3.

Hallowell, Massachusetts

Hallowell, a part of Massachusetts until March 15, 1820, is now in the state of Maine. The community is located in Kennebec County on the west bank of the Kennebec River. Settlers were in the district in the 17th century, but most development took place later. The town was incorporated on April 6, 1771, including at that time parts of what later became Augusta, Chelsea, Farmington, and Manchester. In the 1790s Charles Vaughan, a prosperous merchant of Boston and one of the owners of the land, sought to develop the village of Hallowell. He designed it to be an important town at the head of navigation on the Kennebec River and built a distillery and brewery with the capacity to supply all residents in New England. A flour mill was built, as were wharfs, stores, and houses. The scheme was impressive but not financially feasible, and most of the buildings decayed and were abandoned. Hallowell was chartered as a city on August 29, 1850, and divided into four wards. In 1850 the population was 4,769, reducing to an estimated 2,400 by 1857. In later years it had three shipyards, two tanneries, two machine shops, a linseed oil factory, four pail factories, two brickyards, and other enterprises including three banks.

See also Hallowell, Maine.

Hallowell and Augusta Bank {1st}

1804–1812

W-MA-1810 • W-ME-910

History: There were two entities named the Hallowell and Augusta Bank. The first was chartered on March 6, 1804, by the Massachusetts General Court and went out of business in October 1814 when its charter expired. It seems that many of its activities were deceptive if not downright fraudulent. On June 23, 1812, *The* Hallowell and Augusta Bank was chartered by the Massachusetts General Court. Although similar in name, the official addition of the word *The* made it a different corporation rather than a renewal. The new bank held that it was not in any way responsible for the paper money, debts, or obligations of the old.

In accordance with prevailing law, the first Hallowell and Augusta Bank was prohibited from issuing bills of denominations less than $5 in an effort to keep coins in circulation. While the bank was intended to benefit residents of Hallowell, it was required that at least one-eighth of the loan funds be made available to citizens of the Commonwealth who were involved in agriculture. It had a capital of $200,000.[18]

The bank ran into difficulties after the Embargo Act of 1807 and the resulting financial distress, and it was discovered that the whole capital stock of the bank was invested in real estate and in permanent loans. It became insolvent by 1812 if not before.[19]

The Hallowell and Augusta Bank {2nd}

1812–1829

W-MA-1820 • W-ME-920

History: On June 23, 1812, *The* Hallowell and Augusta Bank was chartered by the Massachusetts General Court. The word *The* was added to the title for the legal purpose of making this a new bank and not a continuation or renewal of the old. However, many of the people involved were the same as in the former bank. The capital was authorized at $150,000. On March 15, 1820, Maine became a state; thus, The Hallowell and Augusta Bank had a new address. Nevertheless, the bank was in trouble. In early May it stopped redeeming its notes. On May 13, the president and cashier issued a directive for all debtors to pay immediately and that the bank's real estate would be sold. The resultant cash would be used to redeem notes. A statement of June 22, 1820, showed $106,061 of bills in circulation but just $238 in specie on hand. Finally, the Legislature revoked the bank's charter. In the first issue of *Bicknell's Counterfeit Detector*, July 31, 1830, this bank was on its "List of Broken Banks."

Numismatic Commentary: All issues are of the PSSP style. Issues list the title of the bank two different ways: Hallowell & Aug. Bank, and Hallo & Augusta Bank, with a small, superior letter "o" after the last "L" in "Hall."

Valid Issues

Notes With Massachusetts Address

$1 • W-MA-1820-001-G010

Left: 1 / 1. ***Center:*** Flower garlands, ONE. ***Right:*** 1 / 1. ***Engraver:*** PSSP. ***Comments:*** H-Unlisted, Wait-33.

Rarity: —

$1 • W-MA-1820-001-G020

Left: 1 / 1. ***Center:*** Flower garlands, ONE. ***Right:*** 1 / 1. ***Engraver:*** PSSP. ***Comments:*** H-MA-655-G10, Wait-Unlisted. 1800s.

Rarity: —

$1 • W-MA-1820-001-G030

Left: 1 / 1. ***Center:*** Flower garlands, ONE. ***Right:*** 1 / 1. ***Engraver:*** PSSP. ***Comments:*** H-MA-655-G12, Wait-Unlisted. 1807–1809.

Rarity: —

$1 • W-MA-1820-001-G040
Engraver: PSSP. ***Comments:*** H-MA-655-G14, Wait-Unlisted. Similar to W-MA-1820-001-G030 but without ONE. 1809–1812.
Rarity: —

$1 • W-MA-1820-001-G050
CJF

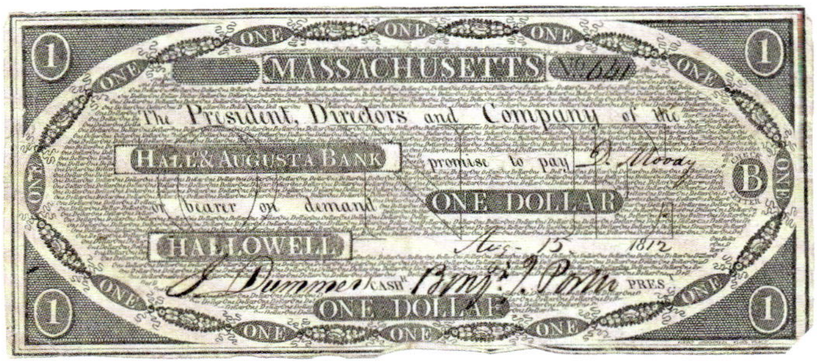

Comments: H-MA-655-G16, Wait-Unlisted. Similar to W-MA-1820-001-G030. 18__. 1810s.
Rarity: URS-7
F $100

$2 • W-MA-1820-002-G060
Left: 2 / 2. ***Center:*** Flower garlands, TWO. ***Right:*** 2 / 2. ***Engraver:*** PSSP. ***Comments:*** H-Unlisted, Wait-34.
Rarity: —

$2 • W-MA-1820-002-G070
Engraver: PSSP. ***Comments:*** H-MA-655-G20, Wait-Unlisted. Similar to W-MA-1820-001-G020 but with different denomination. 1800s.
Rarity: —

$2 • W-MA-1820-002-G080
Center: TWO. ***Engraver:*** PSSP. ***Comments:*** H-MA-655-G22, Wait-Unlisted. Similar to W-MA-1820-001-G030 but with different denomination. 1807–1809.
Rarity: —

$2 • W-MA-1820-002-G090
Engraver: PSSP. ***Comments:*** H-MA-655-G24, Wait-Unlisted. Similar to W-MA-1820-002-G080 but without TWO. 1809–1812.
Rarity: URS-4
F $250

$2 • W-MA-1820-002-G100
CJF

Engraver: PSSP. ***Comments:*** H-MA-655-G26, Wait-Unlisted. Similar to W-MA-1820-002-G080. 18__. 1810s.
Rarity: URS-9
F $60

$3 • W-MA-1820-003-G110
Left: 3 / 3. ***Center:*** Flower garlands, THREE. ***Right:*** 3 / 3. ***Engraver:*** PSSP. ***Comments:*** H-Unlisted, Wait-35.
Rarity: —

$3 • W-MA-1820-003-G120
Engraver: PSSP. ***Comments:*** H-MA-655-G28, Wait-Unlisted. Similar to W-MA-1820-001-G020 but with different denomination. 1800s.
Rarity: —

$3 • W-MA-1820-003-G130
Engraver: Unverified, but likely PSSP. ***Comments:*** H-MA-655-G30, Wait-Unlisted. No description available. 1800s.
Rarity: *None known*

$3 • W-MA-1820-003-G140
Engraver: PSSP. ***Comments:*** H-MA-655-G32, Wait-Unlisted. Similar to W-MA-1820-001-G030 but with different denomination. 1807–1809.
Rarity: —

$3 • W-MA-1820-003-G150
CJF

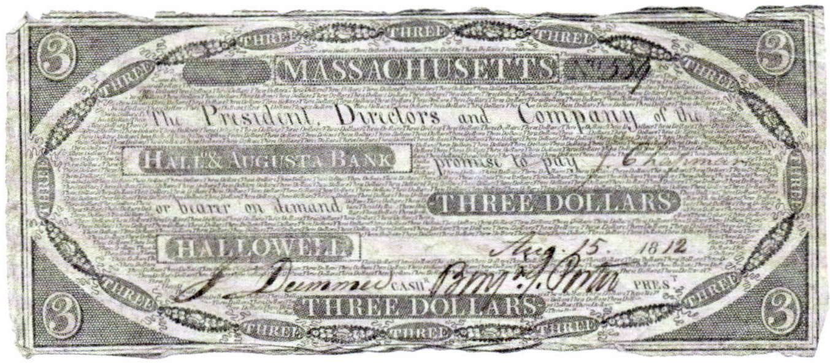

Engraver: PSSP. ***Comments:*** H-MA-655-G34, Wait-Unlisted. Similar to W-MA-1820-001-G030 but with different denomination. 18__. 1810s.
Rarity: URS-8
F $80

$5 • W-MA-1820-005-G160
Left: State arms / 5, Plate letter, 5. ***Center:*** FIVE DOLLARS, Text. ***Right:*** 5, Plate letter, 5. ***Engraver:*** PSSP. ***Comments:*** H-Unlisted, Wait-37.
Rarity: —

$5 • W-MA-1820-005-G170
Left: MASSACHUSETTS vertically / 5, Plate letter, 5. ***Center:*** FIVE DOLLARS, Text. ***Right:*** 5, Plate letter, 5. ***Engraver:*** PSSP. ***Comments:*** H-MA-655-G36, Wait-Unlisted. 18__. 1800s.
Rarity: —

$5 • W-MA-1820-005-G180
QDB

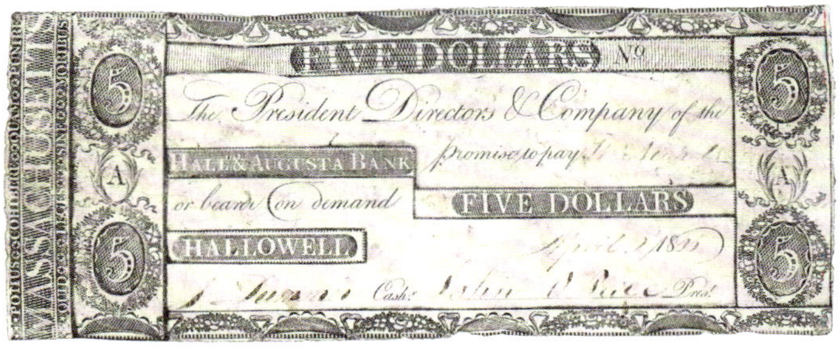

Engraver: PSSP. ***Comments:*** H-MA-655-G38, Wait-Unlisted. 18__. 1806–1809.
Rarity: URS-9
F $60

$5 • W-MA-1820-005-G190

QDB

Back: Stereotype Steel Check Plate. ***Engraver:*** PSSP. ***Comments:*** H-MA-655-G40, Wait-Unlisted. 18__. 1810s.

Rarity: URS-9
F $60

$10 • W-MA-1820-010-G200

Left: State arms / 10, Plate letter, 10. ***Center:*** TEN DOLLARS, Text. ***Right:*** 10, Plate letter, 10. ***Engraver:*** PSSP. ***Comments:*** H-Unlisted, Wait-39. 18__.

Rarity: —

$10 • W-MA-1820-010-G210

Back: Stereotype Steel Check Plate. ***Engraver:*** PSSP. ***Comments:*** H-MA-655-G42, Wait-38. 18__. 1800s.

Rarity: —

$10 • W-MA-1820-010-G220

QDB

Back: Stereotype Steel Check Plate. ***Engraver:*** PSSP. ***Comments:*** H-MA-655-G44, Wait-Unlisted. Similar to W-MA-1820-010-G210. 18__. 1800s.

Rarity: URS-9
VG $75; **F** $125

$10 • W-MA-1820-010-G230

QDB

Back: Stereotype Steel Check Plate. ***Engraver:*** PSSP. ***Comments:*** H-MA-655-G46, Wait-Unlisted. Similar to W-MA-1820-010-G220 but with state arms and no TEN. 18__. 1809–1812.

Rarity: URS-9
VG $75; **F** $125

$10 • W-MA-1820-010-G240

Engraver: PSSP. ***Comments:*** H-MA-655-G48, Wait-Unlisted. Similar to W-MA-1820-010-G230 but with TEN. 1810s.

Rarity: —

$20 • W-MA-1820-020-G250

HA

Engraver: PSSP. ***Comments:*** H-MA-655-G50, Wait-40. 18__. 1800s.

Rarity: URS-8
F $400

$20 • W-MA-1820-020-G260

Back: Stereotype Steel Check Plate. ***Engraver:*** PSSP. ***Comments:*** H-MA-655-G52, Wait-Unlisted. Similar to W-MA-1820-020-G250 but with state arms. 1809–1810s.

Rarity: —

Non-Valid Issues

$3 • W-MA-1820-003-C130

Engraver: PSSP. ***Comments:*** H-MA-655-C30, Wait-Unlisted. Counterfeit of W-MA-1820-003-G130. 1807.

Rarity: —

Kennebec Bank

1812–1820 • 1820–1826

W-MA-1825 • W-ME-930

History: The Kennebec Bank in Augusta (W-MA-110) was incorporated on June 12, 1812, following an effort to establish it in Hallowell. As this was a small community and the Hallowell and Augusta Bank was already chartered there, a second bank in Hallowell was not allowed. However, in 1816 the Legislature responded to a petition and allowed the move. Henceforth paper money of the institution bore the Hallowell address. In June 1818, bills in circulation totaled $139,025. In 1818 and 1819 the directors declared a three percent dividend every three months on the par value of shares. These were difficult times in the American economy, and rumors swirled about the bank, but it was able to meet its obligations. The *Report of the Maine District Banks to the Commonwealth of Massachusetts*, January 1820, gave the capital stock paid in as $100,000 and the bills in circulation as $128,513. In the *History of Augusta*, James W. North noted: "The bank failed May 1, 1826." Other accounts state that the bank suspended the redemption of its notes on May 1 and failed soon afterward. See also listing under Maine.

Numismatic Commentary: All of this bank's issues were of the PSSP variety. Enough remain in the marketplace to satisfy collector demand.

Valid Issues

Notes With Massachusetts Address

$1 • W-MA-1825-001-G010

Engraver: PSSP. ***Comments:*** H-MA-50-G24, Wait-Unlisted. Similar to W-MA-110-001-G010 but with different city (see W-MA-110). 1810s.

Rarity: —

$2 • W-MA-1825-002-G020

QDB

Engraver: PSSP. ***Comments:*** H-MA-50-G26, Wait-Unlisted. Similar to W-MA-110-002-G020 but with different city (see W-MA-110). 18__. 1810s.

Rarity: URS-6
VF $150

$3 • W-MA-1825-003-G030

MC

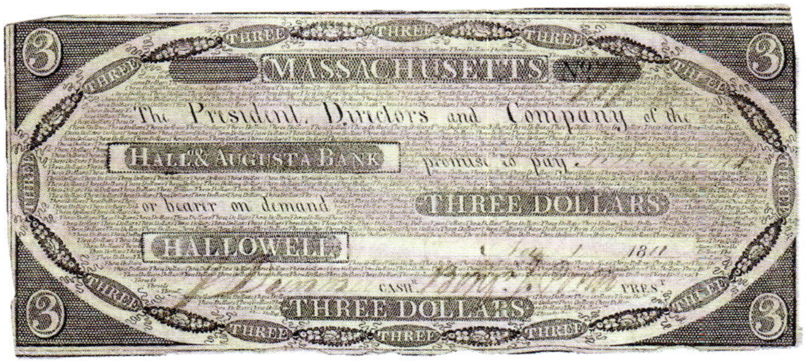

Engraver: PSSP. ***Comments:*** H-MA-50-G28, Wait-Unlisted Similar to W-MA-110-003-G030 but with different city (see W-MA-110). 18__. 1810s.

Rarity: —

$5 • W-MA-1825-005-G040

HA

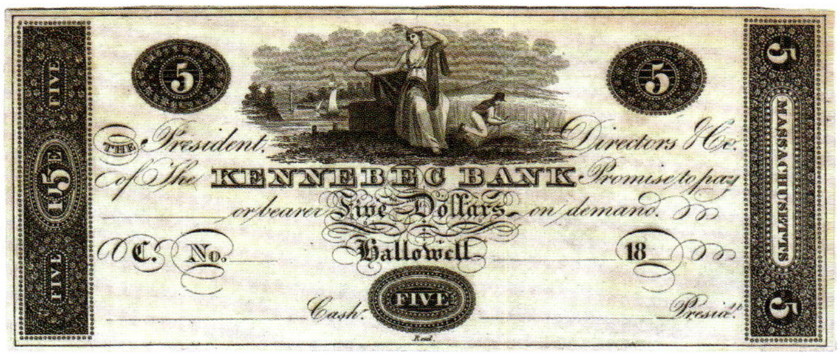

Comments: H-MA-50-G32, Wait-Unlisted. Similar to W-MA-110-003-G040 but with different city (see W-MA-110). 18__. 1810s.

Rarity: URS-6
VF $150; **Proof** $900

$10 • W-MA-1825-010-G050

Left: TEN, 10, TEN across. ***Center:*** 10 / Woman seated with shield bearing 10, Houses / 10 / X. ***Right:*** 10, MASSACHUSETTS, 10. ***Comments:*** H-MA-50-G36, Wait-Unlisted. Similar to W-MA-110-003-G050 but with different city (see W-MA-110). 1810s.

Rarity: —

Notes With Maine Address

$1 • W-ME-930-001-G010

CJF

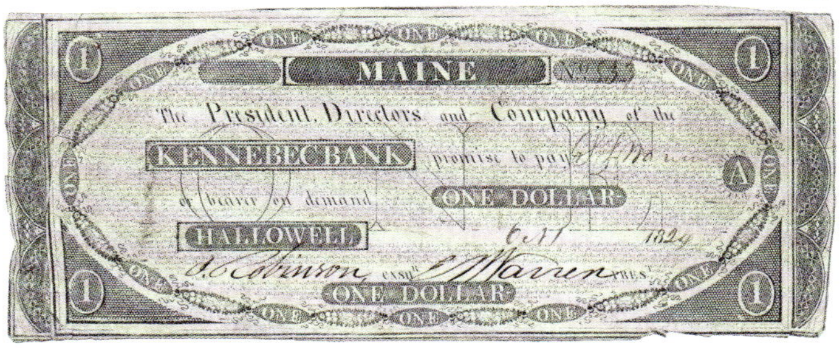

Engraver: PSSP. ***Comments:*** H-ME-365-G4, Wait-41. 18__. 1820s.

Rarity: URS-6
VG $60; **VF** $100

$1 • W-ME-930-001-G020

CJF

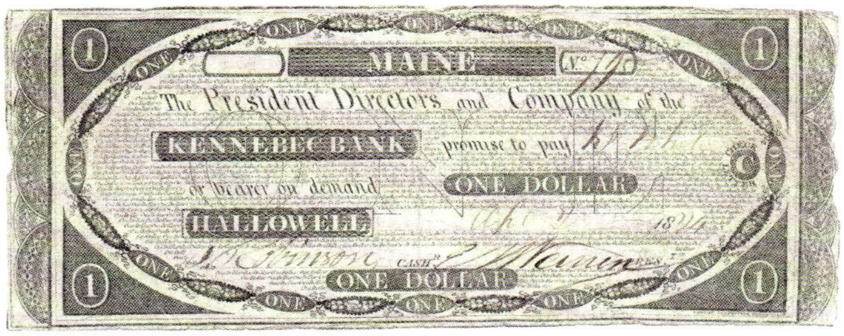

Comments: H-ME-365-G6, Wait-Unlisted. Similar to W-ME-930-001-G010. 18__. 1820s.

Rarity: URS-6
VG $60; **VF** $100

$2 • W-ME-930-002-G030

CJF

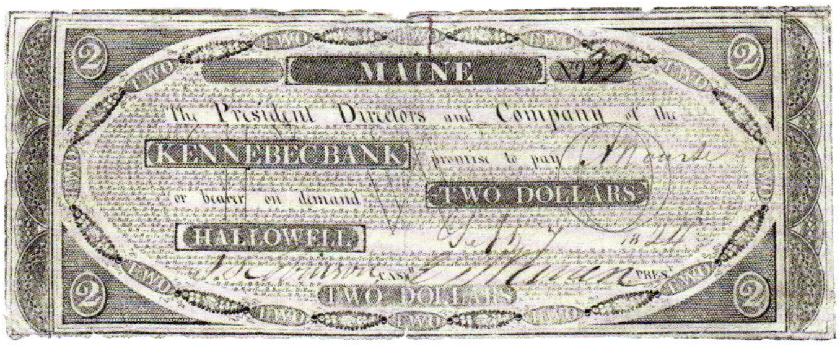

Engraver: PSSP. ***Comments:*** H-ME-365-G10, Wait-42. 18__. 1820s.

Rarity: URS-6
VG $75; **VF** $100

$2 • W-ME-930-002-G040

Comments: H-ME-365-G12, Wait-Unlisted. Similar to W-ME-930-002-G030. 1820s.

Rarity: —

$3 • W-ME-930-003-G050

QDB

Engraver: PSSP. ***Comments:*** H-ME-365-G16, Wait-43. 18__. 1820s.

Rarity: URS-6
VG $85; **VF** $140

$3 • W-ME-930-003-G060

Comments: H-ME-365-G18, Wait-44. Similar to W-ME-930-003-G050. 1820s.

Rarity: —

$5 • W-ME-930-005-G070

Center: Grids flanking MAINE. ***Back:*** Black. ***Engraver:*** PSSP. ***Comments:*** H-ME-365-G22a, Wait-Unlisted. 1820s.

Rarity: URS-6
VG $50; **VF** $75

$5 • W-ME-930-005-G080

Left: MAINE vertically / 5, Plate letter, 5. ***Center:*** FIVE DOLLARS, Text. ***Right:*** 5, Plate letter, 5. ***Back:*** Brown. ***Engraver:*** PSSP. ***Comments:*** H-ME-365-G24a, Wait-46. 1820s.

Rarity: URS-6
VG $75; **VF** $125

$5 • W-ME-930-005-G080a

CJF

Back: Black Stereotype Steel Check Plate. ***Comments:*** H-ME-365-G24b, Wait-Unlisted. Similar to W-ME-930-005-G080. 18__. 1820s.

Rarity: URS-6
VG $75; **VF** $150

$10 • W-ME-930-010-G090

CJF

Back: Black Stereotype Steel Check Plate. ***Engraver:*** PSSP. ***Comments:*** H-ME-365-G28a, Wait-Unlisted. 18__. 1820s.

Rarity: URS-6
VG $100; **VF** $250

$10 • W-ME-930-010-G100

Left: MAINE vertically / 10, Plate letter, 10. ***Center:*** TEN DOLLARS, Text. ***Right:*** 10, Plate letter, 10. ***Back:*** Brown Stereotype Steel Check Plate. ***Engraver:*** PSSP. ***Comments:*** H-ME-365-G30a, Wait-Unlisted. 1820s.

Rarity: —

Non-Valid Issues
Notes With Massachusetts Address

$5 • W-MA-1825-005-C040

CJF

Comments: H-MA-50-C32, Wait-45. Counterfeit of W-MA-1825-005-G040. 18__.

Rarity: —

$10 • W-MA-1825-010-C050

Comments: H-MA-50-C36, Wait-47. Counterfeit of W-MA-1825-010-G050.

Rarity: —

Harwich, Massachusetts

Located on the south side of Cape Cod, Harwich used to be called Satucket. It was originally a part of Yarmouth but was incorporated in 1694, including the lands which now make up the town of Brewster. Seven villages make up the town of Harwich: Harwich, North, East, South, and West Harwich, Harwich Port, and Pleasant Lake.

Industry in early times was comprised of fishing and farming. During the time of the American Revolution, Harwich was considered the chief fishing port in the Cape. Schooners travelled to the Grand Banks to catch fish and then headed south to the West Indies to trade cod and herring for rum and molasses. In 1845 Alvin Cahoon planted cranberries at Pleasant Lake, establishing the nation's first cranberry bog. Cahoon's cousin soon followed suit in 1847 and began growing cranberries at Pleasant Lake.

Bank of Cape Cod
1856–1865
W-MA-1830

History: The Bank of Cape Cod was incorporated on May 21, 1855, with an authorized capital of $100,000, increased to $150,000 in 1858. Circulation in 1857 was $131,800. The bank's highest record of this value was $153,843 in 1858. Selected figures for 1857 included: bills of this bank and other New England states $2,580; specie $71,090.95; real estate $3,625.81. The bank, although in sound condition, ran into trouble in 1862 and was censured for charging a fee to redeem its own notes.

The business of the Bank of Cape Cod was succeeded by the Cape Cod National Bank of Harwich in 1865.

Numismatic Commentary: Notes from this bank are hard to locate, but a lucky collector may be able to purchase one with a nice historical vignette of the "Landing of the Pilgrims" or even the "Signing of the First Constitution" on board the *Mayflower*. The popularity of these vignettes, plus the fact that notes from the Cape are in high demand, will make this acquisition somewhat of a challenge.

VALID ISSUES

$1 • W-MA-1830-001-G010

Left: 1 / Male portrait. ***Center:*** Lighthouse, Brig, Merchant ship, and Man-of-war, Ships. ***Bottom center:*** Codfish. ***Right:*** 1 / Woman with spyglass seated on barrel. ***Engraver:*** Toppan, Carpenter & Co. ***Comments:*** H-MA-660-G2. 18__. 1850s.

Rarity: —

$2 • W-MA-1830-002-G020

Left: 2 / Sailor seated with U.S. flag, anchor, cask, and sextant. ***Center:*** "Landing of the Pilgrims". ***Bottom center:*** Codfish. ***Right:*** 2 / Portrait of girl. ***Engraver:*** Toppan, Carpenter & Co. ***Comments:*** H-MA-660-G4. 18__. 1850s.

Rarity: —

$3 • W-MA-1830-003-G030

Left: Female portrait / 3. ***Center:*** Three sailors, one seated smoking pipe, one standing, one seated on anchor. ***Right:*** 3 / Portrait of child. ***Engraver:*** Toppan, Carpenter & Co. ***Comments:*** H-MA-660-G6. 18__. 1850s.

Rarity: —

$4 • W-MA-1830-004-G040

Left: Portrait of boy / 4 / FOUR. ***Center:*** "Presentation of the Declaration of Independence". ***Bottom center:*** Codfish. ***Right:*** 4 / Woman with trident seated in floating shell. ***Engraver:*** Toppan, Carpenter & Co. ***Comments:*** H-MA-660-G8. 18__. 1850s.

Rarity: —

$4 • W-MA-1830-004-G040a

JF

Overprint: 4 / 4. ***Engraver:*** Toppan, Carpenter & Co. ***Comments:*** H-Unlisted. Similar to W-MA-1830-004-G040. 18__. 1850s.

Rarity: URS-2
G $2,000; **F** $7,500

Collectors and Researchers:

If you have new information about any banks or notes listed in this volume, contact Whitman Publishing, Attn: Obsolete Paper Money, 3101 Clairmont Road, Suite G, Atlanta, GA 30329.

$5 • W-MA-1830-005-G050

CJF

Engraver: Toppan, Carpenter & Co. ***Comments:*** H-MA-660-G10. Proof. 18__. 1850s.

Rarity: URS-1
Proof $15,000

$10 • W-MA-1830-010-G060

Left: 10 / Sailor leaning on capstan by barrel and bale. ***Center:*** "Signing of the First Constitution" on board the Mayflower in Cape Cod Harbor, 1620 / Indian woman with bow and quiver. ***Bottom center:*** Codfish. ***Right:*** 10 / Portrait of John Quincy Adams / TEN. ***Engraver:*** Toppan, Carpenter & Co. ***Comments:*** H-MA-660-G12. 18__. 1850s.

Rarity: —

$20 • W-MA-1830-020-G070

Left: 20 / Scene on Marshfield farm, Two cows standing in stream, two on bank. ***Right:*** 20 / Portrait of Daniel Webster. ***Engraver:*** Toppan, Carpenter & Co. ***Comments:*** H-MA-660-G14. 18__. 1850s.

Rarity: —

$50 • W-MA-1830-050-G080

Left: Female portrait / 50. ***Center:*** Sailor standing on board ship. ***Bottom center:*** Codfish. ***Right:*** 50 / Anchor, box, barrel, and bale. ***Engraver:*** Toppan, Carpenter & Co. ***Comments:*** H-MA-660-G16. 18__. 1850s.

Rarity: —

$100 • W-MA-1830-100-G090

Left: Woman seated and sailor standing with flag. ***Center:*** 100 / 100 / Portrait of George Washington. ***Right:*** Justice draped in U.S. flag. ***Engraver:*** Toppan, Carpenter & Co. ***Comments:*** H-MA-660-G18. 18__. 1850s.

Rarity: —

NON-VALID ISSUES

$5 • W-MA-1830-005-R010

Engraver: Toppan, Carpenter & Co. ***Comments:*** H-MA-660-R5. Raised from W-MA-1830-001-G010. 18__. 1850s.

Rarity: —

$10 • W-MA-1830-010-R020

Engraver: Toppan, Carpenter & Co. ***Comments:*** H-MA-660-R10. Raised from W-MA-1830-001-G010. 18__. 1850s.

Rarity: —

$10 • W-MA-1830-010-R030

Engraver: Toppan, Carpenter & Co. ***Comments:*** H-MA-660-R15. Raised from W-MA-1830-001-G010. 18__. 1850s.

Rarity: —

Haverhill, Massachusetts

Located on the Merrimack River, Haverhill is bordered by Methuen, Groveland, and Boxford, as well as West Newbury and the state of New Hampshire to the north. Its name was taken from a city in England.

In the early days, the town was now and then raided by Indians, who were sometimes attended by French troops. Originally a farming community, Haverhill soon became an industrial area with saw mills and grist mills generated by water power. Tanneries, shipping, and shipbuilding were influential during the 18th century, as was shoemaking and hat making.

Essex Bank

1851–1864

W-MA-1840

History: The Essex Bank was incorporated on May 24, 1851, with an authorized capital of $100,000. On June 19, 1852, William H. Hewes was elected president of the Essex Bank, replacing J.A. Brodhead, who had resigned. William Caldwell was cashier. James Gale then became president in 1855.

Circulation ranged from $63,582 in 1857 to $76,340 in 1863. Selected figures for 1857 included: bills of this bank and other New England states $140; specie $5,465.59; real estate $8,000.

In 1850 there was scandal when the cashier and the clerk stole $32,000 in gold coins placed for safekeeping by a customer of the bank. The matter did not involve any directors and was satisfactorily adjusted amid much embarrassment.

The Essex Bank wound down its affairs after the Essex National Bank of Haverhill was chartered on November 7, 1864.

Numismatic Commentary: Genuine notes are available for certain issues, as indicated by the rarity listings. Counterfeits of a nice quality are also available in the current marketplace.

Valid Issues

$1 • W-MA-1840-001-G010

CC

Engraver: Rawdon, Wright, Hatch & Edson / New England Bank Note Co. ***Comments:*** H-MA-665-G2. 18__. 1850s.

Rarity: URS-3

VF $700

$1 • W-MA-1840-001-G010a

Left: Woman seated with 1 / 1. ***Center:*** 1 bearing 1. ***Right:*** 1 / Woman seated holding 1. ***Tint:*** Brown-orange lathework. ***Engraver:*** Rawdon, Wright, Hatch & Edson / New England Bank Note Co. / ABNCo. monogram. ***Comments:*** H-MA-665-G2b. Similar to W-MA-1840-001-G010 but with additional engraver imprint. 18__. 1860s.

Rarity: —

$2 • W-MA-1840-002-G020

Left: Two women flanking shield surmounted by eagle, Steamboat / 2. ***Center:*** 2. ***Right:*** 2 / Woman seated with stalk of grain, Cornucopia. ***Engraver:*** Rawdon, Wright, Hatch & Edson / New England Bank Note Co. ***Comments:*** H-MA-665-G4. 18__. 1850s.

Rarity: —

$2 • W-MA-1840-002-G020a

SN

Tint: Brown-orange lathework. ***Engraver:*** Rawdon, Wright, Hatch & Edson / New England Bank Note Co. / ABNCo. monogram. ***Comments:*** H-MA-665-G4b. Similar to W-MA-1840-002-G020 but with additional engraver imprint. 18__. 1860s.

Rarity: URS-2

VF $1,000

$3 • W-MA-1840-003-G030

Left: Train / THREE. ***Center:*** 3. ***Right:*** 3 / Blacksmith, sailor, and farmer standing with 3. ***Engraver:*** Rawdon, Wright, Hatch & Edson / New England Bank Note Co. ***Comments:*** H-MA-665-G6. 18__. 1850s.

Rarity: —

$3 • W-MA-1840-003-G030a

Tint: Brown-orange lathework. ***Engraver:*** Rawdon, Wright, Hatch & Edson / New England Bank Note Co. / ABNCo. monogram. ***Comments:*** H-MA-665-G6b. Similar to W-MA-1840-003-G030 but with additional engraver imprint. 18__. 1860s.

Rarity: —

$5 • W-MA-1840-005-G040

Left: Two women flanking shield, Man plowing / Train and factory / 5. ***Center:*** FIVE on 5. ***Right:*** 5 / Five women in and around 5. ***Engraver:*** Rawdon, Wright, Hatch & Edson / New England Bank Note Co. ***Comments:*** H-MA-665-G8. 18__. 1850s.

Rarity: —

$5 • W-MA-1840-005-G040a

CJF

Engraver: Rawdon, Wright, Hatch & Edson / New England Bank Note Co. / ABNCo. monogram. ***Comments:*** H-Unlisted. Similar to W-MA-1840-005-G040 but with additional engraver imprint. 18__. 1860s.

Rarity: URS-3
F $500

$5 • W-MA-1840-005-G040b

Tint: Brown-orange lathework. ***Engraver:*** Rawdon, Wright, Hatch & Edson / New England Bank Note Co. / ABNCo. monogram. ***Comments:*** H-MA-665-G8b. Similar to W-MA-1840-005-G040 but with additional engraver imprint. 18__. 1860s.

Rarity: —

$10 • W-MA-1840-010-G050

Left: Two women with shield surmounted by bust / TEN. ***Center:*** X. ***Right:*** 10 / Portrait of Indian. ***Engraver:*** Rawdon, Wright, Hatch & Edson / New England Bank Note Co. ***Comments:*** H-MA-665-G10. 18__. 1850s.

Rarity: —

$10 • W-MA-1840-010-G050a

Engraver: Rawdon, Wright, Hatch & Edson / New England Bank Note Co. / ABNCo. monogram. ***Comments:*** H-MA-665-G10a. Similar to W-MA-1840-010-G050 but with additional engraver imprint. 18__. 1860s.

Rarity: —

$20 • W-MA-1840-020-G060

Left: 20 / Anchor. ***Center:*** Sailing ships / Eagle. ***Right:*** 20 / Boy. ***Tint:*** Orange die bearing 20 and TWENTY. ***Engraver:*** American Bank Note Co. ***Comments:*** H-MA-665-G12a. Oct. 1, 1860.

Rarity: —

$50 • W-MA-1840-050-G070

SI

Tint: Green. ***Engraver:*** American Bank Note Co. ***Comments:*** H-MA-665-G14a. Oct. 1, 1860.

Rarity: URS-2
Proof $6,500

$100 • W-MA-1840-100-G080

Left: 100 / Vulcan seated with sledge and anchor. ***Center:*** Train on bridge, Eagle on limb, Canal locks. ***Bottom center:*** 100. ***Right:*** 100 / Ceres seated, Cornucopia. ***Engraver:*** Rawdon, Wright, Hatch & Edson. ***Comments:*** H-MA-665-G16. 18__. 1850s.

Rarity: —

$100 • W-MA-1840-100-G090

Left: 100 / Woman seated at sewing machine. ***Center:*** Black horse and white horse frightened by lightning, Cattle. ***Right:*** 100 / Portrait of girl. ***Tint:*** Color unknown. ***Engraver:*** American Bank Note Co. ***Comments:*** H-MA-665-G18a. Oct. 1, 1860.

Rarity: —

Non-Valid Issues

$2 • W-MA-1840-002-S010

CJF

Engraver: Toppan, Carpenter & Co. ***Comments:*** H-MA-665-S5. May 1, 1863. 1860s.

Rarity: URS-7
F $75

$10 • W-MA-1840-010-C050a

CJF

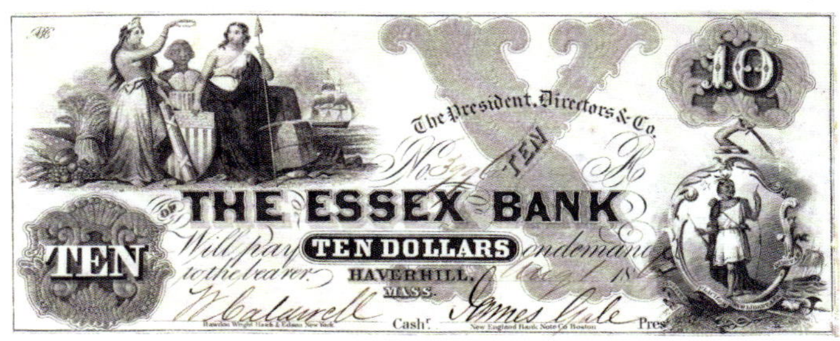

Engraver: Rawdon, Wright, Hatch & Edson / New England Bank Note Co. / ABNCo. monogram. ***Comments:*** H-MA-665-C10a. Counterfeit of W-MA-1840-010-G050a. 18__. 1860s.

Rarity: URS-7
F $80

Haverhill Bank

1836–1864

W-MA-1850

History: The Haverhill Bank was chartered on April 1, 1836, with an authorized capital of $100,000. It was directed by Enoch Silsbee, James Noyes, and Hiram Plummer. The capital was increased to $150,000 in 1850, later to $200,000, and eventually to $500,000.

Circulation was $24,191.25 in 1842, but it reached its highest of $118,027 in 1863. Selected figures for 1857 included: bills of this bank and other New England states $1,155.81; specie $5,465.59; real estate $6,050.

The business of the Haverhill Bank was succeeded by the Haverhill National Bank, chartered in July 1864.

Numismatic Commentary: Genuine notes from this bank are hard to locate, but fortunately some that do make an appearance show a street scene in downtown Haverhill. Notes showing local scenery have always been popular.

Valid Issues

$1 • W-MA-1850-001-G010

Left: 1 / Children sailing boats in tub / ONE. ***Center:*** Steamboat and other ships / Plow and sheaf. ***Right:*** 1 / Blacksmith, anvil, and forge / ONE. ***Engraver:*** New England Bank Note Co. ***Comments:*** H-MA-670-G2. 18__. 1836–1850s.

Rarity: —

$1 • W-MA-1850-001-G020

CC

Engraver: Danforth, Wright & Co. ***Comments:*** H-MA-670-G4. Proof. January 1, 18__. 1850s.

Rarity: URS-2
Proof $3,000

$1 • W-MA-1850-001-G020a

SN

Overprint: Red ONE. ***Engraver:*** Danforth, Wright & Co. ***Comments:*** H-MA-670-G4a. Similar to W-MA-1850-001-G020. January 1, 18__. 1850s.

Rarity: URS-2
Proof $3,250

$1.25 • W-MA-1850-001.25-G030

Left: 1 25/100 / Train / 1 25/100. ***Center:*** Sloop and other ships at sea / $1.25 cts. ***Right:*** 1 25/100 / Eagle. ***Engraver:*** New England Bank Note Co. ***Comments:*** H-MA-670-G6. 18__. 1830s.

Rarity: —

$1.50 • W-MA-1850-001.50-G040

Left: 1 Doll. 50 Cts. vertically. ***Center:*** Eagle on rock in ocean / $1 50/100. ***Right:*** 1 50/100 / Justice. ***Engraver:*** New England Bank Note Co. ***Comments:*** H-MA-670-G8. 18__. 1830s.

Rarity: —

$1.75 • W-MA-1850-001.75-G050

Left: $1.75 Cts. / Woman watering eagle / 1 75/100. ***Center:*** Three sloops at sea. ***Right:*** $1.75 Cts. / Dog, Woman seated with grain / 1 75/100. ***Engraver:*** New England Bank Note Co. ***Comments:*** H-MA-670-G10. 18__. 1830s.

Rarity: —

$2 • W-MA-1850-002-G060

Left: 2 / Indian man with bow / TWO. ***Center:*** Train passing between cliffs / Woman and shield. ***Right:*** 2 / Ship / TWO. ***Engraver:*** New England Bank Note Co. ***Comments:*** H-MA-670-G12. 18__. 1836–1850s.

Rarity: —

$2 • W-MA-1850-002-G070

Left: Man / TWO. ***Center:*** TWO over $, Buildings and street. ***Right:*** 2 / Woman. ***Engraver:*** Danforth, Wright & Co. ***Comments:*** H-MA-670-G14. 18__. 1850s.

Rarity: URS-2
Proof $2,000

$2 • W-MA-1850-002-G070a

SN

Overprint: Red TWO. ***Engraver:*** Danforth, Wright & Co. ***Comments:*** H-MA-670-G14a. Similar to W-MA-1850-002-G070. January 1, 18__. 1850s.

Rarity: URS-2
VF $1,500

$3 • W-MA-1850-003-G080

Left: 3 / Shipyard / THREE. ***Center:*** Farmer sowing grain / Cattle. ***Right:*** 3 / Indian man / THREE. ***Engraver:*** New England Bank Note Co. ***Comments:*** H-MA-670-G16. 18__. 1836–1850s.

Rarity: —

$3 • W-MA-1850-003-G090

JF

Engraver: Danforth, Wright & Co. ***Comments:*** H-MA-670-G18. Proof. January 1, 18__. 1850s.

Rarity: URS-1
Proof $5,000

$3 • W-MA-1850-003-G090a
Left: Street scene in Haverhill / 3. ***Center:*** THREE across 3. ***Right:*** 3 / Woman with fruit. ***Overprint:*** Red. ***Engraver:*** Danforth, Wright & Co. ***Comments:*** H-MA-670-G18a. Similar to W-MA-1850-003-G090. 18__. 1850s.

Rarity: —

$5 • W-MA-1850-005-G100
Left: FIVE / Milkmaid. ***Center:*** State arms / Farming scene / State arms. ***Right:*** 5 / Woman / FIVE. ***Engraver:*** New England Bank Note Co. ***Comments:*** H-MA-670-G20. 18__. 1836–1850s.

Rarity: —

$5 • W-MA-1850-005-G110
Left: Dog, Man seated with girl on knee, Woman and boy / FIVE. ***Center:*** Street scene in Haverhill. ***Right:*** 5 / Woman sewing shoes, Box of shoes. ***Engraver:*** Danforth, Wright & Co. ***Comments:*** H-MA-670-G22. 18__. 1850s.

Rarity: —

$5 • W-MA-1850-005-G110a
Overprint: Red. ***Engraver:*** Danforth, Wright & Co. ***Comments:*** H-MA-670-G22a. Similar to W-MA-1850-005-G110. 18__. 1850s.

Rarity: —

$10 • W-MA-1850-010-G120
Left: Machine. ***Engraver:*** New England Bank Note Co. ***Comments:*** H-MA-670-G24. 18__. 1836–1850s.

Rarity: —

$10 • W-MA-1850-010-G130
Left: Man holding bull, Two men and boy standing, Sheep / TEN across X. ***Center:*** TEN across X. ***Right:*** 10 / Woman feeding fowl. ***Engraver:*** Danforth, Wright & Co. ***Comments:*** H-MA-670-G26. 18__. 1850s.

Rarity: —

$10 • W-MA-1850-010-G130a
Overprint: Red. ***Engraver:*** Danforth, Wright & Co. ***Comments:*** H-MA-670-G26a. Similar to W-MA-1850-010-G130. 18__. 1850s.

Rarity: —

$20 • W-MA-1850-020-G140
Left: Steamboat / XX / Train. ***Center:*** Three women seated with eagle, pole and cap, shield, scales and book / 20 / Panel outlining white TWENTY. ***Right:*** XX / Milkmaid standing with pail. ***Engraver:*** New England Bank Note Co. / PSSP. ***Comments:*** H-MA-670-G28. 18__. 1830s–1840s.

Rarity: —

$20 • W-MA-1850-020-G150
Left: 20 / Minerva standing with spear. ***Center:*** Woman seated between 2 and 0. ***Right:*** 20 / Woman reclining on cornucopia / 20. ***Engraver:*** Rawdon, Wright, Hatch & Edson. ***Comments:*** H-MA-670-G32. 18__. 1850s.

Rarity: —

$20 • W-MA-1850-020-G160
Left: XX / View of buildings. ***Right:*** 20 / View of buildings. ***Tint:*** Red lathework panel bearing 20. ***Engraver:*** American Bank Note Co. ***Comments:*** H-MA-670-G34a. 1860s.

Rarity: —

$50 • W-MA-1850-050-G170
Left: 50 / Steamboat and schooner. ***Center:*** Farmyard scene, Load of hay with two men on it, Man with rake and pail. ***Right:*** L / Justice kneeling. ***Engraver:*** New England Bank Note Co. ***Comments:*** H-MA-670-G36. 18__. 1830s–1840s.

Rarity: —

$50 • W-MA-1850-050-G180
Left: 50 / Minerva standing by column. ***Center:*** Ceres and Vulcan flanking cornucopia. ***Right:*** 50 / Cherub in sailboat / 50. ***Engraver:*** Rawdon, Wright, Hatch & Edson. ***Comments:*** H-MA-670-G40. 18__. 1850s.

Rarity: —

$50 • W-MA-1850-050-G190

CC

Tint: Red lathework panel. ***Engraver:*** American Bank Note Co. ***Comments:*** H-MA-670-G42a. 18__. 1860s.

Rarity: URS-1
Proof $9,400

$100 • W-MA-1850-100-G200
Engraver: Unverified, but likely New England Bank Note Co. ***Comments:*** H-MA-670-G44. No description available. 18__. 1830s–1840s.

Rarity: *None known*

$100 • W-MA-1850-100-G210
Left: 100 / Vulcan seated with sledge and anchor. ***Center:*** Train on bridge, Eagle on limb, Canal locks / C C. ***Bottom center:*** 100 ***Right:*** 100 / Ceres seated, Cornucopia. ***Engraver:*** Rawdon, Wright, Hatch & Edson. ***Comments:*** H-MA-670-G46. 18__ 1850s.

Rarity: —

$100 • W-MA-1850-100-G220
Left: 100 / Old man with tablet and compass instructing child seated at his feet. ***Center:*** C. ***Right:*** 100 / Medallion head / 100. ***Tint:*** Red. ***Engraver:*** American Bank Note Co. ***Comments:*** H-MA-670-G48a. 1860s.

Rarity: —

$500 • W-MA-1850-500-G230
Engraver: Unverified, but likely New England Bank Note Co. ***Comments:*** H-MA-670-G50. No description available. 18__. 1830s–1840s.

Rarity: *None known*

$500 • W-MA-1850-500-G240
Left: 500 / Classical scholar seated with tablet and stylus. ***Center:*** Portrait of George Washington / Two women leaning over beehive. ***Right:*** 500 / Portrait of Martha Washington. ***Engraver:*** Rawdon, Wright, Hatch & Edson. ***Comments:*** H-MA-670-G54. 18__. 1850s.

Rarity: —

$1,000 • W-MA-1850-1000-G250

Engraver: Unverified, but likely New England Bank Note Co. ***Comments:*** H-MA-670-G56. No description available. 18__. 1830s–1840s.

Rarity: *None known*

Uncut Sheets

$1-$1-$2-$3 • W-MA-1850-001.001.002.003-US010

Vignette(s): ($1) Girl / Buildings and street / Male portrait. ***($1)*** Girl / Buildings and street / Male portrait. ***($2)*** Man / Buildings and street / Woman. ***($3)*** Street scene in Haverhill / Woman with fruit. ***Comments:*** H-MA-670-G4, G4, G14, G18. January 1, 18__. 1850s.

Rarity: —

$5-$10 • W-MA-1850-005.010-US020

Vignette(s): ($5) Dog, Man seated with girl on knee, Woman and boy / Street scene in Haverhill / Woman sewing shoes, Box of shoes. ***($10)*** Man holding bull, Two men and boy standing, Sheep / Woman feeding fowl. ***Comments:*** H-MA-670-G22, G26. Partial sheet. January 1, 18__. 1850s.

Rarity: —

$20-$50 • W-MA-1850-020.050-US030

Vignette(s): ($20) View of buildings / View of buildings. ***($50)*** View of buildings / State arms. ***Tint(s):*** Red. ***Comments:*** All unlisted in Haxby. Similar to H-MA-670-G34a, G42a but with additional engraver imprint. Partial sheet. 18__. 1860s.

Rarity: —

Non-Valid Issues

$1 • W-MA-1850-001-N010

Center: Two women, Train. ***Right:*** Globe. ***Comments:*** H-MA-670-N5.

Rarity: —

$1 • W-MA-1850-001-N020

Center: Indian man and settler flanking shield surmounted by eagle, Train. ***Comments:*** H-MA-670-N10.

Rarity: —

$1 • W-MA-1850-001-A010 SN

Comments: H-Unlisted. 18__. 1840s.

Rarity: URS-5

$2 • W-MA-1850-002-A020 SN

Engraver: Boston Bank Note Co. ***Comments:*** H-MA-670-A5. Altered from $2 Bank of Owasso, Owasso, Michigan. 18__. 1830s.

Rarity: URS-5
F $150

$3 • W-MA-1850-003-A030 SN

Engraver: Boston Bank Note Co. ***Comments:*** H-MA-670-A10. 18__. 1840s.

Rarity: URS-5
F $165

$3 • W-MA-1850-003-A040

Left: Lathework panel bearing THREE vertically. ***Center:*** 3 / Group of milkmaids, One standing with bucket on head / 3. ***Bottom center:*** Shield. ***Right:*** 3 / Woman standing, Eagle, Shield surmounted by eagle / 3. ***Engraver:*** Rawdon, Wright, Hatch & Edson. ***Comments:*** H-MA-670-A15. Altered from $3 Monmouth Bank, 2nd, Freehold, New Jersey. 18__. 1840s.

Rarity: —

$5 • W-MA-1850-005-R010

Engraver: New England Bank Note Co. ***Comments:*** H-MA-670-R5. Raised from W-MA-1850-001-G010. 18__. 1840s.

Rarity: —

$5 • W-MA-1850-005-A050 SN

Engraver: Rawdon, Wright & Hatch. ***Comments:*** H-Unlisted. 18__. 1840s.

Rarity: URS-6
F $100

$5 • W-MA-1850-005-A050a

SN

Overprint: Red FIVE. ***Engraver:*** Rawdon, Wright & Hatch. ***Comments:*** H-Unlisted. Similar to W-MA-1850-005-A050. 18__. 1840s.

Rarity: URS-5

F $150

$10 • W-MA-1850-010-R020

Engraver: New England Bank Note Co. ***Comments:*** H-MA-670-R10. Raised from W-MA-1850-002-G060. 18__. 1840s.

Rarity: —

$10 • W-MA-1850-010-A060

Left: TEN vertically. ***Center:*** 10 / Ship / Man / 10. ***Right:*** Woman standing / TEN. ***Comments:*** H-MA-670-A20. Altered from $10 Bank of Lower Canada, Quebec, Canada. 18__. 1840s

Rarity: —

$20 • W-MA-1850-020-A070

Left: 20 / Train / XX. ***Center:*** Diagonal 20 on medallion head / Pat Lyon standing by forge / Diagonal 20 on medallion head. ***Right:*** 20 / Cattle, Man / XX. ***Engraver:*** Draper, Underwood & Co. / Underwood, Bald, Spencer & Hufty. ***Comments:*** H-MA-670-A25. Altered from $20 Tenth Ward Bank, New York City, New York. 18__. 1840s.

Rarity: —

$100 • W-MA-1850-100-N030

Back: Check Plate. ***Comments:*** H-MA-670-N15.

Rarity: —

$500 • W-MA-1850-500-C240

SI

Engraver: Rawdon, Wright, Hatch & Edson. ***Comments:*** H-Unlisted. Counterfeit of W-MA-1850-500-G240. 18__. 1850s.

Rarity: URS-3

F $250

$500 • W-MA-1850-500-N040

Comments: H-MA-670-N20. No description available.

Rarity: *None known*

$1,000 • W-MA-1850-1000-N050

Comments: H-MA-670-N25. No description available.

Rarity: *None known*

Merrimack Bank

1814–1864

W-MA-1860

History: The Merrimack Bank was chartered in 1814 with an authorized capital of $100,000. The economy was difficult, and in October of that year, the Legislature allowed the bank to postpone the deadline for receiving 25 percent of that sum. The bank began business in 1815. In 1818 the capital was increased to $150,000. It was raised to $360,000 in 1839 but lowered again to $180,000 between 1850 and 1864.

Circulation was listed at $52,273 in 1839, $42,295 in 1849, $48,316 in 1854, $65,820 in 1857, $67,821 in 1860, and $74,201 in 1863.

Selected figures for 1857 included: bills of this bank and other New England states $4,393.32; specie $5,668.37; real estate $2,000.

The business of the Merrimack Bank was succeeded by the Merrimack National Bank of Haverhill in 1864.

An unrelated Merrimack Bank, W-MA-2430, was chartered in Newburyport in 1795.

Numismatic Commentary: Although this bank had a long history, most of the available notes in the current marketplace are of the early PSSP type. One design, a combination PSSP and New England Bank Note Co. $500 note, is the only of that design produced for any bank and is unique in that regard.

Valid Issues

$1 • W-MA-1860-001-G010

Center: 1 / 1 / Flower garlands and gridwork segments / ONE / 1 / 1. ***Engraver:*** PSSP. ***Comments:*** H-MA-675-G2. 18__. 1814–1820s.

Rarity: —

$1 • W-MA-1860-001-G010a

Left: Panel of lathework circle segments. ***Right:*** Panel of lathework circle segments. ***Engraver:*** PSSP. ***Comments:*** H-MA-675-G4. Similar to W-MA-1860-001-G010. 18__. 1820s.

Rarity: —

$1 • W-MA-1860-001-G010b

SN

Engraver: PSSP. ***Comments:*** H-MA-675-G6. Similar to W-MA-1860-001-G010. 18__. 1820s–1830s.

Rarity: URS-2

VG $100

$1 • W-MA-1860-001-G010c

CJF

Engraver: PSSP. ***Comments:*** H-MA-675-G8. Similar to W-MA-1860-001-G010. Remainder. 18__. 1830s.

Rarity: URS-3
VF $250

$1 • W-MA-1860-001-G020

CC

Engraver: New England Bank Note Co. ***Comments:*** H-MA-675-G10. 18__. 1830s–1850s.

Rarity: URS-3
Proof $1,600

$1 • W-MA-1860-001-G020a

CJF

Overprint: Green ONE. ***Engraver:*** New England Bank Note Co. ***Comments:*** H-Unlisted. Similar to W-MA-1860-001-G020. May 1, 18__. 1830s–1850s.

Rarity: URS-3
VF $1,000

$2 • W-MA-1860-002-G030

Center: 2 / 2 / Oval of flower garlands and gridwork segments / TWO / 2 / 2. ***Engraver:*** PSSP. ***Comments:*** H-MA-675-G14. 18__. 1814–1820s.

Rarity: —

$2 • W-MA-1860-002-G030a

Left: Panel of lathework circle segments. ***Right:*** Panel of lathework circle segments. ***Engraver:*** PSSP. ***Comments:*** H-MA-675-G16. Similar to W-MA-1860-002-G030. 18__. 1820s.

Rarity: —

$2 • W-MA-1860-002-G030b

Left: Panel of lathework circle segments. ***Right:*** Panel of lathework circle segments. ***Engraver:*** PSSP. ***Comments:*** H-MA-675-G18. Similar to W-MA-1860-002-G030. 18__. 1820s–1830s.

Rarity: —

$2 • W-MA-1860-002-G030c

Left: Five TWOs vertically. ***Right:*** Five TWOs vertically. ***Engraver:*** PSSP. ***Comments:*** H-MA-675-G20. Similar to W-MA-1860-002-G030. 18__. 1830s.

Rarity: —

$2 • W-MA-1860-002-G040

Left: 2 / TWO / 2. ***Center:*** Cornucopia, Woman reclining in clouds, Cherub / TWO. ***Right:*** 2 / Ship on stocks. ***Engraver:*** PSSP. ***Comments:*** H-MA-675-G22. 18__. 1830s–1850s.

Rarity: —

$2 • W-MA-1860-002-G040a

CJF

Overprint: Red TWO. ***Engraver:*** PSSP. ***Comments:*** H-Unlisted. Similar to W-MA-1860-002-G040. 18__. 1830s–1850s.

Rarity: URS-3
VF $750

$3 • W-MA-1860-003-G050

Center: 3 / 3 / Oval of flower garlands and gridwork segments / 3 / 3. ***Engraver:*** PSSP. ***Comments:*** H-MA-675-G26. 18__. 1814–circa 1820.

Rarity: —

How to Read the Whitman Numbering System

$1 • W-MA-010-001-G010a

Denomination: Value of the note shown.

W: Whitman number. This number is a sortable code unique to each bank and note.

MA: Abbreviation for the state under study.

010: Numerical designation specific to each bank.

001: The denomination in dollars.

G010a: G indicates a good or valid note. Other categories are indicated thus: C (counterfeit); R (raised); S (spurious); N (not-attributed); A (altered). Numbers are assigned starting with 010, 020, et seq. Terminal letters following the number indicate variations of a note: a series of different colored overprints, tints, payees, etc., all on the same design of note. For more information, see the "How to Use This Book" section at the front of the volume, page xiv.

$3 • W-MA-1860-003-G050a

Left: Panel of lathework circle segments. ***Right:*** Panel of lathework circle segments. ***Engraver:*** PSSP. ***Comments:*** H-MA-675-G28. Similar to W-MA-1860-003-G050. 18__. 1820s.

Rarity: —

$3 • W-MA-1860-003-G050b

Left: Panel of lathework circle segments. ***Right:*** Panel of lathework circle segments. ***Engraver:*** PSSP. ***Comments:*** H-MA-675-G30. Similar to W-MA-1860-003-G050. 18__. 1820s–1830s.

Rarity: —

$3 • W-MA-1860-003-G050c

SN

Engraver: PSSP. ***Comments:*** H-MA-675-G32. Similar to W-MA-1860-003-G050. 18__. 1830s.

Rarity: URS-2
Proof $1,000

$3 • W-MA-1860-003-G060

Left: THREE vertically. ***Center:*** Wharf scene, Men loading barrels, Wagons, horses, ships / 3. ***Right:*** Woman carrying hat and sheaf. ***Engraver:*** New England Bank Note Co. ***Comments:*** H-MA-675-G34. 18__. 1830s–1850s.

Rarity: —

$3 • W-MA-1860-003-G060a

CJF

Overprint: Red THREE. ***Engraver:*** New England Bank Note Co. ***Comments:*** H-Unlisted. Similar to W-MA-1860-003-G060. 18__. 1830s–1850s.

Rarity: URS-3
VF $1,500

$5 • W-MA-1860-005-G070

Left: Panel bearing state arms / 5 / 5. ***Center:*** Alternating flower garlands and gridwork segments. ***Right:*** 5 / 5. ***Engraver:*** PSSP. ***Comments:*** H-MA-675-G40. 18__. 1810s–1820s.

Rarity: —

$5 • W-MA-1860-005-G070a

Left: Panel bearing lathework chain with MASSACHUSETTS vertically. ***Engraver:*** PSSP. ***Comments:*** H-MA-675-G42. Similar to W-MA-1860-005-G070. 18__. 1820s.

Rarity: —

$5 • W-MA-1860-005-G070b

Left: Panel bearing lathework chain with MASSACHUSETTS vertically. ***Engraver:*** PSSP. ***Comments:*** H-MA-675-G44. Similar to W-MA-1860-005-G070. 18__. 1820s.

Rarity: —

$5 • W-MA-1860-005-G070c

Left: Panel bearing lathework chain with MASSACHUSETTS vertically. ***Center:*** FIVE DOLLARS lined by zigzag ruled lines. ***Engraver:*** PSSP. ***Comments:*** H-MA-675-G46. Similar to W-MA-1860-005-G070. 18__. 1820s–1830s.

Rarity: —

$5 • W-MA-1860-005-G070d

CJF

Engraver: PSSP. ***Comments:*** H-MA-675-G48. Similar to W-MA-1860-005-G070 but with spiral lathework lines. 18__. 1830s.

Rarity: URS-2
Proof $750

$5 • W-MA-1860-005-G080

Left: 5 / FIVE / Woman holding sheaf and leaning on fence. ***Center:*** Train. ***Right:*** 5 / Urn. ***Engraver:*** New England Bank Note Co. ***Comments:*** H-MA-675-G50. Beware of spurious W-MA-1860-005-S010 resembling the genuine. 18__. 1830s–1850s.

Rarity: —

$10 • W-MA-1860-010-G090

Left: Panel bearing state arms / 10 / 10 vertically. ***Center:*** Alternating flower garlands and gridwork segments. ***Right:*** 10 / 10 vertically. ***Engraver:*** Perkins. ***Comments:*** H-MA-675-G54. 18__. 1810s–1820s.

Rarity: —

$10 • W-MA-1860-010-G90a

Left: Panel bearing lathework chain with MASSACHUSETTS vertically. ***Engraver:*** Perkins. ***Comments:*** H-MA-675-G56. Similar to W-MA-1860-010-G090. 18__. 1820s.

Rarity: —

$10 • W-MA-1860-010-G090b

Left: Panel bearing lathework chain with MASSACHUSETTS vertically. ***Engraver:*** Perkins. ***Comments:*** H-MA-675-G58. Similar to W-MA-1860-010-G090. 18__. 1820s.

Rarity: —

$10 • W-MA-1860-010-G090c

Engraver: Perkins. ***Comments:*** H-MA-675-G60. Similar to W-MA-1860-010-G090 but with zigzag ruled lines. 18__. 1820s–1830s.

Rarity: —

$10 • **W-MA-1860-010-G090d** CJF

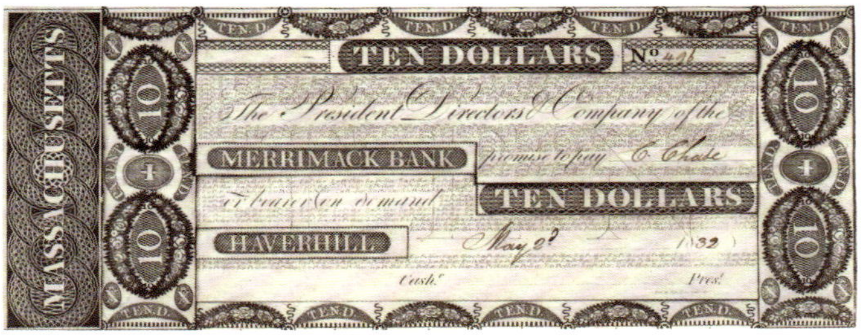

Engraver: New England Bank Note Co. ***Comments:*** H-MA-675-G62. Similar to W-MA-1860-010-G090 but with spiral lathework lines. 18__. 1830s.

Rarity: URS-2
Proof $750

$10 • **W-MA-1860-010-G100** QDB

Engraver: New England Bank Note Co. ***Comments:*** H-MA-675-G64. 18__. 1830s–1850s.

Rarity: URS-2
Proof $1,500

$20 • **W-MA-1860-020-G110**

Left: Panel bearing state arms / 20 / 20 vertically. ***Center:*** Text. ***Right:*** 20 / 20 vertically. ***Engraver:*** Perkins. ***Comments:*** H-MA-675-G66. 18__. 1810s–1820s.

Rarity: —

$20 • **W-MA-1860-020-G110a**

Left: Lathework chain bearing MASSACHUSETTS vertically. ***Engraver:*** PSSP. ***Comments:*** H-MA-675-G68. Similar to W-MA-1860-020-G110. 18__. 1820s–1830s.

Rarity: —

$20 • **W-MA-1860-020-G120**

Left: 20 / XX / 20. ***Center:*** 20 / Men plowing, Woman seated with scales, Sheaf and bales, Ship. ***Right:*** TWENTY vertically. ***Engraver:*** New England Bank Note Co. / PSSP. ***Comments:*** H-MA-675-G74. 18__. 1830s–1840s.

Rarity: —

$20 • **W-MA-1860-020-G130**

Left: 20 / Woman seated with book on lap, opening chest. ***Center:*** XX / Eagle on rock / XX. ***Right:*** 20 / Ship in harbor. ***Engraver:*** New England Bank Note Co. ***Comments:*** H-MA-675-G76. 18__. 1830s–1840s.

Rarity: —

$20 • **W-MA-1860-020-G140**

Left: Pilot boat, tugboat, and ships / 20. ***Center:*** Woman seated on sheaves holding sickle, Sheep, Farmhouse. ***Right:*** 20 / Old man seated showing bust of George Washington to child. ***Engraver:*** American Bank Note Co. ***Comments:*** H-MA-675-G78. 1860s.

Rarity: —

$50 • **W-MA-1860-050-G150**

Left: Panel bearing state arms / 50 / 50 vertically. ***Center:*** Alternating flower garlands and gridwork segments. ***Right:*** 50 / 50 vertically. ***Engraver:*** Perkins. ***Comments:*** H-MA-675-G80. 18__. 1810s–1820s.

Rarity: —

$50 • **W-MA-1860-050-G150a**

Left: Lathework chain bearing MASSACHUSETTS vertically. ***Engraver:*** PSSP. ***Comments:*** H-MA-675-G82. Similar to W-MA-1860-050-G150. 18__. 1820s–1830s.

Rarity: —

$50 • **W-MA-1860-050-G160**

Left: 50 / Woman standing with ankles crossed, Staff, Cornucopia / FIFTY. ***Center:*** FIFTY DOLLARS / 50. ***Right:*** FIFTY vertically. ***Engraver:*** New England Bank Note Co. / PSSP. ***Comments:*** H-MA-675-G86. 18__. 1830s–1840s.

Rarity: —

$50 • **W-MA-1860-050-G170**

Left: FIFTY / Woman standing with wreath and flowers / FIFTY. ***Center:*** 50 / Man restraining prancing horse / 50. ***Right:*** FIFTY / Woman standing with cornucopia / FIFTY. ***Engraver:*** New England Bank Note Co. ***Comments:*** H-MA-675-G88. 18__. 1840s–1850s.

Rarity: —

$50 • **W-MA-1860-050-G180**

Left: Portrait of two girls / 50. ***Center:*** 50 / Two blacksmiths working by anvil, Farmer watching. ***Right:*** 50 / Woman at sewing machine. ***Engraver:*** American Bank Note Co. ***Comments:*** H-MA-675-G90. 1860s.

Rarity: —

$100 • **W-MA-1860-100-G190**

Left: Panel bearing state arms / 100 / 100 vertically. ***Center:*** Alternating flower garlands and gridwork segments. ***Right:*** 100 / 100 vertically. ***Engraver:*** Perkins. ***Comments:*** H-MA-675-G92. 18__. 1810s–1820s.

Rarity: —

$100 • **W-MA-1860-100-G190a**

Left: Lathework chain bearing MASSACHUSETTS vertically. ***Engraver:*** Perkins. ***Comments:*** H-MA-675-G94. Similar to W-MA-1860-100-G190. 18__. 1820s–1830s.

Rarity: —

$100 • **W-MA-1860-100-G200**

Left: ONE HUNDRED on 100 / Portrait of William Henry Harrison. ***Center:*** Wharf scene, Men loading wagon with barrel. ***Right:*** ONE HUNDRED on 100 / Portrait of Christopher Columbus. ***Engraver:*** New England Bank Note Co. ***Comments:*** H-MA-675-G98. 18__. 1840s–1850s.

Rarity: —

$100 • **W-MA-1860-100-G210**

Left: C / Men with fishing boat at shore / 100. ***Center:*** Cornucopia, Eagle perched on bale, Sheaf / 100. ***Right:*** 100 / Ceres / 100. ***Engraver:*** New England Bank Note Co. / ABNCo. monogram. ***Comments:*** H-MA-675-G100. 18__. 1860s.

Rarity: —

$100 • W-MA-1860-100-G220
Left: 100 / Girl and boy drinking at well. ***Center:*** Yoke, plow, harrow, and sheaf. ***Right:*** 100 / Eagle on shield. ***Engraver:*** American Bank Note Co. ***Comments:*** H-MA-675-G102. 1860s.

Rarity: —

$500 • W-MA-1860-500-G230
CJF

Engraver: PSSP / New England Bank Note Co. ***Comments:*** H-MA-675-G106. 18__. 1830s–1850s.

Rarity: URS-1
Proof $5,000

$500 • W-MA-1860-500-G240
Left: Indian paddling canoe, Forest and mountains / 500 / D. ***Right:*** 500 / Justice. ***Engraver:*** New England Bank Note Co. / ABNCo. monogram. ***Comments:*** H-MA-675-G108. 18__. 1860.

Rarity: —

NON-VALID ISSUES

$3 • W-MA-1860-003-C060
Engraver: New England Bank Note Co. ***Comments:*** H-MA-675-C34. Counterfeit of W-MA-1860-003-G060. 18__. 1830s–1850s.

Rarity: —

$5 • W-MA-1860-005-C080
Engraver: New England Bank Note Co. ***Comments:*** H-MA-675-C50. Counterfeit of W-MA-1860-005-G080. 18__. 1830s–1850s.

Rarity: —

$5 • W-MA-1860-005-S010
SN

Engraver: New England Bank Note Co. ***Comments:*** H-MA-675-S5. Spurious design imitating a rough verbal description of W-MA-1860-005-G080. 18__. 1850s.

Rarity: URS-5
F $150

$10 • W-MA-1860-010-R010
Engraver: New England Bank Note Co. ***Comments:*** H-MA-675-R5. Raised from W-MA-1860-001-G020. 18__. 1830s–1850s.

Rarity: —

$10 • W-MA-1860-010-A010
Left: 10 / Hebe watering eagle in clouds / TEN. ***Center:*** Harbor scene / Portrait of Benjamin Franklin flanked by scientific instruments / Harvesting scene. ***Right:*** 10 / Dog, Woman standing with grain / TEN. ***Engraver:*** New England Bank Note Co. / PSSP. ***Comments:*** H-MA-675-A5. Altered from W-MA-520-010-G100. 18__. 1830s–1840s.

Rarity: —

$100 • W-MA-1860-100-R020
Engraver: New England Bank Note Co. ***Comments:*** H-MA-675-R10. Raised from W-MA-1860-003-G060. 18__. 1830s–1840s.

Rarity: —

$100 • W-MA-1860-100-N010
Left: 100. ***Center:*** Eagle on bale. ***Right:*** 100. ***Comments:*** H-MA-675-N10.

Rarity: —

Union Bank
1849–1864
W-MA-1870

History: The Union Bank was chartered in 1849 with an authorized capital of $100,000. George Cogswell was the first president of the Union Bank, and James Noyes was the first cashier. These two men served together until 1863, when Elbridge G. Wood became cashier.

The authorized capital was $150,000 in 1856 and $200,000 in 1860. Circulation was listed at $58,942 in 1851 before it reached a high of $126,488 in 1863. Real estate was valued at $3,300 in 1851, and specie totaled $2,517.68 the same year.

Selected figures for 1857 included: bills of this bank and other New England states $3,100; specie $11,365.43; real estate $3,000.

The business of the Union Bank was succeeded by the First National Bank of Haverhill, chartered June 23, 1864.

Numismatic Commentary: Genuine notes from this bank are very hard to locate, while some non-valid or counterfeit issues are fairly easy to obtain.

VALID ISSUES

$1 • W-MA-1870-001-G010
Left: Two women flanking shield / ONE. ***Center:*** 1 / Portrait of Benjamin Franklin. ***Bottom center:*** Eagle. ***Right:*** 1 / Female portrait / ONE. ***Engraver:*** Rawdon, Wright, Hatch & Edson / New England Bank Note Co. ***Comments:*** H-MA-680-G2. 18__. 1849–1850s.

Rarity: —

$1 • W-MA-1870-001-G010a
Overprint: Red ONE. ***Engraver:*** Rawdon, Wright, Hatch & Edson / New England Bank Note Co. ***Comments:*** H-MA-680-G2a. Similar to W-MA-1870-001-G010. 18__. 1850s.

Rarity: —

$1 • W-MA-1870-001-G010b
Overprint: Red ONE. ***Engraver:*** Rawdon, Wright, Hatch & Edson / New England Bank Note Co. / ABNCo. monogram. ***Comments:*** H-MA-680-G2b. Similar to W-MA-1870-001-G010 but with additional engraver imprint. 18__. 1850s–1860s.

Rarity: URS-5
VG $750; **VF** $1,250

$2 • W-MA-1870-002-G020

Left: Farm woman and man reclining, Three men, one with scythe, one with sickle, and one lying down, Hay wagon / TWO. ***Center:*** 2. ***Bottom center:*** Clasped hands. ***Right:*** 2 / Portrait of boy. ***Engraver:*** Rawdon, Wright, Hatch & Edson / New England Bank Note Co. ***Comments:*** H-MA-680-G4. 18__. 1849–1850s.

Rarity: —

$2 • W-MA-1870-002-G020a

Overprint: Red TWO. ***Engraver:*** Rawdon, Wright, Hatch & Edson / New England Bank Note Co. ***Comments:*** H-MA-680-G4a. Similar to W-MA-1870-002-G020. 18__. 1850s.

Rarity: —

$2 • W-MA-1870-002-G020b

Overprint: Red TWO. ***Engraver:*** Rawdon, Wright, Hatch & Edson / New England Bank Note Co. / ABNCo. monogram. ***Comments:*** H-MA-680-G4b. Similar to W-MA-1870-002-G020 but with additional engraver imprint. 18__. 1850s–1860s.

Rarity: —

$3 • W-MA-1870-003-G030

Left: Woman seated with caduceus and cornucopia, Steamship, factory, and train / THREE. ***Center:*** 3. ***Bottom center:*** Wheels and bale. ***Right:*** 3 / Indian woman holding baby. ***Engraver:*** Rawdon, Wright, Hatch & Edson / New England Bank Note Co. ***Comments:*** H-MA-680-G6. 18__. 1849–1850s.

Rarity: —

$3 • W-MA-1870-003-G030a

CC

Overprint: Red THREE. ***Engraver:*** Rawdon, Wright, Hatch & Edson / New England Bank Note Co. ***Comments:*** H-MA-680-G6a. Similar to W-MA-1870-003-G030. 18__. 1849–1850s.

Rarity: URS-3
VF $1,100

$3 • W-MA-1870-003-G030b

Overprint: Red THREE. ***Engraver:*** Rawdon, Wright, Hatch & Edson / New England Bank Note Co. / ABNCo. monogram. ***Comments:*** H-MA-680-G6b. Similar to W-MA-1870-003-G030 but with additional engraver imprint. 18__. 1850s–1860s.

Rarity: —

$5 • W-MA-1870-005-G040

Left: Two women flanking female portrait surmounted by eagle / 5. ***Center:*** 5. ***Bottom center:*** Farm tools and produce. ***Right:*** 5 bearing FIVE and portrait of George Washington. ***Engraver:*** Rawdon, Wright, Hatch & Edson / New England Bank Note Co. ***Comments:*** H-MA-680-G8. 18__. 1849–1850s.

Rarity: —

$5 • W-MA-1870-005-G040a

Overprint: Red FIVE. ***Engraver:*** Rawdon, Wright, Hatch & Edson / New England Bank Note Co. ***Comments:*** H-MA-680-G8a. Similar to W-MA-1870-005-G040. 18__. 1850s.

Rarity: —

$5 • W-MA-1870-005-G040b

SBG

Overprint: Red FIVE. ***Engraver:*** Rawdon, Wright, Hatch & Edson / New England Bank Note Co. / ABNCo. monogram. ***Comments:*** H-MA-680-G8b. Similar to W-MA-1870-005-G040 but with additional engraver imprint. 18__. 1850s–1860s.

Rarity: URS-3
VF $750
Selected auction price: Stack's Bowers Galleries, August 2012, Lot 3244, F $940

$10 • W-MA-1870-010-G050

Left: Blacksmith shoeing horse, Donkey tied to anvil, Train / TEN. ***Center:*** Medallion X bearing female portrait. ***Bottom center:*** State arms. ***Right:*** 10 / Woman with flag and three cherubs flying in clouds. ***Engraver:*** Rawdon, Wright, Hatch & Edson / New England Bank Note Co. ***Comments:*** H-MA-680-G10. 18__. 1849–1850s.

Rarity: —

$10 • W-MA-1870-010-G050a

Overprint: Red TEN. ***Engraver:*** Rawdon, Wright, Hatch & Edson / New England Bank Note Co. ***Comments:*** H-MA-680-G10a. Similar to W-MA-1870-010-G050. 18__. 1849–1850s.

Rarity: —

$10 • W-MA-1870-010-G050b

Overprint: Red TEN. ***Engraver:*** Rawdon, Wright, Hatch & Edson / New England Bank Note Co. / ABNCo. monogram. ***Comments:*** H-MA-680-G10b. Similar to W-MA-1870-010-G050 but with additional engraver imprint. 18__. 1850s–1860s.

Rarity: —

$20 • W-MA-1870-020-G060

Left: 20 / Minerva standing with spear. ***Center:*** Woman seated between 2 and 0. ***Right:*** 20 / Woman reclining on cornucopia / 20. ***Engraver:*** Rawdon, Wright, Hatch & Edson. ***Comments:*** H-MA-680-G12. 18__. 1849–1850s.

Rarity: —

$20 • W-MA-1870-020-G070

Left: Man holding 2 and 0 / 20. ***Center:*** Woman with distaff reclining on cornucopia, Ship. ***Right:*** 20 / Dolphin / Steamship. ***Engraver:*** Rawdon, Wright, Hatch & Edson / New England Bank Note Co. ***Comments:*** H-MA-680-G14. 18__. 1850s–1860s.

Rarity: —

$50 • W-MA-1870-050-G080

Left: 50 / Minerva standing by column. ***Center:*** Ceres and Vulcan flanking cornucopia. ***Right:*** 50 / Cherub in sailboat. ***Engraver:*** Rawdon, Wright, Hatch & Edson. ***Comments:*** H-MA-680-G16. 18__. 1849–1850s.

Rarity: —

$50 • W-MA-1870-050-G090

Left: Cherub and dolphin / 50. ***Center:*** Indian woman seated, Deer and hills. ***Right:*** 50 / Justice seated. ***Engraver:*** ABNCo. monogram. ***Comments:*** H-MA-680-G18. 18__. 1850s–1860s.

Rarity: —

$100 • W-MA-1870-100-G100

Left: 100 / Vulcan seated with sledge and anchor. ***Center:*** Train on bridge, Eagle on limb, Canal locks / C C. ***Bottom center:*** 100. ***Right:*** 100 / Ceres seated, Cornucopia. ***Engraver:*** Rawdon, Wright, Hatch & Edson. ***Comments:*** H-MA-680-G20. 18__. 1849–1850s.

Rarity: —

$100 • W-MA-1870-100-G110

Left: State arms / 100. ***Center:*** Indian man reclining with deer. ***Bottom center:*** 100. ***Right:*** 100 / Ceres seated. ***Engraver:*** American Bank Note Co. ***Comments:*** H-MA-680-G22. 18__. 1850s–1860s.

Rarity: —

$500 • W-MA-1870-500-G120

Left: Woman seated on sheaves, Men reaping, Man on horse / 500. ***Center:*** 500 / D. ***Right:*** 500 vertically. ***Engraver:*** Rawdon, Wright, Hatch & Edson. ***Comments:*** H-MA-680-G24. 18__. 1849–1850s.

Rarity: —

$500 • W-MA-1870-500-G130

Left: Indian paddling canoe, Forest and mountains / 500 / D D / 500. ***Right:*** 500 / Justice. ***Engraver:*** New England Bank Note Co. ***Comments:*** H-MA-680-G26. 18__. 1850s.

Rarity: —

$1,000 • W-MA-1870-1000-G140

Left: Laocoon and sons strangled by serpents / 1000. ***Center:*** THOUSAND / Train. ***Right:*** 1000 / Ships / 1000. ***Engraver:*** Rawdon, Wright, Hatch & Edson. ***Comments:*** H-MA-680-G28. 18__. 1850s–1860s.

Rarity: —

Non-Valid Issues

$1 • W-MA-1870-001-A010

Left: ONE / Hebe seated on sheaf watering eagle perched on her shoulder / ONE. ***Center:*** Eagle on shield, Ships. ***Right:*** 1 / Ceres kneeling, Sheaf, Farm. ***Engraver:*** Danforth, Bald & Co. ***Comments:*** H-MA-680-A5. Altered from $1 Columbia Bank, Washington, D.C. 18__. 1850s.

Rarity: —

Collectors and Researchers:

If you have new information about any banks or notes listed in this volume, contact Whitman Publishing, Attn: Obsolete Paper Money, 3101 Clairmont Road, Suite G, Atlanta, GA 30329.

$1 • W-MA-1870-001-A020

Left: 1 on ONE / Covered wagon drawn by four horses / ONE. ***Center:*** Three women loading sugar cane into cart drawn by four mules, Two men in cart and one standing. ***Bottom center:*** Eagle. ***Right:*** 1 / Dog, Two farmers carrying rakes, Man and boy and trees. ***Engraver:*** Danforth, Wright & Co. ***Comments:*** H-MA-680-A10. Altered from $1 Central Bank of Tennessee, Nashville, Tennessee. 1850s.

Rarity: —

$2 • W-MA-1870-002-S010

Center: Woman / 2 / Woman. ***Comments:*** H-MA-680-S5. 1850s.

Rarity: —

$2 • W-MA-1870-002-S020

CJF

Tint: Green. ***Engraver:*** American Bank Note Co. ***Comments:*** H-MA-680-S10. Dec. 1, 1859.

Rarity: URS-8
VG $75

$2 • W-MA-1870-002-S020a

SN

Tint: Red. ***Engraver:*** American Bank Note Co. ***Comments:*** H-Unlisted. Similar to W-MA-1870-002-S020. Dec. 1, 1859.

Rarity: URS-8
F $75

$2 • W-MA-1870-002-S030

Center: Mechanic seated, City. ***Comments:*** H-MA-680-S15. 1850s.

Rarity: —

$3 • W-MA-1870-003-S040

Center: Mechanic seated, City. ***Comments:*** H-MA-680-S20. 1850s.

Rarity: —

$3 • W-MA-1870-003-N010

Left: Foliage and 3. ***Center:*** 3 / Woman kneeling / 3. ***Right:*** Woman and 3. ***Comments:*** H-MA-680-N10. 1850s.

Rarity: —

$3 • W-MA-1870-003-A030

SN

Engraver: Danforth, Wright & Co. ***Comments:*** H-MA-680-A15. Altered from $3 Brownville Bank and Land Co., Omaha City, Nebraska series. August 12, 185_. 1850s.

Rarity: URS-8
F $75

$5 • W-MA-1870-005-C040b

QDB

Engraver: Rawdon, Wright, Hatch & Edson / New England Bank Note Co. / ABNCo. monogram. ***Comments:*** H-MA-680-C8b. Counterfeit of W-MA-1870-005-G040b. 18__. 1863.

Rarity: URS-8
F $75

$5 • W-MA-1870-005-S050

CJF

Engraver: Draper, Underwood, Bald & Spencer. ***Comments:*** H-MA-680-S25. From a modified, fraudulent plate originally for a counterfeit $5 Harrisburg Bank, Harrisburg, Pennsylvania. 18__. 1849.

Rarity: URS-6
F $100

$5 • W-MA-1870-005-S060

SI

Engraver: Toppan, Carpenter & Co. ***Comments:*** H-MA-680-S30. From a modified, fraudulent plate originally for a counterfeit $5 National Bank, Providence, Rhode Island. 185_. 1850s.

Rarity: URS-7
F $75

$5 • W-MA-1870-005-S060a

SN

Engraver: Toppan, Carpenter & Co. ***Comments:*** H-Unlisted. Similar to W-MA-1870-005-S060 but printed in blue. 185_. 1850s.

Rarity: URS-7
F $75

$5 • W-MA-1870-005-S070

Center: Mechanic seated, City. ***Comments:*** H-MA-680-S35. 1850s.

Rarity: —

$5 • W-MA-1870-005-N020

Left: Girl and boy. ***Center:*** Steamboat. ***Right:*** Woman. ***Comments:*** H-MA-680-N15. 1850s.

Rarity: —

$5 • W-MA-1870-005-A040

Left: FIVE / Minerva standing / FIVE. ***Center:*** Two women seated, one woman reclining / FIVE. ***Right:*** 5 / Portrait of George Washington. ***Overprint:*** Red FIVE. ***Engraver:*** Danforth, Bald & Co. ***Comments:*** H-MA-680-A20. Altered from $5 Columbia Bank, Washington, D.C. 18__. 1860s.

Rarity: —

$5 • W-MA-1870-005-A040a

CC

Overprint: Green FIVE. ***Engraver:*** Danforth, Bald & Co. ***Comments:*** H-Unlisted. Similar to W-MA-1870-005-A040. 18__. 1860s.

Rarity: URS-7
F $100

$10 • W-MA-1870-010-S080

Center: Mechanic seated, City. ***Comments:*** H-MA-680-S40. 1850s.

Rarity: —

$10 • W-MA-1870-010-N030

Left: Dog's head. ***Center:*** Group of women, Ships. ***Right:*** Female portrait. ***Comments:*** H-MA-680-N20. 1850s.

Rarity: —

$10 • W-MA-1870-010-N040

Center: Man plowing with horses. ***Comments:*** H-MA-680-N25. 1850s.

Rarity: —

$10 • W-MA-1870-010-A050 CJF

Engraver: Danforth, Wright & Co. ***Comments:*** H-MA-680-A25. Altered from $10 Brownville Bank and Land Co., Omaha City, Nebraska series. August 12, 185_. 1850s.

Rarity: URS-4
F $200

$10 • W-MA-1870-010-A060

Left: 10 / Allegorical woman and Justice flanking shield bearing anchor. ***Center:*** Man standing over boy gathering corn. Horse-drawn wagon. ***Right:*** 10 / Portrait of girl with ringlets. ***Overprint:*** Red X X. ***Engraver:*** Toppan, Carpenter & Co. ***Comments:*** H-MA-680-A30. Altered from $10 Farmers Bank, Wickford, Rhode Island. 18__. 1855.

Rarity: —

$20 • W-MA-1870-020-A070 CJF

Engraver: Rawdon, Wright, Hatch & Edson. ***Comments:*** H-MA-680-A35. 18__. 1850s.

Rarity: URS-3
F $200

$50 • W-MA-1870-050-R010

Engraver: Rawdon, Wright, Hatch & Edson / New England Bank Note Co. ***Comments:*** H-MA-680-R5. Raised from W-MA-1870-001-G010 or G010a. 18__. 1850s.

Rarity: —

Hingham, Massachusetts

Named after Hingham, England, the land on which this town was founded was first visited by colonists in 1633. A settlement was established two years later, and in 1665 the Massachusetts Indians gave the land to the settlers.

Fishing, farming, shipping, and milling were important industries in the early days. The first co-educational school in the United States was established in 1784 and later became the Derby Academy. In the 19th century, the fishing industry was a prime activity, with 65 ships fishing as the fourth largest mackerel fleet in the country. For more than four decades Hingham was marked as an official port of entry to the United States.

The population reached 2,000 during the American Revolution, of which about 600 served as soldiers. By the Civil War era the population had doubled.

Hingham Bank
1833–1865
W-MA-1880

History: The Hingham Bank was incorporated on March 25, 1833, with an authorized capital of $100,000. Capital was $105,000 from 1847 to 1851 and then $140,000 in 1855. Circulation ranged from a high of $134,927 in 1845 to $49,708 in 1857. Selected figures for 1857 included: bills of this bank and other New England states $2,804.77; specie $14,875.10; real estate $5,500.

The business of the Hingham Bank was succeeded by the Hingham National Bank in 1865.

Numismatic Commentary: Genuine notes from this Boston suburb bank are hard to find. The collector might have to settle for a non-valid issue such as a $5 note with various tints and overprints showing a large eagle.

Valid Issues

$1 • W-MA-1880-001-G010

Back: Check Plate. ***Engraver:*** PSSP. ***Comments:*** H-MA-685-G4. 18__. 1833–1835.

Rarity: —

$1 • W-MA-1880-001-G010a

Back: Plain. ***Engraver:*** PSSP. ***Comments:*** H-MA-685-G4a. Similar to W-MA-1880-001-G010. 18__. 1830s–1840s.

Rarity: —

$1 • W-MA-1880-001-G020 TD

Engraver: New England Bank Note Co. ***Comments:*** H-MA-685-G8. 18__. 1840s–1850s.

Rarity: URS-3
VF $1,000

$1 • W-MA-1880-001-G030

Left: ONE on 1 / Sailor with sextant beside capstan. ***Center:*** View of fishing schooners in calm. ***Right:*** 1 / Female portrait. ***Tint:*** Red die. ***Engraver:*** American Bank Note Co. ***Comments:*** H-MA-685-G12a. 1860s.

Rarity: —

$2 • W-MA-1880-002-G040

Back: Check Plate. ***Engraver:*** PSSP. ***Comments:*** H-MA-685-G16. 18__. 1833–1835.

Rarity: —

$2 • W-MA-1880-002-G040a

Back: Plain. ***Engraver:*** PSSP. ***Comments:*** H-MA-685-G16a. Similar to W-MA-1880-002-G040. 18__. 1830s–1840s.

Rarity: —

$2 • W-MA-1880-002-G050

Left: Panel bearing 2 / TWO / 2. ***Center:*** Sailing ship and ships / 2. ***Right:*** TWO / Woman drawing water from well / TWO. ***Engraver:*** New England Bank Note Co. ***Comments:*** H-MA-685-G20. 18__. 1840s–1850s.

Rarity: —

$2 • W-MA-1880-002-G060

Left: 2 / Woman, man, child, horse drinking from trough, house. ***Right:*** 2 / Female portrait. ***Tint:*** Red die. ***Engraver:*** American Bank Note Co. ***Comments:*** H-MA-685-G24a. 1860s.

Rarity: —

$3 • W-MA-1880-003-G070

Back: Check Plate. ***Engraver:*** PSSP. ***Comments:*** H-MA-685-G28. 18__. 1833–1835.

Rarity: —

$3 • W-MA-1880-003-G070a

Back: Plain. ***Engraver:*** PSSP. ***Comments:*** H-MA-685-G28a. Similar to W-MA-1880-003-G070. 18__. 1830s–1840s.

Rarity: —

$3 • W-MA-1880-003-G080

Left: Panel bearing THREE vertically. ***Center:*** Man reaping with sickle, Woman standing with hat and sheaf / 3. ***Right:*** THREE / Steamship / 3 on THREE. ***Engraver:*** New England Bank Note Co. ***Comments:*** H-MA-685-G32. 18__. 1840s–1850s.

Rarity: —

$3 • W-MA-1880-003-G090

Left: Two cows in stream, Girl and boy seated on bank, Cow. ***Right:*** THREE / Milkmaid standing, Boy pointing, Tree. ***Tint:*** Red 3. ***Engraver:*** American Bank Note Co. ***Comments:*** H-MA-685-G36a. 1860s.

Rarity: —

$5 • W-MA-1880-005-G100

Back: Check Plate. ***Engraver:*** PSSP. ***Comments:*** H-MA-685-G40. 18__. 1833–1835.

Rarity: —

$5 • W-MA-1880-005-G100a

Back: Plain. ***Engraver:*** PSSP. ***Comments:*** H-MA-685-G40a. Similar to W-MA-1880-005-G100. 18__. 1830s–1840s.

Rarity: URS-5

$5 • W-MA-1880-005-G110

TD

Overprint: Red FIVE. ***Engraver:*** New England Bank Note Co. ***Comments:*** H-MA-685-G44. Beware of spurious W-MA-1880-005-S010 similar to genuine. 18__. 1850s.

Rarity: URS-7

F $100; **CU** $400

$5 • W-MA-1880-005-G120

Left: Scene on seashore, Woman, men, and boat, diagonal FIVE. ***Right:*** Portrait of sailor boy with oar. ***Tint:*** Green 5s. ***Engraver:*** American Bank Note Co. ***Comments:*** H-MA-685-G48a. 1860s.

Rarity: —

$10 • W-MA-1880-010-G130

Back: Check Plate. ***Engraver:*** PSSP. ***Comments:*** H-MA-685-G52. 18__. 1833–1835.

Rarity: —

$10 • W-MA-1880-010-G130a

Back: Plain. ***Engraver:*** PSSP. ***Comments:*** H-MA-685-G52a. Similar to W-MA-1880-010-G130. 18__. 1830s–1840s.

Rarity: —

$10 • W-MA-1880-010-G140

Left: Train, Mechanic seated with tools, Building / TEN. ***Center:*** X. ***Right:*** 10 / Reaper standing with sheaf and stone. ***Engraver:*** New England Bank Note Co. ***Comments:*** H-MA-685-G56. 18__. 1850s.

Rarity: —

$10 • W-MA-1880-010-G140a

JF

Overprint: Red TEN. ***Engraver:*** New England Bank Note Co. ***Comments:*** H-Unlisted. Similar to W-MA-1880-010-G140. 18__. 1850s.

Rarity: URS-5

VF $200

$10 • W-MA-1880-010-G140b

Tint: Green 10s. ***Engraver:*** American Bank Note Co. ***Comments:*** H-MA-685-G60a. Similar to W-MA-1880-010-G140. 1860s.

Rarity: —

$20 • W-MA-1880-020-G150

Left: 20 / XX vertically / 20. ***Center:*** 20 / Men plowing, Woman seated with scales, Sheaf and bales, Ship / 20. ***Right:*** TWENTY vertically. ***Engraver:*** PSSP / New England Bank Note Co. ***Comments:*** H-MA-685-G64. 18__. 1830s.

Rarity: —

$20 • W-MA-1880-020-G160

Left: 20 / Woman seated with book on lap, opening chest. ***Center:*** XX / Eagle on rock / XX. ***Right:*** 20 / Ship in harbor. ***Engraver:*** New England Bank Note Co. ***Comments:*** H-MA-685-G68. 18__. 1840s–1850s.

Rarity: —

$20 • W-MA-1880-020-G160a

JF

Overprint: Red TWENTY. ***Engraver:*** New England Bank Note Co. / ABNCo. monogram. ***Comments:*** H-Unlisted. Similar to W-MA-1880-020-G160 but with additional engraver imprint. 18__. 1850s–1860s.

Rarity: URS-4
VF $1,250

$20 • W-MA-1880-020-G170

TD

Tint: Color unknown. ***Engraver:*** American Bank Note Co. ***Comments:*** H-MA-685-G72a. Sept. 1, 18__. 1860s.

Rarity: —

$50 • W-MA-1880-050-G180

Left: 50 / Cornucopia, Woman standing with ankles crossed, Staff, Anchor / 50. ***Center:*** FIFTY DOLLARS / 50. ***Right:*** FIFTY vertically. ***Engraver:*** New England Bank Note Co. / PSSP. ***Comments:*** H-MA-685-G76. 18__. 1830s.

Rarity: —

$50 • W-MA-1880-050-G190

Engraver: Unverified, but likely New England Bank Note Co. ***Comments:*** H-MA-685-G80. No description available. 18__. 1830s–1840s.

Rarity: *None known*

$50 • W-MA-1880-050-G200

TD

Tint: Color unknown. ***Engraver:*** American Bank Note Co. ***Comments:*** H-MA-685-G84a. Sept. 1, 18__. 1860s.

Rarity: —

$100 • W-MA-1880-100-G210

Left: Lathework panel bearing C / Portrait of George Washington / C. ***Center:*** 100 / Manhattan reclining pouring water, Ship / 100. ***Right:*** Lathework panel bearing ONE HUNDRED vertically. ***Engraver:*** New England Bank Note Co. / PSSP. ***Comments:*** H-MA-685-G88. 18__. 1830s–1840s.

Rarity: —

$100 • W-MA-1880-100-G220

Left: ONE HUNDRED on 100 / Portrait of William Henry Harrison. ***Center:*** Wharf scene, Men loading wagon with barrels. ***Right:*** ONE HUNDRED on 100 / Portrait of Christopher Columbus. ***Engraver:*** New England Bank Note Co. ***Comments:*** H-MA-685-G92. 18__. 1840s–1850s.

Rarity: —

$100 • W-MA-1880-100-G230

Left: ONE HUNDRED on 100 vertically. ***Center:*** C / Clipper ship under sail / C. ***Right:*** 100 / Spread eagle on rock. ***Tint:*** Color unknown. ***Engraver:*** American Bank Note Co. ***Comments:*** H-MA-685-G96a. 1860s.

Rarity: —

$500 • W-MA-1880-500-G240

Engraver: Unverified, but likely New England Bank Note Co. ***Comments:*** H-MA-685-G100. No description available. 18__. 1830s–1840s.

Rarity: *None known*

Uncut Sheets

$20-$50 • W-MA-1880-020.050-US010

TD

Engraver: American Bank Note Co. ***Comments:*** H-MA-685-G72a, G84a. Sept. 1, 18__. 1860s.

Rarity: —

Non-Valid Issues

$5 • W-MA-1880-005-S010

TD

Tint: Green. ***Engraver:*** New England Bank Note Co. / ABNCo. monogram. ***Comments:*** H-MA-685-S5a. Spurious design imitating a rough verbal description of W-MA-1880-005-G110. Aug. 1, 1860.

Rarity: URS-8
F $75; **CU** $300

$5 • W-MA-1880-005-S010a

CJF

Overprint: Red panel outlining white FIVE. ***Engraver:*** New England Bank Note Co. / ABNCo. monogram. ***Comments:*** H-Unlisted. Similar to W-MA-1880-005-S010. Aug. 1, 1860.

Rarity: URS-6
F $350

$5 • W-MA-1880-005-S010b

TD

Overprint: Red end panels outlining white V / 5. ***Engraver:*** New England Bank Note Co. / ABNCo. monogram. ***Comments:*** H-Unlisted. Similar to W-MA-1880-005-S010. Aug. 1, 1860.

Rarity: URS-4
F $150

$10 • W-MA-1880-010-R010

Engraver: PSSP. ***Comments:*** H-MA-685-R5. Raised from W-MA-1880-001-G010. 18__. 1830s.

Rarity: —

$100 • W-MA-1880-100-R020

Engraver: PSSP. ***Comments:*** H-MA-685-R10. Raised from W-MA-1880-001-G010. 18__. 1830s.

Rarity: —

Holliston, Massachusetts

Settled in 1659 by the Massachusetts Bay Puritans, Holliston was incorporated on December 3, 1724. It was named after Thomas Hollis of London, one of the benefactors of Harvard College. Shoemaking was a huge industry in Holliston, making it the largest producer of shoes in the United States at one time.

Holliston Bank

1854–1865

W-MA-1890

History: The Holliston Bank was incorporated on March 28, 1854, with an authorized capital of $100,000. It opened its doors for business on October 20.

Circulation averaged at about $60,000 throughout the bank's existence. The president was William S. Batchelder, and the cashier was Rufus F. Brewer during the time the bank was in business.

Selected figures for 1857 included: bills of this bank and other New England states $2,940.79; specie $5,029.43.

The business of the Holliston Bank was succeeded by the Holliston National Bank, chartered on February 14, 1865.

Numismatic Commentary: Thankfully, a good amount of Proof issues entered the market through a memorable Stack's sale. Otherwise, issues from this bank would be extremely hard to locate.

Valid Issues

$1 • W-MA-1890-001-G010

CC

Engraver: Baldwin, Adams & Co. ***Comments:*** H-MA-690-G2. Proof. Aug. 1, 1854. 1854–1860s.

Rarity: URS-4
Proof $1,000

$1 • W-MA-1890-001-G010a

CC

Overprint: Red ONE. ***Engraver:*** Baldwin, Adams & Co. ***Comments:*** H-Unlisted. Similar to W-MA-1890-001-G010. Proof. Aug. 1, 1854. 1854–1860s.

Rarity: URS-4
Proof $1,050

$2 • W-MA-1890-002-G020

JF

Engraver: Baldwin, Adams & Co. ***Comments:*** H-MA-690-G4. Proof. Aug. 1, 1854. 1854–1860s.

Rarity: URS-5
Proof $750

$2 • W-MA-1890-002-G020a

SBG

Overprint: Red 2 / 2. ***Engraver:*** Baldwin, Adams & Co. ***Comments:*** H-Unlisted. Similar to W-MA-1890-002-G020. Proof. Aug. 1, 1854. 1854–1860s.

Rarity: URS-5
Proof $750

$3 • W-MA-1890-003-G030

Left: 3 / Portrait of Charles Sumner. ***Center:*** Four women tending looms. ***Right:*** 3 / Boy. ***Engraver:*** Baldwin, Adams & Co. ***Comments:*** H-Unlisted. Proof. Aug. 1, 1854. 1854–1860s.

Rarity: —

$3 • W-MA-1890-003-G030a

Overprint: Red 3 / 3. ***Engraver:*** Baldwin, Adams & Co. ***Comments:*** H-Unlisted. Similar to W-MA-1890-003-G030. Proof. Aug. 1, 1854. 1854–1860s.

Rarity: —

$3 • W-MA-1890-003-G030b

CC

Engraver: Bald, Adams & Co. / Bald, Cousland & Co. ***Comments:*** H-MA-690-G6. Similar to W-MA-1890-003-G030 but with different engraver imprint. Proof. October 18, 1854. 1854–1860s.

Rarity: URS-4
Proof $1,000
Selected auction price: Heritage, April 2012, Lot 15242, Gem New $546

$3 • W-MA-1890-003-G030c

SBG

Overprint: Red 3 / 3. ***Engraver:*** Bald, Adams & Co. / Bald, Cousland & Co. ***Comments:*** H-Unlisted. Similar to W-MA-1890-003-G030 but with different engraver imprint. Proof. October 18, 1854. 1854–1860s.

Rarity: URS-6
Proof $600

$5 • W-MA-1890-005-G040

JF

Engraver: Baldwin, Adams & Co. ***Comments:*** H-MA-690-G8. Proof. August 1, 1854. 1854–1860s.

Rarity: URS-5
Proof $800

$5 • W-MA-1890-005-G040a

SBG

Overprint: Red FIVE. ***Engraver:*** Baldwin, Adams & Co. ***Comments:*** H-Unlisted. Similar to W-MA-1890-005-G040. Proof. August 1, 1854. 1854–1860s.

Rarity: URS-6
F $200

$5 • W-MA-1890-005-G040b

Left: V / Portrait of Thomas Hollis. ***Center:*** Train passing through deep cut. ***Right:*** V, 5, V / Portrait of Daniel Webster. ***Engraver:*** Bald, Adams & Co. / Bald, Cousland & Co. ***Comments:*** H-Unlisted. Similar to W-MA-1890-005-G040 but with different engraver imprint. Proof. October 18, 1854. 1854–1860s.

Rarity: —

$5 • W-MA-1890-005-G040c

SBG

Overprint: Red FIVE. ***Engraver:*** Bald, Adams & Co. / Bald, Cousland & Co. ***Comments:*** H-Unlisted. Similar to W-MA-1890-005-G040 but with different engraver imprint. Proof. Oct. 18, 1854. 1854–1860s.

Rarity: URS-5
F $300

$10 • W-MA-1890-010-G050

Left: TEN / Portrait of Lewis Cass. ***Center:*** Spread eagle on shield flanked by clouds and flags of the states, Stars. ***Right:*** X / Portrait of Thomas Hollis. ***Engraver:*** Baldwin, Adams & Co. ***Comments:*** H-Unlisted. Proof. Aug. 1, 1854. 1854–1860s.

Rarity: —

$10 • W-MA-1890-010-G050a

Overprint: Red TEN. ***Engraver:*** Baldwin, Adams & Co. ***Comments:*** H-Unlisted. Similar to W-MA-1890-010-G050. Proof. Aug. 1, 1854. 1854–1860s.

Rarity: —

$10 • W-MA-1890-010-G050b

CC

Engraver: Bald, Adams & Co. / Bald, Cousland & Co. ***Comments:*** H-MA-690-G10. Similar to W-MA-1890-010-G050 but with different engraver imprint. Proof. Oct. 18, 1854. 1854–1860s.

Rarity: URS-5
Proof $1,000

$10 • W-MA-1890-010-G050c

SBG

Overprint: Red TEN. ***Engraver:*** Bald, Adams & Co. / Bald, Cousland & Co. ***Comments:*** H-Unlisted. Similar to W-MA-1890-010-G050 but with different engraver imprint. Proof. Oct. 18, 1854. 1854–1860s.

Rarity: URS-4
Proof $1,100

$20 • W-MA-1890-020-G060

Left: 20 / Portrait of John Quincy Adams. ***Center:*** Train at depot. ***Right:*** 20 / Woman seated with child. ***Engraver:*** Baldwin, Adams & Co. ***Comments:*** H-Unlisted. Proof. Aug. 1, 1854. 1854–1860s.

Rarity: —

$20 • W-MA-1890-020-G060a

Overprint: Red XX. ***Engraver:*** Baldwin, Adams & Co. ***Comments:*** H-Unlisted. Similar to W-MA-1890-020-G060. Proof. Aug. 1, 1854. 1854–1860s.

Rarity: —

$20 • W-MA-1890-020-G060b

QDB

Engraver: Bald, Adams & Co. / Bald, Cousland & Co. ***Comments:*** H-MA-690-G12. Similar to W-MA-1890-020-G060 but with different engraver imprint. Proof. Oct. 18, 1854. 1854–1860s.

Rarity: URS-5
Proof $950

$20 • W-MA-1890-020-G060c

SBG

Overprint: Red XX. ***Engraver:*** Bald, Adams & Co. / Bald, Cousland & Co. ***Comments:*** H-Unlisted. Similar to W-MA-1890-020-G060 but with different engraver imprint. Proof. Oct. 18, 1854. 1854–1860s.

Rarity: URS-5
Proof $600

$50 • W-MA-1890-050-G070

Left: 50 / Portrait of Charles Sumner. ***Center:*** Cattle and sheep, some lying down. ***Right:*** 50 / Portrait of George Washington. ***Engraver:*** Baldwin, Adams & Co. ***Comments:*** H-Unlisted. Proof. Aug. 1, 1854. 1854–1860s.

Rarity: URS-5
Proof $1,000

$50 • W-MA-1890-050-G070a

QDB

Engraver: Bald, Adams & Co. / Bald, Cousland & Co. ***Comments:*** H-MA-690-G14. Similar to W-MA-1890-050-G070 but with different engraver imprint. Proof. Oct. 18, 1854. 1854–1860s.

Rarity: URS-5
Proof $1,000

$100 • W-MA-1890-100-G080

Left: C / Farmer sowing seed. ***Center:*** Indian family in canoe, man paddling, woman and two children. ***Right:*** 100 / Portrait of Charles Sumner. ***Engraver:*** Baldwin, Adams & Co. ***Comments:*** H-Unlisted. Proof. Aug. 1, 1854. 1854–1860s.

Rarity: URS-5
Proof $1,000

$100 • W-MA-1890-100-G080a

CC

Engraver: Bald, Adams & Co. / Bald, Cousland & Co. ***Comments:*** H-MA-690-G16. Similar to W-MA-1890-100-G080 but with different engraver imprint. Proof. Oct. 18, 1854. 1854–1860s.

Rarity: URS-4
Proof $1,500

Uncut Sheets

$1-$2-$5 • W-MA-1890-001.002.005-US010

JF

Overprint(s): None. ***Engraver:*** Baldwin, Adams & Co. ***Comments:*** H-MA-690-G2, G4, G8. Partial sheet. August 1, 1854. 1854–1860s.

Rarity: URS-4
Proof $2,400

$1-$1-$2-$5 • W-MA-1890-001.001.002.005-US020

Vignette(s): ($1) Portrait of Thomas Hollis / Milkmaid and two cows, one lying down / Portrait of Henry Clay. ***($1)*** Portrait of Thomas Hollis / Milkmaid and two cows, one lying down / Portrait of Henry Clay. ***($2)*** Portrait of Thomas Hollis / Two girls holding sheaf of wheat above them / Girl shading eyes. ***($5)*** Portrait of Thomas Hollis / Train passing through deep cut / Portrait of Daniel Webster. ***Overprint(s):*** None. ***Engraver:*** Baldwin, Adams & Co. ***Comments:*** H-MA-690-G2, G2, G4, G8. August 1, 1854. 1854–1860s.

Rarity: —

$1-$1-$2-$5 • W-MA-1890-001.001.002.005-US020a SBG

Overprint(s): Red. ***Engraver:*** Baldwin, Adams & Co. ***Comments:*** All unlisted in Haxby. Similar to W-MA-1890-001.001.002.005-US020. August 1, 1854. 1854–1860s.

Rarity: URS-4
Proof $4,000

$3-$5-$10-$20 • W-MA-1890-003.005.010.020-US030

Vignette(s): ($3) Portrait of Charles Sumner / Four women tending looms / Boy. ***($5)*** Portrait of Thomas Hollis / Train passing through deep cut / Portrait of Daniel Webster. ***($10)*** Portrait of Lewis Cass / Spread eagle on shield flanked by clouds and flags of the states, Stars / Portrait of Thomas Hollis. ***($20)*** Portrait of John Quincy Adams / Train at depot / Woman seated with child. ***Overprint(s):*** None. ***Engraver:*** Baldwin, Adams & Co. ***Comments:*** H-MA-690-G6, G8, G10, G12. Aug. 1, 1854. 1854–1860s.

Rarity: —

$3-$5-$10-$20 • W-MA-1890-003.005.010.020-US030a

Overprint(s): Red. ***Engraver:*** Baldwin, Adams & Co. ***Comments:*** All unlisted in Haxby. Similar to W-MA-1890-003.005.010.020-US030. Aug. 1, 1854. 1854–1860s.

Rarity: —

$3-$5-$10-$20 • W-MA-1890-003.005.010.020-US030b

Engraver: Bald, Adams & Co. / Bald, Cousland & Co. ***Comments:*** All unlisted in Haxby. Similar to W-MA-1890-003.005.010.020-US030 but with different engraver imprint. October 18, 1854. 1854–1860s.

Rarity: URS-4
Proof $1,200

How to Read the Whitman Numbering System

$1 • W-MA-010-001-G010a

Denomination: Value of the note shown.

W: Whitman number. This number is a sortable code unique to each bank and note.

MA: Abbreviation for the state under study.

010: Numerical designation specific to each bank.

001: The denomination in dollars.

G010a: G indicates a good or valid note. Other categories are indicated thus: C (counterfeit); R (raised); S (spurious); N (not-attributed); A (altered). Numbers are assigned starting with 010, 020, et seq. Terminal letters following the number indicate variations of a note: a series of different colored overprints, tints, payees, etc., all on the same design of note. For more information, see the "How to Use This Book" section at the front of the volume, page xiv.

$3-$5-$10-$20 • W-MA-1890-003.005.010.020-US030c

SBG

Overprint(s): Red. ***Engraver:*** Bald, Adams & Co. / Bald, Cousland & Co. ***Comments:*** All unlisted in Haxby. Similar to W-MA-1890-003.005.010.020-US030 but with different engraver imprint. October 18, 1854. 1854–1860s.

Rarity: URS-3

Proof $6,000

$50-$100 • W-MA-1890-050.100-US040

Vignette(s): ***($50)*** Portrait of Charles Sumner / Cattle and sheep, some lying down / Portrait of George Washington. ***($100)*** Farmer sowing seed / Indian family in canoe, man paddling, woman and two children / Portrait of Charles Sumner. ***Engraver:*** Baldwin, Adams & Co. ***Comments:*** All unlisted in Haxby. Similar to H-MA-690-G14, G16 but with different engraver imprint. Aug. 1, 1854. 1854–1860s.

Rarity: —

$50-$100 • W-MA-1890-050.100-US040a

JF

Engraver: Bald, Adams & Co. / Bald, Cousland & Co. ***Comments:*** H-MA-690-G14, G16. Similar to W-MA-1890-050.100-US040. Oct. 18, 1854. 1854–1860s.

Rarity: URS-4

Proof $2,200

Non-Valid Issues

$5 • W-MA-1890-005-R010

Engraver: Baldwin, Adams & Co. ***Comments:*** H-MA-690-R5. Raised from W-MA-1890-002-G020. 18__. 1850s.

Rarity: —

$5 • W-MA-1890-005-A010

CC

Overprint: Red FIVE. ***Engraver:*** New England Bank Note Co. / Rawdon, Wright, Hatch & Edson. ***Comments:*** H-MA-690-A5. Altered from $5 Waubeek Bank, De Soto, Nebraska. 18__. 1857.

Rarity: URS-7

F $175

$10 • W-MA-1890-010-R020

Engraver: Baldwin, Adams & Co. ***Comments:*** H-MA-690-R10. Raised from W-MA-1890-002-G020. 18__. 1850s.

Rarity: —

$20 • W-MA-1890-020-R030

Engraver: Baldwin, Adams & Co. ***Comments:*** H-MA-690-R15. Raised from W-MA-1890-002-G020. 18__. 1850s.

Rarity: —

Holyoke, Massachusetts

Settled in 1747, Holyoke was incorporated as a town in 1850. Cotton and silk were primary mill industries in the town, as well as paper. The town gained the nickname "Paper City" for its world-famous paper production. The Parsons Paper Company was the first of such mills, appearing in 1853. Others that followed caused the industrial rise of Holyoke, and by the end of the 19th century, the population was more than 35,000 due to immigrants searching for jobs and housing.

Hadley Falls Bank

1851–1865

W-MA-1900

History: The Hadley Falls Bank was incorporated on May 24, 1851, and began business on November 3 with $100,000 in authorized capital. In 1853 the capital value was $175,000, and by 1855 it had risen to $200,000.

Circulation in 1857 was $124,639 and $195,388 in 1863. Selected figures for 1857 included: bills of this bank and other New England states $150; specie $8,853.53; real estate $2,000.

The business of the Hadley Falls Bank was succeeded by the Hadley Falls National Bank of Holyoke in 1865.

Numismatic Commentary: This bank did not issue a large selection of bank notes. Some of its issues do show interesting vignettes, such as the dam on the Connecticut River at Holyoke. The vignette of this structure reaches across the whole note—an impressive sight.

As of 2003 there was a $1-$1-$2-$3 tint, a $1-$5-$5-$5 tint, and a $5-$5-$5-$10 tint plate remaining at the American Bank Note Co. archives.

Valid Issues

$1 • W-MA-1900-001-G010

Left: 1 / Female portrait. ***Center:*** Woman reclining with easel and brush, Two cherubs, one of them painting / 1. ***Right:*** 1 / Indian woman and child. ***Engraver:*** Danforth, Bald & Co. ***Comments:*** H-MA-695-G2. 18__. 1850s.

Rarity: —

$1 • W-MA-1900-001-G010a

JF

Overprint: Red overall. ***Engraver:*** Danforth, Bald & Co. ***Comments:*** H-MA-695-G2a. Similar to W-MA-1900-001-G010. 18__. 1850s.

Rarity: URS-4
Proof $4,000

$1 • W-MA-1900-001-G020

Left: Portrait of boy with cap / 1. ***Center:*** Man on horseback shooting buffalo. ***Bottom center:*** Dog. ***Right:*** 1 / Female portrait. ***Tint:*** Orange. ***Engraver:*** American Bank Note Co. ***Comments:*** H-MA-695-G4a. Jan. 1, 18__. 1850s–1860s.

Rarity: —

$2 • W-MA-1900-002-G030

CJF

Engraver: Danforth, Bald & Co. ***Comments:*** H-MA-695-G6. 18__. 1850s.

Rarity: URS-3
F $500

$2 • W-MA-1900-002-G030a

JF

Overprint: Red overall. ***Engraver:*** Danforth, Bald & Co. ***Comments:*** H-MA-695-G6a. Similar to W-MA-1900-002-G030. 18__. 1850s.

Rarity: URS-5
VG $375; **Proof** $2,500

$2 • W-MA-1900-002-G030b

TD

Overprint: Red overall. ***Engraver:*** Danforth, Bald & Co. / ABNCo. monogram. ***Comments:*** H-Unlisted. Similar to W-MA-1900-002-G030 but with additional engraver imprint. 18__. 1850s.

Rarity: URS-3
VG $350

$3 • W-MA-1900-003-G040

Left: THREE / Hebe watering eagle from cup / THREE. ***Center:*** 3 / Farmer, sailor, and mechanic / 3. ***Right:*** 3 / Sailor holding flag. ***Engraver:*** Danforth, Bald & Co. ***Comments:*** H-MA-695-G8. 18__. 1850s.

Rarity: —

$3 • W-MA-1900-003-G040a

SBG

Overprint: Red overall. ***Engraver:*** Danforth, Bald & Co. ***Comments:*** H-MA-695-G8a. Similar to W-MA-1900-003-G040. 18__. 1850s.

Rarity: URS-5
Proof $2,500

$5 • W-MA-1900-005-G050

CJF

Engraver: Danforth, Bald & Co. ***Comments:*** H-MA-695-G10. 18__. 1850s.

Rarity: URS-6
AU $300; **Proof** $1,000

$5 • W-MA-1900-005-G050a

SBG

Overprint: Red 5s on dies. ***Engraver:*** Danforth, Bald & Co. ***Comments:*** H-MA-695-G10a. Similar to W-MA-1900-005-G050. Proof. 18__. 1850s.

Rarity: URS-5
Proof $1,000
Selected auction price: Heritage, October 2013, Lot 15862, Superb Gem New $822

$5 • W-MA-1900-005-G060

CJF

Overprint: Red. ***Engraver:*** American Bank Note Co. ***Comments:*** H-MA-695-G12a. January 1, 18__. 1850s–1860s.

Rarity: URS-5
VF $300

$5 • W-MA-1900-005-G070

Left: 5 / Woman standing next to pedestal. ***Center:*** Two men and dog. ***Right:*** 5 / Portrait of girl. ***Tint:*** Orange bank title, dies, and panels of microlettering. ***Engraver:*** American Bank Note Co. ***Comments:*** H-MA-695-G14a. Jan. 1, 18__. 1850s–1860s.

Rarity: —

$5 • W-MA-1900-005-G080

Left: 5 / Male portrait. ***Center:*** Steamship at sea. ***Bottom center:*** Portrait of Indian man. ***Right:*** 5 / Female portrait. ***Tint:*** Orange. ***Engraver:*** American Bank Note Co. ***Comments:*** H-MA-695-G16a. Jan. 1, 18__. 1850s–1860s.

Rarity: —

$10 • W-MA-1900-010-G090

Left: 10 / X. ***Center:*** View of Hadley Falls. ***Right:*** 10 / X. ***Engraver:*** Danforth, Bald & Co. ***Comments:*** H-MA-695-G18. 18__. 1850s.

Rarity: URS-4
Unc-Rem $1,800

$10 • W-MA-1900-010-G090a

CC

Overprint: Red. ***Engraver:*** Danforth, Bald & Co. ***Comments:*** H-Unlisted. Similar to W-MA-1900-010-G090. Proof. 18__. 1850s.

Rarity: URS-1
Proof $4,500

$20 • W-MA-1900-020-G100

Left: XX / Justice. ***Center:*** White horse and black horse flanking state arms. ***Right:*** 20 / Woman seated. ***Engraver:*** Danforth, Bald & Co. ***Comments:*** H-MA-695-G20. 18__. 1850s.

Rarity: URS-4
Proof $3,000

$20 • W-MA-1900-020-G100a SBG

Tint: Red overall. ***Engraver:*** Danforth, Bald & Co. ***Comments:*** H-Unlisted. Similar to W-MA-1900-020-G100. Proof. 18__. 1850s.

Rarity: URS-4
Proof $3,000

$50 • W-MA-1900-050-G110

Left: Indian woman seated with shield and implements / 50. ***Center:*** Two women flanking portrait of Daniel Webster, Ships and reapers. ***Bottom center:*** Horse. ***Right:*** 50 / Blacksmith standing. ***Engraver:*** Danforth, Bald & Co. ***Comments:*** H-MA-695-G22. 18__. 1850s.

Rarity: —

$50 • W-MA-1900-050-G110a JF

Tint: Red overall. ***Engraver:*** Danforth, Bald & Co. ***Comments:*** H-Unlisted. Similar to W-MA-1900-050-G110. Proof. 18__. 1850s.

Rarity: URS-3
Proof $3,250

$100 • W-MA-1900-100-G120

Left: C / River, Train on bridge, Trees, Town. ***Center:*** Three women in clouds. ***Right:*** 100 / Ship under sail, City. ***Engraver:*** Danforth, Bald & Co. ***Comments:*** H-MA-695-G24. 18__. 1850s.

Rarity: —

$100 • W-MA-1900-100-G120a JF

Tint: Red overall. ***Engraver:*** Danforth, Bald & Co. ***Comments:*** H-Unlisted. Similar to W-MA-1900-100-G120. Proof. 18__. 1850s.

Rarity: URS-3
Proof $3,500

Uncut Sheets

$1-$1-$2-$3 • W-MA-1900-001.001.002.003-US010

Vignette(s): ***($1)*** Female portrait / Woman reclining with easel and brush, Two cherubs, one of them painting / Indian woman and child. ***($1)*** Female portrait / Woman reclining with easel and brush, Two cherubs, one of them painting / Indian woman and child. ***($2)*** Indian woman and child with white woman instructing two children flanking U.S. flag and shield surmounted by eagle / Arm, hammer, and anvil. ***($3)*** Woman watering eagle from cup / Farmer, sailor, and mechanic / Sailor holding flag. ***Comments:*** H-MA-695-G2, G2, G6, G8. 18__. 1850s.

Rarity: —

$1-$1-$2-$3 • W-MA-1900-001.001.002.003-US010a JF

Overprint(s): Red overall. ***Comments:*** H-MA-695-G2a, G2a, G6a, G8a. Similar to W-MA-1900-001.001.002.003-US010. 18__. 1850s.

Rarity: URS-3
Proof $10,000

$1-$1-$2-$3 • W-MA-1900-001.001.002.003-US010b

Tint(s): Ochre. ***Comments:*** All unlisted in Haxby. Similar to W-MA-1900-001.001.002.003-US010. 18__. 1850s.

Rarity: —

$5-$5-$5-$10 • **W-MA-1900-005.005.005.010-US020**

Vignette(s): ($5) Woman / Man, Cog wheels. ***($5)*** Woman / Man, Cog wheels. ***($5)*** Woman / Man, Cog wheels. ***($10)*** View of Hadley Falls. ***Comments:*** H-MA-695-G10, G10, G10, G18. 18__. 1850s.

Rarity: —

$5-$5-$5-$10 • **W-MA-1900-005.005.005.010-US020a**

Tint(s): Ochre. ***Comments:*** All unlisted in Haxby. Similar to W-MA-1900-005.005.005.010-US020. 18__. 1850s.

Rarity: —

$20-$50-$100 • **W-MA-1900-020.050.100-US030**

Vignette(s): ($20) Justice / White horse and black horse flanking state arms / Woman seated. ***($50)*** Indian woman seated with shield and implements / Two women flanking portrait of Daniel Webster, Ships and reapers / Horse / Blacksmith standing. ***($100)*** River, Train on bridge, Trees, Town / Three women in clouds / Ship under sail, City. ***Comments:*** H-MA-695-G20, G22, G24 18__. 1850s.

Rarity: —

$20-$50-$100 • **W-MA-1900-020.050.100-US030a**

Tint(s): Ochre. ***Comments:*** All unlisted in Haxby. Similar to W-MA-1900-020.050.100-US030. 18__. 1850s.

Rarity: —

Non-Valid Issues

$2 • **W-MA-1900-002-A010**

Left: 2 / Farmer plowing with black and white horses. ***Center:*** Two men loading wagon with sheaves, Three men cradling and binding. ***Right:*** 2 / Two floating cherubs with caduceus and sheaf. ***Tint:*** Red-brown 2s and TWO DOLLARS. ***Engraver:*** Danforth, Wright & Co. ***Comments:*** H-MA-695-A5. Altered from $2 Southern Bank of Georgia, Bainbridge, Georgia. March 1, 1858.

Rarity: —

$5 • **W-MA-1900-005-C050**

NJW

Engraver: Danforth, Bald & Co. ***Comments:*** H-MA-695-C10. Counterfeit of W-MA-1900-005-G050. 18__. 1850s.

Rarity: —
VF $125

$5 • **W-MA-1900-005-R010**

Engraver: American Bank Note Co. ***Comments:*** H-MA-695-R5. Raised from W-MA-1900-001-G020. Jan. 1, 18__. 1850s–1860s.

Rarity: —

$10 • **W-MA-1900-010-C090**

CJF

Engraver: Danforth, Bald & Co. ***Comments:*** H-MA-695-C18. Counterfeit of W-MA-1900-010-G090. 18__. 1850s.

Rarity: —
F $75; **VF** $125

Holyoke Bank
1848–1864
W-MA-1910

History: The Holyoke Bank was chartered on April 25, 1848, with an authorized capital of $100,000. It opened its doors for business on September 1. The capital was increased to $150,000, then in October 1849 to $200,000. In 1850 John Clarke was the president of the Holyoke Bank, and Thomas Green was the cashier. Irregularities were found in the accounts of 1856, and forfeiture of the charter was threatened, but a decision of the Supreme Court of Massachusetts in early 1857 allowed business to continue. In time, matters became normal. In 1860 the circulation was listed at $123,651, and in 1863 it was $199,892.

In April 1864, the business of the Holyoke Bank was succeeded by the First National Bank of Northampton.

See also listing under Northampton, W-MA-2550.

Numismatic Commentary: Notes from this bank that turn up with the most frequency are the issues showing a central vignette of the town center. Notes showing local scenery as it appeared in the mid-1800s are often a welcome addition to collections.

As of 2003 there was a $1-$1-$1-$2 tint, a $5-$5-$5-$10 tint, and a $5-$5-$5-$10 tint plate remaining at the American Bank Note Co. archives.

Hopkinton, Massachusetts

Incorporated on December 13, 1715, Hopkinton was named after Edward Hopkins, a benefactor of Harvard College. Hopkins had left behind a large sum of money for investment in New England acreage, to be used for the benefit of the college. The trustees of Harvard purchased the land with the proceeds of the fund and incorporated it as Hopkinton.

The first noteworthy crop in town was grain, later followed by fruit and dairy industries. Until 1840 agricultural pursuits were the most profitable and popular, but by 1850 boot and shoe factories had become important. After the Civil War, business declined. The associated village of Woodville was a cotton cloth making center and also the location of one of the major shoe factories, with a grist mill located there in 1714.

Hopkinton Bank
1853–1864
W-MA-1920

History: The Hopkinton Bank was incorporated on April 28, 1853, with an authorized capital of $100,000. Lee Claflin was president and Joseph Whitman was cashier in 1854. The arrangement did not last long, as Whitman died on August 11, 1854. Rufus F. Brewer was appointed assistant-cashier and was authorized to sign the circulating bills of the bank. In October 1854, James S. Tileston was elected cashier. L.H. Bowker became president in 1860.

By 1858 capital had risen to $150,000. Circulation was $99,568 in 1857 and $122,727 in 1863. Selected figures for 1857 included: bills of this bank and other New England states $4,017; specie $5,506.62.

The business of the Hopkinton Bank was succeeded by the Hopkinton National Bank in 1864.

Numismatic Commentary: The vignettes on many of this bank's notes show men working in a shoe and boot manufactory, exemplifying the local factories for these products. There were many such shops in the Boston area catering to the increasing population and the needs of exporters for the foreign market.

Valid Issues

$1 • W-MA-1920-001-G010

Left: 1 / 1. ***Center:*** Six men at work in boot factory / Dog's head / 1 on die. ***Right:*** 1 / ONE / Portrait of Lee Claflin. ***Engraver:*** Rawdon, Wright, Hatch & Edson / New England Bank Note Co. ***Comments:*** H-MA-700-G2. Mar. 1, 185_. 1850s.

Rarity: —

$1 • W-MA-1920-001-G010a

JF

Tint: Green. ***Engraver:*** American Bank Note Co. ***Comments:*** H-MA-700-G2a. Similar to W-MA-1920-001-G010 but with different date and engraver imprint. March 1, 186_. 1860s.

Rarity: URS-2
Proof $4,000

$2 • W-MA-1920-002-G020

Left: 2 / 2. ***Center:*** Six men at work in boot factory / Medallion 2. ***Bottom center:*** Dog's head. ***Right:*** 2 / Portrait of J.P. Hale. ***Engraver:*** Rawdon, Wright, Hatch & Edson / New England Bank Note Co. ***Comments:*** H-MA-700-G4. Mar. 1, 185_. 1850s.

Rarity: —

$2 • W-MA-1920-002-G020a

CJF

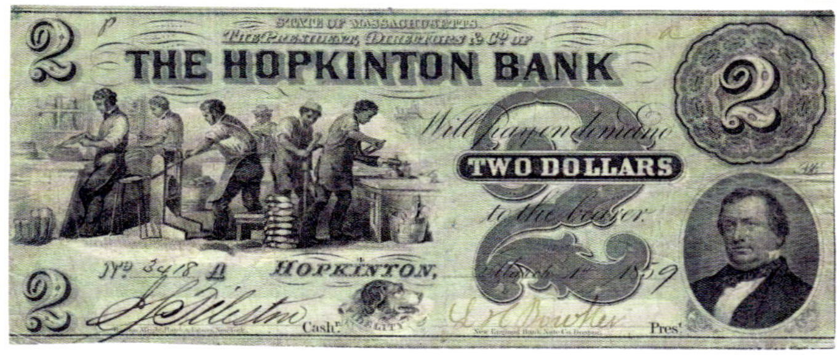

Tint: Green. ***Engraver:*** Rawdon, Wright, Hatch & Edson / New England Bank Note Co. / ABNCo. monogram. ***Comments:*** H-MA-700-G4a. Similar to W-MA-1920-002-G020 but with additional engraver imprint. March 1, 185_. 1850s.

Rarity: URS-3
VF $1,500

$2 • W-MA-1920-002-G020b

Tint: Green. ***Engraver:*** American Bank Note Co. ***Comments:*** H-MA-700-G4a. Similar to W-MA-1920-002-G020 but with different date and engraver imprint. Mar. 1, 186_. 1860s.

Rarity: —

$5 • W-MA-1920-005-G030

HA

Engraver: Rawdon, Wright, Hatch & Edson / New England Bank Note Co. ***Comments:*** H-MA-700-G6. March 1, 185_. 1850s.

Rarity: URS-2
F $750

$5 • W-MA-1920-005-G030a

Left: 5 / 5. ***Center:*** Six men at work in boot factory / FIVE DOLLARS over 5. ***Right:*** 5 / Portrait of Lee Claflin. ***Tint:*** Green. ***Engraver:*** American Bank Note Co. ***Comments:*** H-MA-700-G6a. Similar to W-MA-1920-005-G030 but with different date and engraver imprint. Mar. 1, 186_. 1860s.

Rarity: —

$10 • W-MA-1920-010-G040

CJF

Engraver: Rawdon, Wright, Hatch & Edson / New England Bank Note Co. ***Comments:*** H-MA-700-G8. March 1, 185_. 1850s.

Rarity: URS-3
VF $750

$10 • W-MA-1920-010-G040a

Left: X / 10. ***Center:*** Six men at work in boot factory / TEN DOLLARS over X. ***Right:*** 10 / Portrait of J.P. Hale. ***Tint:*** Green. ***Engraver:*** American Bank Note Co. ***Comments:*** H-MA-700-G8a. Similar to W-MA-1920-010-G040 but with different date and engraver imprint. Mar. 1, 186_. 1860s.

Rarity: —

$50 • W-MA-1920-050-G050

Left: 50 / Male portrait / FIFTY. ***Center:*** Six men at work in boot factory. ***Right:*** 50. ***Engraver:*** Rawdon, Wright, Hatch & Edson / New England Bank Note Co. ***Comments:*** H-MA-700-G10. Mar. 1, 185_. 1850s.

Rarity: —

$100 • W-MA-1920-100-G060

Left: C / Six men at work in boot factory. ***Right:*** 100 / Cog wheels and bale / 100. ***Engraver:*** Rawdon, Wright, Hatch & Edson / New England Bank Note Co. ***Comments:*** H-MA-700-G12. Mar. 1, 185_. 1850s.

Rarity: —

Non-Valid Issues

$2 • W-MA-1920-002-A010

Left: Two girls carrying sheaves / 2. ***Center:*** Sailor and mechanic flanking U.S. shield surmounted by badger. ***Right:*** 2 / Liberty standing, Indian woman kneeling. ***Overprint:*** Red TWO. ***Engraver:*** New England Bank Note Co. / Rawdon, Wright, Hatch & Edson. ***Comments:*** H-MA-700-A5. Altered from $2 Waubeek Bank, De Soto, Nebraska. 1857.

Rarity: —

$3 • W-MA-1920-003-A020

Left: 3 / Portrait of Daniel Webster. ***Center:*** Ceres and Liberty flanking U.S. shield surmounted by eagle. ***Right:*** THREE across 3 / Female portrait. ***Overprint:*** Red THREE. ***Engraver:*** New England Bank Note Co. / Rawdon, Wright, Hatch & Edson. ***Comments:*** H-MA-700-A10. Altered from $3 Waubeek Bank, De Soto, Nebraska. 1857.

Rarity: —

$5 • W-MA-1920-005-R010

Engraver: Rawdon, Wright, Hatch & Edson / New England Bank Note Co. ***Comments:*** H-MA-700-R5. Raised from W-MA-1920-001-G010. Mar. 1, 185_. 1850s.

Rarity: —

$10 • W-MA-1920-010-R020

Engraver: Rawdon, Wright, Hatch & Edson / New England Bank Note Co. ***Comments:*** H-MA-700-R10. Raised from W-MA-1920-001-G010. Mar. 1, 185_. 1850s.

Rarity: —

$10 • W-MA-1920-010-R030

Engraver: Rawdon, Wright, Hatch & Edson / New England Bank Note Co. ***Comments:*** H-MA-700-R15. Raised from W-MA-1920-002-G020. Mar. 1, 185_. 1850s.

Rarity: —

Ipswich, Massachusetts

Founded by John Winthrop the Younger, Ipswich was established in 1630 on land that had once been called Agawam. Ipswich was the town in England from which most of the settlers had come. Bordered by Hamilton, Rowley, Essex, Topsfield, and Boxford, Ipswich was located near natural resources such as fresh water—allowing for waterpower to fuel commerce—good transportation, and fishing. Salt works, tanneries, and shipbuilding were parts of the strong industries of this town, as well as the gathering and distributing of shellfish. Molasses was traded from the West Indies for the fish. Lace- and stocking-making became an important business as well. In fact, the first stocking machine to arrive in Ipswich in 1822 was smuggled there, in direct violation of a British ban against exporting technology.

Ipswich Bank

1833–1841

W-MA-1930

History: The Ipswich Bank was chartered on March 23, 1833, with an authorized capital of $100,000. Thomas Manning was president in 1835. Circulation was reported to be $25,882 in 1839, and on February 20, 1838, the capital was stated to be $30,629. Circulation that year was $14,512, and specie on hand totaled $2,981. In October 1840, the circulation was $26,838, specie was $12,949, and profit on hand was $14,237. The bank also had accrued doubtful debts to the amount of $14,000.

On May 10, 1841, the Ipswich Bank building was to be auctioned off, and on August 10, 1841, a meeting of the stockholders was called by cashier Joseph Lord Jr. to discuss the surrendering of the bank's charter. On August 17, the stockholders voted to close the bank and were given a $25 dividend on December 25, 1841.

Numismatic Commentary: The bank wound down its business in 1840 extending into early 1841 as noted. The bank was solvent and seems to have redeemed its notes, accounting for their unavailability today.

Valid Issues

$1 • W-MA-1930-001-G010

Engraver: Unverified, but likely New England Bank Note Co. ***Comments:*** H-MA-703-G4. No description available. 18__. 1830s.

Rarity: *None known*

$2 • W-MA-1930-002-G020

Engraver: Unverified, but likely New England Bank Note Co. ***Comments:*** H-MA-703-G8. No description available. 18__. 1830s.

Rarity: *None known*

$3 • W-MA-1930-003-G030

Engraver: Unverified, but likely New England Bank Note Co. ***Comments:*** H-MA-703-G12. No description available. 18__. 1830s.

Rarity: *None known*

$5 • W-MA-1930-005-G040

Engraver: Unverified, but likely New England Bank Note Co. ***Comments:*** H-MA-703-G16. No description available. 18__. 1830s.

Rarity: *None known*

$10 • W-MA-1930-010-G050

Engraver: Unverified, but likely New England Bank Note Co. ***Comments:*** H-MA-703-G20. No description available. 18__. 1830s.

Rarity: *None known*

$10 • W-MA-1930-010-G060

Engraver: Unverified, but likely New England Bank Note Co. ***Comments:*** H-MA-703-G24. No description available. 18__. 1830s.

Rarity: *None known*

$10 • W-MA-1930-010-G070

Engraver: Unverified, but likely New England Bank Note Co. ***Comments:*** H-MA-703-G28. No description available. 18__. 1830s.

Rarity: *None known*

Kennebunkport, Massachusetts

Kennebunkport, in York County on the coast, is separated from Biddeford by the Little River. Until Maine became a state on March 15, 1820, it was in the Maine District of Massachusetts. The town was first known as Cape Porpoise and was settled in the early 17th century, after which it became a prominent fishing village. In 1653 Cape Porpoise was incorporated by Massachusetts, but as it was a place of modest means and low population, it was generally considered a part of Saco. On June 26, 1684, a charter was granted to the area as Kennebunkport. In 1717 the town was reincorporated as Arundel, only to later regain the name of Kennebunkport. During the 1780s, lumbering and shipbuilding brought much prosperity to the town. This success increased until the implementation of the Embargo Act of 1807, which grounded many ships. Business in Kennebunkport declined beginning in 1826 and remained at a low level through the 1850s. In 1850 the population was 2,706. Business areas within the town were known as Kennebunkport, Cape Porpoise, and North Kennebunkport.

See also Kennebunkport, Maine.

Kennebunk Bank

1814–1820 • 1820–1831

W-MA-1940 • W-ME-960

History: In June 1813, the Kennebunk Bank was incorporated with an authorized capital of $100,000. Business commenced on April 1, 1814, and its charter was to expire on October 1, 1831. In January 1820, the capital stock paid in was $100,000; its circulation was $22,573. In that decade the bank sustained great losses on loans and was forced to close. Its charter was surrendered in October 1831. See also listing under Maine.

Numismatic Commentary: All notes for the Kennebunk Bank were of the PSSP engraving.

Valid Issues

Notes With Massachusetts Address

$1 • W-MA-1940-001-G010

Left: 1 / 1. ***Center:*** ONE DOLLAR, Text. ***Right:*** 1 / 1. ***Comments:*** H-MA-705-G10, Wait-Unlisted. 1810s.

Rarity: —

$2 • W-MA-1940-002-G020

Comments: H-MA-705-G12, Wait-Unlisted. Similar to W-MA-1940-001-G010 but with different denomination. 1810s.

Rarity: —

$3 • W-MA-1940-003-G030

Comments: H-MA-705-G14, Wait-Unlisted. Similar to W-MA-1940-001-G010 but with different denomination. 1810s.

Rarity: —

$5 • W-MA-1940-005-G040

Left: State arms / 5, Plate letter, 5. ***Center:*** Flower garlands, FIVE. ***Right:*** 5, Plate letter, 5. ***Comments:*** H-MA-705-G16, Wait-Unlisted. 1810s.

Rarity: —

$10 • W-MA-1940-010-G050

Comments: H-MA-705-G18, Wait-Unlisted. Similar to W-MA-1940-005-G040 but with different denomination. 1810s.

Rarity: —

$20 • W-MA-1940-020-G060

Comments: H-MA-705-G20, Wait-Unlisted. Similar to W-MA-1940-005-G040 but with different denomination. 1810s.

Rarity: —

$50 • W-MA-1940-050-G070

Comments: H-MA-705-G22, Wait-Unlisted. Similar to W-MA-1940-005-G040 but with different denomination. 1810s.

Rarity: —

$100 • W-MA-1940-100-G080

Comments: H-MA-705-G24, Wait-Unlisted. Similar to W-MA-1940-005-G040 but with different denomination. 1810s.

Rarity: —

Notes With Maine Address

$1 • W-ME-960-001-G010

HA

Comments: H-ME-380-G4, Wait-1. 18__. 1820s.

Rarity: URS-3

F $1,500

$2 • W-ME-960-002-G020

Left: 2 / 2. ***Center:*** TWO DOLLARS, Text. ***Right:*** 2 / 2. ***Comments:*** H-ME-380-G8, Wait-12. 1820s.

Rarity: —

$3 • W-ME-960-003-G030

Comments: H-ME-380-G12, Wait-Unlisted. Similar to W-ME-960-002-G020 but with different denomination. 1820s.

Rarity: —

$5 • W-ME-960-005-G040

Comments: H-ME-380-G16, Wait-Unlisted. No description available. 1820s.

Rarity: *None known*

$10 • W-ME-960-010-G050

Comments: H-ME-380-G20, Wait-Unlisted. No description available. 1820s.

Rarity: *None known*

LANCASTER, MASSACHUSETTS

Named after the local Nashaway Indian tribe, what later became Lancaster was settled in 1643. It was renamed Lancaster in 1653, including all of the towns of Harvard, Stow, Bolton, Hudson, Marlborough, Leominster, Clinton, Berlin, and Boylston. Lancaster is made up of three villages: Central, New Boston, and North.

Some of the settlers wished to name Lancaster after its founder, John Prescott, but the request was considered presumptuous by the Massachusetts General Court, and so they named it after Prescott's hometown in England instead.

Lancaster Bank

1836–1864

W-MA-1950

History: The Lancaster Bank was incorporated on April 9, 1836, with an authorized capital of $100,000. This was increased to $125,000 in 1848 and $150,000 by 1850. In 1863 it was reported at $200,000.

Circulation ranged from a low of $37,546 in 1839 to a high of $192,700 in 1863. Overall it averaged about $115,000. Selected figures for 1857 included: bills of this bank and other New England states $1,028; specie $20,058; real estate $1,000.

The business of the Lancaster Bank was succeeded by the Lancaster National Bank, chartered on November 22, 1864.

Numismatic Commentary: The market has been quite stingy in letting notes from this bank appear at auction or in fixed price lists. It is hard to find genuine examples from this bank. As there was a similarly named bank in New Hampshire at the time, certain of the Lancaster Bank's notes had a red overprint of MASSACHUSETTS added to facilitate sorting and redemptions in clearing houses.

VALID ISSUES

$1 • W-MA-1950-001-G010

CJF

Engraver: New England Bank Note Co. ***Comments:*** H-MA-710-G2. 18__. 1830s–1840s.

Rarity: —

$1 • W-MA-1950-001-G020

Left: Arm with sword over state arms / ONE. ***Center:*** Woman seated, Cattle / ONE. ***Right:*** ONE / Woman and cherub holding up 1. ***Engraver:*** Rawdon, Wright, Hatch & Edson / New England Bank Note Co. ***Comments:*** H-MA-710-G6. Oct. 1, 185_. 1850s.

Rarity: —

$1 • W-MA-1950-001-G020a

Overprint: Red ONE. ***Engraver:*** Rawdon, Wright, Hatch & Edson / New England Bank Note Co. ***Comments:*** H-MA-710-G6a. Similar to W-MA-1950-001-G020. Oct. 1, 185_. 1850s.

Rarity: URS-6

VG $250

$1 • W-MA-1950-001-G020b

CC

Overprint: Red ONE. ***Engraver:*** Rawdon, Wright, Hatch & Edson / New England Bank Note Co. / ABNCo. monogram. ***Comments:*** H-Unlisted. Similar to W-MA-1950-001-G020 but with additional engraver imprint. Oct. 1, 185_. 1850s.

Rarity: URS-5

F $650

$1 • W-MA-1950-001-G020c

TD

Overprint: Red MASSACHUSETTS vertically and ornate ONE. ***Engraver:*** Rawdon, Wright, Hatch & Edson / New England Bank Note Co. / ABNCo. monogram. ***Comments:*** H-Unlisted. Similar to W-MA-1950-001-G020 but with different date and additional engraver imprint. Oct. 1, 186_. 1860s.

Rarity: URS-2

VG $750

$2 • W-MA-1950-002-G030

Comments: H-MA-710-G8. No description available. 18__. 1830s–1840s.

Rarity: *None known*

$2 • W-MA-1950-002-G040

Left: Woman seated on bank / TWO. ***Center:*** Woman resting both arms on bale, Barrel and spinning wheel, Village and factory. ***Right:*** 2 / Indian woman and child. ***Engraver:*** Rawdon, Wright, Hatch & Edson / New England Bank Note Co. ***Comments:*** H-MA-710-G12. Oct. 1, 185_. 1850s.

Rarity: —

$2 • W-MA-1950-002-G040a

CC

Overprint: Red TWO. ***Engraver:*** Rawdon, Wright, Hatch & Edson / New England Bank Note Co. ***Comments:*** H-MA-710-G12a. Similar to W-MA-1950-002-G040. Oct. 1, 185_. 1850s.

Rarity: URS-5

F $600; **EF** $1,000

$3 • W-MA-1950-003-G050

Comments: H-MA-710-G14. No description available. 18__. 1830s–1840s.

Rarity: *None known*

$3 • W-MA-1950-003-G060

Left: 3 / Justice seated. ***Center:*** Man drinking, Boy, Two horses and plow. ***Right:*** 3 / Carpenter at work. ***Engraver:*** American Bank Note Co. ***Comments:*** H-MA-710-G20. 1860s.

Rarity: —

$5 • W-MA-1950-005-G070

Comments: H-MA-710-G22. No description available. 18__. 1830s–1840s.

Rarity: *None known*

$5 • W-MA-1950-005-G080

Left: Panel bearing FIVE vertically. ***Center:*** Woman unveiling shield bearing 5 / V. ***Right:*** 5 / Sailing ship. ***Engraver:*** New England Bank Note Co. ***Comments:*** H-MA-710-G26. 18__. 1840s.

Rarity: —

$5 • W-MA-1950-005-G090

CJF

Engraver: Rawdon, Wright, Hatch & Co. / New England Bank Note Co. ***Comments:*** H-MA-710-G28. Oct. 1, 185_. 1850s.

Rarity: URS-4

F $400

$5 • W-MA-1950-005-G090a

Left: FIVE / Woman and cherub holding up 5. ***Center:*** Cattle / FIVE. ***Right:*** FIVE / Indian woman standing. ***Overprint:*** Red FIVE. ***Engraver:*** Rawdon, Wright, Hatch & Co. / New England Bank Note Co. ***Comments:*** H-MA-710-G28a. Similar to W-MA-1950-005-G090. Oct. 1, 185_. 1850s.

Rarity: —

$5 • W-MA-1950-005-G090b

Overprint: Red FIVE. ***Engraver:*** Rawdon, Wright, Hatch & Co. / New England Bank Note Co. / ABNCo. monogram. ***Comments:*** H-Unlisted. Similar to W-MA-1950-005-G090 but with additional engraver imprint. Oct. 1, 185_. 1850s.

Rarity: —

$5 • W-MA-1950-005-G090c

QDB

Overprint: Red ornate FIVE and MASSACHSUETTS vertically. ***Engraver:*** Rawdon, Wright, Hatch & Co. / New England Bank Note Co. / ABNCo. monogram. ***Comments:*** H-Unlisted. Similar to W-MA-1950-005-G090 but with different date and additional engraver imprint. Oct. 1, 186_. 1860s.

Rarity: URS-3

F $750

$10 • W-MA-1950-010-G100

Comments: H-MA-710-G30. No description available. 18__. 1830s–1840s.

Rarity: *None known*

$10 • W-MA-1950-010-G110

Left: Panel bearing 10 / X / 10. ***Center:*** Allegorical man standing by oxen and plow / 10. ***Right:*** TEN / Woman standing with rudder, Cornucopia. ***Engraver:*** New England Bank Note Co. ***Comments:*** H-MA-710-G34. 18__. 1840s.

Rarity: —

$10 • W-MA-1950-010-G120

Left: 10 / Woman reclining on shield holding spear and branch. ***Center:*** Woman seated with infant, Four reapers reclining and standing, Hay wagon. ***Right:*** TEN / Bull's head. ***Engraver:*** Rawdon, Wright, Hatch & Co. / New England Bank Note Co. ***Comments:*** H-MA-710-G36. Oct. 1, 185_. 1850s.

Rarity: —

$10 • W-MA-1950-010-G120a

Overprint: Red. ***Engraver:*** Rawdon, Wright, Hatch & Co. / New England Bank Note Co. ***Comments:*** H-MA-710-G36a. Similar to W-MA-1950-010-G120. Oct. 1, 185_. 1850s.

Rarity: —

$20 • W-MA-1950-020-G130

Comments: H-MA-710-G38. No description available. 18__. 1830s–1840s.

Rarity: *None known*

$20 • W-MA-1950-020-G140

Left: 20 / Woman seated with book on lap, opening chest. ***Center:*** XX / Eagle on rock / XX. ***Right:*** 20 / Ship in harbor. ***Engraver:*** New England Bank Note Co. ***Comments:*** H-MA-710-G42. 18__. 1840s–1850s.

Rarity: —

$20 • W-MA-1950-020-G150

Left: 20 / Woman and man at well, Man drinking. ***Center:*** Dog on strongbox. ***Right:*** 20 / Eagle. ***Tint:*** Green XX / XX. ***Engraver:*** American Bank Note Co. ***Comments:*** H-MA-710-G44a. 1860s.

Rarity: —

$50 • W-MA-1950-050-G160

Comments: H-MA-710-G46. No description available. 18__. 1830s–1840s.

Rarity: *None known*

$50 • W-MA-1950-050-G170

Left: 50 / Woman standing with wreath and flowers / FIFTY. ***Center:*** 50 / Man restraining prancing horse / 50. ***Right:*** FIFTY / Woman standing with cornucopia / FIFTY. ***Engraver:*** New England Bank Note Co. ***Comments:*** H-MA-710-G50. 18__. 1840s–1850s.

Rarity: —

$50 • W-MA-1950-050-G180

Left: 50 / State arms. ***Center:*** Girl and boy seated under tree, Cows and sheep. ***Right:*** 50 / Indian woman by rock. ***Tint:*** Green. ***Engraver:*** New England Bank Note Co. ***Comments:*** H-MA-710-G52a. 1860s.

Rarity: —

$100 • W-MA-1950-100-G190

Comments: H-MA-710-G54. No description available. 18__. 1830s–1840s.

Rarity: *None known*

$100 • W-MA-1950-100-G200

Left: ONE HUNDRED on 100 / Portrait of William Henry Harrison. ***Center:*** Wharf scene, Men loading wagon with barrels. ***Right:*** ONE HUNDRED on 100 / Portrait of Christopher Columbus. ***Engraver:*** New England Bank Note Co. ***Comments:*** H-MA-710-G58. 18__. 1840s–1850s.

Rarity: —

$100 • W-MA-1950-100-G210

Left: C / Men with fishing boat at shore / 100. ***Center:*** Cornucopia, Eagle perched on bale, Sheaf / 100. ***Right:*** 100 / Ceres / 100. ***Engraver:*** New England Bank Note Co. ***Comments:*** H-MA-710-G60. 18__. 1850s.

Rarity: —

$100 • W-MA-1950-100-G220

Left: Woman leaning on pillar / 100. ***Center:*** Liberty holding wreath over state arms. ***Right:*** 100 / Portrait of boy. ***Tint:*** Green C C. ***Engraver:*** American Bank Note Co. ***Comments:*** H-MA-710-G62a. 1860s.

Rarity: —

$500 • W-MA-1950-500-G230

Left: Indian paddling canoe, Forest and mountains / 500 / D D / 500. ***Right:*** 500 / Justice. ***Engraver:*** New England Bank Note Co. ***Comments:*** H-MA-710-G66. 18__. 1850s.

Rarity: —

$1,000 • W-MA-1950-1000-G240

Left: Eagle on cliff, Ship / 1000 / M / 1000. ***Right:*** 1000 / Indian woman with bow and arrows. ***Engraver:*** New England Bank Note Co. ***Comments:*** H-MA-710-G70. A spurious printing from a stolen genuine plate has been recorded. 18__. 1850s.

Rarity: —

Non-Valid Issues

$2 • W-MA-1950-002-C040

Comments: H-MA-710-C12. Counterfeit of W-MA-1950-002-G040 or G040a. Oct. 1, 185_. 1850s.

Rarity: —

$3 • W-MA-1950-003-C060

Engraver: American Bank Note Co. ***Comments:*** H-MA-710-C20. Counterfeit of W-MA-1950-003-G060. 1860s.

Rarity: —

$5 • W-MA-1950-005-R010

CC

Engraver: Rawdon, Wright, Hatch & Co. / New England Bank Note Co. ***Comments:*** H-MA-710-R5. Raised from W-MA-1950-001-G020 or G020a. Oct. 1, 185_. 1850s.

Rarity: URS-6

F $250

$5 • W-MA-1950-005-A010

Left: Indian standing / 5. ***Center:*** V / Building and ship / Train with smoke / Lion and horse's head with V. ***Right:*** Woman standing / FIVE. ***Comments:*** H-MA-710-A5. Altered from $5 Bank of Lower Canada, Quebec, Canada. 18__. 1840s.

Rarity: —

$10 • W-MA-1950-010-A020

Left: TEN vertically. ***Center:*** 10 / Ship, Mercury seated on shore with caduceus / 10. ***Bottom center:*** Royal crest. ***Right:*** Minerva standing with staff / TEN. ***Comments:*** H-MA-710-A10. Altered from $10 Bank of Lower Canada, Quebec, Canada. 18__. 1840s.

Rarity: —

Lawrence, Massachusetts

First settled in 1640 and made up of parts of Andover and Methuen, this district was purchased in 1845 by Boston industrialists led by Abbott Lawrence. The city was named after him and incorporated in 1853.

Lawrence's close proximity to Lowell and Boston, as well as its location on the Merrimack River to provide a power source, proved to be ideal. In 1860 the Pemberton Mill collapsed from unsafe conditions, killing 145 workers. Despite this, Lawrence was a strong wool processing town through the turn of the 20th century. Immigrants came to the United States in droves in the mid-19th century with the result that the population of Lawrence was mostly made up of workers from all over Europe. As such, Lawrence became known as the "Immigrant City."

Bay State Bank

1847–1865

W-MA-1960

History: The Bay State Bank, to be located in Methuen, was chartered on February 10, 1847, with an authorized capital of $100,000. This was increased to $241,900 by 1849 and had risen to $300,000 by 1851. It got as high as $500,000 in 1852. In December 1860, it was back down to $375,000. Charles L. Storrow was the president of the bank, and Nathaniel White was cashier.

Circulation in 1849 was $133,930, experiencing a high of $245,934 in 1863. Real estate was valued at $20,000 and specie at $7,852.96. The same increased to $16,953.09 by 1858.

The business of the Bay State Bank was succeeded by the Bay State National Bank of Lawrence, chartered April 10, 1865.

Numismatic Commentary: On occasion, collectors may be able to purchase a genuine note from this bank, but more likely a counterfeit $10 note will be offered.

As of 2003 there was a $5-$5-$5-$10 back plate remaining at the American Bank Note Co. archives.

Valid Issues

$1 • W-MA-1960-001-G010

QDB

Engraver: Toppan, Carpenter & Co. ***Comments:*** H-MA-715-G2. Proof. 18__. 1847–1860s.

Rarity: URS-4
Proof $2,250

$1 • W-MA-1960-001-G010a

CC

Overprint: Red 1 / 1. ***Engraver:*** Toppan, Carpenter & Co. ***Comments:*** H-Unlisted. 18__. 1847–1860s.

Rarity: URS-4
Proof $2,500

$2 • W-MA-1960-002-G020

QDB

Engraver: Toppan, Carpenter & Co. ***Comments:*** H-MA-715-G4. Proof. 18__. 1847–1860s.

Rarity: URS-4
Proof $2,500

$3 • W-MA-1960-003-G030

QDB

Engraver: Toppan, Carpenter & Co. ***Comments:*** H-MA-715-G6. 18__. 1847–1860s.

Rarity: URS-4
Proof $2,500
Selected auction price: Heritage, January 2014, Lot 15355, New $2,232

$3 • W-MA-1960-003-G030a

CJF

Overprint: Red 3 / 3. ***Engraver:*** Toppan, Carpenter & Co. / ABNCo. monogram. ***Comments:*** H-Unlisted. Similar to W-MA-1960-003-G030 but with additional engraver imprint. 18__. 1847–1860s.

Rarity: URS-3
Proof $3,000

Collectors and Researchers:

If you have new information about any banks or notes listed in this volume, contact Whitman Publishing, Attn: Obsolete Paper Money, 3101 Clairmont Road, Suite G, Atlanta, GA 30329.

$5 • W-MA-1960-005-G040

CJF

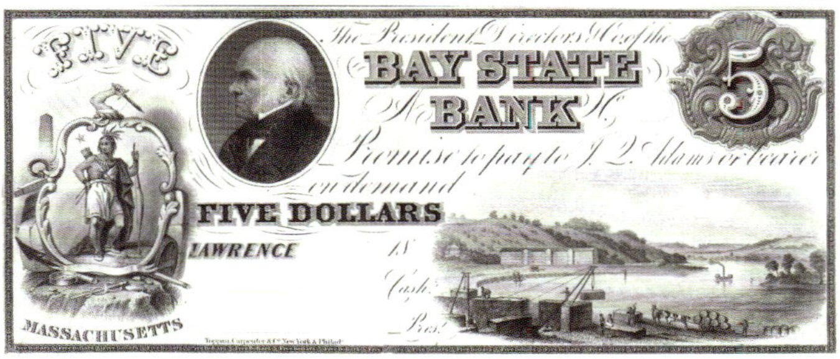

Engraver: Toppan, Carpenter & Co. ***Comments:*** H-MA-715-G8. Proof. 18__. 1847–1860s.

Rarity: —

$10 • W-MA-1960-010-G050

Engraver: Toppan, Carpenter & Co. ***Comments:*** H-MA-715-G12. Similar to W-MA-1960-010-C050. 18__. 1847–1860s.

Rarity: —

$20 • W-MA-1960-020-G060

Left: 20 / Man with sledge over shoulder and cannon. ***Center:*** State arms. ***Right:*** 20 / Woman seated with pole. ***Engraver:*** Toppan, Carpenter & Co. ***Comments:*** H-MA-715-G14. 18__. 1847–1860s.

Rarity: —

$50 • W-MA-1960-050-G070

Left: FIFTY / State arms. ***Right:*** 50 / Scene with men and horses. ***Engraver:*** Toppan, Carpenter & Co. ***Comments:*** H-MA-715-G16. 18__. 1847–1860s.

Rarity: —

$100 • W-MA-1960-100-G080

JF

Engraver: Toppan, Carpenter & Co. ***Comments:*** H-MA-715-G18 Proof. 18__. 1847–1860s.

Rarity: URS-4

Proof $3,500

$500 • W-MA-1960-500-G090

CC

Engraver: Toppan, Carpenter & Co. ***Comments:*** H-MA-715-G20. Proof. 18__. 1847–1860s.

Rarity: URS-3

Proof $5,500

Uncut Sheets

$1-$1-$2-$3 • W-MA-1960-001.001.002.003-US010

Vignette(s): ($1) State arms / Woman seated with merchandise, Ship and factories / Indian woman as Liberty. ***($1)*** State arms / Woman seated with merchandise, Ship and factories / Indian woman as Liberty. ***($2)*** State arms / Dog and strongbox. ***($3)*** State arms / Men chopping log / Helmeted medallion head. ***Engraver:*** Toppan, Carpenter & Co. ***Comments:*** H-MA-715-G2, G2, G4, G6.

Rarity: —

Non-Valid Issues

$5 • W-MA-1960-005-A010

Left: 5 / Blacksmith at anvil / FIVE. ***Center:*** Mercury standing with 5, Cornucopia and merchandise, Factories and ship. ***Right:*** 5 / Ceres kneeling / FIVE. ***Engraver:*** New England Bank Note Co. ***Comments:*** H-MA-715-A5. Altered from $5 Washington County Bank, Calais, Maine, or from notes of other failed banks using the same plate. 18__. 1840s–1850s.

Rarity: —

$10 • W-MA-1960-010-C050

SN

Engraver: Toppan, Carpenter & Co. ***Comments:*** H-MA-715-C12. Counterfeit of W-MA-1960-010-G050. 18__. 1860s.

Rarity: URS-7

VF $175

$10 • W-MA-1960-010-R010

Engraver: Toppan, Carpenter & Co. ***Comments:*** H-MA-715-R5. Raised from W-MA-1960-001-G010. 18__. 1850s.

Rarity: —

$10 • W-MA-1960-010-A020

Left: 10 / Farmer sowing / TEN. ***Center:*** Mercury standing with 10, Cornucopia and merchandise, Factories and ship, Canal scene. ***Right:*** 10 / Ship / TEN. ***Engraver:*** New England Bank Note Co. ***Comments:*** H-MA-715-A10. Altered from $10 Washington County Bank, Calais, Maine, or from notes of other failed banks using the same plate. 18__. 1840s–1850s.

Rarity: —

Pemberton Bank

1854–1865

W-MA-1970

History: The Pemberton Bank was incorporated on March 28, 1854, with an authorized capital of $100,000. It began business on October 13. The bank's annual expenses in 1851 were reported to be about $1,800.[20] Its circulation was $100,614 in 1863. Real estate was valued at $10,700.49, and specie was listed at $4,970.97.

The business of the Pemberton Bank was succeeded by the National Pemberton Bank of Lawrence, chartered on April 24, 1865.

Numismatic Commentary: Genuine notes are hard to locate, especially in denominations higher than $5.

Valid Issues

$1 • W-MA-1970-001-G010

Left: 1 / Woman with veil / ONE. ***Center:*** Trees / Train / ONE. ***Right:*** 1 / Portrait of Daniel Webster / ONE. ***Overprint:*** Red ONE. ***Engraver:*** Toppan, Carpenter, Casilear & Co. ***Comments:*** H-MA-720-G2a. Oct. 2, 18__. 1850s.

Rarity: —

$2 • W-MA-1970-002-G020

Left: 2 / Woman with flowers. ***Center:*** Two women tending looms. ***Right:*** 2 / Portrait of George Washington. ***Overprint:*** Red TWO. ***Engraver:*** Toppan, Carpenter, Casilear & Co. ***Comments:*** H-MA-720-G4a. Oct. 2, 18__. 1850s.

Rarity: —

$3 • W-MA-1970-003-G030

CJF

Overprint: Red THREE. ***Engraver:*** Toppan, Carpenter, Casilear & Co. ***Comments:*** H-MA-720-G6a. October 2, 18__. 1850s.

Rarity: URS-4

F $1,000

$5 • W-MA-1970-005-G040

CC

Engraver: Toppan, Carpenter, Casilear & Co. ***Comments:*** H-MA-720-G8a. Proof. October 2, 18__. 1850s.

Rarity: URS-3

Proof $3,500

$10 • W-MA-1970-010-G050

Left: X / Three women standing / TEN. ***Center:*** Woman with state arms, Sailing ship. ***Right:*** 10 / Blacksmith with anvil. ***Engraver:*** Toppan, Carpenter, Casilear & Co. ***Comments:*** H-MA-720-G10. Oct. 2, 18__. 1850s.

Rarity: URS-3

Proof $2,000

$20 • W-MA-1970-020-G060

JF

Engraver: Toppan, Carpenter, Casilear & Co. ***Comments:*** H-MA-720-G12. Proof. October 2, 18__. 1850s.

Rarity: URS-4

Proof $3,000

$50 • W-MA-1970-050-G070

Left: 50 / Portrait of Henry Clay. ***Center:*** Liberty seated with shield, pole and cap / U.S. Capitol. ***Right:*** 50 / Female portrait. ***Engraver:*** Toppan, Carpenter, Casilear & Co. ***Comments:*** H-MA-720-G14. Oct. 2, 18__. 1850s.

Rarity: —

$100 • W-MA-1970-100-G080

Left: C / Anchor and bale. ***Center:*** Woman seated with shield, pole and cap, Eagle and fasces. ***Right:*** 100 / Eagle. ***Engraver:*** Toppan, Carpenter, Casilear & Co. ***Comments:*** H-MA-720-G16. Oct. 2, 18__. 1850s.

Rarity: —

$500 • W-MA-1970-500-G090

Left: 500 / Scene on Dorchester Heights. ***Center:*** "Landing of the Pilgrims". ***Right:*** 500 / D. ***Engraver:*** Toppan, Carpenter, Casilear & Co. ***Comments:*** H-MA-720-G18. Oct. 2, 18__. 1850s.

Rarity: —

Non-Valid Issues

$2 • W-MA-1970-002-N010

Center: Woman and child floating in clouds above river. ***Right:*** Portrait. ***Comments:*** H-MA-720-N5.

Rarity: —

$10 • W-MA-1970-010-S010

CJF

Overprint: Red outlining white TEN. ***Engraver:*** Toppan, Carpenter & Co. ***Comments:*** H-MA-720-S5. 18__. 1850s.

Rarity: URS-6

F $75

$10 • W-MA-1970-010-N020

Center: Commerce seated on wharf with goods. ***Comments:*** H-MA-720-N10.

Rarity: —

Lee, Massachusetts

The land that was part of the territory of the Mohegan Indians was incorporated under the name of Lee in 1777. It was named after General Charles Lee, was made up from parts of Great Barrington and Washington, and includes the villages of South and East Lee.

Industries during the early years of the town included agriculture and lumbering, as well as the making of lime in kilns. Lee is located on the Housatonic River, which provided power for textile mills and wire mills. Papermaking rose to prominence when the first paper mill was built in 1806. The next mill was set up in 1827. By 1857 Lee claimed 25 paper mills, including the one that served the *New York Times*, which published its first issue in 1851.

Other manufacturing industries included cotton and woolen goods, leather, hats, boots, shoes, iron, iron castings, axes, shovels, spades, hoes, forks, ploughs, chairs, tin, wooden wares, and carriages. Marble also became a profitable business after the first quarry was established in 1852. The Housatonic Railroad carried nearly 500,000 cubic feet of marble in 1857. Lee marble was used in constructing part of the U.S. Capitol.

Lee Bank

1835–1865

W-MA-1980

History: The Lee Bank was incorporated on March 27, 1835, with an authorized capital of $100,000. The capital was increased to $200,000 by 1851. In 1854 it was $300,000, and it fluctuated between $200,000 and $300,000 for the remainder of the bank's existence.

The Lee Bank's circulation was $89,166 in 1837 and $226,420 in 1863. Real estate was valued at $2,330 and specie at $5,955.18.

The business of the Lee Bank was succeeded by the Lee National Bank, chartered on March 14, 1865.

Numismatic Commentary: Genuine notes are hard to locate in the marketplace but not impossible. The note that shows up most often is a spurious $5 with red-orange lathework covering the entire face.

Valid Issues

$1 • W-MA-1980-001-G010

Left: 1 / Woman wearing bonnet with pail / ONE. ***Center:*** Machinery and merchandise flanking Ceres seated holding sickle and rake, Factories and harbor / ONE / Panel outlining white ONE. ***Right:*** 1 / Ship / ONE. ***Engraver:*** PSSP / New England Bank Note Co. ***Comments:*** H-MA-725-G2. 18__. 1830s–1840s.

Rarity: —

$1 • W-MA-1980-001-G020

CJF

Engraver: Rawdon, Wright, Hatch & Edson. ***Comments:*** H-MA-725-G4. 18__. 1830s–1850s.

Rarity: URS-5

VG $500; **VF** $1,250

$1 • W-MA-1980-001-G020a

Left: ONE / Woman / ONE. ***Center:*** 1 with cherub / Ship, Woman with shield bearing eagle / 1 with cherub. ***Right:*** ONE / Portrait of George Washington / ONE. ***Engraver:*** Rawdon, Wright, Hatch & Edson. ***Comments:*** H-MA-725-G4a. Similar to W-MA-1980-001-G020 but with engraved payee W. Porter, Jr. 18__. 1830s–1840s.

Rarity: —

$1 • W-MA-1980-001-G020b

CC

Overprint: Green panel outlining ONE. ***Engraver:*** Rawdon, Wright, Hatch & Edson / ABNCo. monogram. ***Comments:*** H-MA-725-G4e. Similar to W-MA-1980-001-G020 but with additional engraver imprint. Jan. 1, 18__. 1850s.

Rarity: URS-3

EF $800

$1 • W-MA-1980-001-G020c

CJF

Overprint: Green ONE. ***Engraver:*** Rawdon, Wright, Hatch & Edson / ABNCo. monogram. ***Comments:*** H-MA-725-G4f. Similar to W-MA-1980-001-G020 but with additional engraver imprint. October 1, 18__. 1850s.

Rarity: URS-3

EF $800

$1 • W-MA-1980-001-G030

CC

Tint: Red lathework. *Engraver:* Danforth, Wright & Co. *Comments:* H-MA-725-G6a. April 1, 18__. 1850s.

Rarity: URS-2

VG $1,500; **EF** $3,000

$2 • W-MA-1980-002-G040

Left: 2 / Woman standing with staff, Cornucopia / TWO. *Center:* TWO / Machinery and merchandise flanking Ceres seated holding sickle and rake, Factories and harbor / Panel outlining white TWO. *Right:* 2 / Woman wearing hat, Trees / TWO. *Engraver:* New England Bank Note Co. / PSSP. *Comments:* H-MA-725-G8a. 18__. 1830s–1840s.

Rarity: —

$2 • W-MA-1980-002-G050

CC

Engraver: Rawdon, Wright, Hatch & Edson. *Comments:* H-MA-725-G10. 18__. 1830s–1840s.

Rarity: URS-3

F $800

$2 • W-MA-1980-002-G050a

CJF

Overprint: Green TWO. *Engraver:* Rawdon, Wright, Hatch & Edson. *Comments:* H-Unlisted. Similar to W-MA-1980-002-G050. October 1, 18__. 1850s.

Rarity: URS-2

F $2,000

$2 • W-MA-1980-002-G050b

Left: TWO / Woman / TWO. *Center:* 2 / Two women flanking 2 / 2. *Bottom center:* State arms. *Right:* 2 with woman standing inside. *Overprint:* Green TWO. *Engraver:* Rawdon, Wright, Hatch & Edson / ABNCo. monogram. *Comments:* H-MA-725-G10a. Similar to W-MA-1980-002-G050 but with additional engraver imprint. October 1, 18__. 1850s.

Rarity: —

$2 • W-MA-1980-002-G060

Left: 2 / Female portrait. *Center:* Three women with bust of George Washington / TWO. *Right:* TWO / 2 inside 2. *Tint:* Brown lathework. *Engraver:* Danforth, Wright & Co. *Comments:* H-MA-725-G12a. Apr. 1, 18__. 1850s.

Rarity: —

$3 • W-MA-1980-003-G070

Left: THREE / Beehive and foliage / THREE. *Center:* Machinery and merchandise flanking Ceres seated holding sickle and rake, Factories and harbor / THREE / Panel outlining the white THREE. *Right:* 3 on THREE / Two reapers / 3 on THREE. *Engraver:* New England Bank Note Co. / PSSP. *Comments:* H-MA-725-G14. 18__. 1830s–1840s.

Rarity: —

$5 • W-MA-1980-005-G080

Left: 5 / Blacksmith at anvil / FIVE. *Center:* Mercury standing with 5, Cornucopia and merchandise, Factories and ship / V / Panel outlining white FIVE. *Right:* 5 / Ceres kneeling / FIVE. *Engraver:* New England Bank Note Co. / PSSP. *Comments:* H-MA-725-G16. 18__. 1830s–1850s.

Rarity: —

$5 • W-MA-1980-005-G090

Left: 5 / Female portrait / 5. *Center:* 5 / Woman / 5. *Right:* Die / Cherub / Die. *Engraver:* Rawdon, Wright, Hatch & Edson. *Comments:* H-MA-725-G18. 18__. 1830s–1840s.

Rarity: —

$5 • W-MA-1980-005-G090a

SI

Overprint: Green ornate FIVE. *Engraver:* Rawdon, Wright, Hatch & Edson / ABNCo. monogram. *Comments:* H-MA-725-G18a. Similar to W-MA-1980-005-G090 but with additional engraver imprint. October 1, 18__. 1850s.

Rarity: URS-3

VG $500; **F** $800

$5 • W-MA-1980-005-G100

Left: 5 / Female portrait. *Center:* 5. *Right:* 5 / Woman seated with sword, balance, eagle, and strongbox. *Tint:* Brown. *Engraver:* Danforth, Wright & Co. *Comments:* H-MA-725-G20a. Apr. 1, 18__. 1850s.

Rarity: —

$10 • W-MA-1980-010-G110

Engraver: Unverified, but likely New England Bank Note Co. ***Comments:*** H-MA-725-G21. No description available. 18__. 1830s.

Rarity: *None known*

$10 • W-MA-1980-010-G120

Left: Panel bearing 10 / X / 10. ***Center:*** Allegorical man standing by oxen and plow / 10. ***Right:*** TEN / Woman standing with rudder, Cornucopia. ***Engraver:*** New England Bank Note Co. ***Comments:*** H-MA-725-G22. 18__. 1840s–1850s.

Rarity: —

$10 • W-MA-1980-010-G130

Left: 10 / Woman seated with pen, scroll, harp, and palette. ***Center:*** Medallion. ***Bottom center:*** Beehive. ***Right:*** Indian woman as Liberty. ***Tint:*** Brown. ***Engraver:*** Danforth, Wright & Co. ***Comments:*** H-MA-725-G24a. 18__. 1850s.

Rarity: —

$10 • W-MA-1980-010-G140

Left: 10 / Woman seated on box. ***Center:*** Two women seated with dog / X X. ***Right:*** 10 / Female portrait. ***Overprint:*** Green TEN. ***Engraver:*** Rawdon, Wright, Hatch & Edson. ***Comments:*** H-MA-725-G26a. Oct. 1, 1857.

Rarity: —

$20 • W-MA-1980-020-G150

Engraver: Unverified, but likely New England Bank Note Co. ***Comments:*** H-MA-725-G28. No description available. 18__. 1830s–1840s.

Rarity: *None known*

$20 • W-MA-1980-020-G160

Left: 20 / Woman seated with book on lap, opening chest. ***Center:*** XX / Eagle on rock / XX. ***Right:*** 20 / Ship in harbor. ***Engraver:*** New England Bank Note Co. / PSSP. ***Comments:*** H-MA-725-G30. 18__. 1840s–1850s.

Rarity: —

$20 • W-MA-1980-020-G170

JF

Overprint: Green TWENTY. ***Engraver:*** Rawdon, Wright, Hatch & Edson. ***Comments:*** H-MA-725-G32a. Proof. October 1, 1857.

Rarity: URS-4
Proof $3,250

$50 • W-MA-1980-050-G180

Engraver: Unverified, but likely New England Bank Note Co. ***Comments:*** H-MA-725-G34. No description available. 18__. 1830s–1840s.

Rarity: *None known*

$50 • W-MA-1980-050-G190

Left: FIFTY / Woman standing with wreath and flowers / FIFTY. ***Center:*** 50 / Man restraining prancing horse / 50. ***Right:*** FIFTY / Woman standing with cornucopia / FIFTY. ***Engraver:*** New England Bank Note Co. / PSSP. ***Comments:*** H-MA-725-G36. 18__. 1840s–1850s.

Rarity: —

$50 • W-MA-1980-050-G200

Left: Woman standing. ***Center:*** 50 / Three women seated. ***Right:*** 50 / FIFTY / Portrait of Andrew Jackson. ***Overprint:*** Green FIFTY. ***Engraver:*** Rawdon, Wright, Hatch & Edson. ***Comments:*** H-MA-725-G38a. Oct. 1, 1857.

Rarity: —

$100 • W-MA-1980-100-G210

CC

Overprint: Green HUNDRED. ***Engraver:*** Rawdon, Wright, Hatch & Edson. ***Comments:*** H-MA-725-G40a. Proof. October 1, 1857.

Rarity: URS-3
Proof $4,500

$500 • W-MA-1980-500-G220

Left: Woman seated on sheaves, Men reaping, Man on horse / 500. ***Center:*** 500 / D. ***Right:*** 500 vertically. ***Overprint:*** Green. ***Engraver:*** Rawdon, Wright, Hatch & Edson. ***Comments:*** H-MA-725-G44a. 18__. 1850s.

Rarity: —

Uncut Sheets

$1-$1-$2-$5 • W-MA-1980-001.001.002.005-US010

Vignette(s): ***($1)*** Woman / Woman with frame / Portrait of George Washington. ***($1)*** Woman / Woman with frame / Portrait of George Washington. ***($2)*** Woman / Woman / Woman / State arms / 2 with woman standing inside. ***($5)*** Female portrait / Woman / Die / Cherub / Die. ***Engraver:*** Rawdon, Wright, Hatch & Edson. ***Comments:*** H-MA-725-G4, G4, G10, G18.

Rarity: —

$1-$1-$2-$5 • W-MA-1980-001.001.002.005-US010a

Tint(s): Brown. ***Engraver:*** Rawdon, Wright, Hatch & Edson. ***Comments:*** H-MA-725-G6a, G6a, G12a, G20a. Similar to W-MA-1980-001.001.002.005-US010. April 1, 18__. 1850s.

Rarity: —

$10-$20-$50-$100 • W-MA-1980-010.020.050.100-US020

Vignette(s): ***($10)*** Woman seated on box / Two women seated with dog / Female portrait. ***($20)*** Female portrait / Two women seated / Two cherubs. ***($50)*** Woman standing / Three women seated / Portrait of Andrew Jackson. ***($100)*** State arms / Woman seated with C / Male portrait. ***Overprint(s):*** Green. ***Engraver:*** Rawdon, Wright, Hatch & Edson. ***Comments:*** H-MA-725-G26a, G32a, G38a, G40a.

Rarity: —

Non-Valid Issues

$1 • W-MA-1980-001-C010

Engraver: PSSP / New England Bank Note Co. ***Comments:*** H-MA-725-C2. Counterfeit of W-MA-1980-001-G010. 18__. 1840s.

Rarity: —

$1 • W-MA-1980-001-S010

CJF

Engraver: Hatch & Co. ***Comments:*** H-MA-725-S5. 18__. 1849.

Rarity: URS-8

VG $75

$5 • W-MA-1980-005-R010

Engraver: New England Bank Note Co. ***Comments:*** H-MA-725-R5. Raised from W-MA-1980-001-G010. 18__. 1830s–1840s.

Rarity: —

$5 • W-MA-1980-005-S020

CJF

Tint: Orange lathework. ***Engraver:*** Danforth, Wright & Co. ***Comments:*** H-MA-725-S10. July 1, 1857. 1850s.

Rarity: URS-6

F $150

$5 • W-MA-1980-005-N010

Center: Sailing ship, Steamboat and sloop. ***Comments:*** H-MA-725-N5.

Rarity: —

$20 • W-MA-1980-020-R020

Engraver: Danforth, Wright & Co. ***Comments:*** H-MA-725-R10. Raised from W-MA-1980-001-G030. 18__. 1850s.

Rarity: —

Leicester, Massachusetts

A group of men purchased land in 1686 that in 1713 was settled, first under the name of Towtaid, which had been given by the Nipmuc Indians who sold the land. Later the name changed to Strawberry Hill and then finally to Leicester. Leicester Centre, Cherry Valley, Rochdale, Brick City, Greenville, and Manville make up the villages of Leicester.

During the Revolutionary War, militia from Leicester fought at the battles of Lexington and Concord, and a freed slave from Leicester fought at the Battle of Bunker Hill.

Leicester's mills were important in the production of the country's carding tools for wool and weaving cloth.

Leicester Bank

1826–1865

W-MA-1990

History: The Leicester Bank was chartered on March 4, 1826, with an authorized capital of $100,000. On Monday, March 27, the subscription books were opened at Howard's Hotel in Leicester. John Clapp was elected president, and John A. Smith was appointed cashier. The bank opened for business on June 1.

Sylvester's Reporter noted the following about counterfeits in 1838:

> $10s of this bank dated July 14, 1836, payable to E. Field, signed by H.G. Henshaw, cashier, and V.P. Denny, President. Not having seen one, we are unable to give a particular description. Henshaw was cashier of the Leicester Bank for more than 20 years.[21]

By 1854 the capital had increased to $150,000, and in 1855 it was $200,000. Circulation was $35,198.28 in 1839 and $200,117 in 1863.

The Leicester Bank was succeeded by the Leicester National Bank, chartered on March 21, 1865.

Numismatic Commentary: Genuine notes are very hard to locate, but counterfeit notes of the PSSP design are plentiful. These, plus a counterfeit New England Bank Note Co. issue, become available regularly.

Valid Issues

$1 • W-MA-1990-001-G010

Left: Narrow panel of lathework circle segments. ***Center:*** 1 / 1 / Flower garlands and gridwork segments / 1 / 1. ***Right:*** Narrow panel of lathework circle segments. ***Engraver:*** PSSP. ***Comments:*** H-MA-730-G2. 18__. 1820s–1830s.

Rarity: —

$1 • W-MA-1990-001-G010a

Left: ONE / D / ONE vertically. ***Right:*** ONE / D / ONE vertically. ***Engraver:*** PSSP. ***Comments:*** H-MA-730-G4. Similar to W-MA-1990-001-G010. 18__. 1830s.

Rarity: —

$1 • W-MA-1990-001-G020

Left: ONE / Profile of George Washington / ONE. ***Center:*** 1 / Two blacksmiths at anvil / 1 / Panel outlining white ONE. ***Right:*** ONE / Woman / ONE. ***Engraver:*** New England Bank Note Co. ***Comments:*** H-MA-730-G8. 18__. 1840s.

Rarity: —

$1 • W-MA-1990-001-G030

Left: Two women flanking state arms, Train and steamboat / 1. ***Center:*** 1 on 1. ***Right:*** 1 / Liberty seated with hand on 1. ***Engraver:*** New England Bank Note Co. ***Comments:*** H-MA-730-G10. 18__. 1840s.

Rarity: —

$1 • W-MA-1990-001-G030a

CJF

Overprint: Red ONE. ***Engraver:*** New England Bank Note Co / ABNCo. monogram. ***Comments:*** H-Unlisted. Similar to W-MA-1990-001-G030 but with additional engraver imprint. January 1, 18__. 1840s.

Rarity: URS-5
F $750

$2 • W-MA-1990-002-G040

Left: Narrow panel of lathework circle segments. ***Center:*** 2 / 2 / Flower garlands and gridwork segments / 2 / 2. ***Right:*** Narrow panel of lathework circle segments. ***Comments:*** H-MA-730-G14. 18__. 1840s.

Rarity: URS-3
F $1,250

$2 • W-MA-1990-002-G040a

Left: Five TWOs vertically. ***Right:*** Five TWOs vertically. ***Comments:*** H-MA-730-G16. Similar to W-MA-1990-002-G040. 18__. 1840s.

Rarity: —

$2 • W-MA-1990-002-G050

Left: TWO / Female portrait / 2. ***Center:*** 2 / Woman giving drink to one of two seated men / 2 / Panel outlining white TWO. ***Right:*** TWO / Bust of female reaper. ***Engraver:*** New England Bank Note Co. ***Comments:*** H-MA-730-G18. 18__. 1840s.

Rarity: —

$2 • W-MA-1990-002-G060

Left: 2 / TWO vertically / Portrait of Millard Fillmore. ***Center:*** Justice and cherub flanking shield / 2. ***Right:*** 2 / Portrait of Daniel Webster. ***Engraver:*** Rawdon, Wright, Hatch & Edson. ***Comments:*** H-MA-730-G20. 18__. 1850s.

Rarity: —

$2 • W-MA-1990-002-G060a

CJF

Overprint: Red TWO. ***Engraver:*** Rawdon, Wright, Hatch & Edson / New England Bank Note Co. / ABNCo. monogram. ***Comments:*** H-Unlisted. Similar to W-MA-1990-002-G060 but with additional engraver imprint. January 1, 18__. 1850s.

Rarity: URS-3
F $1,250

$3 • W-MA-1990-003-G070

Left: Narrow panel of lathework circle segments. ***Center:*** 3 / 3 / Flower garlands and gridwork segments / 3 / 3. ***Right:*** Narrow panel of lathework circle segments. ***Engraver:*** PSSP. ***Comments:*** H-MA-730-G24. 18__. 1820s–1830s.

Rarity: —

$3 • W-MA-1990-003-G070a

Left: THREE vertically. ***Right:*** THREE vertically. ***Engraver:*** PSSP. ***Comments:*** H-MA-730-G26. Similar to W-MA-1990-003-G070. 18__. 1830s.

Rarity: —

$3 • W-MA-1990-003-G080

Left: THREE / Farmer sharpening scythe / 3 across THREE. ***Center:*** 3 / Beehive and cornucopia, Woman placing garland on eagle / 3 / Panel outlining white THREE. ***Right:*** THREE / Sailor standing on wharf with hat / 3 across THREE. ***Engraver:*** New England Bank Note Co. ***Comments:*** H-MA-730-G30. 18__. 1840s.

Rarity: —

$3 • W-MA-1990-003-G090

Left: 3 / THREE / Portrait of Henry Clay. ***Center:*** Farmer and milkmaid flanking shield. ***Right:*** 3 / Portrait of Zachary Taylor. ***Engraver:*** Rawdon, Wright, Hatch & Edson. ***Comments:*** H-MA-730-G32. 18__. 1850s.

Rarity: —

$5 • W-MA-1990-005-G100

Left: Lathework chain bearing MASSACHUSETTS / 5 / 5. ***Center:*** Alternating flower garlands and gridwork segments. ***Right:*** 5 / 5. ***Engraver:*** PSSP. ***Comments:*** H-MA-730-G36. 18__. 1820s.

Rarity: —

$5 • W-MA-1990-005-G100a

Engraver: PSSP. ***Comments:*** H-MA-730-G38. Similar to W-MA-1990-005-G100 but with zigzag ruled lines. 18__. 1820s–1830s.

Rarity: —

$5 • W-MA-1990-005-G100b

Engraver: PSSP. ***Comments:*** H-MA-730-G40. Similar to W-MA-1990-005-G100 but with spiral lathework lines. 18__. 1830s.

Rarity: —

$5 • W-MA-1990-005-G110

Left: 5 / FIVE / 5. ***Center:*** V / Eagle / V. ***Right:*** 5 / FIVE / 5. ***Engraver:*** New England Bank Note Co. ***Comments:*** H-MA-730-G44. 18__. 1840s–1850s.

Rarity: —

$5 • W-MA-1990-005-G120

CJF

Overprint: Red FIVE. ***Engraver:*** Rawdon, Wright, Hatch & Edson. ***Comments:*** H-MA-730-G46. January 1, 18__. 1850s.

Rarity: URS-5
F $750

$10 • W-MA-1990-010-G130

Left: MASSACHUSETTS vertically / 10 / 10 vertically. ***Center:*** Text. ***Right:*** 10 / 10 vertically. ***Engraver:*** Perkins. ***Comments:*** H-MA-730-G50. 18__. 1820s.

Rarity: —

$10 • W-MA-1990-010-G130a

Engraver: PSSP. ***Comments:*** H-MA-730-G52. Similar to W-MA-1990-010-G130 but with zigzag ruled lines. 18__. 1820s–1830s.

Rarity: —

$10 • W-MA-1990-010-G130b

Engraver: PSSP. ***Comments:*** H-MA-730-G54. Similar to W-MA-1990-010-G130 but with spiral lathework lines. 18__. 1830s.

Rarity: —

$10 • W-MA-1990-010-G140

Left: 10 / X / 10. ***Center:*** Allegorical man standing by oxen and plow / 10. ***Right:*** TEN / Woman standing with rudder, Cornucopia. ***Engraver:*** New England Bank Note Co. ***Comments:*** H-MA-730-G58. 18__. 1840s.

Rarity: —

$10 • W-MA-1990-010-G150

Left: X bearing TEN. ***Center:*** Woman seated between 1 and 0 holding key and cornucopia. ***Right:*** X / Female portrait. ***Engraver:*** Rawdon, Wright, Hatch & Edson. ***Comments:*** H-MA-730-G60. 18__. 1850s.

Rarity: —

$20 • W-MA-1990-020-G160

Left: Lathework chain with MASSACHUSETTS / 20 / 20 vertically. ***Center:*** Alternating flower garlands and gridwork segments. ***Right:*** 20 / 20 vertically. ***Engraver:*** PSSP. ***Comments:*** H-MA-730-G64. 18__. 1820s–1840s.

Rarity: —

$20 • W-MA-1990-020-G170

Left: 20 / Woman seated with book on lap, opening chest. ***Center:*** XX / Eagle on rock / XX. ***Right:*** 20 / Ship in harbor. ***Engraver:*** New England Bank Note Co. ***Comments:*** H-MA-730-G68. 18__. 1840s–1850s.

Rarity: —

$20 • W-MA-1990-020-G180

Left: 20 / Minerva standing with spear. ***Center:*** Woman seated between 2 and 0. ***Bottom center:*** XX. ***Right:*** 20 / Woman reclining on cornucopia / 20. ***Engraver:*** Rawdon, Wright, Hatch & Edson. ***Comments:*** H-MA-730-G70. 18__. 1850s.

Rarity: —

$20 • W-MA-1990-020-G190

Left: 20 / TWENTY / XX. ***Center:*** 20 / Woman seated with eagle and shield, House, trees, and steamship. ***Right:*** 20 / Female portrait. ***Tint:*** Color unknown. ***Engraver:*** American Bank Note Co. ***Comments:*** H-MA-730-G72a. 1860s.

Rarity: —

$50 • W-MA-1990-050-G200

Left: Lathework chain with MASSACHUSETTS / 50 / 50 vertically. ***Center:*** Alternating flower garlands and gridwork segments. ***Right:*** 50 / 50 vertically. ***Engraver:*** PSSP. ***Comments:*** H-MA-730-G76. 18__. 1820s–1840s.

Rarity: —

$50 • W-MA-1990-050-G210

Left: FIFTY / Woman standing with wreath and flowers / FIFTY. ***Center:*** 50 / Man restraining prancing horse / 50. ***Right:*** FIFTY / Woman standing with cornucopia / FIFTY. ***Engraver:*** New England Bank Note Co. ***Comments:*** H-MA-730-G80. 18__. 1840s–1850s.

Rarity: —

$50 • W-MA-1990-050-G220

Left: 50 / Minerva standing by column. ***Center:*** Ceres and Vulcan flanking cornucopia. ***Right:*** 50 / Cherub in sailboat / 50. ***Engraver:*** Rawdon, Wright, Hatch & Edson. ***Comments:*** H-MA-730-G82. 18__. 1850s.

Rarity: —

$50 • W-MA-1990-050-G230

Left: 50 / Boy and dog, House. ***Center:*** Two horses frightened by lightning, Cattle. ***Right:*** 50 / Woman reclining with basket of fruit and flowers. ***Engraver:*** American Bank Note Co. ***Comments:*** H-MA-730-G84a. 1860s.

Rarity: —

$100 • W-MA-1990-100-G240

Left: Lathework chain with MASSACHUSETTS / 100 / 100 vertically. ***Center:*** Alternating flower garlands and gridwork segments. ***Right:*** 100 / 100 vertically. ***Engraver:*** Perkins. ***Comments:*** H-MA-730-G86. 18__. 1820s–1840s.

Rarity: —

$100 • W-MA-1990-100-G250

Left: ONE HUNDRED on 100 / Portrait of William Henry Harrison. ***Center:*** Wharf scene, Men loading wagon with barrels. ***Right:*** ONE HUNDRED on 100 / Portrait of Christopher Columbus. ***Engraver:*** New England Bank Note Co. ***Comments:*** H-MA-730-G90. 18__. 1840s–1850s.

Rarity: —

$100 • W-MA-1990-100-G260

Left: 100 / Vulcan seated with sledge and anchor. ***Center:*** Train on bridge, Eagle on limb, Canal locks / C. ***Bottom center:*** 100. ***Right:*** 100 / Ceres seated, Cornucopia. ***Engraver:*** Rawdon, Wright, Hatch & Edson. ***Comments:*** H-MA-730-G92. 18__. 1850s.

Rarity: —

$100 • W-MA-1990-100-G270

Left: Street scene, Men loading express wagon, Omnibus / C. ***Center:*** Eagle and shield. ***Right:*** 100 / Portrait of girl. ***Tint:*** Color unknown. ***Engraver:*** American Bank Note Co. ***Comments:*** H-MA-730-G94a. 1860s.

Rarity: —

$500 • W-MA-1990-500-G280

Left: Two mermaids, Rock, Ships / D. ***Center:*** Eagle on rock. ***Right:*** 500. ***Tint:*** Color unknown. ***Engraver:*** American Bank Note Co. ***Comments:*** H-MA-730-G98a. 1860s.

Rarity: —

Non-Valid Issues

$1 • W-MA-1990-001-C010a

Engraver: PSSP. ***Comments:*** H-MA-730-C4. Counterfeit of W-MA-1990-001-G010a. 18__. 1830s.

Rarity: —

$2 • W-MA-1990-002-C040a

Engraver: PSSP. ***Comments:*** H-MA-730-C16. Counterfeit of W-MA-1990-002-G040a. 18__. 1820s–1830s.

Rarity: —
VG $100

$5 • W-MA-1990-005-C100b HA

Engraver: PSSP. ***Comments:*** H-MA-730-C40. Counterfeit of W-MA-1990-005-G100b. 18__. 1830s.

Rarity: —
AU $110

$5 • W-MA-1990-005-C110 CC

Engraver: New England Bank Note Co. ***Comments:*** H-MA-730-C44. Counterfeit of W-MA-1990-005-G110. 18__. 1840s–1850s.

Rarity: URS-7
F $100

$5 • W-MA-1990-005-C120

Engraver: Rawdon, Wright, Hatch & Edson. ***Comments:*** H-MA-730-C46. Counterfeit of W-MA-1990-005-G120. 18__. 1850s.

Rarity: —

$10 • W-MA-1990-010-C130a QDB

Engraver: PSSP. ***Comments:*** H-MA-730-C52. Counterfeit of W-MA-1990-010-G130a. 18__. 1830s.

Rarity: —
VF $95

Lifton, Massachusetts

This town does not exist. It appeared as an imprint on a made-up Proof sample by the American Bank Note Co. titled with the similarly non-existent Thames Bank.

Thames Bank

Circa 1858–1862

W-MA-1995

History: The Thames Bank was a non-existent entity. This bank was only represented by a made-up Proof sample titled with the similarly non-existent Lifton, Massachusetts.

Numismatic Commentary: Vignettes include a portrait of Judge Story, a U.S. Supreme Court justice born in Massachusetts.

Issues

$500 • W-MA-1995-500-G010 PEM

Engraver: American Bank Note Co. ***Comments:*** H-Unlisted. Fantasy trial note. 18__.

Rarity: URS-1
Proof $5,000

Lowell, Massachusetts

The Pennacook tribe used the land that became Lowell as access to a fishing ground, relying on the same waterways that would later power the factories of Lowell for a century. In 1655 the towns of Chelmsford and Billerica were incorporated out of land that would one day be Lowell. On March 1, 1826, the city of Lowell was incorporated with a population of 2,500.

The city was created as "The Lowell Experiment" and became the nation's most profitable textile center. It heralded the Industrial Revolution in America as the first large factory town. Lowell's population was 33,000 by 1850, and the extended canals, which had been widened and fortified by Irish-immigrant work crews, allowed the mills to produce 50,000 miles of cloth each year. The first belt-driven power system was put into place in Lowell, as was the first turbine. Business fell off sharply during the Civil War, and many mills were closed.

Appleton Bank

1847–1865

W-MA-2000

History: The Appleton Bank was chartered on March 6, 1847, with an authorized capital of $100,000. It opened its doors on May 14. In 1849 the capital was increased to $150,000. The circulation of the bank was $125,385 in 1849 and $197,698 in 1863. Real estate of the bank was valued at $15,000.

The Appleton Bank was succeeded by the Appleton National Bank of Lowell, chartered on April 7, 1865.

Numismatic Commentary: Although this bank can boast to having issued a note showing "Columbus Discovering the New World," bills of this bank are very hard to come by.

Valid Issues

$1 • W-MA-2000-001-G010

CJF

Engraver: New England Bank Note Co. ***Comments:*** H-MA-735-G2. May 1, 18__. 1847–1850s.

Rarity: URS-6
F $500

$1 • W-MA-2000-001-G010a

Left: Eagle / ONE / Shield bearing ONE. ***Center:*** Man seated at bench / 1. ***Right:*** 1 / Man standing. ***Engraver:*** New England Bank Note Co. / ABNCo. monogram. ***Comments:*** H-MA-735-G2a. Similar to W-MA-2000-001-G010 but with additional engraver imprint. May 1, 18__. 1850s–1860s.

Rarity: —

$1 • W-MA-2000-001-G020

Left: Woman standing with arm on pedestal holding torch / ONE. ***Center:*** 1 / Mechanic seated with hammer, anvil, wheel, and bales, Train and factories. ***Right:*** ONE across 1. ***Tint:*** Green. ***Engraver:*** American Bank Note Co. ***Comments:*** H-MA-735-G4a. May 1, 1862.

Rarity: —

$2 • W-MA-2000-002-G030

Left: Man and boy driving sheep across stream / 2. ***Center:*** Medallion 2. ***Bottom center:*** Cow and fence. ***Right:*** 2 / Train. ***Engraver:*** New England Bank Note Co. ***Comments:*** H-MA-735-G6. 18__. 1847–1850s.

Rarity: —

$2 • W-MA-2000-002-G040

Left: Two women beside machine. ***Center:*** Portrait of F.C. Lowell. ***Right:*** 2 / Male portrait. ***Tint:*** Green TWO and 2. ***Engraver:*** American Bank Note Co. ***Comments:*** H-MA-735-G8a. May 1, 1862.

Rarity: —

$3 • W-MA-2000-003-G050

Left: Blacksmith's shop, Smith at anvil, Man with horse, Boy at forge / 3. ***Center:*** Medallion 3. ***Right:*** 3 / Male portrait. ***Engraver:*** New England Bank Note Co. ***Comments:*** H-MA-735-G10. 18__. 1847–1850s.

Rarity: —

$3 • W-MA-2000-003-G050a

Engraver: New England Bank Note Co. / ABNCo. monogram. ***Comments:*** H-MA-735-G10a. Similar to W-MA-2000-003-G050 but with additional engraver imprint. 18__. 1850s–1860s.

Rarity: —

$3 • W-MA-2000-003-G050b

CJF

Overprint: Red ornate THREE. ***Engraver:*** New England Bank Note Co. / ABNCo. monogram. ***Comments:*** H-Unlisted. Similar to W-MA-2000-003-G050 but with additional engraver imprint. May 1, 18__. 1850s–1860s.

Rarity: URS-3
F $1,000

$3 • W-MA-2000-003-G060

Left: 3 on die. ***Center:*** Landing of Christopher Columbus. ***Right:*** 3 / Blacksmith. ***Tint:*** Green 3 on die and panel of 3s. ***Engraver:*** American Bank Note Co. ***Comments:*** H-MA-735-G12a. May 1, 1862.

Rarity: URS-3
G $900

$5 • W-MA-2000-005-G070

Left: Phaeton in chariot of the sun surrounded by women, Cherub with torch above horses / 5. ***Center:*** Medallion 5 with woman and cherub. ***Right:*** FIVE / Medallion head / 5. ***Engraver:*** New England Bank Note Co. ***Comments:*** H-MA-735-G14. 18__. 1847–1850s.

Rarity: —

How to Read the Whitman Numbering System

$1 • W-MA-010-001-G010a

Denomination: Value of the note shown.

W: Whitman number. This number is a sortable code unique to each bank and note.

MA: Abbreviation for the state under study.

010: Numerical designation specific to each bank.

001: The denomination in dollars.

G010a: G indicates a good or valid note. Other categories are indicated thus: C (counterfeit); R (raised); S (spurious); N (not-attributed); A (altered). Numbers are assigned starting with 010, 020, et seq. Terminal letters following the number indicate variations of a note: a series of different colored overprints, tints, payees, etc., all on the same design of note. For more information, see the "How to Use This Book" section at the front of the volume, page xiv.

$5 • W-MA-2000-005-G070a

CC

Overprint: Red ornate FIVE. ***Engraver:*** New England Bank Note Co. ***Comments:*** H-Unlisted. Similar to W-MA-2000-005-G070. May 1, 18__. 1850s–1860s.

Rarity: URS-3
VG $750

$5 • W-MA-2000-005-G070b

Engraver: New England Bank Note Co. / ABNCo. monogram. ***Comments:*** H-MA-735-G14a. Similar to W-MA-2000-005-G070 but with additional engraver imprint. 18__. 1850s–1860s.

Rarity: —

$10 • W-MA-2000-010-G080

Left: Factory, Train on bridge, Man with wheel barrow, Church / X. ***Center:*** Medallion X. ***Right:*** TEN / Indian woman / TEN. ***Engraver:*** New England Bank Note Co. ***Comments:*** H-MA-735-G16. 18__. 1847–1850s.

Rarity: —

$10 • W-MA-2000-010-G080a

Engraver: New England Bank Note Co. / ABNCo. monogram. ***Comments:*** H-MA-735-G16a. Similar to W-MA-2000-010-G080 but with additional engraver imprint. 18__. 1850s–1860s.

Rarity: —

$20 • W-MA-2000-020-G090

Left: 20 / Woman seated with book on lap, opening chest. ***Center:*** XX / Eagle on rock / XX. ***Right:*** 20 / Ship in harbor. ***Engraver:*** New England Bank Note Co. ***Comments:*** H-MA-735-G18. 18__. 1847–1850s.

Rarity: —

$20 • W-MA-2000-020-G100

SI

Tint: Red-orange. ***Engraver:*** American Bank Note Co. ***Comments:*** H-MA-735-G20a. Proof. 1860s.

Rarity: URS-2
Proof $6,000

$50 • W-MA-2000-050-G110

Left: FIFTY / Woman standing with wreath and flowers / FIFTY. ***Center:*** 50 / Man restraining prancing horse / 50. ***Right:*** FIFTY / Woman standing with cornucopia / FIFTY. ***Engraver:*** New England Bank Note Co. ***Comments:*** H-MA-735-G22. 18__. 1847–1850s.

Rarity: —

$50 • W-MA-2000-050-G120

Left: L / Portrait of George Washington. ***Center:*** 50 DOLL'S. ***Right:*** 50 / Portrait of Martha Washington. ***Tint:*** Red-orange. ***Engraver:*** American Bank Note Co. ***Comments:*** H-MA-735-G24a. 1860s.

Rarity: —

$100 • W-MA-2000-100-G130

Left: ONE HUNDRED on 100 / Portrait of William Henry Harrison. ***Center:*** Wharf scene, Men loading wagon with barrels. ***Right:*** ONE HUNDRED on 100 / Portrait of Christopher Columbus. ***Engraver:*** New England Bank Note Co. ***Comments:*** H-MA-735-G26. 18__. 1847–1850s.

Rarity: —

$100 • W-MA-2000-100-G140

SI

Tint: Red-orange. ***Engraver:*** American Bank Note Co. ***Comments:*** H-MA-735-G28a. Proof. 1860s.

Rarity: URS-1
Proof $10,000

$500 • W-MA-2000-500-G150

Left: Woman seated on sheaves, Men reaping, Man on horse / 500. ***Center:*** 500 / D. ***Right:*** 500 vertically. ***Engraver:*** Rawdon, Wright, Hatch & Edson. ***Comments:*** H-MA-735-G30. 18__. 1850s.

Rarity: —

$500 • W-MA-2000-500-G160

SI

Tint: Red-orange. ***Engraver:*** American Bank Note Co. ***Comments:*** H-MA-735-G32. Proof. 1860s.

Rarity: URS-1
Proof $10,000

Non-Valid Issues

$1 • W-MA-2000-001-S010

CJF

Engraver: Rawdon, Wright & Hatch. ***Comments:*** H-MA-735-S5. 18__. 1847.

Rarity: —

$5 • W-MA-2000-005-N010

Center: Harbor scene. ***Comments:*** H-MA-735-N5. 18__. 1840s–1850s.

Rarity: —

$10 • W-MA-2000-010-R010

Engraver: American Bank Note Co. ***Comments:*** H-MA-735-R5. Raised from W-MA-2000-001-G020. May 1, 1862.

Rarity: —

$10 • W-MA-2000-010-R020

Engraver: American Bank Note Co. ***Comments:*** H-MA-735-R10. Raised from W-MA-2000-002-G040. May 1, 1862.

Rarity: —

$10 • W-MA-2000-010-N020

Center: Harbor scene. ***Comments:*** H-MA-735-N10. 18__. 1840s–1850s.

Rarity: —

City Bank

1836–1841

W-MA-2010

History: The City Bank was incorporated on March 31, 1836, with an authorized capital of $150,000, all of which was to be paid in by January 1837, half in the form of specie. The directors falsified their records and borrowed $43,000 of this from Boston banks and $20,000 elsewhere, all of which was soon returned. As a result the capital was mostly fictitious.

This fraudulent bank was closed by receivership in February 1841. In the meantime it issued worthless paper money.

Numismatic Commentary: This bank never opened, but it is possible that notes were printed in anticipation and never circulated. All described notes bear the imprint of the New England Bank Note Co.

Valid Issues

$1 • W-MA-2010-001-G010

Comments: H-MA-740-G2. No description available. 18__.

Rarity: *None known*

$1.25 • W-MA-2010-001.25-G020

Left: 1 25/100 / Train / 1 25/100. ***Center:*** Sloop and other ships at sea / $1.25 cts. ***Right:*** 1 25/100 / Eagle. ***Comments:*** H-MA-740-G4. 18__.

Rarity: —

$1.50 • W-MA-2010-001.50-G030

Left: 1 Doll. 50 Cts. vertically. ***Center:*** Eagle on rock in ocean / $1 50/100. ***Right:*** 1 50/100 / Justice. ***Comments:*** H-MA-740-G6. 18__.

Rarity: —

$1.75 • W-MA-2010-001.75-G040

Left: $1. 75 Cts. / Hebe watering eagle / 175/100. ***Center:*** Three sloops at sea. ***Right:*** $1.75 Cts. / Dog, Ceres seated with grain / 175/100. ***Comments:*** H-MA-740-G8. 18__.

Rarity: —

$2 • W-MA-2010-002-G050

Comments: H-MA-740-G10. No description available. 18__.

Rarity: *None known*

$3 • W-MA-2010-003-G060

Comments: H-MA-740-G12. No description available. 18__.

Rarity: *None known*

$5 • W-MA-2010-005-G070

Comments: H-MA-740-G14. No description available. 18__.

Rarity: *None known*

$10 • W-MA-2010-010-G080

Comments: H-MA-740-G16. No description available. 18__.

Rarity: *None known*

$20 • W-MA-2010-020-G090

Comments: H-MA-740-G18. No description available. 18__.

Rarity: *None known*

$50 • W-MA-2010-050-G100

Comments: H-MA-740-G20. No description available. 18__.

Rarity: *None known*

$100 • W-MA-2010-100-G110

Comments: H-MA-740-G22. No description available. 18__.

Rarity: *None known*

Lowell Bank

1829–1865

W-MA-2020

History: On March 3, 1829, the Lowell Bank was incorporated with an authorized capital of $200,000. By 1839 it had a capital of $250,000, but by 1850 it had dropped back to $200,000. Circulation was $89,991 in 1839 and $165,009 in 1845. Between 1849 and 1863 it fluctuated between $123,986 and $118,806.

In 1865 the business of this bank was succeeded by the Old Lowell National Bank.

Numismatic Commentary: Genuine notes from this bank make an appearance from time to time, so collectors should be able to eventually obtain a circulated example. Many of these notes show a distant view of Lowell and the mills that were so important during the Industrial Revolution.

Valid Issues

$1 • W-MA-2020-001-G010

Left: 1 / Portrait of woman with wreath on head. ***Center:*** Woman working at loom, Overseer. ***Right:*** 1 / Man examining fabric, Man seated. ***Comments:*** H-MA-745-G2.

Rarity: —

$1 • W-MA-2020-001-G020

Left: Narrow panel of lathework circle segments. ***Center:*** 1 / 1 / Flower garlands and gridwork segments / 1 / 1. ***Right:*** Narrow panel of lathework circle segments. ***Engraver:*** PSSP. ***Comments:*** H-MA-745-G4. 18__. 1820s–1830s.

Rarity: —

$1 • W-MA-2020-001-G020a

Left: ONE / D / ONE vertically. ***Right:*** ONE / D / ONE vertically. ***Engraver:*** PSSP. ***Comments:*** H-MA-745-G8. Similar to W-MA-2020-001-G020. 18__. 1830s.

Rarity: —

$1 • W-MA-2020-001-G030

Left: Woman standing / ONE. ***Center:*** Village scene with trees. ***Right:*** Woman standing / 1. ***Engraver:*** New England Bank Note Co. ***Comments:*** H-MA-745-G12. Jan. 1, 18__. 1830s–1850s.

Rarity: —

$1 • W-MA-2020-001-G030a

CJF

Engraver: New England Bank Note Co. / ABNCo. monogram. ***Comments:*** H-MA-745-G12a. Similar to W-MA-2020-001-G030 but with additional engraver imprint. Jan. 1, 18__. 1850s–1860s.

Rarity: URS-4
F $500

$1 • W-MA-2020-001-G040

CJF

Tint: Green. ***Engraver:*** American Bank Note Co. ***Comments:*** H-MA-745-G16a. April 1, 1864. 1860s.

Rarity: URS-4
VG $500; **F** $1,000; **VF** $2,000

$2 • W-MA-2020-002-G050

Left: Narrow panel of lathework circle segments. ***Center:*** 2 / 2 / Flower garlands and gridwork segments / 2 / 2. ***Right:*** Narrow panel of lathework circle segments. ***Engraver:*** PSSP. ***Comments:*** H-MA-745-G20. 18__. 1820s–1830s.

Rarity: —

$2 • W-MA-2020-002-G050a

Left: Five TWOs vertically. ***Right:*** Five TWOs vertically. ***Engraver:*** PSSP. ***Comments:*** H-MA-745-G24. Similar to W-MA-2020-002-G050. 18__. 1830s.

Rarity: —

$2 • W-MA-2020-002-G060

Left: TWO / Woman standing / 2. ***Center:*** Village scene with trees. ***Right:*** TWO / Woman standing / 2. ***Engraver:*** New England Bank Note Co. ***Comments:*** H-MA-745-G28. Jan. 1, 18__. 1830s–1850s.

Rarity: —

$2 • W-MA-2020-002-G060a

CJF

Engraver: New England Bank Note Co. / ABNCo. monogram. ***Comments:*** H-MA-745-G28a. Similar to W-MA-2020-002-G060 but with additional engraver imprint. Jan. 1, 18__. 1850s–1860s.

Rarity: URS-4
VG $600; **F** $1,000

$2 • W-MA-2020-002-G070

CJF, CJF

Tint: Green. ***Engraver:*** American Bank Note Co. ***Comments:*** H-MA-745-G32a. 1860s.

Rarity: URS-3
VG $750; **F** $1,500

$3 • W-MA-2020-003-G080

Left: Narrow panel of lathework circle segments. ***Center:*** 3 / 3 / Flower garlands and gridwork segments / 3 / 3. ***Right:*** Narrow panel of lathework circle segments. ***Engraver:*** PSSP. ***Comments:*** H-MA-745-G36. 18__. 1820s–1830s.

Rarity: —

$3 • W-MA-2020-003-G080a

Left: THREE vertically. ***Right:*** THREE vertically. ***Engraver:*** PSSP. ***Comments:*** H-MA-745-G40. Similar to W-MA-2020-003-G080. 18__. 1830s.

Rarity: —

$3 • W-MA-2020-003-G090

Left: THREE / Woman standing / 3 on THREE. ***Center:*** Village scene with buildings. ***Bottom center:*** Building. ***Right:*** THREE / Woman standing / 3 on THREE. ***Engraver:*** New England Bank Note Co. ***Comments:*** H-MA-745-G44. Jan. 1, 18__. 1830s–1850s.

Rarity: —

$3 • W-MA-2020-003-G090a

Engraver: New England Bank Note Co. / ABNCo. monogram. ***Comments:*** H-MA-745-G44a. Similar to W-MA-2020-003-G090 but with additional engraver imprint. Jan. 1, 18__. 1850s–1860s.

Rarity: —

$3 • W-MA-2020-003-G100

CJF, CJF

Tint: Green. ***Engraver:*** American Bank Note Co. ***Comments:*** H-MA-745-G48a. April 1, 1864. 1860s.

Rarity: URS-3

VG $1,000; **F** $2,000

$5 • W-MA-2020-005-G110

Left: Lathework chain bearing MASSACHUSETTS / 5 / 5 vertically. ***Center:*** Alternating flower garlands and gridwork segments / FIVE DOLLARS lined by zigzag ruled lines. ***Right:*** 5 / 5 vertically. ***Engraver:*** PSSP. ***Comments:*** H-MA-745-G50. 18__. 1820s–1830s.

Rarity: —

$5 • W-MA-2020-005-G110a

Engraver: PSSP. ***Comments:*** H-MA-745-G52. Similar to W-MA-2020-005-G110 but with spiral lathework lines. 18__. 1830s.

Rarity: —

$5 • W-MA-2020-005-G120

Left: Lathework panel bearing MASSACHUSETTS vertically. ***Center:*** 5 / Woman seated / 5 / Text. ***Right:*** 5 / 5. ***Back:*** Green. ***Engraver:*** PSSP. ***Comments:*** H-MA-745-G56a. 18__. 1830s–1840s.

Rarity: —

$5 • W-MA-2020-005-G120a

Overprint: Red FIVE. ***Engraver:*** PSSP. ***Comments:*** H-MA-745-G56b. Similar to W-MA-2020-005-G120. 18__. 1850s.

Rarity: —

$5 • W-MA-2020-005-G120b

Overprint: Red FIVE. ***Engraver:*** PSSP / ABNCo. monogram. ***Comments:*** H-MA-745-G56c. Similar to W-MA-2020-005-G120 but with additional engraver imprint. 18__. 1850s–1860s.

Rarity: —

$5 • W-MA-2020-005-G120c

CC, CC

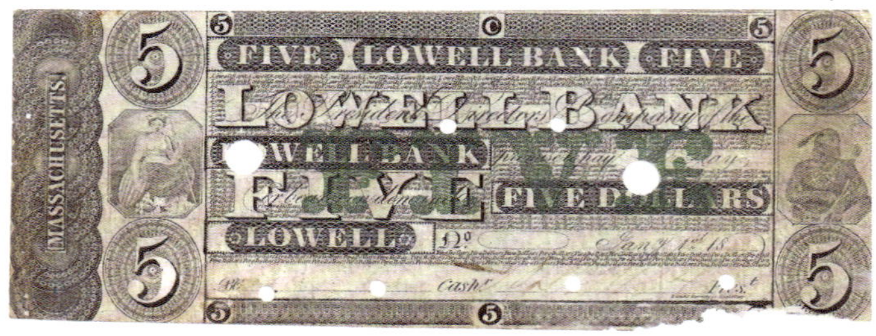

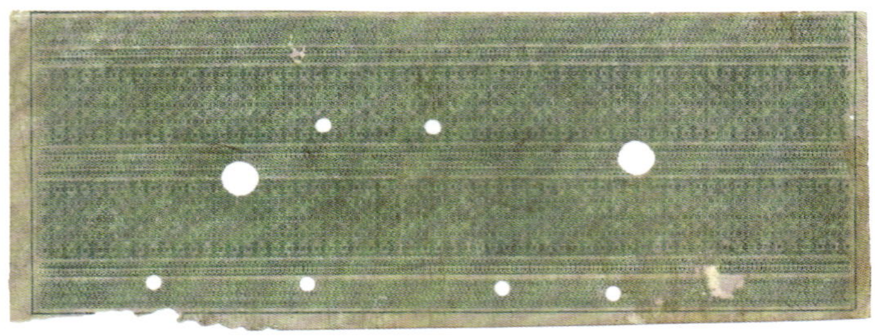

Overprint: Green ornate FIVE. ***Engraver:*** PSSP / ABNCo. monogram. ***Comments:*** H-Unlisted. Similar to W-MA-2020-005-G120 but with additional engraver imprint. Jan. 1, 18__. 1850s–1860s.

Rarity: URS-4

F $350

$10 • W-MA-2020-010-G130

Left: Lathework chain bearing MASSACHUSETTS / 10 / 10 vertically. ***Center:*** Alternating flower garlands and gridwork segments / TEN DOLLARS with zigzag ruled lines. ***Right:*** 10 / 10 vertically. ***Engraver:*** PSSP. ***Comments:*** H-MA-745-G58. 18__. 1820s–1830s.

Rarity: —

$10 • W-MA-2020-010-G130a

Engraver: PSSP. ***Comments:*** H-MA-745-G60. Similar to W-MA-2020-010-G130 but with spiral lathework lines. 18__. 1830s.

Rarity: —

$10 • W-MA-2020-010-G140

Left: Lathework chain with MASSACHUSETTS / 10 / Woman seated with shield and spear / 10. ***Center:*** Text / TEN. ***Right:*** 10 / Indian / 10. ***Back:*** Green. ***Engraver:*** PSSP. ***Comments:*** H-MA-745-G64. 18__. 1830s–1840s.

Rarity: —

$10 • W-MA-2020-010-G140a

Overprint: Red TEN. ***Engraver:*** PSSP. ***Comments:*** H-MA-745-G64b. Similar to W-MA-2020-010-G140. 18__. 1850s.

Rarity: —

$10 • W-MA-2020-010-G140b

CJF

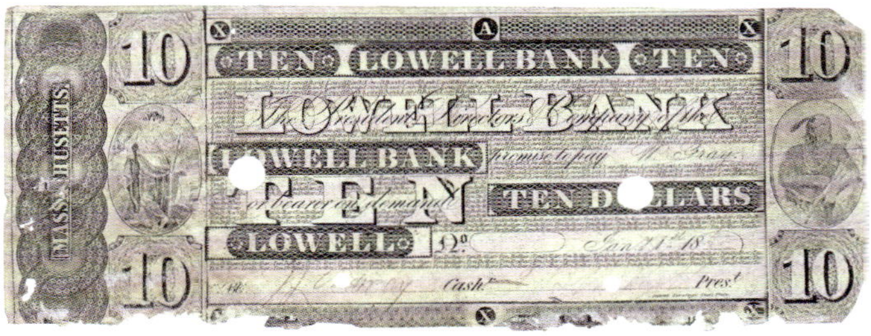

Engraver: PSSP / ABNCo. monogram. ***Comments:*** H-Unlisted. Similar to W-MA-2020-010-G140 but with additional engraver imprint. Jan. 1, 18__. 1860s.

Rarity: —

$10 • W-MA-2020-010-G140c

SN

Overprint: Green ornate TEN. ***Engraver:*** PSSP / ABNCo. monogram. ***Comments:*** H-MA-745-G64c. Similar to W-MA-2020-010-G140 but with additional engraver imprint. Jan. 1, 18__. 1850s–1860s.

Rarity: URS-2
G $500

$20 • W-MA-2020-020-G150

Left: Lathework chain bearing MASSACHUSETTS / 20 / 20 vertically. ***Center:*** Alternating flower garlands and gridwork segments. ***Right:*** 20 / 20 vertically. ***Engraver:*** PSSP. ***Comments:*** H-MA-745-G66. 18__. 1820s–1830s.

Rarity: —

$20 • W-MA-2020-020-G160

Left: 20 / Woman seated. ***Center:*** XX / Eagle / XX. ***Right:*** 20 / Sailing ship. ***Engraver:*** New England Bank Note Co. ***Comments:*** H-MA-745-G72. 18__. 1840s–1850s.

Rarity: —

$20 • W-MA-2020-020-G160a

CJF

Engraver: New England Bank Note Co. / ABNCo. monogram. ***Comments:*** H-Unlisted. Similar to W-MA-2020-020-G160 but with additional engraver imprint. Proof. 18__. 1840s–1850s.

Rarity: URS-4
Proof $2,000

$20 • W-MA-2020-020-G170

Left: 20 / State arms. ***Center:*** TWENTY. ***Right:*** 20 / Woman seated with spinning wheel. ***Engraver:*** American Bank Note Co. ***Comments:*** H-MA-745-G76. 1860s.

Rarity: —

$50 • W-MA-2020-050-G180

Left: Lathework chain bearing MASSACHUSETTS / 50 / 50 vertically. ***Center:*** Alternating flower garlands and gridwork segments. ***Right:*** 50 / 50 vertically. ***Engraver:*** PSSP. ***Comments:*** H-MA-745-G78. 18__. 1830s.

Rarity: —

$50 • W-MA-2020-050-G190

Left: FIFTY / Woman standing with wreath and flowers / FIFTY. ***Center:*** 50 / Man restraining prancing horse / 50. ***Right:*** FIFTY / Woman standing with cornucopia / FIFTY. ***Engraver:*** New England Bank Note Co. ***Comments:*** H-MA-745-G84. 18__. 1840s–1850s.

Rarity: —

$50 • W-MA-2020-050-G200

Left: 50 / Justice leaning on pedestal. ***Center:*** FIFTY. ***Right:*** 50 / Eagle on shield. ***Engraver:*** American Bank Note Co. ***Comments:*** H-MA-745-G88. 1860s.

Rarity: —

$100 • W-MA-2020-100-G210

Left: Lathework chain bearing MASSACHUSETTS / 100 / 100 vertically. ***Center:*** Alternating flower garlands and gridwork segments. ***Right:*** 100 / 100 vertically. ***Engraver:*** Perkins. ***Comments:*** H-MA-745-G90. 18__. 1820s–1830s.

Rarity: —

$100 • W-MA-2020-100-G220

Left: ONE HUNDRED on 100 / Portrait of William Henry Harrison. ***Center:*** Wharf scene, Men loading wagon with barrels. ***Right:*** ONE HUNDRED on 100 / Portrait of Christopher Columbus. ***Engraver:*** New England Bank Note Co. ***Comments:*** H-MA-745-G96. 18__. 1840s–1850s.

Rarity: —

$100 • W-MA-2020-100-G230

Left: 100 / Mechanic resting hammer on anvil. ***Center:*** ONE HUNDRED. ***Right:*** 100 / Dog lying by strongbox. ***Engraver:*** American Bank Note Co. ***Comments:*** H-MA-745-G100. 1860s.

Rarity: —

$500 • W-MA-2020-500-G240

Left: Woman seated on sheaves, Men reaping, Man on horse. ***Center:*** 500 / D. ***Right:*** 500 vertically. ***Engraver:*** Rawdon, Wright, Hatch & Edson. ***Comments:*** H-MA-745-G108. 18__. 1850s.

Rarity: —

$500 • W-MA-2020-500-G250

Left: Woman leaning on column holding torch / 500. ***Center:*** 500. ***Right:*** 500 / Eagle on rock. ***Engraver:*** American Bank Note Co. ***Comments:*** H-MA-745-G112. 1860s.

Rarity: —

Non-Valid Issues

$1 • W-MA-2020-001-A010

Left: 5 / Blacksmith at anvil / FIVE. ***Center:*** Mercury standing with 5, Cornucopia and merchandise, Factories and ship / V / Panel outlining white FIVE. ***Right:*** 5 / Ceres kneeling / FIVE. ***Engraver:*** New England Bank Note Co. / PSSP. ***Comments:*** H-MA-745-A5. Altered from $5 Farmers Bank of Sandstone, Barry, Michigan. 18__. 1830s.

Rarity: —

$5 • W-MA-2020-005-N010

Center: Woman, Sailing ship. ***Comments:*** H-MA-745-N5. 1850s.

Rarity: —

$10 • W-MA-2020-010-R010

Engraver: New England Bank Note Co. ***Comments:*** H-MA-745-R5. Raised from W-MA-2020-001-G030. 18__. 1840s.

Rarity: —

Manufacturers Bank

Circa 1860

W-MA-2030

History: The Manufacturers Bank never had an issued charter, and thus it is likely that the bank never even opened. Any notes in existence are presumed to be Proofs made in anticipation of a business that never materialized.

Numismatic Commentary: There is no record of the Manufacturers Bank of Lowell, either as a genuine bank or a spurious bank. However, the National Bank Note Co. issued mock-up notes with this imprint as samples of their work. They are very collectible.

Valid Issues

$1 • W-MA-2030-001-G010

CJF

Engraver: National Bank Note Co. ***Comments:*** H-MA-750-G2. Mock-up note. 18__.

Rarity: —

$5 • W-MA-2030-005-G020

CJF

Engraver: National Bank Note Co. ***Comments:*** H-MA-750-G8. Mock-up note. 18__.

Rarity: —

Merchants Bank

1854–1864

W-MA-2040

History: The Merchants Bank was incorporated on March 28, 1854, with an authorized capital of $100,000. Capital fluctuated between $100,000 and $150,000 for the entirety of the bank's existence. Circulation was $66,590 in 1857, $103,500 in 1858, $66,590 in 1860, and $97,372 in 1863.

The business of the Merchants Bank was succeeded by the Merchants National Bank of Lowell, chartered on August 30, 1864.

Numismatic Commentary: It should be easy to locate non-valid issues of this bank, but valid or genuine notes are hard to come by in the marketplace.

Valid Issues

$1 • W-MA-2040-001-G010

Left: Factories, Woman reclining with arm on bale, Train and ships / 1. ***Center:*** 1. ***Right:*** 1 / Female portrait. ***Engraver:*** Rawdon, Wright, Hatch & Edson. ***Comments:*** H-MA-755-G2. 18__. 1850s.

Rarity: —

$2 • W-MA-2040-002-G020

Left: Two women seated. ***Center:*** 2. ***Right:*** 2 / Woman seated between shield and 2. ***Engraver:*** Rawdon, Wright, Hatch & Edson. ***Comments:*** H-MA-755-G4. 18__. 1850s.

Rarity: —

$3 • W-MA-2040-003-G030

Left: Justice seated with scales and bale / 3. ***Center:*** Woman with staff and two women with money bag and cornucopia flanking 3 on bale. ***Right:*** 3 / Male portrait. ***Engraver:*** Rawdon, Wright, Hatch & Edson. ***Comments:*** H-MA-755-G6. 18__. 1850s.

Rarity: —

$5 • W-MA-2040-005-G040

Left: 5 / 5. ***Center:*** Woman and eagle, Ship. ***Right:*** 5 / Ships / FIVE. ***Engraver:*** Rawdon, Wright, Hatch & Edson. ***Comments:*** H-MA-755-G8. 18__. 1850s.

Rarity: —

$10 • W-MA-2040-010-G050

Left: 10 / Barrels, bales, and anchor / TEN. ***Center:*** Woman reclining holding Liberty cap, Eagle and globe, Ships. ***Right:*** 10 / Portrait of girl. ***Engraver:*** Rawdon, Wright, Hatch & Edson. ***Comments:*** H-MA-755-G10. 18__. 1850s.

Rarity: —

$20 • W-MA-2040-020-G060

Left: 20 / XX. ***Center:*** XX / Female portrait / XX. ***Right:*** 20 / XX. ***Engraver:*** Rawdon, Wright, Hatch & Edson. ***Comments:*** H-MA-755-G12. 18__. 1850s.

Rarity: —

$50 • W-MA-2040-050-G070

Left: 50 / Woman. ***Center:*** Shipping, City. ***Right:*** 50 / Portrait of George Washington. ***Engraver:*** Rawdon, Wright, Hatch & Edson. ***Comments:*** H-MA-755-G14. 18__. 1850s.

Rarity: —

$100 • W-MA-2040-100-G080

Left: 100 / Portrait / C. ***Center:*** Railroad depot, Train, Wharf. ***Right:*** 100 / C. ***Engraver:*** Rawdon, Wright, Hatch & Edson. ***Comments:*** H-MA-755-G16. 18__. 1850s.

Rarity: —

$500 • W-MA-2040-500-G090

Left: D / State arms. ***Center:*** FIVE HUNDRED DOLLARS. ***Right:*** 500 / Male portrait. ***Engraver:*** American Bank Note Co. ***Comments:*** H-MA-755-G18. 1850s–1860s.

Rarity: —

$500 • W-MA-2040-500-G100

Left: D / State arms. ***Right:*** 500 / Justice seated on bale. ***Engraver:*** American Bank Note Co. ***Comments:*** H-MA-755-G20. 1850s–1860s.

Rarity: —

Non-Valid Issues

$1 • W-MA-2040-001-N010

Left: Two women. ***Center:*** Farmer seated on sheaf. ***Right:*** Two women with flowers. ***Comments:*** H-MA-755-N5.

Rarity: —

$1 • W-MA-2040-001-N020

Center: Three women. ***Right:*** Two women. ***Comments:*** H-MA-755-N10.

Rarity: —

$1 • W-MA-2040-001-A010

CJF

Engraver: Danforth, Bald & Co. ***Comments:*** H-MA-755-A5. Altered from $1 Mechanics and Traders Bank, Georgetown, D.C. November 14, 1852. 1850s.

Rarity: URS-6
F $75

$1 • W-MA-2040-001-A020

Left: Laureate woman leaning on shield bearing 1. ***Center:*** 1 / Bull in field / Horse, Trees. ***Bottom center:*** Road, Trees, Sign post. ***Right:*** Indian man / 1. ***Engraver:*** W.L. Ormsby. ***Comments:*** H-MA-755-A10. Altered from $1 Merchants Bank, Stillwater, Minnesota. Nov. 14, 1852.

Rarity: —

$1 • W-MA-2040-001-A030

Left: ONE / Woman with eagle and shield / ONE. ***Center:*** Eagle perched on shield. ***Right:*** 1 / Woman seated. ***Engraver:*** Doty & Bergen. ***Comments:*** H-MA-755-A15. Altered from $1 Columbia Bank, Washington, D.C. Oct. 20, 1854.

Rarity: —

$2 • W-MA-2040-002-S010

CJF

Tint: Red-orange TWO. ***Comments:*** H-MA-755-S5. 18__. Circa 1860.

Rarity: URS-6
F $100

$2 • W-MA-2040-002-S020

SI

Tint: Green TWO. ***Comments:*** H-MA-755-S10. 18__. Circa 1860.

Rarity: URS-5
F $100

$2 • W-MA-2040-002-N030

BC

Comments: H-MA-755-N15. 185_. 1850s.

Rarity: —

$2 • W-MA-2040-002-N040

Center: Woman and sheaf. ***Right:*** Indian man. ***Comments:*** H-MA-755-N20.

Rarity: —

$2 • W-MA-2040-002-N050

Center: Woman / 2 / Woman. ***Comments:*** H-MA-755-N25.

Rarity: —

$2 • W-MA-2040-002-A040

Left: 2 / TWO / 2. ***Center:*** 2 / Ceres seated, Train on bridge, Sheaf and canal lock. ***Bottom center:*** Road, Trees, Sign post. ***Right:*** Indian man / 2. ***Engraver:*** Doty & Bergen. ***Comments:*** H-MA-755-A20. Altered from $2 Merchants Bank, Stillwater, Minnesota. Oct. 20, 1854.

Rarity: —

$3 • W-MA-2040-003-S030 NJW

Engraver: Rawdon, Wright & Hatch. ***Comments:*** H-MA-755-S15. Oct. 8, 185_. 1850s.

Rarity: URS-8
F $75

$3 • W-MA-2040-003-S040

Left: 3 / Woman standing with sheaf / THREE. ***Center:*** Girl standing with sheaf on head, Dog seated under tree. ***Bottom center:*** Dog and strongbox. ***Right:*** THREE / Milkmaid seated with bucket. ***Tint:*** Brown or green lathework. ***Comments:*** H-MA-755-S20. Sept. 10, 18__. 1850s.

Rarity: —

$3 • W-MA-2040-003-S050

Center: Woman and man under tree. ***Comments:*** H-MA-755-S25. 18__. 1850s.

Rarity: —

$3 • W-MA-2040-003-N060

Center: Two women with 3. ***Comments:*** H-MA-755-N30.

Rarity: —

$3 • W-MA-2040-003-N070

Center: Steamship and sailing ship. ***Comments:*** H-MA-755-N35.

Rarity: —

$3 • W-MA-2040-003-A050

Left: 3 / Portrait of Andrew Jackson / 3. ***Center:*** 3 / Indian woman with frame bearing coat of arms / 3. ***Bottom center:*** Train at station. ***Right:*** THREE / Ceres seated with caduceus / 3. ***Engraver:*** Rawdon, Wright, Hatch & Edson. ***Comments:*** H-MA-755-A25. Altered from $3 Merchants Bank, Washington, D.C. Dec. 1, 1852.

Rarity: —

$3 • W-MA-2040-003-A060

Left: 3 / Helmeted medallion head. ***Center:*** Mechanic seated, Forge, anvil, and cogwheel. ***Right:*** 3 / Portrait of William Henry Harrison. ***Engraver:*** W.L. Ormsby. ***Comments:*** H-MA-755-A30. Altered from $3 Merchants Bank, Ft. Leavenworth, Kansas. 185_. 1850s.

Rarity: —

$5 • W-MA-2040-005-C040

Engraver: Rawdon, Wright, Hatch & Edson. ***Comments:*** H-MA-755-C8. Counterfeit of W-MA-2040-005-G040. 18__. 1850s.

Rarity: —

$5 • W-MA-2040-005-S060 CJF

Tint: Red-orange end panels outlining white Vs and FIVE. ***Comments:*** H-MA-755-S30. 18__. Circa 1860.

Rarity: URS-5
F $100

$5 • W-MA-2040-005-S070

Center: Ship under sail, Brig. ***Comments:*** H-MA-755-S35. 18__. 1840.

Rarity: —

$5 • W-MA-2040-005-S080

Center: Two people seated, Griffin on chest. ***Comments:*** H-MA-755-S40.

Rarity: —

$5 • W-MA-2040-005-N080

Left: FIVE vertically. ***Center:*** 5 / Eagle and shield, Train. ***Right:*** Indian woman with bow / FIVE. ***Overprint:*** Red FIVE. ***Comments:*** H-MA-755-N38. 18__. 1850s.

Rarity: —

$5 • W-MA-2040-005-A070 CC

Engraver: W.L. Ormsby. ***Comments:*** H-MA-755-A35. Altered from $5 Merchants Bank, Ft. Leavenworth, Kansas. 185_. 1850s.

Rarity: URS-7
F $100

$5 • W-MA-2040-005-A080

Left: Indian woman holding bow / FIVE. ***Center:*** Eagle on branch / Indian man standing on cliff watching train. ***Bottom center:*** Indian in canoe. ***Right:*** 5 / Woman seated with anchor, Ship. ***Engraver:*** Doty & Bergen. ***Comments:*** H-MA-755-A40. Altered from $5 Merchants Bank, Mankato City, Minnesota. Sept. 1, 185_. 1850s.

Rarity: —

$5 • W-MA-2040-005-A090

Left: FIVE vertically. ***Center:*** 5 / Spread eagle on U.S. shield holding banner in its beak. ***Bottom center:*** Road, Trees, Sign post. ***Right:*** Indian woman standing holding bow. ***Engraver:*** Doty & Bergen. ***Comments:*** H-MA-755-A45. Altered from $5 Merchants Bank, Stillwater, Minnesota. Oct. 20, 1854.

Rarity: —

$10 • **W-MA-2040-010-S090**

Left: X / Child standing with pitcher. ***Center:*** X / Sailor with flag seated on bales, Two ships / X. ***Bottom center:*** Ship. ***Right:*** X / Shipyard scene. ***Engraver:*** Rawdon, Wright & Hatch. ***Comments:*** H-MA-755-S45. 18__. 1850s.

Rarity: —

$10 • **W-MA-2040-010-S100**

Center: Two people seated, Griffin on chest. ***Comments:*** H-MA-755-S50.

Rarity: —

$10 • **W-MA-2040-010-N090**

CJF

Comments: H-MA-755-N40. 185_. 1850s.

Rarity: URS-7

F $125

$10 • **W-MA-2040-010-N100**

Center: Woman seated on rock. ***Tint:*** Red. ***Comments:*** H-MA-755-N45.

Rarity: —

$10 • **W-MA-2040-010-N110**

Left: Train. ***Center:*** Woman with sheaf. ***Comments:*** H-MA-755-N50.

Rarity: —

$10 • **W-MA-2040-010-N120**

Center: Eagle and shield. ***Comments:*** H-MA-755-N55.

Rarity: —

$10 • **W-MA-2040-010-A100**

Left: X / Eagle surmounting frame bearing arm and hammer. ***Center:*** Woman seated on bale, Spinning wheel / 10. ***Right:*** Panel of flowers and fruit bearing horizontal medallion portrait of George Washington. ***Engraver:*** W.L. Ormsby. ***Comments:*** H-MA-755-A50. Altered from $10 Merchants Bank, Ft. Leavenworth, Kansas. 18__. 1850s.

Rarity: —

$20 • **W-MA-2040-020-C060**

Engraver: Rawdon, Wright, Hatch & Edson. ***Comments:*** H-MA-755-C12. Counterfeit of W-MA-2040-020-G060. 18__. 1850s.

Rarity: —

$20 • **W-MA-2040-020-S110**

Center: Two people seated, Griffin on chest. ***Comments:*** H-MA-755-S55.

Rarity: —

$50 • **W-MA-2040-050-S120**

Center: Two people seated, Griffin on chest. ***Comments:*** H-MA-755-S60.

Rarity: —

Prescott Bank

1850–1865

W-MA-2050

History: The Prescott Bank was incorporated in 1850 with $100,000 in authorized capital. Shortly after its opening, many counterfeit $100 notes with its imprint made the news. In 1851 the capital was increased by $50,000, to be paid in before May 1, 1852. By 1854 the capital was $200,000.

Circulation from 1857 to 1860 was $122,712. In 1861 it was $116,613, and in 1863 it was $190,695.

The business of the Prescott Bank was succeeded by the Prescott National Bank of Lowell, chartered on March 31, 1865.

Numismatic Commentary: Fortunately for collectors, both genuine and fine-quality, low-denomination counterfeits are available with minimum searching. Higher-denomination, genuine notes are very hard to locate.

Valid Issues

$1 • **W-MA-2050-001-G010**

Left: Women flanking frame bearing scene / 1. ***Center:*** 1. ***Right:*** 1 / Woman standing with 1 bearing ONE. ***Engraver:*** Rawdon, Wright, Hatch & Edson / New England Bank Note Co. ***Comments:*** H-MA-760-G2. July 1, 185_. 1850s.

Rarity: —

$1 • **W-MA-2050-001-G010a**

CJF

Overprint: Red ONE. ***Engraver:*** Rawdon, Wright, Hatch & Edson / New England Bank Note Co. ***Comments:*** H-MA-760-G2a. Similar to W-MA-2050-001-G010. July 1, 185_. 1850s.

Rarity: URS-5

VF $750

$1 • **W-MA-2050-001-G010b**

Overprint: Red ONE. ***Engraver:*** Rawdon, Wright, Hatch & Edson / New England Bank Note Co. / ABNCo. monogram. ***Comments:*** H-MA-760-G2b. Similar to W-MA-2050-001-G010 but with additional engraver imprint. July 1, 185_. 1850s.

Rarity: —

$2 • **W-MA-2050-002-G020**

Left: Mechanic reclining with hammer, Factory and train / 2. ***Center:*** Cherub and woman supporting die bearing 2. ***Right:*** TWO. ***Engraver:*** Rawdon, Wright, Hatch & Edson / New England Bank Note Co. ***Comments:*** H-MA-760-G4. July 1, 185_. 1850s.

Rarity: —

$2 • W-MA-2050-002-G020a

Overprint: Red TWO. ***Engraver:*** Rawdon, Wright, Hatch & Edson / New England Bank Note Co. ***Comments:*** H-MA-760-G4a. Similar to W-MA-2050-002-G020. July 1, 185_. 1850s.

Rarity: —

$2 • W-MA-2050-002-G020b

CJF

Overprint: Red TWO. ***Engraver:*** Rawdon, Wright, Hatch & Edson / New England Bank Note Co. / ABNCo. monogram. ***Comments:*** H-MA-760-G4b. Similar to W-MA-2050-002-G020 but with additional engraver imprint. July 1, 185_. 1850s.

Rarity: URS-5
VF $1,250

$3 • W-MA-2050-003-G030

Left: Man plowing with oxen and horse, Dog, Cart, Man on horse, Train going under bridge / 3. ***Center:*** 3. ***Right:*** THREE / Two women. ***Engraver:*** Rawdon, Wright, Hatch & Edson / New England Bank Note Co. ***Comments:*** H-MA-760-G6. July 1, 185_. 1850s.

Rarity: URS-4
VF $1,500

$3 • W-MA-2050-003-G030a

Overprint: Red THREE. ***Engraver:*** Rawdon, Wright, Hatch & Edson / New England Bank Note Co. ***Comments:*** H-MA-760-G6a. Similar to W-MA-2050-003-G030. July 1, 185_. 1850s.

Rarity: —

$3 • W-MA-2050-003-G030b

Overprint: Red THREE. ***Engraver:*** Rawdon, Wright, Hatch & Edson / New England Bank Note Co. / ABNCo. monogram. ***Comments:*** H-MA-760-G6b. Similar to W-MA-2050-003-G030 but with additional engraver imprint. July 1, 185_. 1850s.

Rarity: —

$5 • W-MA-2050-005-G040

Left: Woman reclining with bale, cotton plant, and spinning wheel, Factories / 5. ***Center:*** 5 bearing FIVE. ***Right:*** FIVE / Woman standing with wreath, pole and cap, 5, and cornucopia. ***Engraver:*** Rawdon, Wright, Hatch & Edson / New England Bank Note Co. ***Comments:*** H-MA-760-G8. July 1, 185_. 1850s.

Rarity: URS-4
F $495

Collectors and Researchers:

If you have new information about any banks or notes listed in this volume, contact Whitman Publishing, Attn: Obsolete Paper Money, 3101 Clairmont Road, Suite G, Atlanta, GA 30329.

$5 • W-MA-2050-005-G040a

Overprint: Red FIVE. ***Engraver:*** Rawdon, Wright, Hatch & Edson / New England Bank Note Co. ***Comments:*** H-MA-760-G8a. Similar to W-MA-2050-005-G040. July 1, 185_. 1850s.

Rarity: —

$5 • W-MA-2050-005-G040b

CJF

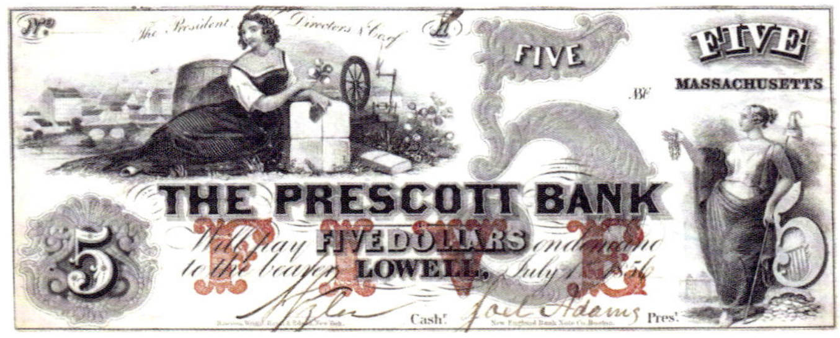

Overprint: Red FIVE. ***Engraver:*** Rawdon, Wright, Hatch & Edson / New England Bank Note Co. / ABNCo. monogram. ***Comments:*** H-MA-760-G8b. Similar to W-MA-2050-005-G040 but with additional engraver imprint. July 1, 185_. 1850s.

Rarity: URS-5
VF $750

$5 • W-MA-2050-005-G050

Left: 5 on dies vertically and inverted. ***Center:*** Girl at loom, Man and boy. ***Right:*** 5. ***Tint:*** Green. ***Back:*** Plain. ***Engraver:*** National Bank Note Co. ***Comments:*** H-MA-760-G10a. Oct. 1, 18__. 1860s.

Rarity: —

$5 • W-MA-2050-005-G050a

HA, HA

Tint: Green. ***Back:*** Green. ***Engraver:*** National Bank Note Co. ***Comments:*** H-MA-760-G10b. Similar to W-MA-2050-005-G050. October 1, 18__. 1860s.

Rarity: URS-2
Proof $5,000

$10 • W-MA-2050-010-G060

Left: Woman with eagle and shield / TEN. ***Center:*** X bearing TEN. ***Right:*** 10 / State arms. ***Engraver:*** Rawdon, Wright, Hatch & Edson / New England Bank Note Co. ***Comments:*** H-MA-760-G12. July 1, 185_. 1850s.

Rarity: —

$10 • W-MA-2050-010-G060a

CJF

Overprint: Red TEN. ***Engraver:*** Rawdon, Wright, Hatch & Edson / New England Bank Note Co. ***Comments:*** H-MA-760-G12a. Similar to W-MA-2050-010-G060. July 1, 185_. 1850s.

Rarity: URS-7

VG $125; **VF** $250

$10 • W-MA-2050-010-G060b

Overprint: Red TEN. ***Engraver:*** Rawdon, Wright, Hatch & Edson / New England Bank Note Co. / ABNCo. monogram. ***Comments:*** H-MA-760-G12b. Similar to W-MA-2050-010-G060 but with additional engraver imprint. July 1, 185_. 1850s.

Rarity: —

$10 • W-MA-2050-010-G070

Left: Herd of deer grazing by stream in forest, Trees and waterfall / 10. ***Right:*** Female portrait. ***Tint:*** Green panel of lathework and microlettering, Die bearing 5. ***Back:*** Plain. ***Engraver:*** National Bank Note Co. ***Comments:*** H-MA-760-G14a. Oct. 1, 18__. 1860s.

Rarity: —

$10 • W-MA-2050-010-G070a

Back: Color unknown. ***Engraver:*** National Bank Note Co. ***Comments:*** H-MA-760-G14b. Similar to W-MA-2050-010-G070. Oct. 1, 18__. 1860s.

Rarity: —

$20 • W-MA-2050-020-G080

Left: 20 / Minerva standing with spear. ***Center:*** Woman seated between 2 and 0. ***Right:*** 20 / Woman reclining on cornucopia / 20. ***Engraver:*** Rawdon, Wright, Hatch & Edson. ***Comments:*** H-MA-760-G16. 18__. 1850s.

Rarity: —

$20 • W-MA-2050-020-G090

Left: 20 / Female portrait. ***Center:*** Man reclining with globe. ***Right:*** 20 / Male portrait. ***Tint:*** Red-orange. ***Engraver:*** National Bank Note Co. ***Comments:*** H-MA-760-G18a. 186_. 1860s.

Rarity: —

$50 • W-MA-2050-050-G100

Left: 50 / Minerva standing by column. ***Center:*** Ceres and Vulcan flanking cornucopia. ***Right:*** 50 / Cherub in sailboat / 50. ***Engraver:*** Rawdon, Wright, Hatch & Edson. ***Comments:*** H-MA-760-G20. 18__. 1850s.

Rarity: —

$50 • W-MA-2050-050-G110

JF

Tint: Red-orange. ***Engraver:*** National Bank Note Co. ***Comments:*** H-MA-760-G22a. Proof. July 2, 1860.

Rarity: URS-1

Proof $7,500

$100 • W-MA-2050-100-G120

Left: 100 / Vulcan seated with sledge and anchor. ***Center:*** Train on bridge, Eagle on limb, Canal locks / C C. ***Bottom center:*** 100. ***Right:*** 100 / Ceres seated, Cornucopia. ***Engraver:*** Rawdon, Wright, Hatch & Edson. ***Comments:*** H-MA-760-G24. 18__. 1850s.

Rarity: —

$100 • W-MA-2050-100-G130

CC

Tint: Red-orange. ***Engraver:*** American Bank Note Co. ***Comments:*** H-MA-760-G26a. July 2, 1860.

Rarity: URS-1

Proof $11,000

Selected auction price: Stack's Bowers Galleries, August 2014, Lot 2084, Proof $10,575

$500 • W-MA-2050-500-G140

Left: Woman seated on sheaves, Men reaping, Man on horse / 500. ***Center:*** 500 / D. ***Right:*** 500 vertically. ***Engraver:*** Rawdon, Wright, Hatch & Edson. ***Comments:*** H-MA-760-G28. 18__. 1850s.

Rarity: —

$500 • W-MA-2050-500-G150

JF

Tint: Red-orange. ***Engraver:*** American Bank Note Co. ***Comments:*** H-MA-760-G30a. 186_. 1860s.

Rarity: URS-1
Proof $10,000

Uncut Sheets

$20-$50 • W-MA-2050-020.050-US010

Vignette(s): ***($20)*** Female portrait / Man reclining with globe / Male portrait. ***($50)*** Fifty on die / Woman seated with globe / Male portrait. ***Tint(s):*** Red-orange. ***Engraver:*** National Bank Note Co. ***Comments:*** H-MA-760-G18a, G22a.

Rarity: —

Non-Valid Issues

$5 • W-MA-2050-005-C040

CC

Engraver: Rawdon, Wright, Hatch & Edson / New England Bank Note Co. ***Comments:*** H-MA-760-C8. Counterfeit of W-MA-2050-005-G040. July 1, 185_.

Rarity: URS-6
VF $250

$5 • W-MA-2050-005-C040b

Engraver: Rawdon, Wright, Hatch & Edson / New England Bank Note Co. / ABNCo. monogram. ***Comments:*** H-MA-760-C8b. Counterfeit of W-MA-2050-005-G040b.

Rarity: URS-7
F $75

$5 • W-MA-2050-005-A010

Left: Several men with sticks driving herd of cattle into stream / 5. ***Center:*** Five men raking and loading hay, Ox wagon. ***Right:*** 5. ***Tint:*** Red-brown lathework outlining white 5. ***Engraver:*** Bald, Cousland & Co. ***Comments:*** H-MA-760-A5. Altered from $5 Pioneer Association, Lafayette, Indiana. 18__. 1850s.

Rarity: —

$10 • W-MA-2050-010-C060

Engraver: Rawdon, Wright, Hatch & Edson / New England Bank Note Co. ***Comments:*** H-MA-760-C12. Counterfeit of W-MA-2050-010-G060 or variety.

Rarity: —

$100 • W-MA-2050-100-C120

Engraver: Rawdon, Wright, Hatch & Edson. ***Comments:*** H-MA-760-C24. Counterfeit of W-MA-2050-100-G120.

Rarity: —

Rail Road Bank

1831–1865

W-MA-2060

History: The Rail Road Bank was chartered on March 19, 1831, with an authorized capital of $200,000. It went into operation in the autumn of that year.

The capital of the bank in 1839 was $800,000, but it was reduced to $600,000 by 1845. Circulation was $285,661 in 1839 and rose up to $489,146 in 1845. By 1863 it had leveled out at $383,968.

The business of the Rail Road Bank was succeeded by the Railroad National Bank of Lowell, chartered on January 25, 1865.

Numismatic Commentary: Genuine notes are hard to locate. Notes with local scenery or structures are always in great demand. The bank's first currency issue comprised of $5 notes with a steam locomotive vignette.

Valid Issues

$1 • W-MA-2060-001-G010

Left: Lathework panel bearing MASSACHUSETTS vertically. ***Center:*** 1 / 1 / Alternating flower garlands and gridwork segments / ONE / 1 / 1. ***Right:*** Lathework panel bearing ONE / D / ONE vertically. ***Engraver:*** PSSP. ***Comments:*** H-MA-765-G2. 18__. 1830s.

Rarity: —

$1 • W-MA-2060-001-G020

Back: Congreve Check Plate. ***Engraver:*** PSSP. ***Comments:*** H-MA-765-G4. 18__. 1830s.

Rarity: —

$1 • W-MA-2060-001-G030

Left: 1 / Woman seated / 1. ***Center:*** 1 / Woman seated with shield / 1. ***Right:*** ONE vertically. ***Back:*** Congreve Check Plate. ***Engraver:*** New England Bank Note Co. / PSSP. ***Comments:*** H-MA-765-G8. 18__. 1830s.

Rarity: —

$1 • W-MA-2060-001-G030a

BC

Back: Plain. ***Engraver:*** New England Bank Note Co. / PSSP. ***Comments:*** H-MA-765-G8a. Similar to W-MA-2060-001-G030. 18__. 1830s–1850s.

Rarity: —

$1 • W-MA-2060-001-G030b

Overprint: Red ONE. ***Back:*** Plain. ***Engraver:*** New England Bank Note Co. / PSSP. ***Comments:*** H-MA-765-G8b. Similar to W-MA-2060-001-G030. 18__. 1850s.

Rarity: —

$1 • W-MA-2060-001-G030c

Overprint: Red ONE. ***Back:*** Plain. ***Engraver:*** New England Bank Note Co. / PSSP / ABNCo. monogram. ***Comments:*** H-MA-765-G8c. Similar to W-MA-2060-001-G030 but with additional engraver imprint. 18__. 1850s–1860s.

Rarity: —

$2 • W-MA-2060-002-G040

Left: Lathework panel bearing MASSACHUSETTS vertically. ***Center:*** 2 / 2 / Alternating flower garlands and gridwork segments / TWO / 2 / 2. ***Right:*** Lathework panel bearing five TWOs vertically. ***Engraver:*** PSSP. ***Comments:*** H-MA-765-G10. 18__. 1830s.

Rarity: —

$2 • W-MA-2060-002-G050

Back: Congreve Check Plate. ***Engraver:*** PSSP. ***Comments:*** H-MA-765-G12. 18__. 1830s.

Rarity: —

$2 • W-MA-2060-002-G060

Left: TWO / Archimedes / 2. ***Center:*** 2 / Crowned woman seated with shield, Caduceus, Cornucopia and sheaf, Train / 2 / Panel of microlettering. ***Right:*** Lathework panel bearing TWO vertically. ***Back:*** Congreve Check Plate. ***Engraver:*** New England Bank Note Co. / PSSP. ***Comments:*** H-MA-765-G16. 18__. 1830s.

Rarity: —

$2 • W-MA-2060-002-G060a

Back: Plain. ***Engraver:*** New England Bank Note Co. / PSSP. ***Comments:*** H-MA-765-G16a. Similar to W-MA-2060-002-G060. 18__. 1830s–1850s.

Rarity: —

$2 • W-MA-2060-002-G060b

Overprint: Red TWO. ***Back:*** Plain. ***Engraver:*** New England Bank Note Co. / PSSP. ***Comments:*** H-MA-765-G16b. Similar to W-MA-2060-002-G060. 18__. 1850s.

Rarity: —

$2 • W-MA-2060-002-G060c

HA

Overprint: Red TWO. ***Back:*** Plain. ***Engraver:*** New England Bank Note Co. / PSSP / ABNCo. monogram. ***Comments:*** H-MA-765-G16c. Similar to W-MA-2060-002-G060 but with additional engraver imprint. 18__. 1850s–1860s.

Rarity: URS-4
VF $1,250
Selected auction price: Heritage, January 2014, Lot 15356, VF $1,233

$3 • W-MA-2060-003-G070

Left: Lathework panel bearing MASSACHUSETTS vertically. ***Center:*** 3 / 3 / Alternating flower garlands and gridwork segments / THREE / 3 / 3. ***Right:*** Lathework panel bearing THREE vertically. ***Engraver:*** PSSP. ***Comments:*** H-MA-765-G18. 18__. 1830s.

Rarity: —

$3 • W-MA-2060-003-G080

Back: Congreve Check Plate. ***Engraver:*** PSSP. ***Comments:*** H-MA-765-G20. 18__. 1830s.

Rarity: —

$3 • W-MA-2060-003-G090

Left: 3 / Vulcan standing with hammer / 3. ***Center:*** THREE / Crowned woman seated with shield, Caduceus, Cornucopia and sheaf, Train / 3. ***Right:*** Lathework panel bearing THREE vertically. ***Back:*** Congreve Check Plate. ***Engraver:*** New England Bank Note Co. / PSSP. ***Comments:*** H-MA-765-G24. 18__. 1830s.

Rarity: —

$3 • W-MA-2060-003-G090a

Back: Plain. ***Engraver:*** New England Bank Note Co. / PSSP. ***Comments:*** H-MA-765-G24a. Similar to W-MA-2060-003-G090. 18__. 1830s–1850s.

Rarity: —

$3 • W-MA-2060-003-G090b

Overprint: Red THREE. ***Back:*** Plain. ***Engraver:*** New England Bank Note Co. / PSSP. ***Comments:*** H-MA-765-G24b. Similar to W-MA-2060-003-G090. 18__. 1830s–1850s.

Rarity: —

$3 • W-MA-2060-003-G090c

Overprint: Red THREE. ***Back:*** Plain. ***Engraver:*** New England Bank Note Co. / PSSP / ABNCo. monogram. ***Comments:*** H-MA-765-G24c. Similar to W-MA-2060-003-G090 but with additional engraver imprint. 18__. 1850s–1860s.

Rarity: —

$5 • W-MA-2060-005-G100

Center: Train. ***Comments:*** H-Unlisted. 18__. 1830s.

Rarity: —

$5 • W-MA-2060-005-G110

Left: Lathework chain bearing MASSACHUSETTS / 5 / 5. ***Center:*** Alternating flower garlands and gridwork segments / FIVE DOLLARS lined by spiral lathework lines. ***Right:*** 5 / 5. ***Engraver:*** PSSP. ***Comments:*** H-MA-765-G28. 18__. 1830s.

Rarity: —

$5 • W-MA-2060-005-G110a

Back: Plain. ***Engraver:*** New England Bank Note Co. / PSSP. ***Comments:*** H-MA-765-G28a. Similar to W-MA-2060-005-G110. 18__. 1830s–1850s.

Rarity: —

$5 • W-MA-2060-005-G120

Left: Male portrait / 5. ***Center:*** Train at depot, Church. ***Right:*** 5 / Five women surrounding 5. ***Engraver:*** Rawdon, Wright, Hatch & Edson / New England Bank Note Co. ***Comments:*** H-MA-765-G32. 18__. 1850s.

Rarity: —

$5 • W-MA-2060-005-G120a

HA

Overprint: Red FIVE. ***Engraver:*** Rawdon, Wright, Hatch & Edson / New England Bank Note Co. / ABNCo. monogram. ***Comments:*** H-Unlisted. Similar to W-MA-2060-005-G120 but with additional engraver imprint. 18__. 1850s.

Rarity: URS-2
F $2,250

$10 • W-MA-2060-010-G130

Left: Lathework chain bearing MASSACHUSETTS / 10 / 10 vertically. ***Center:*** Alternating flower garlands and gridwork segments / TEN DOLLARS lined by spiral lathework lines. ***Right:*** 10 / 10 vertically. ***Engraver:*** PSSP. ***Comments:*** H-MA-765-G34. 18__. 1830s.

Rarity: —

$10 • W-MA-2060-010-G140

Left: MASSACHUSETTS vertically. ***Center:*** 10 / Woman standing / 10 / Train. ***Right:*** 10 / State arms / 10. ***Back:*** Congreve Check Plate. ***Engraver:*** New England Bank Note Co. / PSSP. ***Comments:*** H-MA-765-G36. 18__. 1830s.

Rarity: —

$10 • W-MA-2060-010-G140a

CC

Back: Plain. ***Engraver:*** New England Bank Note Co. / PSSP. ***Comments:*** H-MA-765-G36a. Similar to W-MA-2060-010-G140. 18__. 1830s–1850s.

Rarity: URS-5
VG $150; **VF** $400

$10 • W-MA-2060-010-G150

Left: 10 / X. ***Center:*** Street scene, Buildings and pedestrians. ***Right:*** X / Male portrait. ***Engraver:*** Rawdon, Wright, Hatch & Edson / New England Bank Note Co. ***Comments:*** H-MA-765-G40. 18__. 1850s.

Rarity: —

$20 • W-MA-2060-020-G160

Left: Lathework chain bearing MASSACHUSETTS / 20 / 20 vertically. ***Center:*** Alternating flower garlands and gridwork segments / XX. ***Right:*** 20 / 20 vertically. ***Engraver:*** PSSP. ***Comments:*** H-MA-765-G42. 18__. 1830s.

Rarity: —

$20 • W-MA-2060-020-G170

Left: 20 / Woman seated with book on lap, opening chest. ***Center:*** XX / Eagle on rock / XX. ***Right:*** 20 / Ship in harbor. ***Engraver:*** New England Bank Note Co. / ABNCo. monogram. ***Comments:*** H-MA-765-G44a. 18__. Circa 1860.

Rarity: —

$20 • W-MA-2060-020-G180

Left: XX / 20. ***Center:*** Male portrait. ***Right:*** 20 / Woman seated by spindle, Factory. ***Tint:*** Red TWENTY / XX / TWENTY. ***Engraver:*** American Bank Note Co. ***Comments:*** H-MA-765-G48. 1860s.

Rarity: —

$50 • W-MA-2060-050-G190

Left: Lathework chain bearing MASSACHUSETTS / 50 / 50 vertically. ***Center:*** Alternating flower garlands and gridwork segments / FIFTY. ***Right:*** 50 / 50 vertically. ***Engraver:*** PSSP. ***Comments:*** H-MA-765-G50. 18__. 1830s.

Rarity: —

$50 • W-MA-2060-050-G200

Left: FIFTY / Woman standing with wreath and flowers / FIFTY. ***Center:*** 50 / Man restraining prancing horse / 50. ***Right:*** FIFTY / Woman standing with cornucopia / FIFTY. ***Engraver:*** New England Bank Note Co. / ABNCo. monogram. ***Comments:*** H-MA-765-G52a. 18__. Circa 1860.

Rarity: —

$50 • W-MA-2060-050-G210

Left: View of cotton factories at Lowell / 50. ***Right:*** 50 / Male portrait. ***Tint:*** Red FIFTY / 50 / FIFTY. ***Engraver:*** American Bank Note Co. ***Comments:*** H-MA-765-G56. 1860s.

Rarity: —

$100 • W-MA-2060-100-G220

Left: Lathework chain bearing MASSACHUSETTS / 100 / 100 vertically. ***Center:*** Alternating flower garlands and gridwork segments with 100. ***Right:*** 100 / 100 vertically. ***Engraver:*** Perkins. ***Comments:*** H-MA-765-G58. 18__. 1830s.

Rarity: —

$100 • W-MA-2060-100-G230

Left: ONE HUNDRED on 100 / Portrait of William Henry Harrison. ***Center:*** Wharf scene, Men loading wagon with barrels. ***Right:*** ONE HUNDRED on 100 / Portrait of Christopher Columbus. ***Engraver:*** New England Bank Note Co. / ABNCo. monogram. ***Comments:*** H-MA-765-G64a. 18__. Circa 1860.

Rarity: —

$100 • W-MA-2060-100-G240

Left: 100 / Woman seated on bale with spool. ***Center:*** View of factories at Lowell. ***Right:*** 100 / Male portrait. ***Engraver:*** American Bank Note Co. ***Comments:*** H-MA-765-G68. 1860s.

Rarity: —

$500 • W-MA-2060-500-G250

Engraver: Unverified, but likely PSSP. ***Comments:*** H-MA-765-G72. No description available. 18__. 1830s–1850s.

Rarity: *None known*

$500 • **W-MA-2060-500-G260**

Left: Woman seated on sheaves, Men reaping, Man on horse. ***Center:*** 500 / D. ***Right:*** 500 vertically. ***Engraver:*** New England Bank Note Co. / ABNCo. monogram. ***Comments:*** H-MA-765-G76a. 18__. Circa 1860.

Rarity: —

$500 • **W-MA-2060-500-G270**

Left: Train emerging from depot, Church and buildings / 500. ***Center:*** Male portrait. ***Right:*** 500 / State arms. ***Tint:*** Red D. ***Engraver:*** American Bank Note Co. ***Comments:*** H-MA-765-G80. 1860s.

Rarity: —

Non-Valid Issues

$1 • **W-MA-2060-001-N010**

Left: Male portrait. ***Center:*** Train and trees. ***Right:*** Woman. ***Comments:*** H-MA-765-N5.

Rarity: —

$1 • **W-MA-2060-001-A010**

CJF

Overprint: Red ONE. ***Engraver:*** Toppan, Carpenter, Casilear & Co. ***Comments:*** H-MA-765-A5. Altered from $1 Erie and Kalamazoo R. R. Bank, Adrian, Michigan. August 1, 1853 or 1854. 9 handwritten over 3 in date. 1850s.

Rarity: URS-7

F $100

$2 • **W-MA-2060-002-A020**

Left: 2 / Man with sickle. ***Center:*** Man on horseback, Man standing nearby, Bridge. ***Right:*** 2 / Portrait of Lewis Cass. ***Overprint:*** Red TWO. ***Engraver:*** Toppan, Carpenter, Casilear & Co. ***Comments:*** H-MA-765-A10. Altered from $2 Erie and Kalamazoo R. R. Bank, Adrian, Michigan. Aug. 1, 1853 or 1854.

Rarity: —

$3 • **W-MA-2060-003-C090**

Engraver: New England Bank Note Co. / PSSP. ***Comments:*** H-MA-765-C24. Counterfeit of W-MA-2060-003-G090 or variety. 18__. 1840s.

Rarity: —

$3 • **W-MA-2060-003-A030**

CJF

Overprint: Red THREE. ***Engraver:*** New England Bank Note Co. / Rawdon, Wright, Hatch & Edson. ***Comments:*** H-MA-765-A15. Altered from $3 Waubeek Bank, De Soto, Nebraska. 1857.

Rarity: URS-6

VG $125; **VF** $250

$5 • **W-MA-2060-005-R010**

Engraver: New England Bank Note Co. / PSSP. ***Comments:*** H-MA-765-R5. Raised from W-MA-2060-001-G030 or G030a. 18__. 1840s.

Rarity: —

$5 • **W-MA-2060-005-R020**

Engraver: New England Bank Note Co. / PSSP. ***Comments:*** H-MA-765-R10. Raised from W-MA-2060-002-G060. 18__. 1840s.

Rarity: —

$5 • **W-MA-2060-005-S010**

CJF

Engraver: Danforth, Wright & Co. ***Comments:*** H-MA-765-S5. 18__. 1850s.

Rarity: URS-6

VG $125; **F** $135; **VF** $175

$5 • **W-MA-2060-005-N020**

Left: 5 / Man. ***Center:*** Bridge and train. ***Right:*** 5 / Woman. ***Comments:*** H-MA-765-N10.

Rarity: —

$5 • **W-MA-2060-005-A040**

SI

Overprint: Red. ***Engraver:*** Toppan, Carpenter, Casilear & Co. ***Comments:*** H-MA-765-A20. Altered from $5 Erie and Kalamazoo R. R. Bank, Adrian, Michigan series. August 1, 1853.

Rarity: URS-7

F $100

$10 • **W-MA-2060-010-R030**

Engraver: New England Bank Note Co. / PSSP. ***Comments:*** H-MA-765-R15. Raised from W-MA-2060-001-G030 or G030a. 18__. 1840s.

Rarity: —

$10 • W-MA-2060-010-R040

Engraver: New England Bank Note Co. / PSSP. ***Comments:*** H-MA-765-R20. Raised from W-MA-2060-002-G060. 18__. 1840s.

Rarity: —

$10 • W-MA-2060-010-R050

Engraver: New England Bank Note Co. / PSSP. ***Comments:*** H-MA-765-R25. Raised from W-MA-2060-005-G110 or G110a. 18__. 1840s.

Rarity: —

$10 • W-MA-2060-010-A050

Left: X / Indian kneeling. ***Center:*** Steamboat, Schooner and boats, City / X / Panel outlining white TEN. ***Right:*** 10 / Woman with bonnet and sheaf. ***Engraver:*** New England Bank Note Co. ***Comments:*** H-MA-765-A25. Altered from $10 Hamilton Bank, Scituate, Rhode Island, or from notes of other failed banks using the same plate. 18__. 1840s.

Rarity: —

$20 • W-MA-2060-020-N030

Left: Woman. ***Center:*** Train. ***Engraver:*** Underwood, Bald, Spencer & Hufty. ***Comments:*** H-MA-765-N15. 18__. 1840s.

Rarity: —

$20 • W-MA-2060-020-A060

CC

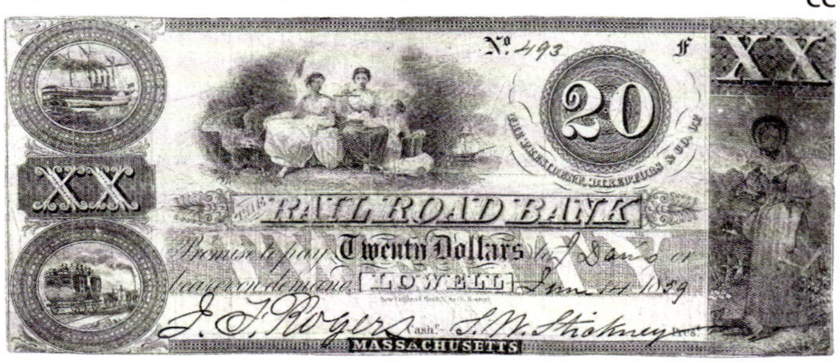

Engraver: New England Bank Note Co. ***Comments:*** H-MA-765-A30. Altered from $20 Hamilton Bank, Scituate, Rhode Island, or from notes of other failed banks using the same plate. 18__. 1840s–1850s.

Rarity: URS-6
VG $125; **VF** $175

Wamesit Bank
1853–1865
W-MA-2070

History: The Wamesit Bank was chartered on April 28, 1853, with an authorized capital of $100,000. It opened its doors for business on November 1. The capital was increased to $150,000 in 1855. Circulation from 1857 to 1860 was $88,373. In 1862 it was $89,909, and in 1863 it was $128,311. Real estate was valued at $12,822.46.

The Wamesit Bank was succeeded by the Wamesit National Bank of Lowell, chartered on February 3, 1865.

Numismatic Commentary: Both genuine and non-valid notes of this bank are hard to find in today's marketplace.

Valid Issues

$1 • W-MA-2070-001-G010

Left: 1 / Indian man with bow and tomahawk. ***Center:*** Bricklayers at work on scaffold / 1. ***Right:*** 1 / Stonecutter. ***Engraver:*** Danforth, Wright & Co. ***Comments:*** H-MA-770-G2. Oct. 1, 18__. 1850s.

Rarity: —

$2 • W-MA-2070-002-G020

CC

Engraver: Danforth, Wright & Co. ***Comments:*** H-MA-770-G4. October 1, 18__. 1850s.

Rarity: URS-1
Proof $4,200

$3 • W-MA-2070-003-G030

Left: 3 / THREE. ***Center:*** Indian family on cliff overlooking city / 3 bearing state arms. ***Right:*** 3 / Two farmers walking with dog. ***Engraver:*** Danforth, Wright & Co. ***Comments:*** H-MA-770-G6. Oct. 1, 18__. 1850s.

Rarity: —

$5 • W-MA-2070-005-G040

Left: FIVE / Train passing under arched bridge. ***Center:*** FIVE / Farmer with sickle and sheaf seated in V. ***Right:*** 5 / Road scene, Cattle, Bridge and train. ***Engraver:*** Danforth, Wright & Co. ***Comments:*** H-MA-770-G8. Oct. 1, 18__. 1850s.

Rarity: —

$10 • W-MA-2070-010-G050

Left: Two women seated with book, Chest and spinning wheel, Sailor and mechanic / TEN. ***Center:*** TEN / Two women seated, Oxen, Farmer and dog. ***Right:*** TEN. ***Engraver:*** Danforth, Wright & Co. ***Comments:*** H-MA-770-G10. Whole-note vignette. Oct. 1, 18__. 1850s.

Rarity: —

$20 • W-MA-2070-020-G060

CJF

Engraver: Danforth, Wright & Co. ***Comments:*** H-MA-770-G12. Proof. October 1, 18__. 1850s.

Rarity: URS-2

$50 • W-MA-2070-050-G070 JF

Engraver: Danforth, Wright & Co. ***Comments:*** H-MA-770-G14. Whole-note vignette. Proof. October 1, 18__. 1850s.

Rarity: URS-2

Proof $5,000

$100 • W-MA-2070-100-G080

Left: 100 / Two men loading wagon with sheaves, Man holding horse. ***Center:*** ONE HUNDRED on lathework strip. ***Right:*** 100 / Two women, one kneeling with sickle and grain, one standing behind her. ***Engraver:*** Danforth, Wright & Co. ***Comments:*** H-MA-770-G16. Oct. 1, 18__. 1850s.

Rarity: URS-1

Proof $5,500

$500 • W-MA-2070-500-G090

Left: D / Three women in clouds. ***Right:*** Minerva standing / 500. ***Engraver:*** Danforth, Wright & Co. ***Comments:*** H-MA-770-G13. Oct. 1, 18__. 1850s.

Rarity: —

Uncut Sheets

$50-$100 • W-MA-2070-050.100-US010

Vignette(s): ($50) Liberty with pole and cap, Shield and eagle / Two women, one kneeling with sickle and grain, one standing behind her. ***($100)*** Two men loading wagon with sheaves, Man holding horse / Two women, one kneeling with sickle and grain, one standing behind her. ***Comments:*** H-MA-770-G14, G16. October 1, 18__. 1850s.

Rarity: —

Non-Valid Issues

$2 • W-MA-2070-002-C020

Engraver: Danforth, Wright & Co. ***Comments:*** H-MA-770-C4. Counterfeit of W-MA-2070-002-G020. Oct. 1, 18__. 1850s.

Rarity: —

$2 • W-MA-2070-002-A010

Left: 2 / Farmer plowing with black and white horses. ***Center:*** Two men loading wagon with sheaves, Three men cradling and binding. ***Right:*** 2 / Two floating cherubs with caduceus and sheaf. ***Tint:*** Red-brown 2s and TWO DOLLARS. ***Engraver:*** Danforth, Wright & Co. ***Comments:*** H-MA-770-A5. Altered from $2 Southern Bank of Georgia, Bainbridge, Georgia. March 1, 1858.

Rarity: —

$5 • W-MA-2070-005-N010

Center: Man in 5, Mountain view. ***Right:*** Woman and child. ***Comments:*** H-MA-770-N5.

Rarity: —

$5 • W-MA-2070-005-A020 CJF

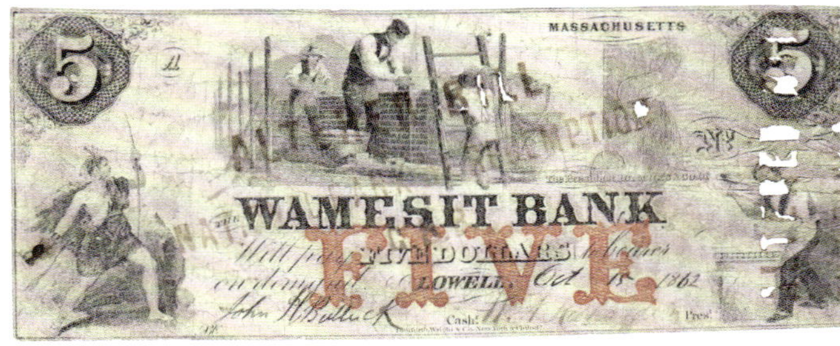

Overprint: Red FIVE. ***Engraver:*** Danforth, Wright & Co. / ABNCo. monogram. ***Comments:*** H-Unlisted. 18__. 1860s.

Rarity: URS-7

F $75

Lynn, Massachusetts

In 1629 Edmund Ingalls settled on the land owned by the Sagamore Indians. The town that became Lynn was incorporated in 1631 as Saugus. Later it was renamed after King's Lynn, Norfolk, England.

Most of the town's centers slowly separated into independent towns, including Reading, Lynnfield, Saugus, Swampscott, and Nahant. Lynn was incorporated as a city in 1850.

The tannery and shoemaking industries were important in Lynn from the Revolutionary War era into the early 20th century.

City Bank
1854–1864
W-MA-2080

History: The City Bank, also listed as the City Bank of Lynn, was chartered on March 28, 1854, with an authorized capital of $100,000. It commenced operations on October 5. The capital was increased to $150,000 in 1861. Circulation in 1860 was $78,582, $95,129 in 1862, and $129,475 in 1863.

The City Bank was succeeded by the National City Bank of Lynn in 1865.

Numismatic Commentary: Collectors should be able to secure an example or two of genuine notes from this bank without too much trouble. Some of the issues show the city green with a picture of a bank on the right.

Valid Issues

$1 • W-MA-2080-001-G010 CJF

Overprint: Red 1 / 1. ***Engraver:*** Danforth, Wright & Co. ***Comments:*** H-MA-775-G2a. September __, 18__. 1850s–1860s.

Rarity: URS-4

VF $500; **Unc-S&D** $1,750

$2 • W-MA-2080-002-G020

CJF

Overprint: Red 2 / 2. ***Engraver:*** Danforth, Wright & Co. ***Comments:*** H-MA-775-G4a. September __, 18__. 1850s–1860s.

Rarity: URS-3
F $1,000

$3 • W-MA-2080-003-G030

Left: 3. ***Center:*** Yacht race, Group of women and men on beach with basket and dog. ***Right:*** THREE 3 / Two mechanics. ***Engraver:*** American Bank Note Co. ***Comments:*** H-MA-775-G6. 1850s–1860s.

Rarity: —

$5 • W-MA-2080-005-G040

Left: Woman with flowers / 5. ***Center:*** View of Lynn Common. ***Right:*** V / Ship / FIVE. ***Overprint:*** Red 5 / 5. ***Engraver:*** Danforth, Wright & Co. ***Comments:*** H-MA-775-G8a. 18__. 1850s.

Rarity: —

$5 • W-MA-2080-005-G050

Left: FIVE / 5 / FIVE. ***Center:*** View of Lynn Common. ***Right:*** 5 / V in FIVE / 5. ***Engraver:*** American Bank Note Co. ***Comments:*** H-MA-775-G10. 1850s–1860s.

Rarity: —

$10 • W-MA-2080-010-G060

CC

Overprint: Red X X. ***Engraver:*** Danforth, Wright & Co. ***Comments:*** H-MA-775-G12. September __, 18__. 1850s–1860s.

Rarity: URS-1
Proof $5,000

$20 • W-MA-2080-020-G070

Left: 20 / Woman with scroll and woman with rod flanking state arms. ***Right:*** TWENTY / 20 / TWENTY. ***Engraver:*** Danforth, Wright & Co. ***Comments:*** H-MA-775-G14. 18__. 1850s–1860s.

Rarity: —

$50 • W-MA-2080-050-G080

Left: Train, trees, and factories / 50. ***Right:*** 50 / Portrait of Daniel Webster. ***Engraver:*** Danforth, Wright & Co. ***Comments:*** H-MA-775-G16. 18__. 1850s–1860s.

Rarity: —

$100 • W-MA-2080-100-G090

Left: C / Three cherubs, one turning screw, one splitting stone, one lifting stone with lever. ***Right:*** 100 / Sailing ship. ***Engraver:*** Danforth, Wright & Co. ***Comments:*** H-MA-775-G18. 18__. 1850s–1860s.

Rarity: —

Non-Valid Issues

$1 • W-MA-2080-001-A010

CJF

Engraver: Doty & Bergen. ***Comments:*** H-MA-775-A5. Altered from $1 Delaware City Bank, Delaware, Kansas. Dec. 20, 1854. 1850s.

Rarity: —

$1 • W-MA-2080-001-A020

Left: 1 / View of port city. ***Center:*** Steamship sailing. ***Bottom center:*** Spread eagle. ***Right:*** 1 / View of man with two horses and canal locks / KANSAS. ***Engraver:*** Doty & Bergen. ***Comments:*** H-MA-775-A10. Altered from $1 Delaware City Bank, Delaware, Kansas. July 1, 185_. 1850s.

Rarity: —

$2 • W-MA-2080-002-A030

Left: Laureate woman leaning on shield bearing TWO vertically. ***Center:*** 2 / Indian men standing on cliff watching train. ***Bottom center:*** Bear leaning against tree. ***Right:*** 2 on oval die, KANSAS / Stag on hill facing viewer. ***Engraver:*** Doty & Bergen. ***Comments:*** H-MA-775-A15. Altered from $2 Delaware City Bank, Delaware, Kansas. Dec. 20, 1854. 1850s.

Rarity: —

$5 • W-MA-2080-005-R010

Engraver: Danforth, Wright & Co. ***Comments:*** H-MA-775-R5. Raised from W-MA-2080-002-G020. 18__. 1850s.

Rarity: —

$5 • W-MA-2080-005-A040

Left: Die bearing 5. ***Center:*** Farmer plowing with two oxen, House, Trees. ***Bottom center:*** Bear leaning against tree. ***Right:*** 5 on die, KANSAS / FIVE / Portrait of George Washington. ***Engraver:*** Doty & Bergen. ***Comments:*** H-MA-775-A20. Altered from $5 Delaware City Bank, Delaware, Kansas. Dec. 20, 1854. 1850s.

Rarity: —

$5 • W-MA-2080-005-A050

Left: FIVE / State arms vertically. ***Center:*** Farmer, sailor, and mechanic. ***Right:*** 5 / Portrait of Franklin Pierce. ***Engraver:*** Danforth, Wright & Co. ***Comments:*** H-MA-775-A25. Altered from $5 Bank of Washtenaw, Washtenaw, Michigan series. 1850s.

Rarity: —

$5 • **W-MA-2080-005-A060**

Left: V / Portrait of Henry Clay. ***Center:*** Western river steamboat, Wharf. ***Right:*** 5 / Portrait of George Washington. ***Overprint:*** Red FIVE. ***Engraver:*** New England Bank Note Co. / Rawdon, Wright, Hatch & Edson. ***Comments:*** H-MA-775-A30. Altered from $5 Waubeek Bank, De Soto, Nebraska. 1857.

Rarity: —

$10 • **W-MA-2080-010-R020**

Engraver: Danforth, Wright & Co. ***Comments:*** H-MA-775-R10. Raised from W-MA-2080-002-G020. 18__. 1850s.

Rarity: —

$10 • **W-MA-2080-010-A070**

Left: Diagonal X / TEN. ***Center:*** Woman leaning on rock, Train / Ceres with sheaf on back. ***Right:*** 10 / Portrait of George Washington. ***Overprint:*** Red TEN. ***Engraver:*** Bald, Cousland & Co. / Baldwin, Bald & Cousland. ***Comments:*** H-MA-775-A35. Altered from $10 Southern Bank of Georgia, Bainbridge, Georgia. 18__. 1860s.

Rarity: —

Laighton Bank

1849–1865

W-MA-2090

History: The Laighton Bank, named after early settler Thomas Laighton, was chartered in 1849 with an authorized capital of $100,000 and began operations in August.[22] The capital was increased to $150,000 in 1851 and then to $200,000 in 1854. It was $100,000 in 1855.

The bank's circulation was $75,135 in 1851, $67,912 in 1857, $47,739 in 1852, and $105,808 in 1863. Selected figures for 1857 included: bills of this bank and other New England states $7,833; specie $15,599.69; real estate $5,371.42.

In 1865 the interests of the Laighton Bank were succeeded by the Central National Bank of Lynn.

Numismatic Commentary: Valid issues are extremely hard to locate. There are records in the *Banker's Magazine* of a framed set of notes consisting of the $1, $2, $3, $5, and $10 issues as having been saved. Collectors will probably have to settle for a counterfeit or spurious note to fill this bank's place in a collection.

Valid Issues

$1 • **W-MA-2090-001-G010**

QDB

Engraver: Rawdon, Wright, Hatch & Edson / New England Bank Note Co. ***Comments:*** H-MA-780-G2. July 1, 18__. 1849–1850s.

Rarity: —

$1 • **W-MA-2090-001-G010a**

Left: Woman reclining with 1, Fruit / ONE on medallion. ***Center:*** 1 / Portrait of Benjamin Franklin. ***Bottom center:*** 1. ***Right:*** 1 / Portrait of boy. ***Overprint:*** Red ONE. ***Engraver:*** Rawdon, Wright, Hatch & Edson / New England Bank Note Co. ***Comments:*** H-MA-780-G2a. Similar to W-MA-2090-001-G010. 18__. 1850s.

Rarity: —

$1 • **W-MA-2090-001-G010b**

Overprint: Red ONE. ***Engraver:*** Rawdon, Wright, Hatch & Edson / New England Bank Note Co. / ABNCo. monogram. ***Comments:*** H-MA-780-G2b. Similar to W-MA-2090-001-G010 but with additional engraver imprint. 18__. 1850s–1860s.

Rarity: —

$2 • **W-MA-2090-002-G020**

Left: Man shoeing horse, Forge, Colt tied to anvil, Train / 2. ***Center:*** 2. ***Bottom center:*** State arms. ***Right:*** 2 / Minerva seated with spear and shield. ***Engraver:*** Rawdon, Wright, Hatch & Edson / New England Bank Note Co. ***Comments:*** H-MA-780-G4. 18__. 1849–1850s.

Rarity: —

$2 • **W-MA-2090-002-G020a**

Overprint: Red. ***Engraver:*** Rawdon, Wright, Hatch & Edson / New England Bank Note Co. ***Comments:*** H-MA-780-G4a. Similar to W-MA-2090-002-G020. 18__. 1850s.

Rarity: —

$2 • **W-MA-2090-002-G020b**

Overprint: Red. ***Engraver:*** Rawdon, Wright, Hatch & Edson / New England Bank Note Co. / ABNCo. monogram. ***Comments:*** H-MA-780-G4b. Similar to W-MA-2090-002-G020 but with additional engraver imprint. 18__. 1850s–1860s.

Rarity: —

$3 • **W-MA-2090-003-G030**

Left: Liberty and eagle flanking shield bearing 3 / Bale and barrel / 3. ***Center:*** 3 / Portrait of George Washington. ***Right:*** THREE / Indian woman with child. ***Engraver:*** Rawdon, Wright, Hatch & Edson / New England Bank Note Co. ***Comments:*** H-MA-780-G6. 18__. 1849–1850s.

Rarity: —

$3 • **W-MA-2090-003-G030a**

Overprint: Red. ***Engraver:*** Rawdon, Wright, Hatch & Edson / New England Bank Note Co. ***Comments:*** H-MA-780-G6a. Similar to W-MA-2090-003-G030. 18__. 1850s.

Rarity: —

$3 • **W-MA-2090-003-G030b**

Overprint: Red. ***Engraver:*** Rawdon, Wright, Hatch & Edson / New England Bank Note Co. / ABNCo. monogram. ***Comments:*** H-MA-780-G6b. Similar to W-MA-2090-003-G030 but with additional engraver imprint. 18__. 1850s–1860s.

Rarity: —

$5 • **W-MA-2090-005-G040**

Left: Two women flanking shield bearing Indian man, Fruit and shield. ***Center:*** 5. ***Bottom center:*** Wheels and bales. ***Right:*** 5 / Portrait of Daniel Webster. ***Engraver:*** Rawdon, Wright, Hatch & Edson / New England Bank Note Co. ***Comments:*** H-MA-780-G8. Beware of spurious W-MA-2090-005-S010 similar to genuine. 18__. 1849–1850s.

Rarity: —

$5 • W-MA-2090-005-G040a

Overprint: Red. ***Engraver:*** Rawdon, Wright, Hatch & Edson / New England Bank Note Co. ***Comments:*** H-MA-780-G8a. Similar to W-MA-2090-005-G040. 18__. 1850s.

Rarity: —

$5 • W-MA-2090-005-G040b

Overprint: Red. ***Engraver:*** Rawdon, Wright, Hatch & Edson / New England Bank Note Co. / ABNCo. monogram. ***Comments:*** H-MA-780-G8b. Similar to W-MA-2090-005-G040 but with additional engraver imprint. 18__. 1850s.

Rarity: —

$10 • W-MA-2090-010-G050

Left: TEN / Woman seated on bank holding trident. ***Center:*** Woman seated holding child, Four reapers reclining and standing, Hay wagon. ***Bottom center:*** Wheels and bales. ***Right:*** 10 / Portrait of John Quincy Adams. ***Engraver:*** Rawdon, Wright, Hatch & Edson / New England Bank Note Co. ***Comments:*** H-MA-780-G10. 18__. 1849–1850s.

Rarity: —

$10 • W-MA-2090-010-G050a

Overprint: Red. ***Engraver:*** Rawdon, Wright, Hatch & Edson / New England Bank Note Co. ***Comments:*** H-MA-780-G10a. Similar to W-MA-2090-010-G050. 18__. 1850s.

Rarity: —

$10 • W-MA-2090-010-G050b

Overprint: Red. ***Engraver:*** Rawdon, Wright, Hatch & Edson / New England Bank Note Co. / ABNCo. monogram. ***Comments:*** H-MA-780-G10b. Similar to W-MA-2090-010-G050 but with additional engraver imprint. 18__. 1850s–1860s.

Rarity: —

$20 • W-MA-2090-020-G060

Left: 20 / Minerva standing with spear. ***Center:*** Woman seated between 2 and 0. ***Right:*** 20 / Woman reclining on cornucopia / 20. ***Engraver:*** Rawdon, Wright, Hatch & Edson / New England Bank Note Co. ***Comments:*** H-MA-780-G12. 18__. 1850s.

Rarity: —

$20 • W-MA-2090-020-G060a

Overprint: Red. ***Engraver:*** Rawdon, Wright, Hatch & Edson / New England Bank Note Co. ***Comments:*** H-MA-780-G12a. Similar to W-MA-2090-020-G060. 18__. 1850s.

Rarity: —

$20 • W-MA-2090-020-G070

Left: 20 / Man dressing leather. ***Center:*** Male portrait. ***Right:*** 20 / Woman at sewing machine. ***Tint:*** Green 20 / 20. ***Engraver:*** American Bank Note Co. ***Comments:*** H-MA-780-G14a. 1860s.

Rarity: —

$50 • W-MA-2090-050-G080

Left: 50 / Minerva standing by column. ***Center:*** Ceres and Vulcan flanking cornucopia. ***Right:*** 50 / Cherub in sailboat / 50. ***Engraver:*** Rawdon, Wright, Hatch & Edson. ***Comments:*** H-MA-780-G16. 18__. 1850s.

Rarity: —

$50 • W-MA-2090-050-G080a

Overprint: Red. ***Engraver:*** Rawdon, Wright, Hatch & Edson / New England Bank Note Co. ***Comments:*** H-MA-780-G16a. Similar to W-MA-2090-050-G080. 18__. 1850s.

Rarity: —

$50 • W-MA-2090-050-G090

Left: 50 / Eagle on shield. ***Center:*** Male portrait. ***Right:*** 50 / Portrait of girl. ***Tint:*** Green. ***Engraver:*** American Bank Note Co. ***Comments:*** H-MA-780-G18a. 1860s.

Rarity: —

$100 • W-MA-2090-100-G100

Left: 100 / Vulcan seated with sledge and anchor. ***Center:*** Train on bridge, Eagle on limb, Canal locks / C C. ***Bottom center:*** 100. ***Right:*** 100 / Ceres seated, Cornucopia. ***Engraver:*** Rawdon, Wright, Hatch & Edson. ***Comments:*** H-MA-780-G20. 18__. 1850s.

Rarity: —

$100 • W-MA-2090-100-G100a

Overprint: Red. ***Engraver:*** Rawdon, Wright, Hatch & Edson. ***Comments:*** H-MA-780-G20a. Similar to W-MA-2090-100-G100. 18__. 1850s.

Rarity: —

$100 • W-MA-2090-100-G110

Left: C / Woman seated on box, Merchandise, Schooner and ship. ***Center:*** Portrait. ***Right:*** 100 / Sailor standing with sextant, Capstan. ***Tint:*** Green. ***Engraver:*** American Bank Note Co. ***Comments:*** H-MA-780-G22a. 1860s.

Rarity: —

$500 • W-MA-2090-500-G120

Left: Indian paddling canoe, Forest and mountains / 500 / D D / 500. ***Right:*** 500 / Justice. ***Engraver:*** New England Bank Note Co. ***Comments:*** H-MA-780-G24. 18__. 1840s–1850s.

Rarity: —

$500 • W-MA-2090-500-G130

Left: D / Male portrait / D. ***Center:*** 500 / Eagle, Woman and two men at work in shoe factory. ***Tint:*** Green. ***Engraver:*** American Bank Note Co. ***Comments:*** H-MA-780-G26a. 1860s.

Rarity: —

NON-VALID ISSUES

$5 • W-MA-2090-005-S010

CJF

Engraver: New England Bank Note Co. ***Comments:*** H-MA-780-S5. Spurious design imitating a rough verbal description of W-MA-2090-005-G040. July 1, 18__. 1850s.

Rarity: —
VG $75

$10 • W-MA-2090-010-R010

Engraver: Rawdon, Wright, Hatch & Edson / New England Bank Note Co. ***Comments:*** H-MA-780-R5. Raised from W-MA-2090-001-G010. 18__. 1850s.

Rarity: —

$100 • W-MA-2090-100-C100

Engraver: Rawdon, Wright, Hatch & Edson. ***Comments:*** H-MA-780-C20. Counterfeit of W-MA-2090-100-G100. 18__. 1850s.

Rarity: —

Lynn Mechanics Bank

1814–1864

W-MA-2100

History: The Lynn Mechanics Bank was incorporated on February 28, 1814, with an authorized capital of $100,000.

By 1839 the bank's capital was $250,000; it fluctuated between $150,000 and $250,000 during the life of the bank. Circulation ranged from $60,547 in 1839 to $181,657 in 1863. Figures for 1857 included: bills of this bank and other New England states $7,246; specie $17,163.57; real estate $12,000.

On December 20, 1864, the business of the Lynn Mechanics Bank was succeeded by the First National Bank of Lynn.

Numismatic Commentary: Genuine notes become available from time to time, so collectors should not have to search very long for one. However, non-valid issues appear much more often.

Valid Issues

$1 • W-MA-2100-001-G010

Center: 1 / 1 / Flower garlands and gridwork segments / ONE / 1 / 1. ***Engraver:*** PSSP. ***Comments:*** H-MA-785-G20. 18__. 1814–1820s.

Rarity: —

$1 • W-MA-2100-001-G010a

Left: Panel of lathework circle segments. ***Right:*** Panel of lathework circle segments. 18__. 1820s. ***Comments:*** H-MA-785-G24. Similar to W-MA-2100-001-G010. 18__. 1820s.

Rarity: —

$1 • W-MA-2100-001-G010b

Left: Panel of lathework circle segments. ***Right:*** Panel of lathework circle segments. ***Engraver:*** PSSP. ***Comments:*** H-MA-785-G28. Similar to W-MA-2100-001-G010. 18__. 1820s–1830s.

Rarity: —

$1 • W-MA-2100-001-G010c

Left: ONE / D / ONE vertically. ***Right:*** ONE / D / ONE vertically. ***Engraver:*** PSSP. ***Comments:*** H-MA-785-G32. Similar to W-MA-2100-001-G010. 18__. 1830s.

Rarity: —

$1 • W-MA-2100-001-G020

Left: 1 / Minerva standing with 1 / 1. ***Center:*** ONE / Commerce seated with caduceus and cornucopia, Plow and ships / ONE. ***Right:*** 1 / Eagle / 1. ***Engraver:*** PSSP. ***Comments:*** H-MA-785-G36. 18__. 1830s.

Rarity: —

$1 • W-MA-2100-001-G030

Left: 1 / Woman wearing bonnet with pail / ONE. ***Center:*** Machinery and merchandise flanking Ceres seated holding sickle and rake, Factories and harbor / ONE / Panel outlining white ONE. ***Right:*** 1 / Ship / ONE. ***Engraver:*** PSSP / New England Bank Note Co. ***Comments:*** H-MA-785-G40. 18__. 1830s–1840s.

Rarity: —

$1 • W-MA-2100-001-G040

Left: 1 / Portrait of George Washington. ***Center:*** Woman seated with rudder / 1 / Woman seated. ***Right:*** 1 / Portrait of Benjamin Franklin. ***Engraver:*** New England Bank Note Co. ***Comments:*** H-MA-785-G44. Beware of spurious W-MA-2100-001-S010 resembling the genuine. 18__. 1850s.

Rarity: —

$1 • W-MA-2100-001-G050

Left: Woman standing, Woman kneeling. ***Center:*** 1 on die / Woman standing, Woman seated, flanking shield bearing farm implements / ONE. ***Right:*** 1 / Female portrait. ***Tint:*** Brown-orange. ***Engraver:*** Danforth, Wright & Co. ***Comments:*** H-MA-785-G48a. January 1, 18__. 1850s.

Rarity: URS-4

Proof $3,500

$1 • W-MA-2100-001-G050a

CJF

Tint: Brown-orange. ***Engraver:*** Danforth, Wright & Co. / ABNCo. monogram. ***Comments:*** H-MA-785-G48b. Similar to W-MA-2100-001-G050 but with additional engraver imprint. January 1, 18__. 1850s–1860s.

Rarity: URS-4

EF $3,000

$1 • W-MA-2100-001-G060

CJF, CJF

Overprint: Red ONE. ***Back:*** Brown. ***Engraver:*** New England Bank Note Co. ***Comments:*** H-Unlisted. 18__. 1850s.

Rarity: URS-4

VF $750; **CU** $1,750

$2 • W-MA-2100-002-G070

Center: 2 / 2 / Flower garlands and gridwork segments / TWO / 2 / 2. ***Engraver:*** PSSP. ***Comments:*** H-MA-785-G52. 18__. 1810s–1820s.

Rarity: —

$2 • W-MA-2100-002-G070a

Left: Panel of lathework circle segments. ***Right:*** Panel of lathework circle segments. ***Engraver:*** PSSP. ***Comments:*** H-MA-785-G56. Similar to W-MA-2100-002-G070. 18__. 1820s.

Rarity: —

$2 • W-MA-2100-002-G070b

Left: Panel of lathework circle segments. ***Right:*** Panel of lathework circle segments. ***Engraver:*** PSSP / New England Bank Note Co. ***Comments:*** H-MA-785-G60. Similar to W-MA-2100-002-G070. 18__. 1820s–1830s.

Rarity: —

$2 • W-MA-2100-002-G070c

Left: Five TWOs vertically. ***Right:*** Five TWOs vertically. ***Engraver:*** PSSP. ***Comments:*** H-MA-785-G64. Similar to W-MA-2100-002-G070. 18__. 1830s.

Rarity: —

$2 • W-MA-2100-002-G080

Left: 2 / Hebe watering eagle / 2. ***Center:*** 2 / Plow, Commerce seated with caduceus and cornucopia, Ships / 2. ***Right:*** 2 / Justice standing / 2. ***Engraver:*** PSSP. ***Comments:*** H-MA-785-G68. 18__. 1830s.

Rarity: —

$2 • W-MA-2100-002-G090

Left: 2 / Woman standing with staff, Cornucopia / TWO. ***Center:*** TWO / Machinery and merchandise flanking Ceres seated holding sickle and rake, Factories and harbor / Panel outlining white TWO. ***Right:*** 2 / Woman wearing hat, Trees / TWO. ***Engraver:*** New England Bank Note Co. / PSSP. ***Comments:*** H-MA-785-G72. 18__. 1830s.

Rarity: —

$2 • W-MA-2100-002-G100

Left: 2 / Portrait of Christopher Columbus. ***Center:*** Woman standing with cornucopia / 2 / Justice seated. ***Right:*** 2 / Male portrait. ***Engraver:*** New England Bank Note Co. ***Comments:*** H-MA-785-G76. 18__. 1850s.

Rarity: —

$2 • W-MA-2100-002-G110

Left: Woman with cornucopia / 2. ***Center:*** Horses flanking state arms surmounted by eagle. ***Right:*** 2 / Woman with cornucopia and flowers. ***Tint:*** Brown-orange. ***Engraver:*** Danforth, Wright & Co. ***Comments:*** H-MA-785-G80a. Jan. 1, 18__. 1850s.

Rarity: URS-5
Proof $4,500

$2 • W-MA-2100-002-G110a

Tint: Brown-orange. ***Engraver:*** Danforth, Wright & Co. / ABNCo. monogram. ***Comments:*** H-MA-785-G80b. Similar to W-MA-2100-002-G110 but with additional engraver imprint. Jan. 1, 18__. 1850s–1860s.

Rarity: —

$2 • W-MA-2100-002-G120

CC

Tint: Red-orange. ***Engraver:*** Danforth, Wright & Co. ***Comments:*** H-Unlisted. Remainder. January 1, 18__.

Rarity: URS-1
Proof $4,500

$2 • W-MA-2100-002-G130

JF

Engraver: New England Bank Note Co. ***Comments:*** H-Unlisted. 18__. 1850s.

Rarity: URS-3
VG $500

$3 • W-MA-2100-003-G140

Center: 3 / 3 / Oval of flower garlands and gridwork segments / 3 / 3. ***Engraver:*** PSSP. ***Comments:*** H-MA-785-G84. 18__. 1814–circa 1820s.

Rarity: —

$3 • W-MA-2100-003-G140a

Left: Panel of lathework circle segments. ***Right:*** Panel of lathework circle segments. ***Engraver:*** PSSP. ***Comments:*** H-MA-785-G88. Similar to W-MA-2100-003-G140. 18__. 1820s.

Rarity: —

$3 • W-MA-2100-003-G140b

Left: Panel of lathework circle segments. ***Right:*** Panel of lathework circle segments. ***Engraver:*** PSSP. ***Comments:*** H-MA-785-G92. Similar to W-MA-2100-003-G140. 18__. 1820s–1830s.

Rarity: —

$3 • W-MA-2100-003-G140c

Left: THREE vertically. ***Right:*** THREE vertically. ***Engraver:*** PSSP. ***Comments:*** H-MA-785-G96. Similar to W-MA-2100-003-G140. 18__. 1830s.

Rarity: —

$3 • W-MA-2100-003-G150

Left: 3 / Eagle on rock / 3. ***Center:*** 3 / Plow, Commerce seated with caduceus and cornucopia, Ships / 3 / Panel bearing THREE. ***Right:*** 3 / Woman standing with cornucopia / 3. ***Engraver:*** PSSP. ***Comments:*** H-MA-785-G100. 18__. 1830s.

Rarity: —

$3 • W-MA-2100-003-G160

Left: THREE / Beehive and foliage / THREE. ***Center:*** Machinery and merchandise flanking Ceres seated holding sickle and rake, Factories and harbor / THREE / Panel outlining white THREE. ***Right:*** 3 on THREE / Two reapers / 3 on THREE. ***Engraver:*** New England Bank Note Co. / PSSP. ***Comments:*** H-MA-785-G104. 18__. 1830s.

Rarity: —

$3 • W-MA-2100-003-G170

Left: 3 / George Washington standing by horse. ***Center:*** Female portrait / 3 / Girl with ringlets. ***Right:*** 3 / Vulcan standing with sledge. ***Engraver:*** New England Bank Note Co. ***Comments:*** H-MA-785-G108. Beware of spurious W-MA-2100-003-S020 resembling the genuine. 18__. 1850s.

Rarity: —

$3 • W-MA-2100-003-G180

CC

Tint: Brown-orange. ***Engraver:*** Danforth, Wright & Co. ***Comments:*** H-MA-785-G112a. Beware of spurious W-MA-2100-003-S030 resembling the genuine. Remainder. January 1, 18__. 1850s.

Rarity: URS-1
Proof $5,250

$3 • W-MA-2100-003-G180a

Left: 3 / Portrait of John C. Fremont. ***Center:*** Three horses drinking from trough, Farmer, Goats and sheep, Farmhouse ***Right:*** THREE / Two cherubs flying with grain, purse, and wand. ***Tint:*** Brown-orange. ***Engraver:*** Danforth, Wright & Co. / ABNCo. monogram. ***Comments:*** H-MA-785-G112b. Similar to W-MA-2100-003-G180 but with additional engraver imprint. Jan. 1, 18__. 1850s–1860s.

Rarity: —

$5 • W-MA-2100-005-G190

Comments: H-Unlisted.

Rarity: —
Selected auction price: Heritage, January 2011, Lot 15551, VF $690

$5 • W-MA-2100-005-G200

Left: Panel bearing state arms / 5 / 5. ***Center:*** Alternating flower garlands and gridwork segments. ***Right:*** 5 / 5. ***Engraver:*** PSSP. ***Comments:*** H-MA-785-G114. 18__. 1810s–1820s.

Rarity: —

$5 • W-MA-2100-005-G200a

Left: Lathework chain bearing MASSACHUSETTS vertically. ***Right:*** Panel of lathework circle segments. ***Engraver:*** PSSP. ***Comments:*** H-MA-785-G116. Similar to W-MA-2100-005-G200. 18__. 1820s.

Rarity: —

$5 • W-MA-2100-005-G200b

Left: Lathework chain bearing MASSACHUSETTS vertically. ***Right:*** Panel of lathework circle segments. ***Engraver:*** PSSP. ***Comments:*** H-MA-785-G118. Similar to W-MA-2100-005-G200. 18__. 1820s.

Rarity: —

$5 • W-MA-2100-005-G200c

Engraver: PSSP. ***Comments:*** H-MA-785-G120. Similar to W-MA-2100-005-G200 but with zigzag ruled lines. 18__. 1820s–1830s.

Rarity: —

$5 • W-MA-2100-005-G200d

Engraver: PSSP. ***Comments:*** H-MA-785-G122. Similar to W-MA-2100-005-G200 but with spiral lathework lines. 18__. 1830s.

Rarity: —

$5 • W-MA-2100-005-G210

Left: Panel bearing FIVE / Plenty and Minerva seated / V. ***Center:*** FIVE / Allegorical woman seated / FIVE / Panel of microletters. ***Right:*** 5 / Eagle / 5. ***Engraver:*** PSSP. ***Comments:*** H-MA-785-G136. 18__. 1830s.

Rarity: —

$5 • W-MA-2100-005-G220

Left: 5 / Blacksmith at anvil / FIVE. ***Center:*** Mercury standing with 5, Cornucopia and merchandise, Factories and ship / V / Panel outlining white FIVE. ***Right:*** 5 / Ceres kneeling / FIVE. ***Engraver:*** New England Bank Note Co. / PSSP. ***Comments:*** H-MA-785-G140. 18__. 1830s–1850s.

Rarity: —

$5 • W-MA-2100-005-G230

Left: FIVE vertically. ***Center:*** Woman seated / V. ***Right:*** 5 / Sailing ship. ***Engraver:*** New England Bank Note Co. ***Comments:*** H-MA-785-G144. Beware of spurious W-MA-2100-005-S040 resembling the genuine. 18__. 1840s–1850s.

Rarity: —

$5 • W-MA-2100-005-G240

CC

Tint: Brown-orange. ***Engraver:*** Danforth, Wright & Co. ***Comments:*** H-MA-785-G148a. January 1, 18__. 1850s.

Rarity: URS-3
Proof $3,250

$5 • W-MA-2100-005-G240a

Left: 5 on die / Justice seated. ***Center:*** Three women with bust of George Washington / FIVE. ***Right:*** 5 on FIVE / Woman seated. ***Tint:*** Brown-orange. ***Engraver:*** Danforth, Wright & Co. / ABNCo. monogram. ***Comments:*** H-MA-785-G148b. Similar to W-MA-2100-005-G240 but with additional engraver imprint. Jan. 1, 18__. 1850s–1860s.

Rarity: —

$10 • W-MA-2100-010-G250

Left: Panel bearing state arms / 10 / 10 vertically. ***Center:*** Alternating flower garlands and gridwork segments. ***Right:*** 10 / 10 vertically. ***Engraver:*** Perkins. ***Comments:*** H-MA-785-G150. 18__. 1820s–1830s.

Rarity: —

$10 • W-MA-2100-010-G250a

Left: Lathework chain bearing MASSACHUSETTS vertically. ***Right:*** Panel of lathework circle segments. ***Engraver:*** Perkins. ***Comments:*** H-MA-785-G152. Similar to W-MA-2100-010-G250. 18__. 1820s.

Rarity: —

$10 • W-MA-2100-010-G250b

Left: Lathework chain bearing MASSACHUSETTS vertically. ***Right:*** Panel of lathework circle segments. ***Engraver:*** Perkins. ***Comments:*** H-MA-785-G154. Similar to W-MA-2100-010-G250. 18__. 1820s.

Rarity: —

$10 • W-MA-2100-010-G250c

Left: Lathework chain bearing MASSACHUSETTS vertically. ***Right:*** Panel of lathework circle segments. ***Engraver:*** PSSP. ***Comments:*** H-MA-785-G156. Similar to W-MA-2100-010-G250 but with zigzag ruled lines. 18__. 1820s–1830s.

Rarity: —

$10 • W-MA-2100-010-G250d

Engraver: PSSP. ***Comments:*** H-MA-785-G158. Similar to W-MA-2100-010-G250 but with spiral lathework lines. 18__. 1830s.

Rarity: —

$10 • W-MA-2100-010-G260

Left: Panel bearing TEN / Manhattan with spilling water jug / TEN. ***Center:*** TEN / Ceres seated / TEN / Panel of microletters. ***Right:*** Panel bearing 10 / Portrait of Indian / 10. ***Engraver:*** PSSP. ***Comments:*** H-MA-785-G168. 18__. 1830s.

Rarity: —

$10 • W-MA-2100-010-G270

Left: 10 / Farmer sowing / TEN. ***Center:*** Mercury standing with 10, Cornucopia and merchandise, Factories and ship, Canal scene / Panel outlining white TEN. ***Right:*** 10 / Ship / TEN. ***Engraver:*** New England Bank Note Co. ***Comments:*** H-MA-785-G172. 18__. 1830s.

Rarity: —

$10 • W-MA-2100-010-G280

Left: 10 / X / 10. ***Center:*** Man with cow / 10. ***Right:*** TEN / Woman standing. ***Engraver:*** New England Bank Note Co. ***Comments:*** H-MA-785-G176. 18__. 1840s–1850s.

Rarity: —

$10 • W-MA-2100-010-G290 CC

Tint: Brown-orange. ***Engraver:*** Danforth, Wright & Co. ***Comments:*** H-MA-785-G180a. Proof. January 1, 18__. 1850s.

Rarity: URS-1
Proof $5,250

$10 • W-MA-2100-010-G290a ANS

Tint: Brown-orange. ***Engraver:*** Danforth, Wright & Co. / ABNCo. monogram. ***Comments:*** H-MA-785-G180b. Similar to W-MA-2100-010-G290 but with additional engraver imprint. January 1, 18__. 1850s–1860s.

Rarity: URS-3
F $1,000

$20 • W-MA-2100-020-G300

Left: Panel bearing state arms / 20 / 20 vertically. ***Center:*** Alternating flower garlands and gridwork segments. ***Right:*** 20 / 20 vertically. ***Engraver:*** Perkins. ***Comments:*** H-MA-785-G182. 18__. 1810s–1820s.

Rarity: —

$20 • W-MA-2100-020-G300a

Left: Lathework chain bearing MASSACHUSETTS vertically. ***Right:*** Panel of lathework circle segments. ***Engraver:*** PSSP. ***Comments:*** H-MA-785-G184. Similar to W-MA-2100-020-G300. 18__. 1820s–1830s.

Rarity: —

$20 • W-MA-2100-020-G310

Left: 20 / XX / 20. ***Center:*** 20 / Woman seated with scales, sheaf, and bales. ***Right:*** TWENTY vertically. ***Engraver:*** New England Bank Note Co. / PSSP. ***Comments:*** H-MA-785-G188. 18__. 1830s.

Rarity: —

$20 • W-MA-2100-020-G320

Left: 20 / Woman seated with book on lap, opening chest. ***Center:*** XX / Eagle on rock / XX. ***Right:*** 20 / Ship in harbor. ***Engraver:*** New England Bank Note Co. ***Comments:*** H-MA-785-G192. 18__. 1840s–1850s.

Rarity: —

$20 • W-MA-2100-020-G330 CC

Tint: Brown-red. ***Engraver:*** Danforth, Wright & Co. ***Comments:*** H-MA-785-G196a. January 1, 18__. 1850s.

Rarity: URS-1
Proof $6,250

$20 • W-MA-2100-020-G330a

Left: XX / Man dressing leather. ***Center:*** Indian family with woman and three children flanking portrait of William Penn. ***Right:*** 20 / Female portrait. ***Tint:*** Likely yellow. ***Engraver:*** Danforth, Wright & Co. / ABNCo. monogram. ***Comments:*** H-MA-785-G196b. Similar to W-MA-2100-020-G330 but with additional engraver imprint. Jan. 1, 18__. 1850s–1860s.

Rarity: —

$50 • W-MA-2100-050-G340

Left: Panel bearing oval seal of Massachusetts across / 50 / 50 vertically. ***Center:*** Alternating flower garlands and gridwork segments. ***Right:*** 50 / 50 vertically. ***Engraver:*** Perkins. ***Comments:*** H-MA-785-G198. 18__. 1810s–1820s.

Rarity: —

$50 • W-MA-2100-050-G340a

Left: Lathework chain bearing MASSACHUSETTS vertically. ***Engraver:*** PSSP. ***Comments:*** H-MA-785-G200. Similar to W-MA-2100-050-G340. 18__. 1820s–1830s.

Rarity: —

$50 • W-MA-2100-050-G350

Left: 50 / Cornucopia, Woman standing with ankles crossed, Staff, Anchor / 50. ***Center:*** FIFTY DOLLARS / 50. ***Right:*** FIFTY vertically. ***Engraver:*** New England Bank Note Co. / PSSP. ***Comments:*** H-MA-785-G208. 18__. 1830s.

Rarity: —

$50 • W-MA-2100-050-G360

Left: FIFTY / Woman standing with wreath and flowers / FIFTY. ***Center:*** 50 / Man restraining prancing horse / 50. ***Right:*** FIFTY / Woman standing with cornucopia / FIFTY. ***Engraver:*** New England Bank Note Co. ***Comments:*** H-MA-785-G212. 18__. 1840s–1850s.

Rarity: —

$50 • W-MA-2100-050-G370

CC

Tint: Red-brown. ***Engraver:*** Danforth, Wright & Co. ***Comments:*** H-MA-785-G216a. January 1, 18__. 1850s.

Rarity: URS-1

Proof $6,500

$50 • W-MA-2100-050-G370a

Left: L / Female portrait. ***Center:*** Hunter shooting stag. ***Right:*** 50 / Indian man seated. ***Tint:*** Yellow outlining white THREE. ***Engraver:*** Danforth, Wright & Co. / ABNCo. monogram. ***Comments:*** H-MA-785-G216b. Similar to W-MA-2100-050-G370 but with additional engraver imprint. Jan. 1, 18__. 1850s–1860s.

Rarity: —

$100 • W-MA-2100-100-G380

Left: Panel bearing state arms / 100 / 100 vertically. ***Center:*** Alternating flower garlands and gridwork segments. ***Right:*** 100 / 100 vertically. ***Engraver:*** Perkins. ***Comments:*** H-MA-785-G218. 18__. 1810s–1820s.

Rarity: —

$100 • W-MA-2100-100-G380a

Left: Lathework chain bearing MASSACHUSETTS vertically. ***Engraver:*** Perkins. ***Comments:*** H-MA-785-G220. Similar to W-MA-2100-100-G380. 18__. 1820s–1830s.

Rarity: —

$100 • W-MA-2100-100-G390

Left: 100 / Eagle / 100. ***Center:*** C / Phoebus in the Chariot of the Sun / 100. ***Right:*** C / Portrait of George Washington / C. ***Engraver:*** New England Bank Note Co. ***Comments:*** H-MA-785-G224. 18__. 1840s–1850s.

Rarity: —

$100 • W-MA-2100-100-G400

Left: ONE HUNDRED on 100 / Portrait of William Henry Harrison. ***Center:*** Wharf scene, Men loading wagon with barrels. ***Right:*** ONE HUNDRED on 100 / Portrait of Christopher Columbus. ***Engraver:*** New England Bank Note Co. ***Comments:*** H-MA-785-G228. 18__. 1840s–1850s.

Rarity: —

$100 • W-MA-2100-100-G410

CC

Tint: Ochre. ***Engraver:*** Danforth, Wright & Co. ***Comments:*** H-MA-785-G232a. January 1, 18__. 1850s.

Rarity: URS-2

Proof $5,000

$100 • W-MA-2100-100-G410a

Tint: Likely yellow. ***Engraver:*** Danforth, Wright & Co. / ABNCo. monogram. ***Comments:*** H-MA-785-G232b. Similar to W-MA-2100-100-G410. Jan. 1, 18__. 1850s–1860s.

Rarity: —

$500 • W-MA-2100-500-G420

Left: 500 / Classical scholar seated with stylus and tablet. ***Center:*** Portrait of George Washington, Two women leaning over beehive. ***Bottom center:*** Machinery. ***Right:*** 500 / Portrait of Martha Washington. ***Comments:*** H-MA-785-G244. 18__. 1850s.

Rarity: —

Gem $1,050

$500 • W-MA-2100-500-G430

Left: 500. ***Center:*** Spread eagle on shield, Fort. ***Right:*** 500. ***Tint:*** Green die bearing white D. ***Engraver:*** American Bank Note Co. ***Comments:*** H-MA-785-G248a. 1860s.

Rarity: —

Payable at Phoenix Bank, Hartford, Connecticut

$1 • W-MA-2100-001-G440

Left: TEN on lathework. ***Center:*** 1 / Text / 1. ***Right:*** 1 / MASSACHUSETTS / 1. ***Engraver:*** Reed. ***Comments:*** H-MA-785-G260. Nov. 1, 1816.

Rarity: —

Uncut Sheets

$1-$1-$2-$3 • W-MA-2100-001.001.002.003-US010 CJF

Tint(s): Brown-orange. ***Comments:*** H-MA-785-G48a, G48a, H-Unlisted, G112a. Remainder.

Rarity: URS-2
Unc-Rem $2,200; **Proof** $6,000

$5-$5-$5-$10 • W-MA-2100-005.005.005.010-US020

Vignette(s): ***($5)*** Woman seated / Three women with bust of George Washington / Woman seated. ***($5)*** Woman seated / Three women with bust of George Washington / Woman seated. ***($5)*** Woman seated / Three women with bust of George Washington / Woman seated. ***($10)*** Woman with four cherubs / Woman with three cherubs. ***Comments:*** H-MA-785-G148a, G148a, G148a, G180a. January 1, 18__. 1850s.

Rarity: —

$50-$20-$100 • W-MA-2100-050.020.100-US030

Vignette(s): ***($50)*** Female portrait / Hunter shooting stag / Woman seated. ***($20)*** Man dressing leather / Indian family with white woman and three children flanking portrait of William Penn / Female portrait. ***($100)*** Two medallion heads / Three women seated, Woman reading from book / Two medallion heads. ***Tint(s):*** Ochre. ***Comments:*** All unlisted in Haxby. Similar to H-MA-785-G216a, G196a, G232a. January 1, 18__. 1850s.

Rarity: —

Non-Valid Issues

$1 • W-MA-2100-001-S010 NJW

Engraver: New England Bank Note Co. / ABNCo. monogram. ***Comments:*** H-MA-785-S5. Spurious design imitating a rough verbal description of W-MA-2100-001-G040. June 1, 1862. 1860s.

Rarity: URS-7
F $75

$3 • W-MA-2100-003-S020 SI

Overprint: Red THREE. ***Comments:*** H-MA-785-S10. Roughly similar to W-MA-2100-003-G170. Jan. __, 18__. 1850s.

Rarity: URS-7
F $75

$3 • W-MA-2100-003-S030 SI

Tint: Green. ***Engraver:*** American Bank Note Co. / ABNCo. monogram. ***Comments:*** H-MA-785-S12. Similar to W-MA-2100-003-G180. June 1, 1864. 1860s.

Rarity: URS-7
F $75

$5 • W-MA-2100-005-S040 ANS

Engraver: New England Bank Note Co. ***Comments:*** H-MA-785-S15. Similar to W-MA-2100-005-G230. 185_. 1850s.

Rarity: —

Nahant Bank

1833–1836

W-MA-2110

History: The Nahant Bank was incorporated on March 28, 1833, with a starting capital of $150,000. Hezekiah Chase, Henry A. Breed, and William Chase were the founders of the bank. In 1836 the bank had a "run" on it by holders of bills and depositors who wanted specie, and it was forced to suspend payments. An investigation revealed that bank president Breed and another director had become bankrupt, but the bank itself was solvent. Notwithstanding this, the reputation of the bank was destroyed. The bank failed soon afterward, and more than $200,000 in notes became worthless. The Legislature voided its charter in 1837.

Numismatic Commentary: All issues from this bank are printed with either plain backs or bi-colored Congreve Check Plate backs, giving today's collector the opportunity to acquire a note with this anti-counterfeiting device. Three or four different colors were used for the various backs across the board. Only two of these colors would appear on the back of any particular note.

All notes are of the PSSP style.

How to Read the Whitman Numbering System

$1 • W-MA-010-001-G010a

Denomination: Value of the note shown.

W: Whitman number. This number is a sortable code unique to each bank and note.

MA: Abbreviation for the state under study.

010: Numerical designation specific to each bank.

001: The denomination in dollars.

G010a: G indicates a good or valid note. Other categories are indicated thus: C (counterfeit); R (raised); S (spurious); N (not-attributed); A (altered). Numbers are assigned starting with 010, 020, et seq. Terminal letters following the number indicate variations of a note: a series of different colored overprints, tints, payees, etc., all on the same design of note. For more information, see the "How to Use This Book" section at the front of the volume, page xiv.

Valid Issues

$1 • W-MA-2110-001-G010 TD, TD

Back: Green and brown Check Plate. ***Comments:*** H-MA-790-G4. 18__. 1830s.

Rarity: URS-6
VG $300

$1 • W-MA-2110-001-G010a CJF, CJF

Back: Red and brown Check Plate. ***Comments:*** H-Unlisted. Similar to W-MA-2110-001-G010. 18__. 1830s.

Rarity: URS-7
F $125; **VF** $250

$2 • **W-MA-2110-002-G020**

QDB, QDB

Back: Green and brown Check Plate. ***Comments:*** H-MA-790-G8. 18__. 1830s.

Rarity: URS-5
F $500

$3 • **W-MA-2110-003-G030**

Left: MASSACHUSETTS vertically. ***Center:*** 3 / Female portrait / 3 / THREE. ***Right:*** 3 / Indian chief / 3. ***Back:*** Green and brown Check Plate. ***Comments:*** H-MA-790-G12. 18__. 1830s.

Rarity: —

$5 • **W-MA-2110-005-G040**

Left: MASSACHUSETTS vertically. ***Center:*** 5 / Female portrait / 5 / FIVE. ***Right:*** 5 / Indian chief / 5. ***Back:*** Green and brown Check Plate. ***Comments:*** H-MA-790-G16. 18__. 1830s.

Rarity: —

$5 • **W-MA-2110-005-G040a**

Back: Plain. ***Comments:*** H-MA-790-G16b. Similar to W-MA-2110-005-G040. 18__. 1830s.

Rarity: —

$10 • **W-MA-2110-010-G050**

Left: MASSACHUSETTS vertically. ***Center:*** 10 / Woman with cornucopia / 10 / TEN / Cherubs. ***Right:*** 10 / State arms / 10. ***Back:*** Green and brown Check Plate. ***Comments:*** H-MA-790-G20. 18__. 1830s.

Rarity: —

$10 • **W-MA-2110-010-G050a**

CJF, CJF

Back: Red and brown Check Plate. ***Comments:*** H-Unlisted. Similar to W-MA-2110-010-G050. 18__. 1830s.

Rarity: URS-4
F $200

$10 • **W-MA-2110-010-G050b**

Back: Plain. ***Comments:*** H-MA-790-G20b. Similar to W-MA-2110-010-G050. 18__. 1830s.

Rarity: —

$20 • **W-MA-2110-020-G060**

CJF, CJF

Back: Red and brown Check Plate. ***Comments:*** H-MA-790-G24. 18__. 1830s.

Rarity: —

$20 • **W-MA-2110-020-G060a**

Back: Plain. ***Comments:*** H-MA-790-G24b. Similar to W-MA-2110-020-G060. 18__. 1830s.

Rarity: URS-4
F $250

$50 • W-MA-2110-050-G070

Left: MASSACHUSETTS vertically. ***Center:*** 50 / Woman seated / 50. ***Right:*** 50 / State arms / 50. ***Back:*** Check Plate. ***Comments:*** H-MA-790-G28. 18__. 1830s.

Rarity: —

$50 • W-MA-2110-050-G070a

Back: Plain. ***Comments:*** H-MA-790-G28b. Similar to W-MA-2110-050-G070. 18__. 1830s.

Rarity: —

$100 • W-MA-2110-100-G080

Left: MASSACHUSETTS vertically. ***Center:*** 100 / Woman seated / 100. ***Right:*** 100 / State arms / 100. ***Back:*** Check Plate. ***Comments:*** H-MA-790-G32. 18__. 1830s.

Rarity: —

$100 • W-MA-2110-100-G080a

Back: Plain. ***Comments:*** H-MA-790-G32b. Similar to W-MA-2110-100-G080. 18__. 1830s.

Rarity: —

$500 • W-MA-2110-500-G090

CC

Back: Check Plate. ***Comments:*** H-MA-790-G36. 18__. 1830s.

Rarity: —

$500 • W-MA-2110-500-G090a

CJF

Back: Plain. ***Comments:*** H-MA-790-G36b. Similar to W-MA-2110-500-G090. 18__. 1830s.

Rarity: URS-4

VF $3,300

Malden, Massachusetts

The district that later became Malden was purchased from the local Indians in 1629 and settled in 1640 by Puritans. It was originally part of Charlestown and was incorporated as a stand-alone town in 1649, named after *Maldon*, England. The nearby cities of Melrose and Everett used to be a part of Malden. During the American Revolution, the population was about 1,000. In 1770 citizens of the town stopped using tea in protest of a tax levied by the British crown. They were the first town to petition a withdrawal from Britain.

Textiles, a rubber factory, a tannery for fancy leathers, shoe-lasts, machinery, brass work, tinware, wire, carriages, furniture, emery cloth, bleachery goods, cordage, twine, and food preparations were part of the industries of Malden.

Malden Bank

1851–1864

W-MA-2120

History: The Malden Bank was incorporated on May 24, 1851, with an authorized capital of $100,000. The bank commenced business in September. The capital remained constant throughout the existence of the bank. In 1851 circulation was valued at $88,440, and in 1863 it was $96,575. Real estate was valued at $5,602.64, and specie totaled $6,803.74. Selected figures for 1857 included: bills of this bank and other New England states $880; specie $13,009.30; real estate $5,602.64. Tragedy struck on December 23, 1863, when a customer came in and fatally shot 17-year old Frank Converse, the only son of the bank president, and stole $5,000. The murderer was later identified as the postmaster of Malden, and he was arrested and convicted.

The business of the Malden Bank was succeeded by the First National Bank of Malden in 1864.

Numismatic Commentary: This is another bank which will prove difficult for collectors to find an example from. Many of the banks that reorganized into the National Banking system redeemed the state bank note issues for many years after. Proof notes may be all that are available from this bank.

Valid Issues

$1 • W-MA-2120-001-G010

Left: 1 / Woman seated. ***Center:*** Train. ***Bottom center:*** Arm and hammer. ***Right:*** 1 / State arms. ***Engraver:*** Rawdon, Wright, Hatch & Edson. ***Comments:*** H-MA-795-G2. 18__. 1850s.

Rarity: —

$1 • W-MA-2120-001-G020

Left: Liberty standing. ***Center:*** Farmer seated with cradle and basket of corn. ***Right:*** 1 / Two girls. ***Engraver:*** American Bank Note Co. ***Comments:*** H-MA-795-G4. 1860s.

Rarity: —

$2 • W-MA-2120-002-G030

Left: Indian woman with bow and spear / TWO. ***Center:*** Blacksmith seated with hammer, Train and factory. ***Bottom center:*** Wheels and bale. ***Right:*** 2 / Cherub riding on dolphin / TWO. ***Engraver:*** Rawdon, Wright, Hatch & Edson. ***Comments:*** H-MA-795-G6. 18__. 1850s.

Rarity: —

$3 • W-MA-2120-003-G040

Left: Liberty seated / THREE. ***Center:*** Haying scene, Reapers and cattle. ***Right:*** 3 / Woman and cherubs in clouds. ***Engraver:*** Rawdon, Wright, Hatch & Edson. ***Comments:*** H-MA-795-G8. 18__. 1850s.

Rarity: —

$5 • W-MA-2120-005-G050

Left: 5 / Female portrait / FIVE. ***Center:*** Woman reclining on bale, Cotton plant and wheels, Factories and village. ***Bottom center:*** State arms. ***Right:*** FIVE / Portrait of Zachary Taylor / FIVE. ***Engraver:*** Rawdon, Wright, Hatch & Edson. ***Comments:*** H-MA-795-G10. 18__. 1850s.

Rarity: —

$10 • W-MA-2120-010-G060

Left: 10 / Blacksmith standing by anvil and forge. ***Center:*** Woman holding cornucopia and key seated between 1 and 0. ***Bottom center:*** Train. ***Right:*** 10 / Person holding cornucopia and anchor. ***Engraver:*** Rawdon, Wright, Hatch & Edson. ***Comments:*** H-MA-795-G12. 18__. 1850s.

Rarity: —

$20 • W-MA-2120-020-G070

Left: 20 / Female portrait. ***Center:*** Woman placing wreath on eagle, Train and ships. ***Right:*** 20 / Woman holding figures 2 and 0. ***Engraver:*** Rawdon, Wright, Hatch & Edson. ***Comments:*** H-MA-795-G14. 18__. 1850s.

Rarity: —

$50 • W-MA-2120-050-G080

Left: 50 / Minerva standing by column. ***Center:*** Ceres and Vulcan flanking cornucopia. ***Right:*** 50 / Cherub in sailboat / 50. ***Engraver:*** Rawdon, Wright, Hatch & Edson. ***Comments:*** H-MA-795-G16. 18__. 1850s.

Rarity: —

$100 • W-MA-2120-100-G090

Left: 100 / Vulcan seated with sledge and anchor. ***Center:*** Train on bridge, Eagle on limb, Canal locks / C C. ***Bottom center:*** 100. ***Right:*** 100 / Ceres seated, Cornucopia. ***Engraver:*** Rawdon, Wright, Hatch & Edson. ***Comments:*** H-MA-795-G18. 18__. 1850s.

Rarity: —

$100 • W-MA-2120-100-G100

Left: C / Sailboat. ***Center:*** Cattle. ***Right:*** 100 / Portrait of girl. ***Tint:*** Green frame, die bearing C, and panel of 100s. ***Engraver:*** American Bank Note Co. ***Comments:*** H-MA-795-G20a. Oct. 1, 186_. 1860s.

Rarity: —

Non-Valid Issues

$5 • W-MA-2120-005-R010

Engraver: Rawdon, Wright, Hatch & Edson. ***Comments:*** H-MA-795-R5. Raised from W-MA-2120-001-G010. 18__. 1850s.

Rarity: —

$10 • W-MA-2120-010-S010

Left: TEN on three dies. ***Center:*** 10 / Steamboat, Sailing ships / 10. ***Right:*** TEN / Portrait of George Washington / TEN. ***Engraver:*** Rawdon, Wright, Hatch & Edson. ***Comments:*** H-MA-795-S5. Aug. 1, 1849.

Rarity: —

Marblehead, Massachusetts

In 1629 the land that would later be known as Marblehead was a plantation within Salem. It incorporated as a town in 1648. The town has at other times been known as Marvell Head, Marble Harbour, and Foy. It gained its name from settlers who mistakenly thought its natural resource of granite was marble.

Cod were exported from this fishing village early on, and as a result rope making, sail making, ship's block making, carpentry, and other water related industries sprang up to bolster the fleets that brought in the fish. In exchange for the fish and salt products including hemp, items such as rum, sugar, molasses, fruits, and other tidbits were obtained from the West Indies and traded to coastal America and other European markets.

A hurricane in 1846 destroyed 11 ships and damaged others, killing several sailors. The fishing industry declined in Marblehead after that time.

Grand Bank

1831–1865

W-MA-2130

History: The Grand Bank was chartered in the spring of 1831 with an authorized capital of $100,000. It took its name from the Grand Banks fishing area in the North Atlantic Ocean, a destination for ships sailing out of this famous port. In 1839 the bank's capital was $125,000, and in 1845 it was $100,000. Circulation was $34,395 in 1839, but it reached a high of $92,415 during the period of 1857 to 1860.

The bank's real estate was valued at $8,700, and specie was at $5,107.96 in 1851.

In 1864 the business of the Grand Bank was succeeded by the National Grand Bank of Marblehead with the same officers.

Numismatic Commentary: Early notes of the PSSP design are the most frequently encountered for this bank.

Valid Issues

$1 • W-MA-2130-001-G010

Left: Lathework panel bearing MASSACHUSETTS vertically. ***Center:*** 1 / 1 / Alternating flower garlands and gridwork segments / ONE / 1 / 1. ***Right:*** Lathework panel bearing ONE / D / ONE vertically. ***Engraver:*** PSSP. ***Comments:*** H-MA-800-G2. 18__. 1830s.

Rarity: —

$1 • W-MA-2130-001-G020

Left: ONE on 1 / Scene / ONE. ***Center:*** 1 / Ships / 1 / ONE. ***Right:*** ONE on 1 / Woman seated / ONE. ***Engraver:*** New England Bank Note Co. / PSSP. ***Comments:*** H-MA-800-G4. 18__. 1830s–1850s.

Rarity: —

$1 • W-MA-2130-001-G020a

Overprint: Red. ***Engraver:*** New England Bank Note Co. / PSSP. ***Comments:*** H-MA-800-G4a. Similar to W-MA-2130-001-G020. 18__. 1850s.

Rarity: —

$1 • W-MA-2130-001-G020b

Overprint: Red. ***Engraver:*** New England Bank Note Co. / PSSP / ABNCo. monogram. ***Comments:*** H-MA-800-G4b. Similar to W-MA-2130-001-G020 but with additional engraver imprint. 18__. 1850s–1860s.

Rarity: —

$2 • W-MA-2130-002-G030

Left: Lathework panel bearing MASSACHUSETTS vertically. ***Center:*** 2 / 2 / Alternating flower garlands and gridwork segments / TWO / 2 / 2. ***Right:*** Lathework panel bearing five TWOs vertically. ***Engraver:*** PSSP. ***Comments:*** H-MA-800-G6. 18__. 1830s.

Rarity: —

$2 • W-MA-2130-002-G040

Left: 2 / Ship / 2. ***Center:*** 2 / Woman leaning on fence, Dog / 2. ***Right:*** 2 / Farm tools / 2. ***Engraver:*** New England Bank Note Co. / PSSP. ***Comments:*** H-MA-800-G8. 18__. 1830s–1850s.

Rarity: —

$2 • W-MA-2130-002-G040a

Overprint: Red. ***Engraver:*** New England Bank Note Co. / PSSP. ***Comments:*** H-MA-800-G8a. Similar to W-MA-2130-002-G040. 18__.

Rarity: —

$2 • W-MA-2130-002-G040b

Overprint: Red. ***Engraver:*** New England Bank Note Co. / PSSP / ABNCo. monogram. ***Comments:*** H-MA-800-G8b. Similar to W-MA-2130-002-G040 but with additional engraver imprint 18__. 1850s–1860s.

Rarity: —

$3 • W-MA-2130-003-G050

Left: Lathework panel bearing MASSACHUSETTS vertically. ***Center:*** 3 / 3 / Alternating flower garlands and gridwork segments / THREE / 3 / 3. ***Right:*** Lathework panel bearing THREE vertically. ***Engraver:*** PSSP. ***Comments:*** H-MA-800-G10. 18__. 1830s.

Rarity: —

$5 • W-MA-2130-005-G060

Left: Lathework panel bearing MASSACHUSETTS vertically. ***Center:*** 5 / 5 / Alternating flower garlands and gridwork segments. ***Right:*** 5 / 5. ***Back:*** Black Check Plate. ***Engraver:*** PSSP. ***Comments:*** H-MA-800-G12. 18__. 1830s.

Rarity: —

$5 • W-MA-2130-005-G060a

NJW

Back: Plain. ***Engraver:*** PSSP. ***Comments:*** H-MA-800-G12a. Similar to W-MA-2130-005-G060. 18__. 1830s–1840s.

Rarity: URS-4
VF $750

$5 • W-MA-2130-005-G070

Left: Eagle on cliff / FIVE. ***Center:*** 5 on FIVE / Four women with anchor and plow / 5 on FIVE. ***Right:*** Statue of George Washington. ***Engraver:*** New England Bank Note Co. ***Comments:*** H-MA-800-G16. 18__. 1840s–1850s.

Rarity: —

$5 • W-MA-2130-005-G070a

Overprint: Red. ***Engraver:*** New England Bank Note Co. ***Comments:*** H-MA-800-G16a. Similar to W-MA-2130-005-G070. 18__. 1850s.

Rarity: —

$5 • W-MA-2130-005-G070b

Overprint: Red. ***Engraver:*** New England Bank Note Co. / ABNCo. monogram. ***Comments:*** H-MA-800-G16b. Similar to W-MA-2130-005-G070 but with additional engraver imprint. 18__. 1850s–1860s.

Rarity: —

$10 • W-MA-2130-010-G080

Left: Lathework chain bearing MASSACHUSETTS / 10 / 10 vertically. ***Center:*** Alternating flower garlands and gridwork segments / TEN DOLLARS lined by zigzag ruled lines. ***Right:*** 10 / 10 vertically. ***Engraver:*** PSSP. ***Comments:*** H-MA-800-G18. 18__. 1830s.

Rarity: —

$10 • W-MA-2130-010-G090

Left: 10 / Sailor standing with one foot on cannon holding sextant / 10. ***Center:*** X / Ship under sail / X. ***Right:*** 10 / Beehive / 10. ***Engraver:*** New England Bank Note Co. / PSSP. ***Comments:*** H-MA-800-G20. 18__. 1830s–1850s.

Rarity: —

$10 • W-MA-2130-010-G090a

Overprint: Red. ***Engraver:*** New England Bank Note Co. / PSSP. ***Comments:*** H-MA-800-G20a. Similar to W-MA-2130-010-G090. 18__. 1850s.

Rarity: —

$10 • W-MA-2130-010-G090b

Overprint: Red. ***Engraver:*** New England Bank Note Co. / PSSP / ABNCo. monogram. ***Comments:*** H-MA-800-G20b. Similar to W-MA-2130-010-G090 but with additional engraver imprint. 18__. 1850s–1860s.

Rarity: —

$20 • W-MA-2130-020-G100

Left: Lathework chain bearing MASSACHUSETTS / 20 / 20 vertically. ***Center:*** Alternating flower garlands and gridwork segments. ***Right:*** 20 / 20 vertically. ***Engraver:*** PSSP. ***Comments:*** H-MA-800-G22. 18__. 1830s.

Rarity: —

$20 • W-MA-2130-020-G110

Left: Steamboat / XX / Train. ***Center:*** Three women seated with eagle, pole and cap, shield, scales, and book / 20 / Panel outlining white TWENTY. ***Right:*** XX / Milkmaid standing with pail. ***Engraver:*** New England Bank Note Co. ***Comments:*** H-MA-800-G24. Beware altered W-MA-2130-020-A010 of this design. 18__. 1830s–1840s.

Rarity: —

$20 • W-MA-2130-020-G120

Left: 20 / Minerva standing with spear. ***Center:*** Woman seated between 2 and 0. ***Bottom center:*** XX. ***Right:*** 20 / Woman reclining on cornucopia / 20. ***Engraver:*** Rawdon, Wright, Hatch & Edson. ***Comments:*** H-MA-800-G28. 18__. 1850s.

Rarity: —

$20 • W-MA-2130-020-G130

Left: 20 / Sailor throwing line. ***Center:*** Steamship and other ships at sea. ***Right:*** 20 / Pilot-boat under sail. ***Tint:*** Green TWENTY / TWENTY. ***Engraver:*** American Bank Note Co. ***Comments:*** H-MA-800-G32. 1860s.

Rarity: —

$50 • W-MA-2130-050-G140

Left: Lathework chain bearing MASSACHUSETTS / 50 / 50 vertically. ***Center:*** Alternating flower garlands and gridwork segments. ***Right:*** 50 / 50 vertically. ***Engraver:*** PSSP. ***Comments:*** H-MA-800-G34. 18__. 1830s.

Rarity: —

$50 • W-MA-2130-050-G150

Left: River scene, Ships. ***Right:*** 50 / Male portrait. ***Tint:*** Green 50 / 50 / FIFTY. ***Engraver:*** American Bank Note Co. ***Comments:*** H-MA-800-G40. 1860s.

Rarity: —

$100 • W-MA-2130-100-G160

Left: Lathework chain bearing MASSACHUSETTS / 100 / 100 vertically. ***Center:*** Alternating flower garlands and gridwork segments. ***Right:*** 100 / 100 vertically. ***Engraver:*** Perkins. ***Comments:*** H-MA-800-G42. 18__. 1830s.

Rarity: —

$500 • W-MA-2130-500-G170

Comments: H-MA-800-G48. No description available. 18__. 1830s.

Rarity: *None known*

Non-Valid Issues

$10 • W-MA-2130-010-R010

Engraver: New England Bank Note Co. / PSSP. ***Comments:*** H-MA-800-R5. Raised from W-MA-2130-001-G020. 18__. 1840s–1850s.

Rarity: —

$20 • W-MA-2130-020-A010

Left: Scene / XX / Scene. ***Center:*** Two women seated / 20. ***Right:*** XX / Woman standing. ***Comments:*** H-MA-800-A5.

Rarity: —

$50 • W-MA-2130-050-R020

Engraver: New England Bank Note Co. / PSSP. ***Comments:*** H-MA-800-R10. Raised from W-MA-2130-001-G020. 18__. 1840s–1850s.

Rarity: —

Marblehead Bank

1804–1865

W-MA-2145

History: The Marblehead Bank was incorporated on June 23, 1804, with $100,000 in authorized capital. The amount was increased to $120,000 by 1839.

Circulation was $51,425 in 1839; it reached a high of $59,998 from 1857 to 1860. The bank's real estate was valued at $6,333.33 in 1857, and specie totaled $9,877 at the same time.

On January 30, 1865, the business of this venerable bank was succeeded by the Marblehead National Bank.

Numismatic Commentary: Although the early issues of the PSSP design show up with regularity, later issues by the American Bank Note Co. become available from time to time. One of the most historic vignettes on American paper money appears on such a later issue: that of John Paul Jones fighting on board the *Bonhomme Richard*.

Valid Issues

$1 • W-MA-2145-001-G010

Center: 1 / 1 / Black oval bearing white flower buds / 1 / 1. ***Engraver:*** Perkins. ***Comments:*** H-MA-805-G20. 18__. 1800s.

Rarity: —

$1 • W-MA-2145-001-G020

Center: 1 / 1 / Double oval of flower garlands and gridwork segments / ONE / 1 / 1. ***Engraver:*** PSSP. ***Comments:*** H-MA-805-G24. 18__. 1807–1809.

Rarity: —

$1 • W-MA-2145-001-G030

Center: 1 / 1 / Oval of flower garlands and gridwork segments / 1 / 1. ***Engraver:*** PSSP. ***Comments:*** H-MA-805-G26. 18__. 1809–circa 1812.

Rarity: —

$1 • W-MA-2145-001-G030a

Center: 1 / 1 / Oval of flower garlands and gridwork segments / ONE / 1 / 1. ***Engraver:*** PSSP. ***Comments:*** H-MA-805-G28. Similar to W-MA-2145-001-G030. 18__. Circa 1812–1820s.

Rarity: —

$1 • W-MA-2145-001-G030b

Left: Panel of lathework circle segments. ***Right:*** Panel of lathework circle segments. ***Engraver:*** PSSP. ***Comments:*** H-MA-805-G30. Similar to W-MA-2145-001-G030. 18__. 1820s.

Rarity: —

$1 • W-MA-2145-001-G030c

Left: Panel of lathework circle segments. ***Right:*** Panel of lathework circle segments. ***Engraver:*** PSSP. ***Comments:*** H-MA-805-G32. Similar to W-MA-2145-001-G030. 18__. 1820s–1830s.

Rarity: —

$1 • W-MA-2145-001-G030d

Left: ONE / D / ONE vertically. ***Right:*** ONE / D / ONE vertically. ***Engraver:*** PSSP. ***Comments:*** H-MA-805-G34. Similar to W-MA-2145-001-G030. 18__. 1830s.

Rarity: —

$1 • W-MA-2145-001-G030e

Left: ONE / D / ONE vertically. ***Right:*** ONE / D / ONE vertically. ***Engraver:*** PSSP. ***Comments:*** H-MA-805-G36. Similar to W-MA-2145-001-G030. 18__. 1830s–1840s.

Rarity: —

$1 • W-MA-2145-001-G040

Left: 1 / Portrait of George Washington. ***Center:*** Woman seated with rudder / 1 / Woman seated. ***Right:*** 1 / Portrait of Benjamin Franklin. ***Engraver:*** New England Bank Note Co. ***Comments:*** H-MA-805-G40. 18__. 1850s.

Rarity: —

$1 • W-MA-2145-001-G050

CJF

Engraver: New England Bank Note Co. ***Comments:*** H-Unlisted. 18__. 1850s.

Rarity: URS-2
VF $1,500

$1 • W-MA-2145-001-G050a

Left: 1 / Bales, cornucopia, and caduceus. ***Center:*** 1 / Commerce reclining against bale, Ships / 1. ***Right:*** 1 / Farm implements / 1. ***Overprint:*** Red ONE. ***Engraver:*** New England Bank Note Co. ***Comments:*** H-MA-805-G44a. Similar to W-MA-2145-001-G050. 18__. 1850s.

Rarity: —

$1 • W-MA-2145-001-G060

CJF

Tint: Green. ***Engraver:*** American Bank Note Co. ***Comments:*** H-MA-805-G48a. 18__. 1860s.

Rarity: URS-1
Proof $5,750

$2 • W-MA-2145-002-G070

Center: 2 / 2 / Black oval bearing white flower buds / 2 / 2. ***Engraver:*** Perkins. ***Comments:*** H-MA-805-G58. 18__. 1800s.

Rarity: —

$2 • W-MA-2145-002-G070a

Center: 2 / 2 / Black oval bearing white flower buds / TWO / 2 / 2. ***Engraver:*** PSSP. ***Comments:*** H-MA-805-G60. Similar to W-MA-2145-002-G070. 18__. 1807–1809.

Rarity: —

$2 • W-MA-2145-002-G080

Center: 2 / 2 / Oval of flower garlands and gridwork segments / 2 / 2. ***Engraver:*** PSSP. ***Comments:*** H-MA-805-G62. 18__. 1809–circa 1812.

Rarity: —

$2 • W-MA-2145-002-G080a

Center: 2 / 2 / Oval of flower garlands and gridwork segments / TWO / 2 / 2. ***Engraver:*** PSSP. ***Comments:*** H-MA-805-G64. Similar to W-MA-2145-002-G080. 18__. Circa 1812–1820s.

Rarity: —

$2 • W-MA-2145-002-G080b

Left: Panel of lathework circle segments. ***Right:*** Panel of lathework circle segments. ***Engraver:*** PSSP. ***Comments:*** H-MA-805-G66. Similar to W-MA-2145-002-G080. 18__. 1820s.

Rarity: —

$2 • W-MA-2145-002-G080c

Left: Panel of lathework circle segments. ***Right:*** Panel of lathework circle segments. ***Engraver:*** PSSP. ***Comments:*** H-MA-805-G68. Similar to W-MA-2145-002-G080. 18__. 1820s–1830s.

Rarity: —

$2 • W-MA-2145-002-G080d

Left: Five TWOs vertically. ***Right:*** Five TWOs vertically. ***Engraver:*** PSSP. ***Comments:*** H-MA-805-G70. Similar to W-MA-2145-002-G080. 18__. 1830s.

Rarity: —

$2 • W-MA-2145-002-G080e

Left: Five TWOs vertically. ***Right:*** Five TWOs vertically. ***Engraver:*** PSSP. ***Comments:*** H-MA-805-G72. Similar to W-MA-2145-002-G080. 18__. 1830s–1840s.

Rarity: —

$2 • W-MA-2145-002-G090

Left: 2 / Portrait of Christopher Columbus. ***Center:*** Woman seated with cornucopia / 2 / Justice seated. ***Right:*** 2 / Male portrait. ***Engraver:*** New England Bank Note Co. ***Comments:*** H-MA-805-G76. 18__. 1850s.

Rarity: —

$2 • W-MA-2145-002-G100

Left: 2 / George Washington on horse / 2. ***Center:*** 2 / Woman seated with shield bearing 2, Cornucopia / 2. ***Right:*** 2 / George Washington on horse / 2. ***Overprint:*** Red TWO. ***Engraver:*** New England Bank Note Co. ***Comments:*** H-MA-805-G80a. 18__. 1850s.

Rarity: —

$2 • W-MA-2145-002-G110

CC

Tint: Green. ***Engraver:*** American Bank Note Co. ***Comments:*** H-MA-805-G84a. Proof. 18__. 1860s.

Rarity: URS-1
Proof $5,750

$3 • W-MA-2145-003-G120

Center: 3 / 3 / Black oval bearing white flower buds / 3 / 3. ***Engraver:*** Perkins. ***Comments:*** H-MA-805-G90. 18__. 1800s.

Rarity: —

$3 • W-MA-2145-003-G120a

Center: 3 / 3 / Black oval bearing white flower buds / THREE / 3 / 3. ***Engraver:*** PSSP. ***Comments:*** H-MA-805-G92. Similar to W-MA-2145-003-G120. 18__. 1807–1809.

Rarity: —

$3 • W-MA-2145-003-G130

Center: 3 / 3 / Oval of flower garlands and gridwork segments / 3 / 3. ***Engraver:*** PSSP. ***Comments:*** H-MA-805-G94 18__. 1809–1820s.

Rarity: —

$3 • W-MA-2145-003-G130a

Left: Panel of lathework circle segments. ***Right:*** Panel of lathework circle segments. ***Engraver:*** PSSP. ***Comments:*** H-MA-805-G96. Similar to W-MA-2145-003-G130. 18__. 1820s.

Rarity: —

$3 • W-MA-2145-003-G130b

Left: Panel of lathework circle segments. ***Right:*** Panel of lathework circle segments. ***Engraver:*** PSSP. ***Comments:*** H-MA-805-G98. Similar to W-MA-2145-003-G130. 18__. 1820s–1830s.

Rarity: —

$3 • W-MA-2145-003-G130c

Left: THREE vertically. ***Right:*** THREE vertically. ***Engraver:*** PSSP. ***Comments:*** H-MA-805-G100. Similar to W-MA-2145-003-G130. 18__. 1830s.

Rarity: —

$3 • W-MA-2145-003-G130d

CJF

Engraver: PSSP. ***Comments:*** H-MA-805-G102. Similar to W-MA-2145-003-G130. 18__. 1830s–1840s.

Rarity: URS-5

F $300

$3 • W-MA-2145-003-G140

Left: 3 / George Washington standing by horse. ***Center:*** Female portrait / 3 / Girl with ringlets. ***Right:*** 3 / Vulcan standing with sledge. ***Engraver:*** New England Bank Note Co. ***Comments:*** H-MA-805-G106. 18__. 1850s.

Rarity: —

$3 • W-MA-2145-003-G150

Left: 3 / Portrait of cherub / 3. ***Center:*** 3 / Woman seated with lyre and shield bearing 3 / 3. ***Right:*** 3 / Portrait of cherub / 3. ***Overprint:*** Red THREE. ***Engraver:*** New England Bank Note Co. ***Comments:*** H-MA-805-G110a. 18__. 1850s.

Rarity: —

$5 • W-MA-2145-005-G160

Left: Narrow panel bearing MASSACHUSETTS vertically. ***Center:*** 5 / 5 / Black circles bearing white lettering / 5 / 5. ***Engraver:*** Perkins. ***Comments:*** H-MA-805-G120. 18__. 1850s.

Rarity: —

$5 • W-MA-2145-005-G170

Left: Narrow panel bearing MASSACHUSETTS / 5 / 5. ***Center:*** Alternating flower garlands and gridwork segments. ***Right:*** 5 / 5. ***Engraver:*** Perkins. ***Comments:*** H-MA-805-G122. 18__. 1806–1809.

Rarity: —

$5 • W-MA-2145-005-G170a

Center: Rose-covered FIVE. ***Engraver:*** Perkins. ***Comments:*** H-MA-805-G124. Similar to W-MA-2145-005-G170. 18__. Circa 1808 and 1809.

Rarity: —

$5 • W-MA-2145-005-G170b

Left: Narrow panel bearing MASSACHUSETTS / State arms / 5 / 5. ***Engraver:*** PSSP. ***Comments:*** H-MA-805-G126. Similar to W-MA-2145-005-G170. 18__. 1809–1820s.

Rarity: —

$5 • W-MA-2145-005-G170c

Left: Lathework chain bearing MASSACHUSETTS vertically. ***Right:*** Panel of lathework circle segments. ***Engraver:*** PSSP. ***Comments:*** H-MA-805-G128. Similar to W-MA-2145-005-G170. 18__. 1820s.

Rarity: —

$5 • W-MA-2145-005-G170d

Left: Lathework chain bearing MASSACHUSETTS vertically. ***Right:*** Panel of lathework circle segments. ***Engraver:*** PSSP. ***Comments:*** H-MA-805-G130. Similar to W-MA-2145-005-G170. 18__. 1820s.

Rarity: —

$5 • W-MA-2145-005-G170e

Engraver: PSSP. ***Comments:*** H-MA-805-G132. Similar to W-MA-2145-005-G170 but with zigzag rules lines. 18__. 1820s–1830s.

Rarity: —

$5 • W-MA-2145-005-G170f

Engraver: PSSP. ***Comments:*** H-MA-805-G134. Similar to W-MA-2145-005-G170 but with spiral lathework lines. 18__. 1830s.

Rarity: —

$5 • W-MA-2145-005-G180

Comments: H-MA-805-G138. No description available. 18__. 1830s–1840s.

Rarity: *None known*

$5 • W-MA-2145-005-G190

Left: Eagle on shield and anchor, Factories and ships / FIVE. ***Center:*** V with woman, cornucopia, and cherub. ***Right:*** 5 / Girl with ringlets holding basket. ***Engraver:*** New England Bank Note Co. ***Comments:*** H-MA-805-G142. 18__. 1850s.

Rarity: —

$5 • W-MA-2145-005-G200

CC

Tint: Green. ***Engraver:*** American Bank Note Co. ***Comments:*** H-MA-805-G146a. 18__. 1860s.

Rarity: URS-1
Proof $3,000

$10 • W-MA-2145-010-G210

Left: Narrow panel bearing MASSACHUSETTS vertically. ***Center:*** 10 / 10 / Black circles bearing white lettering / 10. ***Engraver:*** Perkins. ***Comments:*** H-MA-805-G156. 18__. 1800s.

Rarity: —

$10 • W-MA-2145-010-G220

Left: Narrow panel bearing MASSACHUSETTS / 10 / 10 vertically. ***Center:*** Alternating flower garlands and gridwork segments. ***Right:*** 10 / 10 vertically. ***Engraver:*** Perkins. ***Comments:*** H-MA-805-G158. 18__. 1800s.

Rarity: —

$10 • W-MA-2145-010-G220a

Center: Rose-covered TEN. ***Engraver:*** Perkins. ***Comments:*** H-MA-805-G160. Similar to W-MA-2145-010-G220. 18__ Circa 1808 and 1809.

Rarity: —

$10 • W-MA-2145-010-G220b

Left: Narrow panel bearing MASSACHUSETTS / State arms / 10 / 10. ***Engraver:*** Perkins. ***Comments:*** H-MA-805-G162. Similar to W-MA-2145-010-G220. 18__. 1809–circa 1812.

Rarity: —

$10 • W-MA-2145-010-G220c

Left: Narrow panel bearing MASSACHUSETTS / State arms / 10 / 10. ***Center:*** Alternating flower garlands and gridwork segments / TEN. ***Engraver:*** Perkins. ***Comments:*** H-MA-805-G164. Similar to W-MA-2145-010-G220. 18__. 1810s.

Rarity: —

$10 • W-MA-2145-010-G220d

Left: Lathework chain bearing MASSACHUSETTS vertically. ***Right:*** Panel of lathework circle segments. ***Engraver:*** Perkins. ***Comments:*** H-MA-805-G166. Similar to W-MA-2145-010-G220. 18__. 1820s.

Rarity: —

$10 • W-MA-2145-010-G220e

Left: Lathework chain bearing MASSACHUSETTS vertically. ***Right:*** Panel of lathework circle segments. ***Engraver:*** Perkins. ***Comments:*** H-MA-805-G168. Similar to W-MA-2145-010-G220. 18__. 1820s.

Rarity: —

$10 • W-MA-2145-010-G220f

Engraver: PSSP. ***Comments:*** H-MA-805-G170. Similar to W-MA-2145-010-G220 but with zigzag ruled lines. 18__. 1820s–1830s.

Rarity: —

$10 • W-MA-2145-010-G220g

Engraver: PSSP. ***Comments:*** H-MA-805-G172. Similar to W-MA-2145-010-G220 but with spiral lathework lines. 18__. 1830s.

Rarity: —

$10 • W-MA-2145-010-G230

Left: Mechanic seated with tools, Train and building / TEN. ***Center:*** X. ***Right:*** 10 / Reaper standing with sheaf and stone. ***Engraver:*** New England Bank Note Co. ***Comments:*** H-MA-805-G176. 18__. 1850s.

Rarity: —

$10 • W-MA-2145-010-G240

CJF

Tint: Green. ***Engraver:*** American Bank Note Co. ***Comments:*** H-MA-805-G180a. 18__. 1860s.

Rarity: URS-4
Proof $3,500

$20 • W-MA-2145-020-G250

Left: Narrow panel bearing MASSACHUSETTS / 20 / 20 vertically. ***Center:*** Alternating flower garlands and gridwork segments. ***Right:*** 20 / 20 vertically. ***Engraver:*** PSSP. ***Comments:*** H-MA-805-G190. 18__. 1806–1809.

Rarity: —

$20 • W-MA-2145-020-G250a

Left: Narrow panel bearing MASSACHUSETTS / State arms / 20 / 20 vertically. ***Engraver:*** Perkins. ***Comments:*** H-MA-805-G192. Similar to W-MA-2145-020-G250. 18__. 1809–1820s.

Rarity: —

$20 • W-MA-2145-020-G250b

Left: Lathework chain bearing MASSACHUSETTS vertically. ***Engraver:*** PSSP. ***Comments:*** H-MA-805-G194. Similar to W-MA-2145-020-G250. 18__. 1820s–1830s.

Rarity: —

$20 • W-MA-2145-020-G260

Left: 20 / Woman seated with book on lap, opening chest. ***Center:*** XX / Eagle on rock / XX. ***Right:*** 20 / Ship in harbor. ***Engraver:*** New England Bank Note Co. ***Comments:*** H-MA-805-G198. 18__. 1840s–1850s.

Rarity: —

$20 • W-MA-2145-020-G270

Left: 20 / Portrait of two children with grapes / TWENTY. ***Center:*** Man-of-war under sail, Ships. ***Right:*** 20 / Indian woman, Lake and trees. ***Tint:*** Green. ***Engraver:*** American Bank Note Co. ***Comments:*** H-MA-805-G202a. 18__. 1860s.

Rarity: —

$50 • W-MA-2145-050-G280
Left: Panel bearing state arms / 50 / 50 vertically. ***Center:*** Alternating flower garlands and gridwork segments. ***Right:*** 50 / 50 vertically. ***Engraver:*** Perkins. ***Comments:*** H-MA-805-G208. 18__. 1809–1820s.

Rarity: —

$50 • W-MA-2145-050-G280a
Left: Lathework chain bearing MASSACHUSETTS vertically. ***Engraver:*** PSSP. ***Comments:*** H-MA-805-G210. Similar to W-MA-2145-050-G280. 18__. 1820s–1830s.

Rarity: —

$50 • W-MA-2145-050-G290
Left: FIFTY / Woman standing with wreath and flowers / FIFTY. ***Center:*** 50 / Man restraining prancing horse / 50. ***Right:*** FIFTY / Woman standing with cornucopia / FIFTY. ***Comments:*** H-MA-805-G214. 18__. 1840s–1850s.

Rarity: —

$50 • W-MA-2145-050-G300
Left: FIFTY / Woman with child / FIFTY. ***Center:*** Man with horse and pig, Pillar with light atop / FIFTY FIFTY. ***Right:*** 50 / Female portrait. ***Tint:*** Green. ***Engraver:*** American Bank Note Co. ***Comments:*** H-MA-805-G218a. 18__. 1860s.

Rarity: —

$100 • W-MA-2145-100-G310
Left: Panel bearing state arms / 100 / 100 vertically. ***Center:*** Alternating flower garlands and gridwork segments. ***Right:*** 100 / 100 vertically. ***Engraver:*** Perkins. ***Comments:*** H-MA-805-G224. 18__. 1809–1820s.

Rarity: —

$100 • W-MA-2145-100-G310a
Left: Lathework chain bearing MASSACHUSETTS vertically. ***Engraver:*** Perkins. ***Comments:*** H-MA-805-G226. Similar to W-MA-2145-100-G310. 18__. 1820s–1830s.

Rarity: —

$100 • W-MA-2145-100-G320
Left: 100 / Benjamin Franklin seated in study. ***Center:*** C. ***Right:*** 100 / Old man showing bust of George Washington to child. ***Tint:*** Green. ***Engraver:*** American Bank Note Co. ***Comments:*** H-MA-805-G230a. 18__. 1860s.

Rarity: —

Non-Valid Issues

$2 • W-MA-2145-002-C080e

CJF

Engraver: PSSP. ***Comments:*** H-MA-805-C72. Counterfeit of W-MA-2145-002-G080e. 18__. 1846.

Rarity: —

$3 • W-MA-2145-003-C130d

NJW

Engraver: PSSP. ***Comments:*** H-MA-805-C102. Counterfeit of W-MA-2145-003-G130d. 18__. 1845.

Rarity: —

$5 • W-MA-2145-005-C170f
Engraver: PSSP. ***Comments:*** H-MA-805-C134. Counterfeit of W-MA-2145-005-G170f. 18__. 1830s.

Rarity: —

$10 • W-MA-2145-010-N010
Left: Panel bearing 10 / X / 10. ***Center:*** Allegorical man standing by oxen and plow / 10. ***Right:*** TEN / Woman standing with rudder, Cornucopia. ***Engraver:*** New England Bank Note Co. ***Comments:*** H-MA-805-N5. 18__. 1840s.

Rarity: —

Mendon, Massachusetts

Mendon was settled when locals in nearby Braintree petitioned for their own land grant west of Medfield. A deed was signed in 1662 and the land was purchased from the Nipmuc tribe. It was incorporated as the town of Mendon on May 15, 1667.

Mendon was first considered part of Essex County in 1667, then as Suffolk County in 1671, and finally Worcester County in 1731. Towns that sprang from Mendon included Milford, Hopedale, Bellingham, Upton, Uxbridge, Northbridge, Blackstone, and Millville. Bellingham broke away first in 1719.

Honeoye Falls, Mendon Center, and Sibleyville were Mendon's three villages. The first water-powered mill was built in 1664, but it was destroyed in 1675 during King Philip's War. The town was mostly destroyed by fire in 1676, but it was rebuilt by 1680.

Mendon Bank
1824–1837
W-MA-2160

History: The Mendon Bank was chartered on February 7, 1824, with an authorized capital of $100,000. By 1837 its charter had expired, but its bills were still traded for a short time afterward.

Numismatic Commentary: All issues are of the PSSP design are are extremely hard to locate.

Valid Issues

$1 • W-MA-2160-001-G010
Left: Lathework panel. ***Center:*** 1 / 1 / Oval of flower garlands and gridwork segments / 1 / 1. ***Right:*** Lathework panel. ***Engraver:*** PSSP. ***Comments:*** H-MA-810-G2. 18__. 1820s.

Rarity: —

$1 • W-MA-2160-001-G010a

Left: Panel of lathework circle segments. ***Right:*** Panel of lathework circle segments. ***Engraver:*** PSSP. ***Comments:*** H-MA-810-G4. Similar to W-MA-2160-001-G010. 18__. 1820s–1830s.

Rarity: —

$1 • W-MA-2160-001-G010b

Left: ONE / D / ONE vertically. ***Right:*** ONE / D / ONE vertically. ***Engraver:*** PSSP. ***Comments:*** H-MA-810-G6. Similar to W-MA-2160-001-G010. 18__. 1830s.

Rarity: —

$2 • W-MA-2160-002-G020

Left: Lathework panel. ***Center:*** 2 / 2 / Flower garlands and gridwork segments / 2 / 2. ***Right:*** Lathework panel. ***Engraver:*** PSSP. ***Comments:*** H-MA-810-G8. 18__. 1820s.

Rarity: —

$2 • W-MA-2160-002-G020a

Left: Panel of lathework circle segments. ***Right:*** Panel of lathework circle segments. ***Engraver:*** PSSP. ***Comments:*** H-MA-810-G10. Similar to W-MA-2160-002-G020. 18__. 1820s–1830s.

Rarity: —

$2 • W-MA-2160-002-G020b

Left: Five TWOs vertically. ***Right:*** Five TWOs vertically ***Engraver:*** PSSP. ***Comments:*** H-MA-810-G12. Similar to W-MA-2160-002-G020. 18__. 1830s.

Rarity: —

$3 • W-MA-2160-003-G030

Left: Lathework panel. ***Center:*** 3 / 3 / Flower garlands and gridwork segments / 3 / 3. ***Right:*** Lathework panel. ***Engraver:*** PSSP. ***Comments:*** H-MA-810-G14. 18__. 1820s.

Rarity: —

$3 • W-MA-2160-003-G030a

Left: Panel of lathework circle segments. ***Right:*** Panel of lathework circle segments. ***Engraver:*** PSSP. ***Comments:*** H-MA-810-G16. Similar to W-MA-2160-003-G030. 18__. 1820s–1830s.

Rarity: —

$3 • W-MA-2160-003-G030b

Left: THREE vertically. ***Right:*** THREE vertically. ***Engraver:*** PSSP. ***Comments:*** H-MA-810-G18. Similar to W-MA-2160-003-G030. 18__. 1830s.

Rarity: —

$5 • W-MA-2160-005-G040

Left: Lathework chain bearing MASSACHUSETTS / 5 / 5. ***Center:*** Alternating flower garlands and gridwork segments. ***Right:*** 5 / 5. ***Engraver:*** PSSP. ***Comments:*** H-MA-810-G20. 18__. 1820s.

Rarity: —

$5 • W-MA-2160-005-G040a

CJF

Engraver: PSSP. ***Comments:*** H-MA-810-G22. Similar to W-MA-2160-005-G040 but with zigzag ruled lines. 18__. 1820s–1830s.

Rarity: —

$5 • W-MA-2160-005-G040b

Engraver: PSSP. ***Comments:*** H-MA-810-G24. Similar to W-MA-2160-005-G040 but with spiral lathework lines. 18__. 1830s.

Rarity: —

$10 • W-MA-2160-010-G050

Left: Lathework chain bearing MASSACHUSETTS / 10 / 10 vertically. ***Center:*** Alternating flower garlands and gridwork segments / TEN DOLLARS. ***Right:*** 10 / 10 vertically. ***Engraver:*** Perkins. ***Comments:*** H-MA-810-G26. 18__. 1820s.

Rarity: —

$10 • W-MA-2160-010-G050a

Engraver: PSSP. ***Comments:*** H-MA-810-G28. Similar to W-MA-2160-010-G050 but with zigzag ruled lines. 18__. 1820s–1830s.

Rarity: —

$10 • W-MA-2160-010-G050b

Engraver: PSSP. ***Comments:*** H-MA-810-G30. Similar to W-MA-2160-010-G050 but with spiral lathework lines. 18__. 1830s.

Rarity: —

$20 • W-MA-2160-020-G060

Left: Lathework chain bearing MASSACHUSETTS / 20 / 20 vertically. ***Center:*** Alternating flower garlands and gridwork segments / FIFTY. ***Right:*** 20 / 20 vertically. ***Engraver:*** PSSP. ***Comments:*** H-MA-810-G32. 18__. 1820s–1830s.

Rarity: —

$50 • W-MA-2160-050-G070

Left: Lathework chain bearing MASSACHUSETTS / 50 / 50 vertically. ***Center:*** Alternating flower garlands and gridwork segments / FIFTY. ***Right:*** 50 / 50 vertically. ***Engraver:*** PSSP. ***Comments:*** H-MA-810-G34. 18__. 1820s–1830s.

Rarity: —

$100 • W-MA-2160-100-G080

Left: Lathework chain bearing MASSACHUSETTS / 100 / 100 vertically. ***Center:*** Alternating flower garlands and gridwork segments / 100. ***Right:*** 100 / 100 vertically. ***Engraver:*** Perkins. ***Comments:*** H-MA-810-G36. 18__. 1820s–1830s.

Rarity: —

METHUEN, MASSACHUSETTS

Originally known as Haverhill in the 17th century, Methuen was settled in 1642 and incorporated in 1726. It was named after Lord Methuen, a friend of the governor.

The first military company was organized in Methuen in 1774, and its members marched to Lexington in 1775 for the first strike in the Revolutionary War. 47 men from Methuen fought at the Battle of Bunker Hill, including Robert Rogers, who was the leader of the famed Rogers's Rangers.

Methuen once included a portion of Salem, New Hampshire, and also a portion of Windham, New Hampshire. In 1741 Massachusetts and New Hampshire were separated, determining not only the border between the states but also the northern border of the city of Methuen. By 1847 the city of Lawrence had separated from Methuen to the south.

Cattle, hogs, sheep, and chickens were raised in Methuen, as well as honey bees. The first white potatoes were brought by the Scotch-Irish in 1718 and became one of the main food sources in New England. A tannery and a grist mill were located here, and brick making was also a source of industry. An iron works was created in the mid-1700s and a nickel mine is said to have existed.

Spicket Falls Bank
1853–1865
W-MA-2180

History: The Spicket Falls Bank was chartered on May 25, 1853, with an authorized capital of $100,000. It commenced operations on November 15. Joseph W. Carleton was the founding president, and George Foot was the first cashier.

Circulation was $45,225 in 1857, and the same was $60,238 in 1863.

The business of the Spicket Falls Bank was succeeded by the National Bank of Methuen in 1865.

Numismatic Commentary: Circulated, genuine notes are very hard to locate, but Proofs from the Christie's Sale in 1990 will turn up with some regularity. This landmark auction event rearranged the rarity landscape for many obsolete notes from various states.

All valid notes bear the imprint of Baldwin, Adams & Co.

Valid Issues

$1 • W-MA-2180-001-G010

CJF

Comments: H-Unlisted. Proof. October 1, 1853.

Rarity: URS-2

Proof $4,500

$1 • W-MA-2180-001-G010a

Left: ONE / Arm and hammer. ***Center:*** View of six-story factory, Trees and mill dam, Men, horses, and wagons. ***Right:*** 1 / Portrait of Daniel Webster. ***Overprint:*** Red. ***Comments:*** H-MA-815-G2a. Similar to W-MA-2180-001-G010. October 1, 1853.

Rarity: URS-2

Proof $4,000

$2 • W-MA-2180-002-G020

CJF

Comments: H-Unlisted. Proof. October 1, 1853.

Rarity: URS-5

Proof $1,500

Selected auction price: Heritage, January 2011, Lot 15553, Choice AN $1,035

$2 • W-MA-2180-002-G020a

Left: View of six-story factory, Trees and mill dam, Men, horses, and wagons / TWO. ***Center:*** Portrait of John Quincy Adams. ***Right:*** 2 / 2. ***Overprint:*** Red. ***Comments:*** H-MA-815-G4a. Similar to W-MA-2180-002-G020. October 1, 1853.

Rarity: —

$3 • W-MA-2180-003-G030

CJF

Comments: H-Unlisted. Proof. October 1, 1853.

Rarity: URS-5

Proof $1,500

$3 • W-MA-2180-003-G030a

Left: 3 / 3. ***Center:*** Train at depot, People on platform, Train. ***Right:*** 3 / Mechanic seated with hammer. ***Overprint:*** Red. ***Comments:*** H-MA-815-G6a. Similar to W-MA-2180-003-G030. October 1, 1853.

Rarity: —

$5 • W-MA-2180-005-G040

Left: 5 / Woman binding hats. ***Center:*** Two shoemakers at work, Woman binding shoes, Boy standing. ***Right:*** V / Dog's head. ***Overprint:*** Red. ***Comments:*** H-MA-815-G8a. Oct. 1, 1853.

Rarity: —

$10 • W-MA-2180-010-G050

CJF

Overprint: Red TEN. ***Comments:*** H-MA-815-G10a. Proof. October 1, 1853.

Rarity: —

$20 • W-MA-2180-020-G060

Left: XX / Man picking corn. ***Center:*** 20 / XX. ***Right:*** 20 / Portrait of Lewis Cass. ***Overprint:*** Red XX. ***Comments:*** H-MA-815-G12a. Oct. 1, 1853.

Rarity: —

$50 • W-MA-2180-050-G070

Left: 50. ***Center:*** Cattle and sheep in pasture. ***Right:*** 50 / Ceres. ***Overprint:*** Red. ***Comments:*** H-MA-815-G14a. Oct. 1, 1853.

Rarity: —

$100 • W-MA-2180-100-G080

Left: 100. ***Center:*** Santa Claus in sleigh drawn by reindeer above rooftops. ***Right:*** C / Santa Claus seated by fire. ***Overprint:*** Red. ***Comments:*** H-MA-815-G16a. A popular "Santa Claus" note. Oct. 1, 1853.

Rarity: —

Uncut Sheets

$1-$1-$2-$3 • W-MA-2180-001.001.002.003-US010

CJF

Overprint(s): None. ***Comments:*** All unlisted in Haxby. Similar to H-MA-815-G2a, G2a, G4a, G6a. October 1, 1853.

Rarity: URS-4
Proof $4,200

Non-Valid Issues

$1 • W-MA-2180-001-A010

Left: 1 / State arms / ONE. ***Center:*** Three allegorical women reclining around shield surmounted by eagle, Ship. ***Right:*** 1 / Two farmers walking, Dog. ***Engraver:*** Danforth, Wright & Co. ***Comments:*** H-MA-815-A5. Altered from $1 Bank of Washtenaw, Washtenaw, Michigan series. 1850s.

Rarity: —

How to Read the Whitman Numbering System

$1 • W-MA-010-001-G010a

Denomination: Value of the note shown.

W: Whitman number. This number is a sortable code unique to each bank and note.

MA: Abbreviation for the state under study.

010: Numerical designation specific to each bank.

001: The denomination in dollars.

G010a: G indicates a good or valid note. Other categories are indicated thus: C (counterfeit); R (raised); S (spurious); N (not-attributed); A (altered). Numbers are assigned starting with 010, 020, et seq. Terminal letters following the number indicate variations of a note: a series of different colored overprints, tints, payees, etc., all on the same design of note. For more information, see the "How to Use This Book" section at the front of the volume, page xiv.

$2 • **W-MA-2180-002-A020**

SN

Engraver: Doty & Bergen. ***Comments:*** H-MA-815-A10. Altered from $2 Delaware City Bank, Delaware, Kansas. July 1, 185_. 1850s.

Rarity: URS-5
VF $300; **AU** $500

$3 • **W-MA-2180-003-S010**

JF

Comments: H-Unlisted. Jan. __, 185_. 1850s.

Rarity: URS-5
VF $300; **AU** $500

$3 • **W-MA-2180-003-A030**

Left: THREE / Woman seated / THREE. ***Center:*** Woman with eagle / Shield / Steamboat. ***Right:*** Woman leaning on shield bearing 3. ***Engraver:*** W.L. Ormsby. ***Comments:*** H-MA-815-A15. Altered from $3 Potomac River Bank, Georgetown, D.C. 185_. 1850s.

Rarity: —

$3 • **W-MA-2180-003-A040**

SN, CJF

Back: Orange. ***Engraver:*** Rawdon, Wright, Hatch & Edson. ***Comments:*** H-MA-815-A20. Altered from $3 Bank of West Union, West Union, Ohio. 18__. 1850s.

Rarity: —

$3 • **W-MA-2180-003-A050**

Left: 3 / Portrait of George Washington / THREE. ***Center:*** Woman seated on wharf with caduceus, Ship. ***Bottom center:*** Strongbox and cornucopia with coins. ***Right:*** 3 / Mechanic, sailor, and farmer standing with 3. ***Overprint:*** THREE. ***Engraver:*** Rawdon, Wright, Hatch & Edson. ***Comments:*** H-MA-815-A25. Altered from $3 Farmers and Merchants Bank of Memphis, Memphis, Tennessee series. 1850s.

Rarity: —

$5 • **W-MA-2180-005-A060**

SN

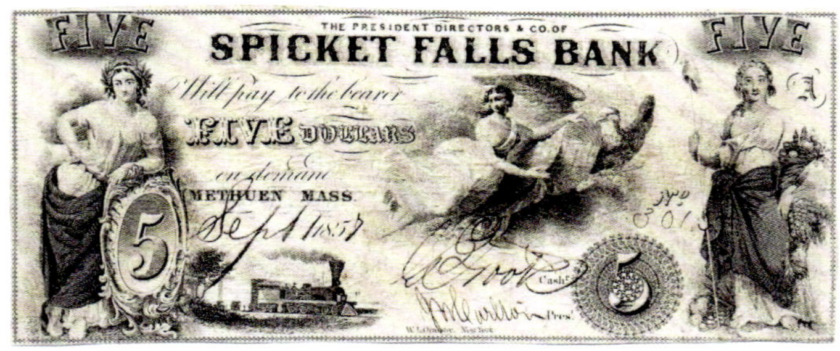

Engraver: W.L. Ormsby. ***Comments:*** H-MA-815-A30. 185_. 1850s.

Rarity: URS-5
F $250; **VF** $350

Milford, Massachusetts

Milford was incorporated as a town in 1780 and was originally part of Mendon. Farming fulfilled the major commercial needs until shoe manufacturing was introduced. More than 11 shops ended up producing shoes in Milford. Other businesses included a spindle factory, a machinery shop, an iron foundry, hat manufacturing, and the quarrying of pink granite. Pear and apple trees provided products for wide sale.

Bank of Milford

1850s

W-MA-2200

History: A non-existent bank represented only by notes altered from those of other banks.

Numismatic Commentary: This being a non-existent bank, only notes altered from other institutions will be found. Even these are not easy to locate.

All notes bear the imprint of Danforth, Bald & Co.

Issues

$1 • **W-MA-2200-001-A010**

Left: ONE / Hebe seated on bale watering eagle / ONE. ***Center:*** Indian man and sailor flanking shield bearing bull and grain, surmounted by eagle. ***Bottom center:*** Two men repairing boat. ***Right:*** 1 / Ship. ***Overprint:*** Red ONE. ***Comments:*** H-MA-825-A5. Altered from $1 Bank of Milford, Milford, Delaware. 18__. 1850s.

Rarity: —

$2 • **W-MA-2200-002-A020**

Left: Curved TWO and 2 on die / Arm and hammer. ***Center:*** Three allegorical women flanking shield bearing bull and grain, surmounted by eagle. ***Bottom center:*** Schooner. ***Right:*** 2 / Liberty seated on 2. ***Overprint:*** Red TWO. ***Comments:*** H-MA-825-A10. Altered from $2 Bank of Milford, Milford, Delaware. 18__. 1850s.

Rarity: —

$3 • **W-MA-2200-003-A030**

Left: 3 / Pat Lyon at the Forge. ***Center:*** Woman reclining on strongbox, Shield bearing bull and grain, surmounted by eagle, Sheep. ***Bottom center:*** Wheel barrow, plow, and sheaf. ***Right:*** 3 / Kneeling woman with grain and sickle. ***Overprint:*** Red THREE. ***Comments:*** H-MA-825-A15. Altered from $3 Bank of Milford, Milford, Delaware. 18__. 1850s.

Rarity: —

$5 • **W-MA-2200-005-A040**

Center: 5 / Farmer with grain, Farm scene / 5. ***Right:*** Milkmaid and cow. ***Comments:*** H-MA-825-A20. 18__. 1850s.

Rarity: —

Milford Bank

1849–1865

W-MA-2220

History: The Milford Bank was chartered on May 1, 1849, with an authorized capital of $100,000. By 1857 the capital was $250,000.

The business of the Milford Bank was succeeded by the Milford National Bank, chartered on March 7, 1865.

Numismatic Commentary: On occasion, a note from this bank will show up in the marketplace. Some have an interesting vignette of shoemakers plying their trade.

Valid Issues

$1 • **W-MA-2220-001-G010** CJF

Engraver: Toppan, Carpenter & Co. ***Comments:*** H-MA-820-G2. Oct. 15, 18__. 1849–1850s.

Rarity: URS-6
VF $300

$1 • **W-MA-2220-001-G010a**

Left: Woman holding up 1 / ONE. ***Center:*** Men at work in shop / ONE on 1. ***Bottom center:*** Train. ***Right:*** 1 / George Washington on horseback. ***Tint:*** Yellow. ***Engraver:*** Toppan, Carpenter & Co. ***Comments:*** H-MA-820-G2a. Similar to W-MA-2220-001-G010. Oct. 15, 18__. 1850s.

Rarity: —

$1 • **W-MA-2220-001-G010b**

Tint: Yellow. ***Engraver:*** American Bank Note Co. ***Comments:*** H-MA-820-G2c. Similar to W-MA-2220-001-G010 but with different engraver imprint. Oct. 15, 18__. 1860s.

Rarity: —

$2 • **W-MA-2220-002-G020** CJF

Engraver: Toppan, Carpenter & Co. ***Comments:*** H-MA-820-G4. 15 Oct. 18__. 1849–1850s.

Rarity: URS-5
VF $300

$2 • **W-MA-2220-002-G020a**

Left: Scene in boot shop, Two men at work / Portrait of Henry Clay. ***Center:*** 2. ***Bottom center:*** Horses pulling wagon. ***Right:*** 2 / Portrait of Zachary Taylor. ***Engraver:*** American Bank Note Co. ***Comments:*** H-MA-820-G4c. Similar to W-MA-2220-002-G020 but with different engraver imprint. Oct. 15, 18__. 1860s.

Rarity: —
Selected auction price: Heritage, January 2011, Lot 15554, VF $1,035

$2 • **W-MA-2220-002-G020b** JF

Overprint: Green TWO. ***Engraver:*** American Bank Note Co. ***Comments:*** H-Unlisted. Similar to W-MA-2220-002-G020 but with different engraver imprint. 15 Oct. 18__. 1860s.

Rarity: URS-5
VF $400

$3 • **W-MA-2220-003-G030**

Left: Woman with cattle / Portrait of Andrew Jackson. ***Center:*** 3. ***Bottom center:*** Building. ***Right:*** 3 / Three cherubs around 3. ***Engraver:*** Toppan, Carpenter & Co. ***Comments:*** H-MA-820-G6. Oct. 15, 18__. 1849–1850s.

Rarity: —

$3 • **W-MA-2220-003-G030a**

Engraver: American Bank Note Co. ***Comments:*** H-MA-820-G6c. Similar to W-MA-2220-003-G030 but with different engraver imprint. Oct. 15, 18__. 1860s.

Rarity: URS-5
VF $500

$5 • W-MA-2220-005-G040

CC

Engraver: Toppan, Carpenter & Co. ***Comments:*** H-MA-820-G8. Oct. 15, 18__. 1849–1850s.

Rarity: URS-5
VG $200; **VF** $500

$5 • W-MA-2220-005-G050

Left: 5 / Male portrait. ***Center:*** Woman seated in 5. ***Right:*** 5 / Portrait of Daniel Webster. ***Tint:*** Green. ***Engraver:*** American Bank Note Co. ***Comments:*** H-MA-820-G10. 1860s.

Rarity: —

$10 • W-MA-2220-010-G060

Left: X / Female portrait / 10. ***Center:*** Spread eagle / X. ***Bottom center:*** Horses pulling wagon. ***Right:*** 10 / Male portrait. ***Engraver:*** Toppan, Carpenter & Co. ***Comments:*** H-MA-820-G12. Oct. 15, 18__. 1849–1850s.

Rarity: —

$10 • W-MA-2220-010-G060a

Engraver: American Bank Note Co. ***Comments:*** H-MA-820-G12c. Similar to W-MA-2220-010-G060 but with different engraver imprint. Oct. 15, 18__. 1860s.

Rarity: —

$10 • W-MA-2220-010-G060b

CJF

Overprint: Green TEN. ***Engraver:*** American Bank Note Co. ***Comments:*** H-Unlisted. Similar to W-MA-2220-010-G060 but with different engraver imprint. Oct. 15, 18__. 1860s.

Rarity: URS-5
VF $400

$20 • W-MA-2220-020-G070

Left: 20 / Train and depot. ***Center:*** Woman flanked by two cherubs seated with balance, pole and cap. ***Bottom center:*** Steamship and ship. ***Right:*** 20 / Woman with sheaf. ***Engraver:*** Toppan, Carpenter & Co. ***Comments:*** H-MA-820-G14. 18__. 1850s.

Rarity: —

$20 • W-MA-2220-020-G080

Left: Girl holding hen and chicks. ***Center:*** Man holding black horse and white horse, Train and house. ***Right:*** 20 / Male portrait. ***Tint:*** Green die bearing 20. ***Engraver:*** American Bank Note Co. ***Comments:*** H-MA-820-G16. 1860s.

Rarity: —

$50 • W-MA-2220-050-G090

Left: 50 / Woman with sickle / 50. ***Center:*** Two women seated, Factories and train, Ship. ***Bottom center:*** Train and tender. ***Right:*** 5 / Farmer picking corn. ***Engraver:*** Toppan, Carpenter & Co. ***Comments:*** H-MA-820-G18. 18__. 1850s.

Rarity: —

$50 • W-MA-2220-050-G100

Left: 50 / Girl and boy at well. ***Center:*** Woman and two men making shoes. ***Right:*** 50 / Woman seated at sewing machine. ***Tint:*** Green 50 50. ***Engraver:*** American Bank Note Co. ***Comments:*** H-MA-820-G20. 1860s.

Rarity: —

$100 • W-MA-2220-100-G110

Left: 100 / Sailor seated with hat and flag. ***Center:*** Woman and cherubs scattering flowers in clouds above city. ***Bottom center:*** Machinery. ***Right:*** 100 / Female portrait / 100. ***Engraver:*** Toppan, Carpenter & Co. ***Comments:*** H-MA-820-G22. 18__. 1850s.

Rarity: —

$100 • W-MA-2220-100-G120

Left: Corn husking scene. ***Center:*** Female portrait. ***Right:*** 100 / Male portrait. ***Tint:*** Green die bearing 100 and green C C. ***Engraver:*** American Bank Note Co. ***Comments:*** H-MA-820-G24. 1860s.

Rarity: —

$500 • W-MA-2220-500-G130

Left: 500 / Indian woman seated with bow. ***Center:*** 500 / Three allegorical women on wharf, one reclining with lyre, one seated with staff, one kneeling with sheaf / 500. ***Bottom center:*** Eagle. ***Engraver:*** Toppan, Carpenter & Co. ***Comments:*** H-MA-820-G26. 18__. 1850s.

Rarity: —

Non-Valid Issues

$1 • W-MA-2220-001-A010

Left: ONE / Hebe seated on bale watering eagle / ONE. ***Center:*** Indian man and sailor flanking shield bearing bull and grain, surmounted by eagle. ***Bottom center:*** Two men repairing boat. ***Right:*** 1 / Ship. ***Overprint:*** Red ONE. ***Engraver:*** Danforth, Bald & Co. ***Comments:*** H-MA-820-A5. Altered from $1 Bank of Milford, Milford, Delaware. 18__. 1850s.

Rarity: —

$2 • W-MA-2220-002-A020

Left: Curved TWO and 2 on die / Arm and hammer. ***Center:*** Three allegorical women flanking shield bearing bull and grain, surmounted by eagle. ***Bottom center:*** Schooner. ***Right:*** 2 / Liberty seated on 2. ***Overprint:*** Red TWO. ***Engraver:*** Danforth, Bald & Co. ***Comments:*** H-MA-820-A10. Altered from $2 Bank of Milford, Milford, Delaware. 18__. 1850s.

Rarity: —

$3 • W-MA-2220-003-A030

Left: 3 / Pat Lyon at the Forge. ***Center:*** Woman reclining on strongbox, Shield bearing bull and grain, surmounted by eagle, Sheep. ***Bottom center:*** Wheelbarrow, plow, and sheaf. ***Right:*** 3 / Kneeling woman with grain and sickle. ***Overprint:*** Red THREE. ***Engraver:*** Danforth, Bald & Co. ***Comments:*** H-MA-820-A15. Altered from $3 Bank of Milford, Milford, Delaware. 18__. 1850s.

Rarity: —

$5 • W-MA-2220-005-A040

Left: Farmer and frontiersman flanking shield bearing bull and grain, surmounted by ship. ***Center:*** 5. ***Bottom center:*** Woman swimming. ***Right:*** FIVE / Milkmaid standing with pail. ***Overprint:*** Red FIVE. ***Engraver:*** Danforth, Bald & Co. ***Comments:*** H-MA-820-A20. Altered from $5 Bank of Milford, Milford, Delaware. 18__. 1850s.

Rarity: —

$5 • W-MA-2220-005-A050

Center: 5 / Farmer with grain, Farm scene. ***Right:*** Milkmaid and cow. ***Comments:*** H-MA-820-A25. 18__. 1850s.

Rarity: —

$10 • W-MA-2220-010-R010

Engraver: Toppan, Carpenter & Co. ***Comments:*** H-MA-820-R5. Raised from W-MA-2220-001-G010 or variety. Oct. 15, 18__. 1850s.

Rarity: —

Millbury, Massachusetts

The Blackstone River flows through the town of Millbury, which was settled in 1716 and incorporated in 1813. The water power gained from the river fueled many textile mills and factories, from which the name of the town is derived.

The earliest mill in the area was operated in 1735 and continued in use for many years afterward, up to modern times. Firearms production began at the turn of the century when Asa and Elijah Waters built factories to produce guns, scythes, and mill saws. An armory was built in 1808, closing in 1841 and opening up again at the onset of the Civil War in 1861.

Millbury Bank
1825–1864
W-MA-2230

History: The Millbury Bank was chartered on June 18, 1825, with $50,000 capital. The capital was increased to $100,000 in 1839, although the bank was experiencing the effects of the Panic of 1837. Troubles continued through the early 1840s, after which the bank prospered. Circulation was $34,498 in 1839 and $76,535 in 1863.

The business of the Millbury Bank was succeeded by the Millbury National Bank, chartered on October 25, 1864.

Numismatic Commentary: The paper money marketplace has been very stingy over the years in giving up any genuine examples from this bank. Notes from this small town are very hard to locate.

Valid Issues

$1 • W-MA-2230-001-G010

Left: Narrow panel of lathework circle segments. ***Center:*** 1 / 1 / Flower garlands and gridwork segments / 1 / 1. ***Right:*** Narrow panel of lathework circle segments. ***Engraver:*** PSSP. ***Comments:*** H-MA-830-G2. 18__. 1820s–1830s.

Rarity: —

$1 • W-MA-2230-001-G010a

Left: ONE / D / ONE vertically. ***Right:*** ONE / D / ONE vertically. ***Engraver:*** PSSP. ***Comments:*** H-MA-830-G4. Similar to W-MA-2230-001-G010. 18__. 1830s.

Rarity: —

$1 • W-MA-2230-001-G020

Engraver: Unverified, but likely New England Bank Note Co. ***Comments:*** H-MA-830-G8. No description available. 18__. 1830s.

Rarity: *None known*

$1 • W-MA-2230-001-G030

Engraver: Unverified, but likely Terry, Pelton & Co. ***Comments:*** H-MA-830-G12. No description available. 18__. 1830s.

Rarity: *None known*

$1 • W-MA-2230-001-G040

Left: ONE / Bust of George Washington / ONE. ***Center:*** 1 / Two blacksmiths at anvil in front of forge / 1 / Panel outlining white ONE. ***Right:*** ONE / Woman / ONE. ***Engraver:*** New England Bank Note Co. ***Comments:*** H-MA-830-G16. 18__. 1840s–1850s.

Rarity: —

$1 • W-MA-2230-001-G050

Left: Commerce seated with rudder leaning on barrel / 1. ***Center:*** 1 bearing "Presentation of the Declaration of Independence". ***Right:*** 1 / Woman standing with apron full of grain. ***Engraver:*** New England Bank Note Co. ***Comments:*** H-MA-830-G20. 18__. 1840s–1850s

Rarity: —

$1 • W-MA-2230-001-G060

Left: ONE / Indian man seated with 1. ***Center:*** Woman seated with cog wheel, Train and factories. ***Right:*** 1 / Blacksmith standing by anvil. ***Engraver:*** American Bank Note Co. ***Comments:*** H-MA-830-G24. 18__. 1850s–1860s.

Rarity: —

$1.25 • W-MA-2230-001.25-G070

Left: 1 25/100 / Train / 1 25/100. ***Center:*** Sloop and other ships at sea / $1.25 Cts. ***Right:*** 1 25/100 / Eagle. ***Engraver:*** New England Bank Note Co. ***Comments:*** H-MA-830-G28. 18__. 1830s.

Rarity: —

$1.50 • W-MA-2230-001.50-G080

Left: 1 Doll 50 Cts. vertically. ***Center:*** Eagle on rock in ocean / $1 50/100. ***Right:*** 1 50/100 / Justice. ***Engraver:*** New England Bank Note Co. ***Comments:*** H-MA-830-G30. 18__. 1830s.

Rarity: —

$1.75 • W-MA-2230-001.75-G090

Left: $1.75 Cts. / Hebe watering eagle / 1 75/100. ***Center:*** Three sloops at sea. ***Right:*** $1.75 Cts. / Woman seated with grain, Dog / 1 75/100. ***Engraver:*** New England Bank Note Co. ***Comments:*** H-MA-830-G32. 18__. 1830s.

Rarity: —

$2 • W-MA-2230-002-G100

Left: Narrow panel of lathework circle segments. ***Center:*** 2 / 2 / Flower garlands and gridwork segments / 2 / 2. ***Right:*** Narrow panel of lathework circle segments. ***Engraver:*** PSSP. ***Comments:*** H-MA-830-G34. 18__. 1820s–1830s.

Rarity: —

$2 • **W-MA-2230-002-G100a**

Left: Five TWOs vertically. ***Right:*** Five TWOs vertically. ***Engraver:*** PSSP. ***Comments:*** H-MA-830-G36. Similar to W-MA-2230-002-G100. 18__. 1830s.

Rarity: —

$2 • **W-MA-2230-002-G110**

Engraver: Unverified, but likely New England Bank Note Co. ***Comments:*** H-MA-830-G40. No description available. 18__. 1830s.

Rarity: *None known*

$2 • **W-MA-2230-002-G120**

Engraver: Unverified, but likely Terry, Pelton & Co. ***Comments:*** H-MA-830-G44. No description available. 18__. 1830s.

Rarity: *None known*

$2 • **W-MA-2230-002-G130**

Left: TWO / Female portrait / 2. ***Center:*** 2 / Woman giving drink to one of two seated men / 2 / Panel outlining white TWO. ***Right:*** TWO / Bust of female reaper. ***Engraver:*** New England Bank Note Co. ***Comments:*** H-MA-830-G48. 18__. 1840s.

Rarity: —

$2 • **W-MA-2230-002-G140**

Left: Men driving sheep into stream / 2. ***Center:*** 2 bearing "Presentation of the Declaration of Independence". ***Right:*** TWO / Woman seated with wreath of flowers / TWO. ***Engraver:*** New England Bank Note Co. ***Comments:*** H-MA-830-G52. 18__. 1840s.

Rarity: —

$2 • **W-MA-2230-002-G140a** JF

Engraver: New England Bank Note Co. / ABNCo. monogram. ***Comments:*** H-MA-830-G52a. Similar to W-MA-2230-002-G140 but with additional engraver imprint. 18__. 1850s.

Rarity: URS-3
Proof $2,000

$2 • **W-MA-2230-002-G150**

Left: 2 / Cowboy lassoing steer. ***Center:*** Women feeding looms. ***Right:*** 2 / Portrait of Benjamin Franklin. ***Engraver:*** American Bank Note Co. ***Comments:*** H-MA-830-G54. 18__. 1850s–1860s.

Rarity: —

$3 • **W-MA-2230-003-G160**

Left: Narrow panel of lathework circle segments. ***Center:*** 3 / 3 / Flower garlands and gridwork segments / 3 / 3. ***Right:*** Narrow panel of lathework circle segments. ***Engraver:*** PSSP. ***Comments:*** H-MA-830-G56. 18__. 1820s–1830s.

Rarity: —

$3 • **W-MA-2230-003-G160a**

Left: THREE vertically. ***Right:*** THREE vertically. ***Engraver:*** PSSP. ***Comments:*** H-MA-830-G58. Similar to W-MA-2230-003-G160. 18__. 1830s.

Rarity: —

$3 • **W-MA-2230-003-G170**

Engraver: Unverified, but likely New England Bank Note Co. ***Comments:*** H-MA-830-G60. No description available. 18__. 1830s.

Rarity: *None known*

$3 • **W-MA-2230-003-G180**

Left: THREE vertically. ***Center:*** Ship, Ships. ***Right:*** 3 / Cow / 3. ***Engraver:*** Terry, Pelton & Co. ***Comments:*** H-MA-830-G64. 18__. 1830s.

Rarity: —

$3 • **W-MA-2230-003-G190**

Left: THREE / Farmer sharpening scythe / 3 across THREE. ***Center:*** 3 / Woman placing garland on eagle, Beehive and cornucopia / 3 / Panel outlining white THREE. ***Right:*** THREE / Sailor standing on wharf with hat / 3 across THREE. ***Engraver:*** New England Bank Note Co. ***Comments:*** H-MA-830-G68. 18__. 1840s.

Rarity: —

$3 • **W-MA-2230-003-G200**

Left: Barnyard scene, Man on horse, Boy and cattle / 3. ***Center:*** 3. ***Right:*** 3 on THREE / Woman with flowers / THREE. ***Engraver:*** New England Bank Note Co. ***Comments:*** H-MA-830-G72. 18__. 1840s–1850s.

Rarity: —

$3 • **W-MA-2230-003-G200a**

Engraver: New England Bank Note Co. / ABNCo. monogram. ***Comments:*** H-MA-830-G72a. Similar to W-MA-2230-003-G200 but with additional engraver imprint. 18__. 1850s.

Rarity: —

$3 • **W-MA-2230-003-G210**

Left: 3 / Woodsman chopping tree. ***Center:*** Steamship at sea. ***Right:*** THREE across 3 / 3. ***Engraver:*** American Bank Note Co. ***Comments:*** H-MA-830-G76. 18__. 1850s–1860s.

Rarity: —

$5 • **W-MA-2230-005-G220**

Left: Lathework chain bearing MASSACHUSETTS / 5 / 5. ***Center:*** Alternating flower garlands and gridwork segments. ***Right:*** 5 / 5. ***Engraver:*** PSSP. ***Comments:*** H-MA-830-G78. 18__. 1820s.

Rarity: —

$5 • **W-MA-2230-005-G220a**

Engraver: PSSP. ***Comments:*** H-MA-830-G80. Similar to W-MA-2230-005-G220 but with zigzag ruled lines. 18__. 1820s–1830s.

Rarity: —

$5 • **W-MA-2230-005-G220b**

Engraver: PSSP. ***Comments:*** H-MA-830-G82. Similar to W-MA-2230-005-G220 but with spiral lathework lines. 18__. 1830s.

Rarity: —

$5 • **W-MA-2230-005-G230**

Engraver: Unverified, but likely New England Bank Note Co. ***Comments:*** H-MA-830-G84. No description available. 18__. 1830s.

Rarity: *None known*

$5 • **W-MA-2230-005-G240**

Left: 5 / FIVE / 5. ***Center:*** V / Eagle on wharf with plow, Cannon and anchor, Ships / V / Panel outlining white FIVE. ***Right:*** 5 / FIVE / 5. ***Engraver:*** New England Bank Note Co. ***Comments:*** H-MA-830-G88. 18__. 1840s.

Rarity: —

$5 • **W-MA-2230-005-G250**

Left: FIVE / Woman placing wreath on bust of George Washington, Eagle and shield. ***Center:*** 5 / Blacksmith's shop, Man at work / V. ***Right:*** 5 / Ship on stocks. ***Engraver:*** New England Bank Note Co. ***Comments:*** H-MA-830-G92. 18__. 1850s.

Rarity: —

$10 • **W-MA-2230-010-G260**

Left: Lathework chain bearing MASSACHUSETTS / 10 / 10 vertically. ***Center:*** Alternating flower garlands and gridwork segments. ***Right:*** 10 / 10 vertically. ***Engraver:*** Perkins. ***Comments:*** H-MA-830-G94. 18__. 1820s.

Rarity: —

$10 • **W-MA-2230-010-G260a**

Engraver: PSSP. ***Comments:*** H-MA-830-G96. Similar to W-MA-2230-010-G260 but with zigzag ruled lines. 18__. 1820s–1830s.

Rarity: —

$10 • **W-MA-2230-010-G260b**

Engraver: PSSP. ***Comments:*** H-MA-830-G98. Similar to W-MA-2230-010-G260 but with spiral lathework lines. 18__. 1830s.

Rarity: —

$10 • **W-MA-2230-010-G270**

Engraver: Unverified, but likely New England Bank Note Co. ***Comments:*** H-MA-830-G100. No description available. 18__. 1830s.

Rarity: *None known*

$10 • **W-MA-2230-010-G280**

Left: TEN / George Washington standing by horse / 10. ***Center:*** X / Farm scene, Men working, Hay wagon / 10. ***Bottom center:*** Canal scene. ***Right:*** TEN / Male portrait. ***Engraver:*** New England Bank Note Co. ***Comments:*** H-MA-830-G104. 18__. 1850s.

Rarity: —

$20 • **W-MA-2230-020-G290**

Left: Lathework chain bearing MASSACHUSETTS / 20 / 20 vertically. ***Center:*** Alternating flower garlands and gridwork segments. ***Right:*** 20 / 20 vertically. ***Engraver:*** PSSP. ***Comments:*** H-MA-830-G106. 18__. 1820s–1830s.

Rarity: —

$20 • **W-MA-2230-020-G300**

Left: 20 / XX / 20 vertically. ***Center:*** 20 / Woman seated with scales, Sheaf and bales, Men plowing, Ship / 20. ***Right:*** TWENTY vertically. ***Engraver:*** PSSP. ***Comments:*** H-MA-830-G112. 18__. 1830s.

Rarity: —

$20 • **W-MA-2230-020-G310**

Engraver: Unverified, but likely New England Bank Note Co. ***Comments:*** H-MA-830-G116. No description available. 18__. 1830s–1840s.

Rarity: *None known*

$20 • **W-MA-2230-020-G320**

Left: Woman standing with eagle / 20. ***Center:*** TWENTY across 20 / Female portrait. ***Right:*** 20 / Portrait of Benjamin Franklin. ***Engraver:*** New England Bank Note Co. ***Comments:*** H-MA-830-G120. 18__. 1840s–1850s.

Rarity: —

$50 • **W-MA-2230-050-G330**

Left: Lathework chain bearing MASSACHUSETTS / 50 / 50 vertically. ***Center:*** Alternating flower garlands and gridwork segments. ***Right:*** 50 / 50 vertically. ***Engraver:*** PSSP. ***Comments:*** H-MA-830-G124. 18__. 1820s–1830s.

Rarity: —

$50 • **W-MA-2230-050-G340**

Left: 50 / Woman standing with ankles crossed, Staff, Cornucopia / 50. ***Center:*** FIFTY DOLLARS / 50. ***Right:*** FIFTY vertically. ***Engraver:*** New England Bank Note Co. / PSSP. ***Comments:*** H-MA-830-G128. 18__. 1820s.

Rarity: —

$50 • **W-MA-2230-050-G350**

Left: FIFTY / Sheaves and fruit / 50. ***Center:*** 50 / Three women seated with eagle, pole and cap, shield, scales, and book. ***Right:*** FIFTY across 50 / Vulcan seated with tools, Train. ***Engraver:*** New England Bank Note Co. ***Comments:*** H-MA-830-G132. 18__. 1840s–1850s.

Rarity: —

$50 • **W-MA-2230-050-G360**

Left: 50. ***Center:*** George Washington on horse flanked by soldiers. ***Right:*** 500 / Portrait of General Winfield Scott. ***Tint:*** Green die bearing 50 and green dies bearing L L. ***Engraver:*** American Bank Note Co. ***Comments:*** H-MA-830-G136. 1860s.

Rarity: —

$100 • **W-MA-2230-100-G370**

Left: Lathework chain bearing MASSACHUSETTS / 100 / 100 vertically. ***Center:*** Alternating flower garlands and gridwork segments. ***Right:*** 100 / 100 vertically. ***Engraver:*** Perkins. ***Comments:*** H-MA-830-G138. 18__. 1820s–1830s.

Rarity: —

$100 • **W-MA-2230-100-G380**

Left: Lathework panel bearing C / Portrait of George Washington. ***Center:*** 100 / Manhattan reclining, pouring water, Ship / 100. ***Right:*** Lathework panel bearing ONE HUNDRED vertically. ***Engraver:*** New England Bank Note Co. ***Comments:*** H-MA-830-G144. 18__. 1830s–1840s.

Rarity: —

$100 • **W-MA-2230-100-G390**

Left: ONE HUNDRED on 100 / Portrait of William Henry Harrison. ***Center:*** Wharf scene, Men loading wagon with barrels. ***Right:*** ONE HUNDRED on 100 / Portrait of Christopher Columbus. ***Engraver:*** New England Bank Note Co. ***Comments:*** H-MA-830-G148. 18__. 1840s–1850s.

Rarity: —

$100 • **W-MA-2230-100-G400**

Left: C. ***Center:*** Farmyard scene, Man watering horses at trough, Pig, cows, and poultry. ***Right:*** 100 / Portrait of Daniel Webster. ***Tint:*** Green die bearing 100. ***Engraver:*** American Bank Note Co. ***Comments:*** H-MA-830-G152. 1860s.

Rarity: —

$500 • W-MA-2230-500-G410
Engraver: Unverified, but likely New England Bank Note Co. ***Comments:*** H-MA-830-G156. No description available. 18__. 1830s–1840s.
Rarity: *None known*

$500 • W-MA-2230-500-G420
Left: 500 / 500 vertically. ***Center:*** 500 / Woman seated with shield bearing D, Fasces, cornucopia, lyre, and sheaf / 500. ***Right:*** 500 / D / 500. ***Engraver:*** PSSP / New England Bank Note Co. ***Comments:*** H-MA-830-G160. 1850s.
Rarity: —

Non-Valid Issues

$3 • W-MA-2230-003-N010
Left: Train. ***Center:*** Steamboat and ships. ***Comments:*** H-MA-830-N5.
Rarity: —

$5 • W-MA-2230-005-S010
Comments: H-Unlisted.
Rarity: —
VF $295

Monson, Massachusetts

Settled in 1715 and incorporated in 1775, Monson was named after Sir John Monson, who was a friend of the governor. In the 19th century a few mills were located here, but none had any lasting importance. A granite quarry owned by the Flynt family provided a secondary industry which operated until the 20th century.

Monson Bank
1854–1864
W-MA-2240

History: The Monson Bank was chartered on March 28, 1854, with an authorized capital of $100,000. Its first day of business was October 5. The capital was raised to $150,000 in 1857. Bills in circulation amounted to $77,940 in 1862 and $149,903 in 1863. Real estate was valued at $6,626.62.

The business of the Monson Bank was succeeded by the Monson National Bank, chartered in August 1864.

Numismatic Commentary: Genuine notes from this bank are very hard to locate, but altered or spurious issues are seen with some frequency.

Valid Issues

$1 • W-MA-2240-001-G010
Left: ONE / Justice standing. ***Center:*** 1 / Indian man seated on cliff, holding bow and arrows, gazing at city / 1. ***Right:*** 1 / Female portrait. ***Engraver:*** American Bank Note Co. / Jocelyn, Draper, Welsh & Co. ***Comments:*** H-MA-835-G2. 18__. 1850s.
Rarity: —

$1 • W-MA-2240-001-G020
Left: ONE / Woman standing / 1. ***Center:*** Woman kneeling with shield. ***Right:*** 1 / ONE / Horse. ***Engraver:*** American Bank Note Co. / Jocelyn, Draper, Welsh & Co. ***Comments:*** H-MA-835-G4. 18__. 1850s.
Rarity: —

$1 • W-MA-2240-001-G020a
Overprint: Red 1 1. ***Engraver:*** American Bank Note Co. / Jocelyn, Draper, Welsh & Co. ***Comments:*** H-MA-835-G4a. Similar to W-MA-2240-001-G020. 18__. 1850s.
Rarity: —

$2 • W-MA-2240-002-G030
Left: Female portrait / 2. ***Center:*** Mechanic and farmer, Horse, Factories. ***Right:*** 2 / Shield, Scroll, E PLURIBUS UNUM. ***Engraver:*** American Bank Note Co. / Jocelyn, Draper, Welsh & Co. ***Comments:*** H-MA-835-G6. 18__. 1850s.
Rarity: —

$2 • W-MA-2240-002-G030a
Overprint: Red. ***Engraver:*** American Bank Note Co. / Jocelyn, Draper, Welsh & Co. ***Comments:*** H-MA-835-G6a. Similar to W-MA-2240-002-G030. 18__. 1850s.
Rarity: —

$3 • W-MA-2240-003-G040
Left: 3 / Male portrait. ***Center:*** 3 / Two allegorical women and one man reclining in clouds with pole and cap, Cornucopia and anvil / 3. ***Right:*** 3 / Blacksmith at work. ***Engraver:*** American Bank Note Co. / Jocelyn, Draper, Welsh & Co. ***Comments:*** H-MA-835-G8. 18__. 1850s.
Rarity: —

$3 • W-MA-2240-003-G040a
Overprint: Red. ***Engraver:*** American Bank Note Co. / Jocelyn, Draper, Welsh & Co. ***Comments:*** H-MA-835-G8a. Similar to W-MA-2240-003-G040. 18__. 1850s.
Rarity: —

$5 • W-MA-2240-005-G050
Left: 5 / Train, buildings, and chimneys. ***Right:*** 5 / Indian woman standing with hand on bank. ***Engraver:*** American Bank Note Co. / Jocelyn, Draper, Welsh & Co. ***Comments:*** H-MA-835-G10. 18__. 1850s.
Rarity: —

$5 • W-MA-2240-005-G060
Left: 5 / Portrait of George Washington. ***Center:*** Train on viaduct, Train, bridge, and village. ***Right:*** 5 / 5. ***Engraver:*** American Bank Note Co. / Jocelyn, Draper, Welsh & Co. ***Comments:*** H-MA-835-G12. 18__. 1850s.
Rarity: —

$5 • W-MA-2240-005-G070
Left: FIVE / Farmer seated between two sheaves, Sickle / 5. ***Center:*** Two women with distaff and spinning wheel, Train on bridge. ***Right:*** 5. ***Engraver:*** American Bank Note Co. / Jocelyn, Draper, Welsh & Co. ***Comments:*** H-MA-835-G14. 18__. 1850s.
Rarity: —

$10 • W-MA-2240-010-G080
Left: Team of oxen with horse, Men loading wagon with sheaves. ***Center:*** 10. ***Right:*** X / Woman reclining with shield, Pole and cap, scroll, Ships, train, and buildings. ***Engraver:*** American Bank Note Co. / Jocelyn, Draper, Welsh & Co. ***Comments:*** H-MA-835-G16. 18__. 1850s.
Rarity: —

$20 • W-MA-2240-020-G090

JF

Engraver: American Bank Note Co. / Jocelyn, Draper, Welsh & Co. ***Comments:*** H-MA-835-G18. 18__. 1850s.

Rarity: —

$50 • W-MA-2240-050-G100

JF

Engraver: American Bank Note Co. / Jocelyn, Draper, Welsh & Co. ***Comments:*** H-MA-835-G20. 18__. 1850s.

Rarity: —

Uncut Sheets

$1-$1-$2-$5 • W-MA-2240-001.001.002.005-US010

Vignette(s): ***($1)*** Justice standing / Indian man seated on cliff, holding bow and arrows, gazing at city / Female portrait. ***($1)*** Woman standing / Woman kneeling with shield / Horse. ***($2)*** Female portrait / Mechanic and farmer, Horse, Factories/ Shield, Scroll, E PLURIBUS UNUM. ***($5)*** Train, buildings, and chimneys / Indian woman standing with hand on bank. ***Comments:*** H-MA-835-G2, G4, G6, G10. 18__. 1850s.

Rarity: —

$1-$1-$2-$5 • W-MA-2240-001.001.002.005-US010a

Overprint(s): Red. ***Comments:*** All unlisted in Haxby. Similar to H-MA-835-G2, G4a, G6a, G10. 18__. 1850s.

Rarity: —

$5-$5-$3-$10 • W-MA-2240-005.005.003.010-US020

Vignette(s): ***($5)*** Portrait of George Washington / Train on viaduct, Train, bridge, and village. ***($5)*** Farmer seated between two sheaves, Sickle / Two women with distaff and spinning wheel, Train on bridge. ***($3)*** Male portrait / Two allegorical women and one man reclining in clouds with pole and cap, Cornucopia and anvil / Blacksmith at work. ***($10)*** Team of oxen with horse, Men loading wagon with sheaves / Woman reclining with shield, Pole and cap, scroll, Ships, train, and buildings. ***Comments:*** H-MA-835-G12, G14, G8, G16. 18__. 1850s.

Rarity: —

$20-$50 • W-MA-2240-020.050-US030

JF

Comments: H-MA-835-G18, G20. Partial sheet. 18__. 1850s.

Rarity: —

Non-Valid Issues

$1 • W-MA-2240-001-A010

Left: ONE on die vertically. ***Center:*** Overseer on horse and men picking cotton / Indian stalking two deer. ***Bottom center:*** Sleeping dog. ***Right:*** 1 / Female portrait. ***Overprint:*** Red ONE. ***Engraver:*** Bald, Cousland & Co. / Baldwin, Bald & Cousland. ***Comments:*** H-MA-835-A5. Altered from $1 Southern Bank of Georgia, Bainbridge, Georgia. 18__. 1860s.

Rarity: —

$2 • W-MA-2240-002-C030

Engraver: American Bank Note Co. / Jocelyn, Draper, Welsh & Co. ***Comments:*** H-MA-835-C6. Counterfeit of W-MA-2240-002-G030 or G030a. 18__. 1850s.

Rarity: —

$2 • W-MA-2240-002-N010

Left: Farmer driving cattle into stream. ***Right:*** Haying scene, Men loading ox wagon. ***Engraver:*** New England Bank Note Co. ***Comments:*** H-MA-835-N5.

Rarity: —

$5 • W-MA-2240-005-S010

CJF

Tint: Red-orange. ***Comments:*** H-MA-835-S5. 18__. 1860s.

Rarity: URS-5

F $500

$5 • W-MA-2240-005-N020

Left: FIVE vertically. ***Right:*** Portrait. ***Comments:*** H-MA-835-N10.

Rarity: —

$5 • W-MA-2240-005-N030

SI

Overprint: Red ONE outlined in black. ***Comments:*** H-Unlisted. Hand-made note with pasted on end panels. October 1, 1854.

Rarity: —

$5 • W-MA-2240-005-A020

Left: 5 / Male portrait. ***Center:*** Train / FIVE. ***Right:*** 5 / Woman standing / FIVE. ***Engraver:*** American Bank Note Co. ***Comments:*** H-MA-835-A10. Altered from $5 Clinton Bank, Westernport, Maryland series. 18__. 1860.

Rarity: —

$20 • W-MA-2240-020-R010

Engraver: American Bank Note Co. / Jocelyn, Draper, Welsh & Co. ***Comments:*** H-MA-835-R5. Raised from W-MA-2240-001-G020 or G020a. 18__. 1850s.

Rarity: —

NANTUCKET, MASSACHUSETTS

Nantucket is made up of the islands Tuckernuck and Muskeget. It is also known as Canopache, which means "place of peace" in the native Wampanoag language. The first English settlers arrived in 1602.

The whaling industry had its start in Nantucket after a whale swam into the harbor and was killed. During the whaling era of the town, Nantucket was the third largest city in Massachusetts, with a population of about 10,000. As many as 88 whaling ships from Nantucket sailed across the globe at the height of this industry, and for four decades Nantucket Island was foremost in this industry. Herman Melville's novel *Moby-Dick* was based on the tale of the *Essex*, a Nantucket whaling ship that was rammed by a whale off the coast of South America in 1820.

In 1837 the main road in Nantucket was paved with Gloucester cobblestones. 1850 saw the downward slide of whaling, and the economic struggles for the island only grew worse when the great fire of 1846, fueled by whale oil and lumber, destroyed the main town. The popularity of the railroad on the mainland further isolated the island, as shipping by train to domestic locations was easier, more convenient, and ultimately more desirable than by sea. After the 1850s, petroleum derivatives took most of the market that had earlier been enjoyed by whale oil.

Citizens Bank
1831–1842
W-MA-2250

History: The Citizens Bank was incorporated on March 18, 1831, with an authorized capital of $100,000. James Mitchell was the first president, and W.C. Starbank was the founding cashier. Circulation in 1839 was calculated at $22,920.50. In 1842 there was a rash of notes altered from the Citizens Bank of Augusta, Maine.

In 1842 the bank discontinued business, but notes continued to be redeemed for a time afterward. The bank building was destroyed by fire on July 13, 1846.

Numismatic Commentary: As are all issues from the off-shore islands, these notes are extremely hard to find. Bank notes from the islands, small fishing ports, and tourist destinations are in great demand. At least one issue shows the view as you approach the landing, and if you have ever taken the ferry to Nantucket, this scene will be very familiar to you.

VALID ISSUES

$1 • W-MA-2250-001-G010

Left: Eagle / 1. ***Center:*** Portrait of George Washington / Cherubs, bales / Portrait of Marquis de Lafayette. ***Right:*** Eagle / 1. ***Engraver:*** PSSP. ***Comments:*** H-MA-840-G2. 18__. 1830s.

Rarity: —

$1 • W-MA-2250-001-G020

Engraver: Unverified, but likely New England Bank Note Co. ***Comments:*** H-MA-840-G4. No description available. 18__. 1830s–1840s.

Rarity: *None known*

$1.25 • W-MA-2250-001.25-G030

Left: 1 25/100 / Train / 1 25/100. ***Center:*** Sloop and other ships at sea / $1.25 cts. ***Right:*** 1 25/100 / Eagle. ***Engraver:*** New England Bank Note Co. ***Comments:*** H-MA-840-G6. 18__. 1830s.

Rarity: —

$1.50 • W-MA-2250-001.50-G040

Left: 1 Doll. 50 Cts. vertically. ***Center:*** Eagle on rock in ocean / $1 50/100. ***Right:*** 1 50/100 / Justice. ***Engraver:*** New England Bank Note Co. ***Comments:*** H-MA-840-G7. 18__. 1830s.

Rarity: —

$1.75 • W-MA-2250-001.75-G050

Left: $1.75 Cts. / Hebe watering eagle / 1 75/100. ***Center:*** Three sloops at sea. ***Right:*** $1.75 Cts. / Dog, Woman seated with grain / 1 75/100. ***Engraver:*** New England Bank Note Co. ***Comments:*** H-MA-840-G8. 18__. 1830s.

Rarity: —
F $695

$2 • W-MA-2250-002-G060

Left: Eagle / 2. ***Center:*** Portrait of George Washington / Cherubs, bales / Portrait of Marquis de Lafayette. ***Right:*** Eagle / 2. ***Engraver:*** PSSP. ***Comments:*** H-MA-840-G10. 18__. 1820s–1830s.

Rarity: —

$2 • W-MA-2250-002-G070

Engraver: Unverified, but likely New England Bank Note Co. ***Comments:*** H-MA-840-G12. No description available. 18__. 1830s–1840s.

Rarity: *None known*

$3 • W-MA-2250-003-G080

CJF

Engraver: PSSP. ***Comments:*** H-MA-840-G14. 18__. 1830s.

Rarity: —

$3 • W-MA-2250-003-G090

Engraver: Unverified, but likely New England Bank Note Co. ***Comments:*** H-MA-840-G16. No description available. 18__. 1830s–1840s.

Rarity: *None known*

$5 • W-MA-2250-005-G100

Left: Narrow lathework panel / 5 / Portrait of George Washington / 5. ***Center:*** Text on a microletter background. ***Right:*** 5 / Portrait of Marquis de Lafayette / 5 / Panel. ***Engraver:*** PSSP. ***Comments:*** H-MA-840-G18. 18__. 1820s–1830s.

Rarity: —

$5 • W-MA-2250-005-G110

CJF

Engraver: New England Bank Note Co. ***Comments:*** H-MA-840-G20. 18__. 1830s–1840s.

Rarity: —

$10 • W-MA-2250-010-G120

Left: Narrow lathework panel / 10 / Portrait of George Washington / 10. ***Center:*** Text on a microletter background. ***Right:*** 10 / Portrait of Marquis de Lafayette / 10 / Narrow lathework panel. ***Engraver:*** PSSP. ***Comments:*** H-MA-840-G22. 18__. 1820s–1830s.

Rarity: —

$20 • W-MA-2250-020-G130

Left: Lathework chain bearing MASSACHUSETTS / 20 / 20 vertically. ***Center:*** Alternating flower garlands and gridwork segments. ***Right:*** 20 / 20 vertically. ***Engraver:*** PSSP. ***Comments:*** H-MA-840-G24. 18__. 1830s.

Rarity: —

$50 • W-MA-2250-050-G140

Left: Lathework chain bearing MASSACHUSETTS / 50 / 50 vertically. ***Center:*** Alternating flower garlands and gridwork segments. ***Right:*** 50 / 50 vertically. ***Engraver:*** PSSP. ***Comments:*** H-MA-840-G26. 18__. 1830s.

Rarity: —

$100 • W-MA-2250-100-G150

Left: Lathework chain bearing MASSACHUSETTS / 100 / 100 vertically. ***Center:*** Alternating flower garlands and gridwork segments. ***Right:*** 100 / 100 vertically. ***Engraver:*** Perkins. ***Comments:*** H-MA-840-G28. 18__. 1830s.

Rarity: —

Non-Valid Issues

$1 • W-MA-2250-001-A010

CJF

Engraver: Terry, Pelton & Co. ***Comments:*** H-MA-840-A5. Altered from $1 Citizens Bank, Augusta, Maine, or from notes of other failed banks using the same plate. 18__. 1840s.

Rarity: —

$2 • W-MA-2250-002-A020

Left: TWO / Portrait of cherub / 2. ***Center:*** 2 / Ceres giving grain to seated Liberty / 2. ***Bottom center:*** Anchor and implements. ***Right:*** 2 / Female portrait / TWO. ***Engraver:*** Terry, Pelton & Co. ***Comments:*** H-MA-840-A10. Altered from $2 Citizens Bank, Augusta, Maine, or from notes of other failed banks using the same plate. 18__.

Rarity: —

$3 • W-MA-2250-003-A030

Left: 3 / Woman standing with branch, trident, and THREE / THREE. ***Center:*** Female portrait / Ceres and Justice flanking shield bearing anchor and surmounted by eagle / Portrait of cherub. ***Bottom center:*** Anchor and implements. ***Right:*** 3 / Ceres seated in grain field / THREE. ***Engraver:*** Terry, Pelton & Co. ***Comments:*** H-MA-840-A15. Altered from $3 Citizens Bank, Augusta, Maine, or from notes of other failed banks using the same plate. 18__. 1840s.

Rarity: —

$5 • W-MA-2250-005-A040

Left: FIVE / Portrait of Benjamin Franklin / V. ***Center:*** 5 / Two allegorical women standing and one seated / Agricultural items and ship. ***Bottom center:*** Anchor and implements. ***Right:*** V / Portrait of Marquis de Lafayette / FIVE. ***Engraver:*** Terry, Pelton & Co. ***Comments:*** H-MA-840-A20. Altered from $5 Citizens Bank, Augusta, Maine, or from notes of other failed banks using the same plate. 18__. 1840s.

Rarity: —

$10 • W-MA-2250-010-A050

Left: 10 / Portrait of George Washington held by cherub / 10. ***Center:*** X / Spread eagle with shield and arrows, E PLURIBUS UNUM / X. ***Bottom center:*** Ship. ***Right:*** 10 / Standing Indian man / 10. ***Engraver:*** Terry, Pelton & Co. ***Comments:*** H-MA-840-A25. Altered from $10 Citizens Bank, Augusta, Maine, or from notes of other failed banks using the same plate. 18__. 1840s.

Rarity: —

Manufacturers and Mechanics Bank

1825–1846

W-MA-2270

History: The Manufacturers and Mechanics Bank was chartered on June 18, 1825, with an authorized capital of $100,000. It had a circulation of $63,464 in 1845. All was not well, and the bank failed in February 1846 due to embezzlement by the cashier. The bank building was destroyed in the disastrous fire of July 13 that year.

Numismatic Commentary: One of the most interesting "whaling" scenes on a bank note appears on some of this bank's issues. A sperm whale attacked by whalers is reminiscent of the story *Moby-Dick*.

All notes bear the imprint of the New England Bank Note Co. The books of the bank reside with the Nantucket Historical Association.

Valid Issues

$1 • W-MA-2270-001-G010

Left: Lathework panel. ***Center:*** 1 / 1 / Oval of flower garlands and gridwork segments / 1 / 1. ***Right:*** Lathework panel. ***Engraver:*** PSSP. ***Comments:*** H-MA-845-G2. 18__. 1820s.

Rarity: —
AG $175

$1 • W-MA-2270-001-G010a

QDB

Engraver: PSSP. ***Comments:*** H-Unlisted. Similar to W-MA-2270-001-G010. 18__. 1840s.

Rarity: —

$1 • W-MA-2270-001-G020

Left: Eagle / 1. ***Center:*** Portrait of George Washington / Cherubs, bales / Portrait of Marquis de Lafayette. ***Right:*** Eagle / 1. ***Engraver:*** PSSP. ***Comments:*** H-MA-845-G4. 18__. 1820s–1830s.

Rarity: —

$1 • W-MA-2270-001-G030

CJF

Engraver: New England Bank Note Co. ***Comments:*** H-MA-845-G6. 18__. 1830s–1840s.

Rarity: URS-5
VG $500; **F** $750; **VF** $950

$2 • W-MA-2270-002-G040

Left: Lathework panel. ***Center:*** 2 / 2 / Oval of flower garlands and gridwork segments / 2 / 2. ***Right:*** Lathework panel. ***Engraver:*** PSSP. ***Comments:*** H-MA-845-G8. 18__. 1820s.

Rarity: —

$2 • W-MA-2270-002-G050

Left: Eagle / 2. ***Center:*** Portrait of George Washington / Cherubs, bales / Portrait of Marquis de Lafayette. ***Right:*** Eagle / 2. ***Engraver:*** PSSP. ***Comments:*** H-MA-845-G10. 18__. 1820s–1830s.

Rarity: —

$2 • W-MA-2270-002-G060

Left: TWO / Sailing ship / 2. ***Center:*** Ship at sea, Whaling scene / TWO. ***Right:*** 2 / Man standing / TWO. ***Engraver:*** New England Bank Note Co. ***Comments:*** H-MA-845-G12. 18__. 1830s–1840s.

Rarity: —

$3 • W-MA-2270-003-G070

Left: Lathework panel. ***Center:*** 3 / 3 / Oval of flower garlands and gridwork segments / 3 / 3. ***Right:*** Lathework panel. ***Engraver:*** PSSP. ***Comments:*** H-MA-845-G14. 18__. 1820s–1830s.

Rarity: —

$3 • W-MA-2270-003-G080

Left: Eagle / 3. ***Center:*** Portrait of George Washington / Cherubs, bales / Portrait of Marquis de Lafayette. ***Right:*** Eagle / 3. ***Engraver:*** PSSP. ***Comments:*** H-MA-845-G16. 18__. 1820s–1830s.

Rarity: —
Selected auction price: Stack's Bowers Galleries, March 2013, Choice F $6,462

$3 • W-MA-2270-003-G090

Engraver: Unverified, but likely New England Bank Note Co. ***Comments:*** H-MA-845-G18. No description available. 18__. 1830s–1840s.

Rarity: *None known*

Collectors and Researchers:

If you have new information about any banks or notes listed in this volume, contact Whitman Publishing, Attn: Obsolete Paper Money, 3101 Clairmont Road, Suite G, Atlanta, GA 30329.

$3 • W-MA-2270-003-G100

SBG

Engraver: PSSP. ***Comments:*** H-Unlisted. 18__. 1840s.

Rarity: URS-2
F $9,000

$5 • W-MA-2270-005-G110

Left: Lathework panel. ***Center:*** 5 / 5 / Oval of flower garlands and gridwork segments / 5 / 5. ***Right:*** Lathework panel. ***Engraver:*** PSSP. ***Comments:*** H-MA-845-G20. 18__. 1820s.

Rarity: —
VG $750

$5 • W-MA-2270-005-G120

Left: 5 / Portrait of George Washington / 5. ***Right:*** 5 / Portrait of Marquis de Lafayette / 5. ***Engraver:*** PSSP. ***Comments:*** H-MA-845-G22. 18__. 1820s–1830s.

Rarity: —

$5 • W-MA-2270-005-G130

CJF

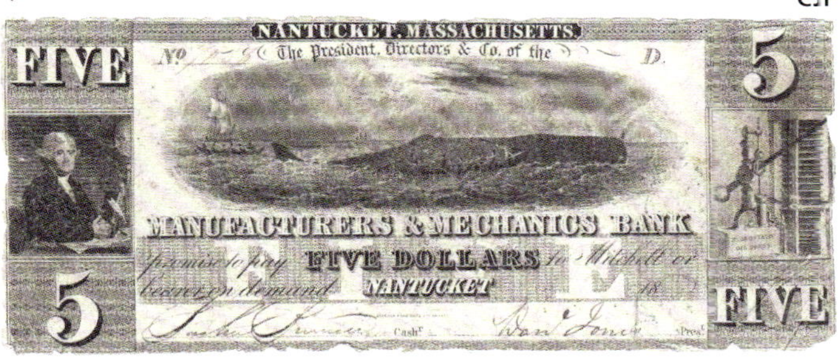

Engraver: New England Bank Note Co. ***Comments:*** H-MA-845-G24. 18__. 1830s–1840s.

Rarity: URS-2
F $11,000

$10 • W-MA-2270-010-G140

Left: Lathework chain bearing MASSACHUSETTS / 10 / 10 vertically. ***Center:*** Alternating flower garlands and gridwork segments / TEN DOLLARS with zigzag ruled lines. ***Right:*** 10 / 10 vertically. ***Engraver:*** PSSP. ***Comments:*** H-MA-845-G26. 18__. 1820s.

Rarity: —

$10 • W-MA-2270-010-G150

CC

Engraver: PSSP. ***Comments:*** H-MA-845-G28. 18__. 1820s–1830s.

Rarity: URS-3
VF $1,200

$10 • W-MA-2270-010-G160

Engraver: Unverified, but likely New England Bank Note Co. ***Comments:*** H-MA-845-G30. No description available. 18__. 1830s–1840s.

Rarity: *None known*

$20 • W-MA-2270-020-G170

Left: Lathework chain bearing MASSACHUSETTS / 20 / 20 vertically. ***Center:*** Alternating flower garlands and gridwork segments. ***Right:*** 20 / 20 vertically. ***Engraver:*** PSSP. ***Comments:*** H-MA-845-G32. 18__. 1820s–1830s.

Rarity: —

$20 • W-MA-2270-020-G180

Engraver: Unverified, but likely New England Bank Note Co. ***Comments:*** H-MA-845-G34. No description available. 18__. 1830s–1840s.

Rarity: *None known*

$50 • W-MA-2270-050-G190

Left: Lathework chain bearing MASSACHUSETTS / 50 / 50 vertically. ***Center:*** Alternating flower garlands and gridwork segments. ***Right:*** 50 / 50 vertically. ***Engraver:*** PSSP. ***Comments:*** H-MA-845-G36. 18__. 1820s–1830s.

Rarity: —

$50 • W-MA-2270-050-G200

Engraver: Unverified, but likely New England Bank Note Co. ***Comments:*** H-MA-845-G38. No description available. 18__. 1830s–1840s.

Rarity: *None known*

$100 • W-MA-2270-100-G210

Left: Lathework chain bearing MASSACHUSETTS / 100 / 100 vertically. ***Center:*** Alternating flower garlands and gridwork segments. ***Right:*** 100 / 100 vertically. ***Engraver:*** Perkins. ***Comments:*** H-MA-845-G40. 18__. 1820s–1830s.

Rarity: —

$100 • W-MA-2270-100-G220

Engraver: Unverified, but likely New England Bank Note Co. ***Comments:*** H-MA-845-G42. No description available. 18__. 1830s–1840s.

Rarity: *None known*

Nantucket Bank

1795–1816

W-MA-2290

History: The Nantucket Bank was incorporated on February 27, 1795, with $40,000 in authorized capital, a figure that was later increased to $100,000.

On June 20, 1795, the bank was robbed of more than $20,000. On June 17, 1816, an act was passed allowing the bank two more years to close its affairs and settle the concerns of the stockholders.

Numismatic Commentary: Findings from this bank are limited to very early notes. Most if not all of these existing in collections are counterfeits. Some of the issues show a primitive engraving of a whale.

VALID ISSUES

$1 • W-MA-2290-001-G010
Left: Carved letters vertically. ***Center:*** 1 / 1 / ONE. ***Right:*** 1. ***Engraver:*** Perkins. ***Comments:*** H-MA-855-G2. 1___. 1790s–1800s.

Rarity: *None known*

$1 • W-MA-2290-001-G020
Comments: H-MA-855-G6. No description available. 1800s.

Rarity: *None known*

$2 • W-MA-2290-002-G030
Left: Carved letters vertically. ***Center:*** 2 / 2 / TWO. ***Right:*** 2. ***Engraver:*** Perkins. ***Comments:*** H-MA-855-G8. 1___. 1790s–1800s.

Rarity: *None known*

$2 • W-MA-2290-002-G040
Comments: H-MA-855-G12. No description available. 1800s.

Rarity: *None known*

$3 • W-MA-2290-003-G050
Left: Carved letters vertically. ***Center:*** III / 3 on vertical whale / 3 / THREE. ***Right:*** 3. ***Engraver:*** Perkins. ***Comments:*** H-MA-855-G14. 1___. 1790s–1800s.

Rarity: *None known*

$3 • W-MA-2290-003-G060
Comments: H-MA-855-G18. No description available. 1800s.

Rarity: *None known*

$4 • W-MA-2290-004-G070
Left: Carved letters / IV vertically. ***Center:*** 4 in diamond / FOUR DOLLARS. ***Right:*** 4 vertically. ***Engraver:*** Perkins. ***Comments:*** H-MA-855-G20. 1___. 1790s–1800s.

Rarity: *None known*

$5 • W-MA-2290-005-G080
Left: Carved letters vertically. ***Center:*** 5 / 5 / FIVE. ***Right:*** 5. ***Engraver:*** Perkins. ***Comments:*** H-MA-855-G24. 1___. 1790s–1800s.

Rarity: *None known*

$5 • W-MA-2290-005-G090
Comments: H-MA-855-G28. No description available. 1800s.

Rarity: *None known*

$10 • W-MA-2290-010-G100
Left: Carved letters vertically. ***Center:*** 10 / 10 / TEN. ***Right:*** 10. ***Engraver:*** Perkins. ***Comments:*** H-MA-855-G60. 1___. 1790s–1800s.

Rarity: *None known*

$10 • W-MA-2290-010-G110
Comments: H-MA-855-G64. No description available. 1800s.

Rarity: *None known*

$20 • W-MA-2290-020-G120
Left: Carved letters vertically. ***Center:*** 20 / 20 / TWENTY. ***Right:*** 20. ***Engraver:*** Perkins. ***Comments:*** H-MA-855-G66. 1___. 1790s–1800s.

Rarity: *None known*

$20 • W-MA-2290-020-G130
Comments: H-MA-855-G70. No description available. 1800s.

Rarity: *None known*

$50 • W-MA-2290-050-G140
Left: Carved letters vertically. ***Center:*** 50 / 50 / FIFTY. ***Right:*** 50. ***Engraver:*** Perkins. ***Comments:*** H-MA-855-G84. 1___. 1790s–1800s.

Rarity: *None known*

$50 • W-MA-2290-050-G150
Comments: H-MA-855-G88. No description available. 1800s.

Rarity: *None known*

$100 • W-MA-2290-100-G160
Left: Carved letters vertically. ***Center:*** 100 / 100 / ONE HUNDRED. ***Right:*** 100. ***Engraver:*** Perkins. ***Comments:*** H-MA-855-G90. 1___. 1790s–1800s.

Rarity: *None known*

$100 • W-MA-2290-100-G170
Comments: H-MA-855-G94. No description available. 1800s.

Rarity: *None known*

NON-VALID ISSUES

$3 • W-MA-2290-003-C050
CC

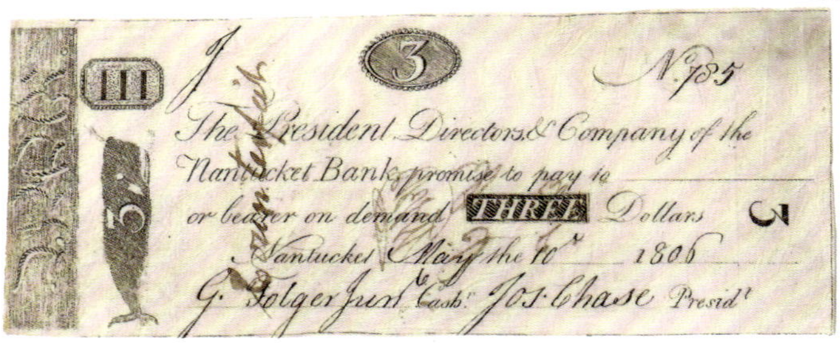

Comments: H-MA-855-C14. Counterfeit of W-MA-2290-003-G050. 1___. 1800s.

Rarity: URS-3
F $565; **EF** $1,700

$4 • W-MA-2290-004-C070
CC

Comments: H-MA-855-C20. Counterfeit of W-MA-2290-004-G070. 1___. 1800s.

Rarity: URS-3
EF $1,250

Pacific Bank

1804–1865

W-MA-2310

History: The Pacific Bank was chartered on March 3, 1804, with $100,000 in authorized capital, a figure which later increased to $200,000. In the enabling legislation and in some scattered early accounts, the bank was listed as the "Nantucket Pacific Bank," but Nantucket was not a part of the bank title. It served as an adjective to identify the location. In 1837 there was a major scandal when the president, who also served as cashier (a rare situation), was found to owe the bank more than $185,000. The debt was secured, and no loss was taken. The president was removed from the office.

Circulation in 1839 was $62,607.25, from which it reached a high of $165,994 in 1854. The bank's real estate was valued at $10,000 in 1854, and specie amounted to $15,031.90 that same year. The bank was located in an imposing, two-story brick building at 51 Main Street.

In 1865 the business of the Pacific Bank was succeeded by the Pacific National Bank of Nantucket.

Numismatic Commentary: As the waters in the Atlantic were becoming crowded with whalers, some captains opted for the richer fisheries in the distant Pacific Ocean. Subsequently, a bank was established to support these ships. Notes from this bank are hard to find. The bank continued to redeem its state bank notes after it morphed into a national bank, resulting in their scarcity for today's collectors.

Valid Issues

$1 • W-MA-2310-001-G010

Center: 1 / 1 / Black oval bearing white flower buds / 1 / 1. ***Engraver:*** Perkins. ***Comments:*** H-MA-865-G10. 18__. 1800s.

Rarity: —

$1 • W-MA-2310-001-G020

Center: 1 / 1 / Double oval flower garlands and gridwork segments / ONE / 1 / 1. ***Engraver:*** PSSP. ***Comments:*** H-MA-865-G12. 18__. 1807–1809.

Rarity: —

$1 • W-MA-2310-001-G030

Center: 1 / 1 / Oval flower garlands and gridwork segments / 1 / 1. ***Engraver:*** PSSP. ***Comments:*** H-MA-865-G14. 18__. 1809–circa 1812.

Rarity: —

$1 • W-MA-2310-001-G030a

Center: 1 / 1 / Oval flower garlands and gridwork segments / ONE / 1 / 1. ***Engraver:*** PSSP. ***Comments:*** H-MA-865-G16. Similar to W-MA-2310-001-G030. 18__. Circa 1812–1820s.

Rarity: —

$1 • W-MA-2310-001-G030b

Left: Panel of lathework circle segments. ***Right:*** Panel of lathework circle segments. ***Engraver:*** PSSP. ***Comments:*** H-MA-865-G18. Similar to W-MA-2310-001-G030. 18__. 1820s.

Rarity: —

$1 • W-MA-2310-001-G030c

Left: Panel of lathework circle segments. ***Right:*** Panel of lathework circle segments. ***Engraver:*** PSSP. ***Comments:*** H-MA-865-G20. Similar to W-MA-2310-001-G030. 18__. 1820s–1830s.

Rarity: —

$1 • W-MA-2310-001-G030d

Left: ONE / D / ONE vertically. ***Right:*** ONE / D / ONE vertically. ***Engraver:*** PSSP. ***Comments:*** H-MA-865-G22. Similar to W-MA-2310-001-G030. 18__. 1830s.

Rarity: —

$1 • W-MA-2310-001-G040

Engraver: Unverified, but likely New England Bank Note Co. ***Comments:*** H-MA-865-G24. No description available. 18__. 1830s–1840s.

Rarity: *None known*

$1 • W-MA-2310-001-G050

Left: Sailboats / 1. ***Center:*** 1 / ONE. ***Right:*** ONE / Ship with whale / ONE. ***Engraver:*** New England Bank Note Co. ***Comments:*** H-MA-865-G28. 18__. 1840s.

Rarity: —

$1 • W-MA-2310-001-G050a

Overprint: Red ONE. ***Engraver:*** New England Bank Note Co. ***Comments:*** H-MA-865-G28a. Similar to W-MA-2310-001-G050. 18__. 1850s.

Rarity: —

$1 • W-MA-2310-001-G050b

ANS

Overprint: Red ONE. ***Engraver:*** New England Bank Note Co. / ABNCo. monogram. ***Comments:*** H-MA-865-G28b. Similar to W-MA-2310-001-G050 but with additional engraver imprint. 18__. 1850s–1860s.

Rarity: URS-4
F $750

$1.25 • W-MA-2310-001.25-G060

Left: 1 25/100. ***Center:*** Sloop and other ships at sea / $1.25 cts. ***Right:*** 1 25/100 / Eagle. ***Engraver:*** New England Bank Note Co. ***Comments:*** H-MA-865-G30. 18__. 1830s.

Rarity: —

$1.50 • W-MA-2310-001.50-G070

Left: 1 Doll 50 Cts. vertically. ***Center:*** Eagle on rock in ocean / $1 50/100. ***Right:*** 1 50/100 / Justice. ***Engraver:*** New England Bank Note Co. ***Comments:*** H-MA-865-G32. 18__. 1830s.

Rarity: —

$1.75 • W-MA-2310-001.75-G080

Left: $1.75 Cts. / Hebe watering eagle / 1 75/100. ***Center:*** Three sloops at sea. ***Right:*** $1.75 Cts. / Dog, Woman seated with grain / 1 75/100. ***Engraver:*** New England Bank Note Co. ***Comments:*** H-MA-865-G34. 18__. 1830s.

Rarity: —

$2 • W-MA-2310-002-G090

Center: 2 / 2 / Black oval bearing white flower buds / 2 / 2. ***Engraver:*** Perkins. ***Comments:*** H-MA-865-G40. 18__. 1800s.

Rarity: —

$2 • W-MA-2310-002-G100

Center: 2 / 2 / Black oval bearing white flower buds / TWO / 2 / 2. ***Engraver:*** PSSP. ***Comments:*** H-MA-865-G42. 18__. 1807–1809.

Rarity: —

$2 • W-MA-2310-002-G110

Center: 2 / 2 / Oval of flower garlands and gridwork segments / 2 / 2. ***Engraver:*** PSSP. ***Comments:*** H-MA-865-G44. 18__. 1809–circa 1812.

Rarity: —

$2 • W-MA-2310-002-G110a

Center: 2 / 2 / Oval of flower garlands and gridwork segments / TWO / 2 / 2. ***Engraver:*** PSSP. ***Comments:*** H-MA-865-G46. Similar to W-MA-2310-002-G110. 18__. 1809–circa 1812.

Rarity: —

$2 • W-MA-2310-002-G110b

Left: Panel of lathework circle segments. ***Right:*** Panel of lathework circle segments. ***Engraver:*** PSSP. ***Comments:*** H-MA-865-G48. Similar to W-MA-2310-002-G110. 18__. 1820s.

Rarity: —

$2 • W-MA-2310-002-G110c

Left: Panel of lathework circle segments. ***Right:*** Panel of lathework circle segments. ***Engraver:*** PSSP. ***Comments:*** H-MA-865-G50. Similar to W-MA-2310-002-G110. 18__. 1820s–1830s.

Rarity: —

$2 • W-MA-2310-002-G110d

Left: Five TWOs vertically. ***Right:*** Five TWOs vertically. ***Engraver:*** PSSP. ***Comments:*** H-MA-865-G52. Similar to W-MA-2310-002-G110. 18__. 1830s.

Rarity: —

$2 • W-MA-2310-002-G120

Engraver: Unverified, but likely New England Bank Note Co. ***Comments:*** H-MA-865-G54. No description available. 18__. 1830s–1840s.

Rarity: *None known*

$2 • W-MA-2310-002-G130

Left: Whaling scene / 2. ***Right:*** 2 / Ship under full sail. ***Engraver:*** New England Bank Note Co. ***Comments:*** H-MA-865-G58. 18__. 1840s.

Rarity: —

$2 • W-MA-2310-002-G130a

Overprint: Red TWO. ***Engraver:*** New England Bank Note Co. ***Comments:*** H-MA-865-G58a. Similar to W-MA-2310-002-G130. 18__. 1850s.

Rarity: —

$2 • W-MA-2310-002-G130b

Overprint: Red TWO. ***Engraver:*** New England Bank Note Co. / ABNCo. monogram. ***Comments:*** H-MA-865-G58b. Similar to W-MA-2310-002-G130 but with additional engraver imprint. 18__. 1850s–1860s.

Rarity: —

$3 • W-MA-2310-003-G140

Center: 3 / 3 / Black oval bearing white flower buds / 3 / 3. ***Engraver:*** Perkins. ***Comments:*** H-MA-865-G64. 18__. 1800s.

Rarity: —

$3 • W-MA-2310-003-G150

Center: 3 / 3 / Black oval bearing white flower buds / THREE / 3 / 3. ***Engraver:*** PSSP. ***Comments:*** H-MA-865-G66. 18__. 1807–1809.

Rarity: —

$3 • W-MA-2310-003-G160

Center: 3 / 3 / Oval of flower garlands and gridwork segments / 3 / 3. ***Engraver:*** PSSP. ***Comments:*** H-MA-865-G68. 18__. 1809–1820s.

Rarity: —

$3 • W-MA-2310-003-G160a

Left: Panel of lathework circle segments. ***Right:*** Panel of lathework circle segments. ***Engraver:*** PSSP. ***Comments:*** H-MA-865-G70. Similar to W-MA-2310-003-G160. 18__. 1820s.

Rarity: —

$3 • W-MA-2310-003-G160b

Left: Panel of lathework circle segments. ***Right:*** Panel of lathework circle segments. ***Comments:*** H-MA-865-G72. Similar to W-MA-2310-003-G160. 18__. 1820s–1830s.

Rarity: —

$3 • W-MA-2310-003-G160c

Left: Panel of lathework circle segments. ***Right:*** Panel of lathework circle segments. ***Engraver:*** PSSP. ***Comments:*** H-MA-865-G74. Similar to W-MA-2310-003-G160. 18__. 1830s.

Rarity: —

$3 • W-MA-2310-003-G170

Engraver: Unverified, but likely New England Bank Note Co. ***Comments:*** H-MA-865-G76. No description available. 18__. 1830s–1840s.

Rarity: *None known*

$3 • W-MA-2310-003-G180

Left: Ships at sea / 3. ***Right:*** 3 / Boy driving sheep intro stream, Man standing. ***Engraver:*** New England Bank Note Co. ***Comments:*** H-MA-865-G80. 18__. 1840s.

Rarity: —

$3 • W-MA-2310-003-G180a

Overprint: Red THREE. ***Engraver:*** New England Bank Note Co. ***Comments:*** H-MA-865-G80a. Similar to W-MA-2310-003-G180. 18__. 1850s.

Rarity: —

$3 • W-MA-2310-003-G180b

Overprint: Red THREE. ***Engraver:*** New England Bank Note Co. / ABNCo. monogram. ***Comments:*** H-MA-865-G80b. Similar to W-MA-2310-003-G180 but with additional engraver imprint. 18__. 1850s–1860s.

Rarity: —

$5 • W-MA-2310-005-G190

Left: Narrow panel bearing MASSACHUSETTS vertically. ***Center:*** 5 / 5 / Black circles bearing white lettering / 5 / 5. ***Engraver:*** Perkins. ***Comments:*** H-MA-865-G82. 18__. 1800s.

Rarity: —

$5 • W-MA-2310-005-G200

Left: Narrow panel bearing MASSACHUSETTS / 5 / 5. ***Center:*** Alternating flower garlands and gridwork segments. ***Right:*** 5 / 5. ***Engraver:*** Perkins. ***Comments:*** H-MA-865-G84. 18__. 1806 and 1807.

Rarity: —

$5 • W-MA-2310-005-G200a

Center: Rose-covered FIVE. ***Engraver:*** PSSP. ***Comments:*** H-MA-865-G86. Similar to W-MA-2310-005-G200. 18__. Circa 1808 and 1809.

Rarity: —

$5 • W-MA-2310-005-G200b

Left: Narrow panel bearing MASSACHUSETTS / 5 / State arms / 5. ***Engraver:*** PSSP. ***Comments:*** H-MA-865-G88. Similar to W-MA-2310-005-G200. 18__. 1809–1820s.

Rarity: —

$5 • W-MA-2310-005-G200c

Left: Lathework chain bearing MASSACHUSETTS vertically. ***Right:*** Panel of lathework circle segments. ***Engraver:*** PSSP. ***Comments:*** H-MA-865-G90. Similar to W-MA-2310-005-G200. 18__. 1820s.

Rarity: —

$5 • W-MA-2310-005-G200d

Left: Lathework chain bearing MASSACHUSETTS vertically. ***Right:*** Panel of lathework circle segments. ***Engraver:*** PSSP. ***Comments:*** H-MA-865-G92. Similar to W-MA-2310-005-G200. 18__. 1820s.

Rarity: —

$5 • W-MA-2310-005-G200e

Left: Lathework chain bearing MASSACHUSETTS vertically. ***Right:*** Panel of lathework circle segments. ***Engraver:*** PSSP. ***Comments:*** H-MA-865-G94. Similar to W-MA-2310-005-G200 but with zigzag ruled lines. 18__. 1820s–1830s.

Rarity: —

$5 • W-MA-2310-005-G200f

Left: Lathework chain bearing MASSACHUSETTS vertically. ***Right:*** Panel of lathework circle segments. ***Engraver:*** PSSP. ***Comments:*** H-MA-865-G96. Similar to W-MA-2310-005-G200 but with spiral lathework lines. 18__. 1830s.

Rarity: —

$5 • W-MA-2310-005-G210

Engraver: Unverified, but likely New England Bank Note Co. ***Comments:*** H-MA-865-G98. No description available. 18__. 1830s–1840s.

Rarity: *None known*

$5 • W-MA-2310-005-G220

CJF

Engraver: Rawdon, Wright, Hatch & Edson. ***Comments:*** H-MA-865-G102. Proof. 18__. 1850s.

Rarity: —

$10 • W-MA-2310-010-G230

Left: Narrow panel bearing MASSACHUSETTS vertically. ***Center:*** 10 / 10 / Black circles bearing white lettering. ***Engraver:*** Perkins. ***Comments:*** H-MA-865-G104. 18__. 1800s.

Rarity: —

$10 • W-MA-2310-010-G240

Left: Narrow panel bearing MASSACHUSETTS / 10 / 10 vertically. ***Center:*** Alternating flower garlands and gridwork segments. ***Right:*** 10 / 10 vertically. ***Engraver:*** Perkins. ***Comments:*** H-MA-865-G106. 18__. 1806 and 1807.

Rarity: —

$10 • W-MA-2310-010-G240a

Center: Rose-covered TEN. ***Engraver:*** Perkins. ***Comments:*** H-MA-865-G108. Similar to W-MA-2310-010-G240. 18__. Circa 1808 and 1809.

Rarity: —

$10 • W-MA-2310-010-G240b

Left: Narrow panel bearing MASSACHUSETTS / 10 / State arms / 10 vertically. ***Engraver:*** Perkins. ***Comments:*** H-MA-865-G110. Similar to W-MA-2310-010-G240. 18__. 1809–circa 1812.

Rarity: —

$10 • W-MA-2310-010-G240c

Left: Narrow panel bearing MASSACHUSETTS / 10 / State arms / 10 vertically. ***Center:*** Alternating flower garlands and gridwork segments / TEN. ***Engraver:*** Perkins. ***Comments:*** H-MA-865-G112. Similar to W-MA-2310-010-G240. 18__. Circa 1812–1820s.

Rarity: —

$10 • W-MA-2310-010-G240d

Left: Lathework chain bearing MASSACHUSETTS vertically. ***Right:*** Panel of lathework circle segments. ***Engraver:*** Perkins. ***Comments:*** H-MA-865-G114. Similar to W-MA-2310-010-G240. 18__. 1820s.

Rarity: —

$10 • W-MA-2310-010-G240e

Left: Lathework chain bearing MASSACHUSETTS vertically. ***Right:*** Panel of lathework circle segments. ***Engraver:*** Perkins. ***Comments:*** H-MA-865-G116. Similar to W-MA-2310-010-G240. 18__. 1820s.

Rarity: —

$10 • W-MA-2310-010-G240f

Left: Lathework chain bearing MASSACHUSETTS vertically. ***Right:*** Panel of lathework circle segments. ***Engraver:*** PSSP. ***Comments:*** H-MA-865-G118. Similar to W-MA-2310-010-G240. 18__. 1820s–1830s.

Rarity: —

$10 • W-MA-2310-010-G240g

Left: Lathework chain bearing MASSACHUSETTS vertically. ***Right:*** Panel of lathework circle segments. ***Engraver:*** PSSP. ***Comments:*** H-MA-865-G120. Similar to W-MA-2310-010-G240. 18__. 1830s.

Rarity: —

$10 • W-MA-2310-010-G250

Engraver: Unverified, but likely New England Bank Note Co. ***Comments:*** H-MA-865-G122. No description available. 18__. 1830s–1840s.

Rarity: *None known*

$10 • W-MA-2310-010-G260
Left: 10 / Mermaid and Triton / Steamship. ***Center:*** Eagle on shield / Ships. ***Bottom center:*** State arms. ***Right:*** 10 / Female portrait / TEN. ***Engraver:*** Rawdon, Wright, Hatch & Edson. ***Comments:*** H-MA-865-G126. 18__. 1850s.

Rarity: —

$20 • W-MA-2310-020-G270
Left: Narrow panel bearing MASSACHUSETTS / 20 / 20 vertically. ***Center:*** Alternating flower garlands and gridwork segments. ***Right:*** 20 / 20 vertically. ***Engraver:*** Perkins. ***Comments:*** H-MA-865-G128. 18__. 1806–1809.

Rarity: —

$20 • W-MA-2310-020-G280
Left: Panel bearing state arms / 20 / 20 vertically. ***Center:*** Alternating flower garlands and gridwork segments. ***Right:*** 20 / 20 vertically. ***Engraver:*** Perkins. ***Comments:*** H-MA-865-G130. 18__. 1810s–1820s.

Rarity: —

$20 • W-MA-2310-020-G280a
Left: Lathework chain bearing MASSACHUSETTS vertically. ***Engraver:*** PSSP. ***Comments:*** H-MA-865-G132. Similar to W-MA-2310-020-G280. 18__. 1820s–1830s.

Rarity: —

$20 • W-MA-2310-020-G290
Left: 20 / Cherub in sailboat / 20. ***Center:*** Medallion head / Neptune / Medallion head. ***Right:*** 20 / Woman. ***Engraver:*** Rawdon, Wright, Hatch & Edson. ***Comments:*** H-MA-865-G136. 18__. 1850s.

Rarity: —

$50 • W-MA-2310-050-G300
Left: Panel bearing state arms / 50 / 50 vertically. ***Center:*** Alternating flower garlands and gridwork segments. ***Right:*** 50 / 50 vertically. ***Engraver:*** Perkins. ***Comments:*** H-MA-865-G138. 18__. 1810s–1820s.

Rarity: —

$50 • W-MA-2310-050-G300a
Left: Lathework chain bearing MASSACHUSETTS vertically. ***Engraver:*** PSSP. ***Comments:*** H-MA-865-G140. Similar to W-MA-2310-050-G300. 18__. 1820s–1830s.

Rarity: —

$50 • W-MA-2310-050-G310
Left: 50 / Medallion head / 50. ***Center:*** Medallion head / Neptune and allegorical woman / Medallion head. ***Right:*** 50 / Female portrait / FIFTY. ***Engraver:*** Rawdon, Wright, Hatch & Edson. ***Comments:*** H-MA-865-G146. 18__. 1850s.

Rarity: —

$100 • W-MA-2310-100-G320
Left: Panel bearing state arms / 100 / 100 vertically. ***Center:*** Alternating flower garlands and gridwork segments. ***Right:*** 100 / 100 vertically. ***Engraver:*** Perkins. ***Comments:*** H-MA-865-G148. 18__. 1810s–1820s.

Rarity: —

$100 • W-MA-2310-100-G320a
Left: Lathework chain bearing MASSACHUSETTS vertically. ***Engraver:*** Perkins. ***Comments:*** H-MA-865-G150. Similar to W-MA-2310-100-G320. 18__. 1820s–1830s.

Rarity: —

$100 • W-MA-2310-100-G330
Left: 100 / Shipyard scene / 100. ***Center:*** C / Two women, Shipping / C. ***Right:*** 100 / Ships. ***Engraver:*** Rawdon, Wright, Hatch & Edson. ***Comments:*** H-MA-865-G156. 18__. 1850s.

Rarity: —

Non-Valid Issues

$2 • W-MA-2310-002-N010
Center: Woman seated. ***Bottom center:*** Anchor. ***Comments:*** H-MA-865-N5.

Rarity: —

$3 • W-MA-2310-003-N020
Left: Sailor. ***Center:*** Train. ***Comments:*** H-MA-865-N10.

Rarity: —

$5 • W-MA-2310-005-N030
CJF

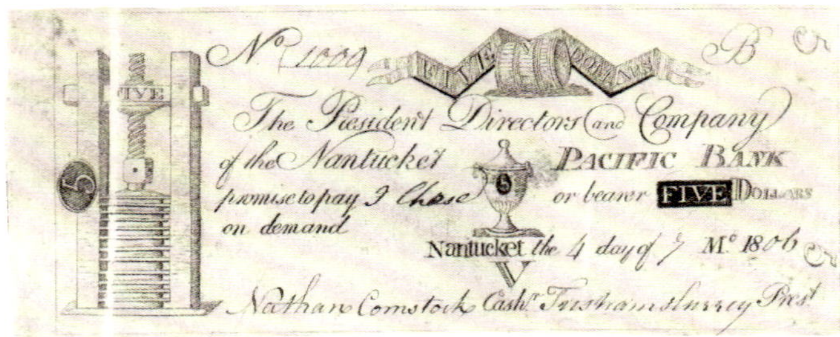

Comments: H-Unlisted. 18__. 1800s.

Rarity: —

$5 • W-MA-2310-005-A010
Left: Sailing ships at sea / 5. ***Center:*** Four women seated on globe. ***Right:*** 5 / Woman standing with 5. ***Engraver:*** New England Bank Note Co. ***Comments:*** H-MA-865-A5. Altered from $5 Globe Bank, Bangor, Maine. 18__. 1840s.

Rarity: —

F $635

$10 • W-MA-2310-010-A020
Left: Train passing cliffs, Men with wheelbarrow and picks / Benjamin Franklin reading. ***Center:*** Four women seated on globe. ***Right:*** 10 / 10. ***Engraver:*** New England Bank Note Co. ***Comments:*** H-MA-865-A10. Altered from $10 Globe Bank, Bangor, Maine. 18__. 1840s.

Rarity: —

Phoenix Bank
1812–1842
W-MA-2320

History: The Phoenix Bank was chartered on June 23, 1812, with an authorized capital of $100,000. In 1818 the capital of the bank was increased to $200,000, rising still further to $350,000 by 1832. On March 31, 1836, the Phoenix Bank was authorized to increase its capital stock by $150,000. The bank experienced difficulty during the Hard Times period. By 1842 its bills were worthless. On July 13, 1846, the bank building was destroyed by fire.

There was a bank of similar name but unrelated charter in Charlestown, W-MA-1330.

Numismatic Commentary: Most of the genuine issues collectors are likely to find are of the PSSP design. It is fortunate that a number of uncut sheets escaped destruction after the bank closed. These sheets, and examples cut from the same, have supplied collectors for decades.

VALID ISSUES

$1 • W-MA-2320-001-G010

CC

Engraver: PSSP. ***Comments:*** H-MA-870-G10. Remainder. 18__. 1810s.

Rarity: URS-7

VG $100; **VF** $200; **Unc-Rem** $150

$1 • W-MA-2320-001-G020

Left: ONE vertically. ***Center:*** 1 / Spread eagle / 1. ***Bottom center:*** I. ***Right:*** NANTUCKET vertically. ***Engraver:*** Murray, Draper, Fairman & Co. ***Comments:*** H-MA-870-G12. 181_. 1810s.

Rarity: —

$1 • W-MA-2320-001-G020a

Engraver: Murray, Draper, Fairman & Co. ***Comments:*** H-MA-870-G12a. Similar to W-MA-2320-001-G020 but with different date. 182_. 1820s.

Rarity: —

$2 • W-MA-2320-002-G030

CJF

Engraver: PSSP. ***Comments:*** H-MA-870-G16. Remainder. 18__. 1810s.

Rarity: URS-7

VG $100; **VF** $225

$2 • W-MA-2320-002-G040

Left: TWO vertically. ***Center:*** 2 / Spread eagle / 2. ***Bottom center:*** II. ***Right:*** NANTUCKET vertically. ***Engraver:*** Murray, Draper, Fairman & Co. ***Comments:*** H-MA-870-G18. 181_. 1810s.

Rarity: —

$2 • W-MA-2320-002-G040a

Engraver: Murray, Draper, Fairman & Co. ***Comments:*** H-MA-870-G18a. Similar to W-MA-2320-002-G040 but with different date. 182_. 1820s.

Rarity: —

$3 • W-MA-2320-003-G050

CJF

Engraver: PSSP. ***Comments:*** H-MA-870-G20. Remainder. 18__. 1810s.

Rarity: URS-7

Unc-Rem $200

$3 • W-MA-2320-003-G060

Left: THREE vertically. ***Center:*** 3 / Spread eagle / 3. ***Bottom center:*** III. ***Right:*** NANTUCKET vertically. ***Engraver:*** Murray, Draper, Fairman & Co. ***Comments:*** H-MA-870-G22. 181_. 1810s.

Rarity: —

$3 • W-MA-2320-003-G060a

Engraver: Murray, Draper, Fairman & Co. ***Comments:*** H-MA-870-G22a. Similar to W-MA-2320-003-G060 but with different date. 182_. 1820s.

Rarity: —

$3 • W-MA-2320-003-G070

CC

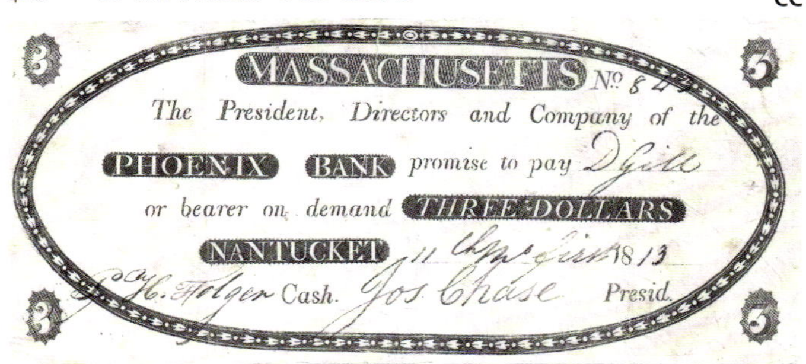

Comments: H-Unlisted. 18__. 1810s.

Rarity: URS-5

F $450

$5 • W-MA-2320-005-G080

Left: Panel bearing state arms / 5 / 5. ***Center:*** Alternating flower garlands and gridwork segments. ***Right:*** 5 / 5. ***Engraver:*** PSSP. ***Comments:*** H-MA-870-G26. 18__. 1810s.

Rarity: —

$5 • W-MA-2320-005-G090

Left: FIVE vertically. ***Center:*** 5 / Spread eagle / 5. ***Bottom center:*** V. ***Right:*** NANTUCKET vertically. ***Engraver:*** Murray, Draper, Fairman & Co. ***Comments:*** H-MA-870-G28. 181_. 1810s.

Rarity: —

$5 • W-MA-2320-005-G090a

Engraver: Murray, Draper, Fairman & Co. ***Comments:*** H-MA-870-G28a. Similar to W-MA-2320-005-G090 but with different date. 182_. 1820s.

Rarity: —

$10 • **W-MA-2320-010-G100**

Left: Panel bearing state arms / 10 / 10 vertically. ***Center:*** Alternating flower garlands and gridwork segments / TEN. ***Right:*** 10 / 10 vertically. ***Engraver:*** Perkins. ***Comments:*** H-MA-870-G36. 18__. 1810s.

Rarity: —

$10 • **W-MA-2320-010-G110**

Left: TEN vertically. ***Center:*** 10 / Spread eagle / 10. ***Bottom center:*** X. ***Right:*** NANTUCKET vertically. ***Engraver:*** Murray, Draper, Fairman & Co. ***Comments:*** H-MA-870-G38. 181_. 1810s.

Rarity: —

$10 • **W-MA-2320-010-G110a**

Engraver: Murray, Draper, Fairman & Co. ***Comments:*** H-MA-870-G38a. Similar to W-MA-2320-010-G110 but with different date. 182_. 1820s.

Rarity: —

$20 • **W-MA-2320-020-G120**

Left: Panel bearing state arms / 20 / 20 vertically. ***Center:*** Alternating flower garlands and gridwork segments. ***Right:*** 20 / 20 vertically. ***Engraver:*** Perkins. ***Comments:*** H-MA-870-G46. 18__. 1810s.

Rarity: —

$50 • **W-MA-2320-050-G130**

Left: Panel bearing state arms / 50 / 50 vertically. ***Center:*** Alternating flower garlands and gridwork segments. ***Right:*** 50 / 50 vertically. ***Engraver:*** Perkins. ***Comments:*** H-MA-870-G52. 18__. 1810s.

Rarity: —

$100 • **W-MA-2320-100-G140**

Left: Panel bearing state arms / 100 / 100 vertically. ***Center:*** Alternating flower garlands and gridwork segments. ***Right:*** 100 / 100 vertically. ***Engraver:*** Perkins. ***Comments:*** H-MA-870-G58. 18__. 1810s.

Rarity: —

Uncut Sheets

$1-$1-$2-$3 • **W-MA-2320-001.001.002.003-US010** CJF

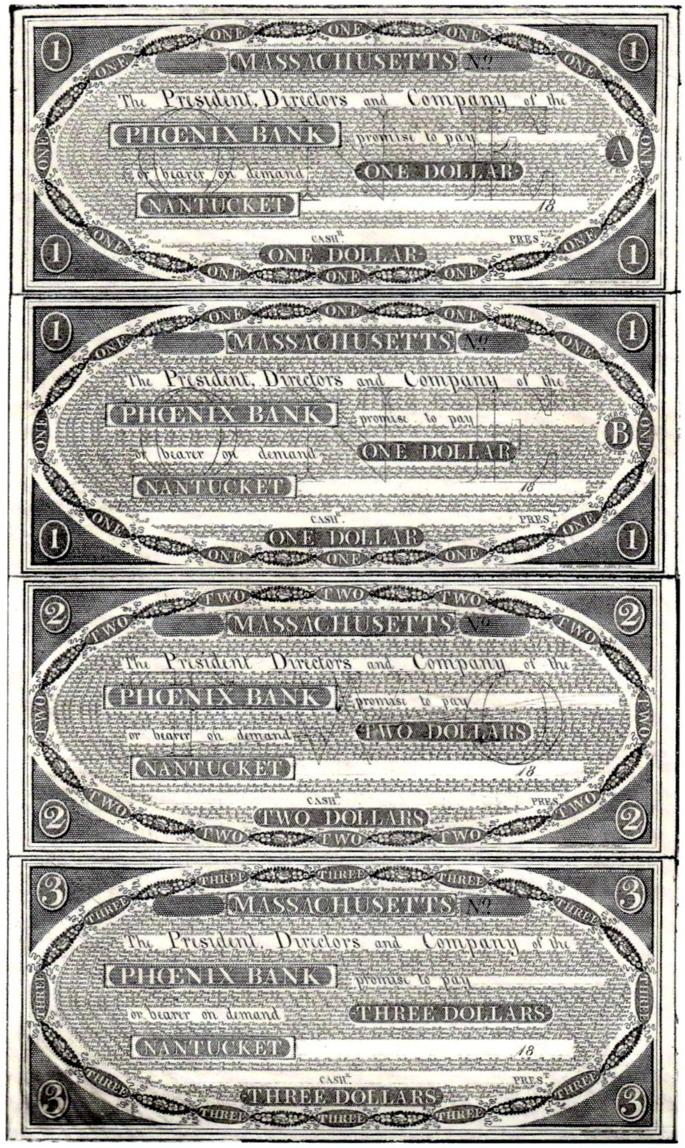

Engraver: PSSP. ***Comments:*** H-MA-870-G10, G10, G16, G20. 18__. 1810s.

Rarity: —

How to Read the Whitman Numbering System

$1 • **W-MA-010-001-G010a**

Denomination: Value of the note shown.

W: Whitman number. This number is a sortable code unique to each bank and note.

MA: Abbreviation for the state under study.

010: Numerical designation specific to each bank.

001: The denomination in dollars.

G010a: G indicates a good or valid note. Other categories are indicated thus: C (counterfeit); R (raised); S (spurious); N (not-attributed); A (altered). Numbers are assigned starting with 010, 020, et seq. Terminal letters following the number indicate variations of a note: a series of different colored overprints, tints, payees, etc., all on the same design of note. For more information, see the "How to Use This Book" section at the front of the volume, page xiv.

Non-Valid Issues

$1 • W-MA-2320-001-C010

Engraver: PSSP. ***Comments:*** H-MA-870-C10. Counterfeit of W-MA-2320-001-G010. 18__. 1813.

Rarity: —

$3 • W-MA-2320-003-C050

Engraver: PSSP. ***Comments:*** H-MA-870-C20. Counterfeit of W-MA-2320-003-G050. 18__. 1813.

Rarity: —

$3 • W-MA-2320-003-C060a

CJF

Engraver: Murray, Draper, Fairman & Co. ***Comments:*** H-MA-870-C22a. Counterfeit of W-MA-2320-003-G060a. 182_. 1820s.

Rarity: —

VG $595

New Bedford, Massachusetts

New Bedford was the town that became more important than Nantucket in the whaling industry. Plymouth Colony settlers bought the land from the chief of the Wampanoag tribe. Beginning in 1652, Europeans settled there. Coincidentally, this was also the year of the first New England silver coinage.

The first town in the district was Old Dartmouth, including the areas later known as Dartmouth, New Bedford, Acushnet, Fairhaven, and Westport. The area of Old Dartmouth near the Acushnet River was incorporated as the town of New Bedford in 1787, as the name "Bedford" was already taken. Fairhaven separated from New Bedford in 1812. It became the nation's best and largest whaling port, with a deep harbor and excellent location on the mainland.

Textiles including cotton goods also made up a large part of the New Bedford economy. As whaling declined with the advent of petroleum derivatives after the 1850s, the textile business boomed.

Bedford Bank

1803–1816

W-MA-2330

History: The Bedford Bank was incorporated on March 7, 1803, with an authorized capital of $60,000, soon increased to $150,000. The charter expired in 1812 and was replaced by a new corporation that lasted until 1816, after which the Legislature did not extend it. The bank was given three years to settle and close its concerns.

The principals reorganized under a new charter as the Bedford Commercial Bank, W-MA-2340.

Numismatic Commentary: One issue bears the motto "Peace to the World," seemingly more pertinent in today's world than the early 1800s. It is very hard to locate any note from this bank.

Valid Issues

$1 • W-MA-2330-001-G010

Comments: H-MA-875-G4. No description available. 1803.

Rarity: *None known*

$2 • W-MA-2330-002-G020

Comments: H-MA-875-G8. No description available. 1803.

Rarity: *None known*

$3 • W-MA-2330-003-G030

Comments: H-MA-875-G12. No description available. 1803.

Rarity: *None known*

$5 • W-MA-2330-005-G040

Comments: H-MA-875-G16. No description available. 1803.

Rarity: *None known*

$10 • W-MA-2330-010-G050

Left: Scrollwork panel. ***Center:*** Barrel bearing 10 / X / Banner bearing woman seated with olive branch / Globe and PEACE TO THE WORLD. ***Comments:*** H-MA-875-G20. 1803.

Rarity: —

$20 • W-MA-2330-020-G060

Comments: H-MA-875-G24. No description available. 1803.

Rarity: *None known*

Bedford Commercial Bank

1816–1864

W-MA-2340

History: The Bedford Commercial Bank was established by the principals of the former Bedford Bank, W-MA-2330. The new bank was incorporated on February 10, 1816, with the authorized capital of $100,000, to be paid in gold and silver coins—a provision that reflected monetary stress in America at the time and the scarcity of such coins in circulation. The capital was later increased and reached $600,000 in 1852. Circulation in 1839 was $80,582. In 1858 it reached a high of $215,635. Real estate of the bank was valued at $16,800. Specie amounted to $20,171.04.

The business of the Bedford Commercial Bank was succeeded by the National Bank of Commerce of New Bedford, chartered on January 9, 1865.

Numismatic Commentary: Collectors will find it relatively easy to obtain genuine issues from this bank. The bank used a number of engraving companies. Examples of certain issues from the 1820s through the 1860s can be found.

Valid Issues

$1 • W-MA-2340-001-G010

Left: Panel bearing 1 / ONE / 1 vertically. ***Center:*** 1 / Woman seated on shore / 1. ***Right:*** Panel bearing MASSACHUSETTS vertically. ***Engraver:*** Leney & Rollinson. ***Comments:*** H-MA-880-G2. 18__. 1810s–1820s.

Rarity: —

$1 • W-MA-2340-001-G020

QDB

Engraver: Draper, Toppan & Co. ***Comments:*** H-MA-880-G6. 18__. 1840s.

Rarity: —

$1 • W-MA-2340-001-G030

CJF

Engraver: Rawdon, Wright, Hatch & Edson / New England Bank Note Co. ***Comments:*** H-MA-880-G8. 18__. 1850s.

Rarity: URS-5

F $500

$1 • W-MA-2340-001-G030a

Left: ONE / Sailor hoisting U.S. flag. ***Center:*** Ships. ***Bottom center:*** ONE / Liberty / ONE. ***Right:*** 1. ***Overprint:*** Red 1 1. ***Engraver:*** Rawdon, Wright, Hatch & Edson / New England Bank Note Co. ***Comments:*** H-MA-880-G8a. Similar to W-MA-2340-001-G030. 18__. 1850s.

Rarity: —

$1 • W-MA-2340-001-G030b

CJF

Overprint: Red 1 1. ***Engraver:*** Rawdon, Wright, Hatch & Edson / New England Bank Note Co. / ABNCo. monogram. ***Comments:*** H-MA-880-G8b. Similar to W-MA-2340-001-G030 but with additional engraver imprint. 18__. 1850s–1860s.

Rarity: URS-5

F $500

$1 • W-MA-2340-001-G030c

CJF

Overprint: Green 1 1. ***Engraver:*** Rawdon, Wright, Hatch & Edson / New England Bank Note Co. / ABNCo. monogram. ***Comments:*** H-MA-880-G8c. Similar to W-MA-2340-001-G030 but with additional engraver imprint. 18__. 1860s.

Rarity: URS-5

F $500

$2 • W-MA-2340-002-G040

Left: 2 / TWO / 2 vertically. ***Center:*** 2 / Woman seated / 2. ***Bottom center:*** 2. ***Right:*** MASSACHUSETTS vertically. ***Engraver:*** Leney & Rollinson. ***Comments:*** H-MA-880-G10. 18__. 1810s–1820s.

Rarity: —

$2 • W-MA-2340-002-G050

CJF

Engraver: Draper, Toppan & Co. ***Comments:*** H-MA-880-G14. 18__. 1840s.

Rarity: URS-5

F $500

$2 • W-MA-2340-002-G060

Left: 2 / Woman with flowers. ***Center:*** Woman with spyglass seated by shield and sheaf, Ship / 2. ***Right:*** Ship under full sail / TWO. ***Engraver:*** Rawdon, Wright, Hatch & Edson / New England Bank Note Co. ***Comments:*** H-MA-880-G16. 18__. 1850s.

Rarity: —

$2 • W-MA-2340-002-G060a

Overprint: Red. ***Engraver:*** Rawdon, Wright, Hatch & Edson / New England Bank Note Co. ***Comments:*** H-MA-880-G16a. Similar to W-MA-2340-002-G060. 18__. 1850s.

Rarity: —

$2 • W-MA-2340-002-G060b

Overprint: Red. ***Engraver:*** Rawdon, Wright, Hatch & Edson / New England Bank Note Co. / ABNCo. monogram. ***Comments:*** H-MA-880-G16b. Similar to W-MA-2340-002-G060 but with additional engraver imprint. 18__. 1850s–1860s.

Rarity: —

$2 • W-MA-2340-002-G060c

Overprint: Green. ***Engraver:*** Rawdon, Wright, Hatch & Edson / New England Bank Note Co. / ABNCo. monogram. ***Comments:*** H-MA-880-G16c. Similar to W-MA-2340-002-G060 but with additional engraver imprint. 18__. 1860s.

Rarity: —

$3 • W-MA-2340-003-G070

Left: Panel bearing 3 / THREE / 3 vertically. ***Center:*** 3 / Woman seated on shore / 3. ***Right:*** Panel bearing MASSACHUSETTS vertically. ***Engraver:*** Leney & Rollinson. ***Comments:*** H-MA-880-G18. 18__. 1810s–1820s.

Rarity: —

$3 • W-MA-2340-003-G080

Left: THREE / Woman standing. ***Center:*** Spread eagle, THREE / THREE. ***Right:*** 3. ***Engraver:*** Rawdon, Wright, Hatch & Edson / New England Bank Note Co. ***Comments:*** H-MA-880-G22. 18__. 1850s.

Rarity: —

$3 • W-MA-2340-003-G080a

Overprint: Red THREE. ***Engraver:*** Rawdon, Wright, Hatch & Edson / New England Bank Note Co. ***Comments:*** H-MA-880-G22a. Similar to W-MA-2340-003-G080. 18__. 1850s.

Rarity: —

$3 • W-MA-2340-003-G080b

Overprint: Red 3 3. ***Engraver:*** Rawdon, Wright, Hatch & Edson / New England Bank Note Co. ***Comments:*** H-Unlisted. Similar to W-MA-2340-003-G080.

Rarity: —
VG $1,250

$3 • W-MA-2340-003-G080c

Overprint: Red THREE. ***Engraver:*** Rawdon, Wright, Hatch & Edson / New England Bank Note Co. / ABNCo. monogram. ***Comments:*** H-MA-880-G22b. Similar to W-MA-2340-003-G080 but with additional engraver imprint. 18__. 1850s–1860s.

Rarity: —

$3 • W-MA-2340-003-G080d

Overprint: Green THREE. ***Engraver:*** Rawdon, Wright, Hatch & Edson / New England Bank Note Co. / ABNCo. monogram. ***Comments:*** H-MA-880-G22c. Similar to W-MA-2340-003-G080 but with additional engraver imprint. 18__. 1860s.

Rarity: —

$5 • W-MA-2340-005-G090

QDB

Engraver: Leney & Rollinson. ***Comments:*** H-MA-880-G24. Proof. 18__. 1810s–1820s.

Rarity: URS-2
Proof $3,000

$5 • W-MA-2340-005-G090a

Left: V / FIVE / V vertically. ***Center:*** 5 / Woman seated next to parcels, Ship / V. ***Bottom center:*** V. ***Right:*** MASSACHUSETTS vertically. ***Overprint:*** Red 5 / 5. ***Engraver:*** Leney & Rollinson. ***Comments:*** H-MA-880-G24a. Similar to W-MA-2340-005-G090. 18__. 1820s.

Rarity: —

$5 • W-MA-2340-005-G100

Left: 5 / Man seated under tree / FIVE. ***Center:*** 5 / Perched eagle / 5 / FIVE. ***Right:*** FIVE vertically. ***Engraver:*** Draper, Toppan & Co. ***Comments:*** H-MA-880-G26. 18__. 1840s–1850s.

Rarity: —

$5 • W-MA-2340-005-G100a

Overprint: Red FIVE / FIVE. ***Engraver:*** Draper, Toppan & Co. ***Comments:*** H-MA-880-G26a. Similar to W-MA-2340-005-G100. 18__. 1850s.

Rarity: —

$5 • W-MA-2340-005-G100b

Overprint: Red FIVE / FIVE. ***Engraver:*** Draper, Toppan & Co. / ABNCo. monogram. ***Comments:*** H-MA-880-G26c. Similar to W-MA-2340-005-G100 but with additional engraver imprint. 18__. 1860s.

Rarity: —
F $1,150

$10 • W-MA-2340-010-G110

CC

Engraver: Leney & Rollinson. ***Comments:*** H-MA-880-G28. 18__. 1810s–1820s.

Rarity: URS-3
Proof $1,000

$10 • W-MA-2340-010-G120

CJF

Engraver: Draper, Toppan & Co. ***Comments:*** H-MA-880-G32. 18__. 1840s.

Rarity: URS-6
F $250

$10 • W-MA-2340-010-G120a

CJF

Overprint: Red TEN. ***Engraver:*** Draper, Toppan & Co. ***Comments:*** H-MA-880-G32a. Similar to W-MA-2340-010-G120. 18__. 1850s–1860s.

Rarity: URS-5
F $300

$10 • W-MA-2340-010-G120b

CJF

Overprint: Green TEN. ***Engraver:*** Draper, Toppan & Co. / ABNCo. monogram. ***Comments:*** H-MA-880-G32c. Similar to W-MA-2340-010-G120 but with additional engraver imprint. 18__. 1860s.

Rarity: URS-5
F $300

$20 • W-MA-2340-020-G130

CC

Engraver: Leney & Rollinson. ***Comments:*** H-MA-880-G34. Proof. Plate note. 18__. 1810s–1820s.

Rarity: URS-3
Proof $1,200

$20 • W-MA-2340-020-G140

JF

Engraver: Draper, Toppan & Co. ***Comments:*** H-MA-880-G38. 18__. 1840s.

Rarity: —

$20 • W-MA-2340-020-G150

Left: Cherub / 20. ***Center:*** Sailing ship and steamship. ***Bottom center:*** Wheels. ***Right:*** 20. ***Engraver:*** Rawdon, Wright, Hatch & Edson / New England Bank Note Co. ***Comments:*** H-MA-880-G40. 18__. 1850s–1860s.

Rarity: —

$30 • W-MA-2340-030-G160

Left: THIRTY vertically. ***Center:*** 30 / Woman seated with parcels, Ship / 30. ***Right:*** MASSACHUSETTS. ***Engraver:*** Leney & Rollinson. ***Comments:*** H-MA-880-G42. 18__. 1810s–1820s.

Rarity: —

$50 • W-MA-2340-050-G170

Left: Panel bearing L / FIFTY / L vertically. ***Center:*** 50 / Woman seated on shore / L. ***Bottom center:*** L. ***Right:*** Panel bearing MASSACHUSETTS vertically. ***Engraver:*** Leney & Rollinson. ***Comments:*** H-MA-880-G46. 18__. 1810s–1820s.

Rarity: —

$50 • W-MA-2340-050-G180

Left: FIFTY / Woman / FIFTY. ***Center:*** Woman, child, and merchandise on shore, Ship. ***Bottom center:*** Building. ***Right:*** 50. ***Comments:*** H-MA-880-G50. 18__. 1860s.

Rarity: URS-5
Proof $2,250

$100 • W-MA-2340-100-G190

Left: Panel bearing C / HUNDRED / C vertically. ***Center:*** 100 / Woman seated on shore / C. ***Bottom center:*** C. ***Right:*** Panel bearing MASSACHUSETTS vertically. ***Engraver:*** Leney & Rollinson. ***Comments:*** H-MA-880-G54. 18__. 1810s–1820s.

Rarity: —

$100 • W-MA-2340-100-G200

Engraver: Unverified, but likely New England Bank Note Co. ***Comments:*** H-MA-880-G58. No description available. 18__. 1840s.

Rarity: *None known*

$100 • W-MA-2340-100-G210

Left: 100 / Steamship. ***Center:*** Ships, City. ***Bottom center:*** Justice. ***Right:*** 100. ***Comments:*** H-MA-880-G62. 18__. 1860s.

Rarity: —

$500 • W-MA-2340-500-G220

Engraver: Unverified, but likely New England Bank Note Co. ***Comments:*** H-MA-880-G66. No description available. 18__. 1840s.

Rarity: *None known*

$500 • W-MA-2340-500-G230

Left: Indian paddling canoe, Forest and mountains / 500 / D. ***Right:*** 500 / Justice. ***Engraver:*** New England Bank Note Co. ***Comments:*** H-MA-880-G70. 18__. 1840s–1860s.

Rarity: —

Non-Valid Issues

$1 • W-MA-2340-001-C010

Engraver: Leney & Rollinson. ***Comments:*** H-MA-880-C2. Counterfeit of W-MA-2340-001-G010. 18__. 1810s–1820s.

Rarity: URS-4
F $750

$2 • W-MA-2340-002-C040

HA

Engraver: Leney & Rollinson. ***Comments:*** H-MA-880-C10. Counterfeit of W-MA-2340-002-G040. 18__. 1820s.

Rarity: —
F $105

$2 • W-MA-2340-002-C060

Engraver: Rawdon, Wright, Hatch & Edson / New England Bank Note Co. ***Comments:*** H-MA-880-C16. Counterfeit of W-MA-2340-002-G060 or variety. 18__. 1850s–1860s.

Rarity: —

$3 • W-MA-2340-003-C070

Engraver: Leney & Rollinson. ***Comments:*** H-MA-880-C18. Counterfeit of W-MA-2340-003-G070. 18__. 1810s–1820s.

Rarity: —

$5 • W-MA-2340-005-C090a

PEM

Overprint: Grey 5 / 5. ***Engraver:*** Leney & Rollinson. ***Comments:*** H-MA-880-C24a. Counterfeit of W-MA-2340-005-G090a. 18__. 1820s.

Rarity: —

$10 • W-MA-2340-010-C110

CJF

Engraver: Leney & Rollinson. ***Comments:*** H-MA-880-C28. Counterfeit of W-MA-2340-010-G110. 18__. 1820s.

Rarity: —

$20 • W-MA-2340-020-C140

Comments: H-MA-880-C38. Counterfeit of W-MA-2340-020-G140. 18__. 1850s.

Rarity: —

$50 • W-MA-2340-050-C180

Comments: H-MA-880-C50. Counterfeit of W-MA-2340-050-G180. 18__. 1850s–1860s.

Rarity: —

Marine Bank

1832–1863

W-MA-2350

History: The Marine Bank was incorporated on March 3, 1832, with an authorized capital of $250,000, a figure which later was increased to $300,000 in 1833. Circulation in 1839 was $55,056, but it reached a high of $287,296 in 1863.

The Marine Bank was succeeded by the Marine National Bank of New Bedford in 1864.

Numismatic Commentary: It is possible, over a period of time, to obtain a few different denominations from this bank. Great patience will be an asset to collectors attempting to do so.

Valid Issues

$1 • W-MA-2350-001-G010

SBG

Engraver: PSSP. ***Comments:*** H-MA-885-G2. 18__. 1830s.

Rarity: URS-4
F $850

$1 • W-MA-2350-001-G020

Engraver: Unverified, but likely New England Bank Note Co. ***Comments:*** H-MA-885-G4. No description available. 18__. 1830s–1840s.

Rarity: *None known*

$1 • W-MA-2350-001-G030

CJF

Engraver: New England Bank Note Co. ***Comments:*** H-MA-885-G8. 18__. 1850s.

Rarity: —

$1 • W-MA-2350-001-G030a

Left: Ships / 1. ***Center:*** 1 / ONE. ***Right:*** 1 / Female portrait. ***Overprint:*** Red ONE. ***Engraver:*** New England Bank Note Co. ***Comments:*** H-MA-885-G8a. Similar to W-MA-2350-001-G030.

Rarity: —

$1 • W-MA-2350-001-G030b

Overprint: Red ONE. ***Engraver:*** New England Bank Note Co. / ABNCo. monogram. ***Comments:*** H-MA-885-G8b. Similar to W-MA-2350-001-G030 but with different date and additional engraver imprint.

Rarity: —

$2 • W-MA-2350-002-G040

Left: Lathework panel bearing MASSACHUSETTS vertically. ***Center:*** 2 / 2 / Alternating flower garlands and gridwork segments / TWO / 2 / 2. ***Right:*** Lathework panel bearing five TWOs vertically. ***Engraver:*** PSSP. ***Comments:*** H-MA-885-G10. 18__. 1830s.

Rarity: —

$2 • W-MA-2350-002-G050

Engraver: Unverified, but likely New England Bank Note Co. ***Comments:*** H-MA-885-G12. No description available. 18__. 1830s–1840s.

Rarity: *None known*

$2 • W-MA-2350-002-G060

Left: Ships at sea / 2. ***Center:*** 2. ***Right:*** 2 / Whaling scene. ***Engraver:*** New England Bank Note Co. ***Comments:*** H-MA-885-G16. 18__. 1840s–1850s.

Rarity: —

$2 • W-MA-2350-002-G060a

Overprint: Red TWO. ***Engraver:*** New England Bank Note Co. ***Comments:*** H-MA-885-G16a. Similar to W-MA-2350-002-G060. 18__. 1850s.

Rarity: —

$2 • W-MA-2350-002-G060b

CJF

Overprint: Red TWO. ***Engraver:*** New England Bank Note Co. / ABNCo. monogram. ***Comments:*** H-MA-885-G16b. Similar to W-MA-2350-002-G060 but with different date and additional engraver imprint. January __, 186_. 1860s.

Rarity: URS-5
VF $600

$3 • W-MA-2350-003-G070

Left: Lathework panel bearing MASSACHUSETTS vertically. ***Center:*** 3 / 3 / Alternating flower garlands and gridwork segments / THREE / 3 / 3. ***Right:*** Lathework panel bearing THREE vertically. ***Engraver:*** PSSP. ***Comments:*** H-MA-885-G18. 18__. 1830s.

Rarity: —

$3 • W-MA-2350-003-G080

Left: Steamship, Ships / THREE vertically. ***Center:*** 3. ***Right:*** 3 / Girl. ***Engraver:*** New England Bank Note Co. ***Comments:*** H-MA-885-G24. 18__. 1840s–1850s.

Rarity: —

$3 • W-MA-2350-003-G080a

Overprint: Red. ***Engraver:*** New England Bank Note Co. ***Comments:*** H-MA-885-G24a. Similar to W-MA-2350-003-G080. 18__. 1850s.

Rarity: —

$3 • W-MA-2350-003-G080b

Engraver: New England Bank Note Co. / ABNCo. monogram. ***Comments:*** H-MA-885-G24b. Similar to W-MA-2350-003-G080 but with different date and additional engraver imprint. Jan. __, 1860.

Rarity: —

$5 • W-MA-2350-005-G090

Left: Lathework chain bearing MASSACHUSETTS / 5 / 5. ***Center:*** Alternating flower garlands and gridwork segments / FIVE. ***Right:*** 5 / 5. ***Engraver:*** PSSP. ***Comments:*** H-MA-885-G26. 18__. 1830s.

Rarity: —

$5 • W-MA-2350-005-G100

Engraver: Unverified, but likely New England Bank Note Co. ***Comments:*** H-MA-885-G28. No description available. 18__. 1830s–1840s.

Rarity: *None known*

$5 • W-MA-2350-005-G110

Center: V / Eagle on wharf with plow, Cannon and anchor, Ships / V / Panel outlining white FIVE. ***Engraver:*** New England Bank Note Co. ***Comments:*** H-MA-885-G32. 18__. 1840s.

Rarity: —

$5 • W-MA-2350-005-G120

Left: Wharf scene, Steamboat, Row boats and other ships / 5. ***Center:*** V. ***Right:*** 5 / Sailor standing with anchor / FIVE. ***Engraver:*** New England Bank Note Co. ***Comments:*** H-MA-885-G34. 18__. 1840s–1850s.

Rarity: —

$5 • W-MA-2350-005-G120a

Overprint: Red. ***Engraver:*** New England Bank Note Co. ***Comments:*** H-MA-885-G34a. Similar to W-MA-2350-005-G120. 18__. 1850s.

Rarity: —

$5 • W-MA-2350-005-G120b

Overprint: Red. ***Engraver:*** New England Bank Note Co. / ABNCo. monogram. ***Comments:*** H-MA-885-G34b. Similar to W-MA-2350-005-G120 but with different date and additional engraver imprint. Jan. __, 1860.

Rarity: —

$10 • W-MA-2350-010-G130

Left: Lathework chain bearing MASSACHUSETTS / 10 / 10 vertically. ***Center:*** Alternating flower garlands and gridwork segments / TEN. ***Right:*** 10 / 10 vertically. ***Engraver:*** PSSP. ***Comments:*** H-MA-885-G36. 18__. 1830s.

Rarity: —

$10 • W-MA-2350-010-G140

Engraver: Unverified, but likely New England Bank Note Co. ***Comments:*** H-MA-885-G38. No description available. 18__. 1830s–1840s.

Rarity: *None known*

$10 • W-MA-2350-010-G150

Left: X / Indian kneeling after shooting arrow. ***Center:*** Steamboat, Schooner and boats, City / X / Panel outlining white TEN. ***Right:*** 10 / Woman with bonnet and sheaf. ***Engraver:*** New England Bank Note Co. ***Comments:*** H-MA-885-G42. 18__. 1840s.

Rarity: —

$10 • W-MA-2350-010-G160

Left: Cherub and woman flanking state arms, Train and shipping / 10. ***Center:*** X. ***Right:*** 10 / Woman seated with barrel. ***Engraver:*** New England Bank Note Co. ***Comments:*** H-MA-885-G44. 18__. 1840s–1850s.

Rarity: —

$10 • W-MA-2350-010-G160a

Overprint: Red. ***Engraver:*** New England Bank Note Co. ***Comments:*** H-MA-885-G44a. Similar to W-MA-2350-010-G160. 18__. 1850s.

Rarity: —

$10 • W-MA-2350-010-G160b

Engraver: New England Bank Note Co. / ABNCo. monogram. ***Comments:*** H-MA-885-G44b. Similar to W-MA-2350-010-G160 but with different date and additional engraver imprint. Jan. __, 1860.

Rarity: —

$20 • W-MA-2350-020-G170

Left: Lathework chain bearing MASSACHUSETTS / 20 / 20 vertically. ***Center:*** Alternating flower garlands and gridwork segments / TWENTY. ***Right:*** 20 / 20 vertically. ***Engraver:*** PSSP. ***Comments:*** H-MA-885-G46. 18__. 1830s.

Rarity: —

$20 • W-MA-2350-020-G180

Engraver: Unverified, but likely New England Bank Note Co. ***Comments:*** H-MA-885-G48. No description available. 18__. 1830s–1840s.

Rarity: *None known*

$20 • W-MA-2350-020-G190

Left: Woman, canal, and train / 20. ***Center:*** 20. ***Right:*** XX / Portrait of Christopher Columbus. ***Engraver:*** New England Bank Note Co. ***Comments:*** H-MA-885-G52. 18__. 1840s–1850s.

Rarity: —

$20 • W-MA-2350-020-G190a

Overprint: Red. ***Engraver:*** New England Bank Note Co. ***Comments:*** H-MA-885-G52a. Similar to W-MA-2350-020-G190. 18__. 1850s.

Rarity: —

$50 • W-MA-2350-050-G200

Left: Lathework chain bearing MASSACHUSETTS / 50 / 50 vertically. ***Center:*** Alternating flower garlands and gridwork segments / FIFTY. ***Right:*** 50 / 50 vertically. ***Engraver:*** PSSP. ***Comments:*** H-MA-885-G54. 18__. 1830s.

Rarity: —

$50 • W-MA-2350-050-G210

Engraver: Unverified, but likely New England Bank Note Co. ***Comments:*** H-MA-885-G56. No description available. 18__. 1830s–1840s.

Rarity: *None known*

$50 • W-MA-2350-050-G220

Left: Eagle on limb, Train and canal / FIFTY across 50. ***Center:*** 50. ***Right:*** 50 / Ship at sea. ***Engraver:*** New England Bank Note Co. ***Comments:*** H-MA-885-G58. 18__. 1840s–1850s.

Rarity: —

$50 • W-MA-2350-050-G220a

Overprint: Red. ***Engraver:*** New England Bank Note Co. ***Comments:*** H-MA-885-G58a. Similar to W-MA-2350-050-G220. 18__. 1850s.

Rarity: —

$100 • W-MA-2350-100-G230

Left: Lathework chain bearing MASSACHUSETTS / 100 / 100 vertically. ***Center:*** Alternating flower garlands and gridwork segments / 100. ***Right:*** 100 / 100 vertically. ***Engraver:*** PSSP. ***Comments:*** H-MA-885-G60. 18__. 1830s.

Rarity: —

$100 • W-MA-2350-100-G240

Engraver: Unverified, but likely New England Bank Note Co. ***Comments:*** H-MA-885-G62. No description available. 18__. 1830s–1840s.

Rarity: *None known*

$100 • W-MA-2350-100-G250

Left: 100 / Portrait of George Washington. ***Center:*** Ship and steamship. ***Right:*** 100 / Woman seated in C. ***Engraver:*** New England Bank Note Co. ***Comments:*** H-MA-885-G64. 18__. 1840s–1850s.

Rarity: —

$100 • W-MA-2350-100-G250a

Overprint: Red. ***Engraver:*** New England Bank Note Co. ***Comments:*** H-MA-885-G64a. Similar to W-MA-2350-100-G250. 18__. 1850s.

Rarity: —

$500 • W-MA-2350-500-G260

Engraver: Unverified, but likely New England Bank Note Co. ***Comments:*** H-MA-885-G66. No description available. 18__. 1830s–1840s.

Rarity: *None known*

$500 • W-MA-2350-500-G270

Left: Woman seated on sheaves, Men reaping, Man on horse / D D. ***Center:*** 500 / D. ***Right:*** 500 vertically. ***Engraver:*** Rawdon, Wright, Hatch & Edson. ***Comments:*** H-MA-885-G68. 18__. 1850s.

Rarity: —

$500 • W-MA-2350-500-G280

Left: Shipping scene / 500. ***Center:*** D. ***Right:*** 500 / Sailor standing at helm. ***Engraver:*** American Bank Note Co. ***Comments:*** H-MA-885-G70. 18__. 1860s.

Rarity: —

Non-Valid Issues

$3 • W-MA-2350-003-S010

CJF

Overprint: Red. ***Engraver:*** New England Bank Note Co. ***Comments:*** H-Unlisted. Jan. 1, 1856.

Rarity: URS-4
VF $750

$3 • W-MA-2350-003-S010a

Left: THREE / 3. ***Center:*** Ships in harbor / 3. ***Right:*** Woman standing / THREE. ***Overprint:*** Red. ***Engraver:*** New England Bank Note Co. / ABNCo. monogram. ***Comments:*** H-MA-885-S5. Similar to W-MA-2350-003-S010 but with additional engraver imprint. Jan. 1, 1856.

Rarity: —

$3 • W-MA-2350-003-N010

Left: Two women. ***Center:*** Three sailing ships. ***Comments:*** H-MA-885-N5.

Rarity: —

$5 • W-MA-2350-005-C110

Engraver: New England Bank Note Co. ***Comments:*** H-MA-885-C32. Counterfeit of W-MA-2350-005-G110. 18__. 1840s.

Rarity: —

$5 • W-MA-2350-005-N020

Center: Man plowing with two oxen. ***Comments:*** H-MA-885-N10.

Rarity: —

$10 • W-MA-2350-010-C160

Engraver: New England Bank Note Co. ***Comments:*** H-MA-885-C44. Counterfeit of W-MA-2350-010-G160 or G160a. 18__. 1850s.

Rarity: —

$10 • W-MA-2350-010-N030

Left: Ship. ***Center:*** Man seated. ***Right:*** Medallion head. ***Comments:*** H-MA-885-N15. 18__. 1840s.

Rarity: —

$10 • W-MA-2350-010-A010

Left: 10 / Farmer sowing / TEN. ***Center:*** Mercury seated with 10, Merchandise, factories, and ship / Canal scene. ***Right:*** 10 / Ship / TEN. ***Engraver:*** New England Bank Note Co. ***Comments:*** H-MA-885-A5. Altered from $10 Washington County Bank, Calais, Maine, or from notes of other failed banks using the same plate. 18__. Circa 1840.

Rarity: —

$20 • W-MA-2350-020-A020

CJF

Engraver: Durand & Co. ***Comments:*** H-MA-885-A10. Altered from $20 Globe Bank, New York City, New York. 18__. 1840s.

Rarity: URS-6
F $300

Mechanics Bank

1831–1864

W-MA-2360

History: The Mechanics Bank was chartered on June 10, 1831, with an authorized capital of $200,000. In 1855 it was $400,000, and it increased to $600,000 in 1857. Circulation in 1839 was $41,236; it reached $261,649 in 1863. Specie amounted to $17,733.54 in 1857, and the bank's real estate was worth $9,000.

On January 23, 1865, the business of the Mechanics Bank was succeeded by the Mechanics National Bank of Bedford, which had a capital of $600,000, the same impressive amount that the state-charted institution had achieved.

Numismatic Commentary: It is not easy to locate genuine issues from this bank. Rare survivors with whaling vignettes are in special demand.

Valid Issues

$1 • W-MA-2360-001-G010

Left: Lathework panel bearing MASSACHUSETTS vertically. ***Center:*** 1 / 1 / Alternating flower garlands and gridwork segments / ONE / 1 / 1. ***Right:*** Lathework panel bearing ONE / D / ONE vertically. ***Engraver:*** PSSP. ***Comments:*** H-MA-890-G2. 18__. 1830s.

Rarity: —

$1 • W-MA-2360-001-G020

CC

Comments: H-MA-890-G4. 18__. 1830s–1840s.

Rarity: URS-6
VG $150; **F** $350

$1 • W-MA-2360-001-G030
Left: 1. ***Center:*** Whaling scene / ONE. ***Right:*** 1. ***Engraver:*** Toppan, Carpenter & Co. ***Comments:*** H-MA-890-G6. 18__. 1850s.

Rarity: —

$1 • W-MA-2360-001-G030a
Overprint: Green ONE. ***Engraver:*** Toppan, Carpenter & Co. ***Comments:*** H-MA-890-G6a. Similar to W-MA-2360-001-G030. 18__. 1850s–1860s.

Rarity: —

$1 • W-MA-2360-001-G030b
CJF

Overprint: Red ONE. ***Engraver:*** Toppan, Carpenter & Co. ***Comments:*** H-Unlisted. Similar to W-MA-2360-001-G030. 18__ 1860s.

Rarity: URS-6
F $350

$2 • W-MA-2360-002-G040
Left: Lathework panel bearing MASSACHUSETTS vertically. ***Center:*** 2 / 2 / Alternating flower garlands and gridwork segments / TWO / 2 / 2. ***Right:*** Lathework panel bearing five TWOs vertically. ***Engraver:*** PSSP. ***Comments:*** H-MA-890-G8. 18__. 1830s.

Rarity: —

$2 • W-MA-2360-002-G050
Comments: H-MA-890-G12. No description available. 18__. 1830s–1840s.

Rarity: *None known*

$2 • W-MA-2360-002-G060
Left: 2 / Mechanic seated. ***Center:*** Sailor seated on rudder holding spyglass and resting on bale. ***Bottom center:*** Train. ***Right:*** 2 / Dog and strongbox. ***Engraver:*** Toppan, Carpenter & Co. ***Comments:*** H-MA-890-G14. 18__. 1850s.

Rarity: —

$2 • W-MA-2360-002-G060a
Overprint: Green. ***Engraver:*** Toppan, Carpenter & Co. ***Comments:*** H-MA-890-G14a. Similar to W-MA-2360-002-G060. 18__. 1850s–1860s.

Rarity: —

$2 • W-MA-2360-002-G060b
CJF

Overprint: Red TWO. ***Engraver:*** Toppan, Carpenter & Co. ***Comments:*** H-Unlisted. Similar to W-MA-2360-002-G060. 18__. 1850s–1860s.

Rarity: URS-6
VF $500

$3 • W-MA-2360-003-G070
Left: Lathework panel bearing MASSACHUSETTS vertically. ***Center:*** 3 / 3 / Alternating flower garlands and gridwork segments / 3 / 3. ***Right:*** Lathework panel bearing THREE vertically. ***Engraver:*** PSSP. ***Comments:*** H-MA-890-G16. 18__. 1830s.

Rarity: —

$3 • W-MA-2360-003-G080
Left: 3 / Two children. ***Center:*** 3 / Three sailing ships / 3. ***Right:*** 3 / Sailor with hand on capstan holding sextant, Ships. ***Engraver:*** American Bank Note Co. ***Comments:*** H-MA-890-G20. 1860s.

Rarity: —

$5 • W-MA-2360-005-G090
Left: Lathework chain bearing MASSACHUSETTS / 5 / 5. ***Center:*** Alternating flower garlands and gridwork segments / FIVE lined by spiral lathework lines. ***Right:*** 5 / 5. ***Engraver:*** PSSP. ***Comments:*** H-MA-890-G22. 18__. 1830s.

Rarity: —

$5 • W-MA-2360-005-G100
Comments: H-MA-890-G26. No description available. 18__. 1830s–1840s.

Rarity: *None known*

$5 • W-MA-2360-005-G110
CJF

Engraver: Toppan, Carpenter & Co. ***Comments:*** H-MA-890-G30. 18__. 1850s.

Rarity: URS-5
F $400

$5 • W-MA-2360-005-G110a
Left: 5. ***Center:*** Whaling scene / Three female portraits. ***Right:*** 5. ***Overprint:*** Green. ***Engraver:*** Toppan, Carpenter & Co. ***Comments:*** H-MA-890-G30a. Similar to W-MA-2360-005-G110. 18__. 1850s–1860s.

Rarity: —

$10 • W-MA-2360-010-G120
Left: Lathework chain bearing MASSACHUSETTS / 10 / 10 vertically. ***Center:*** Alternating flower garlands and gridwork segments / TEN lined by spiral lathework lines. ***Right:*** 10 / 10 vertically. ***Engraver:*** PSSP. ***Comments:*** H-MA-890-G32. 18__. 1830s.

Rarity: —

$10 • W-MA-2360-010-G130
Comments: H-MA-890-G34. No description available. 18__. 1830s–1840s.

Rarity: *None known*

$10 • W-MA-2360-010-G140

CJF

Engraver: Toppan, Carpenter & Co. ***Comments:*** H-MA-890-G36. 18__. 1850s.

Rarity: URS-6
VF $400

$10 • W-MA-2360-010-G140a

Left: 10 / Blacksmith at work. ***Center:*** Train at depot in city. ***Bottom center:*** Ships. ***Right:*** 10 / Sailor with spyglass. ***Overprint:*** Green. ***Engraver:*** Toppan, Carpenter & Co. ***Comments:*** H-MA-890-G36a. Similar to W-MA-2360-010-G140. 18__. 1850s–1860s.

Rarity: —

$20 • W-MA-2360-020-G150

Left: Lathework chain bearing MASSACHUSETTS / 20 / 20 vertically. ***Center:*** Alternating flower garlands and gridwork segments / XX. ***Right:*** 20 / 20 vertically. ***Engraver:*** PSSP. ***Comments:*** H-MA-890-G38. 18__. 1830s.

Rarity: —

$20 • W-MA-2360-020-G160

Comments: H-MA-890-G40. No description available. 18__. 1830s.

Rarity: *None known*

$20 • W-MA-2360-020-G170

Left: 20 / Medallion head / 20. ***Center:*** 20 / Child, Dog and strongbox. ***Bottom center:*** Ships. ***Right:*** 20. ***Engraver:*** Draper, Toppan & Co. ***Comments:*** H-MA-890-G44. 18__. 1840s–1850s.

Rarity: —

$50 • W-MA-2360-050-G180

Left: Lathework chain bearing MASSACHUSETTS / 50 / 50 vertically. ***Center:*** Alternating flower garlands and gridwork segments / FIFTY. ***Right:*** 50 / 50 vertically. ***Engraver:*** PSSP. ***Comments:*** H-MA-890-G46. 18__. 1830s.

Rarity: —

$50 • W-MA-2360-050-G190

Comments: H-MA-890-G48. No description available. 18__. 1830s.

Rarity: *None known*

$50 • W-MA-2360-050-G200

Left: 50 / Medallion head / 50. ***Center:*** 50 / View of New Bedford City Hall. ***Bottom center:*** Portrait. ***Right:*** 50. ***Engraver:*** Draper, Toppan & Co. ***Comments:*** H-MA-890-G52. 18__. 1840s–1850s.

Rarity: —

$100 • W-MA-2360-100-G210

Left: Lathework chain bearing MASSACHUSETTS / 100 / 100 vertically. ***Center:*** Alternating flower garlands and gridwork segments / 100. ***Right:*** 100 / 100 vertically. ***Engraver:*** Perkins. ***Comments:*** H-MA-890-G54. 18__. 1830s.

Rarity: —

$500 • W-MA-2360-500-G220

Left: Indian paddling canoe, Forest and mountains / 500 / D D / 500. ***Right:*** 500 / Justice. ***Engraver:*** New England Bank Note Co. ***Comments:*** H-MA-890-G58. 18__. 1840s–1850s.

Rarity: —

Non-Valid Issues

$1 • W-MA-2360-001-A010

Left: ONE / Hebe seated on sheaf watering eagle / ONE. ***Center:*** Eagle on shield / Ships. ***Right:*** 1 / Ceres kneeling with sheaf, Farm. ***Engraver:*** Danforth, Bald & Co. ***Comments:*** H-MA-890-A5. Altered from $1 Columbia Bank, Washington, D.C. 18__. 1830s.

Rarity: —

$1 • W-MA-2360-001-A020

Left: Panel bearing portrait of Zachary Taylor. ***Center:*** 1 / Woman in clouds holding shield, Eagle / 1 / ONE. ***Right:*** Panel bearing Ceres. ***Engraver:*** W.L. Ormsby. ***Comments:*** H-MA-890-A10. Altered from $1 Mechanics and Traders Bank, Georgetown, D.C. Nov. 14, 1852.

Rarity: —

$1 • W-MA-2360-001-A030

Left: Woman leaning on 1. ***Center:*** 1 / Cow in field. ***Right:*** Indian man standing / 1. ***Engraver:*** Doty & Bergen. ***Comments:*** H-MA-890-A15. Altered from $1 Merchants Bank, Stillwater, Minnesota. October 20, 1854.

Rarity: —

$2 • W-MA-2360-002-A040

Left: 2 / Portrait of George Washington / TWO. ***Center:*** Woman seated with scroll, U.S. shield, globe, and sheaves. ***Right:*** TWO / Mercury in clouds with caduceus and cornucopia of coins. ***Overprint:*** Red TWO. ***Engraver:*** Wellstood, Hanks, Hay & Whiting. ***Comments:*** H-MA-890-A20. Altered from $2 Mechanics Bank (2nd), Georgetown, D.C. 18__. 1850s.

Rarity: —

$5 • W-MA-2360-005-C110

Engraver: Toppan, Carpenter & Co. ***Comments:*** H-MA-890-C30. Counterfeit of W-MA-2360-005-G110 or G110a. 18__. 1850s.

Rarity: —

$5 • W-MA-2360-005-A050

Left: FIVE vertically. ***Center:*** 5 / Farmer plowing with two horses. ***Bottom center:*** Steamboat. ***Right:*** Ceres and Vulcan flanking anvil, Mercury / V. ***Engraver:*** Rawdon, Wright & Hatch. ***Comments:*** H-MA-890-A25. Altered from $5 Mechanics Bank of St. John's, St. John's, Canada. 18__. 1830s.

Rarity: —

$5 • W-MA-2360-005-A060

Left: Indian man standing with rocks, holding bow / FIVE. ***Center:*** Eagle / Indian man standing on cliff, holding bow, watching train. ***Bottom center:*** Indian in canoe. ***Right:*** 5 / Man seated on anchor, Ship. ***Engraver:*** Doty & Bergen. ***Comments:*** H-MA-890-A30. Altered from $5 Merchants Bank, Mankato City, Minnesota. Sept. 1, 185_. 1850s.

Rarity: —

$10 • W-MA-2360-010-R010

Engraver: Toppan, Carpenter & Co. ***Comments:*** H-MA-890-R5. Raised from W-MA-2360-001-G030. 18__. 1850s.

Rarity: —

$10 • W-MA-2360-010-R020
Engraver: Toppan, Carpenter & Co. ***Comments:*** H-MA-890-R10. Raised from W-MA-2360-002-G060. 18__. 1850s.

Rarity: —

$10 • W-MA-2360-010-S010

NJW

Engraver: Rawdon, Wright, Hatch & Edson. ***Comments:*** H-MA-890-S10. Aug. 1, 1849.

Rarity: —

$10 • W-MA-2360-010-A070
Left: 10. ***Center:*** X. ***Right:*** 10 / Men working. ***Engraver:*** Danforth, Wright & Co. ***Comments:*** H-MA-890-A35. Altered from $10 Mechanics Bank of Memphis, Memphis, Tennessee series. 1850s.

Rarity: —

$20 • W-MA-2360-020-C170
Engraver: Draper, Toppan & Co. ***Comments:*** H-MA-890-C44. Counterfeit of W-MA-2360-020-G170. 18__. 1840s–1850s.

Rarity: —

Merchants Bank
1825–1865

W-MA-2370

History: The Merchants Bank was chartered on June 28, 1825, with an authorized capital of $150,000, a figure which increased to $250,000 in 1827. Capital rose to $400,000 in 1849 and increased further to $600,000 in 1855. Circulation was $75,178 in 1839, $137,951 in 1845, $122,610 in 1849, $228,851 in 1857, $389,552 in 1858, $228,851 in 1860, and $449,969 in 1863.

The business of the Merchants Bank was succeeded by the Merchants National Bank of New Bedford, chartered on February 14, 1865.

Numismatic Commentary: It will probably take some time to locate genuine examples from this bank. Non-valid issues are plentiful in the marketplace.

Valid Issues

$1 • W-MA-2370-001-G010
Left: Narrow panel of lathework circle segments. ***Center:*** 1 / 1 / Flower garlands and gridwork segments / 1 / 1. ***Right:*** Narrow panel of lathework circle segments. ***Engraver:*** PSSP. ***Comments:*** H-MA-895-G2. 18__. 1820s–1830s.

Rarity: —

$1 • W-MA-2370-001-G010a
Left: ONE / D / ONE vertically. ***Right:*** ONE / D / ONE vertically. ***Engraver:*** PSSP. ***Comments:*** H-MA-895-G4. Similar to W-MA-2370-001-G010. 18__. 1830s.

Rarity: —

$1 • W-MA-2370-001-G020
Engraver: Unverified, but likely New England Bank Note Co. ***Comments:*** H-MA-895-G6. No description available. 18__. 1830s.

Rarity: *None known*

$1 • W-MA-2370-001-G030
Left: Portrait of Indian / ONE. ***Center:*** Man seated, Woman standing / ONE. ***Right:*** 1 / Woman seated with staff. ***Engraver:*** Toppan, Carpenter & Co. ***Comments:*** H-MA-895-G10. 18__. 1840s–1850s.

Rarity: —

$1 • W-MA-2370-001-G030a
Overprint: Red. ***Engraver:*** Toppan, Carpenter & Co. ***Comments:*** H-MA-895-G10a. Similar to W-MA-2370-001-G030. 18__. 1850s.

Rarity: —

$1 • W-MA-2370-001-G030b
Overprint: Red. ***Engraver:*** Toppan, Carpenter & Co. / ABNCo. monogram. ***Comments:*** H-MA-895-G10b. Similar to W-MA-2370-001-G030 but with additional engraver imprint. 18__. 1840s–1850s.

Rarity: —

$1 • W-MA-2370-001-G030c
Overprint: Red panel outlining white ONE. ***Engraver:*** American Bank Note Co. ***Comments:*** H-MA-895-G10c. Similar to W-MA-2370-001-G030 but with different date and different engraver imprint. March 4, 186_. 1860s.

Rarity: —

$2 • W-MA-2370-002-G040
Left: Narrow panel of lathework circle segments. ***Center:*** 2 / 2 / Flower garlands and gridwork segments / 2 / 2. ***Right:*** Narrow panel of lathework circle segments. ***Engraver:*** PSSP. ***Comments:*** H-MA-895-G12. 18__. 1820s–1830s.

Rarity: —

$2 • W-MA-2370-002-G040a
Left: Five TWOs across. ***Right:*** Five TWOs across. ***Engraver:*** PSSP. ***Comments:*** H-MA-895-G14. Similar to W-MA-2370-002-G040. 18__. 1830s.

Rarity: —

$2 • W-MA-2370-002-G050
Engraver: Unverified, but likely New England Bank Note Co. ***Comments:*** H-MA-895-G16. No description available. 18__. 1830s–1840s.

Rarity: *None known*

$2 • W-MA-2370-002-G060
Left: 2 / Female portrait / TWO. ***Center:*** Woman seated on bale, Steamboat and factory. ***Bottom center:*** Steamboat. ***Right:*** 2 / Ship / TWO. ***Engraver:*** Toppan, Carpenter & Co. ***Comments:*** H-MA-895-G20. 18__. 1840s–1850s.

Rarity: —

$2 • W-MA-2370-002-G060a

Overprint: Red TWO. ***Engraver:*** Toppan, Carpenter & Co. ***Comments:*** H-MA-895-G20a. Similar to W-MA-2370-002-G060. 18__. 1850s.

Rarity: —

$2 • W-MA-2370-002-G060b

Overprint: Red TWO. ***Engraver:*** Toppan, Carpenter & Co. / ABNCo. monogram. ***Comments:*** H-MA-895-G20b. Similar to W-MA-2370-002-G060 but with different date and additional engraver imprint. 18__. 1850s–1860s.

Rarity: —

$2 • W-MA-2370-002-G060c

Overprint: Red panel outlining white TWO. ***Engraver:*** American Bank Note Co. ***Comments:*** H-MA-895-G20c. Similar to W-MA-2370-002-G060 but with different date and different engraver imprint. Mar. 4, 186_. 1860s.

Rarity: —

$3 • W-MA-2370-003-G070

Left: Narrow panel of lathework circle segments. ***Center:*** 3 / 3 / Flower garlands and gridwork segments / 3 / 3. ***Right:*** Narrow panel of lathework circle segments. ***Engraver:*** PSSP. ***Comments:*** H-MA-895-G22. 18__. 1820s–1830s.

Rarity: —

$3 • W-MA-2370-003-G070a

Left: THREE vertically. ***Right:*** THREE vertically. ***Engraver:*** PSSP. ***Comments:*** H-MA-895-G24. Similar to W-MA-2370-003-G070. 18__. 1830s.

Rarity: —

$3 • W-MA-2370-003-G080

Left: Two women, Canal, Shipping and train / 3. ***Center:*** 3. ***Bottom center:*** Beehive. ***Right:*** 3 / Female portrait. ***Engraver:*** Toppan, Carpenter & Co. ***Comments:*** H-MA-895-G26. 18__. 1840s–1850s.

Rarity: —

$3 • W-MA-2370-003-G080a

Overprint: Red THREE. ***Engraver:*** Toppan, Carpenter & Co. ***Comments:*** H-MA-895-G26a. Similar to W-MA-2370-003-G080. 18__. 1850s.

Rarity: —

$3 • W-MA-2370-003-G080b

Overprint: Red THREE. ***Engraver:*** Toppan, Carpenter & Co. / ABNCo. monogram. ***Comments:*** H-MA-895-G26b. Similar to W-MA-2370-003-G080 but with additional engraver imprint. 18__. 1850s–1860s.

Rarity: —

$3 • W-MA-2370-003-G080c

Overprint: Red panel outlining white THREE. ***Engraver:*** American Bank Note Co. ***Comments:*** H-MA-895-G26c. Similar to W-MA-2370-003-G080 but with different date and different engraver imprint. Mar. 4, 186_. 1860s.

Rarity: —

$5 • W-MA-2370-005-G090

Left: Lathework chain bearing MASSACHUSETTS / 5 / 5. ***Center:*** Alternating flower garlands and gridwork segments / FIVE. ***Right:*** 5 / 5. ***Engraver:*** PSSP. ***Comments:*** H-MA-895-G28. 18__. 1820s.

Rarity: —

$5 • W-MA-2370-005-G090a

Engraver: PSSP. ***Comments:*** H-MA-895-G30. Similar to W-MA-2370-005-G090 but with zigzag ruled lines. 18__. 1820s–1830s.

Rarity: —

$5 • W-MA-2370-005-G090b

Engraver: PSSP. ***Comments:*** H-MA-895-G32. Similar to W-MA-2370-005-G090 but with spiral lathework lines. 18__. 1830s.

Rarity: —

$5 • W-MA-2370-005-G100

Engraver: Unverified, but likely New England Bank Note Co. ***Comments:*** H-MA-895-G34. No description available. 18__. 1830s–1840s.

Rarity: *None known*

$5 • W-MA-2370-005-G110

Left: 5 / Woman seated. ***Center:*** 5 / Woman seated. ***Right:*** 5 / Woman seated. ***Engraver:*** Toppan, Carpenter & Co. ***Comments:*** H-MA-895-G36. March 1, 186_. 1840s–1850s.

Rarity: —

$5 • W-MA-2370-005-G110a

Overprint: Red FIVE. ***Engraver:*** Toppan, Carpenter & Co. ***Comments:*** H-MA-895-G36a. Similar to W-MA-2370-005-G110. 18__. 1850s.

Rarity: —

$5 • W-MA-2370-005-G110b

Overprint: Red FIVE. ***Engraver:*** Toppan, Carpenter & Co. / ABNCo. monogram. ***Comments:*** H-MA-895-G36b. Similar to W-MA-2370-005-G110 but with additional engraver imprint. 18__. 1850s–1860s.

Rarity: —

$5 • W-MA-2370-005-G110c

CJF

Overprint: Red panel outlining white FIVE. ***Engraver:*** American Bank Note Co. ***Comments:*** H-MA-895-G36c. Similar to W-MA-2370-005-G110 but with different date and different engraver imprint. March 4, 186_. 1860s.

Rarity: URS-5
F $350

$10 • W-MA-2370-010-G120

Comments: H-MA-895-G38. No description available. 18__. 1820s.

Rarity: *None known*

$10 • W-MA-2370-010-G130

Center: Sailing ship / Brig crossing wake. ***Bottom center:*** Brig. ***Engraver:*** New England Bank Note Co. ***Comments:*** H-MA-895-G42. 18__. 1830s–1840s.

Rarity: —

$10 • W-MA-2370-010-G140

Left: TEN / Shipyard scene / TEN. ***Center:*** 10 / Interior of blacksmith shop, Men at work / X. ***Right:*** 10 / Whaling ship / TEN ***Comments:*** H-MA-895-G46. 18__. 1840s–1850s.

Rarity: —

$10 • W-MA-2370-010-G150

Left: Lathework chain bearing MASSACHUSETTS / 10 / 10 vertically. ***Center:*** Alternating flower garlands and gridwork segments. ***Right:*** 10 / 10 vertically. ***Engraver:*** Perkins. ***Comments:*** H-MA-895-G48. 18__. 1820s.

Rarity: —

$10 • W-MA-2370-010-G160

Engraver: PSSP. ***Comments:*** H-MA-895-G50. 18__. 1820s–1830s.

Rarity: —

$10 • W-MA-2370-010-G160a

Engraver: PSSP. ***Comments:*** H-MA-895-G52. Similar to W-MA-2370-010-G160. 18__. 1830s.

Rarity: —

$10 • W-MA-2370-010-G170

Left: 10 / State arms. ***Center:*** Woman seated on strongbox with dog and child. ***Bottom center:*** Eagle. ***Right:*** TEN / Woman with sheaf / 10. ***Engraver:*** Toppan, Carpenter, Casilear & Co. ***Comments:*** H-MA-895-G54. 18__. 1850s.

Rarity: —

$10 • W-MA-2370-010-G170a

Overprint: Red. ***Engraver:*** Toppan, Carpenter, Casilear & Co. ***Comments:*** H-MA-895-G54a. Similar to W-MA-2370-010-G170. 18__. 1850s.

Rarity: —

$20 • W-MA-2370-020-G180

Left: Lathework chain bearing MASSACHUSETTS / 20 / 20 vertically. ***Center:*** Alternating flower garlands and gridwork segments / XX. ***Right:*** 20 / 20 vertically. ***Engraver:*** PSSP. ***Comments:*** H-MA-895-G56. 18__. 1830–1840s.

Rarity: —

$20 • W-MA-2370-020-G190

Engraver: Unverified, but likely New England Bank Note Co. ***Comments:*** H-MA-895-G58. No description available. 18__. 1840.

Rarity: *None known*

$20 • W-MA-2370-020-G200

Left: 20 / Woman seated with book on lap, opening chest. ***Center:*** XX / Eagle on rock / XX. ***Right:*** 20 / Ship in harbor. ***Engraver:*** New England Bank Note Co. ***Comments:*** H-MA-895-G60. 18__. 1840s–1850s.

Rarity: —

$20 • W-MA-2370-020-G210

Left: TWENTY / Ceres. ***Center:*** Woman and Indian man flanking eagle and globe, Building. ***Bottom center:*** Woman and ship. ***Right:*** 20 / Two ships. ***Engraver:*** Toppan, Carpenter, Casilear & Co. ***Comments:*** H-MA-895-G62. 18__. 1850s.

Rarity: —

$20 • W-MA-2370-020-G210a

Overprint: Red. ***Engraver:*** Toppan, Carpenter, Casilear & Co. ***Comments:*** H-MA-895-G62a. Similar to W-MA-2370-020-G210. 18__. 1850s.

Rarity: —

$20 • W-MA-2370-020-G220

Left: TWENTY / Justice. ***Center:*** Cattle / 20. ***Right:*** XX / Woman binding grain / XX. ***Engraver:*** American Bank Note Co. ***Comments:*** H-MA-895-G64. 1860s.

Rarity: —

$50 • W-MA-2370-050-G230

Left: Lathework chain bearing MASSACHUSETTS / 50 / 50 vertically. ***Center:*** Alternating flower garlands and gridwork segments / FIFTY. ***Right:*** 50 / 50 vertically. ***Engraver:*** PSSP. ***Comments:*** H-MA-895-G66. 18__. 1820s–1830s.

Rarity: —

$50 • W-MA-2370-050-G240

Comments: H-MA-895-G70. No description available.

Rarity: *None known*

$50 • W-MA-2370-050-G250

Left: L / Woman. ***Center:*** Farmer with rake, Hay wagon / FIFTY. ***Right:*** 50 / Two ships. ***Comments:*** H-MA-895-G74. 18__. 1830s–1840s.

Rarity: —

$50 • W-MA-2370-050-G260

Left: FIFTY / Woman standing with wreath and flowers / FIFTY. ***Center:*** 50 / Man restraining prancing horse / 50. ***Right:*** FIFTY / Woman standing with cornucopia / FIFTY. ***Engraver:*** New England Bank Note Co. ***Comments:*** H-MA-895-G78. 18__. 1840s.

Rarity: —

$50 • W-MA-2370-050-G270

Left: Female portrait / 50. ***Center:*** Three women seated with staff and shield, fasces, sickle, and sheaf, Train and ships. ***Bottom center:*** Customs house. ***Right:*** 50 / Female portrait. ***Engraver:*** Toppan, Carpenter & Co. ***Comments:*** H-MA-895-G80. 18__. 1840s–1850s.

Rarity: —

$100 • W-MA-2370-100-G280

Left: Lathework chain bearing MASSACHUSETTS / 100 / 100 vertically. ***Center:*** Alternating flower garlands and gridwork segments / 100. ***Right:*** 100 / 100 vertically. ***Engraver:*** Perkins. ***Comments:*** H-MA-895-G82. 18__. 1820s–1830s.

Rarity: —

$100 • W-MA-2370-100-G290

Engraver: Unverified, but likely New England Bank Note Co. ***Comments:*** H-MA-895-G86. No description available. 18__. 1830s–1840s.

Rarity: *None known*

$100 • W-MA-2370-100-G300

Left: 100 / Portrait of George Washington / 100. ***Center:*** Woman seated on bale with sheaf. ***Bottom center:*** Mansion. ***Right:*** 100 / Woman standing by anchor pointing at distant ship, City. ***Engraver:*** Toppan, Carpenter & Co. ***Comments:*** H-MA-895-G90. 18__. 1840s–1850s.

Rarity: —

$500 • **W-MA-2370-500-G310**

Engraver: Unverified, but likely New England Bank Note Co. ***Comments:*** H-MA-895-G96. No description available. 18__. 1830s–1840s.

Rarity: *None known*

$500 • **W-MA-2370-500-G320**

Left: 500 / Women and man seated with sheaf, Hammer and anvil / D. ***Center:*** Two women flanking state arms surmounted by eagle, City and steamboat. ***Bottom center:*** Public building. ***Right:*** 500 / Woman seated by strongbox / 500. ***Engraver:*** Toppan, Carpenter, Casilear & Co. ***Comments:*** H-MA-895-G100. 18__. 1850s.

Rarity: —

Non-Valid Issues

$1 • **W-MA-2370-001-N010**

Left: Two women. ***Center:*** Farmer seated on sheaf. ***Right:*** Two women with flowers. ***Comments:*** H-MA-895-N5.

Rarity: —

$1 • **W-MA-2370-001-A010**

Left: ONE / Hebe seated on sheaf watering eagle / ONE. ***Center:*** Eagle on shield, Ships. ***Right:*** 1 / Ceres kneeling with sheaf, Farm. ***Engraver:*** Danforth, Bald & Co. ***Comments:*** H-MA-895-A5. Altered from $1 Columbia Bank, Washington, D.C. 18__. 1850s.

Rarity: —

$1 • **W-MA-2370-001-A020**

Left: Panel bearing portrait of Zachary Taylor. ***Center:*** 1 / Woman in clouds holding shield, Eagle / 1 / ONE. ***Right:*** Panel bearing Ceres. ***Engraver:*** W.L. Ormsby. ***Comments:*** H-MA-895-A10. Altered from $1 Mechanics and Traders Bank, Georgetown, D.C. Nov. 14, 1852.

Rarity: —

$1 • **W-MA-2370-001-A030**

CJF

Engraver: Doty & Bergen. ***Comments:*** H-MA-895-A15. Altered from $1 Merchants Bank, Stillwater, Minnesota. October 20, 1854.

Rarity: —

$1 • **W-MA-2370-001-A030a**

Overprint: Red ONE. ***Comments:*** H-MA-895-A15a. Similar to W-MA-2370-001-A030. Oct. 20, 1854.

Rarity: —

$1 • **W-MA-2370-001-A040**

Left: 1 / State arms / ONE. ***Center:*** Three allegorical women reclining around shield surmounted by eagle, Ship. ***Right:*** 1 / Two farmers walking, Dog. ***Engraver:*** Danforth, Wright & Co. ***Comments:*** H-MA-895-A20. Altered from $1 Bank of Washtenaw, Washtenaw, Michigan series. 1850s.

Rarity: —

$2 • **W-MA-2370-002-S010**

Center: Woman / 2 / Woman. ***Comments:*** H-MA-895-S5.

Rarity: —

$2 • **W-MA-2370-002-N020**

Center: Two horses flanking shield bearing scene with canal lock. ***Comments:*** H-MA-895-N10.

Rarity: —

$2 • **W-MA-2370-002-N030**

Center: Train. ***Comments:*** H-MA-895-N20.

Rarity: —

$2 • **W-MA-2370-002-N040**

Center: Woman seated with sheaf. ***Right:*** Indian man. ***Comments:*** H-MA-895-N25.

Rarity: —

$2 • **W-MA-2370-002-A050**

CJF

Overprint: Red lazy 2. ***Engraver:*** Doty & Bergen. ***Comments:*** H-MA-895-A25a. Altered from $2 Delaware City Bank, Delaware, Kansas. July 1, 185_. 1850s.

Rarity: URS-7

VG $125; **VF** $175

$2 • **W-MA-2370-002-A060**

Left: 2 / TWO / 2. ***Center:*** 2 / Ceres seated, Train on bridge, Sheaf and canal lock. ***Bottom center:*** Road, Trees, Sign post. ***Right:*** Indian man standing / 2. ***Engraver:*** Doty & Bergen. ***Comments:*** H-MA-895-A30. Altered from $2 Merchants Bank, Stillwater, Minnesota. Oct. 20, 1854.

Rarity: —

$3 • **W-MA-2370-003-A070**

Left: 3 / Portrait of Andrew Jackson / 3. ***Center:*** 3 / Indian woman with bow / Flags, drums / 3. ***Bottom center:*** Train at station. ***Right:*** THREE / Ceres seated with caduceus / 3. ***Engraver:*** Rawdon, Wright, Hatch & Edson. ***Comments:*** H-MA-895-A35. Altered from $3 Merchants Bank, Washington, D.C. Dec. 1, 1852.

Rarity: —

$3 • **W-MA-2370-003-A080**

Left: 3 on panel bearing dolphins. ***Center:*** 3 / Roman scholar seated, Building / 3. ***Bottom center:*** Clasped hands. ***Right:*** Cherub with flowers in clouds. ***Engraver:*** Rawdon, Wright & Hatch. ***Comments:*** H-MA-895-A40. Altered from $3 Lower Canada Bank, Montreal, Canada. 18__. 1830s.

Rarity: —

$5 • **W-MA-2370-005-C110c**

Engraver: American Bank Note Co. ***Comments:*** H-MA-895-C36c. Counterfeit of W-MA-2370-005-G110c. Mar. 4, 186_. 1860s.

Rarity: —

VF $90

$5 • W-MA-2370-005-R010

Engraver: New England Bank Note Co. ***Comments:*** H-MA-895-R5. Raised from W-MA-2370-001-G020. 18__. 1830s.

Rarity: —

$5 • W-MA-2370-005-S020

Comments: H-Unlisted. October 20, 1854.

Rarity: —

$5 • W-MA-2370-005-N050

Center: Two sailing ships. ***Comments:*** H-MA-895-N30. 18__ Circa 1840.

Rarity: —

$5 • W-MA-2370-005-N060

Center: Woman and agricultural implements. ***Comments:*** H-MA-895-N35.

Rarity: —

$5 • W-MA-2370-005-A090

Left: 5 / Woman seated on rocks with shield, Tools. ***Center:*** Ceres standing and Liberty seated. ***Right:*** 5 / Portrait of Zachary Taylor. ***Engraver:*** W.L. Ormsby. ***Comments:*** H-MA-895-A45. Altered from $5 Merchants Bank, Fort Leavenworth, Kansas. 18__. 1850s.

Rarity: —

$10 • W-MA-2370-010-C130

Engraver: New England Bank Note Co. ***Comments:*** H-MA-895-C42. Counterfeit of W-MA-2370-010-G130. 18__. 1840s.

Rarity: —

$10 • W-MA-2370-010-R020

Engraver: New England Bank Note Co. ***Comments:*** H-MA-895-R10. Raised from W-MA-2370-001-G020. 18__. 1830s.

Rarity: —

$10 • W-MA-2370-010-N070

Left: Ships and bridge. ***Center:*** State House. ***Right:*** Woman and eagle. ***Comments:*** H-MA-895-N40.

Rarity: —

$20 • W-MA-2370-020-R030

Engraver: New England Bank Note Co. ***Comments:*** H-MA-895-R15. Raised from W-MA-2370-001-G020. 18__. 1830s.

Rarity: —

$20 • W-MA-2370-020-S030

Left: 20 / XX. ***Center:*** XX / Female portrait / XX. ***Right:*** 20 / XX. ***Comments:*** H-MA-895-S10.

Rarity: —

$50 • W-MA-2370-050-A100

Left: 50 on die / Portrait of Benjamin Franklin. ***Center:*** Sailor seated on bale, Flag, Ships. ***Bottom center:*** Eagle. ***Right:*** 50 on die / Portrait of George Washington. ***Engraver:*** Boston Bank Note Co. ***Comments:*** H-MA-895-A50. Altered from $50 Bank of Vernon, Vernon, Texas. 18__. 1840s.

Rarity: —

Newburyport, Massachusetts

What later became Newburyport was known earlier as the Newberry Plantation. It was land originally dwelt on by the Pawtucket natives, and it was settled in 1635. In 1764 the General Court of Massachusetts incorporated the town under the name of Newburyport, which included part of Plum Island.

The town became a city in 1851 and was a center for fishing, shipbuilding, shipping, and the manufacturing of silverware. Distilleries made rum from molasses imported from the West Indies, and privateering occurred here during the Revolutionary War and the War of 1812. A terrible fire destroyed the downtown area in 1811. As a result of the destruction, the city suffered an economic decline which was only exacerbated by the embargoes brought on by the War of 1812 and the financial panic of 1816. Nevertheless, by 1832 the town had recovered enough to build ships for the whaling trade. By 1851 Newburyport had annexed part of Newbury and incorporated as a city. The area also saw the construction of steam-powered mills, allowing a margin of growth for the city's industries.

From the early 19th century until 1832, Newburyport was home to engraver and bank-note printer Jacob Perkins. Later, his brother also moved to Newburyport and issued bills of the PSSP type.

Chemical Bank

Circa 1831

W-MA-2390

History: A non-existent bank represented only by fraudulent notes.

Numismatic Commentary: The only issue known from this fantasy bank is the $3 denomination. Interestingly, it has a signed vignette by H. Inman, del. as delineator and A.B. Durand, sc. as sculptor. This issue is very rare.

Collectors and Researchers:

If you have new information about any banks or notes listed in this volume, contact Whitman Publishing, Attn: Obsolete Paper Money, 3101 Clairmont Road, Suite G, Atlanta, GA 30329.

Issues

$3 • W-MA-2390-003-G010

CJF

Engraver: Durand, Perkins & Co. ***Comments:*** H-MA-900-G6. From a modified plate originally for a counterfeit $3 of the Chemical Bank, New York City, New York. 18__. Circa 1831.

Rarity: —

Mechanics Bank

1812–1864

W-MA-2400

History: The Mechanics Bank (also sometimes seen as Mechanicks) was chartered on June 23, 1812, with an authorized capital of $200,000. John Wood was the first president, and John Andrews Jr. was the founding cashier. On June 12, 1813, an act was passed extending the time by which the installments of capital stock had to be paid in, giving the bank until July 1, 1813, to make the first payment. The second was to occur by October 1, 1813, the third by January 1, 1814, and the fourth by April 1, 1814. These were difficult times in the American economy.

Circulation in 1839 was $45,630.50. It reached $114,723 in 1863. Capital was $200,000 in 1845 and $210,000 in 1849.

On November 23, 1864, the business of the Mechanics Bank was succeeded by the Mechanics National Bank of Newburyport.

Numismatic Commentary: Genuine issues from this bank seldom turn up in the marketplace. Counterfeit PSSP design notes are occasionally available.

Valid Issues

$1 • W-MA-2400-001-G010

Center: 1 / 1 / Flower garlands and gridwork segments / ONE / 1 / 1. ***Engraver:*** PSSP. ***Comments:*** H-MA-905-G10. 18__. 1812–1820s.

Rarity: URS-6
F $100

$1 • W-MA-2400-001-G010a

Left: Panel of lathework circle segments. ***Right:*** Panel of lathework circle segments. ***Engraver:*** PSSP. ***Comments:*** H-MA-905-G12. Similar to W-MA-2400-001-G010. 18__. 1820s.

Rarity: —

$1 • W-MA-2400-001-G010b

Left: Panel of lathework circle segments. ***Right:*** Panel of lathework circle segments. ***Engraver:*** PSSP. ***Comments:*** H-MA-905-G14. Similar to W-MA-2400-001-G010. 18__. 1820s–1830s.

Rarity: —

$1 • W-MA-2400-001-G010c

Left: ONE / D / ONE vertically. ***Right:*** ONE / D / ONE vertically. ***Engraver:*** PSSP. ***Comments:*** H-MA-905-G16. Similar to W-MA-2400-001-G010. 18__. 1830s.

Rarity: —

$1 • W-MA-2400-001-G020

CC

Overprint: Red ONE. ***Engraver:*** Rawdon, Wright, Hatch & Edson / New England Bank Note Co. ***Comments:*** H-MA-905-G20. 18__. 1850s.

Rarity: URS-2
VF $1,000

$2 • W-MA-2400-002-G030

Center: 2 / 2 / Oval of flower garlands and gridwork segments / TWO / 2 / 2. ***Engraver:*** PSSP. ***Comments:*** H-MA-905-G26. 18__. 1812–1820s.

Rarity: —

$2 • W-MA-2400-002-G030a

Left: Panel of lathework circle segments. ***Right:*** Panel of lathework circle segments. ***Engraver:*** PSSP. ***Comments:*** H-MA-905-G28. Similar to W-MA-2400-002-G030. 18__. 1820s.

Rarity: —

$2 • W-MA-2400-002-G030b

Left: Panel of lathework circle segments. ***Right:*** Panel of lathework circle segments. ***Engraver:*** PSSP. ***Comments:*** H-MA-905-G30. Similar to W-MA-2400-002-G030. 18__. 1820s–1830s.

Rarity: —

$2 • W-MA-2400-002-G030c

SI

Engraver: PSSP. ***Comments:*** H-MA-905-G32. Similar to W-MA-2400-002-G030. 18__. 1830s.

Rarity: URS-5
F $150

$2 • W-MA-2400-002-G040

Left: Shipyard scene, Ship on stocks / 2. ***Center:*** 2 bearing female portrait. ***Right:*** 2 / Eagle in 2. ***Engraver:*** Rawdon, Wright, Hatch & Edson / New England Bank Note Co. ***Comments:*** H-MA-905-G36. 18__. 1850s.

Rarity: —

$3 • W-MA-2400-003-G050

Center: 3 / 3 / Oval of flower garlands and gridwork segments / 3 / 3. ***Engraver:*** PSSP. ***Comments:*** H-MA-905-G38. 18__. 1810s–1820s.

Rarity: —

$3 • W-MA-2400-003-G050a

Left: Panel of lathework circle segments. ***Right:*** Panel of lathework circle segments. ***Engraver:*** PSSP. ***Comments:*** H-MA-905-G40. Similar to W-MA-2400-003-G050. 18__. 1820s.

Rarity: —

$3 • W-MA-2400-003-G050b

Left: Panel of lathework circle segments. ***Right:*** Panel of lathework circle segments. ***Engraver:*** PSSP. ***Comments:*** H-MA-905-G42. Similar to W-MA-2400-003-G050. 18__. 1820s–1830s.

Rarity: —

$3 • W-MA-2400-003-G050c

Left: THREE vertically. ***Right:*** THREE vertically. ***Engraver:*** PSSP. ***Comments:*** H-MA-905-G44. Similar to W-MA-2400-003-G050. 18__. 1830s.

Rarity: —

$3 • W-MA-2400-003-G060

Left: Wharf scene and ships / 3. ***Right:*** 3 / Mechanic seated. ***Engraver:*** Rawdon, Wright, Hatch & Edson / New England Bank Note Co. ***Comments:*** H-MA-905-G48. 18__. 1850s.

Rarity: —

$5 • W-MA-2400-005-G070

Left: Panel bearing state arms / 5 / 5. ***Center:*** Alternating flower garlands and gridwork segments. ***Right:*** 5 / 5. ***Engraver:*** PSSP. ***Comments:*** H-MA-905-G50. 18__. 1810s–1820s.

Rarity: —

$5 • W-MA-2400-005-G070a

Left: Lathework chain bearing MASSACHUSETTS vertically. ***Right:*** Panel of lathework circle segments. ***Engraver:*** PSSP. ***Comments:*** H-MA-905-G52. Similar to W-MA-2400-005-G070. 18__. 1820s.

Rarity: —

$5 • W-MA-2400-005-G070b

Engraver: PSSP. ***Comments:*** H-MA-905-G54. Similar to W-MA-2400-005-G070. 18__. 1820s.

Rarity: —

$5 • W-MA-2400-005-G070c

Engraver: PSSP. ***Comments:*** H-MA-905-G56. Similar to W-MA-2400-005-G070 but with zigzag ruled lines. 18__. 1820s–1830s.

Rarity: —

$5 • W-MA-2400-005-G070d

Engraver: PSSP. ***Comments:*** H-MA-905-G58. Similar to W-MA-2400-005-G070 but with spiral lathework lines. 18__. 1830s.

Rarity: —

$5 • W-MA-2400-005-G080

Left: Train / 5. ***Center:*** V. ***Right:*** 5 / Portrait of Benjamin Franklin. ***Engraver:*** Rawdon, Wright, Hatch & Edson / New England Bank Note Co. ***Comments:*** H-MA-905-G62. 18__. 1850s.

Rarity: —

$10 • W-MA-2400-010-G090

Left: Panel bearing state arms / 10 / 10 vertically. ***Center:*** Alternating flower garlands and gridwork segments / TEN. ***Right:*** 10 / 10 vertically. ***Engraver:*** Perkins. ***Comments:*** H-MA-905-G64. 18__. 1810s–1820s.

Rarity: —

$10 • W-MA-2400-010-G090a

Left: Lathework chain bearing MASSACHUSETTS vertically. ***Right:*** Panel of lathework circle segments. ***Engraver:*** Perkins. ***Comments:*** H-MA-905-G66. Similar to W-MA-2400-010-G090. 18__. 1820s.

Rarity: —

$10 • W-MA-2400-010-G090b

Engraver: Perkins. ***Comments:*** H-MA-905-G68. Similar to W-MA-2400-010-G090. 18__. 1820s.

Rarity: —

$10 • W-MA-2400-010-G090c

Engraver: PSSP. ***Comments:*** H-MA-905-G70. Similar to W-MA-2400-010-G090. 18__. 1820s–1830s.

Rarity: —

$10 • W-MA-2400-010-G090d

Engraver: PSSP. ***Comments:*** H-MA-905-G72. Similar to W-MA-2400-010-G090. 18__. 1830s.

Rarity: —

$10 • W-MA-2400-010-G100

Center: Steamship and sailing ship at sea / 10. ***Right:*** 10 / Portrait of George Washington. ***Engraver:*** Rawdon, Wright, Hatch & Edson / New England Bank Note Co. ***Comments:*** H-MA-905-G76. 18__. 1850s.

Rarity: —

$20 • W-MA-2400-020-G110

Left: Panel bearing state arms / 20 / 20 vertically. ***Center:*** Alternating flower garlands and gridwork segments. ***Right:*** 20 / 20 vertically. ***Engraver:*** Perkins. ***Comments:*** H-MA-905-G78. 18__. 1810s–1820s.

Rarity: —

$20 • W-MA-2400-020-G110a

Left: Lathework chain bearing MASSACHUSETTS vertically. ***Engraver:*** PSSP. ***Comments:*** H-MA-905-G80. Similar to W-MA-2400-020-G110. 18__. 1820s–1830s.

Rarity: —

$20 • W-MA-2400-020-G120

Left: 20 / Woman seated with book on lap, opening chest. ***Center:*** XX / Eagle on rock / XX. ***Right:*** 20 / Ship in harbor. ***Engraver:*** New England Bank Note Co. ***Comments:*** H-MA-905-G84. 18__. 1840s–1850s.

Rarity: —

$20 • W-MA-2400-020-G130

Left: 20 / Minerva standing with spear. ***Center:*** Woman seated between 2 and 0. ***Right:*** 20 / Woman reclining on cornucopia / 20. ***Engraver:*** Rawdon, Wright, Hatch & Edson. ***Comments:*** H-MA-905-G86. 18__. 1850s.

Rarity: —

$20 • W-MA-2400-020-G140
Left: 20 / TWENTY / 20. ***Center:*** Arctic scene, Four men in boat attacked by polar bear. ***Right:*** 20 / Female portrait. ***Tint:*** Green. ***Engraver:*** American Bank Note Co. ***Comments:*** H-MA-905-G88a. 1860s.
Rarity: —

$50 • W-MA-2400-050-G150
Left: Panel bearing state arms / 50 / 50 vertically. ***Center:*** Alternating flower garlands and gridwork segments. ***Right:*** 50 / 50 vertically. ***Engraver:*** Perkins. ***Comments:*** H-MA-905-G90. 18__. 1810s–1820s.
Rarity: —

$50 • W-MA-2400-050-G150a
Left: Lathework chain bearing MASSACHUSETTS vertically. ***Engraver:*** PSSP. ***Comments:*** H-MA-905-G92. Similar to W-MA-2400-050-G150. 18__. 1820s–1830s.
Rarity: —

$50 • W-MA-2400-050-G160
Left: 50 / Woman standing with ankles crossed, Staff, cornucopia, and anchor. ***Center:*** FIFTY DOLLARS / 50. ***Right:*** FIFTY vertically. ***Engraver:*** New England Bank Note Co. / PSSP. ***Comments:*** H-MA-905-G94. 18__. 1830s.
Rarity: —

$50 • W-MA-2400-050-G170
Left: FIFTY / Woman standing with wreath and flowers / FIFTY. ***Center:*** 50 / Man restraining prancing horse / 50. ***Right:*** FIFTY / Woman standing with cornucopia / FIFTY. ***Engraver:*** New England Bank Note Co. ***Comments:*** H-MA-905-G96. 18__. 1840s–1850s.
Rarity: —

$50 • W-MA-2400-050-G180
Left: Portrait of two children. ***Center:*** 50 / Two sailors, one seated on bale with anchor, rope, and flag / 50. ***Right:*** Woman blowing on dandelion. ***Tint:*** Green. ***Engraver:*** American Bank Note Co. ***Comments:*** H-MA-905-G98a. 1860s.
Rarity: —

$100 • W-MA-2400-100-G190
Left: Panel bearing state arms / 100 / 100 vertically. ***Center:*** Alternating flower garlands and gridwork segments. ***Right:*** 100 / 100 vertically. ***Engraver:*** Perkins. ***Comments:*** H-MA-905-G100. 18__. 1810s–1820s.
Rarity: —

$100 • W-MA-2400-100-G190a
Left: Lathework chain bearing MASSACHUSETTS vertically. ***Engraver:*** Perkins. ***Comments:*** H-MA-905-G102. Similar to W-MA-2400-100-G190. 18__. 1820s–1820s.
Rarity: —

$100 • W-MA-2400-100-G200
Left: Lathework chain with C / Portrait of George Washington / C. ***Center:*** 100 / Manhattan reclining pouring water, Ship / 100. ***Right:*** Lathework panel bearing ONE HUNDRED vertically. ***Engraver:*** New England Bank Note Co. / PSSP. ***Comments:*** H-MA-905-G104. 18__. 1830s.
Rarity: —

$100 • W-MA-2400-100-G210
Left: ONE HUNDRED on 100 / Portrait of William Henry Harrison. ***Center:*** Wharf scene, Men loading wagon with barrels. ***Right:*** ONE HUNDRED on 100 / Portrait of Christopher Columbus. ***Engraver:*** New England Bank Note Co. ***Comments:*** H-MA-905-G106. 18__. 1840s–1850s.
Rarity: —

$100 • W-MA-2400-100-G220
Left: 100. ***Center:*** Train / Ships at sea. ***Right:*** 100 / Sailor seated on yard-arm with spyglass. ***Tint:*** Green C. ***Engraver:*** American Bank Note Co. ***Comments:*** H-MA-905-G108a. 1860s.
Rarity: —

$500 • W-MA-2400-500-G230
Left: 500 / 500 / 500. ***Center:*** 500 / Woman seated with shield bearing D, Fasces, cornucopia, lyre, and sheaf / 500. ***Right:*** 500 / D / 500. ***Engraver:*** PSSP / New England Bank Note Co. ***Comments:*** H-MA-905-G110. 18__. 1830s.
Rarity: —

$1,000 • W-MA-2400-1000-G240
Left: THOUSAND vertically. ***Center:*** 1000 / Woman standing with legs crossed, Lyre, Cornucopia / 1000. ***Right:*** 1000 / M / 1000. ***Engraver:*** PSSP / New England Bank Note Co. ***Comments:*** H-MA-905-G112. 18__. 1830s.
Rarity: —

Non-Valid Issues

$1 • W-MA-2400-001-C010c

SN

Engraver: PSSP. ***Comments:*** H-MA-905-C16. Counterfeit of W-MA-2400-001-G010c. 18__. 1840s.
Rarity: —

$1 • W-MA-2400-001-A010
Left: ONE / Woman standing, Pitcher on pedestal / ONE. ***Center:*** 1 / Woman seated with vase of flowers / 1. ***Right:*** ONE / Steamboat / ONE. ***Engraver:*** Mason & Taylor. ***Comments:*** H-MA-905-A5. Altered from $1 Pennsylvania Savings Bank, Philadelphia, Pennsylvania. 183_. 1830s.
Rarity: —

$2 • W-MA-2400-002-C030c
Engraver: PSSP. ***Comments:*** H-MA-905-C32. Counterfeit of W-MA-2400-002-G030c. 18__. 1840s.
Rarity: —

$3 • W-MA-2400-003-C050c
Engraver: PSSP. ***Comments:*** H-MA-905-C44. Counterfeit of W-MA-2400-003-G050c. 18__. 1840s.
Rarity: —

$3 • W-MA-2400-003-A020
Left: 3 / 3 with woman seated at its base, Lighthouse. ***Center:*** Eagle on shield / 3. ***Right:*** Woman seated with barrel / 3. ***Engraver:*** Wellstood, Hanks, Hay & Whiting. ***Comments:*** H-MA-905-A10. Altered from $3 Metropolitan Bank, Washington, D.C. series. 18__. 1850s.
Rarity: —

$5 • W-MA-2400-005-N010
Left: Portrait of George Washington. ***Center:*** 5 / Hebe watering eagle / 5. ***Bottom center:*** Female portrait. ***Right:*** Woman. ***Comments:*** H-MA-905-N5. 18__. 1850s.
Rarity: —

$5 • W-MA-2400-005-A030
Left: FIVE vertically. ***Center:*** 5 / Spread eagle on U.S. shield holding banner in its beak. ***Bottom center:*** Road, Trees, Sign post. ***Right:*** Indian woman holding bow. ***Engraver:*** Doty & Bergen. ***Comments:*** H-MA-905-A15. Altered from $5 Merchants Bank, Stillwater, Minnesota. Oct. 20, 1854.
Rarity: —

$10 • W-MA-2400-010-S010
Left: TEN on three dies. ***Center:*** 10 / Steamboat, Sailing ships / 10. ***Right:*** TEN / Portrait of George Washington / TEN. ***Engraver:*** Rawdon, Wright & Hatch. ***Comments:*** H-MA-905-S5. Aug. 1, 1849.
Rarity: —

Merchants Bank
1831–1865
W-MA-2420

History: The Merchants Bank was chartered on March 18, 1831, with an authorized capital of $225,000. In 1839 the capital had risen to $300,000, but by 1845 it had dropped to $210,000. Circulation was $58,111.75 in 1845. In 1863 it was $72,356.

The business of the Merchants Bank was succeeded by the Merchants National Bank in 1865.

Numismatic Commentary: Genuine notes are hard to come by. Counterfeits are plentiful. Historical vignettes appear on some of these notes, such as "Washington Crossing the Delaware" and the "Death of General Montgomery at Quebec."

Valid Issues

$1 • W-MA-2420-001-G010
Left: Lathework panel bearing ONE / D / ONE vertically. ***Center:*** 1 / 1 / Alternating flower garlands and gridwork segments / ONE / 1 / 1. ***Right:*** Lathework panel bearing ONE / D / ONE vertically. ***Engraver:*** PSSP. ***Comments:*** H-MA-910-G2. 18__. 1830s.
Rarity: —

$1 • W-MA-2420-001-G020
Left: 1 / Ship / 1. ***Center:*** ONE / Whaling scene / Woman seated with shield bearing 1. ***Right:*** 1 / Ship / 1. ***Engraver:*** New England Bank Note Co. ***Comments:*** H-MA-910-G6. 18__. 1830s–1850s.
Rarity: —

$1.25 • W-MA-2420-001.25-G030
Left: 1 25/100 / Train / 1 25/100. ***Center:*** Sloop and other ships at sea / $1.25 cts. ***Right:*** 1 25/100 / Eagle. ***Engraver:*** New England Bank Note Co. ***Comments:*** H-MA-910-G8. 18__. 1830s.
Rarity: —

$1.50 • W-MA-2420-001.50-G040
Left: 1 Doll. 50 Cts. vertically. ***Center:*** Eagle on rock in ocean / $1 50/100. ***Right:*** 1 50/100 / 100 / Justice. ***Engraver:*** New England Bank Note Co. ***Comments:*** H-MA-910-G10. 18__. 1830s.
Rarity: —

$1.75 • W-MA-2420-001.75-G050
Left: $1.75 Cts. / Hebe watering eagle / 1 75/100. ***Center:*** Three sloops at sea. ***Right:*** $1.75 Cts. / Dog, Woman seated with grain / 1 75/100. ***Engraver:*** New England Bank Note Co. ***Comments:*** H-MA-910-G12. 18__. 1830s.
Rarity: —

$2 • W-MA-2420-002-G060
Left: Lathework panel bearing MASSACHUSETTS vertically. ***Center:*** 2 / 2 / Alternating flower garlands and gridwork segments / TWO / 2 / 2. ***Right:*** Lathework panel bearing five TWOs vertically. ***Engraver:*** PSSP. ***Comments:*** H-MA-910-G14. 18__. 1830s.
Rarity: —

$2 • W-MA-2420-002-G070
Left: TWO / Train / TWO. ***Center:*** 2 / Ships sailing / 2. ***Right:*** 2 / Manhattan reclining, pouring water from jar / 2. ***Engraver:*** New England Bank Note Co. ***Comments:*** H-MA-910-G18. 18__. 1830s–1850s.
Rarity: —

$2 • W-MA-2420-002-G070a

CJF

Overprint: Red TWO. ***Engraver:*** New England Bank Note Co. / PSSP. ***Comments:*** H-Unlisted. Similar to W-MA-2420-002-G070. 18__. 1860s.
Rarity: URS-5
F $350

$3 • W-MA-2420-003-G080
Left: Lathework panel bearing MASSACHUSETTS vertically. ***Center:*** 3 / 3 / Alternating flower garlands and gridwork segments / THREE / 3 / 3. ***Right:*** Lathework panel bearing THREE vertically. ***Engraver:*** PSSP. ***Comments:*** H-MA-910-G20. 18__. 1830s.
Rarity: —

$3 • W-MA-2420-003-G090
Left: THREE / Steamboat / THREE. ***Center:*** Woman / Shipyard scene / Sailor. ***Right:*** 3 / Ship / 3. ***Engraver:*** New England Bank Note Co. ***Comments:*** H-MA-910-G24. 18__. 1830s–1850s.
Rarity: —

$5 • W-MA-2420-005-G100

CC

Overprint: Red FIVE. ***Engraver:*** PSSP. ***Comments:*** H-MA-910-G26. 18__. 1830s.

Rarity: URS-3
Proof $3,000

$5 • W-MA-2420-005-G110

Left: Eagle on rock. ***Center:*** Ship / George Washington and troops crossing the Delaware. ***Right:*** Axe and cornucopia / FIVE. ***Engraver:*** New England Bank Note Co. ***Comments:*** H-MA-910-G30. 18__. 1830s–1850s.

Rarity: —

$5 • W-MA-2420-005-G110a

CJF

Overprint: Red FIVE. ***Engraver:*** New England Bank Note Co. / PSSP. ***Comments:*** H-Unlisted. Similar to W-MA-2420-005-G110. 18__.

Rarity: URS-4
Proof $1,500

$10 • W-MA-2420-010-G120

Left: Lathework chain bearing MASSACHUSETTS / 10 / 10 vertically. ***Center:*** Alternating flower garlands and gridwork segments / Spiral lathework lines. ***Right:*** 10 / 10 vertically. ***Engraver:*** PSSP. ***Comments:*** H-MA-910-G32. 18__. 1830s.

Rarity: —

$10 • W-MA-2420-010-G130

Left: 10 / Surrender of Cornwallis / TEN. ***Center:*** Ship / Allegorical man standing in chariot drawn by three horses / Ship. ***Right:*** 10 / George Washington and troops crossing the Delaware / TEN. ***Engraver:*** New England Bank Note Co. ***Comments:*** H-MA-910-G36. 18__. 1830s–1850s.

Rarity: URS-3
Proof $1,500

$10 • W-MA-2420-010-G130a

CC

Overprint: Red TEN. ***Engraver:*** New England Bank Note Co. / PSSP. ***Comments:*** H-Unlisted. Similar to W-MA-2420-010-G130. 18__.

Rarity: URS-3
Proof $1,600

$20 • W-MA-2420-020-G140

Left: Lathework chain bearing MASSACHUSETTS / 20 / 20 vertically. ***Center:*** Alternating flower garlands and gridwork segments. ***Right:*** 20 / 20 vertically. ***Engraver:*** PSSP. ***Comments:*** H-MA-910-G38. 18__. 1830s.

Rarity: —

$20 • W-MA-2420-020-G150

Engraver: Unverified, but likely New England Bank Note Co. ***Comments:*** H-MA-910-G42. No description available. 18__. 1830s–1840s.

Rarity: *None known*

$20 • W-MA-2420-020-G160

Left: TWENTY / Justice standing. ***Center:*** Cattle and sheep / 20. ***Right:*** XX / Woman binding wheat. ***Engraver:*** American Bank Note Co. ***Comments:*** H-MA-910-G44. 18__. 1860s.

Rarity: —

$50 • W-MA-2420-050-G170

Left: Lathework chain bearing MASSACHUSETTS / 50 / 50 vertically. ***Center:*** Alternating flower garlands and gridwork segments. ***Right:*** 50 / 50 vertically. ***Engraver:*** PSSP. ***Comments:*** H-MA-910-G46. 18__. 1830s.

Rarity: —

$50 • W-MA-2420-050-G180

Left: FIFTY / Man / 50. ***Center:*** FIFTY / Steamboat, City / Woman. ***Right:*** 50 / Bust / FIFTY. ***Engraver:*** New England Bank Note Co. ***Comments:*** H-MA-910-G50. 18__. 1830s–1850s.

Rarity: —

$100 • W-MA-2420-100-G190

Left: Lathework chain bearing MASSACHUSETTS / 100 / 100 vertically. ***Center:*** Alternating flower garlands and gridwork segments. ***Right:*** 100 / 100 vertically. ***Engraver:*** Perkins. ***Comments:*** H-MA-910-G52. 18__. 1830s.

Rarity: —

$100 • W-MA-2420-100-G200 CJF

Overprint: Red HUNDRED. ***Engraver:*** New England Bank Note Co. ***Comments:*** H-MA-910-G56. 18__. 1830s–1850s.

Rarity: URS-3
Proof $3,000

$500 • W-MA-2420-500-G210

Left: 500 / 500 / 500. ***Center:*** 500 / Woman seated with shield bearing D, Fasces, cornucopia, lyre, and sheaf / 500. ***Right:*** 500 / D / 500. ***Engraver:*** PSSP / New England Bank Note Co. ***Comments:*** H-MA-910-G60. 18__. 1830s–1840s.

Rarity: —

$1,000 • W-MA-2420-1000-G220

Left: THOUSAND vertically. ***Center:*** 1000 / Woman standing with legs crossed, Lyre, Cornucopia / 1000. ***Right:*** 1000 / M / 1000. ***Engraver:*** PSSP / New England Bank Note Co. ***Comments:*** H-MA-910-G64. 18__. 1830s–1840s.

Rarity: —

Non-Valid Issues

$1 • W-MA-2420-001-A010

Left: ONE / Hebe seated on sheaf, watering eagle / ONE. ***Center:*** Eagle on shield, Ships. ***Right:*** 1 / Ceres kneeling with sheaf, Farm. ***Engraver:*** Danforth, Bald & Co. ***Comments:*** H-MA-910-A5. Altered from $1 Columbia Bank, Washington, D.C. 18__. 1850s.

Rarity: —

$1 • W-MA-2420-001-A020

Left: Panel bearing portrait of Zachary Taylor. ***Center:*** 1 / Woman in clouds holding shield, Eagle / 1 / ONE. ***Right:*** Panel bearing Ceres. ***Engraver:*** W.L. Ormsby. ***Comments:*** H-MA-910-A10. Altered from $1 Mechanics and Traders Bank, Georgetown, D.C. Nov. 14, 1852.

Rarity: —

$1 • W-MA-2420-001-A030

Left: Laureate woman leaning on shield bearing 1. ***Center:*** 1 / Bull in field, Horse, Trees. ***Bottom center:*** Road, Trees, Sign post. ***Right:*** Indian man standing / 1. ***Engraver:*** Doty & Bergen. ***Comments:*** H-MA-910-A15. Altered from $1 Merchants Bank, Stillwater, Minnesota. Oct. 20, 1854.

Rarity: —

$1 • W-MA-2420-001-A040

Left: 1 / State arms / ONE. ***Center:*** Three allegorical women reclining around shield surmounted by eagle, Ship. ***Right:*** 1 / Two farmers walking, Dog. ***Engraver:*** Danforth, Wright & Co. ***Comments:*** H-MA-910-A20. Altered from $1 Bank of Washtenaw, Washtenaw, Michigan series. 1850s.

Rarity: —

$2 • W-MA-2420-002-S010 CJF

Engraver: Danforth, Wright & Co. ***Comments:*** H-MA-910-S5. 18__. 1850s.

Rarity: URS-8
F $50; **VF** $125

$2 • W-MA-2420-002-S020

Center: Woman / 2 / Woman. ***Comments:*** H-MA-910-S10.

Rarity: —

$2 • W-MA-2420-002-N010

Center: Train. ***Comments:*** H-MA-910-N5.

Rarity: —

$3 • W-MA-2420-003-N020 CC

Comments: H-MA-910-N10. 18__. 1840s.

Rarity: URS-6
F $100; **VF** $250

$3 • W-MA-2420-003-A050

Left: 3 / Portrait of Andrew Jackson / 3. ***Center:*** 3 / Indian woman with bow / Coats of arms, Flags, Drums / 3. ***Bottom center:*** Train at station. ***Right:*** THREE / Ceres seated with caduceus / 3. ***Engraver:*** Rawdon, Wright, Hatch & Edson. ***Comments:*** H-MA-910-A25. Altered from $3 Merchants Bank, Washington, D.C. Dec. 1, 1852.

Rarity: —

$3 • W-MA-2420-003-A060

Left: 3 / Helmeted medallion head. ***Center:*** Mechanic seated, Forge, anvil, and cogwheel. ***Right:*** 3 / Portrait of William Henry Harrison. ***Engraver:*** W.L. Ormsby. ***Comments:*** H-MA-910-A30. Altered from $3 Merchants Bank, Ft. Leavenworth, Kansas. 185_. 1850s.

Rarity: —

$5 • W-MA-2420-005-S030

Center: Two people seated. ***Comments:*** H-MA-910-S15.

Rarity: —

$5 • W-MA-2420-005-S040

Center: Two sailing ships. ***Comments:*** H-MA-910-S20. 18__. 1840s.

Rarity: —

$5 • W-MA-2420-005-N030
Left: Portrait of Zachary Taylor. ***Center:*** Woman. ***Comments:*** H-MA-910-N15.
Rarity: —

$5 • W-MA-2420-005-A070
Left: FIVE vertically. ***Center:*** 5 / Spread eagle on U.S. shield holding banner in its beak. ***Bottom center:*** Road, Trees, Sign post. ***Right:*** Indian woman holding bow. ***Engraver:*** Doty & Bergen. ***Comments:*** H-MA-910-A35. Altered from $5 Merchants Bank, Stillwater, Minnesota. Oct. 20, 1854.
Rarity: —

$5 • W-MA-2420-005-A080
Left: Indian man seated on rock with bow, Dog. ***Center:*** Ships in harbor, Warehouse / 5. ***Right:*** FIVE on die on panel of wheat ears and fruit. ***Engraver:*** Durand & Co. ***Comments:*** H-MA-910-A40. Altered from $5 Globe Bank, New York City, New York. 1840s.
Rarity: —

$10 • W-MA-2420-010-S050
Center: Two people seated. ***Comments:*** H-MA-910-S25.
Rarity: —

$10 • W-MA-2420-010-N040
Comments: H-MA-910-N20. No description available. Printed on pink paper. 18__. 1850s.
Rarity: *None known*

$10 • W-MA-2420-010-A090
Left: X / Eagle surmounting frame bearing arm and hammer. ***Center:*** Woman seated on bale, Spinning wheel / 10. ***Right:*** Panel of flowers and fruit bearing medallion portrait of George Washington. ***Engraver:*** W.L. Ormsby. ***Comments:*** H-MA-910-A45. Altered from $10 Merchants Bank, Ft. Leavenworth, Kansas. 18__. 1850s.
Rarity: —

$20 • W-MA-2420-020-S060
Center: Two people seated. ***Comments:*** H-MA-910-S30.
Rarity: —

$50 • W-MA-2420-050-S070
Center: Two people seated. ***Comments:*** H-MA-910-S35.
Rarity: —

Merrimac Bank
1795–1805
W-MA-2430

History: The Merrimac Bank (also preferably spelled Merrimack) was chartered in 1795 with an authorized capital of no less than $70,000 and no more than $150,000. The name was taken from the river that flows through the town and empties into the Atlantic Ocean. No loans were to be made to shareholders until they had paid their shares in full. If the $150,000 capital was chosen, the shareholders could borrow from the bank any amount above the minimum capital of $70,000.[23]

On February 21, 1800, the bank was authorized to increase its capital to $250,000. William Bartlet was president of the bank at that time, and Joseph Cutler was cashier.[24] On June 25, 1805, the shareholders met, and after that date the business was wound down.

An unrelated Merrimack Bank, W-MA-1860, was chartered in Haverhill in 1814.

Numismatic Commentary: Notes of this bank are so rare as to be non-collectible. None are represented in the collections surveyed.

Valid Issues

$1 • W-MA-2430-001-G010
Comments: H-MA-915-G20. Similar to W-MA-2430-010-R010. 179_. 1790s.
Rarity: —

$1 • W-MA-2430-001-G020
Comments: H-MA-915-G24. No description available. 179_. 1790s.
Rarity: *None known*

$2 • W-MA-2430-002-G030
Comments: H-MA-915-G28. Similar to W-MA-2430-010-R010. 179_. 1790s.
Rarity: —

$2 • W-MA-2430-002-G040
Comments: H-MA-915-G32. No description available. 18__. 1800s.
Rarity: *None known*

$3 • W-MA-2430-003-G050
Comments: H-MA-915-G36. Similar to W-MA-2430-010-R010. 179_. 1790s.
Rarity: —

$3 • W-MA-2430-003-G060
Comments: H-MA-915-G40. No description available. 18__. 1800s.
Rarity: *None known*

$5 • W-MA-2430-005-G070
Comments: H-MA-915-G42. No description available. 18__. 1800s.
Rarity: *None known*

$5 • W-MA-2430-005-G080
Comments: H-MA-915-G44. Similar to W-MA-2430-010-R010. 179_. 1790s.
Rarity: —

$10 • W-MA-2430-010-G090
Comments: H-MA-915-G52. Similar to W-MA-2430-010-R010. 179_. 1790s.
Rarity: —

$10 • W-MA-2430-010-G100
Comments: H-MA-915-G56. No description available. 18__. 1800s
Rarity: *None known*

Non-Valid Issues

$10 • W-MA-2430-010-R010
Center: Tree / Ship / Die. ***Comments:*** H-MA-915-R5. Raised from note of unknown denomination. 179_. 1790s.
Rarity: —

Newburyport Bank {1st}
1803–1812
W-MA-2445

History: The Newburyport Bank was chartered on March 8, 1803, with $200,000 capital to be divided into shares of $100 each. Micajah Sawyer, Michael Hodge, John Greenleaf, Joshua

Carter, Israel Young, Thomas Cary Jr., Charles Jackson, Samuel Allyne Otis, and Dudley Atkins Tyng were incorporated by the name of "The President, Directors and Company of the Newbury Port Bank."

In 1805 the capital was approved to be increased to $250,000.[25] In 1812 the bank's charter expired. A new corporation under the name of the Newburyport Bank, W-MA-2460, took the place of the bank with most of the same stockholders and principals.

Numismatic Commentary: Genuine notes from the first Newburyport Bank are unknown. Pictured is a reprint taken from an original plate.

Valid Issues

$5 • W-MA-2445-005-G010

CJF

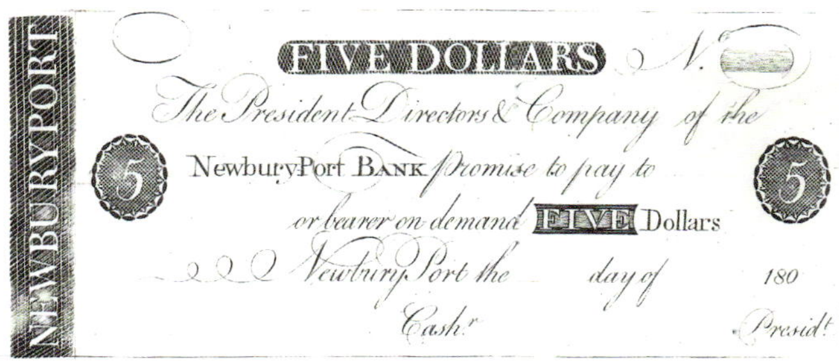

Comments: H-Unlisted. Reprint. 180_.
Rarity: URS-1

$10 • W-MA-2445-010-G020

CJF

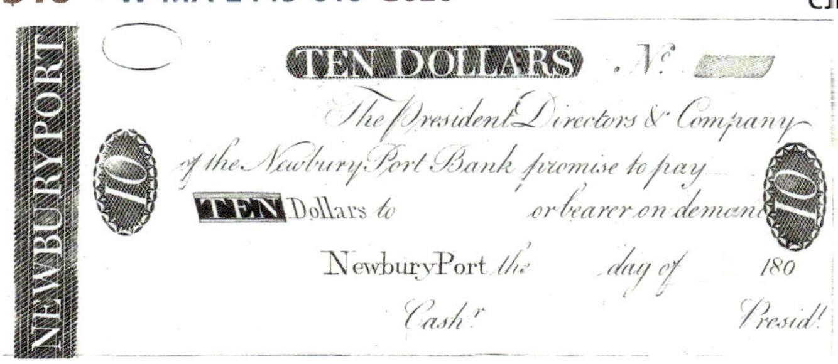

Comments: H-Unlisted. Reprint. 180_.
Rarity: URS-1

$40 • W-MA-2445-040-G030

CJF

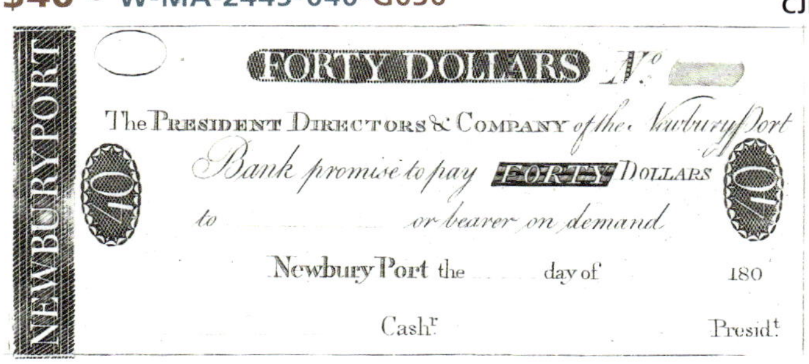

Comments: H-Unlisted. Reprint. 180_.
Rarity: URS-1

$50 • W-MA-2445-050-G040

CJF

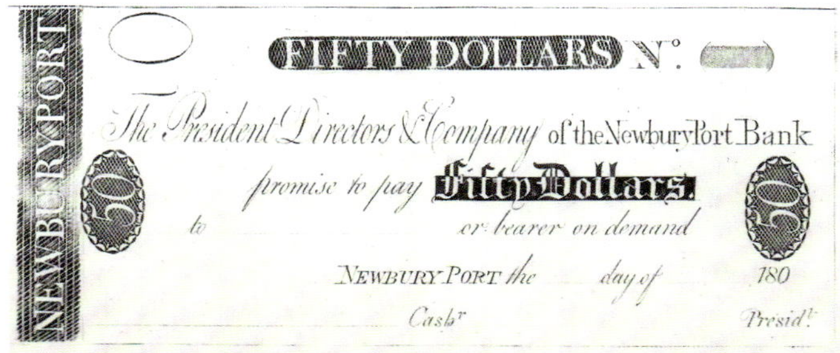

Comments: H-Unlisted. Reprint. 180_.
Rarity: URS-1

Uncut Sheets

$5-$10-$40-$50 • W-MA-2445-005.010.040.050-US010

CJF

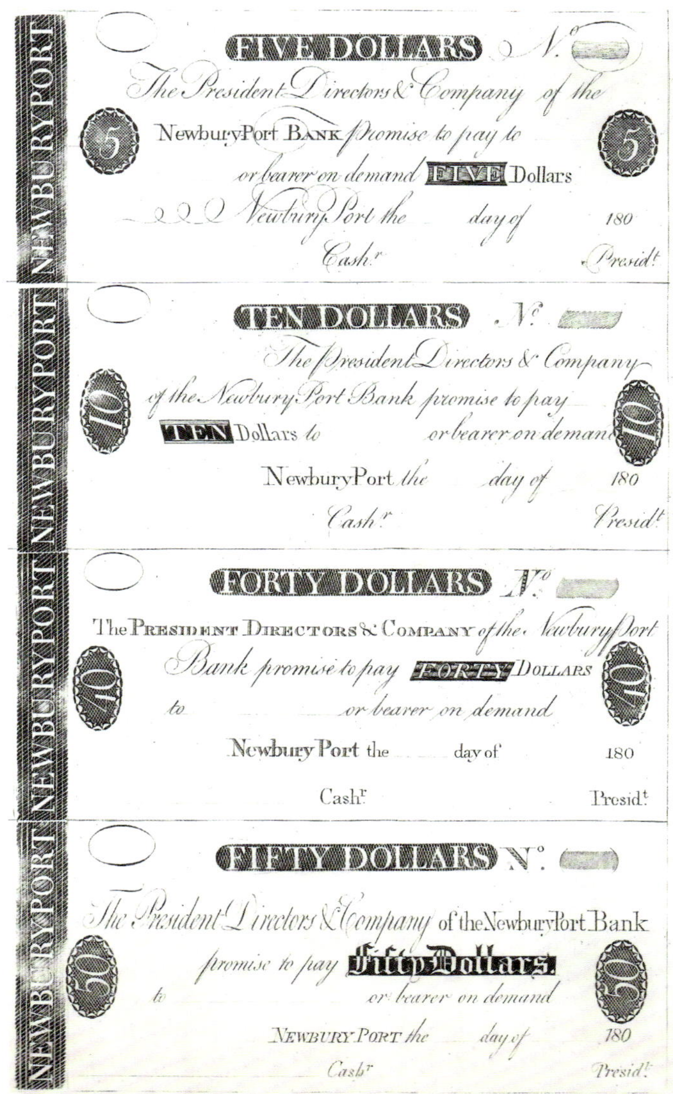

Comments: All unlisted in Haxby. Reprint. 180_.
Rarity: URS-1

Newburyport Bank {2nd}

1812–1831

W-MA-2460

History: On the expiration of the charter of the first Newburyport Bank, W-MA-2445, in 1812, a new act of incorporation was obtained for the Newburyport Bank. It was set up by most of the former principals in succeeding the business of its predecessor. The charter was given on June 23, 1812, with an authorized capital of $350,000.

On October 13, 1814, the capital stock of the bank was reduced to $210,000. William Bartlet was elected president, and Samuel Mulliken was cashier. On June 15, 1831, the president and directors of the bank were authorized and directed to reduce the bank's liabilities and settle all outstanding accounts within three years, "in the same manner, and to every intent and purpose, as if the act incorporating said company had expired by its own limitation."[26]

Valid Issues

$5 • W-MA-2460-005-G010 CJF

Engraver: PSSP. ***Comments:*** H-Unlisted. 18__. 1820s.

Rarity: —

Newburyport Bank {3rd}

1836–1841

W-MA-2470

History: Another Newburyport Bank, unrelated to the earlier entities with the same name, was chartered on April 9, 1836, with an authorized capital of $100,000. The bank was star-crossed, as by the time it was underway, with some stock subscriptions still unpaid, the Panic of 1837 took place.

The bank was unable to do business and suspended payment in 1841. In 1845 its affairs were wound up, and the bank redeemed every bill in full. Those who had bought stock lost their investment.

Numismatic Commentary: Among the notes of this bank, collectors have a choice of interesting vignettes to choose from. The town square and harbor are popular, as they look almost identical today as when the notes were engraved in the 1830s and 1840s. There are also some partially vignette PSSP style notes from the era after the New England Bank Note Co. absorbed the Perkins engraving plant.

Valid Issues

$1 • W-MA-2470-001-G010 CC

Engraver: PSSP / New England Bank Note Co. ***Comments:*** H-MA-921-G4. 18__. 1830s.

Rarity: URS-5

VG $250

$1 • W-MA-2470-001-G020 AAS

Engraver: New England Bank Note Co. ***Comments:*** H-MA-921-G8. 18__. Circa 1840.

Rarity: URS-6

F $350; **VF** $500

$1.25 • W-MA-2470-001.25-G030

Left: 1 25/100 / Train / 1 25/100. ***Center:*** Sloop and other ships at sea / $1.25 cts. ***Right:*** 1 25/100 / Eagle. ***Engraver:*** New England Bank Note Co. ***Comments:*** H-MA-921-G12. 18__. 1830s.

Rarity: —

How to Read the Whitman Numbering System

$1 • W-MA-010-001-G010a

Denomination: Value of the note shown.

W: Whitman number. This number is a sortable code unique to each bank and note.

MA: Abbreviation for the state under study.

010: Numerical designation specific to each bank.

001: The denomination in dollars.

G010a: G indicates a good or valid note. Other categories are indicated thus: C (counterfeit); R (raised); S (spurious); N (not-attributed); A (altered). Numbers are assigned starting with 010, 020, et seq. Terminal letters following the number indicate variations of a note: a series of different colored overprints, tints, payees, etc., all on the same design of note. For more information, see the "How to Use This Book" section at the front of the volume, page xiv.

$1.50 • W-MA-2470-001.50-G040

Left: 1 Doll. 50 Cts. vertically. ***Center:*** Eagle on rock in ocean / $1 50/100. ***Right:*** 1 50/100 / Justice. ***Engraver:*** New England Bank Note Co. ***Comments:*** H-MA-921-G14. 18__. 1830s.

Rarity: —

$1.75 • W-MA-2470-001.75-G050

Left: $1.75 Cts. / Hebe watering eagle / 1 75/100. ***Center:*** Three sloops at sea. ***Right:*** $1.75 Cts. / Dog, Woman seated with grain / 1 75/100. ***Engraver:*** New England Bank Note Co. ***Comments:*** H-MA-921-G16. 18__. 1830s.

Rarity: —

$2 • W-MA-2470-002-G060

Left: 2 / Woman standing with staff, Cornucopia / TWO. ***Center:*** TWO / Machinery and merchandise flanking Ceres seated holding sickle and rake, Factories and harbor / Panel outlining white TWO. ***Right:*** 2 / Woman wearing hat, Trees / TWO. ***Engraver:*** New England Bank Note Co. / PSSP. ***Comments:*** H-MA-921-G20. 18__. 1830s.

Rarity: —

$2 • W-MA-2470-002-G070

CJF

Engraver: New England Bank Note Co. ***Comments:*** H-MA-921-G24. 18__. Circa 1840.

Rarity: URS-5

F $500

$3 • W-MA-2470-003-G080

Left: THREE / Beehive / THREE. ***Center:*** Woman with shield / THREE. ***Right:*** 3 on THREE / Two figures / 3 on THREE. ***Engraver:*** New England Bank Note Co. / PSSP. ***Comments:*** H-MA-921-G28. 18__. 1830s.

Rarity: —

$3 • W-MA-2470-003-G090

Left: THREE vertically. ***Center:*** View of Newburyport Harbor. ***Right:*** THREE / Eagle perched on 3 / THREE. ***Engraver:*** New England Bank Note Co. ***Comments:*** H-MA-921-G32. 18__. Circa 1840.

Rarity: URS-4

F $300; **VF** $500

$5 • W-MA-2470-005-G100

Left: 5 / Blacksmith at anvil / FIVE. ***Center:*** Mercury standing with 5, Cornucopia and merchandise, Factories and ship / V / Panel outlining white FIVE. ***Right:*** 5 / Ceres kneeling / FIVE. ***Engraver:*** New England Bank Note Co. / PSSP. ***Comments:*** H-MA-921-G36. 18__. 1830s.

Rarity: —

$5 • W-MA-2470-005-G110

CC

Engraver: New England Bank Note Co. ***Comments:*** H-MA-921-G40. 18__. Circa 1840.

Rarity: URS-5

F $550; **EF** $1,100

$10 • W-MA-2470-010-G120

Left: 10 / Man standing / TEN. ***Center:*** 10 / Two figures / Scene. ***Right:*** 10 / Scene / TEN. ***Engraver:*** New England Bank Note Co. ***Comments:*** H-MA-921-G44. 18__. 1830s.

Rarity: —

$10 • W-MA-2470-010-G130

Engraver: Unverified, but likely New England Bank Note Co. ***Comments:*** H-MA-921-G48. No description available. 18__. Circa 1840.

Rarity: *None known*

$20 • W-MA-2470-020-G140

CJF

Engraver: PSSP / New England Bank Note Co. ***Comments:*** H-MA-921-G52. 18__. 1830s.

Rarity: URS-5

F $400; **VF** $600

$50 • W-MA-2470-050-G150

Left: 50 / Cornucopia, Woman standing with ankles crossed, Staff, Anchor / 50. ***Center:*** FIFTY DOLLARS / 50. ***Right:*** FIFTY vertically. ***Engraver:*** New England Bank Note Co. / PSSP. ***Comments:*** H-MA-921-G56. 18__. 1830s.

Rarity: —

$100 • W-MA-2470-100-G160

Left: Lathework panel bearing C / Portrait of George Washington / C. ***Center:*** 100 / Manhattan reclining, pouring water, Ship / 100. ***Right:*** Lathework panel bearing ONE HUNDRED vertically. ***Engraver:*** New England Bank Note Co. / PSSP. ***Comments:*** H-MA-921-G60. 18__. 1830s.

Rarity: —

$500 • **W-MA-2470-500-G170**

Left: 500 / 500 vertically. ***Center:*** 500 / Woman seated with shield bearing D, Fasces, cornucopia, lyre, and sheaf / 500. ***Right:*** 500 / D / 500. ***Engraver:*** New England Bank Note Co. / PSSP. ***Comments:*** H-MA-921-G64. 18__. 1830s.

Rarity: —

Non-Valid Issues

$10 • **W-MA-2470-010-R010**

Engraver: New England Bank Note Co. ***Comments:*** H-MA-921-R5. Raised from W-MA-2470-002-G060. 18__. 1830s.

Rarity: —

Ocean Bank

1833–1865

W-MA-2480

History: The Ocean Bank was chartered on March 20, 1833, with an authorized capital of $200,000. In 1844 the capital was reduced to $100,000. Circulation of the Ocean Bank ranged from a low of $69,411 in 1839 to a high of $158,191 in 1863.

The business of the Ocean Bank was succeeded by the Ocean National Bank, chartered on April 14, 1865.

Numismatic Commentary: All of the genuine Ocean Bank notes are of the PSSP design, some showing the American Bank Note Co. monogram. These are scarce, but with a little time and effort, a note should be found.

Valid Issues

$1 • **W-MA-2480-001-G010**

Left: MASSACHUSETTS vertically / 1 / Female portrait / 1. ***Center:*** 1 / ONE / 1 / Ship. ***Right:*** 1 / Portrait of Indian / 1 / ONE DOLLAR vertically. ***Engraver:*** PSSP. ***Comments:*** H-MA-925-G2. 18__. 1830s–1850s.

Rarity: —

$1 • **W-MA-2480-001-G010a**

Overprint: Red ONE. ***Engraver:*** PSSP. ***Comments:*** H-MA-925-G2a. Similar to W-MA-2480-001-G010. 18__. 1850s.

Rarity: —

$1 • **W-MA-2480-001-G010b** CC

Engraver: PSSP / ABNCo. monogram. ***Comments:*** H-MA-925-G2b. Similar to W-MA-2480-001-G010 but with additional engraver imprint. Proof. 18__.

Rarity: URS-4
Proof $2,100

$1 • **W-MA-2480-001-G010c**

Overprint: Red ONE. ***Engraver:*** PSSP / ABNCo. monogram. ***Comments:*** H-MA-925-G2c. Similar to W-MA-2480-001-G010 but with additional engraver imprint. 18__. 1850s–1860s.

Rarity: —

$2 • **W-MA-2480-002-G020**

Left: MASSACHUSETTS vertically / 2 / Female portrait / 2. ***Center:*** 2 / TWO / 2 / Ship. ***Right:*** 2 / Portrait of Indian / 2 / TWO DOLLARS vertically. ***Engraver:*** PSSP. ***Comments:*** H-MA-925-G4. 18__. 1830s–1850s.

Rarity: —

$2 • **W-MA-2480-002-G020a** JF

Overprint: Red TWO. ***Engraver:*** PSSP. ***Comments:*** H-MA-925-G4a. Similar to W-MA-2480-002-G020. Proof. 18__. 1850s.

Rarity: URS-3
Proof $2,500

$2 • **W-MA-2480-002-G020b** CC

Engraver: PSSP / ABNCo. monogram. ***Comments:*** H-MA-925-G4b. Similar to W-MA-2480-002-G020 but with additional engraver imprint. Proof. 18__.

Rarity: URS-4
Proof $2,100

$2 • **W-MA-2480-002-G020c**

Overprint: Red TWO. ***Engraver:*** PSSP / ABNCo. monogram. ***Comments:*** H-MA-925-G4c. Similar to W-MA-2480-002-G020 but with additional engraver imprint. 18__. 1850s–1860s.

Rarity: —

$3 • **W-MA-2480-003-G030**

Left: MASSACHUSETTS / 3 / Female portrait / 3. ***Center:*** 3 / THREE / 3 / Ship. ***Right:*** 3 / Portrait of Indian / 3 / THREE DOLLARS vertically. ***Engraver:*** PSSP. ***Comments:*** H-MA-925-G6. 18__. 1830s–1850s.

Rarity: —

$3 • **W-MA-2480-003-G030a**

Overprint: Red THREE. ***Engraver:*** PSSP. ***Comments:*** H-MA-925-G6a. Similar to W-MA-2480-003-G030. 18__. 1850s.

Rarity: —

$3 • W-MA-2480-003-G030b

CJF

Engraver: PSSP / ABNCo. monogram. ***Comments:*** H-MA-925-G6b. Similar to W-MA-2480-003-G030 but with additional engraver imprint. Might have been made only as Proof. 18__.

Rarity: URS-4
Proof $2,500

$3 • W-MA-2480-003-G030c

CJF

Overprint: Red THREE. ***Engraver:*** PSSP / ABNCo. monogram. ***Comments:*** H-MA-925-G6c. Similar to W-MA-2480-003-G030 but with additional engraver imprint. 18__. 1850s–1860s.

Rarity: URS-5
VF $750

$5 • W-MA-2480-005-G040

Engraver: PSSP. ***Comments:*** H-MA-925-G8. 18__. 1830s–1850s.

Rarity: —

$5 • W-MA-2480-005-G040a

Overprint: Red FIVE. ***Engraver:*** PSSP. ***Comments:*** H-MA-925-G8a. Similar to W-MA-2480-005-G040. 18__. 1850s.

Rarity: URS-5
VF $500

$5 • W-MA-2480-005-G040b

Overprint: Red FIVE. ***Engraver:*** PSSP / ABNCo. monogram. ***Comments:*** H-MA-925-G8c. Similar to W-MA-2480-005-G040 but with additional engraver imprint. 18__. 1850s–1860s.

Rarity: —

$10 • W-MA-2480-010-G050

Engraver: PSSP. ***Comments:*** H-MA-925-G10. 18__. 1830s–1850s.

Rarity: —

$10 • W-MA-2480-010-G050a

Overprint: Red TEN. ***Engraver:*** PSSP. ***Comments:*** H-MA-925-G10a. Similar to W-MA-2480-010-G050. 18__. 1850s.

Rarity: —

$10 • W-MA-2480-010-G050b

Overprint: Red TEN. ***Engraver:*** PSSP / ABNCo. monogram. ***Comments:*** H-MA-925-G10c. Similar to W-MA-2480-010-G050 but with additional engraver imprint. 18__. 1850s–1860s.

Rarity: —

$20 • W-MA-2480-020-G060

Engraver: PSSP. ***Comments:*** H-MA-925-G12. 18__. 1830s–1850s.

Rarity: URS-4
Proof $2,500

$50 • W-MA-2480-050-G070

Engraver: PSSP. ***Comments:*** H-MA-925-G14. 18__. 1830s–1850s.

Rarity: —

$100 • W-MA-2480-100-G080

Engraver: PSSP. ***Comments:*** H-MA-925-G16. 18__. 1830s–1850s.

Rarity: —

$500 • W-MA-2480-500-G090

Engraver: PSSP. ***Comments:*** H-MA-925-G18. 18__. 1830s–1850s.

Rarity: —

Non-Valid Issues

$5 • W-MA-2480-005-C040

Engraver: PSSP. ***Comments:*** H-MA-925-C8. Counterfeit of W-MA-2480-005-G040. 18__. 1840s.

Rarity: —

$5 • W-MA-2480-005-N010

Center: Drove of cattle, Train. ***Comments:*** H-MA-925-N5.

Rarity: —

$10 • W-MA-2480-010-A010

Left: Train / Portrait of George Washington. ***Center:*** Three women. ***Right:*** 10 / X / 10. ***Engraver:*** New England Bank Note Co. ***Comments:*** H-MA-925-A10. 18__. Circa 1840.

Rarity: —

Newton, Massachusetts

Taking its name from "new town," Newton was settled in 1630 and renamed Cambridge in 1638. In 1688 it was incorporated as Cambridge Village, but it was renamed Newtown in 1691. In 1766 the name was shortened to Newton. It was incorporated as a city in 1873.

13 villages make up the city of Newton: Auburndale, Chestnut Hill, Newton Centre, Newton Corner, Newton Highlands, Newton Lower Falls, Newton Upper Falls, Newtonville, Nonantum, Oak Hill, Thompsonville, Waban, and West Newton.

Early industries included mills that were powered by the river and falls, producing chocolate, glue, paper, and tobacco. However, the water power was not sufficient to make Newton a major manufacturing city. It instead became a commuter town: starting in 1834, a large number of workers from Newton took the Boston and Worcester Railroad into the nearby towns to work the factories.

Newton Bank

1848–1865

W-MA-2490

History: The Newton Bank was chartered on April 17, 1848, with an authorized capital of $200,000. It opened its doors on October 14. By February 1849, the capital had been reduced to $100,000. By 1851 it was $150,000. Circulation was $89,445 in 1849.[27] It reached a high of $110,574 in 1857.

The business of the Newton Bank was succeeded by the Newton National Bank, chartered on February 8, 1865.

Numismatic Commentary: Many of the notes from this bank show preacher John Eliot speaking to the local Nonantum Indians. History tells us that he converted many Indians to Christianity and set up "praying towns" for them. There were 14 such villiages in southern New England. In the process, he also translated the Bible into the local Indian dialect. The historical context of these vignettes will not be lost on those informed of this man's work, and subsequently these notes are sought after not only by state collectors but also collectors of historical vignettes, making them very hard to obtain casually.

Valid Issues

$1 • W-MA-2490-001-G010

Left: "John Eliot Preaching to Indians". ***Center:*** Portrait of Benjamin Franklin. ***Right:*** Portrait of John Quincy Adams. ***Engraver:*** New England Bank Note Co. / Rawdon, Wright, Hatch & Edson. ***Comments:*** H-MA-930-G2. Oct. 7, 18__. 1848–1850s.

Rarity: —

$1 • W-MA-2490-001-G010a

Overprint: Red ONE. ***Engraver:*** New England Bank Note Co. / Rawdon, Wright, Hatch & Edson. ***Comments:*** H-MA-930-G2a. Similar to W-MA-2490-001-G010. Oct. 7, 18__. 1850s.

Rarity: —

$1 • W-MA-2490-001-G010b

Overprint: Red ONE. ***Engraver:*** New England Bank Note Co. / American Bank Note Co. / ABNCo. monogram. ***Comments:*** H-MA-930-G2b. Similar to W-MA-2490-001-G010 but with additional engraver imprint. Oct. 7, 18__. 1850s–1860s.

Rarity: URS-3
Proof $2,000

$2 • W-MA-2490-002-G020

CJF

Engraver: New England Bank Note Co. / Rawdon, Wright, Hatch & Edson. ***Comments:*** H-MA-930-G4. October 7, 18__. 1848–1850s.

Rarity: URS-3
VF $4,000

$2 • W-MA-2490-002-G020a

Left: "John Eliot Preaching to Indians" / 2. ***Center:*** 2. ***Right:*** 2 / Portrait of George Washington / TWO. ***Overprint:*** Red TWO. ***Engraver:*** New England Bank Note Co. / Rawdon, Wright, Hatch & Edson. ***Comments:*** H-MA-930-G4a. Similar to W-MA-2490-002-G020. Oct. 7, 18__. 1850s.

Rarity: —

$2 • W-MA-2490-002-G020b

JF

Overprint: Red TWO. ***Engraver:*** New England Bank Note Co. / Rawdon, Wright, Hatch & Edson / ABNCo. monogram. ***Comments:*** H-MA-930-G4b. Similar to W-MA-2490-002-G020 but with additional engraver imprint. October 7, 18__. 1850s–1860s.

Rarity: URS-2
VF $6,000

$3 • W-MA-2490-003-G030

Left: "John Eliot Preaching to Indians". ***Center:*** 3. ***Bottom center:*** Farm tools and cornucopia. ***Right:*** 3 / Indian woman with bow and arrows / THREE / 3. ***Engraver:*** New England Bank Note Co. / Rawdon, Wright, Hatch & Edson. ***Comments:*** H-MA-930-G6. Oct. 7, 18__. 1848–1850s.

Rarity: —

$3 • W-MA-2490-003-G030a

Overprint: Red THREE. ***Engraver:*** New England Bank Note Co. / Rawdon, Wright, Hatch & Edson. ***Comments:*** H-MA-930-G6a. Similar to W-MA-2490-003-G030. Oct. 7, 18__. 1850s.

Rarity: —

$3 • W-MA-2490-003-G030b

Overprint: Red THREE. ***Engraver:*** New England Bank Note Co. / Rawdon, Wright, Hatch & Edson / ABNCo. monogram. ***Comments:*** H-MA-930-G6b. Similar to W-MA-2490-003-G030 but with additional engraver imprint. Oct. 7, 18__. 1850s–1860s.

Rarity: —

$5 • W-MA-2490-005-G040

Left: "John Eliot Preaching to Indians" / 5. ***Center:*** 5. ***Bottom center:*** Train. ***Right:*** 5 / Cattle, sheep, and pigs / FIVE. ***Engraver:*** New England Bank Note Co. / Rawdon, Wright, Hatch & Edson. ***Comments:*** H-MA-930-G8. Oct. 7, 18__. 1848–1850s.

Rarity: —

$5 • W-MA-2490-005-G040a

Overprint: Red FIVE. ***Engraver:*** New England Bank Note Co. / Rawdon, Wright, Hatch & Edson. ***Comments:*** H-MA-930-G8a. Similar to W-MA-2490-005-G040. Oct. 7, 18__. 1850s.

Rarity: —

$5 • W-MA-2490-005-G040b

Overprint: Red FIVE. ***Engraver:*** New England Bank Note Co. / Rawdon, Wright, Hatch & Edson / ABNCo. monogram. ***Comments:*** H-MA-930-G8b. Similar to W-MA-2490-005-G040 but with additional engraver imprint. Oct. 7, 18__. 1850s–1860s.

Rarity: —

$10 • W-MA-2490-010-G050

Left: "John Eliot Preaching to Indians" / 10. ***Center:*** X. ***Bottom center:*** Farmer seated on plow. ***Right:*** 10 / Indian woman standing with ear of corn and X / X. ***Engraver:*** New England Bank Note Co. / Rawdon, Wright, Hatch & Edson. ***Comments:*** H-MA-930-G10. Oct. 7, 18__. 1848–1850s.

Rarity: —

$10 • W-MA-2490-010-G050a

Overprint: Red TEN. ***Engraver:*** New England Bank Note Co. / Rawdon, Wright, Hatch & Edson. ***Comments:*** H-MA-930-G10a. Similar to W-MA-2490-010-G050. Oct. 7, 18__. 1848–1850s.

Rarity: —

$10 • W-MA-2490-010-G050b

Overprint: Red TEN. ***Engraver:*** New England Bank Note Co. / Rawdon, Wright, Hatch & Edson / ABNCo. monogram. ***Comments:*** H-MA-930-G10b. Similar to W-MA-2490-010-G050 but with additional engraver imprint. Oct. 7, 18__. 1850s–1860s.

Rarity: —

$20 • W-MA-2490-020-G060

Left: Shield bearing TWENTY / Woman seated on bale with shield / 20. ***Center:*** "John Eliot Preaching to Indians". ***Bottom center:*** Train. ***Right:*** 20 / State arms. ***Engraver:*** New England Bank Note Co. / Rawdon, Wright, Hatch & Edson. ***Comments:*** H-MA-930-G12. Oct. 7, 18__. 1848–1850s.

Rarity: —

$20 • W-MA-2490-020-G060a

Overprint: Red TWENTY. ***Engraver:*** New England Bank Note Co. / Rawdon, Wright, Hatch & Edson. ***Comments:*** H-MA-930-G12a. Similar to W-MA-2490-020-G060. Oct. 7, 18__. 1850s.

Rarity: —

$20 • W-MA-2490-020-G060b

Overprint: Red TWENTY. ***Engraver:*** New England Bank Note Co. / Rawdon, Wright, Hatch & Edson / ABNCo. monogram. ***Comments:*** H-MA-930-G12b. Similar to W-MA-2490-020-G060 but with additional engraver imprint. Oct. 7, 18__. 1850s–1860s.

Rarity: —

$50 • W-MA-2490-050-G070

Left: 50 / Minerva standing by column. ***Center:*** Ceres and Vulcan flanking cornucopia. ***Right:*** 50 / Cherub in sailboat / 50. ***Engraver:*** Rawdon, Wright, Hatch & Edson. ***Comments:*** H-MA-930-G14. 18__. 1848–1850s.

Rarity: —

$50 • W-MA-2490-050-G080

CJF

Tint: Green. ***Engraver:*** American Bank Note Co. ***Comments:*** H-MA-930-G16a. 18__. 1860s.

Rarity: URS-3
Proof $6,500
Selected auction price: Stack's Bowers Galleries, August 2014, Lot 2088, Proof $6,462

$100 • W-MA-2490-100-G090

Left: 100 / Vulcan seated with sledge and anchor. ***Center:*** Train on bridge, Eagle on limb, Canal locks / C. ***Bottom center:*** 100. ***Right:*** 100 / Ceres seated, Cornucopia. ***Engraver:*** Rawdon, Wright, Hatch & Edson. ***Comments:*** H-MA-930-G18. 18__. 1848–1850s.

Rarity: —

$100 • W-MA-2490-100-G100

CJF

Tint: Green. ***Engraver:*** American Bank Note Co. ***Comments:*** H-MA-930-G20a. 18__. 1860s.

Rarity: URS-3
Proof $10,000
Selected auction price: Stack's Bowers Galleries, August 2014, Lot 1089, Proof $12,925

$500 • W-MA-2490-500-G110

Left: Woman seated on sheaves, Men reaping, Man on horse / 500. ***Center:*** 500 / D. ***Right:*** 500 vertically. ***Engraver:*** Rawdon, Wright, Hatch & Edson. ***Comments:*** H-MA-930-G22. 18__. 1850s–1860s.

Rarity: —

Uncut Sheets

$50-$100 • W-MA-2490-050.100-US010

CJF

Tint(s): Green. ***Comments:*** H-MA-930-G16a, G20a. 18__. 1860s.

Rarity: —

Non-Valid Issues

$3 • **W-MA-2490-003-N010**

Center: 3 / Woman and man seated under tree / 3. ***Right:*** Three women seated. ***Comments:*** H-MA-930-N5. 1850s.

Rarity: —

$10 • **W-MA-2490-010-R010**

Engraver: New England Bank Note Co. / Rawdon, Wright, Hatch & Edson. ***Comments:*** H-MA-930-R5. Raised from W-MA-2490-001-G010 or G010a. Oct. 7, 18__. 1850s.

Rarity: —

$100 • **W-MA-2490-100-C090**

Engraver: Rawdon, Wright, Hatch & Edson. ***Comments:*** H-MA-930-C18. Counterfeit of W-MA-2490-100-G090. 18__. 1850s.

Rarity: —

North Adams, Massachusetts

Originally settled in 1737, the land that would become Adams was purchased by Nathan Jones in 1762 when it was still known as East Hoosac. It was incorporated in 1778. Named in honor of Samuel Adams, a signer of the Declaration of Independence and later governor of the province (today a popular beer bears his name), the farmland was mostly divided into lots along the Hoosic River. Later that river would turn water power into mills for woolen, cotton, lumber, and plastic products. Water power provided the opportunity to build a variety of mills.

Before the American Revolution, manufacturing in the form of mills brought prosperity to North Adams. Its prime location between two branches of the Hoosic River provided ample water power to the entire area. Shoe manufacturers, brick makers, saw mills, cabinet makers, hat manufacturers, marble works, machine shops, wagon makers, sleigh makers, flax seed oil extraction, and iron works made up some of the industries. Armor plates for the *Monitor*, the famous Civil War ironclad ship, were made in this town.

See also Adams, Adams South Village, and South Adams, Massachusetts.

Adams Bank

1831–1865

W-MA-2510

History: The Adams Bank was chartered in June 1831 with an authorized capital of $100,000. In 1837 the capital was increased to $200,000. On November 2, 1839, the circulation of bills $5 and higher in value was $39,930, and the circulation of smaller denomination bills was $13,942. By 1840 the Adams Bank was using a North Adams address.

In 1845 the capital was reduced to $100,000, and by 1851 it was $150,000. By that time the circulation of higher denomination bills had increased to $83,520; the circulation of bills valued less than $5 had decreased to $12,110.

Capital was increased to $300,000 in 1856. In 1857 it was $350,000. Bills in circulation were listed at $193,248, specie was $7,080.54, and real estate was valued at $8,815. In October 1849, circulation was at $83,510. On January 3, 1863, it was reported at $339,697.

On May 4, 1865, the bank was succeeded by the Adams National Bank of North Adams.

See also listing under Adams, W-MA-025.

Numismatic Commentary: Genuine notes from this western Massachusetts bank are very hard to locate. Non-valid issues appear with some regularity.

As of 2003 there were two $20-$50 tint plates remaining at the American Bank Note Co. archives. Modern proprietary Proofs have been made of these.

Valid Issues

$1 • **W-MA-2510-001-G010**

Left: Lathework panel bearing MASSACHUSETTS vertically. ***Center:*** 1 / 1 / Alternating flower garlands and gridwork segments / ONE / 1 / 1. ***Right:*** Narrow lathework panel bearing ONE / D / ONE vertically. ***Engraver:*** PSSP. ***Comments:*** H-MA-935-G2. 18__. 1830s.

Rarity: —

$1 • **W-MA-2510-001-G020**

Engraver: Unverified, but likely Boston Bank Note Co. ***Comments:*** H-MA-935-G4. No description available. Nov. 15, 1837.

Rarity: *None known*

$1 • **W-MA-2510-001-G030**

Left: ONE / 1. ***Center:*** Farmer sowing, Man. ***Right:*** 1 / Ship / ONE. ***Engraver:*** New England Bank Note Co. ***Comments:*** H-MA-935-G6. 18__. 1840s.

Rarity: —

$1 • **W-MA-2510-001-G040**

Left: 1 / Portrait of George Washington. ***Center:*** Woman seated with rudder / 1 / Woman seated. ***Right:*** 1 / Portrait of Benjamin Franklin. ***Engraver:*** New England Bank Note Co. ***Comments:*** H-MA-935-G8. 18__. 1850s.

Rarity: —

$1 • **W-MA-2510-001-G050** CC

Engraver: Rawdon, Wright, Hatch & Edson. ***Comments:*** H-MA-935-G10. June 17, 1855. 1850s–1860s.

Rarity: URS-5

VG $150; **VF** $350; **Proof** $750

$1 • W-MA-2510-001-G050a

JF

Overprint: Red ONE. ***Engraver:*** Rawdon, Wright, Hatch & Edson. ***Comments:*** H-Unlisted. Similar to W-MA-2510-001-G050. June 17, 1857. 1850s–1860s.

Rarity: URS-4

VF $1,500

$1 • W-MA-2510-001-G050b

CJF

Overprint: Red lathework outlining white ONE. ***Engraver:*** Rawdon, Wright, Hatch & Edson. / ABNCo. monogram. ***Comments:*** H-Unlisted. Similar to W-MA-2510-001-G050 but with additional engraver imprint. June 17, 1857. 1850s–1860s.

Rarity: URS-3

VG $600; **F** $1,000

$2 • W-MA-2510-002-G060

Left: Lathework panel bearing MASSACHUSETTS vertically. ***Center:*** 2 / 2 / Alternating flower garlands and gridwork segments / TWO / 2 / 2. ***Right:*** Lathework panel bearing five TWOs vertically. ***Engraver:*** PSSP. ***Comments:*** H-MA-935-G12. 18__. 1830s.

Rarity: —

$2 • W-MA-2510-002-G070

SI

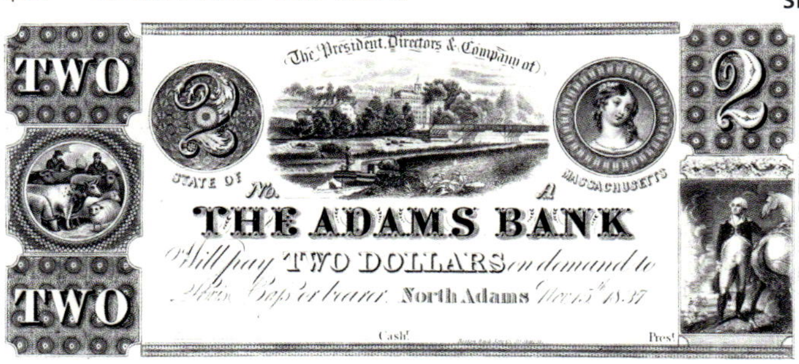

Engraver: New England Bank Note Co. ***Comments:*** H-MA-935-G14. Nov. 15, 1837.

Rarity: —

$2 • W-MA-2510-002-G080

Left: TWO / 2. ***Center:*** Eagle on bale, Cannon balls and machinery / 2. ***Right:*** 2 / TWO / Schooner. ***Engraver:*** New England Bank Note Co. ***Comments:*** H-MA-935-G16. 18__. 1840s.

Rarity: —

$2 • W-MA-2510-002-G090

Left: 2 / Portrait of Christopher Columbus. ***Center:*** Woman standing with cornucopia / 2 / Justice seated. ***Right:*** 2 / Male portrait. ***Engraver:*** New England Bank Note Co. ***Comments:*** H-MA-935-G18. 18__. 1850s.

Rarity: —

$2 • W-MA-2510-002-G100

Left: Two women standing / 2. ***Center:*** Two cherubs with two silver dollars, Train. ***Right:*** 2 / Sailor and Indian man flanking shield bearing TWO. ***Engraver:*** Rawdon, Wright, Hatch & Edson. ***Comments:*** H-MA-935-G20. 1850s–1860s.

Rarity: —

$3 • W-MA-2510-003-G110

Left: Lathework panel bearing MASSACHUSETTS vertically. ***Center:*** 3 / 3 / Alternating flower garlands and gridwork segments / THREE / 3 / 3. ***Right:*** Lathework panel bearing THREE vertically. ***Engraver:*** PSSP. ***Comments:*** H-MA-935-G22. 18__. 1830s.

Rarity: —

$3 • W-MA-2510-003-G120

Engraver: Unverified, but likely Boston Bank Note Co. ***Comments:*** H-MA-935-G24. No description available. Nov. 15, 1837.

Rarity: *None known*

$3 • W-MA-2510-003-G130

Left: THREE / 3. ***Center:*** Sailor standing with hat in hand, Bales and harbor / 3. ***Right:*** 3 / THREE / Train. ***Engraver:*** New England Bank Note Co. ***Comments:*** H-MA-935-G26. 18__. 1840s.

Rarity: —

$3 • W-MA-2510-003-G140

Left: 3 / George Washington standing by horse. ***Center:*** Female portrait / 3 / Portrait of girl with ringlets. ***Right:*** 3 / Vulcan standing with sledge. ***Engraver:*** New England Bank Note Co. ***Comments:*** H-MA-935-G28. 18__. 1850s.

Rarity: —

$5 • W-MA-2510-005-G150

Left: Lathework chain bearing MASSACHUSETTS / 5 / 5. ***Center:*** Alternating flower garlands and gridwork segments / FIVE. ***Right:*** 5 / 5. ***Engraver:*** PSSP. ***Comments:*** H-MA-935-G30. 18__. 1830s.

Rarity: —

$5 • W-MA-2510-005-G160

Left: Indian with bow drawn / V. ***Center:*** 5 / Man and woman seated with Mercury / 5. ***Right:*** V / Train / V. ***Engraver:*** Rawdon, Wright & Hatch. ***Comments:*** H-MA-935-G32. 18__. 1830s–1850s.

Rarity: —

$5 • W-MA-2510-005-G160a

Overprint: Red FIVE. ***Engraver:*** Rawdon, Wright & Hatch / ABNCo. monogram. ***Comments:*** H-MA-935-G32a. Similar to W-MA-2510-005-G160 but with additional engraver imprint. 18__. 1850s–1860s.

Rarity: URS-5

F $750; **VF** $1,250

$5 • W-MA-2510-005-G170

Left: Woman standing / FIVE. ***Center:*** 5 / Woman standing with staff and woman seated. ***Right:*** 5. ***Engraver:*** American Bank Note Co. ***Comments:*** H-MA-935-G36. Jan. 1, 1864.

Rarity: —

$10 • W-MA-2510-010-G180

Left: Lathework chain bearing MASSACHUSETTS vertically. ***Center:*** Alternating flower garlands and gridwork segments / TEN. ***Right:*** 10 / 10 vertically. ***Engraver:*** PSSP. ***Comments:*** H-MA-935-G38. 18__. 1830s.

Rarity: —

$10 • W-MA-2510-010-G190

Left: 10 / Train / 10. ***Center:*** X / Archimedes in clouds raising globe with lever / X. ***Right:*** Woman with cornucopia and liberty cap / 10. ***Engraver:*** Rawdon, Wright & Hatch. ***Comments:*** H-MA-935-G40. 18__. 1840s–1860s.

Rarity: —

$10 • W-MA-2510-010-G200

Left: Three deer / TEN. ***Center:*** X / Woman at well with urn, Sheep drinking / X. ***Right:*** 10 / Girl with puppies. ***Engraver:*** American Bank Note Co. ***Comments:*** H-MA-935-G42. Jan. 1, 1864.

Rarity: —

$20 • W-MA-2510-020-G210

Left: Lathework chain bearing MASSACHUSETTS / 20 / 20 vertically. ***Center:*** Alternating flower garlands and gridwork segments / TWENTY. ***Right:*** 20 / 20 vertically. ***Engraver:*** PSSP. ***Comments:*** H-MA-935-G44. 18__. 1830s.

Rarity: URS-5
Proof $1,500

$20 • W-MA-2510-020-G220

Left: 20 / Minerva standing with spear. ***Center:*** Woman seated between 2 and 0 / TWENTY. ***Bottom center:*** XX. ***Right:*** 20 / Woman reclining on cornucopia / 20. ***Engraver:*** Rawdon, Wright, Hatch & Edson. ***Comments:*** H-MA-935-G48. 18__. 1850s.

Rarity: —

$20 • W-MA-2510-020-G230

JF

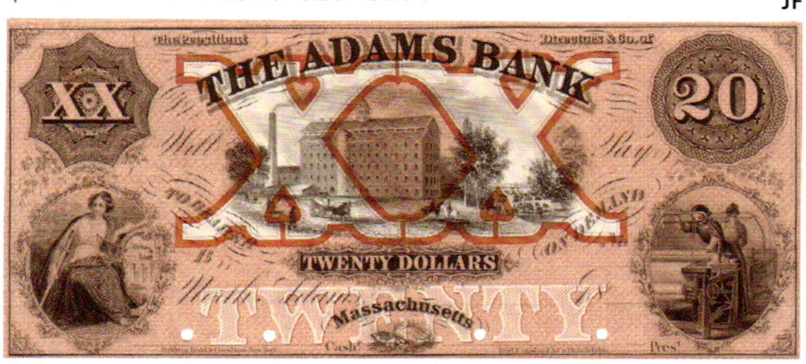

Tint: Red outlining white XX. ***Engraver:*** Baldwin, Bald & Cousland / Bald, Cousland & Co. ***Comments:*** H-Unlisted. Proof. 18__. 1850s.

Rarity: URS-3
Proof $1,400

$50 • W-MA-2510-050-G240

CC

Tint: Red outlining white 50. ***Comments:*** H-Unlisted. 18__. 1850s.

Rarity: URS-3
Proof $1,500
Selected auction price: Heritage, January 2013, Lot 15820, Gem New $616

$50 • W-MA-2510-050-G250

Left: Lathework chain bearing MASSACHUSETTS / 50 / 50 vertically. ***Center:*** Alternating flower garlands and gridwork segments / FIFTY. ***Right:*** 50 / 50 vertically. ***Engraver:*** PSSP. ***Comments:*** H-MA-935-G50. 18__. 1830s.

Rarity: —

$50 • W-MA-2510-050-G260

Left: 50 / Minerva standing by column. ***Center:*** Ceres and Vulcan flanking cornucopia. ***Bottom center:*** 50. ***Right:*** 50 / Cherub in sailboat / 50. ***Engraver:*** Rawdon, Wright, Hatch & Edson. ***Comments:*** H-MA-935-G56. 18__. 1850s.

Rarity: —

$100 • W-MA-2510-100-G270

Left: Lathework chain bearing MASSACHUSETTS / 100 / 100 vertically. ***Center:*** Alternating flower garlands and gridwork segments / HUNDRED. ***Right:*** 100 / 100 vertically. ***Engraver:*** PSSP. ***Comments:*** H-MA-935-G60. 18__. 1830s.

Rarity: —

$100 • W-MA-2510-100-G280

Left: 100 / Vulcan seated, Cornucopia. ***Center:*** Train on bridge, Eagle on limb, Canal locks / C. ***Bottom center:*** 100. ***Right:*** 100 / Ceres seated, Cornucopia. ***Engraver:*** Rawdon, Wright, Hatch & Edson. ***Comments:*** H-MA-935-G64. 18__. 1850s.

Rarity: —

Uncut Sheets

$20-$50 • W-MA-2510-020.050-US010

JF

Tint(s): Red. ***Comments:*** All unlisted in Haxby. 18__. 1850s.

Rarity: URS-3
Proof $2,900

Non-Valid Issues

$1 • W-MA-2510-001-S010

CJF

Engraver: Boston Bank Note Co. ***Comments:*** H-MA-935-S5. Nov. 15, 1845.

Rarity: —

$2 • W-MA-2510-002-N010

Left: Two women flanking sheaf. ***Right:*** Woman and two men. ***Comments:*** H-MA-935-N5.

Rarity: —

$3 • W-MA-2510-003-S020

SI

Engraver: New England Bank Note Co. ***Comments:*** H-MA-935-S10. 18__. 1840s.

Rarity: URS-7

F $75

$3 • W-MA-2510-003-S030

Left: Man plowing with ox, Trees, House / 3. ***Center:*** 3. ***Right:*** 3 / Woman seated with cornucopia / THREE. ***Engraver:*** New England Bank Note Co. ***Comments:*** H-MA-935-S15. March 1, 1858

Rarity: —

$5 • W-MA-2510-005-C160a

NJW

Overprint: Red FIVE. ***Engraver:*** Rawdon, Wright & Hatch / ABNCo. monogram. ***Comments:*** H-MA-935-C32a. Counterfeit of W-MA-2510-005-G160a. 18__. 1860s.

Rarity: URS-7

F $75

$5 • W-MA-2510-005-S040

Left: V / Ox / V. ***Center:*** 5 / Ceres seated, Train on bridge, Sheaf and canal lock / 5. ***Bottom center:*** Sheaf, Plow. ***Right:*** Lathework panel bearing FIVE vertically. ***Comments:*** H-MA-935-S20. 184_. 1840s.

Rarity: —

$10 • W-MA-2510-010-R010

Comments: H-MA-935-R5. Raised from W-MA-2510-001-G020 or W-MA-2510-001-G030. 18__. 1840s.

Rarity: —

$10 • W-MA-2510-010-S050

Left: Die / Scene vertically / Die. ***Center:*** 10 / Indian man standing / Dog and strongbox. ***Right:*** X / Two figures next to building / X. ***Engraver:*** Rawdon, Clark & Co. ***Comments:*** H-MA-935-S25. 18__. 1840s.

Rarity: —

North Andover, Massachusetts

In 1634 the General Court of Massachusetts set aside the land around Lake Cochichewick to be used as a plantation. Part of this land included areas which are now Andover, North Andover, and South Lawrence. The first settlement in Andover of permanent nature was established by John Woodbridge in 1641.

In May 1646, the area was incorporated as an official town, named after Andover, England, which was the birthplace of some of the settlers. In 1778 Samuel Phillips Jr. began a school for boys in a remodeled carpenter's shop, and today Phillips Academy is one of the premier private schools in the nation. Mills were built to process corn and wood, and in 1775 a powder mill produced gunpowder for the Continental Army. Textile mills were prevalent through the 1780s and later. By 1835 there were six mill districts in existence: Sutton Mills and Stevens Mills on the Cochichewick River, and Ballardvale, Abbot Village, Marland Mills, and Frye Village adjacent to the Shawsheen River.

In 1854 the town was divided into political halves, with Andover representing the west and south and North Andover representing the north.

See also Andover, Massachusetts.

Essex Bank

1836–1847

W-MA-2520

History: Chartered on April 1, 1836, with $100,000 capital, the Essex Bank was incorporated in the Andover North Parish. In May 1836, the directors were elected and listed as: Dr. Joseph Kittredge, Gayton P. Osgood, Nathaniel Stevens, John Tenny, Nathaniel Swift, George Hodges, William Johnson, James Stevens 2nd, and N.W. Hazen. The bank opened for business on July 1, 1836, with William Stevens as cashier. In November 1839, the Essex Bank's capital was $100,000, and its circulation was $46,753. On March 25, 1845, the Legislature passed an act to close its business, allowing extra time for a period of two years after December 1, 1845, to accomplish this. Accordingly, 1847 was the last year of its activity.

See also listing under Andover, W-MA-070.

Numismatic Commentary: All notes bear the New England Bank Note Co. imprint.

Valid Issues

$5 • W-MA-2520-005-G010

SN

Engraver: New England Bank Note Co. / PSSP. ***Comments:*** H-Unlisted. 18__. 1830s.

Rarity: —

North Bridgewater, Massachusetts

Settled in 1650 at what is now West Bridgewater, North Bridgewater was originally known as the Duxbury New Plantation. It was incorporated as Bridgewater in June 1656. By 1683 the town had divided into four parts. In 1817 the General Court was petitioned, and on June 15, 1821, despite opposition from the township of Bridgewater, North Bridgewater was incorporated as a separate entity.

Shoemaking was a large industry in North Bridgewater, with more than 100,000 pairs being distributed annually by 1837. A furnace and forge, grist and saw mills, and textile manufacturing also existed here. In 1846 the Old Colony Railroad made a stop in North Bridgewater, and by the 1860s a new and improved, patented machine spurred the shoe industry to new heights in the town, making North Bridgewater the heart of shoe production in the nation by the close of the Civil War. As a result, North Bridgewater was nicknamed "Shoe City."

See also Bridgewater and East Bridgewater, Massachusetts.

North Bridgewater Bank
1854–1860s
W-MA-2530

History: The North Bridgewater Bank was chartered on March 28, 1854, with an authorized capital of $100,000. The first president was Martin Wales, and the first cashier was Rufus P. Kingman. The banking rooms were in the Brett & Kingman Block. The first bills were issued on September 4, 1854. President Wales was pictured on certain of the smaller denomination notes.

Circulation ranged from $72,464 in 1853 to $87,529 in 1858. Specie ranged from $4,734 to $6,837.35 during the same time.

In September 1866, the North Bridgewater Bank was the last of the state-chartered banks in operation. It declared a final dividend and asked the shareholders to surrender their stock.

See also listing under Bridgewater, W-MA-1110.

Numismatic Commentary: This is another hard bank to collect. The vignette of the town center on a few of its notes makes it a collectible with local interest.

Valid Issues

$1 • W-MA-2530-001-G010

CJF

Overprint: Red 1. ***Engraver:*** Rawdon, Wright, Hatch & Edson / New England Bank Note Co. ***Comments:*** H-MA-940-G2a. Sept. 4, 18__. 1850s.

Rarity: URS-4
F $400; **CU** $1,000

$1 • W-MA-2530-001-G010a

Left: 1 / Street scene in North Bridgewater. ***Center:*** Male portrait / ONE. ***Right:*** 1. ***Engraver:*** Rawdon, Wright, Hatch & Edson / New England Bank Note Co. / ABNCo. monogram. ***Comments:*** H-MA-940-G2b. Similar to W-MA-2530-001-G010 but with additional engraver imprint. 18__. 1850s–1860s.

Rarity: —

$2 • W-MA-2530-002-G020

Left: Street scene in North Bridgewater / 2. ***Center:*** 1 / Male portrait. ***Bottom center:*** Woman. ***Overprint:*** Red. ***Engraver:*** Rawdon, Wright, Hatch & Edson / New England Bank Note Co. ***Comments:*** H-MA-940-G4a. Sept. 4, 18__. 1850s.

Rarity: —

$2 • W-MA-2530-002-G020a

Engraver: Rawdon, Wright, Hatch & Edson / New England Bank Note Co. / ABNCo. monogram. ***Comments:*** H-MA-940-G4b. Similar to W-MA-2530-002-G020 but with additional engraver imprint. Sept. 4, 18__. 1850s–1860s.

Rarity: —

$3 • W-MA-2530-003-G030

Left: Woman / 3. ***Center:*** Street scene in North Bridgewater / THREE. ***Right:*** 3 / Male portrait. ***Overprint:*** Red THREE. ***Engraver:*** Rawdon, Wright, Hatch & Edson / New England Bank Note Co. ***Comments:*** H-MA-940-G6a. Sept. 4, 18__. 1850s.

Rarity: —

Collectors and Researchers:

If you have new information about any banks or notes listed in this volume, contact Whitman Publishing, Attn: Obsolete Paper Money, 3101 Clairmont Road, Suite G, Atlanta, GA 30329.

$3 • **W-MA-2530-003-G030a** SI

Overprint: Red THREE. ***Engraver:*** Rawdon, Wright, Hatch & Edson / New England Bank Note Co. / ABNCo. monogram. ***Comments:*** H-MA-940-G6b. Similar to W-MA-2530-003-G030 but with additional engraver imprint. Sept. 4, 18__. 1850s–1860s.

Rarity: URS-4
F $500; **VF** $750

$5 • **W-MA-2530-005-G040** CJF

Overprint: Red FIVE. ***Engraver:*** Rawdon, Wright, Hatch & Edson / New England Bank Note Co. ***Comments:*** H-MA-940-G8a. Sept. 4, 18__. 1850s.

Rarity: URS-5
F $600

$5 • **W-MA-2530-005-G040a**

Left: 5 / Male portrait. ***Center:*** FIVE / Five women with 5. ***Right:*** FIVE / Five women in 5. ***Engraver:*** Rawdon, Wright, Hatch & Edson / New England Bank Note Co. / ABNCo. monogram. ***Comments:*** H-MA-940-G8b. Similar to W-MA-2530-005-G040 but with additional engraver imprint. Sept. 4, 18__. 1850s–1860s.

Rarity: —

$10 • **W-MA-2530-010-G050**

Left: TEN / 10. ***Center:*** Train. ***Bottom center:*** Hay wagon. ***Right:*** 1 / Indian woman standing with ear of corn and X. ***Overprint:*** Red. ***Engraver:*** Rawdon, Wright, Hatch & Edson / New England Bank Note Co. ***Comments:*** H-MA-940-G10a. Sept. 4, 18__. 1850s.

Rarity: —

$10 • **W-MA-2530-010-G050a**

Engraver: Rawdon, Wright, Hatch & Edson / New England Bank Note Co. / ABNCo. monogram. ***Comments:*** H-MA-940-G10b. Similar to W-MA-2530-010-G050 but with additional engraver imprint. Sept. 4, 18__. 1850s–1860s.

Rarity: —

$20 • **W-MA-2530-020-G060**

Left: Woman with basket of fruit and flowers / XX. ***Center:*** Woman reclining by shield, Train and factory, Milkmaid and cows. ***Bottom center:*** Man and horses. ***Right:*** 20 / Woman seated between 2 and 0 / TWENTY. ***Engraver:*** Rawdon, Wright, Hatch & Edson / New England Bank Note Co. ***Comments:*** H-MA-940-G12. Sept. 4, 18__. 1850s.

Rarity: —

$20 • **W-MA-2530-020-G060a**

Engraver: American Bank Note Co. ***Comments:*** H-MA-940-G12b. Similar to W-MA-2530-020-G060 but with different engraver imprint. 1860s.

Rarity: —

$50 • **W-MA-2530-050-G070**

Left: Woman. ***Center:*** 50 / Two women with eagle and state arms, Train and steamboat / 50. ***Right:*** Woman. ***Engraver:*** Rawdon, Wright, Hatch & Edson / New England Bank Note Co. ***Comments:*** H-MA-940-G14. Sept. 4, 18__. 1850s.

Rarity: —

$50 • **W-MA-2530-050-G070a**

Engraver: American Bank Note Co. ***Comments:*** H-MA-940-G14b. Similar to W-MA-2530-050-G070 but with different engraver imprint. 1860s.

Rarity: —

$100 • **W-MA-2530-100-G080**

Left: Female portrait / 100. ***Center:*** View of U.S. Capitol. ***Right:*** 100 / Blacksmith, anvil, and forge / 100. ***Engraver:*** Rawdon, Wright, Hatch & Edson / New England Bank Note Co. ***Comments:*** H-MA-940-G16. Sept. 4, 18__. 1850s.

Rarity: —

$100 • **W-MA-2530-100-G080a**

Engraver: American Bank Note Co. ***Comments:*** H-MA-940-G16b. Similar to W-MA-2530-100-G080 but with different engraver imprint. 1860s.

Rarity: —

Uncut Sheets

$20-$50-$100 • **W-MA-2530-020.050.100-US010**

Vignette(s): ($20) Woman with basket of fruit and flowers / Woman reclining by shield, Train and factory, Milkmaid and cows / Man and horses / Woman seated between 2 and 0. ***($50)*** Woman / Two women with eagle and state arms, Train and steamboat / Woman. ***($100)*** Female portrait / View of U.S. Capitol / Blacksmith, anvil, and forge. ***Engraver:*** American Bank Note Co. ***Comments:*** H-MA-940-G12b, G14b, G16b.

Rarity: —

Non-Valid Issues

$5 • **W-MA-2530-005-R010**

Engraver: Rawdon, Wright, Hatch & Edson / New England Bank Note Co. ***Comments:*** H-MA-940-R5. Raised from W-MA-2530-001-G010. Sept. 4, 18__. 1850s.

Rarity: —

Northampton, Massachusetts

Originally known as Nonotuck by the Pocumtuc Indians, the area that later became Northampton was sold to settlers in 1653 and occupied in 1654. Mohawk hostilities escalated a decade later against neighboring tribes, and the relationship between the natives and the colonists took a turn for the worse, expanding into King Philip's War.

Southampton, Westhampton, and Easthampton all separated from Northampton between 1775 and 1809, and another section of Northampton was split apart by the division of Easthampton. A canal connected Northampton and the sea in 1835, but when the railroad came along the same course, the canal business declined. Northampton was also home to abolitionists between 1832 and 1846. For a time, silk and mulberry trees were an important industry.

Hampshire Bank
1813–1837
W-MA-2540

History: The Hampshire Bank was chartered on June 16, 1813, with $100,000 in authorized capital. The first president was Joseph Lyman, and F.H. Wright was the first cashier.

The charter for the Hampshire Bank was annulled in 1837, after which time the Northampton Bank was appointed to receive its bills as affairs were being settled.

Numismatic Commentary: Genuine notes are very hard to locate. Early counterfeits abound.

Valid Issues

$1 • W-MA-2540-001-G010
Left: ONE vertically. *Center:* 1 / Woman seated / I. *Right:* HAMPSHIRE vertically. *Engraver:* Murray, Draper, Fairman & Co. *Comments:* H-MA-945-G20. 181_. 1810s.

Rarity: —

$1 • W-MA-2540-001-G020
Left: ONE / 1 / ONE. *Center:* 1 / Woman seated with anchor / 1. *Bottom center:* ONE. *Right:* 1 / MASSACHUSETTS / 1. *Engraver:* A. Reed / Reed. *Comments:* H-MA-945-G24. 18__. 1810s.

Rarity: —

$1 • W-MA-2540-001-G030
Left: 1 / Woman wearing bonnet with pail / ONE. *Center:* Machinery and merchandise flanking Ceres seated holding sickle and rake, Factories and harbor / ONE / Panel outlining white ONE. *Right:* 1 / Ship / ONE. *Engraver:* PSSP / New England Bank Note Co. *Comments:* H-MA-945-G28. 18__. 1830s.

Rarity: —

$1 • W-MA-2540-001-G040
Comments: H-MA-945-G32. No description available. 18__. 1820s.

Rarity: *None known*

$2 • W-MA-2540-002-G050
Left: TWO vertically. *Center:* 2 / Woman seated / II. *Right:* HAMPSHIRE vertically. *Engraver:* Murray, Draper, Fairman & Co. *Comments:* H-MA-945-G36. 181_. 1810s.

Rarity: —

$2 • W-MA-2540-002-G060
Left: TWO / 2 / TWO. *Center:* 2 / Woman seated with anchor / 2. *Bottom center:* TWO. *Right:* 2 / MASSACHUSETTS / 2. *Engraver:* A. Reed / Reed. *Comments:* H-MA-945-G40. 18__. 1810s.

Rarity: —

$2 • W-MA-2540-002-G070
Comments: H-MA-945-G44. No description available. 18__. 1820s.

Rarity: *None known*

$3 • W-MA-2540-003-G080
Left: THREE vertically. *Center:* 3 / Woman seated / III. *Right:* HAMPSHIRE vertically. *Engraver:* Murray, Draper, Fairman & Co. *Comments:* H-MA-945-G48. 181_. 1810s.

Rarity: —

$3 • W-MA-2540-003-G090
Left: THREE / 3 / THREE. *Center:* 3 / Woman seated with anchor / 3. *Bottom center:* THREE. *Right:* 3 / MASSACHUSETTS / 3. *Engraver:* A. Reed / Reed. *Comments:* H-MA-945-G52. 18__. 1810s.

Rarity: —

$3 • W-MA-2540-003-G100
Comments: H-MA-945-G56. No description available. 18__. 1820s.

Rarity: *None known*

$5 • W-MA-2540-005-G110
Left: FIVE vertically. *Center:* 5 / Woman seated / V. *Right:* HAMPSHIRE vertically. *Engraver:* Murray, Draper, Fairman & Co. *Comments:* H-MA-945-G64. 181_. 1810s.

Rarity: —

$5 • W-MA-2540-005-G120

CC

Engraver: A. Reed / Reed. *Comments:* H-MA-945-G68. 18__. 1810s.

Rarity: —

$5 • W-MA-2540-005-G130
Left: 5 / Blacksmith at anvil / FIVE. *Center:* Mercury standing with 5, Cornucopia and merchandise, Factories and ship / V / Panel outlining white FIVE. *Right:* 5 / Ceres kneeling / FIVE. *Engraver:* New England Bank Note Co. / PSSP. *Comments:* H-MA-945-G72. 18__. 1830s.

Rarity: —

$5 • W-MA-2540-005-G140
Comments: H-MA-945-G76. No description available. 18__. 1820s.

Rarity: *None known*

$10 • W-MA-2540-010-G150

CJF

Engraver: PSSP. ***Comments:*** H-Unlisted. 18__.

Rarity: —

$10 • W-MA-2540-010-G160

Left: TEN vertically. ***Center:*** 10 / Woman seated / X. ***Right:*** HAMPSHIRE vertically. ***Engraver:*** Murray, Draper, Fairman & Co. ***Comments:*** H-MA-945-G80. 181_. 1810s.

Rarity: —

$10 • W-MA-2540-010-G170

Left: TEN / X / TEN. ***Center:*** 10 / Woman seated / 10. ***Bottom center:*** X. ***Right:*** 10 / MASSACHUSETTS / 10 vertically. ***Engraver:*** A. Reed / Reed. ***Comments:*** H-MA-945-G82. 18__. 1810s.

Rarity: —

$10 • W-MA-2540-010-G180

Left: 10 / Farmer sowing / TEN. ***Center:*** Mercury standing with 10, Cornucopia and merchandise, Factories and ship, Canal scene / Panel outlining white TEN. ***Right:*** 10 / Ship / TEN. ***Engraver:*** New England Bank Note Co. ***Comments:*** H-MA-945-G84. 18__. 1830s.

Rarity: —

$10 • W-MA-2540-010-G190

Comments: H-MA-945-G88. No description available. 18__. 1820s.

Rarity: *None known*

$20 • W-MA-2540-020-G200

Comments: H-MA-945-G96. No description available. 18__. 1820s.

Rarity: *None known*

$20 • W-MA-2540-020-G210

Comments: H-MA-945-G104. No description available. 18__. 1820s.

Rarity: *None known*

$50 • W-MA-2540-050-G220

Left: 50 / Cornucopia, Woman standing with ankles crossed, Staff, Anchor / 50. ***Center:*** FIFTY DOLLARS / 50. ***Right:*** FIFTY vertically. ***Engraver:*** New England Bank Note Co. / PSSP. ***Comments:*** H-MA-945-G108. 18__. 1830s.

Rarity: —

$100 • W-MA-2540-100-G230

Left: Lathework panel bearing C / Portrait of George Washington / C. ***Center:*** 100 / Manhattan reclining pouring water, Ship / 100. ***Right:*** Lathework panel bearing ONE HUNDRED vertically. ***Engraver:*** New England Bank Note Co. / PSSP. ***Comments:*** H-MA-945-G112. 18__. 1830s.

Rarity: —

Payable at Bank of the New York Manufacturing Company, New York City

$5 • W-MA-2540-005-G240

Left: FIVE vertically. ***Center:*** 5 / Woman seated / V. ***Right:*** HAMPSHIRE vertically. ***Engraver:*** Murray, Draper, Fairman & Co. ***Comments:*** H-MA-945-G130. 181_. 1810s.

Rarity: —

Payable at the Phenix Bank, New York City

$5 • W-MA-2540-005-G250

CC

Engraver: A. Reed / Reed. ***Comments:*** H-MA-945-G140. 18__. 1810s.

Rarity: URS-4
VF $450

Non-Valid Issues

$1 • W-MA-2540-001-C020

Engraver: A. Reed / Reed. ***Comments:*** H-MA-945-C24. Counterfeit of W-MA-2540-001-G020. 18__. 1810s.

Rarity: —
F $80

$2 • W-MA-2540-002-C070

Comments: H-MA-945-C44. Counterfeit of W-MA-2540-002-G070. 18__. 1810s–1820s.

Rarity: —

$5 • W-MA-2540-005-C120

CJF

Engraver: A. Reed / Reed. ***Comments:*** H-MA-945-C68. Counterfeit of W-MA-2540-005-G120. 18__. Circa 1819.

Rarity: —

Holyoke Bank

1848–1864

W-MA-2550

History: The Holyoke Bank was chartered on April 25, 1848, with an authorized capital of $100,000. It opened its doors for business on September 1. The capital was increased to $150,000 and then in October 1849 to $200,000. In 1850 John Clarke was the president of the Holyoke Bank, and Thomas Green was the cashier. Irregularities were found in the accounts of 1856, and forfeiture of the charter was threatened, but a decision of the Supreme Court of Massachusetts in early 1857 allowed business to continue. In time, matters became normal. In 1860 the circulation was listed at $123,651, and in 1863 it was $199,892.

In April 1864, the business of the Holyoke Bank was succeeded by the First National Bank of Northampton.

See also listing under Holyoke, W-MA-1910.

Numismatic Commentary: Quite a few different issues were printed for this bank, making it somewhat easier to obtain genuine examples. Some notes are colorful and exhibit pleasant local scenery.

VALID ISSUES

$1 • W-MA-2550-001-G010

CC

Engraver: Danforth & Hufty. ***Comments:*** H-MA-950-G2. 18__. 1848–1850s.

Rarity: URS-4
Proof $1,750

$1 • W-MA-2550-001-G020

CC

Tint: Red-brown lathework and panel of microlettering outlining white ONE. ***Back:*** Plain. ***Engraver:*** American Bank Note Co. / Jocelyn, Draper, Welsh & Co. ***Comments:*** H-MA-950-G4a. October 4, 1858.

Rarity: URS-4
VG $75; **F** $225; **VF** $310; **Proof** $3,750

$1 • W-MA-2550-001-G020a

Left: 1 / Man standing. ***Center:*** Man with horse and sheep. ***Right:*** 1 / State Hospital at Northampton. ***Tint:*** Brown lathework and panel of microlettering outlining white ONE. ***Back:*** Plain. ***Engraver:*** American Bank Note Co. / Jocelyn, Draper, Welsh & Co. ***Comments:*** H-MA-950-G4b. Similar to W-MA-2550-001-G020. Handwritten 62 over engraved 58 in date. Oct. 4, 1862.

Rarity: —

$1 • W-MA-2550-001-G020b

CC

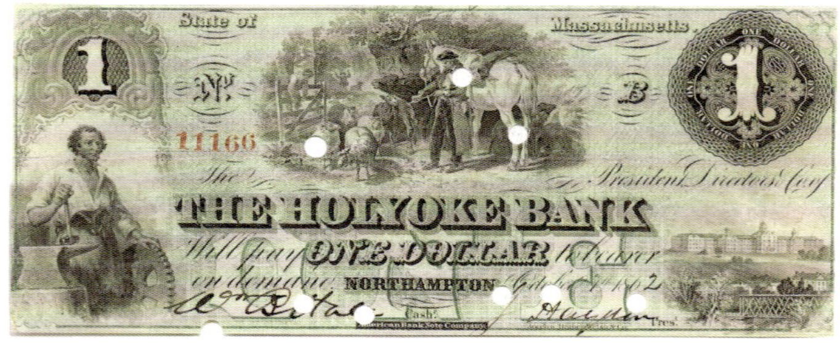

Tint: Green lathework and panel of microlettering outlining white ONE. ***Back:*** Green. ***Engraver:*** American Bank Note Co. / Jocelyn, Draper, Welsh & Co. ***Comments:*** H-MA-950-G4d. Similar to W-MA-2550-001-G020 but with different date. October 7, 186_. 1860s.

Rarity: URS-6
VF $350

$2 • W-MA-2550-002-G030

CC

Engraver: Danforth & Hufty. ***Comments:*** H-MA-950-G6. Proof. 18__. 1848–1850s.

Rarity: URS-4
Proof $1,750

$2 • W-MA-2550-002-G040

CC

Tint: Red-brown lathework and panel of microlettering outlining white TWO. ***Back:*** Plain. ***Engraver:*** American Bank Note Co. / Jocelyn, Draper, Welsh & Co. ***Comments:*** H-MA-950-G8a. Handwritten 62 over 58 in date. October 4, 1858.

Rarity: URS-5
F $250; **VF** $400

$2 • W-MA-2550-002-G040a

Left: TWO / State Hospital at Northampton. ***Center:*** Two women seated. ***Right:*** 2 / Woman with cow and calf. ***Tint:*** Brown lathework and panel of microlettering outlining white TWO. ***Back:*** Plain. ***Engraver:*** American Bank Note Co. / Jocelyn, Draper, Welsh & Co. ***Comments:*** H-MA-950-G8b. Similar to W-MA-2550-002-G040. Handwritten 62 over engraved 58 in date. Oct. 4, 1862.

Rarity: URS-5
F $250; **VF** $400

$2 • W-MA-2550-002-G040b

Tint: Brown lathework and panel of microlettering outlining white TWO. ***Back:*** Plain. ***Engraver:*** American Bank Note Co. / Jocelyn, Draper, Welsh & Co. ***Comments:*** H-MA-950-G8c. Similar to W-MA-2550-002-G040. Oct. 4, 1858.

Rarity: URS-3
Proof $3,750

$2 • W-MA-2550-002-G040c

CJF, CJF

Tint: Green lathework and panel of microlettering outlining white TWO. ***Back:*** Green. ***Engraver:*** American Bank Note Co. / Jocelyn, Draper, Welsh & Co. ***Comments:*** H-MA-950-G8d. Similar to W-MA-2550-002-G040 but with different date. October 7, 186_. 1860s.

Rarity: URS-6
F $250; **VF** $400

$5 • W-MA-2550-005-G050

CJF

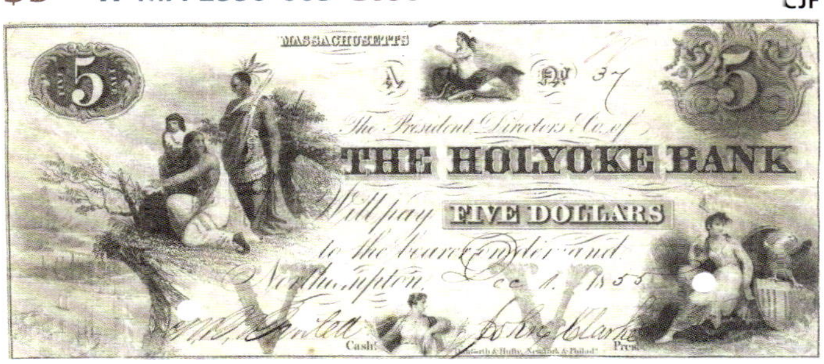

Engraver: Danforth & Hufty. ***Comments:*** H-MA-950-G10. 18__. 1848–1850s.

Rarity: URS-6
F $150; **VF** $250

$5 • W-MA-2550-005-G060

CJF

Engraver: Danforth & Hufty. ***Comments:*** H-MA-950-G12. 18__. 1850s.

Rarity: URS-6
F $150; **VF** $250

$5 • W-MA-2550-005-G070

QDB

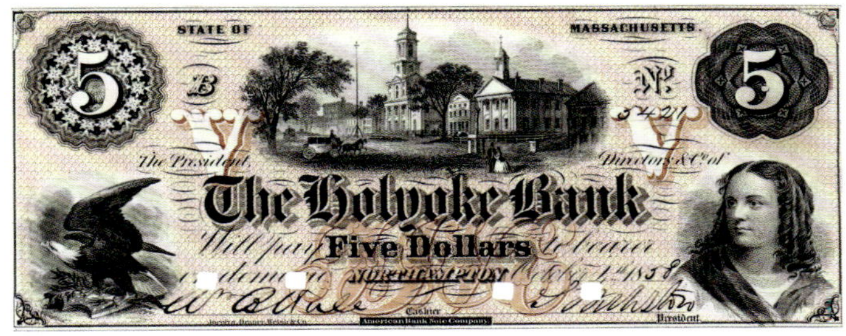

Tint: Brown lathework outlining white Vs, Brown FIVE. ***Back:*** Plain. ***Engraver:*** Jocelyn, Draper, Welsh & Co. / American Bank Note Co. ***Comments:*** H-MA-950-G14a. October 4, 18__. 1850s.

Rarity: URS-5
VG $150; **F** $250; **VF** $375; **Proof** $3,000

$5 • W-MA-2550-005-G070a

SI, SI

Tint: Green lathework outlining white Vs, Green FIVE. ***Back:*** Green. ***Engraver:*** Jocelyn, Draper, Welsh & Co. / American Bank Note Co. ***Comments:*** H-MA-950-G14c. Similar to W-MA-2550-005-G070 but with different date. Remainder. October 7, 186_. 1860s.

Rarity: URS-3
Proof $1,500

$5 • W-MA-2550-005-G070b

CC

Tint: Green lathework outlining white Vs, Green FIVE. ***Back:*** Green. ***Engraver:*** Jocelyn, Draper, Welsh & Co. / American Bank Note Co. ***Comments:*** H-MA-950-G14d. Similar to W-MA-2550-005-G070. October 7, 186_. 1860s.

Rarity: URS-4
Proof $1,250

$10 • W-MA-2550-010-G080

CJF

Engraver: Danforth & Hufty. ***Comments:*** H-MA-950-G16. 18__. 1848–1850s.

Rarity: URS-5
F $200; **VF** $400

$10 • W-MA-2550-010-G090

CC

Tint: Brown lathework outlining white Xs, White TEN. ***Back:*** Plain. ***Engraver:*** Jocelyn, Draper, Welsh & Co. / American Bank Note Co. ***Comments:*** H-MA-950-G18a. October 4, 18__. 1850s.

Rarity: URS-3
Proof $6,000

$10 • W-MA-2550-010-G090a

CC

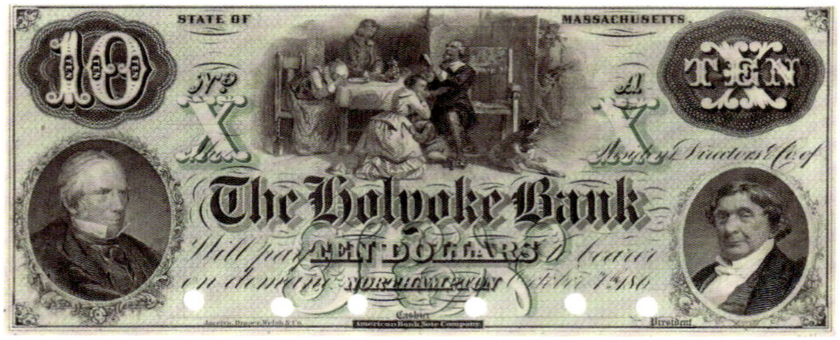

Tint: Green lathework outlining white Xs, White TEN. ***Back:*** Plain. ***Engraver:*** Jocelyn, Draper, Welsh & Co. / American Bank Note Co. ***Comments:*** H-MA-950-G18c. Similar to W-MA-2550-010-G090 but with different date. Remainder. October 7, 186_. 1860s.

Rarity: URS-3
Proof $6,000

$10 • W-MA-2550-010-G090b

Left: 10 / Portrait of Henry Clay. ***Center:*** X / Man preaching to family / X / TEN. ***Right:*** TEN on X / Male portrait. ***Tint:*** Green lathework outlining white Xs, Green TEN. ***Back:*** Green. ***Engraver:*** Jocelyn, Draper, Welsh & Co. / American Bank Note Co. ***Comments:*** H-MA-950-G18d. Similar to W-MA-2550-010-G090. Oct. 4, 186_. 1860s.

Rarity: —

$20 • W-MA-2550-020-G100

CC

Engraver: Danforth & Hufty. ***Comments:*** H-MA-950-G20. Proof. 18__. 1848–1850s.

Rarity: URS-1
Proof $3,500

How to Read the Whitman Numbering System

$1 • W-MA-010-001-G010a

Denomination: Value of the note shown.

W: Whitman number. This number is a sortable code unique to each bank and note.

MA: Abbreviation for the state under study.

010: Numerical designation specific to each bank.

001: The denomination in dollars.

G010a: G indicates a good or valid note. Other categories are indicated thus: C (counterfeit); R (raised); S (spurious); N (not-attributed); A (altered). Numbers are assigned starting with 010, 020, et seq. Terminal letters following the number indicate variations of a note: a series of different colored overprints, tints, payees, etc., all on the same design of note. For more information, see the "How to Use This Book" section at the front of the volume, page xiv.

$20 • W-MA-2550-020-G100a

CC

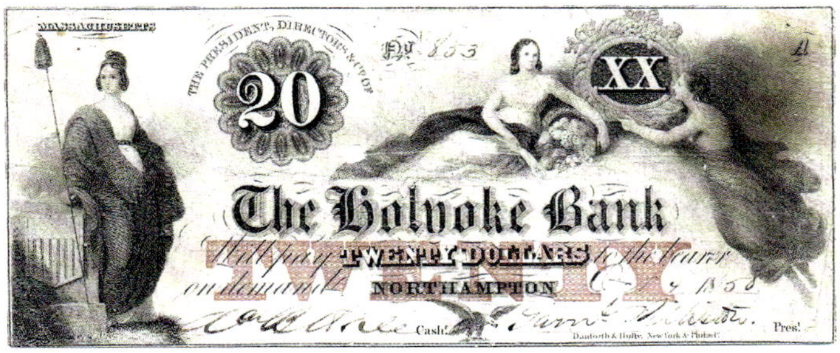

Overprint: Red TWENTY. ***Engraver:*** Danforth & Hufty. ***Comments:*** H-MA-950-G20a. Similar to W-MA-2550-020-G100. 18__. 1850s.

Rarity: URS-5

F $500

$20 • W-MA-2550-020-G110

JF

Tint: Green. ***Back:*** Plain. ***Engraver:*** American Bank Note Co. ***Comments:*** H-MA-950-G22a. Proof. Oct. 7, 186_. 1860s.

Rarity: URS-2

Proof $3,000

$20 • W-MA-2550-020-G110a

CJF, CJF

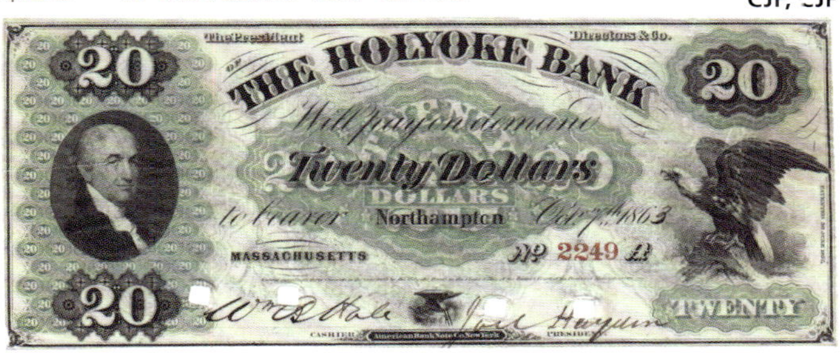

Tint: Green. ***Back:*** Green. ***Engraver:*** American Bank Note Co. ***Comments:*** H-MA-950-G22b. Similar to W-MA-2550-020-G110. Oct. 7, 186_. 1860s.

Rarity: URS-3

F $1,000; **VF** $1,500

$50 • W-MA-2550-050-G120

CC

Back: Plain. ***Engraver:*** Danforth & Hufty. ***Comments:*** H-MA-950-G24. Proof. 18__. 1848–1850s.

Rarity: URS-1

Proof $4,000

$50 • W-MA-2550-050-G120a

Left: Woman standing with pole and cap, Shield. ***Center:*** 50 on medallion head / Woman with wings reaching out to two women in clouds / Ship. ***Right:*** 50. ***Tint:*** Green panel of microletters outlining white 50, Green dies bearing white 50s. ***Back:*** Plain. ***Engraver:*** Danforth & Hufty. ***Comments:*** H-MA-950-G24b. Similar to W-MA-2550-050-G120. 18__. 1850s.

Rarity: —

$50 • W-MA-2550-050-G120b

JF

Tint: Green panel of microletters outlining white 50, Green dies bearing white 50s. ***Back:*** Green. ***Engraver:*** Danforth & Hufty / ABNCo. monogram. ***Comments:*** H-MA-950-G24c. Similar to W-MA-2550-050-G120 but with different date and additional engraver imprint. Oct. 7, 186_. 1860s.

Rarity: URS-4

F $1,250; **VF** $2,000

$100 • W-MA-2550-100-G130

CC

Back: Plain. ***Engraver:*** Danforth & Hufty. ***Comments:*** H-MA-950-G26. Proof. Plate note. 18__. 1848–1850s.

Rarity: URS-2

Proof $3,750

$100 • W-MA-2550-100-G130a

Left: Medallion head with 100 / Trees and bridge. ***Center:*** Three women / 100. ***Right:*** Medallion head with 100 / Ship. ***Tint:*** Green $100s, Green Cs, Green die bearing 100. ***Back:*** Plain. ***Engraver:*** Danforth & Hufty. ***Comments:*** H-MA-950-G26b. Similar to W-MA-2550-100-G130. 18__. 1850s.

Rarity: —

$100 • W-MA-2550-100-G130b

Tint: Green $100s, Green Cs, Green die bearing 100. ***Back:*** Green. ***Engraver:*** Danforth & Hufty / ABNCo. monogram. ***Comments:*** H-MA-950-G26c. Similar to W-MA-2550-100-G130 but with different date and additional engraver imprint. Oct. 1, 186_. 1860s.

Rarity: —

Uncut Sheets

$1-$1-$1-$2 • W-MA-2550-001.001.001.002-US010

Vignette(s): ($1) Woman standing / Man with horse / State Hospital at Northampton. ***($1)*** Woman standing / Man with horse / State Hospital at Northampton. ***($1)*** Woman standing / Man with horse / State Hospital at Northampton. ***($2)*** State Hospital at Northampton / Man and woman seated / Woman with calf. ***Tint(s):*** Red. ***Engraver:*** American Bank Note Co. / Jocelyn, Draper, Welsh & Co. ***Comments:*** All unlisted in Haxby. Similar to H-MA-950-G4a, G4a, G4a, G8a. October 4, 1858.

Rarity: —

$1-$1-$2-$5 • W-MA-2550-001.001.002.005-US020

Vignette(s): ($1) Portrait of George Washington / White horse, Black horse rearing / Medallion head of William Shakespeare / Man standing. ***($1)*** Portrait of George Washington / White horse, Black horse rearing / Medallion head of William Shakespeare / Man standing. ***($2)*** Portrait of John Quincy Adams / Woman seated with shield / Portrait of John Hancock. ***($5)*** Two women with Indian man standing / Woman reclining / Woman / Woman seated next to shield. ***Engraver:*** Danforth & Hufty. ***Comments:*** H-MA-950-G2, G2, G6, G10. 18__. 1850s.

Rarity: —

$5-$5-$5-$10 • W-MA-2550-005.005.005.010-US030

Vignette(s): ($5) Perched eagle / Street scene in Northampton / Female portrait. ***($5)*** Perched eagle / Street scene in Northampton / Female portrait. ***($5)*** Perched eagle / Street scene in Northampton / Female portrait. ***($10)*** Portrait of Henry Clay / Men working in shop / Male portrait. ***Tint(s):*** Red. ***Back(s):*** Green. ***Engraver:*** American Bank Note Co. / Jocelyn, Draper, Welsh & Co. ***Comments:*** All unlisted in Haxby. Similar to H-MA-950-G14a, G14a, G14a, G18a.

Rarity: —

$5-$5-$5-$10 • W-MA-2550-005.005.005.010-US030a JF

Tint(s): Green. ***Back(s):*** Green. ***Engraver:*** American Bank Note Co. / Jocelyn, Draper, Welsh & Co. ***Comments:*** H-MA-950-G14d, G14d, G14d, G18d. October 7, 186_. 1860s.

Rarity: —

$5-$5-$10-$20 • W-MA-2550-005.005.010.020-US040

Vignette(s): ($5) Two women with Indian man standing / Woman reclining / Woman / Woman seated next to shield. ***($5)*** Two women with Indian man standing / Woman reclining / Woman / Woman seated next to shield. ***($10)*** Portrait of Benjamin Franklin / Female portrait / Woman with wings / Woman swimming / Woman with wings reaching out to another woman. ***($20)*** Woman standing with pole and cap next to shield / Woman reclining / Perched eagle / Woman holding up XX. ***Engraver:*** Danforth & Hufty. ***Comments:*** H-MA-950-G10, G10, G16, G20. 18__. 1848–1850s.

Rarity: —

$50-$100 • W-MA-2550-050.100-US050

Vignette(s): ($50) Woman standing with pole and cap, Shield / Two women with wings in clouds / Woman with wings. ***($100)*** Medallion head with 100 / Trees and bridge / Three women / Medallion head with 100 / Ship. ***Engraver:*** Danforth & Hufty ***Comments:*** H-MA-950-G24, G26. 18__. 1848–1850s.

Rarity: —

Non-Valid Issues

$3 • W-MA-2550-003-R010

Engraver: American Bank Note Co. / Jocelyn, Draper, Welsh & Co. ***Comments:*** H-MA-950-R5. Raised from W-MA-2550-001-G020b. The bank issued no $3 notes. Oct. 7, 186_. 1860s.

Rarity: —

$3 • W-MA-2550-003-S010

Left: THREE / State arms / THREE. ***Center:*** 3 / Woman seated next to shield, Plow and implements. ***Right:*** Flower / Die / Flower. ***Engraver:*** Rawdon, Wright & Hatch. ***Comments:*** H-MA-950-S5. 18__. 1850.

Rarity: —

$5 • W-MA-2550-005-C050

Engraver: Danforth & Hufty. ***Comments:*** H-MA-950-C10. Counterfeit of W-MA-2550-005-G050. 18__. 1850s.

Rarity: —

$5 • W-MA-2550-005-R020

Engraver: Danforth & Hufty. ***Comments:*** H-MA-950-R10. Raised from W-MA-2550-001-G010. 18__. 1850s.

Rarity: —

$10 • W-MA-2550-010-R030

Engraver: Danforth & Hufty. ***Comments:*** H-MA-950-R15. Raised from W-MA-2550-001-G010. 18__. 1850s.

Rarity: —

$10 • W-MA-2550-010-R040

Engraver: American Bank Note Co. / Jocelyn, Draper, Welsh & Co. ***Comments:*** H-MA-950-R20. Raised from W-MA-2550-002-G040 series. Oct. 4, 1858.

Rarity: —

Northampton Bank

1803–1865

W-MA-2565

History: The Northampton Bank was chartered on March 1, 1803, with an authorized capital of $75,000. The cashier and others engaged in questionable manipulations of the bank stock, discounted quantities of bills to exchange with banks in other locations, and engaged in other irregularities. Normal banking business seems to have ended in 1809, although the bills were traded for some time afterward. An advertisement of one of the principals in 1810 stated that he wanted to buy $20,000 worth of bills in exchange for merchandise he offered for sale. Stockholders' meetings continued to be held.

On June 11, 1813, the Legislature extended the charter for five years. The bank officers changed over time, normal practices were resumed, and it continued in business for years afterward. In 1819, during a nationwide shortage of coins in circulation, the bank suspended specie payments. During the Panic of 1837, the bank again suspended specie payments for a time, as did most banks in the state.

The bank's circulation in 1839 was $113,518, reaching a high of $216,233 in 1845.

In 1865 the business of the Northampton Bank was succeeded by the Northampton National Bank.

Numismatic Commentary: Charles White, cashier of the Northampton Bank in Massachusetts, is little remembered today.[28] However, White, who apparently later moved to New York City, was also a coin collector, and like many numismatists he could not resist some hoarding. His collection was cataloged and sold by one Harlan P. Smith in 1886.

As of 2003 there remained a $1-$1-$1-$2 tint and a $5-$5-$10-$10 tint plate of this bank at the American Bank Note Co. archives.

Valid Issues

$1 • W-MA-2565-001-G010

Comments: H-MA-955-G2. 180_. 1800s.

Rarity: —

$1 • W-MA-2565-001-G020

CJF

Engraver: PSSP. ***Comments:*** H-MA-955-G6. 18__. 1807–1809.

Rarity: —

$1 • W-MA-2565-001-G030

Engraver: PSSP. ***Comments:*** H-MA-955-G8. 18__. 1809–circa 1812.

Rarity: —

$1 • W-MA-2565-001-G040

QDB

Engraver: PSSP. ***Comments:*** H-MA-956-G2. 18__. 1830s.

Rarity: URS-4

F $350

$1 • W-MA-2565-001-G050

CC

Engraver: PSSP / New England Bank Note Co. ***Comments:*** H-MA-956-G4. Beware of altered W-MA-2565-001-A010 from the same plate as the genuine. 18__. 1830s–1840s.

Rarity: URS-4
F $400

$1 • W-MA-2565-001-G060

Left: ONE / Bust of George Washington / ONE. ***Center:*** 1 / Men on each side of workbench / 1. ***Right:*** ONE / Female portrait / ONE. ***Engraver:*** New England Bank Note Co. ***Comments:*** H-MA-956-G6. 18__. 1840s–1850s.

Rarity: —

$1 • W-MA-2565-001-G070

Left: 1 / Portrait of George Washington. ***Center:*** Woman seated with rudder / 1 / Woman seated. ***Right:*** 1 / Portrait of Benjamin Franklin. ***Engraver:*** New England Bank Note Co. ***Comments:*** H-MA-956-G8. 18__. 1850s.

Rarity: —

$1 • W-MA-2565-001-G080

Left: Commerce seated with rudder, leaning on barrel / 1. ***Center:*** 1 bearing "Presentation of the Declaration of Independence". ***Right:*** 1 / Woman standing with apron full of grain. ***Overprint:*** Red ONE. ***Engraver:*** New England Bank Note Co. ***Comments:*** H-MA-956-G10a. 18__. 1850s.

Rarity: —

$1 • W-MA-2565-001-G090

CC

Tint: Green. ***Engraver:*** American Bank Note Co. ***Comments:*** H-MA-956-G12a. Jan. 2, 186_. 1860s.

Rarity: URS-4
VG $1,000; **F** $1,500

$2 • W-MA-2565-002-G100

Center: Alternating flower garlands and gridwork segments. ***Comments:*** H-MA-955-G14. 180_. 1800s.

Rarity: —

$2 • W-MA-2565-002-G110

Center: 2 / 2 / Black oval bearing white flower buds / TWO / 2 / 2. ***Engraver:*** PSSP. ***Comments:*** H-MA-955-G18. 18__. 1807–1809.

Rarity: —

$2 • W-MA-2565-002-G120

CJF

Engraver: PSSP. ***Comments:*** H-MA-955-G20. 18__. 1809–circa 1812.

Rarity: —

$2 • W-MA-2565-002-G130

Left: 2 / Hebe watering eagle / 2. ***Center:*** 2 / Commerce seated on shore, Plow and cornucopia / 2. ***Right:*** 2 / Justice standing / 2. ***Engraver:*** PSSP. ***Comments:*** H-MA-956-G14. 18__. 1830s.

Rarity: —

$2 • W-MA-2565-002-G140

Left: 2 / Woman standing with staff, Cornucopia / TWO. ***Center:*** TWO / Machinery and merchandise flanking Ceres seated holding sickle and rake, Factories and harbor / Panel outlining white TWO. ***Right:*** 2 / Woman wearing hat, Trees / TWO. ***Engraver:*** New England Bank Note Co. / PSSP. ***Comments:*** H-MA-956-G16. Beware of altered W-MA-2565-002-A020 from the same plate as the genuine. 18__. 1830s–1840s.

Rarity: —

$2 • W-MA-2565-002-G150

Left: TWO / Female portrait / 2. ***Center:*** 2 / Woman giving drink to one of two seated men / 2 / Panel outlining white TWO. ***Right:*** TWO / Bust of female reaper. ***Engraver:*** New England Bank Note Co. ***Comments:*** H-MA-956-G18. 18__. 1840s–1850s.

Rarity: —

$2 • W-MA-2565-002-G160 CJF

Engraver: New England Bank Note Co. ***Comments:*** H-MA-956-G20. 18__. 1840s–1850s.

Rarity: URS-5
F $250; **VF** $400

$2 • W-MA-2565-002-G170 CJF

Engraver: New England Bank Note Co. ***Comments:*** H-Unlisted. 18__. 1850s.

Rarity: —

$2 • W-MA-2565-002-G170a

Left: Men driving sheep into stream / 2. ***Center:*** 2 bearing "Presentation of the Declaration of Independence". ***Right:*** TWO / Woman seated with wreath of flowers / TWO. ***Overprint:*** Red TWO. ***Engraver:*** New England Bank Note Co. ***Comments:*** H-MA-956-G22a. Similar to W-MA-2565-002-G170. 18__. 1850s.

Rarity: —

$2 • W-MA-2565-002-G180

Left: Stonecutter. ***Tint:*** Green panel of micro-TWOs. ***Engraver:*** American Bank Note Co. ***Comments:*** H-MA-956-G24a. Jan. 2, 186_. 1860s.

Rarity: —

$3 • W-MA-2565-003-G190

Center: Alternating flower garlands and gridwork segments. ***Comments:*** H-MA-955-G24. 180_. 1800s.

Rarity: —

$3 • W-MA-2565-003-G200

Center: 3 / 3 / Black oval bearing white flower buds / THREE / 3 / 3. ***Engraver:*** PSSP. ***Comments:*** H-MA-955-G28. 18__. 1807–1809.

Rarity: —

$3 • W-MA-2565-003-G210

Center: 3 / 3 / Oval of flower garlands and gridwork segments / 3 / 3. ***Engraver:*** PSSP. ***Comments:*** H-MA-955-G30. 18__. 1809–1810s.

Rarity: —

$3 • W-MA-2565-003-G220

Left: 3 / Eagle on rock / 3. ***Center:*** 3 / Plow, Commerce seated with caduceus and cornucopia, Ships / 3 / Panel bearing THREE. ***Right:*** 3 / Woman standing with cornucopia / 3. ***Engraver:*** PSSP. ***Comments:*** H-MA-956-G26. 18__. 1830s.

Rarity: —

$3 • W-MA-2565-003-G230

Left: THREE / Farmer sharpening scythe / 3 across THREE. ***Center:*** 3 / Woman placing garland on eagle, Beehive and cornucopia 3 / Panel outlining white THREE. ***Right:*** THREE / Sailor standing on wharf with hat / 3 across THREE. ***Engraver:*** New England Bank Note Co. ***Comments:*** H-MA-956-G30. 18__. 1840s–1850s.

Rarity: —

$3 • W-MA-2565-003-G240

Left: Barnyard scene, Man on horse, Boy and cattle / 3. ***Center:*** 3. ***Right:*** 3 on THREE / Woman with flowers / THREE. ***Overprint:*** Red THREE. ***Engraver:*** New England Bank Note Co. ***Comments:*** H-MA-956-G32a. 18__. 1850s.

Rarity: —

$5 • W-MA-2565-005-G250

Left: FIVE vertically. ***Center:*** Woman holding frame bearing river scene / FIVE. ***Right:*** 5 / FIVE. ***Comments:*** H-MA-955-G34. 180_. 1800s.

Rarity: —

$5 • W-MA-2565-005-G260 CJF

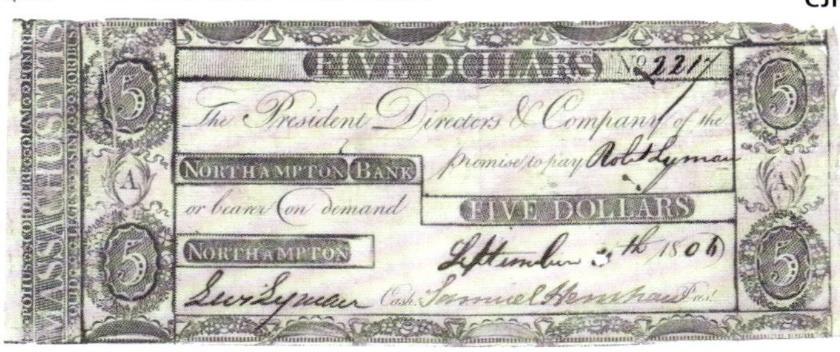

Engraver: Perkins. ***Comments:*** H-MA-955-G38. 18__. 1806 and 1807.

Rarity: —

$5 • W-MA-2565-005-G260a CJF

Engraver: Perkins. ***Comments:*** H-MA-955-G40. Similar to W-MA-2565-005-G260. 18__. Circa 1808 and 1809.

Rarity: —

$5 • W-MA-2565-005-G270

Left: Panel bearing FIVE / Plenty and Minerva seated / V. ***Center:*** FIVE / Allegorical woman seated / FIVE / Panel of microletters. ***Right:*** 5 / Eagle / 5. ***Engraver:*** PSSP. ***Comments:*** H-MA-956-G34. 18__. 1830s.

Rarity: —

$5 • W-MA-2565-005-G270a

Back: Congreve Check Plate. ***Engraver:*** PSSP. ***Comments:*** H-MA-956-G34a. Similar to W-MA-2565-005-G270. 18__. 1830s.

Rarity: —

$5 • W-MA-2565-005-G280

CC

Engraver: PSSP / New England Bank Note Co. ***Comments:*** H-MA-956-G36. Beware of altered W-MA-2565-005-A040 from the same plate as the genuine. 18__. 1830s.

Rarity: URS-7
VG $100; **VF** $175

$5 • W-MA-2565-005-G290

Left: 5 / FIVE / 5. ***Center:*** V / Eagle on wharf with plow, Cannon and anchor, Ships / V / Panel outlining white FIVE. ***Right:*** 5 / FIVE / 5. ***Engraver:*** New England Bank Note Co. ***Comments:*** H-MA-956-G38. 18__. 1840s–1850s.

Rarity: —

$5 • W-MA-2565-005-G300

Left: Eagle on shield and anchor, Factories and ships / FIVE. ***Center:*** Woman with cornucopia and cherub in V. ***Right:*** 5 / Girl with ringlets holding basket. ***Overprint:*** Red FIVE. ***Engraver:*** New England Bank Note Co. ***Comments:*** H-MA-956-G40a. 18__. 1850s.

Rarity: —

$5 • W-MA-2565-005-G310

Left: 5 / Woman seated with flowers / FIVE. ***Center:*** 5 / State arms. ***Right:*** 5. ***Tint:*** Green. ***Engraver:*** American Bank Note Co. ***Comments:*** H-MA-956-G42a. Jan. 2, 186_. 1860s.

Rarity: —

$10 • W-MA-2565-010-G320

CJF

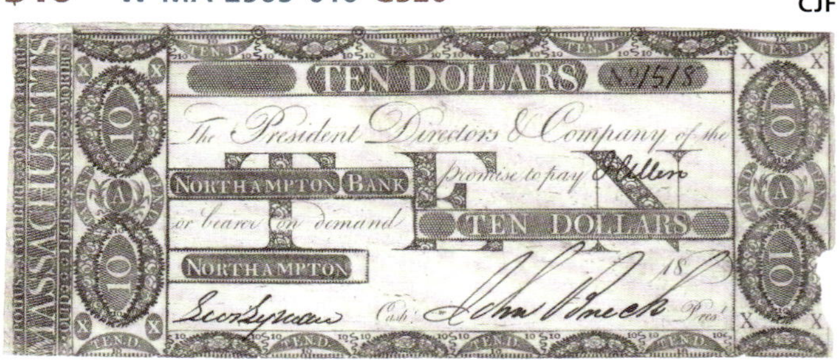

Comments: H-MA-955-G44. 18__. 1800s.

Rarity: —

$10 • W-MA-2565-010-G330

Left: Narrow panel bearing MASSACHUSETTS / 10 / 10. ***Center:*** Alternating flower garlands and gridwork segments. ***Right:*** 10 / 10. ***Engraver:*** Perkins. ***Comments:*** H-MA-955-G48. 18__. 1806 and 1807.

Rarity: —
F $60

$10 • W-MA-2565-010-G330a

Center: Rose-covered TEN. ***Engraver:*** PSSP. ***Comments:*** H-MA-955-G50. Similar to W-MA-2565-010-G330. 18__. Circa 1808 and 1809.

Rarity: —

$10 • W-MA-2565-010-G340

Left: Panel bearing TEN / Manhattan spilling water jug / TEN. ***Center:*** TEN / Ceres seated / TEN / Panel bearing microletters. ***Right:*** Panel bearing 10 / Portrait of Indian / 10. ***Engraver:*** PSSP. ***Comments:*** H-MA-956-G44. 18__. 1830s.

Rarity: —

$10 • W-MA-2565-010-G340a

Back: Congreve Check Plate. ***Engraver:*** PSSP. ***Comments:*** H-MA-956-G44a. Similar to W-MA-2565-010-G340. 18__. 1830s.

Rarity: —

$10 • W-MA-2565-010-G350

Engraver: Unverified, but likely New England Bank Note Co. ***Comments:*** H-MA-956-G46. No description available. 18__. 1830s.

Rarity: *None known*

$10 • W-MA-2565-010-G360

Left: Panel bearing 10 / X / 10. ***Center:*** Allegorical male standing by oxen and plow / 10. ***Right:*** TEN / Woman standing with rudder, Cornucopia. ***Engraver:*** New England Bank Note Co. ***Comments:*** H-MA-956-G48. 18__. 1840s–1850s.

Rarity: —

$10 • W-MA-2565-010-G370

Left: Mechanic seated with tools, Train and buildings / TEN. ***Center:*** X. ***Right:*** 10 / Reaper standing with sheaf and stone. ***Overprint:*** Red. ***Engraver:*** New England Bank Note Co. ***Comments:*** H-MA-956-G50. 18__. 1850s.

Rarity: —

$10 • W-MA-2565-010-G380

Left: Old man showing bust of George Washington to child / 10. ***Center:*** Eagle on rock. ***Right:*** 10. ***Tint:*** Green. ***Engraver:*** American Bank Note Co. ***Comments:*** H-MA-956-G52a. Jan. 2, 186_. 1860s.

Rarity: —

$20 • W-MA-2565-020-G390

Center: Alternating flower garlands and gridwork segments. ***Comments:*** H-MA-955-G54. 180_. 1800s.

Rarity: —

$20 • **W-MA-2565-020-G400**

Left: Narrow panel bearing MASSACHUSETTS / 20 / 20 vertically. ***Center:*** Alternating flower garlands and gridwork segments. ***Right:*** 20 / 20 vertically. ***Engraver:*** Perkins. ***Comments:*** H-MA-955-G58. 18__. 1806–1809.

Rarity: —

$20 • **W-MA-2565-020-G410**

Left: 20 / XX / 20. ***Center:*** 20 / Woman seated with scales, Sheaf and bales, Men plowing, Ship / 20. ***Right:*** TWENTY vertically. ***Back:*** Congreve Check Plate. ***Engraver:*** New England Bank Note Co. / PSSP. ***Comments:*** H-MA-956-G54. 18__. 1830s.

Rarity: —

$20 • **W-MA-2565-020-G420**

Left: Steamboat / XX / Train. ***Center:*** Three women seated with eagle, pole and cap, shield, scales, and book / 20 / Panel outlining white TWENTY. ***Right:*** XX / Milkmaid standing with pail. ***Engraver:*** New England Bank Note Co. ***Comments:*** H-MA-956-G56. 18__. 1830s–1840s.

Rarity: —

$20 • **W-MA-2565-020-G430**

Left: 20 / Woman seated with book on lap, opening chest. ***Center:*** XX / Eagle on rock / XX. ***Right:*** 20 / Ship in harbor. ***Engraver:*** New England Bank Note Co. ***Comments:*** H-MA-956-G58. 18__. 1840s–1850s.

Rarity: —

$20 • **W-MA-2565-020-G440**

CJF

Tint: Green lathework die bearing TWENTY DOLLARS. ***Engraver:*** American Bank Note Co. ***Comments:*** H-MA-956-G60a. Jan. 2, 1861. 1860s.

Rarity: URS-3
Proof $2,500

$50 • **W-MA-2565-050-G450**

Left: 50 / Cornucopia, Woman standing with ankles crossed, Staff, Anchor / 50. ***Center:*** FIFTY DOLLARS / 50. ***Right:*** FIFTY vertically. ***Back:*** Congreve Check Plate. ***Engraver:*** New England Bank Note Co. / PSSP. ***Comments:*** H-MA-956-G62. 18__. 1830s–1840s.

Rarity: —

$50 • **W-MA-2565-050-G460**

Left: FIFTY / Woman standing with wreath and flowers / FIFTY. ***Center:*** 50 / Man restraining prancing horse / 50. ***Right:*** FIFTY / Woman standing with cornucopia / FIFTY. ***Engraver:*** New England Bank Note Co. ***Comments:*** H-MA-956-G64. 18__. 1840s–1850s.

Rarity: —

$50 • **W-MA-2565-050-G470**

CJF

Tint: Green lathework panel bearing FIFTY DOLLARS. ***Engraver:*** American Bank Note Co. ***Comments:*** H-MA-956-G66. Jan. 2, 1861. 1860s.

Rarity: URS-2
Proof $3,500

$100 • **W-MA-2565-100-G480**

Left: Lathework panel bearing C / Portrait of George Washington / C. ***Center:*** 100 / Manhattan reclining, pouring water, Ship / 100. ***Right:*** Lathework panel bearing ONE HUNDRED vertically. ***Engraver:*** New England Bank Note Co. / PSSP. ***Comments:*** H-MA-956-G68. 18__. 1830s–1840s.

Rarity: —

$100 • **W-MA-2565-100-G490**

Left: ONE HUNDRED on 100 / Portrait of William Henry Harrison. ***Center:*** Wharf scene, Men loading wagon with barrel. ***Right:*** ONE HUNDRED on 100 / Portrait of Christopher Columbus. ***Engraver:*** New England Bank Note Co. ***Comments:*** H-MA-956-G70. 18__. 1840s–1850s.

Rarity: —

$100 • **W-MA-2565-100-G500**

CJF

Tint: Green. ***Engraver:*** American Bank Note Co. ***Comments:*** H-MA-956-G72a. Jan. 2, 1861. 1860s.

Rarity: URS-2
Proof $5,000

Uncut Sheets

$20-$50-$100 • W-MA-2565-020.050.100-US010 CJF

Tint(s): Green. ***Comments:*** H-MA-956-G60a, G66, G72a. Jan. 2, 1861. 1860s.

Rarity: URS-1
Proof $10,000

Non-Valid Issues

$1 • W-MA-2565-001-S010 NJW

Engraver: New England Bank Note Co. ***Comments:*** H-MA-956-S5. May 25, 1863.

Rarity: URS-7
VG $125; **VF** $175; **CU** $215

$1 • W-MA-2565-001-A010 SI

Engraver: New England Bank Note Co. ***Comments:*** H-MA-956-A5. Altered from $1 Washington County Bank, Calais, Maine, or from notes of other failed banks using the same plate. Genuine notes from this plate were issued, W-MA-2565-001-G050. 18__. 1840s.

Rarity: —

$2 • W-MA-2565-002-S020 HA

Engraver: Rawdon, Wright & Hatch. ***Comments:*** H-MA-956-S10. From a fraudulently modified plate originally for $2 Havre-De-Grace Bank, Havre-De-Grace, Maryland. Nov. 18, 18__. 1850s.

Rarity: —

$2 • W-MA-2565-002-A020

Left: 2 / Woman standing with staff, Cornucopia / TWO. ***Center:*** TWO / Machinery and merchandise flanking Ceres seated holding sickle and rake, Factories and harbor. ***Engraver:*** New England Bank Note Co. ***Comments:*** H-MA-956-A10. Altered from $2 Washington County Bank, Calais, Maine, or from notes of other failed banks using the same plate. Genuine notes W-MA-2565-002-G140 from this plate were issued. 18__. 1840s.

Rarity: —

$3 • W-MA-2565-003-C230

Engraver: New England Bank Note Co. ***Comments:*** H-MA-956-C30. Counterfeit of W-MA-2565-003-G230. 18__. Circa 1850.

Rarity: —

$3 • W-MA-2565-003-A030

Left: THREE / Beehive and foliage / THREE. ***Center:*** Machinery and merchandise flanking Ceres seated holding sickle and rake, Factories and harbor / THREE. ***Right:*** 3 on THREE / Two reapers / 3 on THREE. ***Engraver:*** New England Bank Note Co. ***Comments:*** H-MA-956-A15. Altered from $3 Washington County Bank, Calais, Maine, or from notes of other failed banks using the same plate. 18__. 1840s

Rarity: —

$5 • W-MA-2565-005-C290

SI

Engraver: New England Bank Note Co. ***Comments:*** H-MA-956-C38. Counterfeit of W-MA-2565-005-G290. 18__. 1840s–1850s.

Rarity: URS-7
F $75

$5 • W-MA-2565-005-N010

Center: Beehive. ***Comments:*** H-MA-956-N10.

Rarity: —

$5 • W-MA-2565-005-A040

Left: 5 / Blacksmith / FIVE. ***Center:*** Laureate man holding shield bearing 5 / Ship / 5. ***Right:*** 5 / Woman seated / FIVE. ***Engraver:*** New England Bank Note Co. ***Comments:*** H-MA-956-A20. Altered from $5 Washington County Bank, Calais, Maine, or from notes of other failed banks using the same plate. Genuine notes W-MA-2565-005-G280 from this plate were issued. 18__. 1840s.

Rarity: —

$10 • W-MA-2565-010-A050

Left: 10 / Farmer sowing / TEN. ***Center:*** Mercury standing with 10 / Merchandise, factories, and ship / Canal scene. ***Right:*** 10 / Ship / TEN. ***Engraver:*** New England Bank Note Co. ***Comments:*** H-MA-956-A25. Altered from $10 Washington County Bank, Calais, Maine, or from notes of other failed banks using the same plate. 18__. 1840s.

Rarity: —

NORTHBOROUGH, MASSACHUSETTS

Originally a part of Marlboro (also spelled Marlborough) at the time of its settlement in 1672, Northborough separated in 1717. It became its own town in 1775, and on June 20, 1807, a section of Marlboro was annexed to Northborough. Industries of the town included grist and saw mills, iron works, brick works, and later cotton mills, woolen mills, and boot and shoemaking.

Northborough Bank
1854–1865
W-MA-2580

History: The Northborough Bank was incorporated on March 28, 1854, with an authorized capital of $100,000. It opened for business in June 1855. Circulation in 1857 amounted to $73,263. It reached a high of $93,213 in 1863.

The business of the Northborough Bank was succeeded by the Northborough National Bank in 1865.

Numismatic Commentary: This is another extremely hard bank to collect. As with most state banks that reorganized into the national banking system, their notes were redeemed for many years to come, reducing the quantity available for today's collectors.

VALID ISSUES

$1 • W-MA-2580-001-G010

Left: 1 / Portrait of Governor Edmund J. Davis / ONE. ***Center:*** Train. ***Right:*** 1 / Woman seated on plow with sheaf, sickle, and basket of fruit. ***Engraver:*** Rawdon, Wright, Hatch & Edson. ***Comments:*** H-MA-960-G2. 18__. 1850s.

Rarity: —

$1 • W-MA-2580-001-G010a

CJF

Overprint: Red ONE. ***Engraver:*** Rawdon, Wright, Hatch & Edson. ***Comments:*** H-Unlisted. Similar to W-MA-2580-001-G010. Dec. 1, 18__. 1850s.

Rarity: URS-6
F $300; **VF** $500

$2 • W-MA-2580-002-G020

Left: 2 / Portrait of Governor Edmund J. Davis. ***Center:*** Woman reclining by plow, Milkmaid and cows, Train, factory, and ships. ***Bottom center:*** Man plowing. ***Right:*** 2 / Two boot makers at work. ***Engraver:*** Rawdon, Wright, Hatch & Edson. ***Comments:*** H-MA-960-G4. 18__. 1850s.

Rarity: —

$3 • W-MA-2580-003-G030

Left: 3 / Portrait of Governor Edmund J. Davis. ***Center:*** Man making horn combs in a comb press, Basket of horns. ***Right:*** 3 / Farmer, sailor, and mechanic standing with 3. ***Engraver:*** American Bank Note Co. ***Comments:*** H-MA-960-G6. 18__. 1850s–1860s.

Rarity: —

$5 • W-MA-2580-005-G040

Left: 5 / Farmer with scythe, keg, and basket, Farmhouse. ***Center:*** Angel with trumpet and cherub flanking portrait of Governor Edmund J. Davis. ***Right:*** 5 / Five women with 5. ***Engraver:*** Rawdon, Wright, Hatch & Edson. ***Comments:*** H-MA-960-G8. 18__. 1850s.

Rarity: —

$10 • W-MA-2580-010-G050

Left: 10 / Portrait of John Quincy Adams. ***Center:*** Woman reclining with shield, Cornucopia and ten gold dollars, Nine cherubs. ***Right:*** X / Woman seated with shield and globe. ***Engraver:*** Rawdon, Wright, Hatch & Edson. ***Comments:*** H-MA-960-G10. 18__. 1850s.

Rarity: —

$20 • W-MA-2580-020-G060

Left: XX / Portrait of George Washington. ***Center:*** Liberty reclining with eagle and globe, Ships. ***Bottom center:*** Farm tools and products. ***Right:*** 20 / Cattle, sheep, and hogs, Two men. ***Engraver:*** Rawdon, Wright, Hatch & Edson. ***Comments:*** H-MA-960-G12. 18__. 1850s.

Rarity: —

$50 • W-MA-2580-050-G070

Left: L / Portrait of Charles Sumner. ***Center:*** Drover on horse with cattle and sheep. ***Bottom center:*** Horses. ***Right:*** 50 / Woman churning butter. ***Engraver:*** American Bank Note Co. ***Comments:*** H-MA-960-G14. 18__. 1850s–1860s.

Rarity: —

$100 • W-MA-2580-100-G080

Left: 100 / Portrait of Zachary Taylor / HUNDRED. ***Center:*** Blacksmith shoeing horse held by boy, Boy fanning fire and man on horse. ***Engraver:*** American Bank Note Co. ***Comments:*** H-MA-960-G16. 18__. 1850s–1860s.

Rarity: —

Non-Valid Issues

$20 • W-MA-2580-020-R010

Engraver: Rawdon, Wright, Hatch & Edson. ***Comments:*** H-MA-960-R5. Raised from W-MA-2580-002-G020. 18__. 1850s.

Rarity: —

North Danvers, Massachusetts

This was a village within Danvers.

See also Danvers and South Danvers, Massachusetts.

Village Bank

1850s

W-MA-2590

History: A non-existent bank represented only by fraudulent notes intended to pass for those of the Village Bank, W-MA-1400.

Issues

$3 • W-MA-2590-003-S010

CJF

Overprint: Red THREE. ***Engraver:*** Danforth, Underwood & Co. ***Comments:*** H-MA-943-S5. October. 1, 18__. 1850s.

Rarity: URS-8

F $100; **VF** $150

Oxford, Massachusetts

Settled by the Huguenots in 1686, the area which became Oxford had an uncertain beginning. The first residents were killed by the local Nipmuc Indians. John Johnson and his three children were killed, but his wife was saved by her brother, who dragged her out via the back door, saving another child. They fled to the garrison at Woodstock, Connecticut. The settlement at Oxford was abandoned and later resettled, incorporating officially as Oxford in 1713. Cotton, woolen, and shoe manufactories existed here during the note-issuing era.

Oxford Bank

1823–1865

W-MA-2600

History: The Oxford Bank was chartered on February 8, 1823, with an authorized capital of $100,000. Its circulation ranged from a low of $50,259.25 in 1839 to a high of $106,680 in 1851. In later years there was an attempt by two fraudsters to gain control of the bank through stock purchases, and afterwards they issued large amounts of bills. The plot was discovered and thwarted.

The business of the Oxford Bank was succeeded by the Oxford National Bank, chartered on January 28, 1865.

Numismatic Commentary: Not many genuine notes remain in the marketplace for today's collectors. There is mention of one nice example showing the Battle of Bunker Hill on a $5 denomination note that some lucky collector will one day own.

Valid Issues

$1 • W-MA-2600-001-G010

Left: Lathework panel. ***Center:*** 1 / 1 / Flower garlands and gridwork segments / 1 / 1. ***Right:*** Lathework panel. ***Engraver:*** PSSP. ***Comments:*** H-MA-965-G2. 18__. 1820s.

Rarity: —

$1 • W-MA-2600-001-G010a

Left: Panel of lathework circle segments. ***Right:*** Panel of lathework circle segments. ***Engraver:*** PSSP. ***Comments:*** H-MA-965-G4. Similar to W-MA-2600-001-G010. 18__. 1820s–1830s.

Rarity: —

$1 • W-MA-2600-001-G010b

Left: ONE / D / ONE vertically. ***Right:*** ONE / D / ONE vertically. ***Engraver:*** PSSP. ***Comments:*** H-MA-965-G6. Similar to W-MA-2600-001-G010. 18__. 1830s.

Rarity: —

$1 • W-MA-2600-001-G020

Comments: H-MA-965-G8. No description available. 18__. 1830s.

Rarity: *None known*

$1 • W-MA-2600-001-G030

Left: ONE / Eagle / ONE. ***Center:*** 1 / Farm woman giving cup to one of two seated men, Hay wagon / ONE. ***Right:*** 1 / Three women seated. ***Engraver:*** New England Bank Note Co. / PSSP. ***Comments:*** H-MA-965-G12. 18__. 1850s.

Rarity: URS-5

VG $750; **VF** $1,250

$1 • W-MA-2600-001-G030a CC

Overprint: Red ONE. ***Engraver:*** New England Bank Note Co. / PSSP / ABNCo. monogram. ***Comments:*** H-Unlisted. Similar to W-MA-2600-001-G030 but with additional engraver imprint. June 12, 18__. 1860s.

Rarity: URS-5
VG $800; **VF** $1,500

$1.25 • W-MA-2600-001.25-G040

Left: 1 25/100 / Train / 1 25/100. ***Center:*** Sloop and other ships at sea / $1.25 cts. ***Right:*** 1 25/100 / Eagle. ***Engraver:*** New England Bank Note Co. ***Comments:*** H-MA-965-G14. 18__. 1830s.

Rarity: —

$1.50 • W-MA-2600-001.50-G050

Left: 1 Doll. 50 Cts. vertically. ***Center:*** Eagle on rock in ocean / $1 50/100. ***Right:*** 1 50/100 / Justice. ***Engraver:*** New England Bank Note Co. ***Comments:*** H-MA-965-G16. 18__. 1830s.

Rarity: —

$2 • W-MA-2600-002-G060

Left: Lathework panel. ***Center:*** 2 / 2 / Oval of flower garlands and gridwork segments / 2 / 2. ***Right:*** Lathework panel. ***Engraver:*** PSSP. ***Comments:*** H-MA-965-G18. 18__. 1820s.

Rarity: —

$2 • W-MA-2600-002-G060a

Left: Panel of lathework circle segments. ***Right:*** Panel of lathework circle segments. ***Engraver:*** PSSP. ***Comments:*** H-MA-965-G20. Similar to W-MA-2600-002-G060. 18__. 1820s–1830s.

Rarity: —

$2 • W-MA-2600-002-G060b

Left: Five TWOs vertically. ***Right:*** Five TWOs vertically. ***Engraver:*** PSSP. ***Comments:*** H-MA-965-G22. Similar to W-MA-2600-002-G060. 18__. 1830s.

Rarity: —

$2 • W-MA-2600-002-G070

Comments: H-MA-965-G24. No description available. 18__. 1830s.

Rarity: *None known*

$2 • W-MA-2600-002-G080

Left: 2 / Justice / 2. ***Center:*** Cattle and sheep, Man on horse, Man standing with dog / 2. ***Right:*** TWO / George Washington standing by horse / 2. ***Comments:*** H-MA-965-G28. 18__. 1850s.

Rarity: —

$3 • W-MA-2600-003-G090

Left: Lathework panel. ***Center:*** 3 / 3 / Oval of flower garlands and gridwork segments / 3 / 3. ***Right:*** Lathework panel. ***Engraver:*** PSSP. ***Comments:*** H-MA-965-G30. 18__. 1820s.

Rarity: —

$3 • W-MA-2600-003-G090a

Left: Panel of lathework circle segments. ***Right:*** Panel of lathework circle segments. ***Engraver:*** PSSP. ***Comments:*** H-MA-965-G32. Similar to W-MA-2600-003-G090. 18__. 1820s–1830s.

Rarity: —

$3 • W-MA-2600-003-G090b

Left: THREE vertically. ***Right:*** THREE vertically. ***Engraver:*** PSSP. ***Comments:*** H-MA-965-G34. Similar to W-MA-2600-003-G090. 18__. 1830s.

Rarity: —

$3 • W-MA-2600-003-G100

Comments: H-MA-965-G36. No description available. 18__. 1830s.

Rarity: *None known*

$3 • W-MA-2600-003-G110

Left: 3 / Woman seated / 3. ***Center:*** THREE / Surrender of Lord Cornwallis to George Washington / 3. ***Right:*** THREE / Farm tools / 3. ***Engraver:*** Toppan, Carpenter, Casilear & Co. ***Comments:*** H-MA-965-G40. 18__. 1850s.

Rarity: —

$5 • W-MA-2600-005-G120

Left: Lathework chain bearing MASSACHUSETTS / 5 / 5. ***Center:*** Text on microletter background. ***Right:*** 5 / 5. ***Engraver:*** PSSP. ***Comments:*** H-MA-965-G42. 18__. 1820s.

Rarity: —

$5 • W-MA-2600-005-G130

Engraver: PSSP. ***Comments:*** H-MA-965-G44. Similar to W-MA-2600-005-G120. 18__. 1820s.

Rarity: —

$5 • W-MA-2600-005-G130a

Engraver: PSSP. ***Comments:*** H-MA-965-G46. Similar to W-MA-2600-005-G120 but with zigzag ruled lines. 18__. 1820s–1830s.

Rarity: —

$5 • W-MA-2600-005-G130b

Engraver: PSSP. ***Comments:*** H-MA-965-G48. Similar to W-MA-2600-005-G120 but with spiral lathework lines. 18__. 1830s.

Rarity: —

$5 • W-MA-2600-005-G140

Comments: H-MA-965-G50. No description available. 18__. 1830s.

Rarity: *None known*

$5 • W-MA-2600-005-G150

Engraver: Unverified, but likely New England Bank Note Co. ***Comments:*** H-MA-965-G52. No description available. 18__. 1840s.

Rarity: *None known*

$5 • W-MA-2600-005-G160

Left: FIVE / Minerva standing. ***Center:*** V / "The Death of General Warren at Battle of Bunker Hill" / 5. ***Right:*** FIVE / Portrait of George Washington / 5. ***Engraver:*** New England Bank Note Co. / PSSP. ***Comments:*** H-MA-965-G56. 18__. 1850s.

Rarity: —

$5 • W-MA-2600-005-G160a

CJF

Overprint: Red FIVE. ***Engraver:*** New England Bank Note Co. / PSSP / ABNCo. monogram. ***Comments:*** H-Unlisted. Similar to W-MA-2600-005-G160 but with additional engraver imprint. June 12, 18__. 1860s.

Rarity: URS-4
F $750; **VF** $1,250

$10 • W-MA-2600-010-G170

Left: Lathework chain bearing MASSACHUSETTS / 10 / 10 vertically. ***Center:*** Alternating flower garlands and gridwork segments. ***Right:*** 10 / 10 vertically. ***Engraver:*** Perkins. ***Comments:*** H-MA-965-G58. 18__. 1810s–1820s.

Rarity: —

$10 • W-MA-2600-010-G170a

Engraver: Perkins. ***Comments:*** H-MA-965-G60. Similar to W-MA-2600-010-G170. 18__. 1820s.

Rarity: —

$10 • W-MA-2600-010-G170b

Engraver: PSSP. ***Comments:*** H-MA-965-G62. Similar to W-MA-2600-010-G170. 18__. 1820s–1830s.

Rarity: —

$10 • W-MA-2600-010-G170c

Engraver: PSSP. ***Comments:*** H-MA-965-G64. Similar to W-MA-2600-010-G170. 18__. 1830s.

Rarity: —

$10 • W-MA-2600-010-G180

Comments: H-MA-965-G66. No description available. 18__. 1830s.

Rarity: *None known*

$10 • W-MA-2600-010-G190

Engraver: Unverified, but likely New England Bank Note Co. ***Comments:*** H-MA-965-G68. No description available. 18__. 1840s.

Rarity: *None known*

$10 • W-MA-2600-010-G200

Left: Statue of George Washington. ***Center:*** 10 / George Washington crossing the Delaware / 10. ***Right:*** TEN / Male portrait / X. ***Comments:*** H-MA-965-G72. 18__. 1850s.

Rarity: —

$20 • W-MA-2600-020-G210

Left: Lathework chain bearing MASSACHUSETTS / 20 / 20 vertically. ***Center:*** Alternating flower garlands and gridwork segments. ***Right:*** 20 / 20 vertically. ***Engraver:*** PSSP. ***Comments:*** H-MA-965-G74. 18__. 1820s–1830s.

Rarity: —

$20 • W-MA-2600-020-G220

Left: Steamboat / XX / Train. ***Center:*** Three women seated with eagle, pole and cap, shield, scales, and book / 20 / Panel outlining white TWENTY. ***Right:*** XX / Milkmaid standing with pail. ***Engraver:*** New England Bank Note Co. ***Comments:*** H-MA-965-G78. Beware of altered W-MA-2600-020-A040 from the same plate as the genuine. 18__. 1840s–1850s.

Rarity: —

$20 • W-MA-2600-020-G230

Left: 20 / Two children with butterfly. ***Center:*** Indian family reclining, Woman with infant, Man and boy, City and ship. ***Right:*** 20 / U.S. shield. ***Overprint:*** Red TWENTY. ***Engraver:*** American Bank Note Co. ***Comments:*** H-MA-965-G80. 1860s.

Rarity: URS-3
F $750; **VF** $1,250

$50 • W-MA-2600-050-G240

Left: Lathework chain bearing MASSACHUSETTS / 50 / 50 vertically. ***Center:*** Alternating flower garlands and gridwork segments. ***Right:*** 50 / 50 vertically. ***Engraver:*** PSSP. ***Comments:*** H-MA-965-G82. 18__. 1820s–1830s.

Rarity: —

$50 • W-MA-2600-050-G250

Left: FIFTY / Sheaves and fruit / 50. ***Center:*** 50 / Three women seated with eagle, pole and cap, shield, scales, and book. ***Right:*** FIFTY across 50 / Vulcan seated with tools, Train. ***Overprint:*** Red FIFTY. ***Engraver:*** New England Bank Note Co. ***Comments:*** H-MA-965-G86. 18__. 1850s.

Rarity: URS-3
F $750; **VF** $1,000

$50 • W-MA-2600-050-G260

Left: State arms. ***Center:*** Girl and boy under tree, Cow in stream. ***Right:*** 50 / Woman seated at sewing machine. ***Tint:*** Green die bearing 50. ***Engraver:*** American Bank Note Co. ***Comments:*** H-MA-965-G88. 1860s.

Rarity: —

$100 • W-MA-2600-100-G270

Left: Lathework chain bearing MASSACHUSETTS / 100 / 100 vertically. ***Center:*** Alternating flower garlands and gridwork segments. ***Right:*** 100 / 100 vertically. ***Engraver:*** Perkins. ***Comments:*** H-MA-965-G90. 18__. 1820s–1830s.

Rarity: —

$100 • W-MA-2600-100-G280

Left: 100 / Eagle / 100. ***Center:*** C / Phoebus in the Chariot of the Sun / 100. ***Right:*** C / Portrait of George Washington / C. ***Engraver:*** New England Bank Note Co. ***Comments:*** H-MA-965-G94. 18__. 1840s–1850s.

Rarity: —

$100 • W-MA-2600-100-G290

Left: C / Men with fishing boat at shore / 100. ***Center:*** Eagle perched on bale, Cornucopia and sheaf / 100. ***Right:*** 100 / Ceres / 100. ***Engraver:*** New England Bank Note Co. ***Comments:*** H-MA-965-G96. 18__. 1850s.

Rarity: —

$100 • W-MA-2600-100-G300

Left: Man drinking from jug, Woman at well. ***Center:*** Two horses startled by lightning, Cows in stream. ***Right:*** C / 100. ***Tint:*** Green die bearing 100. ***Engraver:*** American Bank Note Co. ***Comments:*** H-MA-965-G98. 1860s.

Rarity: —

Non-Valid Issues

$5 • W-MA-2600-005-A010

Left: 5 / Blacksmith at anvil / FIVE. ***Center:*** Mercury standing with 5, Cornucopia and merchandise, Factories and ship / V. ***Right:*** 5 / Ceres kneeling / FIVE. ***Engraver:*** New England Bank Note Co. ***Comments:*** H-MA-965-A5. Altered from $5 Oxford Bank, Fryeburg, Maine. 18__. 1830s.

Rarity: —

$10 • W-MA-2600-010-N010

Left: Trains. ***Center:*** Commerce seated on wharf with goods. ***Comments:*** H-MA-965-N5. 18__. 1840s.

Rarity: —

$10 • W-MA-2600-010-N020

Center: Woman reclining on hill, Town and train. ***Comments:*** H-MA-965-N10. 18__. 1840s.

Rarity: —

$10 • W-MA-2600-010-A020

Left: 10 / Farmer sowing / TEN. ***Center:*** Mercury standing with right hand on 10, Merchandise, Factories and ship / X / Panel outlining white TEN. ***Right:*** 10 / Ship / TEN. ***Engraver:*** PSSP / New England Bank Note Co. ***Comments:*** H-MA-965-A10 Altered from $10 Oxford Bank, Fryeburg, Maine. 18__. 1830s.

Rarity: —

$10 • W-MA-2600-010-A030

Left: X / Indian kneeling with bow. ***Center:*** Steamboat, Schooner and boats, City / X / Panel outlining white TEN. ***Right:*** 10 / Woman with bonnet and sheaf. ***Engraver:*** New England Bank Note Co. ***Comments:*** H-MA-965-A15. Altered from $10 Hamilton Bank, Scituate, Rhode Island, or from notes of other failed banks using the same plate. 18__. 1840s.

Rarity: —

$20 • W-MA-2600-020-A040

CJF

Engraver: New England Bank Note Co. ***Comments:*** H-MA-965-A20. Altered from $20 Hamilton Bank, Scituate, Rhode Island, or from notes of other failed banks using the same plate. Genuine notes of this design were issued. W-MA-2600-020-G220. 18__. 1840s.

Rarity: URS-6
F $150; **VF** $250

Pawtucket, Massachusetts

Pawtucket, a village of North Providence, means "little falls" in the native tongue, referring to the 50 foot falls of the local river. It was originally known as Rehoboth in 1651 and was comprised of 600 acres. In 1671 Joseph Jenks settled across the river and erected a forge and shop. In the same place, Samuel Slater opened the country's first cotton mill in 1793. Iron workers produced farm tools, anchors, cannons, and muskets. 12 cotton mills, a print works, and manufacturers of cotton machinery, bobbins, spools, shoes, boots, ships, carriages, chairs, and cabinets were also located here. In 1862 the entire area was ceded to Rhode Island.

See also Pawtucket, Rhode Island.

Pawtucket Bank

1814–1850

W-MA-2610

History: The Pawtucket Bank was located across the Blackstone River from Rhode Island. It was situated in a town that was located in Massachusetts at the time.

The Pawtucket Bank was chartered on June 13, 1814, with an authorized capital of $100,000. Circulation was $18,084 in 1839, $57,750 in 1848, and $32,165 in 1849. In October 1850, the Bank Commissioners visited the Pawtucket Bank and found that the cashier had been engaging in unlawful activity, had given unrecorded loans, and had incurred losses of over $200,000. The bank was forced into liquidation. All submitted currency was redeemed at par, and the depositors were safe. However, the stockholders lost their investment.

Numismatic Commentary: Examples of issues from this bank turn up in the marketplace at widely spaced intervals. All the genuine issues were engraved in the PSSP style, including others also engraved by the New England Bank Note Co.

Valid Issues

$1 • W-MA-2610-001-G010

Center: 1 / 1 / Flower garlands and gridwork segments / ONE / 1 / 1. ***Engraver:*** PSSP. ***Comments:*** H-MA-970-G10. 18__. Circa 1812–1820s.

Rarity: *None known*

$1 • W-MA-2610-001-G010a

Left: Panel of lathework circle segments. ***Right:*** Panel of lathework circle segments. ***Engraver:*** PSSP. ***Comments:*** H-MA-970-G12. Similar to W-MA-2610-001-G010. 18__. 1820s.

Rarity: *None known*

$1 • W-MA-2610-001-G010b

Left: Panel of lathework circle segments. ***Right:*** Panel of lathework circle segments. ***Engraver:*** PSSP. ***Comments:*** H-MA-970-G14. Similar to W-MA-2610-001-G010. 18__. 1820s–1830s.

Rarity: *None known*

$1 • W-MA-2610-001-G010c

Left: ONE / D / ONE vertically. ***Right:*** ONE / D / ONE vertically. ***Engraver:*** PSSP. ***Comments:*** H-MA-970-G16. Similar to W-MA-2610-001-G010. 18__. 1830s.

Rarity: *None known*

$1 • W-MA-2610-001-G010d CJF

Engraver: PSSP. ***Comments:*** H-Unlisted. Similar to W-MA-2610-001-G010. 18__. 1840s.

Rarity: —

$1 • W-MA-2610-001-G020

Engraver: Unverified, but likely New England Bank Note Co. ***Comments:*** H-MA-970-G18. No description available. 18__. 1830s.

Rarity: *None known*

$1 • W-MA-2610-001-G030

Left: Panel bearing ONE vertically. ***Center:*** Sloop and other ships, 1. ***Right:*** ONE / Indian woman seated with bow and arrow / ONE. ***Engraver:*** New England Bank Note Co. ***Comments:*** H-MA-970-G22. 18__. 1840s.

Rarity: *None known*

$2 • W-MA-2610-002-G040

Center: 2 / 2 / Flower garlands and gridwork segments / TWO / 2 / 2. ***Engraver:*** PSSP. ***Comments:*** H-MA-970-G26. 18__. Circa 1812–1820s.

Rarity: *None known*

$2 • W-MA-2610-002-G040a

Left: Panel of lathework circle segments. ***Right:*** Panel of lathework circle segments. ***Engraver:*** PSSP. ***Comments:*** H-MA-970-G28. Similar to W-MA-2610-002-G040. 18__. 1820s.

Rarity: *None known*

$2 • W-MA-2610-002-G040b

Left: Panel of lathework circle segments. ***Right:*** Panel of lathework circle segments. ***Engraver:*** PSSP. ***Comments:*** H-MA-970-G30. Similar to W-MA-2610-002-G040. 18__. 1820s–1830s.

Rarity: *None known*

$2 • W-MA-2610-002-G040c

Left: Five TWOs vertically. ***Right:*** Five TWOs vertically. ***Engraver:*** PSSP. ***Comments:*** H-MA-970-G32. Similar to W-MA-2610-002-G040. 18__. 1830s.

Rarity: *None known*

$2 • W-MA-2610-002-G050

Engraver: Unverified, but likely New England Bank Note Co. ***Comments:*** H-MA-970-G34. No description available. 18__. 1830s.

Rarity: *None known*

$2 • W-MA-2610-002-G060 CC

Engraver: New England Bank Note Co. ***Comments:*** H-MA-970-G38. 18__. 1840s.

Rarity: URS-3

F $1,100; **Proof** $1,250

$3 • W-MA-2610-003-G070

Center: 3 / 3 / Oval of flower garlands and gridwork segments / 3 / 3. ***Engraver:*** PSSP. ***Comments:*** H-MA-970-G40. 18__. 1810s–1820s.

Rarity: *None known*

$3 • W-MA-2610-003-G070a

Left: Panel of lathework circle segments. ***Right:*** Panel of lathework circle segments. ***Engraver:*** PSSP. ***Comments:*** H-MA-970-G42. Similar to W-MA-2610-003-G070. 18__. 1820s.

Rarity: *None known*

$3 • W-MA-2610-003-G070b

Left: Panel of lathework circle segments. ***Right:*** Panel of lathework circle segments. ***Engraver:*** PSSP. ***Comments:*** H-MA-970-G44. Similar to W-MA-2610-003-G070. 18__. 1820s–1830s.

Rarity: *None known*

$3 • W-MA-2610-003-G070c

Left: THREE vertically. ***Right:*** THREE vertically. ***Engraver:*** PSSP. ***Comments:*** H-MA-970-G46. Similar to W-MA-2610-003-G070. 18__. 1830s.

Rarity: *None known*

$3 • W-MA-2610-003-G080

Engraver: Unverified, but likely New England Bank Note Co. ***Comments:*** H-MA-970-G48. No description available. 18__. 1830s.

Rarity: *None known*

$3 • W-MA-2610-003-G090 CC

Engraver: New England Bank Note Co. ***Comments:*** H-MA-970-G52. 18__. 1840s.

Rarity: URS-4

VG $450; **F** $900

$5 • **W-MA-2610-005-G100**

Left: Panel bearing state arms / 5 / 5. ***Center:*** Alternating flower garlands and gridwork segments. ***Right:*** 5 / 5. ***Engraver:*** PSSP. ***Comments:*** H-MA-970-G54. 18__. 1810s–1820s.

Rarity: *None known*

$5 • **W-MA-2610-005-G100a**

Left: Lathework chain bearing MASSACHUSETTS vertically. ***Right:*** Panel of lathework circle segments. ***Engraver:*** PSSP. ***Comments:*** H-MA-970-G56. Similar to W-MA-2610-005-G100. 18__. 1820s.

Rarity: *None known*

$5 • **W-MA-2610-005-G100b**

Engraver: PSSP. ***Comments:*** H-MA-970-G58. Similar to W-MA-2610-005-G100. 18__. 1820s.

Rarity: *None known*

$5 • **W-MA-2610-005-G100c**

Engraver: PSSP. ***Comments:*** H-MA-970-G60. Similar to W-MA-2610-005-G100 but with zigzag ruled lines. 18__. 1820s–1830s.

Rarity: *None known*

$5 • **W-MA-2610-005-G100d**

Engraver: PSSP. ***Comments:*** H-MA-970-G62. Similar to W-MA-2610-005-G100 but with spiral lathework lines. 18__. 1830s.

Rarity: *None known*

$5 • **W-MA-2610-005-G110**

Engraver: Unverified, but likely New England Bank Note Co. ***Comments:*** H-MA-970-G64. No description available. 18__. 1830s.

Rarity: *None known*

$5 • **W-MA-2610-005-G120**

CJF

Engraver: New England Bank Note Co. ***Comments:*** H-MA-970-G68. 18__. 1840s.

Rarity: URS-4
F $500; **VF** $600

$10 • **W-MA-2610-010-G130**

Left: Panel bearing state arms / 10 / 10 vertically. ***Center:*** Text on microletter background / TEN. ***Right:*** 10 / 10 vertically. ***Engraver:*** Perkins. ***Comments:*** H-MA-970-G70. 18__. 1810s–1820s.

Rarity: *None known*

$10 • **W-MA-2610-010-G130a**

Left: Lathework chain bearing MASSACHUSETTS vertically. ***Right:*** Panel of lathework circle segments. ***Engraver:*** Perkins. ***Comments:*** H-MA-970-G72. Similar to W-MA-2610-010-G130. 18__. 1820s.

Rarity: *None known*

$10 • **W-MA-2610-010-G130b**

Engraver: Perkins. ***Comments:*** H-MA-970-G74. Similar to W-MA-2610-010-G130. 18__. 1820s.

Rarity: *None known*

$10 • **W-MA-2610-010-G130c**

Engraver: PSSP. ***Comments:*** H-MA-970-G76. Similar to W-MA-2610-010-G130. 18__. 1820s–1830s.

Rarity: *None known*

$10 • **W-MA-2610-010-G130d**

Engraver: PSSP. ***Comments:*** H-MA-970-G78. Similar to W-MA-2610-010-G130 but with spiral lathework lines. 18__. 1830s.

Rarity: *None known*

$10 • **W-MA-2610-010-G140**

Engraver: Unverified, but likely New England Bank Note Co. ***Comments:*** H-MA-970-G80. No description available. 18__. 1830s.

Rarity: *None known*

$10 • **W-MA-2610-010-G150**

Left: Panel bearing 10 / X / 10. ***Center:*** Allegorical male standing by oxen and plow / 10. ***Right:*** TEN / Woman standing with rudder, Cornucopia. ***Engraver:*** New England Bank Note Co. ***Comments:*** H-MA-970-G84. 18__. 1840s.

Rarity: *None known*

$20 • **W-MA-2610-020-G160**

Left: Panel bearing state arms / 20 / 20 vertically. ***Center:*** Alternating flower garlands and gridwork segments. ***Right:*** 20 / 20 vertically. ***Engraver:*** Perkins. ***Comments:*** H-MA-970-G86. 18__. 1810s–1820s.

Rarity: *None known*

$20 • **W-MA-2610-020-G160a**

Left: Lathework chain bearing MASSACHUSETTS vertically. ***Engraver:*** PSSP. ***Comments:*** H-MA-970-G88. Similar to W-MA-2610-020-G160. 18__. 1820s–1830s.

Rarity: *None known*

$20 • **W-MA-2610-020-G170**

Engraver: Unverified, but likely New England Bank Note Co. ***Comments:*** H-MA-970-G90. No description available. 18__. 1830s.

Rarity: *None known*

$50 • **W-MA-2610-050-G180**

Left: Panel bearing state arms / 50 / 50 vertically. ***Center:*** Alternating flower garlands and gridwork segments. ***Right:*** 50 / 50 vertically. ***Engraver:*** Perkins. ***Comments:*** H-MA-970-G94. 18__. 1810s–1820s.

Rarity: *None known*

$50 • **W-MA-2610-050-G180a**

Left: Lathework chain bearing MASSACHUSETTS vertically. ***Engraver:*** PSSP. ***Comments:*** H-MA-970-G96. Similar to W-MA-2610-050-G180. 18__. 1820s–1830s.

Rarity: *None known*

$50 • **W-MA-2610-050-G190**

Engraver: Unverified, but likely New England Bank Note Co. ***Comments:*** H-MA-970-G98. No description available. 18__. 1830s.

Rarity: *None known*

$100 • W-MA-2610-100-G200

Left: Panel bearing state arms / 100 / 100 vertically. ***Center:*** Alternating flower garlands and gridwork segments. ***Right:*** 100 / 100 vertically. ***Engraver:*** Perkins. ***Comments:*** H-MA-970-G102. 18__. 1810s–1820s.

Rarity: *None known*

$100 • W-MA-2610-100-G200a

Left: Lathework chain bearing MASSACHUSETTS vertically. ***Engraver:*** Perkins. ***Comments:*** H-MA-970-G104. Similar to W-MA-2610-100-G200. 18__. 1820s–1830s.

Rarity: *None known*

$100 • W-MA-2610-100-G210

Engraver: Unverified, but likely New England Bank Note Co. ***Comments:*** H-MA-970-G106. No description available. 18__. 1830s.

Rarity: *None known*

Non-Valid Issues

$1 • W-MA-2610-001-A010

Left: 1 / Steamboat / 1. ***Center:*** Medallion head with 1 / Train backed up to wharf, People standing, Train / Medallion head with 1. ***Bottom center:*** Dog and strongbox. ***Right:*** 1 / Cherub with arms upraised seated on lion / 1. ***Comments:*** H-MA-970-A5. Altered from $1 Geauga Insurance Co., Painesville, Ohio. 18__. 1840s.

Rarity: *None known*

$2 • W-MA-2610-002-N010

Center: Indian man, Ship at anchor. ***Comments:*** H-MA-970-N5. 18__. 1840s.

Rarity: *None known*

$5 • W-MA-2610-005-N020

Center: Train. ***Comments:*** H-MA-970-N10. 18__. 1840s.

Rarity: *None known*

$5 • W-MA-2610-005-A020

Left: FIVE / Roman senator seated with scroll / 5. ***Center:*** FIVE on helmeted medallion head / Woman seated holding infant, Sheaf / Five on helmeted medallion head. ***Bottom center:*** Train. ***Right:*** FIVE / Woman seated with closed book / 5. ***Engraver:*** Danforth, Underwood & Co. / Underwood, Bald, Spencer & Hufty. ***Comments:*** H-MA-970-A10. Altered from $5 Tenth Ward Bank New York City, New York. 18__. 1840s.

Rarity: *None known*

$5 • W-MA-2610-005-A030

CJF

Comments: H-MA-970-A15. Altered from $5 Geauga Insurance Co., Painesville, Ohio. 18__. Circa 1850.

Rarity: URS-3
F $300; **VF** $500

$10 • W-MA-2610-010-A040

Left: 10 / Sailor standing with U.S. flag / X. ***Center:*** Diagonal 10 on medallion head / "Presentation of the Declaration of Independence" / Diagonal 10 medallion head. ***Bottom center:*** Eagle. ***Right:*** X / Pat Lyon at Forge / 10. ***Engraver:*** Danforth, Underwood & Co. / Underwood, Bald, Spencer & Hufty. ***Comments:*** H-MA-970-A20. Altered from $10 Tenth Ward Bank, New York City, New York. 18__. 1840s.

Rarity: *None known*

$50 • W-MA-2610-050-A050

Left: 50 / Woman standing, Bowl of fruit, Shield bearing anchor / 50. ***Center:*** L / Hebe watering eagle / L. ***Bottom center:*** Anchor and implements. ***Right:*** 50 / Farmer holding grain / 50. ***Engraver:*** Terry, Pelton & Co. ***Comments:*** H-MA-970-A25. Altered from $50 Citizens Bank, Augusta, Maine, or from notes of other failed banks using the same plate. 18__. Circa 1840.

Rarity: *None known*

Pittsfield, Massachusetts

The Mohican tribe resided in the area that later became Pittsfield and continued to be active there after settlement by the colonists. The first land was purchased in 1738 by Colonel Jacob Wendell, who bought 24,000 acres that belonged to land once known as Pontoosuck, meaning "field or haven for winter deer." The French and Indian War caused conflict and concern over the area, and as a result the land was uninhabited for several years. A village began to rise when settlers from Westfield arrived, and soon the land was incorporated in 1753 as the Pontoosuck Plantation, incorporating as the town of Pittsfield in 1761. It was named after a British nobleman and politician, William Pitt, who later was recognized as being favorable to the concerns voiced by American colonists against the British Crown. The 1766 Pitt halfpenny bears his image.

At the end of the American Revolution, Pittsfield claimed 2,000 occupants. Agriculture was the mainstay of the town, and the area also claimed a few mills that worked lumber, grist, paper, and textiles. Merino sheep from Spain came in 1807, after which, in time, Pittsfield became the woolen manufacturing center of the country. Snare drums were also constructed here by the Stevens family.

Agricultural Bank

1818–1865

W-MA-2620

History: The Agricultural Bank was chartered on February 20, 1818, with an authorized capital of $100,000, to be paid in gold and silver coins. This was a difficult time in the economy, and such coins were scarce. In 1819, after the first installment of $45,000 was placed in the vault, the bank was permitted to open. However, it was found that $32,000 of this was on loan and had been taken back the next day. Such shenanigans were very common at the time, and many requirements that capital be paid in specie were ignored. Paper IOUs were accepted instead. Most often, such activities were not acted upon by the Legislature.

The bank's capital was $150,000 in 1839 and increased to $200,000 in 1855. Circulation was at a low of $92,745 in 1839 but reached a high of $198,989 in 1863. The bank's real estate was valued at $8,800.

In April 1849, the *Banker's Magazine* reported this:

> It is just *thirty* years since the Agricultural Bank in Pittsfield, (Mass.) went into operation. For the same period of thirty years the present highly respected incumbent, Ezekiel R. Colt, Esq., has been its only cashier. Besides making dividends averaging eight percent per annum for the whole period of its existence, it has accumulated a surplus of *thirty* thousand dollars. It would be difficult to produce better evidence of the good management of such an institution than the facts above stated, and of the worthiness of the persons with whom it has had to deal. The Hon. Nathan Appleton was one of its founders.

The business of the Agricultural Bank was succeeded by the Agricultural National Bank of Pittsfield in 1865.

Numismatic Commentary: Genuine notes that become available will most likely be the early Abner Reed designs. Counterfeits of these are fairly plentiful in the marketplace. Later issues will be harder to locate due to the bank reorganizing into a national bank and continuing to redeem its issues.

As of 2003 there was a $20-$50 tint plate remaining at the American Bank Note Co. archives.

VALID ISSUES

$1 • W-MA-2620-001-G010

Left: ONE ONE ONE vertically. ***Center:*** 1 / Woman seated / 1. ***Bottom center:*** ONE. ***Right:*** 1 MASSACHUSETTS 1. ***Engraver:*** A. Reed / Reed. ***Comments:*** H-MA-975-G4. 18__. 1818–1820s.

Rarity: URS-2
Proof $1,000

$1 • W-MA-2620-001-G020

Comments: H-MA-975-G8. No description available. 18__. 1820s.

Rarity: *None known*

$1 • W-MA-2620-001-G030

Left: 1 / Woman wearing bonnet with pail / ONE. ***Center:*** Machinery and merchandise flanking Ceres seated holding sickle and rake, Factories and harbor, ONE / Panel outlining white ONE. ***Right:*** 1 / Ship / ONE. ***Engraver:*** PSSP / National Bank Note Co. ***Comments:*** H-MA-975-G12. 18__. 1830s.

Rarity: —

$1 • W-MA-2620-001-G040

CC

Engraver: Rawdon, Wright & Hatch. ***Comments:*** H-MA-975-G16. 18__. 1840s–1850s.

Rarity: URS-3
Proof $2,500

$1 • W-MA-2620-001-G050

Left: 1 / Woman seated with children and globe. ***Center:*** 1 / Man with horse and wagon / Two men / 1. ***Bottom center:*** ONE. ***Right:*** 1 / Indian woman seated with child. ***Engraver:*** Danforth, Bald & Co. ***Comments:*** H-MA-975-G20. 18__. 1850s.

Rarity: —

$1 • W-MA-2620-001-G050a

CJF

Overprint: Red 1 1 / ONE. ***Engraver:*** Danforth, Bald & Co. / ABNCo. monogram. ***Comments:*** H-MA-975-G20b. Similar to W-MA-2620-001-G050 but with additional engraver imprint. 18__. 1850s–1860s.

Rarity: URS-4
VG $400; **F** $600; **VF** $1,000

$2 • W-MA-2620-002-G060

Left: Panel bearing 2 / TWO / 2 vertically. ***Center:*** 2 / 2. ***Bottom center:*** 2 on die. ***Right:*** Panel bearing 2 / MASSACHUSETTS / 2 vertically. ***Engraver:*** A. Reed / Reed. ***Comments:*** H-MA-975-G24. 18__. 1818–1820s.

Rarity: —

$2 • W-MA-2620-002-G070

Comments: H-MA-975-G28. No description available. 18__. 1820s.

Rarity: *None known*

$2 • W-MA-2620-002-G080

Left: 2 / Woman standing with staff, Cornucopia / TWO. ***Center:*** TWO / Machinery and merchandise flanking Ceres seated holding sickle and rake, Factories and harbor / Panel outlining white TWO. ***Right:*** 2 / Woman wearing hat, Trees / TWO. ***Engraver:*** New England Bank Note Co. / PSSP. ***Comments:*** H-MA-975-G32. 18__. 1830s.

Rarity: —

$2 • W-MA-2620-002-G090

Left: TWO vertically. ***Center:*** 2 / Two men and two women. ***Right:*** 2 / Man plowing with two horses. ***Engraver:*** Rawdon, Wright & Hatch. ***Comments:*** H-MA-975-G36. 18__. 1840s–1850s.

Rarity: —

$2 • W-MA-2620-002-G100

Left: Woman kneeling with sheaf, Woman with spear. ***Center:*** 2 / Woman seated in 2, Farm scene / 2. ***Right:*** 2 / State arms. ***Engraver:*** Danforth, Bald & Co. ***Comments:*** H-MA-975-G40. 18__. 1850s.

Rarity: —

$2 • W-MA-2620-002-G100a

Overprint: Red. ***Engraver:*** Danforth, Bald & Co. / ABNCo. monogram. ***Comments:*** H-MA-975-G40b. Similar to W-MA-2620-002-G100 but with additional engraver imprint. 18__. 1850s–1860s.

Rarity: —

$3 • W-MA-2620-003-G110

QDB

Engraver: Reed. ***Comments:*** H-MA-975-G44. Proof. 18__. 1818–1820s.

Rarity: URS-2
Unc-S&D $2,000

$3 • W-MA-2620-003-G120

Comments: H-MA-975-G48. No description available. 18__. 1820s.

Rarity: *None known*

$3 • W-MA-2620-003-G130

Left: THREE / Beehive and foliage / THREE. ***Center:*** Machinery and merchandise flanking Ceres seated holding sickle and rake, Factories and harbor / THREE / Panel outlining white THREE. ***Right:*** 3 on THREE / Two reapers / 3 on THREE. ***Engraver:*** New England Bank Note Co. / PSSP. ***Comments:*** H-MA-975-G52. 18__. 1830s.

Rarity: —

$3 • W-MA-2620-003-G140

Left: Woman kneeling with sickle and cornucopia, Ship / THREE vertically. ***Center:*** White horse and black horse flanking shield bearing Indian man surmounted by eagle. ***Right:*** 3 / Milkmaid, train, and house. ***Engraver:*** Danforth, Bald & Co. ***Comments:*** H-MA-975-G60. 18__. 1850s.

Rarity: —

$3 • W-MA-2620-003-G140a

Overprint: Red. ***Engraver:*** Danforth, Bald & Co. / ABNCo. monogram. ***Comments:*** H-MA-975-G60b. Similar to W-MA-2620-003-G140 but with additional engraver imprint. 18__. 1850s–1860s.

Rarity: —

$5 • W-MA-2620-005-G150

Left: 5 FIVE 5 vertically. ***Center:*** 5 / Farmer with oxen plowing / 5. ***Bottom center:*** FIVE. ***Right:*** V Massachusetts V vertically. ***Engraver:*** Reed. ***Comments:*** H-MA-975-G64. 18__. 1818–1820s.

Rarity: URS-3
Proof $750

$5 • W-MA-2620-005-G160

Comments: H-MA-975-G68. No description available. 18__. 1820s.

Rarity: *None known*

$5 • W-MA-2620-005-G170

Comments: H-MA-975-G72. No description available. 18__. 1830s.

Rarity: *None known*

$5 • W-MA-2620-005-G180

Left: Man and woman / FIVE / 5. ***Center:*** 5 / Street scene with buildings and tree / 5. ***Bottom center:*** Arm and hammer. ***Right:*** FIVE vertically. ***Engraver:*** Rawdon, Wright & Hatch. ***Comments:*** H-MA-975-G76. 18__. 1840s–1850s.

Rarity: —

$5 • W-MA-2620-005-G190

Left: V in FIVE / Train passing under bridge. ***Center:*** Woman reclining with chest, Shield bearing scene. ***Right:*** 5 / Woodcutter. ***Engraver:*** Danforth, Bald & Co. ***Comments:*** H-MA-975-G80. 18__. 1850s.

Rarity: —

$5 • W-MA-2620-005-G190a

Overprint: Red. ***Engraver:*** Danforth, Bald & Co. / ABNCo. monogram. ***Comments:*** H-MA-975-G80b. Similar to W-MA-2620-005-G190 but with additional engraver imprint. 18__. 1850s–1860s.

Rarity: —

$10 • W-MA-2620-010-G200

Left: 10 TEN 10. ***Center:*** 10 / Man plowing, Sheaf / 10. ***Bottom center:*** TEN. ***Right:*** X MASSACHUSETTS X. ***Engraver:*** A. Reed / Reed. ***Comments:*** H-MA-975-G84. 18__. 1818–1820s.

Rarity: —

$10 • W-MA-2620-010-G210

Comments: H-MA-975-G92. No description available. 18__. 1830s.

Rarity: *None known*

$10 • W-MA-2620-010-G220

Left: Panel bearing 10 / X / 10. ***Center:*** Allegorical male standing by oxen and plow / 10. ***Right:*** TEN / Woman standing with rudder, Cornucopia. ***Engraver:*** New England Bank Note Co. ***Comments:*** H-MA-975-G96. 18__. 1840s–1850s.

Rarity: —

$10 • W-MA-2620-010-G230

Left: 10 / Portrait of Daniel Webster. ***Center:*** Train, trees, and factories. ***Right:*** TEN and X across 10 / Two farmers and dog. ***Engraver:*** Danforth, Bald & Co. ***Comments:*** H-MA-975-G100. 18__. 1850s.

Rarity: —

$10 • W-MA-2620-010-G230a

Overprint: Red. ***Engraver:*** Danforth, Bald & Co. / ABNCo. monogram. ***Comments:*** H-MA-975-G100b. Similar to W-MA-2620-010-G230 but with additional engraver imprint. 18__. 1850s–1860s.

Rarity: —

$20 • W-MA-2620-020-G240

Left: Panel bearing 20 / TWENTY / 20 vertically. ***Center:*** 20 / 20. ***Bottom center:*** XX on die. ***Right:*** Panel bearing XX / MASSACHUSETTS / 20 vertically. ***Engraver:*** A. Reed / Reed. ***Comments:*** H-MA-975-G104. 18__. 1818–1820s.

Rarity: —

$20 • W-MA-2620-020-G250

Left: Steamboat / XX / Train. ***Center:*** Three women seated with eagle, pole and cap, shield, scales, and book / 20 / Panel outlining white TWENTY. ***Right:*** XX / Milkmaid standing with pail. ***Engraver:*** New England Bank Note Co. ***Comments:*** H-MA-975-G112. 18__. 1830s.

Rarity: —

$20 • W-MA-2620-020-G260

Left: 20 / Woman seated with book on lap, opening chest. ***Center:*** XX / Eagle on rock / XX. ***Right:*** 20 / Ship in harbor. ***Engraver:*** New England Bank Note Co. ***Comments:*** H-MA-975-G116. 18__. 1840s–1850s.

Rarity: —

$20 • W-MA-2620-020-G270

Left: TWENTY / 20. ***Center:*** Farmer grinding scythe, Boy turning stone / Horses drinking at trough, Woman and boy. ***Right:*** TWENTY / 20. ***Tint:*** Green XX. ***Engraver:*** American Bank Note Co. ***Comments:*** H-MA-975-G120. 1860s.

Rarity: —

$50 • W-MA-2620-050-G280

Left: 50 / Steamboat and schooner. ***Center:*** Farmyard scene, Load of hay with two men on it, Man with rake and pail. ***Right:*** L / Justice kneeling. ***Engraver:*** New England Bank Note Co. ***Comments:*** H-MA-975-G130. 18__. 1830s.

Rarity: —

$50 • W-MA-2620-050-G290

Left: Woman holding shield bearing words INCORPORATED A.D. 1818. ***Center:*** 50 / Farming implements. ***Right:*** 50 / Dog lying on strongbox. ***Tint:*** Green. ***Engraver:*** American Bank Note Co. ***Comments:*** H-MA-975-G140. 1860s.

Rarity: —

$100 • W-MA-2620-100-G300

Engraver: Unverified, but likely New England Bank Note Co. ***Comments:*** H-MA-975-G150. No description available. 18__. 1830s–1840s.

Rarity: *None known*

Uncut Sheets

$1-$1-$2-$3 • W-MA-2620-001.001.002.003-US010

Vignette(s): ***($1)*** No description available. ***($1)*** No description available. ***($2)*** Woman kneeling with sheaf, Woman with spear / Woman seated in 2, Farm scene / State arms. ***($3)*** Woman kneeling with sickle and cornucopia, Ship / White horse and black horse flanking shield bearing Indian man and surmounted by eagle / Milkmaid, train, and house. ***Comments:*** H-Unlisted, H-Unlisted, H-MA-975-G40, G60. 18__. 1850s.

Rarity: *None known*

$1-$3-$5-$5 • W-MA-2620-001.003.005.005-US020

Vignette(s): No description available. ***Comments:*** H-MA-975-G8, G48, G68, G68. 18__. 1820s.

Rarity: *None known*

$5-$5-$5-$10 • W-MA-2620-005.005.005.010-US030

Vignette(s): ***($5)*** Train passing under bridge / Woman reclining with chest, Shield bearing scene / Woodcutter. ***($5)*** Train passing under bridge / Woman reclining with chest, Shield bearing scene / Woodcutter. ***($5)*** Train passing under bridge / Woman reclining with chest, Shield bearing scene / Woodcutter. ***($10)*** Portrait of Daniel Webster / Train, trees, and factories / Two farmers and dog. ***Comments:*** All unlisted in Haxby. Similar to H-MA-975-G80, G80, G80, G100 but with different engraver imprint. 18__. 1850s.

Rarity: —

Non-Valid Issues

$1 • W-MA-2620-001-C010

Engraver: A. Reed / Reed. ***Comments:*** H-MA-975-C4. Counterfeit of W-MA-2620-001-G010. 18__. 1818.

Rarity: —

$1 • W-MA-2620-001-A010

CJF

Engraver: Burton & Gurley. ***Comments:*** H-MA-975-A5. Altered from $1 Agricultural Bank, Montreal, Canada. 18__. 1840s.

Rarity: URS-5

F $100

$2 • W-MA-2620-002-C060

Engraver: A. Reed / Reed. ***Comments:*** H-MA-975-C24. Counterfeit of W-MA-2620-002-G060. 18__. 1820s.

Rarity: —

$2 • W-MA-2620-002-S010

CJF

Engraver: Spencer, Hufty & Danforth. ***Comments:*** H-MA-975-S5. January 1, 1852.

Rarity: URS-5

F $125

$2 • W-MA-2620-002-S020

Left: TWO / Two men holding up two women / TWO. ***Center:*** 2 / Women flanking shield / 2. ***Bottom center:*** Woman with sheaf. ***Right:*** TWO / Woman seated / TWO. ***Engraver:*** Rawdon, Wright & Hatch. ***Comments:*** H-MA-975-S10. From a fraudulently modified plate originally for a $1 Havre-De-Grace Bank, Havre-De-Grace, Maryland. Nov. 18, 18__. 1850s.

Rarity: URS-5

F $125; **VF** $175

$2 • W-MA-2620-002-A020

Left: DEUX / Farmer standing under tree holding sheaf / 2 DOLLARS. ***Center:*** 2 / Ceres seated, Sheaves and plow, Two cows / 2. ***Bottom center:*** Bear. ***Right:*** Helmeted woman standing / TWO. ***Engraver:*** Burton, Gurley & Edmonds. ***Comments:*** H-MA-975-A10. Altered from $2 Agricultural Bank, Montreal, Canada. 18__. 1840s.

Rarity: —

$3 • W-MA-2620-003-A030

Left: TROIS / Woman standing / 3. ***Center:*** 3 / Woman seated with shield bearing 3, Ships / 3. ***Bottom center:*** Crown. ***Right:*** TROIS / Farmer plowing with two oxen / 3. ***Engraver:*** Burton & Gurley. ***Comments:*** H-MA-975-A15. 18__. 1840s.

Rarity: —

$3 • W-MA-2620-003-A030a

CJF

Engraver: Burton & Gurley. ***Comments:*** H-Unlisted. Similar to W-MA-2620-003-A030. Altered from $3 Agricultural Bank, Montreal, Canada. 18__. 1840s.

Rarity: URS-5
F $125

$5 • W-MA-2620-005-C150

TD

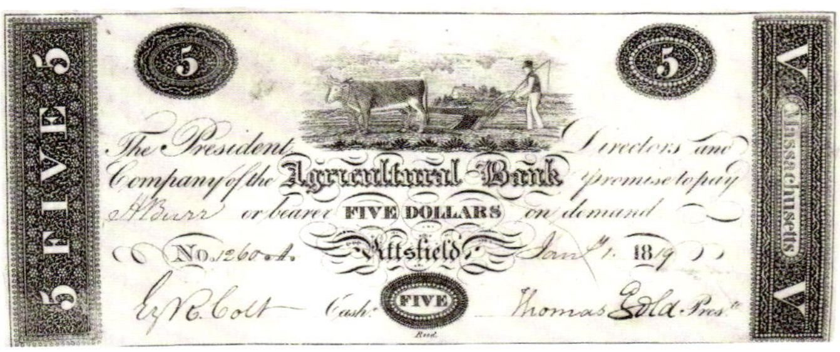

Engraver: A. Reed / Reed. ***Comments:*** H-MA-975-C64. Counterfeit of W-MA-2620-005-G150. 18__. 1819.

Rarity: URS-3
F $125; **VF** $175

$5 • W-MA-2620-005-S030

Left: 5 / Woman scattering flowers while being carried by two men / FIVE. ***Center:*** 5 or V / Minerva seated and Justice standing flanking shield surmounted by sheaf / 5 or V. ***Bottom center:*** Woman seated. ***Right:*** FIVE / Ceres seated with sheaf and cornucopia / FIVE. ***Engraver:*** Rawdon, Wright & Hatch. ***Comments:*** H-MA-975-S15. From a modified plate originally for $1 Havre-De-Grace Bank, Havre-De-Grace, Maryland. Nov. 18, 18__. 1850s.

Rarity: —

$5 • W-MA-2620-005-N010

Left: Woman with rake. ***Center:*** Woman seated with farm implements, Ships. ***Comments:*** H-MA-975-N5.

Rarity: —

$5 • W-MA-2620-005-A040

Engraver: PSSP. ***Comments:*** H-MA-975-A20. Altered from W-MA-175-005-G040 or G040a. 18__. 1820s.

Rarity: —

$5 • W-MA-2620-005-A050

Left: 5 / State arms / FIVE. ***Center:*** View of U.S. Capitol, Figures / Portrait of Zachary Taylor / FIVE. ***Bottom center:*** Two quail. ***Right:*** 5 / Liberty seated looking, Train and building. ***Engraver:*** Danforth, Bald & Co. ***Comments:*** H-MA-975-A25. Altered from $5 Government Stock Bank, Ann Arbor, Michigan. June 1, 1852.

Rarity: —

$10 • W-MA-2620-010-S040

CJF

Engraver: Rawdon, Wright & Hatch. ***Comments:*** H-MA-975-S20. Nov. 18, 18__. 1850s.

Rarity: URS-5
F $100; **VF** $125

Belvidere Bank

1850s

W-MA-2625

History: A non-existent bank represented only by notes altered from other banks.

Issues

$5 • W-MA-2625-005-A010

CJF

Engraver: Rawdon, Wright, Hatch & Edson. ***Comments:*** H-Unlisted. Altered from a note from Pittsfield, Illinois. 18__. 1850s.

Rarity: URS-3
F $300

Berkshire Bank

1806–1809

W-MA-2630

History: The Berkshire Bank was chartered on February 25, 1806, with an authorized capital of $75,000. It was controlled by Andrew Dexter Jr., a fraudster who operated the Boston Exchange Office and, famously, the Farmers Exchange Bank of Gloucester, Rhode Island, a phony bank that issued large amounts of worthless paper notes that were conveniently supplied by Jacob Perkins, who asked no questions. The scheme gained recognition as America's first large bank fraud. The deception was aided by advertisements in 1807, 1808, and early 1809, stating that dividends were being paid regularly to stockholders.

The bank failed in 1809 and left behind no assets of value. Dexter was never convicted of his crimes with the Berkshire Bank, the Farmers Exchange Bank, the Penobscot Bank in

Maine, or his other frauds. He went to the South, where he profited in land investment. In Montgomery, the capital of Alabama, Dexter Avenue bears his name.

Numismatic Commentary: Because of the fraudulent nature of this bank controlled by Andrew Dexter, there are plenty of bank notes available today. The prime activity of fraudulent banks was to circulate paper money. Subsequently, these could not be redeemed, and quantities remained outstanding for today's collector.

As of 2003 there was a $1-$5 face plate remaining at the American Bank Note Co. archives.

Valid Issues

$1 • W-MA-2630-001-G010

CC

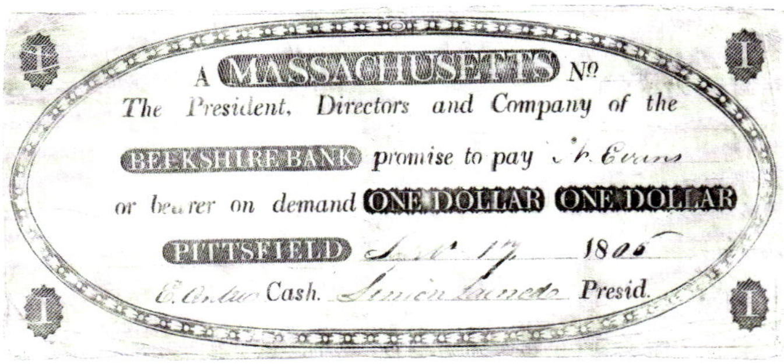

Engraver: Perkins. ***Comments:*** H-MA-980-G2. 18__. 1800s.

Rarity: URS-7
VG $175; **F** $325

$1 • W-MA-2630-001-G020

Center: 1 / 1 / Double oval of flower garlands and gridwork segments / ONE / 1 / 1. ***Engraver:*** PSSP. ***Comments:*** H-MA-980-G4. 18__. 1807–1809.

Rarity: —

$1 • W-MA-2630-001-G030

Center: 1 / 1 / Oval of flower garlands and gridwork segments / ONE / 1 / 1. ***Engraver:*** PSSP. ***Comments:*** H-MA-980-G6. 18__. 1809–circa 1812.

Rarity: —

$2 • W-MA-2630-002-G040

CJF

Engraver: Perkins. ***Comments:*** H-MA-980-G8. 18__. 1800s.

Rarity: URS-5
VG $300; **VF** $500

$2 • W-MA-2630-002-G050

Center: 2 / 2 / Black oval bearing white flower buds / TWO / 2 / 2. ***Engraver:*** PSSP. ***Comments:*** H-MA-980-G10. 18__. 1807–1809.

Rarity: —

$2 • W-MA-2630-002-G060

CJF

Engraver: PSSP. ***Comments:*** H-MA-980-G12. 18__. 1809–circa 1812.

Rarity: URS-6
F $150; **VF** $200

$3 • W-MA-2630-003-G070

Center: 3 / 3 / Black oval bearing white flower buds / 3 / 3. ***Engraver:*** Perkins. ***Comments:*** H-MA-980-G14. 18__. 1800s.

Rarity: —

$3 • W-MA-2630-003-G080

Center: 3 / 3 / Black oval bearing white flower buds / THREE / 3 / 3. ***Engraver:*** PSSP. ***Comments:*** H-MA-980-G16. 18__. 1807–1809.

Rarity: —

$3 • W-MA-2630-003-G090

Center: 3 / 3 / Oval of flower garlands and gridwork segments / 3 / 3. ***Engraver:*** PSSP. ***Comments:*** H-MA-980-G18. 18__. 1809–1820s.

Rarity: —

$5 • W-MA-2630-005-G100

NJW

Engraver: Perkins. ***Comments:*** H-MA-980-G20. 18__. 1806–1809.

Rarity: URS-6
VF $100

$10 • W-MA-2630-010-G110

QDB

Engraver: Perkins. ***Comments:*** H-MA-980-G22. 18__. Circa 1806 and 1807.

Rarity: URS-7
F $75; **VF** $100

$20 • W-MA-2630-020-G120

CJF

Engraver: Perkins. ***Comments:*** H-MA-980-G24. 18__. Circa 1806 and 1807.

Rarity: URS-7
F $75; **VF** $100

$100 • W-MA-2630-100-G130

CJF

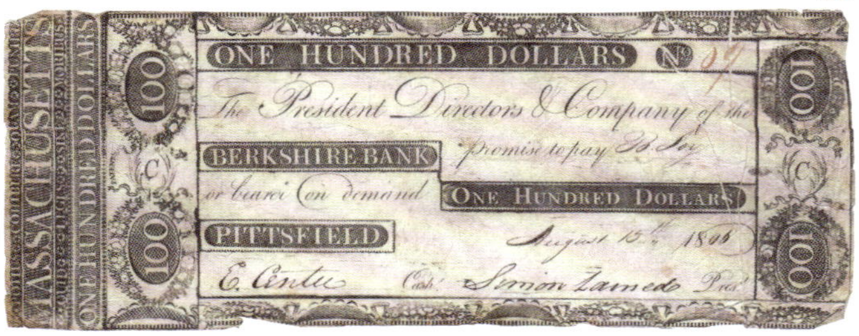

Engraver: Perkins. ***Comments:*** H-Unlisted. 18__. Circa 1806 and 1807.

Rarity: URS-5
F $150; **VF** $250

Lincoln and Kennebec Bank
1806
W-MA-2640

History: A non-existent bank represented only by notes altered from those of other banks. The notes were intended to pass for the Lincoln and Kennebec Bank, W-MA-3360.

Issues

$5 • W-MA-2640-005-A010

Left: MASSACHUSETTS vertically / 5 / 5. ***Center:*** Text. ***Right:*** 5 / 5. ***Engraver:*** Perkins. ***Comments:*** H-MA-985-A5. Altered from W-MA-2630-005-G100. 18__. Circa 1806 and 1807.

Rarity: —

Pittsfield Bank
1853–1865
W-MA-2650

History: The Pittsfield Bank was chartered on April 28, 1853, with an authorized capital of $150,000. It opened for business on June 18. The capital was increased to $300,000 in 1857. In 1860 it was $500,000. The circulation of the bank was $449,008 in 1857. Its real estate was valued at $13,767.14.

In 1865 the business of the Pittsfield Bank was succeeded by the Pittsfield National Bank.

Numismatic Commentary: A fair amount of genuine issues remain in the marketplace for today's collectors. Two issues of the $20 denomination have an elusive vignette of Santa Claus in his sleigh, a very coveted design. Some Uncut Sheets also with the Santa Claus vignette have made it to the marketplace.

Valid Issues

$1 • W-MA-2650-001-G010

SBG

Engraver: Baldwin, Adams & Co. ***Comments:*** H-Unlisted. Proof. June 1, 1853.

Rarity: URS-7
Proof $500

$1 • W-MA-2650-001-G010a

QDB

Overprint: Red ONE. ***Engraver:*** Baldwin, Adams & Co. ***Comments:*** H-MA-990-G2a. Similar to W-MA-2650-001-G010. Proof. June 1, 1853.

Rarity: URS-5
VG $275; **F** $450; **CU** $795; **Proof** $1,100

$1 • W-MA-2650-001-G010b

JF

Tint: Red-orange lathework outlining white ONE. ***Engraver:*** Bald, Cousland & Co. ***Comments:*** H-MA-990-G2c. Similar to W-MA-2650-001-G010 but with different date and engraver imprint. Proof. June 1, 1857.

Rarity: URS-4
CU $750; **Proof** $1,000

$1 • W-MA-2650-001-G010c

Left: 1 / Men building furniture. ***Center:*** ONE. ***Right:*** ONE / Male portrait. ***Tint:*** Red-orange lathework outlining white ONE. ***Engraver:*** American Bank Note Co. ***Comments:*** H-MA-990-G2d. Similar to W-MA-2650-001-G010 but with different date and engraver imprint. June 1, 1957.

Rarity: —

$1 • W-MA-2650-001-G020

CJF

Tint: Green. ***Engraver:*** American Bank Note Co. ***Comments:*** H-MA-990-G4a. Red serial number. June 10, 1861.

Rarity: URS-2

VF $1,600

$1 • W-MA-2650-001-G020a

CJF

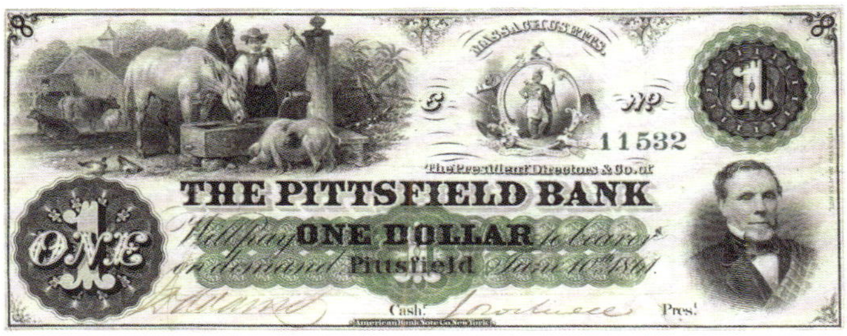

Tint: Green. ***Engraver:*** American Bank Note Co. ***Comments:*** H-Unlisted. Similar to W-MA-2650-001-G020. Green serial number. June 10, 1861.

Rarity: URS-3

VF $1,500

$2 • W-MA-2650-002-G030

CC

Engraver: Baldwin, Adams & Co. ***Comments:*** H-Unlisted. Proof. June 1, 1853.

Rarity: URS-3

Proof $1,100

Selected auction price: Stack's Bowers Galleries, June 2010, Lot 5359, Proof $850

$2 • W-MA-2650-002-G030a

CC

Overprint: Red 2 / 2. ***Engraver:*** Baldwin, Adams & Co. ***Comments:*** H-MA-990-G6a. Similar to W-MA-2650-002-G030. Proof. June 1, 1853.

Rarity: URS-2

Proof $1,600

$2 • W-MA-2650-002-G030b

CC

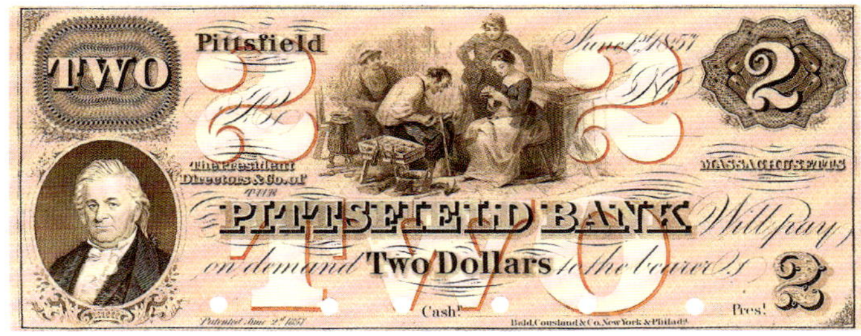

Tint: Red-orange lathework outlining white 2 2 / TWO. ***Engraver:*** Bald, Cousland & Co. ***Comments:*** H-MA-990-G6c. Similar to W-MA-2650-002-G030 but with different date and engraver imprint. Proof. June 1, 1857.

Rarity: —

$2 • W-MA-2650-002-G030c

Left: TWO / Male portrait. ***Center:*** 2 / Men building furniture / 2. ***Right:*** 2 / 2. ***Tint:*** Red-orange lathework outlining white 2 2 / TWO. ***Engraver:*** American Bank Note Co. ***Comments:*** H-MA-990-G6d. Similar to W-MA-2650-002-G030 but with different date and engraver imprint. June 1, 1857.

Rarity: —

$2 • W-MA-2650-002-G040

CJF

Tint: Green. ***Engraver:*** American Bank Note Co. ***Comments:*** H-MA-990-G8. June 10, 1861.

Rarity: URS-5

VG $800

$2 • W-MA-2650-002-G040a

Left: Male portrait / TWO on 2. ***Center:*** TWO DOLLARS across 2 / Portrait of two girls / TWO DOLLARS across 2. ***Bottom center:*** 2s around 2. ***Right:*** 2 / Male portrait. ***Engraver:*** American Bank Note Co. ***Comments:*** H-Unlisted. Similar to W-MA-2650-002-G040. June 10, 1861.

Rarity: URS-3

Proof $1,750

$5 • W-MA-2650-005-G050

QDB

Overprint: Red 5. ***Engraver:*** Baldwin, Adams & Co. ***Comments:*** H-MA-990-G10a. Proof. June 1, 1853.

Rarity: URS-3
Proof $1,500

$5 • W-MA-2650-005-G050a

Left: Spread eagle / V. ***Center:*** 5. ***Right:*** 5 / Male portrait. ***Overprint:*** None. ***Engraver:*** Baldwin, Adams & Co. ***Comments:*** H-MA-990-G10b. Similar to W-MA-2650-005-G050 but with different date. There may have been no genuine notes with this date. June 1, 1854.

Rarity: —

$5 • W-MA-2650-005-G060

JF

Tint: Red-orange lathework outlining white 5 / V / 5. ***Engraver:*** Bald, Cousland & Co. ***Comments:*** H-MA-990-G12. June 1, 1857.

Rarity: URS-3
AU $305; **CU** $795; **Proof** $3,000

$5 • W-MA-2650-005-G060a

Left: Male portrait / 5. ***Center:*** Two women seated. ***Right:*** 5 / 5. ***Engraver:*** American Bank Note Co. ***Comments:*** H-MA-990-G12a. Similar to W-MA-2650-005-G060 but with different date and engraver imprint. June 1, 1857.

Rarity: URS-3
Proof $3,000

$10 • W-MA-2650-010-G070

JF

Overprint: Red X. ***Engraver:*** Baldwin, Adams & Co. ***Comments:*** H-MA-990-G16a. June 1, 1853.

Rarity: URS-3
Proof $3,000

$10 • W-MA-2650-010-G070a

QDB

Tint: Red-orange lathework outlining white 10 / TEN / TEN. ***Engraver:*** Bald, Cousland & Co. ***Comments:*** H-MA-990-G16c. Similar to W-MA-2650-010-G070 but with different date and engraver imprint. June 1, 1857.

Rarity: URS-3
Proof $3,000

$10 • W-MA-2650-010-G070b

Tint: Red-orange lathework outlining white 10. ***Engraver:*** American Bank Note Co. ***Comments:*** H-MA-990-G16d. Similar to W-MA-2650-010-G070 but with different date and engraver imprint. June 1, 1857.

Rarity: —

$10 • W-MA-2650-010-G080

Left: X / Male portrait. ***Center:*** Man whittling, standing by horse, sheep, Boy on gate, Two men and cattle / X. ***Right:*** 10 / Male portrait. ***Tint:*** Green. ***Engraver:*** American Bank Note Co. ***Comments:*** H-MA-990-G18. June 10, 1861.

Rarity: —

$20 • W-MA-2650-020-G090

JF

Overprint: Red XX. ***Engraver:*** Baldwin, Adams & Co. ***Comments:*** H-MA-990-G20a. A coveted Santa Claus note. June 1, 1853.

Rarity: URS-3
Proof $8,000

$20 • W-MA-2650-020-G090a

QDB

Tint: Red-orange lathework outlining white 20. ***Engraver:*** Bald, Cousland & Co. ***Comments:*** H-MA-990-G20c. Similar to W-MA-2650-020-G090 but with different date and engraver imprint. A coveted Santa Claus note. Proof. June 1, 1857.

Rarity: URS-3
Proof $7,000

$20 • **W-MA-2650-020-G090b**

Tint: Red-orange lathework outlining white 20. ***Engraver:*** American Bank Note Co. ***Comments:*** H-MA-990-G20d. Similar to W-MA-2650-020-G090 but with different date and engraver imprint. A coveted Santa Claus note. June 1, 1857.

Rarity: —

$50 • **W-MA-2650-050-G100**

JF

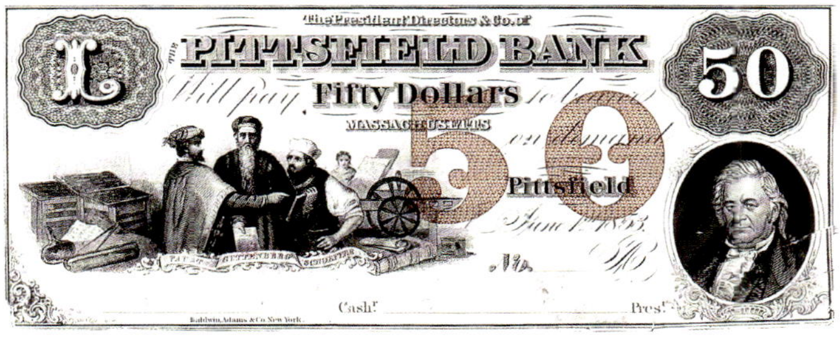

Overprint: Red 50. ***Engraver:*** Baldwin, Adams & Co. ***Comments:*** H-MA-990-G22a. June 1, 1853.

Rarity: URS-3
Proof $4,000

$50 • **W-MA-2650-050-G100a**

QDB

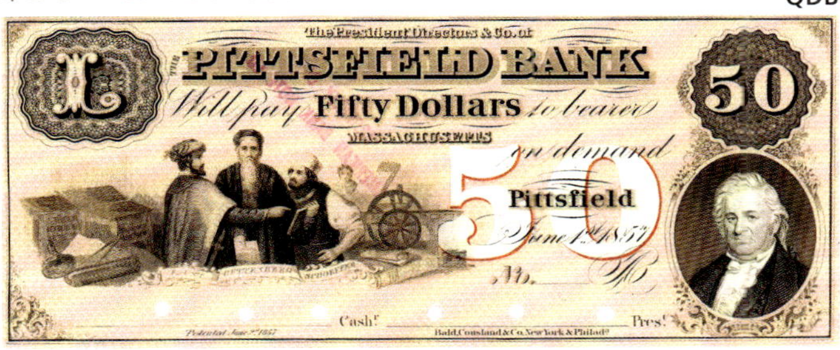

Tint: Red-orange lathework outlining white 50. ***Engraver:*** Bald, Cousland & Co. ***Comments:*** H-MA-990-G22c. Similar to W-MA-2650-050-G100 but with different date and engraver imprint. Proof. June 1, 1857.

Rarity: URS-3
Proof $4,000

$50 • **W-MA-2650-050-G100b**

Tint: Red-orange lathework outlining white 50. ***Engraver:*** American Bank Note Co. ***Comments:*** H-MA-990-G22d. Similar to W-MA-2650-050-G100 but with different date and engraver imprint. June 1, 1857.

Rarity: —

Uncut Sheets

$1-$1-$2-$5 • **W-MA-2650-001.001.002.005-US010**

Vignette(s): ***($1)*** Men building furniture / Male portrait. ***($1)*** Men building furniture / Male portrait. ***($2)*** Male portrait / Men building furniture. ***($5)*** Spread eagle / Male portrait. ***Overprint(s):*** None. ***Engraver:*** Baldwin, Adams & Co. ***Comments:*** All unlisted in Haxby.

Rarity: —

$1-$1-$2-$5 • **W-MA-2650-001.001.002.005-US010a**

Overprint(s): Red. ***Engraver:*** Baldwin, Adams & Co. ***Comments:*** H-MA-990-G2a, G2a, G6a, G10a. Similar to W-MA-2650-001.001.002.005-US010.

Rarity: —

$1-$1-$2-$5 •
W-MA-2650-001.001.002.005-US020

JF

Tint(s): Red-orange. ***Engraver:*** Baldwin, Adams & Co. ***Comments:*** H-MA-990-G2c, G2c, G6c, G12. Similar to W-MA-2650-001.001.002.005-US010 but with different bottom note. June 1, 1857.

Rarity: URS-4
Proof $3,000

$5-$10-$20-$50 •

W-MA-2650-005.010.020.050-US030

JF

Overprint(s): Red. ***Engraver:*** Baldwin, Adams & Co. ***Comments:*** H-MA-990-G10a, G16a, G20a, G22a. June 1, 1853.

Rarity: —

Proof $16,000

$5-$10-$20-$50 •

W-MA-2650-005.010.020.050-US040

JF

Tint(s): Red-orange. ***Engraver:*** Bald, Cousland & Co. ***Comments:*** H-MA-990-G12, G16c, G20c, G22c. Similar to W-MA-2650-005.010.020.050-US030 but with different top note. June 1, 1857.

Rarity: —

Proof $20,000

How to Read the Whitman Numbering System

$1 • W-MA-010-001-G010a

Denomination: Value of the note shown.

W: Whitman number. This number is a sortable code unique to each bank and note.

MA: Abbreviation for the state under study.

010: Numerical designation specific to each bank.

001: The denomination in dollars.

G010a: G indicates a good or valid note. Other categories are indicated thus: C (counterfeit); R (raised); S (spurious); N (not-attributed); A (altered). Numbers are assigned starting with 010, 020, et seq. Terminal letters following the number indicate variations of a note: a series of different colored overprints, tints, payees, etc., all on the same design of note. For more information, see the “How to Use This Book” section at the front of the volume, page xiv.

Non-Valid Issues

$2 • W-MA-2650-002-R010

Engraver: Baldwin, Adams & Co. ***Comments:*** H-MA-990-R5. Raised from W-MA-2650-001-G010a or variety. June 1, 1853.

Rarity: —

$5 • W-MA-2650-005-C050a

CJF

Engraver: Baldwin, Adams & Co. ***Comments:*** H-MA-990-C10b. Counterfeit of W-MA-2650-005-G050a. Some counterfeit notes of this design bear the engraved date June 1, 1862. It is unlikely that any genuine notes were so dated. June 1, 1854.

Rarity: URS-6

F $150

$5 • W-MA-2650-005-R020

Engraver: Baldwin, Adams & Co. ***Comments:*** H-MA-990-R10. Raised from W-MA-2650-001-G010a or variety. June 1, 1853.

Rarity: —

$5 • W-MA-2650-005-R030

Engraver: American Bank Note Co. ***Comments:*** H-MA-990-R11. Raised from W-MA-2650-001-G020. June 10, 1857.

Rarity: —

$5 • W-MA-2650-005-A010

Left: Portrait of Henry Clay / V. ***Center:*** Farmer feeding hogs. ***Bottom center:*** Dog lying down. ***Right:*** 5 / Farmer carrying basket of corn. ***Overprint:*** Red FIVE. ***Engraver:*** Wellstood, Hay & Whiting. ***Comments:*** H-MA-990-A5. Altered from $1 Thames Bank, Laurel, Indiana. 1850s.

Rarity: —

$10 • W-MA-2650-010-R040

Engraver: Baldwin, Adams & Co. ***Comments:*** H-MA-990-R15. Raised from W-MA-2650-001-G010a or variety. June 1, 1853.

Rarity: —

$10 • W-MA-2650-010-R050

Engraver: American Bank Note Co. ***Comments:*** H-MA-990-R16. Raised from W-MA-2650-001-G020. June 1, 1861.

Rarity: —

$20 • W-MA-2650-020-R060

Engraver: Baldwin, Adams & Co. ***Comments:*** H-MA-990-R20. Raised from W-MA-2650-001-G010a or variety. June 1, 1853.

Rarity: —

Plymouth, Massachusetts

Historical spellings of this area's name include Plimouth and Plimoth. It was named after a port city in Devon, England. Plymouth Rock was the original landing place of the Pilgrims on December 21, 1620, making Plymouth the first establishment of colonists in New England. It was merged with the Massachusetts Bay Colony in 1691. Help from the natives was crucial for the beginnings of the Plymouth colony, including the raising of crops, establishment of trade, ambassadorship between other tribes, and forming peace with the locals. The celebration of a plentiful harvest in 1621 was celebrated by the Pilgrims and several Wampanoag men and is still known as the first Thanksgiving today.

In the early 19th century, Plymouth became a regional center for shipbuilding and fishing, and the construction of rope and cordage products made it one of the world's largest cordage providers. The Plymouth Cordage Company was founded in 1824 and held the longest ropewalk in the entire world.

Old Colony Bank

1832–1865

W-MA-2660

History: The Old Colony Bank was chartered on March 3, 1832, with an authorized capital of $100,000. This was increased to $150,000 in 1854 and then to $210,000 in 1857. In 1847 the bank had dividends of four percent, equaling $4,000.[29] The circulation of the bank went from a low of $73,698 in 1839 to a high of $154,872 in 1863.

The Old Colony Bank was succeeded by the Old Colony National Bank of Plymouth, chartered on April 8, 1865.

Numismatic Commentary: With such a quaint title, one would almost expect to see something historical appear in this bank's vignettes. Some issues from this bank will not disappoint in this regard. On one there is a somewhat realistic view of Pilgrims unloading supplies on their new home shore while others prepare a meal under a shelter. A Native American approaches from the right. High in a tree and with a watchful eye, an osprey surveys the scene below. On another there is a different version of the same event: a small landing boat of Pilgrims set foot in their new world while a small group of Native Americans look on. Historical vignettes such as these are high on the list of popular collecting topics.

On occasion, genuine notes from this bank will appear at auction and are vigorously pursued.

Valid Issues

$1 • W-MA-2660-001-G010

Left: Lathework panel bearing MASSACHUSETTS vertically. ***Center:*** 1 / 1 / Alternating flower garlands and gridwork segments / ONE / 1 / 1. ***Right:*** Lathework panel bearing ONE / D / ONE vertically. ***Engraver:*** PSSP. ***Comments:*** H-MA-995-G2. 18__. 1830s.

Rarity: —

$1 • W-MA-2660-001-G020

Left: ONE on 1 / Justice / ONE. ***Center:*** 1 / "Landing of the Pilgrims" / 1. ***Right:*** ONE on 1 / Portrait of George Washington / ONE. ***Engraver:*** New England Bank Note Co. / PSSP. ***Comments:*** H-MA-995-G4. 18__. 1830s–1850s.

Rarity: —

$1 • W-MA-2660-001-G020a

CJF

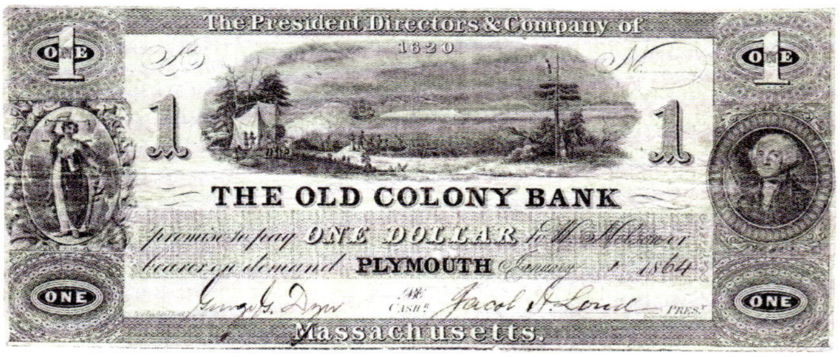

Engraver: New England Bank Note Co. / PSSP / ABNCo. monogram. ***Comments:*** H-MA-995-G4a. Similar to W-MA-2660-001-G020 but with additional engraver imprint. January __, 18__. 1850s–1860s.

Rarity: URS-3
VF $1,500; **Proof** $3,000

$1 • W-MA-2660-001-G020b

JF

Engraver: New England Bank Note Co. / PSSP. ***Comments:*** H-Unlisted. Similar to W-MA-2660-001-G020. Made from original plates for celebration some years after 1864. Printed on yellow paper. 18__. 1860s.

Rarity: URS-4
Proof $2,000

$1 • W-MA-2660-001-G020c

JF

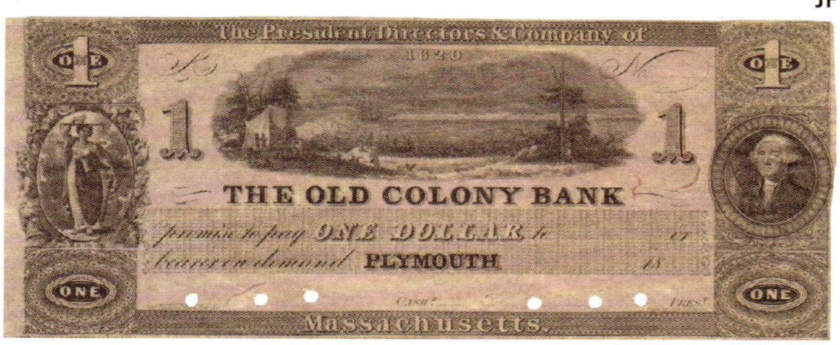

Engraver: New England Bank Note Co. / PSSP. ***Comments:*** H-Unlisted. Similar to W-MA-2660-001-G020. Made from original plates for celebration some years after 1864. Printed on pink paper. 18__. 1860s.

Rarity: URS-2
Proof $5,000

$1 • W-MA-2660-001-G020d

JF

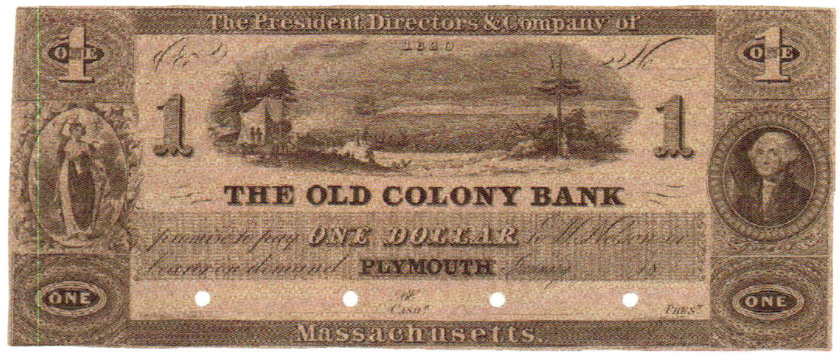

Tint: Red. ***Engraver:*** New England Bank Note Co. / PSSP / ABNCo. monogram. ***Comments:*** H-Unlisted. Similar to W-MA-2660-001-G020 but with additional engraver imprint. Made from original plates for celebration some years after 1864. Printed on pink paper. January __, 18__. 1860s.

Rarity: URS-2
Proof $5,000

$2 • W-MA-2660-002-G030

Left: Lathework panel bearing MASSACHUSETTS vertically. ***Center:*** 2 / 2 / Alternating flower garland and gridwork segments / TWO / 2 / 2. ***Right:*** Lathework panel bearing five TWOs vertically. ***Engraver:*** PSSP. ***Comments:*** H-MA-995-G6. 18__. 1830s.

Rarity: —

$2 • W-MA-2660-002-G040

Left: TWO / Justice seated / TWO. ***Center:*** 2 / "Landing of the Pilgrims" / 2. ***Right:*** 2 / Woman standing / TWO. ***Engraver:*** New England Bank Note Co. ***Comments:*** H-MA-995-G8. 18__. 1830s–1850s.

Rarity: —

$2 • W-MA-2660-002-G040a

Engraver: New England Bank Note Co. / PSSP / ABNCo. monogram. ***Comments:*** H-MA-995-G8a. Similar to W-MA-2660-002-G040 but with additional engraver imprint. 18__. 1850s–1860s.

Rarity: —

$2 • W-MA-2660-002-G040b

CJF

Overprint: Red TWO. ***Engraver:*** New England Bank Note Co. / PSSP / ABNCo. monogram. ***Comments:*** H-Unlisted. Similar to W-MA-2660-002-G040 but with additional engraver imprint. Remainder. April 1, 18__. 1850s–1860s.

Rarity: URS-3
Proof $3,500

$2 • W-MA-2660-002-G040c

JF

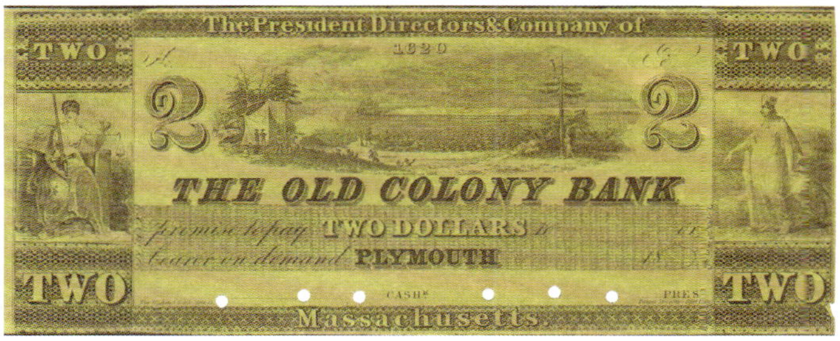

Engraver: New England Bank Note Co. / PSSP. ***Comments:*** H-Unlisted. Similar to W-MA-2660-002-G040. Made from original plates for celebration some years after 1864. Printed on yellow paper. Remainder. 18__. 1860s.

Rarity: URS-4
Proof $2,500

$2 • W-MA-2660-002-G040d

JF

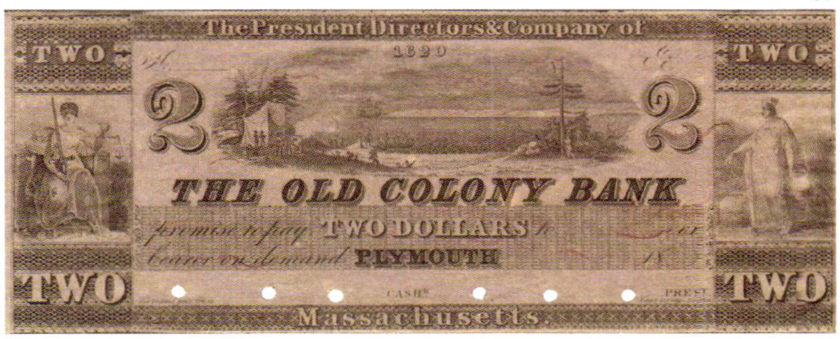

Engraver: New England Bank Note Co. / PSSP. ***Comments:*** H-Unlisted. Similar to W-MA-2660-002-G040. Made from original plates for celebration some years after 1864. Printed on pink paper. Remainder. 18__. 1860s.

Rarity: URS-4
Proof $2,500

$3 • W-MA-2660-003-G050

Left: Lathework panel bearing MASSACHUSETTS vertically. ***Center:*** 3 / 3 / Alternating flower garlands and gridwork segments / THREE / 3 / 3. ***Right:*** Lathework panel bearing THREE vertically. ***Engraver:*** PSSP. ***Comments:*** H-MA-995-G10. 18__. 1830s.

Rarity: —

$3 • W-MA-2660-003-G060

Left: 3 / Portrait of George Washington / 3. ***Center:*** THREE / "Landing of the Pilgrims" / 3. ***Right:*** Panel bearing THREE vertically. ***Engraver:*** New England Bank Note Co. / PSSP. ***Comments:*** H-MA-995-G12. 18__. 1830s–1850s.

Rarity: —

$3 • W-MA-2660-003-G060a

Engraver: New England Bank Note Co. / PSSP / ABNCo. monogram. ***Comments:*** H-MA-995-G12a. Similar to W-MA-2660-003-G060 but with additional engraver imprint. 18__. 1850s–1860s.

Rarity: —

$3 • W-MA-2660-003-G060b

TD

Overprint: Red THREE. ***Engraver:*** New England Bank Note Co. / PSSP / ABNCo. monogram. ***Comments:*** H-Unlisted. Similar to W-MA-2660-003-G060 but with additional engraver imprint. July __, 18__.

Rarity: URS-3
Proof $3,500

$3 • W-MA-2660-003-G060c

JF

Engraver: New England Bank Note Co. / PSSP. ***Comments:*** H-Unlisted. Similar to W-MA-2660-003-G060. Made from original plates for celebration some years after 1864. Printed on yellow paper. Remainder. 18__. 1860s.

Rarity: URS-4
Proof $3,000

$3 • W-MA-2660-003-G060d

JF

Engraver: New England Bank Note Co. / PSSP. ***Comments:*** H-Unlisted. Similar to W-MA-2660-003-G060. Made from original plates for celebration some years after 1864. Printed on pink paper. Remainder. 18__. 1860s.

Rarity: URS-4
Proof $3,000

$5 • W-MA-2660-005-G070

Left: Lathework chain bearing MASSACHUSETTS / 5 / 5. ***Center:*** Alternating flower garlands and gridwork segments / FIVE. ***Right:*** 5 / 5. ***Engraver:*** PSSP. ***Comments:*** H-MA-995-G14. 18__. 1830s.

Rarity: —

$5 • W-MA-2660-005-G080

Left: Statue of George Washington. ***Center:*** 5 / "Landing of the Pilgrims" / 5. ***Right:*** Eagle on rock above ocean / FIVE. ***Engraver:*** New England Bank Note Co. / PSSP. ***Comments:*** H-MA-995-G16. 18__. 1830s–1850s.

Rarity: —

$5 • W-MA-2660-005-G080a

Engraver: New England Bank Note Co. / PSSP / ABNCo. monogram. ***Comments:*** H-MA-995-G16a. Similar to W-MA-2660-005-G080 but with additional engraver imprint. 18__. 1850s–1860s.

Rarity: —

$10 • W-MA-2660-010-G090

Left: Lathework chain bearing MASSACHUSETTS / 10 / 10 vertically. ***Center:*** Alternating flower garlands and gridwork segments / TEN. ***Right:***10 / 10. ***Engraver:*** PSSP. ***Comments:*** H-MA-995-G18. 18__. 1830s.

Rarity: —

$10 • W-MA-2660-010-G100

Left: Eagle on rock above ocean / TEN. ***Center:*** 10 / "Landing of the Pilgrims" / X. ***Right:*** Minerva standing / TEN. ***Engraver:*** New England Bank Note Co. / PSSP. ***Comments:*** H-MA-995-G20. 18__. 1830s–1850s.

Rarity: —

$10 • W-MA-2660-010-G100a

Engraver: New England Bank Note Co. / PSSP / ABNCo. monogram. ***Comments:*** H-MA-995-G20a. Similar to W-MA-2660-010-G100 but with additional engraver imprint. 18__. 1850s–1860s.

Rarity: —

$20 • W-MA-2660-020-G110

Left: Lathework chain bearing MASSACHUSETTS / 20 / 20 vertically. ***Center:*** Alternating flower garlands and gridwork segments / TWENTY. ***Right:*** 20 / 20 vertically. ***Engraver:*** PSSP. ***Comments:*** H-MA-995-G22. 18__. 1830s.

Rarity: —

$20 • W-MA-2660-020-G120

Engraver: Unverified, but likely New England Bank Note Co. ***Comments:*** H-MA-995-G24. No description available. 18__. 1830s.

Rarity: *None known*

$20 • W-MA-2660-020-G130

CJF

Engraver: New England Bank Note Co. / PSSP. ***Comments:*** H-MA-995-G26. Proof. 18__. 1840s–1850s.

Rarity: URS-3
Proof $6,500

$20 • W-MA-2660-020-G130a

Left: 20 / Indian man. ***Center:*** "Landing of the Pilgrims". ***Right:*** 20 / Portrait of George Washington / XX. ***Engraver:*** New England Bank Note Co. / PSSP / ABNCo. monogram. ***Comments:*** H-MA-995-G26a. Similar to W-MA-2660-020-G130 but with additional engraver imprint. 18__. 1830s–1850s.

Rarity: —

$50 • W-MA-2660-050-G140

Left: Lathework chain bearing MASSACHUSETTS / 50 / 50 vertically. ***Center:*** Alternating flower garlands and gridwork segments / FIFTY. ***Right:*** 50 / 50 vertically. ***Engraver:*** PSSP. ***Comments:*** H-MA-995-G28. 18__. 1830s.

Rarity: —

$50 • W-MA-2660-050-G150

Left: 50 / Cornucopia, Woman standing with ankles crossed, Staff, Anchor / 50. ***Center:*** FIFTY DOLLARS / 50. ***Right:*** FIFTY vertically. ***Engraver:*** New England Bank Note Co. / PSSP. ***Comments:*** H-MA-995-G30. 18__. 1830s.

Rarity: —

$50 • W-MA-2660-050-G160

JF

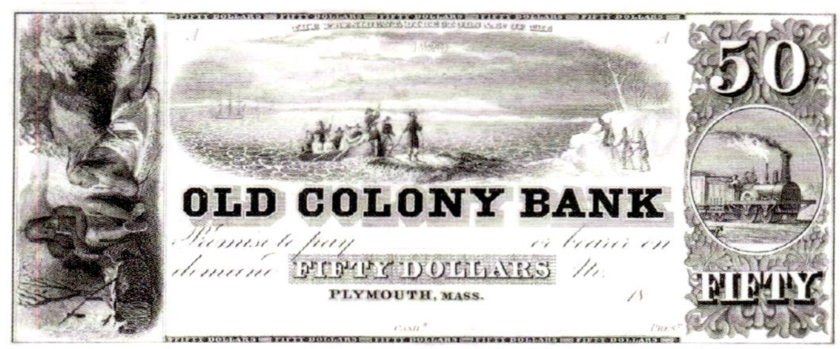

Engraver: New England Bank Note Co. / PSSP. ***Comments:*** H-Unlisted. Proof. 18__.

Rarity: URS-2
Proof $7,500

$50 • W-MA-2660-050-G160a

CC

Overprint: Red FIFTY. ***Engraver:*** New England Bank Note Co. / PSSP. ***Comments:*** H-MA-995-G32. Similar to W-MA-2660-050-G160. Proof. 18__. 1840s–1850s.

Rarity: URS-1
Proof $18,500

$50 • W-MA-2660-050-G160b

Left: Indians vertically. ***Center:*** "Landing of the Pilgrims". ***Right:*** 50 / Train / FIFTY. ***Engraver:*** New England Bank Note Co. / PSSP / ABNCo. monogram. ***Comments:*** H-MA-995-G32a. Similar to W-MA-2660-050-G160 but with additional engraver imprint. 18__. 1850s–1860s.

Rarity: —

$100 • **W-MA-2660-100-G170**

Left: Lathework chain bearing MASSACHUSETTS / 100 / 100 vertically. ***Center:*** Alternating flower garlands and gridwork segments / 100. ***Right:*** 100 / 100 vertically. ***Engraver:*** PSSP ***Comments:*** H-MA-995-G34. 18__. 1830s.

Rarity: —

$100 • **W-MA-2660-100-G180**

Left: Lathework panel bearing C / Portrait of George Washington / C. ***Center:*** 100 / Manhattan reclining, pouring water, Ship / 100. ***Right:*** Lathework panel bearing ONE HUNDRED vertically. ***Engraver:*** New England Bank Note Co. / PSSP. ***Comments:*** H-MA-995-G36. 18__. 1830s.

Rarity: —

$100 • **W-MA-2660-100-G190**

CC

Engraver: New England Bank Note Co. / PSSP. ***Comments:*** H-MA-995-G38. Proof. 18__. 1830s–1850s.

Rarity: URS-2
Proof $10,000

$100 • **W-MA-2660-100-G190a**

Left: 100 / Reaper. ***Center:*** "Landing of the Pilgrims". ***Right:*** 100 / Woman and eagle. ***Engraver:*** New England Bank Note Co. / PSSP / ABNCo. monogram. ***Comments:*** H-MA-995-G38a. Similar to W-MA-2660-100-G190 but with additional engraver imprint. 18__. 1850s–1860s.

Rarity: —

$500 • **W-MA-2660-500-G200**

Left: 500 / 500 / 500. ***Center:*** 500 / Woman seated with shield bearing D, Fasces, cornucopia, lyre, and sheaf / 500. ***Right:*** 500 / D / 500. ***Engraver:*** New England Bank Note Co. / PSSP. ***Comments:*** H-MA-995-G40. 18__. 1830s–1840s.

Rarity: —

$500 • **W-MA-2660-500-G210**

Left: Indian paddling canoe, Forest and mountains / 500 / D D / 500. ***Right:*** 500 / Justice. ***Engraver:*** New England Bank Note Co. / ABNCo. monogram. ***Comments:*** H-MA-995-G40a. 18__. 1850s–1860s.

Rarity: —

Uncut Sheets

$1-$2-$3 • **W-MA-2660-001.002.003-US010**

JF

Engraver: New England Bank Note Co. / PSSP. ***Comments:*** All unlisted in Haxby. Made from original plates for celebration some years after 1864. Printed on yellow paper. Partial sheet. 18__. 1860s.

Rarity: URS-1
Proof $10,000

$1-$1-$2-$3 • W-MA-2660-001.001.002.003-US020 JF

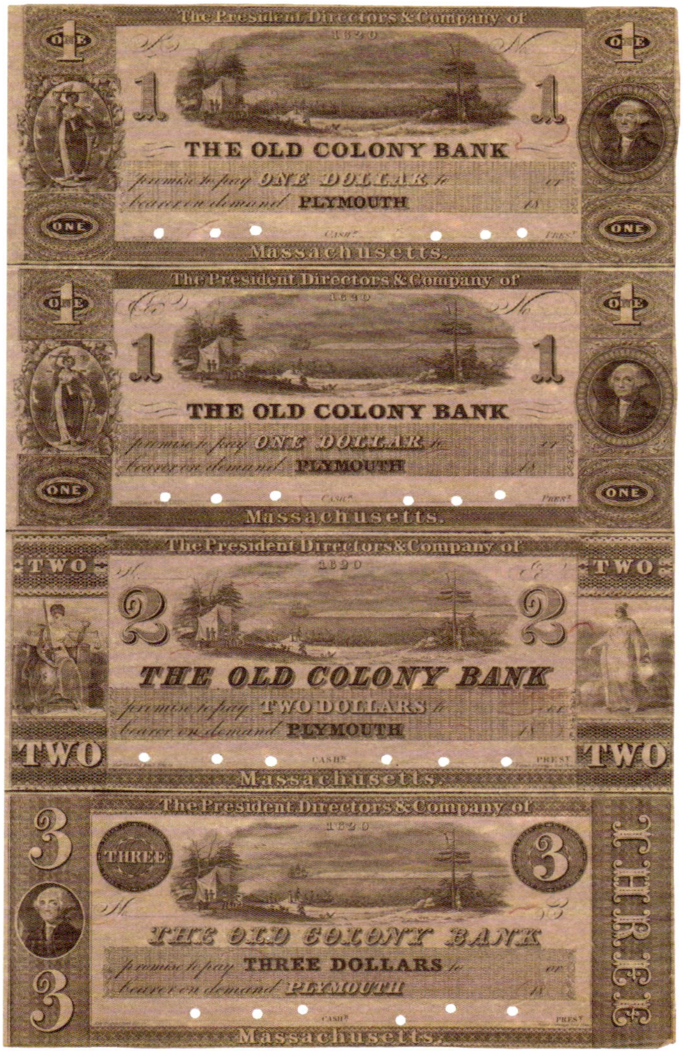

Engraver: New England Bank Note Co. / PSSP. ***Comments:*** All unlisted in Haxby. Made from original plates for celebration some years after 1864. Printed on pink paper. 18__. 1860s.

Rarity: URS-1
Proof $10,000

Non-Valid Issues

$5 • W-MA-2660-005-C080

Engraver: New England Bank Note Co. / PSSP. ***Comments:*** H-MA-995-C16. Counterfeit of W-MA-2660-005-G080. 18__. Circa 1850s.

Rarity: —

$10 • W-MA-2660-010-N010

Left: Train. ***Center:*** Commerce seated on shore with goods. ***Comments:*** H-MA-995-N5.

Rarity: —

$50 • W-MA-2660-050-R010

Engraver: New England Bank Note Co. / PSSP. ***Comments:*** H-MA-995-R10. Raised from W-MA-2660-001-G020. 18__. Circa 1840s.

Rarity: —

Old Colony Bank at Plymouth
1850s
W-MA-2670

History: A non-existent bank represented only by notes altered from those of other banks. The notes were intended to pass for those of the Old Colony Bank, W-MA-2660.

Numismatic Commentary: All notes bear the imprint of Rawdon, Wright & Hatch.

Issues

$1 • W-MA-2670-001-A010 TD

Comments: H-MA-996-A5. Altered from $1 Wayne County Bank at Plymouth, Michigan. 18__. 1830s–1850s.

Rarity: URS-7
VG $125; **VF** $175

$2 • W-MA-2670-002-A020 CJF

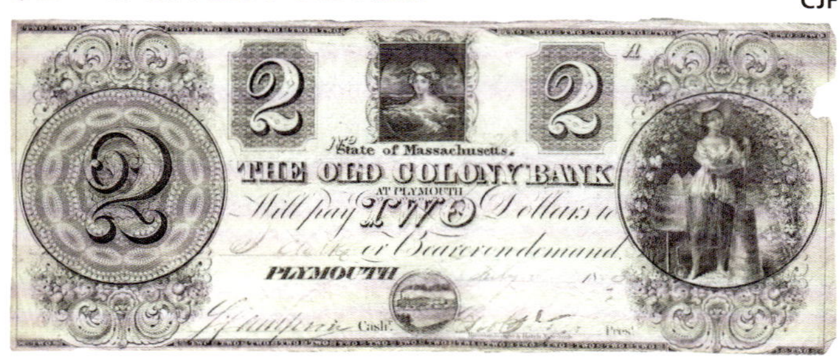

Comments: H-MA-996-A10. Altered from $2 Wayne County Bank at Plymouth, Michigan. 18__. 1830s–1850s.

Rarity: URS-6
VG $125; **F** $175; **VF** $200

$3 • W-MA-2670-003-A030

Left: 3 on die and panel. ***Center:*** 3 / Man plowing with two horses / 3. ***Bottom center:*** Pledge. ***Right:*** Girl and boy on die and panel. ***Comments:*** H-MA-996-A15. Altered from $3 Wayne County Bank at Plymouth, Michigan. 18__. 1830s–1850s.

Rarity: —

Collectors and Researchers:

If you have new information about any banks or notes listed in this volume, contact Whitman Publishing, Attn: Obsolete Paper Money, 3101 Clairmont Road, Suite G, Atlanta, GA 30329.

$5 • W-MA-2670-005-A040

HA

Comments: H-Unlisted. Altered from $5 Wayne County Bank at Plymouth, Michigan. 18__. 1830s–1850s.

Rarity: URS-7

F $100; **VF** $150

Plymouth Bank

1803–1865

W-MA-2680

History: The Plymouth Bank was chartered on June 13, 1803, with an authorized capital of $100,000. It was required to gather at least one-eighth of its capital for the exclusive use of agricultural interests, to be given in loans of no less than $100 and no greater than $500, for the period of a year.[30] Circulation in 1839 was $41,658, and in 1857 it was $120,010. The capital was increased to $150,000 in 1855.

This business of the Plymouth Bank was succeeded by the Plymouth National Bank, chartered on February 7, 1865.

Numismatic Commentary: Genuine early notes of the PSSP design are quite hard to locate, while later issues by Toppan, Carpenter & Co. appear at auction from time to time. The Toppan, Carpenter & Co. issues carry a vignette of the "Landing of the Pilgrims" taken from a Henry Sargent painting that can be seen at the Pilgrim Hall Museum in Plymouth.

VALID ISSUES

$1 • W-MA-2680-001-G010

Left: ONE vertically. ***Center:*** 1 on shield. ***Right:*** 1 on shield vertically. ***Comments:*** H-MA-1000-G20. 18__. 1800s.

Rarity: —

$1 • W-MA-2680-001-G020

Center: 1 / 1 / Oval of flower garlands and gridwork segments / 1 / 1. ***Engraver:*** PSSP. ***Comments:*** H-MA-1000-G26. 18__. 1809–circa 1812.

Rarity: —

$1 • W-MA-2680-001-G020a

Center: 1 / 1 / Oval of flower garlands and gridwork segments / ONE / 1 / 1. ***Engraver:*** PSSP. ***Comments:*** H-MA-1000-G28. Similar to W-MA-2680-001-G020. 18__. Circa 1812–1820s.

Rarity: —

$1 • W-MA-2680-001-G020b

Left: Panel of lathework circle segments. ***Right:*** Panel of lathework circle segments. ***Engraver:*** PSSP. ***Comments:*** H-MA-1000-G30. Similar to W-MA-2680-001-G020. 18__. 1820s.

Rarity: —

$1 • W-MA-2680-001-G020c

Left: Panel of lathework circle segments. ***Right:*** Panel of lathework circle segments. ***Engraver:*** PSSP. ***Comments:*** H-MA-1000-G32. Similar to W-MA-2680-001-G020. 18__. 1820s–1830s.

Rarity: —

$1 • W-MA-2680-001-G020d

CJF

Engraver: PSSP. ***Comments:*** H-MA-1000-G34. Similar to W-MA-2680-001-G020. 18__. 1830s.

Rarity: URS-7

F $100; **VF** $150

$1 • W-MA-2680-001-G030

Left: 1 / Minerva standing with / 1. ***Center:*** ONE / Commerce seated with caduceus and cornucopia, Plow and ships / ONE. ***Right:*** 1 / Eagle / 1. ***Engraver:*** PSSP. ***Comments:*** H-MA-1000-G36. 18__. 1830s.

Rarity: —

$1 • W-MA-2680-001-G040

Left: ONE / D / ONE vertically. ***Right:*** ONE / D / ONE vertically. ***Engraver:*** PSSP. ***Comments:*** H-MA-1000-G38. 18__. 1830s–1840s.

Rarity: —

$1 • W-MA-2680-001-G050

Left: Four cherubs placing 1 on base bearing ONE. ***Center:*** "Landing of the Pilgrims". ***Right:*** Woman seated on bale supporting die bearing 1. ***Engraver:*** Toppan, Carpenter & Co. ***Comments:*** H-MA-1000-G40. 18__. 1840s–1850s.

Rarity: —

$1 • W-MA-2680-001-G060

CJF

Engraver: Toppan, Carpenter & Co. ***Comments:*** H-MA-1000-G42. 18__. 1840s–1850s.

Rarity: URS-3

VF $3,000

$2 • W-MA-2680-002-G070

Left: TWO vertically. ***Center:*** 2 on shield. ***Right:*** 2 on shield vertically. ***Comments:*** H-MA-1000-G48. 18__. 1800s.

Rarity: —

$2 • **W-MA-2680-002-G080**

Center: 2 / 2 / Oval of flower garlands and gridwork segments / 2 / 2. ***Engraver:*** PSSP. ***Comments:*** H-MA-1000-G54. 18__. 1809–circa 1812.

Rarity: —

$2 • **W-MA-2680-002-G080a**

Center: 2 / 2 / Oval of flower garlands and gridwork segments / TWO / 2 / 2. ***Engraver:*** PSSP. ***Comments:*** H-MA-1000-G56. Similar to W-MA-2680-002-G080. 18__. Circa 1812–1820s.

Rarity: —

$2 • **W-MA-2680-002-G080b**

Center: 2 / 2 / Oval of flower garlands and gridwork segments / TWO / 2 / 2. ***Engraver:*** PSSP. ***Comments:*** H-MA-1000-G58. Similar to W-MA-2680-002-G080. 18__. 1820s.

Rarity: —

$2 • **W-MA-2680-002-G080c**

Left: Panel of lathework circle segments. ***Right:*** Panel of lathework circle segments. ***Engraver:*** PSSP. ***Comments:*** H-MA-1000-G60. Similar to W-MA-2680-002-G080. 18__. 1820s–1830s.

Rarity: —

$2 • **W-MA-2680-002-G080d**

Left: Five TWOs vertically. ***Right:*** Five TWOs vertically. ***Engraver:*** PSSP. ***Comments:*** H-MA-1000-G62. Similar to W-MA-2680-002-G080. 18__. 1830s.

Rarity: —

$2 • **W-MA-2680-002-G090**

Left: 2 / Hebe watering eagle / 2. ***Center:*** 2 / Plow, Commerce seated with caduceus and cornucopia, Ships / 2. ***Right:*** 2 / Justice standing / 2. ***Engraver:*** PSSP. ***Comments:*** H-MA-1000-G64. 18__. 1830s.

Rarity: —

$2 • **W-MA-2680-002-G100**

Left: Five TWOs vertically. ***Right:*** Five TWOs vertically. ***Engraver:*** PSSP. ***Comments:*** H-MA-1000-G66. 18__. 1830s–1840s.

Rarity: —

$2 • **W-MA-2680-002-G110**

Left: 2 / Portrait of Benjamin Franklin. ***Center:*** "Landing of the Pilgrims". ***Right:*** 2 / Two cherubs in 2. ***Engraver:*** Toppan, Carpenter & Co. ***Comments:*** H-MA-1000-G68. 18__. 1840s–1850s.

Rarity: —

$3 • **W-MA-2680-003-G120**

Left: THREE vertically. ***Center:*** 3 on shield. ***Right:*** 3 on shield vertically. ***Comments:*** H-MA-1000-G70. 18__. 1800s.

Rarity: —

$3 • **W-MA-2680-003-G130**

Center: 3 / 3 / Oval of flower garlands and gridwork segments / 3 / 3. ***Engraver:*** PSSP. ***Comments:*** H-MA-1000-G72. 18__. 1809–1820s.

Rarity: —

$3 • **W-MA-2680-003-G130a**

Left: Panel of lathework circle segments. ***Right:*** Panel of lathework circle segments. ***Engraver:*** PSSP. ***Comments:*** H-MA-1000-G74. Similar to W-MA-2680-003-G130. 18__. 1820s.

Rarity: —

$3 • **W-MA-2680-003-G130b**

Left: Panel of lathework circle segments. ***Right:*** Panel of lathework circle segments. ***Engraver:*** PSSP. ***Comments:*** H-MA-1000-G76. Similar to W-MA-2680-003-G130. 18__. 1820s–1830s.

Rarity: —

$3 • **W-MA-2680-003-G130c**

Left: THREE vertically. ***Right:*** THREE vertically. ***Engraver:*** PSSP. ***Comments:*** H-MA-1000-G78. Similar to W-MA-2680-003-G130. 18__. 1830s.

Rarity: —

$3 • **W-MA-2680-003-G140**

Left: 3 / Eagle on rock / 3. ***Center:*** 3 / Commerce seated with caduceus and cornucopia / Plow, Ships / 3 / Panel bearing THREE. ***Right:*** 3 / Woman standing with cornucopia / 3. ***Engraver:*** PSSP. ***Comments:*** H-MA-1000-G80. 18__. 1830s.

Rarity: —

$3 • **W-MA-2680-003-G150**

Left: THREE vertically. ***Right:*** THREE vertically. ***Engraver:*** PSSP. ***Comments:*** H-MA-1000-G82. 18__. 1830s–1840s.

Rarity: —

$5 • **W-MA-2680-005-G160**

Left: FIVE vertically. ***Center:*** 5 on shield. ***Right:*** 5 on shield vertically. ***Comments:*** H-MA-1000-G84. 18__. 1800s.

Rarity: —

$5 • **W-MA-2680-005-G170**

Center: 5 / 5 / Oval of flower garlands and gridwork segments / 5 / 5. ***Engraver:*** PSSP. ***Comments:*** H-MA-1000-G86. 18__. 1809–1820s.

Rarity: —

$5 • **W-MA-2680-005-G170a**

Left: Lathework chain bearing MASSACHUSETTS vertically. ***Engraver:*** PSSP. ***Comments:*** H-MA-1000-G88. Similar to W-MA-2680-005-G170. 18__. 1820s.

Rarity: —

$5 • **W-MA-2680-005-G170b**

Left: Lathework chain bearing MASSACHUSETTS vertically. ***Right:*** Panel of lathework circle segments. ***Engraver:*** PSSP. ***Comments:*** H-MA-1000-G90. Similar to W-MA-2680-005-G170. 18__. 1820s.

Rarity: —

$5 • **W-MA-2680-005-G170c**

Engraver: PSSP. ***Comments:*** H-MA-1000-G92. Similar to W-MA-2680-005-G170 but with zigzag ruled lines. 18__. 1820s–1830s.

Rarity: —

$5 • **W-MA-2680-005-G170d**

Engraver: PSSP. ***Comments:*** H-MA-1000-G94. Similar to W-MA-2680-005-G170 but with spiral lathework lines. 18__. 1830s.

Rarity: —

$5 • **W-MA-2680-005-G180**

Comments: H-MA-1000-G96. No description available. 18__. 1830s.

Rarity: *None known*

$5 • W-MA-2680-005-G190

Left: 5 / Portrait of George Washington / FIVE. ***Center:*** "Landing of the Pilgrims". ***Right:*** 5 / Woman standing / FIVE. ***Engraver:*** Toppan, Carpenter & Co. ***Comments:*** H-MA-1000-G100. 18__. 1840s–1850s.

Rarity: —

$10 • W-MA-2680-010-G200

Left: TEN vertically. ***Center:*** 10 on shield. ***Right:*** 10 on shield vertically. ***Comments:*** H-MA-1000-G104. 18__. 1800s.

Rarity: —

$10 • W-MA-2680-010-G210

TD

Engraver: Perkins. ***Comments:*** H-MA-1000-G108. 18__. 1809–circa 1812.

Rarity: URS-3
Proof $350

$10 • W-MA-2680-010-G210a

Left: State arms / 10 / 10 vertically. ***Center:*** 10 / 10 / Flower garlands and gridwork segments / TEN / 10 / 10. ***Engraver:*** Perkins. ***Comments:*** H-MA-1000-G110. Similar to W-MA-2680-010-G210. 18__. Circa 1812–1820s.

Rarity: —

$10 • W-MA-2680-010-G210b

Left: Lathework chain bearing MASSACHUSETTS vertically. ***Right:*** Panel of lathework circle segments. ***Engraver:*** Perkins. ***Comments:*** H-MA-1000-G112. Similar to W-MA-2680-010-G210. 18__. 1820s.

Rarity: —

$10 • W-MA-2680-010-G210c

Left: Lathework chain bearing MASSACHUSETTS vertically. ***Right:*** Panel of lathework circle segments. ***Engraver:*** Perkins. ***Comments:*** H-MA-1000-G114. Similar to W-MA-2680-010-G210. 18__. 1820s.

Rarity: —

$10 • W-MA-2680-010-G210d

Engraver: PSSP. ***Comments:*** H-MA-1000-G116. Similar to W-MA-2680-010-G210 but with zigzag ruled lines. 18__. 1820s–1830s.

Rarity: —

$10 • W-MA-2680-010-G210e

Engraver: PSSP ***Comments:*** H-MA-1000-G118. Similar to W-MA-2680-010-G210 but with spiral lathework lines. 18__. 1830s.

Rarity: —

$10 • W-MA-2680-010-G220

Comments: H-MA-1000-G120. No description available 18__. 1830s–1840s.

Rarity: *None known*

$10 • W-MA-2680-010-G230

CJF

Engraver: Toppan, Carpenter & Co. ***Comments:*** H-MA-1000-G124. 18__. 1840s–1850s.

Rarity: URS-3
Proof $5,000
Selected auction price: Stack's Bowers Galleries, March 2012, Lot 5181, EF $4,887

$20 • W-MA-2680-020-G240

Left: Panel bearing state arms / 20 / 20 vertically. ***Center:*** Alternating flower garlands and gridwork segments. ***Right:*** 20 / 20 vertically. ***Engraver:*** Perkins. ***Comments:*** H-MA-1000-G128. 18__. 1810s–1820s.

Rarity: —

$20 • W-MA-2680-020-G240a

Left: Lathework chain bearing MASSACHUSETTS vertically. ***Engraver:*** PSSP. ***Comments:*** H-MA-1000-G130. Similar to W-MA-2680-020-G240. 18__. 1820s–1840s.

Rarity: —

$20 • W-MA-2680-020-G250

JF

Engraver: Toppan, Carpenter & Co. ***Comments:*** H-MA-1000-G134. 18__. 1840s–1850s.

Rarity: URS-2
Proof $7,000

$50 • W-MA-2680-050-G260

Left: Panel bearing state arms / 50 / 50 vertically. ***Center:*** Alternating flower garlands and gridwork segments. ***Right:*** 50 / 50 vertically. ***Engraver:*** Perkins. ***Comments:*** H-MA-1000-G138. 18__. 1810s–1820s.

Rarity: —

$50 • W-MA-2680-050-G260a

Left: Lathework chain bearing MASSACHUSETTS vertically. ***Engraver:*** PSSP. ***Comments:*** H-MA-1000-G140. Similar to W-MA-2680-050-G260. 18__. 1820s–1840s.

Rarity: —

$50 • W-MA-2680-050-G270

Left: Woman with sickle and sheaf / FIFTY. ***Center:*** 50 / "Landing of the Pilgrims". ***Right:*** 50. ***Engraver:*** Toppan, Carpenter & Co. ***Comments:*** H-MA-1000-G144. 18__. 1840s–1850s.

Rarity: —

$100 • W-MA-2680-100-G280

Left: Panel bearing state arms / 100 / 100 vertically. ***Center:*** Alternating flower garlands and gridwork segments. ***Right:*** 100 / 100 vertically. ***Engraver:*** Perkins. ***Comments:*** H-MA-1000-G148. 18__. 1810s–1820s.

Rarity: —

$100 • W-MA-2680-100-G280a

Left: Lathework chain bearing MASSACHUSETTS vertically. ***Engraver:*** Perkins. ***Comments:*** H-MA-1000-G150. Similar to W-MA-2680-100-G280. 18__. 1820s–1840s.

Rarity: —

$100 • W-MA-2680-100-G290

Left: ONE HUNDRED across 100 / Woman reclining on bale, Ship. ***Center:*** "Landing of the Pilgrims". ***Bottom center:*** Eagle. ***Right:*** 100 / 100. ***Engraver:*** Toppan, Carpenter & Co. ***Comments:*** H-MA-1000-G154. 18__. 1840s–1850s.

Rarity: —

$500 • W-MA-2680-500-G300

Left: Lathework chain bearing MASSACHUSETTS / 500 / 500 vertically. ***Center:*** Alternating flower garlands and gridwork segments. ***Right:*** 500 / 500 vertically. ***Engraver:*** PSSP. ***Comments:*** H-MA-1000-G158. 18__. 1820s–1830s.

Rarity: —

Non-Valid Issues

$1 • W-MA-2680-001-C040

Engraver: PSSP. ***Comments:*** H-MA-1000-C38. Counterfeit of W-MA-2680-001-G040. 18__. Circa 1840.

Rarity: —

$2 • W-MA-2680-002-C100

Engraver: PSSP. ***Comments:*** H-MA-1000-C66. Counterfeit of W-MA-2680-002-G100. 18__. Circa 1840.

Rarity: URS-6
F $100

$2 • W-MA-2680-002-R010

Engraver: Toppan, Carpenter & Co. ***Comments:*** H-MA-1000-R5. Raised from W-MA-2680-001-G050 or W-MA-2680-001-G060. 18__. 1840s.

Rarity: —

$3 • W-MA-2680-003-C150

CJF

Engraver: PSSP. ***Comments:*** H-MA-1000-C82. Counterfeit of W-MA-2680-003-G150. 18__. Circa 1840.

Rarity: URS-7
VG $75; **VF** $150

$5 • W-MA-2680-005-C160

TD

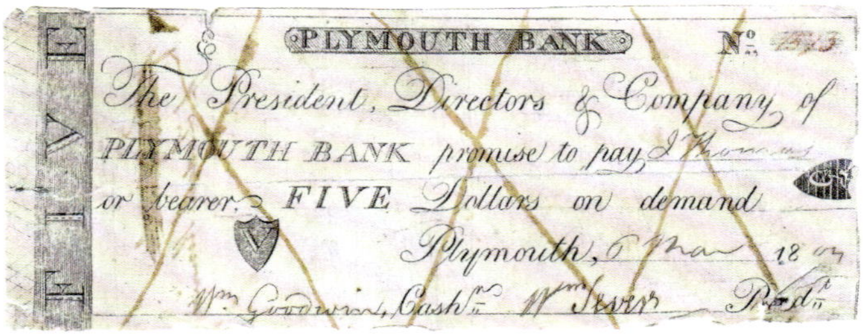

Comments: H-MA-1000-C84. Counterfeit of W-MA-2680-005-G160. 18__. 1800s.

Rarity: —

$10 • W-MA-2680-010-N010

Center: Spread eagle. ***Comments:*** H-MA-1000-N10.

Rarity: —

Plymouth Bank at Plymouth

1850s

W-MA-2690

History: A non-existent bank represented only by notes altered from those of other banks. The notes were intended to pass for those of the Plymouth Bank, W-MA-2680.

Issues

$5 • W-MA-2690-005-A010

CC

Engraver: Rawdon, Wright & Hatch. ***Comments:*** H-MA-1001-A5. Altered from $5 Wayne County Bank at Plymouth, Michigan. 18__. 1830s–1850s.

Rarity: URS-7
VG $100; **VF** $175

Portland, Massachusetts

Portland, in Cumberland County on Casco Bay, was originally a part of the town of Falmouth, as were Westbrook, Cape Elizabeth, and a number of islands. Until March 15, 1820, it was in the Maine District of Massachusetts. After that time, it was in the new state of Maine. The first settlement was made there in 1630. What became Portland was first known as Machigonne, then Cleeves's Neck, then Munjoy Neck, and sometimes as Casco and Old Casco. In July 1658, it was called Falmouth. The settlement grew with shipbuilding, maritime trade, and other activities. Principal articles of export were lumber, fish, and produce. By 1749 the greater district had an estimated 2,346 employees. Portland was separated from Falmouth on July 4, 1786. In 1814, with British forces on land in Maryland and Washington, the Portland banks removed their specie to safe places, and some residents left the city. No invasion ever occurred. In 1832 Portland, Maine, was incorporated as a city.

See also Portland, Maine.

Bank of Portland

1819–1820 • 1820–1843

W-MA-2700 • W-ME-1140

History: The Bank of Portland was chartered in 1819 with $200,000 in authorized capital to be paid in gold and silver coins. Once $134,900 of the stock was paid in by January 1820, the bank began issuing paper money. In the same year, Maine became a state of its own as part of the Missouri Compromise. The year 1820 saw a circulation of $38,098. The *Bank Commissioners' Report*, February 5, 1838, gave this information: capital $300,000; circulation in bills of $5 upward $22,675; $975 in bills of $1, $2, and $3; specie in the vault $3,080.26; bills of banks outside of Maine $3,757; and real estate $7,000. By late 1839 figures were: capital $225,000; bills in circulation $22,095; specie $8,023.34; and real estate $13,470. In 1843 the bank's capital was $100,000; it liquidated its affairs this year. The bank surrendered its charter to the last legislature and closed its concerns.[31] See also listing under Maine.

Numismatic Commentary: The note listing for this bank is replete with issues that are not known. The $100 issue, however, stands out not only for its claim to be engraved by Underwood, Bald, Spencer & Hufty—as are other high denominations of this bank—but for the engraving itself. Depicted is the likeness of George Gordon (Lord Byron), a British Romantic poet.

Valid Issues

Notes With Massachusetts Address

$1 • W-MA-2700-001-G010

Left: 1 / 1. ***Center:*** ONE DOLLAR, Text. ***Right:*** 1 / 1. ***Engraver:*** PSSP. ***Comments:*** H-MA-1015-G2, Wait-Unlisted. 1819.

Rarity: —

$2 • W-MA-2700-002-G020

Engraver: PSSP. ***Comments:*** H-MA-1015-G4, Wait-Unlisted. Similar to W-MA-2700-001-G010 but with different denomination. 1819.

Rarity: —

$3 • W-MA-2700-003-G030

Engraver: PSSP. ***Comments:*** H-MA-1015-G6, Wait-Unlisted. Similar to W-MA-2700-001-G010 but with different denomination. 1819.

Rarity: —

$5 • W-MA-2700-005-G040

Left: MASSACHUSETTS vertically / 5, Plate letter, 5. ***Center:*** Flower garlands, FIVE. ***Right:*** 5, Plate letter, 5. ***Engraver:*** PSSP. ***Comments:*** H-MA-1015-G8, Wait-Unlisted. 1819.

Rarity: —

$10 • W-MA-2700-010-G050

Engraver: PSSP. ***Comments:*** H-MA-1015-G10, Wait-Unlisted. Similar to W-MA-2700-005-G040 but with different denomination. 1819.

Rarity: —

$20 • W-MA-2700-020-G060

Left: State arms / 20, Plate letter, 20. ***Center:*** Flower garlands, TWENTY. ***Right:*** 20, Plate letter, 20. ***Engraver:*** PSSP. ***Comments:*** H-MA-1015-G12, Wait-Unlisted. 1819.

Rarity: —

$50 • W-MA-2700-050-G070

Engraver: PSSP. ***Comments:*** H-MA-1015-G14, Wait-Unlisted. Similar to W-MA-2700-020-G060 but with different denomination. 1819.

Rarity: —

$100 • W-MA-2700-100-G080

Engraver: PSSP. ***Comments:*** H-MA-1015-G16, Wait-Unlisted. Similar to W-MA-2700-020-G060 but with different denomination. 1819.

Rarity: —

Notes With Maine Address

$1 • W-ME-1140-001-G010

Left: 1 / 1. ***Center:*** ONE DOLLAR, Text. ***Right:*** 1 / 1. ***Engraver:*** PSSP. ***Comments:*** H-ME-490-G2, Wait-Unlisted. 1820s.

Rarity: —

$1 • W-ME-1140-001-G020

Comments: H-ME-490-G8, Wait-Unlisted. No description available. 1830s.

Rarity: *None known*

$2 • W-ME-1140-002-G030

Engraver: PSSP. ***Comments:*** H-ME-490-G10, Wait-Unlisted. Similar to W-ME-1140-001-G010 but with different denomination. 1820s.

Rarity: —

$2 • W-ME-1140-002-G040

Comments: H-ME-490-G16, Wait-Unlisted. No description available. 1830s.

Rarity: *None known*

$3 • W-ME-1140-003-G050

Engraver: PSSP. ***Comments:*** H-ME-490-G18, Wait-Unlisted. Similar to W-ME-1140-001-G010 but with different denomination. 1820s.

Rarity: —

$3 • W-ME-1140-003-G060

Comments: H-ME-490-G24, Wait-Unlisted. No description available. 1830s.

Rarity: *None known*

$5 • W-ME-1140-005-G070

Left: MAINE vertically / 5, Plate letter, 5. ***Center:*** FIVE DOLLARS, Text. ***Right:*** 5, Plate letter, 5. ***Engraver:*** PSSP. ***Comments:*** H-ME-490-G26, Wait-Unlisted. 1820s.

Rarity: —

$5 • W-ME-1140-005-G080

Comments: H-ME-490-G32, Wait-Unlisted. No description available. 1830s.

Rarity: *None known*

$10 • W-ME-1140-010-G090

Engraver: PSSP. ***Comments:*** H-ME-490-G36, Wait-Unlisted. Similar to W-ME-1140-005-G070 but with different denomination. 1820s.

Rarity: —

$10 • W-ME-1140-010-G100

Comments: H-ME-490-G40, Wait-Unlisted. No description available. 1830s.

Rarity: *None known*

$20 • W-ME-1140-020-G110

Engraver: PSSP. ***Comments:*** H-ME-490-G42, Wait-Unlisted. Similar to W-ME-1140-005-G070 but with different denomination. 1820s–1830s.

Rarity: —

$20 • W-ME-1140-020-G120

Comments: H-ME-490-G46, Wait-Unlisted. No description available. 1830s.

Rarity: *None known*

$50 • W-ME-1140-050-G130

Engraver: PSSP. ***Comments:*** H-ME-490-G48, Wait-Unlisted. Similar to W-ME-1140-005-G070 but with different denomination. 1820s–1830s.

Rarity: —

$50 • W-ME-1140-050-G140

Comments: H-ME-490-G52, Wait-Unlisted. No description available. 1830s.

Rarity: *None known*

$100 • W-ME-1140-100-G150

QDB

Engraver: Underwood, Bald & Spencer. ***Comments:*** H-ME-490-G56, Wait-Unlisted. 18__. 1830s.

Rarity: URS-1
Proof $5,000

$500 • W-ME-1140-500-G160

Comments: H-ME-490-G60, Wait-Unlisted. No description available. 1830s.

Rarity: *None known*

$1,000 • W-ME-1140-1000-G170

Comments: H-ME-490-G64, Wait-Unlisted. No description available. 1830s.

Rarity: *None known*

Non-Valid Issues

$5 • W-ME-1140-005-C075

Engraver: PSSP. ***Comments:*** H-ME-490-N5, Wait-47. 1834.

Rarity: —

$5 • W-ME-1140-005-N010

Comments: H-Unlisted, Wait-48. Similar to W-ME-1140-005-C075 but with different date.

Rarity: —

$5 • W-ME-1140-005-A010

Left: FIVE vertically. ***Center:*** 5 / Four women under tree, Village, farm, and harbor / 5. ***Bottom center:*** 5. ***Right:*** FIVE vertically. ***Comments:*** H-ME-490-A5, Wait-46. Altered from Passamaquoddy Bank, Eastport, Massachusetts. 1819.

Rarity: —

$100 • W-ME-1140-100-N020

Left: 100 / C / 100 vertically. ***Center:*** Urn / Sailor standing with flag, Ship and buildings / Urn / Male portrait. ***Right:*** 100 / Male portrait with helmet / 100. ***Comments:*** H-Unlisted, Wait-48a.

Rarity: —

Cumberland Bank

1812–1820 • 1820–1831

W-MA-2710 • W-ME-1190

History: The Cumberland Bank was chartered on June 23, 1812, with an authorized capital of $300,000 to be paid in silver and gold coins. It succeeded certain interests of the Maine Bank, whose charter expired in 1812. In 1818 the bank suffered a massive robbery of more than $200,000 in gold, silver, and bills of other banks. A reward of $1,500 was issued regarding information and the return of the stolen money, and after a long search, the accomplice was apprehended. He dispatched himself during the search for the stolen funds, having been deceived by the main perpetrator in regards to the location of the monetary deposits. Daniel Manly, the perpetrator of the robbery, was caught, examined, and brought to terms for the renewal of the money. This done, Manly was jailed and the bank's stolen funds restored.

The bank's capital was $200,000 in 1819. On September 23, 1820, the Cumberland Bank was in "bad repute," at between 55 and 70 percent discount. Its charter expired in 1831. See also listing under Maine.

Numismatic Commentary: This bank was in business for just more than 20 years—as such, its earliest notes are dated in the state of Massachusetts. All of the notes with the Massachusetts address are of the PSSP type. These are so rare as to be essentially uncollectible.

Valid Issues

Notes With Massachusetts Address

$1 • W-MA-2710-001-G010

Left: 1 / 1. ***Center:*** ONE DOLLAR, Text. ***Right:*** 1 / 1. ***Comments:*** H-MA-1005-G10, Wait-Unlisted. 1810s.

Rarity: —

$2 • W-MA-2710-002-G020

Comments: H-MA-1005-G14, Wait-Unlisted. Similar to W-MA-2710-001-G010 but with different denomination. 1810s.

Rarity: —

$3 • W-MA-2710-003-G030

Comments: H-MA-1005-G16, Wait-Unlisted. Similar to W-MA-2710-001-G010 but with different denomination. 1810s.

Rarity: —

$5 • W-MA-2710-005-G040

CJF, CJF

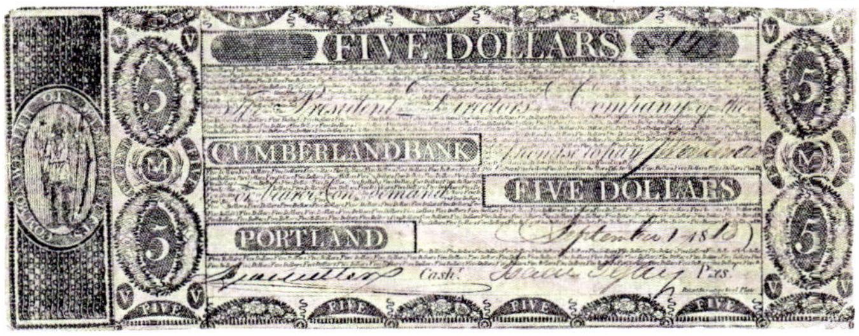

Back: Black Stereotype Steel Check Plate. ***Engraver:*** PSSP. ***Comments:*** H-MA-1005-G18, Wait-Unlisted. 18__ 1810s.

Rarity: URS-1
F $3,000

$10 • W-MA-2710-010-G050

Comments: H-MA-1005-G20, Wait-Unlisted. Similar to W-MA-2710-005-G040 but with different denomination. 1810s.

Rarity: URS-2
EF $800

$20 • W-MA-2710-020-G060

Comments: H-MA-1005-G22, Wait-Unlisted. Similar to W-MA-2710-005-G040 but with different denomination. 1810s.

Rarity: —

$50 • W-MA-2710-050-G070

Comments: H-MA-1005-G24, Wait-Unlisted. Similar to W-MA-2710-005-G040 but with different denomination. 1810s.

Rarity: —

$100 • W-MA-2710-100-G080

Comments: H-MA-1005-G26, Wait-Unlisted. Similar to W-MA-2710-005-G040 but with different denomination. 1810s.

Rarity: —

Notes With Maine Address

$1 • W-ME-1190-001-G010

Left: 1 / 1. ***Center:*** MAINE, Text. ***Right:*** 1 / 1. ***Comments:*** H-ME-450-G2, Wait-106. 1820s.

Rarity: —

$2 • W-ME-1190-002-G020

Comments: H-ME-450-G6, Wait-106. Similar to W-ME-1190-001-G010 but with different denomination. 1820s.

Rarity: —

$3 • W-ME-1190-003-G030

Comments: H-ME-450-G10, Wait-106. Similar to W-ME-1190-001-G010 but with different denomination. 1820s.

Rarity: —

$5 • W-ME-1190-005-G040

Left: State arms / 5, Plate letter, 5. ***Center:*** FIVE DOLLARS, Text. ***Right:*** 5, Plate letter, 5. ***Comments:*** H-ME-450-G14, Wait-106. 1820s.

Rarity: —

$10 • W-ME-1190-010-G050

Comments: H-ME-450-G18, Wait-106. Similar to W-ME-1190-005-G040 but with different denomination. 1820s.

Rarity: —

$20 • W-ME-1190-020-G060

Comments: H-ME-450-G22, Wait-106. Similar to W-ME-1190-005-G040 but with different denomination. 1820s.

Rarity: —

Non-Valid Issues

$3 • W-ME-1190-003-S010

QDB

Comments: H-Unlisted, Wait-Unlisted. 18__. 1840s.

Rarity: —

John Taber and Son

Circa 1802–1810

W-MA-2715 • W-ME-1215

History: John Taber & Son was a merchant cargo shipper and owned a sailing ship named the *Mac*, which plied its trade along the east coast to New Orleans, the West Indies, etc.

Numismatic Commentary: Although this is a strictly merchant scrip issuing entity, John Taber & Son notes are similar to and collectible as bank notes. They were engraved early on by Perkins prior to his PSSP style.

Valid Issues

$1 • W-MA-2715-001-G010

CJF

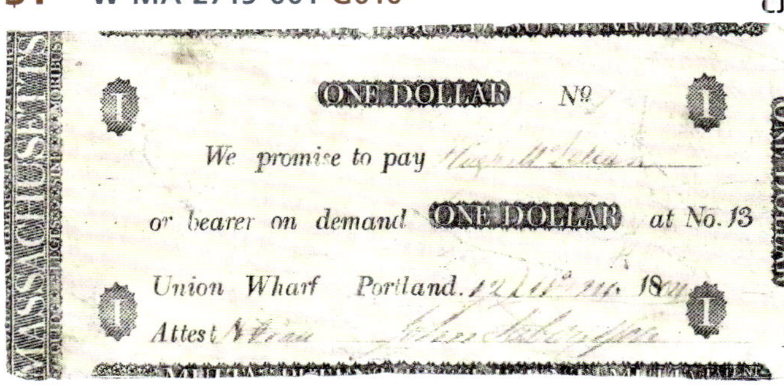

Engraver: Perkins. ***Comments:*** H-Unlisted, Wait-241. 18__. 1800s.

Rarity: URS-10
EF $150

$2 • W-MA-2715-002-G020

CJF

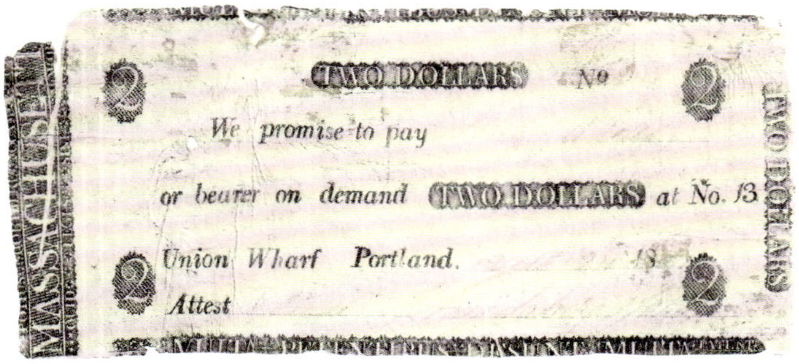

Engraver: Perkins. ***Comments:*** H-Unlisted, Wait-242. Similar to W-MA-2715-001-G010 but with different denomination. 18__.

Rarity: URS-10
EF $150

$3 • W-MA-2715-003-G030

Left: MASSACHUSETTS vertically. ***Center:*** III, III / THREE DOLLARS, Text / III, III. ***Right:*** THREE DOLLARS vertically. ***Engraver:*** Perkins. ***Comments:*** H-Unlisted, Wait-243. Similar to W-MA-2715-001-G010 but with different denomination. 18__.

Rarity: URS-10
EF $150

$4 • W-MA-2715-004-G040

CJF

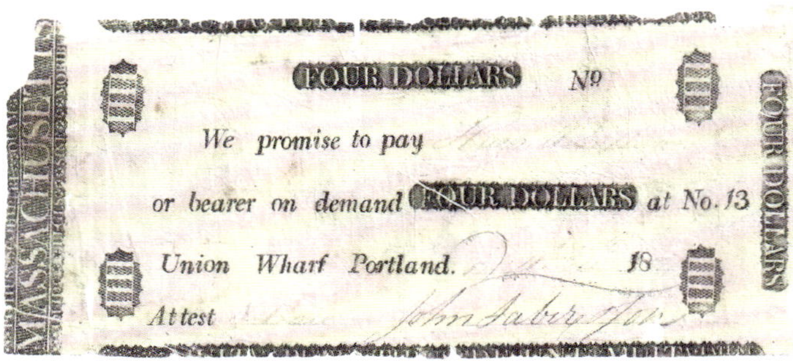

Engraver: Perkins. ***Comments:*** H-Unlisted, Wait-244. Similar to W-MA-2715-001-G010 but with different denomination. 18__.

Rarity: URS-7
EF $200

Maine Bank {1st}

1802–1812

W-MA-2720 • W-ME-1220

History: The Maine Bank was organized on June 23, 1802, in the district of Maine. It commenced business on April 1, 1803. The capital was reported as paid-in at $300,000 but was later reduced to $200,000. After the payment of one-fourth of the capital, loans were made to stockholders. It was afterwards shown that within a year, discounts to stockholders on pledge of stock amounted to $137,750, although the total stock was only $150,000.

The bank had an uneventful career and ceased to do business at the expiration of its charter, leaving a good record behind it. It closed on the first Monday in October 1812.[32] Certain of its interests were succeeded in that year by the Cumberland Bank, incorporated in 1812.

Numismatic Commentary: This bank did all of its business when Maine was still part of Massachusetts. Remaining issues in the marketplace will show the location as the State of Massachusetts above the title of the bank. Notes of odd denominations may be found on some issues, and counterfeits have been noted.

Valid Issues

$1 • W-MA-2720-001-G010

Left: 1 / 1. ***Center:*** Flower garlands, ONE. ***Right:*** 1 / 1. ***Comments:*** H-MA-1010-G20, Wait-Unlisted. 1800s.

Rarity: —

$1 • W-MA-2720-001-G020

Engraver: PSSP. ***Comments:*** H-MA-1010-G22, Wait-Unlisted. Similar to W-MA-2720-001-G010 but with different denomination. 1809–1810s.

Rarity: —

$2 • W-MA-2720-002-G030

Comments: H-MA-1010-G28, Wait-Unlisted. Similar to W-MA-2720-001-G010 but with different denomination. 1800s.

Rarity: —

$2 • W-MA-2720-002-G040

Engraver: PSSP. ***Comments:*** H-MA-1010-G36, Wait-Unlisted. Similar to W-MA-2720-001-G010 but with different denomination. 1809–1810s.

Rarity: —

$3 • W-MA-2720-003-G050

Engraver: PSSP. ***Comments:*** H-MA-1010-G40, Wait-Unlisted. Similar to W-MA-2720-001-G010 but with different denomination. 1800s.

Rarity: —

$3 • W-MA-2720-003-G060

QDB

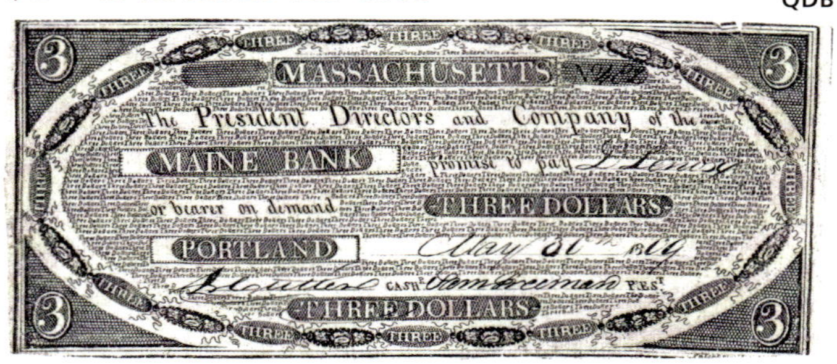

Engraver: PSSP. ***Comments:*** H-MA-1010-G44, Wait-Unlisted. Similar to W-MA-2720-001-G010 but with different denomination. 18__. 1800s.

Rarity: URS-4
EF $500

$5 • W-MA-2720-005-G070

Comments: H-MA-1010-G48, Wait-Unlisted. Similar to W-MA-2720-005-C070. 1800s.

Rarity: —

$5 • W-MA-2720-005-G070a

Comments: H-MA-1010-G48a, Wait-Unlisted. Similar to W-MA-2720-005-C070 but with FIVE. 1800s.

Rarity: —

$5 • W-MA-2720-005-G080

Left: State arms / 5, Plate letter, 5. ***Center:*** FIVE DOLLARS, Text. ***Right:*** 5, Plate letter, 5. ***Engraver:*** PSSP. ***Comments:*** H-MA-1010-G52, Wait-Unlisted. 1809–1810s.

Rarity: —

$6 • W-MA-2720-006-G090

Comments: H-MA-1010-G56, Wait-Unlisted. Similar to W-MA-2720-005-C070. 1800s.

Rarity: —

$6 • W-MA-2720-006-G090a

Comments: H-MA-1010-G56a, Wait-Unlisted. Similar to W-MA-2720-005-C070 but with SIX. 1800s.

Rarity: —

$7 • W-MA-2720-007-G100

Comments: H-MA-1010-G58, Wait-Unlisted. Similar to W-MA-2720-005-C070. 1800s.

Rarity: —

$7 • W-MA-2720-007-G100a

Comments: H-MA-1010-G58a, Wait-Unlisted. Similar to W-MA-2720-005-C070 but with SEVEN. 1800s.

Rarity: —

$7 • W-MA-2720-007-G110

Left: 7 vertically / Ship. ***Center:*** Potted plant, tree, cow / SEVEN. ***Comments:*** H-Unlisted, Wait-153.

Rarity: —

$8 • W-MA-2720-008-G120

Left: 8 vertically. ***Center:*** 8 on shield / Sheaf / EIGHT DOLLARS / Tree. ***Right:*** 8 vertically. ***Comments:*** H-Unlisted, Wait-154.

Rarity: —

$8 • W-MA-2720-008-G130

Comments: H-MA-1010-G60, Wait-Unlisted. Similar to W-MA-2720-008-C130. 1800s.

Rarity: —

$8 • W-MA-2720-008-G130a

Comments: H-MA-1010-G60a, Wait-Unlisted. Similar to W-MA-2720-008-C130 but with EIGHT. 1800s.

Rarity: —

$9 • W-MA-2720-009-G140

Comments: H-MA-1010-G62, Wait-Unlisted. Similar to W-MA-2720-009-C140. 1800s.

Rarity: —

$9 • W-MA-2720-009-G140a

Comments: H-MA-1010-G62a, Wait-Unlisted. Similar to W-MA-2720-009-C140 but with NINE. 1800s.

Rarity: —

$10 • W-MA-2720-010-G150

Comments: H-MA-1010-G66, Wait-Unlisted. Similar to W-MA-2720-005-C070. 1800s.

Rarity: —

$10 • W-MA-2720-010-G150a

Comments: H-MA-1010-G66a, Wait-Unlisted. Similar to W-MA-2720-005-C070 but with TEN. 1800s.

Rarity: —

$10 • W-MA-2720-010-G160

Engraver: PSSP. ***Comments:*** H-MA-1010-G70, Wait-Unlisted. Similar to W-MA-2720-005-G080 but with different denomination. 1809–1810s.

Rarity: —

$20 • W-MA-2720-020-G170

Comments: H-MA-1010-G74, Wait-Unlisted. Similar to W-MA-2720-005-C070. 1800s.

Rarity: —

$20 • W-MA-2720-020-G170a

Comments: H-MA-1010-G74a, Wait-Unlisted. Similar to W-MA-2720-005-C070 but with TWENTY. 1800s.

Rarity: —

$20 • W-MA-2720-020-G180

Engraver: PSSP. ***Comments:*** H-MA-1010-G78, Wait-Unlisted Similar to W-MA-2720-005-G080 but with different denomination. 1809–1810s.

Rarity: —

$50 • W-MA-2720-050-G190

Comments: H-MA-1010-G82, Wait-Unlisted. W-MA-2720-005-C070. 1800s.

Rarity: —

$50 • W-MA-2720-050-G190a

Comments: H-MA-1010-G82a, Wait-Unlisted. W-MA-2720-005-C070 but with FIFTY. 1800s.

Rarity: —

$50 • W-MA-2720-050-G200

Engraver: PSSP. ***Comments:*** H-MA-1010-G86, Wait-Unlisted. Similar to W-MA-2720-005-G080 but with different denomination. 1809–1810s.

Rarity: —

$100 • W-MA-2720-100-G210

Engraver: PSSP. ***Comments:*** H-MA-1010-G90, Wait-Unlisted. Similar to W-MA-2720-005-G080 but with different denomination. 1809–1810s.

Rarity: —

Non-Valid Issues

$3 • W-MA-2720-003-C050

C. F

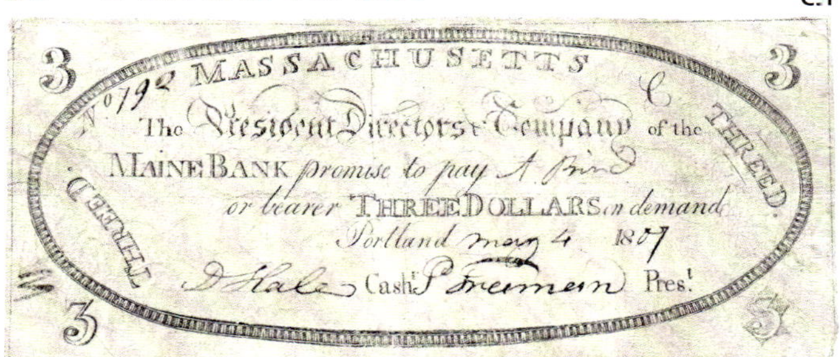

Comments: H-MA-1010-C40, Wait-Unlisted. Counterfeit of W-MA-2720-003-G050. 18__. 1800s.

Rarity: URS-5

F $200

$5 • W-MA-2720-005-C070

QDB

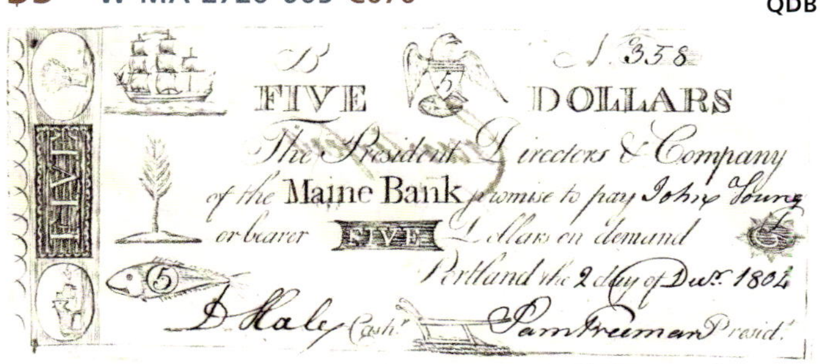

Comments: H-MA-1010-C48, Wait-Unlisted. Counterfeit of W-MA-2720-005-G070. 1800s.

Rarity: URS-6

F $150

$8 • W-MA-2720-008-C130

Left: 8 / 8. ***Center:*** Indian portrait / Shield / Banner. ***Comments:*** H-MA-1010-C60, Wait-Unlisted. Counterfeit of W-MA-2720-008-G130. 1800s.

Rarity: —

$9 • W-MA-2720-009-C140 CJF

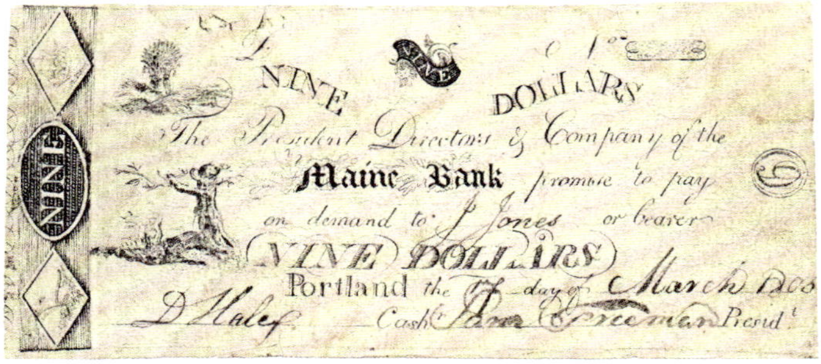

Comments: H-MA-1010-C62, Wait-Unlisted. Counterfeit of W-MA-2720-009-G140. 1800s.

Rarity: URS-4
VF $250

$9 • W-MA-2720-009-C140a CJF

Comments: H-MA-1010-C62a, Wait-Unlisted. Counterfeit of W-MA-2720-009-G140a. 1800s.

Rarity: URS-4
VF $250

$50 • W-MA-2720-050-C190

Comments: H-MA-1010-C82, Wait-Unlisted. Counterfeit of W-MA-2720-050-G190 or W-MA-2720-050-G190a. 1800s.

Rarity: —

Portland Bank

1799–1815

W-MA-2730 • W-ME-1270

History: The Portland Bank was chartered on June 15, 1799, the first in the district that is now the State of Maine. The capital was authorized at $200,000, but paid-in subscriptions arrived slowly.

According to the February 17, 1812, issue of the *Boston Gazette*, counterfeit $7 bills of this bank were being circulated. The bank's original charter provided that all bills issued must have a minimum denomination of $5. The lower denominations were authorized by an act of Massachusetts Legislature on June 5, 1805. The bank was liquidated in 1815. See also listing under Maine.

VALID ISSUES

$1 • W-MA-2730-001-G010

Comments: H-MA-1020-G20, Wait-Unlisted. No description available. 1800s.

Rarity: *None known*

$1 • W-MA-2730-001-G020

Left: 1 / 1. ***Center:*** ONE DOLLAR, Text. ***Right:*** 1 / 1. ***Engraver:*** PSSP. ***Comments:*** H-MA-1020-G24, Wait-Unlisted. 1809–1812.

Rarity: —

$1 • W-MA-2730-001-G030

Comments: H-MA-1020-G26, Wait-Unlisted. Similar to W-MA-2730-001-G020 but with ONE. 1810s.

Rarity: —

$1 • W-MA-2730-001-G040

Left: 1 / 1. ***Center:*** Watermelon design. ***Right:*** 1 / 1. ***Engraver:*** PSSP. ***Comments:*** H-Unlisted, Wait-232.

Rarity: —

$2 • W-MA-2730-002-G050

Comments: H-MA-1020-G32, Wait-Unlisted. No description available. 1800s.

Rarity: *None known*

$2 • W-MA-2730-002-G060

Engraver: PSSP. ***Comments:*** H-MA-1020-G36, Wait-Unlisted. Similar to W-MA-2730-001-G020 but with different denomination. 1809–1812.

Rarity: URS-2
EF $800

$2 • W-MA-2730-002-G070

Comments: H-MA-1020-G38, Wait-Unlisted. Similar to W-MA-2730-002-G060 but with TWO. 1810s.

Rarity: —

$2 • W-MA-2730-002-G080

Left: 2 / 2. ***Center:*** Watermelon design. ***Right:*** 2 / 2. ***Engraver:*** PSSP. ***Comments:*** H-Unlisted, Wait-233.

Rarity: —

$3 • W-MA-2730-003-G090

Comments: H-MA-1020-G44, Wait-Unlisted. No description available. 1800s.

Rarity: *None known*

$3 • W-MA-2730-003-G100

Left: 3 / 3. ***Center:*** MASSACHUSETTS, Text. ***Right:*** 3 / 3. ***Engraver:*** PSSP. ***Comments:*** H-MA-1020-G48, Wait-Unlisted. 1809–1810s.

Rarity: URS-2
EF $800

$5 • W-MA-2730-005-G110

Comments: H-MA-1020-G52, Wait-Unlisted. No description available. 1800s.

Rarity: *None known*

$5 • W-MA-2730-005-G120

Left: State arms / 5, Plate letter, 5. ***Center:*** FIVE DOLLARS, Text. ***Right:*** 5, Plate letter, 5. ***Engraver:*** PSSP. ***Comments:*** H-MA-1020-G56, Wait-Unlisted. 1800s.

Rarity: —

$6 • W-MA-2730-006-G130

Comments: H-MA-1020-G60, Wait-Unlisted. No description available. 1800s.

Rarity: *None known*

$7 • W-MA-2730-007-G140
Comments: H-MA-1020-G62, Wait-Unlisted. No description available. 1800s.
Rarity: *None known*

$8 • W-MA-2730-008-G150
Comments: H-MA-1020-G64, Wait-Unlisted. No description available. 1800s.
Rarity: *None known*

$9 • W-MA-2730-009-G160
Comments: H-MA-1020-G66, Wait-Unlisted. No description available. 1800s.
Rarity: *None known*

$10 • W-MA-2730-010-G170
Comments: H-MA-1020-G70, Wait-Unlisted. No description available. 1800s.
Rarity: *None known*

$10 • W-MA-2730-010-G180
Engraver: PSSP. ***Comments:*** H-MA-1020-G74, Wait-Unlisted. Similar to W-MA-2730-005-G120 but with different denomination. 1809–1812.
Rarity: —

$10 • W-MA-2730-010-G190
Comments: H-MA-1020-G76, Wait-Unlisted. Similar to W-MA-2730-005-G120 but with different denomination and TEN. 1810s.
Rarity: —

$20 • W-MA-2730-020-G200
Engraver: PSSP. ***Comments:*** H-MA-1020-G80, Wait-Unlisted. Similar to W-MA-2730-005-G120 but with different denomination. 1809–1810s.
Rarity: —

$50 • W-MA-2730-050-G210
Engraver: PSSP. ***Comments:*** H-MA-1020-G84, Wait-Unlisted. Similar to W-MA-2730-005-G120 but with different denomination. 1809–1810s.
Rarity: —

$100 • W-MA-2730-100-G220
Engraver: PSSP. ***Comments:*** H-MA-1020-G88, Wait-Unlisted. Similar to W-MA-2730-005-G120 but with different denomination. 1809–1810s.
Rarity: —

Non-Valid Issues

$7 • W-MA-2730-007-C140
Comments: H-MA-1020-C62, Wait-Unlisted. Counterfeit of W-MA-2730-007-G140. 1800s.
Rarity: —

Providence, Massachusetts

Providence was never a part of Massachusetts. This imprint appears only on an issue from a non-existent bank meant to imitate Pawtuxet, Rhode Island.

Pawtuxet Bank
1840s–1850s
W-MA-2740

History: A non-existent bank represented only by fraudulent notes. These notes were intended to pass for those of the Pawtuxet Bank in Pawtuxet, Rhode Island.

Issues

$20 • W-MA-2740-020-G010
Left: 20 / Woman seated. ***Center:*** XX / Eagle / XX. ***Right:*** 20 / Ship. ***Engraver:*** New England Bank Note Co. ***Comments:*** H-MA-1025-G10. 18__. 1840s–1850s.
Rarity: —

Provincetown, Massachusetts

Located at the tip of Cape Cod, Provincetown was originally known by the local tribe as Chequocket or Coatuit. It was organized by colonists as part of Truro in 1714 and incorporated in 1727. It became well known for the prosperity of its fishing grounds, although it remained a small town throughout the 19th century. Ship and boat building occurred here, as well as cordage making, carriage making, the construction of machinery and metallic items, clothes making, and other establishments for food preparation, including salt and cod liver oil. Sails, boots, shoes, lumber, and wrought stone were also manufactured.

Cape Cod Bank
1860
W-MA-2750

History: The Cape Cod Bank was incorporated in 1860 but never went into operation. It had an approved capital of $300,000.[33] This bank had no relation to the Bank of Cape Cod, W-MA-1830, in Harwich, Massachusetts.

Provincetown Bank
1854–1865
W-MA-2760

History: The Provincetown Bank was incorporated on March 28, 1854, with an authorized capital of $100,000. Circulation averaged at $100,000 during the bank's short existence. The real estate of the bank was valued at $3,000, and specie was $7,112.65 in 1857.

The business of the Provincetown Bank was succeeded by the Provincetown National Bank, chartered on January 21, 1865.

Numismatic Commentary: Genuine signed and dated issues from this geographical "last bank on the cape" will be hard to locate. Fortunately, some Proof sheets surfaced some decades ago and since then have appeared in the marketplace on occasion.

Valid Issues

$1 • W-MA-2760-001-G010

CC

Engraver: Bald, Adams & Co. / Bald, Cousland & Co. ***Comments:*** H-MA-1030-G2. Proof. Dec. 1, 1854.

Rarity: URS-3

Gem $895; **Proof** $1,100

$1 • W-MA-2760-001-G010a

CJF

Overprint: Red ONE. ***Engraver:*** Bald, Adams & Co. / Bald, Cousland & Co. ***Comments:*** H-MA-1030-G2a. Similar to W-MA-2760-001-G010. Dec. 1, 1854. 1850s.

Rarity: URS-4

Proof $1,250

$2 • W-MA-2760-002-G020

JF

Engraver: Bald, Adams & Co. / Bald, Cousland & Co. ***Comments:*** H-MA-1030-G4. Proof. Dec. 1, 1854.

Rarity: URS-4

Proof $1,000

$2 • W-MA-2760-002-G020a

SBG

Overprint: Red TWO. ***Engraver:*** Bald, Adams & Co. / Bald, Cousland & Co. ***Comments:*** H-MA-1030-G4a. Similar to W-MA-2760-002-G020. Proof. Dec. 1, 1854. 1850s.

Rarity: URS-4

Proof $1,100

$3 • W-MA-2760-003-G030

CJF

Engraver: Bald, Adams & Co. / Bald, Cousland & Co. ***Comments:*** H-MA-1030-G6. Proof. 185_. 1850s.

Rarity: URS-4

Proof $1,100

$3 • W-MA-2760-003-G030a

Left: 3 / Sailor and mechanic, Ship. ***Center:*** 3 on die. ***Right:*** 3 / Ship. ***Overprint:*** Red THREE. ***Engraver:*** Bald, Adams & Co. / Bald, Cousland & Co. ***Comments:*** H-MA-1030-G6a. Similar to W-MA-2760-003-G030. 185_. 1850s.

Rarity: —

$5 • W-MA-2760-005-G040

JF

Engraver: Bald, Adams & Co. / Bald, Cousland & Co. ***Comments:*** H-MA-1030-G8. Proof. 185_. 1850s.

Rarity: URS-4

Proof $1,000

$5 • W-MA-2760-005-G040a

CC

Overprint: Red FIVE. ***Engraver:*** Bald, Adams & Co. / Bald, Cousland & Co. ***Comments:*** H-MA-1030-G8a. Similar to W-MA-2760-005-G040. Proof. Dec. 1, 1854. 1850s.

Rarity: URS-4

Proof $1,100

$10 • W-MA-2760-010-G050

CC

Engraver: Bald, Adams & Co. / Bald, Cousland & Co. ***Comments:*** H-MA-1030-G10. Proof. 185_. 1850s.

Rarity: URS-4
Proof $1,000

$10 • W-MA-2760-010-G050a

Left: Woman standing with staff and shield. ***Center:*** TEN / Sailing ship. ***Right:*** 10 / X. ***Overprint:*** Red TEN. ***Engraver:*** Bald, Adams & Co. / Bald, Cousland & Co. ***Comments:*** H-MA-1030-G10a. Similar to W-MA-2760-010-G050. 185_. 1850s.

Rarity: URS-4
Proof $1,000

$20 • W-MA-2760-020-G060

S3G

Engraver: Bald, Adams & Co. / Bald, Cousland & Co. ***Comments:*** H-MA-1030-G12. Proof. 185_. 1850s.

Rarity: URS-4
Proof $1,000

$20 • W-MA-2760-020-G060a

Left: XX / Massachusetts / Portrait of John Quincy Adams. ***Center:*** Three men on beach. ***Right:*** XX / 20. ***Overprint:*** Red. ***Engraver:*** Bald, Adams & Co. / Bald, Cousland & Co. ***Comments:*** H-MA-1030-G12a. Similar to W-MA-2760-020-G060. 185_. 1850s.

Rarity: —

$50 • W-MA-2760-050-G070

QDB

Engraver: Bald, Adams & Co. / Bald, Cousland & Co. ***Comments:*** H-MA-1030-G14. Proof. Dec. 1, 1854.

Rarity: URS-3
CU $1,195; **Proof** $1,250

$50 • W-MA-2760-050-G070a

Left: L / Female portrait. ***Center:*** Woman reclining against packages. ***Right:*** 50. ***Overprint:*** Red. ***Engraver:*** Bald, Adams & Co. / Bald, Cousland & Co. ***Comments:*** H-MA-1030-G14a. Similar to W-MA-2760-050-G070. Dec. 1, 1854.

Rarity: —

$100 • W-MA-2760-100-G080

JF

Engraver: Bald, Adams & Co. / Bald, Cousland & Co. ***Comments:*** H-MA-1030-G16. Proof. December 1, 1854.

Rarity: URS-2
Proof $1,200

$100 • W-MA-2760-100-G080a

Left: C / Clipper ship with topsails / C. ***Right:*** 100 / Sailor leaning on capstan. ***Overprint:*** Red C. ***Engraver:*** Bald, Adams & Co. / Bald, Cousland & Co. ***Comments:*** H-MA-1030-G16a. Similar to W-MA-2760-100-G080. 1850s.

Rarity: —

Uncut Sheets

$1-$2 • W-MA-2760-001.002-US010

JF

Engraver: Bald, Adams & Co. / Bald, Cousland & Co. ***Comments:*** H-MA-1030-G2, G4. Partial sheet. Proof. Dec. 1, 1854.

Rarity: —

$1-$1-$2-$5 • W-MA-2760-001.001.002.005-US020

Vignette(s): ($1) Man holding axe / Ships on ocean / Girl shading eyes with hand. ***($1)*** Man holding gun / Ships on ocean / Girl shading eyes with hand. ***($2)*** Building with steeple / Ships on ocean. ***($5)*** Woman seated in clouds with sword, balance, and eagle / Portrait of Daniel Webster / Portrait of boy. ***Engraver:*** Bald, Adams & Co. / Bald, Cousland & Co. ***Comments:*** H-MA-1030-G2, G2, G4, G8. December 1, 1854.

Rarity: —

$1-$1-$2-$5 • W-MA-2760-001.001.002.005-US020a

Overprint(s): Red. ***Engraver:*** Bald, Adams & Co. / Bald, Cousland & Co. ***Comments:*** H-MA-1030-G2a, G2a, G4a, G8a. Similar to W-MA-2760-001.001.002.005-US020a. Dec. 1, 1854. 1850s.

Rarity: —

$3-$5-$10-$20 • W-MA-2760-003.005.010.020-US030

Engraver: Bald, Adams & Co. / Bald, Cousland & Co. ***Comments:*** H-MA-1030-G6, G8, G10, G12. 185_. 1850s.

Rarity: URS-4
Proof $3,000

$3-$5-$10-$20 • W-MA-2760-003.005.010.020-US030a

Vignette(s): ($3) Two men, one seated, one standing / Ship. ***($5)*** Woman seated in clouds with sword, balance, and eagle / Portrait of Daniel Webster / Portrait of boy. ***($10)*** Woman standing with staff and shield / Sailing ship. ***($20)*** Portrait of John Quincy Adams / Three men on beach. ***Overprint(s):*** Red. ***Engraver:*** Bald, Adams & Co. / Bald, Cousland & Co. ***Comments:*** H-MA-1030-G6a, G8a, G10a, G12a. Similar to W-MA-2760-003.005.010.020-US030. 185_. 1850s.

Rarity: —

$50-$100 • W-MA-2760-050.100-US040 JF

Engraver: Bald, Adams & Co. / Bald, Cousland & Co. ***Comments:*** H-MA-1030-G14, G16. Partial sheet. Proof. December 1, 1854.

Rarity: URS-3
Proof $2,500

$50-$100 • W-MA-2760-050.100-US040a

Vignette(s): ($50) Female portrait / Woman reclining against packages. ***($100)*** Clipper ship with topsails / Sailor leaning on capstan. ***Overprint(s):*** Red. ***Engraver:*** Bald, Adams & Co. / Bald, Cousland & Co. ***Comments:*** H-MA-1030-G14a, G16a. Similar to W-MA-2760-050.100-US040. Partial sheet. December 1, 1854.

Rarity: —

NON-VALID ISSUES

$5 • W-MA-2760-005-R010

Engraver: Bald, Adams & Co. / Bald, Cousland & Co. ***Comments:*** H-MA-1030-R5. Raised from W-MA-2760-001-G010 or G010a. Dec. 1, 1854.

Rarity: —

QUINCY, MASSACHUSETTS

Named after Colonel John Quincy, Quincy is the birthplace of presidents John Adams and his son John Quincy Adams. It was originally incorporated as a part of Dorchester in 1630 and then annexed to Boston in 1634. Later it was reorganized as Braintree in 1640 and incorporated as the town of Quincy in 1792.

The first commercial railroad in the United States was constructed in order to carry granite from a quarry in Quincy to Milton. The granite attracted a strong demand and thus stonecutting became the primary industry for the town. The first iron furnace in the United States was also invented here. Shipbuilding followed as a profitable commerce, producing sailing ships including the only seven-masted schooner ever to be built. By 1845 the Old Colony Railroad had been established here.

Mount Wollaston Bank
1853–1864
W-MA-2775

History: The Mount Wollaston Bank commenced operations on August 12, 1853, with an authorized capital of $100,000. In 1857 capital was raised to $150,000. Circulation was $51,694 in 1857, $48,277 in 1858, and $68,598 in 1863.

In October 1864, the business of the bank was succeeded by the Mount Wollaston National Bank of Quincy.

Numismatic Commentary: This bank is another example of an entity having a fair amount of Proof issues available while genuine signed and dated notes are rare.

All notes bear the engraving of Baldwin, Adams & Co.

VALID ISSUES

$1 • W-MA-2775-001-G010 TD

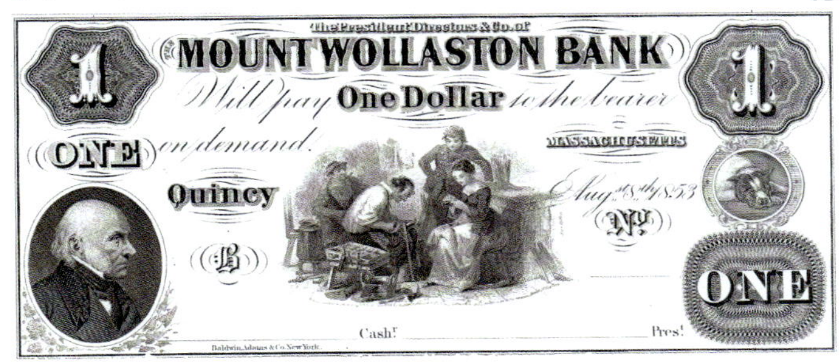

Comments: H-MA-1035-G2. Proof. Aug. 8, 1853. 1850s.

Rarity: URS-7
Proof $200

How to Read the Whitman Numbering System

$1 • W-MA-010-001-G010a

Denomination: Value of the note shown.

W: Whitman number. This number is a sortable code unique to each bank and note.

MA: Abbreviation for the state under study.

010: Numerical designation specific to each bank.

001: The denomination in dollars.

G010a: G indicates a good or valid note. Other categories are indicated thus: C (counterfeit); R (raised); S (spurious); N (not-attributed); A (altered). Numbers are assigned starting with 010, 020, et seq. Terminal letters following the number indicate variations of a note: a series of different colored overprints, tints, payees, etc., all on the same design of note. For more information, see the "How to Use This Book" section at the front of the volume, page xiv.

$1 • **W-MA-2775-001-G010a** TD

Overprint: Red 1 / 1. ***Comments:*** H-Unlisted. Similar to W-MA-2775-001-G010. Proof. Aug. 8, 1853. 1850s.

Rarity: URS-6
Proof $250

$2 • **W-MA-2775-002-G020** TD

Comments: H-MA-1035-G4. Proof. August 8, 1853. 1850s.

Rarity: URS-7
Proof $250

$2 • **W-MA-2775-002-G020a** TD

Overprint: Red 2. ***Comments:*** H-Unlisted. Similar to W-MA-2775-002-G020. Proof. August 8, 1853. 1850s.

Rarity: URS-7
Proof $300

$3 • **W-MA-2775-003-G030**

Left: 3 / 3. ***Center:*** Portrait of Charles F. Adams. ***Right:*** 3 / Stonemason working / 3. ***Comments:*** H-MA-1035-G6. 18__. 1850s.

Rarity: URS-7
Proof $300

$3 • **W-MA-2775-003-G030a** TD

Overprint: Lazy red 3. ***Comments:*** H-Unlisted. Similar to W-MA-2775-003-G030. Proof. August 8, 1853. 1850s.

Rarity: URS-6
Proof $350

$3 • **W-MA-2775-003-G030b** TD

Comments: H-Unlisted. Similar to W-MA-2775-003-G030 but with different center portrait. Proof. August 8, 1853. 1850s.

Rarity: URS-7
Proof $300

$5 • **W-MA-2775-005-G040**

Left: V / View of church. ***Center:*** View John Quincy Adams's residence. ***Right:*** 5 / Portrait of Charles F. Adams. ***Comments:*** H-MA-1035-G8. 18__. 1850s.

Rarity: URS-7
Proof $200

$10 • **W-MA-2775-010-G050**

Left: TEN / Dog's head / TEN. ***Center:*** Ocean scene with yacht *America*. ***Right:*** X / View of church. ***Comments:*** H-MA-1035-G10. 18__. 1850s.

Rarity: URS-6
Proof $250

$20 • **W-MA-2775-020-G060**

Left: XX / Hunter seated on log, warming hands by fire, Dog and gun. ***Center:*** Woman, View of houses. ***Right:*** 20 / Portrait of John Quincy Adams. ***Comments:*** H-MA-1035-G12. 18__. 1850s.

Rarity: URS-7
Proof $300

$50 • **W-MA-2775-050-G070** CC

Comments: H-MA-1035-G14. Proof. August 8, 1853. 1850s.

Rarity: URS-4
CU $1,050; **Proof** $1,200

$100 • W-MA-2775-100-G080 JF

Comments: H-MA-1035-G16. Proof. August 8, 1853. 1850s.

Rarity: URS-4

CU $1,125; **Proof** $1,200

Uncut Sheets

$1-$1-$2-$3 • W-MA-2775-001.001.002.003-US010

Vignette(s): ($1) Portrait of John Quincy Adams / Shoemaker's shop, Two men and woman working, Boy standing / Dog's head. ***($1)*** Portrait of John Quincy Adams / Shoemaker's shop, Two men and woman working, Boy standing / Dog's head. ***($2)*** Portrait of John Quincy Adams / Three stonecutters at work / View of church. ***($3)*** Portrait of Charles F. Adams. ***Comments:*** H-MA-1035-G2, G2, G4, G6. August 8, 1853.

Rarity: —

$1-$1-$2-$3 • W-MA-2775-001.001.002.003-US010a

Overprint(s): Red. ***Comments:*** All unlisted in Haxby. Similar to W-MA-2775-001.001.002.003-US010. August 8, 1853.

Rarity: —

$50-$100 • W-MA-2775-050.100-US020 QDB

Comments: H-MA-1035-G14, G16. Partial sheet. August 8, 1853.

Rarity: URS-4

Proof $2,400

Non-Valid Issues

$3 • W-MA-2775-003-N010

Left: Woman. ***Center:*** Eagle and shield. ***Right:*** Woman. ***Comments:*** H-MA-1035-N5.

Rarity: —

$5 • W-MA-2775-005-R010

Comments: H-MA-1035-R5. Raised from W-MA-2775-001-G010. 18__. 1850s.

Rarity: —

Quincy Stone Bank
1836–1865
W-MA-2790

History: The Quincy Stone Bank was incorporated on March 31, 1836, with an authorized capital of $100,000, a figure which was increased to $150,000 in 1860. Circulation in 1839 was $59,056; it reached $77,548 in 1863. Specie totaled $7,508.46 in 1857.

On February 23, 1865, the National Granite Bank of Quincy was chartered, succeeding the interests of the Quincy Stone Bank.

Numismatic Commentary: Genuine notes are hard to locate. Some of the issues show Quincy granite being loaded on specially built boats for delivery to the Boston area. The Bunker Hill Monument as seen on notes of Charlestown, Massachusetts, was built with stone from this site.

Valid Issues

$1 • W-MA-2790-001-G010 CC

Engraver: PSSP / New England Bank Note Co. ***Comments:*** H-MA-1040-G2. 18__. 1830s.

Rarity: URS-6

VG $100; **F** $175; **VF** $250

$1 • W-MA-2790-001-G020

Left: 1 / Portrait of John Adams / ONE. ***Center:*** Granite Quarry in Quincy. ***Right:*** 1 / Portrait of John Hancock / ONE. ***Engraver:*** New England Bank Note Co. ***Comments:*** H-MA-1040-G4. Jany. 1, 186_. 1840s–1850s.

Rarity: —

$1 • W-MA-2790-001-G020a

Overprint: Red ONE. ***Engraver:*** New England Bank Note Co. ***Comments:*** H-MA-1040-G4a. Similar to W-MA-2790-001-G020. 18__. 1850s.

Rarity: —

$1 • W-MA-2790-001-G020b

CJF

Overprint: Red ONE. ***Engraver:*** New England Bank Note Co. / ABNCo. monogram. ***Comments:*** H-MA-1040-G4b. Similar to W-MA-2790-001-G020 but with additional engraver imprint and different date. Jany. 1, 186_. 1860s.

Rarity: URS-5
F $300; **VF** $500

$2 • W-MA-2790-002-G030

Left: 2 / Woman standing with staff, Cornucopia / TWO. ***Center:*** TWO / Machinery and merchandise flanking Ceres seated holding sickle and rake, Factories and harbor / Panel outlining white TWO. ***Right:*** 2 / Woman wearing hat, Trees / TWO. ***Engraver:*** PSSP / New England Bank Note Co. ***Comments:*** H-MA-1040-G6. 18__. 1830s.

Rarity: —

$2 • W-MA-2790-002-G040

Left: TWO / Portrait of John Hancock / 2. ***Center:*** Scene in Quincy. ***Right:*** 2 / Portrait of John Adams. ***Engraver:*** New England Bank Note Co. ***Comments:*** H-MA-1040-G8. 18__. 1840s–1850s.

Rarity: —

$2 • W-MA-2790-002-G040a

Overprint: Red TWO. ***Engraver:*** New England Bank Note Co. ***Comments:*** H-MA-1040-G8a. Similar to W-MA-2790-002-G040. 18__. 1850s.

Rarity: —

$2 • W-MA-2790-002-G040b

Overprint: Red TWO. ***Engraver:*** New England Bank Note Co. / ABNCo. monogram. ***Comments:*** H-MA-1040-G8b. Similar to W-MA-2790-002-G040 but with additional engraver imprint and different date. Jan. 1, 186_. 1860s.

Rarity: —

$3 • W-MA-2790-003-G050

Left: THREE / Beehive and foliage / THREE. ***Center:*** Machinery and merchandise flanking Ceres seated holding sickle and rake, Factories and harbor / THREE / Panel outlining white THREE. ***Right:*** 3 on THREE / Two reapers / 3 on THREE. ***Engraver:*** New England Bank Note Co. / PSSP. ***Comments:*** H-MA-1040-G10. 18__. 1830s.

Rarity: —

$3 • W-MA-2790-003-G060

Left: THREE / Portrait of John Adams / 3. ***Center:*** Scene in Quincy. ***Right:*** 3 / Portrait of John Hancock. ***Engraver:*** New England Bank Note Co. ***Comments:*** H-MA-1040-G12. 18__. 1840s–1850s.

Rarity: —

$3 • W-MA-2790-003-G060a

Overprint: Red THREE. ***Engraver:*** New England Bank Note Co. ***Comments:*** H-MA-1040-G12a. Similar to W-MA-2790-003-G060. 18__. 1850s.

Rarity: —

$3 • W-MA-2790-003-G060b

Overprint: Red THREE. ***Engraver:*** New England Bank Note Co. / ABNCo. monogram. ***Comments:*** H-MA-1040-G12b. Similar to W-MA-2790-003-G060 but with additional engraver imprint and different date. Jan. 1, 186_. 1860s.

Rarity: —

$5 • W-MA-2790-005-G070

Left: 5 / Blacksmith at anvil / FIVE. ***Center:*** Mercury standing with 5 / Cornucopia and merchandise, Factories and ship / V / Panel outlining white FIVE. ***Right:*** 5 / Ceres kneeling / FIVE. ***Engraver:*** New England Bank Note Co. / PSSP. ***Comments:*** H-MA-1040-G14. 18__. 1830s.

Rarity: —

$5 • W-MA-2790-005-G080

Left: 5 / Portrait of John Hancock. ***Center:*** Scene in Quincy. ***Right:*** 5 / Portrait of John Adams / FIVE. ***Engraver:*** New England Bank Note Co. ***Comments:*** H-MA-1040-G16. 18__. 1840s–1850s.

Rarity: —

$5 • W-MA-2790-005-G080a

Overprint: Red FIVE. ***Engraver:*** New England Bank Note Co. ***Comments:*** H-MA-1040-G16a. Similar to W-MA-2790-005-G080. 18__. 1850s.

Rarity: —

$5 • W-MA-2790-005-G080b

Overprint: Red FIVE. ***Engraver:*** New England Bank Note Co. / ABNCo. monogram. ***Comments:*** H-MA-1040-G16b. Similar to W-MA-2790-005-G080 but with different date and additional engraver imprint. Jan. 1, 186_. 1860s.

Rarity: —

$10 • W-MA-2790-010-G090

Engraver: Unverified, but likely New England Bank Note Co. ***Comments:*** H-MA-1040-G18. No description available. 18__. 1830s.

Rarity: *None known*

$10 • W-MA-2790-010-G100

Left: X / Portrait of John Hancock / TEN. ***Center:*** Scene in Quincy. ***Right:*** 10 / Portrait of John Adams / TEN. ***Engraver:*** New England Bank Note Co. ***Comments:*** H-MA-1040-G20. 18__. 1840s–1850s.

Rarity: —

$10 • W-MA-2790-010-G100a

Overprint: Red. ***Engraver:*** New England Bank Note Co. ***Comments:*** H-MA-1040-G20a. Similar to W-MA-2790-010-G100. 18__. 1850s.

Rarity: —

$10 • W-MA-2790-010-G100b

Overprint: Red. ***Engraver:*** New England Bank Note Co. / ABNCo. monogram. ***Comments:*** H-MA-1040-G20b. Similar to W-MA-2790-010-G100 but with different date and additional engraver imprint. Jan. 1, 186_. 1860s.

Rarity: —

$20 • W-MA-2790-020-G110

Left: Steamboat / XX / Train. ***Center:*** Three women seated with eagle, pole and cap, shield, scales, and book / 20 / Panel outlining white TWENTY. ***Right:*** XX / Milkmaid standing with pail. ***Engraver:*** New England Bank Note Co. ***Comments:*** H-MA-1040-G22. 18__. 1830s.

Rarity: —

$20 • W-MA-2790-020-G120

Left: 20 / Portrait of John Adams / TWENTY. ***Center:*** Scene in Quincy. ***Right:*** 20 / Portrait of John Hancock / TWENTY. ***Engraver:*** New England Bank Note Co. ***Comments:*** H-MA-1040-G24. 18__. 1840s–1850s.

Rarity: —

$20 • W-MA-2790-020-G120a

Overprint: Red. ***Engraver:*** New England Bank Note Co. ***Comments:*** H-MA-1040-G24a. Similar to W-MA-2790-020-G120. 18__. 1850s.

Rarity: —

$20 • W-MA-2790-020-G120b

Overprint: Red. ***Engraver:*** New England Bank Note Co. / ABNCo. monogram. ***Comments:*** H-MA-1040-G24b. Similar to W-MA-2790-020-G120 but with different date and additional engraver imprint. Jan. 1, 186_. 1860s.

Rarity: —

$50 • W-MA-2790-050-G130

Engraver: Unverified, but likely New England Bank Note Co. ***Comments:*** H-MA-1040-G26. No description available. 18__. 1830s.

Rarity: *None known*

$50 • W-MA-2790-050-G140

Left: 50 / Woman standing with wreath and flowers / FIFTY. ***Center:*** 50 / Man restraining prancing horse / 50. ***Right:*** FIFTY / Woman standing with cornucopia / FIFTY. ***Engraver:*** New England Bank Note Co. ***Comments:*** H-MA-1040-G28. 18__. 1840s–1850s.

Rarity: —

$50 • W-MA-2790-050-G150

Left: Granite Quarry in Quincy / 50. ***Center:*** L. ***Right:*** 50 / Male portrait. ***Tint:*** Green. ***Engraver:*** American Bank Note Co. ***Comments:*** H-MA-1040-G30. 1860s.

Rarity: —

$100 • W-MA-2790-100-G160

Left: ONE HUNDRED on 100 / Portrait of William Henry Harrison. ***Center:*** Wharf scene, Men loading wagon with barrels. ***Right:*** ONE HUNDRED on 100 / Portrait of Christopher Columbus. ***Engraver:*** New England Bank Note Co. ***Comments:*** H-MA-1040-G32. 18__. 1840s–1850s.

Rarity: —

$100 • W-MA-2790-100-G170

Left: 100 / Eagle / 100. ***Center:*** C / Horses, Man with hand truck / 100. ***Right:*** C / Portrait of George Washington / C. ***Engraver:*** New England Bank Note Co. ***Comments:*** H-MA-1040-G34. 18__. 1850s.

Rarity: —

$100 • W-MA-2790-100-G180

Left: C / State arms. ***Center:*** Benjamin Franklin seated in study. ***Right:*** 100 / Female portrait. ***Tint:*** Green C C. ***Engraver:*** American Bank Note Co. ***Comments:*** H-MA-1040-G36. 1860s.

Rarity: —

$500 • W-MA-2790-500-G190

Left: Indian paddling canoe, Forest and mountains / 500 / D D / 500. ***Right:*** 500 / Justice. ***Engraver:*** New England Bank Note Co. ***Comments:*** H-MA-1040-G38. 18__. 1840s–1850s.

Rarity: —

$500 • W-MA-2790-500-G200

Left: 500 / D. ***Center:*** Eagle. ***Right:*** 500 / D. ***Engraver:*** American Bank Note Co. ***Comments:*** H-MA-1040-G40. 1860s.

Rarity: —

Selected auction price: Stack's Bowers Galleries, 2013, Lot 24317, Unc $18,800

$1,000 • W-MA-2790-1000-G210

Left: Eagle on cliff, Ship / 1000 / M / 1000. ***Right:*** 1000 / Indian woman with bow and arrows. ***Engraver:*** New England Bank Note Co. ***Comments:*** H-MA-1040-G44. 18__. 1850s.

Rarity: —

NON-VALID ISSUES

$1 • W-MA-2790-001-A010

Left: 1 / Woman standing / ONE. ***Center:*** Woman holding rake, Buildings. ***Right:*** 1 / Ship / ONE. ***Engraver:*** New England Bank Note Co. ***Comments:*** H-MA-1040-A5. Altered from $1 Washington County Bank, Calais, Maine, or from notes of other failed banks using the same plate. 18__. 1830s.

Rarity: —

$3 • W-MA-2790-003-N010

Center: Woman, sailor, and eagle. ***Comments:*** H-MA-1040-N5.

Rarity: —

$5 • W-MA-2790-005-R010

Engraver: New England Bank Note Co. ***Comments:*** H-MA-1040-R5. Raised from W-MA-2790-001-G020. 18__. 1850s.

Rarity: —

$5 • W-MA-2790-005-R010a

CC

Overprint: Red FIVE. ***Engraver:*** New England Bank Note Co. / ABNCo. monogram. ***Comments:*** H-MA-1040-R5b. Raised from W-MA-2790-001-G020b. Jany. 1, 186_. 1860s.

Rarity: URS-6
VG $50; **F** $100; **VF** $150

$5 • W-MA-2790-005-A020

Left: FIVE / Portrait of Benjamin Franklin / V. ***Center:*** 5 / Two allegorical women standing and one seated, Agricultural items and ship. ***Bottom center:*** Anchor and implements. ***Right:*** V / Portrait of Marquis de Lafayette / FIVE. ***Engraver:*** Terry, Pelton & Co. ***Comments:*** H-MA-1040-A10. Altered from $5 Citizens Bank, Augusta, Maine, or from notes of other failed banks using the same plate. 18__. 1840s.

Rarity: —

$10 • W-MA-2790-010-A030

CC

Engraver: Terry, Pelton & Co. ***Comments:*** H-MA-1040-A15. 18__. 1840s.

Rarity: URS-6
VG $50; **F** $100; **VF** $150

$20 • W-MA-2790-020-R020

Engraver: New England Bank Note Co. ***Comments:*** H-MA-1040-R10. Raised from W-MA-2790-002-G040. 18__. 1840s

Rarity: —

$50 • W-MA-2790-050-R030

Engraver: New England Bank Note Co. ***Comments:*** H-MA-1040-R15. Raised from a note of unknown denomination. 18__. 1840s.

Rarity: —

Randolph, Massachusetts

Randolph was incorporated in 1793 on land divided from the southern portion of Braintree. The name is assumed to have come from Peyton Randolph, the first president of the Continental Congress. A need for income during the winter months spawned the cottage industry of sewing shoes in the home. As a result, year-round factories in the trade developed, specializing in boots.

Randolph Bank

1836–1864

W-MA-2800

History: The Randolph Bank was incorporated in 1836 with an authorized capital of $150,000. Seth Mann, Royal Turner, and Jonathan Wales were the founders. Circulation was $21,078 in 1839 and $88,908 in 1857. Specie was $14,078.15 also in 1857.

In 1854 this was published:

> We copied yesterday from a contemporary, a statement that one of our city banks had loaned from fifteen to eighteen millions of dollars during the last five years, and had lost but $191.22. We have now another illustration of the safety of business paper, and of prudent management on the part of the officers of a bank. The Randolph Bank, with a capital of $150,000, has loaned during the past seven years, between six and seven millions of dollars, *and has not lost a dollar during the whole period!* Royal Turner is President of this bank, and Seth Turner, Cashier.[34]

The business of the Randolph Bank was succeeded by the Randolph National Bank after it was chartered on October 29, 1864.

Numismatic Commentary: Notes from this well-run bank are very hard to locate, as most were redeemed after conversion to national bank status.

Valid Issues

$1 • W-MA-2800-001-G010

CJF

Engraver: New England Bank Note Co. ***Comments:*** H-MA-1045-G2. 18__. 1830s–1850s.

Rarity: URS-3
VG $300; **VF** $750

$1 • W-MA-2800-001-G010a

JF

Overprint: Red ONE. ***Engraver:*** New England Bank Note Co. / ABNCo. monogram. ***Comments:*** H-Unlisted. Similar to W-MA-2800-001-G010 but with additional engraver imprint. 18__. 1860s.

Rarity: URS-2
VG $600; **VF** $1,000

$2 • W-MA-2800-002-G020

TD

Engraver: New England Bank Note Co. ***Comments:*** H-MA-1045-G4. 18__. 1830s–1850s.

Rarity: URS-2
VG $750; **VF** $1,250

$3 • W-MA-2800-003-G030

Left: THREE / Portrait of Thomas Jefferson / 3. ***Center:*** THREE / Eagle standing on globe / THREE. ***Bottom center:*** Reaping scene. ***Right:*** 3 / George Washington standing by horse / THREE. ***Engraver:*** New England Bank Note Co. ***Comments:*** H-MA-1045-G6. 18__. 1830s–1850s.

Rarity: —

$5 • W-MA-2800-005-G040

Left: 5 / Woman kneeling on ground under trees. ***Center:*** Three women seated with pole and cap, Shield and book, Eagle, Ship / V. ***Bottom center:*** Dog and strongbox. ***Right:*** 5 / Boots and shoes / FIVE. ***Engraver:*** New England Bank Note Co. ***Comments:*** H-MA-1045-G8. 18__. 1830s–1850s.

Rarity: —

$10 • W-MA-2800-010-G050

Left: 10 / Woman pouring water from pitcher. ***Center:*** 10 / Blacksmith shoeing horse held by man / X. ***Bottom center:*** Sheaves. ***Right:*** 10 / Boots and shoes. ***Engraver:*** New England Bank Note Co. ***Comments:*** H-MA-1045-G10. 18__. 1830s–1850s.

Rarity: —

$20 • W-MA-2800-020-G060

Left: Steamboat / XX / Train. ***Center:*** Three women seated with eagle, pole and cap, shield, scales, and book / 20 / Panel outlining white TWENTY. ***Right:*** XX / Milkmaid standing with pail. ***Engraver:*** New England Bank Note Co. ***Comments:*** H-MA-1045-G12. 18__. 1830s.

Rarity: —

$20 • W-MA-2800-020-G070

Left: 20 / Minerva standing with spear. ***Center:*** Woman seated between 2 and 0. ***Right:*** 20 / Woman reclining on cornucopia / 20. ***Engraver:*** Rawdon, Wright, Hatch & Edson. ***Comments:*** H-MA-1045-G14. 18__. 1840s–1850s.

Rarity: —

$20 • W-MA-2800-020-G080

Left: Liberty standing with flag and shield, Indian woman seated ***Center:*** 20 / Two shoemakers at work, Woman. ***Right:*** 20 / Cattle and telegraph poles, Train on bridge. ***Engraver:*** American Bank Note Co. ***Comments:*** H-MA-1045-G16. 1860s.

Rarity: —

$50 • W-MA-2800-050-G090

Left: 50 / Steamboat and schooner. ***Center:*** Farmyard scene, Load of hay with two men on it, Man with rake and pail. ***Right:*** L / Justice kneeling. ***Engraver:*** New England Bank Note Co. ***Comments:*** H-MA-1045-G18. 18__. 1830s–1840s.

Rarity: —

$50 • W-MA-2800-050-G100

Left: 50 / Minerva standing by column. ***Center:*** Ceres and Vulcan flanking cornucopia / FIFTY. ***Right:*** 50 / Cherub in sailboat / 50. ***Engraver:*** Rawdon, Wright, Hatch & Edson. ***Comments:*** H-MA-1045-G20. 18__. 1850s.

Rarity: —

$50 • W-MA-2800-050-G110

Left: FIFTY / Ceres / 50. ***Center:*** 50 / Farmer seated with farm tools and products, Hay wagon and buildings / 50. ***Right:*** 50 / Female portrait. ***Engraver:*** American Bank Note Co. ***Comments:*** H-MA-1045-G22. 1860s.

Rarity: —

$100 • W-MA-2800-100-G120

Left: Lathework panel bearing C / Portrait of George Washington / C. ***Center:*** 100 / Manhattan reclining, pouring water, Ship / 100. ***Right:*** Lathework panel bearing ONE HUNDRED vertically. ***Engraver:*** New England Bank Note Co. / PSSP. ***Comments:*** H-MA-1045-G24. 18__. 1830s–1840s.

Rarity: —

$100 • W-MA-2800-100-G130

Left: 100 / Vulcan seated with sledge and anchor. ***Center:*** Train on bridge, Eagle on limb, Canal locks / C. ***Bottom center:*** 100. ***Right:*** 100 / Ceres seated, Cornucopia. ***Engraver:*** Rawdon, Wright, Hatch & Edson. ***Comments:*** H-MA-1045-G26. 18__. 1850s.

Rarity: —

$100 • W-MA-2800-100-G140

Left: 100 / Female portrait. ***Center:*** Two women seated, Steamship, Buildings and monument. ***Right:*** 100 / Train on bridge. ***Engraver:*** American Bank Note Co. ***Comments:*** H-MA-1045-G28. 1860s.

Rarity: —

$500 • W-MA-2800-500-G150

Left: 500 / 500 / 500. ***Center:*** 500 / Woman seated with shield bearing D, Fasces, cornucopia, lyre, and sheaf / 500. ***Right:*** 500 / D / 500. ***Engraver:*** PSSP / New England Bank Note Co. ***Comments:*** H-MA-1045-G30. 18__. 1830s–1840s.

Rarity: —

$500 • W-MA-2800-500-G160

Left: Woman seated on sheaves, Men reaping, Man on horse. ***Center:*** 500 / D. ***Right:*** 500 vertically. ***Engraver:*** Rawdon, Wright, Hatch & Edson. ***Comments:*** H-MA-1045-G32. 18__. 1850s–1860s.

Rarity: —

Non-Valid Issues

$1 • W-MA-2800-001-A010

SI

Engraver: Underwood, Bald, Spencer & Hufty. ***Comments:*** H-MA-1045-A5. Altered from $1 Bank of Superior, Superior, Michigan. 18__. 1840s.

Rarity: URS-6
F $75

$2 • W-MA-2800-002-A020

Left: 2 / Liberty standing. ***Center:*** 2 on medallion head / Ceres, Indian woman, and sailor / 2 on medallion head. ***Right:*** 2 / Minerva standing. ***Engraver:*** Underwood, Bald, Spencer & Hufty. ***Comments:*** H-MA-1045-A10. Altered from $2 Bank of Superior, Superior, Michigan. 18__. 1840s.

Rarity: —

$3 • W-MA-2800-003-A030

Left: 3 / Hunter with gun / 3. ***Center:*** 3 / Indian man seated on cliff / 3. ***Bottom center:*** Stag. ***Right:*** 3 / Man standing with gun and dog / 3. ***Engraver:*** Underwood, Bald, Spencer & Hufty. ***Comments:*** H-MA-1045-A15. Altered from $3 Bank of Superior, Superior, Michigan. 18__. 1840s.

Rarity: —

$5 • W-MA-2800-005-A040

Left: FIVE / Roman senator seated with scroll / 5. ***Center:*** FIVE on helmeted medallion head / Woman seated holding infant, Sheaf / FIVE on helmeted medallion head. ***Bottom center:*** Train. ***Right:*** FIVE / Woman seated with closed book / 5. ***Engraver:*** Danforth, Underwood & Co. / Underwood, Bald, Spencer & Hufty. ***Comments:*** H-MA-1045-A20. Altered from $5 Tenth Ward Bank, New York City, New York. 18__. 1840s.

Rarity: —

$10 • W-MA-2800-010-A050

TD

Engraver: Danforth, Underwood & Co. / Underwood, Bald, Spencer & Hufty. ***Comments:*** H-MA-1045-A25. Altered from $10 Tenth Ward Bank, New York City, New York. 18__. 1840s.

Rarity: URS-5

F $100; **VF** $150

$20 • W-MA-2800-020-A060

Left: 20 / Train / XX. ***Center:*** Diagonal 20 on medallion head / Pat Lyon standing by Forge / Diagonal 20 on medallion head. ***Right:*** 20 / Cattle, Man / XX. ***Engraver:*** Danforth, Underwood & Co. / Underwood, Bald, Spencer & Hufty. ***Comments:*** H-MA-1045-A30. 18__. 1840s.

Rarity: —

Rockport, Massachusetts

An undeveloped part of Gloucester comprised the land that made up Rockport, which was established in 1840. In the early days, the uninhabited area was a source of pine timber for shipbuilding. In 1743 a dock was built in the fertile fishing grounds of Rockport Harbor, and granite quarries were formed in the early 19th century. The stone found a ready market along the East Coast.

Rockport Bank

1850–1865

W-MA-2810

History: The Rockport Bank was incorporated on April 6, 1850, with an authorized capital of $100,000, an amount that increased to $150,000 in 1857. The circulation of the bank was $82,678 in 1857 and $86,455 in 1863.

The business of the Rockport Bank was succeeded by the Rockport National Bank after it was chartered in 1865.

Numismatic Commentary: Genuine notes from this bank, located at one of the country's tiniest seaports, are extremely hard to locate. At least one issue shows an engraving of granite quarrying that took place in the vicinity.

Valid Issues

$1 • W-MA-2810-001-G010

CJF

Engraver: New England Bank Note Co. ***Comments:*** H-MA-1050-G2. 18__. 1850s.

Rarity: URS-3

VF $1,500

$1 • W-MA-2810-001-G020

HA

Overprint: Red ONE. ***Engraver:*** Rawdon, Wright, Hatch & Edson / New England Bank Note Co. ***Comments:*** H-MA-1050-G4. 18__. 1850s.

Rarity: URS-2

VF $2,500

$2 • W-MA-2810-002-G030

Left: TWO / 2. ***Center:*** Eagle on bale, Cannonballs and machinery / 2. ***Right:*** 2 / TWO / Schooner. ***Engraver:*** New England Bank Note Co. ***Comments:*** H-MA-1050-G6. 18__. 1850s.

Rarity: —

$2 • W-MA-2810-002-G040

Left: Sailor with capstan, Masts, barrels, and bales / 2. ***Center:*** View of stone quarry, Oxen, wagon, men. ***Bottom center:*** Men loading wagon. ***Right:*** 2 / Two women. ***Overprint:*** Red TWO. ***Engraver:*** Rawdon, Wright, Hatch & Edson / New England Bank Note Co. ***Comments:*** H-MA-1050-G8. 18__. 1850s.

Rarity: —

$3 • W-MA-2810-003-G050

Left: THREE / 3. ***Center:*** Sailor standing with hat, Bales and harbor / 3. ***Right:*** 3 / THREE / Train. ***Engraver:*** New England Bank Note Co. ***Comments:*** H-MA-1050-G10. 18__. 1850s.

Rarity: —

$3 • W-MA-2810-003-G060

Left: THREE / Old man with cane. ***Center:*** View of stone quarry, Oxen, wagon, men. ***Bottom center:*** Eagle. ***Right:*** 3 / Two women, one standing with rake, one pitching hay. ***Overprint:*** Red. ***Engraver:*** Rawdon, Wright, Hatch & Edson / New England Bank Note Co. ***Comments:*** H-MA-1050-G12. 18__. 1850s.

Rarity: —

$5 • W-MA-2810-005-G070

Left: Eagle on shield and anchor, Factories and ships / FIVE. ***Center:*** V with woman, cornucopia, and cherub. ***Right:*** 5 / Girl with ringlets holding basket. ***Overprint:*** Red FIVE. ***Engraver:*** New England Bank Note Co. ***Comments:*** H-MA-1050-G14a. 18__. 1850s.

Rarity: —

$5 • W-MA-2810-005-G080

Left: Farmer with grain cradle / 5. ***Center:*** View of stone quarry Oxen, wagon, men. ***Right:*** 5 / Woman. ***Overprint:*** Red. ***Engraver:*** Rawdon, Wright, Hatch & Edson / New England Bank Note Co. ***Comments:*** H-MA-1050-G16. 18__. 1850s.

Rarity: —

$10 • W-MA-2810-010-G090

Left: Mechanic seated with tools, Train and building / TEN. ***Center:*** X. ***Right:*** 10 / Reaper standing with sheaf and stone. ***Overprint:*** Red TEN. ***Engraver:*** New England Bank Note Co. ***Comments:*** H-MA-1050-G18a. 18__. 1850s.

Rarity: —

$10 • W-MA-2810-010-G100

Left: Soldier with sword / TEN. ***Center:*** View of stone quarry, Oxen, wagon, men. ***Right:*** 10 / Female portrait. ***Overprint:*** Red. ***Engraver:*** Rawdon, Wright, Hatch & Edson / New England Bank Note Co. ***Comments:*** H-MA-1050-G20. 18__. 1850s.

Rarity: —

$20 • W-MA-2810-020-G110

Left: 20 / Woman seated with book on lap, opening chest. ***Center:*** XX / Eagle on rock / XX. ***Right:*** 20 / Ship in harbor. ***Engraver:*** New England Bank Note Co. ***Comments:*** H-MA-1050-G22. 18__. 1850s.

Rarity: —

$20 • W-MA-2810-020-G120

Left: Female portrait / XX. ***Center:*** View of stone quarry, Oxen, wagon, men. ***Bottom center:*** Cow and calf. ***Right:*** 20 / Male portrait. ***Overprint:*** Red. ***Engraver:*** Rawdon, Wright, Hatch & Edson / New England Bank Note Co. ***Comments:*** H-MA-1050-G24. 18__. 1850s.

Rarity: —

$50 • W-MA-2810-050-G130

Left: FIFTY / Woman standing with wreath and flowers / FIFTY. ***Center:*** 50 / Man restraining prancing horse / 50. ***Right:*** FIFTY / Woman standing with cornucopia / FIFTY. ***Engraver:*** New England Bank Note Co. ***Comments:*** H-MA-1050-G26. 18__. 1850s.

Rarity: —

$50 • W-MA-2810-050-G140

Left: Portrait of Benjamin Franklin / 50. ***Center:*** View of stone quarry, Oxen, wagons, men. ***Bottom center:*** Shield bearing sunrise. ***Right:*** 50 / Male portrait. ***Engraver:*** Rawdon, Wright, Hatch & Edson / New England Bank Note Co. ***Comments:*** H-MA-1050-G28. 18__. 1850s.

Rarity: —

$100 • W-MA-2810-100-G150

Left: ONE HUNDRED on 100 / Portrait of William Henry Harrison. ***Center:*** Wharf scene, Men loading wagon with barrels. ***Right:*** ONE HUNDRED on 100 / Portrait of Christopher Columbus. ***Engraver:*** New England Bank Note Co. ***Comments:*** H-MA-1050-G30. 18__. 1850s.

Rarity: —

$100 • W-MA-2810-100-G160

Left: Male portrait / 100. ***Center:*** View of stone quarry, Oxen, wagon, men. ***Bottom center:*** Dog's head. ***Right:*** 100 / Portrait of Daniel Webster. ***Engraver:*** Rawdon, Wright, Hatch & Edson / New England Bank Note Co. ***Comments:*** H-MA-1050-G32. 18__. 1850s.

Rarity: —

Non-Valid Issues

$2 • W-MA-2810-002-A010

Left: Two girls carrying sheaves / 2. ***Center:*** Sailor and mechanic flanking U.S. shield surmounted by badger. ***Right:*** 2 / Liberty standing, Indian woman kneeling. ***Overprint:*** Red TWO. ***Engraver:*** New England Bank Note Co. / Rawdon, Wright, Hatch & Edson. ***Comments:*** H-MA-1050-A5. Altered from $2 Waubeek Bank, De Soto, Nebraska.

Rarity: —

$5 • W-MA-2810-005-S010

Center: Mercury on wharf, Shipping. ***Comments:*** H-MA-1050-S5.

Rarity: —

$5 • W-MA-2810-005-S020

Left: Portrait of Benjamin Franklin. ***Center:*** Canal scene, Woman and man under tree, Man holding two horses. ***Right:*** Liberty leaning on 5. ***Comments:*** H-MA-1050-S10.

Rarity: —

$5 • W-MA-2810-005-A020

Left: Several men with sticks driving herd of cattle into stream / 5. ***Center:*** Five men raking and loading hay, Ox wagon. ***Right:*** 5. ***Tint:*** Red-brown lathework outlining white 5. ***Engraver:*** Bald, Cousland & Co. ***Comments:*** H-MA-1050-A10. Altered from $5 Pioneer Association, Lafayette, Indiana. 1850s.

Rarity: —

$5 • W-MA-2810-005-A030

Left: 5 / FIVE / FIVE. ***Center:*** Indian woman and frontiersman flanking five silver dollars, Three cherubs. ***Bottom center:*** Steamboat. ***Right:*** 5 / Female portrait / FIVE. ***Overprint:*** FIVE. ***Engraver:*** Rawdon, Wright, Hatch & Edson. ***Comments:*** H-MA-1050-A15. Altered from $5 Farmers and Merchants Bank of Memphis, Memphis, Tennessee series. 1850s.

Rarity: —

Rowley, Massachusetts

Incorporated on September 4, 1639, Rowley included towns that later split away to become Byfield, Haverhill, Bradford, Groveland, Georgetown, and a section of Boxford. It was named after a parish in York, England, the hometown of Rowley's first minister. Blacksmithing, butchering, and clam harvesting were important industries. There was also a fulling mill, a grist mill, and the production of hemp, flax cloth, and cotton.

Manufacturers Bank

1836–1855

W-MA-2820

History: On April 1, 1836, the Manufacturers Bank was chartered with an authorized capital of $100,000. In 1845 the Legislature passed an act that stated, in part, "The Manufacturers Bank, heretofore in Rowley, but to be called now in Georgetown, shall heareafter be known by the name of the Manufacturers Bank in Georgetown."[35] From then on the bank was located in Georgetown, W-MA-1700.

See also listing under Georgetown, W-MA-1700.

Numismatic Commentary: Genuine notes dated at Rowley are extremely hard to find. Only slightly less so are the issues dated at Georgetown.

VALID ISSUES

$1 • W-MA-2820-001-G010

Engraver: Unverified, but likely New England Bank Note Co. ***Comments:*** H-MA-1055-G4. No description available. 18__. 1830s.

Rarity: *None known*

$2 • W-MA-2820-002-G020

Engraver: Unverified, but likely New England Bank Note Co. ***Comments:*** H-MA-1055-G8. No description available. 18__. 1830s.

Rarity: *None known*

$3 • W-MA-2820-003-G030

Engraver: Unverified, but likely New England Bank Note Co. ***Comments:*** H-MA-1055-G12. No description available. 18__. 1830s.

Rarity: *None known*

$5 • W-MA-2820-005-G040

Engraver: Unverified, but likely New England Bank Note Co. ***Comments:*** H-MA-1055-G16. No description available. 18__. 1830s.

Rarity: *None known*

$10 • W-MA-2820-010-G050

Engraver: Unverified, but likely New England Bank Note Co. ***Comments:*** H-MA-1055-G20. No description available. 18__. 1830s.

Rarity: *None known*

$20 • W-MA-2820-020-G060

Engraver: Unverified, but likely New England Bank Note Co. ***Comments:*** H-MA-1055-G24. No description available. 18__. 1830s.

Rarity: *None known*

$50 • W-MA-2820-050-G070

Engraver: Unverified, but likely New England Bank Note Co. ***Comments:*** H-MA-1055-G28. No description available. 18__. 1830s.

Rarity: *None known*

$100 • W-MA-2820-100-G080

Engraver: Unverified, but likely New England Bank Note Co. ***Comments:*** H-MA-1055-G32. No description available. 18__. 1830s.

Rarity: *None known*

NON-VALID ISSUES

$1 • W-MA-2820-001-A010 SI

Engraver: New England Bank Note Co. / PSSP. ***Comments:*** H-MA-1055-A5. 18__. 1840s.

Rarity: URS-6

VG $50; **VF** $100

$2 • W-MA-2820-002-A020 CJF

Engraver: New England Bank Note Co. / PSSP. ***Comments:*** H-MA-1055-A10. 18__. 1840s.

Rarity: URS-4

VG $75; **VF** $125

ROXBURY, MASSACHUSETTS

Roxbury was settled by English colonists in 1630. It was linked to Boston by a spit of land and became a city in 1846. It was annexed by Boston in 1868.

Roxbury originally included towns and areas that were later known as Jamaica Plain, Roslindale, West Roxbury, South End, and most of Back Bay. W. Elliot Woodward, America's most accomplished numismatic auction cataloger from 1860 through the 1880s, conducted his business in Roxbury.

Bank of Norfolk

1826–1838

W-MA-2830

History: The Norfolk Bank was incorporated on March 4, 1826, with an authorized capital of $200,000. The bank opened for business on May 15. The City Bank announced that it would also receive and pay out the bank's bills. In 1827 the bank advertised that notes bearing interest could be obtained from the cashier.

In January 1838, the Legislature appointed a committee to examine the affairs of the bank. The findings were unsatisfactory, and the charter of the bank was repealed, after which the bank closed. Its notes continued to be redeemed for a time. Circulation in 1841 was reported as $18,638, and by February 1842, it had dropped to $6,601.

Numismatic Commentary: Genuine notes from this bank are very hard to locate. However, with some luck a collector may come across a nice example with a Congreve Check Plate back.

Valid Issues

$1 • W-MA-2830-001-G010

Left: Narrow panel of lathework circle segments. ***Center:*** 1 / 1 / Flower garlands and gridwork segments / 1 / 1. ***Right:*** Narrow panel of lathework circle segments. ***Engraver:*** PSSP. ***Comments:*** H-MA-1060-G2. 18__. 1820s–1830s.

Rarity: —

$1 • W-MA-2830-001-G010a

Left: ONE / D / ONE vertically. ***Right:*** ONE / D / ONE vertically. ***Engraver:*** PSSP. ***Comments:*** H-MA-1060-G4. Similar to W-MA-2830-001-G010. 18__. 1830s.

Rarity: —

$1 • W-MA-2830-001-G020

Left: 1 / Minerva standing with 1 / 1. ***Center:*** ONE / Commerce seated with caduceus and cornucopia, Plow and ships / ONE. ***Right:*** 1 / Eagle / 1. ***Engraver:*** PSSP. ***Comments:*** H-MA-1060-G6. 18__. 1830s.

Rarity: —

$1 • W-MA-2830-001-G030

CC

Engraver: New England Bank Note Co. ***Comments:*** H-MA-1060-G8. 18__. 1830s.

Rarity: URS-6
F $200; **VF** $350

$2 • W-MA-2830-002-G040

Left: Narrow panel of lathework circle segments. ***Center:*** 2 / 2 / Flower garlands and gridwork segments / 2 / 2. ***Right:*** Narrow panel of lathework circle segments. ***Engraver:*** PSSP. ***Comments:*** H-MA-1060-G10. 18__. 1820s–1830s.

Rarity: —

$2 • W-MA-2830-002-G040a

Left: Five TWOs vertically. ***Right:*** Five TWOs vertically. ***Engraver:*** PSSP. ***Comments:*** H-MA-1060-G12. Similar to W-MA-2830-002-G040. 18__. 1830s.

Rarity: —

$2 • W-MA-2830-002-G050

Left: 2 / Hebe watering eagle / 2. ***Center:*** 2 / Plow, Commerce seated with caduceus and cornucopia, Ships / 2. ***Right:*** 2 / Justice standing / 2. ***Engraver:*** PSSP. ***Comments:*** H-MA-1060-G14. 18__. 1830s.

Rarity: —

$2 • W-MA-2830-002-G060

CJF

Engraver: New England Bank Note Co. ***Comments:*** H-MA-1060-G16. 18__. 1830s.

Rarity: URS-5
F $250; **VF** $400

$3 • W-MA-2830-003-G070

Left: 3 / Eagle on rock / 3. ***Center:*** 3 / Plow / Commerce seated with caduceus and cornucopia / Ships. ***Right:*** 3 / Woman standing with cornucopia / 3. ***Engraver:*** PSSP. ***Comments:*** H-MA-1060-G22. 18__. 1830s.

Rarity: —

$3 • W-MA-2830-003-G080

CJF

Engraver: New England Bank Note Co. ***Comments:*** H-MA-1060-G24. 18__. 1830s.

Rarity: URS-2
F $400; **VF** $750

$3 • W-MA-2830-003-G090

Left: Narrow panel of lathework circle segments. ***Center:*** 3 / 3 / Flower garlands and gridwork segments / 3 / 3. ***Right:*** Narrow panel of lathework circle segments. ***Engraver:*** PSSP. ***Comments:*** H-MA-1060-G26. 18__. 1820s–1830s.

Rarity: —

$3 • W-MA-2830-003-G090a

Left: THREE vertically. ***Right:*** THREE vertically. ***Engraver:*** PSSP. ***Comments:*** H-MA-1060-G28. Similar to W-MA-2830-003-G090. 18__. 1830s.

Rarity: —

$5 • W-MA-2830-005-G100

Left: Lathework chain bearing MASSACHUSETTS / 5 / 5. ***Center:*** Alternating flower garlands and gridwork segments. ***Right:*** 5 / 5. ***Engraver:*** PSSP. ***Comments:*** H-MA-1060-G30. 18__. 1820s.

Rarity: —

$5 • W-MA-2830-005-G100a

Engraver: PSSP. ***Comments:*** H-MA-1060-G32. Similar to W-MA-2830-005-G100 but with zigzag ruled lines. 18__. 1820s–1830s.

Rarity: —

$5 • W-MA-2830-005-G100b

Engraver: PSSP. ***Comments:*** H-MA-1060-G34. Similar to W-MA-2830-005-G100 but with spiral lathework lines. 18__. 1830s.

Rarity: —

$5 • W-MA-2830-005-G110

Back: Plain. ***Engraver:*** New England Bank Note Co. ***Comments:*** H-MA-1060-G36. 18__. 1830s.

Rarity: —

$5 • W-MA-2830-005-G110a

Back: Red and brown Congreve Check Plate. ***Engraver:*** New England Bank Note Co. ***Comments:*** H-MA-1060-G36a. Similar to W-MA-2830-005-G110. 18__. 1830s.

Rarity: —

$10 • W-MA-2830-010-G120

Left: Lathework chain bearing MASSACHUSETTS / 10 / 10 vertically. ***Center:*** Alternating flower garlands and gridwork segments. ***Right:*** 10 / 10 vertically. ***Engraver:*** Perkins. ***Comments:*** H-MA-1060-G38. 18__. 1820s.

Rarity: —

$10 • W-MA-2830-010-G120a

Engraver: PSSP. ***Comments:*** H-MA-1060-G40. Similar to W-MA-2830-010-G120 but with zigzag ruled lines. 18__. 1820s–1830s.

Rarity: —

$10 • W-MA-2830-010-G120b

Engraver: PSSP. ***Comments:*** H-MA-1060-G42. Similar to W-MA-2830-010-G120 but with spiral lathework lines. 18__. 1830s.

Rarity: —

$10 • W-MA-2830-010-G130

Left: TEN / Woman standing with staff / 10. ***Center:*** 10 / Man standing, Plow / 10. ***Bottom center:*** Dog and strongbox. ***Right:*** 10 / Woman standing / TEN. ***Back:*** Plain. ***Engraver:*** New England Bank Note Co. ***Comments:*** H-MA-1060-G44. 18__. 1830s.

Rarity: —

$10 • W-MA-2830-010-G130a

Back: Red and brown Congreve Check Plate. ***Engraver:*** New England Bank Note Co. ***Comments:*** H-MA-1060-G44a. Similar to W-MA-2830-010-G130. 18__. 1830s.

Rarity: —

$20 • W-MA-2830-020-G140

Left: Lathework chain bearing MASSACHUSETTS / 20 / 20 vertically. ***Center:*** Alternating flower garlands and gridwork segments. ***Right:*** 20 / 20 vertically. ***Engraver:*** PSSP. ***Comments:*** H-MA-1060-G46. 18__. 1820s–1830s.

Rarity: —

$20 • W-MA-2830-020-G150

CC

Back: Plain. ***Engraver:*** New England Bank Note Co. ***Comments:*** H-MA-1060-G48. 18__. 1830s.

Rarity: URS-4
F $300; **VF** $500

$20 • W-MA-2830-020-G150a

Left: Die / Portrait of George Washington / Die. ***Center:*** XX / Three cows and two sheep. ***Right:*** Die / Portrait of Benjamin Franklin / Die. ***Back:*** Red and brown Congreve Check Plate. ***Engraver:*** New England Bank Note Co. ***Comments:*** H-MA-1060-G48a. Similar to W-MA-2830-020-G150. 18__. 1830s.

Rarity: —

$50 • W-MA-2830-050-G160

Left: Lathework chain bearing MASSACHUSETTS / 50 / 50 vertically. ***Center:*** Alternating flower garlands and gridwork segments. ***Right:*** 50 / 50 vertically. ***Engraver:*** PSSP. ***Comments:*** H-MA-1060-G50. 18__. 1820s–1830s.

Rarity: —

$100 • W-MA-2830-100-G170

Left: Lathework chain bearing MASSACHUSETTS / 100 / 100 vertically. ***Center:*** Alternating flower garlands and gridwork segments. ***Right:*** 100 / 100 vertically. ***Engraver:*** Perkins. ***Comments:*** H-MA-1060-G52. 18__. 1820s–1830s.

Rarity: —

$100 • W-MA-2830-100-G180

Left: Lathework panel bearing C / Portrait of George Washington / C. ***Center:*** 100 / Woman seated with right arm on shield bearing C, Fasces, cornucopia, lyre, and sheaf / 100. ***Right:*** Lathework panel bearing ONE HUNDRED vertically. ***Engraver:*** PSSP. ***Comments:*** H-MA-1060-G54. 18__. 1830s.

Rarity: —

$500 • W-MA-2830-500-G190

Left: 500 / 500 vertically. ***Center:*** 500 / Woman seated with right arm on shield bearing D, fasces, cornucopia, lyre, and sheaf / 500. ***Right:*** 500 / D / 500. ***Engraver:*** PSSP. ***Comments:*** H-MA-1060-G56. 18__. 1830s.

Rarity: —

$1,000 • W-MA-2830-1000-G200

Left: THOUSAND vertically. ***Center:*** 1000 / Woman standing with legs crossed, Lyre, Cornucopia / 1000. ***Right:*** 1000 / M / 1000. ***Engraver:*** PSSP. ***Comments:*** H-MA-1060-G58. 18__. 1830s.

Rarity: —

Non-Valid Issues

$5 • W-MA-2830-005-C015

CC

Comments: H-Unlisted. Counterfeit from plate used for multiple banks. 18__. 1820s.

Rarity: URS-6
F $400

Peoples Bank

1833–1864

W-MA-2840

History: The Peoples Bank was chartered on March 25, 1833, with an authorized capital of $100,000, a figure that was later raised to $150,000 in 1847. Circulation was $54,570 in 1851; it reached a high of $119,010 in 1863. The bank's specie amounted to $48,061.36 in 1851. Real estate was valued at $2,500 in 1856 and at $3,772.68 in 1857.

The business of the Peoples Bank was succeeded by the Peoples National Bank of Roxbury when it was chartered in 1864.

Numismatic Commentary: Genuine issues are quite hard to locate. Non-valid issues are, however, abundant in the marketplace.

VALID ISSUES

$1 • W-MA-2840-001-G010

Left: Lathework panel bearing MASSACHUSETTS vertically. ***Center:*** 1 / 1 / Alternating flower garlands and gridwork segments / ONE / 1 / 1. ***Right:*** Lathework panel bearing ONE / D / ONE vertically. ***Engraver:*** PSSP. ***Comments:*** H-MA-1065-G2. 18__. 1830s.

Rarity: —

$1 • W-MA-2840-001-G010a

CJF

Engraver: PSSP. ***Comments:*** H-MA-1065-G4. Similar to W-MA-2840-001-G010. 18__. 1830s.

Rarity: URS-6
F $75; **VF** $150

$1 • W-MA-2840-001-G020

Left: ONE / Two Indians reclining and smoking. ***Center:*** 1 / Three allegorical women with eagle, pole and cap, shield, scales, and book / 1. ***Bottom center:*** Cattle. ***Right:*** 1 / Portrait of George Washington / ONE. ***Engraver:*** Terry, Pelton & Co. ***Comments:*** H-MA-1065-G6. Beware of altered W-MA-2840-001-A010 from the same plate as the genuine. 18__. 1830s.

Rarity: —

$1 • W-MA-2840-001-G030

CJF

Engraver: New England Bank Note Co. ***Comments:*** H-MA-1065-G8. 18__. 1840s–1850s.

Rarity: URS-4
F $400; **VF** $600

$1 • W-MA-2840-001-G030a

Left: ONE / Woman standing with staff / ONE. ***Center:*** Farmer loading hay onto cart drawn by two oxen. ***Right:*** Justice standing in niche inside 1 / ONE / ONE vertically. ***Overprint:*** Likely red. ***Engraver:*** New England Bank Note Co. ***Comments:*** H-MA-1065-G8a. Similar to W-MA-2840-001-G030. 18__. 1850s.

Rarity: —

$1 • W-MA-2840-001-G030b

Overprint: Likely red. ***Engraver:*** New England Bank Note Co. / ABNCo. monogram. ***Comments:*** H-MA-1065-G8b. Similar to W-MA-2840-001-G030 but with additional engraver imprint. 1860s.

Rarity: —

$2 • W-MA-2840-002-G040

Left: Lathework panel bearing MASSACHUSETTS vertically. ***Center:*** 2 / 2 / Alternating flower garlands and gridwork segments / TWO / 2 / 2. ***Right:*** Lathework panel bearing five TWOs vertically. ***Engraver:*** PSSP. ***Comments:*** H-MA-1065-G10. 18__. 1830s.

Rarity: —

$2 • W-MA-2840-002-G040a

Left: Lathework panel bearing five TWOs vertically. ***Right:*** Lathework panel bearing five TWOs vertically. ***Engraver:*** PSSP. ***Comments:*** H-MA-1065-G12. Similar to W-MA-2840-002-G040. 18__. 1830s–1840s.

Rarity: —

$2 • W-MA-2840-002-G050

Left: TWO / Portrait of cherub / 2. ***Center:*** 2 / Ceres giving grain to seated Liberty / 2. ***Bottom center:*** Anchor and implements. ***Right:*** 2 / Female portrait / TWO. ***Engraver:*** Terry, Pelton & Co. ***Comments:*** H-MA-1065-G14. Beware of altered W-MA-2840-002-A040 from the same plate as the genuine. Impaired Proof. 18__. 1830s–1840s.

Rarity: —

$2 • W-MA-2840-002-G060

Left: TWO / Woman standing holding wreath. ***Center:*** Train. ***Right:*** TWO / Medallion head and 2. ***Engraver:*** New England Bank Note Co. ***Comments:*** H-MA-1065-G16. Beware of spurious W-MA-2840-002-S010 and S010a roughly similar to genuine. 18__. 1840s–1850s.

Rarity: —

$2 • W-MA-2840-002-G060a

Overprint: Likely red. ***Engraver:*** New England Bank Note Co. ***Comments:*** H-MA-1065-G16a. Similar to W-MA-2840-002-G060. 18__. 1850s.

Rarity: —

$2 • W-MA-2840-002-G060b

Overprint: Likely red. ***Engraver:*** New England Bank Note Co. / ABNCo. monogram. ***Comments:*** H-MA-1065-G16b. Similar to W-MA-2840-002-G060 but with additional engraver imprint. 1860s.

Rarity: —

$2 • W-MA-2840-002-G070 CC

Engraver: PSSP. ***Comments:*** H-Unlisted. 18__.

Rarity: URS-3

F $850

$3 • W-MA-2840-003-G080

Left: Lathework panel bearing MASSACHUSETTS vertically. ***Center:*** 3 / 3 / Alternating flower garlands and gridwork segments / THREE / 3 / 3. ***Right:*** Lathework panel bearing THREE vertically. ***Engraver:*** PSSP. ***Comments:*** H-MA-1065-G18. 18__. 1830s.

Rarity: —

$3 • W-MA-2840-003-G080a

Left: Lathework panel bearing THREE vertically. ***Right:*** Lathework panel bearing THREE vertically. ***Engraver:*** PSSP. ***Comments:*** H-MA-1065-G20. Similar to W-MA-2840-003-G080. 18__. 1830s–1840s.

Rarity: —

$3 • W-MA-2840-003-G090

Left: 3 / Woman seated with branch, trident, and THREE / THREE. ***Center:*** Female portrait / Ceres and Justice flanking shield bearing anchor and surmounted by eagle / Portrait of cherub. ***Bottom center:*** Anchor and implements. ***Right:*** 3 / Ceres seated in grain field / THREE. ***Engraver:*** Terry, Pelton & Co. ***Comments:*** H-MA-1065-G22. Beware of altered W-MA-2840-003-A050 from the same plate as the genuine. 18__. 1830s.

Rarity: —

$3 • W-MA-2840-003-G100

Left: 3 on THREE / Indian woman seated on rock / THREE. ***Center:*** Eagle on limb, Train and canal scene / 3. ***Right:*** 3 on THREE / George Washington standing by horse / THREE. ***Engraver:*** New England Bank Note Co. ***Comments:*** H-MA-1065-G24. 18__. 1840s–1850s.

Rarity: —

$3 • W-MA-2840-003-G100a

Overprint: Likely red. ***Engraver:*** New England Bank Note Co. ***Comments:*** H-MA-1065-G24a. Similar to W-MA-2840-003-G100. 18__. 1850s.

Rarity: —

$3 • W-MA-2840-003-G100b

Overprint: Likely red. ***Engraver:*** New England Bank Note Co. / ABNCo. monogram. ***Comments:*** H-MA-1065-G24b. Similar to W-MA-2840-003-G100 but with additional engraver imprint. 1860s.

Rarity: —

$3 • W-MA-2840-003-G110 CC

Engraver: PSSP. ***Comments:*** H-Unlisted. 18__.

Rarity: URS-3

VG $600

$5 • W-MA-2840-005-G120

Left: Panel bearing FIVE / Plenty and Minerva seated / V. ***Center:*** FIVE / Allegorical woman seated / FIVE / Panel of microletters. ***Right:*** 5 / Eagle / 5. ***Engraver:*** PSSP. ***Comments:*** H-MA-1065-G26. 18__. 1830s.

Rarity: —

$5 • W-MA-2840-005-G130

Engraver: Unverified, but likely PSSP. ***Comments:*** H-MA-1065-G28. No description available. 18__. 1830s.

Rarity: *None known*

$5 • W-MA-2840-005-G140

Left: FIVE / Portrait of Benjamin Franklin / V. ***Center:*** 5 in die / Three women standing / 5 in die. ***Right:*** V / Portrait of Marquis de Lafayette / FIVE. ***Engraver:*** Terry, Pelton & Co. ***Comments:*** H-MA-1065-G30. 18__. 1830s.

Rarity: —

$5 • W-MA-2840-005-G150

Left: 10 / Portrait of George Washington held by cherub / 10. ***Center:*** X / Spread eagle with shield and arrows, E PLURIBUS UNUM / X. ***Bottom center:*** Ship. ***Right:*** 10 / Seated woman with hand on shoulder of Indian / 10. ***Engraver:*** Terry, Pelton & Co. ***Comments:*** H-MA-1065-G32. 18__. 1830s.

Rarity: —

$5 • W-MA-2840-005-G160

Left: FIVE / Woman pouring water from pitcher into cup. ***Center:*** Eagle on rock, Steamship / V. ***Right:*** 5 / Male portrait. ***Engraver:*** New England Bank Note Co. ***Comments:*** H-MA-1065-G34. 18__. 1840s–1850s.

Rarity: —

$5 • W-MA-2840-005-G160a

Overprint: Likely red. ***Engraver:*** New England Bank Note Co. ***Comments:*** H-MA-1065-G34a. Similar to W-MA-2840-005-G160. 18__. 1850s.

Rarity: —

$5 • W-MA-2840-005-G160b

Overprint: Likely red. ***Engraver:*** New England Bank Note Co. / ABNCo. monogram. ***Comments:*** H-MA-1065-G34b. Similar to W-MA-2840-005-G160 but with additional engraver imprint. 1860s.

Rarity: —

$10 • W-MA-2840-010-G170

Left: Panel bearing TEN / Manhattan and spilling water jug / TEN. ***Center:*** TEN / Ceres seated / TEN / Panel of microletters. ***Right:*** Panel bearing 10 / Portrait of Indian / 10. ***Engraver:*** PSSP. ***Comments:*** H-MA-1065-G36. 18__. 1830s.

Rarity: —

$10 • W-MA-2840-010-G180

Left: Allegorical woman seated in chariot drawn by two horses surrounded by group of women, Cherub flying. ***Center:*** 10. ***Right:*** TEN / Portrait of George Washington / TEN. ***Engraver:*** New England Bank Note Co. ***Comments:*** H-MA-1065-G38. 18__. 1840s–1850s.

Rarity: —

$10 • W-MA-2840-010-G180a

Overprint: Likely red. ***Engraver:*** New England Bank Note Co. ***Comments:*** H-MA-1065-G38a. Similar to W-MA-2840-010-G180. 18__. 1850s.

Rarity: —

$10 • W-MA-2840-010-G180b

Overprint: Likely red. ***Engraver:*** New England Bank Note Co. / ABNCo. monogram. ***Comments:*** H-MA-1065-G38b. Similar to W-MA-2840-010-G180 but with additional engraver imprint. 1860s.

Rarity: —

$20 • W-MA-2840-020-G190

Engraver: Unverified, but likely PSSP. ***Comments:*** H-MA-1065-G40. No description available. 18__. 1830s.

Rarity: *None known*

$20 • W-MA-2840-020-G200

Left: 20 / Woman seated with book on lap, opening chest. ***Center:*** XX / Eagle on rock / XX. ***Right:*** 20 / Ship in harbor. ***Engraver:*** New England Bank Note Co. ***Comments:*** H-MA-1065-G42. 18__. 1840s–1850s.

Rarity: —

$50 • W-MA-2840-050-G210

Engraver: Unverified, but likely PSSP. ***Comments:*** H-MA-1065-G44. No description available. 18__. 1830s.

Rarity: *None known*

$50 • W-MA-2840-050-G220

Left: FIFTY / Woman standing with wreath and flowers / FIFTY. ***Center:*** 50 / Man restraining prancing horse / 50. ***Right:*** FIFTY / Woman standing with cornucopia / FIFTY. ***Engraver:*** New England Bank Note Co. ***Comments:*** H-MA-1065-G46. 18__. 1840s–1850s.

Rarity: —

$50 • W-MA-2840-050-G230

Left: Soldier loading gun. ***Center:*** Indian woman seated with eagle and shield. ***Right:*** 50 / Male portrait. ***Tint:*** Green die bearing 50. ***Engraver:*** American Bank Note Co. ***Comments:*** H-MA-1065-G48. 1860s.

Rarity: —

$100 • W-MA-2840-100-G240

Engraver: Unverified, but likely PSSP. ***Comments:*** H-MA-1065-G50. No description available. 18__. 1830s.

Rarity: *None known*

$100 • W-MA-2840-100-G250

Left: ONE HUNDRED on 100 / Portrait of William Henry Harrison. ***Center:*** Wharf scene, Men loading wagon with barrels. ***Right:*** ONE HUNDRED on 100 / Portrait of Christopher Columbus. ***Engraver:*** New England Bank Note Co. ***Comments:*** H-MA-1065-G52. 18__. 1840s–1850s.

Rarity: —

$100 • W-MA-2840-100-G260

Left: State arms. ***Center:*** "Landing of the Pilgrims". ***Right:*** 100 / Portrait of Benjamin Franklin. ***Tint:*** Green die bearing 100. ***Engraver:*** American Bank Note Co. ***Comments:*** H-MA-1065-G54. 1860s.

Rarity: —

$500 • W-MA-2840-500-G270

Left: Portrait of George Washington. ***Center:*** Boy holding black horse and white horse, Train and farm. ***Right:*** 500 / Eagle on rock. ***Tint:*** Green die bearing D. ***Engraver:*** American Bank Note Co. ***Comments:*** H-MA-1065-G56. 1860s.

Rarity: —

$1,000 • W-MA-2840-1000-G280

Left: THOUSAND vertically. ***Center:*** 1000 / Woman standing with legs crossed, Lyre, Cornucopia / 1000. ***Right:*** 1000 / M / 1000. ***Back:*** Check Plate. ***Engraver:*** PSSP / New England Bank Note Co. ***Comments:*** H-MA-1065-G58. 18__. 1830s.

Rarity: —

Non-Valid Issues

$1 • W-MA-2840-001-A010

Left: ONE / Two Indians reclining and smoking. ***Center:*** 1 / Three allegorical women with eagle, pole and cap, shield, scales, and book / 1. ***Bottom center:*** Cattle. ***Right:*** 1 / Portrait of George Washington / ONE. ***Engraver:*** Terry, Pelton & Co. ***Comments:*** H-MA-1065-A5. Altered from W-MA-2840-001-G020. 18__. 1830s.

Rarity: —

$1 • W-MA-2840-001-A020

JF

Engraver: Danforth, Bald & Co. ***Comments:*** H-Unlisted. December 1, 1852.

Rarity: URS-7
VG $75; **VF** $150

$2 • W-MA-2840-002-S010

SI

Overprint: Green TWO. ***Engraver:*** New England Bank Note Co. / ABNCo. monogram. ***Comments:*** H-MA-1065-S5. Spurious design imitating a rough verbal description of W-MA-2840-002-G060. April 1, 1862.

Rarity: URS-7
VG $100; **VF** $200

$2 • W-MA-2840-002-S010a

Overprint: Blue TWO. ***Engraver:*** New England Bank Note Co. / ABNCo. monogram. ***Comments:*** H-MA-1065-S5a. Similar to W-MA-2840-002-S010. April 1, 1862.

Rarity: —

$2 • W-MA-2840-002-A030

Left: 2 / Boy with tool. ***Center:*** 2 on shield / Woman seated with plow and sheaf. ***Bottom center:*** Strongbox. ***Right:*** 2 / Man. ***Engraver:*** Danforth, Bald & Co. ***Comments:*** H-MA-1065-A10. Altered from $2 Peoples Bank, Georgetown, D.C. Dec. 1, 1852.

Rarity: URS-7
VG $100; **VF** $200

$2 • W-MA-2840-002-A040

Left: TWO / Portrait of cherub / 2. ***Center:*** 2 / Ceres giving grain to seated Liberty / 2. ***Bottom center:*** Anchor and implements. ***Right:*** 2 / Female portrait / TWO. ***Engraver:*** Terry, Pelton & Co. ***Comments:*** H-MA-1065-A15. Altered from W-MA-2840-002-G050. Genuine notes of this design were issued. 18__. 1830s.

Rarity: URS-7
VG $100; **VF** $200

$3 • W-MA-2840-003-A050

Left: 3 / Woman standing with branch, trident, and THREE / THREE. ***Center:*** Female portrait / Ceres and Justice flanking shield bearing anchor surmounted by eagle / Portrait of cherub. ***Bottom center:*** Anchor and implements. ***Right:*** 3 / Ceres seated in grain field / THREE. ***Engraver:*** Terry, Pelton & Co. ***Comments:*** H-MA-1065-A20. Altered from W-MA-2840-003-G090. Genuine notes of this design were issued. 18__. 1830s.

Rarity: —

$3 • W-MA-2840-003-A060

CC

Overprint: Red THREE. ***Engraver:*** New England Bank Note Co. / Rawdon, Wright, Hatch & Edson. ***Comments:*** H-MA-1065-A25. Altered from $3 Waubeek Bank, De Soto, Nebraska. 1857.

Rarity: URS-7
F $250

$5 • W-MA-2840-005-A070

CC

Engraver: PSSP / New England Bank Note Co. ***Comments:*** H-MA-1065-A30. Altered from W-MA-2860-005-G100. Genuine notes of this design were issued. 18__. 1830s.

Rarity: URS-6
F $300

$5 • W-MA-2840-005-A080

CJF

Overprint: Red FIVE. ***Engraver:*** New England Bank Note Co. / Rawdon, Wright, Hatch & Edson. ***Comments:*** H-MA-1065-A40. Altered from $5 Waubeek Bank, De Soto, Nebraska. 1857.

Rarity: URS-4
F $400; **VF** $600

$10 • W-MA-2840-010-AR010

Left: 10 / Sailing ship. ***Center:*** Three men forging iron / 10 on medallion shield. ***Bottom center:*** Woman swimming. ***Right:*** TEN / Ceres kneeling, Indian woman standing behind her. ***Engraver:*** Danforth, Bald & Co. ***Comments:*** H-MA-1065-A45. Altered and raised from $1 Peoples Bank, Georgetown, D.C. Dec. 1, 1852.

Rarity: —

$20 • W-MA-2840-020-N010

Center: Woman seated with sheaf, Building and train. ***Right:*** Portrait of Daniel Webster. ***Comments:*** H-MA-1065-N5. 1850s.

Rarity: —

Rockland Bank

1853–1864

W-MA-2850

History: The Rockland Bank was chartered on April 28, 1853, with an authorized capital of $100,000. It commenced business on Wednesday, October 19. The capital was raised to $150,000 in 1854. Circulation in 1854 was at $68,675; it reached a high of $147,576 in 1863. Specie amounted to $10,303.28 in 1854 and $15,973.68 in 1857.

The business of the Rockland Bank was succeeded by the National Rockland Bank of Roxbury after it was chartered 1864.

Numismatic Commentary: There are enough genuine issues in the marketplace to yield the occasional buying opportunity. Non-valid examples are even more numerous and may have to do until the opportunity to secure a valid issue presents itself.

Valid Issues

$1 • W-MA-2850-001-G010

Left: Women flanking shield bearing seated woman / 1. ***Right:*** 1 / Man reclining with rake and ONE. ***Engraver:*** Rawdon, Wright, Hatch & Edson / New England Bank Note Co. ***Comments:*** H-MA-1070-G2. 18__. 1850s.

Rarity: —

$1 • W-MA-2850-001-G010a

Engraver: Rawdon, Wright, Hatch & Edson / New England Bank Note Co. / ABNCo. monogram. ***Comments:*** H-MA-1070-G2a. Similar to W-MA-2850-001-G010 but with additional engraver imprint. 18__. 1850s–1860s.

Rarity: —

$1 • W-MA-2850-001-G010b

JF

Tint: Orange lathework outlining white 1 and ONE ONE. ***Engraver:*** Rawdon, Wright, Hatch & Edson / New England Bank Note Co. / ABNCo. monogram. ***Comments:*** H-MA-1070-G2b. Similar to W-MA-2850-001-G010 but with additional engraver imprint. March 1, 1860.

Rarity: URS-4

F $750; **VF** $1,250

$1 • W-MA-2850-001-G010c

Tint: Orange lathework outlining white 1 and ONE ONE. ***Engraver:*** Rawdon, Wright, Hatch & Edson / New England Bank Note Co. / ABNCo. monogram. ***Comments:*** H-MA-1070-G2c. Similar to W-MA-2850-001-G010 but with additional engraver imprint and different date. Oct. 1, 186_. 1860s.

Rarity: —

$1 • W-MA-2850-001-G010d

CC

Tint: Green lathework outlining white 1 and ONE ONE. ***Engraver:*** Rawdon, Wright, Hatch & Edson / New England Bank Note Co. / ABNCo. monogram. ***Comments:*** H-MA-1070-G2d. Similar to W-MA-2850-001-G010 but with additional engraver imprint and different date. Oct. 1, 186_. Circa 1863.

Rarity: URS-3

EF $1,500

$2 • W-MA-2850-002-G020

Left: Female portrait / 2. ***Center:*** Boy pushing sheep into stream, Man watching / 2. ***Right:*** 2 / Woman seated between shield and 2. ***Engraver:*** Rawdon, Wright, Hatch & Edson / New England Bank Note Co. ***Comments:*** H-MA-1070-G4. 18__. 1850s.

Rarity: —

$2 • W-MA-2850-002-G020a

JF

Tint: Orange lathework outlining white 2 and TWO TWO. ***Engraver:*** Rawdon, Wright, Hatch & Edson / New England Bank Note Co. / ABNCo. monogram. ***Comments:*** H-MA-1070-G4a. Similar to W-MA-2850-002-G020 but with additional engraver imprint. 18__. 1850s–1860s.

Rarity: URS-3

F $1,000; **VF** $1,500

$2 • W-MA-2850-002-G020b

Tint: Orange lathework outlining white 2 and TWO TWO. ***Engraver:*** Rawdon, Wright, Hatch & Edson / New England Bank Note Co. / ABNCo. monogram. ***Comments:*** H-MA-1070-G4b. Similar to W-MA-2850-002-G020 but with additional engraver imprint and different date. March 1, 1860.

Rarity: —

$2 • W-MA-2850-002-G020c

Tint: Orange lathework outlining white 2 and TWO TWO. ***Engraver:*** Rawdon, Wright, Hatch & Edson / New England Bank Note Co. / ABNCo. monogram. ***Comments:*** H-MA-1070-G4c. Similar to W-MA-2850-002-G020 but with additional engraver imprint and different date. Oct. 1, 186_. 1862 and 1863.

Rarity: —

$2 • W-MA-2850-002-G020d

Tint: Green lathework outlining white 2 and TWO TWO. ***Engraver:*** Rawdon, Wright, Hatch & Edson / New England Bank Note Co. / ABNCo. monogram. ***Comments:*** H-MA-1070-G4d. Similar to W-MA-2850-002-G020 but with additional engraver imprint and different date. Oct. 1, 186_. Circa 1863.

Rarity: —

$3 • W-MA-2850-003-G030

Left: Farmer, sailor, and mechanic seated with scythe, spyglass, hammer, and anvil, Three gold dollars. ***Center:*** THREE. ***Right:*** 3 / Dog's head. ***Engraver:*** Rawdon, Wright, Hatch & Edson / New England Bank Note Co. ***Comments:*** H-MA-1070-G6. 18__. 1850s.

Rarity: URS-4
F $1,500; **VF** $2,000

$3 • W-MA-2850-003-G030a

Tint: Orange lathework outlining white 3 and THREE DOLLARS. ***Engraver:*** Rawdon, Wright, Hatch & Edson / New England Bank Note Co. / ABNCo. monogram. ***Comments:*** H-MA-1070-G6a. Similar to W-MA-2850-003-G030 but with additional engraver imprint. 18__. 1850s–1860s.

Rarity: —

$3 • W-MA-2850-003-G030b

Tint: Orange lathework outlining white 3 and THREE DOLLARS. ***Engraver:*** Rawdon, Wright, Hatch & Edson / New England Bank Note Co. / ABNCo. monogram. ***Comments:*** H-MA-1070-G6b. Similar to W-MA-2850-003-G030 but with additional engraver imprint and different date. March 1, 1860.

Rarity: —

$3 • W-MA-2850-003-G030c

Tint: Orange lathework outlining white 3 and THREE DOLLARS. ***Engraver:*** Rawdon, Wright, Hatch & Edson / New England Bank Note Co. / ABNCo. monogram. ***Comments:*** H-MA-1070-G6c. Similar to W-MA-2850-003-G030 but with additional engraver imprint and different date. Oct. 1, 186_. 1860s.

Rarity: —

$3 • W-MA-2850-003-G030d

Tint: Green lathework outlining white 3 and THREE DOLLARS. ***Engraver:*** Rawdon, Wright, Hatch & Edson / New England Bank Note Co. / ABNCo. monogram. ***Comments:*** H-MA-1070-G6d. Similar to W-MA-2850-003-G030 but with additional engraver imprint and different date. Oct. 1, 186_. 1850s–1860s.

Rarity: —

$5 • W-MA-2850-005-G040

Left: 5 / Male portrait / FIVE. ***Center:*** Indian woman and hunter flanking five gold dollars and three cherubs. ***Right:*** 5. ***Engraver:*** Rawdon, Wright, Hatch & Edson / New England Bank Note Co. ***Comments:*** H-MA-1070-G8. 18__. 1850s.

Rarity: —

$5 • W-MA-2850-005-G040a

Tint: Orange. ***Engraver:*** Rawdon, Wright, Hatch & Edson / New England Bank Note Co. / ABNCo. monogram. ***Comments:*** H-MA-1070-G8a. Similar to W-MA-2850-005-G040 but with additional engraver imprint. 18__. Circa 1860.

Rarity: —

$10 • W-MA-2850-010-G050

Left: X / Two women embracing. ***Center:*** Farm woman and man seated, Three men, one with sickle, one sharpening scythe, one lying down, Hay wagon. ***Right:*** X / Portrait of George Washington. ***Engraver:*** Rawdon, Wright, Hatch & Edson / New England Bank Note Co. ***Comments:*** H-MA-1070-G10. 18__. 1850s.

Rarity: —

$10 • W-MA-2850-010-G050a

Tint: Orange. ***Engraver:*** Rawdon, Wright, Hatch & Edson / New England Bank Note Co. / ABNCo. monogram. ***Comments:*** H-MA-1070-G10b. Similar to W-MA-2850-010-G050 but with additional engraver imprint. 18__. 1860s.

Rarity: —

$20 • W-MA-2850-020-G060

Left: State arms / XX. ***Center:*** Farmer plowing with two oxen and horse, Livestock, River and city. ***Right:*** 20 / Male portrait. ***Engraver:*** Rawdon, Wright, Hatch & Edson / New England Bank Note Co. ***Comments:*** H-MA-1070-G12. 18__. 1850s.

Rarity: —

$20 • W-MA-2850-020-G060a

Tint: Orange. ***Engraver:*** Rawdon, Wright, Hatch & Edson / New England Bank Note Co. / ABNCo. monogram. ***Comments:*** H-MA-1070-G12b. Similar to W-MA-2850-020-G060 but with additional engraver imprint. 18__. 1860s.

Rarity: —

$50 • W-MA-2850-050-G070

Left: 50 / Portrait of Daniel Webster. ***Center:*** Ships, City. ***Right:*** 50 / 50. ***Engraver:*** Rawdon, Wright, Hatch & Edson / New England Bank Note Co. ***Comments:*** H-MA-1070-G14. 18__. 1850s.

Rarity: URS-3
F $1,750; **VF** $2,500

$50 • W-MA-2850-050-G070a

Tint: Orange. ***Engraver:*** Rawdon, Wright, Hatch & Edson / New England Bank Note Co. / ABNCo. monogram. ***Comments:*** H-MA-1070-G14a. Similar to W-MA-2850-050-G070 but with additional engraver imprint. 18__. 1860s.

Rarity: —

$100 • W-MA-2850-100-G080

Left: C / Fountain. ***Center:*** Farm scene, Women, men, and children. ***Right:*** 100 / Portrait of Thomas Jefferson. ***Engraver:*** Rawdon, Wright, Hatch & Edson / New England Bank Note Co. ***Comments:*** H-MA-1070-G16. 18__. 1850s.

Rarity: —

$100 • W-MA-2850-100-G090

Left: D / Woman and horse. ***Center:*** 500 / Woman reclining with eagle and globe, Ship and steamer. ***Right:*** 500 / 500. ***Engraver:*** Rawdon, Wright, Hatch & Edson / New England Bank Note Co. ***Comments:*** H-MA-1070-G18. 18__. 1850s.

Rarity: —

Non-Valid Issues

$1 • W-MA-2850-001-A010

Left: 1 / Cattle and telegraph poles, Train on bridge. ***Center:*** Young woman seated with two calves, Trees and river. ***Right:*** 1 / Female portrait. ***Tint:*** Red-brown 1s and panel outlining white ONE DOLLAR. ***Engraver:*** Danforth, Wright & Co. ***Comments:*** H-MA-1070-A5. Altered from $1 Southern Bank of Georgia, Bainbridge, Georgia. March 1, 1858.

Rarity: —

$2 • **W-MA-2850-002-A020**

CJF

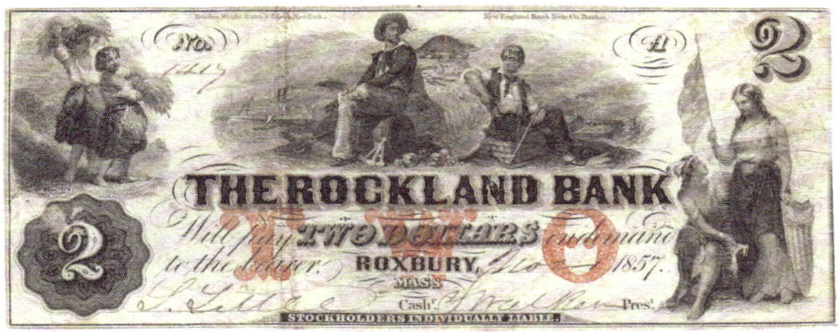

Overprint: Red TWO. ***Engraver:*** New England Bank Note Co. / Rawdon, Wright, Hatch & Edson. ***Comments:*** H-MA-1070-A10. Altered from $2 Waubeek Bank, De Soto, Nebraska. 1857.

Rarity: URS-3
F $1,250; **VF** $1,750

$5 • **W-MA-2850-005-A030**

HA

Overprint: Red FIVE. ***Engraver:*** New England Bank Note Co. / Rawdon, Wright, Hatch & Edson. ***Comments:*** H-MA-1070-A15. Altered from $5 Waubeek Bank, De Soto, Nebraska. 1857.

Rarity: URS-6
VG $50; **F** $75

$5 • **W-MA-2850-005-A040**

CC

Overprint: Blue FIVE. ***Engraver:*** Rawdon, Wright, Hatch & Edson. ***Comments:*** H-MA-1070-A20. Altered from $5 Farmers and Merchants Bank of Memphis, Memphis, Tennessee series. 1850s.

Rarity: URS-7
VG $50; **F** $75

$5 • **W-MA-2850-005-A050**

Left: Men leading herd of cattle / 5. ***Center:*** 5 / Men raking and loading hay into wagon with oxen. ***Right:*** 5. ***Tint:*** Red-brown lathework outlining white 5. ***Engraver:*** Bald, Cousland & Co. ***Comments:*** H-MA-1070-A25. Altered from $5 Pioneer Association, Lafayette, Indiana. 1850s–1860s.

Rarity: —

$10 • **W-MA-2850-010-R010**

Engraver: Rawdon, Wright, Hatch & Edson / New England Bank Note Co. ***Comments:*** H-MA-1070-R5. Raised from W-MA-2850-001-G010. 18__. 1850s.

Rarity: —

Roxbury Bank
1836–1838
W-MA-2860

History: The Roxbury Bank was incorporated on April 13, 1836, with an authorized capital of $100,000. It was controlled by speculators in New York City and never legitimately opened.

The Boston *Saturday Morning Transcript* published this on July 1, 1837:

> The *Washington Globe* publishes a list of specie-paying banks. Amongst them the Roxbury Bank at Roxbury and the Yarmouth Bank at Barnstable [the *Globe* probably means the Barnstable Bank at Yarmouth] are mentioned. The value and importance of this list may be judged from the fact that the Roxbury Bank *has never been in operation*, and if the Barnstable Bank pays specie it must be whilst the cashier is asleep.

It was announced elsewhere that the capital had been paid in full in 1836, but the bank did not open for business until October 17, 1837. Notwithstanding such notices, the bank had issued a large amount of paper money that was not received by other banks.

Numismatic Commentary: This bank's failure proved to be good fortune for today's collector, as various issues from the bank note inventory that were once worthless are readily available today.

Valid Issues

$1 • **W-MA-2860-001-G010**

QDB

Engraver: PSSP / New England Bank Note Co. ***Comments:*** H-MA-1075-G2. 18__. 1830s.

Rarity: URS-7
F $100; **VF** $150

$1 • **W-MA-2860-001-G020**

Left: ONE / Man seated / 1. ***Center:*** 1 / Two women seated with shield and child / 1. ***Right:*** 1 / Portrait of George Washington / ONE. ***Engraver:*** Terry, Pelton & Co. ***Comments:*** H-MA-1075-G4. 18__. 1830s.

Rarity: —

$1.25 • W-MA-2860-001.25-G030

QDB

Engraver: New England Bank Note Co. ***Comments:*** H-MA-1075-G6. 18__. 1830s.

Rarity: URS-6

VF $350

$1.50 • W-MA-2860-001.50-G040

ANS

Engraver: New England Bank Note Co. ***Comments:*** H-MA-1075-G8. 18__. 1830s.

Rarity: URS-6

F $350

$1.75 • W-MA-2860-001.75-G050

Left: $1.75 Cts. / Woman watering eagle / 1 75/100. ***Center:*** Three sloops at sea. ***Right:*** $1.75 Cts. / Dog, Woman seated with grain / 1 75/100. ***Engraver:*** New England Bank Note Co. ***Comments:*** H-MA-1075-G10. 18__. 1830s.

Rarity: —

$2 • W-MA-2860-002-G060

Left: 2 / Man standing / TWO. ***Center:*** TWO / Woman seated with shield and rake / TWO. ***Right:*** 2 / Woman / TWO. ***Engraver:*** New England Bank Note Co. ***Comments:*** H-MA-1075-G12. 18__. 1830s.

Rarity: —

$2 • W-MA-2860-002-G070

CC

Engraver: Terry, Pelton & Co. ***Comments:*** H-MA-1075-G14. 18__. 1830s.

Rarity: URS-6

F $350

$3 • W-MA-2860-003-G080

Left: THREE / Beehive and foliage / THREE. ***Center:*** Machinery and merchandise flanking Ceres seated holding sickle and rake, Factories and harbor / Panel outlining white THREE. ***Right:*** 3 on THREE / Two reapers / 3 on THREE. ***Engraver:*** New England Bank Note Co. / PSSP. ***Comments:*** H-MA-1075-G16. 18__. 1830s.

Rarity: —

$3 • W-MA-2860-003-G090

CJF

Engraver: Terry, Pelton & Co. ***Comments:*** H-MA-1075-G18. 18__. 1830s.

Rarity: URS-6

EF $350

$5 • W-MA-2860-005-G100

Left: 5 / Blacksmith at anvil / FIVE. ***Center:*** Mercury standing with 5, Cornucopia and merchandise, Factories and ship / V / Panel outlining white FIVE. ***Right:*** 5 / Ceres kneeling / FIVE. ***Engraver:*** New England Bank Note Co. / PSSP. ***Comments:*** H-MA-1075-G20. 18__. 1830s.

Rarity: —

$5 • W-MA-2860-005-G110

CJF

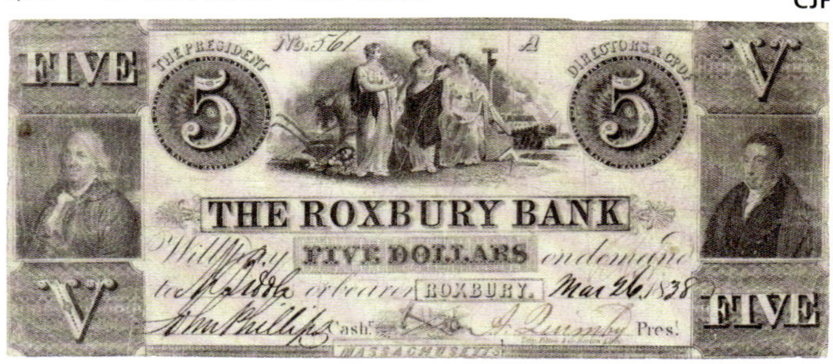

Engraver: Terry, Pelton & Co. ***Comments:*** H-MA-1075-G22. 18__. 1830s.

Rarity: URS-6

VG $100; **VF** $350

$10 • W-MA-2860-010-G120

Engraver: Unverified, but likely New England Bank Note Co. ***Comments:*** H-MA-1075-G24. No description available. 18__. 1830s.

Rarity: *None known*

$20 • W-MA-2860-020-G130

Left: 20 / XX / 20. ***Center:*** 20 / Woman seated with scales, Sheaf and bales, Men plowing, Ship / 20. ***Right:*** TWENTY vertically. ***Engraver:*** PSSP / New England Bank Note Co. ***Comments:*** H-MA-1075-G30. 18__. 1830s.

Rarity: —

$50 • W-MA-2860-050-G140

Left: 50 / Cornucopia, Woman standing with ankles crossed, Staff, Anchor / 50. ***Center:*** FIFTY DOLLARS / 50. ***Right:*** FIFTY vertically. ***Engraver:*** New England Bank Note Co. / PSSP. ***Comments:*** H-MA-1075-G34. 18__. 1830s.

Rarity: —

$100 • W-MA-2860-100-G150

Left: Lathework panel bearing C / Portrait of George Washington / C. ***Center:*** 100 / Manhattan reclining, pouring water, Ship / 100. ***Right:*** Lathework panel bearing ONE HUNDRED vertically. ***Engraver:*** New England Bank Note Co. / PSSP. ***Comments:*** H-MA-1075-G38. 18__. 1830s.

Rarity: —

$100 • W-MA-2860-100-G160 CJ

Engraver: Terry, Pelton & Co. ***Comments:*** H-Unlisted. 18__. 1830s.

Rarity: URS-3
F $250; **VF** $400

NON-VALID ISSUES

$10 • W-MA-2860-010-A010

Left: 10 / Portrait of George Washington held by cherub / 10. ***Center:*** X / Spread eagle with shield and arrows, E PLURIBUS UNUM / X. ***Bottom center:*** Ship. ***Right:*** 10 / White woman seated and Indian man standing / 10. ***Engraver:*** Terry, Pelton & Co. ***Comments:*** H-MA-1075-G26. Actually an altered note from $10 Citizens Bank, Augusta, Maine, or from notes of other failed banks using the same plate. 18__. 1830s.

Rarity: —

Winthrop Bank

1836–1840

W-MA-2870

History: The Winthrop Bank was incorporated on April 16, 1836, with an authorized capital of $100,000. In 1839 the bank had a circulation of $29,212.75. These were difficult economic times, and the bank's charter was surrendered in December 1840.

See also listing under Winthrop, W-MA-3350.

Numismatic Commentary: Genuine issues from this bank are all but impossible to locate. At least one variety shows a portrait of John Winthrop, the first governor of the Massachusetts Bay Colony.

VALID ISSUES

$1 • W-MA-2870-001-G010

Engraver: Unverified, but likely New England Bank Note Co. ***Comments:*** H-MA-1080-G2. No description available. 18__. 1830s.

Rarity: *None known*

$1.25 • W-MA-2870-001.25-G020

Left: 1 25/100 / Train / 1 25/100. ***Center:*** Sloop and other ships at sea / $1.25 cts. ***Right:*** 1 25/100 / Eagle. ***Engraver:*** New England Bank Note Co. ***Comments:*** H-MA-1080-G6. 18__. 1830s.

Rarity: —

$1.50 • W-MA-2870-001.50-G030

Left: 1 Doll. 50 Cts. vertically. ***Center:*** Eagle on rock in ocean / $1 50/100. ***Right:*** 1 50/100 / Justice. ***Engraver:*** New England Bank Note Co. ***Comments:*** H-MA-1080-G8. 18__. 1830s.

Rarity: —

$1.75 • W-MA-2870-001.75-G040

Left: $1.75 Cts. / Hebe watering eagle / 1 75/100. ***Center:*** Three sloops at sea. ***Right:*** $1.75 Cts. / Dog, Ceres seated with grain / 1 75/100. ***Engraver:*** New England Bank Note Co. ***Comments:*** H-MA-1080-G10. 18__. 1830s.

Rarity: —

$2 • W-MA-2870-002-G050

Engraver: Unverified, but likely New England Bank Note Co. ***Comments:*** H-MA-1080-G12. No description available. 18__. 1830s.

Rarity: *None known*

$3 • W-MA-2870-003-G060

Engraver: Unverified, but likely New England Bank Note Co. ***Comments:*** H-MA-1080-G16. No description available. 18__. 1830s.

Rarity: *None known*

$5 • W-MA-2870-005-G070 CC

Comments: H-Unlisted. Remainder. 18__.

Rarity: URS-2
Proof $2,200

$5 • W-MA-2870-005-G080

Engraver: Unverified, but likely New England Bank Note Co. ***Comments:*** H-MA-1080-G20. No description available. 18__. 1830s.

Rarity: *None known*

$10 • W-MA-2870-010-G090

Engraver: Unverified, but likely New England Bank Note Co. ***Comments:*** H-MA-1080-G24. No description available. 18__. 1830s.

Rarity: *None known*

$20 • W-MA-2870-020-G100

Engraver: Unverified, but likely New England Bank Note Co. ***Comments:*** H-MA-1080-G28. No description available. 18__. 1830s.

Rarity: *None known*

$50 • W-MA-2870-050-G110

Engraver: Unverified, but likely New England Bank Note Co. ***Comments:*** H-MA-1080-G32. No description available. 18__. 1830s.

Rarity: *None known*

$100 • W-MA-2870-100-G120

Engraver: Unverified, but likely New England Bank Note Co. ***Comments:*** H-MA-1080-G36. No description available. 18__. 1830s.

Rarity: *None known*

$500 • W-MA-2870-500-G130

Engraver: Unverified, but likely New England Bank Note Co. ***Comments:*** H-MA-1080-G40. No description available. 18__. 1840.

Rarity: *None known*

Non-Valid Issues

$2 • W-MA-2870-002-S010

CC

Comments: H-MA-1080-S5. 18__. 1830s.

Rarity: URS-7
F $150

$5 • W-MA-2870-005-A010

Left: FIVE / Portrait of Benjamin Franklin / V. ***Center:*** 5 / Two allegorical women standing and one seated, Agricultural items, Ship. ***Bottom center:*** Anchor and implements. ***Right:*** V / Portrait of Marquis de Lafayette / FIVE. ***Engraver:*** Terry, Pelton & Co. ***Comments:*** H-MA-1080-A5. Altered from $5 Citizens Bank, Augusta, Maine, or from notes of other failed banks using the same plate. 18__. 1830s.

Rarity: —

$10 • W-MA-2870-010-A020

Left: 10 / Portrait of George Washington held by cherub / 10. ***Center:*** X / Spread eagle with shield and arrows, E PLURIBUS UNUM / X. ***Bottom center:*** Ship. ***Right:*** 10 / Standing Indian man / 10. ***Engraver:*** Terry, Pelton & Co. ***Comments:*** H-MA-1080-A10. Altered from $10 Citizens Bank, Augusta, Maine, or from notes of other failed banks using the same plate. 18__. 1830s.

Rarity: —

$100 • W-MA-2870-100-A030

Left: 100 / Man carrying rake / 100. ***Center:*** C / Hercules wrestling with Nemean lion / C. ***Bottom center:*** Men in boat. ***Right:*** 100 / George Washington standing by horse / 100. ***Engraver:*** Terry, Pelton & Co. ***Comments:*** H-MA-1080-A15. Altered from $100 Citizens Bank, Augusta, Maine, or from notes of other failed banks using the same plate. 18__. 1830s.

Rarity: —

Sunderland, Massachusetts

Settled in 1713 and officially incorporated on November 12, 1718, Sunderland was initially known as Swampfield. The name was eventually changed in an attempt to attract more settlers, and the name was chosen in honor of the Earl of Sunderland, Charles Spencer. The land has an agricultural history, and before it was incorporated in 1774, the town of Levertt used to be included in the Sunderland territory.

In 1832 a bridge was built in the central village, spanning 858 feet in length across the Connecticut River. Early industries for the town included the raising of sheep, pigs, horses, cattle, and even geese. There was an active river trade, allowing logging to become a popular industry. Broom corn was the primary agricultural pursuit for the town, which produced more than 130,000 pounds of broom corn in 1845. During the 1830s, sugar maples were planted. The town borders Whately, Deerfield, Montague, Levertt, Amherst, and Hadley. Nearby, the Sugarloaf Mountain and Mount Toby frame the horizon of Sunderland.

Sunderland Bank
1825–1831
W-MA-2880

History: The Sunderland Bank was incorporated on February 26, 1825, with an authorized capital of $100,000. On June 13, 1831, the General Court passed an act approving the removal of

How to Read the Whitman Numbering System

$1 • W-MA-010-001-G010a

Denomination: Value of the note shown.

W: Whitman number. This number is a sortable code unique to each bank and note.

MA: Abbreviation for the state under study.

010: Numerical designation specific to each bank.

001: The denomination in dollars.

G010a: G indicates a good or valid note. Other categories are indicated thus: C (counterfeit); R (raised); S (spurious); N (not-attributed); A (altered). Numbers are assigned starting with 010, 020, et seq. Terminal letters following the number indicate variations of a note: a series of different colored overprints, tints, payees, etc., all on the same design of note. For more information, see the "How to Use This Book" section at the front of the volume, page xiv.

the Sunderland Bank to Amherst, as well as a change in name to the Amherst Bank, W-MA-050. The same officers that founded the Sunderland Bank transferred along with the bank.

Numismatic Commentary: This listing is speculative in the absence of specific information. The name Sunderland was possibly used for a short time after the move to Amherst, but no notes with this name or location are known.

VALID ISSUES

$1 • W-MA-2880-001-G010
Comments: H-Unlisted. No description available. 1820s–1830s.
Rarity: *None known*

$2 • W-MA-2880-002-G020
Comments: H-Unlisted. No description available. 1820s–1830s.
Rarity: *None known*

$3 • W-MA-2880-003-G030
Comments: H-Unlisted. No description available. 1820s–1830s.
Rarity: *None known*

$5 • W-MA-2880-005-G040
Comments: H-Unlisted. No description available. 1820s–1830s.
Rarity: *None known*

$10 • W-MA-2880-010-G050
Comments: H-Unlisted. No description available. 1820s–1830s.
Rarity: *None known*

$20 • W-MA-2880-020-G060
Comments: H-Unlisted. No description available. 1820s–1830s.
Rarity: *None known*

$50 • W-MA-2880-050-G070
Comments: H-Unlisted. No description available. 1820s–1830s.
Rarity: *None known*

$100 • W-MA-2880-100-G080
Comments: H-Unlisted. No description available. 1820s–1830s.
Rarity: *None known*

SACO, MASSACHUSETTS

Saco, in York County, is located on the eastern bank of the Saco River. Settlement began in 1640. Around 1653 commissioners were sent from Massachusetts and declared that Saco should be a township with the privileges thereof. However, it was not represented in the General Court until 1659 and again in 1675, in which year the town was totally destroyed by Indians. In the meantime, the district later known as Biddeford was added to Saco until 1718, when inhabitants on both sides of the river agreed to use the old name of Saco for the entire territory. This resulted in an opposing petition in 1718 in which the town on the west side of the Saco River was called Biddeford and the remaining part Saco. Inhabitants petitioned for an act of incorporation, which took place in June 1762, changing the name to Pepperrellborough (also Pepperrellboro) in memory of General Pepperell. This name does not seem to have been embraced warmly by the inhabitants, and in 1805 they eliminated it and returned to the name of Saco. On March 15, 1820, the Maine District of Massachusetts became the state of Maine.

See also Saco, Maine.

Saco Bank

1803–1820 • 1820–1831

W-MA-2890 • W-ME-1350

History: The Saco Bank was organized on March 8, 1803, in Pepperrellboro (known two years later as Saco).[36] It is not known if any issues bear the address of Pepperrellboro. Capital totaled $120,000. In January 1820, circulation was $10,014. Its charter expired in 1831. See also listing under Maine.

Numismatic Commentary: Some of the early notes of this bank with the Massachusetts address will be found to have been printed on fine-quality laid paper and without an engraver's imprint. The clarity of the engravings on these notes, while primitive and uncomplicated, must point to an engraver with some experience in this business.

VALID ISSUES

Notes With Massachusetts Address

$1 • W-MA-2890-001-G010
Comments: H-MA-1085-G24, Wait-Unlisted. No description available. 1800s.
Rarity: *None known*

$1 • W-MA-2890-001-G020
Comments: H-MA-1085-G28, Wait-Unlisted. No description available. 1810s.
Rarity: *None known*

$2 • W-MA-2890-002-G030
Comments: H-MA-1085-G32, Wait-Unlisted. No description available. 1800s.
Rarity: *None known*

$2 • W-MA-2890-002-G040
Comments: H-MA-1085-G36, Wait-Unlisted. No description available. 1810s.
Rarity: *None known*

$3 • W-MA-2890-003-G050
Center: MASSACHUSETTS, Text. ***Comments:*** H-MA-1085-G40, Wait-Unlisted. 1800s.
Rarity: URS-3
EF $600

$3 • W-MA-2890-003-G060
Comments: H-MA-1085-G44, Wait-Unlisted. No description available. 1810s.
Rarity: *None known*

$5 • W-MA-2890-005-G070
Comments: H-MA-1085-G48, Wait-Unlisted. No description available. 1800s.
Rarity: *None known*

$5 • W-MA-2890-005-G080
Comments: H-MA-1085-G52, Wait-Unlisted. No description available. 1810s.
Rarity: *None known*

$6 • W-MA-2890-006-G090

CJF

Comments: H-MA-1085-G56, Wait-Unlisted. 180_. 1800s.

Rarity: URS-3

EF $600

$7 • W-MA-2890-007-G100

Comments: H-MA-1085-G60, Wait-Unlisted. No description available. 1800s. **Rarity:** *None known*

$8 • W-MA-2890-008-G110

CJF

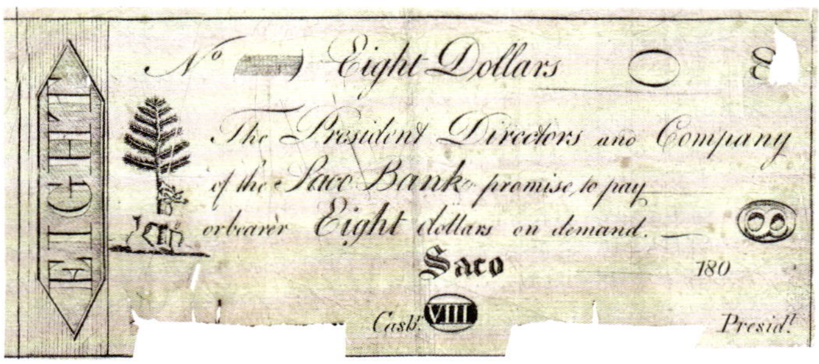

Comments: H-MA-1085-G64, Wait-Unlisted. 180_. 1800s.

Rarity: URS-3

EF $600

$9 • W-MA-2890-009-G120

QDB

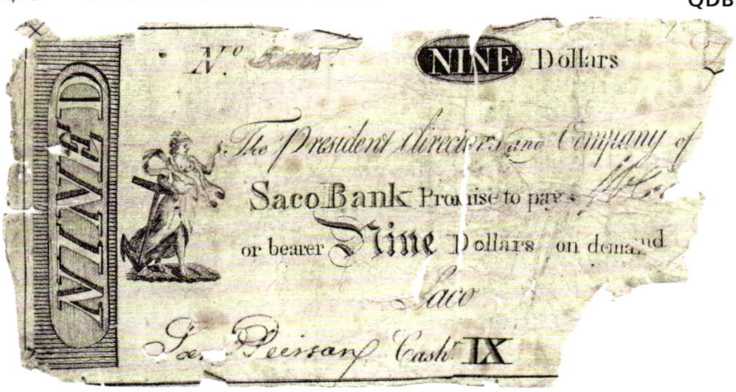

Comments: H-MA-1085-G68, Wait-Unlisted. 1800s.

Rarity: URS-2

AG $350; **VF** $800

$10 • W-MA-2890-010-G130

Comments: H-MA-1085-G72, Wait-Unlisted. No description available. 1800s. **Rarity:** *None known*

$10 • W-MA-2890-010-G140

Comments: H-MA-1085-G76, Wait-Unlisted. No description available. 1810s. **Rarity:** *None known*

$20 • W-MA-2890-020-G150

Comments: H-MA-1085-G80, Wait-Unlisted. No description available. 1800s. **Rarity:** *None known*

$20 • W-MA-2890-020-G160

Comments: H-MA-1085-G84, Wait-Unlisted. No description available. 1810s. **Rarity:** *None known*

Notes With Maine Address

$1 • W-ME-1350-001-G010

Comments: H-ME-520-G4, Wait-Unlisted. No description available. 1820s. **Rarity:** *None known*

$2 • W-ME-1350-002-G020

Comments: H-ME-520-G8, Wait-Unlisted. No description available. 1820s. **Rarity:** *None known*

$3 • W-ME-1350-003-G030

Center: MAINE, Text. ***Comments:*** H-ME-520-G12, Wait-20. 1820s. **Rarity:** *None known*

$5 • W-ME-1350-005-G040

Comments: H-ME-520-G16, Wait-Unlisted. No description available. 1820s. **Rarity:** *None known*

$10 • W-ME-1350-010-G050

Comments: H-ME-520-G20, Wait-Unlisted. No description available. 1820s. **Rarity:** *None known*

Salem, Massachusetts

Founded as the town of Naumkeag in this area in 1626, Salem was incorporated in 1629. It was comprised of what later became Peabody and sections of Beverly, Middleton, Topsfield, Wenham, and Manchester-by-the-Sea. The Salem Witch Trials took place mostly in nearby Salem Village, now known as Danvers. The trials occurred in 1692, causing the deaths of 20 people.

In 1775 the British troops were prevented from capturing ammunition in North Salem by patriots who raised the North River drawbridge. Merchants from Salem soon published a pamphlet professing their colonial leanings and refuting Loyalist behaviors.

The town became a privateering center during the Revolutionary War, with almost 800 ships capturing or destroying 600 enemy vessels. For the China trade, Salem was the most famous seaport in the world, exporting codfish to the West Indies and Europe in return for sugar, molasses, tea, and pepper. Africa, Russia, Japan, and Australia were also destinations to which Salem ships sailed. The War of 1812 saw the continuation of privateering. With the decline of shipping in the 19th century, manufacturing became the means of industry in Salem, including tanneries, shoemaking, and cotton manufacturing.

Asiatic Bank

1824–1865

W-MA-2900

History: The Asiatic Bank was chartered on June 12, 1824, with an authorized capital of $200,000, increased to $315,000 by the time the bank opened for business in July on Central Street. The bank later moved to the East India Marine Building and in 1855 to the Asiatic Building on Washington Street.

Circulation in 1839 was $48,346; it reached a high of $118,151 in 1863. Real estate of the bank was valued at $24,120.41.

The business of the Asiatic Bank was succeeded by the Asiatic National Bank of Salem after it was chartered on December 20, 1864, and went into operation in early 1865.

Numismatic Commentary: This is a very hard bank to obtain genuine notes from. Some of its issues show a street scene in Salem along with the building housing the bank. On these same issues is a smaller vignette of elephants carrying passengers to some unknown location. Elephants appearing on obsolete bank notes are a rare occurrence.

Valid Issues

$1 • W-MA-2900-001-G010

Left: Lathework panel. ***Center:*** 1 / 1 / Oval of flower garlands and gridwork segments / 1 / 1. ***Right:*** Lathework panel. ***Engraver:*** PSSP. ***Comments:*** H-MA-1080-G2. 18__. 1820s.

Rarity: —

$1 • W-MA-2900-001-G010a

Left: Panel of lathework circle segments. ***Right:*** Panel of lathework circle segments. ***Engraver:*** PSSP. ***Comments:*** H-MA-1080-G4. Similar to W-MA-2900-001-G010. 18__. 1820s–1830s.

Rarity: —

$1 • W-MA-2900-001-G010b

Left: ONE / D / ONE vertically. ***Right:*** ONE / D / ONE vertically. ***Engraver:*** PSSP. ***Comments:*** H-MA-1080-G6. Similar to W-MA-2900-001-G010. 18__. 1830s.

Rarity: —

$1 • W-MA-2900-001-G020

Left: Female portrait / ONE. ***Center:*** View of Essex Street, Salem. ***Right:*** 1 / Two elephants. ***Engraver:*** Terry, Pelton & Co. ***Comments:*** H-MA-1080-G10. 18__. 1830s–1850s.

Rarity: —

$1 • W-MA-2900-001-G020a

PEM

Overprint: Red ONE. ***Engraver:*** Terry, Pelton & Co. ***Comments:*** H-MA-1080-G10a. Similar to W-MA-2900-001-G020. 18__. 1850s.

Rarity: —

$1 • W-MA-2900-001-G020b

Overprint: Red. ***Engraver:*** Terry, Pelton & Co. / ABNCo. monogram. ***Comments:*** H-MA-1080-G10b. Similar to W-MA-2900-001-G020 but with additional engraver imprint. 18__. 1850s–1860s.

Rarity: —

$2 • W-MA-2900-002-G030

Left: Lathework panel. ***Center:*** 2 / 2 / Oval of flower garlands and gridwork segments / 2 / 2. ***Right:*** Lathework panel. ***Engraver:*** PSSP. ***Comments:*** H-MA-1080-G12. 18__. 1820s.

Rarity: —

$2 • W-MA-2900-002-G030a

Left: Panel of lathework circle segments. ***Right:*** Panel of lathework circle segments. ***Engraver:*** PSSP. ***Comments:*** H-MA-1080-G14. Similar to W-MA-2900-002-G030. 18__. 1820s–1830s.

Rarity: —

$2 • W-MA-2900-002-G030b

Left: Five TWOs vertically. ***Right:*** Five TWOs vertically. ***Engraver:*** PSSP. ***Comments:*** H-MA-1080-G16. Similar to W-MA-2900-002-G030. 18__. 1830s.

Rarity: —

$2 • W-MA-2900-002-G040

Left: TWO / Two elephants / TWO. ***Center:*** View of Essex St., Salem. ***Right:*** TWO / Woman / TWO. ***Comments:*** H-MA-1080-G20. 18__. 1830s–1850s.

Rarity: —

$2 • W-MA-2900-002-G040a

Overprint: Red. ***Engraver:*** Terry, Pelton & Co. ***Comments:*** H-MA-1080-G20a. Similar to W-MA-2900-002-G040. 18__. 1850s.

Rarity: —

$2 • W-MA-2900-002-G040b

Overprint: Red. ***Engraver:*** Terry, Pelton & Co. / ABNCo. monogram. ***Comments:*** H-MA-1080-G20b. Similar to W-MA-2900-002-G040 but with additional engraver imprint. 18__. 1850s–1860s.

Rarity: —

$3 • W-MA-2900-003-G050

Left: Lathework panel. ***Center:*** 3 / 3 / Oval of flower garlands and gridwork segments / 3 / 3. ***Right:*** Lathework panel. ***Engraver:*** PSSP. ***Comments:*** H-MA-1080-G22. 18__. 1820s.

Rarity: —

$3 • W-MA-2900-003-G050a

Left: Panel of lathework circle segments. ***Right:*** Panel of lathework circle segments. ***Engraver:*** PSSP. ***Comments:*** H-MA-1080-G24. Similar to W-MA-2900-003-G050. 18__. 1820s–1830s.

Rarity: —

$3 • W-MA-2900-003-G050b

Left: THREE vertically. ***Right:*** THREE vertically. ***Engraver:*** PSSP. ***Comments:*** H-MA-1080-G26. Similar to W-MA-2900-003-G050. 18__. 1830s.

Rarity: —

$3 • W-MA-2900-003-G060

Left: THREE / Woman / THREE. ***Center:*** View of Essex St., Salem / THREE. ***Right:*** 3 / Two elephants / THREE. ***Engraver:*** Terry, Pelton & Co. ***Comments:*** H-MA-1080-G30. 18__. 1830s–1850s.

Rarity: —

$3 • W-MA-2900-003-G060a
Overprint: Red THREE. ***Engraver:*** Terry, Pelton & Co. ***Comments:*** H-MA-1080-G30a. Similar to W-MA-2900-003-G060. 18__. 1850s.

Rarity: —

$3 • W-MA-2900-003-G060b
Overprint: Red THREE. ***Engraver:*** Terry, Pelton & Co. / ABNCo. monogram. ***Comments:*** H-MA-1080-G30b. Similar to W-MA-2900-003-G060 but with additional engraver imprint and printed serial number. 18__. 1850s–1860s.

Rarity: —

$5 • W-MA-2900-005-G070
Left: Lathework chain bearing MASSACHUSETTS / 5 / 5. ***Center:*** Alternating flower garlands and gridwork segments. ***Right:*** 5 / 5. ***Engraver:*** PSSP. ***Comments:*** H-MA-1080-G32. 18__. 1820s.

Rarity: —

$5 • W-MA-2900-005-G070a
Engraver: PSSP. ***Comments:*** H-MA-1080-G34. Similar to W-MA-2900-005-G070 but with zigzag ruled lines. 18__. 1820s–1830s.

Rarity: —

$5 • W-MA-2900-005-G070b
Engraver: PSSP. ***Comments:*** H-MA-1080-G36. Similar to W-MA-2900-005-G070 but with spiral lathework lines. 18__. 1830s.

Rarity: —

$5 • W-MA-2900-005-G080

PEM

Engraver: Terry, Pelton & Co. ***Comments:*** H-MA-1080-G40. 18__. 1830s–1850s.

Rarity: —

$5 • W-MA-2900-005-G080a
Left: Female portrait / FIVE. ***Center:*** View of Essex St., Salem. ***Right:*** V / Two elephants / FIVE. ***Overprint:*** Red. ***Engraver:*** Terry, Pelton & Co. ***Comments:*** H-MA-1080-G40a. Similar to W-MA-2900-005-G080. 18__. 1850s.

Rarity: —

$5 • W-MA-2900-005-G080b
Overprint: Red. ***Engraver:*** Terry, Pelton & Co. / ABNCo. monogram. ***Comments:*** H-MA-1080-G40b. Similar to W-MA-2900-005-G080 but with additional engraver imprint. 18__. 1850s–1860s.

Rarity: —

$10 • W-MA-2900-010-G090
Left: Lathework chain bearing MASSACHUSETTS / 10 / 10 vertically. ***Center:*** Alternating flower garlands and gridwork segments. ***Right:*** 10 / 10 vertically. ***Engraver:*** Perkins. ***Comments:*** H-MA-1080-G42. 18__. 1820s.

Rarity: —

$10 • W-MA-2900-010-G090a
Engraver: PSSP. ***Comments:*** H-MA-1080-G44. Similar to W-MA-2900-010-G090 but with zigzag ruled lines. 18__. 1820s–1830s.

Rarity: —

$10 • W-MA-2900-010-G090b
Engraver: PSSP. ***Comments:*** H-MA-1080-G46. Similar to W-MA-2900-010-G090 but with spiral lathework lines. 18__. 1830s.

Rarity: —

$10 • W-MA-2900-010-G100
Left: TEN vertically. ***Center:*** 10 / View of Essex St., Salem / X. ***Right:*** 10 / Female portrait. ***Engraver:*** Terry, Pelton & Co. ***Comments:*** H-MA-1080-G50. 18__. 1830s–1850s.

Rarity: —

$10 • W-MA-2900-010-G100a
Overprint: Red. ***Engraver:*** Terry, Pelton & Co. ***Comments:*** H-MA-1080-G50a. Similar to W-MA-2900-010-G100. 18__. 1850s.

Rarity: —

$10 • W-MA-2900-010-G100b
Overprint: Red. ***Engraver:*** Terry, Pelton & Co. / ABNCo. monogram. ***Comments:*** H-MA-1080-G50b. Similar to W-MA-2900-010-G100 but with additional engraver imprint. 18__. 1850s–1860s.

Rarity: —

$20 • W-MA-2900-020-G110
Left: Lathework chain bearing MASSACHUSETTS / 20 / 20 vertically. ***Center:*** Alternating flower garlands and gridwork segments. ***Right:*** 20 / 20 vertically. ***Engraver:*** PSSP. ***Comments:*** H-MA-1080-G52. 18__. 1820s–1830s.

Rarity: —

$20 • W-MA-2900-020-G120
Left: 20 / Man plowing with horses / 20. ***Center:*** 20 / Group of milkmaids. ***Right:*** 20 / Ship / XX. ***Comments:*** H-MA-1080-G56. 18__. 1830s–1840s.

Rarity: —

$20 • W-MA-2900-020-G130
Left: 20 / Woman seated with book on lap, opening chest. ***Center:*** XX / Eagle on rock / XX. ***Right:*** 20 / Ship in harbor. ***Engraver:*** New England Bank Note Co. ***Comments:*** H-MA-1080-G58. 18__. 1840s–1850s.

Rarity: —

$20 • W-MA-2900-020-G140
Left: 20 / Minerva standing with spear. ***Center:*** Woman seated between 2 and 0. ***Bottom center:*** XX. ***Right:*** 20 / Woman reclining on cornucopia / 20. ***Engraver:*** Rawdon, Wright, Hatch & Edson. ***Comments:*** H-MA-1080-G60. 18__. 1850s.

Rarity: —

$50 • W-MA-2900-050-G150

Left: Lathework chain bearing MASSACHUSETTS / 50 / 50 vertically. ***Center:*** Alternating flower garlands and gridwork segments. ***Right:*** 50 / 50 vertically. ***Engraver:*** PSSP. ***Comments:*** H-MA-1080-G62. 18__. 1820s–1830s.

Rarity: —

$50 • W-MA-2900-050-G160

Left: FIFTY / Woman standing with wreath and flowers / FIFTY. ***Center:*** 50 / Man restraining prancing horse / 50. ***Right:*** FIFTY / Woman standing with cornucopia / FIFTY. ***Engraver:*** New England Bank Note Co. ***Comments:*** H-MA-1080-G66. 18__ 1840s–1850s.

Rarity: —

$50 • W-MA-2900-050-G170

Left: 50 / Minerva standing by column. ***Center:*** Ceres and Vulcan flanking cornucopia. ***Right:*** 50 / Cherub in sailboat / 50. ***Engraver:*** Rawdon, Wright, Hatch & Edson. ***Comments:*** H-MA-1080-G68. 18__. 1850s.

Rarity: —

$100 • W-MA-2900-100-G180

Left: Lathework chain bearing MASSACHUSETTS / 100 / 100 vertically. ***Center:*** Alternating flower garlands and gridwork segments. ***Right:*** 100 / 100 vertically. ***Engraver:*** Perkins. ***Comments:*** H-MA-1080-G70. 18__. 1820s–1830s.

Rarity: —

$100 • W-MA-2900-100-G190

Left: ONE HUNDRED on 100 / Portrait of William Henry Harrison. ***Center:*** Wharf scene, Men loading wagon with barrels. ***Right:*** ONE HUNDRED on 100 / Portrait of Christopher Columbus. ***Engraver:*** New England Bank Note Co. ***Comments:*** H-MA-1080-G74. 18__. 1840s–1850s.

Rarity: —

$100 • W-MA-2900-100-G200

Left: 100 / Vulcan seated with sledge and anchor. ***Center:*** Train on bridge, Eagle on limb, Canal locks / C C. ***Right:*** 100 / Ceres seated, Cornucopia. ***Engraver:*** Rawdon, Wright, Hatch & Edson. ***Comments:*** H-MA-1080-G76. 18__. 1850s–1860s.

Rarity: —

$100 • W-MA-2900-100-G210

CC

Engraver: Rawdon, Wright, Hatch & Edson. ***Comments:*** H-Unlisted. 18__.

Rarity: URS-2
Proof $1,500

$500 • W-MA-2900-500-G220

Left: Woman seated on sheaves, Men reaping, Man on horse / 500. ***Center:*** 500 / D. ***Right:*** 500 vertically. ***Engraver:*** Rawdon, Wright, Hatch & Edson. ***Comments:*** H-MA-1080-G80. 18__. 1850s–1860s.

Rarity: —

$1,000 • W-MA-2900-1000-G230

Left: Laocoon and sons strangled by serpents / 1000. ***Center:*** THOUSAND / Train. ***Right:*** 1000 / Ships / 1000. ***Engraver:*** Rawdon, Wright, Hatch & Edson. ***Comments:*** H-MA-1080-G84. 18__. 1850s–1860s.

Rarity: —

Non-Valid Issues

$5 • W-MA-2900-005-A010

Left: Several men with sticks driving herd of cattle into stream / 5. ***Center:*** Five men raking and loading hay, Ox wagon. ***Right:*** 5. ***Tint:*** Red-brown lathework outlining white 5. ***Engraver:*** Bald, Cousland & Co. ***Comments:*** H-MA-1080-A5. Altered from $5 Pioneer Association, Lafayette, Indiana. 1850s.

Rarity: —

$10 • W-MA-2900-010-R010

Engraver: Terry, Pelton & Co. ***Comments:*** H-MA-1080-R5. Raised from W-MA-2900-001-G020. 18__. 1840s.

Rarity: —

Bank of General Interest

1831–1839

W-MA-2910

History: The Bank of General Interest was chartered on March 13, 1831, with an authorized capital of $200,000, a figure which was raised to $400,000 in 1839. Its office was at 172 Essex Street in 1842.

Circulation in 1839 was $21,748. During this year the stockholders voted unanimously to surrender the charter of the bank. The losses of the bank in this difficult economic era were estimated at $70,000.[37]

Numismatic Commentary: Genuine notes from this bank are especially hard to locate. Most issues are of the PSSP design, but the Boston Bank Note Co. designs are the most interesting and will offer a vignette not seen on notes from other banks.

Valid Issues

$1 • W-MA-2910-001-G010

Left: Lathework panel bearing MASSACHUSETTS vertically. ***Center:*** 1 / 1 / Alternating flower garlands and gridwork segments / ONE / 1 / 1. ***Right:*** Lathework panel bearing ONE / D / ONE vertically. ***Engraver:*** PSSP. ***Comments:*** H-MA-1110-G2. 18__. 1830s.

Rarity: —

$1 • W-MA-2910-001-G020

CJF

Engraver: Boston Bank Note Co. ***Comments:*** H-MA-1110-G4. 18__. 1830s–1840s.

Rarity: —

$2 • W-MA-2910-002-G030

Left: Lathework panel bearing MASSACHUSETTS vertically. ***Center:*** 2 / 2 / Alternating flower garlands and gridwork segments / TWO / 2 / 2. ***Right:*** Lathework panel bearing five TWOs vertically. ***Engraver:*** PSSP. ***Comments:*** H-MA-1110-G8. 18__. 1830s.

Rarity: —

$2 • W-MA-2910-002-G040

Engraver: Unverified, but likely Boston Bank Note Co. ***Comments:*** H-MA-1110-G10. No description available. 18__. 1830s–1840s.

Rarity: *None known*

$3 • W-MA-2910-003-G050

Left: Lathework panel bearing MASSACHUSETTS vertically. ***Center:*** 3 / 3 / Alternating flower garlands and gridwork segments / THREE / 3 / 3. ***Right:*** Lathework panel bearing THREE vertically. ***Engraver:*** PSSP. ***Comments:*** H-MA-1110-G12. 18__. 1830s.

Rarity: —

$5 • W-MA-2910-005-G060

Left: Lathework chain bearing MASSACHUSETTS / 5 / 5. ***Center:*** Alternating flower garlands and gridwork segments / FIVE DOLLARS lined by spiral lathework lines. ***Right:*** 5 / 5. ***Engraver:*** PSSP. ***Comments:*** H-MA-1110-G16. 18__. 1830s.

Rarity: —

$10 • W-MA-2910-010-G070

Left: Lathework chain bearing MASSACHUSETTS / 10 / 10 vertically. ***Center:*** Alternating flower garlands and gridwork segments / TEN DOLLARS lined by spiral lathework lines. ***Right:*** 10 / 10 vertically. ***Engraver:*** PSSP. ***Comments:*** H-MA-1110-G20. 18__. 1830s.

Rarity: —

$20 • W-MA-2910-020-G080

Left: Lathework chain bearing MASSACHUSETTS / 20 vertically. ***Center:*** Alternating flower garlands and gridwork segments. ***Right:*** 20 / 20 vertically. ***Engraver:*** PSSP. ***Comments:*** H-MA-1110-G24. 18__. 1830s.

Rarity: —

$50 • W-MA-2910-050-G090

Left: Lathework chain bearing MASSACHUSETTS / 50 / 50 vertically. ***Center:*** Alternating flower garlands and gridwork segments. ***Right:*** 50 / 50 vertically. ***Engraver:*** PSSP. ***Comments:*** H-MA-1110-G28. 18__. 1830s.

Rarity: —

$100 • W-MA-2910-100-G100

Left: Lathework chain MASSACHUSETTS / 100 / 100 vertically. ***Center:*** Alternating flower garlands and gridwork segments. ***Right:*** 100 / 100 vertically. ***Engraver:*** Perkins. ***Comments:*** H-MA-1110-G32. 18__. 1830s.

Rarity: —

Commercial Bank

1819–1864

W-MA-2920

History: The Commercial Bank was chartered on February 12, 1819, with an authorized capital of $300,000, reduced by 1827 to $200,000 but later restored to $300,000. Circulation of the bank in 1839 was $30,851; it reached a high of $95,045 in 1857. Real estate was valued at $4,500 in 1857.

In 1864 the business of the Commercial Bank was succeeded by the First National Bank of Salem, chartered on April 30, 1864. Throughout its existence, the bank was in the same location in its own building on Central Street.

Numismatic Commentary: Genuine notes from this bank are very hard to locate in the marketplace.

VALID ISSUES

$1 • W-MA-2920-001-G010

Center: 1 / 1 / Oval of flower garlands and gridwork segments / ONE / 1 / 1. ***Engraver:*** PSSP. ***Comments:*** H-MA-1095-G2. 18__. 1819–1820s.

Rarity: —

$1 • W-MA-2920-001-G010a

Left: Panel of lathework circle segments. ***Right:*** Panel of lathework circle segments. ***Engraver:*** PSSP. ***Comments:*** H-MA-1095-G4. Similar to W-MA-2920-001-G010. 18__. 1820s.

Rarity: —

$1 • W-MA-2920-001-G010b

Left: Panel of lathework circle segments. ***Right:*** Panel of lathework circle segments. ***Engraver:*** PSSP. ***Comments:*** H-MA-1095-G6. Similar to W-MA-2920-001-G010. 18__. 1820s–1830s.

Rarity: —

$1 • W-MA-2920-001-G010c

Left: ONE / D / ONE vertically. ***Right:*** ONE / D / ONE vertically. ***Engraver:*** PSSP. ***Comments:*** H-MA-1095-G8. Similar to W-MA-2920-001-G010. 18__. 1830s.

Rarity: —

$1 • W-MA-2920-001-G020

Left: 1 / Woman leaning on rock / ONE. ***Center:*** Spread eagle, Farm implements, Shipping / ONE. ***Right:*** 1 / Woman leaning on cornucopia. ***Engraver:*** New England Bank Note Co. ***Comments:*** H-MA-1095-G10. 18__. 1830s–1850s.

Rarity: —

$1 • W-MA-2920-001-G030

CJF

Tint: Red. ***Engraver:*** American Bank Note Co. ***Comments:*** H-MA-1095-G12a. Jan. 1, 18__. 1850s–1860s.

Rarity: URS-3

VF $2,500

$2 • W-MA-2920-002-G040

Center: 2 / 2 / Oval of flower garlands and gridwork segments / TWO / 2 / 2. ***Engraver:*** PSSP. ***Comments:*** H-MA-1095-G14. 18__. 1819–1820s.

Rarity: —

$2 • W-MA-2920-002-G040a

Left: Panel of lathework circle segments. ***Right:*** Panel of lathework circle segments. ***Engraver:*** PSSP. ***Comments:*** H-MA-1095-G16. Similar to W-MA-2920-002-G040. 18__. 1820s.

Rarity: —

$2 • W-MA-2920-002-G040b

Left: Five TWOs vertically. ***Right:*** Five TWOs vertically. ***Engraver:*** PSSP. ***Comments:*** H-MA-1095-G18. Similar to W-MA-2920-002-G040. 18__. 1820s–1830s.

Rarity: —

$2 • W-MA-2920-002-G040c

Left: Five TWOs vertically. ***Right:*** Five TWOs vertically. ***Engraver:*** PSSP. ***Comments:*** H-MA-1095-G20. Similar to W-MA-2920-002-G040. 18__. 1830s.

Rarity: —

$2 • W-MA-2920-002-G050

Left: TWO / Ship / TWO. ***Center:*** 2 / Commerce seated on bale, Ship / 2. ***Right:*** TWO / Portrait of Indian / TWO. ***Engraver:*** New England Bank Note Co. ***Comments:*** H-MA-1095-G22. 18__. 1830s–1850s.

Rarity: —

$2 • W-MA-2920-002-G060

Left: 2 / Two Indians viewing city. ***Center:*** Woman seated with bolt of cloth pointing to mills, Village and falls. ***Right:*** 2 / Woman with spyglass. ***Tint:*** Red or green. ***Engraver:*** American Bank Note Co. ***Comments:*** H-MA-1095-G24a. Jan. 1, 18__ 1850s–1860s.

Rarity: —

$3 • W-MA-2920-003-G070

Center: 3 / 3 / Oval of flower garlands and gridwork segments / 3 / 3. ***Engraver:*** PSSP. ***Comments:*** H-MA-1095-G26. 18__. 1819–1820s.

Rarity: —

$3 • W-MA-2920-003-G070a

Left: Panel of lathework circle segments. ***Right:*** Panel of lathework circle segments. ***Engraver:*** PSSP. ***Comments:*** H-MA-1095-G28. Similar to W-MA-2920-003-G070. 18__. 1820s.

Rarity: —

$3 • W-MA-2920-003-G070b

Left: Panel of lathework circle segments. ***Right:*** Panel of lathework circle segments. ***Engraver:*** PSSP. ***Comments:*** H-MA-1095-G30. Similar to W-MA-2920-003-G070. 18__. 1820s–1830s.

Rarity: —

$3 • W-MA-2920-003-G070c

Left: THREE vertically. ***Right:*** THREE vertically. ***Engraver:*** PSSP. ***Comments:*** H-MA-1095-G32. Similar to W-MA-2920-003-G070. 18__. 1830s.

Rarity: —

$3 • W-MA-2920-003-G080

Left: 3 / Mercury / THREE. ***Center:*** THREE / Indian man seated on rock with gun / THREE. ***Right:*** 3 / Ship / THREE. ***Engraver:*** New England Bank Note Co. ***Comments:*** H-MA-1095-G34. 18__. 1830s–1850s.

Rarity: —

$3 • W-MA-2920-003-G090

Left: Man with horses / 3. ***Center:*** 3 / THREE. ***Right:*** 3 / Portrait of George Washington. ***Tint:*** Green 3, THREE. ***Engraver:*** American Bank Note Co. ***Comments:*** H-MA-1095-G36a. Jan. 1, 18__. 1850s–1860s.

Rarity: —

$5 • W-MA-2920-005-G100

Left: Lathework panel bearing MASSACHUSETTS / 5 / 5. ***Center:*** Alternating flower garlands and gridwork segments. ***Right:*** 5 / 5. ***Engraver:*** PSSP. ***Comments:*** H-MA-1095-G38. 18__. 1819–1820s.

Rarity: —

$5 • W-MA-2920-005-G100a

Left: Lathework chain bearing MASSACHUSETTS vertically. ***Right:*** Panel of lathework circle segments. ***Engraver:*** PSSP. ***Comments:*** H-MA-1095-G40. Similar to W-MA-2920-005-G100. 18__. 1820s.

Rarity: —

$5 • W-MA-2920-005-G100b

Engraver: PSSP. ***Comments:*** H-MA-1095-G42. Similar to W-MA-2920-005-G100 but with zigzag ruled lines. 18__. 1820s–1830s.

Rarity: —

$5 • W-MA-2920-005-G100c

Engraver: PSSP. ***Comments:*** H-MA-1095-G44. Similar to W-MA-2920-005-G100 but with spiral lathework lines. 18__. 1830s.

Rarity: —

$5 • W-MA-2920-005-G110

Left: 5 / Cattle / FIVE. ***Center:*** Woman / River scene, Steamboat, ship, and bridge / V. ***Right:*** 5 / Cattle / FIVE. ***Engraver:*** New England Bank Note Co. ***Comments:*** H-MA-1095-G46. 18__. 1830s–1850s.

Rarity: —

$5 • W-MA-2920-005-G120

Left: FIVE / Justice seated / FIVE. ***Center:*** 5 / Steamboat and schooner, Men on wharf / 5. ***Right:*** FIVE / State arms / FIVE. ***Engraver:*** New England Bank Note Co. ***Comments:*** H-MA-1095-G48. 18__. 1830s–1850s.

Rarity: —

$5 • W-MA-2920-005-G130

Left: 5 / Male portrait. ***Center:*** Two sailors with bales and anchor, Ships. ***Right:*** 5 / Woman kneeling with chart, globe, and sextant. ***Tint:*** Red or green. ***Engraver:*** American Bank Note Co. ***Comments:*** H-MA-1095-G50a. Jan. 1, 18__. 1850s–1860s.

Rarity: —

$10 • W-MA-2920-010-G140

Left: Lathework panel bearing MASSACHUSETTS / 10 / 10 vertically. ***Center:*** Alternating flower garlands and gridwork segments / TEN. ***Right:*** 10 / 10 vertically. ***Engraver:*** Perkins. ***Comments:*** H-MA-1095-G52. 18__. 1819–1820s.

Rarity: —

$10 • W-MA-2920-010-G140a

Left: Lathework chain bearing MASSACHUSETTS vertically. ***Right:*** Panel of lathework circle segments. ***Engraver:*** Perkins. ***Comments:*** H-MA-1095-G54. Similar to W-MA-2920-010-G140. 18__. 1820s.

Rarity: —

$10 • W-MA-2920-010-G140b

Engraver: PSSP. ***Comments:*** H-MA-1095-G56. Similar to W-MA-2920-010-G140. 18__. 1820s–1830s.

Rarity: —

$10 • W-MA-2920-010-G140c

Engraver: PSSP. ***Comments:*** H-MA-1095-G58. Similar to W-MA-2920-010-G140 but with zigzag ruled lines. 18__. 1830s.

Rarity: —

$10 • W-MA-2920-010-G150

Left: 10 / Ship / TEN. ***Center:*** 10 / Whaling ships and rowboats / Woman seated with cornucopia and shield bearing X. ***Right:*** 10 / Ship / TEN. ***Engraver:*** New England Bank Note Co. ***Comments:*** H-MA-1095-G60. 18__. 1830s–1850s.

Rarity: —

$20 • W-MA-2920-020-G160

Left: Panel bearing state arms / 20 / 20 vertically. ***Center:*** Alternating flower garlands and gridwork segments. ***Engraver:*** Perkins. ***Comments:*** H-MA-1095-G62. 18__. 1819–1820s.

Rarity: —

$20 • W-MA-2920-020-G160a

Left: Lathework chain bearing MASSACHUSETTS vertically. ***Engraver:*** PSSP. ***Comments:*** H-MA-1095-G64. Similar to W-MA-2920-020-G160. 18__. 1820s–1830s.

Rarity: —

$20 • W-MA-2920-020-G170

Left: 20 / XX / 20. ***Center:*** 20 / Woman seated with balance, Sheaf and bales, Men plowing and ship / 20. ***Right:*** TWENTY vertically. ***Engraver:*** PSSP / New England Bank Note Co. ***Comments:*** H-MA-1095-G66. 18__. 1830s–1840s.

Rarity: —

$20 • W-MA-2920-020-G180

Left: 20 / Minerva standing with spear. ***Center:*** Woman seated between 2 and 0. ***Right:*** 20 / Woman reclining on cornucopia / 20. ***Engraver:*** Rawdon, Wright, Hatch & Edson. ***Comments:*** H-MA-1095-G68. 18__. 1840s–1850s.

Rarity: —

$20 • W-MA-2920-020-G190

Left: Woman standing with eagle / 20. ***Center:*** TWENTY across 20 / Female portrait. ***Right:*** 20 / Portrait of Benjamin Franklin. ***Engraver:*** New England Bank Note Co. ***Comments:*** H-MA-1095-G70. 18__. 1850s.

Rarity: —

$50 • W-MA-2920-050-G200

Left: Panel bearing state arms / 50 / 50 vertically. ***Center:*** Text with a microletter background. ***Right:*** 50 / 50 vertically. ***Engraver:*** Perkins. ***Comments:*** H-MA-1095-G72. 18__. 1819–1820s.

Rarity: —

$50 • W-MA-2920-050-G200a

Left: Lathework chain bearing MASSACHUSETTS vertically. ***Engraver:*** PSSP. ***Comments:*** H-MA-1095-G74. Similar to W-MA-2920-050-G200. 18__. 1820s–1830s.

Rarity: —

$50 • W-MA-2920-050-G210

Left: 50 / Woman standing on shore with staff and cornucopia. ***Center:*** 50. ***Right:*** FIFTY vertically. ***Engraver:*** New England Bank Note Co. ***Comments:*** H-MA-1095-G76. 18__. 1830s–1840s.

Rarity: —

$50 • W-MA-2920-050-G220

Left: FIFTY / Woman standing with wreath and flowers / FIFTY. ***Center:*** 50 / Man restraining prancing horse / 50. ***Right:*** FIFTY / Woman standing with cornucopia / FIFTY. ***Engraver:*** New England Bank Note Co. ***Comments:*** H-MA-1095-G78. 18__. 1840s.

Rarity: —

$50 • W-MA-2920-050-G230

Left: 50 / Minerva standing by column. ***Center:*** Ceres and Vulcan flanking cornucopia. ***Right:*** 50 / Cherub in sailboat / 50. ***Engraver:*** Rawdon, Wright, Hatch & Edson. ***Comments:*** H-MA-1095-G80. 18__. 1840s–1850s.

Rarity: —

$50 • W-MA-2920-050-G240

SBG

Tint: Green. ***Engraver:*** American Bank Note Co. ***Comments:*** H-MA-1095-G82a. Sept. 1, 1860.

Rarity: URS-3

Proof $6,000

$100 • W-MA-2920-100-G250

Left: Panel bearing state arms / 100 / 100 vertically. ***Center:*** Alternating flower garlands and gridwork segments. ***Right:*** 100 / 100 vertically. ***Engraver:*** Perkins. ***Comments:*** H-MA-1095-G84. 18__. 1819–1820s.

Rarity: —

$100 • W-MA-2920-100-G250a

Left: Lathework chain bearing MASSACHUSETTS vertically. ***Engraver:*** Perkins. ***Comments:*** H-MA-1095-G86. Similar to W-MA-2920-100-G250. 18__. 1820s–1830s.

Rarity: —

$100 • W-MA-2920-100-G260

Left: C / Portrait of George Washington / C. ***Center:*** 100 / Manhattan reclining pouring water, Ship / 100. ***Right:*** ONE HUNDRED vertically. ***Engraver:*** New England Bank Note Co. ***Comments:*** H-MA-1095-G88. 18__. 1830s–1840s.

Rarity: —

$100 • W-MA-2920-100-G270

Left: 100 / Eagle / 100. ***Center:*** C / Phoebus in the Chariot of the Sun / 100. ***Right:*** C / Portrait of George Washington / C. ***Engraver:*** New England Bank Note Co. ***Comments:*** H-MA-1095-G90. 18__. 1840s–1850s.

Rarity: —

$100 • W-MA-2920-100-G280

Left: C / Men with fishing boat at shore / 100. ***Center:*** Eagle perched on bale, Cornucopia and Sheaf / 100. ***Right:*** 100 / Ceres / 100. ***Engraver:*** New England Bank Note Co. ***Comments:*** H-MA-1095-G92. 18__. 1850s.

Rarity: —

$100 • W-MA-2920-100-G290

Left: 100 / Vulcan seated with sledge and anchor. ***Center:*** Eagle on limb, Train on bridge, Canal locks. ***Bottom center:*** 100. ***Right:*** 100 / Ceres seated with cornucopia. ***Engraver:*** Rawdon, Wright, Hatch & Edson. ***Comments:*** H-MA-1095-G94. 18__. 1850s–1860s.

Rarity: —

$100 • W-MA-2920-100-G300

Left: 100 / Woman standing with headdress. ***Center:*** C / C. ***Right:*** 100 / Two men with guns. ***Tint:*** Green. ***Engraver:*** American Bank Note Co. ***Comments:*** H-MA-1095-G96a. Sept. 1, 1860.

Rarity: —

$500 • W-MA-2920-500-G310

Left: 500 / 500 / 500. ***Center:*** 500 / Woman seated with shield bearing D, Fasces, cornucopia, lyre, and sheaf / 500. ***Right:*** 500 / D / 500. ***Engraver:*** PSSP / New England Bank Note Co. ***Comments:*** H-MA-1095-G98. 18__. 1830s–1840s.

Rarity: —

$500 • W-MA-2920-500-G320

Left: Indian paddling canoe, Forest and mountains / 500 / D D / 500. ***Right:*** 500 / Justice. ***Engraver:*** New England Bank Note Co. ***Comments:*** H-MA-1095-G100. 18__. 1840s–1850s.

Rarity: —

$500 • W-MA-2920-500-G330

Left: Woman seated on sheaves, Men reaping, Man on horse / 500. ***Center:*** 500 / D. ***Right:*** 500 vertically. ***Engraver:*** Rawdon, Wright, Hatch & Edson. ***Comments:*** H-MA-1095-G102. 18__. 1850s–1860s.

Rarity: —

Non-Valid Issues

$1 • W-MA-2920-001-A010

Left: ONE / Hebe seated on sheaf, watering eagle / ONE. ***Center:*** Ships / Eagle on shield. ***Right:*** 1 / Ceres kneeling, Sheaf, Farm. ***Engraver:*** Danforth, Bald & Co. ***Comments:*** H-MA-1095-A5. Altered from $1 Columbia Bank, Washington, D.C. 18__. 1850s.

Rarity: —

$1 • W-MA-2920-001-A020

Left: 1 / Man seated with hat under tree. ***Center:*** Horses / ONE. ***Right:*** 1 / Man seated. ***Engraver:*** Danforth, Wright & Co. ***Comments:*** H-MA-1095-A10. Altered from $1 Commercial Bank of New Jersey, Perth Amboy, New Jersey series. July 10, 1856.

Rarity: —

$2 • W-MA-2920-002-A030

Left: 2 / Man on horse, Boy standing with scythe, Dog and cow / TWO. ***Center:*** Train passing cliffs, Men with wheelbarrow and picks. ***Bottom center:*** Sailboat. ***Right:*** 2 / Ships near shore. ***Engraver:*** New England Bank Note Co. ***Comments:*** H-MA-1095-A15. Altered from $2 Commercial Bank, Gratiot, Michigan. 18__. 1840s.

Rarity: —

$2 • W-MA-2920-002-A040

Left: TWO / Woman standing. ***Center:*** Sailing ships at sea / TWO. ***Right:*** 2 / Woman seated. ***Engraver:*** Danforth, Wright & Co. ***Comments:*** H-MA-1095-A20. Altered from $2 Commercial Bank of New Jersey, Perth Amboy, New Jersey series. July 10, 1856.

Rarity: —

$2 • W-MA-2920-002-A050

CJF

Engraver: Toppan & Co. ***Comments:*** H-MA-1095-A25. Altered from $2 Pennsylvania Savings Bank, Philadelphia, Pennsylvania. 185_. 1850s.

Rarity: URS-6
F $100; **VF** $150

$3 • W-MA-2920-003-N010

Center: Woman seated, Ship. ***Right:*** Portrait of George Washington. ***Comments:*** H-MA-1095-N5.

Rarity: —

$3 • W-MA-2920-003-A060

Left: 3 / Portrait of Benjamin Franklin. ***Center:*** Woman reclining with strongbox / 3 on shield, Produce. ***Right:*** 3 / Indian woman seated under tree. ***Engraver:*** Danforth, Bald & Co. ***Comments:*** H-MA-1095-A30. Altered from $3 Columbia Bank, Washington, D.C. 18__. 1850s.

Rarity: —

$3 • W-MA-2920-003-A070

Left: 3 / Portrait of George Washington / THREE. ***Center:*** Steamship and other ships at sea. ***Right:*** 3 / Hebe watering eagle. ***Engraver:*** New England Bank Note Co. ***Comments:*** H-MA-1095-A35. Altered from $3 Commercial Bank, Gratiot, Michigan. 18__. 1840s.

Rarity: —

$5 • W-MA-2920-005-S010

CC

Comments: H-MA-1095-N10. Spurious note. June 15, 1852.

Rarity: URS-6
F $300

$5 • W-MA-2920-005-A080
Left: 5 / Train / 5. ***Center:*** 5 / Ship / FIVE. ***Right:*** 5 / George Washington standing by horse. ***Engraver:*** New England Bank Note Co. ***Comments:*** H-MA-1095-A40. Altered from $5 Commercial Bank, Gratiot, Michigan. 18__. 1840s.

Rarity: —

$5 • W-MA-2920-005-A090
Left: 5 / Sailing ship. ***Center:*** Whale blowing through spout, Ship. ***Right:*** 5 / Sailor. ***Engraver:*** Danforth, Wright & Co. ***Comments:*** H-MA-1095-A45. Altered from $5 Commercial Bank of New Jersey, Perth Amboy, New Jersey series. Sept. 1, 1856.

Rarity: —
F $310

$5 • W-MA-2920-005-A090a
SI

Overprint: Red 5 / 5. ***Comments:*** H-Unlisted. Similar to W-MA-2920-005-A090. September 1, 1856.

Rarity: URS-3
F $250

$10 • W-MA-2920-010-R010
Engraver: New England Bank Note Co. ***Comments:*** H-MA-1095-R5. Raised from W-MA-2920-001-G020. 18__. 1840s.

Rarity: —

$10 • W-MA-2920-010-A100
Left: TEN / Helmeted woman standing with lyre. ***Center:*** Sailing ship, Gears and produce. ***Right:*** 10 / Wharf scene. ***Engraver:*** New England Bank Note Co. ***Comments:*** H-MA-1095-A50. Altered from $10 Commercial Bank, Gratiot, Michigan. 18__. 1840s.

Rarity: —

$20 • W-MA-2920-020-AR010
QDB

Engraver: Danforth, Wright & Co. ***Comments:*** H-MA-1095-A55. Altered and raised from $1 Commercial Bank of New Jersey, Perth Amboy, New Jersey series. July 10, 1856.

Rarity: —

$20 • W-MA-2920-020-A110
Left: XX / Portrait of George Washington / 20. ***Center:*** XX / Steamship / XX. ***Bottom center:*** Buffalo. ***Right:*** Jupiter in clouds, Staff, Thunderbolts / 20. ***Engraver:*** Rawdon, Wright, Hatch & Edson. ***Comments:*** H-MA-1095-A60. Altered from $20 Commercial Bank of Buffalo, New York. 18__. 1840s.

Rarity: —

Essex Bank
1792–1819
W-MA-2930

History: The Essex Bank was chartered on June 18, 1792, with an authorized capital to be no less than $100,000 and no more than $400,000. Paper money could be issued up to twice the amount of paid-in capital. The bank began business on July 2, 1792, in a building on Central Street, then known as Bank Street. By 1812 the bank had a capital of $300,000.

The celebrated case of Foster v. the Essex Bank involved a depositor, Israel Foster, who left kegs filled with $32,000 in gold coins with the cashier and president of the bank and received a receipt for them. The coins were stolen by the cashier and chief clerk in August 1818, and the court held the bank responsible for their loss. The bank slowed down its operations afterward. Its charter expired in 1819, after which its bills and obligations were settled for several years by the Commercial Bank.

Numismatic Commentary: This entity was one of the state's earliest banks. When notes are found, they are usually of the PSSP design or early non-valid issues.

Valid Issues

$1 • W-MA-2930-001-G010
Comments: H-MA-1100-G20. No description available. 1800s.

Rarity: *None known*

$1 • W-MA-2930-001-G020
Center: 1 / 1 / Double oval of flower garlands and gridwork segments / ONE / 1 / 1. ***Engraver:*** PSSP. ***Comments:*** H-MA-1100-G26. 18__. 1807–1809.

Rarity: —

$1 • W-MA-2930-001-G030
Center: 1 / 1 / Oval of flower garlands and gridwork segments / ONE / 1 / 1. ***Engraver:*** PSSP. ***Comments:*** H-MA-1100-G28. 18__. 1809–circa 1812.

Rarity: —

$1 • W-MA-2930-001-G040
Center: 1 / 1 / Flower garlands and gridwork segments / ONE / 1 / 1. ***Engraver:*** PSSP. ***Comments:*** H-MA-1100-G30. 18__. 1810s–1820s.

Rarity: —

$2 • W-MA-2930-002-G050
Comments: H-MA-1100-G40. 1800s.

Rarity: URS-2
Proof $1,500

$2 • W-MA-2930-002-G060
Center: 2 / 2 / Double oval of flower garlands and gridwork segments / TWO / 2 / 2. ***Engraver:*** PSSP. ***Comments:*** H-MA-1100-G46. 18__. 1807–1809.
Rarity: —

$2 • W-MA-2930-002-G070
Center: 2 / 2 / Oval of flower garlands and gridwork segments / TWO / 2 / 2. ***Engraver:*** PSSP. ***Comments:*** H-MA-1100-G48. 18__. 1809–circa 1812.
Rarity: —

$2 • W-MA-2930-002-G080
Center: 2 / 2 / Flower garlands and gridwork segments / TWO / 2 / 2. ***Engraver:*** PSSP. ***Comments:*** H-MA-1100-G50. 18__. 1810s–1820s.
Rarity: —

$3 • W-MA-2930-003-G090
Comments: H-MA-1100-G60. No description available. 1800s.
Rarity: *None known*

$3 • W-MA-2930-003-G100
Center: 3 / 3 / Black oval bearing white flower buds / THREE / 3 / 3. ***Engraver:*** PSSP. ***Comments:*** H-MA-1100-G66. 18__. 1807–1809.
Rarity: —

$3 • W-MA-2930-003-G110 CJF

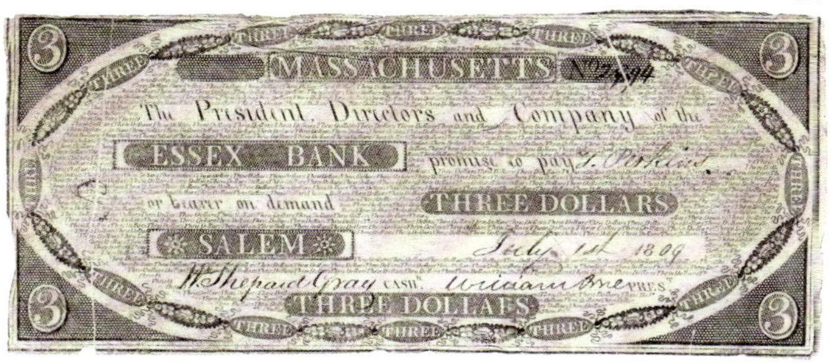

Engraver: PSSP. ***Comments:*** H-MA-1100-G68. 18__. 1809–1820s.
Rarity: —

$5 • W-MA-2930-005-G120
Comments: H-MA-1100-G76. No description available. 1800s.
Rarity: *None known*

$5 • W-MA-2930-005-G130
Left: Gridwork panel bearing MASSACHUSETTS / 5 / 5. ***Center:*** Alternating flower garlands and gridwork segments. ***Right:*** 5 / 5. ***Engraver:*** Perkins. ***Comments:*** H-MA-1100-G82. 18__. Circa 1806 and 1807.
Rarity: —

$5 • W-MA-2930-005-G130a
Center: Rose-covered FIVE. ***Engraver:*** Perkins. ***Comments:*** H-MA-1100-G84. Similar to W-MA-2930-005-G130. 18__. Circa 1808 and 1809.
Rarity: —

$5 • W-MA-2930-005-G130b
Left: Gridwork panel bearing MASSACHUSETTS / State arms / 5 / 5. ***Engraver:*** PSSP. ***Comments:*** H-MA-1100-G86. Similar to W-MA-2930-005-G130. 18__. 1809–1820s.
Rarity: —

$10 • W-MA-2930-010-G140
Comments: H-MA-1100-G92. No description available. 1800s.
Rarity: *None known*

$10 • W-MA-2930-010-G150
Left: Gridwork panel bearing MASSACHUSETTS / 10 / 10 vertically. ***Center:*** Alternating flower garlands and gridwork segments. ***Right:*** 10 / 10 vertically. ***Engraver:*** Perkins. ***Comments:*** H-MA-1100-G98. 18__. Circa 1806 and 1807.
Rarity: —

$10 • W-MA-2930-010-G150a
Center: Rose-covered TEN. ***Engraver:*** Perkins. ***Comments:*** H-MA-1100-G100. Similar to W-MA-2930-010-G150. 18__. Circa 1808 and 1809.
Rarity: —

$10 • W-MA-2930-010-G150b
Left: Gridwork panel bearing MASSACHUSETTS / State arms / 10 / 10 vertically. ***Engraver:*** Perkins. ***Comments:*** H-MA-1100-G102. Similar to W-MA-2930-010-G150. 18__. 1809–circa 1812.
Rarity: —

$10 • W-MA-2930-010-G150c
Left: Gridwork panel bearing MASSACHUSETTS / State arms / 10 / 10 vertically. ***Center:*** Alternating flower garlands and gridwork segments / TEN. ***Engraver:*** Perkins. ***Comments:*** H-MA-1100-G104. Similar to W-MA-2930-010-G150. 18__. Circa 1812–1820s.
Rarity: —

$20 • W-MA-2930-020-G160
Comments: H-MA-1100-G110. No description available. 1800s.
Rarity: *None known*

$20 • W-MA-2930-020-G170
Left: Narrow gridwork panel bearing MASSACHUSETTS / 20 / 20 vertically. ***Center:*** Alternating flower garlands and gridwork segments. ***Right:*** 20 / 20 vertically. ***Engraver:*** Perkins. ***Comments:*** H-MA-1100-G116. 18__. Circa 1806–1809.
Rarity: —

$20 • W-MA-2930-020-G170a
Left: Gridwork panel bearing MASSACHUSETTS / State arms / 20 / 20 vertically. ***Engraver:*** Perkins. ***Comments:*** H-MA-1100-G118. Similar to W-MA-2930-020-G170. 18__. 1809–1810s.
Rarity: —

$50 • W-MA-2930-050-G180
Left: Panel bearing state arms / 50 / 50 vertically. ***Center:*** Alternating flower garlands and gridwork segments. ***Right:*** 50 / 50 vertically. ***Engraver:*** Perkins. ***Comments:*** H-MA-1100-G126. 18__. 1809–1810s.
Rarity: —

$100 • W-MA-2930-100-G190
Left: Panel bearing state arms / 100 / 100 vertically. ***Center:*** Alternating flower garlands and gridwork segments. ***Right:*** 100 / 100 vertically. ***Engraver:*** Perkins. ***Comments:*** H-MA-1100-G130. 18__. 1809–1810s.
Rarity: —

Non-Valid Issues

$3 • W-MA-2930-003-N010

Center: Train. ***Engraver:*** Rawdon, Wright & Hatch. ***Comments:*** H-MA-1100-N5. 18__. 1841.

Rarity: —

$3 • W-MA-2930-003-N020

Center: Manhattan reclining with water jug. ***Right:*** Woman and Indian man with eagle. ***Comments:*** H-MA-1100-N10.

Rarity: —

$5 • W-MA-2930-005-N030

Center: 5 / Three women / 5. ***Comments:*** H-MA-1100-N15.

Rarity: —

$8 • W-MA-2930-008-N040

PEM

Comments: H-Unlisted. 180_. 1800s.

Rarity: —

$10 • W-MA-2930-010-S010

Left: TEN on three dies. ***Center:*** 10 / Steamboat, Sailing ships / 10. ***Right:*** TEN / Portrait of George Washington / TEN. ***Engraver:*** Rawdon, Wright & Hatch. ***Comments:*** H-MA-1100-S5. Aug. 1, 1849.

Rarity: —

Exchange Bank
1823–1865
W-MA-2940

History: The Exchange Bank was chartered on January 31, 1823, with an authorized capital of $200,000. The bank opened for business at No. 172 Essex Street and remained there until it moved to the First Church Building on December 8, 1864.

Circulation in 1839 was $27,172; it reached a high of $74,856 in 1857. The specie of the Exchange Bank totaled $6,376.75. Real estate was valued at $3,000.

The business of the Exchange Bank was succeeded by the National Exchange Bank of Salem after it was chartered on February 18, 1865.

Numismatic Commentary: Genuine issues are hard to locate. Fortunately, some striking examples of state-chartered bank notes redeemed after this bank was succeeded by a national bank survived and are illustrated here. Non-valid issues may be found with relative ease in the marketplace.

Valid Issues

$1 • W-MA-2940-001-G010

Left: Lathework panel. ***Center:*** 1 / 1 / Oval of flower garlands and gridwork segments / 1 / 1. ***Right:*** Lathework panel. ***Engraver:*** PSSP. ***Comments:*** H-MA-1105-G2. 18__. 1820s.

Rarity: —

$1 • W-MA-2940-001-G010a

Left: Panel of lathework circle segments. ***Right:*** Panel of lathework circle segments. ***Engraver:*** PSSP. ***Comments:*** H-MA-1105-G4. Similar to W-MA-2940-001-G010. 18__. 1820s–1830s.

Rarity: —

$1 • W-MA-2940-001-G010b

Left: ONE / D / ONE vertically. ***Right:*** ONE / D / ONE vertically. ***Engraver:*** PSSP. ***Comments:*** H-MA-1105-G6. Similar to W-MA-2940-001-G010. 18__. 1830s.

Rarity: —

$1 • W-MA-2940-001-G020

Left: 1 / Male portrait / ONE. ***Center:*** 1 / Woman seated on throne with spear and shield, City and river. ***Right:*** 1 / Woman seated / 1. ***Engraver:*** New England Bank Note Co. / PSSP. ***Comments:*** H-MA-1105-G8. 18__. 1830s–1850s.

Rarity: —

$1 • W-MA-2940-001-G020a

PEM

Overprint: Red ONE. ***Engraver:*** New England Bank Note Co. / PSSP / ABNCo. monogram. ***Comments:*** H-Unlisted. Similar to W-MA-2940-001-G020 but with additional engraver imprint. 18__. 1860s.

Rarity: —

$2 • W-MA-2940-002-G030

Left: Lathework panel. ***Center:*** 2 / 2 / Oval of flower garlands and gridwork segments / 2 / 2. ***Right:*** Lathework panel. ***Engraver:*** PSSP. ***Comments:*** H-MA-1105-G10. 18__. 1820s.

Rarity: —

$2 • W-MA-2940-002-G030a

Left: Panel of lathework circle segments. ***Right:*** Panel of lathework circle segments. ***Engraver:*** PSSP. ***Comments:*** H-MA-1105-G12. Similar to W-MA-2940-002-G030. 18__. 1820s–1830s.

Rarity: —

$2 • W-MA-2940-002-G030b

Left: Five TWOs vertically. ***Right:*** Five TWOs vertically. ***Engraver:*** PSSP. ***Comments:*** H-MA-1105-G14. Similar to W-MA-2940-002-G030. 18__. 1830s.

Rarity: —

$2 • W-MA-2940-002-G040

Left: 2 / Woman standing with shield / TWO. ***Center:*** 2 / Woman seated on throne with spear and shield, City and river / 2. ***Right:*** TWO / Woman standing with cornucopia / 2. ***Engraver:*** New England Bank Note Co. / PSSP. ***Comments:*** H-MA-1105-G16. 18__. 1830s–1850s.

Rarity: —

$2 • W-MA-2940-002-G040a

PEM

Overprint: Red TWO. ***Engraver:*** New England Bank Note Co. / PSSP / ABNCo. monogram. ***Comments:*** H-Unlisted. Similar to W-MA-2940-002-G040 but with additional engraver imprint. 18__. 1860s.

Rarity: —

$3 • W-MA-2940-003-G050

Left: Lathework panel. ***Center:*** 3 / 3 / Oval of flower garlands and gridwork segments / 3 / 3. ***Right:*** Lathework panel. ***Engraver:*** PSSP. ***Comments:*** H-MA-1105-G18. 18__. 1820s.

Rarity: —

$3 • W-MA-2940-003-G050a

Left: Panel of lathework circle segments. ***Right:*** Panel of lathework circle segments. ***Engraver:*** PSSP. ***Comments:*** H-MA-1105-G20. Similar to W-MA-2940-003-G050. 18__. 1820s–1830s.

Rarity: —

$3 • W-MA-2940-003-G050b

Left: THREE vertically. ***Right:*** THREE vertically. ***Engraver:*** PSSP. ***Comments:*** H-MA-1105-G22. Similar to W-MA-2940-003-G050. 18__. 1830s.

Rarity: —

$3 • W-MA-2940-003-G060

Left: 3 / Justice seated / THREE. ***Center:*** 3 / Woman seated on throne with spear and shield, City and river / 3. ***Right:*** III / Woman standing with anchor / 3. ***Engraver:*** New England Bank Note Co / PSSP. ***Comments:*** H-MA-1105-G24. 18__. 1830s–1850s.

Rarity: —

$3 • W-MA-2940-003-G060a

PEM

Overprint: Red THREE. ***Engraver:*** New England Bank Note Co. / PSSP / ABNCo. monogram. ***Comments:*** H-Unlisted. Similar to W-MA-2940-003-G060 but with additional engraver imprint. 18__. 1860s.

Rarity: —

$5 • W-MA-2940-005-G070

Left: Lathework chain bearing MASSACHUSETTS / 5 / 5. ***Center:*** Alternating flower garlands and gridwork segments. ***Right:*** 5 / 5. ***Engraver:*** PSSP. ***Comments:*** H-MA-1105-G28. 18__. 1820s.

Rarity: —

$5 • W-MA-2940-005-G070a

Left: Lathework chain bearing MASSACHUSETTS vertically. ***Right:*** Panel of lathework circle segments. ***Engraver:*** PSSP. ***Comments:*** H-MA-1105-G30. Similar to W-MA-2940-005-G070. 18__. 1820s.

Rarity: —

$5 • W-MA-2940-005-G070b

Engraver: PSSP. ***Comments:*** H-MA-1105-G32. Similar to W-MA-2940-005-G070 but with zigzag ruled lines. 18__. 1820s–1830s.

Rarity: —

$5 • W-MA-2940-005-G070c

Engraver: PSSP. ***Comments:*** H-MA-1105-G34. Similar to W-MA-2940-005-G070 but with spiral lathework lines. 18__. 1830s.

Rarity: —

$5 • W-MA-2940-005-G080

Left: 5 / Woman seated with distaff / V. ***Center:*** 5 / Woman seated on throne with spear and shield, City and river / 5. ***Right:*** FIVE / Justice kneeling / 5. ***Engraver:*** New England Bank Note Co. / PSSP. ***Comments:*** H-MA-1105-G36. 18__. 1830s–1840s.

Rarity: —

$5 • W-MA-2940-005-G080a

PEM

Overprint: Red FIVE. ***Engraver:*** New England Bank Note Co. / PSSP / ABNCo. monogram. ***Comments:*** H-Unlisted. Similar to W-MA-2940-005-G080 but with additional engraver imprint. 18__. 1860s.

Rarity: —

$10 • W-MA-2940-010-G090

Left: Lathework chain bearing MASSACHUSETTS / 10 / 10 vertically. ***Center:*** Alternating flower garlands and gridwork segments. ***Right:*** 10 / 10 vertically. ***Engraver:*** Perkins. ***Comments:*** H-MA-1105-G38. 18__. 1820s.

Rarity: —

$10 • W-MA-2940-010-G090a

Left: Lathework chain bearing MASSACHUSETTS vertically. ***Right:*** Panel of lathework circle segments. ***Engraver:*** Perkins. ***Comments:*** H-MA-1105-G40. Similar to W-MA-2940-010-G090. 18__. 1820s.

Rarity: —

$10 • W-MA-2940-010-G090b

Engraver: PSSP. ***Comments:*** H-MA-1105-G42. Similar to W-MA-2940-010-G090 but with spiral lathework lines. 18__. 1820s–1830s.

Rarity: —

$10 • **W-MA-2940-010-G090c**

Engraver: PSSP. ***Comments:*** H-MA-1105-G44. Similar to W-MA-2940-010-G090 but with spiral lathework lines. 18__. 1830s.

Rarity: —

$10 • **W-MA-2940-010-G100**

Left: X / Portrait of George Washington / TEN. ***Center:*** Woman seated on throne with spear and shield, City and river. ***Right:*** TEN / Male portrait / 10. ***Engraver:*** New England Bank Note Co. / PSSP. ***Comments:*** H-MA-1105-G46. 18__. 1830s–1850s.

Rarity: —

$10 • **W-MA-2940-010-G100a** PEM

Overprint: Red TEN. ***Engraver:*** New England Bank Note Co. / PSSP / ABNCo. monogram. ***Comments:*** H-Unlisted. Similar to W-MA-2940-010-G100 but with additional engraver imprint. 18__. 1860s.

Rarity: —

$20 • **W-MA-2940-020-G110**

Left: Panel bearing state arms / 20 / 20 vertically. ***Center:*** Alternating flower garlands and gridwork segments. ***Right:*** 20 / 20 vertically. ***Engraver:*** Perkins. ***Comments:*** H-MA-1105-G48. 18__. 1820s.

Rarity: —

$20 • **W-MA-2940-020-G110a**

Left: Lathework chain bearing MASSACHUSETTS vertically. ***Engraver:*** PSSP. ***Comments:*** H-MA-1105-G50. Similar to W-MA-2940-020-G110. 18__. 1820s–1830s.

Rarity: —

$20 • **W-MA-2940-020-G120**

Left: 20 / Woman seated with book on lap, opening chest. ***Center:*** XX / Eagle on rock / XX. ***Right:*** 20 / Ship in harbor. ***Engraver:*** New England Bank Note Co. ***Comments:*** H-MA-1105-G54. 18__. 1840s–1850s.

Rarity: —

$50 • **W-MA-2940-050-G130**

Left: Panel bearing state arms / 50 / 50 vertically. ***Center:*** Alternating flower garlands and gridwork segments. ***Right:*** 50 / 50 vertically. ***Engraver:*** Perkins. ***Comments:*** H-MA-1105-G56. 18__. 1820s.

Rarity: —

$50 • **W-MA-2940-050-G130a**

Left: Lathework chain bearing MASSACHUSETTS vertically. ***Engraver:*** PSSP. ***Comments:*** H-MA-1105-G58. Similar to W-MA-2940-050-G130. 18__. 1820s–1830s.

Rarity: —

$50 • **W-MA-2940-050-G140** ABNCo

Tint: Green. ***Engraver:*** American Bank Note Co. ***Comments:*** H-MA-1105-G62a. April 1, 18__. 1860s.

Rarity: URS-3
Proof $4,000

$100 • **W-MA-2940-100-G150**

Left: Panel bearing state arms / 100 / 100 vertically. ***Center:*** Alternating flower garlands and gridwork segments. ***Right:*** 100 / 100 vertically. ***Engraver:*** Perkins. ***Comments:*** H-MA-1105-G64. 18__. 1820s.

Rarity: —

$100 • **W-MA-2940-100-G150a**

Left: Lathework chain bearing MASSACHUSETTS vertically. ***Engraver:*** Perkins. ***Comments:*** H-MA-1105-G66. Similar to W-MA-2940-100-G150. 18__. 1820s–1830s.

Rarity: —

$100 • **W-MA-2940-100-G160**

Left: 100 / Man dressing leather. ***Center:*** Two women seated on bale, Factories. ***Right:*** 100 / Two girls. ***Tint:*** Green. ***Engraver:*** American Bank Note Co. ***Comments:*** H-MA-1105-G68a. 1860s.

Rarity: —

$500 • **W-MA-2940-500-G170**

Left: Female portrait / D / 500 / D. ***Center:*** Dog lying on strongbox. ***Right:*** D / 500. ***Tint:*** Green. ***Engraver:*** American Bank Note Co. ***Comments:*** H-MA-1105-G72a. 1860s.

Rarity: —

Non-Valid Issues

$1 • **W-MA-2940-001-A010**

Left: ONE across 1 / Dog holding key in mouth. ***Center:*** Man binding sheaf, Woman holding sheaf. ***Right:*** ONE across 1 / Female portrait. ***Engraver:*** W.L. Ormsby. ***Comments:*** H-MA-1105-A5. Altered from a spurious issue of Exchange Bank, Hartford, Connecticut. Dec. 1, 1856.

Rarity: —

$1 • **W-MA-2940-001-A020**

Left: ONE / Hebe seated on sheaf, watering eagle / ONE. ***Center:*** Eagle on shield, Ships. ***Right:*** 1 / Ceres kneeling, Sheaf, Farm. ***Engraver:*** Danforth, Bald & Co. ***Comments:*** H-MA-1105-A10. Altered from $1 Columbia Bank, Washington, D.C. 185_. 1850s.

Rarity: —

$2 • W-MA-2940-002-A030

CC

Engraver: W.L. Ormsby. ***Comments:*** H-MA-1105-A15. Altered from a spurious $2 Exchange Bank, Hartford, Connecticut. Dec. 1, 1856.

Rarity: URS-6
F $175

$3 • W-MA-2940-003-S010

CC

Engraver: Rawdon, Wright & Hatch. ***Comments:*** H-Unlisted. 18__. 1840s.

Rarity: URS-6
VF $300

$3 • W-MA-2940-003-S020

SI

Comments: H-Unlisted. 18__. 1850s.

Rarity: URS-6
F $75; **VF** $100

$5 • W-MA-2940-005-A040

Left: 5 / 5. ***Center:*** Two identical allegorical women in clouds, U.S. shield and eagle. ***Right:*** 5 / 5. ***Engraver:*** W.L. Ormsby. ***Comments:*** H-MA-1105-A20. Altered from a spurious $5 Exchange Bank, Hartford, Connecticut. Dec. 1, 1856.

Rarity: —

$5 • W-MA-2940-005-A050

CC

Engraver: Danforth, Underwood & Co. ***Comments:*** H-MA-1105-A25. 18__. 1840s.

Rarity: URS-6
VG $150

$5 • W-MA-2940-005-A060

Left: V / Portrait of Henry Clay. ***Center:*** Western river steamboat, Wharf. ***Right:*** 5 / Portrait of George Washington. ***Overprint:*** Red FIVE. ***Engraver:*** New England Bank Note Co. / Rawdon, Wright, Hatch & Edson. ***Comments:*** H-MA-1105-A30. Altered from $5 Waubeek Bank, De Soto, Nebraska. 1857.

Rarity: —

$10 • W-MA-2940-010-R010

Engraver: New England Bank Note Co. / PSSP. ***Comments:*** H-MA-1105-R5. Raised from W-MA-2940-001-G020. 18__. 1840s.

Rarity: —

$10 • W-MA-2940-010-R020

Engraver: New England Bank Note Co. / PSSP. ***Comments:*** H-MA-1105-R10. Raised from W-MA-2940-002-G040. 18__. 1840s.

Rarity: —

$10 • W-MA-2940-010-S030

CC

Engraver: Rawdon, Wright & Hatch. ***Comments:*** H-Unlisted. July 1, 1850.

Rarity: URS-6
VF $250

$10 • W-MA-2940-010-A070

Left: 10 / 10. ***Center:*** Indian man on horseback spearing bison, Bison and trees. ***Right:*** 10 / 10. ***Engraver:*** W.L. Ormsby. ***Comments:*** H-MA-1105-A35. Altered from a spurious $10 Exchange Bank, Hartford, Connecticut. Dec. 1, 1856.

Rarity: —

$20 • W-MA-2940-020-C110a

Engraver: PSSP. ***Comments:*** H-MA-1105-C50. Counterfeit of W-MA-2940-020-G110a. 18__. 1830s.

Rarity: —

George Washington Bank

19th Century

W-MA-2943

History: A non-existent bank represented only by notes altered from other banks.

Issues

$5 • W-MA-2943-005-A010

CC

Engraver: Underwood, Bald, Spencer & Hufty / Danforth, Underwood & Co. ***Comments:*** H-Unlisted. 18__.

Rarity: URS-3

Proof $900

Mechanics and Traders Bank

1827

W-MA-2945

History: The Mechanics and Traders Bank was chartered on March 10, 1827, with an authorized capital of $200,000. It never went into business.

Mercantile Bank

1826–1865

W-MA-2950

History: On May 8, 1826, the Mercantile Bank was chartered with an authorized capital of $200,000, which remained constant throughout the bank's existence. Its first office was in a room shared with John W. Fenno, a broker, in the Central Building. In early 1827 it was relocated to larger premises, where the bank remained for the rest of the period under study here.

The capital of the bank in 1839 was $200,000. Circulation was $36,798 in 1839, and it reached a high of $67,179 in 1863. Real estate of the Mercantile Bank was valued at $5,000.

After January 10, 1865, the business of the bank was succeeded by the Mercantile National Bank of Salem.

Numismatic Commentary: Genuine issues are somewhat easier to obtain from this bank than from many other banks whose interests were succeeded by national banks.

Valid Issues

$1 • W-MA-2950-001-G010

Left: Lathework panel bearing MASSACHUSETTS vertically. ***Center:*** 1 / 1 / Alternating flower garlands and gridwork segments / ONE / 1 / 1. ***Right:*** Lathework panel bearing ONE / D / ONE vertically. ***Engraver:*** PSSP. ***Comments:*** H-MA-1115-G2. 18__. 1820s–1830s.

Rarity: —

$1 • W-MA-2950-001-G010a

Left: ONE / D / ONE vertically. ***Right:*** ONE / D / ONE vertically. ***Engraver:*** PSSP. ***Comments:*** H-MA-1115-G4. Similar to W-MA-2950-001-G010. 18__. 1830s.

Rarity: URS-4

Proof $2,500

$1 • W-MA-2950-001-G020

Engraver: Unverified, but likely New England Bank Note Co. ***Comments:*** H-MA-1115-G6. No description available. 18__. 1830s–1840s.

Rarity: *None known*

$1 • W-MA-2950-001-G030

Left: ONE / 1. ***Center:*** Farmer sowing, Man harrowing / 1. ***Right:*** 1 / Ship / ONE. ***Engraver:*** New England Bank Note Co. ***Comments:*** H-MA-1115-G8. 18__. 1830s–1840s.

Rarity: —

$1 • W-MA-2950-001-G030a

Overprint: Red. ***Engraver:*** New England Bank Note Co. ***Comments:*** H-MA-1115-G8a. Similar to W-MA-2950-001-G030. 18__. 1850s.

Rarity: —

$1 • W-MA-2950-001-G040

Left: Sailing ship / 1. ***Center:*** 1 on die. ***Right:*** 1 / Woman standing / ONE. ***Engraver:*** American Bank Note Co. ***Comments:*** H-MA-1115-G10. Might have been made only as Proofs. 186_.

Rarity: —

How to Read the Whitman Numbering System

$1 • W-MA-010-001-G010a

Denomination: Value of the note shown.

W: Whitman number. This number is a sortable code unique to each bank and note.

MA: Abbreviation for the state under study.

010: Numerical designation specific to each bank.

001: The denomination in dollars.

G010a: G indicates a good or valid note. Other categories are indicated thus: C (counterfeit); R (raised); S (spurious); N (not-attributed); A (altered). Numbers are assigned starting with 010, 020, et seq. Terminal letters following the number indicate variations of a note: a series of different colored overprints, tints, payees, etc., all on the same design of note. For more information, see the "How to Use This Book" section at the front of the volume, page xiv.

$1 • W-MA-2950-001-G040a

CJF

Overprint: Green panel outlining white ONE. ***Engraver:*** American Bank Note Co. ***Comments:*** H-MA-1115-G10a. Similar to W-MA-2950-001-G040. Jan. __, 186_. 1860s.

Rarity: URS-5
F $300; **VF** $500

$1 • W-MA-2950-001-G040b

CJF

Overprint: Green ONE. ***Engraver:*** American Bank Note Co. ***Comments:*** H-MA-1115-G10b. Similar to W-MA-2950-001-G040. Jan. __, 186_. 1860s.

Rarity: URS-5
F $300; **VF** $500

$2 • W-MA-2950-002-G050

Left: Narrow panel of lathework circle segments. ***Center:*** 2 / 2 / Flower garlands and gridwork segments / 2 / 2. ***Right:*** Narrow panel of lathework circle segments. ***Engraver:*** PSSP. ***Comments:*** H-MA-1115-G12. 18__. 1820s–1830s.

Rarity: —

$2 • W-MA-2950-002-G050a

Left: Five TWOs vertically. ***Right:*** Five TWOs vertically. ***Engraver:*** PSSP. ***Comments:*** H-MA-1115-G14. Similar to W-MA-2950-002-G050. 18__. 1830s.

Rarity: —

$2 • W-MA-2950-002-G060

Engraver: Unverified, but likely New England Bank Note Co. ***Comments:*** H-MA-1115-G16. No description available. 18__. 1830s–1840s.

Rarity: *None known*

$2 • W-MA-2950-002-G070

Left: TWO / 2. ***Center:*** Eagle on bale, Cannon balls and machinery / 2. ***Right:*** 2 / TWO / Schooner. ***Engraver:*** New England Bank Note Co. ***Comments:*** H-MA-1115-G18. 18__. 1840s–1850s.

Rarity: —

$2 • W-MA-2950-002-G070a

Overprint: Red. ***Engraver:*** New England Bank Note Co. ***Comments:*** H-MA-1115-G18a. Similar to W-MA-2950-002-G070. 18__. 1850s.

Rarity: —

$2 • W-MA-2950-002-G080

Left: Woman writing on scroll, Child / TWO. ***Center:*** Three women reclining with sextant, anvil, and wheel, Ship. ***Right:*** 2 / Portrait of girl. ***Engraver:*** American Bank Note Co. ***Comments:*** H-MA-1115-G20. Might have been made only as Proofs. Jan. __, 186_.

Rarity: —

$2 • W-MA-2950-002-G080a

Overprint: Green panel outlining white TWO. ***Engraver:*** American Bank Note Co. ***Comments:*** H-MA-1115-G20a. Similar to W-MA-2950-002-G080. Jan. __, 186_. 1860s.

Rarity: —

$2 • W-MA-2950-002-G080b

CJF

Overprint: Green TWO. ***Engraver:*** American Bank Note Co. ***Comments:*** H-MA-1115-G20b. Similar to W-MA-2950-002-G080. Jan. __, 186_. 1860s.

Rarity: URS-4
Proof $2,000

$3 • W-MA-2950-003-G090

Left: Narrow panel of lathework circle segments. ***Center:*** 3 / 3 / Flower garlands and gridwork segments / 3 / 3. ***Right:*** Narrow panel of lathework circle segments. ***Engraver:*** PSSP. ***Comments:*** H-MA-1115-G22. 18__. 1820s–1830s.

Rarity: —

$3 • W-MA-2950-003-G090a

Left: THREE vertically. ***Right:*** THREE vertically. ***Engraver:*** PSSP. ***Comments:*** H-MA-1115-G24. Similar to W-MA-2950-003-G090. 18__. 1830s.

Rarity: —

$3 • W-MA-2950-003-G100

Engraver: Unverified, but likely New England Bank Note Co. ***Comments:*** H-MA-1115-G26. No description available. 18__. 1830s–1840s.

Rarity: *None known*

$3 • W-MA-2950-003-G110

Left: THREE / 3. ***Center:*** Sailor standing with hat in hand, Bales and harbor / 3. ***Right:*** 3 / THREE / Train. ***Engraver:*** New England Bank Note Co. ***Comments:*** H-MA-1115-G28. 18__. 1840s–1850s.

Rarity: —

$3 • W-MA-2950-003-G110a CJF

Overprint: Red THREE. ***Engraver:*** New England Bank Note Co. ***Comments:*** H-MA-1115-G28a. Similar to W-MA-2950-003-G110. 18__. 1850s.

Rarity: —

$5 • W-MA-2950-005-G120

Left: Lathework chain bearing MASSACHUSETTS / 5 / 5. ***Center:*** Alternating flower garlands and gridwork segments. ***Right:*** 5 / 5. ***Engraver:*** PSSP. ***Comments:*** H-MA-1115-G30. 18__. 1820s.

Rarity: URS-4
Proof $2,500

$5 • W-MA-2950-005-G120a

Engraver: PSSP. ***Comments:*** H-MA-1115-G32. Similar to W-MA-2950-005-G120 but with spiral lathework lines. 18__. 1820s–1830s.

Rarity: —

$5 • W-MA-2950-005-G120b

Engraver: PSSP. ***Comments:*** H-MA-1115-G34. Similar to W-MA-2950-005-G120 but with spiral lathework lines. 18__. 1830s.

Rarity: —

$5 • W-MA-2950-005-G130

Left: Panel bearing FIVE / Plenty and Minerva seated / V. ***Center:*** FIVE / Allegorical woman seated / FIVE / Panel of microletters. ***Right:*** 5 / Eagle / 5. ***Engraver:*** PSSP. ***Comments:*** H-MA-1115-G36. 18__. 1830s–1840s.

Rarity: —

$5 • W-MA-2950-005-G140

Left: FIVE across V / FIVE across V. ***Center:*** Ceres seated on wharf with rake, Sickle and implements, Factories and harbor / Indian woman with bow seated in V. ***Right:*** 5 / Portrait of George Washington. ***Engraver:*** New England Bank Note Co. ***Comments:*** H-MA-1115-G38. 18__. 1840s–1850s.

Rarity: —

$5 • W-MA-2950-005-G140a

Overprint: Red. ***Engraver:*** New England Bank Note Co. ***Comments:*** H-MA-1115-G38a. Similar to W-MA-2950-005-G140. 18__. 1850s.

Rarity: —

$5 • W-MA-2950-005-G150

Left: 5 / Sailor and mechanic. ***Center:*** Woman reclining on shield, Eagle, Steamer. ***Right:*** 5 / FIVE / Sailor standing with hand on capstan. ***Engraver:*** American Bank Note Co. ***Comments:*** H-MA-1115-G40. Might have been made only as Proofs. Jan. __, 186_.

Rarity: —

$5 • W-MA-2950-005-G150a

Overprint: Green panel outlining white FIVE. ***Engraver:*** American Bank Note Co. ***Comments:*** H-MA-1115-G40a. Similar to W-MA-2950-005-G150. Jan. __, 186_. 1860s.

Rarity: —

$10 • W-MA-2950-010-G160

Left: Lathework chain bearing MASSACHUSETTS / 10 / 10 vertically. ***Center:*** Alternating flower garlands and gridwork segments. ***Right:*** 10 / 10 vertically. ***Engraver:*** Perkins. ***Comments:*** H-MA-1115-G42. 18__. 1820s.

Rarity: —

$10 • W-MA-2950-010-G160a

Engraver: PSSP. ***Comments:*** H-MA-1115-G44. Similar to W-MA-2950-010-G160. 18__. 1820s–1830s.

Rarity: —

$10 • W-MA-2950-010-G160b

Engraver: PSSP. ***Comments:*** H-MA-1115-G46. Similar to W-MA-2950-010-G160. 18__. 1830s.

Rarity: —

$10 • W-MA-2950-010-G170

Left: Panel bearing TEN / Manhattan and spilling water jug / TEN. ***Center:*** TEN / Ceres seated / TEN / Panel of microletters. ***Right:*** Panel bearing 10 / Portrait of Indian / 10. ***Engraver:*** PSSP. ***Comments:*** H-MA-1115-G48. 18__. 1830s–1840s.

Rarity: —

$10 • W-MA-2950-010-G180

Left: Mechanic seated with tools, Train and building / TEN. ***Center:*** X. ***Right:*** 10 / Reaper standing with sheaf and stone. ***Engraver:*** New England Bank Note Co. ***Comments:*** H-MA-1115-G50. 18__. 1840s–1850s.

Rarity: —

$10 • W-MA-2950-010-G180a

Overprint: Red. ***Engraver:*** New England Bank Note Co. ***Comments:*** H-MA-1115-G50a. Similar to W-MA-2950-010-G180. 18__. 1850s.

Rarity: —

$10 • W-MA-2950-010-G190

Left: 10 / Pilot boat under sail. ***Center:*** Sailor seated on rail of ship holding spyglass. ***Right:*** 10 / Female portrait. ***Engraver:*** American Bank Note Co. ***Comments:*** H-MA-1115-G52. Might have been made only as Proofs. Jan. __, 186_.

Rarity: —

$10 • W-MA-2950-010-G190a

Overprint: Green panel outlining white TEN. ***Engraver:*** American Bank Note Co. ***Comments:*** H-MA-1115-G52a. Similar to W-MA-2950-010-G190. Jan. __, 186_. 1860s.

Rarity: —

$20 • W-MA-2950-020-G200

Left: Lathework chain bearing MASSACHUSETTS / 20 / 20 vertically. ***Center:*** Alternating flower garlands and gridwork segments. ***Right:*** 20 / 20 vertically. ***Engraver:*** PSSP. ***Comments:*** H-MA-1115-G54. 18__. 1820s–1830s.

Rarity: —

$20 • W-MA-2950-020-G210

Engraver: Unverified, but likely New England Bank Note Co. ***Comments:*** H-MA-1115-G58. No description available. 18__. 1840s.

Rarity: *None known*

$20 • W-MA-2950-020-G220

Left: 20 / Woman seated with book on lap, opening chest. ***Center:*** XX / Eagle on rock / XX. ***Right:*** 20 / Ship in harbor. ***Engraver:*** New England Bank Note Co. ***Comments:*** H-MA-1115-G60. 18__. 1840s–1850s.

Rarity: —

$50 • W-MA-2950-050-G230

Left: Lathework chain bearing MASSACHUSETTS / 50 / 50 vertically. ***Center:*** Alternating flower garlands and gridwork segments. ***Right:*** 50 / 50 vertically. ***Engraver:*** PSSP. ***Comments:*** H-MA-1115-G62. 18__. 1820s–1830s.

Rarity: —

$50 • W-MA-2950-050-G240

Engraver: Unverified, but likely New England Bank Note Co. ***Comments:*** H-MA-1115-G66. No description available. 18__. 1840s.

Rarity: *None known*

$50 • W-MA-2950-050-G250

Left: FIFTY / Woman standing with wreath and flowers. ***Center:*** 50 / Man restraining prancing horse / 50. ***Right:*** FIFTY / Woman standing with cornucopia / FIFTY. ***Engraver:*** New England Bank Note Co. ***Comments:*** H-MA-1115-G68. 18__. 1840s–1850s.

Rarity: —

$50 • W-MA-2950-050-G260

Left: 50 / Justice. ***Center:*** Wharf scene, Men rolling barrels from ship. ***Right:*** 50 / Two sailors. ***Engraver:*** American Bank Note Co. ***Comments:*** H-MA-1115-G70. Jan. __, 186_. 1860s.

Rarity: —

$100 • W-MA-2950-100-G270

Left: Lathework chain bearing MASSACHUSETTS / 100 / 100 vertically. ***Center:*** Alternating flower garlands and gridwork segments. ***Right:*** 100 / 100 vertically. ***Engraver:*** Perkins. ***Comments:*** H-MA-1115-G72. 18__. 1820s–1830s.

Rarity: —

$100 • W-MA-2950-100-G280

Engraver: Unverified, but likely New England Bank Note Co. ***Comments:*** H-MA-1115-G76. No description available. 18__. 1840s.

Rarity: *None known*

$100 • W-MA-2950-100-G290

Left: ONE HUNDRED on 100 / Portrait of William Henry Harrison. ***Center:*** Wharf scene, Men loading wagon with barrel. ***Right:*** ONE HUNDRED on 100 / Portrait of Christopher Columbus. ***Engraver:*** New England Bank Note Co. ***Comments:*** H-MA-1115-G78. 18__. 1840s–1850s.

Rarity: —

$100 • W-MA-2950-100-G300

Left: C / Woman leaning on pedestal holding torch. ***Center:*** Woman seated on wharf surrounded by bales and bags. ***Right:*** 100 / State arms / 100. ***Engraver:*** American Bank Note Co. ***Comments:*** H-MA-1115-G80. Jan. __, 186_. 1860s.

Rarity: —

$500 • W-MA-2950-500-G310

Left: Woman seated on sheaves, Men reaping, Man on horse / 500. ***Center:*** 500 / D. ***Right:*** 500 vertically. ***Engraver:*** Rawdon, Wright, Hatch & Edson. ***Comments:*** H-MA-1115-G84. 18__. 1850s.

Rarity: —

Non-Valid Issues

$1 • W-MA-2950-001-A010

Left: ONE / Hebe seated on sheaf, watering eagle / ONE. ***Center:*** Ships / Eagle on shield. ***Right:*** 1 / Ceres kneeling, Sheaf, Farm. ***Engraver:*** New England Bank Note Co. ***Comments:*** H-MA-1115-A5. Altered from $1 Columbia Bank, Washington, D.C. 18__. 1850s.

Rarity: —

$1 • W-MA-2950-001-A020

Left: Panel bearing portrait of Zachary Taylor. ***Center:*** 1 / Woman in clouds holding shield, Eagle / 1 / ONE. ***Right:*** Panel bearing Ceres. ***Engraver:*** W.L. Ormsby. ***Comments:*** H-MA-1115-A10. Altered from $1 Mechanics and Traders Bank, Georgetown, D.C. Nov. 14, 1852.

Rarity: —

$3 • W-MA-2950-003-S010

Left: 3 / View of woman standing with sheaf / THREE. ***Center:*** Girl standing with sheaf on head, Dog seated under tree. ***Bottom center:*** Dog and strongbox. ***Right:*** THREE / Milkmaid seated with bucket. ***Tint:*** Brown or green lathework. ***Comments:*** H-MA-1115-S5. Sept. 10, 18__. 1850s.

Rarity: —

$3 • W-MA-2950-003-N010

CJF

Comments: H-MA-1115-N5. May 1, 18__. 1850s.

Rarity: —

$5 • W-MA-2950-005-A030

Left: V / Portrait of Henry Clay. ***Center:*** Western river steamboat, Wharf. ***Right:*** 5 / Portrait of George Washington. ***Overprint:*** Red FIVE. ***Engraver:*** New England Bank Note Co. / Rawdon, Wright, Hatch & Edson. ***Comments:*** H-MA-1115-A15 Altered from $5 Waubeek Bank, De Soto, Nebraska. 1857.

Rarity: —

$10 • **W-MA-2950-010-S020** CC

Overprint: Red TEN. ***Comments:*** H-MA-1115-N10. Spurious note. June 1, 1818.

Rarity: URS-7
VG $125; **VF** $175

$50 • **W-MA-2950-050-A040**

Left: 50 on die / Portrait of Benjamin Franklin. ***Center:*** Sailor seated on bale, Flag, Ships. ***Bottom center:*** Eagle. ***Right:*** 50 on die / Portrait of George Washington. ***Engraver:*** Boston Bank Note Co. ***Comments:*** H-MA-1115-A20. Altered from $50 Bank of Vernon, Vernon, Texas. 18__. 1840s.

Rarity: —

Merchants Bank
1811–1865
W-MA-2960

History: The Merchants Bank of Salem was chartered on June 26, 1811, with an authorized capital of $200,000, later increased to $400,000 and then reduced in 1845 to $200,000. The bank opened for business in 1811 in rooms in the Union Building on the corner of Union and Essex streets. Later it moved to the Bowker Building, and in 1855 it was finally relocated to the Asiatic Building. In 1817 the cashier for the bank was J.W. Treadwell. By 1848 Treadwell had become president and his position as cashier was filled by F.H. Silsbee. Circulation in 1839 was $272,904. Its lowest point occurred in 1845 when it was $57,663. The same was $116,658 in 1863.

After January 19, 1865, the business of the Merchants Bank was succeeded by the Merchants National Bank of Salem.

Numismatic Commentary: Genuine notes are hard to locate with the exception of one or two Proof issues that appear from time to time.

Valid Issues

$1 • **W-MA-2960-001-G010**

Center: 1 / 1 / Oval of flower garlands and gridwork segments / 1 / 1. ***Engraver:*** PSSP. ***Comments:*** H-MA-1120-G12. 18__. 1811.

Rarity: —

$1 • **W-MA-2960-001-G010a**

Center: 1 / 1 / Oval of flower garlands and gridwork segments / ONE / 1 / 1. ***Engraver:*** PSSP. ***Comments:*** H-MA-1120-G14. Similar to W-MA-2960-001-G010. 18__. Circa 1812–1820s.

Rarity: —

$1 • **W-MA-2960-001-G010b**

Left: Panel of lathework circle segments. ***Right:*** Panel of lathework circle segments. ***Engraver:*** PSSP. ***Comments:*** H-MA-1120-G16. Similar to W-MA-2960-001-G010. 18__. 1820s.

Rarity: —

$1 • **W-MA-2960-001-G010c**

Left: Panel of lathework circle segments. ***Right:*** Panel of lathework circle segments. ***Engraver:*** PSSP. ***Comments:*** H-MA-1120-G18. Similar to W-MA-2960-001-G010. 18__. 1820s–1830s.

Rarity: —

$1 • **W-MA-2960-001-G010d**

Left: ONE / D / ONE vertically. ***Right:*** ONE / D / ONE vertically. ***Engraver:*** PSSP. ***Comments:*** H-MA-1120-G20. Similar to W-MA-2960-001-G010. 18__. 1830s.

Rarity: —

$1 • **W-MA-2960-001-G020**

Left: 1 / Woman wearing bonnet with pail / ONE. ***Center:*** Machinery and merchandise flanking Ceres seated holding sickle and rake, Factories and harbor / ONE / Panel outlining white ONE. ***Right:*** 1 / Ship / ONE. ***Engraver:*** PSSP / New England Bank Note Co. ***Comments:*** H-MA-1120-G22. 18__. 1830s.

Rarity: —

$1 • **W-MA-2960-001-G030**

Left: ONE / D / ONE vertically. ***Center:*** 1 / 1 / Oval of flower garlands and gridwork segments / ONE / 1 / 1. ***Right:*** ONE / D / ONE vertically. ***Engraver:*** PSSP. ***Comments:*** H-MA-1120-G24. 18__. 1830s–1840s.

Rarity: —

$1 • **W-MA-2960-001-G030a**

Overprint: Red. ***Engraver:*** PSSP. ***Comments:*** H-MA-1120-G24a. Similar to W-MA-2960-001-G030. 18__. 1840s–1850s.

Rarity: —

$1 • **W-MA-2960-001-G040** SN

Engraver: New England Bank Note Co. / PSSP. ***Comments:*** H-Unlisted. 18__.

Rarity: URS-1
Proof $3,000

$1 • **W-MA-2960-001-G040a**

Left: ONE / Sailor boy / ONE. ***Right:*** 1 / ONE / 1. ***Tint:*** Red bank title / ONE DOLLAR microlettering. ***Engraver:*** New England Bank Note Co. / PSSP. ***Comments:*** H-MA-1120-G26. Similar to W-MA-2960-001-G040. 18__. 1850s.

Rarity: —

$1.25 • W-MA-2960-001.25-G050

Left: 1 25/100 / Train / 1 25/100. ***Center:*** Sloop and other ships at sea / $1.25 cts. ***Right:*** 1 25/100 / Eagle. ***Engraver:*** New England Bank Note Co. ***Comments:*** H-MA-1120-G28. 18__. 1830s.

Rarity: —

$1.50 • W-MA-2960-001.50-G060

Left: 1 Doll. 50 Cts. vertically. ***Center:*** Eagle on rock in ocean / $1 50/100. ***Right:*** 1 50/100 / Justice. ***Engraver:*** New England Bank Note Co. ***Comments:*** H-MA-1120-G29. 18__. 1830s.

Rarity: —

$1.75 • W-MA-2960-001.75-G070

Left: $1.75 Cts. / Hebe watering eagle / 1 75/100. ***Center:*** Three sloops at sea. ***Right:*** $1.75 Cts. / Dog, Woman seated with grain / 1 75/100. ***Engraver:*** New England Bank Note Co. ***Comments:*** H-MA-1120-G30. 18__. 1830s.

Rarity: —

$2 • W-MA-2960-002-G080

Center: 2 / 2 / Oval of flower garlands and gridwork segments / 2 / 2. ***Engraver:*** PSSP. ***Comments:*** H-MA-1120-G32. 18__. 1811.

Rarity: —

$2 • W-MA-2960-002-G080a

Center: 2 / 2 / Oval of flower garlands and gridwork segments / TWO / 2 / 2. ***Engraver:*** PSSP. ***Comments:*** H-MA-1120-G34. Similar to W-MA-2960-002-G080. 18__. Circa 1812–1820.

Rarity: —

$2 • W-MA-2960-002-G080b

Left: Panel of lathework circle segments. ***Right:*** Panel of lathework circle segments. ***Engraver:*** PSSP. ***Comments:*** H-MA-1120-G36. Similar to W-MA-2960-002-G080. 18__. 1820s.

Rarity: —

$2 • W-MA-2960-002-G080c

Left: Panel of lathework circle segments. ***Right:*** Panel of lathework circle segments. ***Engraver:*** PSSP. ***Comments:*** H-MA-1120-G38. Similar to W-MA-2960-002-G080. 18__. 1820s–1830s.

Rarity: —

$2 • W-MA-2960-002-G080d

Left: Five TWOs vertically. ***Right:*** Five TWOs vertically. ***Engraver:*** PSSP. ***Comments:*** H-MA-1120-G40. Similar to W-MA-2960-002-G080. 18__. 1830s.

Rarity: —

$2 • W-MA-2960-002-G090

Left: 2 / Woman standing with staff, Cornucopia / TWO. ***Center:*** TWO / Machinery and merchandise flanking Ceres seated holding sickle and rake, Factories and harbor / Panel outlining white TWO. ***Right:*** 2 / Woman wearing hat, Trees / TWO. ***Engraver:*** New England Bank Note Co. / PSSP. ***Comments:*** H-MA-1120-G42. 18__. 1830s.

Rarity: —

$2 • W-MA-2960-002-G100

Left: Five TWOs vertically. ***Center:*** 2 / 2 / Oval of flower garlands and gridwork segments / TWO / 2 / 2. ***Right:*** Five TWOs vertically. ***Engraver:*** PSSP. ***Comments:*** H-MA-1120-G44. 18__. 1830s–1840s.

Rarity: —

$2 • W-MA-2960-002-G100a

Overprint: Red. ***Engraver:*** PSSP. ***Comments:*** H-MA-1120-G44a. Similar to W-MA-2960-002-G100. 18__. 1840s–1850s.

Rarity: —

$2 • W-MA-2960-002-G110

SN

Engraver: New England Bank Note Co. / PSSP. ***Comments:*** H-Unlisted. 18__.

Rarity: URS-1
Proof $3,000

$2 • W-MA-2960-002-G110a

Left: TWO / Ship on stocks / TWO. ***Right:*** 2 / TWO / 2. ***Tint:*** Red bank title / TWO DOLLARS microlettering. ***Engraver:*** New England Bank Note Co. / PSSP. ***Comments:*** H-MA-1120-G50. Similar to W-MA-2960-002-G110. 18__. 1850s.

Rarity: —

$3 • W-MA-2960-003-G120

Center: 3 / 3 / Oval of flower garlands and gridwork segments / 3 / 3. ***Engraver:*** PSSP. ***Comments:*** H-MA-1120-G52. 18__. 1811–1820s.

Rarity: —

$3 • W-MA-2960-003-G120a

Left: Panel of lathework circle segments. ***Right:*** Panel of lathework circle segments. ***Engraver:*** PSSP. ***Comments:*** H-MA-1120-G54. Similar to W-MA-2960-003-G120. 18__. 1820s.

Rarity: —

$3 • W-MA-2960-003-G120b

Left: Panel of lathework circle segments. ***Right:*** Panel of lathework circle segments. ***Engraver:*** PSSP. ***Comments:*** H-MA-1120-G56. Similar to W-MA-2960-003-G120. 18__. 1820s–1830s.

Rarity: —

$3 • W-MA-2960-003-G120c

Left: THREE vertically. ***Right:*** THREE vertically. ***Engraver:*** PSSP. ***Comments:*** H-MA-1120-G58. Similar to W-MA-2960-003-G120. 18__. 1830s.

Rarity: —

$3 • W-MA-2960-003-G130

Left: THREE / Beehive and foliage / THREE. ***Center:*** Machinery and merchandise flanking Ceres seated holding sickle and rake, Factories and harbor / THREE / Panel outlining white THREE. ***Right:*** 3 on THREE / Two reapers / 3 on THREE. ***Engraver:*** New England Bank Note Co. / PSSP. ***Comments:*** H-MA-1120-G60. 18__. 1830s.

Rarity: —

$3 • W-MA-2960-003-G140

Left: THREE vertically. ***Center:*** 3 / 3 / Oval of flower garlands and gridwork segments / 3 / 3. ***Right:*** THREE vertically. ***Engraver:*** PSSP. ***Comments:*** H-MA-1120-G62. 18__. 1830s.

Rarity: —

$3 • W-MA-2960-003-G140a

Overprint: Red. ***Engraver:*** PSSP. ***Comments:*** H-MA-1120-G62a. Similar to W-MA-2960-003-G140. 18__. 1840s–1850s.

Rarity: —

$5 • W-MA-2960-005-G150

Left: Panel bearing state arms / 5 / 5. ***Center:*** Alternating flower garlands and gridwork segments / FIVE. ***Right:*** 5 / 5. ***Engraver:*** PSSP. ***Comments:*** H-MA-1120-G64. 18__. 1811–1820s.

Rarity: —

$5 • W-MA-2960-005-G150a

Left: Lathework chain bearing MASSACHUSETTS vertically. ***Right:*** Panel of lathework circle segments. ***Engraver:*** PSSP. ***Comments:*** H-MA-1120-G66. Similar to W-MA-2960-005-G150. 18__. 1820s.

Rarity: —

$5 • W-MA-2960-005-G150b

Left: Lathework chain bearing MASSACHUSETTS vertically. ***Right:*** Panel of lathework circle segments. ***Engraver:*** PSSP. ***Comments:*** H-MA-1120-G68. Similar to W-MA-2960-005-G150. 18__. 1820s.

Rarity: —

$5 • W-MA-2960-005-G150c

Engraver: PSSP. ***Comments:*** H-MA-1120-G70. Similar to W-MA-2960-005-G150 but with zigzag ruled lines. 18__. 1820s–1830s.

Rarity: —

$5 • W-MA-2960-005-G150d

Engraver: PSSP. ***Comments:*** H-MA-1120-G72. Similar to W-MA-2960-005-G150 but with spiral lathework lines. 18__. 1830s.

Rarity: —

$5 • W-MA-2960-005-G160

QDB

Tint: Red lathework. ***Engraver:*** PSSP. ***Comments:*** H-Unlisted. 18__.

Rarity: URS-1
Proof $5,500

$5 • W-MA-2960-005-G170

Comments: H-MA-1120-G74. No description available. 18__. 1830s.

Rarity: *None known*

$5 • W-MA-2960-005-G180

CJF

Engraver: Underwood, Bald, Spencer & Hufty / Danforth, Underwood & Co. ***Comments:*** H-MA-1120-G76. Proof. 18__. 1840s–1850s.

Rarity: URS-2
Proof $1,500

$5 • W-MA-2960-005-G190

SN

Engraver: New England Bank Note Co. / PSSP. ***Comments:*** H-Unlisted. 18__.

Rarity: URS-1
Proof $3,000

$5 • W-MA-2960-005-G190a

Left: FIVE / Ship under sail / FIVE. ***Right:*** 5 / FIVE / 5. ***Tint:*** Red bank title and FIVE DOLLARS in microlettering. ***Engraver:*** New England Bank Note Co. / PSSP. ***Comments:*** H-MA-1120-G78. Similar to W-MA-2960-005-G190. 18__. 1850s.

Rarity: —

$10 • W-MA-2960-010-G200

Left: Panel bearing state arms / 10 / 10 vertically. ***Center:*** Alternating flower garlands and gridwork segments. ***Right:*** 10 / 10 vertically. ***Engraver:*** Perkins. ***Comments:*** H-MA-1120-G80. 18__. 1811.

Rarity: —

$10 • W-MA-2960-010-G200a

Center: Alternating flower garlands and gridwork segments / TEN. ***Engraver:*** Perkins. ***Comments:*** H-MA-1120-G82. Similar to W-MA-2960-010-G200. 18__. Circa 1812–1820s.

Rarity: —

$10 • W-MA-2960-010-G200b

Left: Lathework chain bearing MASSACHUSETTS vertically. ***Right:*** Panel of lathework circle segments. ***Engraver:*** Perkins. ***Comments:*** H-MA-1120-G84. Similar to W-MA-2960-010-G200. 18__. 1820s.

Rarity: —

$10 • W-MA-2960-010-G200c

Left: Lathework chain bearing MASSACHUSETTS vertically. ***Right:*** Panel of lathework circle segments. ***Engraver:*** Perkins. ***Comments:*** H-MA-1120-G86. Similar to W-MA-2960-010-G200. 18__. 1820s.

Rarity: —

$10 • W-MA-2960-010-G200d

Engraver: PSSP. ***Comments:*** H-MA-1120-G88. Similar to W-MA-2960-010-G200. 18__. 1820s–1830s.

Rarity: —

$10 • W-MA-2960-010-G200e

Engraver: PSSP. ***Comments:*** H-MA-1120-G90. Similar to W-MA-2960-010-G200. 18__. 1830s.

Rarity: —

$10 • W-MA-2960-010-G210

CJF

Engraver: Underwood, Bald, Spencer & Hufty / Danforth, Underwood & Co. ***Comments:*** H-MA-1120-G94. Proof. 18__. 1840s–1850s.

Rarity: URS-2
Proof $1,500

$10 • W-MA-2960-010-G220

SN

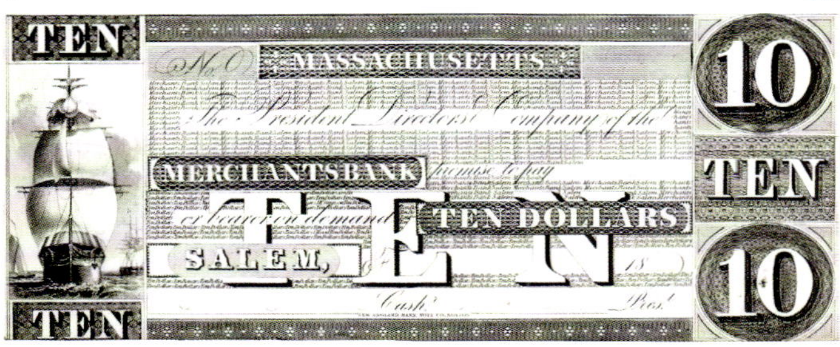

Engraver: New England Bank Note Co. / PSSP. ***Comments:*** H-Unlisted. 18__.

Rarity: URS-2
Proof $1,500

$10 • W-MA-2960-010-G220a

Left: TEN / Front view of ship / TEN. ***Right:*** 10 / TEN / 10. ***Tint:*** Red bank title and TEN DOLLARS in microlettering. ***Engraver:*** New England Bank Note Co. / PSSP. ***Comments:*** H-MA-1120-G96. Similar to W-MA-2960-010-G220. 18__. 1850s.

Rarity: —

$20 • W-MA-2960-020-G230

Left: Panel bearing state arms / 20 / 20 vertically. ***Center:*** Alternating flower garlands and gridwork segments. ***Right:*** 20 / 20 vertically. ***Engraver:*** Perkins. ***Comments:*** H-MA-1120-G98. 18__. 1810s–1820s.

Rarity: —

$20 • W-MA-2960-020-G230a

Left: Panel bearing lathework chain with MASSACHUSETTS. ***Engraver:*** PSSP. ***Comments:*** H-MA-1120-G100. Similar to W-MA-2960-020-G230. 18__. 1820s–1830s.

Rarity: —

$20 • W-MA-2960-020-G240

Left: Panel of lathework chains with MASSACHUSETTS / 20 / Woman seated with cornucopia / 20. ***Center:*** Bank title in microlettering. ***Right:*** 20 / State arms / 20. ***Engraver:*** PSSP. ***Comments:*** H-MA-1120-G104. 18__. 1830s–1840s.

Rarity: —

$50 • W-MA-2960-050-G250

Left: Panel bearing state arms / 50 / 50 vertically. ***Center:*** Alternating flower garlands and gridwork segments. ***Right:*** 50 / 50 vertically. ***Engraver:*** Perkins. ***Comments:*** H-MA-1120-G106. 18__. 1810s–1820s.

Rarity: —

$50 • W-MA-2960-050-G250a

Left: Lathework chain bearing MASSACHUSETTS vertically. ***Engraver:*** PSSP. ***Comments:*** H-MA-1120-G108. Similar to W-MA-2960-050-G250. 18__. 1820s–1830s.

Rarity: —

$50 • W-MA-2960-050-G260

Left: FIFTY / Steamboat / FIFTY. ***Right:*** 50 / FIFTY / 50. ***Tint:*** Red bank title and FIFTY DOLLARS in microlettering. ***Engraver:*** New England Bank Note Co. / PSSP. ***Comments:*** H-MA-1120-G112. 18__. 1850s.

Rarity: —

$100 • W-MA-2960-100-G270

Left: Panel bearing state arms / 100 / 100 vertically. ***Center:*** Alternating flower garlands and gridwork segments. ***Right:*** 100 / 100 vertically. ***Engraver:*** Perkins. ***Comments:*** H-MA-1120-G114. 18__. 1810s–1820s.

Rarity: —

$100 • W-MA-2960-100-G270a

Left: Lathework chain bearing MASSACHUSETTS vertically. ***Engraver:*** Perkins. ***Comments:*** H-MA-1120-G116. Similar to W-MA-2960-100-G270. 18__. 1820s–1830s.

Rarity: —

$100 • W-MA-2960-100-G280

Left: 100 / Sailor, Shipping / 100. ***Right:*** 100 / C / 100. ***Tint:*** Red bank title and HUNDRED DOLLARS in microlettering. ***Engraver:*** New England Bank Note Co. / PSSP. ***Comments:*** H-MA-1120-G120. 18__. 1850s.

Rarity: —

$500 • W-MA-2960-500-G290

Left: Lathework chain bearing MASSACHUSETTS / 500 / 500 vertically. ***Center:*** Alternating flower garlands and gridwork segments. ***Right:*** 500 / 500 vertically. ***Engraver:*** PSSP. ***Comments:*** H-MA-1120-G122. 18__. 1820s–1830s.

Rarity: —

$500 • W-MA-2960-500-G300

Tint: Red bank title and FIVE HUNDRED DOLLARS in microlettering. ***Engraver:*** New England Bank Note Co. / PSSP. ***Comments:*** H-MA-1120-G126. 18__. 1850s.

Rarity: —

Uncut Sheets

$1-$2-$5-$10 • W-MA-2960-001.002.005.010-US010

SN

Comments: All unlisted in Haxby. 18__.

Rarity: URS-1

Proof $10,000

$5-$10 • W-MA-2960-005.010-US020

SN

Comments: H-MA-1120-G76, G94. 18__. 1840s–1850s.

Rarity: —

$5-$5-$10-$10 • W-MA-2960-005.005.010.010-US030

Vignette(s): ($5) Medallion head / 5 on medallion head / Eagle / 5 on medallion head / Dog's head / Medallion head. ***($5)*** Medallion head / 5 on medallion head / Eagle / 5 on medallion head / Dog's head / Medallion head. ***($10)*** Medallion head / Medallion head bearing 10 / Indian woman with shield and bale / Medallion head bearing 10 / Medallion head bearing TEN. ***($10)*** Medallion head / Medallion head bearing 10 / Indian woman with shield and bale / Medallion head bearing 10 / Medallion head bearing TEN. ***Comments:*** H-MA-1120-G76, G76, G94, G94. 18__. 1840s–1850s.

Rarity: —

$__-$5-$10-$10 • W-MA-2960-__.005.010.010-US030a

Comments: H-MA-1120-__, G76, G94, G94. Similar to W-MA-2960-005.005.010.010-US030 but with top note missing. 18__. 1840s–1850s.

Rarity: —

Non-Valid Issues

$1 • W-MA-2960-001-A010

Left: ONE / Hebe seated on sheaf, watering eagle / ONE. ***Center:*** Ships / Eagle on shield. ***Right:*** 1 / Ceres kneeling, Sheaf, Farm. ***Engraver:*** Danforth, Bald & Co. ***Comments:*** H-MA-1120-A5. Altered from $1 Columbia Bank, Washington, D.C. 18__. 1811.

Rarity: —

$1 • W-MA-2960-001-A020

Left: Diagonal ONE / Male portrait / Diagonal ONE. ***Center:*** 1 / Woman reading book / 1. ***Bottom center:*** Train at station. ***Right:*** 1 with woman carrying grain. ***Engraver:*** Rawdon, Wright, Hatch & Edson. ***Comments:*** H-MA-1120-A10. Altered from $1 Merchants Bank, Washington, D.C. July 1, 1852.

Rarity: —

$1 • W-MA-2960-001-A030

Left: Panel bearing portrait of Zachary Taylor. ***Center:*** 1 / Woman in clouds holding shield, Eagle / 1 / ONE. ***Right:*** Panel bearing Ceres. ***Engraver:*** W.L. Ormsby. ***Comments:*** H-MA-1120-A15. Altered from $1 Mechanics and Traders Bank, Georgetown, D.C. Nov. 14, 1852.

Rarity: —

$1 • W-MA-2960-001-A040

Left: 1 / State arms / ONE. ***Center:*** Three allegorical women reclining around shield surmounted by eagle, Ship. ***Right:*** 1 / Two farmers walking, Dog. ***Engraver:*** Danforth, Wright & Co. ***Comments:*** H-MA-1120-A20. Altered from $1 Bank of Washtenaw Washtenaw, Michigan series. 1850s.

Rarity: —

$1 • W-MA-2960-001-A050

Left: Woman leaning on shield bearing 1. ***Center:*** 1 / Animal in field, Trees. ***Right:*** Indian / 1. ***Engraver:*** Doty & Bergen. ***Comments:*** H-MA-1120-A25. Altered from $1 Merchants Bank, Stillwater, Minnesota. Oct. 20, 185_. 1855.

Rarity: —

$2 • W-MA-2960-002-S010

Center: Woman / 2 / Woman. ***Comments:*** H-MA-1120-S5 1850s.

Rarity: —

$2 • W-MA-2960-002-N010

Center: Train. ***Comments:*** H-MA-1120-N5.

Rarity: —

$2 • W-MA-2960-002-A060

Left: 2 / Liberty and Ceres seated with caduceus, shield, sickle and sheaf, Ship. ***Right:*** 2 / Portrait of Zachary Taylor. ***Engraver:*** W.L. Ormsby. ***Comments:*** H-MA-1120-A30. Altered from $2 Merchants Bank, Ft. Leavenworth, Kansas. 18__. 1850s.

Rarity: —

$2 • W-MA-2960-002-A070

S

Overprint: Red TWO. ***Engraver:*** Rawdon, Wright, Hatch & Edson. ***Comments:*** H-MA-1120-A35. Altered from $2 Merchants Bank, Stillwater, Minnesota. October 20, 1854.

Rarity: —

$3 • W-MA-2960-003-S020

CJF

Engraver: Rawdon, Wright & Hatch. ***Comments:*** H-MA-1120-S10. Oct. 8, 1854.

Rarity: URS-7
F $75; **VF** $125; **EF** $250

$3 • W-MA-2960-003-S030

CJF

Tint: Orange bank title and dies. ***Engraver:*** New England Bank Note Co. ***Comments:*** H-MA-1120-S15. Jan. 1, 1859.

Rarity: —

$3 • W-MA-2960-003-A080

Left: 3 / Portrait of Andrew Jackson / 3. ***Center:*** 3 / Indian woman with bow / Flags, drums / 3. ***Bottom center:*** Train at station. ***Right:*** THREE / Ceres seated, Caduceus / 3. ***Engraver:*** Rawdon, Wright, Hatch & Edson. ***Comments:*** H-MA-1120-A40. Altered from $3 Merchants Bank, Washington, D.C. Dec. 1, 1852.

Rarity: —

$5 • W-MA-2960-005-S040

Left: 5 / Classical scholar seated. ***Center:*** Steamship, Sailboat. ***Right:*** 5 / Woman leaning on column. ***Comments:*** H-MA-1120-S20. 18__. 1850s.

Rarity: —

$5 • W-MA-2960-005-S050

CC

Comments: H-MA-1120-N10. Spurious note. 18__. 1839.

Rarity: —

$5 • W-MA-2960-005-A090

Left: FIVE vertically. ***Center:*** 5 / Spread eagle on U.S. shield holding banner in its beak. ***Bottom center:*** Road, Trees, Sign post. ***Right:*** Indian woman holding bow. ***Engraver:*** Doty & Bergen. ***Comments:*** H-MA-1120-A45. Altered from $5 Merchants Bank, Stillwater, Minnesota. Oct. 20, 1854.

Rarity: —

$10 • W-MA-2960-010-S060

Left: X / Girl standing with pitcher. ***Center:*** X / Sailor seated on bale holding flag, Ships / X. ***Bottom center:*** Ship. ***Right:*** X / Ship on stocks. ***Engraver:*** Rawdon, Wright & Hatch. ***Comments:*** H-MA-1120-S25. 18__. 1850s.

Rarity: —

$10 • W-MA-2960-010-A100

Left: X / Eagle surmounting frame bearing arm and hammer. ***Center:*** Woman seated on bale, Spinning wheel / 10. ***Right:*** Panel of flowers and fruit bearing medallion portrait of George Washington. ***Engraver:*** W.L. Ormsby. ***Comments:*** H-MA-1120-A50. Altered from $10 Merchants Bank, Fort Leavenworth, Kansas. 18__. 1850s.

Rarity: —

$50 • W-MA-2960-050-A110

CJF

Engraver: Boston Bank Note Co. ***Comments:*** H-MA-1120-A55. Altered from $50 Bank of Vernon, Vernon, Texas. 18__. 1850s.

Rarity: —

Naumkeag Bank

1831–1865

W-MA-2970

History: The Naumkeag Bank was chartered on March 17, 1831, with an authorized capital of $200,000, later increased to $500,000. It began business in the store of Benjamin Dodge. It moved soon to the Manning Building, later to the East India Marine Building, and then finally to the Asiatic Building on Washington Street. The circulation of the bank was $72,402 in 1839 and $194,231 in 1863. The bank's specie amounted to $16,727.57 in 1857.

The business of the Naumkeag Bank was succeeded by the Naumkeag National Bank of Salem after it was chartered in December 1864 and commenced operations in early 1865.

Numismatic Commentary: The notes that appear the most frequently are the $1 issues showing a street scene in Salem with the bank as the centerpiece. Depictions of local scenery are always popular with paper money collectors. Easily missed under the center vignette are the engraved names of David Pingree, the bank's only president, and J.G. Sprague, the cashier of the bank during its first 17 years.

Valid Issues

$1 • W-MA-2970-001-G010

Left: Lathework panel bearing MASSACHUSETTS vertically. ***Center:*** 1 / 1 / Alternating flower garlands and gridwork segments / ONE / 1 / 1. ***Right:*** Lathework panel bearing ONE / D / ONE vertically. ***Engraver:*** PSSP. ***Comments:*** H-MA-1125-G2. 18__. 1830s.

Rarity: —

$1 • W-MA-2970-001-G020

Left: ONE / Indian on horse with spear raised / ONE. ***Center:*** Building, People. ***Right:*** 1 / People next to grindstone / ONE. ***Back:*** Brown. ***Engraver:*** Terry, Pelton & Co. ***Comments:*** H-MA-1125-G6. 18__.

Rarity: —

$1 • W-MA-2970-001-G020a

Back: Brown. ***Engraver:*** Terry, Pelton & Co. ***Comments:*** H-MA-1125-G6a. Similar to W-MA-2970-001-G020. 18__. 1840s–1850s.

Rarity: —

$1 • W-MA-2970-001-G020b

Back: Plain. ***Engraver:*** Terry, Pelton & Co. / ABNCo. monogram. ***Comments:*** H-MA-1125-G6c. Similar to W-MA-2970-001-G020 but with additional engraver imprint. 18__. 1850s–1860s.

Rarity: —

$1 • W-MA-2970-001-G020c

Overprint: Green panel outlining white ONE. ***Back:*** Plain. ***Engraver:*** Terry, Pelton & Co. / ABNCo. monogram. ***Comments:*** H-MA-1125-G6d. Similar to W-MA-2970-001-G020 but with additional engraver imprint. 18__. 1860s.

Rarity: —

$1 • W-MA-2970-001-G030

Left: ONE / People in factory / ONE. ***Center:*** 1 / Building, People / 1. ***Bottom center:*** Train. ***Right:*** 1 / Indian with rifle / ONE. ***Back:*** Plain. ***Engraver:*** Terry, Pelton & Co. ***Comments:*** H-MA-1125-G8. 18__.

Rarity: —

$1 • W-MA-2970-001-G030a

CJF, CJF

Back: Brown panel bearing CHECK. ***Engraver:*** Terry, Pelton & Co. ***Comments:*** H-MA-1125-G8a. Similar to W-MA-2970-001-G030. 18__. 1840s–1850s.

Rarity: URS-3
VF $1,500

$1 • W-MA-2970-001-G030b

Back: Plain. ***Engraver:*** Terry, Pelton & Co. / ABNCo. monogram. ***Comments:*** H-MA-1125-G8c. Similar to W-MA-2970-001-G030 but with additional engraver imprint. 18__. 1850s–1860s.

Rarity: —

$1 • W-MA-2970-001-G030c

JF

Overprint: Green panel outlining white ONE. ***Back:*** Plain. ***Engraver:*** Terry, Pelton & Co. / ABNCo. monogram. ***Comments:*** H-MA-1125-G8d. Similar to W-MA-2970-001-G030 but with additional engraver imprint. 18__. 1860s.

Rarity: URS-3

VG $750; **VF** $1,250

$1 • W-MA-2970-001-G030d

CJF

Overprint: Red ONE. ***Engraver:*** Terry, Pelton & Co. / ABNCo. monogram. ***Comments:*** H-Unlisted. Similar to W-MA-2970-001-G030 but with additional engraver imprint. 18__. 1860s.

Rarity: URS-2

F $1,000; **VF** $1,500

$1 • W-MA-2970-001-G040

CJF

Engraver: Terry, Pelton & Co. ***Comments:*** H-Unlisted. Proof. 18__.

Rarity: —

$2 • W-MA-2970-002-G050

Left: Lathework panel bearing MASSACHUSETTS vertically. ***Center:*** 2 / 2 / Alternating flower garlands and gridwork segments / TWO / 2 / 2. ***Right:*** Lathework panel bearing five TWOs vertically. ***Engraver:*** PSSP. ***Comments:*** H-MA-1125-G10. 18__. 1830s.

Rarity: —

$2 • W-MA-2970-002-G060

Center: Street scene in Salem. ***Engraver:*** Terry, Pelton & Co. ***Comments:*** H-MA-1125-G14. 18__. 1840s.

Rarity: —

$2 • W-MA-2970-002-G070

Left: TWO / Two Indian men / 2. ***Center:*** Street scene in Salem. ***Bottom center:*** Three men in a boat, Ship and wharf. ***Right:*** 2 / Man leaning on anchor and smoking pipe / TWO. ***Back:*** Brown. ***Engraver:*** Terry, Pelton & Co. ***Comments:*** H-MA-1125-G16. 18__. 1840s–1850s.

Rarity: —

$2 • W-MA-2970-002-G070a

Back: Plain. ***Engraver:*** Terry, Pelton & Co. / ABNCo. monogram. ***Comments:*** H-MA-1125-G16b. Similar to W-MA-2970-002-G070 but with additional engraver imprint. 18__. 1850s–1860s.

Rarity: —

$2 • W-MA-2970-002-G070b

Overprint: Green panel outlining white TWO. ***Back:*** Plain. ***Engraver:*** Terry, Pelton & Co. / ABNCo. monogram. ***Comments:*** H-MA-1125-G16c. Similar to W-MA-2970-002-G070 but with additional engraver imprint. 18__. 1860s.

Rarity: —

$2 • W-MA-2970-002-G070c

JF

Overprint: Red TWO. ***Back:*** Plain. ***Engraver:*** Terry, Pelton & Co. / ABNCo. monogram. ***Comments:*** H-Unlisted. Similar to W-MA-2970-002-G070 but with additional engraver imprint. 18__. 1860s.

Rarity: URS-2

F $1,250; **VF** $2,000

$3 • W-MA-2970-003-G080

Left: Lathework panel bearing MASSACHUSETTS vertically. ***Center:*** 3 / 3 / Alternating flower garlands and gridwork segments / THREE / 3 / 3. ***Right:*** Lathework panel bearing THREE vertically. ***Engraver:*** PSSP. ***Comments:*** H-MA-1125-G20. 18__. 1830s.

Rarity: —

$3 • W-MA-2970-003-G090

Left: 3 / Woman standing / THREE. ***Center:*** Indian standing with staff / THREE. ***Bottom center:*** Train. ***Right:*** 3 / Two men / THREE. ***Back:*** Plain. ***Engraver:*** Terry, Pelton & Co. ***Comments:*** H-MA-1125-G22. 18__. 1840s.

Rarity: —

$3 • W-MA-2970-003-G100

Left: THREE / Ships / 3. ***Center:*** 3 / Street scene in Salem / 3. ***Right:*** 3 / Woman and Indian man / THREE. ***Engraver:*** Terry, Pelton & Co. ***Comments:*** H-MA-1125-G24. 18__. 1840s–1850s.

Rarity: —

$3 • W-MA-2970-003-G100a

Back: Plain. ***Engraver:*** Terry, Pelton & Co. / ABNCo. monogram. ***Comments:*** H-MA-1125-G24b. Similar to W-MA-2970-003-G100 but with additional engraver imprint. 18__. 1850s–1860s.

Rarity: —

$3 • W-MA-2970-003-G100b

Overprint: Green panel outlining white THREE. ***Back:*** Plain. ***Engraver:*** Terry, Pelton & Co. / ABNCo. monogram. ***Comments:*** H-MA-1125-G24c. Similar to W-MA-2970-003-G100 but with additional engraver imprint. 18__. 1860s.

Rarity: —

$5 • W-MA-2970-005-G110

Left: Lathework chain bearing MASSACHUSETTS / 5 / 5. ***Center:*** Alternating flower garlands and gridwork segments / FIVE lined by spiral lathework lines. ***Right:*** 5 / 5. ***Engraver:*** PSSP. ***Comments:*** H-MA-1125-G26. 18__. 1830s.

Rarity: —

$5 • W-MA-2970-005-G120

Left: 5 / Blacksmith at anvil / FIVE. ***Center:*** Mercury standing with 5, Cornucopia and merchandise, Factories and ship / V / Panel outlining white FIVE. ***Right:*** 5 / Ceres kneeling / FIVE. ***Back:*** Check Plate. ***Engraver:*** New England Bank Note Co. / PSSP. ***Comments:*** H-MA-1125-G28. 18__. 1830s.

Rarity: —

$5 • W-MA-2970-005-G130

Left: V / Ships / V. ***Center:*** 5 / Street scene in Salem. ***Bottom center:*** Ships. ***Right:*** 5 / Indian man seated on stump with gun and dog. ***Engraver:*** Terry, Pelton & Co. ***Comments:*** H-MA-1125-G30. 18__. 1840s–1850s.

Rarity: —

$5 • W-MA-2970-005-G130a

Back: Plain. ***Engraver:*** Terry, Pelton & Co. / ABNCo. monogram. ***Comments:*** H-MA-1125-G30b. Similar to W-MA-2970-005-G130 but with additional engraver imprint. 18__. 1850s–1860s.

Rarity: —

$5 • W-MA-2970-005-G130b

Overprint: Green panel outlining white FIVE. ***Back:*** Plain. ***Engraver:*** Terry, Pelton & Co. / ABNCo. monogram. ***Comments:*** H-MA-1125-G30c. Similar to W-MA-2970-005-G130 but with additional engraver imprint. 18__. 1860s.

Rarity: —

$5 • W-MA-2970-005-G140

Left: FIVE / FIVE. ***Center:*** Building. ***Right:*** 5 / FIVE / Female portrait. ***Engraver:*** Terry, Pelton & Co. ***Comments:*** H-MA-1125-G32. 18__. 1840s–1850s.

Rarity: —

$5 • W-MA-2970-005-G140a

Back: Plain. ***Engraver:*** Terry, Pelton & Co. / ABNCo. monogram. ***Comments:*** H-MA-1125-G32b. Similar to W-MA-2970-005-G140 but with additional engraver imprint. 18__. 1850s–1860s.

Rarity: —

$5 • W-MA-2970-005-G140b

Overprint: Green panel outlining white FIVE. ***Back:*** Plain. ***Engraver:*** Terry, Pelton & Co. / ABNCo. monogram. ***Comments:*** H-MA-1125-G32c. Similar to W-MA-2970-005-G140 but with additional engraver imprint. 18__. 1860s.

Rarity: —

$5 • W-MA-2970-005-G150

Left: 5 / FIVE / 5. ***Center:*** Street scene in Salem. ***Right:*** 5 / FIVE / 5. ***Engraver:*** Terry, Pelton & Co. ***Comments:*** H-MA-1125-G34. 18__. 1840s–1850s.

Rarity: —

$5 • W-MA-2970-005-G150a

Back: Plain. ***Engraver:*** Terry, Pelton & Co. / ABNCo. monogram. ***Comments:*** H-MA-1125-G34b. Similar to W-MA-2970-005-G150 but with additional engraver imprint. 18__. 1850s–1860s.

Rarity: —

$5 • W-MA-2970-005-G150b

Overprint: Green panel outlining white FIVE. ***Engraver:*** Terry, Pelton & Co. / ABNCo. monogram. ***Comments:*** H-MA-1125-G34c. Similar to W-MA-2970-005-G150 but with additional engraver imprint. 18__. 1860s.

Rarity: —

$10 • W-MA-2970-010-G160

Left: Lathework chain bearing MASSACHUSETTS / 10 / 10 vertically. ***Center:*** Alternating flower garlands and gridwork segments / TEN lined by spiral lathework lines. ***Right:*** 10 / 10 vertically. ***Engraver:*** PSSP. ***Comments:*** H-MA-1125-G36. 18__. 1830s.

Rarity: —

$10 • W-MA-2970-010-G170

Back: Check Plate. ***Engraver:*** New England Bank Note Co. ***Comments:*** H-MA-1125-G38. 18__. 1830s.

Rarity: —

$10 • W-MA-2970-010-G180

Left: Shipyard scene / Samson. ***Center:*** Street scene in Salem. ***Bottom center:*** Anchor. ***Right:*** 10 / Train / 10. ***Engraver:*** Terry, Pelton & Co. ***Comments:*** H-MA-1125-G40. 18__. 1840s–1850s.

Rarity: —

$10 • W-MA-2970-010-G180a

Back: Plain. ***Engraver:*** Terry, Pelton & Co. / ABNCo. monogram. ***Comments:*** H-MA-1125-G40b. Similar to W-MA-2970-010-G180 but with additional engraver imprint. 18__. 1850s–1860s.

Rarity: —

$10 • W-MA-2970-010-G190

Center: Street scene in Salem. ***Engraver:*** Terry, Pelton & Co. ***Comments:*** H-MA-1125-G42. 18__. 1840s.

Rarity: —

$20 • W-MA-2970-020-G200

Left: Lathework chain bearing MASSACHUSETTS / 20 / 20 vertically. ***Center:*** Alternating flower garlands and gridwork segments. ***Right:*** 20 / 20 vertically. ***Engraver:*** PSSP. ***Comments:*** H-MA-1125-G44. 18__. 1830s.

Rarity: —

$20 • W-MA-2970-020-G210

Left: Steamboat / XX / Train. ***Center:*** Three women seated with eagle, pole and cap, shield, scales, and book / 20 / Panel outlining white TWENTY. ***Right:*** XX / Milkmaid standing with pail. ***Engraver:*** New England Bank Note Co. ***Comments:*** H-MA-1125-G48. Beware of altered W-MA-2970-020-A010 of the same design as the genuine. 18__. 1840s–1850s.

Rarity: —

$20 • W-MA-2970-020-G220
Left: 20 / Woman seated with book on lap, opening chest. ***Center:*** XX / Eagle on rock / XX. ***Right:*** 20 / Ship in harbor. ***Engraver:*** New England Bank Note Co. ***Comments:*** H-MA-1125-G50. 18__. 1850s.
Rarity: —

$20 • W-MA-2970-020-G230
Left: XX / Indian woman standing with bow and arrows. ***Center:*** Two women flanking anvil, Cornucopia and tools, Factory and grain field. ***Right:*** 20 / Indian woman seated. ***Engraver:*** American Bank Note Co. ***Comments:*** H-MA-1125-G52. 1860s.
Rarity: —

$50 • W-MA-2970-050-G240
Left: Lathework chain bearing MASSACHUSETTS / 50 / 50 vertically. ***Center:*** Alternating flower garlands and gridwork segments. ***Right:*** 50 / 50 vertically. ***Engraver:*** PSSP. ***Comments:*** H-MA-1125-G54. 18__. 1830s.
Rarity: —

$50 • W-MA-2970-050-G250
Left: 50 / Steamboat and schooner. ***Center:*** Farmyard scene, Load of hay with two men on it, Man with rake and pail. ***Right:*** L / Justice kneeling. ***Engraver:*** New England Bank Note Co. ***Comments:*** H-MA-1125-G58. 18__. 1840s–1850s.
Rarity: —

$50 • W-MA-2970-050-G260
Left: FIFTY / Woman standing with wreath and flowers / FIFTY. ***Center:*** 50 / Man restraining prancing horse / 50. ***Right:*** FIFTY / Woman standing with cornucopia / FIFTY. ***Engraver:*** New England Bank Note Co. ***Comments:*** H-MA-1125-G60. 18__. 1850s.
Rarity: —

$50 • W-MA-2970-050-G270
Left: FIFTY / Sailor seated with spyglass, Woman with cornucopia / FIFTY. ***Right:*** 50 / Indian woman seated by waterfall with bow and quiver, Rainbow. ***Engraver:*** American Bank Note Co. ***Comments:*** H-MA-1125-G62. 1860s.
Rarity: —

$100 • W-MA-2970-100-G280
Left: Lathework chain bearing MASSACHUSETTS / 100 / 100 vertically. ***Center:*** Alternating flower garlands and gridwork segments. ***Right:*** 100 / 100 vertically. ***Engraver:*** Perkins. ***Comments:*** H-MA-1125-G64. 18__. 1830s.
Rarity: —

$100 • W-MA-2970-100-G290
Left: 100 / Eagle / 100. ***Center:*** C / Phoebus in the Chariot of the Sun / 100. ***Right:*** ONE HUNDRED on 100 / Portrait of Christopher Columbus. ***Engraver:*** New England Bank Note Co. ***Comments:*** H-MA-1125-G68. 18__. 1840s–1850s.
Rarity: —

$100 • W-MA-2970-100-G300
Left: ONE HUNDRED ON 100 / Portrait of William Henry Harrison. ***Center:*** Wharf scene, Men loading wagon with barrels. ***Right:*** ONE HUNDRED on 100 / Portrait of Christopher Columbus. ***Engraver:*** New England Bank Note Co. ***Comments:*** H-MA-1125-G70. 18__. 1850s.
Rarity: —

$100 • W-MA-2970-100-G310
Left: 100 / State arms. ***Center:*** Indian family on cliff viewing city. ***Right:*** 100 / Hay wagon, Farm. ***Engraver:*** American Bank Note Co. ***Comments:*** H-MA-1125-G72. 1860s.
Rarity: —

$500 • W-MA-2970-500-G320
Left: Lathework chain bearing MASSACHUSETTS / 500 / 500 vertically. ***Center:*** Alternating flower garlands and gridwork segments. ***Right:*** 500 / 500 vertically. ***Engraver:*** PSSP. ***Comments:*** H-MA-1125-G74. 18__. 1820s–1830s.
Rarity: —

$500 • W-MA-2970-500-G330
Left: 500 / 500 vertically. ***Center:*** 500 / Woman seated with shield bearing D, Fasces, cornucopia, lyre, and sheaf / 500. ***Right:*** 500 / D / 500. ***Engraver:*** PSSP / New England Bank Note Co. ***Comments:*** H-MA-1125-G76. 18__. 1830s–1840s.
Rarity: —

$500 • W-MA-2970-500-G330a
Overprint: Red. ***Engraver:*** New England Bank Note Co. / PSSP. ***Comments:*** H-MA-1125-G76a. Similar to W-MA-2970-500-G330. 18__. 1850s.
Rarity: —

$500 • W-MA-2970-500-G340
Left: Sailor seated on rail of ship with spyglass / 500. ***Center:*** State arms. ***Right:*** 500 / D. ***Engraver:*** American Bank Note Co. ***Comments:*** H-MA-1125-G78. 1860s.
Rarity: —

$1,000 • W-MA-2970-1000-G350
Left: THOUSAND vertically. ***Center:*** 1000 / Woman standing with legs crossed, Lyre, Cornucopia / 1000. ***Right:*** 1000 / M / 1000. ***Engraver:*** PSSP / New England Bank Note Co. ***Comments:*** H-MA-1125-G80. 18__. 1830s–1840s.
Rarity: —

$1,000 • W-MA-2970-1000-G360
Overprint: Red. ***Engraver:*** New England Bank Note Co. / PSSP. ***Comments:*** H-MA-1125-G82. 18__. 1850s.
Rarity: —

$1,000 • W-MA-2970-1000-G370
Left: Eagle on shield / 1000. ***Center:*** Portrait of George Washington. ***Right:*** 1000 / Woman holding torch, leaning against pedestal. ***Engraver:*** American Bank Note Co. ***Comments:*** H-MA-1125-G84. 1860s.
Rarity: —

NON-VALID ISSUES

$3 • W-MA-2970-003-C100
Engraver: Terry, Pelton & Co. ***Comments:*** H-MA-1125-C24. Counterfeit of W-MA-2970-003-G100. 18__. 1850s.
Rarity: —

$5 • W-MA-2970-005-R010
Engraver: Terry, Pelton & Co. ***Comments:*** H-MA-1125-R5. Raised from W-MA-2970-001-G020 series. 18__. 1840s–1850s.
Rarity: —

$5 • W-MA-2970-005-R020

Engraver: Terry, Pelton & Co. ***Comments:*** H-MA-1125-R10. Raised from W-MA-2970-003-G100. 18__. 1840s.

Rarity: —

$10 • W-MA-2970-010-R030

Engraver: Terry, Pelton & Co. ***Comments:*** H-MA-1125-R15. Raised from W-MA-2970-001-G020 series. 18__. 1840s–1850s.

Rarity: —

$10 • W-MA-2970-010-R040

Engraver: Terry, Pelton & Co. ***Comments:*** H-MA-1125-R20. Raised from W-MA-2970-003-G100. 18__. 1840s.

Rarity: —

$20 • W-MA-2970-020-R050

Engraver: Terry, Pelton & Co. ***Comments:*** H-MA-1125-R25. Raised from W-MA-2970-003-G100. 18__. 1840s.

Rarity: —

$20 • W-MA-2970-020-A010

CJF

Engraver: New England Bank Note Co. ***Comments:*** H-MA-1125-A10. Genuine notes of this design were made, W-MA-2970-020-G210. 18__. 1850s.

Rarity: —

$50 • W-MA-2970-050-R060

Engraver: Terry, Pelton & Co. ***Comments:*** H-MA-1125-R30. Raised from W-MA-2970-003-G100. 18__. 1840s.

Rarity: —

North American Bank

1836

W-MA-2975

History: The North American Bank was chartered on March 17, 1836, with an authorized capital of $200,000. Its advocates failed to raise the necessary funds, and it never went into business.

Salem Bank

1803–1864

W-MA-2980

History: The Salem Bank was chartered on March 8, 1803, with an authorized capital of $200,000. Its first office was in a brick building on the south side of Essex Street, opposite St. Peter's Street. On February 8, 1823, the bank's capital was increased to $250,000. On February 4, 1849, the same was reduced to $187,500.

In early 1853 someone snatched a quantity of bank notes that had been signed by the cashier but not yet by the president. The signature of the latter was forged and the bills exchanged at the Gloucester Bank. The deception was learned, and the Salem Bank refused to honor them, after which the matter landed in court. The Salem Bank was not held responsible, as it was found that the holder of the currency had the obligation to verify the validity of the signatures. The passing of an incompletely signed bill did not obligate the bank.[38]

In 1864 the business of the Salem Bank was succeeded by the Salem National Bank.

Numismatic Commentary: This bank was a prolific issuer of notes by various engravers. One National Bank Note Co. issue shows Civil War action on Roanoke Island, the "Charge of the Zouaves" led by Colonel Rush Hawkins. Historically significant vignettes are very popular with today's numismatists.

Valid Issues

$1 • W-MA-2980-001-G010

Left: Plow / ONE / Grape vine vertically. ***Center:*** 1 / ONE / 1. ***Comments:*** H-MA-1130-G20. 18__. 1800s.

Rarity: —

$1 • W-MA-2980-001-G020

Left: SALEM BANK vertically. ***Center:*** 1 vertically / ONE DOLLAR / ONE. ***Right:*** 1 vertically. ***Engraver:*** PSSP. ***Comments:*** H-MA-1130-G24. 18__. 1800s.

Rarity: —

$1 • W-MA-2980-001-G030

Center: 1 / 1 / Oval of flower garlands and gridwork segments / 1 / 1. ***Engraver:*** PSSP. ***Comments:*** H-MA-1130-G28. 18__. 1809–circa 1812.

Rarity: —

$1 • W-MA-2980-001-G030a

Center: 1 / 1 / Oval of flower garlands and gridwork segments / ONE / 1 / 1. ***Engraver:*** PSSP. ***Comments:*** H-MA-1130-G30. Similar to W-MA-2980-001-G030. 18__. 1812–1820s.

Rarity: —

$1 • W-MA-2980-001-G030b

Left: Panel of lathework circle segments. ***Right:*** Panel of lathework circle segments. ***Engraver:*** PSSP. ***Comments:*** H-MA-1130-G32. Similar to W-MA-2980-001-G030. 18__. 1820s.

Rarity: —

$1 • W-MA-2980-001-G030c

Left: Panel of lathework circle segments. ***Right:*** Panel of lathework circle segments. ***Engraver:*** PSSP. ***Comments:*** H-MA-1130-G34. Similar to W-MA-2980-001-G030. 18__. 1820s–1830s.

Rarity: —

$1 • W-MA-2980-001-G030d

Left: ONE / D / ONE vertically. ***Right:*** ONE / D / ONE vertically. ***Engraver:*** PSSP. ***Comments:*** H-MA-1130-G36. Similar to W-MA-2980-001-G030. 18__. 1830s.

Rarity: —

$1 • W-MA-2980-001-G040
Left: 1 / Three women / 1. ***Center:*** Machinery and factories / Ship / Beehive. ***Right:*** 1 / Portrait of George Washington / 1. ***Engraver:*** New England Bank Note Co. ***Comments:*** H-MA-1130-G38. 18__. 1830s–1850s.

Rarity: —

$1 • W-MA-2980-001-G040a
Engraver: New England Bank Note Co. / ABNCo. monogram. ***Comments:*** H-MA-1130-G38a. Similar to W-MA-2980-001-G040 but with additional engraver imprint. 18__. 1850s–1860s.

Rarity: —

$1 • W-MA-2980-001-G040b
JF

Overprint: Green 1 / ONE / 1. ***Engraver:*** New England Bank Note Co. / ABNCo. monogram. ***Comments:*** H-Unlisted. Similar to W-MA-2980-001-G040 but with additional engraver imprint. 18__. 1850s–1860s.

Rarity: URS-3
F $1,000; **VF** $1,500

$2 • W-MA-2980-002-G050
Left: Plow / TWO / Grape vine vertically. ***Center:*** 2 / TWO / 2. ***Comments:*** H-MA-1130-G44. 18__. 1800s.

Rarity: —

$2 • W-MA-2980-002-G060
Left: SALEM BANK vertically. ***Center:*** 2 vertically / TWO DOLLARS / TWO. ***Right:*** 2 vertically. ***Comments:*** H-MA-1130-G48. 18__. 1800s.

Rarity: —

$2 • W-MA-2980-002-G070
Center: 2 / 2 / Oval of flower garlands and gridwork segments / 2 / 2. ***Engraver:*** PSSP. ***Comments:*** H-MA-1130-G52. 18__ 1809–circa 1812.

Rarity: —

$2 • W-MA-2980-002-G070a
Center: 2 / 2 / Oval of flower garlands and gridwork segments / TWO / 2 / 2. ***Engraver:*** PSSP. ***Comments:*** H-MA-1130-G54. Similar to W-MA-2980-002-G070. 18__. Circa 1812–1820s.

Rarity: —

$2 • W-MA-2980-002-G070b
Left: Panel of lathework circle segments. ***Right:*** Panel of lathework circle segments. ***Engraver:*** PSSP. ***Comments:*** H-MA-1130-G56. Similar to W-MA-2980-002-G070. 18__. 1820s.

Rarity: —

$2 • W-MA-2980-002-G070c
Left: Panel of lathework circle segments. ***Right:*** Panel of lathework circle segments. ***Engraver:*** PSSP. ***Comments:*** H-MA-1130-G58. Similar to W-MA-2980-002-G070. 18__. 1820s–1830s.

Rarity: —

$2 • W-MA-2980-002-G070d
Left: Five TWOs vertically. ***Right:*** Five TWOs vertically. ***Engraver:*** PSSP. ***Comments:*** H-MA-1130-G60. Similar to W-MA-2980-002-G070. 18__. 1830s.

Rarity: —

$2 • W-MA-2980-002-G080
Left: 2 / Cornucopia, barrels, ships / 2. ***Center:*** Two ships / Woman seated with shield bearing state arms / TWO / Men and load of hay. ***Right:*** 2 / Woman placing wreath on bust of George Washington, Eagle with shield / 2. ***Engraver:*** New England Bank Note Co. ***Comments:*** H-MA-1130-G62. 18__. 1830s–1850s.

Rarity: —

$2 • W-MA-2980-002-G080a
Engraver: New England Bank Note Co. / ABNCo. monogram. ***Comments:*** H-MA-1130-G62a. Similar to W-MA-2980-002-G080 but with additional engraver imprint. 18__. 1850s–1860s.

Rarity: —

$2 • W-MA-2980-002-G080b
PEM

Overprint: Green 2 / TWO / 2. ***Engraver:*** New England Bank Note Co. / ABNCo. monogram. ***Comments:*** H-Unlisted. Similar to W-MA-2980-002-G080 but with additional engraver imprint. 18__. 1850s–1860s.

Rarity: URS-3
VF $1,250

$3 • W-MA-2980-003-G090
Left: Plow / THREE / Grape vine vertically. ***Center:*** 3 / THREE / 3. ***Comments:*** H-MA-1130-G66. 18__. 1800s.

Rarity: —

$3 • W-MA-2980-003-G100
Left: SALEM BANK vertically. ***Center:*** 3 vertically / THREE DOLLARS / THREE. ***Right:*** 3 vertically. ***Engraver:*** PSSP. ***Comments:*** H-MA-1130-G70. 18__. 1800s.

Rarity: —

$3 • W-MA-2980-003-G110
Center: 3 / 3 / Oval of flower garlands and gridwork segments / 3 / 3. ***Engraver:*** PSSP. ***Comments:*** H-MA-1130-G72. 18__. 1809–1820s.

Rarity: —

$3 • W-MA-2980-003-G110a
Left: Panel of lathework circle segments. ***Right:*** Panel of lathework circle segments. ***Engraver:*** PSSP. ***Comments:*** H-MA-1130-G74. Similar to W-MA-2980-003-G110. 18__. 1820s.

Rarity: —

$3 • W-MA-2980-003-G110b

Left: Panel of lathework circle segments. ***Right:*** Panel of lathework circle segments. ***Engraver:*** PSSP. ***Comments:*** H-MA-1130-G76. Similar to W-MA-2980-003-G110. 18__. 1820s–1830s.

Rarity: —

$3 • W-MA-2980-003-G110c

Left: THREE vertically. ***Right:*** THREE vertically. ***Engraver:*** PSSP. ***Comments:*** H-MA-1130-G78. Similar to W-MA-2980-003-G110. 18__. 1830s.

Rarity: —

$3 • W-MA-2980-003-G120

PEM

Engraver: New England Bank Note Co. / PSSP. ***Comments:*** H-MA-1130-G80. Remainder. 18__. 1830s–1850s.

Rarity: —

$3 • W-MA-2980-003-G120a

PEM

Engraver: New England Bank Note Co. / ABNCo. monogram. ***Comments:*** H-MA-1130-G80a. Similar to W-MA-2980-003-G120 but with additional engraver imprint. 18__. 1850s–1860s.

Rarity: —

$5 • W-MA-2980-005-G130

Left: Plow / FIVE / Grape vine vertically. ***Center:*** 5 / FIVE / 5. ***Comments:*** H-MA-1130-G84. 18__. 1800s.

Rarity: —

$5 • W-MA-2980-005-G140

Left: SALEM BANK vertically. ***Center:*** 5 vertically / FIVE DOLLARS / FIVE. ***Right:*** 5 vertically. ***Engraver:*** PSSP. ***Comments:*** H-MA-1130-G88. 18__. 1800s.

Rarity: —

$5 • W-MA-2980-005-G150

Left: Panel bearing state arms / 5 / 5. ***Center:*** Text on microletter background. ***Right:*** 5 / 5. ***Engraver:*** PSSP. ***Comments:*** H-MA-1130-G92. 18__. 1809–1820s.

Rarity: —

$5 • W-MA-2980-005-G160

Left: Lathework chain bearing MASSACHUSETTS vertically. ***Engraver:*** PSSP. ***Comments:*** H-MA-1130-G94. 18__. 1820s.

Rarity: —

$5 • W-MA-2980-005-G160a

Left: Lathework chain bearing MASSACHUSETTS vertically. ***Right:*** Panel of lathework circle segments. ***Engraver:*** PSSP. ***Comments:*** H-MA-1130-G96. Similar to W-MA-2980-005-G160. 18__. 1820s.

Rarity: —

$5 • W-MA-2980-005-G160b

Engraver: PSSP. ***Comments:*** H-MA-1130-G98. Similar to W-MA-2980-005-G160 but with zigzag ruled lines. 18__. 1820s–1830s.

Rarity: —

$5 • W-MA-2980-005-G160c

Engraver: PSSP. ***Comments:*** H-MA-1130-G100. Similar to W-MA-2980-005-G160 but with spiral lathework lines. 18__. 1830s.

Rarity: —

$5 • W-MA-2980-005-G170

PEM

Engraver: New England Bank Note Co. / PSSP. ***Comments:*** H-MA-1130-G102. 18__. 1830s–1850s.

Rarity: —

$5 • W-MA-2980-005-G170a

Left: 5 / Woman seated with shield, Ship / 5. ***Center:*** 5 / Woman standing with shield, Ship / 5. ***Right:*** 5 / Woman seated on plow holding sickle / 5. ***Engraver:*** New England Bank Note Co. / ABNCo. monogram. ***Comments:*** H-MA-1130-G102a. Similar to W-MA-2980-005-G170 but with additional engraver imprint. 18__. 1850s–1860s.

Rarity: —

$6 • W-MA-2980-006-G180

Left: Plow / SIX / Grape vine vertically. ***Center:*** 6 / SIX / 6. ***Comments:*** H-MA-1130-G106. 18__. 1800s.

Rarity: —

$6 • W-MA-2980-006-G190

Left: SALEM BANK vertically. ***Center:*** 6 vertically / SIX DOLLARS / SIX. ***Right:*** 6 vertically. ***Engraver:*** PSSP. ***Comments:*** H-MA-1130-G110. 18__. 1800s.

Rarity: —

$7 • W-MA-2980-007-G200

Left: Plow / SEVEN / Grape vine vertically. ***Center:*** 7 / SEVEN / 7. ***Comments:*** H-MA-1130-G112. 18__. 1800s.

Rarity: —

$7 • W-MA-2980-007-G210

Left: SALEM BANK vertically. ***Center:*** 7 vertically / SEVEN DOLLARS / SEVEN. ***Right:*** 7 vertically. ***Engraver:*** PSSP. ***Comments:*** H-MA-1130-G114. 18__. 1800s.

Rarity: —

$8 • W-MA-2980-008-G220
Left: Plow / EIGHT / Grape vine vertically. ***Center:*** 8 / EIGHT / 8. ***Comments:*** H-MA-1130-G118. 18__. 1800s.
Rarity: —

$8 • W-MA-2980-008-G230
Left: SALEM BANK vertically. ***Center:*** 8 vertically / EIGHT DOLLARS / EIGHT. ***Right:*** 8 vertically. ***Engraver:*** PSSP. ***Comments:*** H-MA-1130-G120. 18__. 1800s.
Rarity: —

$9 • W-MA-2980-009-G240
Left: Plow / NINE / Grape vine vertically. ***Center:*** 9 / NINE / 9. ***Comments:*** H-MA-1130-G124. 18__. 1800s.
Rarity: —

$9 • W-MA-2980-009-G250
Left: SALEM BANK vertically. ***Center:*** 9 vertically / NINE DOLLARS / NINE. ***Right:*** 9 vertically. ***Engraver:*** PSSP. ***Comments:*** H-MA-1130-G128. 18__. 1800s.
Rarity: —

$10 • W-MA-2980-010-G260
Left: Plow / TEN / Grape vine vertically. ***Center:*** 10 / TEN / 10. ***Comments:*** H-MA-1130-G132. 18__. 1800s.
Rarity: —

$10 • W-MA-2980-010-G270
Left: SALEM BANK vertically. ***Center:*** 10 vertically / TEN DOLLARS / TEN. ***Right:*** 10 vertically. ***Engraver:*** PSSP. ***Comments:*** H-MA-1130-G136. 18__. 1800s.
Rarity: —

$10 • W-MA-2980-010-G280
Left: Panel bearing state arms / 10 / 10 vertically. ***Center:*** Alternating flower garlands and gridwork segments. ***Right:*** 10 / 10 vertically. ***Engraver:*** Perkins. ***Comments:*** H-MA-1130-G140. 18__. 1809–circa 1812.
Rarity: —

$10 • W-MA-2980-010-G280a
Center: Alternating flower garlands and gridwork segments / TEN. ***Engraver:*** Perkins. ***Comments:*** H-MA-1130-G142. Similar to W-MA-2980-010-G280. 18__. Circa 1812–1820s.
Rarity: —

$10 • W-MA-2980-010-G280b
Left: Lathework chain bearing MASSACHUSETTS vertically. ***Right:*** Panel of lathework circle segments. ***Engraver:*** Perkins. ***Comments:*** H-MA-1130-G144. Similar to W-MA-2980-010-G280. 18__. 1820s.
Rarity: —

$10 • W-MA-2980-010-G280c
Left: Lathework chain bearing MASSACHUSETTS vertically. ***Engraver:*** Perkins. ***Comments:*** H-MA-1130-G146. Similar to W-MA-2980-010-G280. 18__. 1820s.
Rarity: —

$10 • W-MA-2980-010-G280d
Engraver: PSSP. ***Comments:*** H-MA-1130-G148. Similar to W-MA-2980-010-G280. 18__. 1820s–1830s.
Rarity: —

$10 • W-MA-2980-010-G280e
Engraver: PSSP. ***Comments:*** H-MA-1130-G150. Similar to W-MA-2980-010-G280. 18__. 1830s.
Rarity: —

$10 • W-MA-2980-010-G290

CC

Engraver: New England Bank Note Co. ***Comments:*** H-MA-1130-G152. 18__. 1840s–1850s.
Rarity: URS-1
Proof $1,750

$10 • W-MA-2980-010-G290a
Engraver: New England Bank Note Co. / ABNCo. monogram. ***Comments:*** H-MA-1130-G152a. Similar to W-MA-2980-010-G290 but with additional engraver imprint. 18__. 1850s.
Rarity: —

$10 • W-MA-2980-010-G300
Left: 10 / Female portrait / TEN. ***Center:*** Woman seated between 1 and 0 holding cornucopia and key. ***Bottom center:*** TEN. ***Right:*** 10 / Female portrait / TEN. ***Engraver:*** Rawdon, Wright, Hatch & Edson / ABNCo. monogram. ***Comments:*** H-MA-1130-G154. 18__. 1850s.
Rarity: —

$10 • W-MA-2980-010-G310

PEM

Tint: Green. ***Engraver:*** National Bank Note Co. ***Comments:*** H-MA-1130-G156a. April __, 18__. 1860s.
Rarity: URS-3
F $1,000; **VF** $1,500

$20 • W-MA-2980-020-G320
Left: Panel bearing state arms / 20 / 20 vertically. ***Center:*** Alternating flower garlands and gridwork segments. ***Right:*** 20 / 20 vertically. ***Engraver:*** Perkins. ***Comments:*** H-MA-1130-G162. 18__. 1810s–1820s.
Rarity: —

$20 • W-MA-2980-020-G320a
Left: Lathework chain bearing MASSACHUSETTS vertically. ***Engraver:*** PSSP. ***Comments:*** H-MA-1130-G164. Similar to W-MA-2980-020-G320. 18__. 1820s–1830s.
Rarity: —

$20 • **W-MA-2980-020-G330**

Left: Woman seated with book on lap, opening chest. ***Center:*** XX / Eagle on rock / XX. ***Right:*** 20 / Ship in harbor. ***Engraver:*** New England Bank Note Co. ***Comments:*** H-MA-1130-G168. 18__. 1840s–1850s.

Rarity: —

$20 • **W-MA-2980-020-G330a**

Engraver: New England Bank Note Co. / ABNCo. monogram. ***Comments:*** H-MA-1130-G168a. Similar to W-MA-2980-020-G330 but with additional engraver imprint. 18__. 1850s.

Rarity: —

$20 • **W-MA-2980-020-G340**

PEM

Overprint: Red TWENTY. ***Engraver:*** Rawdon, Wright, Hatch & Edson / ABNCo. monogram. ***Comments:*** H-MA-1130-G172a. 18__. 1850s.

Rarity: URS-4
F $750; **VF** $1,000

$50 • **W-MA-2980-050-G350**

Left: Panel bearing state arms / 50 / 50 vertically. ***Center:*** Alternating flower garlands and gridwork segments. ***Right:*** 50 / 50 vertically. ***Engraver:*** Perkins. ***Comments:*** H-MA-1130-G178. 18__. 1810s–1820s.

Rarity: —

$50 • **W-MA-2980-050-G350a**

Left: Lathework chain bearing MASSACHUSETTS vertically. ***Engraver:*** PSSP. ***Comments:*** H-MA-1130-G180. Similar to W-MA-2980-050-G350. 18__. 1820s–1830s.

Rarity: —

$50 • **W-MA-2980-050-G360**

Left: FIFTY / Sheaves and fruit / 50. ***Center:*** 50 / Three women seated with eagle, pole and cap, shield, scales, and book. ***Right:*** FIFTY across 50 / Vulcan seated with tools, Train. ***Engraver:*** New England Bank Note Co. ***Comments:*** H-MA-1130-G184. 18__. 1850s.

Rarity: —

$50 • **W-MA-2980-050-G360a**

Engraver: New England Bank Note Co. / ABNCo. monogram. ***Comments:*** H-MA-1130-G184a. Similar to W-MA-2980-050-G360 but with additional engraver imprint. 18__. 1850s.

Rarity: —

$50 • **W-MA-2980-050-G370**

Left: 50 / Minerva standing by column. ***Center:*** Ceres and Vulcan flanking cornucopia. ***Right:*** 50 / Cherub in sailboat / 50. ***Engraver:*** Rawdon, Wright, Hatch & Edson / ABNCo. monogram. ***Comments:*** H-MA-1130-G186a. 18__. 1850s.

Rarity: —

$50 • **W-MA-2980-050-G380**

PEM

Tint: Green. ***Engraver:*** National Bank Note Co. ***Comments:*** H-MA-1130-G188a. April __, 18__. 1860s.

Rarity: URS-2
VF $2,000

$100 • **W-MA-2980-100-G390**

Left: Panel bearing state arms / 100 / 100 vertically. ***Center:*** Alternating flower garlands and gridwork segments. ***Right:*** 100 / 100 vertically. ***Engraver:*** Perkins. ***Comments:*** H-MA-1130-G192. 18__. 1810s–1820s.

Rarity: —

$100 • **W-MA-2980-100-G390a**

Left: Lathework chain bearing MASSACHUSETTS vertically. ***Engraver:*** Perkins. ***Comments:*** H-MA-1130-G194. Similar to W-MA-2980-100-G390. 18__. 1820s–1830s.

Rarity: —

$100 • **W-MA-2980-100-G400**

Left: C / Men with fishing boat at shore / 100. ***Center:*** Eagle perched on bale, Cornucopia and sheaf / 100. ***Right:*** 100 / Ceres / 100. ***Engraver:*** New England Bank Note Co. ***Comments:*** H-MA-1130-G196. 18__. 1850s.

Rarity: —

$100 • **W-MA-2980-100-G400a**

Engraver: New England Bank Note Co. / ABNCo. monogram. ***Comments:*** H-MA-1130-G196a. Similar to W-MA-2980-100-G400 but with additional engraver imprint. 18__. 1850s.

Rarity: —

$100 • **W-MA-2980-100-G410**

Left: 100 / Vulcan seated with sledge and anchor. ***Center:*** Eagle on limb, Train on bridge. ***Bottom center:*** 100. ***Right:*** 100 / Ceres seated, Cornucopia. ***Engraver:*** Rawdon, Wright, Hatch & Edson / ABNCo. monogram. ***Comments:*** H-MA-1130-G200a. 18__. 1850s.

Rarity: —

$100 • **W-MA-2980-100-G420**

PEM

Tint: Green. ***Engraver:*** National Bank Note Co. ***Comments:*** H-MA-1130-G204a. April __, 18__. 1860s.

Rarity: URS-2
VF $3,500

$500 • **W-MA-2980-500-G430**
Left: Lathework chain bearing MASSACHUSETTS / 500 / 500 vertically. ***Center:*** Alternating flower garlands and gridwork segments. ***Right:*** 500 / 500 vertically. ***Engraver:*** PSSP. ***Comments:*** H-MA-1130-G208. 18__. 1820s–1830s.
Rarity: —

$500 • **W-MA-2980-500-G440**
Left: Indian paddling canoe, Forest and mountains / 500 / D D / 500. ***Right:*** 500 / Justice. ***Engraver:*** New England Bank Note Co. ***Comments:*** H-MA-1130-G216. 18__. 1850s.
Rarity: —

$500 • **W-MA-2980-500-G440a**
Overprint: Red 500. ***Engraver:*** New England Bank Note Co. / ABNCo. monogram. ***Comments:*** H-MA-1130-G216a. Similar to W-MA-2980-500-G440 but with additional engraver imprint. 18__. 1850s–1860s.
Rarity: —

Non-Valid Issues

$3 • **W-MA-2980-003-N010**
Left: Justice with scales. ***Center:*** Man riding in chariot. ***Right:*** Indian man. ***Comments:*** H-MA-1130-N5.
Rarity: —

$3 • **W-MA-2980-003-A010**
Left: 3 on die. ***Center:*** Manhattan reclining, spilling water / 3. ***Right:*** 3 on die on panel of wheat and corn ears. ***Engraver:*** Durand & Co. ***Comments:*** H-MA-1130-A5. Altered from $3 Globe Bank, New York City, New York. 1840.
Rarity: —

$5 • **W-MA-2980-005-A020** CC

Engraver: Durand & Co. ***Comments:*** H-MA-1130-A10. Altered from $5 Globe Bank, New York City, New York. April __, 1840.
Rarity: URS-6
VF $250

$6 • **W-MA-2980-006-C180** CJF

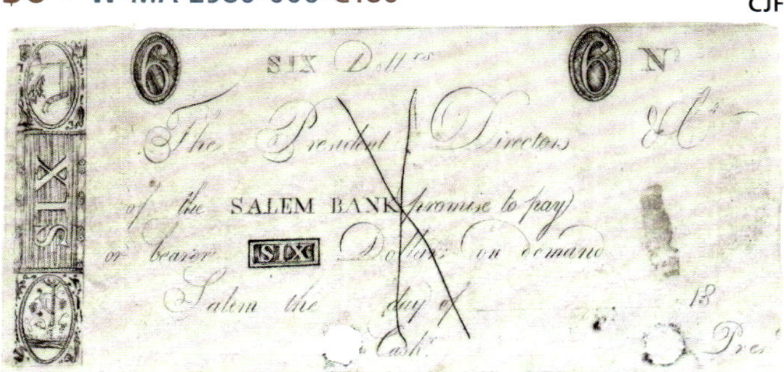

Comments: H-MA-1130-C106. Counterfeit of W-MA-2980-006-G180. 18__. 1800s.
Rarity: —

$8 • **W-MA-2980-008-C230** CC

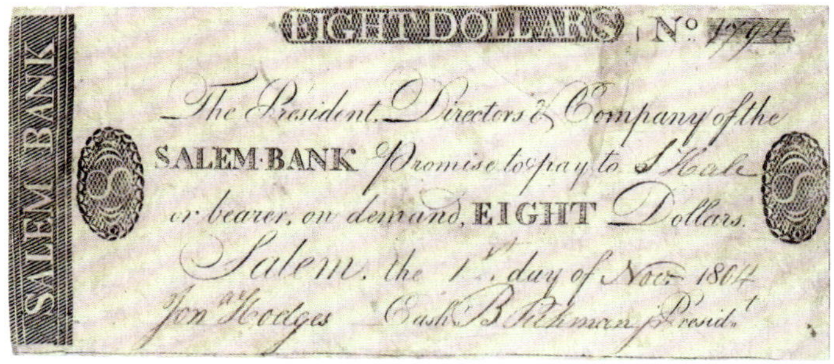

Engraver: PSSP. ***Comments:*** H-MA-1130-C120. Counterfeit of W-MA-2980-008-G230. 18__. 1800s.
Rarity: URS-4
G $225; **VF** $750

$10 • **W-MA-2980-010-A030**
Left: Woman artist resting on easel. ***Center:*** X / Ships in harbor, Warehouse. ***Right:*** 10 / Medallion head / 10. ***Engraver:*** Durand & Co. ***Comments:*** H-MA-1130-A15. Altered from $10 Globe Bank, New York City, New York. 1840.
Rarity: —

Union Bank (branch)
Uncertain
W-MA-2985

History: The Union Bank was incorporated by the general court in 1792 for the purpose of accommodating agricultural interests. The bank was located at 40 State Street, Boston, with branches located in Salem and Worcester. Details of the branches have not been confirmed.

See also listing under Boston, W-MA-1010, and Worcester, W-MA-3440.

Salisbury, Massachusetts

The Pennacook Indians of the Pentucket tribe once lived in this area. It was settled by the English in 1638 under the name of Merrimac. It was incorporated in 1639 as Colchester, and the name changed in 1640 to Salisbury. There were two villages in Salisbury, one of which was located on the Powow River and housed flannel factories, a tannery, and a manufactory of cotton goods, shoes, combs, boats, wherries, and molasses casks. The other was located on the Merrimack River (also spelled as Merrimac) and was known as Webster's Point. Shipbuilding made up the primary industry of this village, as well as fishing for cod and mackerel.

Powow River Bank
1836–1865
W-MA-2990

History: The Powow River Bank was incorporated on March 31, 1836, with an authorized capital of $100,000. The bank enjoyed good business. Its capital was briefly increased to

$250,000 in 1851 then went back down to $100,000 for the remainder of the bank's existence. The circulation of the bank was $66,297 in 1839 and reached its high of $100,890 in 1845. The bank's specie totaled $3,299.31 in 1851.

This bank was succeeded by the Powow River National Bank of Salisbury, which was chartered in April and began business on May 1, 1865.

Numismatic Commentary: Vignettes with various scenes of the city of Salisbury are featured on issues from this bank. Fortunate collectors are able to obtain a note from this bank for a collection.

VALID ISSUES

$1 • W-MA-2990-001-G010

Left: 1 / Woman wearing bonnet with pail / ONE. ***Center:*** Machinery and merchandise flanking Ceres seated holding sickle and rake, Factories and harbor / ONE / Panel outlining white ONE. ***Right:*** 1 / Ship / ONE. ***Engraver:*** PSSP / New England Bank Note Co. ***Comments:*** H-MA-1135-G2. 18__. 1830s.

Rarity: —

$1 • W-MA-2990-001-G020

CJF

Engraver: New England Bank Note Co. ***Comments:*** H-MA-1135-G4. 18__. 1840s–1850s.

Rarity: URS-4
VG $300; **VF** $650

$1 • W-MA-2990-001-G020a

CC

Overprint: Green ONE. ***Engraver:*** New England Bank Note Co. / ABNCo. monogram. ***Comments:*** H-Unlisted. Similar to W-MA-2990-001-G020 but with additional engraver imprint. 18__. 1860s.

Rarity: URS-2
F $1,400

$1.25 • W-MA-2990-001.25-G030

Left: 1 25/100 / Train / 1 25/100. ***Center:*** Sloop and other ships at sea / $1.25 cts. ***Right:*** 1 25/100 / Eagle. ***Engraver:*** New England Bank Note Co. ***Comments:*** H-MA-1135-G6. Printed on white paper. 18__. 1830s.

Rarity: —

$1.25 • W-MA-2990-001.25-G030a

Engraver: New England Bank Note Co. ***Comments:*** H-MA-1135-G6a. Similar to W-MA-2990-001.25-G030 but printed on red paper. 18__. 1830s.

Rarity: —

$1.50 • W-MA-2990-001.50-G040

Left: 1 Doll. 50 Cts. vertically. ***Center:*** Eagle on rock in ocean / $1 50/100. ***Right:*** 1 50/100 / Justice. ***Engraver:*** New England Bank Note Co. ***Comments:*** H-MA-1135-G8. Printed on white paper. 18__. 1830s.

Rarity: URS-2
Unc-Rem $1,250

$1.50 • W-MA-2990-001.50-G040a

Engraver: New England Bank Note Co. ***Comments:*** H-MA-1135-G8a. Similar to W-MA-2990-001.50-G040 but printed on red paper. 18__. 1830s.

Rarity: —

$1.75 • W-MA-2990-001.75-G050

Left: $1.75 Cts. / Hebe watering eagle / 1 75/100. ***Center:*** Three sloops at sea. ***Right:*** $1.75 Cts. / Dog, Woman seated with grain / 1 75/100. ***Engraver:*** New England Bank Note Co. ***Comments:*** H-MA-1135-G10. Printed on white paper. 18__. 1830s.

Rarity: —

$1.75 • W-MA-2990-001.75-G050a

Engraver: New England Bank Note Co. ***Comments:*** H-MA-1135-G10a. Similar to W-MA-2990-001.75-G050 but printed on red paper. 18__. 1830s.

Rarity: —
Selected auction price: Heritage, October 2013, Lot 15863, VF $587

$2 • W-MA-2990-002-G060

Left: 2 / Woman standing with staff, Cornucopia / TWO. ***Center:*** TWO / Machinery and merchandise flanking Ceres seated holding sickle and rake, Factories and harbor / Panel outlining white TWO. ***Right:*** 2 / Woman wearing hat, Trees / TWO. ***Engraver:*** New England Bank Note Co. / PSSP. ***Comments:*** H-MA-1135-G12. 18__. 1830s.

Rarity: —

$2 • W-MA-2990-002-G070

Left: 2 / Interior of blacksmith shop, Two men, dog, horse, and anvil / TWO. ***Center:*** Street scene in Salisbury, Four-story building. ***Right:*** 2 / Schooner and sailboat / TWO. ***Engraver:*** New England Bank Note Co. ***Comments:*** H-MA-1135-G14. 18__. 1840s–1850s.

Rarity: —

$3 • W-MA-2990-003-G080

Left: THREE / Beehive and foliage / THREE. ***Center:*** Machinery and merchandise flanking Ceres seated holding sickle and rake, Factories and harbor / THREE / Panel outlining white THREE. ***Right:*** 3 on THREE / Two reapers / 3 on THREE. ***Engraver:*** New England Bank Note Co. / PSSP. ***Comments:*** H-MA-1135-G16. 18__. 1830s.

Rarity: —

$3 • **W-MA-2990-003-G090**

CJ=

Overprint: Red THREE. ***Engraver:*** Rawdon, Wright, Hatch & Edson / New England Bank Note Co. ***Comments:*** H-MA-1135-G18a. 18__. 1850s.

Rarity: URS-4
F $750; **VF** $1,250

$5 • **W-MA-2990-005-G100**

Left: 5 / Blacksmith at anvil / FIVE. ***Center:*** Mercury standing with 5, Cornucopia and merchandise, Factories and ship / V / Panel outlining white FIVE. ***Right:*** 5 / Ceres kneeling / FIVE. ***Engraver:*** New England Bank Note Co. / PSSP. ***Comments:*** H-MA-1135-G20. 18__. 1830s.

Rarity: —

$5 • **W-MA-2990-005-G110**

Left: 5 / Indian man kneeling on rock with bow / FIVE. ***Center:*** Scene of Salisbury. ***Right:*** 5 / Two farmers, one sharpening scythe / FIVE. ***Engraver:*** New England Bank Note Co. ***Comments:*** H-MA-1135-G22. 18__. 1840s–1850s.

Rarity: URS-4
F $750; **VF** $1,250

$5 • **W-MA-2990-005-G110a**

CC

Overprint: Green FIVE. ***Engraver:*** New England Bank Note Co. / ABNCo. monogram. ***Comments:*** H-Unlisted. Similar to W-MA-2990-005-G110 but with additional engraver imprint. 18__. 1860s.

Rarity: URS-2
VF $950

$10 • **W-MA-2990-010-G120**

Engraver: Unverified, but likely New England Bank Note Co. ***Comments:*** H-MA-1135-G24. No description available. 18__. 1830s.

Rarity: *None known*

$10 • **W-MA-2990-010-G130**

Left: "Presentation of the Declaration of Independence" / X. ***Center:*** X. ***Right:*** 10 / Train passing building with steeple, Man with wheelbarrow. ***Engraver:*** New England Bank Note Co ***Comments:*** H-MA-1135-G26. 18__. 1840s–1850s.

Rarity: —

$10 • **W-MA-2990-010-G140**

Left: 10 / Justice guarding treasury. ***Center:*** Street scene in Salisbury, Bank, Coach. ***Right:*** 10 / Portrait of Henry Clay. ***Tint:*** Red-orange. ***Engraver:*** American Bank Note Co. ***Comments:*** H-MA-1135-G28a. June 1, 1860.

Rarity: —

$20 • **W-MA-2990-020-G150**

Left: Steamboat / XX / Train. ***Center:*** Three women seated with eagle, pole and cap, shield, scales, and book / 20 / Panel outlining white TWENTY. ***Right:*** XX / Milkmaid standing with pail. ***Engraver:*** New England Bank Note Co. ***Comments:*** H-MA-1135-G30. 18__. 1830s.

Rarity: —

$20 • **W-MA-2990-020-G160**

Left: 20 / Woman seated with book on lap, opening chest. ***Center:*** XX / Eagle on rock / XX. ***Right:*** 20 / Ship in harbor. ***Engraver:*** New England Bank Note Co. ***Comments:*** H-MA-1135-G32. 18__. 1840s–1850s.

Rarity: —

$20 • **W-MA-2990-020-G170**

CC

Tint: Red-orange lathework, panel of microlettering, and die bearing 20 Dolls. ***Engraver:*** American Bank Note Co. ***Comments:*** H-MA-1135-G34a. June 1, 1860.

Rarity: URS-1
Proof $5,500

$50 • **W-MA-2990-050-G180**

Left: 50 / Steamboat and schooner. ***Center:*** Farmyard scene, Load of hay with two men on it, Man with rake and pail. ***Right:*** L / Justice kneeling. ***Engraver:*** New England Bank Note Co. ***Comments:*** H-MA-1135-G36. 18__. 1830s.

Rarity: —

$50 • **W-MA-2990-050-G190**

Left: FIFTY / Woman standing with wreath and flowers / FIFTY. ***Center:*** 50 / Man restraining prancing horse / 50. ***Right:*** FIFTY / Woman standing with cornucopia / FIFTY. ***Engraver:*** New England Bank Note Co. ***Comments:*** H-MA-1135-G38. 18__. 1840s–1850s.

Rarity: —

$50 • **W-MA-2990-050-G200**

Left: Woman seated with shield and sheaves / 50. ***Right:*** 50 / Street scene in Salisbury. ***Tint:*** Green L. ***Engraver:*** American Bank Note Co. ***Comments:*** H-MA-1135-G40a. June 1, 1860.

Rarity: —

$100 • **W-MA-2990-100-G210**

Engraver: Unverified, but likely New England Bank Note Co. ***Comments:*** H-MA-1135-G42. No description available. 18__. 1830s.

Rarity: *None known*

$100 • W-MA-2990-100-G220

Left: ONE HUNDRED on 100 / Portrait of William Henry Harrison. ***Center:*** Wharf scene, Men loading wagon with barrels. ***Right:*** ONE HUNDRED on 100 / Portrait of Christopher Columbus. ***Engraver:*** New England Bank Note Co. ***Comments:*** H-MA-1135-G44. 18__. 1840s–1850s.

Rarity: —

$100 • W-MA-2990-100-G230

Left: 100 / Woman with sickle, Grain and dog. ***Center:*** Woman seated with barrels, Bale and wheel, Factories. ***Right:*** 100 / State arms. ***Tint:*** Likely green. ***Engraver:*** American Bank Note Co. ***Comments:*** H-MA-1135-G46a. June 1, 1860.

Rarity: —

$500 • W-MA-2990-500-G240

Left: 500 / 500 / 500. ***Center:*** 500 / Woman seated with shield bearing D, Fasces, cornucopia, lyre, and sheaf / 500. ***Right:*** 500 / D / 500. ***Engraver:*** PSSP / New England Bank Note Co. ***Comments:*** H-MA-1135-G48. 18__. 1830s.

Rarity: —

$500 • W-MA-2990-500-G250

Left: Indian paddling canoe, Forest and mountains / 500 / D D. ***Right:*** 500 / Justice. ***Engraver:*** New England Bank Note Co. ***Comments:*** H-MA-1135-G50. 18__. 1850s.

Rarity: —

$500 • W-MA-2990-500-G260

Left: Train. ***Right:*** 500. ***Tint:*** Green die bearing D. ***Engraver:*** American Bank Note Co. ***Comments:*** H-MA-1135-G52a. June 1, 1860.

Rarity: —

$1,000 • W-MA-2990-1000-G270

Left: THOUSAND vertically. ***Center:*** 1000 / Woman standing with legs crossed, Lyre, Cornucopia / 1000. ***Right:*** 1000 / M / 1000. ***Engraver:*** PSSP / New England Bank Note Co. ***Comments:*** H-MA-1135-G54. 18__. 1830s

Rarity: —

$1,000 • W-MA-2990-1000-G280

Left: Eagle on cliff, Ship / 1000 / M M / 1000. ***Right:*** 1000 / Indian woman with bow and arrows. ***Engraver:*** New England Bank Note Co. ***Comments:*** H-MA-1135-G56. 18__. 1850s.

Rarity: —

$1,000 • W-MA-2990-1000-G280a

Engraver: New England Bank Note Co. / ABNCo. monogram. ***Comments:*** H-MA-1135-G56a. Similar to W-MA-2990-1000-G280 but with additional engraver imprint. 18__. 1850s–1860s.

Rarity: —

Non-Valid Issues

$10 • W-MA-2990-010-R010

Engraver: New England Bank Note Co. ***Comments:*** H-MA-1135-R5. Raised from an unknown denomination. 18__. 1850s.

Rarity: —

$10 • W-MA-2990-010-S010

CJF

Engraver: New England Bank Note Co. ***Comments:*** H-MA-1135-S5. 185_. 1850s.

Rarity: URS-6
VG $125; **F** $200

Shelburne Falls, Massachusetts

Shelburne was initially a part of Deerfield until it was reorganized in 1768 and named in honor of William Petty, second Earl of Shelburne. It was incorporated in 1775 as a town.

The Shelburne Falls were an important fishing location for both the local natives and the colonists. The fertile soils were good for agriculture in terms of crops and grazing herds. Lumbering occurred on a small scale, but saw mills and grist mills were able to utilize the waterfalls more successfully. Agriculture remained the main industry for the town. Cutlery was manufactured beginning in 1837, and a handful of tool-manufacturing shops rose up in Shelburne Falls for the manufacture of farming implements. There were also two fabric mills.

Shelburne Falls Bank
1856–1865
W-MA-3000

History: The Shelburne Falls Bank was incorporated on June 4, 1856, with an authorized capital of $100,000, a figure that was increased to $150,000 in 1860. In 1863 the circulation was $128,890.

The Shelburne Falls Bank was succeeded by the Shelburne Falls National Bank after it was chartered in 1865.

Numismatic Commentary: Genuine notes from this bank are hard to find. Some have a vignette of the river and mill as they were in the mid-19th century. Notes with local scenery are popular and highly sought after.

All valid notes bear the imprints of Rawdon, Wright, Hatch & Edson and the New England Bank Note Co.

Valid Issues

$1 • W-MA-3000-001-G010

Left: Woman standing / ONE on 1. ***Center:*** View of Shelburne Falls. ***Right:*** 1 / Woman churning. ***Overprint:*** Red ONE. ***Comments:*** H-MA-1140-G2a. 18__. 1850s.

Rarity: —

$2 • W-MA-3000-002-G020

Left: 2 / Farmer seated with scythe. ***Center:*** Farm woman and man seated, Three men, one holding sickle, one sharpening scythe, and one lying down, Hay wagon. ***Right:*** 2 / Woman seated on plow, Sheaf and sickle. ***Overprint:*** Red TWO. ***Comments:*** H-MA-1140-G4a. 18__. 1850s.

Rarity: —

$2 • W-MA-3000-002-G020a

CJF

Overprint: Red TWO. ***Engraver:*** ABNCo. monogram. ***Comments:*** H-Unlisted. Similar to W-MA-3000-002-G020 but with additional engraver imprint. 18__. 1860s.

Rarity: URS-4
F $350; **VF** $500

$3 • W-MA-3000-003-G030

Left: 3 / Blacksmith standing by anvil. ***Center:*** View of Shelburne Falls. ***Right:*** 3 / Liberty standing by shield and pedestal. ***Overprint:*** Red THREE. ***Comments:*** H-MA-1140-G6a. 18__. 1850s.

Rarity: —

$3 • W-MA-3000-003-G030a

CJF

Overprint: Red THREE. ***Engraver:*** ABNCo. monogram. ***Comments:*** H-Unlisted. Similar to W-MA-3000-003-G030 but with additional engraver imprint. 18__. 1860s.

Rarity: URS-4
F $400; **VF** $600

$5 • W-MA-3000-005-G040

CJF

Overprint: Red FIVE. ***Comments:*** H-MA-1140-G8a. 18__. 1850s–1860s.

Rarity: URS-5
F $300; **VF** $500

$10 • W-MA-3000-010-G050

CJF

Overprint: Red TEN. ***Comments:*** H-MA-1140-G10a. 18__. 1850s.

Rarity: URS-4
F $400; **VF** $600

$50 • W-MA-3000-050-G060

Left: 50 / Woman with flowers. ***Center:*** View of Shelburne Falls. ***Right:*** 50 / Male portrait. ***Comments:*** H-MA-1140-G12. 18__. 1850s.

Rarity: —

$100 • W-MA-3000-100-G070

Left: 100 / Female portrait. ***Center:*** Agriculture, Commerce, and Manufacture. ***Right:*** 100 / Portrait of Benjamin Franklin. ***Comments:*** H-MA-1140-G14. 18__. 1850s.

Rarity: —

Non-Valid Issues

$2 • W-MA-3000-002-N010

Left: TWO. ***Center:*** Steamship. ***Right:*** Indian woman. ***Comments:*** H-MA-1140-N5. 18__. 1850s.

Rarity: —

How to Read the Whitman Numbering System

$1 • W-MA-010-001-G010a

Denomination: Value of the note shown.

W: Whitman number. This number is a sortable code unique to each bank and note.

MA: Abbreviation for the state under study.

010: Numerical designation specific to each bank.

001: The denomination in dollars.

G010a: G indicates a good or valid note. Other categories are indicated thus: C (counterfeit); R (raised); S (spurious); N (not-attributed); A (altered). Numbers are assigned starting with 010, 020, et seq. Terminal letters following the number indicate variations of a note: a series of different colored overprints, tints, payees, etc., all on the same design of note. For more information, see the "How to Use This Book" section at the front of the volume, page xiv.

$2 • **W-MA-3000-002-A010**

CJF

Tint: Red-brown dies outlining white 2s and TWO DOLLARS. ***Engraver:*** Danforth, Wright & Co. ***Comments:*** H-MA-1140-A5. Altered from $2 Southern Bank of Georgia, Bainbridge, Georgia. March 1, 18__. 1850s–1860s.

Rarity: URS-7
F $100

$2 • **W-MA-3000-002-A020**

Left: Arched TWO and 2 on die / State arms vertically. ***Center:*** Three woodsmen felling and cutting trees. ***Right:*** 2 / Ceres with sheaf. ***Engraver:*** Danforth, Wright & Co. ***Comments:*** H-MA-1140-A10. Altered from $2 Bank of Washtenaw, Washtenaw, Michigan series. 1850s.

Rarity: —

$5 • **W-MA-3000-005-A030**

Left: Horses running / V. ***Center:*** Liberty and Ceres flanking shield surmounted by horse's head. ***Bottom center:*** Sleeping dog. ***Right:*** 5 / Portrait of girl shading eyes. ***Overprint:*** Red FIVE. ***Engraver:*** Bald, Cousland & Co. / Baldwin, Bald & Cousland. ***Comments:*** H-MA-1140-A15. Altered from $5 Bank of Morgan, Morgan, Georgia. 18__. 1850s.

Rarity: —

$5 • **W-MA-3000-005-A040**

Left: 5 / Cattle herd. ***Center:*** 5. ***Right:*** 5 / Man plowing. ***Tint:*** Red-brown lathework outlining white 5. ***Engraver:*** Bald, Cousland & Co. ***Comments:*** H-MA-1140-A20. Altered from $5 Pioneer Association, Lafayette, Indiana. 18__. 1850s.

Rarity: —

$20 • **W-MA-3000-020-A050**

Left: 20 / Woman resting with scroll and chest. ***Center:*** Indian woman reclining on cliff, gazing at canal locks and distant city. ***Right:*** 20 / Train. ***Overprint:*** Red TWENTY. ***Engraver:*** Danforth, Bald & Co. ***Comments:*** H-MA-1140-A25. Altered from $20 Columbia Bank, Washington, D.C. 18__. 1850s.

Rarity: —

South Adams, Massachusetts

Originally settled in 1737, the land that would become Adams was purchased by Nathan Jones in 1762 when it was still known as East Hoosac. It was incorporated in 1778. Named in honor of Samuel Adams, a signer of the Declaration of Independence and later governor of the province (today a popular beer bears his name), the farmland was mostly divided into lots along the Hoosic River. Later that river would turn water power into mills for woolen, cotton, lumber, and plastic products. Water power provided the opportunity to build a variety of mills.

There was never an official, incorporated town of South Adams, but the name was used prior to 1878 to differentiate the southern section of town from the rest of Adams. Farmers moved west for better land during the early 1800s, and the population of the town declined. The industry of textiles grew during the War of 1812, reviving the town to grand proportions. The population doubled to 4,000 between 1820 and 1835 alone.

See also Adams, Adams South Village, and North Adams, Massachusetts.

Berkshire Bank

1860–1865

W-MA-3010

History: The Berkshire Bank was chartered on April 4, 1860, in the village of South Adams within the town of Adams. The authorized capital was $100,000. This bank bore no relation to an earlier bank of the same name in Pittsfield that was fraudulently operated. Circulation amounted to $98,860 in 1863.

The business of the Berkshire Bank was succeeded by the Berkshire National Bank of Adams, chartered on July 15, 1865. The new bank had but a brief existence and later in the year it was consolidated into the First National Bank of Adams.

Numismatic Commentary: The Berkshire Bank was in business for about five years before its interests were succeeded by a national bank. Only one issue of four denominations was engraved and printed by the American Bank Note Co., making this selection one of the smallest offered by any Massachusetts bank. Genuine issues from this bank are thus extremely hard, if not impossible, to acquire.

Valid Issues

$1 • **W-MA-3010-001-G010**

CJF

Tint: Green. ***Engraver:*** American Bank Note Co. ***Comments:*** H-MA-1145-G2a. Aug. 1, 1860.

Rarity: URS-4
F $500; **VF** $750; **EF** $1,000

$2 • **W-MA-3010-002-G020**

Left: Cherub with sheaf / Woman seated with spool, Factory. ***Center:*** 2 / Two women at loom / 2. ***Bottom center:*** 2. ***Right:*** Cherub with cornucopia / Mechanic working at vise. ***Tint:*** Likely green. ***Engraver:*** American Bank Note Co. ***Comments:*** H-MA-1145-G4a. Aug. 1, 1860.

Rarity: —

$5 • **W-MA-3010-005-G030**

Left: 5 / Female portrait. ***Center:*** White horse and black horse frightened by lightning, Cattle and trees. ***Right:*** 5 / Girl holding younger child. ***Tint:*** Likely green. ***Engraver:*** American Bank Note Co. ***Comments:*** H-MA-1145-G6a. Aug. 1, 1860.

Rarity: —

$10 • W-MA-3010-010-G040

Left: 10 / Portrait of Benjamin Franklin seated in his study. ***Center:*** TEN / Woman seated with pen and scroll, Cherub / TEN. ***Right:*** 10 / Woman seated with book, globe, and dividers. ***Tint:*** Red. ***Engraver:*** American Bank Note Co. ***Comments:*** H-MA-1145-G8a. Aug. 1, 1860.

Rarity: —

NON-VALID ISSUES

$3 • W-MA-3010-003-S010

CJF

Tint: Green lathework. ***Comments:*** H-MA-1145-S5a. Sept. 16, 18__. 1860s.

Rarity: URS-6
F $250; **VF** $350

$5 • W-MA-3010-005-N010

Center: Farm scene, Farmers and tools. ***Comments:*** H-MA-1145-N5.

Rarity: —

Farmers and Mechanics Bank

1836 and 1837

W-MA-3020

History: The Farmers and Mechanics Bank was incorporated on April 1, 1836, with an authorized capital of $100,000 to be paid in within a year. An additional act extended the original time limit six months further. Finally, on September 30, 1837, the full capital stock was said to have been paid in. An inspection revealed only $50,000 on hand. However, even that claim was a fraud, as specie had been borrowed from a New York operator who took it way after the audit, leaving just $2,000 in the vault. The president of the bank denied knowledge of the caper. The proper amount of money could not be raised, and the bank was turned over to others who claimed to have provided funds. Circulation at the time was estimated to be $16,011 but may have been much more in the absence of records. The bank was closed by injunction, although in actuality it never operated in a legal manner.

See also listing under Adams South Village, W-MA-040.

Numismatic Commentary: The town of South Adams can boast of having two banks with only four issues: this and the previous listing, the Berkshire Bank. With only a few examples of Proof notes known, notes from this bank are very challenging to find.

As of 2003 there was a $1-$2-$3-$5 face plate remaining at the American Bank Note Co. archives.

VALID ISSUES

$1 • W-MA-3020-001-G010

HA

Engraver: Durand & Co. ***Comments:*** H-MA-15-G50. Proof 18__. 1830s.

Rarity: URS-1
Proof $3,500

$2 • W-MA-3020-002-G020

CJF

Engraver: Durand & Co. ***Comments:*** H-MA-15-G52. Proof. 18__. 1830s.

Rarity: URS-1
Proof $4,250

$3 • W-MA-3020-003-G030

QDB

Engraver: Durand & Co. ***Comments:*** H-MA-15-G54. 18__. 1830s.

Rarity: URS-1
Proof $4,250

$5 • W-MA-3020-005-G040

HA

Engraver: Durand & Co. ***Comments:*** H-MA-15-G56. Proof. 18__. 1830s.

Rarity: URS-1
Proof $4,250

Uncut Sheets

$1-$2-$3-$5 • W-MA-3020-001.002.003.005-US010

Engraver: Durand & Co. ***Comments:*** H-MA-15-G50, G52, G54, G56. 18__.

Rarity: —

South Boston, Massachusetts

The district of South Boston was originally known as Dorchester Neck. In 1624 David Thompson opened a trading post here, and in 1634 the land was officially made a part of Dorchester. Eventually South Boston separated from Dorchester, but the two lands were annexed by Boston in sections during the 1800s.

During the Revolutionary War, George Washington forced the British troops out of Boston from his position in South Boston. In 1809 the Cyrus Alger's Iron Foundry was established and supplied the United States with cannon balls during both the War of 1812 and the Civil War. It became the largest foundry in the country by 1850 and provided the majority of industry and economy to South Boston. The reclamation of the mudflats was taken on in 1836 by the Boston Wharf Company, and in 1855 the Commonwealth Lands were created by filling in a section of the harbor. The *Northern Light*, a clipper ship, was built by the Briggs's shipbuilding company in 1851.

See also Boston and East Boston, Massachusetts.

Broadway Bank
1853–1864
W-MA-3030

History: The Broadway Bank was incorporated on April 28, 1853, with an authorized capital of $100,000. The bank was located at 10 Broadway in South Boston and commenced business in December of the same year. Selected values in 1851 included: capital $150,000; circulation $50,857; specie $5,912.84; real estate $8,644.10.

By 1853 capital had decreased to $100,000, but in 1854 it was back up to $150,000, where it remained. The circulation of the bank amounted to $92,818 in 1857 and was $112,371 in 1863. Specie was $5,401.53 in 1857.

After the charter of the Broadway National Bank on October 25, 1864, the national bank assumed the business of the state bank.

See also listing under Boston, W-MA-380.

Numismatic Commentary: It is unusual to find a bank using an identical vignette on all of its issues as this bank has done. This detail is of little importance in locating a genuine note for a collection. All issues are very hard to locate.

Valid Issues

$1 • W-MA-3030-001-G010

Left: Train, machinery, and cannon / 1. ***Center:*** ONE. ***Right:*** 1 / Woman seated with bow and quiver. ***Overprint:*** Red ONE. ***Engraver:*** Rawdon, Wright, Hatch & Edson / New England Bank Note Co. ***Comments:*** H-MA-1150-G2a. 18__. 1850s.

Rarity: —

$2 • W-MA-3030-002-G020

Left: 2 / Machinery, cannon, and plow. ***Right:*** 2 / Wheels and bale / TWO. ***Overprint:*** Red TWO. ***Engraver:*** Rawdon, Wright, Hatch & Edson / New England Bank Note Co. ***Comments:*** H-MA-1150-G4a. 18__. 1850s.

Rarity: —

$2 • W-MA-3030-002-G020a

Overprint: Red TWO. ***Engraver:*** Rawdon, Wright, Hatch & Edson / New England Bank Note Co. / ABNCo. monogram. ***Comments:*** H-MA-1150-G4b. Similar to W-MA-3030-002-G020 but with additional engraver imprint. 18__. 1850s–1860s.

Rarity: —

$3 • W-MA-3030-003-G030

Left: 3 / Woman seated / THREE. ***Center:*** Machinery, cannon, and plow. ***Right:*** 3. ***Overprint:*** Red THREE. ***Engraver:*** Rawdon, Wright, Hatch & Edson / New England Bank Note Co. ***Comments:*** H-MA-1150-G6a. 18__. 1850s.

Rarity: —

$3 • W-MA-3030-003-G030a

Overprint: Red THREE. ***Engraver:*** Rawdon, Wright, Hatch & Edson / New England Bank Note Co. / ABNCo. monogram. ***Comments:*** H-MA-1150-G6b. Similar to W-MA-3030-003-G030 but with additional engraver imprint. 18__. 1850s–1860s.

Rarity: —

$5 • W-MA-3030-005-G040

Left: 5 / 5. ***Center:*** Train, machinery, and plow / 5. ***Right:*** 5 / Man seated. ***Overprint:*** Red FIVE. ***Engraver:*** Rawdon, Wright, Hatch & Edson / New England Bank Note Co. ***Comments:*** H-MA-1150-G8a. 18__. 1850s.

Rarity: URS-3
F $750

$5 • W-MA-3030-005-G040a

Overprint: Red FIVE. ***Engraver:*** Rawdon, Wright, Hatch & Edson / New England Bank Note Co. / ABNCo. monogram. ***Comments:*** H-MA-1150-G8b. Similar to W-MA-3030-005-G040 but with additional engraver imprint. 18__. 1850s–1860s.

Rarity: —

$10 • W-MA-3030-010-G050

Left: X / Woman and state arms. ***Center:*** Machinery, cannon, and plow. ***Right:*** X / X. ***Overprint:*** Red. ***Engraver:*** Rawdon, Wright, Hatch & Edson / New England Bank Note Co. ***Comments:*** H-MA-1150-G10a. 18__. 1850s.

Rarity: —

$10 • W-MA-3030-010-G050a

Overprint: Red. ***Engraver:*** Rawdon, Wright, Hatch & Edson / New England Bank Note Co. / ABNCo. monogram. ***Comments:*** H-MA-1150-G10b. Similar to W-MA-3030-010-G050 but with additional engraver imprint. 18__. 1850s–1860s.

Rarity: —

$20 • W-MA-3030-020-G060

Left: 20 / XX. ***Center:*** Machinery, cannon, and plow. ***Right:*** 20 / Anchor, bale, and barrels. ***Engraver:*** American Bank Note Co. ***Comments:*** H-MA-1150-G12. 1860s.

Rarity: —

$50 • W-MA-3030-050-G070

Left: 50 / Barrels and bales / FIFTY. ***Center:*** Machinery, cannon, and plow. ***Right:*** 50. ***Engraver:*** Rawdon, Wright, Hatch & Edson / New England Bank Note Co. ***Comments:*** H-MA-1150-G14. 18__. 1850s.

Rarity: —

$100 • W-MA-3030-100-G080

Left: C / Machinery, cannon, and plow. ***Right:*** 100 / Sailor seated on bale. ***Engraver:*** Rawdon, Wright, Hatch & Edson / New England Bank Note Co. ***Comments:*** H-MA-1150-G16. 18__. 1850s.

Rarity: —

$500 • W-MA-3030-500-G090

Left: Machinery, cannon, and plow / 500. ***Right:*** 500 / Woman and swan. ***Engraver:*** American Bank Note Co. ***Comments:*** H-MA-1150-G18. 1860s.

Rarity: —

Non-Valid Issues

$1 • W-MA-3030-001-R010

Engraver: Rawdon, Wright, Hatch & Edson / New England Bank Note Co. ***Comments:*** H-MA-1150-R5. Raised from W-MA-3030-001-G010. 18__. 1850s.

Rarity: —

$20 • W-MA-3030-020-R020

Engraver: Rawdon, Wright, Hatch & Edson / New England Bank Note Co. ***Comments:*** H-MA-1150-R15. Raised from W-MA-3030-001-G010. 18__. 1850s.

Rarity: —

$50 • W-MA-3030-050-R030

Engraver: Rawdon, Wright, Hatch & Edson / New England Bank Note Co. ***Comments:*** H-MA-1150-R20. Raised from W-MA-3030-001-G010. 18__. 1850s.

Rarity: —

Mechanics Bank

1836–1865

W-MA-3040

History: The Mechanics Bank of South Boston was chartered on March 31, 1836, with an authorized capital of $150,000. By 1854 the capital was $200,000. The bank was located at No. 27 Turnpike at the corner of Division Street in 1854. By 1855 it had moved to 95 Dorchester Avenue.

Between the years of 1838 and 1860, circulation fluctuated between a low of $63,875 and a high of $106,970. Selected figures for 1838 included: net profits on hand $3,569.48; cash deposited $4,198.18; total amount due from banks $237,655.66; gold, silver, and other coined metals in the banking house $10,007.78; real estate $13,376.55; bills of other banks incorporated in this state $2,300; balance due from other banks $11,262.85; amount of all debts due $200,708.48; total amount of resources of the bank $237,655.66.

The business of the Mechanics Bank was succeeded by the Mechanics National Bank of Boston, chartered on March 24, 1865.

See also listing under Boston, W-MA-730.

Non-Valid Issues

$1 • W-MA-3040-001-A010

CJF

Engraver: Durand & Co. ***Comments:*** H-Unlisted. Similar to W-MA-730-001-A010 but with different location. Altered from $1 Pennsylvania Savings Bank, Philadelphia, Pennsylvania. 185_. 1850s.

Rarity: URS-6
VG $75

$2 • W-MA-3040-002-A020

CC

Overprint: Brown or red TWO. ***Engraver:*** Wellstood, Hanks, Hay & Whiting. ***Comments:*** H-Unlisted. Similar to W-MA-730-002-A020 but with different location. Altered from $2 Mechanics Bank, Georgetown, D.C. 18__. 1850s.

Rarity: URS-7
VG $100; **F** $200

South Danvers, Massachusetts

This land was settled in 1636 when it was part of the area known as Salem. In 1752 it separated from Salem and was incorporated as a portion of Danvers. It then incorporated as a town on May 18, 1855, under the name of South Danvers. The name was changed to Peabody in 1868. It became the leather tanning center of the region.

See also Danvers and North Danvers, Massachusetts.

Danvers Bank

1855–1865

W-MA-3050

History: The Danvers Bank began business in Danvers, and then without moving it became located in South Danvers in 1855. After this time the bank issued notes with the South Danvers imprint. Selected figures for 1857 included: bills of this bank and other New England states $4,395.52; specie $8,508.43; real estate $6,470.

The interests of the Danvers Bank were succeeded by the Danvers National Bank, chartered on November 30, 1864.

See also listing under Danvers, W-MA-1390.

Valid Issues

$1 • W-MA-3050-001-G010

CC

Overprint: Red ONE. ***Engraver:*** Rawdon, Wright, Hatch & Edson / New England Bank Note Co. ***Comments:*** H-Unlisted. Similar to W-MA-1390-001-G040a but with different location. Oct. __, 18__. 1850s–1860s.

Rarity: URS-2
VF $1,600

Non-Valid Issues

$5 • W-MA-3050-005-R010

CJF

Overprint: Red Five. ***Engraver:*** Rawdon, Wright, Hatch & Edson / New England Bank Note Co. / ABNCo. monogram. ***Comments:*** H-Unlisted. Raised from W-MA-3050-001-G010. Oct. __, 18__. 1860s.

Rarity: URS-7
F $100

Warren Bank

1832–1864

W-MA-3060

History: The Warren Bank was chartered on March 3, 1832, with an authorized capital of $120,000. In 1839 its capital was $150,000. Later, capital ranged from a low of $120,000 in 1845 to a high of $250,000 in 1857. Circulation was listed at $39,290 in 1839. In 1849 it was $60,840, and in 1857 it was $120,265. Selected figures for 1857 included: bills of this bank and other New England states $3,182.54; specie $11,280.79; real estate $6,000.

The business of the Warren Bank was succeeded by the Warren National Bank of Danvers, chartered on November 18, 1864.

See also listing under Danvers, W-MA-1420.

Valid Issues

$1 • W-MA-3060-001-G010

CJF

Engraver: Rawdon, Wright, Hatch & Edson / New England Bank Note Co. / ABNCo. monogram. ***Comments:*** H-Unlisted. 1 Jan. 18__. 1860s.

Rarity: URS-5
F $250; **VF** $400

$10 • W-MA-3060-010-G020

Left: Mechanic seated with tools, Train and building / TEN. ***Center:*** X. ***Right:*** 10 / Woman standing with sheaf and stone. ***Engraver:*** New England Bank Note Co. ***Comments:*** H-MA-515-G74. 18__. 1850s.

Rarity: —

$20 • W-MA-3060-020-G030

Left: XX / Justice with scales. ***Center:*** 20 on die / Portrait of George Peabody / 20 on die. ***Right:*** 20 / Woman churning. ***Tint:*** Red. ***Engraver:*** Rawdon, Wright, Hatch & Edson / New England Bank Note Co. ***Comments:*** H-MA-515-G78. May 1, 18__. 1850s.

Rarity: URS-6
Proof $1,500

$20 • W-MA-3060-020-G030a

CC

Tint: Red dies and panel. ***Engraver:*** American Bank Note Co. / New England Bank Note Co. ***Comments:*** H-MA-515-G78a. Similar to W-MA-3060-020-G030 but with different engraver imprint. May 1, 18__. 1860s.

Rarity: URS-3
Proof $1,500

$50 • W-MA-3060-050-G040

Left: FIFTY / Woman. ***Center:*** 50 on die / Portrait of George Peabody / 50 on die. ***Right:*** FIFTY / Liberty with pole, cap, and shield. ***Tint:*** Red. ***Engraver:*** Rawdon, Wright, Hatch & Edson / New England Bank Note Co. ***Comments:*** H-MA-515-G80. May 1, 18__. 1850s.

Rarity: —

$50 • W-MA-3060-050-G040a CC

Tint: Red dies and panel. ***Engraver:*** American Bank Note Co. / New England Bank Note Co. ***Comments:*** H-MA-515-G80a. Similar to W-MA-3060-050-G040 but with different engraver imprint. May 1, 18__. 1860s.

Rarity: URS-3
CU $1,195; **Proof** $1,600

$100 • W-MA-3060-100-G050

Left: 100 / Farmer carrying rake and pitchfork, Dog. ***Center:*** Portrait of George Peabody. ***Right:*** 100 / Female portrait. ***Tint:*** Red C C. ***Engraver:*** Rawdon, Wright, Hatch & Edson / New England Bank Note Co. ***Comments:*** H-MA-515-G82. 18__. 1850s.

Rarity: —

$100 • W-MA-3060-100-G050a

Tint: Red C C. ***Engraver:*** American Bank Note Co. / New England Bank Note Co. ***Comments:*** H-MA-515-G82a. Similar to W-MA-3060-100-G050 but with different engraver imprint. 18__. 1860s.

Rarity: —

$500 • W-MA-3060-500-G060

Left: 500 / HUNDRED on three dies. ***Center:*** Portrait of George Peabody. ***Right:*** 500 / HUNDRED on three dies. ***Tint:*** Green. ***Engraver:*** American Bank Note Co. ***Comments:*** H-MA-515-G84. 18__. 1850s–1860s.

Rarity: URS-2
Proof $1,600

Uncut Sheets

$20-$50 • W-MA-3060-020.050-US010 CJF

Tint(s): Red dies and panel. ***Comments:*** H-MA-515-G78a, G80a. May 1, 18__. 1860s.

Rarity: URS-3
Proof $3,100

Non-Valid Issues

$2 • W-MA-3060-002-S010 CJF

Tint: Red lathework. ***Engraver:*** American Bank Note Co. ***Comments:*** H-Unlisted. Dec. 1, 1859.

Rarity: URS-5
F $350; **VF** $600

$10 • W-MA-3060-010-S020 CJF

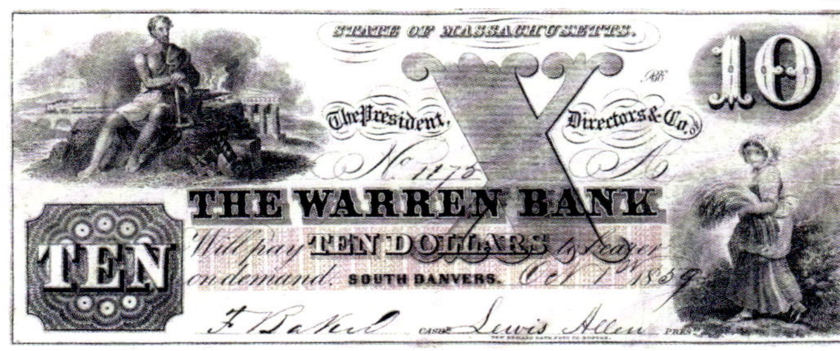

Overprint: Red panel. ***Engraver:*** New England Bank Note Co. / ABNCo. monogram. ***Comments:*** H-Unlisted. 18__. 1850s.

Rarity: URS-5
F $300; **VF** $500

SOUTH READING, MASSACHUSETTS

South Reading was once a part of Reading, which incorporated in 1644. It separated to become its own entity in 1812. The districts of the town are the Common, Fitch's Hill, Leather Street, Side the Pond, Cowdrey's Hill, Lafayette Street, Eaton Street, Water Street, Little World, West Ward, East Ward, and South Ward. Ladies' shoes were created here and remained a main source of industry for the town. Tinware was also a staple in addition to razor straps and shoe tools.

South Reading Bank
1854–1865
W-MA-3070

History: The South Reading Bank was incorporated on March 30, 1854, with an authorized capital of $100,000. The circulation of the bank was $71,771 in 1857, $67,011 in 1862, and $96,414 in 1863. Specie was listed at $5,248.36 in 1862.

In 1865 the business of the South Reading Bank was succeeded by the National Bank of South Reading.

Numismatic Commentary: There are very few genuine notes in the marketplace for this entity, as nearly all were redeemed by the national bank that succeded to its interests.

All valid notes bear the imprint of Rawdon, Wright, Hatch & Edson.

Valid Issues

$1 • W-MA-3070-001-G010

Left: Woman standing with shield and 1 / 1. ***Center:*** Cherub rolling silver dollar, Railroad and village. ***Right:*** 1 / Male portrait. ***Comments:*** H-MA-1155-G2. 18__. 1850s.

Rarity: —

$2 • W-MA-3070-002-G020

JF

Overprint: Red TWO. ***Comments:*** H-MA-1155-G4. 18__. 1850s.

Rarity: URS-2

VG $500; **F** $1,000

$3 • W-MA-3070-003-G030

Left: 3 / Male portrait. ***Center:*** Three cherubs and three silver dollars. ***Right:*** 3 / Blacksmith standing by anvil. ***Comments:*** H-MA-1155-G6. 18__. 1850s.

Rarity: —

$5 • W-MA-3070-005-G040

Left: 5 / Male portrait / 5. ***Center:*** Five cherubs and five silver dollars. ***Right:*** 5 / Woman standing with 5. ***Comments:*** H-MA-1155-G8. 18__. 1850s.

Rarity: —

$10 • W-MA-3070-010-G050

JF

Comments: H-MA-1155-G10. 18__. 1850s.

Rarity: URS-3

F $600; **VF** $1,000

$20 • W-MA-3070-020-G060

Left: XX / Woman. ***Center:*** Woman reclining, Shield, Train and factory, Milkmaid and cows. ***Right:*** 20 / Male portrait. ***Comments:*** H-MA-1155-G12. 18__. 1850s.

Rarity: —

$50 • W-MA-3070-050-G070

Left: Woman with sheaf / 50. ***Center:*** Woman seated on rock, Cherubs playing with dolphins in water. ***Right:*** 50 / Portrait. ***Comments:*** H-MA-1155-G14. 18__. 1850s.

Rarity: —

$100 • W-MA-3070-100-G080

Left: Hebe watering eagle / 100. ***Center:*** View of U.S. Capitol. ***Right:*** 100 / Portrait. ***Comments:*** H-MA-1155-G16. 18__. 1850s.

Rarity: —

Non-Valid Issues

$2 • W-MA-3070-002-R010

Comments: H-MA-1155-R5. Raised from W-MA-3070-001-G010. 18__. 1850s.

Rarity: —

$3 • W-MA-3070-003-R020

Comments: H-MA-1155-R10. Raised from W-MA-3070-001-G010. 18__. 1850s.

Rarity: —

$5 • W-MA-3070-005-R030

Comments: H-MA-1155-R15. Raised from W-MA-3070-001-G010. 18__. 1850s.

Rarity: —

$5 • W-MA-3070-005-R040

Comments: H-MA-1155-R20. Raised from W-MA-3070-002-G020. 18__. 1850s.

Rarity: —

$5 • W-MA-3070-005-S010

CJF

Engraver: Draper, Welsh & Co. ***Comments:*** H-MA-1155-S5. 18__. 1850s.

Rarity: URS-6

VF $350

$10 • W-MA-3070-010-R050

Comments: H-MA-1155-R25. Raised from W-MA-3070-001-G010. 18__. 1850s.

Rarity: —

Southbridge, Massachusetts

The Quinebaug River divided the territories of the Nipmuc and Mohegan tribes who dwelt on this land. It was settled by Europeans in 1730 and incorporated as a town in 1816 under the name of Southbridge. Water power was gained from the river and allowed saw mills, grist mills, and eventually textile mills to spring up. Irish and French-Canadian immigrants came to work in Southbridge after the Civil War. Southbridge also was well-known for the manufacturing of optical products and accessories.

Southbridge Bank
1836–1865
W-MA-3080

History: The Southbridge Bank was chartered on March 31, 1836, with an authorized capital of $100,000, a figure that was raised to $150,000 in 1854. The bank's circulation was $28,295 in 1839. It reached a high of $144,742 in 1851. Specie totaled $7,752.05 in 1851 and $14,080.21 in 1857.

The business of the Southbridge Bank was assumed by the Southbridge National Bank after it was chartered on March 24, 1865.

Numismatic Commentary: Counterfeit and spurious issues are plentiful in the marketplace, but genuine issues are hard to find.

Valid Issues

$1 • W-MA-3080-001-G010
Comments: H-MA-1160-G2. No description available. 18__. 1830s–1840s.

Rarity: *None known*

$1 • W-MA-3080-001-G020
Left: Farmer plowing with two horses, Man sowing, Train / 1. ***Center:*** 1. ***Right:*** 1 / Eagle on shield / ONE. ***Engraver:*** Rawdon, Wright, Hatch & Edson / New England Bank Note Co. ***Comments:*** H-MA-1160-G6. Jan. __, 185_. 1850s.

Rarity: —

$1 • W-MA-3080-001-G020a
Engraver: Rawdon, Wright, Hatch & Edson / New England Bank Note Co. / ABNCo. monogram. ***Comments:*** H-MA-1160-G6a. Similar to W-MA-3080-001-G020 but with additional engraver imprint and different date. July 1, 185_. 1850s.

Rarity: —

$2 • W-MA-3080-002-G030
Left: 2 / Sheaf / TWO. ***Center:*** Archimedes lifting the world with a lever. ***Bottom center:*** Steamboat. ***Right:*** 2 / Beehive / TWO. ***Engraver:*** Rawdon, Wright, Hatch & Edson. ***Comments:*** H-MA-1160-G8. 18__. 1830s–1840s.

Rarity: —

$2 • W-MA-3080-002-G040
Left: Train, Factory, Man with wheelbarrow / 2. ***Center:*** 2 bearing female portrait. ***Right:*** 2 / Farmer loading hay wagon. ***Engraver:*** Rawdon, Wright, Hatch & Edson / New England Bank Note Co. ***Comments:*** H-MA-1160-G12. Jan. __, 185_. 1850s.

Rarity: —

$2 • W-MA-3080-002-G040a
Engraver: Rawdon, Wright, Hatch & Edson / New England Bank Note Co. / ABNCo. monogram. ***Comments:*** H-MA-1160-G12a. Similar to W-MA-3080-002-G040 but with additional engraver imprint and different date. July 1, 185_. 1850s.

Rarity: —

$3 • W-MA-3080-003-G050
Bottom center: Steamboat. ***Comments:*** H-MA-1160-G14. 18__. 1830s–1840s.

Rarity: —

$3 • W-MA-3080-003-G060
CJF

Engraver: Rawdon, Wright, Hatch & Edson / New England Bank Note Co. ***Comments:*** H-MA-1160-G18. 18__. 1850s.

Rarity: URS-4
F $350; **VF** $500

$3 • W-MA-3080-003-G060a
Left: Train, church, and village / 3. ***Center:*** 3. ***Right:*** 3 / Girl with basket. ***Engraver:*** Rawdon, Wright, Hatch & Edson / New England Bank Note Co. / ABNCo. monogram. ***Comments:*** H-MA-1160-G18a. Similar to W-MA-3080-003-G060 but with additional engraver imprint and different date. July 1, 185_. 1850s.

Rarity: —

$5 • W-MA-3080-005-G070
Left: Lathework panel bearing FIVE vertically. ***Center:*** FIVE / Two women flanking shield bearing eagle / FIVE. ***Bottom center:*** Steamboat. ***Right:*** 5 / Male portrait / FIVE. ***Engraver:*** Rawdon, Wright, Hatch & Edson. ***Comments:*** H-MA-1160-G20. 18__. 1830s–1840s.

Rarity: —

$5 • W-MA-3080-005-G080
Left: Lathework panel bearing FIVE vertically. ***Center:*** FIVE / Two women flanking shield bearing eagle / FIVE, Ship and train / FIVE. ***Right:*** 5 / Male portrait / FIVE. ***Engraver:*** New England Bank Note Co. ***Comments:*** H-MA-1160-G22. 18__. 1840s–1850s.

Rarity: —

$5 • W-MA-3080-005-G090
CJF

Engraver: Rawdon, Wright, Hatch & Edson / New England Bank Note Co. ***Comments:*** H-MA-1160-G24. January __, 185_. 1850s.

Rarity: URS-4
F $300; **VF** $400

$5 • W-MA-3080-005-G090a
Engraver: Rawdon, Wright, Hatch & Edson / New England Bank Note Co. / ABNCo. monogram. ***Comments:*** H-MA-1160-G24a. Similar to W-MA-3080-005-G090 but with additional engraver imprint and different date. July 1, 185_. 1850s.

Rarity: URS-4
F $300; **VF** $400

$5 • **W-MA-3080-005-G100**

Left: 5 / Woman standing. ***Center:*** View of Mount Vernon. ***Right:*** 5 / Portrait of General George B. McClellan. ***Overprint:*** Green V V. ***Engraver:*** American Bank Note Co. ***Comments:*** H-MA-1160-G26a. 1860s.

Rarity: —

$10 • **W-MA-3080-010-G110**

Bottom center: Steamboat. ***Engraver:*** Rawdon, Wright, Hatch & Edson. ***Comments:*** H-MA-1160-G28. 18__. 1830s–1840s.

Rarity: —

$10 • **W-MA-3080-010-G120**

Left: 10 / Portrait / 10. ***Center:*** X / Eagle / X. ***Right:*** 10 / Woman. ***Engraver:*** New England Bank Note Co. ***Comments:*** H-MA-1160-G32. 18__. 1840s–1850s.

Rarity: —

$10 • **W-MA-3080-010-G130**

Left: Woman seated between 1 and 0 / TEN. ***Center:*** X. ***Bottom center:*** Shield. ***Right:*** 10 / Portrait of Zachary Taylor / TEN. ***Engraver:*** Rawdon, Wright, Hatch & Edson / New England Bank Note Co. ***Comments:*** H-MA-1160-G34. 18__. 1850s.

Rarity: —

$10 • **W-MA-3080-010-G140**

Left: Woman and sailor flanking bust of George Washington, Train and ship / 10. ***Right:*** 10 / Woman with fruit. ***Overprint:*** Green. ***Engraver:*** American Bank Note Co. ***Comments:*** H-MA-1160-G36a. 1860s.

Rarity: —

$20 • **W-MA-3080-020-G150**

Left: 20 / XX / 20. ***Center:*** 20 / Woman seated with scales, Sheaf and bales, Men plowing, Ship / 20. ***Right:*** TWENTY vertically. ***Engraver:*** PSSP / New England Bank Note Co. ***Comments:*** H-MA-1160-G38. 18__. 1830s–1840s.

Rarity: —

$20 • **W-MA-3080-020-G160**

Left: 20 / Woman seated with book on lap, opening chest. ***Center:*** XX / Eagle on rock / XX. ***Right:*** 20 / Ship in harbor. ***Engraver:*** New England Bank Note Co. ***Comments:*** H-MA-1160-G42. 18__ 1840s–1850s.

Rarity: —

$20 • **W-MA-3080-020-G170**

CC

Tint: Green. ***Engraver:*** American Bank Note Co. ***Comments:*** H-MA-1160-G46a. 18__. 1860s.

Rarity: URS-1

Proof $4,250

$50 • **W-MA-3080-050-G180**

Left: 50 / Cornucopia, Woman standing with ankles crossed, Staff, Anchor / 50. ***Center:*** FIFTY DOLLARS / 50. ***Right:*** FIFTY vertically. ***Engraver:*** New England Bank Note Co. / PSSP. ***Comments:*** H-MA-1160-G48. 18__. 1830s–1840s.

Rarity: —

$50 • **W-MA-3080-050-G190**

Left: FIFTY / Woman standing with wreath and flowers / FIFTY. ***Center:*** 50 / Man restraining prancing horse / 50. ***Right:*** FIFTY / Woman standing with cornucopia / FIFTY. ***Engraver:*** New England Bank Note Co. ***Comments:*** H-MA-1160-G52. 18__. 1830s–1840s.

Rarity: —

$50 • **W-MA-3080-050-G200**

CC

Tint: Green. ***Engraver:*** American Bank Note Co. ***Comments:*** H-MA-1160-G54a. 18__. 1860s.

Rarity: URS-1

Proof $4,500

$100 • **W-MA-3080-100-G210**

Left: Panel bearing C / Portrait of George Washington / C. ***Center:*** 100 / Manhattan reclining pouring water from jug, Ship / 100. ***Right:*** Panel bearing ONE HUNDRED vertically. ***Engraver:*** New England Bank Note Co. / PSSP. ***Comments:*** H-MA-1160-G56. 18__. 1830s–1840s.

Rarity: —

$100 • **W-MA-3080-100-G220**

Left: ONE HUNDRED on 100 / Portrait of William Henry Harrison. ***Center:*** Wharf scene, Men loading wagon with barrels. ***Right:*** ONE HUNDRED on 100 / Portrait of Christopher Columbus. ***Engraver:*** New England Bank Note Co. ***Comments:*** H-MA-1160-G60. 18__. 1840s–1850s.

Rarity: —

$100 • **W-MA-3080-100-G230**

CJF

Tint: Green. ***Engraver:*** American Bank Note Co. ***Comments:*** H-MA-1160-G62a. 18__. 1860s.

Rarity: URS-1

Proof $4,500

$500 • **W-MA-3080-500-G240**

Left: Woman seated on sheaves, Men reaping, Man on horse / 500. ***Center:*** 500 / D. ***Right:*** 500 vertically. ***Engraver:*** New England Bank Note Co. ***Comments:*** H-MA-1160-G68. 18__. 1850s.

Rarity: —

Non-Valid Issues

$5 • **W-MA-3080-005-C090**

Comments: H-MA-1160-C24. Counterfeit of W-MA-3080-005-G090. Jan. __, 185_. 1850s.

Rarity: —

$5 • **W-MA-3080-005-C090a** CC

Engraver: Rawdon, Wright, Hatch & Edson / New England Bank Note Co. / American Bank Note Co. ***Comments:*** H-MA-1160-C24a. Counterfeit of W-MA-3080-005-G090a. July 1, 185_. 1850s.

Rarity: URS-7
F $100

$5 • **W-MA-3080-005-S010** CJF

Engraver: Wellstood, Benson & Hanks. ***Comments:*** H-MA-1160-S5. 18__. 1840s.

Rarity: —

$10 • **W-MA-3080-010-N010**

Left: Justice. ***Right:*** Woman and marine view. ***Comments:*** H-MA-1160-N5.

Rarity: —

Springfield, Massachusetts

The area that became Springfield was originally known as the Agawam Plantation. It was renamed in 1640 after Springfield in Chelmsford, Essex, England. In 1675 there was a tragedy when conflict between the native Wampanoag tribe and the Plymouth colonists resulted in the burning of more than half of the town, including the mills. More than 600 settlers were killed, but about 8,000 natives were also killed or captured during King Philip's War, a conflict that ended in 1677 when the Native Americans surrendered.

George Washington designated Springfield to be the location for the National Armory, producing the first U.S. musket in 1795. Farmers led by Daniel Shays attempted to seize the weapons in Springfield in what was later called Shay's Rebellion. This was an important event leading up to the Constitutional Convention. The facility achieved numismatic fame by being pictured on several varieties of 19th century tokens issued by James A. Bolen.

Springfield also played an important part in the Industrial Revolution with the invention of Thomas Blanchard's lathe in 1819, which made mass production a commonplace article. The first American-English dictionary was published in Springfield in 1806. The first rubber stamp, the first adjustable monkey wrench, and the first post card were also produced in Springfield. Not surprisingly, the town housing the National Armory saw the birth of Smith and Wesson firearms.

Agawam Bank
1846–1860s
W-MA-3090

History: The Agawam Bank was chartered on March 11, 1846, with an authorized capital of $100,000. In later years this value was increased to $300,000. Circulation of the bank was $111,255 in 1849 and $298,682 in 1863.

The business of the Agawam Bank was succeeded by the Agawam National Bank of Springfield after it was chartered on April 26, 1865.

Numismatic Commentary: Examples of the lower denomination notes are available in the marketplace from time to time. One shows a historical vignette of "The Landing of Roger Williams" as he came ashore on the land he later named "Providence Plantation."

Valid Issues

$1 • **W-MA-3090-001-G010** CC

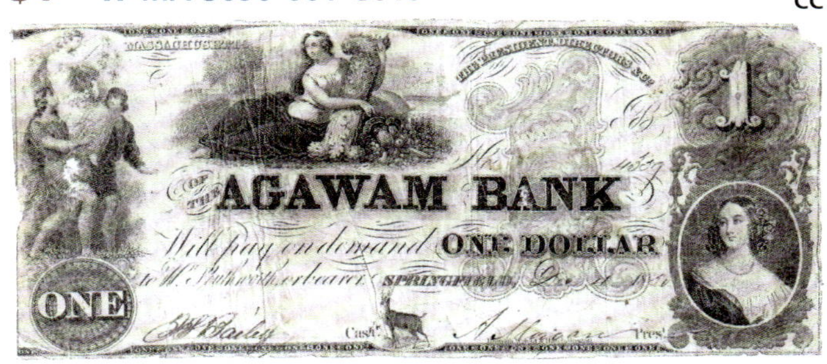

Engraver: Rawdon, Wright & Hatch. ***Comments:*** H-MA-1165-G2. 18__. 1840s–1850s.

Rarity: URS-4
F $600

$1 • **W-MA-3090-001-G010a**

Left: Three men carrying woman / ONE. ***Center:*** Woman holding 1 / 1. ***Right:*** 1 / Female portrait. ***Overprint:*** Red ONE. ***Engraver:*** Rawdon, Wright, Hatch & Edson. ***Comments:*** H-Unlisted. Similar to W-MA-3090-001-G010. 18__. 1840s–1850s.

Rarity: URS-6
F $400

$1 • W-MA-3090-001-G010b

CJF

Overprint: Red ONE. ***Engraver:*** Rawdon, Wright, Hatch & Edson / ABNCo. monogram. ***Comments:*** H-MA-1165-G2b. Similar to W-MA-3090-001-G010 but with additional engraver imprint. October 1, 18__. 1850s–1860s.

Rarity: URS-6
F $400; **VF** $750

$1 • W-MA-3090-001-G010c

Overprint: Green ONE. ***Engraver:*** Rawdon, Wright, Hatch & Edson / ABNCo. monogram. ***Comments:*** H-MA-1165-G2c. Similar to W-MA-3090-001-G010 but with additional engraver imprint, different date, and printed serial number. Oct. 1, 18__. 1860s.

Rarity: —

$2 • W-MA-3090-002-G020

Left: Indian seated with shield bearing 2, Canoe and deer / 2. ***Bottom center:*** State arms. ***Right:*** 2 / Farmer standing with sheaf and stone. ***Engraver:*** Rawdon, Wright & Hatch. ***Comments:*** H-MA-1165-G4. 18__. 1840s–1850s.

Rarity: —

$2 • W-MA-3090-002-G020a

CJF

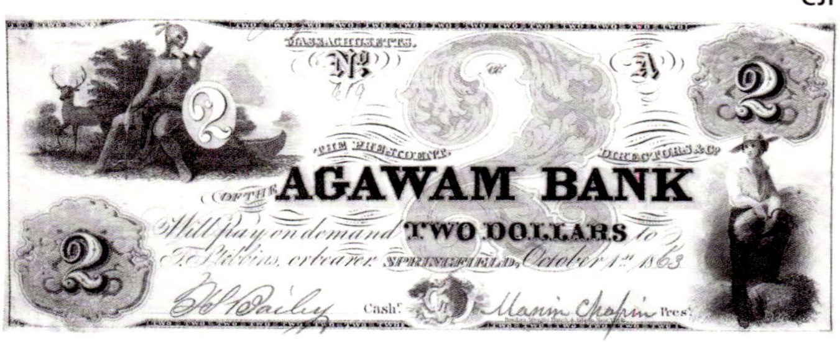

Engraver: Rawdon, Wright & Hatch. / ABNCo. monogram. ***Comments:*** H-Unlisted. Similar to W-MA-3090-002-G020 but with additional engraver imprint. October 1, 18__. 1860s.

Rarity: URS-3
VF $1,000; **Proof** $2,500

$2 • W-MA-3090-002-G020b

Overprint: Red. ***Engraver:*** Rawdon, Wright, Hatch & Edson. ***Comments:*** H-MA-1165-G4b. Similar to W-MA-3090-002-G020. Jan. 1, 18__. 1850s–1860s.

Rarity: —

$2 • W-MA-3090-002-G020c

Overprint: Red. ***Engraver:*** Rawdon, Wright, Hatch & Edson / ABNCo. monogram. ***Comments:*** H-MA-1165-G4c. Similar to W-MA-3090-002-G020 but with additional engraver imprint. Oct. 1, 18__. 1860s.

Rarity: —

$3 • W-MA-3090-003-G030

Left: Two women seated with fruit / 3. ***Center:*** 3. ***Bottom center:*** Cow. ***Right:*** 3 / Portrait of boy. ***Engraver:*** Rawdon, Wright & Hatch. ***Comments:*** H-MA-1165-G6. 18__. 1840s–1850s.

Rarity: —

$3 • W-MA-3090-003-G030a

Overprint: Red. ***Engraver:*** Rawdon, Wright, Hatch & Edson / ABNCo. monogram. ***Comments:*** H-MA-1165-G6b. Similar to W-MA-3090-003-G030 but with additional engraver imprint. Jan. 1, 18__. 1850s–1860s.

Rarity: —

$3 • W-MA-3090-003-G030b

Overprint: Green. ***Engraver:*** Rawdon, Wright, Hatch & Edson / ABNCo. monogram. ***Comments:*** H-MA-1165-G6c. Similar to W-MA-3090-003-G030 but with additional engraver imprint. Oct. 1, 18__. 1860s.

Rarity: —

$5 • W-MA-3090-005-G040

SBG

Engraver: Rawdon, Wright & Hatch. ***Comments:*** H-MA-1165-G8. Plate note. 18__. 1840s–1850s.

Rarity: URS-2
Proof $6,000

$5 • W-MA-3090-005-G040a

CC

Overprint: Red FIVE. ***Engraver:*** Rawdon, Wright, Hatch & Co. ***Comments:*** H-Unlisted. Similar to W-MA-3090-005-G040. Jan. 1, 18__. 1860s.

Rarity: URS-4
F $950

$5 • W-MA-3090-005-G040b

Left: "The Landing of Roger Williams" / 5. ***Center:*** Ceres with sheaf kneeling in V. ***Right:*** FIVE / Woman standing with shield bearing 5. ***Overprint:*** Red FIVE. ***Engraver:*** Rawdon, Wright, Hatch & Co. / ABNCo. monogram. ***Comments:*** H-MA-1165-G8b. Similar to W-MA-3090-005-G040 but with additional engraver imprint. 1850s–1860s.

Rarity: URS-4
VG $350; **F** $950

$10 • W-MA-3090-010-G050

Left: Ceres seated on plow / X. ***Center:*** X. ***Bottom center:*** Farm produce and tools. ***Right:*** 10 / Female portrait. ***Engraver:*** Rawdon, Wright, Hatch & Edson. ***Comments:*** H-MA-1165-G10. 18__. 1840s–1850s.

Rarity: —

$10 • W-MA-3090-010-G050a

Overprint: Red. ***Engraver:*** Rawdon, Wright, Hatch & Co. / ABNCo. monogram. ***Comments:*** H-MA-1165-G10b. Similar to W-MA-3090-010-G050 but with additional engraver imprint. 1850s–1860s.

Rarity: —

$20 • W-MA-3090-020-G060

Left: 20 / Ship / 20. ***Center:*** Ships. ***Right:*** 20 / Eagle perched on shield. ***Engraver:*** Rawdon, Wright & Hatch. ***Comments:*** H-MA-1165-G12. 18__. 1840s–1850s.

Rarity: —

$50 • W-MA-3090-050-G070

Left: 50 / Indian woman with bow and arrows. ***Center:*** Woman with eagle and shield bearing L. ***Bottom center:*** Cow. ***Right:*** 50 / Woman. ***Engraver:*** Rawdon, Wright & Hatch. ***Comments:*** H-MA-1165-G14. 18__. 1840s–1860s.

Rarity: —

$100 • W-MA-3090-100-G080

Left: 100 / Woman standing with hand on capstan. ***Center:*** Horse-drawn wagonload of hay crossing bridge / 100. ***Bottom center:*** Deer. ***Right:*** 100 / Milkmaid. ***Engraver:*** Rawdon, Wright & Hatch. ***Comments:*** H-MA-1165-G16. 18__. 1840s–1860s.

Rarity: URS-3
Proof $3,000

Non-Valid Issues

$2 • W-MA-3090-002-C020

Engraver: Rawdon, Wright & Hatch. ***Comments:*** H-MA-1165-C4. Counterfeit of W-MA-3090-002-G020. 18__. 1850s

Rarity: URS-7
F $50

$2 • W-MA-3090-002-R010

Engraver: Rawdon, Wright & Hatch. ***Comments:*** H-MA-1165-R2. Raised from W-MA-3090-001-G010. 18__. 1840s–1850s.

Rarity: —

$2 • W-MA-3090-002-A010

Left: 2 / Farmer plowing with black and white horses. ***Center:*** Two men loading wagon with sheaves, Three men cradling and binding. ***Right:*** 2 / Two floating cherubs with caduceus and sheaf. ***Tint:*** Red-brown 2s and TWO DOLLARS. ***Engraver:*** Danforth, Wright & Co. ***Comments:*** H-MA-1165-A15. Altered from $2 Southern Bank of Georgia, Bainbridge, Georgia. March 1, 1858.

Rarity: —

$3 • W-MA-3090-003-S010

Left: THREE / Woman reclining / 3. ***Center:*** Woman floating in clouds holding shield, Eagle. ***Right:*** 3 / Ship / THREE. ***Engraver:*** Rawdon, Wright & Hatch. ***Comments:*** H-MA-1165-S5. 18__. 1840s.

Rarity: URS-7
F $75

$5 • W-MA-3090-005-R020

Engraver: Rawdon, Wright & Hatch. ***Comments:*** H-MA-1165-R10. Raised from W-MA-3090-001-G010. 18__. 1840s–1850s.

Rarity: —

$10 • W-MA-3090-010-R030

Engraver: Rawdon, Wright & Hatch. ***Comments:*** H-MA-1165-R15. Raised from W-MA-3090-001-G010. 18__. 1840s–1850s.

Rarity: —

$50 • W-MA-3090-050-R040

Engraver: Rawdon, Wright & Hatch. ***Comments:*** H-MA-1165-R20. Raised from W-MA-3090-002-G020. 18__. 1840s–1850s.

Rarity: —

American Exchange Bank

Circa 1855

W-MA-3100

History: A non-existent bank represented only by fraudulent notes.

Issues

$2 • W-MA-3100-002-A010

CJF

Comments: H-MA-1170-A4. 185_. 1855.

Rarity: —

Cabot Bank

1845–1865

W-MA-3110

History: The Cabot Bank was chartered on January 24, 1845, with an authorized capital of $150,000. Principals included N.P. Ames, John Chase, D.M. Bryant, and Robert Bemis. The president in 1847 was J. Chase, and G. Walker was cashier. In 1851 John Wells became president, and J.L. Warriner became cashier. Circulation in 1849 was $95,935. By 1863 it was $136,133.

On April 26, 1845, the First National Bank of Chicopee was chartered and succeeded the business of the Cabot Bank.

See also listings under Cabotville, W-MA-1180, and Chicopee, W-MA-1360.

Collectors and Researchers:

If you have new information about any banks or notes listed in this volume, contact Whitman Publishing, Attn: Obsolete Paper Money, 3101 Clairmont Road, Suite G, Atlanta, GA 30329.

Chicopee Bank

1836–1860s

W-MA-3120

History: The Chicopee Bank was incorporated on April 9, 1836, with $200,000 authorized capital. This was raised to $300,000 in 1850. Its corporation was to continue until January 1, 1875. Its circulation ranged from a low of $160,329 in 1839 to a high of $299,668 in 1863. Specie was listed at $11,170 in 1854. Real estate was valued at $7,000.

The Chicopee Bank was succeeded by the Chicopee National Bank of Springfield after it was chartered on April 7, 1865.

Numismatic Commentary: Genuine notes turn up with some regularity in the marketplace. There are interesting vignettes on some of these, such as a large oval portrait of Winfield Scott of Mexican War fame, as well as a section of the U.S. Armory in Springfield, known as the Water Shops.

As of 2003 there was a $1-$1-$2-$3 tint, $5-$5-$5-$10 tint, and a $1-$1-$2-$3 back plate remaining at the American Bank Note Co. archives.

Valid Issues

$1 • W-MA-3120-001-G010

Comments: H-MA-1175-G4. 18__. 1830s.

Rarity: —

$1 • W-MA-3120-001-G020

Engraver: Unverified, but likely Terry, Pelton & Co. ***Comments:*** H-MA-1175-G8. No description available. 18__. 1840s.

Rarity: *None known*

$1 • W-MA-3120-001-G030

Left: Train / 1. ***Center:*** 1 bearing house. ***Right:*** 1 / Eagle on shield / ONE. ***Engraver:*** Danforth, Spencer & Hufty / Spencer, Hufty & Danforth. ***Comments:*** H-MA-1175-G12. 18__. 1840s–1850s.

Rarity: —

$1 • W-MA-3120-001-G040

Left: 1 / Soldier with gun and drum. ***Center:*** U.S. Arsenal at Springfield. ***Right:*** Portrait of General George B. McClellan. ***Overprint:*** Green 1 1. ***Back:*** Green. ***Engraver:*** American Bank Note Co. ***Comments:*** H-MA-1175-G14a. Nov. 1, 1862.

Rarity: URS-2
EF $2,200

$1 • W-MA-3120-001-G050

SBG, SBG

Overprint: Green 1 1 and panel. ***Back:*** Green. ***Engraver:*** American Bank Note Co. ***Comments:*** H-MA-1175-G16a. Similar to W-MA-3120-001-G040 but with different right vignette. Nov. 1, 1862. 1860s.

Rarity: URS-3
EF $2,200

$1 • W-MA-3120-001-G060

SBG

Engraver: Terry, Pelton & Co. ***Comments:*** H-Unlisted. 18__. 1830s.

Rarity: URS-2
VF $2,500

$2 • W-MA-3120-002-G065

CC

Tint: Green. ***Engraver:*** American Bank Note Co. ***Comments:*** H-Unlisted. Nov. 1, 1862. 1860s.

Rarity: URS-1
EF $1,750

$2 • W-MA-3120-002-G070

Comments: H-MA-1175-G20. No description available. 18__. 1830s.

Rarity: *None known*

$2 • W-MA-3120-002-G080

Engraver: Unverified, but likely Terry, Pelton & Co. ***Comments:*** H-MA-1175-G24. No description available. 18__. 1840s.

Rarity: *None known*

$2 • W-MA-3120-002-G090

Left: Man standing between two horses, harnessing one of them / 2. ***Center:*** 2 bearing female portrait. ***Right:*** 2 / Farmer loading hay / TWO. ***Engraver:*** Danforth, Spencer & Hufty / Spencer, Hufty & Danforth. ***Comments:*** H-MA-1175-G28. 18__. 1840s–1850s.

Rarity: —

$3 • W-MA-3120-003-G100

Engraver: Unverified, but likely Terry, Pelton & Co. ***Comments:*** H-MA-1175-G36. No description available. 18__. 1840s.

Rarity: *None known*

$3 • W-MA-3120-003-G110

CJF

Engraver: Danforth, Spencer & Hufty / Spencer, Hufty & Danforth. ***Comments:*** H-MA-1175-G40. Beware of spurious W-MA-3120-003-S020 similar to genuine. 18__. 1840s–1850s.

Rarity: URS-4

F $750; **VF** $1,000

$3 • W-MA-3120-003-G120

CJF

Tint: Green. ***Engraver:*** American Bank Note Co. ***Comments:*** H-Unlisted. Nov. 1, 1862. 1860s.

Rarity: URS-3

F $1,500; **VF** $2,500

$5 • W-MA-3120-005-G130

Comments: H-MA-1175-G44. No description available. 18__. 1830s.

Rarity: *None known*

$5 • W-MA-3120-005-G140

Left: FIVE vertically. ***Center:*** 5 / Village square / 5. ***Right:*** 5 / Indian raising tomahawk. ***Engraver:*** Terry, Pelton & Co. ***Comments:*** H-MA-1175-G48. 18__. 1840s.

Rarity: —

$5 • W-MA-3120-005-G150

Left: 5 / Portrait of George Washington. ***Center:*** Man seated in V. ***Right:*** 5 / Portrait of Kate Sevier / 5. ***Engraver:*** Danforth, Spencer & Hufty / Spencer, Hufty & Danforth. ***Comments:*** H-MA-1175-G52. 18__. 1840s–1850s.

Rarity: —

$10 • W-MA-3120-010-G160

Comments: H-MA-1175-G56. No description available. 18__. 1830s.

Rarity: *None known*

$10 • W-MA-3120-010-G170

Engraver: Unverified, but likely Terry, Pelton & Co. ***Comments:*** H-MA-1175-G60. No description available. 18__. 1840s.

Rarity: *None known*

$10 • W-MA-3120-010-G180

CC

Engraver: Danforth, Spencer & Hufty / Spencer, Hufty & Danforth. ***Comments:*** H-MA-1175-G64. 18__. 1840s–1850s.

Rarity: URS-2

Proof $3,000

$20 • W-MA-3120-020-G190

CJF

Engraver: Terry, Pelton & Co. ***Comments:*** H-MA-1175-G72. Proof. 18__.

Rarity: —

$20 • W-MA-3120-020-G200

SBG

Engraver: Danforth, Spencer & Hufty / Spencer, Hufty & Danforth. ***Comments:*** H-MA-1175-G76. Proof. 18__. 1840s–1850s.

Rarity: URS-3

Proof $3,000

$50 • W-MA-3120-050-G210

JF

Engraver: Danforth, Spencer & Hufty / Spencer, Hufty & Danforth. ***Comments:*** H-MA-1175-G88. Proof. 18__. 1840s–1850s.

Rarity: URS-2

Proof $3,000

$100 • W-MA-3120-100-G220

Left: 100 / Medallion head of William Shakespeare / 100. ***Center:*** Woman reclining with cornucopia. ***Right:*** 100 / Medallion head. ***Engraver:*** Danforth, Spencer & Hufty / Spencer, Hufty & Danforth. ***Comments:*** H-MA-1175-G100. 18__. 1840s–1850s.

Rarity: URS-1
Proof $4,000

$100 • W-MA-3120-100-G230

CJF

Engraver: Terry, Pelton & Co. ***Comments:*** H-Unlisted. Proof. 18__.

Rarity: URS-2
Proof $4,000

$500 • W-MA-3120-500-G240

Left: State arms. ***Tint:*** Red 500s. ***Engraver:*** American Bank Note Co. ***Comments:*** H-MA-1175-G112a. 1860s.

Rarity: —

Uncut Sheets

$5-$5-$5-$10 • W-MA-3120-005.005.005.010-US010

Vignette(s): ($5) Portrait of George Washington / Man seated in V / Portrait of Kate Sevier. ***($5)*** Portrait of George Washington / Man seated in V / Portrait of Kate Sevier. ***($5)*** Portrait of George Washington / Man seated in V / Portrait of Kate Sevier. ***($10)*** Portrait of Mrs. Andrew Jackson / Man plowing black and white horses / Two women seated. ***Engraver:*** Danforth, Spencer & Hufty / Spencer, Hufty & Danforth. ***Comments:*** H-MA-1175-G52, G52, G52, G64. 18__. 1840s–1850s.

Rarity: —

$20-$20-$50-$100 • W-MA-3120-020.020.050.100-US020

Vignette(s): ($20) Woman standing with staff and shield / "Presentation of the Declaration of Independence" / Train. ***($20)*** Woman standing with staff and shield / "Presentation of the Declaration of Independence" / Train. ***($50)*** Medallion head / Man on horseback herding sheep / Medallion head. ***($100)*** Medallion head of William Shakespeare / Woman reclining with cornucopia / Medallion head. ***Engraver:*** Danforth, Spencer & Hufty / Spencer, Hufty & Danforth. ***Comments:*** H-MA-1175-G76, G76, G88, G100. 18__. 1840s–1850s.

Rarity: —

Non-Valid Issues

$1 • W-MA-3120-001-A010

CJF

Back: Orange circles consisting of ONEs. ***Engraver:*** W.L. Ormsby. ***Comments:*** H-MA-1175-A5. Altered from $1 Farmers & Drovers Bank, Petersburg, Indiana. Oct. 1, 1858.

Rarity: URS-6
F $75

$2 • W-MA-3120-002-A020

Left: TWO across 2 / Woman reclining. ***Center:*** Reaper with scythe. ***Right:*** TWO across 2 / Woman reclining. ***Back:*** Orange circles consisting of 2s. ***Engraver:*** W.L. Ormsby. ***Comments:*** H-MA-1175-A10. Altered from $2 Farmers and Drovers Bank, Petersburg, Indiana. Oct. 1, 1858.

Rarity: —

$3 • W-MA-3120-003-S010

CC

Engraver: Terry, Pelton & Co. ***Comments:*** H-MA-1175-S5. 18__. 1840s.

Rarity: URS-6
F $100

$3 • W-MA-3120-003-S020

PEM

Back: Green. ***Engraver:*** American Bank Note Co. / ABNCo. monogram. ***Comments:*** H-MA-1175-S10. Spurious design imitating a rough verbal description of W-MA-3120-003-G110. May 1, 1862.

Rarity: —
CU $135

$3 • W-MA-3120-003-N010
Center: Two women flanking shield, Eagle, Building and tree. ***Comments:*** H-MA-1175-N5.

Rarity: —

$5 • W-MA-3120-005-R010
Engraver: Terry, Pelton & Co. ***Comments:*** H-MA-1175-R5. Raised from W-MA-3120-001-G020. 18__. 1840s.

Rarity: —

$5 • W-MA-3120-005-A030 HA

Back: Five portraits of George Washington surrounded by a circle consisting of 5s. ***Engraver:*** W.L. Ormsby. ***Comments:*** H-MA-1175-A15. Altered from $5 Farmers and Drovers Bank, Petersburg, Indiana. Oct. 1, 1858.

Rarity: —

$10 • W-MA-3120-010-A040
Left: 10 / Justice seated. ***Center:*** Indian family, Woman kneeling and pointing at plow. ***Right:*** 10 / Woman reclining on cornucopia. ***Back:*** Ten orange dies with an X in the center. ***Engraver:*** W.L. Ormsby. ***Comments:*** H-MA-1175-A20. Altered from $10 Farmers and Drovers Bank, Petersburg, Indiana. Oct. 1, 1858.

Rarity: —

John Hancock Bank
1851–1865
W-MA-3130

History: The John Hancock Bank was formed on May 18, 1850, with an authorized capital of $100,000, "to be established in the town of Springfield on the south side of State Street upon the hill and near the Armory and arsenals of the United States." It began business on October 15, 1851, when half of the capital had been paid in as provided for by law. The engraved title of the bank, as it appears on its notes, is a facsimile of the signature of John Hancock as it appears on the Declaration of Independence.[39]

The capital of the bank was increased to $150,000 in 1855. Its circulation was $30,658 in 1851 and $149,319 in 1863. In 1856 the Legislature allowed the bank to relocate to a "more convenient and central part of the city."[40]

The business of the John Hancock Bank was succeeded by the John Hancock National Bank of Springfield after it was chartered on April 5, 1865.

Numismatic Commentary: The directors of this bank chose to display the title on some of their issues in a cursive design appearing like the John Hancock signature recognized from the Declaration of Independence. Counterfeiters imitated it successfully. The buildings in the background show the main part of the campus of the U.S. Armory in Springfield.

Valid Issues

$1 • W-MA-3130-001-G010 JF

Engraver: Toppan, Carpenter, Casilear & Co. ***Comments:*** H-MA-1180-G2. 18__. 1850s.

Rarity: URS-6
F $500

$1 • W-MA-3130-001-G010a
Left: 1 / Eagle and shield, View of U.S. Armory at Springfield. ***Right:*** 1 / Female portrait. ***Overprint:*** Red. ***Engraver:*** Toppan, Carpenter, Casilear & Co. ***Comments:*** H-MA-1180-G2a. Similar to W-MA-3130-001-G010. 18__. 1850s.

Rarity: —

$1 • W-MA-3130-001-G010b
Overprint: Red. ***Engraver:*** American Bank Note Co. ***Comments:*** H-MA-1180-G2b. Similar to W-MA-3130-001-G010 but with different engraver imprint. 18__. 1850s–1860s.

Rarity: —

$1 • W-MA-3130-001-G010c CJF

Overprint: Red shield outlining white 1. ***Engraver:*** American Bank Note Co. / ABNCo. monogram. ***Comments:*** H-Unlisted. Similar to W-MA-3130-001-G010 but with additional engraver imprint. 18__. 1860s.

Rarity: URS-5
F $600; **VF** $1,000

$2 • W-MA-3130-002-G020

QDB

Engraver: Toppan, Carpenter, Casilear & Co. ***Comments:*** H-MA-1180-G4. Proof. 18__. 1850s.

Rarity: URS-4
Proof $1,500

$2 • W-MA-3130-002-G020a

Left: 2 / Female portrait. ***Center:*** Eagle and shield, View of U.S. Armory at Springfield. ***Right:*** 2. ***Overprint:*** Red. ***Engraver:*** Toppan, Carpenter, Casilear & Co. ***Comments:*** H-MA-1180-G4a. Similar to W-MA-3130-002-G020. 18__. 1850s.

Rarity: —

$2 • W-MA-3130-002-G020b

Overprint: Red. ***Engraver:*** American Bank Note Co. ***Comments:*** H-MA-1180-G4b. Similar to W-MA-3130-002-G020 but with different engraver imprint. 18__. 1850s–1860s.

Rarity: —

$2 • W-MA-3130-002-G020c

CJF

Overprint: Red shield outlining white 2. ***Engraver:*** American Bank Note Co. / ABNCo. monogram. ***Comments:*** H-Unlisted. Similar to W-MA-3130-002-G020 but with additional engraver imprint. 18__. 1860s.

Rarity: URS-6
VG $500; **F** $750; **VF** $1,200

$3 • W-MA-3130-003-G030

Left: 3 / Woman. ***Center:*** Train. ***Right:*** 3 / Woman. ***Engraver:*** Toppan, Carpenter, Casilear & Co. ***Comments:*** H-MA-1180-G6. 18__. 1850s.

Rarity: —

$3 • W-MA-3130-003-G030a

Overprint: Red THREE. ***Engraver:*** Toppan, Carpenter, Casilear & Co. ***Comments:*** H-MA-1180-G6a. Similar to W-MA-3130-003-G030. 18__. 1850s.

Rarity: —

$3 • W-MA-3130-003-G030b

Overprint: Red THREE. ***Engraver:*** American Bank Note Co. ***Comments:*** H-MA-1180-G6b. Similar to W-MA-3130-003-G030 but with additional engraver imprint. 18__. 1850s–1860s.

Rarity: —

$5 • W-MA-3130-005-G040

QDB

Engraver: Toppan, Carpenter, Casilear & Co. ***Comments:*** H-MA-1180-G8. 18__. 1850s.

Rarity: URS-4
Proof $1,000

$5 • W-MA-3130-005-G040a

Left: 5 / Indian woman seated with shield, Eagle and flag, Steamship. ***Center:*** Portrait of John Hancock. ***Right:*** 5 / Woman seated with shield bearing 5. ***Overprint:*** Red. ***Engraver:*** Toppan, Carpenter, Casilear & Co. ***Comments:*** H-MA-1180-G8a. Similar to W-MA-3130-005-G040. 18__. 1850s.

Rarity: —

$5 • W-MA-3130-005-G040b

Overprint: Red. ***Engraver:*** American Bank Note Co. ***Comments:*** H-MA-1180-G8b. Similar to W-MA-3130-005-G040 but with additional engraver imprint. 18__. 1850s–1860s.

Rarity: —

$10 • W-MA-3130-010-G050

Left: Woman standing with sickle and sheaf / TEN. ***Center:*** 10 / Three women, Ships. ***Bottom center:*** Eagle. ***Right:*** 10 / Female portrait. ***Engraver:*** Toppan, Carpenter, Casilear & Co. ***Comments:*** H-MA-1180-G10. Beware of spurious W-MA-3130-010-S010 resembling the genuine. 18__. 1850s–1860s.

Rarity: —

$20 • W-MA-3130-020-G060

Left: 20 / Portrait of John Hancock / TWENTY. ***Center:*** Woman blowing trumpet, Eagle, Globe and flag. ***Right:*** 20 / State arms. ***Comments:*** H-MA-1180-G14. 18__. 1850s–1860s.

Rarity: —

$50 • W-MA-3130-050-G070

Left: 50 / Woman seated with spool, Factories. ***Center:*** Woman feeding pigs, Man seated on trough watering horses. ***Right:*** 50 / Indian woman as Liberty. ***Engraver:*** Toppan, Carpenter, Casilear & Co. ***Comments:*** H-MA-1180-G16. 18__. 1850s–1860s.

Rarity: —

$100 • W-MA-3130-100-G080

Left: Woman seated in clouds with eagle on globe / 100. ***Center:*** 100 on die. ***Bottom center:*** Dog's head. ***Right:*** 100 / Farmer sharpening scythe, Train and mill. ***Comments:*** H-MA-1180-G18. 18__. 1850s–1860s.

Rarity: —

Non-Valid Issues

$1 • W-MA-3130-001-C010

Engraver: Toppan, Carpenter, Casilear & Co. / American Bank Note Co. ***Comments:*** H-MA-1180-C2. Counterfeit of W-MA-3130-001-G010 or variety. 18__. 1850s–1860s.

Rarity: —

$1 • W-MA-3130-001-A010

Left: 1. ***Center:*** Woodsman kneeling with axe, Log, Gold dollar. ***Right:*** 1 / Ship on stocks. ***Engraver:*** Rawdon, Wright, Hatch & Edson / New England Bank Note Co. ***Comments:*** H-MA-1180-A5. Altered from $1 Hancock Bank, Ellsworth, Maine. July 1, 185_. 1850s.

Rarity: —

$2 • W-MA-3130-002-A020

Left: Milkmaid with pail seated and man with rake reclining, Two gold dollars, Cows / 2. ***Center:*** Fountain in form of cherub. ***Right:*** 2 / Sailor standing with capstan. ***Engraver:*** Rawdon, Wright, Hatch & Edson / New England Bank Note Co. ***Comments:*** H-MA-1180-A10. Altered from $2 Hancock, Ellsworth, Maine. July 1, 185_. 1850s.

Rarity: —

$3 • W-MA-3130-003-C030a CJF

Overprint: Red THREE. ***Engraver:*** Toppan, Carpenter, Casilear & Co. ***Comments:*** H-MA-1180-C6a. Counterfeit of W-MA-3130-003-G030a. 18__. 1857.

Rarity: URS-7
VG $125; **VF** $175

$3 • W-MA-3130-003-A030 HA

Engraver: Rawdon, Wright, Hatch & Edson / New England Bank Note Co. ***Comments:*** H-MA-1180-A15. Altered from $3 Hancock Bank, Ellsworth, Maine. July 1, 185_. 1850s.

Rarity: —

$5 • W-MA-3130-005-R010

Engraver: Toppan, Carpenter, Casilear & Co. ***Comments:*** H-MA-1180-R5. Raised from W-MA-3130-001-G010 or G010a. 18__. 1850s.

Rarity: —

$5 • W-MA-3130-005-A040

Left: 5 / Indian woman and hunter with gun flanking three cherubs above five gold dollars. ***Right:*** 5 / Woman swimming with swan. ***Engraver:*** Rawdon, Wright, Hatch & Edson / New England Bank Note Co. ***Comments:*** H-MA-1180-A20. Altered from $5 Hancock Bank, Ellsworth, Maine. July 1, 185_. 1850s.

Rarity: —

$5 • W-MA-3130-005-A050

Left: U.S. shield, Eagle, U.S. Armory and houses. ***Right:*** Female portrait. ***Engraver:*** Toppan, Carpenter & Co. ***Comments:*** H-Unlisted. Altered from $5 Hancock Bank, Ellsworth, Maine. 1850s.

Rarity: —

$10 • W-MA-3130-010-R020

Engraver: Toppan, Carpenter, Casilear & Co. ***Comments:*** H-MA-1180-R10. Raised from W-MA-3130-001-G010 or G010a. 18__. 1850s.

Rarity: —

$10 • W-MA-3130-010-S010 SI

Engraver: Toppan, Carpenter, Casilear & Co. ***Comments:*** H-MA-1180-S5. Spurious design imitating a rough verbal description of W-MA-3130-010-G050. 18__. 1860s.

Rarity: —

$10 • W-MA-3130-010-A060

Left: U.S. shield, Eagle, U.S. Armory and houses. ***Right:*** Female portrait. ***Engraver:*** Toppan, Carpenter & Co. ***Comments:*** H-Unlisted. Altered from $10 Hancock Bank, Ellsworth, Maine. 1850s.

Rarity: —

How to Read the Whitman Numbering System

$1 • W-MA-010-001-G010a

Denomination: Value of the note shown.

W: Whitman number. This number is a sortable code unique to each bank and note.

MA: Abbreviation for the state under study.

010: Numerical designation specific to each bank.

001: The denomination in dollars.

G010a: G indicates a good or valid note. Other categories are indicated thus: C (counterfeit); R (raised); S (spurious); N (not-attributed); A (altered). Numbers are assigned starting with 010, 020, et seq. Terminal letters following the number indicate variations of a note: a series of different colored overprints, tints, payees, etc., all on the same design of note. For more information, see the "How to Use This Book" section at the front of the volume, page xiv.

Pynchon Bank

1853–1865

W-MA-3140

History: The Pynchon Bank was chartered on April 28, 1853, with an authorized capital of $150,000. It opened its doors for business on October 14. The bank was named after John Pynchon, who in 1660 built the Pynchon House, which stood until 1831. John A. Bolen, numismatist and medalist, created a token depicting it. The circulation of the bank ranged from a low of $103,018 in 1858 to a high of $152,720 in 1863. Specie was listed at $6,412.71 in 1857 and at $9,149.63 in 1864.

The business of the Pynchon Bank was succeeded by the Pynchon National Bank of Springfield after it was chartered on April 7, 1865.

Numismatic Commentary: Named after William Pynchon, the founder of Springfield, the Pynchon Bank issued some notes with vignettes showing the founder's home. All genuine issues are hard to find in the marketplace.

Valid Issues

$1 • W-MA-3140-001-G010

CC

Engraver: Danforth, Wright & Co. ***Comments:*** H-MA-1185-G2. Proof. 18__. 1850s.

Rarity: URS-2
Proof $1,700

$1 • W-MA-3140-001-G010a

Left: Train / ONE on 1. ***Center:*** 1. ***Right:*** 1 / Male portrait with sledge. ***Overprint:*** Red. ***Engraver:*** Danforth, Wright & Co. ***Comments:*** H-MA-1185-G2a. Similar to W-MA-3140-001-G010. 18__. 1850s.

Rarity: —

$1 • W-MA-3140-001-G010b

Overprint: Red. ***Engraver:*** Danforth, Wright & Co. / ABNCo. monogram. ***Comments:*** H-MA-1185-G2b. Similar to W-MA-3140-001-G010 but with additional engraver imprint. 18__. 1850s–1860s.

Rarity: —

$2 • W-MA-3140-002-G020

Left: 2 on TWO / Old Pynchon House / TWO. ***Center:*** Woman seated in 2 / 2. ***Right:*** TWO / Woman with arm raised. ***Engraver:*** Danforth, Wright & Co. ***Comments:*** H-MA-1185-G4. 18__. 1850s.

Rarity: —

$2 • W-MA-3140-002-G020a

Overprint: Red 2 2. ***Engraver:*** Danforth, Wright & Co. ***Comments:*** H-MA-1185-G4a. Similar to W-MA-3140-002-G020. 18__. 1850s.

Rarity: —

$2 • W-MA-3140-002-G020b

CJF

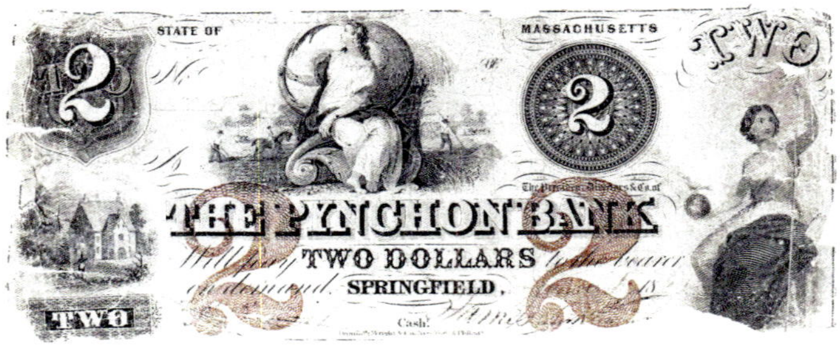

Overprint: Red 2 2. ***Engraver:*** Danforth, Wright & Co. / ABNCo. monogram. ***Comments:*** H-MA-1185-G4b. Similar to W-MA-3140-002-G020 but with additional engraver imprint. 18__. 1860s.

Rarity: URS-4
VG $500; **F** $750

$3 • W-MA-3140-003-G030

CC

Engraver: Danforth, Wright & Co. ***Comments:*** H-MA-1185-G6. Proof. 18__. 1850s.

Rarity: URS-2
Proof $3,000

$3 • W-MA-3140-003-G030a

Left: 3 / Cow's head / THREE. ***Center:*** White horse, 3 on shield surmounted by eagle, Black horse / 3. ***Right:*** THREE vertically. ***Overprint:*** Red. ***Engraver:*** Danforth, Wright & Co. ***Comments:*** H-MA-1185-G6a. Similar to W-MA-3140-003-G030. 18__. 1850s.

Rarity: —

$3 • W-MA-3140-003-G030b

Overprint: Red. ***Engraver:*** Danforth, Wright & Co. / ABNCo. monogram. ***Comments:*** H-MA-1185-G6b. Similar to W-MA-3140-003-G030 but with additional engraver imprint. 18__. 1850s–1860s.

Rarity: —

$5 • W-MA-3140-005-G040

JF

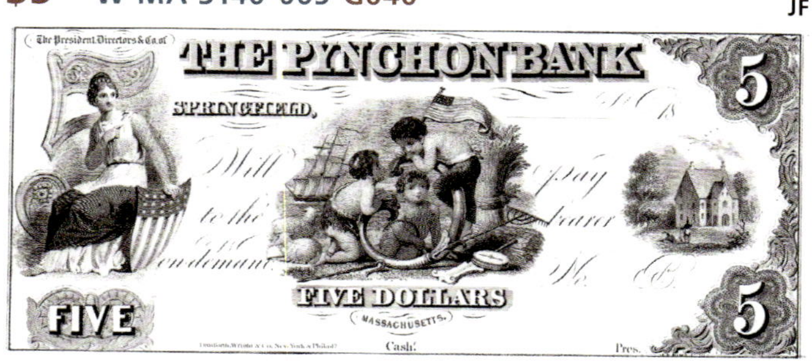

Engraver: Danforth, Wright & Co. ***Comments:*** H-MA-1185-G8. Proof. 18__. 1850s.

Rarity: URS-3
Proof $3,000

$5 • W-MA-3140-005-G040a

Left: Woman seated with shield in 5 / FIVE. ***Center:*** Three boys in 5, Flag, Ship. ***Right:*** 5 / Old Pynchon House / 5. ***Overprint:*** Red 5 5. ***Engraver:*** Danforth, Wright & Co. ***Comments:*** H-MA-1185-G8a. Similar to W-MA-3140-005-G040. 18__. 1850s.

Rarity: —

$5 • W-MA-3140-005-G040b

Overprint: Red 5 5. ***Engraver:*** Danforth, Wright & Co. / ABNCo. monogram. ***Comments:*** H-MA-1185-G8b. Similar to W-MA-3140-005-G040 but with additional engraver imprint. 18__. 1850s–1860s.

Rarity: —

$10 • W-MA-3140-010-G050

CC

Engraver: Danforth, Wright & Co. ***Comments:*** H-MA-1185-G10. Plate note. 18__. 1850s.

Rarity: URS-2
Proof $3,000

$10 • W-MA-3140-010-G050a

Overprint: Red. ***Engraver:*** Danforth, Wright & Co. ***Comments:*** H-MA-1185-G10a. Similar to W-MA-3140-010-G050. 18__. 1850s.

Rarity: —

$10 • W-MA-3140-010-G050b

Overprint: Red. ***Engraver:*** Danforth, Wright & Co. / ABNCo. monogram. ***Comments:*** H-MA-1185-G10b. Similar to W-MA-3140-010-G050 but with additional engraver imprint. 18__. 1850s–1860s.

Rarity: —

$20 • W-MA-3140-020-G060

Left: 20 / Portrait of Daniel Webster. ***Center:*** Indian seated next to plow / 20. ***Bottom center:*** XX. ***Right:*** XX / Boy with shield and flag. ***Engraver:*** Danforth, Wright & Co. ***Comments:*** H-MA-1185-G12. 18__. 1850s.

Rarity: —

$20 • W-MA-3140-020-G060a

Overprint: Red. ***Engraver:*** Danforth, Wright & Co. ***Comments:*** H-MA-1185-G12a. Similar to W-MA-3140-020-G060. 18__. 1850s.

Rarity: —

$20 • W-MA-3140-020-G060b

Overprint: Red. ***Engraver:*** Danforth, Wright & Co. / ABNCo. monogram. ***Comments:*** H-MA-1185-G12b. Similar to W-MA-3140-020-G060 but with additional engraver imprint. 18__. 1850s–1860s.

Rarity: —

$50 • W-MA-3140-050-G070

Left: Woman standing with staff. ***Center:*** 50 / "Presentation of the Declaration of Independence". ***Right:*** 50 / Portrait of George Washington. ***Engraver:*** Danforth, Wright & Co. ***Comments:*** H-MA-1185-G14. 18__. 1850s.

Rarity: —

$50 • W-MA-3140-050-G070a

Overprint: Red. ***Engraver:*** Danforth, Wright & Co. ***Comments:*** H-MA-1185-G14a. Similar to W-MA-3140-050-G070. 18__. 1850s.

Rarity: —

$50 • W-MA-3140-050-G070b

Overprint: Red. ***Engraver:*** Danforth, Wright & Co. / ABNCo. monogram. ***Comments:*** H-MA-1185-G14b. Similar to W-MA-3140-050-G070 but with additional engraver imprint. 18__. 1850s–1860s.

Rarity: —

$100 • W-MA-3140-100-G080

Left: 100 / Woman reclining with shield. ***Center:*** C. ***Right:*** 100 / Woman seated next to crate looking at Old Pynchon House. ***Engraver:*** Danforth, Wright & Co. ***Comments:*** H-MA-1185-G16 18__. 1850s.

Rarity: URS-1
Proof $4,000

$100 • W-MA-3140-100-G080a

Overprint: Red. ***Engraver:*** Danforth, Wright & Co. ***Comments:*** H-MA-1185-G16a. Similar to W-MA-3140-100-G080. 18__. 1850s.

Rarity: —

$100 • W-MA-3140-100-G080b

Overprint: Red. ***Engraver:*** Danforth, Wright & Co. ***Comments:*** H-MA-1185-G16b. Similar to W-MA-3140-100-G080 but with additional engraver imprint. 18__. 1850s–1860s.

Rarity: —

Non-Valid Issues

$1 • W-MA-3140-001-C010

Engraver: Danforth, Wright & Co. ***Comments:*** H-MA-1185-C2. Counterfeit of W-MA-3140-001-G010 or G010a. 18__. 1850s.

Rarity: —

$2 • W-MA-3140-002-A010

CJF

Overprint: Red TWO. ***Engraver:*** Wellstood, Hay & Whiting. ***Comments:*** H-MA-1185-A5. Altered from $2 Thames Bank, Laurel, Indiana. August 12, 1856.

Rarity: URS-7
VG $125; **VF** $175

$3 • W-MA-3140-003-C030
Engraver: Danforth, Wright & Co. ***Comments:*** H-MA-1185-C6. Counterfeit of W-MA-3140-003-G030 or variety. 18__. 1850s.
Rarity: —

$5 • W-MA-3140-005-R010
Engraver: Danforth, Wright & Co. ***Comments:*** H-MA-1185-R5. Raised from W-MA-3140-001-G010 or G010a. 18__. 1850s.
Rarity: —

$5 • W-MA-3140-005-N010
Center: Public building. ***Overprint:*** Red end panels. ***Comments:*** H-MA-1185-N5.
Rarity: —

$5 • W-MA-3140-005-N020
Center: Two women seated, Train. ***Comments:*** H-MA-1185-N10.
Rarity: —

$5 • W-MA-3140-005-A020
Left: Five men haying, Wagon and two oxen. ***Center:*** Men driving cattle into stream / 5. ***Right:*** 5. ***Tint:*** Brown-orange lathework outlining white 5. ***Engraver:*** Bald, Cousland & Co. ***Comments:*** H-MA-1185-A10. Altered from $5 Pioneer Association, Lafayette, Indiana. 18__. 1850s–1860s.
Rarity: —

$5 • W-MA-3140-005-A030
Left: Portrait of Henry Clay / V. ***Center:*** Farmer feeding hogs. ***Bottom center:*** Dog lying down. ***Right:*** 5 / Farmer carrying basket of corn. ***Overprint:*** Red FIVE. ***Engraver:*** Wellstood, Hay & Whiting. ***Comments:*** H-MA-1185-A15. Altered from $5 Thames Bank, Laurel, Indiana. 1850s.
Rarity: —

$10 • W-MA-3140-010-R020
Engraver: Danforth, Wright & Co. ***Comments:*** H-MA-1185-R10. Raised from W-MA-3140-001-G010 or G010a. 18__. 1850s.
Rarity: —

$10 • W-MA-3140-010-N030
Center: Woman seated on bale / 10. ***Comments:*** H-MA-1185-N15.
Rarity: —

$20 • W-MA-3140-020-R030
Engraver: Danforth, Wright & Co. ***Comments:*** H-MA-1185-R15. Raised from W-MA-3140-001-G010 or G010a. 18__. 1850s.
Rarity: —

Springfield Bank
1814–1864
W-MA-3150

History: The Springfield Bank was incorporated on February 4, 1814, with $100,000 in authorized capital. This value was increased to $300,000 in 1831. In 1839 the capital was $250,000, but it was back to $300,000 by 1851. The bank's circulation had a low of $131,130 in 1839 and a high of $286,110 in 1863.

The business of the Springfield Bank was succeeded by the Springfield National Bank of Springfield, chartered on January 2, 1864.

Numismatic Commentary: Most issues are payable in Springfield, but some are payable in New York City. Presently, enough appear in the marketplace to keep collectors interested in the hunt.

Valid Issues

$1 • W-MA-3150-001-G010
Engraver: Unverified, but likely A. Reed / Reed. ***Comments:*** H-MA-1190-G12. No description available. 18__. 1810s.
Rarity: *None known*

$1 • W-MA-3150-001-G020
Left: Narrow panel of lathework circle segments. ***Center:*** 1 / 1 / Flower garlands and gridwork segments / 1 / 1. ***Right:*** Narrow panel of lathework circle segments. ***Engraver:*** PSSP. ***Comments:*** H-MA-1190-G14. 18__. 1820s–1830s.
Rarity: —

$1 • W-MA-3150-001-G020a
Left: ONE / D / ONE vertically. ***Right:*** ONE / D / ONE vertically. ***Engraver:*** PSSP. ***Comments:*** H-MA-1190-G16. Similar to W-MA-3150-001-G020. 18__. 1830s.
Rarity: —

$1 • W-MA-3150-001-G030
Engraver: Unverified, but likely PSSP. ***Comments:*** H-MA-1190-G18. No description available. 18__. 1830s–1840s.
Rarity: *None known*

$1 • W-MA-3150-001-G040 CJF

Engraver: Danforth, Bald & Co. ***Comments:*** H-MA-1190-G22. Plate note. 18__. 1850s.
Rarity: URS-1
Proof $4,000

$1 • W-MA-3150-001-G040a SBG

Tint: Orange lathework and 1 1. ***Engraver:*** Danforth, Bald & Co. ***Comments:*** H-MA-1190-G22a. Similar to W-MA-3150-001-G040. 18__. 1850s.
Rarity: URS-2
Proof $5,000
Selected auction price: Stack's Bowers Galleries, August 2012, Lot 7133, Gem Unc $1,725

$1 • W-MA-3150-001-G040b

Left: 1 / Cattle at river / ONE. ***Center:*** Man seated with dog, ONE. ***Right:*** 1 / Portrait of Jenny Lind. ***Tint:*** Orange lathework and 1 1. ***Engraver:*** Danforth, Bald & Co. / ABNCo. monogram. ***Comments:*** H-MA-1190-G22b. Similar to W-MA-3150-001-G040 but with additional engraver imprint. 18__. 1860s.

Rarity: —

$2 • W-MA-3150-002-G050

Left: Narrow panel of lathework circle segments. ***Center:*** 2 / 2 / Flower garlands and gridwork segments / 2 / 2. ***Right:*** Narrow panel of lathework circle segments. ***Engraver:*** PSSP. ***Comments:*** H-MA-1190-G28. 18__. 1820s–1830s.

Rarity: —

$2 • W-MA-3150-002-G050a

Left: Five TWOs vertically. ***Right:*** Five TWOs vertically. ***Engraver:*** PSSP. ***Comments:*** H-MA-1190-G30. Similar to W-MA-3150-002-G050. 18__. 1830s.

Rarity: —

$2 • W-MA-3150-002-G060

Engraver: Unverified, but likely PSSP. ***Comments:*** H-MA-1190-G32. No description available. 18__. 1830s–1840s.

Rarity: *None known*

$2 • W-MA-3150-002-G070

SBG

Engraver: Danforth, Bald & Co. ***Comments:*** H-MA-1190-G36. Proof. 18__. 1850s.

Rarity: URS-3
Proof $1,000

Selected auction price: Stack's Bowers Galleries, November 2012, Lot 4186, Choice Unc $763

$2 • W-MA-3150-002-G070a

CC

Tint: Orange lathework and 2 2. ***Engraver:*** Danforth, Bald & Co. ***Comments:*** H-MA-1190-G36a. Similar to W-MA-3150-002-G070. Proof. 18__. 1850s.

Rarity: URS-1
Proof $6,000

$2 • W-MA-3150-002-G070b

CJF

Tint: Orange lathework and 2 2. ***Engraver:*** Danforth, Bald & Co. / ABNCo. monogram. ***Comments:*** H-MA-1190-G36b. Similar to W-MA-3150-002-G070 but with additional engraver imprint. 18__. 1860s.

Rarity: URS-2
F $2,000

$3 • W-MA-3150-003-G080

Left: Narrow panel of lathework circle segments. ***Center:*** 3 / 3 / Flower garlands and gridwork segments / 3 / 3. ***Right:*** Narrow panel of lathework circle segments. ***Engraver:*** PSSP. ***Comments:*** H-MA-1190-G40. 18__. 1820s–1830s.

Rarity: —

$3 • W-MA-3150-003-G080a

HA

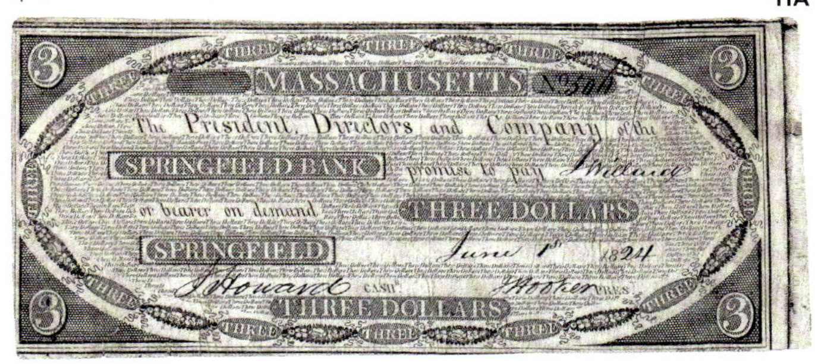

Engraver: PSSP. ***Comments:*** H-Unlisted. Similar to W-MA-3150-003-G080. 18__. 1820s.

Rarity: —

$3 • W-MA-3150-003-G080b

Left: THREE vertically. ***Center:*** 3 / 3 / Flower garlands and gridwork segments / 3 / 3. ***Right:*** THREE vertically. ***Engraver:*** PSSP. ***Comments:*** H-MA-1190-G42. Similar to W-MA-3150-003-G080. 18__. 1830s.

Rarity: —

$3 • W-MA-3150-003-G090

Engraver: Unverified, but likely PSSP. ***Comments:*** H-MA-1190-G44. No description available. 18__. 1830s–1840s.

Rarity: *None known*

$5 • W-MA-3150-005-G100

Left: Lathework chain bearing MASSACHUSETTS / 5 / 5 vertically. ***Center:*** Alternating flower garlands and gridwork segments. ***Right:*** 5 / 5 vertically. ***Engraver:*** PSSP. ***Comments:*** H-MA-1190-G50. 18__. 1820s.

Rarity: —

$5 • W-MA-3150-005-G100a

Engraver: PSSP. ***Comments:*** H-MA-1190-G52. Similar to W-MA-3150-005-G100 but with zigzag ruled lines. 18__. 1820s–1830s.

Rarity: —

$5 • W-MA-3150-005-G100b

Engraver: PSSP. ***Comments:*** H-MA-1190-G54. Similar to W-MA-3150-005-G100 but with spiral lathework lines. 18__. 1830s.

Rarity: —

$5 • W-MA-3150-005-G110

CJF

Engraver: New England Bank Note Co. / PSSP. ***Comments:*** H-MA-1190-G56. 18__. 1830s–1850s.

Rarity: —

$10 • W-MA-3150-010-G120

Comments: H-MA-1190-G62. No description available. 18__. 1810s.

Rarity: *None known*

$10 • W-MA-3150-010-G130

Left: Lathework chain bearing MASSACHUSETTS / 10 / 10 vertically. ***Center:*** Alternating flower garlands and gridwork segments. ***Right:*** 10 / 10 vertically. ***Engraver:*** Perkins. ***Comments:*** H-MA-1190-G66. 18__. 1820s.

Rarity: —

$10 • W-MA-3150-010-G130a

Engraver: PSSP. ***Comments:*** H-MA-1190-G68. Similar to W-MA-3150-010-G130. 18__. 1820s–1830s.

Rarity: —

$10 • W-MA-3150-010-G130b

Engraver: PSSP. ***Comments:*** H-MA-1190-G70. Similar to W-MA-3150-010-G130. 18__. 1830s.

Rarity: —

$10 • W-MA-3150-010-G140

JF

Engraver: New England Bank Note Co. / PSSP. ***Comments:*** H-MA-1190-G72. 18__. 1830s–1850s.

Rarity: URS-5

Proof $1,250

$20 • W-MA-3150-020-G150

Left: Alternating chain with MASSACHUSETTS / 20 / 20 vertically. ***Center:*** Alternating flower garlands and gridwork segments. ***Right:*** 20 / 20 vertically. ***Engraver:*** PSSP. ***Comments:*** H-MA-1190-G78. 18__. 1820s–1830s.

Rarity: —

$20 • W-MA-3150-020-G160

CC

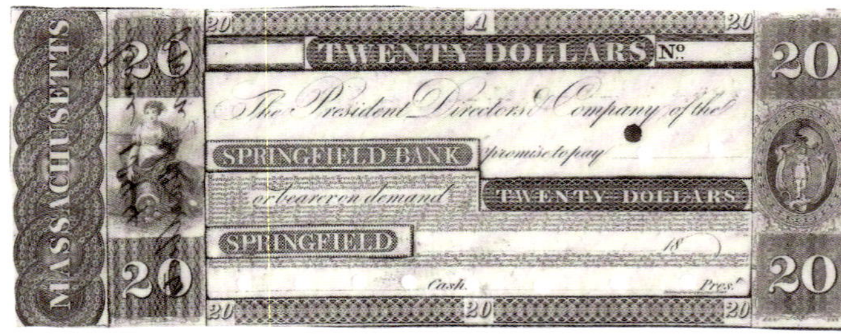

Engraver: New England Bank Note Co. / PSSP. ***Comments:*** H-MA-1190-G82. 18__. 1830s–1850s.

Rarity: URS-3

Proof $950

$50 • W-MA-3150-050-G170

Left: Lathework chain bearing MASSACHUSETTS / 50 / 50 vertically. ***Center:*** Alternating flower garlands and gridwork segments. ***Right:*** 50 / 50 vertically. ***Engraver:*** PSSP. ***Comments:*** H-MA-1190-G86. 18__. 1820s–1830s.

Rarity: —

$50 • W-MA-3150-050-G180

Left: MASSACHUSETTS vertically. ***Center:*** Panel of microlettering, woman seated on bale holding purse. ***Right:*** State arms. ***Engraver:*** New England Bank Note Co. / PSSP. ***Comments:*** H-MA-1190-G88. 18__. 1830s–1850s.

Rarity: —

$100 • W-MA-3150-100-G190

Left: Lathework chain bearing MASSACHUSETTS / 100 / 100 vertically. ***Center:*** Alternating flower garlands and gridwork segments. ***Right:*** 100 / 100 vertically. ***Engraver:*** Perkins. ***Comments:*** H-MA-1190-G92. 18__. 1820s–1830s.

Rarity: URS-3

Proof $2,000

$100 • W-MA-3150-100-G200

Left: MASSACHUSETTS vertically. ***Center:*** Panel of microlettering, woman seated on bale holding purse. ***Right:*** State arms. ***Engraver:*** New England Bank Note Co. / PSSP. ***Comments:*** H-MA-1190-G94. 18__. 1830s–1850s.

Rarity: —

Payable at Mechanics Bank, New York City

$5 • W-MA-3150-005-G210

CJF

Engraver: A. Reed / Reed. ***Comments:*** H-MA-1190-G100. 181_. 1810s.

Rarity: —

$10 • W-MA-3150-010-G220

CC

Engraver: A. Reed / Reed. ***Comments:*** H-MA-1190-G102. 181_. 1810s.

Rarity: URS-2
Proof $1,250

$20 • W-MA-3150-020-G230

CC

Engraver: A. Reed / Reed. ***Comments:*** H-MA-1190-G104. 181_. 1810s.

Rarity: URS-2
Proof $1,250

Uncut Sheets

$1-$1-$1-$2 • W-MA-3150-001.001.001.002-US010

Vignette(s): ($1) Scene with water / Man seated with dog / Portrait of Jenny Lind. ***($1)*** Scene with water / Man seated with dog / Portrait of Jenny Lind. ***($1)*** Scene with water / Man seated with dog / Portrait of Jenny Lind. ***($2)*** Woman standing in niche / Man seated with dog / Two men walking. ***Comments:*** H-MA-1190-G22, G22, G22, G36. 18__. 1850s.

Rarity: —

$1-$1-$1-$2 • W-MA-3150-001.001.001.002-US010a

Tint(s): Ochre. ***Comments:*** All unlisted in Haxby. Similar to W-MA-3150-001.001.001.002-US010. 18__. 1850s.

Rarity: —

Non-Valid Issues

$3 • W-MA-3150-003-N010

Center: Spread eagle with snake in beak. ***Comments:*** H-MA-1190-N5.

Rarity: —

$5 • W-MA-3150-005-S010

Left: 5 / Portrait of William Henry Harrison. ***Center:*** Ship sailing / 5. ***Bottom center:*** Eagle. ***Right:*** Indian woman holding bow / FIVE. ***Engraver:*** Toppan, Carpenter, Casilear & Co. ***Comments:*** H-MA-1190-S5. 18__. 1850s.

Rarity: —

$5 • W-MA-3150-005-S020

CJF

Engraver: Rawon, Wright & Hatch. ***Comments:*** H-Unlisted. 18__. 1840s.

Rarity: —

$10 • W-MA-3150-010-R010

Engraver: Danforth, Bald & Co. ***Comments:*** H-MA-1190-R5. Raised from W-MA-3150-001-G040. 18__. 1850s.

Rarity: —

$10 • W-MA-3150-010-R020

Engraver: Danforth, Bald & Co. ***Comments:*** H-MA-1190-R10. Raised from W-MA-3150-002-G070. 18__. 1850s.

Rarity: —

Western Bank

1849–1858

W-MA-3160

History: The Western Bank was chartered in April 1849 with an authorized capital of $100,000, later increased to $250,000. Circulation was valued at $56,275. The bank suffered from the Panic of 1857 and went into receivership in early 1858, after which normal banking business was discontinued.

Numismatic Commentary: Genuine issues are hard to locate, while non-valid issues appear much more often.

As of 2003 there was a $5-$5-$5-$5 face and a $5-$5-$5-$5 tint plate remaining at the American Bank Note Co. archives.

Valid Issues

$1 • W-MA-3160-001-G010

QDB

Engraver: Rawdon, Wright, Hatch & Edson / New England Bank Note Co. ***Comments:*** H-MA-1195-G4. October 2, 1854. 1849–1850s.

Rarity: URS-5
VG $275; **VF** $650

$1 • **W-MA-3160-001-G010a**

Left: Man with sledge / 1. ***Center:*** ONE / 1 / ONE. ***Bottom center:*** 1. ***Right:*** 1 / Cow's head. ***Engraver:*** Rawdon, Wright, Hatch & Edson / New England Bank Note Co. ***Comments:*** H-MA-1195-G4a. Similar to W-MA-3160-001-G010 but with different date. Oct. 2, 1854.

Rarity: —

$2 • **W-MA-3160-002-G020**

SI

Engraver: Rawdon, Wright, Hatch & Edson / New England Bank Note Co. ***Comments:*** H-MA-1195-G8. 18__. 1849–1850s.

Rarity: —

$2 • **W-MA-3160-002-G020a**

Left: Cattle, Farmers plowing, Train / 2. ***Center:*** 2. ***Right:*** 2 / Cattle and hogs. ***Engraver:*** Rawdon, Wright, Hatch & Edson / New England Bank Note Co. ***Comments:*** H-MA-1195-G8a. Similar to W-MA-3160-002-G020 but with different date. Oct. 2, 1854.

Rarity: —

$3 • **W-MA-3160-003-G030**

CJF

Engraver: Rawdon, Wright, Hatch & Edson / New England Bank Note Co. ***Comments:*** H-MA-1195-G12. 18__. 1849–1850s.

Rarity: —

$3 • **W-MA-3160-003-G030a**

Left: Men driving sheep across stream / 3. ***Center:*** 3. ***Right:*** 3 / Woman standing. ***Engraver:*** Rawdon, Wright, Hatch & Edson / New England Bank Note Co. ***Comments:*** H-MA-1195-G12a. Similar to W-MA-3160-003-G030 but with different date. Oct. 2, 1854.

Rarity: —

Collectors and Researchers:

If you have new information about any banks or notes listed in this volume, contact Whitman Publishing, Attn: Obsolete Paper Money, 3101 Clairmont Road, Suite G, Atlanta, GA 30329.

$5 • **W-MA-3160-005-G040**

CJF

Engraver: Rawdon, Wright, Hatch & Edson / New England Bank Note Co. ***Comments:*** H-MA-1195-G16. 18__. 1849–1850s.

Rarity: —

$5 • **W-MA-3160-005-G050**

SBG

Engraver: Rawdon, Wright, Hatch & Edson / New England Bank Note Co. ***Comments:*** H-MA-1195-G20. Proof. January 1, 1851. 1850s.

Rarity: URS-2
Proof $2,900
Selected auction price: Stack's Bowers Galleries, August 2013, Lot 25, Choice Unc $881

$5 • **W-MA-3160-005-G050a**

CC

Tint: Red lathework. ***Engraver:*** Rawdon, Wright, Hatch & Edson / New England Bank Note Co. ***Comments:*** H-Unlisted. Similar to W-MA-3160-005-G050. Proof. January 1, 1853. 1850s.

Rarity: URS-2
Proof $7,000

$10 • **W-MA-3160-010-G060**

Left: Woman riding on deer / TEN. ***Center:*** X. ***Right:*** 10 / Blacksmith, Anvil and forge. ***Engraver:*** Rawdon, Wright, Hatch & Edson / New England Bank Note Co. ***Comments:*** H-MA-1195-G24. 18__. 1849–1850s.

Rarity: —

$20 • W-MA-3160-020-G070

Left: 20 / Portrait of Daniel Webster / 20. ***Center:*** Woman with cornucopia and merchandise, Factories and shipping. ***Right:*** 20 / Woman seated between 2 and 0. ***Engraver:*** Rawdon, Wright, Hatch & Edson / New England Bank Note Co. ***Comments:*** H-MA-1195-G28. 18__. 1849–1850s.

Rarity: —

$50 • W-MA-3160-050-G080

Left: 50 / Woman. ***Center:*** Blacksmith shoeing horse. ***Bottom center:*** State arms. ***Right:*** Indian woman and child. ***Engraver:*** Rawdon, Wright, Hatch & Edson / New England Bank Note Co. ***Comments:*** H-MA-1195-G32. 18__. 1849–1850s.

Rarity: —

$100 • W-MA-3160-100-G090

Left: 100 / Portrait of Benjamin Franklin. ***Center:*** Two women flanking state arms. ***Right:*** 100 / Portrait of George Washington / 100. ***Engraver:*** Rawdon, Wright, Hatch & Edson / New England Bank Note Co. ***Comments:*** H-MA-1195-G36. 18__. 1849–1850s.

Rarity: —

Uncut Sheets

$5-$5-$5-$5 • W-MA-3160-005.005.005.005-US010

Vignette(s): ($5) Medallion head / Herd of horses running / Liberty. ***($5)*** Medallion head / Herd of horses running / Liberty. ***($5)*** Medallion head / Herd of horses running / Liberty. ***($5)*** Medallion head / Herd of horses running / Liberty. ***Comments:*** All unlisted in Haxby. Similar to MA-1195-G20, G20, G20, G20 but with different engraver imprint. January 1, 1851.

Rarity: —

$5-$5-$5-$5 • W-MA-3160-005.005.005.005-US010a

Tint(s): Red. ***Comments:*** All unlisted in Haxby. Similar to W-MA-3160-005.005.005.005-US010 but with different engraver imprint. January 1, 1851.

Rarity: —

Non-Valid Issues

$1 • W-MA-3160-001-C010

Engraver: Rawdon, Wright, Hatch & Edson / New England Bank Note Co. ***Comments:*** H-MA-1195-C4. Counterfeit of W-MA-3160-001-G010 or G010a. 18__. 1850s.

Rarity: —

$1 • W-MA-3160-001-S010

CJF

Comments: H-MA-1195-S4. 185_. 1850s.

Rarity: URS-7

VG $125; **VF** $175

$2 • W-MA-3160-002-S020

CJF

Comments: H-MA-1195-S5. Some examples have MASSACHUSETTS stamped at top center. 185_. 1850s.

Rarity: URS-7

VG $125; **VF** $175

$3 • W-MA-3160-003-S030

CJF

Engraver: Rawdon, Wright & Hatch. ***Comments:*** H-MA-1195-S10. 18__. Circa 1850.

Rarity: —

$3 • W-MA-3160-003-N010

Center: Women surrounding shield. ***Comments:*** H-MA-1195-N5. 18__. 1850s.

Rarity: —

$5 • W-MA-3160-005-S040

CJF

Engraver: Danforth, Bald & Co. ***Comments:*** H-MA-1195-S15. January 1, 1851.

Rarity: —

$5 • W-MA-3160-005-A010

Left: 5 / Female portrait / 5. ***Center:*** Man reclining with sickle, sheaf, and cornucopia in V. ***Right:*** 5 / Female portrait / FIVE. ***Overprint:*** Red 5 5 or FIVE. ***Engraver:*** Danforth, Bald & Co. ***Comments:*** H-MA-1195-A5. Altered from $5 Eastern Bank, West Killingly, Connecticut. 185_. 1850s.

Rarity: —

$10 • W-MA-3160-010-R010

Engraver: Rawdon, Wright, Hatch & Edson / New England Bank Note Co. ***Comments:*** H-MA-1195-R5. Raised from W-MA-3160-001-G010 or G010a. 18__. 1850s.

Rarity: —

$10 • W-MA-3160-010-A020

Left: Indian man standing with spear and horse, Trains and mountains / X. ***Center:*** Portrait of George Washington. ***Right:*** 10 / Mechanic reclining with sledge, Factory. ***Engraver:*** Danforth, Bald & Co. ***Comments:*** H-MA-1195-A10. Altered from $10 Eastern Bank, West Killingly, Connecticut. 185_. 1850s.

Rarity: —

Stockbridge, Massachusetts

Stockbridge was settled as a mission for the local natives in 1734, and it was chartered as a town in 1737. It was officially incorporated as Stockbridge in 1739, named after the town in England. After the railroad was established in Stockbridge in 1850, the town became a getaway resort for wealthy families. Paper mills, a cotton mill, a tannery, and grist and saw mills were located in town.

Housatonic Bank

1825–1865

W-MA-3170

History: The Housatonic Bank was chartered on February 26, 1825, with an authorized capital of $100,000 to be paid in gold and silver. The bank's circulation in 1839 was $67,830; in 1863 it was $189,337. Specie was listed at $7,130.83 in 1864.

In 1865 the business of the Housatonic Bank was succeeded by the Housatonic National Bank.

Numismatic Commentary: With the coming of the railroad, Stockbridge and close neighbor Lenox became tourist destinations in western Massachusetts. The wealthy from Boston and its suburbs summered here. The bank prospered, and many issues from various engraving companies were circulated. Many of these issues survived and are available for today's numismatists.

As of 2003 there was a $1-$2-$5-$5 tint and a $1-$2-$5-$5 discarded tint plate remaining at the American Bank Note Co. archives.

Valid Issues

$1 • W-MA-3170-001-G010

Left: Narrow panel of lathework circle segments. ***Center:*** 1 / 1 / Flower garlands and gridwork segments / 1 / 1. ***Right:*** Narrow panel of lathework circle segments. ***Engraver:*** PSSP. ***Comments:*** H-MA-1200-G2. 18__. 1820s–1830s.

Rarity: —

$1 • W-MA-3170-001-G010a

Left: ONE / D / ONE vertically. ***Right:*** ONE / D / ONE vertically. ***Engraver:*** PSSP. ***Comments:*** H-MA-1200-G4. Similar to W-MA-3170-001-G010. 18__. 1830s.

Rarity: —

$1 • W-MA-3170-001-G020

Engraver: Unverified, but likely New England Bank Note Co. ***Comments:*** H-MA-1200-G6. No description available. 18__. 1830s.

Rarity: *None known*

$1 • W-MA-3170-001-G030

Left: 1 / Medallion head / 1. ***Center:*** 1 / Woman standing / 1. ***Bottom center:*** Dog's head. ***Right:*** ONE / Woman / ONE. ***Engraver:*** Rawdon, Wright & Hatch. ***Comments:*** H-MA-1200-G8. 18__. 1840s.

Rarity: URS-3
Proof $1,000

$1 • W-MA-3170-001-G030a

Left: 1 / Medallion head bearing ONE / 1. ***Center:*** 1 / Woman standing / ONE / 1. ***Engraver:*** Rawdon, Wright & Hatch. ***Comments:*** H-MA-1200-G8a. Similar to W-MA-3170-001-G030. 18__. 1840s–1850s.

Rarity: —

$1 • W-MA-3170-001-G040

CC

Engraver: Rawdon, Wright, Hatch & Edson. ***Comments:*** H-MA-1200-G10. Proof. Plate note. 18__. 1850s.

Rarity: URS-2
Proof $2,200

$1 • W-MA-3170-001-G040a

CJF

Tint: Red-orange lathework. ***Engraver:*** Rawdon, Wright, Hatch & Edson. ***Comments:*** H-Unlisted. Similar to W-MA-3170-001-G040. Proof. 1 Jan. 1857.

Rarity: URS-3
Proof $2,250

$2 • W-MA-3170-002-G050

Left: Narrow panel of lathework circle segments. ***Center:*** 2 / 2 / Flower garlands and gridwork segments / 2 / 2. ***Right:*** Narrow panel of lathework circle segments. ***Engraver:*** PSSP. ***Comments:*** H-MA-1200-G14. 18__. 1820s–1830s.

Rarity: URS-7
F $300

$2 • W-MA-3170-002-G050a

Left: Five TWOs vertically. ***Right:*** Five TWOs vertically. ***Engraver:*** PSSP. ***Comments:*** H-MA-1200-G16. Similar to W-MA-3170-002-G050. 18__. 1830s.

Rarity: —

$2 • W-MA-3170-002-G060

Engraver: Unverified, but likely New England Bank Note Co. ***Comments:*** H-MA-1200-G18. No description available. 18__. 1830s.

Rarity: *None known*

$2 • W-MA-3170-002-G070

Left: 2 / Liberty / 2. ***Center:*** 2 / Woman, anchor, and spinning wheel, Train and factories. ***Right:*** 2 / Medallion head. ***Engraver:*** Rawdon, Wright, & Hatch. ***Comments:*** H-MA-1200-G22. 18__. 1840s.

Rarity: URS-2
Proof $1,600

$2 • W-MA-3170-002-G070a

CC

Engraver: Rawdon, Wright, & Hatch. ***Comments:*** H-MA-1200-G22a. Similar to W-MA-3170-002-G070. Proof. 18__. 1840s–1850s.

Rarity: URS-2
Proof $1,600

$2 • W-MA-3170-002-G080

CC

Engraver: Rawdon, Wright, Hatch & Edson. ***Comments:*** H-MA-1200-G24. Proof. 18__.

Rarity: URS-2
Proof $1,600

$2 • W-MA-3170-002-G080a

CJF

Tint: Green. ***Engraver:*** Rawdon, Wright, Hatch & Edson / ABNCo. monogram. ***Comments:*** H-MA-1200-G24a. Similar to W-MA-3170-002-G080 but with additional engraver imprint. 1 Jan. 1858.

Rarity: URS-3
F $750; **VF** $1,250

$3 • W-MA-3170-003-G090

Left: Narrow panel of lathework circle segments. ***Center:*** 3 / 3 / Flower garlands and gridwork segments / 3 / 3. ***Right:*** Narrow panel of lathework circle segments. ***Engraver:*** PSSP. ***Comments:*** H-MA-1200-G26. 18__. 1820s–1830s.

Rarity: —

$3 • W-MA-3170-003-G090a

Left: THREE vertically. ***Right:*** THREE vertically. ***Engraver:*** PSSP. ***Comments:*** H-MA-1200-G28. Similar to W-MA-3170-003-G090. 18__. 1830s.

Rarity: —

$3 • W-MA-3170-003-G100

Engraver: Unverified, but likely New England Bank Note Co. ***Comments:*** H-MA-1200-G30. No description available. 18__. 1830s.

Rarity: *None known*

$3 • W-MA-3170-003-G110

CC

Engraver: Rawdon, Wright & Hatch. ***Comments:*** H-MA-1200-G34. 18__. 1840s.

Rarity: URS-2
Proof $2,000

$3 • W-MA-3170-003-G110a

Left: 3 / Medallion head / 3. ***Center:*** 3 / Two men / THREE. ***Bottom center:*** State arms. ***Right:*** 3 / Female portrait / THREE. ***Engraver:*** Rawdon, Wright, Hatch & Edson. ***Comments:*** H-MA-1200-G34a. Similar to W-MA-3170-003-G110. 18__. 1840s–1850s.

Rarity: —

$5 • W-MA-3170-005-G120

Left: Lathework chain bearing MASSACHUSETTS / 5 / 5. ***Center:*** Alternating flower garlands and gridwork segments. ***Right:*** 5 / 5. ***Engraver:*** PSSP. ***Comments:*** H-MA-1200-G36. 18__. 1820s.

Rarity: —

$5 • W-MA-3170-005-G120a

Engraver: PSSP. ***Comments:*** H-MA-1200-G38. Similar to W-MA-3170-005-G120 but with spiral lathework lines. 18__. 1820s–1830s.

Rarity: —

$5 • W-MA-3170-005-G120b

Engraver: PSSP. ***Comments:*** H-MA-1200-G40. Similar to W-MA-3170-005-G120 but with spiral lathework lines. 18__. 1830s.

Rarity: —

$5 • W-MA-3170-005-G130

Comments: H-MA-1200-G42. No description available. 18__. 1830s–1840s.

Rarity: *None known*

$5 • W-MA-3170-005-G140

Left: Panel bearing FIVE DOLLARS vertically. ***Center:*** 5 / Hebe watering eagle / 5. ***Bottom center:*** Drovers and cattle. ***Right:*** Indian man / 5. ***Engraver:*** Rawdon, Wright, Hatch & Edson. ***Comments:*** H-MA-1200-G46. Beware of spurious W-MA-3170-005-S030 resembling the genuine. Jan. 1, 1854.

Rarity: —

$5 • W-MA-3170-005-G150 CC

Tint: Green. ***Engraver:*** Rawdon, Wright, Hatch & Edson. ***Comments:*** H-MA-1200-G48a. Beware of spurious W-MA-3170-005-S040 resembling the genuine. 1 Jan. 1857.

Rarity: URS-2
Proof $1,500
Selected auction price: Stack's Bowers Galleries, August 2013, Lot 24318, AU $940

$5 • W-MA-3170-005-G160

Left: FIVE / Blacksmith with sledge on shoulder, anvil, Train and factory. ***Center:*** 5 / Man plowing with black horse and white horse, Man harrowing, Train. ***Bottom center:*** Arm and hammer. ***Right:*** 5 / Two children holding grapes. ***Tint:*** Color unknown. ***Engraver:*** American Bank Note Co. ***Comments:*** H-MA-1200-G50a. 1860s.

Rarity: URS-3
Proof $3,000

$10 • W-MA-3170-010-G170

Left: Lathework chain bearing MASSACHUSETTS / 10 / 10 vertically. ***Center:*** Alternating flower garlands and gridwork segments. ***Right:*** 10 / 10 vertically. ***Engraver:*** Perkins. ***Comments:*** H-MA-1200-G52. 18__. 1820s.

Rarity: —

$10 • W-MA-3170-010-G170a

Engraver: PSSP. ***Comments:*** H-MA-1200-G54. Similar to W-MA-3170-010-G170. 18__. 1820s–1830s.

Rarity: —

$10 • W-MA-3170-010-G170b

Engraver: PSSP. ***Comments:*** H-MA-1200-G56. Similar to W-MA-3170-010-G170. 18__. 1830s.

Rarity: —

$10 • W-MA-3170-010-G180

Engraver: Unverified, but likely New England Bank Note Co. ***Comments:*** H-MA-1200-G58. No description available. 18__. 1830s.

Rarity: *None known*

$10 • W-MA-3170-010-G190

Left: 10 / Portrait of George Washington / 10. ***Center:*** X / Archimedes raising globe with lever / X. ***Bottom center:*** Ceres. ***Right:*** TEN / Portrait / TEN vertically. ***Engraver:*** Rawdon, Wright & Hatch. ***Comments:*** H-MA-1200-G62. 18__. 1840s.

Rarity: —

$10 • W-MA-3170-010-G200

Left: Liberty standing with pole and cap / TEN. ***Center:*** 10 / Men with animals lying down. ***Bottom center:*** White horse. ***Right:*** 10 / Woman carrying pole and X. ***Engraver:*** Rawdon, Wright, Hatch & Edson. ***Comments:*** H-MA-1200-G64. June 1, 1854.

Rarity: URS-3
Proof $2,000

$20 • W-MA-3170-020-G210

Left: Lathework chain with MASSACHUSETTS / 20 / 20 vertically. ***Center:*** Alternating flower garlands and gridwork segments. ***Right:*** 20 / 20 vertically. ***Engraver:*** PSSP. ***Comments:*** H-MA-1200-G68. 18__. 1820s–1830s.

Rarity: —

$20 • W-MA-3170-020-G220

Engraver: Unverified, but likely New England Bank Note Co. ***Comments:*** H-MA-1200-G70. No description available. 18__. 1830s–1840s.

Rarity: *None known*

$20 • W-MA-3170-020-G230 JF

Engraver: Rawdon, Wright, Hatch & Edson. ***Comments:*** H-MA-1200-G72. Proof. June 1, 1854.

Rarity: URS-3
Proof $2,000

$50 • W-MA-3170-050-G240

Left: Lathework chain bearing MASSACHUSETTS / 50 / 50 vertically. ***Center:*** Alternating flower garlands and gridwork segments. ***Right:*** 50 / 50 vertically. ***Engraver:*** PSSP. ***Comments:*** H-MA-1200-G76. 18__. 1820s–1830s.

Rarity: —

$50 • W-MA-3170-050-G250

Engraver: Unverified, but likely New England Bank Note Co. ***Comments:*** H-MA-1200-G78. No description available. 18__. 1830s–1840s.

Rarity: *None known*

$50 • W-MA-3170-050-G260

Left: 50 / Female portrait. ***Center:*** Indian man and sailor flanking shield, Two women flanking shield surmounted by eagle / 50. ***Right:*** Winged woman standing with trumpet and wreath, Liberty seated with pole and cap, Eagle and cornucopia. ***Engraver:*** Rawdon, Wright, Hatch & Edson. ***Comments:*** H-MA-1200-G82. June 1, 1854.

Rarity: —

$100 • W-MA-3170-100-G270

Left: Lathework chain bearing MASSACHUSETTS / 100 / 100 vertically. ***Center:*** Alternating flower garlands and gridwork segments. ***Right:*** 100 / 100 vertically. ***Engraver:*** Perkins. ***Comments:*** H-MA-1200-G84. 18__. 1820s–1830s.

Rarity: —

$100 • W-MA-3170-100-G280

Engraver: Unverified, but likely New England Bank Note Co. ***Comments:*** H-MA-1200-G86. No description available. 18__. 1830s–1840s.

Rarity: *None known*

Non-Valid Issues

$1 • W-MA-3170-001-N010

Center: Sailor seated by coil of rope and anchor. ***Comments:*** H-MA-1200-N5.

Rarity: —

$1 • W-MA-3170-001-A010

CC

Overprint: Red ONE. ***Engraver:*** Toppan, Carpenter & Co. ***Comments:*** H-Unlisted. Nov. 1, 1852.

Rarity: —

$2 • W-MA-3170-002-A020

Left: 2 / Reaper sharpening scythe. ***Center:*** Canal scene, Man on horse, Men loading hay and train. ***Right:*** Woman / 2 / Portrait of Lewis Cass. ***Overprint:*** Red TWO. ***Engraver:*** Toppan, Carpenter, Casilear & Co. ***Comments:*** H-MA-1200-A5. Altered from $2 Erie and Kalamazoo Railroad Bank, Adrian, Michigan. Aug. 1, 1853 or 1854.

Rarity: —

$2 • W-MA-3170-002-A030

Left: TWO / Woman feeding chickens. ***Center:*** Ships / TWO. ***Right:*** 2 / Portrait of seated woman. ***Engraver:*** Danforth, Wright & Co. ***Comments:*** H-MA-1200-A10. Altered from $2 Commercial Bank of New Jersey, Perth Amboy, New Jersey series. July 10, 1856.

Rarity: —

$3 • W-MA-3170-003-S010

CJF

Engraver: New England Bank Note Co. ***Comments:*** H-MA-1200-S5. Sept. 2, 185_. 1850s.

Rarity: —
VG $110

$3 • W-MA-3170-003-N020

Center: Female portrait / Man holding hat / Female portrait. ***Right:*** Woman. ***Comments:*** H-MA-1200-N10.

Rarity: —

$5 • W-MA-3170-005-R010

Engraver: Rawdon, Wright, Hatch & Edson. ***Comments:*** H-MA-1200-R5. Raised from W-MA-3170-002-G080. Jan. 1, 1854.

Rarity: —

$5 • W-MA-3170-005-S020

CJF

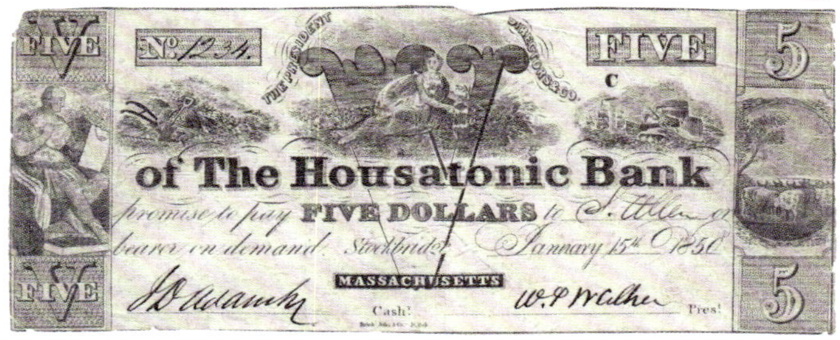

Engraver: Balch, Stiles & Co. ***Comments:*** H-MA-1200-S10. January 15, 1850.

Rarity: —
VG $75

$5 • W-MA-3170-005-S030

CJF

Engraver: Rawdon, Wright, Hatch & Edson. ***Comments:*** H-MA-1200-S15. Spurious design imitating a rough verbal description of W-MA-3170-005-G140. 1 Jan. 1854.

Rarity: —

$5 • W-MA-3170-005-S030a

Left: FIVE vertically. ***Center:*** 5 / Woman with eagle / 5. ***Bottom center:*** Horse's head. ***Right:*** Indian man standing / 5. ***Engraver:*** Rawdon, Wright, Hatch & Edson. ***Comments:*** H-MA-1200-S15a. Similar to W-MA-3170-005-S030 but with female portrait glued over central vignette. Jan. 1, 1854.

Rarity: —

$5 • W-MA-3170-005-S040

CC

Tint: Green lathework. ***Engraver:*** Rawdon, Wright, Hatch & Edson. ***Comments:*** H-MA-1200-S20. Spurious design imitating a rough verbal description of W-MA-3170-005-G150. April 6, 1857.

Rarity: URS-7
VG $125; **VF** $175

$5 • W-MA-3170-005-N030

Left: Indian man. ***Center:*** Farmer sharpening scythe. ***Comments:*** H-MA-1200-N15.

Rarity: —

$5 • W-MA-3170-005-N040

Left: FIVE / Blacksmith. ***Center:*** Man plowing with two horses. ***Right:*** 5 / Two children. ***Tint:*** Green. ***Comments:*** H-MA-1200-N20.

Rarity: —

$5 • W-MA-3170-005-A040

Left: V in FIVE / Man seated with child on knee, Woman and boy standing, Dog. ***Center:*** Man in boat, Men, Woman and boy on raft. ***Right:*** 5 / Ceres kneeling, Woman standing behind her. ***Engraver:*** Danforth, Wright & Co. ***Comments:*** H-MA-1200-A15. Altered from $5 Brownville Bank and Land Co., Omaha City, Nebraska series. Sept. 1, 1857.

Rarity: —

$10 • W-MA-3170-010-R020

Engraver: Rawdon, Wright, Hatch & Edson. ***Comments:*** H-MA-1200-R10. Raised from W-MA-3170-001-G040. 18__. 1850s.

Rarity: —

$10 • W-MA-3170-010-R030

Engraver: Rawdon, Wright, Hatch & Edson. ***Comments:*** H-MA-1200-R15. Raised from W-MA-3170-002-G080. Jan. 1, 1854.

Rarity: —

$20 • W-MA-3170-020-R040

Engraver: Rawdon, Wright, Hatch & Edson. ***Comments:*** H-MA-1200-R20. Raised from W-MA-3170-001-G010a. Jan. 1, 1854.

Rarity: —

Taunton, Massachusetts

Taunton was originally called Cohannet and was incorporated as a town in 1639. Most of the settlers hailed from Taunton, England. It was the site for many battles during King Philip's War and the Revolutionary War.

Taunton was known as the "Silver City" during the 19th century due to the large number of silversmiths and jewelry firms here. The town was also important in the iron industry, taking bog iron from the various swamps in the area. Stoves, tacks, and machinery were made here, as well as machines for textiles and steam locomotives. Textile mills were important as were felt businesses and brick making. Grain was shipped from inland farms to the rest of Massachusetts through Taunton via the Taunton River.

Bristol County Bank

1832–1864

W-MA-3180

History: The Bristol County Bank was incorporated on March 6, 1832, with an authorized capital of $100,000. In later years and in steps this value was increased to $500,000. Circulation in 1839 was $52,334.25. It reached a high of $497,768 in 1863. Specie of the bank amounted to $14,018.79, and real estate was valued at $10,000.

The business of the Bristol County Bank was succeeded by the Bristol County National Bank of Taunton, chartered on January 30, 1865.

Numismatic Commentary: Collectors should not find it hard to secure genuine notes from this bank. Some issues show the village green in Taunton, a view to a bygone era.

Valid Issues

$1 • W-MA-3180-001-G010

Left: Lathework panel bearing MASSACHUSETTS vertically. ***Center:*** 1 / 1 / Alternating flower garlands and gridwork segments / ONE / 1 / 1. ***Right:*** Lathework panel bearing ONE / D / ONE vertically. ***Engraver:*** PSSP. ***Comments:*** H-MA-1205-G2. 18__. 1830s.

Rarity: —

$1 • W-MA-3180-001-G020 CJF

Engraver: PSSP / New England Bank Note Co. ***Comments:*** H-MA-1205-G6. Proof. 18__. 1830s–1840s.

Rarity: —

$1 • W-MA-3180-001-G030

Left: 1 on medallion head / ONE / 1 on medallion head. ***Center:*** Male portrait / Ships / Portrait of George Washington. ***Right:*** 1 on medallion head / ONE / 1 on medallion head. ***Engraver:*** Underwood, Bald, Spencer & Hufty / Danforth, Underwood & Co. ***Comments:*** H-MA-1205-G8. 18__. 1840s.

Rarity: —

$1 • W-MA-3180-001-G030a JF

Overprint: Red ONE. ***Engraver:*** Underwood, Bald, Spencer & Hufty / Danforth, Underwood & Co. ***Comments:*** H-Unlisted. Similar to W-MA-3180-001-G030. 18__. 1850s.

Rarity: —

$1 • W-MA-3180-001-G040

Left: 1 / Man standing next to cogwheel. ***Center:*** Trees with houses behind. ***Right:*** 1 / Female portrait. ***Engraver:*** Toppan, Carpenter, Casilear & Co. ***Comments:*** H-MA-1205-G10. 185_.

Rarity: —

$1 • W-MA-3180-001-G040a

NJW

Overprint: Red lazy 1. ***Engraver:*** Toppan, Carpenter, Casilear & Co. ***Comments:*** H-MA-1205-G10a. Similar to W-MA-3180-001-G040. Proof. 185_. 1850s.

Rarity: URS-3
Proof $2,000

$1 • W-MA-3180-001-G040b

CJF

Overprint: Red panel outlining white ONE. ***Engraver:*** Toppan, Carpenter, Casilear & Co. / ABNCo. monogram. ***Comments:*** H-MA-1205-G10b. Similar to W-MA-3180-001-G040 but with additional engraver imprint. March 4, 1861.

Rarity: URS-4
F $600

$1.25 • W-MA-3180-001.25-G050

Left: 1 25/100 / Train / 1 25/100. ***Center:*** Sloop and other ships at sea / $1.25 cts. ***Right:*** 1 25/100 / Eagle. ***Engraver:*** New England Bank Note Co. ***Comments:*** H-MA-1205-G11. 18__. 1830s.

Rarity: —

$1.50 • W-MA-3180-001.50-G060

Left: 1 Doll. 50 Cts. vertically. ***Center:*** Eagle on rock in ocean / $1 50/100. ***Right:*** 1 50/100 / Justice. ***Engraver:*** New England Bank Note Co. ***Comments:*** H-MA-1205-G12. 18__. 1830s.

Rarity: —

$1.75 • W-MA-3180-001.75-G070

Left: $1.75 Cts. / Hebe watering eagle / 1 75/100. ***Center:*** Three sloops at sea. ***Right:*** $1.75 Cts. / Dog, Woman seated with grain / 1 75/100. ***Engraver:*** New England Bank Note Co. ***Comments:*** H-MA-1205-G13. 18__. 1830s.

Rarity: —

$2 • W-MA-3180-002-G080

Left: Lathework panel bearing MASSACHUSETTS vertically. ***Center:*** 2 / 2 / Alternating flower garlands and gridwork segments / TWO / 2 / 2. ***Right:*** Lathework panel bearing five TWOs vertically. ***Engraver:*** PSSP. ***Comments:*** H-MA-1205-G14. 18__. 1830s.

Rarity: —

$2 • W-MA-3180-002-G090

Left: 2 / Woman standing with staff, Cornucopia / TWO. ***Center:*** TWO / Machinery and merchandise flanking Ceres seated holding sickle and rake, Factories and harbor / Panel outlining white TWO. ***Right:*** 2 / Woman wearing hat, Trees / TWO. ***Engraver:*** PSSP / New England Bank Note Co. ***Comments:*** H-MA-1205-G20. 18__. 1830s–1840s.

Rarity: —

$2 • W-MA-3180-002-G100

Left: 2 / TWO on medallion head / 2. ***Center:*** Portrait of Henry Clay / Woman seated / Portrait of Daniel Webster. ***Right:*** 2 / TWO on medallion head / 2. ***Engraver:*** Underwood, Bald, Spencer & Hufty / Danforth, Underwood & Co. ***Comments:*** H-MA-1205-G22. 18__. 1840s.

Rarity: —

$2 • W-MA-3180-002-G110

Left: TWO / Woman with sheaf and mechanic seated / 2. ***Center:*** Two boilermakers at work, Factories. ***Right:*** 2 / Portrait of Millard Fillmore. ***Engraver:*** Toppan, Carpenter, Casilear & Co. ***Comments:*** H-MA-1205-G24. 185_.

Rarity: —

$2 • W-MA-3180-002-G110a

Overprint: Red lazy 2. ***Engraver:*** Toppan, Carpenter, Casilear & Co. ***Comments:*** H-MA-1205-G24a. Similar to W-MA-3180-002-G110. 185_. 1850s.

Rarity: —

$2 • W-MA-3180-002-G110b

CC

Overprint: Red panel outlining white TWO. ***Engraver:*** Toppan, Carpenter, Casilear & Co. / ABNCo. monogram. ***Comments:*** H-MA-1205-G24b. Similar to W-MA-3180-002-G110 but with additional engraver imprint. March 4, 1861.

Rarity: URS-4
VF $900

$3 • W-MA-3180-003-G120

Left: Lathework panel bearing MASSACHUSETTS vertically. ***Center:*** 3 / 3 / Alternating flower garlands and gridwork segments / THREE / 3 / 3. ***Right:*** Lathework panel bearing THREE vertically. ***Engraver:*** PSSP. ***Comments:*** H-MA-1205-G26. 18__. 1830s.

Rarity: —

$3 • W-MA-3180-003-G130

Left: THREE / Beehive and foliage / THREE. ***Center:*** Machinery and merchandise flanking Ceres seated holding sickle and rake, Factories and harbor / THREE / Panel outlining white THREE. ***Right:*** 3 on THREE / Two reapers / 3 on THREE. ***Engraver:*** PSSP / New England Bank Note Co. ***Comments:*** H-MA-1205-G30. 18__. 1830s–1840s.

Rarity: —

$3 • W-MA-3180-003-G140 CC

Engraver: Underwood, Bald, Spencer & Hufty / Danforth, Underwood & Co. ***Comments:*** H-MA-1205-G32. 18__. 1840s.

Rarity: URS-3
Proof $1,000

$3 • W-MA-3180-003-G150

Left: 3 / Three cherubs playing with 3. ***Center:*** View of Taunton Green. ***Bottom center:*** Farm tools. ***Right:*** 3 / Portrait of Henry Clay. ***Engraver:*** Toppan, Carpenter, Casilear & Co. ***Comments:*** H-MA-1205-G34. 185_.

Rarity: —

$3 • W-MA-3180-003-G150a

Overprint: Red lazy 3. ***Engraver:*** Toppan, Carpenter, Casilear & Co. ***Comments:*** H-MA-1205-G34a. Similar to W-MA-3180-003-G150. 185_. 1850s.

Rarity: —

$3 • W-MA-3180-003-G150b

Overprint: Red panel outlining white THREE. ***Engraver:*** Toppan, Carpenter, Casilear & Co. / ABNCo. monogram. ***Comments:*** H-MA-1205-G34b. Similar to W-MA-3180-003-G150 but with additional engraver imprint. March 4, 1861.

Rarity: —

$5 • W-MA-3180-005-G160

Left: Lathework chain bearing MASSACHUSETTS / 5 / 5. ***Center:*** Alternating flower garlands and gridwork segments / FIVE. ***Right:*** 5 / 5. ***Engraver:*** PSSP. ***Comments:*** H-MA-1205-G36. 18__. 1830s.

Rarity: —

$5 • W-MA-3180-005-G170

Left: 5 / Blacksmith at anvil. ***Center:*** Mercury standing with 5, Cornucopia and merchandise, Factories and ship / V / Panel outlining white FIVE. ***Right:*** 5 / Ceres kneeling / FIVE. ***Engraver:*** PSSP / New England Bank Note Co. ***Comments:*** H-MA-1205-G40. 18__. 1830s–1840s.

Rarity: —

$5 • W-MA-3180-005-G180

Left: 5 / Woman seated with staff. ***Center:*** Men in factory working. ***Right:*** 5 / Train. ***Engraver:*** Toppan, Carpenter, Casilear & Co. ***Comments:*** H-MA-1205-G42. 185_.

Rarity: —

$5 • W-MA-3180-005-G180a

Overprint: Red lazy 5. ***Engraver:*** Toppan, Carpenter, Casilear & Co. ***Comments:*** H-MA-1205-G42a. Similar to W-MA-3180-005-G180. Beware of spurious imitation W-MA-3180-005-S010. 185_. 1850s.

Rarity: URS-5
F $500; **VF** $750

$5 • W-MA-3180-005-G180b

Overprint: Red panel outlining white FIVE. ***Engraver:*** Toppan, Carpenter, Casilear & Co. / ABNCo. monogram. ***Comments:*** H-MA-1205-G42b. Similar to W-MA-3180-005-G180 but with additional engraver imprint. Mar. 4, 1861.

Rarity: —

$10 • W-MA-3180-010-G190

Left: Lathework chain bearing MASSACHUSETTS / 10 / 10 vertically. ***Center:*** Alternating flower garlands and gridwork segments / TEN. ***Right:*** 10 / 10 vertically. ***Engraver:*** PSSP. ***Comments:*** H-MA-1205-G44. 18__. 1830s.

Rarity: —

$10 • W-MA-3180-010-G200

Left: 10 / Farmer sowing / TEN. ***Center:*** Mercury standing with 10, Cornucopia and merchandise, Factories and ship, Canal scene / Panel outlining white TEN. ***Right:*** 10 / Ship / TEN. ***Engraver:*** PSSP / New England Bank Note Co. ***Comments:*** H-MA-1205-G48. 18__. 1830s–1840s.

Rarity: —

$10 • W-MA-3180-010-G210

Left: 10 / Anchor and merchandise. ***Center:*** View of river, Train on bridge, Village and mountains. ***Right:*** 10 / Portrait of Daniel Webster. ***Engraver:*** Toppan, Carpenter, Casilear & Co. ***Comments:*** H-MA-1205-G50. 185_.

Rarity: —

$10 • W-MA-3180-010-G210a

Overprint: Red. ***Engraver:*** Toppan, Carpenter, Casilear & Co. ***Comments:*** H-MA-1205-G50a. Similar to W-MA-3180-010-G210. 185_. 1850s.

Rarity: —

$10 • W-MA-3180-010-G210b

Overprint: Red panel outlining white TEN. ***Engraver:*** Toppan, Carpenter, Casilear & Co. / ABNCo. monogram. ***Comments:*** H-MA-1205-G50b. Similar to W-MA-3180-010-G210 but with additional engraver imprint. Mar. 4, 1861.

Rarity: URS-3
VF $1,250

$20 • W-MA-3180-020-G220

Left: Lathework chain bearing MASSACHUSETTS / 20 / 20 vertically. ***Center:*** Alternating flower garlands and gridwork segments / TWENTY. ***Right:*** 20 / 20 vertically. ***Engraver:*** PSSP. ***Comments:*** H-MA-1205-G52. 18__. 1830s.

Rarity: —

$20 • W-MA-3180-020-G230 JF

Engraver: PSSP. ***Comments:*** H-Unlisted. Proof. 18__.

Rarity: URS-2
Proof $750

$20 • W-MA-3180-020-G240

Left: 20 / Soldier loading gun. ***Center:*** Family at table surprised by Indians entering door. ***Right:*** 20 / Two children. ***Engraver:*** American Bank Note Co. ***Comments:*** H-MA-1205-G58. 1860s.

Rarity: —

$50 • W-MA-3180-050-G250

Left: Lathework chain bearing MASSACHUSETTS / 50 / 50 vertically. ***Center:*** Alternating flower garlands and gridwork segments / FIFTY. ***Right:*** 50 / 50 vertically. ***Engraver:*** PSSP. ***Comments:*** H-MA-1205-G60. 18__. 1830s.

Rarity: —

$50 • W-MA-3180-050-G260

Left: 50 / State arms. ***Center:*** "Landing of the Pilgrims". ***Right:*** 50 / Woman working at sewing machine. ***Engraver:*** American Bank Note Co. ***Comments:*** H-MA-1205-G66. 1860s.

Rarity: —

$100 • W-MA-3180-100-G270

Left: Lathework chain bearing MASSACHUSETTS / 100 / 100 vertically. ***Center:*** Alternating flower garlands and gridwork segments. ***Right:*** 100 / 100 vertically. ***Engraver:*** PSSP. ***Comments:*** H-MA-1205-G68. 18__. 1830s.

Rarity: URS-2
Proof $1,250

$100 • W-MA-3180-100-G280

Left: C / Two children. ***Center:*** Three cows in stream. Girl and boy seated on bank. ***Right:*** 100 / Woman seated with basket of fruit. ***Engraver:*** American Bank Note Co. ***Comments:*** H-MA-1205-G74. 1860s.

Rarity: —

$500 • W-MA-3180-500-G290

Left: Lathework chain bearing MASSACHUSETTS / 500 / 500 vertically. ***Center:*** Alternating flower garlands and gridwork segments. ***Right:*** 500 / 500 vertically. ***Engraver:*** PSSP. ***Comments:*** H-MA-1205-G76. 18__. 1820s–1830s.

Rarity: —

$500 • W-MA-3180-500-G300

Left: Hebe watering eagle, holding pole and cap. ***Center:*** D / View of Niagara Falls. ***Right:*** 500 / D. ***Engraver:*** American Bank Note Co. ***Comments:*** H-MA-1205-G82. 1860s.

Rarity: —

$1,000 • W-MA-3180-1000-G310

Left: Lathework chain bearing MASSACHUSETTS / 1000 / 1000 vertically. ***Center:*** Alternating flower garlands and gridwork segments. ***Right:*** 1000 / 1000 vertically. ***Engraver:*** PSSP. ***Comments:*** H-MA-1205-G84. 18__. 1820s–1830s.

Rarity: —

Uncut Sheets

$1-$1-$2-$3 • W-MA-3180-001.001.002.003-US010

Vignette(s): ($1) 1 on medallion head / 1 on medallion head / Male portrait / Ships / Portrait of George Washington / 1 on medallion head / 1 on medallion head. ***($1)*** 1 on medallion head / 1 on medallion head / Male portrait / Ships / Portrait of George Washington / 1 on medallion head / 1 on medallion head. ***($2)*** TWO on medallion head / Portrait of Henry Clay / Woman seated / Portrait of Daniel Webster / TWO on medallion head. ***($3)*** Medallion head / Male portrait / Three women, one with back to viewer / Portrait of Henry Clay / Medallion head. ***Comments:*** H-MA-1205-G8, G8, G22, G32. 18__. 1840s.

Rarity: —

Non-Valid Issues

$2 • W-MA-3180-002-C100

Engraver: Underwood, Bald, Spencer & Hufty / Danforth, Underwood & Co. ***Comments:*** H-MA-1205-C22. Counterfeit of W-MA-3180-002-G100. 18__. 1840s.

Rarity: —

$5 • W-MA-3180-005-R010

Engraver: Toppan, Carpenter, Casilear & Co. ***Comments:*** H-MA-1205-R5. Raised from W-MA-3180-001-G040a. 18__. 1850s.

Rarity: —

$5 • W-MA-3180-005-S010

CJF

Engraver: American Bank Note Co. ***Comments:*** H-MA-1205-S5. Spurious design imitating a rough verbal description of W-MA-3180-005-G180a. Jan. 1, 1863.

Rarity: URS-7
VF $75; **EF** $100

$5 • W-MA-3180-005-A010

Left: FIVE / Portrait of Benjamin Franklin / V. ***Center:*** 5 / Two allegorical women standing and one seated, Agricultural items and ship. ***Right:*** V / Portrait of Marquis de Lafayette / FIVE. ***Engraver:*** Terry, Pelton & Co. ***Comments:*** H-MA-1205-A5. Altered from $5 Citizens Bank, Augusta, Maine, or from notes of other failed banks using the same plate. 18__. 1840s.

Rarity: —

$10 • W-MA-3180-010-R020

Engraver: Toppan, Carpenter, Casilear & Co. ***Comments:*** H-MA-1205-R10. Raised from W-MA-3180-001-G040a. 18__. 1850s.

Rarity: —

$20 • W-MA-3180-020-R030

Engraver: Toppan, Carpenter, Casilear & Co. ***Comments:*** H-MA-1205-R15. Raised from W-MA-3180-001-G040a. 18__. 1850s.

Rarity: —

Cohannet Bank

1831–1841

W-MA-3190

History: The Cohannet Bank was chartered on March 3, 1829, with an authorized capital of $100,000. Stock subscriptions were slow, and the Legislature allowed the time for organization to be extended to 1831, in which year it opened for business. The bank suffered from the Panic of 1841, was found incapable of conducting business, and was liquidated at that time.

Numismatic Commentary: Valid issues are hard to find. Some have a pleasant view of the bank building beyond the city green, preserving a view of local interest from an era long since gone.

Valid Issues

$1 • W-MA-3190-001-G010

Left: Narrow panel of lathework circle segments. ***Center:*** 1 / 1 / Oval flower garlands and gridwork segments / 1 / 1. ***Right:*** Narrow panel of lathework circle segments. ***Engraver:*** PSSP / New England Bank Note Co. ***Comments:*** H-MA-1210-G2. 18__. 1829–1830s.

Rarity: —

$1 • W-MA-3190-001-G010a

Left: ONE / D / ONE vertically. ***Right:*** ONE / D / ONE vertically. ***Engraver:*** PSSP. ***Comments:*** H-MA-1210-G4. Similar to W-MA-3190-001-G010. 18__. 1830s.

Rarity: —

$1 • W-MA-3190-001-G020

Left: 1 / Minerva standing with 1 / 1. ***Center:*** ONE / Commerce seated with caduceus and cornucopia, Plow and ships / ONE. ***Right:*** 1 / Eagle / 1. ***Engraver:*** PSSP / New England Bank Note Co. ***Comments:*** H-MA-1210-G6. 18__. 1830s.

Rarity: —

$1 • W-MA-3190-001-G030

Left: 1 / Woman wearing bonnet with pail / ONE. ***Center:*** Machinery and merchandise flanking Ceres seated holding sickle and rake, Factories and harbor / ONE / Panel outlining white ONE. ***Right:*** 1 / Ship / ONE. ***Engraver:*** PSSP / New England Bank Note Co. ***Comments:*** H-MA-1210-G8. 18__. 1830s.

Rarity: —

$1 • W-MA-3190-001-G040

Left: ONE / Man with bow. ***Center:*** Building, Trees. ***Right:*** 1 / Man with sheep. ***Engraver:*** New England Bank Note Co. ***Comments:*** H-MA-1210-G10. 18__. 1830s–1840s.

Rarity: —

$1.25 • W-MA-3190-001.25-G050

Left: 1 25/100 / Train / 1 25/100. ***Center:*** Sloop and other ships at sea / $1.25 cts. ***Right:*** 1 / 25/100 / Eagle. ***Engraver:*** New England Bank Note Co. ***Comments:*** H-MA-1210-G12. 18__. 1830s.

Rarity: —

$1.50 • W-MA-3190-001.50-G060

Left: 1 Doll. 50 Cts. vertically. ***Center:*** Eagle on rock in ocean / $1 50/100. ***Right:*** 1 50/100 / Justice. ***Engraver:*** New England Bank Note Co. ***Comments:*** H-MA-1210-G13. 18__. 1830s.

Rarity: —

$1.75 • W-MA-3190-001.75-G070

Left: $1.75 Cts. / Hebe watering eagle / 1 75/100. ***Center:*** Three sloops at sea. ***Right:*** $1.75 Cts. / Dog, Woman seated with grain / 1 75/100. ***Engraver:*** New England Bank Note Co. ***Comments:*** H-MA-1210-G14. 18__. 1830s.

Rarity: —

$2 • W-MA-3190-002-G080

Left: Narrow panel of lathework circle segments. ***Center:*** 2 / 2 / Flower garlands and gridwork segments / 2 / 2. ***Right:*** Narrow panel of lathework circle segments. ***Engraver:*** PSSP. ***Comments:*** H-MA-1210-G16. 18__. 1829–1830s.

Rarity: —

$2 • W-MA-3190-002-G080a

Left: Five TWOs vertically. ***Right:*** Five TWOs vertically. ***Engraver:*** PSSP. ***Comments:*** H-MA-1210-G18. Similar to W-MA-3190-002-G080. 18__. 1830s.

Rarity: —

$2 • W-MA-3190-002-G090

Left: 2 / Hebe watering eagle / 2. ***Center:*** 2 / Plow, Commerce seated with caduceus and cornucopia, Ships / 2. ***Right:*** 2 / Justice standing / 2. ***Engraver:*** PSSP / New England Bank Note Co. ***Comments:*** H-MA-1210-G20. 18__. 1830s.

Rarity: —

$2 • W-MA-3190-002-G100

Left: 2 / Woman standing with staff, Cornucopia / TWO. ***Center:*** TWO / Machinery and merchandise flanking Ceres seated holding sickle and rake, Factories and harbor / Panel outlining white TWO. ***Right:*** 2 / Woman wearing hat, Trees / TWO. ***Engraver:*** PSSP / New England Bank Note Co. ***Comments:*** H-MA-1210-G22. 18__. 1830s.

Rarity: —

$2 • W-MA-3190-002-G110

CJF

Engraver: New England Bank Note Co. ***Comments:*** H-MA-1210-G24. Proof. 18__. 1830s–1840s.

Rarity: URS-3
Proof $2,500

$3 • W-MA-3190-003-G120

Left: Narrow panel of lathework circle segments. ***Center:*** 3 / 3 / Oval of flower garlands and gridwork segments / 3 / 3. ***Right:*** Narrow panel of lathework circle segments. ***Engraver:*** PSSP. ***Comments:*** H-MA-1210-G26. 18__. 1829–1830s.

Rarity: —

$3 • W-MA-3190-003-G120a

Left: THREE vertically. ***Right:*** THREE vertically. ***Engraver:*** PSSP. ***Comments:*** H-MA-1210-G28. Similar to W-MA-3190-003-G120. 18__. 1830s.

Rarity: —

$3 • W-MA-3190-003-G130

Left: 3 / Eagle on rock / 3. ***Center:*** 3 / Commerce seated with caduceus and cornucopia, Plow, Ships / 3 / Panel bearing THREE. ***Right:*** 3 / Woman standing with cornucopia / 3. ***Engraver:*** PSSP / New England Bank Note Co. ***Comments:*** H-MA-1210-G30. 18__. 1830s.

Rarity: —

$3 • W-MA-3190-003-G140

Left: THREE / Beehive and foliage / THREE. ***Center:*** Machinery and merchandise flanking Ceres seated holding sickle and rake, Factories and harbor / THREE / Panel outlining white THREE. ***Right:*** 3 on THREE / Two reapers / 3 on THREE. ***Engraver:*** PSSP / New England Bank Note Co. ***Comments:*** H-MA-1210-G32. 18__. 1830s.

Rarity: —

$3 • W-MA-3190-003-G150

Left: 3 / Indian woman seated on boulder. ***Center:*** Street scene, Public buildings, trees, and pedestrians. ***Right:*** 3 / Train. ***Engraver:*** New England Bank Note Co. ***Comments:*** H-MA-1210-G34. 18__. 1830s–1840s.

Rarity: URS-3
Proof $2,500

$5 • W-MA-3190-005-G160

Left: Lathework chain bearing MASSACHUSETTS / 5 / 5 vertically. ***Center:*** Alternating flower garlands and gridwork segments. ***Right:*** 5 / 5 vertically. ***Engraver:*** PSSP. ***Comments:*** H-MA-1210-G36. 18__. 1829–1830s.

Rarity: —

$5 • W-MA-3190-005-G160a

Engraver: PSSP. ***Comments:*** H-MA-1210-G38. Similar to W-MA-3190-005-G160 but with spiral lathework lines. 18__. 1830s.

Rarity: —

$5 • W-MA-3190-005-G170

Left: 5 / Blacksmith at anvil / FIVE. ***Center:*** Mercury standing with 5, Cornucopia and merchandise, Factories and ship / V / Panel outlining white FIVE. ***Right:*** 5 / Ceres kneeling / FIVE ***Engraver:*** PSSP / New England Bank Note Co. ***Comments:*** H-MA-1210-G40. 18__. 1830s.

Rarity: —

$5 • W-MA-3190-005-G180

JF

Engraver: New England Bank Note Co. ***Comments:*** H-MA-1210-G42. Proof. 18__. 1830s–1840s.

Rarity: URS-3
Proof $2,000

$10 • W-MA-3190-010-G190

Left: Lathework chain bearing MASSACHUSETTS / 10 / 10 vertically. ***Center:*** Alternating flower garlands and gridwork segments / TEN DOLLARS lined by zigzag ruled lines. ***Right:*** 10 / 10 vertically. ***Engraver:*** PSSP / New England Bank Note Co. ***Comments:*** H-MA-1210-G44. 18__. 1829–1830s.

Rarity: —

$10 • W-MA-3190-010-G190a

Engraver: PSSP. ***Comments:*** H-MA-1210-G46. Similar to W-MA-3190-010-G190. 18__. 1830s.

Rarity: —

$10 • W-MA-3190-010-G200

Left: 10 / Farmer sowing / TEN. ***Center:*** Mercury standing with 10, Cornucopia and merchandise, Factories and ship, Canal scene / Panel outlining white TEN. ***Right:*** 10 / Ship / TEN. ***Engraver:*** PSSP / New England Bank Note Co. ***Comments:*** H-MA-1210-G48. 18__. 1830s.

Rarity: —

$10 • W-MA-3190-010-G210

Engraver: Unverified, but likely New England Bank Note Co. ***Comments:*** H-MA-1210-G50. No description available. 18__. 1830s–1840s.

Rarity: *None known*

$20 • W-MA-3190-020-G220

Left: Lathework chain bearing MASSACHUSETTS / 20 / 20 vertically. ***Center:*** Alternating flower garlands and gridwork segments. ***Right:*** 20 / 20 vertically. ***Engraver:*** PSSP / New England Bank Note Co. ***Comments:*** H-MA-1210-G52. 18__. 1829–1830s.

Rarity: —

$50 • W-MA-3190-050-G230

Left: Lathework chain bearing MASSACHUSETTS / 50 / 50 vertically. ***Center:*** Alternating flower garlands and gridwork segments. ***Right:*** 50 / 50 vertically. ***Engraver:*** PSSP / New England Bank Note Co. ***Comments:*** H-MA-1210-G56. 18__. 1829–1830s.

Rarity: —

$100 • W-MA-3190-100-G240

Left: Lathework chain bearing MASSACHUSETTS / 100 / 100 vertically. ***Center:*** Alternating flower garlands and gridwork segments. ***Right:*** 100 / 100 vertically. ***Engraver:*** Perkins. ***Comments:*** H-MA-1210-G60. 18__. 1829–1830s.

Rarity: —

$100 • W-MA-3190-100-G250

Engraver: Unverified, but likely New England Bank Note Co. ***Comments:*** H-MA-1210-G62. No description available. 18__. 1830s.

Rarity: *None known*

$500 • W-MA-3190-500-G260

Engraver: Unverified, but likely New England Bank Note Co. ***Comments:*** H-MA-1210-G66. No description available. 18__. 1830s.

Rarity: *None known*

Non-Valid Issues

$5 • W-MA-3190-005-N010

Comments: H-MA-1210-N5. No description available. 18__. 1842.

Rarity: *None known*

Machinists Bank

1847–1865

W-MA-3200

History: The Machinists Bank was chartered on April 12, 1847, with an authorized capital of $100,000. Business began in an office in the Taunton Hotel. Capital was increased to $200,000 in 1857. Circulation in 1849 was $39,450, rising to $192,182 in 1863. The bank's corporation was to continue until 1875.

The business of the Machinists Bank was succeeded by the Machinists National Bank of Taunton after it was chartered on March 28, 1865.

Numismatic Commentary: Genuine notes from this bank are hard to locate. Nearly all were redeemed and burned, a process that extended into the first several years of operation of the national bank that succeeded its interests.

Valid Issues

$1 • W-MA-3200-001-G010

CJF

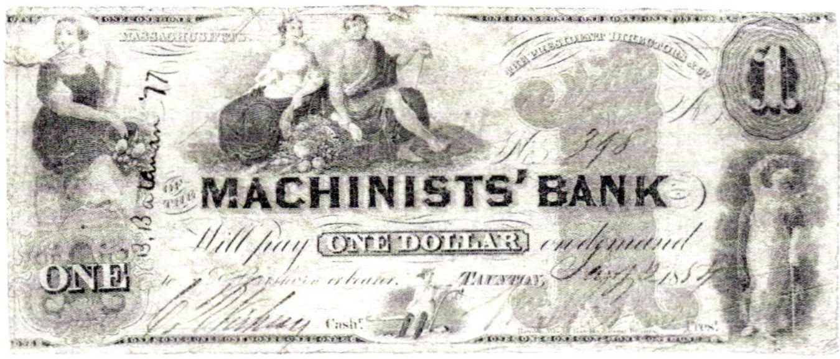

Engraver: Rawdon, Wright, Hatch & Edson. ***Comments:*** H-MA-1215-G2. 18__. 1847–1850s.

Rarity: URS-6
F $150; **VF** $250

$1 • W-MA-3200-001-G010a

Left: Woman seated / ONE. ***Center:*** Man and woman seated / 1. ***Right:*** 1 / Woman standing. ***Overprint:*** Red ONE. ***Engraver:*** Rawdon, Wright, Hatch & Edson. ***Comments:*** H-MA-1215-G2a. Similar to W-MA-3200-001-G010. 18__. 1850s.

Rarity: —

$1 • W-MA-3200-001-G010b

CJF

Overprint: Red ONE. ***Engraver:*** Rawdon, Wright, Hatch & Edson / ABNCo. monogram. ***Comments:*** H-MA-1215-G2b. Similar to W-MA-3200-001-G010 but with additional engraver imprint. 18__. 1850s–1860s.

Rarity: URS-5
F $200; **VF** $400

$1 • W-MA-3200-001-G010c

Overprint: Green ONE. ***Engraver:*** Rawdon, Wright, Hatch & Edson / ABNCo. monogram. ***Comments:*** H-MA-1215-G2c. Similar to W-MA-3200-001-G010 but with additional engraver imprint, different date, and printed serial number. Sept. 1, 1863.

Rarity: —

$2 • W-MA-3200-002-G020

Left: Woman seated / TWO. ***Center:*** TWO / 2. ***Right:*** 2 / Man. ***Engraver:*** Rawdon, Wright, Hatch & Edson. ***Comments:*** H-MA-1215-G4. 18__. 1847–1850s.

Rarity: —

$2 • W-MA-3200-002-G020a

Overprint: Red TWO. ***Engraver:*** Rawdon, Wright, Hatch & Edson. ***Comments:*** H-MA-1215-G4a. Similar to W-MA-3200-002-G020. 18__. 1850s.

Rarity: —

$2 • W-MA-3200-002-G020b

Overprint: Red TWO. ***Engraver:*** Rawdon, Wright, Hatch & Edson / ABNCo. monogram. ***Comments:*** H-MA-1215-G4b. Similar to W-MA-3200-002-G020 but with additional engraver imprint. 18__. 1850s–1860s.

Rarity: —

$2 • W-MA-3200-002-G020c

Overprint: Green TWO. ***Engraver:*** Rawdon, Wright, Hatch & Edson / ABNCo. monogram. ***Comments:*** H-MA-1215-G4c. Similar to W-MA-3200-002-G020 but with additional engraver imprint and different date. Sept. 1, 1863.

Rarity: —

$3 • W-MA-3200-003-G030

Left: Woman seated holding pen, one hand on globe / THREE. ***Center:*** 3. ***Bottom center:*** Indian man. ***Right:*** 3 / Two women standing with caduceus and sickle. ***Engraver:*** Rawdon, Wright, Hatch & Edson. ***Comments:*** H-MA-1215-G6. 18__. 1847–1850s.

Rarity: —

$3 • W-MA-3200-003-G030a

Overprint: Red THREE. ***Engraver:*** Rawdon, Wright, Hatch & Edson. ***Comments:*** H-MA-1215-G6a. Similar to W-MA-3200-003-G030. 18__. 1850s.

Rarity: —

$3 • W-MA-3200-003-G030b

Overprint: Red THREE. ***Engraver:*** Rawdon, Wright, Hatch & Edson / ABNCo. monogram. ***Comments:*** H-MA-1215-G6b. Similar to W-MA-3200-003-G030 but with additional engraver imprint. 18__. 1850s–1860s.

Rarity: —

$3 • W-MA-3200-003-G030c

Overprint: Green THREE. ***Engraver:*** Rawdon, Wright, Hatch & Edson / ABNCo. monogram. ***Comments:*** H-MA-1215-G6c. Similar to W-MA-3200-003-G030 but with additional engraver imprint and different date. Sept. 1, 1863.

Rarity: —

$5 • W-MA-3200-005-G040

Left: Train / FIVE. ***Center:*** V / Ceres kneeling. ***Right:*** 5 / Minerva standing. ***Engraver:*** Rawdon, Wright, Hatch & Edson. ***Comments:*** H-MA-1215-G8. 18__. 1847–1850s.

Rarity: —

$5 • W-MA-3200-005-G040a

Overprint: Red. ***Engraver:*** Rawdon, Wright, Hatch & Edson. ***Comments:*** H-MA-1215-G8a. Similar to W-MA-3200-005-G040. 18__. 1850s.

Rarity: —

$5 • W-MA-3200-005-G040b

Overprint: Red. ***Engraver:*** Rawdon, Wright, Hatch & Edson / ABNCo. monogram. ***Comments:*** H-MA-1215-G8b. Similar to W-MA-3200-005-G040 but with additional engraver imprint. 18__. 1850s–1860s.

Rarity: —

$10 • W-MA-3200-010-G050

Left: Eagle on limb, Canal and train / TEN. ***Right:*** 10 / Woman holding cornucopia, Anchor. ***Engraver:*** Rawdon, Wright, Hatch & Edson. ***Comments:*** H-MA-1215-G10. 18__. 1847–1850s.

Rarity: —

$10 • W-MA-3200-010-G050a

Overprint: Red. ***Engraver:*** Rawdon, Wright, Hatch & Edson. ***Comments:*** H-MA-1215-G10a. Similar to W-MA-3200-010-G050. 18__. 1850s.

Rarity: —

$10 • W-MA-3200-010-G050b

Overprint: Red. ***Engraver:*** Rawdon, Wright, Hatch & Edson / ABNCo. monogram. ***Comments:*** H-MA-1215-G10b. Similar to W-MA-3200-010-G050 but with additional engraver imprint. 18__. 1850s–1860s.

Rarity: —

$20 • W-MA-3200-020-G060

Left: 20 / Minerva standing with spear. ***Center:*** Woman seated between 2 and 0. ***Right:*** 20 / Woman reclining on cornucopia / 20. ***Engraver:*** Rawdon, Wright, Hatch & Edson. ***Comments:*** H-MA-1215-G12. 18__. 1847–1850s.

Rarity: —

$20 • W-MA-3200-020-G070

Left: Woman standing with eagle / 20. ***Center:*** TWENTY across 20 / Female portrait. ***Right:*** 20 / Portrait of Benjamin Franklin. ***Engraver:*** New England Bank Note Co. ***Comments:*** H-MA-1215-G14. 18__. 1850s.

Rarity: —

$20 • W-MA-3200-020-G080 JF

Tint: Green 20, 20, and TWENTY. ***Engraver:*** American Bank Note Co. ***Comments:*** H-MA-1215-G16a. Proof. Plate note. Aug. 1, 1860.

Rarity: URS-1
Proof $5,500
Selected auction price: Stack's Bowers Galleries, August 2014, Lot 2095, Proof $4,993

$50 • W-MA-3200-050-G090

Left: 50 / Minerva standing by column. ***Center:*** Ceres and Vulcan flanking cornucopia. ***Right:*** 50 / Cherub in sailboat / 50. ***Engraver:*** Rawdon, Wright, Hatch & Edson. ***Comments:*** H-MA-1215-G18. 18__. 1847–1850s.

Rarity: —

$50 • W-MA-3200-050-G100

Left: FIFTY / Sheaves and fruit / 50. ***Center:*** 50 / Three women seated with eagle, pole and cap, shield, scales, and book. ***Right:*** FIFTY across 50 / Vulcan seated with tools, Train. ***Engraver:*** New England Bank Note Co. ***Comments:*** H-MA-1215-G20. 18__. 1850s.

Rarity: —

$50 • W-MA-3200-050-G110 CC

Tint: Green dies bearing L and panel of microlettering. ***Engraver:*** American Bank Note Co. ***Comments:*** H-MA-1215-G22a. August 1, 1860.

Rarity: URS-1
Proof $7,700
Selected auction price: Stack's Bowers Galleries, August 2014, Lot 2096, Proof $7,637

$100 • W-MA-3200-100-G120

Left: 100 / Vulcan seated with sledge and anchor. ***Center:*** Train on bridge, Eagle on limb, Canal locks / C C. ***Bottom center:*** 100. ***Right:*** 100 / Ceres seated, Cornucopia. ***Engraver:*** Rawdon, Wright, Hatch & Edson. ***Comments:*** H-MA-1215-G24. 18__. 1847–1850s.

Rarity: —

$100 • W-MA-3200-100-G130

Left: C / Men with fishing boat at shore / 100. ***Center:*** Eagle perched on bale, Cornucopia and sheaf. ***Right:*** 100 / Ceres / 100. ***Engraver:*** New England Bank Note Co. ***Comments:*** H-MA-1215-G26. 18__. 1850s.

Rarity: —

$100 • W-MA-3200-100-G140 CC

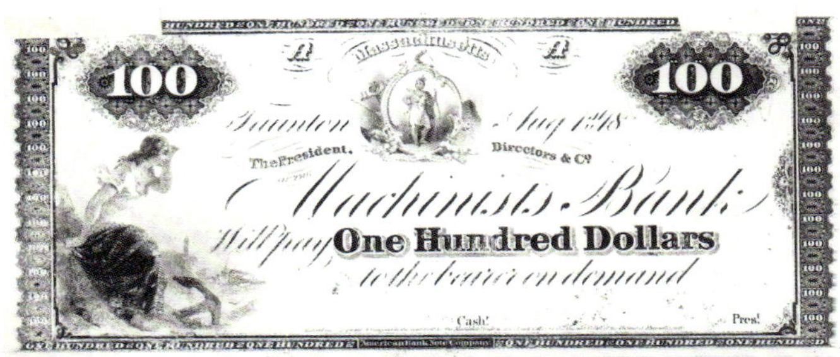

Engraver: American Bank Note Co. ***Comments:*** H-Unlisted. Aug. 1, 18__.

Rarity: URS-1
Proof $2,500

$100 • W-MA-3200-100-G140a

Left: 100 / Woman on rock shading eyes with hand and gazing at steamship. ***Center:*** State arms. ***Right:*** 100. ***Tint:*** Green. ***Engraver:*** American Bank Note Co. ***Comments:*** H-MA-1215-G28a. Similar to W-MA-3200-100-G140. Aug. 1, 1860.

Rarity: URS-1
Proof $10,000

$500 • W-MA-3200-500-G150

Left: Indian paddling canoe, Forest and mountains / 500 / D D. ***Right:*** 500 / Justice. ***Engraver:*** New England Bank Note Co. ***Comments:*** H-MA-1215-G30. 18__. 1847–1850s.

Rarity: —

$500 • W-MA-3200-500-G160

Left: 500 / D. ***Center:*** Two soldiers talking, one seated on gun carriage and one resting on gun, Fort and flags. ***Right:*** 500. ***Tint:*** Green D. ***Engraver:*** American Bank Note Co. ***Comments:*** H-MA-1215-G32a. Aug. 1, 1860.

Rarity: —

Non-Valid Issues

$2 • W-MA-3200-002-S010

Left: TWO. ***Center:*** Flock of sheep drinking at trough. ***Right:*** 2 / Woman with grain. ***Comments:*** H-MA-1215-S5. 1850s.

Rarity: —

$5 • W-MA-3200-005-A010

Left: Portrait of Henry Clay / V. ***Center:*** Farmer feeding hogs. ***Bottom center:*** Dog lying down. ***Right:*** 5 / Farmer carrying basket of corn. ***Overprint:*** Red FIVE. ***Engraver:*** Wellstood, Hay & Whiting. ***Comments:*** H-MA-1215-A5. Altered from $5 Thames Bank, Laurel, Indiana. 1850s.

Rarity: —

$10 • W-MA-3200-010-R010

Engraver: Rawdon, Wright, Hatch & Edson. ***Comments:*** H-MA-1215-R5. Raised from W-MA-3200-001-G010 or G010a. 18__. 1850s.

Rarity: —

Taunton Bank

1812–1865

W-MA-3210

History: The Taunton Bank was incorporated on June 23, 1812, with an authorized capital of $100,000. The bank's capital was $250,000 in 1839 but reduced to $200,000 in 1845. In 1855 it was back up to $350,000, and in 1860 it was $400,000. The circulation of the bank was $64,066.25 in 1839; it reached $389,205 in 1863.

The business of the Taunton Bank was succeeded by the Taunton National Bank after it was chartered on March 31, 1865.

Numismatic Commentary: Examples from this bank can be found in the marketplace. Some of the earlier PSSP designs have a back with the elusive Congreve Check Plate design.

Valid Issues

$1 • W-MA-3210-001-G010

Center: 1 / 1 / Oval flower garlands and gridwork segments / ONE / 1 / 1. ***Engraver:*** PSSP. ***Comments:*** H-MA-1220-G10. 18__. 1850s–1860s.

Rarity: —

$1 • W-MA-3210-001-G010a

Left: Panel of lathework circle segments. ***Right:*** Panel of lathework circle segments. ***Engraver:*** PSSP. ***Comments:*** H-MA-1220-G12. Similar to W-MA-3210-001-G010. 18__. 1820s.

Rarity: —

$1 • W-MA-3210-001-G010b

Left: Panel of lathework circle segments. ***Right:*** Panel of lathework circle segments. ***Engraver:*** PSSP. ***Comments:*** H-MA-1220-G14. Similar to W-MA-3210-001-G010. 18__. 1820s–1830s.

Rarity: —

$1 • W-MA-3210-001-G010c

Left: ONE / D / ONE vertically. ***Right:*** ONE / D / ONE vertically. ***Engraver:*** PSSP. ***Comments:*** H-MA-1220-G16. Similar to W-MA-3210-001-G010. 18__. 1830s.

Rarity: —

$1 • W-MA-3210-001-G020

Left: 1 / Woman leaning on pillar / 1. ***Center:*** ONE / Woman reclining, Plow / ONE. ***Right:*** 1 / 1. ***Engraver:*** PSSP. ***Comments:*** H-MA-1220-G18a. 18__. 1830s.

Rarity: —

$1 • W-MA-3210-001-G020a

Back: Plain. ***Engraver:*** PSSP. ***Comments:*** H-MA-1220-G18b. Similar to W-MA-3210-001-G020. 18__. 1830s.

Rarity: —

$1 • W-MA-3210-001-G030

Left: 1 / Woman wearing bonnet with pail / ONE. ***Center:*** Machinery and merchandise flanking Ceres seated holding sickle and rake, Factories and harbor / ONE / Panel outlining white ONE. ***Right:*** 1 / Ship / ONE. ***Engraver:*** PSSP / New England Bank Note Co. ***Comments:*** H-MA-1220-G20. 18__. 1830s–1840s.

Rarity: —

$1 • W-MA-3210-001-G040

CJF

Engraver: New England Bank Note Co. ***Comments:*** H-MA-1220-G22. 18__. 1840s–1850s.

Rarity: —

How to Read the Whitman Numbering System

$1 • W-MA-010-001-G010a

Denomination: Value of the note shown.

W: Whitman number. This number is a sortable code unique to each bank and note.

MA: Abbreviation for the state under study.

010: Numerical designation specific to each bank.

001: The denomination in dollars.

G010a: G indicates a good or valid note. Other categories are indicated thus: C (counterfeit); R (raised); S (spurious); N (not-attributed); A (altered). Numbers are assigned starting with 010, 020, et seq. Terminal letters following the number indicate variations of a note: a series of different colored overprints, tints, payees, etc., all on the same design of note. For more information, see the "How to Use This Book" section at the front of the volume, page xiv.

$1 • W-MA-3210-001-G040a

Left: 1 / Man / ONE. ***Center:*** Haying scene / 1 / Ships. ***Right:*** 1 / Man. ***Overprint:*** Green ONE. ***Engraver:*** New England Bank Note Co. ***Comments:*** H-MA-1220-G22a. Similar to W-MA-3210-001-G040. 18__. 1850s.

Rarity: —

$1 • W-MA-3210-001-G040b

Overprint: Green ONE. ***Engraver:*** New England Bank Note Co. / ABNCo. monogram. ***Comments:*** H-MA-1220-G22b. Similar to W-MA-3210-001-G040 but with additional engraver imprint. 18__. 1850s–1860s.

Rarity: URS-6
F $950

$1 • W-MA-3210-001-G040c

CC

Overprint: Red ONE. ***Engraver:*** New England Bank Note Co. / ABNCo. monogram. ***Comments:*** H-Unlisted. Similar to W-MA-3210-001-G040 but with additional engraver imprint. 18__. 1850s–1860s.

Rarity: URS-3
F $1,000

$1 • W-MA-3210-001-G050

CC

Tint: Green. ***Engraver:*** National Bank Note Co. ***Comments:*** H-MA-1220-G24a. Proof. 18__. 1860s.

Rarity: URS-1
Proof $9,000

$1.25 • W-MA-3210-001.25-G060

Left: 1 25/100 / Train / 1 25/100. ***Center:*** Sloop and other ships at sea / $1.25 cts. ***Right:*** 1 25/100 / Eagle. ***Engraver:*** New England Bank Note Co. ***Comments:*** H-MA-1220-G26. 18__. 1830s.

Rarity: —

$1.50 • W-MA-3210-001.50-G070

Left: 1 Doll 50 Cts vertically. ***Center:*** Eagle on rock in ocean / $1 50/100. ***Right:*** 1 50/100 / Justice. ***Engraver:*** New England Bank Note Co. ***Comments:*** H-MA-1220-G28. 18__. 1830s.

Rarity: —

$1.75 • W-MA-3210-001.75-G080

Left: $1.75 Cts. / Hebe watering eagle / 1 75/100. ***Center:*** Three sloops at sea. ***Right:*** $1.75 Cts. / Dog, Woman seated with grain / 1 75/100. ***Engraver:*** New England Bank Note Co. ***Comments:*** H-MA-1220-G30. 18__. 1830s.

Rarity: —

$2 • W-MA-3210-002-G090

Center: 2 / 2 / Flower garlands and gridwork segments / TWO / 2 / 2. ***Engraver:*** PSSP. ***Comments:*** H-MA-1220-G32. 18__. 1810s–1820s.

Rarity: —

$2 • W-MA-3210-002-G090a

Left: Panel of lathework circle segments. ***Right:*** Panel of lathework circle segments. ***Engraver:*** PSSP. ***Comments:*** H-MA-1220-G34. Similar to W-MA-3210-002-G090. 18__. 1820s.

Rarity: —

$2 • W-MA-3210-002-G090b

Left: Panel of lathework circle segments. ***Right:*** Panel of lathework circle segments. ***Engraver:*** PSSP. ***Comments:*** H-MA-1220-G36. Similar to W-MA-3210-002-G090. 18__. 1820s–1830s.

Rarity: —

$2 • W-MA-3210-002-G090c

Left: Five TWOs vertically. ***Right:*** Five TWOs vertically. ***Engraver:*** PSSP. ***Comments:*** H-MA-1220-G38. Similar to W-MA-3210-002-G090. 18__. 1830s.

Rarity: —

$2 • W-MA-3210-002-G100

QDB, QDB

Back: Red and brown Check Plate. ***Engraver:*** PSSP. ***Comments:*** H-MA-1220-G40a. Genuine notes with forged signatures have been reported. 18__. 1830s.

Rarity: URS-2
F $2,500

$2 • W-MA-3210-002-G100a

Left: 2 / Hebe watering eagle / 2. ***Center:*** 2 / Ceres seated with plow / 2. ***Right:*** 2 / Justice standing / 2. ***Back:*** Plain. ***Engraver:*** PSSP. ***Comments:*** H-MA-1220-G40b. Similar to W-MA-3210-002-G100. 18__. 1830s.

Rarity: —

$2 • **W-MA-3210-002-G110**
Left: 2 / Woman standing with staff, Cornucopia / TWO. ***Center:*** TWO / Machinery and merchandise flanking Ceres seated holding sickle and rake, Factories and harbor / Panel outlining white TWO. ***Right:*** 2 / Woman wearing hat, Trees / TWO. ***Engraver:*** New England Bank Note Co. / PSSP. ***Comments:*** H-MA-1220-G42. 18__. 1830s–1840s.

Rarity: —

$2 • **W-MA-3210-002-G120**

CJF

Overprint: Red TWO. ***Engraver:*** New England Bank Note Co. ***Comments:*** H-MA-1220-G44. 18__. 1840s–1850s.

Rarity: —

$2 • **W-MA-3210-002-G120a**
Left: TWO / Indian man standing with bow / 2. ***Center:*** Eagle / 2 / George Washington on horseback. ***Right:*** 2 / Train. ***Overprint:*** Green TWO. ***Engraver:*** New England Bank Note Co. ***Comments:*** H-MA-1220-G44a. Similar to W-MA-3210-002-G120. 18__. 1850s.

Rarity: —

$2 • **W-MA-3210-002-G120b**
Overprint: Red TWO. ***Engraver:*** New England Bank Note Co. / ABNCo. monogram. ***Comments:*** H-MA-1220-G44b. Similar to W-MA-3210-002-G120 but with additional engraver imprint. 18__. 1850s–1860s.

Rarity: —

$2 • **W-MA-3210-002-G130**

HA

Tint: Green. ***Engraver:*** National Bank Note Co. ***Comments:*** H-MA-1220-G46a. Proof. March 4, 186_. 1860s.

Rarity: URS-3
Proof $7,500

$3 • **W-MA-3210-003-G140**
Center: 3 / 3 / Oval of flower garlands and gridwork segments / 3 / 3. ***Engraver:*** PSSP. ***Comments:*** H-MA-1220-G48. 18__. 1810s–1820s.

Rarity: —

$3 • **W-MA-3210-003-G140a**
Left: Panel of lathework circle segments. ***Right:*** Panel of lathework circle segments. ***Engraver:*** PSSP. ***Comments:*** H-MA-1220-G50. Similar to W-MA-3210-003-G140. 18__. 1820s.

Rarity: —

$3 • **W-MA-3210-003-G140b**
Left: Panel of lathework circle segments. ***Right:*** Panel of lathework circle segments. ***Engraver:*** PSSP. ***Comments:*** H-MA-1220-G52. Similar to W-MA-3210-003-G140. 18__. 1820s–1830s.

Rarity: —

$3 • **W-MA-3210-003-G140c**
Left: THREE vertically. ***Right:*** THREE vertically. ***Engraver:*** PSSP. ***Comments:*** H-MA-1220-G54. Similar to W-MA-3210-003-G140. 18__. 1830s.

Rarity: —

$3 • **W-MA-3210-003-G150**

TD, TD

Back: Red and brown Check Plate. ***Engraver:*** PSSP. ***Comments:*** H-MA-1220-G56a. Genuine notes with forged signatures have been reported. 18__. 1830s.

Rarity: —

$3 • **W-MA-3210-003-G150a**
Left: 3 / Eagle on rock / 3. ***Center:*** 3 / Plow, Commerce seated with caduceus and cornucopia, Ships / 3 / Panel bearing THREE. ***Right:*** 3 / Woman standing with cornucopia / 3. ***Back:*** Plain. ***Engraver:*** PSSP. ***Comments:*** H-MA-1220-G56b. Similar to W-MA-3210-003-G150. 18__. 1830s.

Rarity: —

$3 • **W-MA-3210-003-G160**
Left: THREE / Beehive and foliage / THREE. ***Center:*** Machinery and merchandise flanking Ceres seated holding sickle and rake, Factories and harbor / THREE / Panel outlining white THREE ***Right:*** 3 on THREE / Two reapers / 3 on THREE. ***Engraver:*** New England Bank Note Co. ***Comments:*** H-MA-1220-G58. 18__. 1830s–1840s.

Rarity: —

$3 • **W-MA-3210-003-G170**

Left: Woman standing with sheaf and hat, Men reaping / THREE. ***Center:*** 3. ***Right:*** 3 / Man leaning on pedestal. ***Engraver:*** New England Bank Note Co. ***Comments:*** H-MA-1220-G60. 18__. 1840s–1850s.

Rarity: —

$3 • **W-MA-3210-003-G170a**

Overprint: Green THREE. ***Engraver:*** New England Bank Note Co. ***Comments:*** H-MA-1220-G60a. Similar to W-MA-3210-003-G170. 18__. 1850s.

Rarity: —

$3 • **W-MA-3210-003-G170b**

Overprint: Red THREE. ***Engraver:*** New England Bank Note Co. / ABNCo. monogram. ***Comments:*** H-MA-1220-G60b. Similar to W-MA-3210-003-G170 but with additional engraver imprint. 18__. 1850s–1860s.

Rarity: —

$3 • **W-MA-3210-003-G180**

JF

Tint: Green. ***Engraver:*** National Bank Note Co. ***Comments:*** H-MA-1220-G62a. Proof. 18__. 1860s.

Rarity: URS-2
Proof $7,500

$5 • **W-MA-3210-005-G190**

Left: Lathework panel bearing MASSACHUSETTS / 5 / 5 vertically. ***Center:*** Alternating flower garlands and gridwork segments / FIVE. ***Right:*** 5 / 5 vertically. ***Engraver:*** PSSP. ***Comments:*** H-MA-1220-G64. 18__. 1810s–1820s.

Rarity: —

$5 • **W-MA-3210-005-G190a**

Left: Lathework chain bearing MASSACHUSETTS vertically. ***Right:*** Panel of lathework circle segments. ***Engraver:*** PSSP. ***Comments:*** H-MA-1220-G66. Similar to W-MA-3210-005-G190. 18__. 1820s.

Rarity: —

$5 • **W-MA-3210-005-G190b**

Engraver: PSSP. ***Comments:*** H-MA-1220-G68. Similar to W-MA-3210-005-G190 but with spiral lathework lines. 18__. 1820s–1830s.

Rarity: —

$5 • **W-MA-3210-005-G190c**

Engraver: PSSP. ***Comments:*** H-MA-1220-G70. Similar to W-MA-3210-005-G190 but with spiral lathework lines. 18__. 1830s.

Rarity: —

$5 • **W-MA-3210-005-G200**

Left: Panel bearing FIVE / Plenty and Minerva seated / V. ***Center:*** FIVE / Allegorical woman seated / FIVE / Panel of microletters. ***Right:*** 5 / Eagle / 5. ***Back:*** Red and brown Check Plate. ***Engraver:*** PSSP. ***Comments:*** H-MA-1220-G72a. 18__. 1830s.

Rarity: —

$5 • **W-MA-3210-005-G210**

Left: 5 / Blacksmith at anvil / FIVE. ***Center:*** Mercury standing with 5, Cornucopia and merchandise, Factories and ship / V / Panel outlining white FIVE. ***Right:*** 5 / Ceres kneeling / FIVE. ***Engraver:*** New England Bank Note Co. / PSSP. ***Comments:*** H-MA-1220-G74. 18__. 1830s–1840s.

Rarity: —

$5 • **W-MA-3210-005-G220**

Engraver: New England Bank Note Co. ***Comments:*** H-MA-1220-G76. 18__. 1840s–1850s.

Rarity: —

$5 • **W-MA-3210-005-G220a**

Overprint: Green FIVE. ***Engraver:*** New England Bank Note Co. ***Comments:*** H-MA-1220-G76a. Similar to W-MA-3210-005-G220. 18__. 1850s.

Rarity: —

$5 • **W-MA-3210-005-G220b**

Overprint: Red FIVE. ***Engraver:*** New England Bank Note Co. / ABNCo. monogram. ***Comments:*** H-MA-1220-G76b. Similar to W-MA-3210-005-G220 but with additional engraver imprint. 18__. 1850s–1860s.

Rarity: —

$5 • **W-MA-3210-005-G230**

QDB

Tint: Green. ***Engraver:*** National Bank Note Co. ***Comments:*** H-MA-1220-G78a. Proof. 18__. 1860s.

Rarity: URS-3
Proof $5,500

$5 • **W-MA-3210-005-G240**

CJF

Overprint: Red FIVE. ***Engraver:*** New England Bank Note Co. ***Comments:*** H-Unlisted. 18__. 1850s.

Rarity: —

$10 • W-MA-3210-010-G250

Left: Lathework panel bearing MASSACHUSETTS / 10 / 10 vertically. ***Center:*** Alternating flower garlands and gridwork segments. ***Right:*** 10 / 10 vertically. ***Engraver:*** Perkins. ***Comments:*** H-MA-1220-G80. 18__. 1810s–1820s.

Rarity: —

$10 • W-MA-3210-010-G250a

Engraver: Perkins. ***Comments:*** H-MA-1220-G82. Similar to W-MA-3210-010-G250. 18__. 1820s.

Rarity: —

$10 • W-MA-3210-010-G250b

Comments: H-MA-1220-G84. Similar to W-MA-3210-010-G250. 18__. 1820s–1830s.

Rarity: —

$10 • W-MA-3210-010-G250c

Engraver: PSSP. ***Comments:*** H-MA-1220-G86. Similar to W-MA-3210-010-G250. 18__. 1830s.

Rarity: —

$10 • W-MA-3210-010-G260

Left: Panel bearing TEN / Manhattan spilling water jug / TEN. ***Center:*** TEN / Ceres seated / TEN / Panel of microletters. ***Right:*** Panel bearing 10 / Portrait of Indian / 10. ***Back:*** Red and brown Check Plate. ***Engraver:*** PSSP. ***Comments:*** H-MA-1220-G88a. 18__. 1830s.

Rarity: —

$10 • W-MA-3210-010-G270

Engraver: Unverified, but likely New England Bank Note Co. ***Comments:*** H-MA-1220-G90. No description available. 18__. 1830s–1840s.

Rarity: *None known*

$10 • W-MA-3210-010-G280

Left: State arms / Train on bridge / 10. ***Center:*** X. ***Right:*** 10 / Farmer standing with sheaf and sickle. ***Engraver:*** New England Bank Note Co. ***Comments:*** H-MA-1220-G92. 18__. 1840s–1850s.

Rarity: —

$10 • W-MA-3210-010-G280a

Overprint: Green TEN. ***Engraver:*** New England Bank Note Co. ***Comments:*** H-MA-1220-G92a. Similar to W-MA-3210-010-G280. 18__. 1850s.

Rarity: —

$10 • W-MA-3210-010-G280b

Overprint: Red TEN. ***Engraver:*** New England Bank Note Co. / ABNCo. monogram. ***Comments:*** H-MA-1220-G92b. Similar to W-MA-3210-010-G280 but with additional engraver imprint. 18__. 1850s–1860s.

Rarity: —

$10 • W-MA-3210-010-G290

JF

Tint: Green. ***Engraver:*** National Bank Note Co. ***Comments:*** H-MA-1220-G94a. March 4, 186_. 1860s.

Rarity: URS-2

Proof $5,750

Selected auction price: Stack's Bowers Galleries, August 2014, Lot 2097, Proof $7,050

$20 • W-MA-3210-020-G300

Left: Panel bearing state arms / 20 / 20 vertically. ***Center:*** Alternating flower garlands and gridwork segments. ***Right:*** 20 / 20 vertically. ***Engraver:*** Perkins. ***Comments:*** H-MA-1220-G96. 18__. 1810s–1820s.

Rarity: —

$20 • W-MA-3210-020-G300a

Left: Lathework chain bearing MASSACHUSETTS vertically. ***Engraver:*** PSSP. ***Comments:*** H-MA-1220-G98. Similar to W-MA-3210-020-G300. 18__. 1820s–1830s.

Rarity: —

$20 • W-MA-3210-020-G310

Left: 20 / XX / 20. ***Center:*** 20 / Woman seated with scales, Sheaf and bales, Men plowing, Ship / 20. ***Right:*** TWENTY vertically. ***Engraver:*** PSSP / New England Bank Note Co. ***Comments:*** H-MA-1220-G100. 18__. 1830s.

Rarity: —

$20 • W-MA-3210-020-G320

Left: 20 / Minerva standing with spear. ***Center:*** Woman seated between 2 and 0. ***Right:*** 20 / Woman reclining on cornucopia / 20. ***Engraver:*** Rawdon, Wright, Hatch & Edson. ***Comments:*** H-MA-1220-G102. 18__. 1850s.

Rarity: —

$20 • W-MA-3210-020-G330

JF

Tint: Green. ***Engraver:*** National Bank Note Co. ***Comments:*** H-MA-1220-G104a. Proof. March 4, 186_. 1860s.

Rarity: URS-2

Proof $8,500

$50 • W-MA-3210-050-G340

Left: Panel bearing state arms / 50 / 50 vertically. ***Center:*** Text with a microletter background. ***Right:*** 50 / 50 vertically. ***Engraver:*** Perkins. ***Comments:*** H-MA-1220-G106. 18__. 1810s–1820s.

Rarity: —

$50 • W-MA-3210-050-G340a

Left: Lathework chain bearing MASSACHUSETTS vertically. ***Engraver:*** PSSP. ***Comments:*** H-MA-1220-G108. Similar to W-MA-3210-050-G340. 18__. 1820s–1830s.

Rarity: —

$50 • W-MA-3210-050-G350

Left: 50 / Cornucopia, Woman standing with ankles crossed, Staff, Anchor / 50. ***Center:*** FIFTY DOLLAR / 50. ***Right:*** FIFTY vertically. ***Engraver:*** New England Bank Note Co. / PSSP. ***Comments:*** H-MA-1220-G110. 18__. 1830s–1840s.

Rarity: —

$50 • W-MA-3210-050-G360

Left: 50 / Minerva standing by column. ***Center:*** Ceres and Vulcan flanking cornucopia. ***Right:*** 50 / Cherub in sailboat / 50. ***Engraver:*** Rawdon, Wright, Hatch & Edson. ***Comments:*** H-MA-1220-G112. 18__. 1850s

Rarity: —

$50 • W-MA-3210-050-G370

Left: Boy on horse at mill door, Two men standing by door, Girl and boy / 50. ***Center:*** Farmer seated on fence holding scythe. ***Right:*** 50 / Male portrait. ***Tint:*** Green. ***Engraver:*** National Bank Note Co. ***Comments:*** H-MA-1220-G114a. 18__. 1860s.

Rarity: —

$100 • W-MA-3210-100-G380

Left: Panel bearing state arms / 100 / 100 vertically. ***Center:*** Alternating flower garlands and gridwork segments. ***Right:*** 100 / 100 vertically. ***Engraver:*** Perkins. ***Comments:*** H-MA-1220-G116. 18__. 1810s–1820s.

Rarity: —

$100 • W-MA-3210-100-G380a

Left: Lathework chain bearing MASSACHUSETTS vertically. ***Engraver:*** Perkins. ***Comments:*** H-MA-1220-G118. Similar to W-MA-3210-100-G380. 18__. 1820s–1830s.

Rarity: —

$100 • W-MA-3210-100-G390

Left: Panel bearing C / Portrait of George Washington / C. ***Center:*** 100 / Manhattan reclining pouring water from jug, Ship / 100. ***Right:*** Panel bearing ONE HUNDRED vertically. ***Engraver:*** New England Bank Note Co. ***Comments:*** H-MA-1220-G120. 18__. 1830s–1840s.

Rarity: —

$100 • W-MA-3210-100-G400

Left: ONE HUNDRED on 100 / Portrait of William Henry Harrison. ***Center:*** Wharf scene, Men loading wagon with barrels. ***Right:*** ONE HUNDRED on 100 / Portrait of Christopher Columbus. ***Engraver:*** New England Bank Note Co. ***Comments:*** H-MA-1220-G124. 18__. 1840s–1850s.

Rarity: —

$100 • W-MA-3210-100-G410

Left: Liberty leaning on column bearing 100. ***Center:*** State arms. ***Right:*** 100 / Male portrait. ***Tint:*** Green. ***Engraver:*** National Bank Note Co. ***Comments:*** H-MA-1220-G126a. 18__. 1860s.

Rarity: —

$500 • W-MA-3210-500-G420

Left: Spread eagle on rock / 500. ***Right:*** 500 / Male portrait. ***Tint:*** Green. ***Engraver:*** National Bank Note Co. ***Comments:*** H-MA-1220-G130a. 18__. 1860s.

Rarity: —

Non-Valid Issues

$2 • W-MA-3210-002-N010

Center: Man and woman flanking shield bearing Indian man. ***Comments:*** H-MA-1220-N5.

Rarity: —

$2 • W-MA-3210-002-A010

CJF

Overprint: Red TWO. ***Engraver:*** Wellstood, Hay & Whiting. ***Comments:*** H-MA-1220-A5. Altered from $2 Thames Bank, Laurel, Indiana. August 12, 185_. 1850s.

Rarity: URS-7
VG $125; **VF** $175

$3 • W-MA-3210-003-N020

Center: Sheaf and farm implements. ***Comments:*** H-MA-1220-N10.

Rarity: —

$5 • W-MA-3210-005-S010

Left: V / Ox / V. ***Center:*** 5 / Ceres seated, Train on bridge, Sheaf and canal lock / 5. ***Bottom center:*** Sheaf, Plow. ***Right:*** Lathework panel bearing FIVE vertically. ***Comments:*** H-MA-1220-S5. 18__. 1840s.

Rarity: —

$5 • W-MA-3210-005-S020

Center: Canal scene, Woman and man under tree, Man holding two horses. ***Right:*** Liberty. ***Comments:*** H-MA-1220-S10.

Rarity: —

$5 • W-MA-3210-005-A020

HA

Overprint: Red FIVE. ***Engraver:*** Wellstood, Hay & Whiting. ***Comments:*** H-MA-1220-A10. Altered from $5 Thames Bank, Laurel, Indiana. August 12, 185_.

Rarity: URS-7
VG $125; **VF** $175

$10 • W-MA-3210-010-R010

Engraver: New England Bank Note Co. ***Comments:*** H-MA-1220-R5. Raised from W-MA-3210-001-G040. 18__. 1840s.

Rarity: —

$10 • W-MA-3210-010-R020

QDB

Tint: Blue. ***Engraver:*** National Bank Note Co. ***Comments:*** H-MA-1220-R10. Raised from W-MA-3210-001-G050. March 4, 186_. 1860s.

Rarity: —

$10 • W-MA-3210-010-R030

Engraver: New England Bank Note Co. ***Comments:*** H-MA-1220-R15. Raised from W-MA-3210-002-G120. 18__. 1840s.

Rarity: —

$10 • W-MA-3210-010-S030

CC

Comments: H-MA-1220-N15. Spurious note. Lithographed. 18__. 1840s.

Rarity: URS-7
VG $100; **VF** $150

$20 • W-MA-3210-020-N030

Center: Train, Tree. ***Bottom center:*** Pelican feeding young. ***Comments:*** H-MA-1220-N20. 18__. 1840s.

Rarity: —

$50 • W-MA-3210-050-A030

Left: 50 / Woman with frame / 50. ***Center:*** L on die / Hebe watering eagle / L on die. ***Right:*** 50 / Man with hat / 50. ***Engraver:*** Terry, Pelton & Co. ***Comments:*** H-MA-1220-A15. Altered from $50 Citizens Bank, Augusta, Maine, or from notes of other failed banks using the same plate. 18__. 1840s.

Rarity: —

$500 • W-MA-3210-500-N040

Center: Woman and agricultural implements. ***Comments:*** H-MA-1220-N25.

Rarity: —

Townsend, Massachusetts

Incorporated in 1732, Townsend was named after a British cabinet minister, Viscount Charles Townshend. The "h" started to be omitted around 1780. In 1733 the first mill was built, followed by the first dam in 1734. The dam also created the Townsend Harbor. Coopering was a large business in Townsend for many years.

Townsend Bank

1854–1865

W-MA-3220

History: The Townsend bank was chartered on March 28, 1854, with an authorized capital of $100,000. Circulation was at its lowest in 1857, amounting to $85,930. The same was at its highest in 1858 at $106,068.

The business of the Townsend Bank was succeeded by the Townsend National Bank after it was chartered in February 1865.

Numismatic Commentary: Genuine notes from this bank are hard to find. $1, $2, $3, and $5 bills all have vignettes of coins showing the equivalent dollar amount of the bill. One reason for this was to deter counterfeiting, and another was to instruct people who could not read the text of the note.

Valid Issues

$1 • W-MA-3220-001-G010

CJF

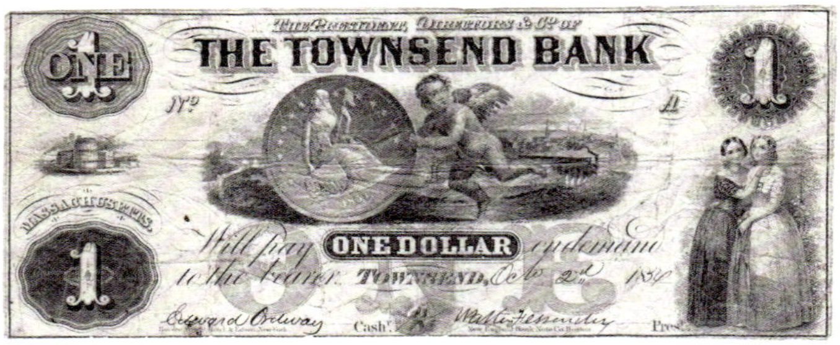

Engraver: Rawdon, Wright, Hatch & Edson. ***Comments:*** H-MA-1225-G2. 18__. 1850s.

Rarity: URS-3
F $1,500

$1 • W-MA-3220-001-G010a

Left: ONE on 1 / Barrel and bales / 1. ***Center:*** Cherub rolling silver dollar, Train and city. ***Bottom center:*** Reaper. ***Right:*** 1 / Two women standing. ***Engraver:*** Rawdon, Wright, Hatch & Edson / ABNCo. monogram. ***Comments:*** H-MA-1225-G2b. Similar to W-MA-3220-001-G010 but with additional engraver imprint. 18__. 1850s–1860s.

Rarity: —

$2 • W-MA-3220-002-G020

Left: 2 / Two women flanking shield. ***Center:*** Two cherubs and two silver dollars. ***Right:*** 2 / Woman seated between shield and 2. ***Engraver:*** Rawdon, Wright, Hatch & Edson. ***Comments:*** H-MA-1225-G4. 18__. 1850s.

Rarity: —

$2 • W-MA-3220-002-G020a

Engraver: Rawdon, Wright, Hatch & Edson / ABNCo. monogram. ***Comments:*** H-MA-1225-G4b. Similar to W-MA-3220-002-G020 but with additional engraver imprint. 18__. 1850s–1860s.

Rarity: —

$3 • W-MA-3220-003-G030

Left: 3 / Male portrait / 3. ***Center:*** Three cherubs and three silver dollars. ***Bottom center:*** Mechanic seated. ***Right:*** 3 / Portrait of girl reading book. ***Engraver:*** Rawdon, Wright, Hatch & Edson. ***Comments:*** H-MA-1225-G6. 18__. 1850s.

Rarity: —

$3 • W-MA-3220-003-G030a

Engraver: Rawdon, Wright, Hatch & Edson / ABNCo. monogram. ***Comments:*** H-MA-1225-G6b. Similar to W-MA-3220-003-G030 but with additional engraver imprint. 18__. 1850s–1860s.

Rarity: —

$5 • W-MA-3220-005-G040

Left: Hebe watering eagle / 5. ***Center:*** Five cherubs and five silver dollars. ***Right:*** 5 / Five women with 5. ***Engraver:*** Rawdon, Wright, Hatch & Edson. ***Comments:*** H-MA-1225-G8. 18__. 1850s.

Rarity: —

$5 • W-MA-3220-005-G040a

Engraver: Rawdon, Wright, Hatch & Edson / ABNCo. monogram. ***Comments:*** H-MA-1225-G8b. Similar to W-MA-3220-005-G040 but with additional engraver imprint. 18__. 1850s–1860s.

Rarity: —

$5 • W-MA-3220-005-G040b

CC

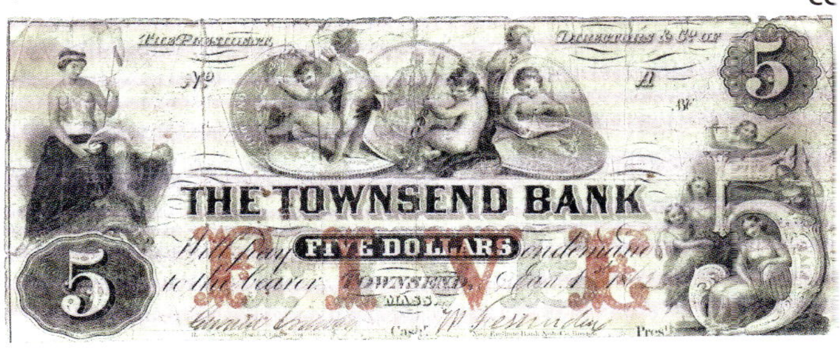

Overprint: Red FIVE. ***Engraver:*** Rawdon, Wright, Hatch & Edson / ABNCo. monogram. ***Comments:*** H-Unlisted. Similar to W-MA-3220-005-G040 but with additional engraver imprint. Jan. 1, 18__. 1860s.

Rarity: URS-3
F $1,200

$10 • W-MA-3220-010-G050

Left: 10 / X. ***Center:*** Farm woman and man seated, Three men, one with sickle, one with scythe, and one lying down. ***Right:*** X / Woman seated with distaff. ***Engraver:*** Rawdon, Wright, Hatch & Edson. ***Comments:*** H-MA-1225-G10. 18__. 1850s.

Rarity: —

$10 • W-MA-3220-010-G050a

Overprint: Red. ***Engraver:*** Rawdon, Wright, Hatch & Edson. ***Comments:*** H-Unlisted. Similar to W-MA-3220-010-G050. 18__. 1850s.

Rarity: URS-3
VF $8,000

$10 • W-MA-3220-010-G050b

Engraver: Rawdon, Wright, Hatch & Edson / ABNCo. monogram. ***Comments:*** H-MA-1225-G10b. Similar to W-MA-3220-010-G050 but with additional engraver imprint. 18__. 1850s–1860s.

Rarity: —

$20 • W-MA-3220-020-G060

Left: TWENTY / Indian woman standing with bow and spear. ***Center:*** Indian man reclining beside slain deer. ***Right:*** 20 / Farmer seated on plow, resting on die bearing XX. ***Engraver:*** Rawdon, Wright, Hatch & Edson. ***Comments:*** H-MA-1225-G12. 18__. 1850s.

Rarity: —

$20 • W-MA-3220-020-G060a

Engraver: Rawdon, Wright, Hatch & Edson / ABNCo. monogram. ***Comments:*** H-MA-1225-G12b. Similar to W-MA-3220-020-G060 but with additional engraver imprint. 18__. 1850s–1860s.

Rarity: —

$50 • W-MA-3220-050-G070

Left: 50 / Woman. ***Center:*** View of U.S. Capitol. ***Right:*** 50 / Woman feeding horse. ***Engraver:*** Rawdon, Wright, Hatch & Edson. ***Comments:*** H-MA-1225-G14. 18__. 1850s.

Rarity: —

$100 • W-MA-3220-100-G080

Left: C / Woman resting arm on tub. ***Center:*** Blacksmith shoeing horse. ***Right:*** 100 / Farm scene, Hay wagon, Tree. ***Engraver:*** Rawdon, Wright, Hatch & Edson. ***Comments:*** H-MA-1225-G16. 18__. 1850s.

Rarity: —

Non-Valid Issues

$10 • W-MA-3220-010-R010

Engraver: Rawdon, Wright, Hatch & Edson. ***Comments:*** H-MA-1225-R5. Raised from W-MA-3220-002-G020. 18__. 1850s.

Rarity: —

Troy, Massachusetts

Fall River separated from Freetown in 1803 and was incorporated on its own. A mere year after that, it changed its name to Troy, which it kept for three decades. On February 12, 1834, it changed its name back to Fall River.

See also Fall River, Massachusetts.

Fall River Bank

1825–1834

W-MA-3230

History: The Fall River Bank of Troy, Massachusetts, was chartered on February 26, 1825, with an authorized capital of $100,000. Bank notes were issued with the Troy address.

In 1834 the charter of the Fall River Bank was modified to change its location and reflect the renaming of the city of Troy to Fall River. From then on the bank was located in Fall River, giving it two locations without actually moving.

See also listing under Fall River, W-MA-1550.

Numismatic Commentary: The Fall River Bank issues with the Troy address are very rare. At least one of the PSSP design issues has a Congreve Check Plate back. Only 15 banks in various states are currently known to have used the Congreve anti-counterfeiting plate, making this a particularly desirable note to obtain.

Valid Issues

$1 • W-MA-3230-001-G010

Left: Narrow panel of lathework circle segments. ***Center:*** 1 / 1 / Oval flower garlands and gridwork segments / 1 / 1. ***Right:*** Narrow panel of lathework circle segments. ***Engraver:*** PSSP. ***Comments:*** H-MA-1230-G2. 18__. 1820s–1830s.

Rarity: —

$1 • **W-MA-3230-001-G010a**

Left: ONE / D / ONE vertically. ***Right:*** ONE / D / ONE vertically. ***Engraver:*** PSSP. ***Comments:*** H-MA-1230-G4. Similar to W-MA-3230-001-G010. 18__. 1830s.

Rarity: —

$2 • **W-MA-3230-002-G020**

Left: Narrow panel of lathework circle segments. ***Center:*** 2 / 2 / Flower garlands and gridwork segments / 2 / 2. ***Right:*** Narrow panel of lathework circle segments. ***Engraver:*** PSSP. ***Comments:*** H-MA-1230-G6. 18__. 1820s–1830s.

Rarity: —

$2 • **W-MA-3230-002-G020a**

Left: Five TWOs vertically. ***Right:*** Five TWOs vertically. ***Engraver:*** PSSP. ***Comments:*** H-MA-1230-G8. Similar to W-MA-3230-002-G020. 18__. 1830s.

Rarity: —

$3 • **W-MA-3230-003-G030**

Left: Narrow panel of lathework circle segments. ***Center:*** 3 / 3 / Flower garlands and gridwork segments / 3 / 3. ***Right:*** Narrow panel of lathework circle segments. ***Engraver:*** PSSP. ***Comments:*** H-MA-1230-G10. 18__. 1820s–1830s.

Rarity: —

$3 • **W-MA-3230-003-G030a**

Left: THREE vertically. ***Right:*** THREE vertically. ***Engraver:*** PSSP. ***Comments:*** H-MA-1230-G12. Similar to W-MA-3230-003-G030. 18__. 1830s.

Rarity: —

$5 • **W-MA-3230-005-G040**

Left: Lathework chain bearing MASSACHUSETTS / 5 / Ceres seated / 5. ***Center:*** Alternating flower garlands and gridwork segments. ***Right:*** 5 / State arms / 5. ***Engraver:*** PSSP. ***Comments:*** H-MA-1230-G14. 18__. 1820s.

Rarity: —

$5 • **W-MA-3230-005-G040a**

Engraver: PSSP. ***Comments:*** H-MA-1230-G16. Similar to W-MA-3230-005-G040 but with zigzag ruled lines. 18__. 1820s–1830s.

Rarity: —

$5 • **W-MA-3230-005-G040b**

CJF, CJF

Back: Congreve Check Plate. ***Engraver:*** PSSP. ***Comments:*** H-MA-1230-G18. Similar to W-MA-3230-005-G040 but with spiral lathework lines. 18__. 1830s.

Rarity: URS-4
F $750; **VF** $1,250

$10 • **W-MA-3230-010-G050**

Left: Lathework chain bearing MASSACHUSETTS / 10 / 10 vertically. ***Center:*** Alternating flower garlands and gridwork segments. ***Right:*** 10 / 10 vertically. ***Engraver:*** Perkins. ***Comments:*** H-MA-1230-G20. 18__. 1820s.

Rarity: —

$10 • **W-MA-3230-010-G050a**

Engraver: PSSP. ***Comments:*** H-MA-1230-G22. Similar to W-MA-3230-010-G050. 18__. 1820s–1830s.

Rarity: —

$10 • **W-MA-3230-010-G050b**

Engraver: PSSP. ***Comments:*** H-MA-1230-G24. Similar to W-MA-3230-010-G050. 18__. 1830s.

Rarity: —

$20 • **W-MA-3230-020-G060**

Left: Lathework chain bearing MASSACHUSETTS / 20 / 20 vertically. ***Center:*** Alternating flower garlands and gridwork segments. ***Right:*** 20 / 20 vertically. ***Engraver:*** PSSP. ***Comments:*** H-MA-1230-G26. 18__. 1820s–1830s.

Rarity: —

$50 • **W-MA-3230-050-G070**

Left: Lathework chain bearing MASSACHUSETTS / 50 / 50 vertically. ***Center:*** Alternating flower garlands and gridwork segments. ***Right:*** 50 / 50 vertically. ***Engraver:*** PSSP. ***Comments:*** H-MA-1230-G28. 18__. 1820s–1830s.

Rarity: —

$100 • **W-MA-3230-100-G080**

Left: Lathework chain bearing MASSACHUSETTS / 100 / 100 vertically. ***Center:*** Alternating flower garlands and gridwork segments. ***Right:*** 100 / 100 vertically. ***Engraver:*** Perkins. ***Comments:*** H-MA-1230-G30. 18__. 1820s–1830s.

Rarity: —

Non-Valid Issues

$1 • **W-MA-3230-001-S010**

Left: ONE / Woman at pedestal / ONE. ***Center:*** Three men around anvil. ***Right:*** One / Portrait of Christopher Columbus / ONE. ***Engraver:*** Draper, Toppan & Co. ***Comments:*** H-MA-1230-S5. From a modified, fraudulent plate originally for a counterfeit $1 State Bank of Indiana, Indiana. July 1, 1859.

Rarity: —

$2 • **W-MA-3230-002-A010**

Left: 2 / Sailing ship / TWO. ***Center:*** 2 / Eagle flying with shield, Ship / 2. ***Bottom center:*** Dog and strongbox. ***Right:*** 2 / Indian man seated / 2 / TWO. ***Comments:*** H-MA-1230-A5. Altered, including replacement of the left and center vignettes, from $2 Geauga Insurance Co., Painsville, Ohio. 18__. 1840s.

Rarity: —

$3 • W-MA-3230-003-A020

Left: 3 / Woman seated with arm around eagle / 3. ***Center:*** Medallion head / Steamboat / Medallion head. ***Bottom center:*** Dog and strongbox. ***Right:*** 3 / Train backed up to wharf, People standing. ***Engraver:*** Chas. E. Ely, Philadelphia. ***Comments:*** H-MA-1230-A10. Altered from $3 Geauga Insurance Co., Painesville, Ohio. 18__. 1840s.

Rarity: —

$5 • W-MA-3230-005-A030

Left: V in FIVE / Man seated with child on knee, Woman and boy standing, Dog. ***Center:*** Man in boat, Men, Woman and boy on raft. ***Bottom center:*** Dog and strongbox. ***Right:*** 5 / Train backed up to wharf, People standing / 5. ***Engraver:*** Danforth, Wright & Co. ***Comments:*** H-MA-1230-A15. Altered from $5 Geauga Insurance Co., Painesville, Ohio. Sept. 1, 1857.

Rarity: —

$5 • W-MA-3230-005-A040

Left: 5 / Train at wharf / 5. ***Center:*** 5 / Indian man seated on cliff observing town / 5. ***Bottom center:*** Dog and strongbox. ***Right:*** 5 / Train backed up to wharf, People standing / 5. ***Engraver:*** Chas E. Ely, Philadelphia. ***Comments:*** H-MA-1230-A20. Altered from $5 Geauga Insurance Co., Painesville, Ohio. 18__. 1840s.

Rarity: —

Uxbridge, Massachusetts

The town of West Mendon became Uxbridge in 1727, after the town of Mendon was burned during King Philip's War. By 1775 the industries of wool manufacturing, linen and cotton cloth, grist mills, saw mills, forges, bog iron, distilleries, and other mills had become active. An 1814 cotton mill owned by William Arnold made blue jeans, and Wheelock and Taft's Central Woolen Company made cloth for the Civil War. A granite quarry was important as well.

Blackstone Bank

1825–1865

W-MA-3240

History: The Blackstone Bank was chartered on July 18, 1825, with an authorized capital of $100,000 to be paid in silver and gold coins. The circulation of the bank was $45,293 in 1839, but it reached $86,495 in 1862. Specie was listed at $8,224.74.

The business of the Blackstone Bank was succeeded by the Blackstone National Bank of Uxbridge after it was chartered in 1865.

Numismatic Commentary: Various non-valid issues are seen on occasion in the marketplace, but genuine notes are extremely hard to locate.

Collectors and Researchers:

If you have new information about any banks or notes listed in this volume, contact Whitman Publishing, Attn: Obsolete Paper Money, 3101 Clairmont Road, Suite G, Atlanta, GA 30329.

Valid Issues

$1 • W-MA-3240-001-G010

Left: Narrow panel of lathework circle segments. ***Center:*** 1 / 1 / Flower garlands and gridwork segments / 1 / 1. ***Right:*** Narrow panel of lathework circle segments. ***Engraver:*** PSSP. ***Comments:*** H-MA-1235-G2. 18__. 1820s–1830s.

Rarity: —

$1 • W-MA-3240-001-G010a

Left: ONE / D / ONE vertically. ***Right:*** ONE / D / ONE vertically. ***Engraver:*** PSSP. ***Comments:*** H-MA-1235-G4. Similar to W-MA-3240-001-G010. 18__. 1830s.

Rarity: —

$1 • W-MA-3240-001-G020

Left: 1 / Minerva standing with 1 / 1. ***Center:*** ONE / Commerce seated with caduceus and cornucopia, Plow and ships / ONE. ***Right:*** 1 / Eagle / 1. ***Engraver:*** PSSP. ***Comments:*** H-MA-1235-G6. 18__. 1830s.

Rarity: —

$1 • W-MA-3240-001-G030

Engraver: Unverified, but likely New England Bank Note Co. ***Comments:*** H-MA-1235-G8. No description available. 18__. 1830s–1840s.

Rarity: *None known*

$1 • W-MA-3240-001-G040

Left: 1 / Portrait of George Washington. ***Center:*** Woman seated with rudder / 1 / Woman seated. ***Right:*** 1 / Portrait of Benjamin Franklin. ***Engraver:*** New England Bank Note Co. ***Comments:*** H-MA-1235-G12. 18__. 1850s.

Rarity: —

$1 • W-MA-3240-001-G050

Left: Commerce seated with rudder / 1 / Woman seated / 1. ***Center:*** 1 bearing "Presentation of the Declaration of Independence". ***Right:*** 1 / Woman standing with apron full of grain. ***Engraver:*** New England Bank Note Co. ***Comments:*** H-MA-1235-G14. 18__. 1850s.

Rarity: —

$1 • W-MA-3240-001-G060 CJF

Tint: Green. ***Engraver:*** American Bank Note Co. ***Comments:*** H-MA-1235-G16a. Jan. 1, 186_. 1860s.

Rarity: URS-6
F $300; **VF** $500

$1.25 • W-MA-3240-001.25-G070

Left: 1 25/100 / Train / 1 25/100. ***Center:*** Sloop and other ships at sea / $1.25 cts. ***Right:*** 1 25/100 / Eagle. ***Engraver:*** New England Bank Note Co. ***Comments:*** H-MA-1235-G18. 18__. 1830s.

Rarity: —

$1.50 • **W-MA-3240-001.50-G080**

Left: 1 Doll 50 Cts vertically. ***Center:*** Eagle on rock in ocean / $1 50/100. ***Right:*** 1 50/100 / Justice. ***Engraver:*** New England Bank Note Co. ***Comments:*** H-MA-1235-G19. 18__. 1830s.

Rarity: —

$1.75 • **W-MA-3240-001.75-G090**

Left: $1.75 Cts. / Hebe watering eagle / 1 75/100. ***Center:*** Three sloops at sea. ***Right:*** $1.75 Cts. / Dog, Woman seated with grain / 1 75/100. ***Engraver:*** New England Bank Note Co. ***Comments:*** H-MA-1235-G20. 18__. 1830s.

Rarity: —

$2 • **W-MA-3240-002-G100**

Left: Narrow panel of lathework circle segments. ***Center:*** 2 / 2 / Flower garlands and gridwork segments / 2 / 2. ***Right:*** Narrow panel of lathework circle segments. ***Engraver:*** PSSP. ***Comments:*** H-MA-1235-G22. 18__. 1820s–1830s.

Rarity: —

$2 • **W-MA-3240-002-G100a**

Left: Five TWOs vertically. ***Right:*** Five TWOs vertically. ***Engraver:*** PSSP. ***Comments:*** H-MA-1235-G24. Similar to W-MA-3240-002-G100. 18__. 1830s.

Rarity: —

$2 • **W-MA-3240-002-G110**

Left: 2 / Hebe watering eagle / 2. ***Center:*** 2 / Plow, Commerce seated with caduceus and cornucopia, Ships / 2. ***Right:*** 2 / Justice standing / 2. ***Engraver:*** PSSP. ***Comments:*** H-MA-1235-G26. 18__. 1830s.

Rarity: —

$2 • **W-MA-3240-002-G120**

Engraver: Unverified, but likely New England Bank Note Co. ***Comments:*** H-MA-1235-G28. No description available. 18__. 1830s–1840s.

Rarity: *None known*

$2 • **W-MA-3240-002-G130**

Left: 2 / Portrait of Christopher Columbus. ***Center:*** Woman standing with cornucopia / 2 / Justice seated. ***Right:*** 2 / Male portrait. ***Engraver:*** New England Bank Note Co. ***Comments:*** H-MA-1235-G32. 18__. 1850s.

Rarity: —

$2 • **W-MA-3240-002-G140**

Left: Men driving sheep into stream / 2. ***Center:*** 2 bearing "Presentation of the Declaration of Independence". ***Right:*** TWO / Woman seated with wreath of flowers / TWO. ***Engraver:*** New England Bank Note Co. ***Comments:*** H-MA-1235-G34. 18__. 1850s.

Rarity: —

$2 • **W-MA-3240-002-G150**

HA

Tint: Green. ***Engraver:*** American Bank Note Co. ***Comments:*** H-MA-1235-G36a. Proof. 186_. 1860s.

Rarity: URS-3
Proof $4,000

$3 • **W-MA-3240-003-G160**

Left: Narrow panel of lathework circle segments. ***Center:*** 3 / 3 / Flower garlands and gridwork segments / 3 / 3. ***Right:*** Narrow panel of lathework circle segments. ***Engraver:*** PSSP. ***Comments:*** H-MA-1235-G38. 18__. 1820s–1830s.

Rarity: —

$3 • **W-MA-3240-003-G160a**

Left: THREE vertically. ***Right:*** THREE vertically. ***Engraver:*** PSSP. ***Comments:*** H-MA-1235-G40. Similar to W-MA-3240-003-G160. 18__. 1830s.

Rarity: —

$3 • **W-MA-3240-003-G170**

Left: 3 / Eagle on rock / 3. ***Center:*** 3 / Plow, Commerce seated with caduceus and cornucopia, Ships / 3 / Panel bearing THREE. ***Right:*** 3 / Woman standing with cornucopia / 3. ***Engraver:*** PSSP. ***Comments:*** H-MA-1235-G42. 18__. 1830s.

Rarity: —

$3 • **W-MA-3240-003-G180**

Left: Portrait of George Washington. ***Center:*** Battle of Bunker Hill. ***Right:*** Portrait of George Washington. ***Engraver:*** New England Bank Note Co. ***Comments:*** H-MA-1235-G44. 18__. 1830s–1840s.

Rarity: —

$3 • **W-MA-3240-003-G190**

Left: 3 / George Washington standing by horse. ***Center:*** Female portrait / 3 / Portrait of girl with ringlets. ***Right:*** 3 / Vulcan standing with sledge. ***Engraver:*** New England Bank Note Co. ***Comments:*** H-MA-1235-G48. Beware of spurious W-MA-3240-003-S010 similar to genuine. 18__. 1850s.

Rarity: —

$3 • **W-MA-3240-003-G200**

Left: Barnyard scene, Man on horse, Boy and cattle. ***Center:*** 3. ***Right:*** 3 on THREE / Woman with flowers / THREE. ***Engraver:*** New England Bank Note Co. ***Comments:*** H-MA-1235-G50. 18__. 1850s.

Rarity: —

$3 • **W-MA-3240-003-G210**

Left: 3 / Portrait of girl. ***Center:*** 3 / Man oiling engine / 3. ***Right:*** 3 / Mechanic working at vice. ***Tint:*** Green. ***Engraver:*** American Bank Note Co. ***Comments:*** H-MA-1235-G52a. 186_. 1860s.

Rarity: —

$5 • **W-MA-3240-005-G220**

Left: Lathework chain bearing MASSACHUSETTS / 5 / 5 vertically. ***Center:*** Alternating flower garlands and gridwork segments. ***Right:*** 5 / 5 vertically. ***Engraver:*** PSSP. ***Comments:*** H-MA-1235-G54. 18__. 1820s.

Rarity: —

$5 • **W-MA-3240-005-G220a**

Engraver: PSSP. ***Comments:*** H-MA-1235-G56. Similar to W-MA-3240-005-G220 but with zigzag ruled lines. 18__. 1820s–1830s.

Rarity: —

$5 • W-MA-3240-005-G220b

Engraver: PSSP. ***Comments:*** H-MA-1235-G58. Similar to W-MA-3240-005-G220 but with spiral lathework lines. 18__. 1830s.

Rarity: —

$5 • W-MA-3240-005-G230

SBG

Engraver: PSSP. ***Comments:*** H-MA-1235-G60. Proof. 18__. 1830s–1840s.

Rarity: —

$5 • W-MA-3240-005-G240

Engraver: Unverified, but likely New England Bank Note Co. ***Comments:*** H-MA-1230-G62. No description available. 18__. 1830s–1840s.

Rarity: *None known*

$5 • W-MA-3240-005-G250

Left: Eagle on shield and anchor, Factories and ships / FIVE. ***Center:*** V with woman, cornucopia, and cherubs. ***Right:*** 5 / Girl with ringlets holding basket. ***Engraver:*** New England Bank Note Co. ***Comments:*** H-MA-1235-G66. Beware of spurious W-MA-3240-005-S020 similar to genuine. 18__. 1850s.

Rarity: —

$5 • W-MA-3240-005-G260

Left: FIVE across 5 / Male portrait. ***Center:*** Two women holding hammer and cornucopia flanking anvil, Factory. ***Right:*** 5 / Portrait of girl. ***Tint:*** Green. ***Engraver:*** American Bank Note Co. ***Comments:*** H-MA-1235-G68a. 1860s.

Rarity: —

$10 • W-MA-3240-010-G270

Left: Lathework chain bearing MASSACHUSETTS / 10 / 10 vertically. ***Center:*** Alternating flower garlands and gridwork segments. ***Right:*** 10 / 10 vertically. ***Engraver:*** Perkins. ***Comments:*** H-MA-1235-G70. 18__. 1820s.

Rarity: —

$10 • W-MA-3240-010-G270a

Engraver: PSSP. ***Comments:*** H-MA-1235-G72. Similar to W-MA-3240-010-G270. 18__. 1820s–1830s.

Rarity: —

$10 • W-MA-3240-010-G270b

Engraver: PSSP. ***Comments:*** H-MA-1235-G74. Similar to W-MA-3240-010-G270. 18__. 1830s.

Rarity: —

$10 • W-MA-3240-010-G280

SBG

Engraver: PSSP. ***Comments:*** H-MA-1235-G76. Proof. 18__. 1830s–1840s.

Rarity: —

$10 • W-MA-3240-010-G290

Left: Mechanic seated with tools, Train and building / TEN. ***Center:*** X. ***Right:*** 10 / Reaper standing with sheaf and stone. ***Engraver:*** New England Bank Note Co. ***Comments:*** H-MA-1235-G80. 18__. 1850s.

Rarity: —

$10 • W-MA-3240-010-G300

Left: 10 / Portrait of girl / TEN. ***Center:*** Train, Factory. ***Right:*** 10 / Male portrait. ***Tint:*** Color unknown. ***Engraver:*** American Bank Note Co. ***Comments:*** H-MA-1235-G82a. 1860s.

Rarity: —

$20 • W-MA-3240-020-G310

Left: Lathework chain bearing MASSACHUSETTS / 20 / 20 vertically. ***Center:*** Alternating flower garlands and gridwork segments. ***Right:*** 20 / 20 vertically. ***Engraver:*** PSSP. ***Comments:*** H-MA-1235-G84. 18__. 1820s–1830s.

Rarity: —

$20 • W-MA-3240-020-G320

Left: 20 / Woman seated with book on lap, opening chest. ***Center:*** XX / Eagle on rock / XX. ***Right:*** 20 / Ship in harbor. ***Engraver:*** New England Bank Note Co. ***Comments:*** H-MA-1235-G86. 18__. 1840s–1850s.

Rarity: —

$20 • W-MA-3240-020-G330

SBG

Tint: Green. ***Engraver:*** American Bank Note Co. ***Comments:*** H-MA-1235-G90a. Proof. 186_. 1860s.

Rarity: URS-1

Proof $8,000

Selected auction price: Stack's Bowers Galleries, November 2012, Lot 4188, Choice AU $7,637

$50 • W-MA-3240-050-G340

Left: Lathework chain bearing MASSACHUSETTS / 50 / 50 vertically. ***Center:*** Alternating flower garlands and gridwork segments. ***Right:*** 50 / 50 vertically. ***Engraver:*** PSSP. ***Comments:*** H-MA-1235-G92. 18__. 1820s–1830s.

Rarity: —

$50 • W-MA-3240-050-G350

Left: 50 / Cornucopia, Woman standing with ankles crossed, Staff, Anchor / 50. ***Center:*** FIFTY DOLLARS / 50. ***Right:*** FIFTY vertically. ***Engraver:*** New England Bank Note Co. / PSSP. ***Comments:*** H-MA-1235-G94. 18__. 1830s–1840s.

Rarity: —

$50 • W-MA-3240-050-G360

Left: FIFTY / Woman standing with wreath and flowers / FIFTY. ***Center:*** 50 / Man restraining prancing horse / 50. ***Right:*** FIFTY / Woman standing with cornucopia / FIFTY. ***Engraver:*** New England Bank Note Co. ***Comments:*** H-MA-1235-G96. 18__. 1840s–1850s.

Rarity: —

$50 • W-MA-3240-050-G370

SBG

Tint: Green. ***Engraver:*** American Bank Note Co. ***Comments:*** H-MA-1235-G100a. Proof. 186_. 1860s.

Rarity: URS-1

Proof $8,500

Selected auction price: Stack's Bowers Galleries, August 2012, Lot 7134, Choice AU $7,762

$100 • W-MA-3240-100-G380

Left: Lathework chain bearing MASSACHUSETTS / 100 / 100 vertically. ***Center:*** Alternating flower garlands and gridwork segments. ***Right:*** 100 / 100 vertically. ***Engraver:*** Perkins. ***Comments:*** H-MA-1235-G102. 18__. 1820s–1830s.

Rarity: —

$100 • W-MA-3240-100-G390

Left: Lathework panel bearing C / Portrait of George Washington / C. ***Center:*** 100 / Manhattan reclining pouring water, Ship / 100. ***Right:*** Lathework panel bearing ONE HUNDRED vertically. ***Engraver:*** New England Bank Note Co. / PSSP. ***Comments:*** H-MA-1235-G104. 18__. 1830s–1840s.

Rarity: —

$100 • W-MA-3240-100-G400

Left: ONE HUNDRED on 100 / Portrait of William Henry Harrison. ***Center:*** Wharf scene, Men loading cart with barrels. ***Right:*** ONE HUNDRED on 100 / Portrait of Christopher Columbus. ***Engraver:*** New England Bank Note Co. ***Comments:*** H-MA-1235-G106. 18__. 1850s.

Rarity: —

$100 • W-MA-3240-100-G410

Left: Male portrait / 100. ***Center:*** Three women seated with sickle, sextant, hammer, and anvil, Ship. ***Right:*** 100 / Sailor boy, Two men with boat. ***Engraver:*** American Bank Note Co. ***Comments:*** H-MA-1235-G108a. 1860s.

Rarity: —

$500 • W-MA-3240-500-G420

Left: Woman seated on sheaves, Men reaping, Man on horse / 500. ***Center:*** 500 / D. ***Right:*** 500 vertically. ***Engraver:*** Rawdon, Wright, Hatch & Edson. ***Comments:*** H-MA-1235-G112. 18__. 1850s–1860s.

Rarity: —

Uncut Sheets

$20-$50 • W-MA-3240-020.050-US010

Vignette(s): ***($20)*** White horse and black horse, Cattle / Male portrait / Dog rescuing child from drowning. ***($50)*** Woman with scroll bearing bank name, Child / Male portrait / L / Male portrait. ***Engraver:*** American Bank Note Co. ***Comments:*** H-MA-1235-G90a, G100a.

Rarity: —

Non-Valid Issues

$2 • W-MA-3240-002-A010

SI

Tint: Red. ***Engraver:*** Bald, Cousland & Co. ***Comments:*** H-MA-1235-A5. Altered from $2 Pioneer Association, Lafayette, Indiana. 18__. 1850s–1860s.

Rarity: —

How to Read the Whitman Numbering System

$1 • W-MA-010-001-G010a

Denomination: Value of the note shown.

W: Whitman number. This number is a sortable code unique to each bank and note.

MA: Abbreviation for the state under study.

010: Numerical designation specific to each bank.

001: The denomination in dollars.

G010a: G indicates a good or valid note. Other categories are indicated thus: C (counterfeit); R (raised); S (spurious); N (not-attributed); A (altered). Numbers are assigned starting with 010, 020, et seq. Terminal letters following the number indicate variations of a note: a series of different colored overprints, tints, payees, etc., all on the same design of note. For more information, see the "How to Use This Book" section at the front of the volume, page xiv.

$3 • W-MA-3240-003-S010 CJF

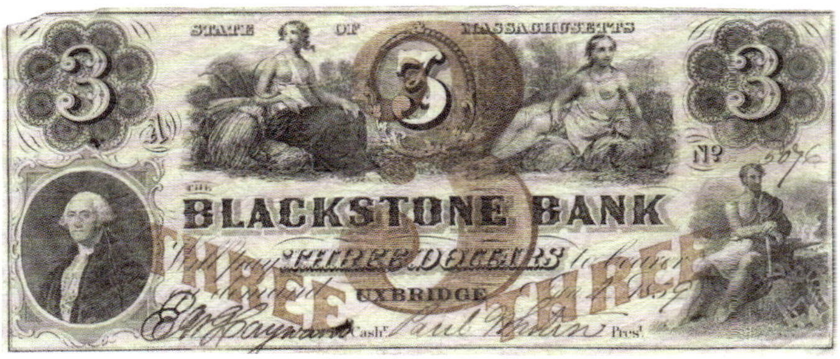

Overprint: Brown 3 / THREE / THREE. ***Comments:*** H-MA-1235-S5. Spurious design imitating a rough verbal description of W-MA-3240-003-G190. Jan. __, 185_. 1850s.

Rarity: —
VF $150

$3 • W-MA-3240-003-N010

Center: Woman seated with sheaf and plow. ***Comments:*** H-MA-1235-N5.

Rarity: —

$3 • W-MA-3240-003-N020

Left: 3. ***Center:*** Woman, Eagle, Train, Steamboat. ***Right:*** 3. ***Comments:*** H-MA-1235-N10.

Rarity: —

$5 • W-MA-3240-005-R010

Engraver: New England Bank Note Co. ***Comments:*** H-MA-1235-R5. Raised from W-MA-3240-001-G030. 18__. 1830s–1840s.

Rarity: —

$5 • W-MA-3240-005-S020 CC

Engraver: Bald, Adams & Co. ***Comments:*** H-MA-1235-S10. Spurious design imitating a rough verbal description of W-MA-3240-005-G250. 185_. 1850s.

Rarity: URS-7
F $175

$10 • W-MA-3240-010-R020

Engraver: New England Bank Note Co. ***Comments:*** H-MA-1235-R10. Raised from W-MA-3240-001-G030. 18__. 1830s–1840s.

Rarity: —

$50 • W-MA-3240-050-R030

Engraver: New England Bank Note Co. ***Comments:*** H-MA-1235-R15. Raised from W-MA-3240-001-G030. 18__. 1830s–1840s.

Rarity: —

$50 • W-MA-3240-050-R040

Engraver: New England Bank Note Co. ***Comments:*** H-MA-1235-R20. Raised from W-MA-3240-003-G180. 18__. 1830s.

Rarity: —

Braintree Bank
1850s
W-MA-3250

History: A non-existent bank represented only by notes altered from other banks.

Issues

$2 • W-MA-3250-002-A010

Left: 2 / Female portrait. ***Center:*** Covered wagon pulled by four horses, Man riding one horse. ***Right:*** 2 / Portrait of Thomas Jefferson. ***Tint:*** Brown-orange lathework outlining white TWO. ***Engraver:*** Bald, Cousland & Co. ***Comments:*** H-MA-1240-A5. Altered from $2 Pioneer Association, LaFayette, Indiana. 18__. 1850s.

Rarity: —

Waltham, Massachusetts

Waltham was once a part of Watertown, established in 1627. Waltham was settled in 1634 and incorporated on January 3, 1738. A dam and a paper mill were built in 1794, followed by another two paper mills in 1801 and 1802. The Boston Manufacturing Company built a mill in 1813 which brought the first power loom to town. It could produce all the various steps of cotton working. Chalk crayons were invented in 1835 in the town of Waltham by Dr. Francis Field. This led to the creation of the American Crayon Company. In 1843 the railways came to Waltham, and an iron and brass foundry was erected in 1846.

Waltham Bank
1836–1865
W-MA-3260

History: The Waltham Bank was incorporated on April 16, 1836, with an authorized capital of $100,000, which was increased to $200,000 in 1854. It had $73,653 bills in circulation in 1837. The same had reached $129,059 in 1863.

The business of the Waltham Bank was succeeded by the Waltham National Bank after it was chartered on December 26, 1864.

Numismatic Commentary: A strong local collector base causes available notes from this bank to be bought quickly when they appear for sale. Many of the signed and dated notes show signs of bank cancellation. Some sheets exist. A local mill of the Boston Manufacturing Co. can be seen on some issues.

Valid Issues

$1 • W-MA-3260-001-G010

QDB

Engraver: New England Bank Note Co. ***Comments:*** H-MA-1245-G4. Remainder. 18__. 1830s–1840s.

Rarity: URS-3
CU $1,400

$1 • W-MA-3260-001-G020

CJF

Engraver: Rawdon, Wright, Hatch & Edson / New England Bank Note Co. ***Comments:*** H-MA-1245-G8. Remainder. Oct. 1, 18__. 1850s.

Rarity: —
Selected auction price: Heritage, April 2013, Lot 15273, Choice New $4,406

$1 • W-MA-3260-001-G020a

HA

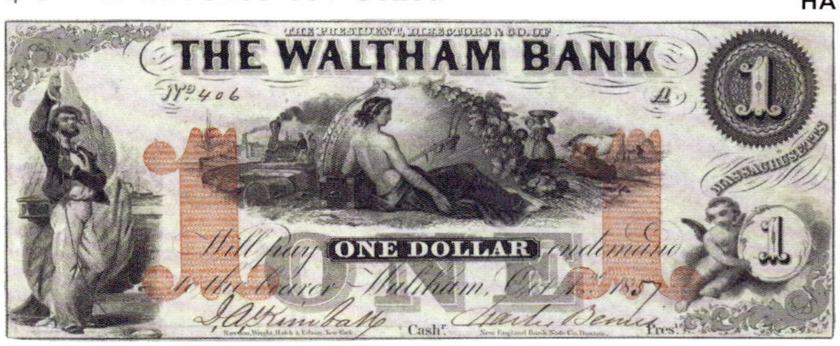

Overprint: Red 1 / 1. ***Engraver:*** Rawdon, Wright, Hatch & Edson / New England Bank Note Co. ***Comments:*** H-Unlisted. Similar to W-MA-3260-001-G020. Oct. 1, 18__. 1850s.

Rarity: URS-4
VG $300; **F** $500; **VF** $1,000; **Unc-S&D** $4,000

$1 • W-MA-3260-001-G020b

CJF

Overprint: Green. ***Engraver:*** Rawdon, Wright, Hatch & Edson / New England Bank Note Co. / ABNCo. monogram. ***Comments:*** H-Unlisted. Similar to W-MA-3260-001-G020 but with additional engraver imprint. Oct. 1, 18__. 1850s.

Rarity: URS-3
VG $400; **VF** $750

$2 • W-MA-3260-002-G030

CC

Engraver: New England Bank Note Co. ***Comments:*** H-MA-1245-G12. Remainder. 18__. 1830s–1840s.

Rarity: URS-4
CU $1,400; **Proof** $2,000

$2 • W-MA-3260-002-G040

CJF

Engraver: Rawdon, Wright, Hatch & Edson / New England Bank Note Co. ***Comments:*** H-MA-1245-G16. Oct. 1, 18__. 1850s.

Rarity: URS-3
Unc-Rem $1,000

$3 • W-MA-3260-003-G050

CJF

Engraver: New England Bank Note Co. ***Comments:*** H-MA-1245-G20. 18__. 1830s–1840s.

Rarity: URS-4
Unc-Rem $1,000

$3 • W-MA-3260-003-G060

Left: 3 / Farmer seated with scythe. ***Center:*** Woman reclining with arm on bale, Spinning wheel, Factories and bridge. ***Right:*** 3 / Mechanic, farmer, and sailor standing with 3. ***Engraver:*** Rawdon, Wright, Hatch & Edson. ***Comments:*** H-MA-1245-G24. 18__. 1850s.

Rarity: —

$5 • W-MA-3260-005-G070

CJF

Engraver: New England Bank Note Co. ***Comments:*** H-MA-1245-G28. 18__. 1830s–1840s.

Rarity: URS-3
CU $1,100; **Proof** $1,500

$5 • W-MA-3260-005-G080

CJF

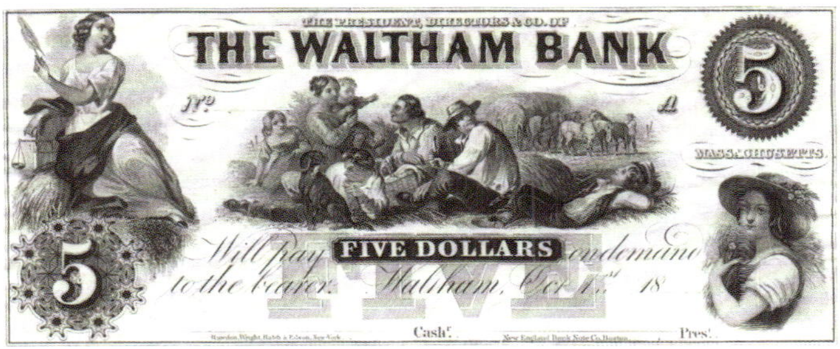

Engraver: Rawdon, Wright, Hatch & Edson / New England Bank Note Co. ***Comments:*** H-MA-1245-G32. Remainder. Oct. 1, 18__. 1850s.

Rarity: URS-3
Unc-Rem $750

$10 • W-MA-3260-010-G090

Engraver: Unverified, but likely New England Bank Note Co. ***Comments:*** H-MA-1245-G36. No description available. 18__. 1830s–1840s.

Rarity: *None known*

$10 • W-MA-3260-010-G100

CJF

Engraver: Rawdon, Wright, Hatch & Edson / New England Bank Note Co. ***Comments:*** H-MA-1245-G40. Oct. 1, 18__. 1850s.

Rarity: URS-4
Proof $1,000

$10 • W-MA-3260-010-G100a

CJF

Overprint: Red TEN. ***Engraver:*** Rawdon, Wright, Hatch & Edson / New England Bank Note Co. ***Comments:*** H-Unlisted. Similar to W-MA-3260-010-G100. Oct. 1, 18__. 1850s.

Rarity: URS-4
F $500

$20 • W-MA-3260-020-G110

Left: Steamboat / XX / Train. ***Center:*** Three women seated with eagle, pole and cap, shield, scales, and book / 20 / Panel outlining white TWENTY. ***Right:*** XX / Milkmaid standing with pail. ***Engraver:*** New England Bank Note Co. ***Comments:*** H-MA-1245-G44. 18__. 1830s–1840s.

Rarity: URS-1
F $1,500

$20 • W-MA-3260-020-G120

Left: 20 / Minerva standing with spear. ***Center:*** Woman seated between 2 and 0. ***Right:*** 20 / Woman reclining on cornucopia / 20. ***Engraver:*** Rawdon, Wright, Hatch & Edson. ***Comments:*** H-MA-1245-G48. 18__. 1850s.

Rarity: —

$20 • W-MA-3260-020-G130

Left: 20 / Two women with sickle and grain. ***Center:*** Man watering two horses at trough, Woman. ***Right:*** 20 / Woman seated by spinning wheel. ***Tint:*** Green. ***Engraver:*** American Bank Note Co. ***Comments:*** H-MA-1245-G52a. 188_. 1860s.

Rarity: URS-1
Proof $4,000

$50 • W-MA-3260-050-G140

Left: 50 / Steamboat and schooner. ***Center:*** Farmyard scene, Load of hay with two men on it, Man with rake and pail. ***Right:*** L / Justice kneeling. ***Engraver:*** New England Bank Note Co. ***Comments:*** H-MA-1245-G56. 18__. 1830s–1840s.

Rarity: —

$50 • W-MA-3260-050-G150

Left: 50 / Minerva standing by column. ***Center:*** Ceres and Vulcan flanking cornucopia. ***Right:*** 50 / Cherub in sailboat / 50. ***Engraver:*** Rawdon, Wright, Hatch & Edson. ***Comments:*** H-MA-1245-G60. 18__. 1850s.

Rarity: —

$50 • W-MA-3260-050-G160

Left: Two women seated on bale, Factories. ***Center:*** State arms. ***Right:*** 50 / Mechanic at work. ***Tint:*** Green. ***Engraver:*** American Bank Note Co. ***Comments:*** H-MA-1245-G64a. 186_. 1860s.

Rarity: URS-1
Proof $5,000

$100 • W-MA-3260-100-G170

Engraver: Unverified, but likely New England Bank Note Co. ***Comments:*** H-MA-1245-G68. No description available. 18__. 1830s–1840s.

Rarity: *None known*

$100 • W-MA-3260-100-G180

Left: 100 / Vulcan seated with sledge and anchor. ***Center:*** Train on bridge, Eagle on limb, Canal locks / C C. ***Bottom center:*** 100. ***Right:*** 100 / Ceres seated, Cornucopia. ***Engraver:*** Rawdon, Wright, Hatch & Edson. ***Comments:*** H-MA-1245-G72. 18__. 1850s.

Rarity: —

$100 • W-MA-3260-100-G180a

Overprint: Red HUNDRED. ***Engraver:*** Rawdon, Wright, Hatch & Edson. ***Comments:*** H-MA-1245-G72a. Similar to W-MA-3260-100-G180. 18__. 1850s.

Rarity: —

$100 • W-MA-3260-100-G190

CC

Tint: Green. ***Engraver:*** American Bank Note Co. ***Comments:*** H-MA-1245-G76a. 186_. 1860s.

Rarity: URS-2
Proof $5,000

$500 • W-MA-3260-500-G200

Left: D / FIVE HUNDRED DOLLARS. ***Center:*** Two soldiers, one seated on cannon, Flag and fort. ***Right:*** 500. ***Tint:*** FIVE HUNDRED on green die. ***Engraver:*** American Bank Note Co. ***Comments:*** H-MA-1245-G84a. 186_. 1860s.

Rarity: URS-1
Proof $10,000

Uncut Sheets

$1-$2-$5-$3 • W-MA-3260-001.002.005.003-US010

CJF

Comments: H-MA-1245-G4, G12, G28, G20. 18__. 1830s–1840s.

Rarity: URS-3
Unc-Rem $3,500

Non-Valid Issues

$3 • W-MA-3260-003-S010

Left: Man plowing with ox, Trees, House / 3. ***Center:*** 3. ***Right:*** 3 / Woman seated with cornucopia / THREE. ***Comments:*** H-MA-1245-S5.

Rarity: —

$5 • W-MA-3260-005-R010

Engraver: New England Bank Note Co. ***Comments:*** H-MA-1245-R5. Raised from W-MA-3260-001-G010. 18__. 1840s.

Rarity: —

$5 • **W-MA-3260-005-A010**

Left: 5 on die / Woman seated on bale holding scales, Ship. ***Center:*** Moneta seated with key receiving bag of coins from Mercury in clouds, Griffin on chest / 5 on die. ***Bottom center:*** Pledge. ***Right:*** FIVE / Two allegorical women seated with caduceus, Shield and cornucopia. ***Engraver:*** Rawdon, Wright & Hatch. ***Comments:*** H-MA-1245-A5. Altered from $5 Chippeway County Bank, Saul De St. Mary, Michigan. 18__. 1830s–1840s.

Rarity: —

$10 • **W-MA-3260-010-R020**

Engraver: New England Bank Note Co. ***Comments:*** H-MA-1245-R10. Raised from W-MA-3260-001-G010. 18__. 1840s.

Rarity: —

$10 • **W-MA-3260-010-A020**

Left: 10 / Portrait of George Washington. ***Center:*** X / Spread eagle with shield and arrows, E PLURIBUS UNUM / X. ***Bottom center:*** Ship. ***Right:*** 10 / Standing Indian man / 10. ***Engraver:*** Terry, Pelton & Co. ***Comments:*** H-MA-1245-A10. Altered from $10 Citizens Bank, Augusta, Maine, or from notes of other failed banks using the same plate. 18__. 1840s.

Rarity: —

$50 • **W-MA-3260-050-R030**

Engraver: Rawdon, Wright, Hatch & Edson. ***Comments:*** H-MA-1245-R15. Raised from W-MA-3260-003-G060. 18__. 1850s.

Rarity: —

$100 • **W-MA-3260-100-C180a**

CJF

Overprint: Red HUNDRED. ***Engraver:*** Rawdon, Wright, Hatch & Edson. ***Comments:*** H-MA-1245-C72a. Counterfeit of W-MA-3260-100-G180a. 18__. 1850s.

Rarity: URS-4
F $200; **VF** $400

WARE, MASSACHUSETTS

Incorporated in 1775, Ware is named after a town in England. In 1729 the first saw and grist mills were built on the Weir River, and by the 1830s textile mills were active.

Hampshire Manufacturers Bank

1825–1865

W-MA-3270

History: The Hampshire Manufacturers Bank was incorporated in February 1825 with $100,000 of authorized capital, which was increased to $150,000 in 1836 and $350,000 by 1860. The circulation of the bank ranged from a low of $57,395 in 1849 to a high of $341,758 in 1863.

The Hampshire Manufacturers Bank was succeeded by the Ware National Bank after it was chartered in 1864.

Numismatic Commentary: Genuine notes are very hard to locate. Many show a vignette of the town of Ware.

VALID ISSUES

$1 • **W-MA-3270-001-G010**

Left: Narrow panel of lathework circle segments. ***Center:*** 1 / 1 / Flower garlands and gridwork segments / 1 / 1. ***Right:*** Narrow panel of lathework circle segments. ***Engraver:*** PSSP. ***Comments:*** H-MA-1250-G2. 18__. 1820s–1830s.

Rarity: —

$1 • **W-MA-3270-001-G010a**

Left: ONE / D / ONE vertically. ***Right:*** ONE / D / ONE vertically. ***Engraver:*** PSSP. ***Comments:*** H-MA-1250-G4. Similar to W-MA-3270-001-G010. 18__. 1830s.

Rarity: —

$1 • **W-MA-3270-001-G020**

JF

Engraver: Toppan, Carpenter & Co. ***Comments:*** H-MA-1250-G8. Proof. 18__. 1840s–1850s.

Rarity: URS-3
Proof $1,000

$1 • **W-MA-3270-001-G020a**

Left: 1 / Female portrait / ONE. ***Center:*** View of Ware. ***Bottom center:*** Dog's head. ***Right:*** Four cherubs holding 1 atop pedestal bearing ONE. ***Overprint:*** Red. ***Engraver:*** Toppan, Carpenter & Co. ***Comments:*** H-MA-1250-G8a. Similar to W-MA-3270-001-G020. 18__. 1850s.

Rarity: —

$2 • **W-MA-3270-002-G030**

Left: Narrow panel of lathework circle segments. ***Center:*** 2 / 2 / Flower garlands and gridwork segments / 2 / 2. ***Right:*** Narrow panel of lathework circle segments. ***Engraver:*** PSSP. ***Comments:*** H-MA-1250-G10. 18__. 1820s–1830s.

Rarity: —

$2 • **W-MA-3270-002-G030a**

Left: Five TWOs vertically. ***Right:*** Five TWOs vertically. ***Engraver:*** PSSP. ***Comments:*** H-MA-1250-G12. Similar to W-MA-3270-002-G030. 18__. 1830s.

Rarity: —

$2 • W-MA-3270-002-G040

JF

Engraver: Toppan, Carpenter & Co. ***Comments:*** H-MA-1250-G16. Proof. 18__. 1840s–1850s.

Rarity: URS-3
Proof $1,500

$2 • W-MA-3270-002-G040a

Overprint: Red panel outlining white TWO. ***Engraver:*** Toppan, Carpenter & Co. / ABNCo. monogram. ***Comments:*** H-MA-1250-G16a. Similar to W-MA-3270-002-G040 but with additional engraver imprint. 18__. 1850s–1860s.

Rarity: —

$3 • W-MA-3270-003-G050

Left: Narrow panel of lathework circle segments. ***Center:*** 3 / 3 / Flower garlands and gridwork segments / 3 / 3. ***Right:*** Narrow panel of lathework circle segments. ***Engraver:*** PSSP. ***Comments:*** H-MA-1250-G18. 18__. 1820s–1830s.

Rarity: —

$3 • W-MA-3270-003-G050a

Left: THREE vertically. ***Right:*** THREE vertically. ***Engraver:*** PSSP. ***Comments:*** H-MA-1250-G20. Similar to W-MA-3270-003-G050. 18__. 1830s.

Rarity: —

$3 • W-MA-3270-003-G060

CC

Engraver: Toppan, Carpenter & Co. ***Comments:*** H-MA-1250-G24. Proof. Plate note. 18__. 1840s–1850s.

Rarity: URS-1
Proof $3,000

$3 • W-MA-3270-003-G060a

CJF

Overprint: Red overall. ***Engraver:*** Toppan, Carpenter & Co. / ABNCo. monogram. ***Comments:*** H-MA-1250-G24a. Similar to W-MA-3270-003-G060 but with additional engraver imprint. 18__. 1850s.

Rarity: URS-4
F $300; **VF** $500

$5 • W-MA-3270-005-G070

Left: Lathework chain bearing MASSACHUSETTS / 5 / 5 vertically. ***Center:*** Alternating flower garlands and gridwork segments. ***Right:*** 5 / 5 vertically. ***Engraver:*** PSSP. ***Comments:*** H-MA-1250-G26. 18__. 1820s.

Rarity: —

$5 • W-MA-3270-005-G070a

Engraver: PSSP. ***Comments:*** H-MA-1250-G28. Similar to W-MA-3270-005-G070 but with zigzag ruled lines. 18__. 1820s–1830s.

Rarity: —

$5 • W-MA-3270-005-G070b

Engraver: PSSP. ***Comments:*** H-MA-1250-G30. Similar to W-MA-3270-005-G070 but with spiral lathework lines. 18__. 1830s.

Rarity: —

$5 • W-MA-3270-005-G080

Center: Bank name repeated in microlettering, Denomination repeated in microlettering. ***Engraver:*** PSSP. ***Comments:*** H-MA-1250-G32. 18__. 1830s–1850s.

Rarity: —

$5 • W-MA-3270-005-G080a

Overprint: Red lazy 5. ***Engraver:*** PSSP. ***Comments:*** H-MA-1250-G32a. Similar to W-MA-3270-005-G080. 18__. 1850s.

Rarity: —

$10 • W-MA-3270-010-G090

Left: Lathework chain bearing MASSACHUSETTS / 10 / 10 vertically. ***Center:*** Alternating flower garlands and gridwork segments. ***Right:*** 10 / 10 vertically. ***Engraver:*** Perkins. ***Comments:*** H-MA-1250-G34. 18__. 1820s.

Rarity: —

$10 • W-MA-3270-010-G090a

Engraver: PSSP. ***Comments:*** H-MA-1250-G36. Similar to W-MA-3270-010-G090 but with zigzag ruled lines. 18__. 1820s–1830s.

Rarity: —

$10 • W-MA-3270-010-G090b

Engraver: PSSP. ***Comments:*** H-MA-1250-G38. Similar to W-MA-3270-010-G090. 18__. 1830s.

Rarity: —

$10 • W-MA-3270-010-G100

Left: MASSACHUSETTS vertically. ***Center:*** 10 / Woman standing / 10 / Text, Train. ***Right:*** 10 / Indian man / 10. ***Engraver:*** PSSP. ***Comments:*** H-MA-1250-G40. 18__. 1830s–1850s.

Rarity: —

$10 • W-MA-3270-010-G100a

Overprint: Red X X. ***Engraver:*** PSSP. ***Comments:*** H-MA-1250-G40a. Similar to W-MA-3270-010-G100. 18__. 1850s.

Rarity: —

$10 • **W-MA-3270-010-G100b**

SBG

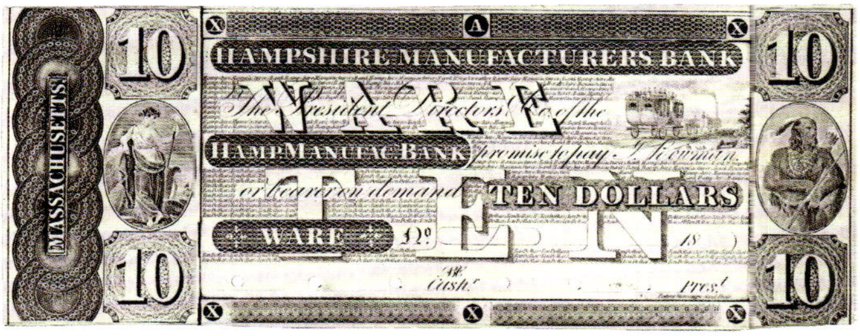

Engraver: PSSP / ABNCo. monogram. ***Comments:*** H-MA-1250-G40b. Similar to W-MA-3270-010-G100 but with additional engraver imprint. 18__. 1850s.

Rarity: URS-2
Proof $1,750

$10 • **W-MA-3270-010-G100c**

Overprint: Red X X. ***Engraver:*** PSSP / ABNCo. monogram. ***Comments:*** H-MA-1250-G40c. Similar to W-MA-3270-010-G100 but with additional engraver imprint. 18__. 1850s–1860s.

Rarity: —

$20 • **W-MA-3270-020-G110**

Left: Lathework chain bearing MASSACHUSETTS / 20 / 20 vertically. ***Center:*** Alternating flower garlands and gridwork segments. ***Right:*** 20 / 20 vertically. ***Engraver:*** PSSP. ***Comments:*** H-MA-1250-G42. 18__. 1820s–1830s.

Rarity: —

$20 • **W-MA-3270-020-G120**

Engraver: PSSP. ***Comments:*** H-MA-1250-G44. 18__. 1830s–1850s.

Rarity: —

$20 • **W-MA-3270-020-G120a**

Overprint: Red XX, 20. ***Engraver:*** PSSP. ***Comments:*** H-MA-1250-G44a. Similar to W-MA-3270-020-G120. 18__. 1850s.

Rarity: URS-2
Unc-Rem $1,250

$50 • **W-MA-3270-050-G130**

Left: Lathework chain bearing MASSACHUSETTS / 50 / 50 vertically. ***Center:*** Alternating flower garlands and gridwork segments. ***Right:*** 50 / 50 vertically. ***Engraver:*** PSSP. ***Comments:*** H-MA-1250-G46. 18__. 1820s–1830s.

Rarity: —

$50 • **W-MA-3270-050-G140**

Left: Lathework chain bearing MASSACHUSETTS / 50 / Ceres seated / 50 vertically. ***Center:*** Text. ***Right:*** 50 / State arms / 50 vertically. ***Engraver:*** PSSP. ***Comments:*** H-MA-1250-G48. 18__. 1830s–1850s.

Rarity: —

$50 • **W-MA-3270-050-G140a**

QDB

Overprint: Red 50. ***Engraver:*** PSSP. ***Comments:*** H-MA-1250-G48a. Similar to W-MA-3270-050-G140. Remainder. 18__. 1850s.

Rarity: URS-1
Proof $4,000

$100 • **W-MA-3270-100-G150**

Left: Lathework chain bearing MASSACHUSETTS / 100 / 100 vertically. ***Center:*** Alternating flower garlands and gridwork segments. ***Right:*** 100 / 100 vertically. ***Engraver:*** Perkins. ***Comments:*** H-MA-1250-G50. 18__. 1820s–1830s.

Rarity: —

$100 • **W-MA-3270-100-G160**

Engraver: Unverified, but likely New England Bank Note Co. ***Comments:*** H-MA-1250-G52. No description available. 18__. 1830s–1840s.

Rarity: *None known*

$100 • **W-MA-3270-100-G170**

Left: 100 / Eagle / 100. ***Center:*** C / Phoebus in the Chariot of the Sun / 100. ***Right:*** C / Portrait of George Washington / C. ***Engraver:*** New England Bank Note Co. ***Comments:*** H-MA-1250-G54. 18__. 1840s–1850s.

Rarity: —

$100 • **W-MA-3270-100-G180**

Left: C / Men with fishing boat at shore / 100. ***Center:*** Eagle perched on bale, Cornucopia and sheaf / 100. ***Right:*** 100 / Ceres / 100. ***Overprint:*** Red HUNDRED. ***Engraver:*** New England Bank Note Co. ***Comments:*** H-MA-1250-G56a. 18__. 1850s.

Rarity: —

Non-Valid Issues

$10 • **W-MA-3270-010-R010**

Engraver: Toppan, Carpenter & Co. ***Comments:*** H-MA-1250-R5. Raised from W-MA-3270-001-G020 or G020a. 18__. 1850s.

Rarity: —

$10 • **W-MA-3270-010-S010**

CJF

Engraver: Draper, Toppan & Co. ***Comments:*** H-MA-1250-S5. June 1, 1848.

Rarity: URS-7
VG $125; **VF** $175

$20 • **W-MA-3270-020-C110**

Engraver: PSSP. ***Comments:*** H-MA-1250-C42. Counterfeit of W-MA-3270-020-G110. 18__. 1833.

Rarity: —

$20 • **W-MA-3270-020-R020**

Engraver: Toppan, Carpenter & Co. ***Comments:*** H-MA-1250-R10. Raised from W-MA-3270-001-G020 or G020a. 18__. 1850s.

Rarity: —

$20 • W-MA-3270-020-R030
Engraver: Toppan, Carpenter & Co. ***Comments:*** H-MA-1250-R15. Raised from W-MA-3270-002-G040 or G040a. 18__. 1850s.
Rarity: —

WAREHAM, MASSACHUSETTS

Agawam was the original name of this land, meaning "a place where fish are caught" in the native tongue. The town of Plymouth bought the land in 1666, and acreage there was later used as payment for soldiers after the French and Indian War. Parts of Rochester and the land of Agawam were combined to create Wareham. It was officially settled in 1678 and incorporated in 1739. Shipbuilding and sister industries made up the main economy. In addition, water-powered mills produced nails, grain, cotton, paper, rails, and iron goods.

Wareham Bank
1833–1865
W-MA-3280

History: The Wareham Bank was chartered on March 22, 1833, with an authorized capital of $100,000. Circulation amounted to $22,822 in 1839. The same was $63,405 in 1849. Specie totaled $5,354.51, and the bank's real estate was valued at $5,000.

In 1865 the business of the Wareham Bank was succeeded by the National Wareham Bank.

Numismatic Commentary: Genuine notes from this bank are very hard to locate. Occasionally a colorful note with a vignette of the local Tremont Nail Works will become available. The vignette of this factory has been used on notes from various other banks across the country.

As of 2003 the American Bank Note Co. archives had a $1-$1-$2-$2 face, a $1-$1-$2-$2 tint, a $50-$100 face, a $50-$100 tint, a $5-$5-$10-$20 face, and a $5-$5-$10-$20 tint plate remaining.

VALID ISSUES

$1 • W-MA-3280-001-G010
Left: MASSACHUSETTS vertically. ***Center:*** 1 / Woman / 1 / 1 / Indian man / 1. ***Right:*** ONE DOLLAR vertically. ***Back:*** Plain. ***Engraver:*** PSSP. ***Comments:*** H-MA-1255-G4. 18__. 1830s–1840s.
Rarity: —

$1 • W-MA-3280-001-G010a
Back: Check Plate. ***Engraver:*** PSSP. ***Comments:*** H-MA-1255-G4a. Similar to W-MA-3280-001-G010. 18__. 1830s.
Rarity: —

$1 • W-MA-3280-001-G020
Left: Commerce seated with rudder leaning on barrel / 1. ***Center:*** 1 bearing "Presentation of the Declaration of Independence". ***Right:*** 1 / Woman standing with apron full of grain. ***Engraver:*** New England Bank Note Co. ***Comments:*** H-MA-1255-G8. 18__. 1850s.
Rarity: —

$1 • W-MA-3280-001-G030 CC

Tint: Green. ***Engraver:*** American Bank Note Co. ***Comments:*** H-MA-1255-G10a. Plate note. Jan. 1, 1862. 1860s.
Rarity: URS-1
VF $8,000

$2 • W-MA-3280-002-G040
Left: MASSACHUSETTS vertically. ***Center:*** 2 / Woman / 2 / 2 / Indian man / 2. ***Right:*** TWO DOLLARS vertically. ***Back:*** Plain. ***Engraver:*** PSSP. ***Comments:*** H-MA-1255-G12. 18__. 1830s–1840s.
Rarity: —

$2 • W-MA-3280-002-G040a
Back: Check Plate. ***Engraver:*** PSSP. ***Comments:*** H-MA-1255-G12a. Similar to W-MA-3280-002-G040. 18__. 1830s–1840s.
Rarity: —

$2 • W-MA-3280-002-G050
Left: Men driving sheep into stream / 2. ***Center:*** 2 bearing "Presentation of the Declaration of Independence". ***Right:*** TWO / Woman seated with wreath of flowers / TWO. ***Overprint:*** Red TWO. ***Engraver:*** New England Bank Note Co. ***Comments:*** H-MA-1255-G16a. 18__. 1850s.
Rarity: —

$2 • W-MA-3280-002-G060
Left: Girl and boy reclining under tree, Cows and sheep / 2. ***Center:*** Eagle on rock. ***Right:*** TWO across 2 / Male portrait. ***Tint:*** Color unknown. ***Engraver:*** American Bank Note Co. ***Comments:*** H-MA-1255-G18a. 18__. 1860s.
Rarity: —

$3 • W-MA-3280-003-G070
Left: MASSACHUSETTS vertically. ***Center:*** 3 / Woman / 3 / 3 / Indian man / 3. ***Right:*** THREE DOLLARS vertically. ***Back:*** Plain. ***Engraver:*** PSSP. ***Comments:*** H-MA-1255-G20. 18__. 1830s–1840s.
Rarity: —

$3 • W-MA-3280-003-G070a
Back: Check Plate. ***Engraver:*** PSSP. ***Comments:*** H-MA-1255-G20a. Similar to W-MA-3280-003-G070. 18__. 1830s.
Rarity: —

$3 • W-MA-3280-003-G080
Left: Barnyard scene, Man on horse, Boy and cattle. ***Center:*** 3. ***Right:*** 3 on THREE / Woman with flowers / THREE. ***Engraver:*** New England Bank Note Co. ***Comments:*** H-MA-1255-G24. 18__. 1850s.
Rarity: —

$5 • W-MA-3280-005-G090

Left: MASSACHUSETTS vertically. ***Center:*** 5 / Woman / 5 / 5 / Indian man / 5. ***Right:*** FIVE DOLLARS vertically. ***Back:*** Plain. ***Engraver:*** PSSP. ***Comments:*** H-MA-1255-G28. 18__. 1830s–1840s.

Rarity: —

$5 • W-MA-3280-005-G090a

Back: Check Plate. ***Engraver:*** PSSP. ***Comments:*** H-MA-1255-G28a. Similar to W-MA-3280-005-G090. 18__. 1830s.

Rarity: —

$5 • W-MA-3280-005-G100

Left: Eagle on shield and anchor, Factories and ships / FIVE. ***Center:*** V with woman, cornucopia, and cherub. ***Right:*** 5 / Girl with ringlets holding basket. ***Engraver:*** New England Bank Note Co. ***Comments:*** H-MA-1255-G32. 18__. 1850s.

Rarity: —

$5 • W-MA-3280-005-G110

Left: V / 5. ***Center:*** Mechanic standing with hammer, Anvils and wheel / V / State arms / V. ***Right:*** 5 / Male portrait. ***Tint:*** 5. ***Engraver:*** American Bank Note Co. ***Comments:*** H-MA-1255-G34a. 18__. 1860s.

Rarity: —

$10 • W-MA-3280-010-G120

Left: MASSACHUSETTS vertically. ***Center:*** 10 / Woman / 10 / 10 / Indian man / 10. ***Right:*** TEN DOLLARS vertically. ***Back:*** Plain. ***Engraver:*** PSSP. ***Comments:*** H-MA-1255-G36. 18__. 1830s–1840s.

Rarity: —

$10 • W-MA-3280-010-G120a

Back: Check Plate. ***Engraver:*** PSSP. ***Comments:*** H-MA-1255-G36a. Similar to W-MA-3280-010-G120. 18__. 1830s.

Rarity: —

$10 • W-MA-3280-010-G130

Left: "Presentation of the Declaration of Independence" / X. ***Center:*** X. ***Right:*** 10 / Train passing building with steeple, Man with wheelbarrow. ***Engraver:*** New England Bank Note Co. ***Comments:*** H-MA-1255-G40. 18__. 1840s–1850s.

Rarity: —

$10 • W-MA-3280-010-G140

Left: Mechanic seated with tools, Train and building / TEN. ***Center:*** X. ***Right:*** 10 / Reaper standing with sheaf and stone. ***Engraver:*** New England Bank Note Co. ***Comments:*** H-MA-1255-G42. 18__. 1850s.

Rarity: —

$10 • W-MA-3280-010-G150

Left: TEN / Woman seated on rock near anchor, Steamship and lighthouse. ***Center:*** State arms / TEN / Male portrait. ***Right:*** 10 / TEN. ***Tint:*** Color unknown. ***Comments:*** H-MA-1255-G44a. 18__. 1860s.

Rarity: —

$20 • W-MA-3280-020-G160

Left: MASSACHUSETTS vertically. ***Center:*** 20 / Woman / 20 / 20 / Indian man / 20. ***Right:*** TWENTY DOLLARS vertically. ***Back:*** Check Plate. ***Engraver:*** PSSP. ***Comments:*** H-MA-1255-G46. 18__. 1830s.

Rarity: —

$20 • W-MA-3280-020-G160a

Back: Plain. ***Engraver:*** PSSP. ***Comments:*** H-MA-1255-G46a. Similar to W-MA-3280-020-G160. 18__. 1830s–1840s.

Rarity: —

$20 • W-MA-3280-020-G170

Left: 20 / Woman seated with book on lap, opening chest. ***Center:*** XX / Eagle on rock / XX. ***Right:*** 20 / Ship in harbor. ***Engraver:*** New England Bank Note Co. ***Comments:*** H-MA-1255-G50. 18__. 1840s–1850s.

Rarity: —

$20 • W-MA-3280-020-G180

Left: View of Tremont Nail Works / 20. ***Center:*** Male portrait. ***Right:*** 20 / 20. ***Tint:*** Color unknown. ***Engraver:*** American Bank Note Co. ***Comments:*** H-MA-1255-G52a. 18__. 1860s.

Rarity: —

$50 • W-MA-3280-050-G190

Left: MASSACHUSETTS vertically. ***Center:*** 50 / Woman / 50 / 50 / Indian man / 50. ***Right:*** FIFTY DOLLARS vertically. ***Back:*** Check Plate. ***Engraver:*** PSSP. ***Comments:*** H-MA-1255-G54. 18__. 1830s.

Rarity: —

$50 • W-MA-3280-050-G190a

Back: Plain. ***Engraver:*** PSSP. ***Comments:*** H-MA-1255-G54a. Similar to W-MA-3280-050-G190. 18__. 1830s–1840s.

Rarity: —

$50 • W-MA-3280-050-G200

Left: FIFTY / Woman standing with wreath and flowers / FIFTY. ***Center:*** 50 / Man restraining prancing horse / 50. ***Right:*** FIFTY / Woman standing with cornucopia / FIFTY. ***Engraver:*** New England Bank Note Co. ***Comments:*** H-MA-1255-G58. 18__. 1840s–1850s.

Rarity: —

$50 • W-MA-3280-050-G210

JF

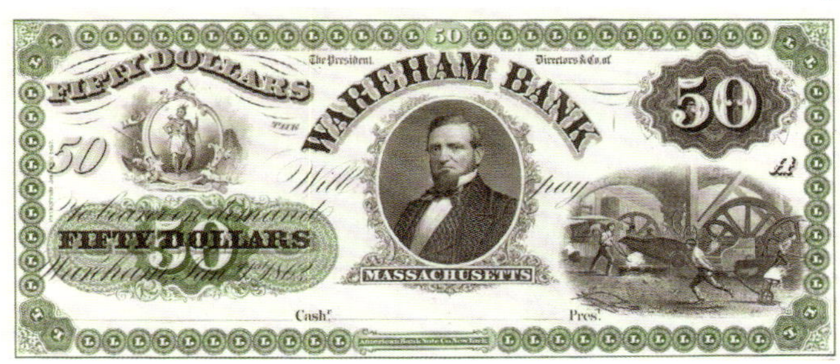

Tint: Green. ***Engraver:*** American Bank Note Co. ***Comments:*** H-MA-1255-G60a. Proof. Jan. 1, 1862. 1860s.

Rarity: URS-4

Proof $2,500

$100 • W-MA-3280-100-G220

Left: MASSACHUSETTS vertically. ***Center:*** 100 / Woman / 100 / 100 / Indian man / 100. ***Right:*** HUNDRED DOLLARS vertically. ***Back:*** Check Plate. ***Engraver:*** PSSP. ***Comments:*** H-MA-1255-G62. 18__. 1830s.

Rarity: —

$100 • W-MA-3280-100-G220a

Back: Plain. ***Engraver:*** PSSP. ***Comments:*** H-MA-1255-G62a. Similar to W-MA-3280-100-G220. 18__. 1830s–1840s.

Rarity: —

$100 • W-MA-3280-100-G230

Left: ONE HUNDRED on 100 / Portrait of William Henry Harrison. ***Center:*** Wharf scene, Men loading wagon with barrels. ***Right:*** ONE HUNDRED on 100 / Portrait of Christopher Columbus. ***Engraver:*** New England Bank Note Co. ***Comments:*** H-MA-1255-G66. 18__. 1840s–1850s.

Rarity: —

$100 • W-MA-3280-100-G240

JF

Tint: Green. ***Engraver:*** American Bank Note Co. ***Comments:*** H-MA-1255-G68a. Proof. Jan. 1, 1862. 1860s.

Rarity: URS-4
Proof $3,500

Uncut Sheets

$50-$100 • W-MA-3280-050.100-US010

JF

Tint(s): Green. ***Engraver:*** American Bank Note Co. ***Comments:*** H-MA-1255-G60a, G68a. Proof. Jan. 1, 1862. 1860s.

Rarity: —

Non-Valid Issues

$1 • W-MA-3280-001-A010

CJF

Engraver: Chas. E. Ely, Philadelphia. ***Comments:*** H-MA-1255-A5. Altered from $1 Geauga Insurance Co., Painesville, Ohio. 18__. 1840s.

Rarity: —

$2 • W-MA-3280-002-A020

CC

Engraver: Chas. E. Ely, Philadelphia. ***Comments:*** H-MA-1255-A10. Altered, including replacement of the left and center vignettes, from $2 Geauga Insurance Co., Painesville, Ohio. 18__. 1840s.

Rarity: URS-7
VG $125; **VF** $175

$3 • W-MA-3280-003-S010

Left: Man plowing with ox, Trees, House / 3. ***Center:*** 3. ***Right:*** 3 / Woman seated with cornucopia / THREE. ***Engraver:*** New England Bank Note Co. ***Comments:*** H-MA-1255-S5. Mar. 1, 1858.

Rarity: —

$3 • W-MA-3280-003-A030

Left: 3 / Woman seated with eagle / 3. ***Center:*** Medallion head / Train / Medallion head. ***Bottom center:*** Dog and strongbox. ***Right:*** 3 / Train backed up to wharf, People standing. ***Engraver:*** Chas. E. Ely, Philadelphia. ***Comments:*** H-MA-1255-A15. Altered from $3 Geauga Insurance Co., Painesville, Ohio. 18__. 1840s.

Rarity: —

$5 • W-MA-3280-005-S020

CJF

Engraver: Draper, Toppan & Co. ***Comments:*** H-MA-1255-S10. From a fraudulently modified plate originally for $5 Lebanon Miami Banking Co., Lebanon, Ohio. 18__. 1850s.

Rarity: URS-7
VG $125; **VF** $175

$5 • W-MA-3280-005-A040

Left: 5 / Train at wharf / 5. ***Center:*** 5 / Indian man seated on cliff observing town / 5. ***Right:*** 5 / Train backed up to wharf, People standing / 5. ***Engraver:*** Chas. E. Ely, Philadelphia. ***Comments:*** H-MA-1255-A20. 18__. 1840s.

Rarity: —

$10 • W-MA-3280-010-R010
Engraver: New England Bank Note Co. ***Comments:*** H-MA-1255-R5. Raised from W-MA-3280-001-G020. 18__. 1850s.
Rarity: —

$10 • W-MA-3280-010-R020
Engraver: New England Bank Note Co. ***Comments:*** H-MA-1255-R10. Raised from W-MA-3280-002-G050. 18__. 1850s.
Rarity: —

WATERVILLE, MASSACHUSETTS

Located on the west side of the Kennebec River, Waterville was earlier part of Winslow but split off and incorporated in 1802. The town was in the Maine District of Massachusetts until Maine achieved statehood on March 15, 1820. Agriculture was the main industry, but the manufacturing of lumber, tools, paper, and the like was also important.

See also Waterville, Maine.

Waterville Bank {1st}
1814–1820 • 1820–1831
W-MA-3290 • W-ME-1510

History: The Waterville Bank was one of six new banks chartered in 1813 in the district of Maine by the Massachusetts General Court. It was incorporated in February 1814 with $100,000 capital. In January 1820, circulation was $97,027. After March 15, 1820, the bank's address was in the state of Maine. A statement of the bank dated December 19, 1827, showed capital stock of $100,000, paper money in circulation of $128,708, real estate of $1,482.50, and currency held in the hands of the president $81,843. The president kept these bills in a vault in the bank. The bank had incurred deep losses in Boston years earlier, with no less than $32,334.46 being carried on the books from September 1818 forward. The bank's charter was to expire on October 31, 1831. In this year the Ticonic Bank succeeded the Waterville Bank, occupying the field alone until 1850 when another bank called the Waterville Bank was started.[41] See also listing under Maine.

Numismatic Commentary: The New England Bank Note Co. was the sole producer of this bank's notes, and enough survive to give collectors a chance to add to their collections. All notes of this bank are of the PSSP type.

VALID ISSUES

Notes With Massachusetts Address

$1 • W-MA-3290-001-G010
Left: 1 / 1. ***Center:*** ONE DOLLAR, Text. ***Right:*** 1 / 1. ***Comments:*** H-MA-1260-G10, Wait-Unlisted. 1810s.
Rarity: —

$2 • W-MA-3290-002-G020
Comments: H-MA-1260-G16, Wait-Unlisted. Similar to W-MA-3290-001-G010 but with different denomination. 1810s.
Rarity: —

$3 • W-MA-3290-003-G030
Comments: H-MA-1260-G18, Wait-Unlisted. Similar to W-MA-3290-001-G010 but with different denomination. 1810s.
Rarity: —

$5 • W-MA-3290-005-G040
Left: State arms / 5, Plate letter, 5. ***Center:*** FIVE DOLLARS, Text. ***Right:*** 5, Plate letter, 5. ***Comments:*** H-MA-1260-G20, Wait-Unlisted. 1810s.
Rarity: —

$10 • W-MA-3290-010-G050
Comments: H-MA-1260-G22, Wait-Unlisted. Similar to W-MA-3290-005-G040 but with different denomination. 1810s.
Rarity: —

$20 • W-MA-3290-020-G060
Comments: H-MA-1260-G24, Wait-Unlisted. Similar to W-MA-3290-005-G040 but with different denomination. 1810s.
Rarity: —

$50 • W-MA-3290-050-G070
Comments: H-MA-1260-G26, Wait-Unlisted. Similar to W-MA-3290-005-G040 but with different denomination. 1810s.
Rarity: —

$100 • W-MA-3290-100-G080
Comments: H-MA-1260-G28, Wait-Unlisted. Similar to W-MA-3290-005-G040 but with different denomination. 1810s.
Rarity: —

Notes With Maine Address

$1 • W-ME-1510-001-G010
Comments: H-ME-600-G4, Wait-Unlisted. No description available. 1820s.
Rarity: *None known*

$2 • W-ME-1510-002-G020
Comments: H-ME-600-G8, Wait-Unlisted. No description available. 1820s.
Rarity: *None known*

$3 • W-ME-1510-003-G030
Comments: H-ME-600-G12, Wait-Unlisted. No description available. 1820s.
Rarity: *None known*

$5 • W-ME-1510-005-G040
Comments: H-ME-600-G16, Wait-Unlisted. No description available. 1820s.
Rarity: *None known*

$10 • W-ME-1510-010-G050
Comments: H-ME-600-G20, Wait-Unlisted. No description available. 1820s.
Rarity: *None known*

WESTFIELD, MASSACHUSETTS

Woronoco was the original name of this district, defined as "winding land" in the original language of the Pocomtuc tribe that lived here. Massachusetts bought Woronoco from the natives to be part of Springfield in 1647. In 1669 the town of Westfield was officially incorporated.

Agriculture dominated the ways of the town for over a century, but mills to produce lumber and flour arrived later. Bricks, whips, and cigars became important in the 19th century. In 1830 a canal connecting to New Haven brought prosperity and increased commerce.

Hampden Bank

1825–1865

W-MA-3300

History: The Hampden Bank was chartered on June 18, 1825, with an authorized capital of $100,000, which was raised to $150,000 in 1854. Its circulation ranged from a low of $79,178 in 1849 to a high of $146,696 in 1863.

The business of the Hampden Bank was succeeded by the Hampden National Bank of Westfield after it was chartered in 1865.

Numismatic Commentary: Notes from this bank are available with some frequency. Many have a vignette of a thoroughfare of the town and presumably the bank building in the distance. Local scenery is always in demand by collectors.

Valid Issues

$1 • W-MA-3300-001-G010

Left: Narrow panel of lathework circle segments. ***Center:*** 1 / 1 / Flower garlands and gridwork segments / 1 / 1. ***Right:*** Narrow panel of lathework circle segments. ***Engraver:*** PSSP. ***Comments:*** H-MA-1265-G2. 18__. 1820s–1830s.

Rarity: —

$1 • W-MA-3300-001-G010a

Left: ONE / D / ONE vertically. ***Right:*** ONE / D / ONE vertically. ***Engraver:*** PSSP. ***Comments:*** H-MA-1265-G4. Similar to W-MA-3300-001-G010. 18__. 1830s.

Rarity: —

$1 • W-MA-3300-001-G020

Left: 1 / Minerva standing with 1 / 1. ***Center:*** ONE / Commerce seated with caduceus and cornucopia, Plow and ships / ONE. ***Right:*** 1 / Eagle / 1. ***Engraver:*** PSSP. ***Comments:*** H-MA-1265-G6. 18__. 1830s–1840s.

Rarity: —

$1 • W-MA-3300-001-G030

Left: ONE / Woman with sickle and sheaf / ONE. ***Center:*** 1 / Street scene in Westfield / 1. ***Right:*** ONE / Two farmers, one sharpening scythe, one reaping. ***Engraver:*** New England Bank Note Co. ***Comments:*** H-MA-1265-G8. 18__. 1840s–1850s.

Rarity: —

$1 • W-MA-3300-001-G040

Left: Justice standing / ONE. ***Center:*** Street scene in Westfield / 1. ***Right:*** 1 / Portrait of Benjamin Franklin. ***Engraver:*** American Bank Note Co. ***Comments:*** H-MA-1265-G10. 18__. 1860s.

Rarity: —

$2 • W-MA-3300-002-G050

Left: Narrow panel of lathework circle segments. ***Center:*** 2 / 2 / Flower garlands and gridwork segments / 2 / 2. ***Right:*** Narrow panel of lathework circle segments. ***Engraver:*** PSSP. ***Comments:*** H-MA-1265-G12. 18__. 1820s–1830s.

Rarity: —

$2 • W-MA-3300-002-G050a

Left: Five TWOs vertically. ***Right:*** Five TWOs vertically. ***Engraver:*** PSSP. ***Comments:*** H-MA-1265-G14. Similar to W-MA-3300-002-G050. 18__. 1830s.

Rarity: —

$2 • W-MA-3300-002-G060

Left: 2 / Hebe watering eagle / 2. ***Center:*** 2 / Plow, Commerce seated with caduceus and cornucopia, Ships / 2. ***Right:*** 2 / Justice standing / 2. ***Engraver:*** PSSP. ***Comments:*** H-MA-1265-G16. 18__. 1830s–1840s.

Rarity: —

$2 • W-MA-3300-002-G070

Left: 2 / Woman with sheaf and hat / Two cherubs. ***Center:*** 2 / Street scene in Westfield. ***Bottom center:*** Steamboat. ***Right:*** 2 / Train / Two cherubs. ***Engraver:*** New England Bank Note Co. ***Comments:*** H-MA-1265-G18. 18__. 1840s–1850s.

Rarity: —

$2 • W-MA-3300-002-G080 NJW

Engraver: American Bank Note Co. ***Comments:*** H-MA-1265-G20. 18__. 1860s.

Rarity: URS-7
F $100; **VF** $200

$3 • W-MA-3300-003-G090

Left: Narrow panel of lathework circle segments. ***Center:*** 3 / 3 / Flower garlands and gridwork segments / 3 / 3. ***Right:*** Narrow panel of lathework circle segments. ***Engraver:*** PSSP. ***Comments:*** H-MA-1265-G22. 18__. 1820s–1830s.

Rarity: —

$3 • W-MA-3300-003-G090a

Left: THREE vertically. ***Right:*** THREE vertically. ***Engraver:*** PSSP. ***Comments:*** H-MA-1265-G24. Similar to W-MA-3300-003-G090. 18__. 1830s.

Rarity: —

$3 • W-MA-3300-003-G100

Left: 3 / Eagle on rock / 3. ***Center:*** 3 / Plow, Commerce seated with caduceus and cornucopia, Ships / 3 / Panel bearing THREE. ***Right:*** 3 / Woman standing with cornucopia / 3. ***Engraver:*** PSSP. ***Comments:*** H-MA-1265-G26. 18__. 1830s–1840s.

Rarity: —

$3 • W-MA-3300-003-G110

Left: THREE / Woman / THREE. ***Center:*** 3 / Street scene in Westfield / 3. ***Bottom center:*** Ship. ***Right:*** 3 / Boy pushing sheep into stream, Man watching / THREE. ***Engraver:*** New England Bank Note Co. ***Comments:*** H-MA-1265-G28. 18__. 1840s–1850s.

Rarity: —

$5 • W-MA-3300-005-G120

Left: Lathework chain bearing MASSACHUSETTS / 5 / 5 vertically. ***Center:*** Alternating flower garlands and gridwork segments. ***Right:*** 5 / 5 vertically. ***Engraver:*** PSSP. ***Comments:*** H-MA-1265-G30. 18__. 1820s.

Rarity: —

$5 • W-MA-3300-005-G120a

Engraver: PSSP. ***Comments:*** H-MA-1265-G32. Similar to W-MA-3300-005-G120 but with zigzag ruled lines. 18__. 1820s–1830s.

Rarity: —

$5 • W-MA-3300-005-G120b

Engraver: PSSP. ***Comments:*** H-MA-1265-G34. Similar to W-MA-3300-005-G120 but with spiral lathework lines. 18__. 1830s.

Rarity: —

$5 • W-MA-3300-005-G130

Left: Panel bearing FIVE / Plenty and Minerva seated / V. ***Center:*** FIVE / Allegorical woman seated / FIVE / Panel of microletters. ***Right:*** 5 / Eagle / 5. ***Engraver:*** PSSP. ***Comments:*** H-MA-1265-G36. 18__. 1830s–1840s.

Rarity: —

$5 • W-MA-3300-005-G140

Left: FIVE / Milkmaid / FIVE. ***Center:*** Street scene in Westfield. ***Right:*** FIVE / Eagle in 5. ***Engraver:*** New England Bank Note Co. ***Comments:*** H-MA-1265-G38. 18__. 1840s–1850s.

Rarity: —

$5 • W-MA-3300-005-G150 HA

Engraver: American Bank Note Co. ***Comments:*** H-MA-1265-G40. 18__. 1860s.

Rarity: URS-7
F $100

$10 • W-MA-3300-010-G160

Left: Lathework chain bearing MASSACHUSETTS / 10 / 10 vertically. ***Center:*** Alternating flower garlands and gridwork segments. ***Right:*** 10 / 10 vertically. ***Engraver:*** Perkins. ***Comments:*** H-MA-1265-G42. 18__. 1820s.

Rarity: —

$10 • W-MA-3300-010-G160a

Engraver: PSSP. ***Comments:*** H-MA-1265-G44. Similar to W-MA-3300-010-G160. 18__. 1820s–1830s.

Rarity: —

$10 • W-MA-3300-010-G160b

Engraver: PSSP. ***Comments:*** H-MA-1265-G46. Similar to W-MA-3300-010-G160. 18__. 1830s.

Rarity: —

$10 • W-MA-3300-010-G170

Left: Panel bearing TEN / Manhattan spilling water jug / TEN. ***Center:*** TEN / Ceres seated / TEN / Panel of microletters. ***Right:*** Panel bearing 10 / Portrait of Indian / 10. ***Engraver:*** PSSP. ***Comments:*** H-MA-1265-G48. 18__. 1830s–1840s.

Rarity: —

$10 • W-MA-3300-010-G180

Left: TEN / Male portrait / TEN. ***Center:*** Street scene in Westfield. ***Right:*** 10 / Woman standing with wreath. ***Engraver:*** New England Bank Note Co. ***Comments:*** H-MA-1265-G50. 18__. 1840s–1850s.

Rarity: —

$20 • W-MA-3300-020-G190

Left: Lathework chain bearing MASSACHUSETTS / 20 / 20 vertically. ***Center:*** Alternating flower garlands and gridwork segments. ***Right:*** 20 / 20 vertically. ***Engraver:*** PSSP. ***Comments:*** H-MA-1265-G52. 18__. 1820s–1830s.

Rarity: —

$20 • W-MA-3300-020-G200

Left: 20 / XX / 20. ***Center:*** 20 / Woman seated with scales, Sheaf and bales, Men plowing, Ship / 20. ***Right:*** TWENTY vertically. ***Engraver:*** PSSP / New England Bank Note Co. ***Comments:*** H-MA-1265-G54. 18__. 1830s.

Rarity: —

$20 • W-MA-3300-020-G210

Left: TWENTY vertically. ***Center:*** 20 / Street scene in Westfield. ***Right:*** TWENTY across 20 / Portrait of George Washington. ***Engraver:*** New England Bank Note Co. ***Comments:*** H-MA-1265-G56. 18__. 1840s–1850s.

Rarity: —

$50 • W-MA-3300-050-G220

Left: Lathework chain bearing MASSACHUSETTS / 50 / 50 vertically. ***Center:*** Alternating flower garlands and gridwork segments. ***Right:*** 50 / 50 vertically. ***Engraver:*** PSSP. ***Comments:*** H-MA-1265-G58. 18__. 1820s–1830s.

Rarity: —

$50 • W-MA-3300-050-G230

Left: 50 / Cornucopia, Woman standing with ankles crossed, Staff, Anchor / 50. ***Center:*** FIFTY DOLLARS / 50. ***Right:*** FIFTY vertically. ***Engraver:*** New England Bank Note Co. / PSSP. ***Comments:*** H-MA-1265-G60. 18__. 1830s.

Rarity: —

$50 • W-MA-3300-050-G240

Left: FIFTY / Medallion head / 50. ***Center:*** Street scene in Westfield. ***Right:*** 50 / Portrait / FIFTY. ***Engraver:*** New England Bank Note Co. ***Comments:*** H-MA-1265-G62. 18__. 1840s–1850s.

Rarity: —

$100 • W-MA-3300-100-G250

Left: Lathework chain bearing MASSACHUSETTS / 100 / 100 vertically. ***Center:*** Alternating flower garlands and gridwork segments. ***Right:*** 100 / 100 vertically. ***Engraver:*** Perkins. ***Comments:*** H-MA-1265-G64. 18__. 1820s–1830s.

Rarity: —

$100 • W-MA-3300-100-G260

Left: Lathework panel bearing C / Portrait of George Washington / C. ***Center:*** 100 / Manhattan reclining pouring water, Ship / 100. ***Right:*** Lathework panel bearing ONE HUNDRED vertically. ***Engraver:*** New England Bank Note Co. / PSSP. ***Comments:*** H-MA-1265-G66. 18__. 1830s.

Rarity: —

$100 • W-MA-3300-100-G270

Left: 100 vertically. ***Center:*** C / Street scene in Westfield. ***Bottom center:*** Dog and strongbox. ***Right:*** 100 / Medallion head. ***Engraver:*** New England Bank Note Co. ***Comments:*** H-MA-1265-G68. 18__. 1840s–1850s.

Rarity: —

Non-Valid Issues

$1 • W-MA-3300-001-A010

Left: ONE on die vertically. ***Center:*** Overseer on horse and men picking cotton / Indian stalking two deer. ***Bottom center:*** Sleeping dog. ***Right:*** 1 / Female portrait. ***Overprint:*** Red ONE. ***Engraver:*** Bald, Cousland & Co. / Baldwin, Bald & Co. ***Comments:*** H-MA-1265-A5. Altered from $1 Southern Bank of Georgia, Bainbridge, Georgia. 18__. 1860s.

Rarity: —

$2 • W-MA-3300-002-A020

Left: 2. ***Center:*** Men haying and loading hay onto wagon. ***Right:*** 2 / Woman with sheaf. ***Tint:*** Red-brown 2s and TWO DOLLARS. ***Engraver:*** Danforth, Wright & Co. ***Comments:*** H-MA-1265-A10. Altered from $2 Southern Bank of Georgia, Bainbridge, Georgia. March 1, 1858.

Rarity: —

$2 • W-MA-3300-002-A030

Left: 2 / Reverses of U.S. and Spanish-American silver dollars. ***Center:*** Man and woman standing by pump and trough. ***Bottom center:*** Bull. ***Right:*** 2 / Allegorical woman seated with 2. ***Overprint:*** Red TWO. ***Engraver:*** Wellstood, Hay & Whiting. ***Comments:*** H-MA-1265-A15. Altered from $2 Thames Bank, Laurel, Indiana. 1850s.

Rarity: —

$3 • W-MA-3300-003-S010

SI

Comments: H-MA-1265-S5. Sept. 10, 18__. 1860s.

Rarity: URS-7

F $50

$5 • W-MA-3300-005-N010

Center: Beehive. ***Comments:*** H-MA-1265-N5.

Rarity: —

$10 • W-MA-3300-010-A040

Left: Diagonal X / TEN. ***Center:*** Woman leaning on rock, Train / Ceres with sheaf on back. ***Right:*** 10 / Portrait of George Washington. ***Overprint:*** Red TEN. ***Engraver:*** Bald, Cousland & Co. / Baldwin, Bald & Cousland. ***Comments:*** H-MA-1265-A20. Altered from $10 Southern Bank of Georgia, Bainbridge, Georgia. 18__. 1860s.

Rarity: —

Westfield Bank

1851–1864

W-MA-3310

History: The Westfield Bank was incorporated on May 24, 1851, with an authorized capital of $100,000. The *Banker's Magazine* reported this in October 1851:

> This institution, incorporated by the last Legislature, has nearly completed its banking-house, and commences operations this week. Messrs. E.D. Beach, S.S. Day, and William Stowe, of this town, commissioners appointed by Governor Boutwell for that purpose, examined and counted the specie in its vaults on Saturday, and, we understand, found matters in good shape. The bills of the new bank are of very elegant design and execution, and cannot fail to be in good demand. The vignette of the *ones* bears a very fine likeness of the late President Taylor.

The capital was to be paid in before May 1, 1852. By 1854 it had increased to $150,000. The circulation of the bank was $56,881 in 1858 and $149,765 in 1863. Real estate was valued at $5,991.54. In 1864 it was $12,651.54. Specie averaged at about $6,000.

The business of the Westfield Bank was succeeded by the First National Bank of Westfield after it was chartered in 1864.

Numismatic Commentary: Genuine notes are available in the marketplace. Some issues show a view of the town green with buildings in the background.

Valid Issues

$1 • W-MA-3310-001-G010

Left: ONE / Portrait of Zachary Taylor / 1. ***Center:*** Indian man seated, Plow / 1 bearing ONE, ONE. ***Right:*** 1 / Medallion head of William Shakespeare bearing ONE / ONE. ***Engraver:*** Danforth, Bald & Co. ***Comments:*** H-MA-1270-G2. 18__. 1850s.

Rarity: —

Collectors and Researchers:

If you have new information about any banks or notes listed in this volume, contact Whitman Publishing, Attn: Obsolete Paper Money, 3101 Clairmont Road, Suite G, Atlanta, GA 30329.

$1 • W-MA-3310-001-G010a

CJF

Engraver: Danforth, Bald & Co. / ABNCo. monogram. ***Comments:*** H-MA-1270-G2a. Similar to W-MA-3310-001-G010 but with additional engraver imprint. 18__. 1850s–1860s.

Rarity: URS-6
F $150; **VF** $250

$2 • W-MA-3310-002-G020

Left: 2 / State arms / TWO. ***Center:*** Two women, one seated holding scroll and pointing upward / 2. ***Bottom center:*** Fish. ***Right:*** TWO / Two Indians / TWO. ***Engraver:*** Danforth, Bald & Co. ***Comments:*** H-MA-1270-G4. 18__. 1850s.

Rarity: —

$2 • W-MA-3310-002-G020a

Engraver: Danforth, Bald & Co. / ABNCo. monogram. ***Comments:*** H-MA-1270-G4a. Similar to W-MA-3310-002-G020 but with additional engraver imprint. 18__. 1850s–1860s.

Rarity: —

$3 • W-MA-3310-003-G030

Left: THREE / Dogs chasing birds under tree. ***Center:*** Farmer, sailor, and mechanic. ***Bottom center:*** Dog, key, and strongbox. ***Right:*** 3 / Woman seated instructing two children / THREE. ***Engraver:*** Danforth, Bald & Co. ***Comments:*** H-MA-1270-G6. 18__. 1850s.

Rarity: —

$3 • W-MA-3310-003-G030a

Engraver: Danforth, Bald & Co. / ABNCo. monogram. ***Comments:*** H-MA-1270-G6a. Similar to W-MA-3310-003-G030 but with additional engraver imprint. 18__. 1850s–1860s.

Rarity: —

$5 • W-MA-3310-005-G040

Left: Two women and boy seated, Two sailors. ***Center:*** FIVE / View of Westfield Green. ***Right:*** 5. ***Engraver:*** Danforth, Bald & Co. ***Comments:*** H-MA-1270-G8. 18__. 1850s.

Rarity: —

$5 • W-MA-3310-005-G040a

Engraver: Danforth, Bald & Co. / ABNCo. monogram. ***Comments:*** H-MA-1270-G8a. Similar to W-MA-3310-005-G040 but with additional engraver imprint. 18__. 1850s–1860s.

Rarity: —

$10 • W-MA-3310-010-G050

Left: 10 / Sloop, train, and bridge. ***Center:*** View of Westfield Green. ***Bottom center:*** Train. ***Right:*** X / Medallion head bearing TEN / 10. ***Engraver:*** Danforth, Bald & Co. ***Comments:*** H-MA-1270-G10. 18__. 1850s.

Rarity: —

$10 • W-MA-3310-010-G050a

Engraver: Danforth, Bald & Co. / ABNCo. monogram. ***Comments:*** H-MA-1270-G10a. Similar to W-MA-3310-010-G050 but with additional engraver imprint. 18__. 1850s–1860s.

Rarity: —

$20 • W-MA-3310-020-G060

JF

Engraver: Danforth, Bald & Co. ***Comments:*** H-MA-1270-G12. Proof. 18__. 1850s.

Rarity: URS-3
Proof $3,500

$20 • W-MA-3310-020-G060a

Left: TWENTY / Woman drawing water from well. ***Center:*** View of Westfield Green. ***Bottom center:*** Hay wagon. ***Right:*** Medallion head bearing 20 / Blacksmith. ***Engraver:*** Danforth, Bald & Co. / ABNCo. monogram. ***Comments:*** H-MA-1270-G12a. Similar to W-MA-3310-020-G060 but with additional engraver imprint. 18__. 1850s–1860s.

Rarity: —

$50 • W-MA-3310-050-G070

Left: 50 / Cattle. ***Center:*** View of Westfield Green. ***Right:*** 50 / Woman tending whip machine in factory. ***Engraver:*** Danforth, Bald & Co. ***Comments:*** H-MA-1270-G14. 18__. 1850s.

Rarity: —

$50 • W-MA-3310-050-G070a

Engraver: Danforth, Bald & Co. / ABNCo. monogram. ***Comments:*** H-MA-1270-G14a. Similar to W-MA-3310-050-G070 but with additional engraver imprint. 18__. 1850s–1860s.

Rarity: —

Uncut Sheets

$1-$2-$3-$5 • W-MA-3310-001.002.003.005-US010

Vignette(s): ($1) Portrait of Zachary Taylor / Man seated, Plow / Portrait of Shakespeare. ***($2)*** State arms / Two women, one seated holding scroll and pointing upward / Fish / Two Indians. ***($3)*** Dogs chasing birds under tree / Farmer, sailor, and mechanic / Dog, key, and strongbox / Woman seated instructing two children. ***($5)*** Two women and boy seated, Two sailors / View of Westfield Green. ***Engraver:*** Danforth, Bald & Co. ***Comments:*** H-MA-1270-G2, G4, G6, G8. 18__. 1850s.

Rarity: —

Non-Valid Issues

$3 • W-MA-3310-003-S010

Left: THREE / State arms / THREE. ***Center:*** 3 / Woman seated with pole and shield. ***Right:*** Panel bearing floral pattern and lathework. ***Engraver:*** Rawdon, Wright & Hatch. ***Comments:*** H-MA-1270-S5. 18__. 1850s.

Rarity: —

$5 • **W-MA-3310-005-C040a** CJF

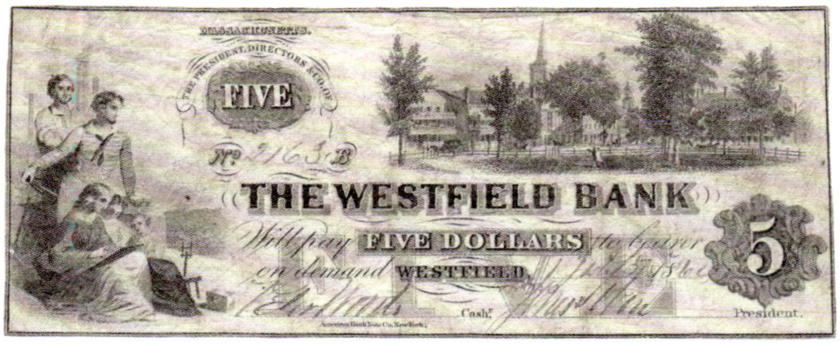

Engraver: American Bank Note Co. ***Comments:*** H-MA-1270-C8a. Counterfeit of W-MA-3310-005-G040a but with different engraver imprint. 18__. 1860s.

Rarity: URS-7
F $100

$5 • **W-MA-3310-005-S020** CJF

Overprint: Red FIVE. ***Engraver:*** New England Bank Note Co. ***Comments:*** H-MA-1270-S10. 18__. 1850s.

Rarity: —
VF $165

Weymouth, Massachusetts

Weymouth was founded as Wessagusset in 1622 and is the second oldest town in the state. It was renamed in 1635 when 100 settlers from Weymouth, England, colonized the area. It was a fishing and agricultural town with a population of 1,470 people by 1776. Bog iron was produced in the Weymouth Iron Works in 1837, and manufacturing and trade were soon the economy of the day, replacing the maritime and agricultural past. Local financial institutions and railways in the mid-19th century made the town economically prosperous.

Union Bank of Weymouth and Braintree

1832–1864

W-MA-3320

History: The Union Bank of Weymouth and Braintree was chartered on March 17, 1832, with an authorized capital of $100,000. Bills in circulation totaled $37,379 in 1839. The capital was raised to $150,000 by 1854. The circulation was $92,032 in 1863.

The interests of the bank were succeeded by the Union National Bank of Weymouth, chartered on September 6, 1864.

See also listing under Braintree, W-MA-1090.

Numismatic Commentary: Genuine notes are hard to locate, as most were redeemed and burned. This process continued several years after the charter of the national bank that succeeded its interests.

Valid Issues

$1 • **W-MA-3320-001-G010**

Left: Lathework panel bearing MASSACHUSETTS vertically. ***Center:*** 1 / 1 / Alternating flower garlands and gridwork segments / ONE / 1 / 1. ***Right:*** Lathework panel bearing ONE / D / ONE vertically. ***Engraver:*** PSSP. ***Comments:*** H-MA-1275-G2. 18__. 1830s.

Rarity: —

$1 • **W-MA-3320-001-G020**

Center: Machinery and merchandise flanking Ceres seated holding sickle and rake, Factories and harbor / ONE / Panel outlining white ONE. ***Right:*** 1 / Ship / ONE. ***Engraver:*** PSSP / New England Bank Note Co. ***Comments:*** H-MA-1275-G4. Beware of altered W-MA-3320-001-A010 from the same plate as the genuine. 18__. 1830s.

Rarity: —

$1 • **W-MA-3320-001-G030**

Left: ONE / Profile of George Washington / ONE. ***Center:*** 1 / Two blacksmiths at anvil in front of forge / 1 / Panel outlining white ONE. ***Right:*** ONE / Woman / ONE. ***Engraver:*** New England Bank Note Co. ***Comments:*** H-MA-1275-G6. 18__. 1840s–1850s.

Rarity: —

$1 • **W-MA-3320-001-G040** TD

Engraver: Baldwin, Adams & Co. ***Comments:*** H-Unlisted. Proof. 18__. 1850s.

Rarity: URS-3
Proof $1,200

$1 • **W-MA-3320-001-G040a** TD

Overprint: Red ONE. ***Engraver:*** Baldwin, Adams & Co. ***Comments:*** H-MA-1275-G8a. Similar to W-MA-3320-001-G040. 18__. 1850s.

Rarity: URS-4
F $1,000; **Proof** $1,500

$2 • W-MA-3320-002-G050

Left: Lathework panel bearing MASSACHUSETTS vertically. ***Center:*** 2 / 2 / Alternating flower garlands and gridwork segments / TWO / 2 / 2. ***Right:*** Lathework panel bearing five TWOs vertically. ***Engraver:*** PSSP. ***Comments:*** H-MA-1275-G10. 18__. 1830s.

Rarity: —

$2 • W-MA-3320-002-G060

Left: 2 / Woman standing with staff, Cornucopia / TWO. ***Center:*** TWO / Machinery and merchandise flanking Ceres seated holding sickle and rake, Factories and harbor / Panel outlining white TWO. ***Right:*** 2 / Woman wearing hat, Trees / TWO. ***Engraver:*** New England Bank Note Co. / PSSP. ***Comments:*** H-MA-1275-G12. 18__. 1830s.

Rarity: —

$2 • W-MA-3320-002-G070

Left: TWO / Female portrait / 2. ***Center:*** 2 / Woman giving drink to one of two seated men / 2 / Panel outlining white TWO. ***Right:*** TWO / Bust of female reaper. ***Engraver:*** New England Bank Note Co. ***Comments:*** H-MA-1275-G14. 18__. 1840s–1850s.

Rarity: —

$2 • W-MA-3320-002-G080

TD

Engraver: Baldwin, Adams & Co. ***Comments:*** H-Unlisted. Proof. 18__. 1850s.

Rarity: URS-4
Proof $2,500

$2 • W-MA-3320-002-G080a

Left: TWO / TWO. ***Center:*** Spread eagle on shield holding arrows and olive branch flanked by state flags. ***Right:*** 2 / Portrait of Zachary Taylor. ***Overprint:*** Red TWO. ***Engraver:*** Baldwin, Adams & Co. ***Comments:*** H-MA-1275-G16a. Similar to W-MA-3320-002-G080. 18__. 1850s.

Rarity: —
Selected auction price: Heritage, September 2011, Lot 15765, Choice AN $2,070

$3 • W-MA-3320-003-G090

Left: Lathework panel bearing MASSACHUSETTS vertically. ***Center:*** 3 / 3 / Alternating flower garlands and gridwork segments / THREE / 3 / 3. ***Right:*** Lathework panel bearing THREE vertically. ***Engraver:*** PSSP. ***Comments:*** H-MA-1275-G18. 18__. 1830s.

Rarity: —

$3 • W-MA-3320-003-G100

CC

Engraver: New England Bank Note Co. / PSSP. ***Comments:*** H-MA-1275-G20. Beware of altered W-MA-3320-003-A020 from the same plate as the genuine. 18__. 1830s.

Rarity: URS-5
VG $250; **F** $575

$3 • W-MA-3320-003-G110

Left: THREE / Farmer sharpening scythe / 3 across THREE. ***Center:*** 3 / Woman placing garland on eagle, Beehive and cornucopia / 3 / Panel outlining white THREE. ***Right:*** THREE / Sailor standing on wharf with hat / 3 across THREE. ***Engraver:*** New England Bank Note Co. ***Comments:*** H-MA-1275-G22. 18__. 1840s–1850s.

Rarity: —

$3 • W-MA-3320-003-G120

TD

Engraver: Baldwin, Adams & Co. ***Comments:*** H-Unlisted. Proof. 18__. 1850s.

Rarity: —

$3 • W-MA-3320-003-G120a

TD

Overprint: Red 3. ***Engraver:*** Baldwin, Adams & Co. ***Comments:*** H-MA-1275-G24a. Similar to W-MA-3320-003-G120. Proof. 18__. 1850s.

Rarity: —

$5 • W-MA-3320-005-G130

Left: Lathework chain bearing MASSACHUSETTS / 5 / 5 vertically. ***Center:*** Alternating flower garlands and gridwork segments / FIVE. ***Right:*** 5 / 5 vertically. ***Engraver:*** PSSP. ***Comments:*** H-MA-1275-G26. 18__. 1830s.

Rarity: —

$5 • W-MA-3320-005-G140
Left: 5 / Blacksmith and anvil / FIVE. ***Center:*** Mercury standing with 5, Cornucopia and merchandise, Factories and ship / V / Panel outlining white FIVE. ***Right:*** 5 / Ceres kneeling / FIVE. ***Engraver:*** New England Bank Note Co. ***Comments:*** H-MA-1275-G28. 18__. 1830s.

Rarity: —

$5 • W-MA-3320-005-G150
Left: 5 / FIVE / 5. ***Center:*** V / Eagle on wharf with plow, cannon, and anchor, Ships / V / Panel outlining white FIVE. ***Right:*** 5 / FIVE / 5. ***Engraver:*** New England Bank Note Co. ***Comments:*** H-MA-1275-G30. 18__. 1840s–1850s.

Rarity: —

$5 • W-MA-3320-005-G160
Left: FIVE / V. ***Center:*** Street in Weymouth, Men, horses, vehicles, and buildings. ***Right:*** V / Portrait of Daniel Webster / V. ***Overprint:*** Red. ***Comments:*** H-MA-1275-G32a. 18__. 1850s.

Rarity: —

$10 • W-MA-3320-010-G170
Left: Lathework chain bearing MASSACHUSETTS / 10 / 10 vertically. ***Center:*** Alternating flower garlands and gridwork segments / TEN. ***Right:*** 10 / 10 vertically. ***Engraver:*** PSSP. ***Comments:*** H-MA-1275-G34. 18__. 1830s.

Rarity: —

$10 • W-MA-3320-010-G180
Engraver: Unverified, but likely New England Bank Note Co. ***Comments:*** H-MA-1275-G36. No description available. 18__. 1830s.

Rarity: *None known*

$10 • W-MA-3320-010-G190
Left: Panel bearing 10 / X / 10. ***Center:*** Allegorical male standing by oxen and plow / 10. ***Right:*** TEN / Woman standing with rudder, Cornucopia. ***Engraver:*** New England Bank Note Co. ***Comments:*** H-MA-1275-G38. 18__. 1840s–1850s.

Rarity: —

$10 • W-MA-3320-010-G200
Left: TEN / Street in Weymouth. ***Right:*** X / Portrait of George Washington. ***Comments:*** H-MA-1275-G40. 18__. 1850s.

Rarity: —

$20 • W-MA-3320-020-G210
Left: Lathework chain bearing MASSACHUSETTS / 20 / 20 vertically. ***Center:*** Alternating flower garlands and gridwork segments / TWENTY. ***Right:*** 20 / 20 vertically. ***Engraver:*** PSSP. ***Comments:*** H-MA-1275-G42. 18__. 1830s.

Rarity: —

$20 • W-MA-3320-020-G220
Left: Steamboat / XX / Train. ***Center:*** Three women seated with eagle, pole and cap, shield, scales, and book / 20 / Panel outlining white TWENTY. ***Right:*** XX / Milkmaid standing with pail. ***Engraver:*** New England Bank Note Co. ***Comments:*** H-MA-1275-G44. 18__. 1830s.

Rarity: —

$20 • W-MA-3320-020-G230
Left: 20 / Woman seated with book on lap, opening chest. ***Center:*** XX / Eagle on rock / XX. ***Right:*** 20 / Ship in harbor. ***Engraver:*** New England Bank Note Co. ***Comments:*** H-MA-1275-G46. 18__. 1840s–1850s.

Rarity: —

$20 • W-MA-3320-020-G240
Left: XX / Portrait of Benjamin Franklin. ***Center:*** Street in Weymouth. ***Right:*** 20. ***Comments:*** H-MA-1275-G48. 18__. 1850s.

Rarity: —

$50 • W-MA-3320-050-G250
Left: Lathework chain bearing MASSACHUSETTS / 50 / 50 vertically. ***Center:*** Alternating flower garlands and gridwork segments / FIFTY. ***Right:*** 50 / 50 vertically. ***Engraver:*** PSSP. ***Comments:*** H-MA-1275-G50. 18__. 1830s.

Rarity: —

$50 • W-MA-3320-050-G260
Left: 50 / Steamboat and schooner. ***Center:*** Farmyard scene, Load of hay with two men on it, Man with rake and pail. ***Right:*** L / Justice kneeling. ***Engraver:*** New England Bank Note Co. ***Comments:*** H-MA-1275-G52. 18__. 1830s.

Rarity: —

$50 • W-MA-3320-050-G270
Left: FIFTY / Woman standing with wreath and flowers / FIFTY. ***Center:*** 50 / Man restraining prancing horse / 50. ***Right:*** FIFTY / Woman standing with cornucopia / FIFTY. ***Engraver:*** New England Bank Note Co. ***Comments:*** H-MA-1275-G54. 18__. 1840s–1850s.

Rarity: —

$100 • W-MA-3320-100-G280
Left: Lathework chain bearing MASSACHUSETTS / 100 / 100 vertically. ***Center:*** Alternating flower garlands and gridwork segments. ***Right:*** 100 / 100 vertically. ***Engraver:*** PSSP. ***Comments:*** H-MA-1275-G56. 18__. 1830s.

Rarity: —

$100 • W-MA-3320-100-G290
Left: ONE HUNDRED on 100 / Portrait of William Henry Harrison. ***Center:*** Wharf scene, Men loading wagon with barrels. ***Right:*** ONE HUNDRED on 100 / Portrait of Christopher Columbus. ***Engraver:*** New England Bank Note Co. ***Comments:*** H-MA-1275-G58. 18__. 1840s–1850s.

Rarity: —

$500 • W-MA-3320-500-G300
Left: Woman seated on sheaves, Men reaping, Man on horse / 500. ***Center:*** 500 / D. ***Right:*** 500 vertically. ***Engraver:*** Rawdon, Wright, Hatch & Edson. ***Comments:*** H-MA-1275-G60. 18__. 1850s.

Rarity: —

$1,000 • W-MA-3320-1000-G310
Left: Laocoon and sons strangled by serpents / 1000. ***Center:*** THOUSAND, Train. ***Right:*** 1000 / Ships / 1000. ***Engraver:*** Rawdon, Wright, Hatch & Edson. ***Comments:*** H-MA-1275-G62. 18__. 1850s.

Rarity: —

Uncut Sheets

$1-$1-$2-$3 • W-MA-3320-001.001.002.003-US010 TD

Overprint(s): None. ***Comments:*** All unlisted in Haxby. Similar to H-MA-1275-G8a, G8a, G16a, G24a. 18__. 1850s.

Rarity: —

Non-Valid Issues

$1 • W-MA-3320-001-A010

Left: 1 / Woman wearing bonnet with pail / ONE. ***Center:*** Machinery and merchandise flanking Ceres seated holding sickle and rake, Factories and harbor / ONE. ***Right:*** 1 / Ship / ONE. ***Engraver:*** New England Bank Note Co. ***Comments:*** H-MA-1275-A5. Altered from $1 Washington County Bank, Calais, Maine, or from notes of other failed banks using the same plate. Genuine notes from this plate were issued, W-MA-3320-001-G020. 18__. Circa 1840.

Rarity: —

$2 • W-MA-3320-002-S010

Left: 2 / TWO / 2. ***Center:*** Portrait of George Washington. ***Right:*** Spread eagle on shield / 2. ***Tint:*** Color unknown. ***Engraver:*** American Bank Note Co. ***Comments:*** H-MA-1275-S5.

Rarity: —

$3 • W-MA-3320-003-C110

Engraver: New England Bank Note Co. ***Comments:*** H-MA-1275-C22. Counterfeit of W-MA-3320-003-G110. 18__. Circa 1850.

Rarity: —

$3 • W-MA-3320-003-A020 CC

Engraver: New England Bank Note Co. ***Comments:*** H-MA-1275-A10. Altered from $3 Washington County Bank, Calais, Maine, or from notes of other failed banks using the same plate. Genuine notes from this plate were issued, W-MA-3320-003-G100. 18__. Circa 1840.

Rarity: —

$5 • W-MA-3320-005-C150

Engraver: New England Bank Note Co. ***Comments:*** H-MA-1275-C30. Counterfeit of W-MA-3320-005-G150. 18__. Circa 1850.

Rarity: —

$5 • W-MA-3320-005-A030 CJ

Overprint: Red FIVE. ***Engraver:*** Bald, Cousland & Co. / ABNCo. monogram. ***Comments:*** H-Unlisted. 18__. 1860s.

Rarity: —

Wilkinsonville, Massachusetts

John Wampas, a Nipmuc Indian, deeded the land that made up Wilkinsonville when he visited England in the 1600s. By 1735 the town of Sutton as well as some northeastern land was incorporated as Grafton. Millbury separated in 1813, and in the 1830s Wilkinsonville took its own official place. A railroad as well as the Blackstone River ran through town.

Sutton Bank
1828–1829
W-MA-3330

History: The Sutton Bank was incorporated on March 11, 1828, with an authorized capital of $100,000, to be divided into shares of $100 each, payable in two installments. The Massachusetts State Legislature granted the request for a delay in raising the additional capital, allowing $25,000 to be paid in on or before June 1, 1829, and the remaining $25,000 on or before October 1, 1829. However, this was never followed through, and the bank floated on little but air. It was discovered that the Sutton Bank had borrowed an amount of $51,000 to be used as the specie under examination, allowing the commissioners to write a report confirming that there was, indeed, $50,000 in specie in the vaults of the Sutton Bank. The Sutton Bank failed that year and never went into normal business.

See also listing under Boston, W-MA-980.

Numismatic Commentary: Genuine issues from this short-lived bank are very hard to locate. All issues are of the PSSP format.

Valid Issues

$1 • W-MA-3330-001-G010

CJF

Engraver: PSSP. ***Comments:*** H-MA-1280-G2. 18__. 1820s–1830s.

Rarity: —

$2 • W-MA-3330-002-G020

Left: Narrow panel of lathework circle segments. ***Center:*** 2 / 2 / Flower garlands and gridwork segments / 2 / 2. ***Right:*** Narrow panel of lathework circle segments. ***Engraver:*** PSSP. ***Comments:*** H-MA-1280-G4. 18__. 1820s–1830s.

Rarity: —

$3 • W-MA-3330-003-G030

CC

Engraver: PSSP. ***Comments:*** H-MA-1280-G6. 18__. 1820s–1830s.

Rarity: URS-7
VG $100; **F** $225

$5 • W-MA-3330-005-G040

Left: Lathework chain with MASSACHUSETTS / 5 / 5. ***Center:*** Alternating flower garlands and gridwork segments / FIVE DOLLARS lined by zigzag ruled lines. ***Right:*** 5 / 5. ***Engraver:*** PSSP. ***Comments:*** H-MA-1280-G8. 18__. 1820s–1830s.

Rarity: —

$10 • W-MA-3330-010-G050

Left: Lathework chain bearing MASSACHUSETTS / 10 / 10 vertically. ***Center:*** Alternating flower garlands and gridwork segments / TEN DOLLARS lined by zigzag ruled lines. ***Right:*** 10 / 10 vertically. ***Engraver:*** PSSP. ***Comments:*** H-MA-1280-G10. 18__. 1820s–1830s.

Rarity: —

$50 • W-MA-3330-050-G060

Left: Lathework chain bearing MASSACHUSETTS / 50 / 50 vertically. ***Center:*** Alternating flower garlands and gridwork segments. ***Right:*** 50 / 50 vertically. ***Engraver:*** PSSP. ***Comments:*** H-MA-1280-G14. 18__. 1820s–1830s.

Rarity: —

$100 • W-MA-3330-100-G070

Left: Lathework chain bearing MASSACHUSETTS / 100 / 100 vertically. ***Center:*** Alternating flower garlands and gridwork segments. ***Right:*** 100 / 100 vertically. ***Engraver:*** Perkins. ***Comments:*** H-MA-1280-G16. 18__. 1820s.

Rarity: —

Winthrop, Massachusetts

English colonists settled the town of Winthrop in the 1630s. Originally a part of Boston, the land was divided into 15 tracts that were distributed among leading men to manage. In 1739 the areas of Chelsea, Revere, and Winthrop separated from Boston and became the town of Chelsea. The residents of this town were prominent in the Revolutionary War.

More local control was the catalyst behind the decision to separate from Chelsea, and Revere and Winthrop did so in 1846 to become North Chelsea. In 1852 the area incorporated and took the name of Winthrop after the first Massachusetts Governor's son, John Winthrop. Villages within Winthrop were Winthrop Highlands, Ocean Spray, Winthrop Beach, and Point Shirley.

Bank of Winthrop
1850s–1860s
W-MA-3340

History: A non-existent bank represented only by fraudulent notes. The notes were meant to pass for and were printed from the same plates as notes of the Bank of Winthrop, Winthrop, Maine.

Numismatic Commentary: These notes are hard to locate. They are sought after by both Maine and Massachusetts collectors.

Issues

$1 • W-MA-3340-001-G010

Left: Lathework panel bearing MASSACHUSETTS / 1 / 1. ***Center:*** Alternating flower garlands and gridwork segments / ONE. ***Right:*** 1 / 1 / Lathework panel bearing ONE vertically. ***Tint:*** Ochre. ***Back:*** Ochre. ***Engraver:*** PSSP. ***Comments:*** H-MA-1285-G4b. 18__. 1850s.

Rarity: —

$1 • W-MA-3340-001-G010a

Tint: Ochre. ***Back:*** Ochre. ***Engraver:*** PSSP / ABNCo. monogram. ***Comments:*** H-MA-1285-G4c. Similar to W-MA-3340-001-G010 but with additional engraver imprint. 18__. 1850s–1860s.

Rarity: —

$2 • W-MA-3340-002-G020 CC

Tint: Ochre. ***Back:*** Ochre. ***Engraver:*** PSSP. ***Comments:*** H-MA-1285-G8b. Remainder. 18__. 1850s.

Rarity: URS-2
Proof $2,200

$2 • W-MA-3340-002-G020a

Left: Lathework panel bearing MASSACHUSETTS / 2 / 2. ***Center:*** Alternating flower garlands and gridwork segments / TWO. ***Right:*** 2 / 2 / Lathework panel bearing TWO vertically. ***Tint:*** Ochre. ***Back:*** Ochre. ***Engraver:*** PSSP / ABNCo. monogram. ***Comments:*** H-MA-1285-G8c. Similar to W-MA-3340-002-G020 but with additional engraver imprint. 18__. 1850s–1860s.

Rarity: —

$3 • W-MA-3340-003-G030

Left: Lathework panel bearing MASSACHUSETTS / 3 / 3. ***Center:*** Alternating flower garlands and gridwork segments / THREE. ***Right:*** 3 / 3 / Lathework panel bearing THREE vertically. ***Tint:*** Ochre. ***Back:*** Ochre. ***Engraver:*** PSSP. ***Comments:*** H-MA-1285-G12b. 18__. 1850s.

Rarity: —

$3 • W-MA-3340-003-G030a

Tint: Ochre. ***Back:*** Ochre. ***Engraver:*** PSSP / ABNCo. monogram. ***Comments:*** H-MA-1285-G12c. Similar to W-MA-3340-003-G030 but with additional engraver imprint. 18__. 1850s–1860s.

Rarity: —

Winthrop Bank

1836–1840

W-MA-3350

History: The Winthrop Bank was incorporated on April 16, 1836, with an authorized capital of $100,000. In 1839 the bank had a circulation of $29,212.75. The bank experienced difficult times and surrendered its charter in 1840.

See also listing under Roxbury, W-MA-2870.

Wiscasset, Massachusetts

Located in Lincoln County, Wiscasset is on the west side of the Sheepscot River, 12 miles from the ocean. The settlement began in 1663 when George Davie purchased a tract of several hundred acres from the Indians. Problems arose with the Indians in due course, causing an abandonment of the town. However, by 1730 new settlers had arrived. By 1740 it was a plantation with 30 families totaling 150 people. In 1760 the town was incorporated as Pownalborough, to honor Governor Pownal of Massachusetts, and within its limits lay what later became the towns of Alna and Dresden.

In 1802 the town was incorporated as Wiscasset. Shipbuilding as well as maritime commerce branched out all over the world, and business prospered. The Embargo Act of 1807 put an end to these trades, never to fully recover. After Maine achieved statehood on March 15, 1820, the town used that address.

See also Wiscasset, Maine.

Lincoln and Kennebec Bank

1802–1812

W-MA-3360 • W-ME-1570

History: The Lincoln and Kennebec Bank, also in print as the Lincoln & Kennebec Bank, was chartered by the General Court of Massachusetts on June 23, 1802, with the provision that up to $20,000 be loaned to the Commonwealth of Massachusetts, if requested. The capital was authorized as $200,000. The charter was to expire by limitation in 1812. Signatures on extant notes suggest that in 1806 H. Roby was cashier and William King was president. The *Massachusetts Manual*, 1814, stated that these men had the same positions at the Lincoln Bank in Bath, Maine. By outward records, the Lincoln and Kennebec Bank conducted its business properly and closed its doors when its charter expired in 1812. After that time, certain people involved with this bank moved to the new Wiscasset Bank chartered on June 23, 1812. The bank experienced difficult times; however, its notes seem to have been redeemed in due course.

Numismatic Commentary: On January 23, 1908, the Maine Historical Society announced that Joseph Wood had presented to the Society an engraved copper plate from which currency of the Lincoln & Kennebec Bank was printed. Wait stated that he had personally seen notes of the $5 (lowest denomination listed by him), $6, $7, $8, $9, $10, $20, and $100 denominations of this bank. Today the notes of the Lincoln & Kennebec Bank are exceedingly rare.

Valid Issues

$1 • W-MA-3360-001-G010

Comments: H-MA-1290-G20, Wait-Unlisted. No description available. 1800s.

Rarity: *None known*

$1 • W-MA-3360-001-G020

Left: 1 / 1. ***Center:*** ONE DOLLAR, Text. ***Right:*** 1 / 1. ***Engraver:*** PSSP. ***Comments:*** H-MA-1290-G26, Wait-Unlisted. 1800s.

Rarity: —

$2 • W-MA-3360-002-G030

Comments: H-MA-1290-G28, Wait-Unlisted. No description available. 1800s.

Rarity: *None known*

$2 • W-MA-3360-002-G040

Engraver: PSSP. ***Comments:*** H-MA-1290-G34, Wait-Unlisted. Similar to W-MA-3360-001-G020 but with different denomination. 1800s.

Rarity: —

$3 • W-MA-3360-003-G050

Comments: H-MA-1290-G36, Wait-Unlisted. No description available. 1800s.

Rarity: *None known*

$3 • W-MA-3360-003-G060

Engraver: PSSP. ***Comments:*** H-MA-1290-G42, Wait-Unlisted. Similar to W-MA-3360-001-G020 but with different denomination. 1800s.

Rarity: —

$5 • W-MA-3360-005-G070

Left: Harbor with ships, Boat building scene, Trees. ***Center:*** FIVE DOLLARS, Text / Fish bearing 5. ***Right:*** 5 vertically. ***Overprint:*** FIVE overprint. ***Comments:*** H-MA-1290-G44, Wait-2. 1800s.

Rarity: —

$5 • W-MA-3360-005-G080

Left: MASSACHUSETTS vertically / 5, Plate letter, 5. ***Center:*** FIVE DOLLARS, Text. ***Right:*** 5, Plate letter, 5. ***Engraver:*** PSSP. ***Comments:*** H-MA-1290-G50, Wait-1. 1809–1810s.

Rarity: —

$6 • W-MA-3360-006-G090

Comments: H-MA-1290-G52, Wait-4. Similar to W-MA-3360-005-G070 but with different denomination. 1800s.

Rarity: —

$7 • W-MA-3360-007-G100

Comments: H-MA-1290-G56, Wait-5. Similar to W-MA-3360-005-G070 but with different denomination. 1800s.

Rarity: —

$8 • W-MA-3360-008-G110

Comments: H-MA-1290-G60, Wait-6. Similar to W-MA-3360-005-G070 but with different denomination. 1800s.

Rarity: URS-2

$9 • W-MA-3360-009-G120

Comments: H-MA-1290-G64, Wait-7. Similar to W-MA-3360-005-G070 but with different denomination. 1800s.

Rarity: —

$10 • W-MA-3360-010-G130

Comments: H-MA-1290-G68, Wait-8. Similar to W-MA-3360-005-G070 but with different denomination. 1800s.

Rarity: —

$10 • W-MA-3360-010-G140

Engraver: PSSP. ***Comments:*** H-MA-1290-G74, Wait-Unlisted. Similar to W-MA-3360-005-G080 but with different denomination. 1809–1810s.

Rarity: —

$20 • W-MA-3360-020-G150

Comments: H-MA-1290-G76, Wait-9. Similar to W-MA-3360-005-G070 but with different denomination. 1800s.

Rarity: —

$100 • W-MA-3360-100-G160

Comments: H-MA-1290-G80, Wait-10. Similar to W-MA-3360-005-G070 but with different denomination. 1800s.

Rarity: —

Non-Valid Issues

$5 • W-MA-3360-005-C070

HA

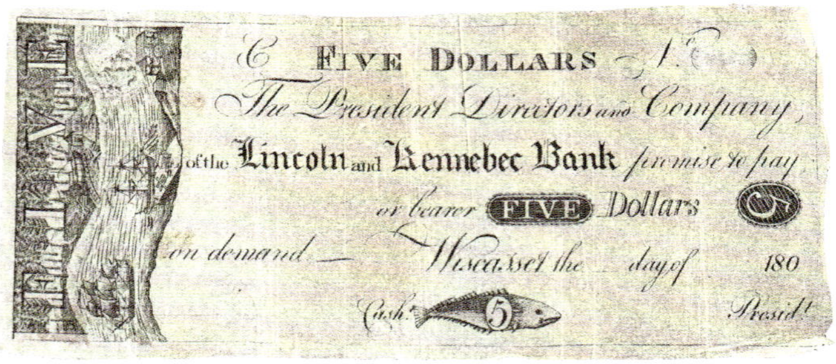

Comments: H-MA-1290-C44, Wait-Unlisted. Counterfeit of W-MA-3360-005-G070. 180_. 1800s.

Rarity: URS-4
VF $250

$8 • W-MA-3360-008-C110

CJF

Comments: H-MA-1290-C60, Wait-Unlisted. Counterfeit of W-MA-3360-008-G110. 180_. 1800s.

Rarity: URS-4
VF $250

$10 • W-MA-3360-010-C130

Comments: H-MA-1290-C68, Wait-Unlisted. Counterfeit of W-MA-3360-010-G130. 1800s.

Rarity: —

Wiscasset Bank

1812–1820

W-MA-3370 • W-ME-1610

History: Following the repeal of the Embargo Act of 1807 and the general restoration of commerce in 1809, by 1812 prosperity had returned to the seacoast towns in the District of Maine.[42] On June 23, 1812, the General Court of Massachusetts chartered 20 banks, six of which were in the District of Maine, the last being the Wiscasset Bank. The authorized capital was "no less" than

$250,000 in gold and silver coins, of which 25 percent was to be paid in by October 1, 1812. On December 8, 1814, the bank ran short of cash and was forced to suspend the redemption of its notes with coins, a situation that lasted until March 28, 1815. On July 20, 1816, there was another shortage, specie payments were again suspended, and it was not until September 20, 1817, that bills could be honored in coins. On February 13, 1818, the bank was permitted to reduce its capital to $100,000. Finally, on May 18, 1820, the bank stopped redeeming its paper money altogether. An audit found $105,553.52 of bills in circulation, against which only $147.92 in coins and $71 in bills of other banks was on hand! It was not until 1829 that the affairs of the Wiscasset Bank were wound up. Large quantities of worthless bills remained in circulation for years afterward.

Numismatic Commentary: As the Wiscasset Bank failed utterly, its notes became worthless and most were later destroyed. Examples come on the market now and again.

Valid Issues

$1 • W-MA-3370-001-G010

CJF

Engraver: PSSP. ***Comments:*** H-MA-1295-G10, Wait-26. 18__. 1810s.

Rarity: URS-6
F $200

$2 • W-MA-3370-002-G020

Engraver: PSSP. ***Comments:*** H-MA-1295-G16, Wait-27. Similar to W-MA-3370-001-G010 but with different denomination. Issued note unverified. 1810s.

Rarity: *None known*

$3 • W-MA-3370-003-G030

QDB

Engraver: PSSP. ***Comments:*** H-MA-1295-G18, Wait-28. Similar to W-MA-3370-001-G010 but with different denomination. 18__. 1810s.

Rarity: URS-6
F $250

$5 • W-MA-3370-005-G040

CJF, CJF

Back: Stereotype Steel Check Plate. ***Engraver:*** PSSP. ***Comments:*** H-MA-1295-G20, Wait-29. 18__. 1810s.

Rarity: URS-7
F $150

$10 • W-MA-3370-010-G050

QDB, QDB

Engraver: PSSP. ***Comments:*** H-MA-1295-G22, Wait-30. Similar to W-MA-3370-005-G040 but with different denomination. 18__. 1810s.

Rarity: URS-7
F $150

$20 • W-MA-3370-020-G060

Engraver: PSSP. ***Comments:*** H-MA-1295-G24, Wait-Unlisted. Similar to W-MA-3370-005-G040 but with different denomination. Issued note unverified. 1809–1820s.

Rarity: *None known*

$50 • W-MA-3370-050-G070

Engraver: PSSP. ***Comments:*** H-MA-1295-G26, Wait-Unlisted. Similar to W-MA-3370-005-G040 but with different denomination. Issued note unverified. 1809–1820s.

Rarity: *None known*

$100 • W-MA-3370-100-G080

Engraver: PSSP. ***Comments:*** H-MA-1295-G28, Wait-Unlisted. Similar to W-MA-3370-005-G040 but with different denomination. 1809–1820s.

Rarity: —

WOBURN, MASSACHUSETTS

Named after Woburn, Bedfordshire, England, Woburn was settled in 1640 and incorporated in 1642. The land included Woburn, Winchester, Burlington, Stoneham, and Wilmington. Lynn Village separated on May 29, 1644. In 1717 the Great Snow brought 20 to 25 feet of snow to the area. By 1730 Wilmington had separated from Woburn, and in 1799 Burlington followed. In 1850 Winchester also separated, and Woburn incorporated as a city on June 12, 1888.

The vulcanization of rubber was discovered by Goodyear in 1839. From 1765 to 1860 the population grew from 1,575 to 6,287. By 1865 there were boot and shoemaking shops as well as tanning and currying shops in town.

Woburn Bank

1853–1865

W-MA-3380

History: The Woburn Bank was incorporated on April 28, 1853, with an authorized capital of $100,000. The circulation of the bank was $70,815 in 1858 and $133,800 in 1864. Specie was $15,388.53 in 1858 and $24,487.05 in 1860. The real estate of the bank was valued at $16,320.40 in 1864.

The interests of the Woburn Bank were succeeded by the First National Bank of Woburn after it was chartered in January 1865.

Numismatic Commentary: A steady but light stream of genuine issues from this bank makes it to the marketplace each year. Many examples show cancellation holes.

VALID ISSUES

$1 • W-MA-3380-001-G010

Left: 1 / 1. ***Center:*** Woman reclining. ***Right:*** 1 / Cherub seated. ***Overprint:*** Green ONE / 1. ***Engraver:*** Rawdon, Wright, Hatch & Edson / New England Bank Note Co. ***Comments:*** H-MA-1295-G2a. Sept. 15, 18__. 1850s.

Rarity: —

$1 • W-MA-3380-001-G010a

SI

Overprint: Red ONE. ***Engraver:*** Rawdon, Wright, Hatch & Edson / New England Bank Note Co. ***Comments:*** H-Unlisted. Similar to W-MA-3380-001-G010. Sept. 15, 18__. 1850s–1860s.

Rarity: URS-5
F $250; **VF** $400

$1 • W-MA-3380-001-G010b

CJF

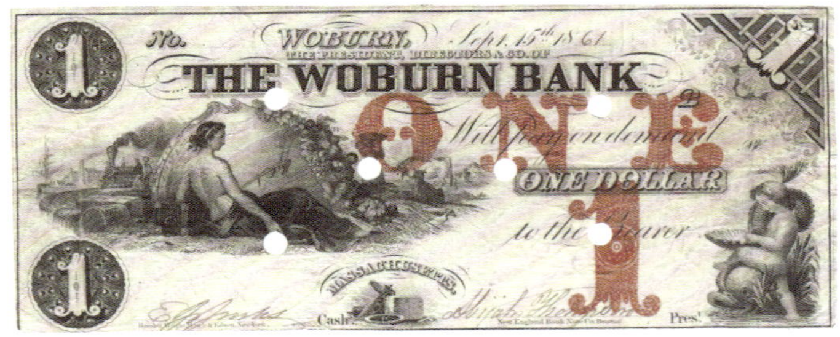

Overprint: Red ONE / 1. ***Engraver:*** Rawdon, Wright, Hatch & Edson / New England Bank Note Co. / ABNCo. monogram. ***Comments:*** H-MA-1295-G2b. Similar to W-MA-3380-001-G010 but with additional engraver imprint. Sept. 15, 18__. 1850s–1860s.

Rarity: URS-4
F $300; **VF** $500

$2 • W-MA-3380-002-G020

CJF

Overprint: Red TWO. ***Engraver:*** Rawdon, Wright, Hatch & Edson / New England Bank Note Co. ***Comments:*** H-MA-1295-G4a. Sept. 15, 18__. 1850s.

Rarity: URS-4
F $400; **VF** $600

$2 • W-MA-3380-002-G020a

Left: Woman and man with two coins, Cattle / 2. ***Center:*** Train. ***Right:*** 2 / Woman with hat and rake. ***Overprint:*** Green. ***Engraver:*** Rawdon, Wright, Hatch & Edson / New England Bank Note Co. / ABNCo. monogram. ***Comments:*** H-MA-1295-G4b. Similar to W-MA-3380-002-G020 but with additional engraver imprint. Sept. 15, 18__. 1850s–1860s.

Rarity: —

$3 • W-MA-3380-003-G030

Left: Liberty holding cap, Globe and eagle, Ship / 3. ***Right:*** 3 / Cherub with shield bearing 3. ***Overprint:*** Green THREE. ***Engraver:*** Rawdon, Wright, Hatch & Edson / New England Bank Note Co. ***Comments:*** H-MA-1295-G6a. Sept. 15, 18__. 1850s.

Rarity: —

$3 • W-MA-3380-003-G030a

Overprint: Green. ***Engraver:*** Rawdon, Wright, Hatch & Edson / New England Bank Note Co. / ABNCo. monogram. ***Comments:*** H-MA-1295-G6b. Similar to W-MA-3380-003-G030 but with additional engraver imprint. Sept. 15, 18__. 1850s–1860s.

Rarity: —

$5 • W-MA-3380-005-G040

Left: Liberty holding cap and watering eagle from cup / 5. ***Center:*** Five women surrounding 5 / Houses and ships. ***Right:*** 5. ***Overprint:*** Green FIVE. ***Engraver:*** Rawdon, Wright, Hatch & Edson / New England Bank Note Co. ***Comments:*** H-MA-1295-G8a. Sept. 15, 18__. 1850s.

Rarity: —

$5 • W-MA-3380-005-G040a

Overprint: Green. ***Engraver:*** Rawdon, Wright, Hatch & Edson / New England Bank Note Co. / ABNCo. monogram. ***Comments:*** H-MA-1295-G8b. Similar to W-MA-3380-005-G040 but with additional engraver imprint. Sept. 15, 18__. 1850s–1860s.

Rarity: —

$10 • W-MA-3380-010-G050

Left: TEN / Liberty standing, Pedestal and shield. ***Center:*** Train. ***Right:*** 10 / Four horses and hay wagon. ***Overprint:*** Green TEN. ***Engraver:*** Rawdon, Wright, Hatch & Edson / New England Bank Note Co. ***Comments:*** H-MA-1295-G10a. Sept. 15, 18__. 1850s.

Rarity: —

$10 • W-MA-3380-010-G050a

CJF

Overprint: Red TEN / X X. ***Engraver:*** Rawdon, Wright, Hatch & Edson / New England Bank Note Co. / ABNCo. monogram. ***Comments:*** H-MA-1295-G10b. Similar to W-MA-3380-010-G050 but with additional engraver imprint. Sept. 15, 18__. 1850s–1860s.

Rarity: URS-3
F $500; **VF** $750

$20 • W-MA-3380-020-G060

Left: 20 / Eagle with one foot on shield, Steamship / U.S. Capitol. ***Center:*** Portrait of George Washington. ***Right:*** 20. ***Overprint:*** Green TWENTY. ***Engraver:*** Rawdon, Wright, Hatch & Edson / New England Bank Note Co. ***Comments:*** H-MA-1295-G12a. Sept. 15, 18__. 1850s.

Rarity: —

$20 • W-MA-3380-020-G060a

Overprint: Green. ***Engraver:*** Rawdon, Wright, Hatch & Edson / New England Bank Note Co. / ABNCo. monogram. ***Comments:*** H-MA-1295-G12b. Similar to W-MA-3380-020-G060 but with additional engraver imprint. Sept. 15, 18__. 1850s–1860s.

Rarity: —

$50 • W-MA-3380-050-G070

Left: 50 / Two women flanking shield surmounted by eagle, Factory, Ships and train. ***Right:*** 50 / Justice seated / FIFTY. ***Overprint:*** Green. ***Engraver:*** Rawdon, Wright, Hatch & Edson / New England Bank Note Co. ***Comments:*** H-MA-1295-G14. Sept. 15, 18__. 1850s.

Rarity: —

$50 • W-MA-3380-050-G070a

Overprint: Green. ***Engraver:*** Rawdon, Wright, Hatch & Edson / New England Bank Note Co. / ABNCo. monogram. ***Comments:*** H-MA-1295-G14b. Similar to W-MA-3380-050-G070 but with additional engraver imprint. Sept. 15, 18__. 1850s–1860s.

Rarity: —

$100 • W-MA-3380-100-G080

Left: 100 / State arms. ***Center:*** 100 / View of U.S. Capitol. ***Right:*** 100. ***Overprint:*** Green. ***Engraver:*** Rawdon, Wright, Hatch & Edson / New England Bank Note Co. ***Comments:*** H-MA-1295-G16a. Sept. 15, 18__. 1850s.

Rarity: —

$100 • W-MA-3380-100-G080a

Overprint: Green. ***Engraver:*** Rawdon, Wright, Hatch & Edson / New England Bank Note Co. / ABNCo. monogram. ***Comments:*** H-MA-1295-G16b. Similar to W-MA-3380-100-G080 but with additional engraver imprint. Sept. 15, 18__. 1850s–1860s.

Rarity: —

Non-Valid Issues

$3 • W-MA-3380-003-R010

Engraver: Rawdon, Wright, Hatch & Edson / New England Bank Note Co. ***Comments:*** H-MA-1295-R5. Raised from W-MA-3380-001-G010. Sept. 15, 18__. 1850s.

Rarity: —

$3 • W-MA-3380-003-S010

Left: Laureate woman standing with ankles crossed and shield bearing 3. ***Center:*** 3 / Horse. ***Right:*** 3 / Indian man. ***Engraver:*** Danforth, Wright & Co. ***Comments:*** H-MA-1295-S5. 18__. 1850s.

Rarity: —

$5 • W-MA-3380-005-C040a

Engraver: Rawdon, Wright, Hatch & Edson / New England Bank Note Co. / ABNCo. monogram. ***Comments:*** H-MA-1295-C8b. Counterfeit of W-MA-3380-005-G040a. Sept. 15, 18__. Circa 1860.

Rarity: —

$5 • W-MA-3380-005-S020

CJF

Engraver: Danforth, Wright & Co. ***Comments:*** H-MA-1295-S10. 18__. 1850s.

Rarity: URS-7
F $75

$5 • W-MA-3380-005-S030 NJW

Overprint: Brown FIVE. ***Engraver:*** Danforth, Bald & Co. ***Comments:*** H-MA-1295-S15. 18__. 1850s.

Rarity: URS-7
F $75

$10 • W-MA-3380-010-S040

Left: Laureate woman standing with ankles crossed and shield bearing 10. ***Center:*** 10 / Horse. ***Right:*** 10 / Indian man standing. ***Engraver:*** Danforth, Wright & Co. ***Comments:*** H-MA-1295-S20. 18__. 1850s.

Rarity: —

$10 • W-MA-3380-010-S050 CJF

Overprint: Red TEN. ***Engraver:*** New England Bank Note Co. ***Comments:*** H-MA-1295-S25. Sept. __, 186_. 1860s.

Rarity: URS-6
F $100; **VF** $150

Worcester, Massachusetts

Natives of the Nipmuc nation were the original settlers of the land that later became Worcester, and they called it Quinsigamond, or "fishing place for pickerel." It was first settled by the English in 1673, but it was destroyed and burned during King Philip's War. The town resettled and incorporated in 1684, named after Worcester, England. It was abandoned a second time in 1702, all save for one man, who was killed along with his wife by natives. In 1713 the town of Worcester was settled for a third and final time and incorporated as a town in 1722. It was then chartered as a city in 1848.

Worcester was well-known for commercial, industrial, and educational innovations, and the town, along with Blackstone Valley, played major parts in the American Industrial Revolution. The Washburn & Moen Company, founded in 1831, developed a means of extruding steel wire, providing barbed wire for westward expansion. The monkey wrench was invented here in 1840 by Loring Coes, and George Crompton and the Knowles brothers set up textile looms in the 1850s. In 1847 the first American Valentine cards were designed here by Esther Howland. The Royal Worcester Corset Factory employed 1,200 women.

Central Bank
1829–1864
W-MA-3390

History: The Central Bank's charter was incorporated on March 12, 1828, with an authorized capital of $100,000. The bank was located at 104 Main Street in 1844. Capital was $350,000 in 1831, reduced to $100,000 by 1847, and then increased to $150,000 in 1849. By 1855 it was back up to $350,000. Circulation in 1831 was $66,716; it reached $119,306 in 1849. Specie was $33,991.35 in 1831, $13,212 in 1854, and $130,120 in 1863.

The business of the Central Bank was succeeded by the Central National Bank of Worcester after it was chartered on June 2, 1864.

Numismatic Commentary: All genuine issues are very hard to find. Non-valid notes permeate the marketplace.

Valid Issues

$1 • W-MA-3390-001-G010

Left: Narrow panel of lathework circle segments. ***Center:*** 1 / 1 / Flower garlands and gridwork segments / 1 / 1. ***Right:*** Narrow panel of lathework circle segments. ***Comments:*** H-MA-1305-G2. 18__. 1829–1830s.

Rarity: —

$1 • W-MA-3390-001-G010a

Left: ONE / D / ONE vertically. ***Right:*** ONE / D / ONE vertically. ***Engraver:*** PSSP. ***Comments:*** H-MA-1305-G4. Similar to W-MA-3390-001-G010. 18__. 1830s.

Rarity: —

$1 • W-MA-3390-001-G020

Engraver: Unverified, but likely New England Bank Note Co. ***Comments:*** H-MA-1305-G6. No description available. 18__. 1830s–1840s.

Rarity: *None known*

$1 • W-MA-3390-001-G030

Left: Woman seated with pen and scroll leaning on column / ONE. ***Center:*** Woman seated on strongbox with child and dog. ***Right:*** 1 / Female portrait. ***Engraver:*** Toppan, Carpenter, Casilear & Co. ***Comments:*** H-MA-1305-G10. Jan. 1, 185_. 1850s.

Rarity: —

$1 • W-MA-3390-001-G030a CJF

Overprint: Red ONE. ***Engraver:*** Toppan, Carpenter, Casilear & Co. / ABNCo. monogram. ***Comments:*** H-MA-1305-G10a. Similar to W-MA-3390-001-G030 but with additional engraver imprint. January 1, 18__. 1850s.

Rarity: —

$1 • W-MA-3390-001-G040

CJF

Engraver: New England Bank Note Co. / PSSP. ***Comments:*** H-Unlisted. 18__. 1830s–1840s.

Rarity: —

$2 • W-MA-3390-002-G050

Left: Narrow panel of lathework circle segments. ***Center:*** 2 / 2 / Flower garlands and gridwork segments / 2 / 2. ***Right:*** Narrow panel of lathework circle segments. ***Engraver:*** PSSP. ***Comments:*** H-MA-1305-G12. 18__. 1829–1830s.

Rarity: —

$2 • W-MA-3390-002-G050a

Left: Five TWOs vertically. ***Right:*** Five TWOs vertically. ***Engraver:*** PSSP. ***Comments:*** H-MA-1305-G14. Similar to W-MA-3390-002-G050. 18__. 1830s.

Rarity: —

$2 • W-MA-3390-002-G060

CJF

Engraver: New England Bank Note Co. / PSSP. ***Comments:*** H-MA-1305-G16. 18__. 1830s–1840s.

Rarity: —

$2 • W-MA-3390-002-G070

Left: Indian man with gun kneeling on rock above waterfall / TWO. ***Center:*** Woman standing by bale, Mechanic seated with dividers and cogwheel, Implements, Train on bridge. ***Right:*** 2 / Woman with sheaf. ***Engraver:*** Toppan, Carpenter, Casilear & Co. ***Comments:*** H-MA-1305-G20. Jan. 1, 185_. 1850s.

Rarity: —

$2 • W-MA-3390-002-G070a

Overprint: Red TWO. ***Engraver:*** Toppan, Carpenter, Casilear & Co. ***Comments:*** H-MA-1305-G20a. Similar to W-MA-3390-002-G070. Jan. 1, 185_. 1850s.

Rarity: —

$3 • W-MA-3390-003-G080

Left: Narrow panel of lathework circle segments. ***Center:*** 3 / 3 / Flower garlands and gridwork segments / 3 / 3. ***Right:*** Narrow panel of lathework circle segments. ***Engraver:*** PSSP. ***Comments:*** H-MA-1305-G22. 18__. 1829–1830s.

Rarity: —

$3 • W-MA-3390-003-G080a

Left: THREE vertically. ***Right:*** THREE vertically. ***Engraver:*** PSSP. ***Comments:*** H-MA-1305-G24. Similar to W-MA-3390-003-G080. 18__. 1830s.

Rarity: —

$3 • W-MA-3390-003-G090

Left: Woman with flowers in basket / 3. ***Center:*** Woman seated on sheaf with shield bearing state arms, Plow and produce. ***Right:*** 3 / Female portrait. ***Engraver:*** Toppan, Carpenter, Casilear & Co. ***Comments:*** H-MA-1305-G28. Jan. 1, 185_. 1850s.

Rarity: —

$3 • W-MA-3390-003-G090a

Overprint: Red THREE. ***Engraver:*** Toppan, Carpenter, Casilear & Co. ***Comments:*** H-MA-1305-G28a. Similar to W-MA-3390-003-G090. Jan. 1, 185_. 1850s.

Rarity: —

$5 • W-MA-3390-005-G100

Left: Lathework chain bearing MASSACHUSETTS / 5 / 5 vertically. ***Center:*** Alternating flower garlands and gridwork segments / FIVE with zigzag ruled lines. ***Right:*** 5 / 5 vertically. ***Engraver:*** PSSP. ***Comments:*** H-MA-1305-G30. 18__. 1829–1830s.

Rarity: —

$5 • W-MA-3390-005-G100a

Engraver: PSSP. ***Comments:*** H-MA-1305-G32. Similar to W-MA-3390-005-G100 but with spiral lathework lines. 18__. 1830s.

Rarity: —

$5 • W-MA-3390-005-G110

Engraver: Unverified, but likely New England Bank Note Co. ***Comments:*** H-MA-1305-G34. No description available. 18__. 1830s–1840s.

Rarity: *None known*

$5 • W-MA-3390-005-G120

Left: Woman with sickle holding die bearing 5 / FIVE. ***Center:*** Horse running, Train. ***Right:*** Woman seated on bale holding die bearing 5 / FIVE. ***Engraver:*** Toppan, Carpenter, Casilear & Co. ***Comments:*** H-MA-1305-G38. Jan. 1, 185_. 1850s.

Rarity: —

$5 • W-MA-3390-005-G120a

Overprint: Red. ***Engraver:*** Toppan, Carpenter, Casilear & Co. ***Comments:*** H-MA-1305-G38a. Similar to W-MA-3390-005-G120. Jan. 1, 185_. 1850s.

Rarity: —

$10 • W-MA-3390-010-G130

Left: Lathework chain bearing MASSACHUSETTS / 10 / 10 vertically. ***Center:*** Alternating flower garlands and gridwork segments / TEN DOLLARS with zigzag ruled lines. ***Right:*** 10 / 10 vertically. ***Engraver:*** PSSP. ***Comments:*** H-MA-1305-G40. 18__. 1829–1830s.

Rarity: —

$10 • W-MA-3390-010-G130a

Engraver: PSSP. ***Comments:*** H-MA-1305-G42. Similar to W-MA-3390-010-G130. 18__. 1830s.

Rarity: —

$10 • **W-MA-3390-010-G140**

Engraver: Unverified, but likely New England Bank Note Co. ***Comments:*** H-MA-1305-G44. No description available. 18__. 1830s–1840s.

Rarity: *None known*

$10 • **W-MA-3390-010-G150**

Left: Three women, one with basket of fruit, one in center pointing to ship / Justice. ***Center:*** X. ***Right:*** TEN / Woman standing beside sickle and sheaf. ***Engraver:*** Toppan, Carpenter, Casilear & Co. ***Comments:*** H-MA-1305-G48. Jan. 1, 18__. 1850s.

Rarity: —

$10 • **W-MA-3390-010-G150a**

Overprint: Red TEN. ***Engraver:*** Toppan, Carpenter, Casilear & Co. ***Comments:*** H-MA-1305-G48a. Similar to W-MA-3390-010-G150. Jan. 1, 18__. 1850s.

Rarity: —

$20 • **W-MA-3390-020-G160**

Left: Lathework chain bearing MASSACHUSETTS / 20 / 20 vertically. ***Center:*** Alternating flower garlands and gridwork segments / XX. ***Right:*** 20 / 20 vertically. ***Engraver:*** PSSP. ***Comments:*** H-MA-1305-G50. 18__. 1829–1830s.

Rarity: —

$20 • **W-MA-3390-020-G170**

Engraver: Unverified, but likely New England Bank Note Co. ***Comments:*** H-MA-1305-G52. No description available. 18__. 1830s–1840s.

Rarity: *None known*

$20 • **W-MA-3390-020-G180**

Left: 20. ***Center:*** Two angels kneeling in clouds holding figures 2 and 0, Two cherubs. ***Right:*** 20. ***Engraver:*** Toppan, Carpenter, Casilear & Co. ***Comments:*** H-MA-1305-G56. Jan. 1, 18__. 1850s.

Rarity: —

$20 • **W-MA-3390-020-G180a**

Overprint: Red. ***Engraver:*** Toppan, Carpenter, Casilear & Co. ***Comments:*** H-MA-1305-G56a. Similar to W-MA-3390-020-G180. Jan. 1, 18__. 1850s.

Rarity: —

$50 • **W-MA-3390-050-G190**

Left: Lathework chain bearing MASSACHUSETTS / 50 / 50 vertically. ***Center:*** Alternating flower garlands and gridwork segments. ***Right:*** 50 / 50 vertically. ***Engraver:*** PSSP. ***Comments:*** H-MA-1305-G60. 18__. 1829–1830s

Rarity: —

$50 • **W-MA-3390-050-G200**

Left: 50 / Woman standing with ankles crossed. ***Center:*** FIFTY DOLLARS / 50. ***Right:*** FIFTY vertically. ***Engraver:*** New England Bank Note Co. / PSSP. ***Comments:*** H-MA-1305-G62. 18__. 1830s–1840s.

Rarity: —

$50 • **W-MA-3390-050-G210**

Left: Two cows standing in water, Two cows and sheep on bank / 50. ***Right:*** 50 / Portrait of George Washington. ***Engraver:*** Toppan, Carpenter, Casilear & Co. ***Comments:*** H-MA-1305-G66. Jan. 1, 18__. 1850s.

Rarity: —

$50 • **W-MA-3390-050-G210a**

Overprint: Red. ***Engraver:*** Toppan, Carpenter, Casilear & Co. ***Comments:*** H-MA-1305-G66a. Similar to W-MA-3390-050-G210. Jan. 1, 18__. 1850s–1860s.

Rarity: —

$100 • **W-MA-3390-100-G220**

Left: Lathework chain bearing MASSACHUSETTS / 100 / 100 vertically. ***Center:*** Alternating flower garlands and gridwork segments. ***Right:*** 100 / 100 vertically. ***Engraver:*** PSSP. ***Comments:*** H-MA-1305-G70. 18__. 1829–1830s.

Rarity: —

$100 • **W-MA-3390-100-G230**

Left: Lathework panel bearing C / Portrait of George Washington / C. ***Center:*** 100 / Manhattan reclining pouring water, Ship / 100. ***Right:*** Lathework panel bearing ONE HUNDRED vertically. ***Engraver:*** New England Bank Note Co. / PSSP. ***Comments:*** H-MA-1305-G72. 18__. 1830s–1840s.

Rarity: —

$100 • **W-MA-3390-100-G240**

Left: Liberty seated / U.S. Capitol / 100. ***Bottom center:*** Horses drinking. ***Right:*** 100 / Portrait of Daniel Webster. ***Engraver:*** Toppan, Carpenter, Casilear & Co. ***Comments:*** H-MA-1305-G76. Jan. 1, 18__. 1850s–1860s.

Rarity: —

$100 • **W-MA-3390-100-G240a**

Overprint: Red. ***Engraver:*** Toppan, Carpenter, Casilear & Co. ***Comments:*** H-MA-1305-G76a. Similar to W-MA-3390-100-G240. Jan. 1, 18__. 1850s–1860s.

Rarity: —

$500 • **W-MA-3390-500-G250**

Left: 500 / 500 / 500. ***Center:*** 500 / Woman seated with shield bearing D, Fasces, cornucopia, lyre, and sheaf / 500. ***Right:*** 500 / D / 500. ***Engraver:*** New England Bank Note Co. / PSSP. ***Comments:*** H-MA-1305-G78. 18__. 1830s–1840s.

Rarity: —

$500 • **W-MA-3390-500-G260** CC

Overprint: Red panel outlining white D / 500 / D. ***Engraver:*** Toppan, Carpenter, Casilear & Co. ***Comments:*** H-MA-1305-G80. Jan. 1, 18__. 1850s–1860s.

Rarity: URS-2
VF $1,400

$1,000 • **W-MA-3390-1000-G270**

Left: THOUSAND vertically. ***Center:*** 1000 / Woman standing with legs crossed, Lyre, Cornucopia / 1000. ***Right:*** 1000 / M / 1000. ***Engraver:*** New England Bank Note Co. / PSSP. ***Comments:*** H-MA-1305-G84. 18__. 1830s–1840s.

Rarity: —

Non-Valid Issues

$1 • W-MA-3390-001-C030

Engraver: Toppan, Carpenter, Casilear & Co. ***Comments:*** H-MA-1305-C10. Counterfeit of W-MA-3390-001-G030. Jan. 1, 185_. 1850s.

Rarity: —

$1 • W-MA-3390-001-A010

SI

Engraver: Danforth, Wright & Co. ***Comments:*** H-MA-1305-A5. Altered from $1 Central Bank of Tennessee, Nashville, Tennessee. June 25, 1855.

Rarity: —

$2 • W-MA-3390-002-C070

Engraver: Toppan, Carpenter, Casilear & Co. ***Comments:*** H-MA-1305-C20. Counterfeit of W-MA-3390-002-G070. Jan. 1, 185_. 1850s.

Rarity: —

$2 • W-MA-3390-002-S010

CJF

Comments: H-MA-1305-N5. Spurious note. 18__.

Rarity: —

$2 • W-MA-3390-002-A020

CC

Engraver: Danforth, Wright & Co. ***Comments:*** H-MA-1305-A10. Altered from $2 Central Bank of Tennessee, Nashville, Tennessee. June 25, 1855.

Rarity: URS-7
VG $125; **VF** $175

$2 • W-MA-3390-002-A020a

Left: 2 on TWO / Man plowing with horses. ***Center:*** Covered wagons. ***Right:*** 2 / Sailor. ***Engraver:*** Danforth, Wright & Co. ***Comments:*** H-MA-1305-A10a. Similar to W-MA-3390-002-A020 but with different date. Jan. 1, 1859.

Rarity: —

$5 • W-MA-3390-005-R010

Comments: H-MA-1305-R5. Raised from W-MA-3390-001-G030. 18__. 1850s.

Rarity: —

$5 • W-MA-3390-005-S020

CJF

Engraver: Wellstood, Hanks & Co. ***Comments:*** H-MA-1305-S5. 18__. 1850s.

Rarity: URS-7
F $150

$5 • W-MA-3390-005-A030

SI

Comments: H-MA-1305-A15. Altered from $5 Bank of Lower Canada, Quebec, Canada. 18__. 1830s.

Rarity: —

$5 • W-MA-3390-005-A040

Left: Male portrait / V. ***Center:*** Man feeding pigs. ***Bottom center:*** Dog lying down. ***Right:*** 5 / Man carrying basket. ***Overprint:*** Red FIVE. ***Engraver:*** Wellstood, Hay & Whiting. ***Comments:*** H-MA-1305-A20. Altered from $5 Thames Bank, Laurel, Indiana. Aug. 12, 1856.

Rarity: —

$10 • W-MA-3390-010-AR010

Left: V / Portrait of Henry Clay. ***Center:*** Western river steamboat, Wharf. ***Right:*** 5 / Portrait of George Washington. ***Overprint:*** Red FIVE. ***Engraver:*** New England Bank Note Co. / Rawdon, Wright, Hatch & Edson. ***Comments:*** H-MA-1305-AR25. Altered and raised from $5 Waubeek Bank, De Soto, Nebraska. 1857.

Rarity: —

$10 • W-MA-3390-010-A050

Left: 10 / X / 10. ***Center:*** Woman reclining, Eagle, Train on arched bridge. ***Bottom center:*** Rooster. ***Right:*** 10 / X / 10. ***Engraver:*** Danforth, Wright & Co. ***Comments:*** H-MA-1305-A30. Altered from $10 Central Bank of Tennessee, Nashville, Tennessee. July 10, 1855.

Rarity: —

$20 • W-MA-3390-020-A060

Left: Woman floating in clouds holding U.S. shield and flowers / XX. ***Center:*** XX / Indian man with headdress reclining, Slain deer. ***Right:*** 20 / Portrait of George Washington. ***Engraver:*** Rawdon, Wright, Hatch & Co. ***Comments:*** H-MA-1305-A35. Altered from $20 New England Bank, Fairmount, Maine. Oct. 1, 1857.

Rarity: —

$500 • W-MA-3390-500-C260

CC

Overprint: Red panel outlining D / 500 / D. ***Engraver:*** Toppan, Carpenter, Casilear & Co. / ABNCo. monogram. ***Comments:*** H-MA-1305-C80. Counterfeit of W-MA-3390-500-G260. Jan. 1, 18__. 1850s–1860s.

Rarity: URS-3
F $650

Citizens Bank
1836–1860s
W-MA-3400

History: The Citizens Bank was incorporated on April 9, 1836, with an authorized capital of $500,000. By 1839 its capital had been reduced to $250,000. Circulation was at $59,653. In 1845 the same was $109,540. Specie was at $12,270.40, and real estate was valued at $16,000 in 1857.

The business of the Citizens Bank was succeeded by the Citizens National Bank of Worcester after it was chartered on January 30, 1865.

Numismatic Commentary: Genuine notes from this bank are hard to find. There are plenty of non-valid issues available.

As of 2003 there was a $1-$2-$3-$5 face plate remaining at the American Bank Note Co. archives.

Valid Issues

$1 • W-MA-3400-001-G010

Left: Woman and 1 / ONE. ***Center:*** Woman holding 1, Train and steamboat. ***Right:*** 1 / Blacksmith and anvil. ***Engraver:*** Rawdon, Wright & Hatch. ***Comments:*** H-MA-1310-G4. 18__. 1830s–1850s.

Rarity: —

$1 • W-MA-3400-001-G020

Left: 1 / Cherub with basket on head / 1. ***Center:*** 1 / Farm tools, Beehive and sheaf / 1. ***Right:*** ONE / Farmer standing with axe and sickle, Beehive and shield / ONE. ***Comments:*** H-MA-1310-G8. 18__. 1850s.

Rarity: —

$2 • W-MA-3400-002-G030

Left: 2 / 2. ***Center:*** Farmer seated with pitcher, sheaf, and dog. ***Right:*** 2 / Cherub riding on dolphin / TWO. ***Engraver:*** Rawdon, Wright & Hatch. ***Comments:*** H-MA-1310-G12. 18__. 1830s–1850s.

Rarity: —

$3 • W-MA-3400-003-G040

Left: 3 / Dolphins / Steamship. ***Center:*** Blacksmith with sledge, Factories and stream. ***Right:*** 3 / State arms. ***Engraver:*** Rawdon, Wright & Hatch. ***Comments:*** H-MA-1310-G16. 18__. 1830s–1850s.

Rarity: —

$3 • W-MA-3400-003-G050

Left: 3 / Medallion head / 3. ***Center:*** 3 / Woman seated on strongbox with sheaf, sickle, and cornucopia, Man plowing, Factory. ***Right:*** 3 / Venus rising from water with shell on head. ***Comments:*** H-MA-1310-G20. 18__. 1850s.

Rarity: —

$5 • W-MA-3400-005-G060

CJF

Engraver: Rawdon, Wright & Hatch. ***Comments:*** H-MA-1310-G24. 18__. 1830s–1850s.

Rarity: —

$5 • W-MA-3400-005-G070

Left: 5 / Medallion head. ***Center:*** Die bearing 5. ***Right:*** 5 / Medallion head. ***Comments:*** H-MA-1310-G28. Beware of spurious W-MA-3400-005-S010 resembling the genuine. 18__. 1850s.

Rarity: —

$10 • W-MA-3400-010-G080

CJF

Engraver: Rawdon, Wright & Hatch. ***Comments:*** H-MA-1310-G32. Beware of spurious W-MA-3400-010-S020 resembling the genuine. 18__. 1830s–1850s.

Rarity: —

$20 • W-MA-3400-020-G090

Left: Panel bearing TWENTY vertically. ***Center:*** 20 / Woman seated in clouds with book / Eagle and portrait of George Washington / 20. ***Right:*** Jupiter holding staff and lightning bolts / 20. ***Engraver:*** Rawdon, Wright & Hatch. ***Comments:*** H-MA-1310-G36. 18__. 1830s–1850s.

Rarity: —

$50 • W-MA-3400-050-G100

Left: Minerva / 50. ***Center:*** L / Train. ***Right:*** Two women / 50. ***Engraver:*** Rawdon, Wright & Hatch. ***Comments:*** H-MA-1310-G40. 18__. 1830s–1850s.

Rarity: —

$100 • W-MA-3400-100-G110

Left: Indian man shooting arrow / 100. ***Center:*** 100 / Neptune / 100. ***Right:*** Statue of George Washington / 100. ***Engraver:*** Rawdon, Wright & Hatch. ***Comments:*** H-MA-1310-G44. 18__. 1830s–1850s.

Rarity: —

Uncut Sheets

$1-$2-$3-$5 • W-MA-3400-001.002.003.005-US010 CC

Comments: H-MA-1310-G8, G12, G20, H-Unlisted. Last note from Newport, Rhode Island. 18__. 1850s.

Rarity: URS-1
Proof $9,500

$5-$5-$10-$__ • W-MA-3400-005.005.010.__-US020 CJF

Comments: H-MA-1310-G24, G24, G32, __. Last note missing. 18__. 1830s–1850s.

Rarity: —

How to Read the Whitman Numbering System

$1 • W-MA-010-001-G010a

Denomination: Value of the note shown.

W: Whitman number. This number is a sortable code unique to each bank and note.

MA: Abbreviation for the state under study.

010: Numerical designation specific to each bank.

001: The denomination in dollars.

G010a: G indicates a good or valid note. Other categories are indicated thus: C (counterfeit); R (raised); S (spurious); N (not-attributed); A (altered). Numbers are assigned starting with 010, 020, et seq. Terminal letters following the number indicate variations of a note: a series of different colored overprints, tints, payees, etc., all on the same design of note. For more information, see the "How to Use This Book" section at the front of the volume, page xiv.

Non-Valid Issues

$1 • W-MA-3400-001-A010

SI

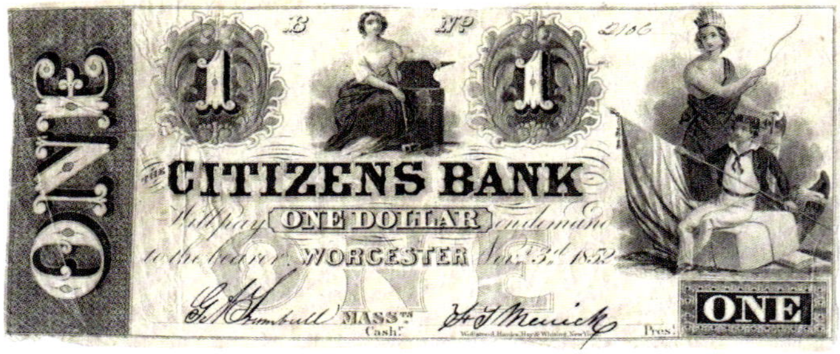

Engraver: Wellstood, Hanks, Hay & Whiting. ***Comments:*** H-MA-1310-A5. Altered from $1 Citizens Bank, Washington, D.C. Nov. 3, 1852.

Rarity: —

$1 • W-MA-3400-001-A020

Left: Laureate woman leaning on shield bearing 1. ***Center:*** 1 / Bull in field / Horse, Trees. ***Bottom center:*** Road, Trees, Sign post. ***Right:*** Indian man standing / 1. ***Engraver:*** Doty & Bergen. ***Comments:*** H-MA-1310-A10. Altered from $1 Merchants Bank, Stillwater, Minnesota. Oct. 20, 185_. 1855.

Rarity: —

$2 • W-MA-3400-002-A030

Left: Panel bearing TWO vertically. ***Center:*** 2 / Roman senator seated, Building / 2 / TWO. ***Right:*** TWO / Woman with shield, Woman reclining with globe. ***Engraver:*** Wellstood, Hanks, Hay & Whiting. ***Comments:*** H-MA-1310-A15. Altered from $2 Citizens Bank, Washington, D.C. 18__. 1850s.

Rarity: —

$2 • W-MA-3400-002-A040

Left: TWO / Portrait of cherub / 2. ***Center:*** 2 / Ceres giving grain to seated Liberty / 2. ***Bottom center:*** Anchor and implements. ***Right:*** 2 / Female portrait / TWO. ***Engraver:*** Terry, Pelton & Co. ***Comments:*** H-MA-1310-A20. Altered from $2 Citizens Bank, Augusta, Maine, or from notes of other failed banks using the same plate. 18__. 1840s.

Rarity: —

$2 • W-MA-3400-002-A050

Left: Arched TWO and 2 on die / State arms vertically. ***Center:*** Three woodsmen felling and cutting trees. ***Right:*** 2 / Ceres with sheaf. ***Engraver:*** Danforth, Wright & Co. ***Comments:*** H-MA-1310-A25. Altered from $2 Bank of Washtenaw, Washtenaw, Michigan series. 1850s.

Rarity: —

$3 • W-MA-3400-003-A060

Left: 3 / Woman standing with branch, Trident and oval bearing THREE / THREE. ***Center:*** Female portrait / Ceres and Justice flanking shield bearing anchor and surmounted by eagle / Portrait of cherub. ***Bottom center:*** Anchor and implements. ***Right:*** 3 / Ceres seated in grain field / THREE. ***Engraver:*** Terry, Pelton & Co. ***Comments:*** H-MA-1310-A30. Altered from $3 Citizens Bank, Augusta, Maine, or from notes of other failed banks using the same plate. 18__. 1840s.

Rarity: —

$5 • W-MA-3400-005-S010

CJF, CJF

Back: Orange. ***Engraver:*** American Bank Note Co. ***Comments:*** H-MA-1310-S5. Spurious design imitating a rough verbal description of W-MA-3400-005-G070. Aug. 10, 1859.

Rarity: —
F $95

$5 • W-MA-3400-005-A070

CJF

Engraver: Wellstood, Hanks, Hay & Whiting. ***Comments:*** H-MA-1310-A35. Altered from $5 Citizens Bank, Washington, D.C. Nov. 3, 1852.

Rarity: —

$5 • W-MA-3400-005-A080

Left: Several men with sticks driving herd of cattle into stream / 5. ***Center:*** Five men raking and loading hay, Ox wagon. ***Right:*** 5. ***Tint:*** Red-brown lathework outlining white 5. ***Engraver:*** Bald, Cousland & Co. ***Comments:*** H-MA-1310-A40. 1850s.

Rarity: —

$5 • W-MA-3400-005-A090

Left: FIVE / Portrait of Benjamin Franklin / V. ***Center:*** 5 / Two allegorical women standing and one seated, Agricultural items and ship. ***Bottom center:*** Anchor and implements. ***Right:*** V / Portrait of Marquis de Lafayette / FIVE. ***Engraver:*** Terry, Pelton & Co. ***Comments:*** H-MA-1310-A45. Altered from $5 Citizens Bank, Augusta, Maine, or from notes of other failed banks using the same plate. 18__. 1840s

Rarity: —

$10 • W-MA-3400-010-S020

CJF

Engraver: Rawdon, Wright & Hatch / ABNCo. monogram. ***Comments:*** H-MA-1310-S10. Spurious design imitating a rough verbal description of W-MA-3400-010-G080. 18__. 1860s.

Rarity: —
F $120

$10 • W-MA-3400-010-A100

Left: TEN vertically. ***Center:*** 10 / Woman standing with X / 10. ***Bottom center:*** Ship. ***Right:*** TEN / Indian man with bow / TEN. ***Engraver:*** Wellstood, Hanks, Hay & Whiting. ***Comments:*** H-MA-1310-A50. Altered from $10 Citizens Bank, Washington, D.C. 18__. 1850s.

Rarity: —

$10 • W-MA-3400-010-A110

Left: 10 / Portrait of George Washington held by cherub / 10. ***Center:*** X / Spread eagle with shield and arrows, E PLURIBUS UNUM / X. ***Bottom center:*** Ship. ***Right:*** 10 / Standing Indian man / 10. ***Engraver:*** Terry, Pelton & Co. ***Comments:*** H-MA-1310-A55. Altered from $10 Citizens Bank, Augusta, Maine, or from notes of other failed banks using the same plate. 18__. 1840s.

Rarity: —

$20 • W-MA-3400-020-A120

Left: Sailing ship. ***Center:*** Mercury with cornucopia, Barrel and bale. ***Bottom center:*** Schooner. ***Right:*** Woman with cornucopia. ***Engraver:*** Wellstood, Hanks, Hay & Whiting. ***Comments:*** H-MA-1310-A60. Altered from $20 Citizens Bank, Washington, D.C. 18__. 1850s.

Rarity: —

City Bank of Worcester

1854–1864

W-MA-3410

History: The City Bank of Worcester was chartered on March 28, 1854, with an authorized capital of $300,000. It went into operation on September 26 at the corner of Main and Pearl streets. The capital of the bank fluctuated between $200,000 and $400,000 for the duration of the bank's existence. Circulation in 1857 was $149,501; it was $217,447 in 1863. Specie was listed at $34,532.56.

The business of the City Bank of Worcester was succeeded by the City National Bank of Worcester after it was chartered on July 2, 1864.

Numismatic Commentary: Many genuine notes show an engraving of the bank building in downtown Worcester. Genuine issues are fairly hard to locate.

Valid Issues

$1 • W-MA-3410-001-G010

Left: 1 / Four story bank building. ***Center:*** ONE / Man working in factory. ***Right:*** 1 on ONE / Panel bearing 1. ***Engraver:*** Danforth, Wright & Co. ***Comments:*** H-MA-1315-G2. 18__. 1850s.

Rarity: —

$1 • W-MA-3410-001-G010a

Overprint: Red ONE. ***Engraver:*** Danforth, Wright & Co. ***Comments:*** H-MA-1315-G2a. Similar to W-MA-3410-001-G010. 18__. 1850s.

Rarity: —

$1 • W-MA-3410-001-G010b

CC

Overprint: Red shield outlining white 1. ***Engraver:*** Danforth, Wright & Co. ***Comments:*** H-Unlisted. Similar to W-MA-3410-001-G010. Proof. 18__. 1850s.

Rarity: URS-2
Proof $4,000

$1 • W-MA-3410-001-G010c

Overprint: Red ONE / Red shield outlining white 1. ***Engraver:*** Danforth, Wright & Co. / ABNCo. monogram. ***Comments:*** H-MA-1315-G2b. Similar to W-MA-3410-001-G010 but with different date and additional engraver imprint. Sept. 1, 18__. 1850s.

Rarity: —

$1 • W-MA-3410-001-G010d

Overprint: Red ONE / Red shield outlining white 1. ***Engraver:*** American Bank Note Co. ***Comments:*** H-MA-1315-G2c. Similar to W-MA-3410-001-G010 but with different date and different engraver imprint. Sept. 1, 18__. 1860s.

Rarity: —

$2 • W-MA-3410-002-G020

Left: 2 / Four story bank building. ***Center:*** TWO / Men haying with horses. ***Right:*** 2 on TWO on shield / 2 on panel. ***Engraver:*** Danforth, Wright & Co. ***Comments:*** H-MA-1315-G4. 18__. 1850s.

Rarity: —

$2 • W-MA-3410-002-G020a

Overprint: Red 2. ***Engraver:*** Danforth, Wright & Co. ***Comments:*** H-MA-1315-G4a. Similar to W-MA-3410-002-G020. 18__. 1850s.

Rarity: —

$2 • W-MA-3410-002-G020b

CC

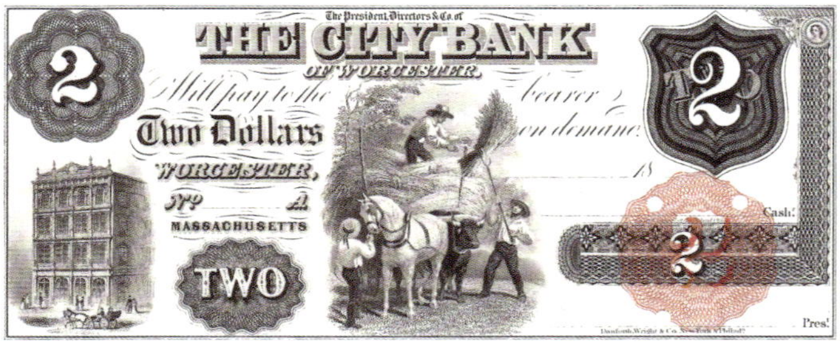

Overprint: Red shield outlining white 2. ***Engraver:*** Danforth, Wright & Co. ***Comments:*** H-Unlisted. Similar to W-MA-3410-002-G020. 18__. 1850s.

Rarity: URS-1
Proof $4,000

$2 • W-MA-3410-002-G020c

CC

Overprint: Red shield outlining white 2. ***Engraver:*** Danforth, Wright & Co. / ABNCo. monogram. ***Comments:*** H-Unlisted. Similar to W-MA-3410-002-G020 but with different date and additional engraver imprint. September 1, 18__. 1850s.

Rarity: URS-3
F $750; **VF** $1,250

$2 • W-MA-3410-002-G020d

Overprint: Red 2 / Red shield outlining white 2. ***Engraver:*** Danforth, Wright & Co. / ABNCo. monogram. ***Comments:*** H-MA-1315-G4b. Similar to W-MA-3410-002-G020 but with different date and additional engraver imprint. Sept. 1, 18__. 1850s.

Rarity: —

$2 • W-MA-3410-002-G020e

Overprint: Red 2 / Red shield outlining white 2. ***Engraver:*** American Bank Note Co. ***Comments:*** H-MA-1315-G4c. Similar to W-MA-3410-002-G020 but with different date and different engraver imprint. Sept. 1, 18__. 1860s.

Rarity: —

$3 • W-MA-3410-003-G030

Left: 3 / Four story bank building. ***Center:*** Woman seated next to strongbox / Shield bearing loom. ***Right:*** 3 on die / 3 on panel. ***Engraver:*** Danforth, Wright & Co. ***Comments:*** H-MA-1315-G6. 18__. 1850s.

Rarity: —

$3 • W-MA-3410-003-G030a

CC

Overprint: Red THREE THREE. ***Engraver:*** Danforth, Wright & Co. ***Comments:*** H-Unlisted. Similar to W-MA-3410-003-G030. Proof. 18__. 1850s.

Rarity: URS-1
Proof $4,700

$3 • W-MA-3410-003-G030b

Overprint: Red 3. ***Engraver:*** Danforth, Wright & Co. ***Comments:*** H-MA-1315-G6a. Similar to W-MA-3410-003-G030. 18__. 1850s.

Rarity: —

$3 • W-MA-3410-003-G030c

CJF

Overprint: Red 3. ***Engraver:*** Danforth, Wright & Co. / ABNCo. monogram. ***Comments:*** H-Unlisted. Similar to W-MA-3410-003-G030 but with different date and additional engraver imprint. September 1, 18__. 1850s.

Rarity: URS-3
F $1,000; **VF** $1,500

$3 • W-MA-3410-003-G030d

CJF

Overprint: Red 3 / Red panel outlining white THREE. ***Engraver:*** Danforth, Wright & Co. / ABNCo. monogram. ***Comments:*** H-MA-1315-G6b. Similar to W-MA-3410-003-G030 but with different date and additional engraver imprint. Proof. September 1, 18__. 1850s.

Rarity: URS-3
F $1,500; **EF** $2,500

$3 • W-MA-3410-003-G030e

Overprint: Red 3 / Red panel outlining white THREE. ***Engraver:*** American Bank Note Co. ***Comments:*** H-MA-1315-G6c. Similar to W-MA-3410-003-G030 but with different date and different engraver imprint. Sept. 1, 18__. 1860s.

Rarity: —

$5 • W-MA-3410-005-G040

Left: Women working in textile factory, Bull's head on shield / V on FIVE. ***Right:*** V on die / 5 on panel. ***Engraver:*** Danforth, Wright & Co. ***Comments:*** H-MA-1315-G8. 18__. 1850s.

Rarity: —

$5 • W-MA-3410-005-G040a

Overprint: Red 5 and lathework end panel outlining white 5. ***Engraver:*** Danforth, Wright & Co. ***Comments:*** H-MA-1315-G8a. Similar to W-MA-3410-005-G040. 18__. 1850s.

Rarity: —

$5 • W-MA-3410-005-G040b CC

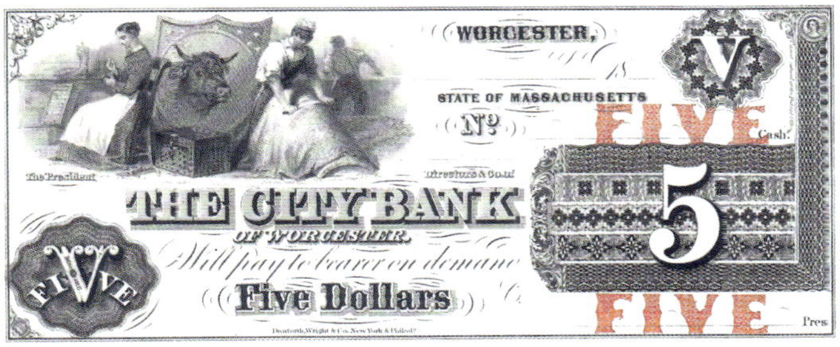

Overprint: Red FIVE FIVE. ***Engraver:*** Danforth, Wright & Co. ***Comments:*** H-Unlisted. Similar to W-MA-3410-005-G040. Proof. 18__. 1850s.

Rarity: URS-1
Proof $4,500

$5 • W-MA-3410-005-G040c

Overprint: Red 5 and lathework end panel outlining white 5 / Red panel outlining white FIVE. ***Engraver:*** Danforth, Wright & Co. / ABNCo. monogram. ***Comments:*** H-MA-1315-G8b. Similar to W-MA-3410-005-G040 but with additional engraver imprint. Sept. 1, 18__. 1850s.

Rarity: —

$5 • W-MA-3410-005-G040d

Overprint: Red 5 and lathework end panel outlining white 5 / Red panel outlining white FIVE. ***Engraver:*** American Bank Note Co. ***Comments:*** H-MA-1315-G8c. Similar to W-MA-3410-005-G040 but with different engraver imprint. Sept. 1, 18__. 1860s.

Rarity: —

$10 • W-MA-3410-010-G050

Left: 10 on TEN on X / Lathework bearing TEN. ***Center:*** Worcester city seal. ***Right:*** 10 / Four story bank building. ***Engraver:*** Danforth, Wright & Co. ***Comments:*** H-MA-1315-G10. 18__. 1850s.

Rarity: —

$10 • W-MA-3410-010-G050a

Overprint: Red X. ***Engraver:*** Danforth, Wright & Co. ***Comments:*** H-MA-1315-G10a. Similar to W-MA-3410-010-G050. 18__. 1850s.

Rarity: —

$10 • W-MA-3410-010-G050b CC

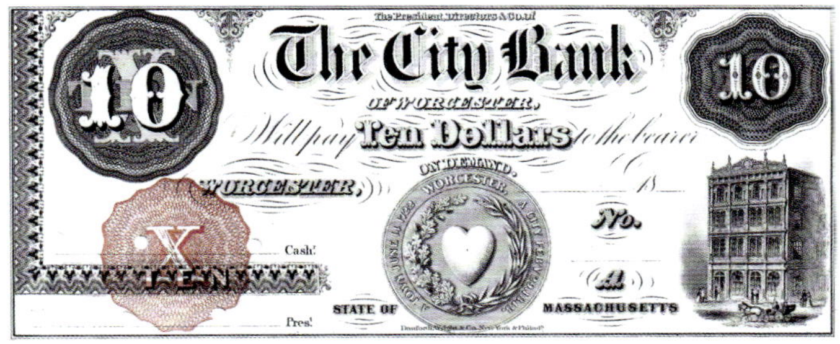

Overprint: Red shield outlining white X. ***Engraver:*** Danforth, Wright & Co. ***Comments:*** H-Unlisted. Similar to W-MA-3410-010-G050. 18__. 1850s.

Rarity: URS-1
Proof $5,500

$10 • W-MA-3410-010-G050c

Overprint: Red X / Red panel outlining white TEN. ***Engraver:*** Danforth, Wright & Co. / ABNCo. monogram. ***Comments:*** H-MA-1315-G10b. Similar to W-MA-3410-010-G050 but with different date and additional engraver imprint. Impaired Proof. Sept. 1, 18__. 1850s.

Rarity: —

$10 • W-MA-3410-010-G050d

Overprint: Red X / Red panel outlining white TEN. ***Engraver:*** American Bank Note Co. ***Comments:*** H-MA-1315-G10c. Similar to W-MA-3410-010-G050 but with different date and different engraver imprint. Sept. 1, 18__. 1860s.

Rarity: —

$20 • W-MA-3410-020-G060 CC

Engraver: Danforth, Wright & Co. ***Comments:*** H-MA-1315-G12. 18__. 1850s.

Rarity: URS-1
Proof $4,000

$20 • W-MA-3410-020-G060a

Overprint: Red XX. ***Engraver:*** Danforth, Wright & Co. ***Comments:*** H-MA-1315-G12a. Similar to W-MA-3410-020-G060. 18__. 1850s.

Rarity: —

$20 • W-MA-3410-020-G060b

Overprint: Red XX. ***Engraver:*** Danforth, Wright & Co. / ABNCo. monogram. ***Comments:*** H-MA-1315-G12b. Similar to W-MA-3410-020-G060 but with additional engraver imprint. 18__. 1850s.

Rarity: —

$50 • W-MA-3410-050-G070

CC

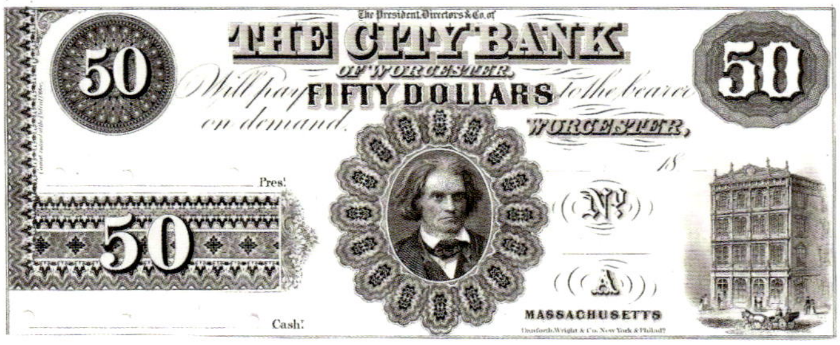

Engraver: Danforth, Wright & Co. ***Comments:*** H-MA-1315-G14. Proof. 18__. 1850s.

Rarity: URS-1
Proof $4,000

$50 • W-MA-3410-050-G070a

Left: 50 / Panel bearing 50. ***Center:*** Portrait of John C. Calhoun. ***Right:*** 50 / Four story bank building. ***Overprint:*** Red. ***Engraver:*** Danforth, Wright & Co. ***Comments:*** H-MA-1315-G14a. Similar to W-MA-3410-050-G070. 18__. 1850s.

Rarity: —

$50 • W-MA-3410-050-G070b

Overprint: Red. ***Engraver:*** Danforth, Wright & Co. / ABNCo. monogram. ***Comments:*** H-MA-1315-G14b. Similar to W-MA-3410-050-G070 but with additional engraver imprint. 18__. 1850s–1860s.

Rarity: —

$100 • W-MA-3410-100-G080

CC

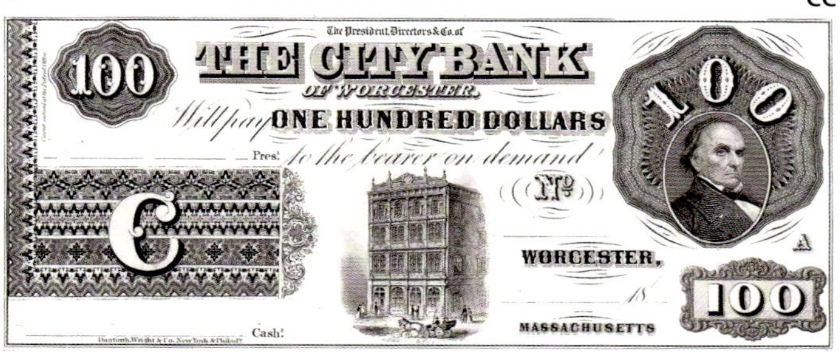

Engraver: Danforth, Wright & Co. ***Comments:*** H-MA-1315-G16. Proof. 18__. 1850s.

Rarity: URS-1
Proof $4,500

$100 • W-MA-3410-100-G080a

Left: 100 / Panel bearing C. ***Center:*** Four story bank building. ***Right:*** 100 / Portrait of Daniel Webster / 100. ***Overprint:*** Red. ***Engraver:*** Danforth, Wright & Co. ***Comments:*** H-MA-1315-G16a. Similar to W-MA-3410-100-G080. 18__. 1850s.

Rarity: —

$100 • W-MA-3410-100-G080b

Overprint: Red. ***Engraver:*** Danforth, Wright & Co. / ABNCo. monogram. ***Comments:*** H-MA-1315-G16b. Similar to W-MA-3410-100-G080 but with additional engraver imprint. 18__. 1850s–1860s.

Rarity: —

$500 • W-MA-3410-500-G090

CC

Engraver: Danforth, Wright & Co. ***Comments:*** H-MA-1315-G18. Proof. 18__. 1850s.

Rarity: URS-1
Proof $6,200

Uncut Sheets

$1-$1-$2-$3 • W-MA-3410-001.001.002.003-US010

Vignette(s): ($1) Building / Man working in factory with wheels / Shield bearing 1. ***($1)*** Building / Man working in factory with wheels / Shield bearing 1. ***($2)*** Building / Men with horses / 2 on shield. ***($3)*** Building / Woman seated next to mirror / Shield bearing machine. ***Tint(s):*** Red. ***Engraver:*** Danforth, Wright & Co. ***Comments:*** All unlisted in Haxby. Similar to H-MA-1315-G2, G2, G4, G6. 18__. 1850s.

Rarity: —

$5-$5-$5-$10 • W-MA-3410-005.005.005.010-US020

Vignette(s): ($5) Women working in textile factory. ***($5)*** Women working in textile factory. ***($5)*** Women working in textile factory. ***($10)*** Worcester city seal / Four story bank building. ***Tint(s):*** Red. ***Engraver:*** Danforth, Wright & Co. ***Comments:*** All unlisted in Haxby. Similar to H-MA-1315-G8, G8, G8, G10. 18__. 1850s.

Rarity: —

$20-$50 • W-MA-3410-020.050-US030

Vignette(s): ($20) Three women in clouds / Four story bank building. ***($50)*** Portrait of John C. Calhoun / Four story bank building. ***Engraver:*** Danforth, Wright & Co. ***Comments:*** H-MA-1315-G12, G14. Partial sheet. 18__. 1850s.

Rarity: —

$100-$500 • W-MA-3410-100.500-US040

Vignette(s): ($100) Four story bank building / Portrait of Daniel Webster. ***($500)*** Four story bank building / Portrait of Henry Clay. ***Engraver:*** Danforth, Wright & Co. ***Comments:*** H-MA-1315-G16, G18. Partial sheet. 18__. 1850s.

Rarity: —

Non-Valid Issues

$1 • W-MA-3410-001-S010

Left: 1 / Woman seated on anchor. ***Center:*** Eagle on U.S. shield, Train. ***Bottom center:*** Sheaf and plow. ***Right:*** ONE / Indian woman pulling arrow from quiver. ***Comments:*** H-MA-1315-S5. 18__. 1850s.

Rarity: —

$2 • W-MA-3410-002-S020

CJF

Comments: H-MA-1315-S10. 185_. 1850s.

Rarity: —

$2 • W-MA-3410-002-S030

CC

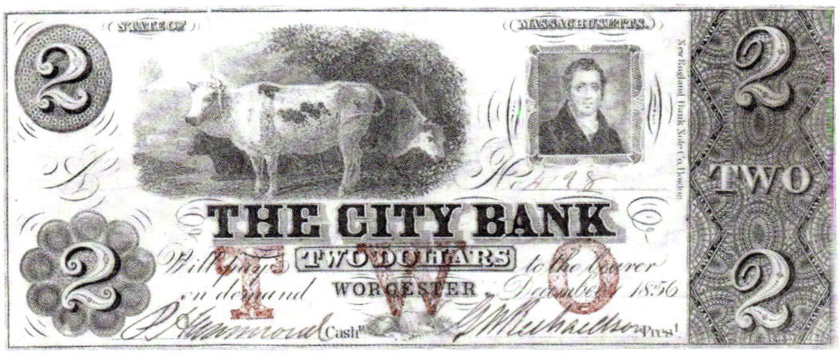

Overprint: Red TWO. ***Engraver:*** New England Bank Note Co ***Comments:*** H-MA-1315-S15. December 1, 1856.

Rarity: URS-8
F $100

$5 • W-MA-3410-005-N010

Left: Woman reclining on rock. ***Center:*** Three women with globe and sheaf. ***Right:*** Woman. ***Comments:*** H-MA-1315-N10. 1850s.

Rarity: —

$10 • W-MA-3410-010-A010

Left: Diagonal X / TEN. ***Center:*** Woman leaning on rock, Train / Ceres with sheaf on back. ***Right:*** 10 / Portrait of George Washington. ***Overprint:*** Red TEN. ***Engraver:*** Bald, Cousland & Co. / Baldwin, Bald & Cousland. ***Comments:*** H-MA-1315-A5. Altered from $10 Southern Bank of Georgia, Bainbridge, Georgia. 18__. 1860s.

Rarity: —

Mechanics Bank

1848–1865

W-MA-3420

History: The Mechanics Bank was chartered on April 18, 1848, with an authorized capital of $100,000, which increased to $300,000 by 1852. In 1856 it was $350,000. The bank was located at the Central Exchange in 1853. Circulation of the bank was $104,305 in 1849 and $214,323 in 1857.

The business of the Mechanics Bank was succeeded by the Mechanics National Bank of Worcester after it was chartered in 1865.

Numismatic Commentary: Genuine notes are hard to find but not impossible to locate.

VALID ISSUES

$1 • W-MA-3420-001-G010

Left: 1 / Portrait of George Washington / ONE. ***Center:*** Interior of blacksmith's shop, Men forging iron. ***Bottom center:*** Loom. ***Right:*** ONE / Liberty, eagle, and shield / ONE. ***Engraver:*** Danforth & Hufty. ***Comments:*** H-MA-1320-G2. 18__. 1848–1850s.

Rarity: —

$1 • W-MA-3420-001-G010a

JF

Overprint: Red ONE. ***Engraver:*** Danforth & Hufty. ***Comments:*** H-MA-1320-G2a. Similar to W-MA-3420-001-G010. July 3, 185_. 1850s–1860s.

Rarity: URS-4
F $1,500; **VF** $2,000

$2 • W-MA-3420-002-G020

Left: TWO / Portrait of Benjamin Franklin / TWO. ***Center:*** Woman / Man on horse, flock of sheep, dog / Mill / Woman. ***Right:*** 2 / Female portrait. ***Engraver:*** Danforth & Hufty. ***Comments:*** H-MA-1320-G4. 18__. 1848–1850s.

Rarity: —

$2 • W-MA-3420-002-G020a

Overprint: Red. ***Engraver:*** Danforth & Hufty. ***Comments:*** H-MA-1320-G4a. Similar to W-MA-3420-002-G020. 18__. 1850s–1860s.

Rarity: —

$3 • W-MA-3420-003-G030

Left: THREE / Female portrait / 3. ***Center:*** One woman and two men flanking shield bearing state arms surmounted by eagle. ***Bottom center:*** Woman. ***Right:*** 3 / Female portrait / 3. ***Engraver:*** Danforth & Hufty. ***Comments:*** H-MA-1320-G6. 18__. 1848–1850s.

Rarity: —

$3 • W-MA-3420-003-G030a

Overprint: Red. ***Engraver:*** Danforth & Hufty. ***Comments:*** H-MA-1320-G6a. Similar to W-MA-3420-003-G030. 18__. 1850s–1860s.

Rarity: —

$5 • W-MA-3420-005-G040

Left: 5 / Ceres / 5. ***Center:*** State arms / Three boys in 5 with flag / Female portrait. ***Right:*** 5 / Portrait of Daniel Webster. ***Engraver:*** Danforth & Hufty. ***Comments:*** H-MA-1320-G8. 18__. 1848–1850s.

Rarity: —

$5 • **W-MA-3420-005-G040a**

CJF

Overprint: Red FIVE. ***Engraver:*** Danforth & Hufty. ***Comments:*** H-MA-1320-G8a. Similar to W-MA-3420-005-G040. 18__. 1850s–1860s.

Rarity: URS-3
F $1,500; **VF** $2,000

$10 • **W-MA-3420-010-G050**

Left: Liberty, shield, and eagle. ***Center:*** 10 / Mechanic seated by anvil, Train and village. ***Bottom center:*** Arm and hammer. ***Right:*** 10 / Portrait of Zachary Taylor. ***Engraver:*** Danforth & Hufty. ***Comments:*** H-MA-1320-G10. 18__. 1848–1850s.

Rarity: —

$10 • **W-MA-3420-010-G050a**

Overprint: Red. ***Engraver:*** Danforth & Hufty. ***Comments:*** H-MA-1320-G10a. Similar to W-MA-3420-010-G050. 18__. 1850s–1860s.

Rarity: —

$20 • **W-MA-3420-020-G060**

Left: XX / Portrait of John Quincy Adams. ***Center:*** Three women floating in clouds / Woman reclining. ***Right:*** 20. ***Engraver:*** Danforth & Hufty. ***Comments:*** H-MA-1320-G12. 18__. 1848–1850s.

Rarity: —

$20 • **W-MA-3420-020-G060a**

SI

Overprint: Red XX. ***Engraver:*** Danforth & Hufty. ***Comments:*** H-MA-1320-G12a. Similar to W-MA-3420-020-G060. 18__. 1850s–1860s.

Rarity: URS-7
VG $100; **VF** $175

$50 • **W-MA-3420-050-G070**

Left: Two women seated, Two men standing, Book, chest, and spinning wheel, Factory chimneys. ***Center:*** 50 / Man plowing with oxen and horse. ***Right:*** 50. ***Engraver:*** Danforth & Hufty. ***Comments:*** H-MA-1320-G14. 18__. 1848–1850s.

Rarity: —

$50 • **W-MA-3420-050-G070a**

Overprint: Red. ***Engraver:*** Danforth & Hufty. ***Comments:*** H-MA-1320-G14a. Similar to W-MA-3420-050-G070. 18__. 1850s–1860s.

Rarity: —

$100 • **W-MA-3420-100-G080**

Left: 100 / Male portrait / 100. ***Center:*** White horse and black horse flanking shield bearing state arms surmounted by eagle. ***Right:*** 100 / Male portrait / 100. ***Engraver:*** Danforth & Hufty. ***Comments:*** H-MA-1320-G16. 18__. 1848–1850s.

Rarity: —

$100 • **W-MA-3420-100-G080a**

Overprint: Red. ***Engraver:*** Danforth & Hufty. ***Comments:*** H-MA-1320-G16a. Similar to W-MA-3420-100-G080. 18__. 1850s–1860s.

Rarity: —

$500 • **W-MA-3420-500-G090**

Left: D. ***Center:*** Woman holding book, Tools / Steamboat and factories. ***Bottom center:*** Dog, key, and strongbox. ***Right:*** 500. ***Engraver:*** American Bank Note Co. ***Comments:*** H-MA-1320-G18. 18__. 1850s–1860s.

Rarity: —

Uncut Sheets

$1-$1-$2-$3 • **W-MA-3420-001.001.002.003-US010**

Vignette(s): ***($1)*** Portrait of George Washington / Interior of blacksmith's shop, Men forging iron / Machine / Liberty, eagle, and shield. ***($1)*** Portrait of George Washington / Interior of blacksmith's shop, Men forging iron / Machine / Liberty, eagle, and shield. ***($2)*** Portrait of Benjamin Franklin / Woman / Man on horse, flock of sheep, dog / Mill / Woman / Female portrait. ***($3)*** Female portrait / One woman and two men flanking shield bearing state arms surmounted by eagle / Woman / Female portrait. ***Engraver:*** Danforth & Hufty. ***Comments:*** H-MA-1320-G2, G2, G4, G6. 18__. 1848–1850s.

Rarity: —

$5-$5-$10-$20 • **W-MA-3420-005.005.010.020-US020**

Vignette(s): ***($5)*** Female portrait / Three boys in 5 with flag / Female portrait / Portrait of Daniel Webster. ***($5)*** Female portrait / Three boys in 5 with flag / Female portrait / Portrait of Daniel Webster. ***($10)*** Liberty, shield, and eagle / Mechanic seated by anvil, Train and village / Arm and hammer / Portrait of Zachary Taylor. ***($20)*** Portrait of John Quincy Adams / Three women floating in clouds / Woman reclining. ***Engraver:*** Danforth & Hufty. ***Comments:*** H-MA-1320-G8, G8, G10, G12. 18__. 1848–1850s.

Rarity: —

$100-$500 • **W-MA-3420-100.500-US030**

Vignette(s): ***($100)*** Male portrait / White horse and black horse flanking shield bearing state arms surmounted by eagle / Male portrait. ***($500)*** Woman holding book, Tools / Steamboat and factories / Dog, key, and strongbox. ***Engraver:*** Danforth & Hufty. ***Comments:*** All unlisted in Haxby. Similar to H-MA-1320-G16, G18 but with different engraver imprint. Partial sheet. 18__. 1848–1850s.

Rarity: —

Non-Valid Issues

$1 • W-MA-3420-001-A010

Left: Panel bearing portrait of Zachary Taylor. ***Center:*** 1 / Woman in clouds holding shield, Eagle / 1 / ONE. ***Right:*** Panel bearing Ceres. ***Engraver:*** W.L. Ormsby. ***Comments:*** H-MA-1320-A5. Altered from $1 Mechanics and Traders Bank, Georgetown, D.C. Nov. 14, 1852.

Rarity: —

$2 • W-MA-3420-002-C020

Engraver: Danforth & Hufty. ***Comments:*** H-MA-1320-C4. Counterfeit of W-MA-3420-002-G020 or G020a. 18__. 1850s.

Rarity: —

$2 • W-MA-3420-002-S010

Center: Hebe watering eagle. ***Engraver:*** Danforth, Wright & Co. ***Comments:*** H-MA-1320-S5. 18__. 1850s.

Rarity: —

$3 • W-MA-3420-003-S020

CJF

Engraver: New England Bank Note Co. ***Comments:*** H-MA-1320-S10. 18__. 1840s.

Rarity: URS-7
F $175

$5 • W-MA-3420-005-S030

CC

Comments: H-MA-1320-S15. July 15, 1852.

Rarity: URS-7
F $175

$5 • W-MA-3420-005-A020

Left: FIVE / Portrait of Benjamin Franklin / FIVE. ***Center:*** Portrait of George Washington flanked by three allegorical women and two men. ***Right:*** 5 / Portrait of Andrew Jackson / 5. ***Engraver:*** Danforth, Wright & Co. ***Comments:*** H-MA-1320-A10. Altered from $5 Mechanics Bank of Memphis, Memphis, Tennessee series. 1850s.

Rarity: —

$10 • W-MA-3420-010-S040

Left: TEN on three dies. ***Center:*** 10 / Steamboat, Sailing ships / 10. ***Right:*** TEN / Portrait of George Washington / TEN ***Engraver:*** Rawdon, Wright & Hatch. ***Comments:*** H-MA-1320-S20. Aug. 1, 1849.

Rarity: —

$10 • W-MA-3420-010-S050

Center: Hebe watering eagle. ***Comments:*** H-MA-1320-S25. 18__. 1850s.

Rarity: —

$20 • W-MA-3420-020-C060a

CJF

Overprint: XX. ***Engraver:*** Danforth & Hufty. ***Comments:*** H-MA-1320-C12a. Counterfeit of W-MA-3420-020-G060a. 18__. 1860s.

Rarity: —

Quinsigamond Bank

1833–1865

W-MA-3430

History: The Quinsigamond Bank, chartered on March 25, 1833, had an authorized capital of $100,000, a figure which was raised to $250,000 in 1854. The circulation of the bank was $56,780 in 1839; it reached $130,155 in 1863. Specie was listed at $13,898.50 in 1854 and at $30,508.19 in 1857.

The business of the Quinsigamond Bank was succeeded by the Quinsigamond National Bank of Worcester after it was chartered on April 28, 1865.

Numismatic Commentary: Genuine notes from this bank are hard to locate. Some issues show a pleasant view of the first Unitarian Church and the Court House on Main Street at Lincoln Square. This bank also offers collectors another chance at obtaining a PSSP design note with a Congreve Check Plate back.

Valid Issues

$1 • W-MA-3430-001-G010

Left: 1 / Minerva standing with 1 / 1. ***Center:*** ONE / Commerce seated with caduceus and cornucopia, Plow and ships / ONE. ***Right:*** 1 / Eagle / 1. ***Back:*** Check Plate. ***Engraver:*** PSSP ***Comments:*** H-MA-1325-G2. 18__. 1830s.

Rarity: —

$1 • W-MA-3430-001-G020

Left: ONE / Bust of George Washington / ONE. ***Center:*** 1 / Two blacksmiths at anvil in forge / 1 / Panel outlining white ONE. ***Right:*** ONE / Woman / ONE. ***Engraver:*** New England Bank Note Co. ***Comments:*** H-MA-1325-G4. 18__. 1840s.

Rarity: —

$1 • W-MA-3430-001-G030

Left: Panel bearing ONE vertically. ***Center:*** Sloop and other ships, 1. ***Right:*** ONE / Indian woman seated with bow and arrow / ONE. ***Engraver:*** New England Bank Note Co. ***Comments:*** H-MA-1325-G6. 18__. 1840s.

Rarity: —

$1 • **W-MA-3430-001-G040**

CJF

Engraver: Toppan, Carpenter, Casilear & Co. ***Comments:*** H-MA-1325-G8. 18__. 1850s.

Rarity: URS-6
F $150

$1 • **W-MA-3430-001-G040a**

CJF

Overprint: Red ONE. ***Engraver:*** Toppan, Carpenter, Casilear & Co. ***Comments:*** H-MA-1325-G8a. Similar to W-MA-3430-001-G040. 18__. 1850s–1860s.

Rarity: —

$2 • **W-MA-3430-002-G050**

Left: 2 / Hebe watering eagle / 2. ***Center:*** 2 / Plow, Commerce seated with caduceus and cornucopia, Ships / 2. ***Right:*** 2 / Justice standing / 2. ***Engraver:*** PSSP. ***Comments:*** H-MA-1325-G10. 18__. 1830s.

Rarity: —

$2 • **W-MA-3430-002-G060**

Left: TWO / Woman / 2. ***Center:*** 2 / Woman giving drink to one of two seated men / 2 / Panel outlining white TWO. ***Right:*** TWO / Bust of female reaper. ***Engraver:*** New England Bank Note Co. ***Comments:*** H-MA-1325-G12. 18__. 1840s.

Rarity: —

$2 • **W-MA-3430-002-G070**

Left: Panel bearing 2 / TWO / 2. ***Center:*** Sailing ship and ships / 2. ***Right:*** Two / Woman drawing water from well / TWO. ***Engraver:*** New England Bank Note Co. ***Comments:*** H-MA-1325-G14. 18__. 1840s.

Rarity: —

$2 • **W-MA-3430-002-G080**

Left: 2 / Scene on plank road, Cattle, wagons, and men. ***Center:*** View of Main Street, Worcester. ***Right:*** 2 / Train, Houses. ***Engraver:*** Toppan, Carpenter, Casilear & Co. ***Comments:*** H-MA-1325-G16. 18__. 1850s.

Rarity: —

$2 • **W-MA-3430-002-G080a**

Overprint: Red TWO. ***Engraver:*** Toppan, Carpenter, Casilear & Co. ***Comments:*** H-MA-1325-G16a. Similar to W-MA-3430-002-G080. 18__. 1850s.

Rarity: —

$3 • **W-MA-3430-003-G090**

CJF

Back: Check Plate. ***Engraver:*** PSSP. ***Comments:*** H-MA-1325-G18. 18__. 1830s.

Rarity: —

$3 • **W-MA-3430-003-G100**

Left: Panel bearing THREE vertically. ***Center:*** Man reaping with sickle, Woman standing with hat and sheaf / 3. ***Right:*** THREE / Steamship / 3 on THREE. ***Engraver:*** New England Bank Note Co. ***Comments:*** H-MA-1325-G20. 18__. 1840s.

Rarity: —

$3 • **W-MA-3430-003-G110**

Left: THREE / Farmer sharpening scythe / 3 across THREE. ***Center:*** 3 / Woman placing garland on eagle, Beehive and cornucopia / 3 / Panel outlining white THREE. ***Right:*** THREE / Sailor standing on wharf with hat / 3 across THREE. ***Engraver:*** New England Bank Note Co. ***Comments:*** H-MA-1325-G22. 18__. 1840s.

Rarity: —

$3 • **W-MA-3430-003-G120**

Left: Mason building brick wall / 3. ***Center:*** View of Main Street, Worcester. ***Right:*** 3 / Woman holding sheaf and shading eyes with hand. ***Engraver:*** Toppan, Carpenter, Casilear & Co. ***Comments:*** H-MA-1325-G24. 18__. 1850s.

Rarity: —

$3 • **W-MA-3430-003-G120a**

Overprint: Red THREE. ***Engraver:*** Toppan, Carpenter, Casilear & Co. ***Comments:*** H-MA-1325-G24a. Similar to W-MA-3430-003-G120. 18__. 1850s.

Rarity: —

$5 • **W-MA-3430-005-G130**

Left: Panel bearing FIVE / Plenty and Minerva seated / V. ***Center:*** FIVE / Allegorical woman seated / FIVE / Panel of microletters. ***Right:*** 5 / Eagle / 5. ***Back:*** Check Plate. ***Engraver:*** PSSP. ***Comments:*** H-MA-1325-G26. 18__. 1830s.

Rarity: —

$5 • **W-MA-3430-005-G140**

Left: 5 / FIVE / 5. ***Center:*** V / Eagle on wharf with plow, Cannon and anchor, Ships / V / Panel outlining white FIVE. ***Right:*** 5 / FIVE / 5. ***Engraver:*** New England Bank Note Co. ***Comments:*** H-MA-1325-G28. 18__. 1840s.

Rarity: —

$5 • W-MA-3430-005-G150

Left: Panel bearing FIVE vertically. ***Center:*** Woman unveiling shield bearing 5 / V. ***Right:*** 5 / Sailing ship. ***Engraver:*** New England Bank Note Co. ***Comments:*** H-MA-1325-G30. 18__. 1840s.

Rarity: —

$5 • W-MA-3430-005-G160

Left: View of Main Street, Worcester / 5. ***Center:*** Male portrait. ***Right:*** 5 / Woman with basket of flowers. ***Engraver:*** Toppan, Carpenter, Casilear & Co. ***Comments:*** H-MA-1325-G32. 18__. 1850s.

Rarity: —

$5 • W-MA-3430-005-G160a

Overprint: Red FIVE. ***Engraver:*** Toppan, Carpenter, Casilear & Co. ***Comments:*** H-MA-1325-G32a. Similar to W-MA-3430-005-G160. 18__. 1850s.

Rarity: —

$10 • W-MA-3430-010-G170

Left: Panel bearing TEN / Manhattan and spilling water jug / TEN. ***Center:*** TEN / Ceres seated / TEN / Panel of microletters. ***Right:*** Panel bearing 10 / Portrait of Indian / 10. ***Back:*** Check Plate. ***Engraver:*** PSSP. ***Comments:*** H-MA-1325-G34. 18__. 1830s.

Rarity: —

$10 • W-MA-3430-010-G180

Left: Panel bearing 10 / X / 10. ***Center:*** Allegorical male standing by oxen and plow / 10. ***Right:*** TEN / Woman standing with rudder and cornucopia. ***Engraver:*** New England Bank Note Co. ***Comments:*** H-MA-1325-G36. 18__. 1840s.

Rarity: —

$10 • W-MA-3430-010-G190

Left: Portrait of William Penn / TEN. ***Center:*** View of Main Street, Worcester. ***Right:*** 10 / Indian man seated. ***Engraver:*** Toppan, Carpenter, Casilear & Co. ***Comments:*** H-MA-1325-G38. 18__. 1850s.

Rarity: —

$10 • W-MA-3430-010-G190a

Overprint: Red TEN. ***Engraver:*** Toppan, Carpenter, Casilear & Co. ***Comments:*** H-MA-1325-G38a. Similar to W-MA-3430-010-G190. 18__. 1850s.

Rarity: —

$20 • W-MA-3430-020-G200

Left: 20 / XX / 20. ***Center:*** 20 / Woman seated with scales, Sheaf and bales, Men plowing and ship. ***Right:*** TWENTY vertically. ***Back:*** Check Plate. ***Engraver:*** PSSP / New England Bank Note Co. ***Comments:*** H-MA-1325-G40. 18__. 1830s–1840s.

Rarity: —

$20 • W-MA-3430-020-G210

Left: State arms / 20. ***Center:*** Angel in clouds blowing trumpet, Globe, Eagle clutching arrows, Flags. ***Right:*** 20 / Portrait of John Quincy Adams. ***Engraver:*** Toppan, Carpenter, Casilear & Co. ***Comments:*** H-MA-1325-G42. 18__. 1850s.

Rarity: URS-3
Proof $2,000

$20 • W-MA-3430-020-G210a

Overprint: Red. ***Engraver:*** Toppan, Carpenter, Casilear & Co. ***Comments:*** H-MA-1325-G42a. Similar to W-MA-3430-020-G210. 18__. 1850s.

Rarity: —

$50 • W-MA-3430-050-G220

Left: 50 / Cornucopia, Woman standing with ankles crossed, Staff, Anchor / 50. ***Center:*** FIFTY DOLLARS / 50. ***Right:*** FIFTY vertically. ***Back:*** Check Plate. ***Engraver:*** New England Bank Note Co. / PSSP. ***Comments:*** H-MA-1325-G44. 18__. 1830s–1840s.

Rarity: —

$50 • W-MA-3430-050-G230

Left: 50 / Portrait of George Washington. ***Center:*** Two cows in stream, one lying down, Three sheep and two cows on shore. ***Right:*** 50. ***Engraver:*** Toppan, Carpenter, Casilear & Co. ***Comments:*** H-MA-1325-G46. 18__. 1850s.

Rarity: —

$100 • W-MA-3430-100-G240

Left: Lathework panel bearing C / Portrait of George Washington / C. ***Center:*** 100 / Manhattan reclining, pouring water, Ship / 100. ***Right:*** Lathework panel bearing ONE HUNDRED vertically. ***Back:*** Check Plate. ***Engraver:*** New England Bank Note Co. / PSSP. ***Comments:*** H-MA-1325-G48. 18__. 1830s–1840s.

Rarity: URS-2
Proof $4,000

$100 • W-MA-3430-100-G250

Left: 100 / Justice seated. ***Center:*** Milkmaid seated with pail, Two cows, Farmhouse. ***Right:*** 100 / Portrait of Benjamin Franklin. ***Engraver:*** Toppan, Carpenter, Casilear & Co. ***Comments:*** H-MA-1325-G50. 18__. 1850s

Rarity: —

$500 • W-MA-3430-500-G260

Left: 500 / 500 vertically. ***Center:*** 500 / Woman seated with shield bearing D, Fasces, cornucopia, lyre, and sheaf. ***Right:*** 500 / D / 500. ***Back:*** Check Plate. ***Engraver:*** PSSP / New England Bank Note Co. ***Comments:*** H-MA-1325-G52. 18__. 1830s–1840s.

Rarity: —

$500 • W-MA-3430-500-G270

JF

Engraver: Toppan, Carpenter, Casilear & Co. ***Comments:*** H-MA-1325-G54. Proof. 18__. 1850s.

Rarity: URS-2
Proof $6,000

$1,000 • W-MA-3430-1000-G280

Left: THOUSAND vertically. ***Center:*** 1000 / Woman standing with legs crossed, Lyre, Cornucopia / 1000. ***Right:*** 1000 / M / 1000. ***Back:*** Check Plate. ***Engraver:*** New England Bank Note Co. / PSSP. ***Comments:*** H-MA-1325-G56. 18__. 1830s–1840s.

Rarity: —

Non-Valid Issues

$1 • W-MA-3430-001-N010

Center: Sailing ship and steamboat. ***Comments:*** H-MA-1325-N5.

Rarity: —

$3 • W-MA-3430-003-C110

CJF

Engraver: New England Bank Note Co. ***Comments:*** H-MA-1325-C22. Counterfeit of W-MA-3430-003-G110. 18__. 1840s–1850s.

Rarity: URS-7
VG $125; **VF** $175

$5 • W-MA-3430-005-C140

SI

Engraver: New England Bank Note Co. ***Comments:*** H-MA-1325-C28. Counterfeit of W-MA-3430-005-G140. 18__. 1840s–1850s.

Rarity: —

$5 • W-MA-3430-005-R010

Engraver: Toppan, Carpenter, Casilear & Co. ***Comments:*** H-MA-1325-R5. Raised from W-MA-3430-001-G040 or G040a. 18__. 1850s.

Rarity: —

$10 • W-MA-3430-010-R020

Engraver: Toppan, Carpenter, Casilear & Co. ***Comments:*** H-MA-1325-R10. Raised from W-MA-3430-001-G040 or G040a. 18__. 1850s.

Rarity: —

$20 • W-MA-3430-020-R030

Engraver: Toppan, Carpenter, Casilear & Co. ***Comments:*** H-MA-1325-R15. Raised from W-MA-3430-001-G040 or G040a. 18__. 1850s.

Rarity: —

Union Bank (branch)

Uncertain

W-MA-3440

History: The Union Bank was incorporated by the general court in 1792 for the purpose of accommodating agricultural interests. The bank was located at 40 State Street, Boston, with branches located in Salem and Worcester. Details of the branches have not been confirmed.

See also listing under Boston, W-MA-1010, and Salem, W-MA-2985.

Worcester Bank

1804–1864

W-MA-3450

History: The Worcester Bank was chartered on March 7, 1804, with an authorized capital of $150,000. The bank was located at 161 Main Street in 1844.

The bank was required to set aside one-eighth of its capital for the exclusive purpose of giving loans, in amounts of no less than $100 and no greater than $500, to agricultural interests. By 1839 the bank's capital was $200,000. In 1852 it was noted that "$75,000 additional capital [was] ascertained to be paid."[43] Capital was $300,000 in 1855, and by 1867 it was $500,000 with a limit of $1,000,000. Circulation was $80,287 in 1839, and by 1863 it had reached $213,810. Specie was $44,094.98, and real estate was valued at $25,000.

The business of the Worcester Bank was succeeded by the Worcester National Bank after it was chartered in 1864.

Numismatic Commentary: This bank used various engravers for their notes, and examples of many of them are still available in the marketplace.

Valid Issues

$1 • W-MA-3450-001-G010

Center: 1 / 1 / Black oval bearing white flower buds / 1 / 1. ***Engraver:*** Perkins. ***Comments:*** H-MA-1330-G10. 18__. 1800s.

Rarity: —

$1 • W-MA-3450-001-G020

Center: 1 / 1 / Double oval of flower garlands and gridwork segments / ONE / 1 / 1. ***Engraver:*** PSSP. ***Comments:*** H-MA-1330-G12. 18__. 1807–1809.

Rarity: —

$1 • W-MA-3450-001-G030

Center: 1 / 1 / Oval of flower garlands and gridwork segments / 1 / 1. ***Engraver:*** PSSP. ***Comments:*** H-MA-1330-G14. 18__. 1809–circa 1812.

Rarity: —

$1 • W-MA-3450-001-G030a

Center: 1 / 1 / Oval of flower garlands and gridwork segments / ONE / 1 / 1. ***Engraver:*** PSSP. ***Comments:*** H-MA-1330-G16. Similar to W-MA-3450-001-G030. 18__. 1810s.

Rarity: —

$1 • **W-MA-3450-001-G040**

Left: ONE vertically. ***Center:*** 1 / 1. ***Bottom center:*** 1. ***Right:*** MASSACHUSETTS vertically. ***Engraver:*** Leney & Rollinson. ***Comments:*** H-MA-1330-G18. 18__. 1810s.

Rarity: —

$1 • **W-MA-3450-001-G050**

Left: Narrow panel of lathework circle segments. ***Center:*** 1 / 1 / Flower garlands and gridwork segments / 1 / 1. ***Right:*** Narrow panel of lathework circle segments. ***Engraver:*** PSSP. ***Comments:*** H-MA-1330-G20. 18__. 1820s–1830s.

Rarity: —

$1 • **W-MA-3450-001-G050a**

Left: ONE / D / ONE vertically. ***Right:*** ONE / D / ONE vertically. ***Engraver:*** PSSP. ***Comments:*** H-MA-1330-G22. Similar to W-MA-3450-001-G050. 18__. 1830s.

Rarity: —

$1 • **W-MA-3450-001-G050b**

Left: ONE / D / ONE vertically. ***Right:*** ONE / D / ONE vertically. ***Engraver:*** PSSP. ***Comments:*** H-MA-1330-G24. Similar to W-MA-3450-001-G050. 18__. 1830s–1840s.

Rarity: —

$1 • **W-MA-3450-001-G060**

Engraver: Unverified, but likely New England Bank Note Co. / PSSP. ***Comments:*** H-MA-1330-G26. No description available. 18__. 1830s.

Rarity: *None known*

$1 • **W-MA-3450-001-G070**

Engraver: Unverified, but likely New England Bank Note Co. / PSSP. ***Comments:*** H-MA-1330-G28. No description available. 18__. 1840s.

Rarity: *None known*

$1 • **W-MA-3450-001-G080**

QDB

Engraver: Toppan, Carpenter & Co. ***Comments:*** H-MA-1330-G30. Proof. 18__. 1840s.

Rarity: —

$1 • **W-MA-3450-001-G080a**

CJF

Overprint: Red ONE. ***Engraver:*** Toppan, Carpenter & Co. ***Comments:*** H-MA-1330-G30a. Similar to W-MA-3450-001-G080. January 1, 18__. 1840s–1850s.

Rarity: —

$2 • **W-MA-3450-002-G090**

Center: 2 / 2 / Black oval bearing white flower buds / 2 / 2. ***Engraver:*** Perkins. ***Comments:*** H-MA-1330-G34. 18__. 1800s.

Rarity: —

$2 • **W-MA-3450-002-G100**

Center: 2 / 2 / Black oval bearing white flower buds / TWO / 2 / 2. ***Engraver:*** PSSP. ***Comments:*** H-MA-1330-G36. 18__. 1807–1809.

Rarity: —

$2 • **W-MA-3450-002-G110**

Center: 2 / 2 / Oval of flower garlands and gridwork segments / 2 / 2. ***Engraver:*** PSSP. ***Comments:*** H-MA-1330-G38. 18__. 1809–circa 1812.

Rarity: —

$2 • **W-MA-3450-002-G110a**

Center: 2 / 2 / Oval of flower garlands and gridwork segments / TWO / 2 / 2. ***Engraver:*** PSSP. ***Comments:*** H-MA-1330-G40. Similar to W-MA-3450-002-G110. 18__. 1810s.

Rarity: —

$2 • **W-MA-3450-002-G120**

Left: 2 vertically. ***Center:*** 2 / 2. ***Bottom center:*** TWO. ***Right:*** MASSACHUSETTS vertically. ***Engraver:*** Leney & Rollinson. ***Comments:*** H-MA-1330-G42. 181_. 1810s.

Rarity: —

$2 • **W-MA-3450-002-G130**

Left: Narrow panel of lathework circle segments. ***Center:*** 2 / 2 / Flower garlands and gridwork segments / 2 / 2. ***Right:*** Narrow panel of lathework circle segments. ***Engraver:*** PSSP. ***Comments:*** H-MA-1330-G44. 18__. 1820s–1830s.

Rarity: —

$2 • **W-MA-3450-002-G130a**

Left: Five TWOs vertically. ***Right:*** Five TWOs vertically. ***Engraver:*** PSSP. ***Comments:*** H-MA-1330-G46. Similar to W-MA-3450-002-G130. 18__. 1830s.

Rarity: —

$2 • **W-MA-3450-002-G130b**

Left: Five TWOs vertically. ***Right:*** Five TWOs vertically. ***Engraver:*** PSSP. ***Comments:*** H-MA-1330-G48. Similar to W-MA-3450-002-G130. 18__. 1830s.

Rarity: —

$2 • **W-MA-3450-002-G130c**

Left: Five TWOs vertically. ***Right:*** Five TWOs vertically. ***Engraver:*** PSSP. ***Comments:*** H-MA-1330-G50. Similar to W-MA-3450-002-G130. 18__. 1830s–1840s.

Rarity: —

$2 • **W-MA-3450-002-G140**

Engraver: Unverified, but likely New England Bank Note Co. / PSSP. ***Comments:*** H-MA-1330-G52. No description available. 18__. 1830s.

Rarity: *None known*

$2 • **W-MA-3450-002-G150**

Engraver: Unverified, but likely New England Bank Note Co. ***Comments:*** H-MA-1330-G54. No description available. 18__. 1840s.

Rarity: *None known*

$2 • **W-MA-3450-002-G160**

QDB

Engraver: Toppan, Carpenter & Co. ***Comments:*** H-MA-1330-G56. Proof. 18__. 1840s.

Rarity: —

$2 • **W-MA-3450-002-G160a**

Left: 2 / Farmer sharpening scythe. ***Center:*** 2 bearing portrait of George Washington. ***Right:*** 2 / Dog and strongbox. ***Overprint:*** Red TWO. ***Engraver:*** Toppan, Carpenter & Co. ***Comments:*** H-MA-1330-G56a. Similar to W-MA-3450-002-G160. Jan. 1, 18__. 1850s.

Rarity: —

$3 • **W-MA-3450-003-G170**

Center: 3 / 3 / Black oval bearing white flower buds / 3 / 3. ***Engraver:*** Perkins. ***Comments:*** H-MA-1330-G60. 18__. 1800s.

Rarity: —

$3 • **W-MA-3450-003-G180**

Center: 3 / 3 / Black oval bearing white flower buds / THREE / 3 / 3. ***Engraver:*** PSSP. ***Comments:*** H-MA-1330-G62. 18__. 1807–1809.

Rarity: —

$3 • **W-MA-3450-003-G190**

Center: 3 / 3 / Oval of flower garlands and gridwork segments / 3 / 3. ***Engraver:*** PSSP. ***Comments:*** H-MA-1330-G64. 18__. 1809–1810s.

Rarity: —

$3 • **W-MA-3450-003-G200**

Left: 3 vertically. ***Center:*** 3 / 3. ***Bottom center:*** 3. ***Right:*** MASSACHUSETTS vertically. ***Engraver:*** Leney & Rollinson. ***Comments:*** H-MA-1330-G66. 181_. 1810s.

Rarity: —

$3 • **W-MA-3450-003-G210**

Left: Narrow panel of lathework circle segments. ***Center:*** 3 / 3 / Flower garlands and gridwork segments / 3 / 3. ***Right:*** Narrow panel of lathework circle segments. ***Engraver:*** PSSP. ***Comments:*** H-MA-1330-G68. 18__. 1820s–1830s.

Rarity: —

$3 • **W-MA-3450-003-G210a**

Left: THREE vertically. ***Right:*** THREE vertically. ***Engraver:*** PSSP. ***Comments:*** H-MA-1330-G70. Similar to W-MA-3450-003-G210. 18__. 1830s.

Rarity: —

$3 • **W-MA-3450-003-G210b**

Left: THREE vertically. ***Right:*** THREE vertically. ***Engraver:*** PSSP. ***Comments:*** H-MA-1330-G72. Similar to W-MA-3450-003-G210. 18__. 1830s–1840s.

Rarity: —

$3 • **W-MA-3450-003-G220**

Engraver: Unverified, but likely New England Bank Note Co. / PSSP. ***Comments:*** H-MA-1330-G74. No description available. 18__. 1830s.

Rarity: *None known*

$3 • **W-MA-3450-003-G230**

Engraver: Unverified, but likely New England Bank Note Co. ***Comments:*** H-MA-1330-G76. No description available. 18__. 1840s.

Rarity: *None known*

$3 • **W-MA-3450-003-G240**

QDB

Engraver: Toppan, Carpenter & Co. ***Comments:*** H-MA-1330-G78. Proof. 18__. 1840s.

Rarity: —

$3 • **W-MA-3450-003-G240a**

Left: 3 / Male portrait. ***Center:*** 3 bearing portrait of John Adams. ***Right:*** 3 / Female portrait. ***Overprint:*** Red THREE. ***Engraver:*** Toppan, Carpenter & Co. ***Comments:*** H-MA-1330-G78a. Similar to W-MA-3450-003-G240. Jan. 1, 18__. 1850s.

Rarity: —

$5 • **W-MA-3450-005-G250**

Left: MASSACHUSETTS vertically. ***Center:*** 5 / 5 / FIVE DOLLARS. ***Right:*** 5. ***Engraver:*** Perkins. ***Comments:*** H-MA-1330-G82. 18__. 1800s.

Rarity: —

$5 • **W-MA-3450-005-G260**

Left: Narrow panel bearing MASSACHUSETTS / 5 / 5 vertically. ***Center:*** Alternating flower garlands and gridwork segments. ***Right:*** 5 / 5 vertically. ***Engraver:*** Perkins. ***Comments:*** H-MA-1330-G84. 18__. 1806 and 1807.

Rarity: —

$5 • **W-MA-3450-005-G260a**

Center: Rose-covered FIVE. ***Engraver:*** Perkins. ***Comments:*** H-MA-1330-G86. Similar to W-MA-3450-005-G260. 18__. Circa 1808 and 1809.

Rarity: —

$5 • **W-MA-3450-005-G260b**

Left: Narrow panel bearing MASSACHUSETTS / 5 / State arms / 5. ***Engraver:*** PSSP. ***Comments:*** H-MA-1330-G88. Similar to W-MA-3450-005-G260. 18__. 1809–1820s.

Rarity: —

$5 • W-MA-3450-005-G260c

Left: Narrow panel bearing MASSACHUSETTS / 5 / State arms / 5. ***Engraver:*** PSSP. ***Comments:*** H-MA-1330-G90. Similar to W-MA-3450-005-G260. 18__. 1809–1810s.

Rarity: —

$5 • W-MA-3450-005-G270

CJF

Engraver: Murray, Draper, Fairman & Co. ***Comments:*** H-MA-1330-G92. Progressive Proof. 181_. 1810s.

Rarity: —

$5 • W-MA-3450-005-G280

Left: Lathework chain bearing MASSACHUSETTS / 5 / 5 vertically. ***Center:*** Alternating flower garlands and gridwork segments. ***Right:*** 5 / 5 vertically. ***Engraver:*** PSSP. ***Comments:*** H-MA-1330-G94. 18__. 1820s.

Rarity: —

$5 • W-MA-3450-005-G280a

Engraver: PSSP. ***Comments:*** H-MA-1330-G96. Similar to W-MA-3450-005-G280 but with zigzag ruled lines. 18__. 1820s–1830s.

Rarity: —

$5 • W-MA-3450-005-G280b

Engraver: PSSP. ***Comments:*** H-MA-1330-G98. Similar to W-MA-3450-005-G280 but with spiral lathework lines. 18__. 1830s.

Rarity: —

$5 • W-MA-3450-005-G290

Engraver: Unverified, but likely New England Bank Note Co. / PSSP. ***Comments:*** H-MA-1330-G100. No description available. 18__. 1830s.

Rarity: *None known*

$5 • W-MA-3450-005-G300

Engraver: Unverified, but likely New England Bank Note Co. ***Comments:*** H-MA-1330-G102. No description available. 18__. 1840s.

Rarity: *None known*

$5 • W-MA-3450-005-G310

Left: 5 / Woman seated with spear. ***Center:*** Female portrait / 5 bearing FIVE / Female portrait. ***Right:*** 5 / Rachel Jackson standing. ***Engraver:*** Toppan, Carpenter & Co. ***Comments:*** H-MA-1330-G104. 18__. 1840s.

Rarity: —

$5 • W-MA-3450-005-G310a

Overprint: Red FIVE. ***Engraver:*** Toppan, Carpenter & Co. ***Comments:*** H-MA-1330-G104a. Similar to W-MA-3450-005-G310. 18__. 1850s.

Rarity: —

$10 • W-MA-3450-010-G320

Left: Narrow panel bearing MASSACHUSETTS vertically. ***Center:*** 10 / 10, 10 / Narrow row of black circles bearing white lettering. ***Engraver:*** Perkins. ***Comments:*** H-MA-1330-G108. 18__. 1800s.

Rarity: —

$10 • W-MA-3450-010-G330

Left: Narrow panel bearing MASSACHUSETTS / 10 / 10 vertically. ***Center:*** Alternating flower garlands and gridwork segments. ***Right:*** 10 / 10 vertically. ***Engraver:*** Perkins. ***Comments:*** H-MA-1330-G110. 18__. 1806 and 1807.

Rarity: —

$10 • W-MA-3450-010-G330a

Center: Rose-covered TEN. ***Engraver:*** Perkins. ***Comments:*** H-MA-1330-G112. Similar to W-MA-3450-010-G330. 18__. Circa 1808 and 1809.

Rarity: —

$10 • W-MA-3450-010-G330b

Left: Narrow panel bearing MASSACHUSETTS / 10 / State arms / 10 vertically. ***Engraver:*** Perkins. ***Comments:*** H-MA-1330-G114. Similar to W-MA-3450-010-G330. 18__. 1809–circa 1812.

Rarity: —

$10 • W-MA-3450-010-G330c

Left: Narrow panel bearing MASSACHUSETTS / 10 / State arms / 10 vertically. ***Center:*** Rose-covered TEN / TEN. ***Engraver:*** Perkins. ***Comments:*** H-MA-1330-G116. Similar to W-MA-3450-010-G330. 18__. 1810s.

Rarity: —

$10 • W-MA-3450-010-G340

Left: TEN vertically. ***Center:*** 10 / 10 / X. ***Right:*** MASSACHUSETTS vertically. ***Engraver:*** Murray, Draper, Fairman & Co. ***Comments:*** H-MA-1330-G118. 181_. 1810s.

Rarity: —

$10 • W-MA-3450-010-G350

Left: Lathework chain bearing MASSACHUSETTS / 10 / 10 vertically. ***Center:*** Alternating flower garlands and gridwork segments. ***Right:*** 10 / 10 vertically. ***Engraver:*** Perkins. ***Comments:*** H-MA-1330-G120. 18__. 1820s.

Rarity: —

$10 • W-MA-3450-010-G350a

Engraver: PSSP. ***Comments:*** H-MA-1330-G122. Similar to W-MA-3450-010-G350. 18__. 1820s–1830s.

Rarity: —

$10 • W-MA-3450-010-G350b

Engraver: PSSP. ***Comments:*** H-MA-1330-G124. Similar to W-MA-3450-010-G350. 18__. 1830s.

Rarity: —

$10 • W-MA-3450-010-G360

Engraver: Unverified, but likely New England Bank Note Co. / PSSP. ***Comments:*** H-MA-1330-G126. No description available. 18__. 1830s.

Rarity: *None known*

$10 • W-MA-3450-010-G370

Engraver: Unverified, but likely New England Bank Note Co. ***Comments:*** H-MA-1330-G128. No description available. 18__. 1840s.

Rarity: *None known*

$10 • W-MA-3450-010-G380

Left: 10 / Blacksmith. ***Center:*** Portrait of James Madison / Woman seated / Portrait of James Monroe / 10. ***Right:*** 10 / Man seated. ***Engraver:*** Toppan, Carpenter & Co. ***Comments:*** H-MA-1330-G130. 18__. 1840s.

Rarity: —

$10 • W-MA-3450-010-G380a

Overprint: Red TEN. ***Engraver:*** Toppan, Carpenter & Co. ***Comments:*** H-MA-1330-G130a. Similar to W-MA-3450-010-G380. 18__. 1850s.

Rarity: —

$20 • W-MA-3450-020-G390

Left: Narrow panel bearing MASSACHUSETTS / 20 / 20 vertically. ***Center:*** Alternating flower garlands and gridwork segments. ***Right:*** 20 / 20 vertically. ***Engraver:*** Perkins. ***Comments:*** H-MA-1330-G134. 18__. 1806–1809.

Rarity: —

$20 • W-MA-3450-020-G390a

Left: Narrow panel bearing MASSACHUSETTS / 20 / State arms / 20 vertically. ***Engraver:*** Perkins. ***Comments:*** H-MA-1330-G136. Similar to W-MA-3450-020-G390. 18__. 1809–1810s.

Rarity: —

$20 • W-MA-3450-020-G400

Left: TWENTY vertically. ***Center:*** 20 / Man working at machine / 20. ***Bottom center:*** Plow and implements. ***Right:*** MASSACHUSETTS vertically. ***Engraver:*** Murray, Draper, Fairman & Co. ***Comments:*** H-MA-1330-G138. 181_. 1810s.

Rarity: —

$20 • W-MA-3450-020-G410

Left: Lathework chain bearing MASSACHUSETTS / 20 / 20 vertically. ***Center:*** Alternating flower garlands and gridwork segments. ***Right:*** 20 / 20 vertically. ***Engraver:*** PSSP. ***Comments:*** H-MA-1330-G140. 18__. 1820s–1830s.

Rarity: —

$20 • W-MA-3450-020-G420

Engraver: Unverified, but likely New England Bank Note Co. / PSSP. ***Comments:*** H-MA-1330-G142. No description available. 18__. 1830s.

Rarity: *None known*

$20 • W-MA-3450-020-G430

Engraver: Unverified, but likely New England Bank Note Co. ***Comments:*** H-MA-1330-G144. No description available. 18__. 1840s.

Rarity: *None known*

$20 • W-MA-3450-020-G440

Left: Woman carrying sheaf and shading eyes with hand / 20. ***Center:*** Indian man and Ceres flanking shield bearing XX surmounted by eagle on globe. ***Right:*** 20 / Man sowing grain. ***Engraver:*** Toppan, Carpenter & Co. ***Comments:*** H-MA-1330-G146. 18__. 1840s.

Rarity: —

$20 • W-MA-3450-020-G440a

Overprint: Red. ***Engraver:*** Toppan, Carpenter & Co. ***Comments:*** H-MA-1330-G146a. Similar to W-MA-3450-020-G440. 18__. 1850s.

Rarity: —

$50 • W-MA-3450-050-G450

Left: Lathework chain bearing MASSACHUSETTS / 50 / 50 vertically. ***Center:*** Alternating flower garlands and gridwork segments. ***Right:*** 50 / 50 vertically. ***Engraver:*** PSSP. ***Comments:*** H-MA-1330-G150. 18__. 1820s–1830s.

Rarity: —

$50 • W-MA-3450-050-G460

Engraver: Unverified, but likely New England Bank Note Co. / PSSP. ***Comments:*** H-MA-1330-G152. No description available. 18__. 1830s.

Rarity: *None known*

$50 • W-MA-3450-050-G470

Engraver: Unverified, but likely New England Bank Note Co. ***Comments:*** H-MA-1330-G154. No description available. 18__. 1840s.

Rarity: *None known*

$50 • W-MA-3450-050-G480

Left: L / 50. ***Center:*** Man reclining next to animals / L. ***Right:*** 50 / Woman seated. ***Engraver:*** Toppan, Carpenter & Co. ***Comments:*** H-MA-1330-G156. 18__. 1840s.

Rarity: —

$50 • W-MA-3450-050-G480a

Overprint: Red. ***Engraver:*** Toppan, Carpenter & Co. ***Comments:*** H-MA-1330-G156a. Similar to W-MA-3450-050-G480. 18__. 1850s.

Rarity: —

$100 • W-MA-3450-100-G490

Left: Lathework chain bearing MASSACHUSETTS / 100 / 100 vertically. ***Center:*** Alternating flower garlands and gridwork segments. ***Right:*** 100 / 100 vertically. ***Engraver:*** Perkins. ***Comments:*** H-MA-1330-G160. 18__. 1820s–1830s.

Rarity: —

How to Read the Whitman Numbering System

$1 • W-MA-010-001-G010a

Denomination: Value of the note shown.

W: Whitman number. This number is a sortable code unique to each bank and note.

MA: Abbreviation for the state under study.

010: Numerical designation specific to each bank.

001: The denomination in dollars.

G010a: G indicates a good or valid note. Other categories are indicated thus: C (counterfeit); R (raised); S (spurious); N (not-attributed); A (altered). Numbers are assigned starting with 010, 020, et seq. Terminal letters following the number indicate variations of a note: a series of different colored overprints, tints, payees, etc., all on the same design of note. For more information, see the "How to Use This Book" section at the front of the volume, page xiv.

$100 • W-MA-3450-100-G500

Engraver: Unverified, but likely New England Bank Note Co. / PSSP. ***Comments:*** H-MA-1330-G162. No description available. 18__. 1830s.

Rarity: *None known*

$100 • W-MA-3450-100-G510

Engraver: Unverified, but likely New England Bank Note Co. ***Comments:*** H-MA-1330-G164. No description available. 18__. 1840s.

Rarity: *None known*

$100 • W-MA-3450-100-G520

Left: 100 / Woman with sickle and sheaf. ***Center:*** Angel in clouds blowing horn with eagle, globe, and flags. ***Right:*** Woman seated on bale holding die bearing C / C. ***Engraver:*** Toppan, Carpenter & Co. ***Comments:*** H-MA-1330-G166. 18__. 1840s.

Rarity: —

$100 • W-MA-3450-100-G520a

Overprint: Red. ***Engraver:*** Toppan, Carpenter & Co. ***Comments:*** H-MA-1330-G166a. Similar to W-MA-3450-100-G520. 18__. 1850s.

Rarity: —

$500 • W-MA-3450-500-G530

Left: Lathework chain bearing MASSACHUSETTS / 500 / 500 vertically. ***Center:*** Alternating flower garlands and gridwork segments. ***Right:*** 500 / 500 vertically. ***Engraver:*** PSSP. ***Comments:*** H-MA-1330-G170. 18__. 1820s–1830s.

Rarity: —

$500 • W-MA-3450-500-G540

Left: 500 / Medallion head. ***Center:*** Eagle on shield, Train, ships, and city. ***Bottom center:*** D. ***Right:*** D / Medallion head. ***Engraver:*** American Bank Note Co. ***Comments:*** H-MA-1330-G174. 1860s.

Rarity: —

Uncut Sheets

$1-$1-$2-$3 • W-MA-3450-001.001.002.003-US010

Vignette(s): ***($1)*** Woman seated / Portrait of George Washington on 1 / Man. ***($1)*** Woman seated / Portrait of George Washington on 1 / Man. ***($2)*** Farmer sharpening scythe / 2 bearing portrait of George Washington / Dog and strongbox. ***($3)*** Male portrait / 3 bearing portrait of John Adams / Female portrait. ***Engraver:*** Toppan, Carpenter & Co. ***Comments:*** H-MA-1330-G30, G30, G56, G78.

Rarity: —

$5-$5-$5-$10 • W-MA-3450-005.005.005.010-US020

Vignette(s): ***($5)*** Woman seated with spear / Female portrait / Female portrait / Mrs. Andrew Jackson standing. ***($5)*** Woman seated with spear / Female portrait / Female portrait / Mrs. Andrew Jackson standing. ***($5)*** Woman seated with spear / Female portrait / Female portrait / Mrs. Andrew Jackson standing. ***($10)*** Blacksmith / Portrait of James Madison / Woman seated / Portrait of James Monroe / Man seated. ***Engraver:*** Toppan, Carpenter & Co. ***Comments:*** H-MA-1330-G104, G104, G104, G130.

Rarity: —

Non-Valid Issues

$1 • W-MA-3450-001-C050b

Engraver: PSSP. ***Comments:*** H-MA-1330-C24. Counterfeit of W-MA-3450-001-G050b. 18__. 1830s.

Rarity: —

$1 • W-MA-3450-001-A010

CC

Engraver: Danforth, Bald & Co. ***Comments:*** H-MA-1330-A5. Altered from $1 Columbia Bank, Washington, D.C. 185_. 1850s.

Rarity: URS-7

VG $125; **VF** $175

$1 • W-MA-3450-001-A020

Left: ONE / Two Indians reclining and smoking. ***Center:*** 1 / Three allegorical women with eagle, pole and cap, shield, balance, and book / 1. ***Bottom center:*** Cattle. ***Right:*** 1 / Portrait of George Washington / ONE. ***Engraver:*** Terry, Pelton & Co. ***Comments:*** H-MA-1330-A10. Altered from $1 Citizens Bank, Augusta, Maine, or from notes of other failed banks using the same plate. 18__. Circa 1840.

Rarity: —

$1 • W-MA-3450-001-A030

CC

Engraver: Terry, Pelton & Co. ***Comments:*** H-Unlisted. 185_. 1850s.

Rarity: —

$2 • W-MA-3450-002-C120

CJF

Engraver: Leney & Rollinson. ***Comments:*** H-MA-1330-C42. Counterfeit of W-MA-3450-002-G120. 181_. 1810s.

Rarity: —

AG $45

$2 • W-MA-3450-002-C130c

CJF

Engraver: PSSP. ***Comments:*** H-MA-1330-C50. Counterfeit of W-MA-3450-002-G130c. 18__. 1840s.

Rarity: —

$2 • W-MA-3450-002-C160

Engraver: Toppan, Carpenter & Co. ***Comments:*** H-MA-1330-C56. Counterfeit of W-MA-3450-002-G160 or G160a. Jan. 1, 18__. 1850s.

Rarity: —

$2 • W-MA-3450-002-A040

Left: 2 / Man carrying basket of cotton. ***Center:*** TWO on die. ***Right:*** 2 / Woman reclining with boulder, Cornucopia. ***Comments:*** H-MA-1330-A15. Altered from $2 Bank of Greensborough, Greensborough, Georgia series. 1850s.

Rarity: —

$2 • W-MA-3450-002-A050

Left: 2 / Farmer plowing with black and white horses. ***Center:*** Two men loading wagon with sheaves, Three men cradling and binding. ***Right:*** 2 / Two floating cherubs with caduceus and sheaf. ***Tint:*** Red-brown 2s and TWO DOLLARS. ***Engraver:*** Danforth, Wright & Co. ***Comments:*** H-MA-1330-A20. Altered from $2 Southern Bank of Georgia, Bainbridge, Georgia. March 1, 1858.

Rarity: —

$2 • W-MA-3450-002-A060

Left: TWO / Portrait of cherub / 2. ***Center:*** 2 / Ceres giving grain to seated Liberty / 2. ***Bottom center:*** Anchor and implements. ***Right:*** 2 / Female portrait / TWO. ***Engraver:*** Terry, Pelton & Co. ***Comments:*** H-MA-1330-A25. Altered from $2 Citizens Bank, Augusta, Maine, or from notes of other failed banks using the same plate. 18__. Circa 1840.

Rarity: —

$3 • W-MA-3450-003-C200

Engraver: Leney & Rollinson. ***Comments:*** H-MA-1330-C66. Counterfeit of W-MA-3450-003-G200. 18__. 1819.

Rarity: —

$3 • W-MA-3450-003-C240

Engraver: Toppan, Carpenter & Co. ***Comments:*** H-MA-1330-C78. Counterfeit of W-MA-3450-003-G240 or G240a. Jan. 1, 18__. 1850s.

Rarity: —

$3 • W-MA-3450-003-A070

Left: 3 / Male portrait. ***Center:*** Woman seated / 3 on shield, THREE. ***Right:*** 3 / Woman seated. ***Engraver:*** Danforth, Bald & Co. ***Comments:*** H-MA-1330-A30. Altered from $3 Columbia Bank, Washington, D.C. 18__. 1850s.

Rarity: —

$3 • W-MA-3450-003-A080

Left: 3 / Women flanking shield bearing anchor surmounted by eagle / Portrait of cherub. ***Center:*** Female portrait / Ceres and Justice flanking shield bearing anchor surmounted by eagle / Portrait of cherub. ***Bottom center:*** Anchor and implements. ***Right:*** 3 / Ceres seated in grain field / THREE. ***Engraver:*** Terry, Pelton & Co. ***Comments:*** H-MA-1330-A35. Altered from $3 Citizens Bank, Augusta, Maine, or from notes of other failed banks using the same plate. 18__. Circa 1840.

Rarity: —

$5 • W-MA-3450-005-C250

PEM

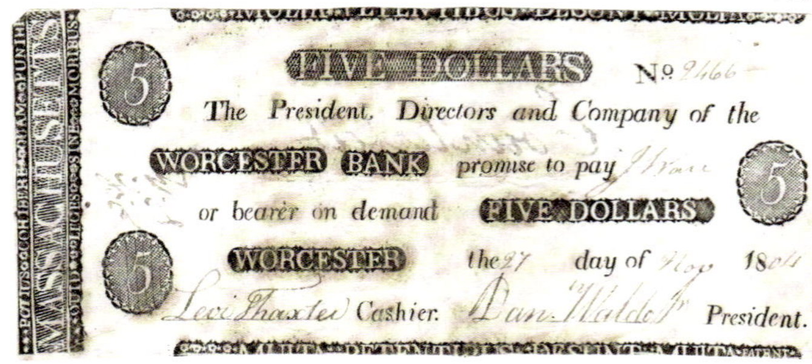

Engraver: Perkins. ***Comments:*** H-MA-1330-C82. Counterfeit of W-MA-3450-005-G250. 18__. 1800s

Rarity: —

$5 • W-MA-3450-005-C270

Engraver: Murray, Draper, Fairman & Co. ***Comments:*** H-MA-1330-C92. Counterfeit of W-MA-3450-005-G270. 181_. 1819.

Rarity: —

$5 • W-MA-3450-005-N010

Left: Portrait. ***Right:*** Portrait. ***Comments:*** H-MA-1330-N5.

Rarity: —

$5 • W-MA-3450-005-A090

Left: FIVE / Portrait of Benjamin Franklin / V. ***Center:*** 5 / Two allegorical women standing and one seated / Agricultural items and ship. ***Bottom center:*** Anchor and implements. ***Right:*** V / Portrait of Marquis de Lafayette / FIVE. ***Engraver:*** Terry, Pelton & Co. ***Comments:*** H-MA-1330-A40. Altered from $5 Citizens Bank, Augusta, Maine, or from notes of other failed banks using the same plate. 18__. Circa 1840.

Rarity: —

$10 • W-MA-3450-010-R010

Engraver: Toppan, Carpenter & Co. ***Comments:*** H-MA-1330-R5. Raised from W-MA-3450-001-G080 or G080a. Jan. 1, 18__. 1850s.

Rarity: —

$20 • W-MA-3450-020-C400

Engraver: Murray, Draper, Fairman & Co. ***Comments:*** H-MA-1330-C138. Counterfeit of W-MA-3450-020-G400. 181_. 1810s.

Rarity: —

$20 • W-MA-3450-020-R020

Engraver: Toppan, Carpenter & Co. ***Comments:*** H-MA-1330-R10. Raised from W-MA-3450-001-G080 or G080a. Jan. 1, 18__. 1850s.

Rarity: —

Wrentham, Massachusetts

Wrentham was incorporated in 1673 after settlers discovered it in 1660. It was burned down during King Philip's War. Originally called Wollomonopoag, or "place of shells," the land of Wrentham was once a part of Dedham. It was named after a town in England. In the 18th century it grew so quickly that two separate towns, Franklin and Foxboro, were set off in 1778.

Straw goods and jewelry comprised the main sources of income for the town, as well as crude woolen goods, saw and grist mills, boots and shoes, leather, furniture, boats, carriages, wrought stone, beverages, and food preparations. In the 19th century the Wrentham-Walpole Turnpike was laid out and aided the most prevalent industries, including Rhodes Sheldon's boatbuilding, Bennett's woodworking, Brown's Straw Shop, textile mills, and the Weber Duck Farm. Other poultry operations also benefited.

Wrentham Bank

1832–1865

W-MA-3460

History: The Wrentham Bank was chartered on March 10, 1832, with an authorized capital of $100,000. It had a capital of $150,000 in 1839 and a circulation of $34,161. In 1863 circulation was up to $82,691. Specie was listed at $11,321.50, and real estate was valued at $1,000.

The business of the Wrentham Bank was succeeded by the National Bank of Wrentham after it was chartered on April 10, 1865.

Numismatic Commentary: Early genuine notes from the various engravers are hard to locate. The later American Bank Note Co. issues appear in the marketplace more often.

Valid Issues

$1 • W-MA-3460-001-G010

Left: Lathework panel bearing MASSACHUSETTS vertically. ***Center:*** 1 / 1 / Alternating flower garlands and gridwork segments / ONE / 1 / 1. ***Right:*** Lathework panel bearing ONE / D / ONE vertically. ***Engraver:*** PSSP. ***Comments:*** H-MA-1335-G2. 18__. 1830s.

Rarity: —

$1 • W-MA-3460-001-G020

Engraver: Unverified, but likely New England Bank Note Co. ***Comments:*** H-MA-1335-G6. No description available. 18__. 1840s.

Rarity: *None known*

$1 • W-MA-3460-001-G030

Left: Commerce seated with rudder leaning on barrel / 1. ***Center:*** 1 bearing "Presentation of the Declaration of Independence". ***Right:*** 1 / Woman standing with apron full of grain. ***Engraver:*** New England Bank Note Co. ***Comments:*** H-MA-1335-G10. 18__. 1850s.

Rarity: —

$1 • W-MA-3460-001-G040

CC

Overprint: Green panel outlining white ONE. ***Engraver:*** American Bank Note Co. ***Comments:*** H-MA-1335-G12a. Oct. 28, 186_. 1860s.

Rarity: URS-3
VF $3,000; **EF** $6,500
Selected auction price: Heritage, January 2011, Lot 15556, VF $1,955

$2 • W-MA-3460-002-G050

Left: Lathework panel bearing MASSACHUSETTS vertically. ***Center:*** 2 / 2 / Alternating flower garlands and gridwork segments / TWO / 2 / 2. ***Right:*** Lathework panel bearing five TWOs vertically. ***Engraver:*** PSSP. ***Comments:*** H-MA-1335-G14. 18__. 1830s.

Rarity: —

$2 • W-MA-3460-002-G060

Engraver: Unverified, but likely New England Bank Note Co. ***Comments:*** H-MA-1335-G18. No description available. 18__. 1840s.

Rarity: *None known*

$2 • W-MA-3460-002-G070

Left: Men driving sheep into stream / 2. ***Center:*** 2 bearing "Presentation of the Declaration of Independence". ***Right:*** TWO / Woman seated with wreath of flowers / TWO. ***Engraver:*** New England Bank Note Co. ***Comments:*** H-MA-1335-G22. Altered notes from the same plate as the genuine have been reported. 18__. 1850s.

Rarity: —

$2 • W-MA-3460-002-G070a

CJF

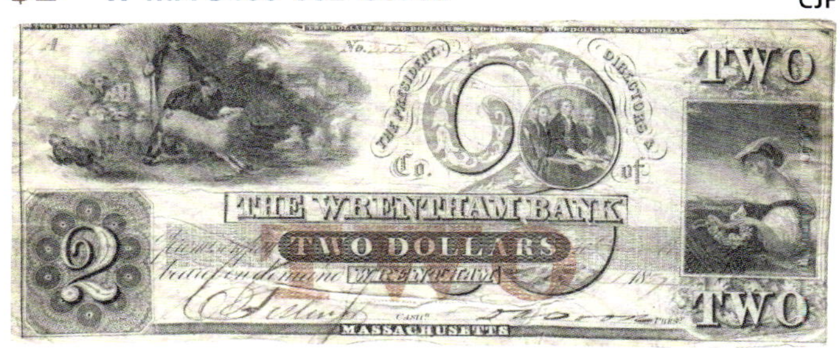

Overprint: Red TWO. ***Engraver:*** New England Bank Note Co. ***Comments:*** H-Unlisted. Similar to W-MA-3460-002-G070. 18__. 1850s.

Rarity: —

$2 • W-MA-3460-002-G080

Left: 2 / Woman leaning on pedestal, Wheel, hammer, and anvil. ***Center:*** Man and boy loading hay onto ox-drawn cart. ***Right:*** 2 / Portrait of Daniel Webster. ***Overprint:*** Green panel outlining white TWO. ***Engraver:*** American Bank Note Co. ***Comments:*** H-MA-1335-G24a. Oct. 28, 186_. 1860s.

Rarity: —

$3 • W-MA-3460-003-G090

Left: Lathework panel bearing MASSACHUSETTS vertically. ***Center:*** 3 / 3 / Alternating flower garlands and gridwork segments / THREE / 3 / 3. ***Right:*** Lathework panel bearing THREE vertically. ***Engraver:*** PSSP. ***Comments:*** H-MA-1335-G26. 18__. 1830s.

Rarity: —

$3 • W-MA-3460-003-G100

Engraver: Unverified, but likely New England Bank Note Co. ***Comments:*** H-MA-1335-G30. No description available. 18__. 1840s.

Rarity: *None known*

$3 • W-MA-3460-003-G110

Left: Barnyard scene, Man on horse, Boy and cattle / 3. ***Center:*** 3. ***Right:*** 3 on THREE / Woman with flowers / THREE. ***Engraver:*** New England Bank Note Co. ***Comments:*** H-MA-1335-G34. Beware of spurious W-MA-3460-003-S010 resembling the genuine. 18__. 1850s.

Rarity: —

$3 • W-MA-3460-003-G120

Left: Man standing / THREE. ***Center:*** Woman seated with urn / THREE. ***Right:*** 3 / Boy seated / THREE. ***Engraver:*** American Bank Note Co. ***Comments:*** H-MA-1335-G36. Might have been made only as Proof. Oct. 28, 18__. 1860s.

Rarity: —

$3 • W-MA-3460-003-G120a

Overprint: Green panel outlining white THREE. ***Engraver:*** American Bank Note Co. ***Comments:*** H-MA-1335-G36a. Similar to W-MA-3460-003-G120. Oct. 28, 18__. 1860s.

Rarity: —

$5 • W-MA-3460-005-G130

Left: Lathework chain bearing MASSACHUSETTS / 5 / 5 vertically. ***Center:*** Alternating flower garlands and gridwork segments / FIVE. ***Right:*** 5 / 5 vertically. ***Engraver:*** PSSP. ***Comments:*** H-MA-1335-G40. 18__. 1830s.

Rarity: —

$5 • W-MA-3460-005-G140

Engraver: Unverified, but likely New England Bank Note Co. ***Comments:*** H-MA-1335-G42. No description available. 18__. 1840s.

Rarity: *None known*

$5 • W-MA-3460-005-G150

Left: Panel bearing FIVE vertically. ***Center:*** Woman unveiling shield bearing 5 / V. ***Right:*** 5 / Sailing ship. ***Engraver:*** New England Bank Note Co. ***Comments:*** H-MA-1335-G44. 18__. 1840s–1850s.

Rarity: —

$5 • W-MA-3460-005-G160

Left: Ceres seated on wharf with rake, sickle, and implements, Factories and harbor / FIVE across V. ***Center:*** Indian woman with bow seated in V. ***Right:*** 5 / Portrait of George Washington. ***Engraver:*** New England Bank Note Co. ***Comments:*** H-MA-1335-G46. Beware of spurious W-MA-3460-005-S020 resembling the genuine. 18__. 1850s.

Rarity: —

$5 • W-MA-3460-005-G170

Left: 5 / Woman. ***Center:*** Black and white horse. ***Right:*** 5 / Male portrait. ***Engraver:*** American Bank Note Co. ***Comments:*** H-MA-1335-G48. Might have been made only as Proof. Oct. 28, 18__. 1860s.

Rarity: —

$10 • W-MA-3460-010-G180

Left: Lathework chain bearing MASSACHUSETTS / 10 / 10 vertically. ***Center:*** Alternating flower garlands and gridwork segments / TEN. ***Right:*** 10 / 10 vertically. ***Engraver:*** PSSP. ***Comments:*** H-MA-1335-G52. 18__. 1830s.

Rarity: —

$10 • W-MA-3460-010-G190

Engraver: Unverified, but likely New England Bank Note Co. ***Comments:*** H-MA-1335-G54. No description available. 18__. 1840s.

Rarity: *None known*

$10 • W-MA-3460-010-G200

Left: Panel bearing 10 / X / 10. ***Center:*** Allegorical male standing by oxen and plow / 10. ***Right:*** TEN / Woman standing with rudder and cornucopia. ***Engraver:*** New England Bank Note Co. ***Comments:*** H-MA-1335-G56. 18__. 1840s–1850s.

Rarity: —

$10 • W-MA-3460-010-G210

Left: "Presentation of the Declaration of Independence" / X. ***Center:*** X. ***Right:*** 10 / Train passing building with steeple, Man with wheelbarrow. ***Engraver:*** New England Bank Note Co. ***Comments:*** H-MA-1335-G58. 18__. 1850s.

Rarity: —

$10 • W-MA-3460-010-G220

Left: 10 / Continental soldier with gun, State arms. ***Center:*** Woman holding bolt of cloth, Barrels and bales, Train and steamboat. ***Right:*** 10 / Man seated showing bust of George Washington to child. ***Engraver:*** American Bank Note Co. ***Comments:*** H-MA-1335-G60. 18__. 1860s.

Rarity: —

$20 • W-MA-3460-020-G230

Left: Lathework chain bearing MASSACHUSETTS / 20 / 20 vertically. ***Center:*** Alternating flower garlands and gridwork segments / TWENTY. ***Right:*** 20 / 20 vertically. ***Engraver:*** PSSP. ***Comments:*** H-MA-1335-G64. 18__. 1830s.

Rarity: —

$20 • W-MA-3460-020-G240

Engraver: Unverified, but likely New England Bank Note Co. ***Comments:*** H-MA-1335-G66. No description available. 18__. 1830s–1840s.

Rarity: *None known*

$20 • W-MA-3460-020-G250

Left: 20 / Woman seated with book on lap, opening chest. ***Center:*** XX / Eagle on rock / XX. ***Right:*** 20 / Ship in harbor. ***Engraver:*** New England Bank Note Co. ***Comments:*** H-MA-1335-G68. 18__. 1840s–1850s.

Rarity: —

$20 • W-MA-3460-020-G260

Left: 20 / Eagle on shield / Two blacksmiths at work on wagon. ***Center:*** 20 / Woman feeding horse, Chickens. ***Right:*** Grain. ***Engraver:*** American Bank Note Co. ***Comments:*** H-MA-1335-G70. 18__. 1860s.

Rarity: —

$50 • W-MA-3460-050-G270

Left: Lathework chain bearing MASSACHUSETTS / 50 / 50 vertically. ***Center:*** Alternating flower garlands and gridwork segments / FIFTY. ***Right:*** 50 / 50 vertically. ***Engraver:*** PSSP. ***Comments:*** H-MA-1335-G74. 18__. 1830s.

Rarity: —

$50 • W-MA-3460-050-G280

Engraver: Unverified, but likely New England Bank Note Co. ***Comments:*** H-MA-1335-G76. No description available. 18__. 1830s–1840s.

Rarity: *None known*

$50 • W-MA-3460-050-G290

Left: Indian woman seated with shield, Eagle, Steamship / 50. ***Center:*** 50. ***Right:*** 50 / Portrait of General Winfield Scott. ***Engraver:*** American Bank Note Co. ***Comments:*** H-MA-1335-G78. 18__. 1860s.

Rarity: —

$100 • W-MA-3460-100-G300

Left: Lathework chain bearing MASSACHUSETTS / 100 / 100 vertically. ***Center:*** Alternating flower garlands and gridwork segments / 100. ***Right:*** 100 / 100 vertically. ***Engraver:*** PSSP. ***Comments:*** H-MA-1335-G82. 18__. 1830s.

Rarity: —

$100 • W-MA-3460-100-G310

Engraver: Unverified, but likely New England Bank Note Co. ***Comments:*** H-MA-1335-G84. No description available. 18__. 1830s–1840s.

Rarity: *None known*

$100 • W-MA-3460-100-G320

Left: ONE HUNDRED on 100 / Portrait of William Henry Harrison. ***Center:*** Wharf scene, Men loading wagon with barrels. ***Right:*** ONE HUNDRED on 100 / Portrait of Christopher Columbus. ***Engraver:*** New England Bank Note Co. ***Comments:*** H-MA-1335-G86. 18__. 1840s–1850s.

Rarity: —

$100 • W-MA-3460-100-G330

Left: 100 / Portrait of girl. ***Center:*** Man standing by horse and whittling, Two men, Cattle and sheep. ***Right:*** 100 / Portrait of girl. ***Engraver:*** American Bank Note Co. ***Comments:*** H-MA-1335-G88. 18__. 1860s.

Rarity: —

Non-Valid Issues

$1 • W-MA-3460-001-A010

Left: 1 / Woman standing / ONE. ***Center:*** Woman holding shield and rake / ONE on die / ONE. ***Right:*** 1 / Ship in storm / ONE. ***Engraver:*** New England Bank Note Co. ***Comments:*** H-MA-1335-A5. Altered from $1 Washington County Bank, Calais, Maine, or from notes of other failed banks using the same plate. 18__. 1830s–1840s.

Rarity: —

$2 • W-MA-3460-002-A020

Left: TWO / Portrait of cherub / 2. ***Center:*** 2 / Ceres giving grain to seated Liberty / 2. ***Bottom center:*** Anchor and implements. ***Right:*** 2 / Female portrait / TWO. ***Engraver:*** Terry, Pelton & Co. ***Comments:*** H-MA-1335-A10. Altered from $2 Citizens Bank, Augusta, Maine, or from notes of other failed banks using the same plate. 18__. Circa 1840.

Rarity: —

$2 • W-MA-3460-002-A030

Left: Men driving sheep into stream / 2. ***Center:*** 2 bearing "Presentation of the Declaration of Independence". ***Right:*** TWO / Woman seated with wreath of flowers / TWO. ***Engraver:*** New England Bank Note Co. ***Comments:*** H-MA-1335-A11. 18__. 1850s.

Rarity: —

$3 • W-MA-3460-003-S010

Left: 3. ***Center:*** Man and cow, Trees / 3. ***Right:*** 3 / Female portrait / THREE. ***Engraver:*** New England Bank Note Co. ***Comments:*** H-MA-1335-S5. Spurious design imitating a rough verbal description of W-MA-3460-003-G110. March 1, 1858.

Rarity: —

$3 • W-MA-3460-003-S010a

CJF

Tint: Brown-orange lathework outlining white ornate THREE. ***Engraver:*** New England Bank Note Co. ***Comments:*** H-MA-1335-S5a. Similar to W-MA-3460-003-S010. March 1, 1858.

Rarity: —

$3 • W-MA-3460-003-A040

Left: 3 / Woman standing with branch, trident, and THREE / THREE. ***Center:*** Female portrait / Ceres and Justice flanking shield bearing anchor and surmounted by eagle / Portrait of cherub. ***Bottom center:*** Anchor and implements. ***Right:*** 3 / Ceres seated in grain field / THREE. ***Engraver:*** Terry, Pelton & Co. ***Comments:*** H-MA-1335-A15. Altered from $3 Citizens Bank, Augusta, Maine, or from notes of other failed banks using the same plate. 18__. Circa 1840.

Rarity: —

$5 • W-MA-3460-005-S020

CJF

Engraver: New England Bank Note Co. ***Comments:*** H-MA-1335-S10. Spurious design imitating a rough verbal description of W-MA-3460-005-G160. May 1, 18__. 1860s.

Rarity: —

$5 • W-MA-3460-005-N010

Center: Woman seated with urn. ***Right:*** Woman. ***Comments:*** H-MA-1335-N5.

Rarity: —

$5 • W-MA-3460-005-N020

Center: Farm scene. ***Right:*** Woman. ***Comments:*** H-MA-1335-N10.

Rarity: —

$5 • W-MA-3460-005-A050

Left: FIVE / Portrait of Benjamin Franklin / V. ***Center:*** 5 / Two allegorical women standing and one seated, Agricultural items and ship. ***Bottom center:*** Anchor and implements. ***Right:*** V / Portrait of Marquis de Lafayette / FIVE. ***Engraver:*** Terry, Pelton & Co. ***Comments:*** H-MA-1335-A20. Altered from $5 Citizens Bank, Augusta, Maine, or from notes of other failed banks using the same plate. 18__. Circa 1840.

Rarity: —

$10 • W-MA-3460-010-R010

Engraver: New England Bank Note Co. ***Comments:*** H-MA-1335-R5. Raised from W-MA-3460-001-G030. 18__. 1850s.

Rarity: —

$10 • W-MA-3460-010-A060

Left: 10 / Portrait of George Washington held by cherub / 10. ***Center:*** X / Spread eagle with shield and arrows, E PLURIBUS UNUM / X. ***Bottom center:*** Ship. ***Right:*** 10 / Standing Indian man / 10. ***Engraver:*** Terry, Pelton & Co. ***Comments:*** H-MA-1335-A25. Altered from $10 Citizens Bank, Augusta, Maine, or from notes of other failed banks using the same plate. 18__. Circa 1840.

Rarity: —

Yarmouth, Massachusetts

Incorporated in September 1639 by John Crowe and Thomas Howes, Yarmouth was originally part of the town of Dennis. The two areas separated in 1793. Named after Great Yarmouth in England, the land was initially home to the native Wampanoag nation.

The town is made up of three villages: Yarmouth Port, South Yarmouth, and West Yarmouth. Salt works, oil cloth works, a stock company, and a stamp cutter were in operation here. A boot and shoe manufactory was begun in 1829 by Elisha Jenkins, and Russel D. Farris began a harness manufacturing business in 1839. It was in operation for 18 years. By 1854 John and Barnabas Sears had built a steam planning mill, adding in machinery for grinding. They were in business until 1865. Grain and flour trade to New York City began in 1860 via Hiram Loring & Co.

Barnstable Bank

1825–1864

W-MA-3470

History: The Barnstable Bank, sometimes listed with a Yarmouth Port address, was chartered on February 16, 1825, with an authorized capital of $100,000. It was to be located in the town of Yarmouth. The circulation of the bank in 1839 was $102,784. It reached $344,387 in 1863. By 1864 the capital had reached $350,000. Real estate was valued at $5,500, and specie was listed at $26,328.87.

The business of the Barnstable Bank was succeeded by the First National Bank of Yarmouth after it was chartered in 1864.

Numismatic Commentary: Bank notes from Cape Cod banks are in great demand. This entity is no exception. It is very hard to locate a genuine note from this bank. Some issues have a vignette of wooden-wheeled traffic travelling east on Main Street (today's Route 6-A) in Yarmouth and passing the bank building on the right, while on the left stands the "Gingerbread House," a fixture on the route for more than 150 years.

Valid Issues

$1 • W-MA-3470-001-G010

Left: Narrow panel of lathework circle segments. ***Center:*** 1 / 1 / Flower garlands and gridwork segments / 1 / 1. ***Right:*** Narrow panel of lathework circle segments. ***Engraver:*** PSSP. ***Comments:*** H-MA-1340-G2. 18__. 1820s–1830s.

Rarity: —

$1 • W-MA-3470-001-G010a

Left: ONE / D / ONE vertically. ***Right:*** ONE / D / ONE vertically. ***Engraver:*** PSSP. ***Comments:*** H-MA-1340-G4. Similar to W-MA-3470-001-G010. 18__. 1830s.

Rarity: —

$1 • W-MA-3470-001-G020

Engraver: Unverified, but likely Terry, Pelton & Co. ***Comments:*** H-MA-1340-G6. No description available. 18__. 1830s–1840s.

Rarity: *None known*

$1 • W-MA-3470-001-G030

Left: ONE / Woman standing / ONE. ***Center:*** Ship / Eagle / Ship. ***Right:*** ONE / Sailboats / ONE. ***Engraver:*** New England Bank Note Co. ***Comments:*** H-MA-1340-G8. 18__. 1840s–1850s.

Rarity: —

$1 • W-MA-3470-001-G030a

Overprint: Red ONE. ***Engraver:*** New England Bank Note Co. ***Comments:*** H-MA-1340-G8a. Similar to W-MA-3470-001-G030. 18__. 1850s.

Rarity: —

$1 • W-MA-3470-001-G030b

CJF

Overprint: Red ONE. ***Engraver:*** New England Bank Note Co. / ABNCo. monogram. ***Comments:*** H-MA-1340-G8b. Similar to W-MA-3470-001-G030 but with additional engraver imprint. 18__. 1850s–1860s.

Rarity: URS-4

F $1,250; **VF** $1,750

$2 • W-MA-3470-002-G040

Left: Narrow panel of lathework circle segments. ***Center:*** 2 / 2 / Flower garlands and gridwork segments / 2 / 2. ***Right:*** Narrow panel of lathework circle segments. ***Engraver:*** PSSP. ***Comments:*** H-MA-1340-G10. 18__. 1820s–1830s.

Rarity: —

$2 • W-MA-3470-002-G040a

Left: Five TWOs vertically. ***Right:*** Five TWOs vertically. ***Engraver:*** PSSP. ***Comments:*** H-MA-1340-G12. Similar to W-MA-3470-002-G040. 18__. 1830s.

Rarity: —

$2 • W-MA-3470-002-G050

Engraver: Unverified, but likely Terry, Pelton & Co. ***Comments:*** H-MA-1340-G14. No description available. 18__. 1830s–1840s.

Rarity: *None known*

$2 • W-MA-3470-002-G060

Left: 2 / Sailor holding flag and seated on barrel / TWO. ***Center:*** Eagle on cliff / TWO / Eagle on cliff. ***Right:*** 2 / Two ships. ***Engraver:*** New England Bank Note Co. ***Comments:*** H-MA-1340-G16. 18__. 1840s–1850s.

Rarity: —

$2 • W-MA-3470-002-G060a

Overprint: Red TWO. ***Engraver:*** New England Bank Note Co. ***Comments:*** H-MA-1340-G16a. Similar to W-MA-3470-002-G060. 18__. 1850s.

Rarity: —

$2 • W-MA-3470-002-G060b

CJF

Overprint: Red TWO. ***Engraver:*** New England Bank Note Co. / ABNCo. monogram. ***Comments:*** H-MA-1340-G16b. Similar to W-MA-3470-002-G060 but with additional engraver imprint. 18__. 1850s–1860s.

Rarity: URS-3

F $1,500; **VF** $2,000

$3 • W-MA-3470-003-G070

Left: Narrow panel of lathework circle segments. ***Center:*** 3 / 3 / Flower garlands and gridwork segments / 3 / 3. ***Right:*** Narrow panel of lathework circle segments. ***Engraver:*** PSSP. ***Comments:*** H-MA-1340-G18. 18__. 1820s–1830s.

Rarity: —

$3 • W-MA-3470-003-G070a

Left: THREE vertically. ***Right:*** THREE vertically. ***Engraver:*** PSSP. ***Comments:*** H-MA-1340-G20. Similar to W-MA-3470-003-G070. 18__. 1830s.

Rarity: —

$3 • W-MA-3470-003-G080

CC

Engraver: Terry, Pelton & Co. ***Comments:*** H-MA-1340-G22. Proof. Plate note. 18__. 1830s–1840s.

Rarity: URS-2

Proof $2,000

$3 • W-MA-3470-003-G090

Left: 3 / Sailor standing. ***Center:*** Main street of Yarmouth. ***Bottom center:*** Sailing ship. ***Right:*** THREE on 3 / Male portrait. ***Overprint:*** Red THREE. ***Comments:*** H-MA-1340-G22a. 1850s.

Rarity: —

$3 • W-MA-3470-003-G090a

CJF

Overprint: Red THREE. ***Engraver:*** Rawdon, Wright, Hatch & Edson / New England Bank Note Co. ***Comments:*** H-MA-1340-G22b. Similar to W-MA-3470-003-G090 but with additional engraver imprint and printed serial number. June 2, 186_. 1860s.

Rarity: URS-3

F $1,500; **VF** $2,000

$5 • W-MA-3470-005-G100

Left: Lathework chain bearing MASSACHUSETTS / 5 / 5 vertically. ***Center:*** Alternating flower garlands and gridwork segments. ***Right:*** 5 / 5 vertically. ***Engraver:*** PSSP. ***Comments:*** H-MA-1340-G24. 18__. 1820s.

Rarity: —

$5 • W-MA-3470-005-G100a

Engraver: PSSP. ***Comments:*** H-MA-1340-G26. Similar to W-MA-3470-005-G100 but with zigzag ruled lines. 18__. 1820s–1830s.

Rarity: —

$5 • W-MA-3470-005-G100b

Engraver: PSSP. ***Comments:*** H-MA-1340-G28. Similar to W-MA-3470-005-G100 but with spiral lathework lines. 18__. 1830s.

Rarity: —

$5 • W-MA-3470-005-G110

Engraver: Unverified, but likely Terry, Pelton & Co. ***Comments:*** H-MA-1340-G30. No description available. 18__. 1830s–1840s

Rarity: *None known*

$5 • W-MA-3470-005-G120

Left: FIVE / Sailor standing with anchor, Masts / FIVE. ***Center:*** Train, Church, Factory. ***Right:*** 5 / Canal boat and schooner / 5. ***Engraver:*** New England Bank Note Co. ***Comments:*** H-MA-1340-G32. 18__. 1840s–1850s.

Rarity: —

$5 • W-MA-3470-005-G120a

Overprint: Red. ***Engraver:*** New England Bank Note Co. ***Comments:*** H-MA-1340-G32a. Similar to W-MA-3470-005-G120. 18__. 1850s.

Rarity: —

$5 • W-MA-3470-005-G120b
Overprint: Red. ***Engraver:*** New England Bank Note Co. / ABNCo. monogram. ***Comments:*** H-MA-1340-G32b. Similar to W-MA-3470-005-G120 but with additional engraver imprint. 18__. 1850s–1860s.

Rarity: —

$5 • W-MA-3470-005-G130

CJF

Engraver: Terry, Pelton & Co. ***Comments:*** H-Unlisted. 18__. 1840s.

Rarity: —

$10 • W-MA-3470-010-G140
Left: Lathework chain bearing MASSACHUSETTS / 10 / 10 vertically. ***Center:*** Alternating flower garlands and gridwork segments. ***Right:*** 10 / 10 vertically. ***Engraver:*** Perkins. ***Comments:*** H-MA-1340-G34. 18__. 1820s.

Rarity: —

$10 • W-MA-3470-010-G140a
Engraver: PSSP. ***Comments:*** H-MA-1340-G36. Similar to W-MA-3470-010-G140. 18__. 1820s–1830s.

Rarity: —

$10 • W-MA-3470-010-G140b
Engraver: PSSP. ***Comments:*** H-MA-1340-G38. Similar to W-MA-3470-010-G140. 18__. 1830s.

Rarity: —

$10 • W-MA-3470-010-G150
Engraver: Unverified, but likely Terry, Pelton & Co. ***Comments:*** H-MA-1340-G40. No description available. 18__. 1830s–1840s.

Rarity: *None known*

$10 • W-MA-3470-010-G160
Left: 10 / Officer seated at table / 10. ***Center:*** TEN / Steamboat and ships / TEN. ***Right:*** 10 / Sailor standing at helm / 10. ***Engraver:*** New England Bank Note Co. ***Comments:*** H-MA-1340-G42. 18__. 1840s–1850s.

Rarity: —

$10 • W-MA-3470-010-G160a
Overprint: Red. ***Engraver:*** New England Bank Note Co. ***Comments:*** H-MA-1340-G42a. Similar to W-MA-3470-010-G160. 18__. 1850s.

Rarity: —

$10 • W-MA-3470-010-G160b
Overprint: Red. ***Engraver:*** New England Bank Note Co. / ABNCo. monogram. ***Comments:*** H-MA-1340-G42b. Similar to W-MA-3470-010-G160 but with additional engraver imprint. 18__. 1850s–1860s.

Rarity: —

$20 • W-MA-3470-020-G170
Left: Lathework chain bearing MASSACHUSETTS / 20 / 20 vertically. ***Center:*** Alternating flower garlands and gridwork segments. ***Right:*** 20 / 20 vertically. ***Engraver:*** PSSP. ***Comments:*** H-MA-1340-G44. 18__. 1820s–1830s.

Rarity: —

$20 • W-MA-3470-020-G180
Left: XX / Sailor leaning on anchor smoking pipe / XX. ***Center:*** Ship and brig, Ships. ***Bottom center:*** Anchor and fishing gear. ***Right:*** 20 / Steamboat, Ship. ***Engraver:*** Terry, Pelton & Co. ***Comments:*** H-MA-1340-G46. 18__. 1830s–1850s.

Rarity: —

$20 • W-MA-3470-020-G190
Left: 20 / TWENTY / Male portrait. ***Center:*** Main street of Yarmouth. ***Right:*** 20 / Liberty seated with globe and shield. ***Engraver:*** Rawdon, Wright, Hatch & Edson / New England Bank Note Co. ***Comments:*** H-MA-1340-G48. 1850s–1860s.

Rarity: —

$50 • W-MA-3470-050-G200
Left: Lathework chain bearing MASSACHUSETTS / 50 / 50 vertically. ***Center:*** Alternating flower garlands and gridwork segments. ***Right:*** 50 / 50 vertically. ***Engraver:*** PSSP. ***Comments:*** H-MA-1340-G50. 18__. 1820s–1830s.

Rarity: —

$50 • W-MA-3470-050-G210
Left: Panel bearing FIFTY vertically. ***Center:*** L / Woman leaning on anchor, Ship / L. ***Bottom center:*** Two men and boats. ***Right:*** 50 / 50. ***Engraver:*** Terry, Pelton & Co. ***Comments:*** H-MA-1340-G52. 18__. 1830s–1850s.

Rarity: —

$50 • W-MA-3470-050-G220
Left: 50 / Bust of sailor boy. ***Center:*** Main street of Yarmouth. ***Bottom center:*** Barrels. ***Right:*** 50 / Male portrait / FIFTY. ***Engraver:*** Rawdon, Wright, Hatch & Edson / New England Bank Note Co. ***Comments:*** H-MA-1340-G54. 1850s–1860s.

Rarity: —

$100 • W-MA-3470-100-G230
Left: Lathework chain bearing MASSACHUSETTS / 100 / 100 vertically. ***Center:*** Alternating flower garlands and gridwork segments. ***Right:*** 100 / 100 vertically. ***Engraver:*** Perkins. ***Comments:*** H-MA-1340-G56. 18__. 1820s–1830s.

Rarity: —

$100 • W-MA-3470-100-G240
Left: Panel bearing ONE HUNDRED vertically. ***Center:*** C / Ceres offering grain to seated Liberty, Ship / C. ***Bottom center:*** Anchor and fishing gear. ***Right:*** 100 / Two ships / 100. ***Engraver:*** Terry, Pelton & Co. ***Comments:*** H-MA-1340-G58. 18__. 1830s–1850s.

Rarity: —

$100 • W-MA-3470-100-G250
Left: 100 / Male portrait. ***Center:*** Main street of Yarmouth. ***Bottom center:*** Ship. ***Right:*** 100 / Female portrait. ***Engraver:*** Rawdon, Wright, Hatch & Edson / New England Bank Note Co. ***Comments:*** H-MA-1340-G60. 1850s–1860s.

Rarity: —

Non-Valid Issues

$5 • W-MA-3470-005-A010

HLA

Engraver: Terry, Pelton & Co. ***Comments:*** H-MA-1340-A5. Altered from $5 Citizens Bank, Augusta, Maine, or from notes of other failed banks using the same plate. 18__. 1830s.

Rarity: —

VF $695

$10 • W-MA-3470-010-R010

Engraver: New England Bank Note Co. ***Comments:*** H-MA-1340-R5. Raised from W-MA-3470-002-G060 or variety. 18__. 1850s.

Rarity: —

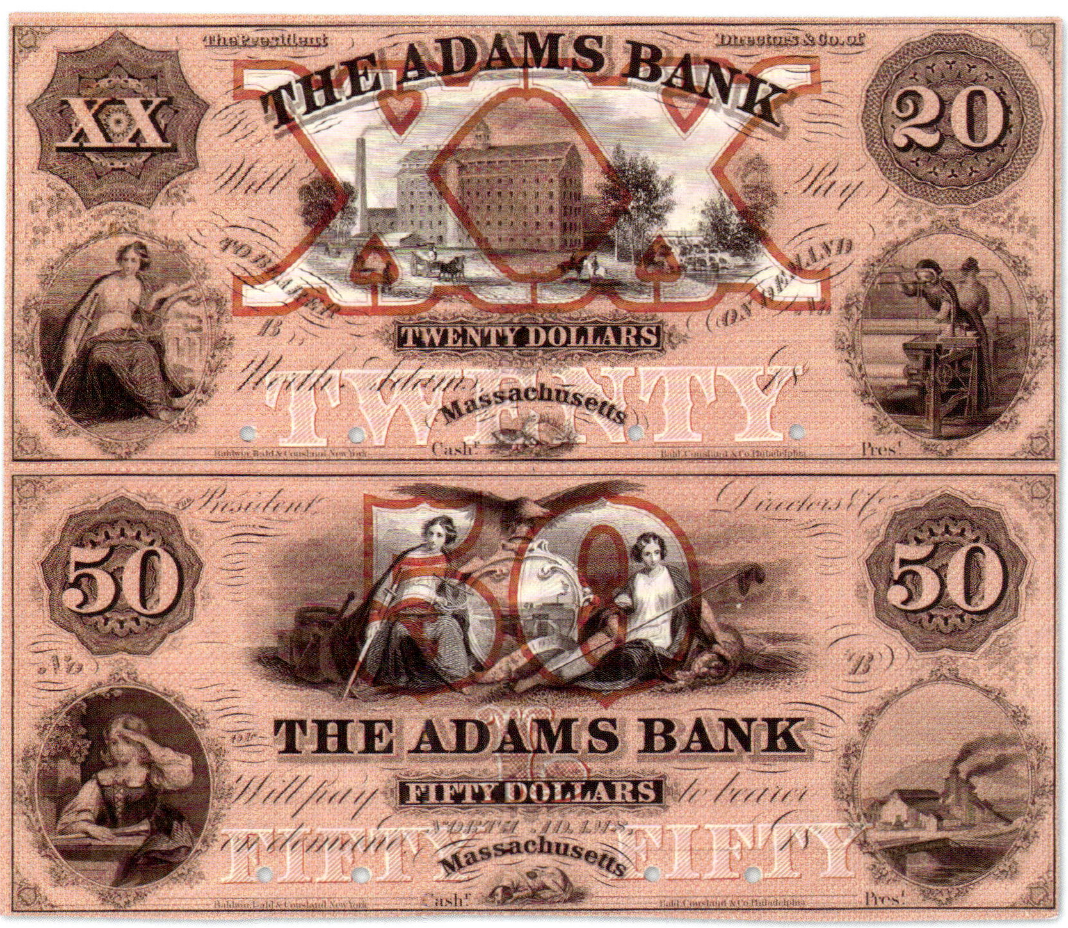

Endnotes

1. J. Hammond Trumbull, *The First Essays at Banking and the First Paper-Money in New England*, 1884, pp. 3–5, 23; Other sources.

2. Andrew McFarland Davis, "Papers Relating to the Land Bank of 1740," 1910.

3. The *Medley*, New Bedford, July 24, 1795.

4. Today a museum with Perkins memorabilia is located there.

5. Secretary of the Treasury William H. Crawford's report to the House of Representatives, February 24, 1820; Other sources.

6. Dudley P. Bailey Jr., "The History of Banking in Massachusetts, No. 2," *Banker's Magazine*, September 1876.

7. D.R. Whitney, *The Suffolk Bank*, 1878.

8. Such as the Farmers Exchange Bank, Gloucester, Rhode Island, and the Hillsborough Bank, Amherst, New Hampshire.

9. Dudley P. Bailey Jr., "The History of Banking in Massachusetts, No. 3," *Banker's Magazine*, October 1876.

10. *Niles' Weekly Register*, April 22, 1837.

11. The *Financial Register*, Volume 1, pp. 304–309.

12. *Niles' National Register*, January 20 and March 11, 1838.

13. Dudley P. Bailey Jr., "The History of Banking in Massachusetts," *Banker's Magazine*, September and October 1876.

14. *Ibid.*

15. *Banker's Magazine*, May 1855.

16. Reported in a letter from the secretary of the Treasury, March 28, 1860, in HR 36th Congress, 1st Sess. Ex. Doc. 49.

17. Dudley P. Bailey Jr., "The History of Banking in Massachusetts, No. 3," *Banker's Magazine*, October 1876.

18. James W. North, *History of Augusta*, Augusta, 1870.

19. James W. North, *History of Augusta*, Augusta, 1870.

20. *Report of the Bank Commissioner*, p. 71.

21. *New England Historical and Genealogical*, Volume 14, p. 287.

22. *History of Lynn*, Volume 1, p. 155.

23. Davis R. Dewey, *State Banking Before the Civil War*, p. 64.

24. John J. Currier, *History of Newburyport, Mass. 1764–1909*, Volume 2, 1909, Newburyport, Massachusetts, Printed for the Author, June 25, 1795.

25. John J. Currier, *History of Newburyport, Mass. 1764–1909*, Volume 2, 1909, Newburyport, Massachusetts, Printed for the author.

26. John J. Currier, *History of Newburyport, Mass. 1764–1909*, Volume 2, 1909, Newburyport, Massachusetts, Printed for the Author.

27. *Annual Report of the Secretary of the Treasury on the Condition of Banks*, 1850.

28. The world of numismatics is full of surprises, including this one, furnished by Karl Moulton, book dealer and collector, who acquainted the author with White and furnished copies of the two auction catalogs quoted.

29. *Banker's Magazine*, Volume 1, p. 318.

30. Davis R. Dewey, *State Banking Before the Civil War*, p. 211.

31. *Annual Report of the Bank Commissioners in 1842.*

32. *Sound Currency*, 1900.

33. Dudley P. Bailey Jr., *Banker's Magazine*: *The History of Banking in Massachusetts*, No. 3, *Concluded.*

34. *Banker's Magazine*, Volume 8, p. 75.

35. *Acts and Resolves Passed by the General Court of Massachusetts*, p. 411.

36. John Jay Knox, *The History of Banking*, 1900, p. 330.

37. *Niles' National Register*, Volume 63, p. 16.

38. *Banker's Magazine*, March 1853; *Gloucester Bank* v. *Salem Bank*, 17 Mass. 33.

39. *Banker's Magazine.*

40. *Acts and Resolves Passed by the General Court of Massachusetts*, p. 418, pp. 765–772.

41. *The Centennial History of Waterville, Kennebec County, Maine.*

42. Massachusetts General Court documents; *Report of the Maine District Banks to the Commonwealth of Massachusetts*, January 1820; *Maine Registry* issues; News accounts; *Sound Currency*, 1900; John Jay Knox, *History of Banking*, 1900. Other sources.

43. *Banker's Magazine and Statistical Register,* Volume 6, p. 84.

Glossary

back—the paper money equivalent of "reverse" used for coins. The front side of a note is called the face.

bank—in the present context, a business set up under a state or federal (e.g. Bank of the United States) charter to engage in the business of receiving and disbursing funds, making loans, issuing paper money, and engaging in related activities.

bank note—a small, rectangular piece of paper money $1 face value or higher issued by a state-chartered bank. Imprinted with a denomination or value and the name/location of the issuing bank. Intended for use in commercial transactions. *Synonyms*: bill, note, bank bill.

bank-note reporter—commercial booklet or publication sold at a premium to bankers, merchants, etc., listing whether banks were solvent or not, descriptions of their notes, and the discounts at which their paper currency traded with exchange brokers and in commerce. *Synonym*: counterfeit detector.

bill—see *bank note.*

blue pup—nickname for a bank that later became insolvent or a circulating note issued by a bank that would not redeem their bills at par. *Synonyms*: owl, red dog.

burin—small, sharp, steel tool, often with a wooden handle, used to carefully engrave on a copper or steel plate. A famous engraving tool.

Canada green—see *Patent green tint.*

capital of a bank—the amount of money authorized by a state charter to be paid in by shareholders and provide funds for a bank's operation.

cashier—in a small bank, the chief operating officer, sometimes the only employee, who opened and closed the bank, signed and supervised the issuance of currency, made loans (often subject to the approval of others), and conducted the business of the bank. The highest-salaried employee. In a large bank, the officer in charge of funds, receipts, and payments, the keeper of bank records.

certified note—a note graded and placed in a sealed holder by a commercial grading service.

charter—operating authorization given by a state legislature to permit a company to engage in banking.

charter expiration—charters were sometimes given to banks for a specific term, such as 20 years, after which a renewal could be applied for. In other instances, a corporation was dissolved and the same people obtained a new charter to continue in business.

circulation of a bank—the total face-value of a given bank's bills in commercial circulation (not including notes held in the bank's vault or not yet issued).

clearing house—a bank or organization that took in bills from various sources and sent them to member banks for exchange or redemption.

counter—technical name for the part of a note showing the denomination in a separate vignette, such as 5, 10, 20, etc., or as a Roman numeral, V, X, M, etc. Some counters are very ornate.

counterfeit—a bill in imitation of an original design but printed from false plates by someone not authorized to do so.

counterfeit detector—see *bank-note reporter*. Often spelled "detecter" in the mid-19th century.

country bank—a bank located in a town or village, not a city or metropolitan area. Sometimes bills of country banks traded at a discount in comparison to banks with large capital located in cities.

cycloidal configuration—latticework, usually printed in color, with arcs and inscriptions said to deter counterfeiting. Also referred to as the "cycloidal" or "kaleidograph counter". Term used by the National Bank Note Company, which utilized James McDonough's patent of March 23, 1860, in which an engraving combined the name of the issuer, the denomination, and geometric, cycloidal, rosette work into a product to prevent alteration or counterfeiting of bank notes.

cylinder die—see *transfer roll.*

date on a note—the time that a note or series of notes was issued. Sometimes a partial date such as 18__ was given, after which the year, month, and day would be added in ink. In other instances a full date was given, such as Jany. 1, 1853, representing the date of a certain series or design. Months were usually abbreviated. Notes with such a printed date could be used for a long time afterward.

denomination—the face or stated value printed on a bill, this being the amount for which the bill could be redeemed in specie or exchanged for other bills. Popular denominations of bills in use in commerce included $1, $2, $3, $5, $10, $20, $50, and $100. Other denominations were occasionally used.

deposit bank—a bank into which the Treasury Department placed federal funds. During the 1830s these were nicknamed "pet banks." Also spelled "deposite."

deuce—numismatic nickname for a $2 bill.

engraver—a skilled artist who, with a burin and other tools, hand-engraved lettering, motifs, and other elements into a printing plate or design element matrix. Various mechanical devices are sometimes used as well.

engraving—intaglio or recessed design elements and lettering engraved by hand or added by the siderographic process to a printing plate. A motif, print, or other reproduction on paper made from an engraved printing plate.

essay—an experimental impression of a partial or completed note printed to test the design or evaluate a concept. The paper money equivalent of a pattern or trial piece coin. French: *essai.*

exchange broker, broker—a person or business specializing in buying and selling current and obsolete paper money and gold and silver coins.

face—the paper money equivalent of "obverse" used for coins. The reverse side of a note is called the back.

free bank—a bank set up under one or another of the state laws enacted from the late 1830s onward whereby any group of people could form a bank providing that assurances were made that sufficient capital would be raised.

geometric lathe—machine that uses gears and linkages to create rosettes, spirals, and other decorative elements on a soft metal plate, which is then hardened and reproduced through siderography for use in creating bank-note printing plates.

grade—designation assigned by numismatists to signify the amount of wear or circulation a note has experienced and its condition today (see chapter 1 for more information). Grading can be expressed by adjectives such as Good, Extremely Fine, and Uncirculated or by abbreviations in combination with numbers from 1 to 70, such as EF-40 or Unc-63 (adapted from the ANA coin grading system).

green tint—see *Patent green tint.*

imprint—printed information added to a bank note, especially the name of an engraver or printer.

ink ball—a porous ball of cloth or other absorbent substance that was charged with ink and then wiped across the face of a printing plate. Superseded by the ink roller.

ink roller—a rubber roller that is partly immersed in a pan or other supply of ink then used to spread the ink across the face of a printing plate.

inked signature—the signature of a bank president or cashier on currency.

launder—often used in a derogatory sense, the cleaning of paper money to enhance its appearance. Careful cleaning, such as to remove grease or grime, can be beneficial but should be done only by experts. In the early 20th century the Treasury Department added several machines to launder soiled paper money, after which the reconditioned notes were again placed into circulation.

legal tender—a bank note that could be used to pay any and all debts except for custom duties. Most notes of state-chartered banks were accepted at par only within the region of issue.

margin—the blank area or white strip beyond the design or printed information at the border of a note. Wide margins are preferred to narrow ones. There are no general rules.

microprint, microprinting—nearly microscopic-size lettering added to a note, such as on Perkins Patent Stereotype Plate notes and related formats.

notaphily—originated by Kenneth R. Lake as a proposal to give a name to the study and appreciation of paper money. Originally found in Yasha Beresiner's "An Introduction to Paper Money," *The Numismatist*, March 1979.

note—see *bank note.*

obverse—see *face.*

overprint—color printing on a note; a design, grill, denomination, or other element intended to defer counterfeiting. Sometimes these were applied before the black section of the note was printed.

owl—nickname for a circulating note issued by a bank that would not redeem them at par or a bank that later became insolvent. Inspired by the worthless bills of the Owl Creek Bank of Mount Vernon, Ohio. *Synonyms*: blue pup, red dog.

panic—an excitement in financial circles caused by unfavorable economic or banking conditions in which holders of bank notes and securities became frightened and rushed to convert paper to gold and silver coins.

par—the value printed on a note.

Patent green tint, green tint, "Canada green"—green imprint, usually called "overprint," of lacy green said to be a deterrent against counterfeiting. Except for paper money sheets that required bronzing, the adding of a green tint was the first printing operation on a blank sheet as reported by S.M. Clark, *Report to the Secretary of the Treasury*, November 26, 1864. As to whether this priority was always followed is not known. The patent was held by Rawdon, Wright, Hatch & Edson, later the American Bank Note Co., having been acquired from a Canadian inventor.

payee—the first person to receive the note when it was issued. This became a nuisance, and many cashiers simply added a short name and used it over and over again. In other instances a name such as Benjamin Franklin or Henry Clay was added to the printing plate.

pet bank—popular nickname for a bank into which the Treasury Department placed federal funds during the second Andrew Jackson administration.

pinhole—in the 19th century it was common practice to stitch several notes together for safekeeping, hiding within a coat's lining, or storing in a small pile. Today, when certain notes are held to the light, tiny holes can be seen.

plate—a rectangle of copper or hardened steel with engraved or otherwise recessed lettering, motifs, and other elements used to print bank notes. Currency of the period under study was often printed four notes to a plate or, if higher denominations, two notes to a plate.

plate letter—a printed letter, often from A to D, signifying the note's position on a four-subject printing plate. In other instances, single plates with various letters were locked into a frame and plate letters were not in any order. If a plate was slightly altered, the plate letter might be given another letter to accompany it, such as Aa, aA, Ab. If a sheet had more than one denomination, each would start anew with A. As examples, a $1-$1-$1-$2 sheet might use A, B, C, A. A four subject sheet of $5 notes would use A, B, C, D.

plate position—the position of a note on a printing plate, sometimes determinable by the plate letter.

post note—a bill imprinted with a statement that it was redeemable at par only at a later specified date.

president—the chairman of the board of directors, presided over board meetings, signed currency. Often engaged in other activities, but visited a bank occasionally. Other times a local person who was on the premises often and made decisions beyond the duties of the cashier.

printer—an individual or firm that prints bank notes using a press, plates, paper, and ink. A printer may or may not have engraving skills. Most if not all printers of bank notes also produced other products such as book plates and decorative prints.

Progressive Proof note—a note printed from a plate which was not completely finished and was absent some lettering, ornaments, or other features. Used to inspect a design as it was being created.

Proof note—a Proof (capitalization optional) note is an impression from a complete or partially complete plate for testing or to illustrate its appearance such as showing to prospective bank clients. Proof notes are usually printed on only one side and show either the front or back. Such Proof notes are highly prized today. Specimen notes are related but were not issued for test purposes. Sometimes printed on ordinary bank-note paper, often on India paper, sometimes on light cardboard or mounted on a thin card. *Synonym*: Proof.

protector—a color overprint or underprint on a note; a design, grill, denomination, or other element intended to defer counterfeiting. *Synonym*: overprint.

rag—nickname for a circulating note that either had no value or was worn to the point of tattering.

ragpicker—nickname in the past for a collector of paper money.

red dog—nickname for a circulating note issued by a bank that would not redeem them at par or a bank that later became insolvent. *Synonyms*: blue pup, owl.

reenter, re-enter—engraving or transfer process whereby original information on a bank-note printing plate is removed and new information is entered in its place. This could permit an old plate to be used for a different bank.

reverse—see *back*.

roll, roller die—see *transfer roll*.

rose machine—a geometric lathe.

run on a bank—see *panic*. Sometimes engineered by profiteers who would encourage a run through rumors of insolvency (which would depreciate the value of a bank's bills), buy up discounted notes, and later redeem them at par as a form of speculation.

safety fund, safety fund bank—a bank chartered with the requirement that it deposit certain of its capital into approved bonds and other securities.

scrip, scrip note—a bill issued by an entity other than a chartered bank, such as a canal, railroad, factory, etc. A bill issued by a bank or other entity with a face value below $1.

security features—aspects of the design or printing of a note intended to deter copying and counterfeiting. In early times, this consisted of minute design elements expertly engraved, as well as printing on special paper. Chapter 7 of volume 1 in this series discusses various methods.

selvage—unused space on a sheet of paper money beyond the normal trim borders of the individual notes.

serial number—a number inked or printed by a numbering machine on a note prior to issuing it. Banks sometimes started serial numbers anew with each day or each month. Serial numbers were kept low by keying them to dates, making them faster to write. For this reason most serial numbers are in the hundreds or low thousands.

sheet of notes, uncut sheet—an uncut group of notes, as printed, usually four subjects with denominations from $1 to $20, usually with more than one denomination per sheet. $50, $100, and higher denominations were printed two to a sheet. Many notes were printed singly in earlier times.

shinplaster—derogatory nickname popular in the early 19th century to denote a scrip note or bank note that had no monetary value, such as an issue of the Hard Times era. Derived from the popular practice of mixing paper sheets and hardener to affix to a person's shins to relieve pain.

siderography, siderographic—the process of engraving a motif, lettering, or other elements on a soft steel plate, then hardening it, after which a cylinder die or transfer roll of soft steel is forcibly rolled into its surface under high pressure in a transfer press, picking up a relief image. The cylinder die is then hardened, placed into a transfer press, and rolled with pressure into a soft steel or copper plate. This transfers the design in recessed form. The plate is then hardened and used to print notes. Lettering, emblems, and other design elements can be added to plates in this manner.

signatures on notes—usually with the cashier's signature in ink at the lower left and the president's at the lower right. Legally a note had no value until signed by both officers.

specie—gold or silver coins.

specie payment—the payment of a gold or silver coin by a bank in exchange for a bank note presented for redemption.

specimen note—a Proof note for examination or display, a plate impression not intended for circulation.

spider press—a rectangular printing press used to make bank notes. The name derives from multiple thin arms extending from the press that are slowly turned by hand to press a sheet of dampened paper into the ink-filled recesses of a printing plate.

surcharge—extra printing or information added to a note after the main printing was finished. *Synonym*: overprint.

suspension, suspension of specie payments—when a bank refuses to redeem its notes in silver or gold coins. This usually happened when a bank had problems or in times of general financial distress. See *run on a bank*.

transfer roll—a hard steel cylinder with a hole at the center for a shaft, on the outside face of which is a raised design, vignette, counter, or other element used in bank-note printing. Transfer rolls are used to imprint a design into a printing plate by the siderographic process. *Synonyms*: cylinder die, roll, roller die.

Unc-Rem—grade designator signifying that an Uncirculated note is an unsigned, undated remainder.

Unc-S&D—grade designator signifying that an Uncirculated note was signed and dated, but never issued.

vignette—an ornamental or illustrative element of a bank note, such as a portrait, allegorical scene, or motif from history. Pronounced "vinn-yet."

wildcat bank—a bank with or without charter that issued paper money with little or no backing. Such banks were often set up in remote locations.

Bibliography

Bailey Jr., Dudley P. "The History of Banking in Massachusetts," *Banker's Magazine*, September and October 1876.

Baker, W.S. *American Engravers and Their Works*. Philadelphia: Gebbie & Barrie, 1875.

Ball, Douglas B. Historical information written for and included in the catalog of the *Abner Reed Sale of United States Paper Money*, NASCA, October 31 to November 2, 1983.

Bank Note Reporter. Iola, Wisconsin: 1990s to date.

Bathe, Greville and Dorothy. *Jacob Perkins: His Inventions, His Times & His Contemporaries*. The Historical Society of Philadelphia, Pennsylvania, 1943.

Berkey, William A. *The Money Question*. The Legal Tender Paper Monetary System of the United States. Grand Rapids, Michigan: Published by the author, 1876.

Blanchard, Julian. "Cycloidal Configurations," *Essay-Proof Journal*, Vol. 20, No. 2 (1963) through Vol. 21, No. 2 (1964). Reprint of Ormsby's circa 1862 pamphlet, with new introductory remarks.

Blanchard, Julian. "Waterman Lily Ormsby, 1809–1883, Bank Note Engraver," commencing in the *Essay-Proof Journal*, January 1957.

Bodenhorn, Howard. *State Banking in Early America: A New Economic History*. Oxford and New York: Oxford University Press, 2003.

Boggs, Winthrop S. *Ten Decades Ago 1840–1850: A Study of the Work of Rawdon, Wright, Hatch & Edson of New York City*. American Philatelic Society, 1949.

Bowers, Q. David and David M. Sundman. *The 100 Greatest American Currency Notes*. Atlanta, Georgia: Whitman Publishing LLC, 2005.

Bowers, Q. David. *Obsolete Paper Money Issued by Banks in the United States, 1782–1866*. Atlanta, Georgia: Whitman Publishing LLC, 2006.

Carpenter, Edward W. *The History of the Town of Amherst, Massachusetts*. Press of Carpenter & Morehouse, 1896.

Chaddock, Robert E. *The Safety Fund Banking System in New York 1829–1866*. Washington, D.C.: Government Printing Office, 1910, for the National Monetary Commission. 61st Congress, 2d Session, Senate, Document No. 581.

Cheap Money. New York City, New York: The Century Co., 1892.

Christie's. "Important Early American Bank Notes, 1810–1874" from the Archives of the American Bank Note Company, catalog of the auction sale held September 14 and 15, 1990.

Currier, John J. *History of Newburyport, Mass. 1764–1909*, Volume 2, 1909. Newburyport, Massachusetts: Published by the author, June 25, 1795.

Davis, Andrew McFarland (introduction by). *Colonial Currency Reprints*. 4 volumes. Boston, Massachusetts: The Prince Society, 1910 and 1911.

Davis, Andrew McFarland. "Papers Relating to the Land Bank of 1740." 1910.

Davis, Andrew McFarland. *Currency and Banking in the Province of the Massachusetts Bay*. New York City, New York: The Macmillan Company, 1901.

Dewey, Davis R. *State Banking Before the Civil War*. Washington, D.C.: Government Printing Office, 1910, for the National Monetary Commission. 61st Congress, 2d Session, Senate, Document No. 581.

Dillistin, William H. *Bank Note Reporters and Counterfeit Detectors, 1826–1866*. New York City, New York: American Numismatic Society, 1949. Numismatic Notes and Monographs No. 114.

Doty, Richard. *Pictures from a Distant Country: Seeing America Through Old Paper Money*. Atlanta, Georgia: Whitman Publishing LLC, 2013.

Dunbar, Charles F. *Chapters on the Theory and History of Banking*. New York and London: G.P. Putnam's Sons, 1892.

Dunbar, Seymour. *A History of Transportation in America*. 4 volumes. Indianapolis, Indiana: The Bobbs-Merrill Company, 1915.

Duncombe, Charles. *Duncombe's Free Banking: An Essay on Banking, Currency, Finance, Exchanges, and Political Economy*. Cleveland, Ohio: Sanford & Co., 1841.

Durand, Roger H. *Interesting Notes* series: *About Denominations* (1988), *About History* (1990), *About Indians* (1991), *About Territories* (1992), *About Christmas* (1993), *About Allegorical Representations* (1994), *About Vignettes* (1995), *About Portraits* (1996), *About Vignettes II* (1996), *About Portraits II* (1997), *About Vignettes III* (2001), *About Portraits III* (2004).

Essay-Proof Journal. New York City, New York: The Essay-Proof Society, 1944.

Financial Register of the United States, The. Vol. 1, July 1837 to July 1838. Philadelphia, Pennsylvania: Wirtz & Tatem, 1838.

Glaser, Lynn. *Counterfeiting in America*. New York City, New York: Clarkson N. Potter, Inc., 1968.

Golembe, Carter H. *State Banks and the Development of the West, 1830–1844*. New York City, New York: Arno Press, 1978. Originally presented as the author's thesis, Columbus University, 1952.

Gouge, William M. *The Curse of Paper-Money and Banking; or a Short History of Banking in the United States of America, with an Account of its Ruinous Effects on Landowners, Farmers, Trades, and on All the Illustrious Classes of the Community*. Philadelphia, Pennsylvania, 1833.

Griffiths, William H. *The Story of the American Bank Note Company*. New York City, New York: American Bank Note Company, 1959.

Harris, Elizabeth M. "Sir William Congreve and His Compound-Plate Printing," *United States National Museum Bulletin 252*, Paper 71 in *Contributions from The Museum of History and Technology*, Washington, D.C., Smithsonian Institution Press, 1967.

Haxby, James A. *Standard Catalog of United States Obsolete Bank Notes 1782–1866*. Krause Publications Inc., 1988.

Hessler, Gene. *The Engraver's Line*. Port Clinton, Ohio: BNR Press, 1993.

Hildreth, Richard. *The History of Banks, to Which is Added a Demonstration of the Advantages and Necessity of Free Competition in the World of Banking*. Boston, Massachusetts: Hilliard, Gray & Company, 1837.

Hunter, Dard. *Papermaking: The History and Technique of an Ancient Craft*. New York City, New York: Dover Publications, Inc., 1978. Reprint of 1943 edition by Alfred A. Knopf, Inc.

Kleeberg, John M. (editor). *Money of Pre-Federal America*. New York City, New York: American Numismatic Society, 1992 (programs presented at the Coinage of the Americas Conference, 1991).

Knapp, Samuel L. "Memoir of Jacob Perkins." Published in 1835 and 1836 in *Family Magazine*, New York. Reprinted with extensive added numismatic commentary in *The Colonial Newsletter*, Volume 27, No. 3, November 1987, Serial No. 77.

Knox, John Jay. *History of Banking*. New York City, New York: Bradford Rhodes & Company, 1900. Anthology of Knox's articles and speeches published posthumously.

Lewis, Lawrence Jr. *A History of the Bank of North America, the First Bank Chartered in the United States*. Philadelphia, Pennsylvania: J.B. Lippincott & Co., 1882.

McCabe, Robert. "Waterman Lilly Ormsby and the Continental Bank Note Co.," *Paper Money*, March–April 2001. Includes much information found in the National Archives by Wayne DeCesar, fully credited by McCabe.

McCulloch, Hugh. *Men and Measures of Half a Century*. New York City, New York: Charles Scribner's Sons, 1889.

McKay, George L. *Early American Currency*. New York City, New York: The Typophiles, 1944.

Mossman, Philip L. *Money of the American Colonies and Confederation: A Numismatic, Economic & Historical Correlation*. New York City, New York: American Numismatic Society, 1993. Magisterial study of early money in America, emphasizing coins, but with a chapter on paper money.

Newman, Eric P. *Early Paper Money of America*. 4th edition. Iola, Wisconsin: Krause Publications, 1997.

Niles' Register. Various issues of *Niles' Weekly Register* 1811 to 1837, title change to *Niles' National Register*, September 2, 1837, continuing to 1849. Baltimore, Maryland, briefly Washington, D.C.

Numismatic Scrapbook Magazine. Hewitt Brothers and Sidney Printing and Publishing Co., 1935–1966.

Numismatist, The. Journal of the American Numismatic Association; established by Dr. George F. Heath in 1888.

O'Brien, Donald C. "Abner Reed: A Connecticut Engraver." *The Connecticut Historical Society Bulletin*, Volume 44, No. 1. Hartford, Connecticut, January 1979.

Ormsby, W.L. *Bank Note Engraving*. New York City, New York: Published by the author, 1852.

Ormsby, W.L. *Cycloidal Configurations, or the Harvest of Counterfeiters, Containing Matter of the Highest Importance concerning Paper Money, also Explaining the Unit System of Bank Note Engraving*. New York City, New York: Published by the author, 1862.

Paper Money. Journal of the Society of Paper Money Collectors: 1960s to date.

Peyton, George. *How to Detect Counterfeit Bank Notes; or, an Illustrated Treatise on the Detection of Counterfeit, Altered, and Spurious Bank Notes, with Original Bank Note Plates and designs, by Rawdon, Wright, Hatch & Edson, Bank Note Engravers, of New-York, the Whole Forming an Unerring Guide, by which Every Person Can, on Examination, Detect Spurious Bank Notes of Every Description, No Matter How Well Executed They May Appear*. New York City, New York: Published by the author, 1856.

Raguet, Condy. *A Treatise on Currency & Banking*. 2nd edition. Philadelphia, Pennsylvania: Grigg & Elliot, 1840.

Rice, Foster Wild. "Antecedents of the American Bank Note Company of 1858," *The Essay-Proof Journal*, Fall 1961.

Scott, Kenneth. *Counterfeiting in Colonial America*. New York City, New York: Oxford University Press, 1957.

Sears, Louis Martin. *Jefferson and the Embargo*. Durham, North Carolina: Duke University Press, 1927.

Stauffer, David McNelly. *American Engravers Upon Copper and Steel*. New York City, New York: The Grolier Club of the City of New York, 1907.

The *Medley*. New Bedford, July 24, 1795.

Tomasko, Mark D. *The Feel of Steel: The Art and History of Bank-Note Engraving in the United States*. 2nd edition. New York City, New York: American Numismatic Society, 2012.

Trumbull, J. Hammond. *The first essays at banking and first paper-money in New-England: from the report of the council of the American Antiquarian society, presented at the annual meeting held in Worcester October 21, 1884*. Worcester: [s.n.]. 1864.

White, Horace. *Money and Banking*. Boston and London: Ginn & Company, 1896.

Whitney, D.R. *The Suffolk Bank*. 1878. Kessinger Publishing, 2010.

About the Author

Q. David Bowers became a professional numismatist as a teenager in 1953, later (1960) earning a B.A. in Finance from Pennsylvania State University, which in 1976 bestowed its Distinguished Alumnus Award on him. He served as president of the Professional Numismatists Guild from 1977 to 1979 and president of the American Numismatic Association from 1983 to 1985. He is a recipient of the Founders Award and Farran Zerbe Award, the highest honors of the PNG and the ANA. He is the author of more than 50 books, including many on paper money, and has received more honors from the Numismatic Literary Guild than has any other person. His column, "The Joys of Collecting," has been a feature of *Coin World* since 1961 and is the longest-running column by any author in the history of numismatics. He may be contacted at P.O. Box 539, Wolfeboro Falls, NH 03896 or by e-mail at qdbarchive@metrocast.net.

About the Foreword Writer

A graduate of Syracuse University, Anne E. Bentley has been with the Massachusetts Historical Society since 1973, first as conservator of manuscripts, then as curator of the art collection. Since 1984 she has been responsible for the Society's numismatic collection. Ms. Bentley has authored papers on the 1776 Massachusetts Pine Tree copper penny and a copper Columbia-Washington medal given to the MHS in 1791 by merchant Joseph Barrell. Along with John W. Adams, she co-wrote *Comitia Americana and Related Medals: Underappreciated Monuments to our Heritage*, and she also contributed to Adams's book, written with Fernando Chao (h), *Medallic Portraits of Admiral Vernon: Medals Sometimes Lie*.

About the State Editor

C. John Ferreri is one of America's most accomplished collectors and researchers in the field of obsolete paper money, having specialized in the series for more than 40 years. In addition he has presented many programs on currency, especially for New England clubs and other organizations. His research has been important in the creation of several specialized texts on the subject.

General Index

Index to Banks, by State

Massachusetts, Book 2

Hallowell through Yarmouth

Found in Massachusetts, Book 1
Abington through Greenfield

Haxby-to-Whitman Numbers Cross-Reference and Index
Massachusetts, Book 2
Hallowell through Yarmouth

Found in Massachusetts, Book 1
Abington through Greenfield